TUTORIAL
Programming Language Design

Anthony I. Wasserman
University of California, San Francisco, California

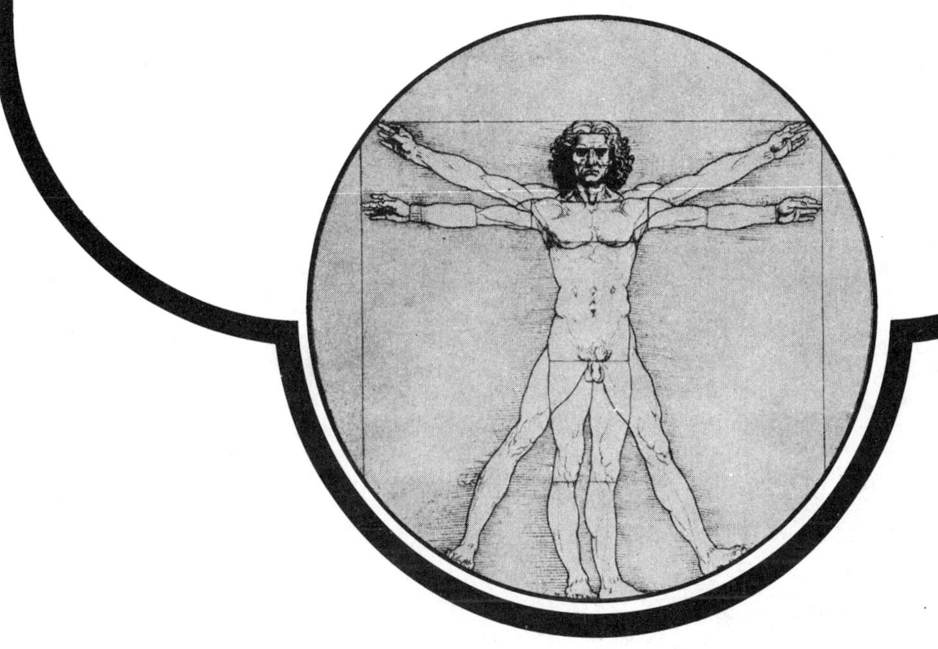

Initially presented at

October 27–31, 1980

compsac80

The IEEE Computer Society's Fourth International
Computer Software & Applications Conference

IEEE Catalog No. EHO 164-4   **Library of Congress No. 80-83087**

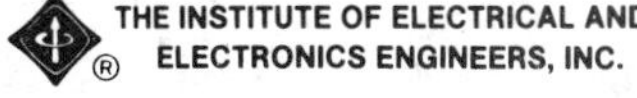

Dedication

To Susan and Mark

Acknowledgments

The willingness of individual authors to allow reprinting of their papers is gratefully acknowledged. Without them, this book would literally not exist. Thanks to Dennis Fife for giving me the opportunity to present the tutorial for which this book was developed.

I am particularly thankful to Christina Taylor and her colleagues at the IEEE Computer Society for their superhuman efforts in coordinating the myriad details associated with production of this book on an extremely tight schedule.

To the Reader

Programming languages have long been among the most popular subjects among programmers and computer scientists. Seemingly endless debates have raged over the relative superiority of various languages, the "best" set of programming language features, and the proper programming style to be used with different languages. The only point that seems clear from the debate is that no agreement exists on this topic, nor is there likely to be in the near future.

Indeed, programming language design remains an extremely popular activity, even given the difficulty of acceptance and use of a new language by a significant number of programmers. After nearly a quarter century of programming in high-level languages, the most dominant ones—FORTRAN, COBOL, and BASIC—are still among the oldest. Other languages—including PL/I, Pascal, LISP, SNOBOL, Bliss, C, MUMPS, and their dialects and descendants—have sizable, identifiable communities of enthusiastic proponents and users as well. New languages are being designed and implemented with great regularity, and the roster of such languages continues to grow.

An observer of this phenomenon might well wonder why people continue to design languages with the knowledge that few languages are likely to have significant impact on computing practices, nor is a sizable percentage of programmers likely to implement and use many new languages. The intent of this volume is to provide some insight into that design activity and to show the challenges presented by the process of language design, as well as to survey a number of languages and language features.

This book, created both as background material for a professional development seminar on recent advances in programming language design and as supplementary reading for university courses on the subject, attempts to present the subject of programming language design in an organized fashion. The initial sections provide some background on programming languages and their history, as well as some philosophical statements on language design. Subsequent sections treat critical language decisions in the areas of control structures and data types. An entire section is then given over to Pascal, including several papers that provide critical evaluation of the language. This section is followed by background and introduction to Ada, a programming language designed to meet U.S. Department of Defense requirements for a high-order language for embedded computer systems. Special attention is given to two language design areas—data base management and exception handling—which are less well established and in which there is little consensus about an appropriate set of language primitives. The last sections deal, respectively, with reported experience in programming language design and with formal definition of programming languages as it impacts the process of language design.

There is a vast amount of literature on programming languages, with several journals devoted almost exclusively to the subject, in addition to newsletters, books, specialized conferences, and technical reports covering this field. As a result, any volume of this size cannot hope to provide thorough coverage of the field, but only a glimpse of a number of key topics.

Accordingly, the editor applied a number of criteria in trying to select an appropriate collection, among them that the papers demonstrate the following qualities:
(1) insight into the language design process, focusing on *why* the author made certain decisions and why they appear to be superior to alternative decisions;
(2) timeliness, showing the state of the art as it exists in 1980, with particular recognition of the relationship between programming languages and the entire software development process;
(3) representation of a number of well-recognized persons in the language design field with an effort to include heavily cited and influential works;
(4) diversity of articles from a variety of publications, including some that are not easily available to most readers.

Some original material, as well as the section overviews, attempt to place the set of papers in perspective and to integrate them. The editor admits to favoring Pascal and Pascal-like languages that support structured programming and type checking and warns the reader that the selection of papers is weighted in that direction. This decision seems justified by the extensive amount of work that has been done recently in this area and by the relative scarcity of papers on other languages.

It seems clear that existing languages will evolve, that new languages will be designed, and that programming languages, far from being a dying field, will continue to be active as a major research area. In the future, more attention will be given to "very-high-level", i.e., non-procedural, languages and to tools that support the programming activity.

It is hoped that this volume will provide a good perspective on the state of the art in programming language design and a framework for understanding future developments as they occur.

Anthony I. Wasserman
August, 1980

TABLE OF CONTENTS

SECTION 9: AXIOMATIC DEFINITION OF PROGRAMMING LANGUAGES

Section 1
Programming Languages

This section provides an introduction to the study of programming language design. The paper by Wasserman focuses on the goals and functions of programming languages, beginning with the initial motivation and historical development of programming languages, then provides a basis for comparison of languages and language features. It concludes with some brief remarks concerning programming language design and implementation.

Wegner's paper provides a thorough survey of the history of programming languages, identifying a number of major milestones in that development. The paper also contains an extensive set of references for additional reading.

The final paper in this section, by Wulf, Shaw, and London, speaks for many of the designers of modern programming languages in laying out the goals of language design in support of the construction of high quality software systems. While their paper is addressed to a particular language, Alphard, it does an excellent job of expressing the aims and objectives of the designers of a number of similar languages.

Introduction to Programming Languages

Anthony I. Wasserman

Motivation for Programming Languages

One of the fundamental attributes of the digital computer is its ability to carry out a computation by following a sequence of steps stored in the computer. This sequence of steps, called a *program,* consists of a number of instructions executed directly by the computer. In general, a different set of instructions exists for every different family of computers. For most computers, these instructions are expressed in binary numbers, 0's and 1's. A complete instruction is comprised of a sequence of 0's and 1's. Although the length of the sequence depends upon the specific machine and the nature of the instruction, typical instruction lengths range from 8 to 64 *bits*. The data manipulated by the instructions are also stored in binary form.

In the early days of the stored program computer, it was necessary to prepare the instructions and data for the machine in binary. The programmer's job was to determine which locations of the computer's memory would be used for each instruction and for each data item. Needless to say, programming was an extremely tedious process. Apart from the problems caused by the unreliability of computer hardware, the programmer had to write instructions in an extremely unnatural notation, often resulting in coding errors. Even the simplest sets of instructions represented a significant investment of coding effort before the desired results could be obtained.

Most important, the coding notation bore no resemblance to the nature of the problem being solved by the programmer: binary notation is oriented to the computer, not to the programmer or to the application being programmed. It soon became apparent that this binary notation did not make effective use of a programmer's time.

Accordingly, alternative languages, better suited to the needs of the programmers, were developed for coding. *Translators* and *interpreters* emerged to process these languages. A translator is a program which takes as input a program written in some other notation and produces as output a set of executable machine instructions. An interpreter is a program which takes as input a program written in some other notation and directly executes the program by interpreting the programmer's commands. Both translators and interpreters provide a mechanism whereby the programmer can escape from coding in binary and yet still be able to write sequences of instructions for the computer.

The alternative notations provided for the programmer differ greatly in compactness, in facility for writing programs, and in suitability for various kinds of programming tasks. One type of notation, still in widespread use, is termed *symbolic assembly language.* The binary machine operations are replaced by symbolic names (mnemonics), so that a programmer can write ADD instead of 001101, for example. In addition, programmers can use symbolic names for storage locations instead of using absolute addresses. The translator, called an *assembler,* converts each instruction in the symbolic assembly language to a machine language instruction, allocating storage as needed for each symbolic name. Furthermore, if the programmer makes mistakes in notation, the assembler will note them; otherwise, the assembler produces executable machine instructions.

From the standpoint of the programmer, assemblers represented a large advance. All physical storage allocation was handled automatically. It became unnecessary to carry a little card showing all of the machine's instructions in binary or octal notation. At the same time, programs written in assembly language executed as if they had been written in machine language, once the translation phase was complete.

Even so, symbolic assembly language was still more oriented to the machine than to the programmer. Each assembly language instruction is mapped into one machine language instruction; assembly language instructions closely resemble basic machine operations involving specific hardware registers.

At the other end of the spectrum of alternative notations were a variety of *problem-oriented* notations, which permitted the programmer to code the steps of the problem solution in a notation related to the task at hand. The language processor, either a translator or an interpreter, acted upon this problem-oriented notation. Various kinds of notational schemes were developed for scientific computation, report generation, decision tables, and other types of problems.

These problem-oriented notations were the forerunner of *programming languages* as we know them today. Because they are problem-oriented, these programming languages bear no direct resemblance to the machine instructions of a given computer; indeed, use of a programming language obviates the need for using an assembly language.

When programs written in a programming language are translated into machine instructions, each programming language statement generally will produce more than one machine language instruction (in contrast to the situation with assembly language, where each symbolic assembly language instruction produces a single machine instruction). Such languages are also called *high-level* languages; the program which translates a high-level language into machine language is called a *compiler*.

Programming languages are dedicated to the notion that efficient use of human resources is more important than efficient use of machine resources. A programming language is intended to make it easier for the programmer to express the solution to a problem for execution by a computer, often saving additional time spent in translation and execution and/or space for memory utilization. When programming languages were first being developed in the late 1950's, these ideas were quite controversial, particularly since computers were much slower and had much less primary memory than is now the case. Considerable effort was made to develop compilers capable of producing machine instructions comparable in efficiency with the set of instructions written by an assembly language programmer. Even now, many applications have severe time or space constraints and must be either programmed in assembly language or compiled very efficiently.

Over the past few years, however, programming languages have become almost universally accepted, and virtually every conceivable type of application has been programmed using some kind of programming language. This range of applications includes not only traditional kinds of systems for scientific computation and business data processing, but also systems for controlling machine tools, for sharing the resources of a computer among a number of concurrent users, and for producing graphical displays.

It is now generally agreed that programming languages are an important part of the total process of solving problems by computer, beginning with the initial statement of a problem and terminating with a reliably executing program for carrying out the steps of the solution to the problem. The ease with which a problem solution can be expressed in a programming language is an important factor in determining the total effort required to complete the problem-solving process.

Programming languages are thus very closely related to the way people think and to the way in which people represent information. A considerable portion of current research in programming languages deals with design of languages and language features that can provide support for the way people solve problems. This relationship helps to show why there are so many different programming languages: different types of problems require different approaches to problem solution because different people tend to think about problems in different ways.

In studying programming languages, then, we must gain some understanding of a number of different languages and must be able to determine which languages are best suited to different types of applications. Because programming is so closely related to human thought processes, the choice of programming languages is highly subjective. Thus, most programmers have one or two favorite programming languages with which they feel most comfortable.

At the same time, however, it is important to gain insight into the *process* of language design. Most languages are designed with a particular set of goals in mind, but there are many ways to achieve these goals. A language designer must choose features from a large number of alternatives and must produce a coherent and consistent notation compatible with the goals set forth. Language design is considerably more difficult than it initially appears to be; there are a number of subtle decisions and tradeoffs to be made.

Despite the proliferation of programming languages, however, almost all share similar functional characteristics. Someone studying any programming language must examine its syntax, its semantics, and its pragmatics. The syntax is the notation used for writing the statements of the language. The semantics is the meaning of the different syntactic constructs. The pragmatics is the informal set of guidelines governing practical use of the language. In combination, these three concepts yield a comprehensive view of the language.

In this book, a number of the underlying concepts of programming languages will be presented, along with their realization in several different programming languages. We will also look carefully at the problems of language design, examining some of the strengths and weaknesses of these languages and considering the issues in designing a new language.

Historical Development of Programming Languages

Programming language design has long been popular with computer scientists. Literally hundreds of distinct programming languages have been designed. Many of these languages were never implemented; others were implemented, but have only been used on a single type of computer or within a small group of programmers; only a handful have become widely used for a significant number of programming problems by different programmers on a variety of computer systems.

It would be nearly impossible to produce a complete listing of programming languages. Any listing becomes obsolete before it can be printed, as new languages appear; furthermore, many of the languages are quite obscure, poorly documented, and confined to a small research group. However, it is possible to identify some historical trends in the design of programming languages, providing a framework for many of these different efforts.

Research and development of programming languages has largely paralleled the state of the art of the digital computer and the range of applications for which use of the computer has been attempted. The predominant considerations at each stage of development often appear in the languages designed and used at that time.

Virtually all of the early applications of computers involved numerical computation problems in astronomy, physics, chemistry, and engineering, for which the results could be obtained more easily with the assistance of a computer. Accordingly, the earliest programming languages were oriented almost exclusively to this class of problems. FORTRAN (for *FOR*mula *TRAN*slation), whose development began in 1954, is easily the best known of this group of languages and remains in widespread use.

ALGOL (for *ALGO*rithmic *L*anguage) was also addressed primarily to the problems of numerical scientific computation, but it also dealt with the need for an unambiguous notation for expressing the steps of a computation. Algol 60 was defined in a published report [Naur, P. (ed.), "Revised Report on the Programming Language ALGOL 60," *Communications of the ACM,* Vol. 6, No. 1 (January, 1963)], with the syntax defined using a formal notation, helping to make Algol 60 an internationally used standard for stating an algorithmic process.

By the mid-1950's, it was apparent that computers were applicable to many other repetitive tasks besides those involving scientific computation. Numerous different input/output and peripheral devices were developed and manufactured, including card readers, printers, magnetic tape units, and magnetic drums. All of these devices made it possible to perform considerably more input/output than had previously been possible. Manufacturers began to produce two kinds of processors: those for scientific computation, and those for business applications. The latter were adapted for tasks involving less computation and more input/output: arithmetic was done in base 10 (decimal), rather than in base 2 (binary), and more input/output devices could be incorporated in a complete system.

Accompanying these developments was the creation of languages for business data processing. The strongest impetus came from the U.S. Department of Defense, which sponsored the formation of the *CO*nference on *D*ata *SY*stems Languages, CODASYL, composed of representatives of many of the largest computer users and manufacturers. CODASYL developed and continues to maintain the programming language COBOL, designed for the needs of business data processing users. One of the major goals of COBOL is that programs be self-documenting, i.e., that a COBOL program be readable and comprehensible without additional documentation.

The increasing availability of computing in the late 1950's and early 1960's attracted a number of applications besides the traditional ones of numerical computation or business data processing. Among these tasks were automatic translation of natural languages (e.g., Russian), mechanical theorem-proving in mathematics, and other efforts at replicating human intelligence. These applications were not well served by languages such as FORTRAN, ALGOL 60, and COBOL. Hence, a number of languages for list-processing and string-processing were devised. Although neither was the first to be developed for its class of applications, LISP (*LIS*t *P*rocessor) and SNOBOL (*StriN*g *O*riented and Sym*BO*lic *L*anguage) have emerged over the years as the most widely used languages produced explicitly for such applications.

The trend toward separate languages and systems for scientific and business computing was interrupted by the introduction of the IBM System/360 series of computers in 1964, along with a "New Programming Language" (then called NPL, now PL/I). IBM announced that it was discontinuing the production of two separate lines of machines and that one machine could be used for both classes of applications. For example, System/360 had machine instructions for both binary and decimal arithmetic. PL/I contained features from FORTRAN, ALGOL, and COBOL, along with many new and untried features, with the intent—not achieved—of making obsolete all previously designed languages.

As the cost of computing continued to fall throughout the 1960's and 70's, the computer was put to more and more uses. Primary memory costs decreased, and the typical size of primary memory on computer systems increased; high-level languages gained wider acceptance. Languages were designed and used for such applications as control of manufacturing processes and computer graphics. Also, "systems programming languages" were invented to write compilers for other languages and for operating systems, the control programs which manage the processing of user programs and the sharing of machine resources. Burroughs developed a dialect of ALGOL as a high level language for writing systems programs; many other such languages now exist. In short, different "special purpose" programming languages have been developed for a variety of uses. Special purpose languages are intended to serve the needs of a narrow scope of problems very well, as opposed to "general purpose" languages such as PL/I.

The trend toward declining computer costs placed greater emphasis upon the costs of people to program the computers. Furthermore, as computers were applied to more and more essential operations, such as air traffic control, concern grew over the correctness of programs and their reliability. This concern is reflected in much current work in language design. New languages now tend to have fewer constructs and a more consistent set of rules for forming statements than do many earlier languages. The objectives are to permit the programmer to understand the language fully, to simplify the problem of constructing a compiler for the language, to permit the programmer to extend the language as needed to suit the particular application being programmed, and to provide a tool that simplifies the process of converting the solution for a problem into a correctly functioning program. Greater care is being taken in language definitions, with efforts being made to formalize both the language syntax and its semantics, in order to facilitate verification of program correctness.

This trend has largely followed from the development of Pascal, which was designed in the late 1960's with the intention of providing a language for teaching systematic thinking about programming and for studying ways of implementing programming languages efficiently. Pascal has acquired a wide following and has been implemented on virtually every kind of computer, from microprocessors to large-scale mainframes. It has been put to uses far beyond the original intent of Niklaus Wirth, its designer.

Pascal has also been extremely influential in the design of other languages. Pascal was designed to be a small language and not specifically to support a diversity of applications in real-time systems, data base management, or other diverse fields. However, it has served as an important foundation for the design of new languages that have addressed these varied applications. The section of this book on Pascal indicates some of the debate over its suitability for various applications, and several of the papers in the section on programming language design experience point out weaknesses or shortcomings of Pascal that led to the design of a new language.

The development of Pascal and other modern languages has paralleled the increasing attention to the programming process itself. The skyrocketing costs of software development, the difficulty of managing the software development process, and the poor quality of the resulting product have all led to interest in the areas of programming methodology and software engineering.

Programming methodology deals with the way in which programs are designed and developed. Software engineering addresses the process by which software is created, from the initial conception of the problem through the entire development process and its maintenance over time. Although software engineering is largely concerned with the management of software development and with tools and procedures in the development environment, these topics have considerable bearing upon programming languages.

The close relationship between programming languages and the problem solving process has been noted. Furthermore, certain programming languages and language features have an impact upon the ease with which one can read, test, and/or maintain a program. This is not to say that it is impossible to write a "good" program in a "bad" programming language or that it is impossible to write a "bad" program in a "good" programming language—it is simply that certain features and certain programming styles can hinder the successful development of good quality programs.

Thus, the notion of programming style is also a major factor in the programming process. The way in which the features of a language are used is just as important as the features of the language themselves. Accordingly, many of the papers in this book give considerable attention to issues of programming style.

In short, the papers selected are largely based upon an awareness of these issues of programming style and software engineering. Although these themes are rarely the predominant notions in the papers, many of the papers are based upon an implicit awareness of these ideas.

Functions of a Programming Language

Although the programming languages we shall examine have different syntaxes and semantics, they have more in common than might immediately be apparent. From a theoretical standpoint, all of the languages are equivalent, in that we may precisely specify a computation in the notation provided by that language. As we shall see, this theoretical result is of little relevance in practice, since the suitability of a language is determined by a number of factors beyond the theoretical possibility of expressing a given algorithm in that language.

Before concentrating on the distinctions among the languages which provide a basis for evaluating the merits of a language for solving a particular problem, or on the factors involved in language design, we shall find it useful to look at some of the common functions of programming languages. Without exception, all programming languages (with their processors) provide these capabilities. Depending upon the language, however, these functions may be directly availble to the programmer or predetermined and outside the programmer's control.

Representation of Information. The first function of a programming language is to provide for the representation of information. With the exception of some trivial examples, all computer programs require access to some *values*. While these may be *constants* with fixed values, in general, there is a need for *variables,* objects whose value may change during the execution of a program. In both cases, the language processor needs to refer to these values within a program and to allocate storage for them.

Variables may be introduced into a program explicitly through declaration, as in Pascal; or implicitly through programmer usage, as in APL; or through a combination of these methods, as in FORTRAN and PL/I. In addition to individual variables, the processor frequently needs to aggregate the variables into groups or structures, so a collection of variables may be referenced by a common name. Different programming languages manifest this aggregative facility in numerous ways, including arrays (in FORTRAN, for example), sets (in Pascal, for example), and records (in COBOL, for example).

Different languages are designed for working with different types of variables. A language such as FORTRAN is intended primarily for numerical scientific computation, so its facilities for representing and handling numerical quantities are relatively powerful. SNOBOL4, on the other hand, is designed primarily for processing character strings and contains powerful features for representing and handling string values. Nonetheless, it remains possible (but inefficient) to carry out string-processing tasks in FORTRAN and numerical computation in SNOBOL4.

Modification of Values. Since a variable may change its value through the execution of a program, it is essential that a programming language provide a means for assigning values to variables and for creating new values from old. In most popular languages, this capability is achieved through a form of *assignment statement,* whereby an expression is evaluated according to a precise set of rules to determine a value which is then assigned to a variable. In general, a set of operations exists which can be performed upon variables. These operations may be used with variables and constants to create complex expressions.

For example, consider a programming language where

variables can assume *integer* values. Then the operations of addition, multiplication, subtraction, and division can be used upon integer variables and integer constants to form an expression which has an integer value. Similarly, relational operators, such as < and >, can be used to produce the logical values *true* and *false*. In this way, it becomes possible to combine existing values and variables into expressions to compute new values.

It should be noted, however, that there is a class of languages, generically termed functional programming languages, that have no variables.

Control Structures. The language must also provide a framework for determining the order in which the statements used in a program will be executed. In most programming languages, statements fall into one of two classes: declarative and executable. Declarations provide information about variables, which the language translator uses to allocate storage, define formats for input/output, or other similar functions. Executable statements direct the computational steps and the logical operations of the program.

Many different types of control structures exist within programming languages. The most common structures are deterministic and sequentially oriented; the order of execution of statements is well defined, and the statements are executed in order unless there is a specific command to the contrary (such as a **goto** statement in some languages). Similarly, one normally thinks of a single program as representing a single computation with a single beginning and a single termination. Virtually all languages incorporate such structures. The most common control structures permit sequential and conditional execution of statements and iteration over a group of statements.

However, there is still a broad range of possibilities with regard to control structures. Some experimentation has been done with nondeterministic control structures, in which the order of execution of statements within a group of statements is determined by a random process.

In Ada and many systems programming languages, one program may initiate the execution of another program in parallel. It is possible for the two programs to communicate with one another and to execute concurrently. These features of parallel processing, co-routines, and interprocess communication are valuable in the development of operating systems and other control programs.

A great deal of controversy appears among programming language designers as to the ''best'' set of control structures to provide in a programming language. As with other programming language features, no solution is always best. The choice is highly dependent upon the intended use(s) for the language and the personal preferences of programmers and language designers.

Abstraction. One of the strongest arguments in favor of high level languages is that they provide a more natural notation for the programmer than that of machine language or assembly language. In other words, high level languages provide a degree of support for the way that people think about the solution to problems.

Because many computational procedures are performed repeatedly, it is convenient to collect frequently used statements and give this grouping a name, which can then be used wherever the collection is needed: when the name of the procedure is invoked, the set of statements is executed. Thus, if one develops a procedure for selecting the largest of a set of numbers S, one might then name this sequence of steps MAX. The use of MAX(S) would then find the maximum value from the set S.

Such a capability exists in virtually all modern programming languages. Depending upon the language, this facility for *operator abstraction* is called a procedure, a subroutine, a function, or a macro. In most languages, the programmer is able to associate a set of parameters with the procedure, such as S in MAX(S) above. For example, if there were a set of numbers T, the operation of finding the maximum value of T could be denoted by MAX (T).

In addition to this facility for naming a computation procedure, a number of newer languages, including Ada, CLU, Alphard, Euclid, and PLAIN, have introduced the notion of a *data abstraction*. In a data abstraction, the programmer is able to group together a collection of variables along with the definitions of the operations which may be performed on this group. This notion is discussed further in the section on data types.

The issue of abstraction is critical in programming languages and their design. We want to be able to organize programs into logical units so that it is easy to understand the operation of the program, to isolate parts of the program from other parts, and to permit the use of names and operations that improve the structure and comprehensibility of the program. The amount of support that a programming language gives to the concept of abstraction is an important determinant of the ease with which programs in the language can be written and understood.

Input/Output. Languages must, in general, provide a means for inputting data to a program and reporting the results of a computation. A simple example of such a facility is the use of a card reader for input and the use of a line printer for output. It is often desirable to specify to the program the format of the input data or the desired format for output. Many applications require the production of reports on preprinted forms or data organized into tables, rather than just a chaotic collection of results. Many applications also need to work with data received from different locations. Input may come from a card reader, a terminal, a magnetic tape, a disk unit, or even several devices during one execution of the program. Similarly, output may be sent to several devices. From a programming language standpoint, it is valuable to be able to designate different logical devices (or files), which in turn correspond to physical devices.

Some languages, particularly those used for the development of systems programs, provide little or no input/output capability. Other languages provide elaborate facilities, which permit the programmer to specify precisely the input and output formats for any number of files on any number of physical devices. In some extreme cases, such as report generation languages, the quantity of language features devoted to the description of these files and the execution of input/output operations exceeds the quantity of other features in the language.

Input/output facilities remain among the least understood aspects of programming languages, primarily as a result of the close relationship between the logical input/output operations and the physical devices upon which they operate.

Syntax and Semantics. Most natural languages entail a great deal of ambiguity. While authors of some textbooks may work to be precise and unambiguous, more casual users of language frequently introduce ambiguity. We commonly use sentences that are meaningful only within a given context. For example, we say, ''He's either thirty-two or three.'' Most listeners understand immediately that we *mean* thirty-two or *thirty*-three, although that is not what was actually said. Natural language, particularly in conversation, also usually permits the opportunity to clarify ambiguous statements.

The situation is different with programming languages. A programming language is a notation for describing to the computer the steps required to carry out the solution to a problem. Such notation must be precise and unambiguous. Each construct in the language must have a single interpretation, both syntactically and semantically. This lack of ambiguity not only assists in specifying the sequence of steps to be performed, but also simplifies (or makes possible) the task of writing a translator for the programming language. Experimentation with ambiguous grammars has shown that while it is possible to conceive of an ambiguous programming language, there are some serious theoretical and practical problems.

As a result, programming languages have specific syntactic and semantic rules, generally specified with a formal notation so as to minimize the possibility of misinterpretation or ambiguity. For this reason, the term "programming language" itself is somewhat misleading, since these languages more closely resemble a mathematical notation than a natural language. It is important to keep this distinction between programming languages and natural languages closely in mind.

Evaluation of Programming Languages and Language Features

With the seemingly endless proliferation of programming languages and the availability of numerous language processors on most computer systems, the developer of a program often has the opportunity to select one of several programming languages for use in a given instance. As a result, it is important to gain an understanding of the relative strengths and weaknesses of various languages. In this way, it becomes possible to make a rational judgment as to the merits of one programming language over others.

The developer of a program must weigh many factors when selecting a particular programming language for use in a given application. Among the most important factors are the following:

(1) *Availability*. Language selection is frequently constrained by the programming languages available on a given computer. Few people have the luxury of being able to acquire a new computer simply because it has a translator for a particular language. Similarly, few people will develop a translator for a language on their own machine. In practice, then, the large number of existing languages is quickly reduced to a relatively small number, depending upon the host machine for a given program. In many organizations, this choice is restricted still further by managerial fiat, for reasons of uniformity.

(2) *Uniformity*. Much of the total costs associated with computer software goes into the costs of programmer training and the costs of modifying and maintaining programs over their lifetimes (frequently as much as 10 years). Thus, it is in the best economic interests of many organizations to minimize the number of programming languages used. For every language used, one needs skilled programmers, complete documentation on the language and its translator, and certainty that a processor for that language is available on any new computers acquired by the organization.

(3) *Portability*. One of the principal advantages of high level languages is that they are largely machine-independent. Unlike assembly language, high-level language use does not require knowledge or use of the individual machine instructions. Thus, a potential benefit of high level languages is that a program written in such a language can execute properly on different, incompatible machines with few modifications to the program. This benefit can only be realized, however, if a translator for the language exists on a variety of machines, because the programmer is effectively "locked into" those machines for which an appropriate language processor exists. If a program is to be used for a long period of time, it almost certainly will be used on more than one type of computer system. This factor weighs in favor of those languages which are available on many different kinds of computers.

Along the same lines, standards have been developed and published for some languages, although most implementations of languages deviate, at least to some degree, from the published standards. If portability is to be a consideration in language choice, one must be careful to base the selection of the language on the standard features, rather than upon the (possibly extended) set of features in a given implementation. (For some languages, less than the full standard is implemented, so that it becomes necessary to identify a commonly available subset.)

(4) *Efficiency*. The quality of processors for languages varies widely. When comparing two different languages on two different computers, one often discovers that one language will perform better on one machine while the other will perform better on the second machine. Considerable differences can emerge in space utilization or processing time by the language processor or by the executing program.

For example, one language processor may attempt to optimize the performance of the resulting machine language program, while another does not. The results may be that the optimized program runs significantly faster or utilizes much less primary memory than does the unoptimized program, but the optimizing processor may take much longer to translate the program into machine language. If the program is to be heavily used, while the translator will be rarely used, it is advantageous to have the optimizing feature. On the other hand, if the language processor is to be used primarily for programs under development or for small, (e.g., student) jobs, the optimizing feature is not always desirable.

As noted above, there are two major approaches to construction of a language processor. One is *interpretation,* in which the program is directly executed. The other is *compilation,* in which the program (source code) is translated into machine language (object code); the object code is loaded into primary memory, and the machine language instructions are then executed.

In general, interpreters require less memory than do compilers, not only because the interpreter is smaller, but also because less space is needed for program storage, since the source code can often be stored more compactly than can the corresponding object code. By contrast, however, compiled programs execute far more rapidly than do interpreted programs unless compiled programs are bound by the speed of input/output operations.

Thus, evaluation based on efficiency requires some type of *benchmarking,* an objective evaluation of the performance of the language processor based on some set of sample programs similar in nature to the programs to be developed. Through benchmarking, one can gather information about the relative space requirements, execution speed, and cost elements for different language processors.

(5) *Language features for specific application.* As noted above, different languages are designed for different types of applications. The design objectives are reflected in the various types of values which can be assumed by variables, the kinds of definable data structures, the extent of input/output operations and format capabilities, and so on. FORTRAN, for example, provides a facility for declaring variables to be complex numbers, making FORTRAN a leading candidate for applications involving complex arithmetic. COBOL, as another example, provides a powerful facility for defining record-oriented data, making it a leading candidate for many business data processing uses. APL has an extensive set of operators for vectors and matrices, along with a compact notation, making it a popular choice for array processing applications.

Beyond these more commonly used languages are a whole range of languages specifically designed for applications such as interactive graphics, manufacturing process control, and algebraic manipulation. Their designers tend to regard languages like FORTRAN and PL/I as being too general for these highly specific applications. The special purpose languages have become popular within their limited areas because they provide the programmer with the facility to express the solution to a problem in a notation which is meaningful in terms of the application and because they serve as a means of communication among researchers and workers in those areas. The desire to have languages for specific applications is a major force in the proliferation of new programming languages and a balancing influence against the languages that try to be all things to all people.

(6) *Personal preferences.* Although virtually all experienced programmers have been exposed to more than one language, everyone seems to have a personal favorite. Many factors go into determining these personal preferences, among them three in particular.

First, since a programming language is nothing more than a notation for expressing the solution to a problem, it is a reflection of the way that people think about programming. Many people tend to think so much about their programs in relation to a certain programming language that they begin to think in that programming language.

Second, many people are strong adherents of whatever language they learned first, since it had an overwhelming influence on their programming habits. Even if they now use a variety of other languages, they remain most comfortable with the notation and features of that first language.

Third, people working on a particular application may find a language to be most suitable for problems in that application, again because it provides the best support for the way they think about the problems.

Many other factors, of course, influence personal preferences in programming languages. These factors are generaly quite arbitrary and difficult to measure, but some casual experiments would indicate that, given equal proficiency in a number of languages, people program better in their chosen language than in any other. These different personal preferences and variations in individual thinking patterns balance against the desire for uniformity in programming languages and help assure that there will be ongoing development of new programming languages.

The existence of individual preferences in programming languages greatly complicates the problem of language evaluation. The subjective feelings that a person has about a given language can often outweigh the objective measures in determining a choice of language for a given problem.

Design of Programming Languages

While much of the day-to-day use of programming languages involves issues of evaluation, much of the research and development involves issues of design and implementation of languages despite the abundance of programming languages, with more being designed all the time. The reasons for designing a language are numerous, but can be summed up by the following four typical goals:

(1) Support for a particular application

New application areas are constantly developing. Each of these areas has its own terminology, its own procedures, and its own requirements in computer utilization. There is a strong temptation to invent a new language for such applications rather than to use or adapt an existing language.

(2) Support for programming methodology

The programming language used for an application is only a small part of the total process of software development, which includes definition of program requirements, design of the program structure, testing and verification of the completed program, and maintenance of the program over a period of time. The features of a language play an important role in simplifying or complicating the transformation of the program design into a running program.

Similarly, language features are critical to the process of testing a program and to the determination of whether or not a program meets the specifications developed at the outset of the development effort.

It is only within the past few years that programming languages have been seen in the context of software development. As a result, much experimentation is still being conducted in language design to discover the role of languages in the overall development process and the impact that various languages and language features have on this process. Thus, languages have been designed to support abstraction, to support modularity, to simplify testing and/or verification, to enhance program readability, or to assist with more than one of these objectives. This area is especially active at present and shows no signs of reduced activity yet.

(3) Personal preference

Some people design programming languages for the sake of designing programming languages. The best way to try to develop a tool which meets one's own approach to problem solving is to design one's own language and then implement it. One of the recurring experiences of language designers is that they are never totally pleased with the result of their efforts, since it is necessary to make compromises in the design goals. Most language designers have worked on several languages; some of these design efforts last several years as minor changes are made to preliminary versions of the language based upon programming and implementation experience.

(4) Research into programming language features

A number of problems in language design have not been solved to the complete satisfaction of researchers in the field. Thus, many experimental languages are devised to explore one of these problems, using standard features for most of the language but examining a new approach for a particular language characteristic. By building an entire language around these features, the designer can examine the ways in which the features affect other aspects of the language.

In studying programming languages, one finds it valuable to understand why certain design decisions were made and how those decisions influence other language characteristics or implementation of the language. Major areas of concern in language design include the types of data objects that will be supported, the notation to be used for expressing programs, and the control structures to be used for directing the flow of program execution.

The presentation of languages and language features in this book focus on the related areas of language design and language evaluation. Particular emphasis is given to languages developed over the last decade, beginning with and influenced by Pascal.

Implementation of Programming Languages

While some languages are of interest from a purely theoretical or historical standpoint, much of the work in programming languages is related to such practical issues as good programming style and effective implementation of languages on different machines. Most language designers aspire to see their languages accepted and used by a large number of people; that goal can only be achieved if the language can be made to execute on a variety of different computers (and if the language is effectively promoted by its developers).

Implementation of languages is a very complex topic, involving a number of different steps. A language compiler must perform several different functions, including the following three:

(1) Input of the source code (lexical analysis)

The source code is read and translated to an internal form suitable for additional processing without having to read the actual program code at subsequent stages of the translation process.

(2) Syntax analysis

The internal form of the program is analyzed to determine if the program is written according to the syntactic rules for the language. Errors are noted and some other kinds of checking are performed to verify that the program conforms to certain semantic rules. Another form of intermediate code is produced by this stage.

(3) Code generation and optimization

The intermediate language is transformed into object code for a particular machine. As a rule, the initial code generated by the compiler is very inefficient in its utilization of machine resources. This code is examined and modified so that it will use less space and will execute more rapidly. This process of code optimization can produce object code comparable in quality with that written by competent assembly language programmers.

The problems of language implementation go well beyond the scope of this book. In fact, they require books of their own. However, it is necessary to gain an understanding of some language implementation issues in order to be a successful language designer. Certain language constructs are difficult to implement efficiently, while others present fewer problems. Some languages are designed with characteristics which make language compilation impossible; it is essential to understand the tradeoff between flexibility for the programmer and efficiency for the implementation.

Thus, while the articles in this book concentrate on comparison of language features and on the understanding of programming language design, the subject of implementation is often present as an influential factor in guiding design decisions.

Programming Languages—The First 25 Years

PETER WEGNER

Reprinted from *IEEE Transactions on Computers,* December 1976, pp. 1207-1225.
Copyright © 1976 by The Institute of Electrical and Electronics Engineers, Inc.

Abstract—The programming language field is certainly one of the most important subfields of computer science. It is rich in concepts, theories, and practical developments. The present paper attempts to trace the 25 year development of programming languages by means of a sequence of 30 milestones (languages and concepts) listed in more or less historical order. The first 13 milestones (M1–M13) are largely concerned with specific programming languages of the 1950's and 1960's such as Fortran, Algol 60, Cobol, Lisp, and Snobol 4. The next ten milestones (M14–M23) relate to concepts and theories in the programming language field such as formal language theory, language definition, program verification, semantics and abstraction. The remaining milestones (M24–M30) relate to the software engineering methodology of the 1970's and include a discussion of structured programming and the life cycle concept. This discussion of programming language development is far from complete and there are both practical developments such as special purpose languages and theoretical topics such as the lambda calculus which are not adequately covered. However, it is hoped that the discussion covers the principal concepts and languages in a reasonably nontrivial way and that it captures the sense of excitement and the enormous variety of activity that was characteristic of the programming language field during its first 25 years.

Index Terms—Abstraction, assemblers, Algol, axioms, Cobol, compilers, Fortran, Lisp, modularity, programming languages, semantics, structures programming, syntax, verification.

I. Three Phases of Programming Language Development

THE 25 year development of programming languages may be characterized by three phases corresponding roughly to the 1950's, 1960's, and 1970's. The 1950's were concerned primarily with the *discovery* and *description* of programming language concepts. The 1960's were concerned primarily with the *elaboration* and *analysis* of concepts developed in the 1950's. The 1970's were concerned with the development of an effective software *technology.* As pointed out in [96], the 1950's emphasized the *empirical* approach to the study of programming language concepts, the 1960's emphasized a *mathematical* approach in its attempts to develop theories and generalizations of concepts developed in the 1950's, and the 1970's emphasized an *engineering* approach in its attempt to harness concepts and theories for the development of software technology.

Manuscript received September 3, 1976; revised August 23, 1976. This work was supported in part by the AFOST, the ARO, and the ONR under Contract N00014-76-C-0160.

The author is with the Division of Applied Mathematics, Brown University, Providence, RI 02912.

1950–1960 Discovery and Description

A remarkably large number of the basic concepts of programming languages had been discovered and implemented by 1960. This period includes the development of symbolic assembly languages, macro-assembly languages, Fortran, Algol 60, Cobol, IPL V, Lisp, and Comit [72]. It includes the discovery of many of the basic implementation techniques such as symbol table construction and look-up techniques for assemblers and macro-assemblers, the stack algorithm for evaluating arithmetic expressions, the activation record stack with display technique for keeping track of accessible identifiers during execution of block structure languages, and marking algorithms for garbage collection in languages such as IPL V and Lisp.

This period was one of discovery and description of programming languages and implementation techniques. Programming languages were regarded solely as tools for facilitating the specification of programs rather than as interesting objects of study in their own right. The development of models, abstractions, and theories concerning programming languages was largely a phenomenon of the 1960's.

1961–1969 Elaboration and Analysis

The 1960's were a period of elaboration of programming languages developed in the 1950's and of analysis for the purpose of constructing models and theories of programming languages.

The languages developed in the 1960's include Jovial, PL/I, Simula 67, Algol 68, and Snobol 4. These languages are, each in a different way, elaborations of languages developed in the 1950's. For example, PL/I is an attempt to combine the "good" features of Fortran, Algol, Cobol, and Lisp into a single language. Algol 68 is an attempt to generalize, as systematically and clearly as possible, the language features of Algol 60. Both the attempt to achieve greater richness by synthesis of existing features and the attempt to achieve greater richness by generalization have led to excessively elaborate languages. We have learned that in order to achieve flexibility and power of expression in programming languages we must pay the price of greater complexity. In the 1970's there is a tendency to retrench towards simpler languages like Pascal, even at the price of restricting flexibility and power of expression.

Theoretical work in the 1960's includes many of the basic results of formal languages and automata theory with applications to parsing and compiling [1]. It includes the development of theories of operational and mathematical semantics, of language definition techniques, and of several frameworks for modeling the compilation and execution process [26]. It includes the development of the basic ideas of program correctness and program verification [54].

Although much of the theoretical work started in the 1960's continued into the 1970's, the emphasis on theoretical research as an end in itself is essentially a phenomenon of the 1960's. In the 1970's theoretical research in areas such as program verification is increasingly motivated by practical technological considerations rather than by the "pure research" objective of advancing our understanding independently of any practical payoff.

In the programming language field the pure research of the 1960's tended to emphasize the study of abstract structures such as the lambda calculus or complex structures such as Algol 68. In the 1970's this emphasis on abstraction and elaboration is gradually being replaced by an emphasis on methodologies aimed at improving the technology of programming.

1970–? Technology

During the 1970's emphasis shifted away from "pure research" towards practical management of the environment, not only in computer science but also in other scientific areas. Decreasing hardware costs and increasingly complex software projects created a "complexity barrier" in software development which caused the management of software-hardware complexity to become the primary practical problem in computer science. Research was directed away from the development of powerful new programming languages and general theories of programming language structure towards the development of tools and methodologies for controlling the complexity, cost, and reliability of large programs.

Research emphasized methodologies such as structured programming, module design and specification, and program verification [41]. Attempts to design verifiable languages which support structured programming and modularity are currently being made. Pascal, Clu, Alphard, Modula, and Euclid are examples of such "methodology-oriented languages."

The technological, methodology-oriented approach to language design results in a very different view of what is important in programming language research. Whereas work in the 1960's was aimed at increasing expressive power, work in the 1970's is aimed at constraining expressive power so as to allow better management of the process of constructing large programs from their components. It remains to be seen whether the management of software complexity can be substantially improved by imposing structure, modularity, and verifiability constraints on program construction.

II. MILESTONES, LANGUAGES, AND CONCEPTS

The body of this paper outlines in greater detail some of the principal milestones of programming language development. The milestones include the development of specific programming languages, and the development of implementation techniques, concepts and theories.

The four most important milestones are probably the following ones.

Fortran, which provided an existence proof for higher level languages, and is still one of the most widely used programming languages.

Algol 60, whose clean design and specification served as an inspiration for the development of a discipline of programming languages.

Cobol, which pioneered the development of data description facilities, was adopted as a required language on department of defense computers and has become the most widely used language of the 1970's.

Lisp, whose unique blend of simplicity and power have caused it to become both the most widely used language in artificial intelligence and the starting point for the development of a mathematical theory of computation.

We shall consider about 30 milestones, and use this section as a vehicle for presenting a brief history of the programming language field. The milestones can be split into three groups. Milestones M1–M13 are concerned largely with specific programming languages developed during the 1950's and 1960's. Milestones M14–M23 consider certain conceptual and theoretical programming language notions. Milestones M24–M30 are concerned with programming languages and methodology of the 1970's.

M1—The EDVAC report, 1944 [81]: This report, written by Von Neumann in September 1944, contains the first description of the stored program computers, subsequently called Von Neumann machines. It develops a (one address) machine language for such computers and some examples of programs in this machine language.

M2—Book by Wilkes, Wheeler, and Gill, 1951 [83]: This is the first book on both application software and system software. It discusses subroutines and subroutine linkage, and develops subroutines for a number of applications. It contains a set of "initial orders" which act like a sophisticated loader, performing decimal to binary conversion for operation codes and addresses, and having relative addressing facilities. Thus, the basic idea of using the computer to translate user specified instructions into a considerably different internal representation was already firmly established by 1951.

M3—The development of assemblers, 1950–1960: The term "assembler" was introduced by Wilkes, Wheeler, and Gill [83] to denote a program which assembles a master program with several subroutines into a single run-time program. The meaning of the term was subsequently narrowed to denote a program which translates from symbolic machine language (with symbolic instruction codes and addresses) into an internal machine representation. Early assemblers include Soap, developed for the IBM 650 in the mid 1950's and Sap developed for the IBM 704 in the late 1950's.

The principal phases of the assembly process are as follows:

   1) scanning of input text;
   2) construction of symbolic address symbol table;

3) transliteration of symbolic instruction and address codes;

4) code generation.

The first assemblers were among the most complex and ingeneous programs of their day. However, during the 1960's the writing of assemblers was transformed from an art into a science, so that an assembler may now be regarded as a "simple" program. The development of an implementation technology for assemblers was an essential prerequisite to the development of an implementation technology for compilers.

M4—Macro assemblers, 1955–1965: Macro-assemblers allow the user to define "macro-instructions" by means of macro-definitions and to call them by means of macro-calls. A macro-facility is effectively a language extension mechanism which allows the user to introduce new language forms (macro-calls) and to define the "meaning" of each new language form by a macro-definition.

A macro-assembler may be implemented by generalizing phases 2 and 3 of the previously discussed assembly process. Phase 2 is generalized by construction of an additional symbol table for macro-definitions. Phase 3 is generalized by requiring table look-up not only for symbolic instruction and address codes but also for macro-calls. The table look-up process for macro-calls is no longer simple transliteration, since the determination of a macro-value may involve parameter substitution and nested macro-calls. However, the implementation technology for macro-assemblers may be regarded as an extension and generalization of the implementation technology for assemblers. The seminal paper on macro-assemblers is the paper by McIlroy [54]. A discussion of implementation technology for macro-assemblers is given in [84].

Macro-systems may be generalized by relaxing restrictions on the form of the text generated as a result of a macro-call. Macro-systems which allow the "value" of a macro-call to be an arbitrary string (as opposed to a sequence of machine language instructions) are called macro-generators. Trac [55] is an interesting example of a macro-generator.

Macro-systems may be generalized even further by generalizing the permitted syntax of macro-calls. Waite's Limp system [85] and Leavenworth's syntax macros [52] are early examples of such generalized macro-systems. Macro-systems of this kind are useful for implementing language preprocessors which translate statement forms and abbreviations of an "extended language" into a "strict language" which generally has a smaller vocabulary but is more verbose.

Generalized macro-systems may be implemented by macro-definition tables which are constructed and used in precisely the same way as for macro-assemblers. Generalized macro "values" require more general macro-body specifications in the macro-definition table while more general syntax for macro-calls requires a more sophisticated scanner for recognizing macro-calls in the source language text.

Assembly and macro-languages have been discussed in some detail because they illustrate how a simple language idea (the idea of transliteration) backed up by a simple implementation mechanism (the symbol table) leads to a class of simple languages (symbolic assembly languages) and how progressive generalization of the language idea together with a corresponding generalization of the implementation technology leads to progressively more complex classes of languages. This example is useful also because it illustrates how the language and implementation mechanism for assemblers are related to the language and implementation mechanisms for compilers.

M5—Fortran, 1954–1958 [27]: Fortran is perhaps the single most important milestone in the development of programming languages. It was developed at a time of considerable scepticism concerning the compile-time and run-time efficiency of higher level languages, and its successful implementation provided an existence proof for both the feasibility and the viability of higher level languages. Important language concepts introduced by Fortran include:

variables, expressions and statements (arithmetic and Boolean);

arrays whose maximum size is known at compile-time;

iterative and conditional branching control structures;

independently compiled (nonrecursive) subroutines;

COMMON and EQUIVALENCE statements for data sharing;

FORMAT directed input-output.

Advances of implementation technology developed in connection with Fortran include the stack model of arithmetic expression evaluation.

Fortran was designed around a model of implementation in which run-time storage requirements for programs, data and working storage was known at compile-time so that relative addresses of entities in all subroutines and COMMON data blocks could be assigned at compile-time and converted to absolute addresses at load time.

This model of implementation required the exclusion from the language of arrays with dynamic bounds and recursive subroutines. Thus, Fortran illustrates the principle that the model of implementation in the mind of the language designers may strongly affect the design of the language. Although Fortran is machine independent in the sense that it is independent of the assembly level instruction set of a specific computer, it is machine dependent in the sense that its design is dependent on a virtual machine that constitutes the model of implementation in the mind of the programming language designer.

M6—Algol 60, 1957–1960: Whereas Fortran is the most important practical milestone in programming language development, Algol 60 is perhaps the most important conceptual milestone. Its defining document, known as the Algol report [62], presents a method of language definition which is an enormous advance over previous definition techniques and allows us for the first time to think of a language as an object of study rather than as a tool in problem solution. Language syntax is defined by a variant of the notation of context-free grammars known as Backus–Naur Form (BNF). The semantics of each syntactic language construct is characterized by an English language description of the execution time effect of the construct.

The Algol report generated a great deal of sometimes heated debate concerning obscurities, ambiguities and trouble spots in the language specification. The revised report [63] corrected many of the less controversial anomalies of the original report. Knuth's 1967 paper on "The remaining trouble spots of Algol 60" [44] illustrates the nature of this great programming language debate. The participants in the debate were at first called Algol lawyers and later called Algol theologians.

Important language constructs introduced by Algol 60 include:

block structure;

explicit type declaration for variables;

scope rules for local variables;

dynamic as opposed to static lifetimes for variables;

nested if-then-else expressions and statements;

call by value and call by name for procedure parameters;

recursive subroutines;

arrays with dynamic bounds.

Algol 60 is carefully designed around a model of implementation in which storage allocation for expression evaluation, block entry and exit and procedure entry and exit can be performed in a single run-time stack. Dijkstra developed an implementation of Algol 60 as early as the fall of 1960 based on this simple model of implementation [23]. However, this semantic model of implementation was implicit rather than explicit in the Algol report. Failure to understand the model led to a widespread view that Algol 60 required a high price in run-time overhead, and to an exaggerated view of the difficulty of implementing Algol 60. An explicit account of the model of implementation is given in [69].

Algol 60 is a good example of a language which becomes semantically very simple if we have the right model of implementation but appears to be semantically complex if we have the wrong model of implementation. The model of implementation is more permissive than Fortran with regard to run-time storage allocation, and can handle arrays with dynamic bounds and recursive procedures. However, it cannot handle certain other language features such as assignment of pointers to pointer valued variables and procedures which return procedures as their result. These language features are accordingly excluded from Algol 60, illustrating again the influence of the model of implementation on the source language.

The Algol 60 notion of block structure quickly became the accepted canonical programming language design folklore and, in spite of its merits, excercised an inhibiting influence on programming language designers during the 1960's. Viewed from the vantage point of the 1970's it appears that nested scope rules for accessibility of identifiers and nested lifetime rules for existence of data structures may be too restrictive a basis for specifying modules and module interconnections in programming languages of the future. Alternatives to block structures are discussed in the sections on Simula 67, Snobol 4, and APL.

M7—Cobol 61, 1959–1961 [12]: Cobol represents the culmination and synthesis of several different projects for the development of business data processing languages, the first of which (flowmatic) was started in the early 1950's by Hopper. See [72] for an account of this development. Important language constructs introduced by Cobol include:

explicit distinction between identification division, environment division, data division, and procedure division;

natural language style of programming;

record data structures;

file description and manipulation facilities.

The two principal contributions of Cobol are its natural language programming style and its greater emphasis on data description. Natural language programming style makes programs more readable (by executives) but does not enhance writability or the ability to find errors. It constitutes a cosmetic change of syntax, sometimes referred to as "syntactic sugaring." It has not been widely adopted in subsequent programming languages but may possibly come into its own if and when the use of computers becomes commonplace in the home and in other nontechnical environments.

The contribution of Cobol to programming language development is probably greater in the area of data description than in the area of natural language programming. By introducing an explicit data division for data description to parallel a procedure division for procedure description Cobol factors out the data description problem as being of equal importance and visibility as the procedure description problem.

The significance of Cobol was greatly enhanced when it was chosen as a required language on DOD computers. Cobol was one of the earliest languages to be standardized, and has provided valuable experience (both positive and negative) concerning the creation and maintenance of programming language standards. It is currently used by more programmers than any other programming language.

Why is it that Cobol, in spite of certain defects in its procedure division, has become the most widely used language among commercial, industrial and government programmers? One reason is perhaps that standardization carries with it advantages that make the use of an imperfect standard more desirable than a more perfect but possibly more volatile alternative. Another perhaps more important reason may be that the advantages of Cobol's powerful facilities in its data division outweigh its imperfections in the procedure division, making it more suitable than languages like Fortran in the large number of medium and large scale data processing applications in business, industry and government. Cobol was behind the state of the art in its procedure division facilities but ahead of the state of the art in its data division facilities. The attractiveness of a language for data processing problems does not appear to depend as critically on its procedure description facilities as on its data description facilities.

M8—PL/I, 1964–1969 [67]: Fortran, Algol 60, and Cobol 61 may be regarded as the three principal first generation higher level languages, while PL/I and Algol 68 may be regarded as the two principal second generation higher level languages. PL/I was developed as a synthesis of Fortran, Algol 60, and Cobol, taking over its expression and statement syntax from Fortran, block structure and type declaration from Algol 60, and data description facilities from Cobol. Additional language features include the following:

programmer defined exception conditions (the ON statement);

based variables (pointers and list processing);

static, automatic and controlled storage;

external (independently compiled) procedures;

multitasking.

PL/I illustrates both the advantages and the problems of developing a rich general purpose language by synthesis of features of existing languages. One of the lessons learned was that greater richness and power of expression led to greater complexity both in language definition and in language use. PL/I is a language in which programming is relatively easy once the language has been mastered, but in which verifiability and subsequent readability of programs may present a problem. Any language definition of PL/I is so complex that its use for the informal or formal verification of correctness for specific programs is intractable.

M9—Algol 68, 1963–1969 [82]: Whereas PL/I was developed by synthesis of the features of a number of existing languages, Algol 68 was developed by systematic generalization of the features of a single language, namely Algol 60. The language contains a relatively small number of "orthogonal" language concepts. The power of the language is obtained by minimizing the restrictions on how features of the language may be combined. Interesting language features of Algol 68 include:

a powerful mechanism for building up composite modes from the five primitive modes *int, real, bool, char, format*;

identity declarations;

pointer values, structures, etc;

carefully designed coercion from one mode to another;

a parallel programming facility.

The generality of the language can be illustrated by considering the mode (type) mechanism. Composite modes can be built up from modes m,n by the mode construction operators [ ] m (multiples), *struct* (m,n) (structures), *proc* $(m)n$ (procedures), *ref* m (references) and *union* (m,n) (unions). Any mode constructed in this way may itself be the "operand" of a further mode construction operator as in *struct* ([ ] *ref* m, *proc* (*ref ref* m) *ref* n). Thus, an infinite number of different modes can be constructed from the primitive ones. Each definable mode has a set of values which must be manipulatable by the assignment operator and other applicable operators. Procedures may have any definable mode as a parameter, so that there must be provision for passing of parameters in any definable mode. The above discussion illustrates how generality in Algol 68 is obtained by starting from a small set of orthogonal concepts (the primitive modes and mode construction operators) and generating a very rich class of objects (modes and mode values) by simply removing all restrictions on the manner of composition.

The defining document for Algol 68 (Algol 68 report) [80], is an important example of a high quality language definition, using a powerful syntactic notation for expressing syntax and semiformal English for expressing semantics. However, the report introduces its own syntactic and semantic terminology and can be read only after a considerable investment of time and effort. The reader must become familiar with syntactic terms such as "notion," "metanotion," and "protonotion," and with semantic terms such as "elaboration," "unit," "closed clause," and "identity declaration."

Algol 68 has not been widely accepted by the programming language community in part because of the lack of adequate implementation and user manuals. However, an ultimately more important reason appears to be that the language constructs of Algol 68 are too general and flexible to be readily assimilated and used by the applications programmer.

M10—Simula 67 1965–1967 [17]: Simula 67 is a milestone in the development of programming languages because it contains an important generalization of the notion of a block, which is called a *class.* A Simula class, just like an Algol block, consists of a set of procedure and data declarations followed by a sequence of executable statements enclosed in begin-end parentheses. However, Simula has a "class" data type and allows the assignment of instances of classes to class-valued variables. Whereas local procedures and data structures of a block are created on entry to the block and disappear on exit from a block, local objects of a class (declared in its outer block) remain in existence independently of whether the class body is being executed as long as the variable to which the instance of the class has been assigned as a value remains in existence.

Classes may function as *coroutines* with interleaved execution of executable instructions of two or more class bodies. Execution of a command "resume C_2" in class C_1 causes the current state of execution of C_1 to be saved followed by transfer of control to the current point of execution of C_2.

The separation between class creation and class execution allows data structures in a class to endure between instances of execution and makes the class more useful than the block as a modeling tool for inventory control systems, operating system modules, data types and other entities which may be characterized by a data structure representing the "current state" and a set of operations for querying and updating the current state.

The usefulness of classes in modeling is enhanced even further by Simula conventions concerning the accessibility of local procedure and data declarations in a class.

If an instance of the class C has been assigned to the variable X, then the local identifier I of this instance of the class C can be accessed as $X \cdot I$. The ability to access local identifiers of a class in this way has both advantages (direct access to class attributes) and disadvantages (not enough control over restricting communication between system modules).

The *subclass* mechanism of Simula 67 allows the procedure and data declarations of a class C to become part of the environment of the class B by means of the declaration "*C class B*." If we think of the procedure and data declarations of a class as its set of attributes, then "*C class B*" causes B to have all the attributes of C plus any additional attributes local to B. B is called a subclass of C since it is the subset of C which has the attributes of B in addition to those of C.

The subclass mechanism is a very effective language extension mechanism. It has been used by the Simula 67 designers to design hierarchies of environments for Simula 67 users. Perhaps the best known of these environments is the simulation environment, which is created by first creating a list processing class containing a set of useful list processing procedures, and then defining a subclass simulation which uses list processing procedures to implement simulation primitives. Thus, Simula is not inherently a simulation language but merely a language which may easily be adapted to simulation by language extension.

A Simula class is a better primitive module for modeling objects or concepts than the Algol procedure because of its ability to remember its data state between instances of execution. It has been used as a starting point for the development of a notion of modularity appropriate to modular programming languages of the 1970's.

M11—IPL V, 1954–1958 [65]: IPL V is a list processing language developed specifically for the solutions of problems in artificial intelligence. It was widely used in the 1950's and 1960's for the programming artificial intelligence applications in areas such as chess, automatic theorem proving and general problem solving.

IPL V has primitive instructions for creating and manipulating list data structures. It is an assembly level list processing language with a $1 + 1$ address code (the first address names an operand and the second address names the next instruction). Both programs and data are represented by lists. There are a number of system cells with reserved names, such as a communication cell for communicating system parameters, a subroutine call stack and a free storage list cell. A large number (over 100) of system defined subroutines (processes) are available to aid the user. The semantics of IPL V instructions is specified by defining an instruction interpreter for IPL V instructions.

IPL V was an important milestone both because it was widely used for a period of over ten years by an important segment of the artificial intelligence community and because it pioneered many of the basic concepts of list processing. For example, the notion of a free storage list serving as a source for storage allocation and as a sink to which cells no longer needed are returned was pioneered in IPL V. IPL V may well have been the first language to define its instructions by a software specified instruction execution cycle (virtual machine).

M12—Lisp, 1959–1960 [56]: Lisp, like IPL V, was developed for the solution of problems in artificial intelligence. However, Lisp may be thought of as a higher level (as opposed to machine level) programming language.

Lisp has two primitive data types referred to as lists and atoms. It has the following simple but powerful set of primitive operations.

A *constructor cons*$[x;y]$ for constructing a composite list from components x and y.

Two *selectors car*$[x]$, *cdr*$[x]$ for, respectively, selecting the first component and remainder of the list.

Two predicates atom$[x]$, eq$[x;y]$ which, respectively, test whether x is an atom and whether two atoms x and y are identical.

A compound conditional of the form $[p_1 \rightarrow a_1; p_2 \rightarrow a_2; \cdots ; p_n \rightarrow a_n]$ which may be read as "*if p_1 then a_1 else if p_2 then a_2 $\cdots$ else if p_n then a_n*" and results in execution of the action a_i corresponding to the first true predicate p_i. Binding operators *lambda*$[x;f]$ and *label*$[x;f]$ which bind free instances of x in f so that they, respectively, denote function arguments and recursive function calls.

The set of primitive Lisp operations have been enumerated explicitly because they exhibit in the simplest terms the essential operators in a nonnumerical processing language. Every nonnumerical processing language must contain constructors for constructing composite structures from their components, selectors for selecting components of composite structures and predicates which permit conditional branching determined by the "value" of the arguments. The compound conditional is a very attractive control structure which was first developed for Lisp and later incorporated into Algol 60. The Lisp binding operators (lambda and label) provide a mechanism for handling functions which have functions as arguments as in the lambda calculus.

Lisp is sufficiently simple to permit the development of a relatively tractable mathematical model. McCarthy used this model as a starting point for the development of a mathematical theory of computation [57]. He considered many of the basic theoretical programming language issues such as mathematical semantics, proofs of program correctness (including compiler correctness) and proofs of program equivalence (by recursion induction) several years before they were considered by anyone else.

McCarthy also developed a definition of Lisp by means of a Lisp interpreter (the APPLY function) which, given an arbitrary Lisp program P with its data D executes the program P with data D. The Lisp APPLY function demonstrated as early as 1960 the technique of defining a programming language L by an interpreter written either in L or in some language definition language. It became the starting point for the subsequent development of theories of operational semantics [95], and for the development of interpreter based language definition languages such as VDL [49].

Lisp contributed a great deal to our understanding of programming language theory. It is also the most influential and widely used artificial intelligence language, its popularity being due in no small measure to its unique blend of simplicity and power. Lisp is certainly among the most important milestones in the development of programming languages.

M13—Snobol 4 1962–1967 [32]: During the 1950's it was felt that mechanical translation and other glamorous language understanding tasks could be greatly facilitated by the development of string manipulation languages with special purpose linguistic transformation aids. The Comit language [99] was developed for this purpose during the period 1957–1961. Comit was a good linguists language with many special purpose linguistic transformation features, but is not a clean programming language because it does not have string-valued variables to which strings may be assigned as values. The deficiencies of Comit led to the development of Snobol 4 during 1962–1967.

Snobol 4 has data values of the type—integer, real, string and pattern, as well as programmer defined data types. However, Snobol 4 has no block structure or declarations. A given variable, say X, may take on string values, numerical values or pattern values at different points of execution. The data type is carried along as part of the Snobol 4 data value and is checked dynamically at execution time to determine whether it is compatible with the operation that is to be applied to it. Dynamic type checking runs counter to the philosophy of static type checking in conventional block structure languages. It introduces additional run-time overhead and increases the proportion of programming errors that will not be discovered until execution time. However, introduction of block structure and explicit type declarations into Snobol 4 would totally change its character, and it is not clear that such a change would be for the better.

The most important programming language contribution of Snobol 4 is the pattern data type. A pattern is an ordered (finite or infinite) set of strings (and string attributes). Snobol 4 has pattern construction operators for constructing composite patterns from their constituents, pattern valued functions, and pattern matching operations which determine if a string S is an instance of the pattern P. The pattern matching process may be extremely complex involving the matching of a sequence of subpatterns, back-tracking if a partial match of subpatterns cannot be completed into a complete match, and possible side effects during pattern matching caused by assignments triggered by subpattern matching. The development of Snobol 4 has considerably advanced both our theoretical understanding of the nature of one dimensional (string) patterns and our ability to manipulate such patterns. A good theoretical discussion of Snobol 4 patterns is given by Gimpel [33].

Another nice feature of Snobol 4 is its programmer defined data types facility which allows selector names for each field of a structured data type to be easily defined. The mechanisms for defining, creating and manipulating data types are greatly simplified because no explicit type information need be specified in the program.

The use of the Snobol 4 data definition mechanism in defining and using Lisp data structures will be briefly illustrated. The data type definition "DATA('CONS-(CAR,CDR)')" defines a new data type called CONS with two subfields called CAR and CDR. The assignment statement "X = CONS('A', 'NIL')" constructs an initialized instance of this data structure and assigns it to X. The expression "CAR(X)" selects the first subfield "A" of the data structure assigned to X. The naturalness of Snobol 4 for specifying nested construction and selection for programmer defined data structures is illustrated by the assignment statement "Y = CONS('B', CONS('A', 'NIL'))" and the expression "CAR(CDR(Y))" which retrieves the CAR subfield of the CDR subfield of Y (which happens again to be the element "A").

Although Snobol 4 is a relatively rich and complex language its implementation appears to be an order of magnitude simpler than PL/I or Algol 68. In order to increase portability of the language, it has been defined in terms of a relatively machine-independent macro-language, and can be implemented on a new machine simply by implementing the macro-language. An efficient compiler—the Spitbol compiler [18]—makes Snobol 4 competitive for a wide range of nonnumerical programming problems.

M14—Language theory, 1948–1962: Whereas milestones M1–M13 were concerned largely with the development of programming languages, milestones M14–M23 will be concerned with concepts and theories in the programming language field. The topics to be considered include language theory, models of implementation, language definition, program verification, semantics and abstraction. The starting point both historically and conceptually, is the development of language theory.

Both natural languages and programming languages are mechanisms for the communication of messages from a "sender" or "generator" to a "receiver" or "recognizer."

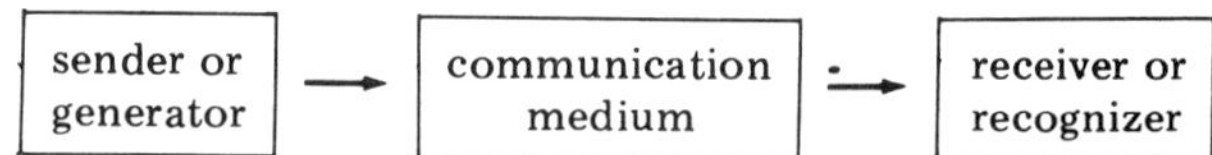

This model of communication was used by Shannon in the late 1940's in developing a mathematical theory of communication [73]. It was used in the late 1950's by linguists and psychologists, such as Chomsky and Miller [16], in the development of a theory of natural languages. In the field of computer science, the great success of the generative (context-free grammar) definition of Algol 60 [63] led to the generative specification of language syntax for all subsequent programming languages, and to the systematic use of recognizers (finite automata and pushdown automata) in implementing translators and interpreters.

The study of natural languages concerns itself with the study of *mental* mechanisms that allow *human* senders and receivers to generate and comprehend a potentially infinite class of sentences after having encountered and learned only a small finite subset of the set of all possible sentences in a language. The study of computer languages is similarly concerned with finite structures that allow languages with an infinite number of sentences to be defined. However, in the case of computer languages, we are not restricted to the study of preexisting human mental mechanisms, but can create language generating and recognition mechanisms with nice mathematical and computational properties. The language generating mechanisms are called *grammars* while the language recognition mechanisms are called *automata.*

One of the most important results in language theory is due to Chomsky, who defined a hierarchy of grammars (type 0, 1, 2, 3 grammars) and a hierarchy of automata (Turing machines, linear bounded automata, pushdown automata, finite automata) and proved the following remarkable four-part result concerning the equivalence of language generating power of grammars and language recognition power of automata.

1) A language L can be generated by a type 0 (unrestricted) grammar iff it can be recognized by a Turing machine.

2) A language L can be generated by a type 1 (context-sensitive) grammar if it can be recognized by a linear bounded automaton.

3) A language L can be generated by a type 2 (context-free) grammar iff it can be recognized by a pushdown automaton.

4) A language L can be generated by a type 3 (finite-state) grammar iff it can be recognized by a finite automaton.

Proof of the above result provides a number of interesting insights concerning the relation between the processes of language generation and language recognition. Moreover, the four part hierarchy allows us to distinguish between type 0 and type 1 grammars and automata, which are primarily of theoretical interest, and type 2 and type 3 grammars and automata, which are occasionally useful in compiler construction. Much of the practical work in language theory is concerned with the characterization and study of subclasses of type 2 and type 3 grammars and automata.

M15—Compiler technology and theory 1960–1970: The notion of a compiler was developed in the early and mid 1950's by Hopper, the developers of Fortran and many others. By the early 1960's the notion that compiling was a three phase process consisting of lexical analysis, parsing and code generation had been firmly established. During the 1960's there was a great deal of both practical and theoretical work on the mechanization of lexical analysis and parsing [28]. Lexical analysis was modeled by finite automata while parsing was modeled by various subclasses of context-free grammars, such as precedence grammars, $LR(k)$ grammars and $LL(k)$ grammars. The mechanization of code generation proved to be more difficult because it was target language dependent but there was some progress in this area also. The cost of building compilers of given complexity decreased considerably in the 1960's as our understanding of compiler structure increased. In the late 1960's and 1970's there was considerable work on program optimization using techniques such as interval analysis for analyzing the flowchart of a program. The state of the art in compiler technology and theory is ably summarized in [1].

M16—Compiler Compilers: Since there is a lot of similarity between compilers for different languages, the notion was developed of a program which, when primed with the syntactic and semantic specification of a given programming language L, would create a compiler for the programming language L. This concept led to interesting work on specifying the compiler-oriented semantics of programming languages by rules for translating source language constituents into the target language. However, the creation of a working compiler compiler which could actually be used in the production of compilers for new languages or new target machines proved to be too ambitious, because the complexity and diversity of languages and machines is simply too great to permit automation. The purely syntactic task of creating an efficient automatic parser from a BNF syntax specification of a language is possible for certain restricted classes of grammars such as precedence grammars, but becomes unmanageable for more ambitious classes of grammars such as $LR(k)$ grammars because of the difficulty of automatically constructing the tables required for automatic parsing. The automation of compiler semantics is even more difficult than the automation of parsing. The best documented example of a compiler compiler (compiler generator) is probably [58].

M17—Models of implementation, interpreters, 1965–1971: Programming languages such as Fortran and Algol 60 have a lot of "surface complexity" but derive their "integrity" from a simple underlying model of implementation, which specifies how programs are to be executed. A model of implementation is a programming language interpreter rather than a compiler. In the early 1960's compiler models of programming languages were emphasized because compiler construction was a pressing technological problem. By the late 1960's it was realized that interpreter models captured the important characteristics of programming languages much more directly than compiler models, so that serious students of programming language structure discarded compiler models in favor of interpreter models.

Fortran is based on a model in which subroutines and COMMON storage areas occupy fixed size blocks, each object is characterized by a relative address relative to the beginning of its block, and no storage allocation is performed during execution. This model gives rise to language restrictions against arrays with dynamic bounds and recursive subroutines.

Algol 60 is based on an activation record stack model of implementation [84] which can handle recursive procedures and arrays with dynamic bounds but cannot handle pointer-valued variables or procedures which return procedures as their values. Algol 68 can be clearly modeled by a run-time environment with two stacks and one heap [86]. Simula 67 requires each created instance of a class to be modeled by a stack. PL/I has no clean model of implementation, and its lack of integrity may be due precisely to the fact that the language designers were more concerned with the synthesis of source language features than with the development of an underlying model of implementation.

The notion of a model of implementation is important because it pinpoints the simple starting point from which the apparent complexity of a programming language is derived. Man is inherently incapable of handling or manipulating great complexity so it stands to reason that there is some simple internalized model that is used as a starting point for designing complex structures such as programming languages. It is argued here that the simple starting point for developing a complex programming language may well be a model of implementation in the mind of the designer.

The 1971 conference on data structures in programming languages [26] contained several papers on models of implementation including a paper on the contour model by Johnston [42], a paper on the B 6700 by Organick and Cleary [66], and a paper on data structure models in programming languages by Wegner [87].

Wegner [86] proposed a class of models called information structure models for characterizing models of implementation by their execution time states and state transitions. An information structure model is a triple $M = (I,I^0,F)$ where I is a set of states $I^0 \subseteq I$ is a set of initial states and F is a state transition function which specifies how a state S can be transformed into a new state S' by the execution of an instruction. A computation in an information structure model is a sequence $S_0 \rightarrow S_1 \rightarrow S_2 \rightarrow \cdots$ where $S_0 \in I^0$ and S_{i+1} is otained from S_i by the execution of an instruction (state transition).

The Lisp APPLY function and the Vienna definition language, discussed in the next section, can be characterized very naturally by information structure models.

Specific assumptions about the structure of the state I and the state transition function F give rise to specific models of implementation. For example states of a Turing machine may be described in terms of three components (t,q,i) where t is the current tape content, q is the current state, and i is the position of the input head. Finite automata are distinguished from Turing machines by the fact that the state transition function F cannot modify the tape component. Pushdown automata have an additional state component called a pushdown tape with characteristic transformation properties.

Programming languages have more complex states and state transitions than automata but may generally be characterized by states with three components (P,C,D) where P is a program component, C is a control component, and D is a data component. Programming languages may be classified in terms of attributes of the P,C,D, components associated with models of implementation. For example the model of implementation of Algol 60 assumes an invariant (reentrant) program component P, a control component C consisting of an instruction pointer ip and an environment pointer ep, and a data component D which is an activation record stack. Fortran does not require P to be reentrant, but requires the size of P,C, and D to be fixed prior to execution.

Information structure models provide a very natural framework for describing programming languages and systems operationally in terms of a specific, possibly abstract, model of implementation. This approach goes against the conventional view that higher level languages should be defined in an implementation-independent way. However, implementation-dependent models reflect the fact that programming-language designers and system programmers think in implementation-dependent ways about programming languages. Implementation-dependent models are therefore valid and important for language designers and system programmers, while implementation independent models are important in other contexts such as program verification.

M18—Language definition, 1960–1970: It is convenient to distinguish between interpreter-oriented language definitions which define the meaning of programs and program constituents in terms of their execution-time effect and compiler-oriented language definitions which define the meaning of source programs in terms of compiled target programs of a target language.

The Algol report is an example of an early (1960) interpreter-oriented language definition with verbal definitions of the meaning of source program constituents. The Lisp APPLY function is an interpreter-oriented language definition in which the execution time effect of source language constructs is rigorously specified by a program.

During the 1960's the interest in compiler technology gave rise to a number of compiler-oriented definitions such as the definition of Euler [89]. Feldman and Gries [28] includes a good review of compiler-oriented language definitions. Knuth [43] proposed an interesting compiler-oriented method of defining the semantics of context-free grammars by associating inherited and synthesized attributes with each vertex of the parse tree of language strings.

During the late 1960's interpreter-oriented definitions of programming languages came back into fashion. The Algol 68 report [80] uses a powerful syntactic notation (VWF notation) to define syntax and semiformal English to define interpreter-oriented semantics. The Vienna definition language [48], [86] is an extension of the Lisp APPLY function definition technique which allows complex languages like PL/I to be defined in terms of an execution-time interpreter.

The Vienna definition language is probably the most practical of the above-mentioned language definition mechanisms. However, it requires approximately 400 pages of "programs" to define PL/I and about 50 pages to define Algol 60. The work on language definition suggests that languages like PL/I are inherently complex in the sense that there simply is no simple way of defining them.

Programming language definitions are intended to serve at least the following two purposes.

1) As a specification of "correctness" for the language implementer.

2) As a specification of "correctness" for the user who wishes to determine whether a program performs its intended task.

The language definition of Algol 60 served as an important frame of reference for a spirited discussion of ambiguities and trouble spots [44]. It was sufficiently precise to serve as an informal tool in checking implementation correctness and program correctness, but was of little help in developing formal methods of program verification. Tools for specifying formal (axiomatic) models of programming languages were developed in the late 1960's and led to an intensive effort in the 1970's to develop tractable formal language definition models [37], [71].

It is important that programming languages of the future have tractable formal language definitions so that program correctness can be formally determined. One of the objectives of programming language design in the 1970's is "simplicity" where simplicity is increasingly defined in terms of ease of developing a formal definition.

M19—Program correctness, 1963–1969: A program is said to be correct if it correctly performs a designated task (computes a designated function). A program may be thought of as a "how" specification and the designated task or function as an associated "what" specification. A correctness demonstration is a demonstration that the how specification determined by the program is a realization (implementation) of the independently given what specification.

Program correctness was considered by McCarthy (1962) [57], Naur (1965) [64], Dijkstra (1966) [19], Floyd (1967) [29] and Hoare (1969) [36]. Floyd developed the axiomatic approach to program correctness which specifies axioms for primitive program statements and a rule of inference for statement composition. Input-output relations of composite programs may be derived as theorems from input-output relations for primitive statements using the rule of inference for statement composition.

Hoare [36] developed a linear notation for the Floyd formalism. Both axioms and theorems have the form $\{P\}S\{Q\}$ where S is a program statement, P is a precondition, and Q is a post condition. Hoare stated axioms for assignment statements, if-then-else statements and while statements, thus producing a formal system sufficient to prove theorems for programs written in a strict structured programming style. Subsequently, Hoare, together with Wirth, developed a formal definition of Pascal [37] which has been widely used as a starting point for correctness proofs by research workers in program verification.

The axiomatic approach has been widely used for proving the correctness of "small" programs [50], but there are some unresolved problems which prevent its being used as a standard tool for program verification in a production environment. One of the principal limitations of correctness proof techniques is that such techniques are applicable only when the what specification of a program can be given in a simple functional form. The majority of large problems have intractable what specifications (requirements specifications) which may be several hundred pages long, and constantly changing. Thus, it may turn out that formal correctness proofs are simply not applicable to "real" problems, being applicable only to "toy" problems with simple functional what specifications.

M20—Verification, testing and symbolic execution: Program verification may be regarded as an ambitious attempt to prove the correctness of program execution for *all* elements of an infinite input domain and may be contrasted with program testing which is concerned with establishing correctness for individual elements of the input domain. Program correctness for subsets of the input domain may be established by a technique called symbolic execution which is intermediate in generality between program verification and program testing.

The concept of symbolic execution arrived on the scene relatively late and was first publicly presented in 1975 at the international conference on reliable software [41] in papers by King [47] and Boyer, Elspas, and Levitt [6]. It involves the tracing of execution paths of a program with symbolic values of program variables. The set of all execution paths of a program may be thought of as a (possibly infinite) execution tree. Terminal nodes of the tree represent completed execution paths. When a terminal node is reached during symbolic execution then symbolic relations between input and output values for that terminal node are available and program correctness (or incorrectness) can be determined for the subset of values of the input domain which cause the particular execution path to be executed.

Symbolic execution is marginally easier than complete program verification because it is unnecessary to determine loop invariants of program loops. However, other problems which arise in program verification such as the algebraic simplification of algebraic expressions along an execution path are, if anything, more acute because "unfolding" of loops in symbolic execution requires longer sequences of algebraic transformations to be handled. The problem of keeping track of the input domain associated with an execution path is also very difficult. The difficulty of this problem is illustrated by the fact that the "emptiness problem" for execution paths is undecidable. That is, we cannot in general determine whether the input domain associated with a given execution path is empty.

Program testing for a particular value of the input domain is clearly easier than symbolic execution or complete verification since it only involves running the program for the particular input value. However, the key problem in testing is to determine "good" test cases by means of a test data selection criterion.

We may think of a "good" test case as a representative of an equivalence class of "similar" data values with the property that correct execution of the test case increases our confidence in the correctness of the program for all data elements in the equivalence class. If we can partition the input domain into a finite, relatively small, number of such equivalence classes then testing of the program for one element of each equivalence class should increase our level of confidence in the correctness of the complete program.

A number of alternative criteria may be used for determining such equivalence classes. For example the set of all data values associated with a given control path is an example of such an equivalence class. Alternatively, we may directly partition the input domain into input equivalence classes (such as large, medium, and small). Equivalence classes based on the internal program structure which systematically select test cases to exercise all control paths are on the whole more effective than arbitrary equivalence classes imposed on the input domain.

Test data selection criteria can be developed by *program*

structure analysis (control path analysis) *operational profile analysis* (classification of inputs by expected frequency of use) and *error analysis* (testing for specific kinds of errors). The papers by Goodenough and Gerhardt [35], Brown and Lipow [7], and Schneiderwind [74], all presented at the International Conference on Reliable Software [41], illustrate these three approaches to test data selection.

M21—Program verification, program synthesis and semantic definition [98]: Program verification is the process of verifying that a given program Prog correctly performs the task specified by a predicate P. If we are given axioms of the form $\{Q\}S\{P\}$ for a set of primitive statement types and an axiom for statement composition then verification that a program Prog correctly performs the task P requires us to prove the theorem $\{true\}\text{Prog}\{P\}$. That is, the postcondition P for the program Prog implies the precondition *true*.

In the case of program synthesis, we are given a specification of a task P and are required to find a program Prog that correctly performs the task. Program synthesis clearly involves program verification of the synthesized program P as a subtask. However, verification need be performed only for the class of programs which can be synthesized and not for all possible programs of a programming language. Systematic (or automatic) program synthesis avoids unnecessary complexity resulting from bad programming and might actually turn out to be easier than the development of a general purpose verifier for both good and bad programs.

The object of program synthesis is to convert a static description P of what is to be computed into a dynamic description Prog of how it is computed. This can be done in a structured way by the stepwise introduction of dynamic features into the static description. At each step one or more statically defined components is expanded into a structure composed of dynamically defined components which may have inner statically defined components as parameters. A structured development of a program Prog from a specification P consists of a sequence $P_0, P_1, \cdots, P_n$ of successively more dynamic descriptions of P where $P_0 = P, P_n = \text{Prog}$ and P_{i+1} is obtained from P_i by "expanding" a component of P_i into a more dynamic form. A formal system such as Hoare [36] may be used to prove that P_{i+1} realizes P if P_i realizes P. Examples of this approach are given by Manna [59], Wirth [90] and Mills [60].

A semantic definition of a programming language L is a mechanism which, given an arbitrary program Prog $\in L$, defines the "meaning" of the program. If the task specification P for a program Prog is taken to be the meaning of Prog, then the semantic definition supplies P given Prog and may be regarded as an inverse process to program synthesis (which supplies Prog given P).

It is very reasonable to think of the input-output predicate P as the meaning of program Prog whenever Prog determines a well defined input-output relation. Unfortunately, there are programs (with an undecidable halting problem) which have no associated input-output predicate

P and therefore would have no "meaning" using this notion semantics. Since a semantic definition of a programming language L should associate a meaning with *all* programs of the programming language, this method of assigning meaning is not altogether satisfactory. The set of meanings expressible by input-output predicates P is restricted to the set of recursive functions while the set of meanings expressible by programs is the richer set of recursively enumerable functions.

Floyd [29] called his seminal paper or program verification "Assigning Meaning to Programs," implying that a formal system for program verification also provides a framework for program semantics. It is often convenient for practical purposes to think of the meaning of a program Prog as its input-output predicate. However, input-output semantics determined by axiomatic models is incomplete because the domain of meanings is not sufficiently rich to express the meaning of all programs. In order to achieve completeness, mathematically more sophisticated semantic theories such as those of Scott [71], [80] must be used which map programs into partial recursive functions rather than total recursive functions.

M22—Semantic models: In order to clarify the notion of semantics, it is convenient to introduce the notion of a semantic model as a triple $M = (E, D, \phi)$ where E is a syntactic domain (of programs) D is a semantic domain of denotations and ϕ is a semantic mapping function which maps elements $e \in E$ of the syntactic domain into their denotations $\phi(e) \in D$.

Semantic models for programming languages may be classified in terms of the nature of the domain D of denotations. In particular it is convenient to distinguish between compiler models in which the semantic domain D is a set of programs in a target language, interpreter models in which the meaning of a program is defined in terms of the computations to which it gives rise, and mathematical models in which the meaning of a program is defined in terms of the mathematical function it denotes. Mathematical models may in turn be subdivided into axiomatic models which restrict the semantic domain to total functions and specify functions by a relation between a precondition (inputs) and a post condition (outputs), and functional models (such as those of Scott [71]) in which the meaning of a program is given by an abstract (partial recursive) function. The relation among these models is given by the following figure:

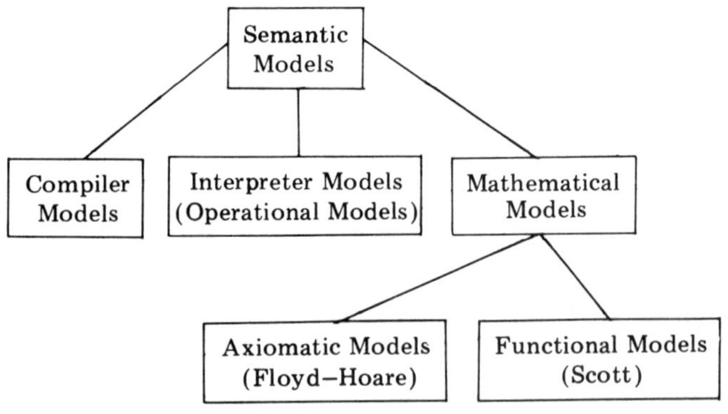

The above discussion makes it clear that the semantics (meaning) of a program is not an absolute (platonic) notion but rather a relative notion which depends on the context of discourse. When we are concerned with compiling, it is natural to think in terms of a compiler oriented semantics for programs. When we are concerned with the process of execution, it is natural to make use of an interpreter oriented semantics. When we are concerned with program verification, then axiomatic semantics is appropriate. When programs are regarded as abstract mathematical objects then the functional semantics of Scott is appropriate.

Each group of semantic models has given rise to a subculture of computer science with its own group of researchers. The subcultures associated with compiler models, interpreter models and axiomatic models have already been discussed (in the sections on compiler methodology, models of implementation and program verification). The Scott approach is the most abstract and Scott's notion of "meaning" has perhaps a greater claim than any other to be considered *the* (platonic) meaning of a program. However, one difficulty with Scott's notion of meaning is that the difference between the how specification of a program and the what specification as an abstract function is so great that the mapping from programs to functions cannot be effectively performed. If it could be effectively performed, then we could decide whether two programs realize the same function by mapping them onto their abstract functions and checking for identity. However, we know that the problem of determining whether two programs realize the same function is undecidable (not even partially decidable) and therefore conclude that the semantic mapping function from programs to abstract functions cannot be constructive.

M23—Abstraction [91]: An abstraction of an object (program) is a characterization of the object by a subset of its attributes. The attribute subset determines an equivalence class objects containing the original object as an element. The objects in the equivalence class are called refinements, realizations or implementations of the abstraction. If the attribute subset captures the "essential" attributes of the object then the user need not be concerned with the object itself but only with the abstract attributes. Moreover, if the attribute subset defining the abstraction is substantially simpler than its realizations then use of the abstraction in place of a realization simplifies the problem addressed by the user.

The input-output relation realized by a program is an example of a program abstraction. It determines an equivalence class of programs (the set of all programs realizing the given input-output relation). Any program in the equivalence class is a realization (refinement) of the abstraction. The input-output relation captures the essential behavior of the program. When the input-output behavior is a simple or well known mathematical function then use of the abstraction in place of a realization serves a useful purpose.

The input-output relation determined by a program may be thought of as a *what* specification (of what the program does) while the program itself is a *how* specification (of how the program is realized). We may, in general, think of an abstraction as a what specification and of its realizations as associated how specifications. The process of abstraction is useful if the what specification characterizing the essential attributes of an object is substantially simpler than the how specification.

Unfortunately, the what specification for programs is not always simpler than the how specification. A program is a relatively compact specification of a functional correspondence between arbitrarily large input and output domains and there is no reason why an explicit description of the input-output relation in a mathematical notation should be simpler than the implicit description by the program. In fact, programs are a more powerful notation for describing functional correspondences than input-output relations because programs can describe recursively enumerable functions (including functions with an undecidable halting problem) while input-output relations can describe only recursive functions (for which the halting problem is decidable).

The equivalence class of all programs (algorithms) associated with a given functional abstraction is studied in the analysis of algorithms. Such equivalence classes can be extraordinarily rich. For example, Knuth in [45] develops an enormous number of different programs for the problem of sorting. It can be shown that the problem of determining whether two programs realize the same abstraction is undecidable (not even partially decidable). The study of the structure of equivalences of how specifications realizing a given what specification is of interest both for programs and other kinds of abstraction.

The notion of abstraction is important in the study of program modularity. All forms of modular programming are concerned with breaking a complex task into modular components where each component has a what specification (abstraction) specifying what the module accomplishes and a how specification (refinement) which specifies how the what specification is realized. If the how specification is specified in terms of a collection of modules which are what specifications to lower level how specifications, then we are led to stepwise abstraction and stepwise refinement. The process of stepwise refinement is illustrated in [88].

The notion of abstraction arises in many different disciplines and may always be characterized in terms of a relation between an equivalence class specification and elements of the equivalence class. The problem of specifying abstractions (equivalence classes) as well as the problem of characterizing the structure of the space of realization (elements) is of interest in many domains of discourse. However, the tools for studying the specification problem and the equivalence problem is determined by the nature of the elements in the domain of discourse. We have already discussed the nature of the specification and equivalence problems when our elements are programs. In the section on "modularity" we will consider the specification and equivalence problems for a class of modules called *data abstractions* which cannot be completely specified by an input-output relation because they have an internal state.

M24—Pascal [92]: Although Pascal was developed in the late 1960's, its structure and design objectives make it a language of the 1970's. Its designer, Wirth, participated in the early stages of design of Algol 68 as a member of the IFIP working group 2.1, but felt that the generality and attendant complexity of the emerging language was a step in the wrong direction. Pascal, like Algol 68, was designed as a successor to Algol 60. However, whereas Algol 68 aimed at generality, Pascal was concerned with simplicity at the conceptual level, the user level and the implementation level. Conceptual simplicity allows simple axiomatization which facilitates verifiability. User simplicity gives the programmer a better understanding of what he is doing and results in more readable, better structured programs with fewer errors. Simplicity of implementation enhances efficiency and portability and ensures simplicity of the associated operational semantic model.

Pascal provides richer data structures than Algol 60, including records, files, sets and programmer defined type specifications but is otherwise as simple as possible. For example, it excludes arrays with dynamic bounds so as to enhance compile time type checking, and excludes pointers and parameters called by name in the interests of conceptual and user simplicity. The notion of compile time checkable data types is central to the structure of Pascal and provides a degree of program redundancy that enhances program reliability. Control structures are designed so as to encourage good programming style such as that advocated in structured programming.

Because Pascal is conceptually simple, it has been possible to develop a fairly complete formal definition for the language [37]. The existence of this formal definition has in turn led to the widespread use of Pascal as a base language for program verification research [50]. The availability of an axiomatized language has removed one of the obstacles to the development of automatic program verification systems, thus allowing researchers to focus more explicitly on other more formidable obstacles such as the handling of tasks with complex or intractable what specifications.

Pascal and Algol 68 represent two very different approaches to the development of a successor to Algol 60. Although the verdict is not yet in, it may turn out that the Pascal approach will turn out to be more relevant to the development of future programming languages than the Algol 68 approach. However, the discussion of "the APL phenomenon" below indicates that the demands of interactive programming may require us to discard notions such as block structure and explicit type declarations which are fundamental to both Pascal and Algol 68.

M25—The APL phenomenon: The idea of time sharing caught the imagination of the computing community as early as 1960, and led to the development of a number of on-line languages in the early 1960's. Quiktran [60] was developed in 1961–1963 by IBM as an on-line dialect of Fortran but never caught on, perhaps because it could not be adequately supported by existing technology. Joss [75] was developed in 1963–1964 by Shaw and others at the Rand Corporation. Basic (beginners all purpose symbolic instruction code) [48] was developed in 1965–1966 at Dartmouth and has had great success in high schools, two year colleges, and other environments concerned with teaching elementary programming.

APL was developed by Iverson in the early 1960's [40], was implemented as an interactive language in 1967 [30], and has proved to be enormously popular in the 1970's among engineers and mathematicians who need a versatile "desk calculator" to aid them in their work.

APL has a richer set of operators than conventional languages like PL/I or Pascal, including ingeneous extensions of scalar operations to vector and matrix operations which allow loop control structures of conventional programming languages to be implicitly specified in APL. Its emphasis on expressive power at the level of expressions is appropriate to on-line languages, since use of on-line languages in the desk calculator mode is largely concerned with the evaluation of expressions. The richness of APL operators and expressions permits a far greater number of essentially different ways of accomplishing a given computation than in conventional languages. The greater scope for programmer ingenuity leads to greater programmer satisfaction but may lead to programs that are more difficult to read, debug, or maintain.

APL has an explicit mechanism for specifying scopes of identifiers, but has a mechanism for specifying local variables of subroutines. Workspaces are a very effective APL mechanism for defining "modules" containing named subroutines and data sets. There are APL extensions such as APL*PLUS and APL SV [34] specifically designed to allow use of APL for large data processing applications.

APL has no explicitly typed variables or block structure and has the *go to* statement as its only form of transfer control. There is not even an "if-then-else" statement, and conditional branching is performed by an implementation trick (branch to a label 0 is interpreted as exit from a subroutine and branch to an ill-formed label is interpreted as a "continue" statement with no effect). In these respects the structure of APL differs markedly from the current conventional wisdom of the software engineering community. However, it nevertheless strikes a strong responsive chord among practical programmers, indicating that explicit type declarations, block structure and control structure might possibly be discarded in future on-line languages, perhaps because the potential gains in program efficiency and reliability are insufficient to offset the extra program complexity resulting from redundant constituents and additional interrelations among program constituents.

Arguments *against* block structure, explicit types and explicit control structures may be formulated as follows.

Argument against block structure: One of the original reasons for block structure was the savings in storage resulting from overlays of variables in disjoint blocks. The price paid for this rather trivial saving is an inflexible set of interrelations among program identifiers which adds greatly to the program complexity. APL has scoping mechanisms at the subroutine and workspace level, but none at the block structure level. This looser scoping mechanism appears to be very appealing to practical programmers. Prior to 1970, we might have dismissed the tendency towards looser scoping as being due to a lack of education. However, now that we have become complexity conscious, we can see that block structure imposes additional complexity on a program and that the desire to ruthlessly prune such complexity by eliminating block structure may be justified by the canons of software engineering.

Argument against explicit type declarations: APL is designed so that types of variables may be determined implicitly by context, and there are in fact many syntactic checks on type compatibility between operators and operands in an APL system. Implicit type definitions may well correspond much more closely to the programmers intuitive thought processes than explicit type definitions. Moreover, explicit type declarations greatly increase the number of interactions among program constituents, and therefore increase the complexity of the program. If the programmer needs explicit information about types, APL has query facilities for providing such information to the programmer.

Argument against explicit control structures: The rich operator structure of APL often allows explicit loops and other explicit control specifications to be avoided. Since control structures are probably the single most significant cause of program complexity, languages which allow control structures to be specified implicitly rather than explicitly clearly give rise to textually simpler programs.

Since language usage in the future is likely to become increasingly interactive, and APL is probably the most widely used interactive language, language designers should analyze very carefully the reasons for the popularity of APL. It is not at present clear how much the popularity of APL is due to the quality of its programming system and how much it is due to the quality of the language design. However, it may well turn out that programming languages of the future will be more APL-like than Pascal-like.

M26—Structured programming: The term "structured programming" was introduced by Dijkstra in 1969 in a seminal paper entitled "Notes on structured programming" [24]. These notes are the culmination of several years of personal development, documented by his 1965 paper entitled "Programming Considered as a Human Activity" [20] which emphasizes the importance of programming style and program verification and contains the observation that "the quality of programmers is inversely proportional to the density of go-to statements in their programs," and by his 1968 letter entitled "Go-to Statement Considered Harmful" [21] which sparked a debate concerning the role of the go-to statements in programming that is ably summarized by Knuth [46]. Dijkstra's recent book entitled *A Discipline of Programming* [22] reflects his current thinking on the subject.

Structured programming in its purest (narrow) form is concerned with the development of programs from assignment statements, conditional branching (if-then-else) statements and iteration (while-do) statements by statement composition. These statement forms can be nicely axiomatized [36] and correspond to "natural" forms of mathematical reasoning (the if-then-else statement corresponds to enumerative (case analysis) reasoning and the while-do statement corresponds to inductive reasoning). It was shown by Bohm and Jacopini [4] that these statement forms are sufficient for expressing any computable function. Moreover, it turns out that these statement forms are appropriate for many practical problems although they must be supplemented by other statement forms in certain cases such as unusual exit from a loop.

Structured programming in its more general meaning is concerned with the better organization of the program development process to achieve objectives such as simplicity, understandability, verifiability, modifiability, maintainability, etc. In order to achieve these objectives it is important to develop a methodology for the modular decomposition of programs into components suitable both for bottom-up and top-down program development. In this connection, it is convenient to distinguish between "programming in the small" concerned with modularity and program structuring at the primitive statement level and "programming in the large" concerned with modularity at a higher (subprogram and data structure) level. The if-then-else and while-do constructs are appropriate module building constructs for programming in the small. The Algol procedure, Simula class and APL workspace are examples of module building constructs for programming in the large. Current research on modularity will be discussed in a separate section.

Structured programming has affected programming language usage in placing greater emphasis on if-then-else and while-do constructs and deemphasizing the go-to statement. It is likely to affect the design of future programming languages by introducing new kinds of program modules for programming in the large, and by placing greater emphasis on verifiability as a programming language design objective. The availability of appropriate concepts of modularity should help the user in systematic modular program development for complex problems. However, there are important areas of program development, such as choice of an appropriate modular data structure where available tools are of little help to the programmer. The influence of the choice of data structure on program structure is discussed in a paper on "top-down program development" by Wirth [90]. The duality between program structure and data structure is discussed in a provocative way by Hoare [38], [39].

The techniques of structured programming have had an impact not only on academic computer science but also on production programming [8]. The chief programmer team approach developed by Mills and Baker [61] is an example of a management structure which makes use of structured programming. The New York Times project [9] is perhaps the most widely advertised success story for the chief programmer team approach, claiming a productivity of 10 000 instructions per man year with only one error per man year. However, the reported success of this project was subsequently challenged, on the basis that maintenance and modifiability of the completed program was unsatisfactory. It appears that the chief programmer team approach is designed to optimize program development but pays insufficient attention to the operations and maintenance part of the life cycle (see the section on life cycle).

M27—Structured model building: Specifications of programming languages are effectively complex programs in some specification language. The notions of abstraction structuring, and stepwise refinement are just as applicable to the construction of semantic models (definitions) of programming languages as they are to the construction of applications programs. Thus, the abstract notion of a semantic model (for a specific language) can be realized by a compiler model, interpreter model, axiomatic model, or functional model (see M22). Once the desired class of models has been chosen, there is enormous scope for "structuring" the language definition by first making "high-level" decisions concerning the overall structure of the model and then filling in lower level details by a process of stepwise refinement. The term "partial model" may be used to describe an intermediate partial language specification in this process of stepwise refinement.

The above structured model building approach will be briefly illustrated by showing how stepwise refinement may be used to build an information structure model (interpreter model) of Algol 60 [97]. In the case of information structure models (I,I°,F) the partial models of the stepwise refinement process will have partial (successively more complete) specifications of the state components I,I°, and the state transition function F. The initial model M_0 would be an arbitrary model with no restriction on I,I°,F. A "first-order" model M, might require states I to be of the form (P,C,D) where P is an invariant (read only) program component, C has the form (ip,ep) where ip is an instruction pointer into P and ep is an environment pointer into D, and D is a stack of activation records. A "second-order" model M_2 might then be introduced which defines the state transitions (instructions) for block entry and exit and procedure call and return. Eventually, a final model M_n would completely define the state structure I and state transitions F for every Algol statement.

The partial models which arise in the above stepwise refinement process specify partial (operational) semantics for partial syntax specifications and may be thought of as defining language classes which are abstractions of the language that is being defined. For example, the abstraction "Algol-like languages" may in principle be defined by a partial information structure model which fixes those semantic and syntactic features that are essential if the language is to be Algol-like and leaves open optional language features of Algol-like languages.

The use of structured techniques of model specification is likely to lead to more understandable definitions of a number of existing programming languages. However, an even more potent way of developing programming languages with simple specifications is to use simplicity of specification as one of the criteria of programming language design, as was done in the case of the programming language Pascal.

M28—The life cycle concept: The software life cycle as formalized by department of defense agencies consists of a *concept formulation* and *requirements specification* stage, a *software development* stage, and an *operations* and *maintenance* stage. These stages may in turn be refined so that the software development stage might consist of a requirements analysis stage, a program design stage, an implementation and debugging stage and a testing and evaluation stage. In analyzing three large military software projects, it was estimated that such systems typically have a life cycle of 16 years, consisting of a concept formulation and requirements stage of 6 years, a software development stage of 2 years, and an operations and maintenance stage of 8 years [70]. Thus, the software development stage comprises only one eighth of the total life cycle of a typical large military software project.

The life cycle concept provides a basis for a more complete analysis of software systems than was previously possible. In the 1960's and early 1970's programming projects were organized to minimize software development costs rather than total life cycle costs. This led to a disproportionate emphasis on program design and implementation and a comparative neglect of both the initial determination of what it is that we really want to accomplish and the long years of program usage in an environment which may involve frequent program modification.

Emphasis on the life cycle as opposed to the software development phase affects both programming language design and programming language usage. For example emphasis on software development requires programming languages to be designed for rapid and correct program development while emphasis on the life cycle requires programs to be readable and modifiable during the long operations and maintenance period, providing a strong argument for simplicity of language design. Language usage should be modular, so that modifications of one part of the program do not have unexpected side effects in another part of the program. Clever tricks which make the program less readable should be avoided like the plague.

The life cycle approach allows the systematic study of cost and effort in all stages of existence of a software system [69]. Bottlenecks can be uncovered in the manner of critical path analysis and tools and techniques may be developed for eliminating such bottlenecks. Studies of software systems have in fact uncovered some quite unexpected facts about system behavior such as the fact that 64 percent of errors are system design errors while only 36 percent are system implementation errors. This suggests that design, rather than implementation, is the bottleneck in software system development and has implications concerning the allocation of funds for research in software engineering.

M29—Modularity: The subroutine mechanism for realizing program modularity was developed as early as 1951 [83]. It was a fundamental feature of Fortran, whose design provided an enormous impetus towards modular programming. Algol 60 was in some ways a backward step from the viewpoint of modularity because its nested module structure discouraged independent module development and because procedure modules could not adequately handle data which remained in existence between instances of execution of a procedure.

The Simula class is a very flexible generalization of the Algol 60 procedure module. It separates creation and deletion of instances of a class from entry and exit for purposes of execution. Coroutine control allows the program and data state at arbitrary points of execution to be preserved and subsequently restored. Access to objects declared in the outermost block of a class provides a more flexible (too flexible) mechanism for module intercommunication. The subclass facility is an ingenious syntactic mechanism for providing the advantages of hierarchical (nested) modular environments while avoiding the need for physical textual nesting of the associated modules. The class concept has served as an inspiration to designers of modular programming languages but is probably too rich in properties to serve as a prototype for modular design.

The collection of declarations in the outer block of a module may be regarded as a set of attributes or resources. One of the purposes of a module is to erect a "fence" around this set of attributes which allows systematic *information hiding* [68] of internal (hidden) attributes of a module and selective specification of a subset of externally known (*exportable*) attributes. Recent research on Clu [51] and Alphard [94] has been concerned with mechanisms for hiding and exporting module attributes.

The experimental language Clu [51] requires its program modules to consist of a collection of exportable procedures operating on a hidden (internal) data structure, and refers to such modules as *clusters*. Clusters are convenient for defining data types (such as stacks) by means of operations (such as push, pop, top, create, testempty) independently of the internal data structure (linear list or array) used to realize the cluster. The user sees an abstraction (the stack abstraction) which is defined by hiding the internal data structure and exporting only the operations. Such an abstraction is called a *data abstraction* because it abstracts from a specific data representation. The effect of the operators is defined by axioms such as "top(push(x,stack)) = x" which defines the effect of the "top" operation in terms of previously executed "push" operations without making any commitment to data representation. Any data structure which causes the defining axioms for the operations to be satisfied is an adequate realization of the data abstraction. Of course, the development of complete and sound sets of axioms for characterizing the set of cluster operations in a data independent way may, in general, be

difficult. However, in most practical cases, we can characterize the behavior of "output" operations of a data abstraction reasonably simply in terms of the effect of previous input operations, and a complete set of axioms can be developed by systematically using our knowledge of what the operations are supposed to accomplish.

The experimental modular programming language Alphard [94] calls its modules *forms*. Recent research on Alphard has emphasized verifiability as an objective of the language. Forms have a *representation* component which defines the representation of hidden data structures, an *implementation* component which defines the implementation of external attributes (operators) of the form and a *specification* component which specifies the "abstract" properties of attributes so that the correctness of their implementation can be verified.

Other work on modular programming languages includes Brinch Hansen's development of *monitors* in concurrent Pascal [9] and Wirth's introduction of *modules* in a Pascal-like language for modular multiprogramming called Modula [97]. Both monitors and modules are motivated by the need to provide the user with machine independent abstractions of machine resources such as disks, user consoles, synchronization primitives, etc. In [9] the relation between the implementation and user abstraction for monitors is described by considering how monitors are implemented. In [97] the relation between abstraction and implementation of modules is described at the language level by introducing notions such as *define list* of objects defined in the module for use outside the module and a *use list* of objects declared outside the module and used inside the module.

Among the problems which must be addressed in any modular programming language are the problems of module interface definition and module interconnection. These problems had already been identified in the 1950's in connection with the development of Fortran (the transfer vector mechanism). One recent example of work in this area is the thesis by Thomas [79] who develops a module interconnection language (MIL) for specifying module interfaces in terms of inherited attributes (use lists), synthesized attributes (define lists), and locally generated attributes using a model similar to Knuth's attribute grammars [43].

Although recent research on modularity and abstraction has greatly increased our understanding of how modules may be designed, it is not yet clear how effectively these notions can be incorporated in future programming languages. The explicit support of clusters or Simula classes introduces extra complexity into a language both at the level of verifiability and at the level of implementation, determining complete and consistent specifications for clusters to serve as a starting point for formal verification. Simula 67 has not become a widely used application language in spite of its superior modularity facilities. The modular programming facilities of a language are clearly among its most important design features, and it is quite likely that future programming languages will contain new kinds of primitives for defining both program and data abstractions. But the precise nature of these primitives has not yet been determined.

M30—Data oriented programming languages: We may distinguish between the program-centered and data-centered views of programming. The program-centered view emphasizes program development and considers data only piecemeal as and when it becomes the object of program transformation. This view is appropriate to numerical problems involving complex functional transformations on simple data structures. The data-centered point of view considers the data structure (data base) as the central part of a problem specification and views programs as "bugs" which crawl around the data base and occasionally query, update or augment the portion of the data base at which they currently reside. This view is appropriate for airline reservation systems, management information systems, information retrieval systems or any other systems whose state description requires a complex data structure and whose operations (transactions) are local queries or perturbations of that data structure.

Bachman in his Turing lecture [11] compares the shift from the program-centered to the data-centered point of view with the shift from an earth-centered to a sun-centered model of the universe brought about by the Copernican revolution. There is no doubt that the increasing importance of the data-centered view of programming will affect the design of future programming languages.

Since programming was initially motivated by numerical problems early programming languages and programming methodology emphasized the programming centered point of view. Algol 60 blocks and procedures are examples of program-centered constructs since internal data structures are forced to disappear between instances of execution. Simula classes generalize block structure so that it becomes appropriate for data-centered programming.

Cobol is an example of an early programming language which allows program and data to be handled in a symmetrical fashion. Programming systems for data-centered programming developed during the 1960's include IDS (integrated data store) [5], and IMS (information management system) [25]. The data-centered view of programming led in the 1970's to the development of database languages and systems [14], [25].

Data-base systems may be classified [25] into *network systems* which require the user to view the data base as a network (spagghetti bowl); *hierarchical systems* which require the data base to be tree structured, and relational data-base systems which permit the user to view the data base as a set of abstract relations. Network and hierarchical systems give rise to "low level" data base languages since they require the user to be explicitly aware of the data structure implementation. Relational systems give rise to high level data base languages which allow programs to specify transactions independently of the internal data structure representation, but lead to formidable implementation problems.

Network systems are a direct outgrowth of the work of the Codasyl data-base task group (DBTG) [14] and were heavily influenced by Bachman's work on IDS [5]. Hierarchical systems are the simplest class of data-base management systems, and most of the practical systems of the 1960's such as IMS were hierarchical. The relational approach to data-base management systems was pioneered by Codd in 1970 [13]. A good recent survey of the state of the art may be found in [77].

There is a great deal of current work on the design and implementation of data-base language. Recently developed relational data-base languages include Sequel [14], Quel [2], and query by example [100].

CONCLUSIONS

The above collection of concepts and milestones is by no means complete, but illustrates the great variety of programming language concepts and products developed during the last 25 years. One of the more interesting facts that emerges from a study of programming language development is the remarkable stability of early programming languages like Fortran and Cobol, and the comparative lack of success of subsequently developed languages like PL/I, Algol 68, Simula 67, and Pascal in capturing significant numbers of adherents in a nonuniversity environment. The exception is perhaps APL which has captured the hearts of a new class of user (the desk calculator user).

All the programming languages described in this paper were developed and implemented in the 1950's and 1960's. Although there have been a number of proposals for general purpose languages in the 1970's such as CS 4 [15] and the Tinman requirements specification for a new DOD-sponsored common higher order language [31], no new general purpose languages comparable to PL/I, Algol 68, or Pascal have been launched during this period. The 1970's have been a period of retrenchment in the development of general purpose languages. A number of new insights have been developed such as the importance of simplicity, readability, verifiability, and maintainability in program design and language design. A better appreciation of the concept of modularity has been developed and we have made some gains in our understanding of program verification. But these insights have led to changes in the mode of use of existing programming languages rather than in the design of a new class of programming languages which are so clearly superior that they are automatically accepted as a replacement for existing programming languages.

The demonstrated reluctance of the programming community to accept a new language is due partly to the costs of a changeover, and partly to the natural resistance to changes in technology. It is due partly to the fact that programming language designers have not been able to come up with an acceptable compromise between simplicity and versatility that is a substantial improvement over Fortran or Cobol. However, a further reason may be that programmer productivity is not as sensitive to language changes as programming language professionals would like to think. Fortran-like languages provided a significant increment of productivity over assembly language but it may well be that further language refinements cause only marginal or even negative increments in programmer productivity. Programming style, structured programming and other methodologies are largely language independent and are probably far more important in increasing programmer productivity than the development of new languages. Ultimately, it is the quality of programming rather than the programming language that determines the cost and reliability of production programs.

The field of programming languages was central to the development of computer science in the 1950's and 1960's, leading to important practical products and to important theoretical advances in our understanding of the nature of computer sciences. It may well be that programming language professionals did their work so well in the 1950's and 1960's that most of the important concepts have already been developed. The programming language field may play a less central (though still important) role in computer science in the 1970's and 1980's than it did in the 1950's and 1960's.

References

Note: OSIPL refers to [25]. ICRS refers to [40].

[1] A. V. Aho and J. R. Ullman, *The Theory of Parsing, Translation and Compiling.* Englewood Cliffs, NJ: Prentice-Hall, vol. I, 1972; vol. II, 1973.

[2] E. Allman, M. Stonebraker, and G. Held, "Embedding a relational sublanguage in a general purpose programming language" *SIGPLAN Notices,* Mar. 1976.

[3] M. M. Astrahan and D. Chamberlin, "Implementation of a structured English query language," *Commun. Ass. Comput. Mach.,* Oct. 1975.

[4] C. Bohm and G. Jacopini, "Flow diagrams, turing machines, and languages with only two formation rules," *Commun. Ass. Comput. Mach.,* May 1966.

[5] C. W. Bachman, "A general purpose system for random access, memories," in *FJCC Proc.,* 1964.

[6] R. S. Boyer, B. Elspas, and K. N. Levitt, "A formal system for testing and debugging programs by symbolic execution," *ICRS,* Apr. 1975.

[7] J. R. Brown and M. Lipow, "Testing for software reliability," *ICRS,* Apr. 1975.

[8] F. T. Baker, "Structured programming in a production programming environment," *ICRS,* Apr. 1975.

[9] P. Brinch Hansen, "The purpose of concurrent PASCAL," *ICRS,* Apr. 1975.

[10] F. T. Baker and H. D. Mills, "Chief programmer teams," *Datamation,* 1973.

[11] C. W. Bachman, "The programmer as navigator," (1973 Turing lecture), *Commun. Ass. Comput. Mach.,* Nov. 1973.

[12] *COBOL 1961: Revised Specifications for a Common Business Oriented Programming Language,* U. S. Govt. Printing Office, 1961.

[13] E. F. Codd, "A relational submodel for large shared data banks," *Commun. Ass. Comput. Mach.,* June 1970.

[14] "CODASYL," Data Base Task Group Rep., Apr. 1971.

[15] *CS-4 Language Reference Manual and Operating System Interface,* Intermetrics Publ., Oct. 1975.

[16] N. Chomsky and G. A. Miller, *Introduction to the Formal Analysis of Natural Languages, Handbook of Mathematical Psychology,* vol. II. New York: Wiley, 1963.

[17] D. Dahl and C. A. R. Hoare, *Hierarchical Program Structures, in Dahl, Dijkstra and Hoare, Structured Programming.* New York: Academic, 1972.

[18] R. Dewar, "SPITBOL 2.0," Illinois Inst. Technol. Rep., 1971.

[19] E. W. Dijkstra, "A constructive approach to the problem of program correctness, *BIT,* Aug. 1968.

[20] ——, "Programming as a human activity," *Proc. IFIP Congress,* 1965.

[21] ——, "Go to statement considered harmful," *Commun. Ass. Comput. Mach.* (Lett.), Mar. 1968.

[22] ——, *A Discipline of Programming.* Englewood Cliffs, NJ: Prentice-Hall, 1976.

[23] ——, "Making a translator for ALGOL 60," *APIC Bull.,* vol. 7, 1961.

[24] ——, *Notes on Structured Programming, in Dahl, Dijkstra and Hoare, Structured Programming.* New York: Academic, 1972.

[25] C. J. Date, *An Introduction to Data Base Systems.* New York: Addison-Wesley, 1975.

[26] *Data Structures in Programming Languages, Proc. of Symp., SIGPLAN Notices,* Feb. 1971.

[27] "FORTRAN vs. basic FORTRAN," *Commun. Ass. Comput. Mach.,* Oct. 1964.

[28] J. Feldman and D. Gries, "Translator writing systems," *Commun. Ass. Comput. Mach.,* Nov. 1968.

[29] R. W. Floyd, *Assigning Meanings to Programs, Proc. Symp. App. Math.* vol XIX, AMS, 1967.

[30] A. D. Falkoff and K. E. Iverson, *The APL Terminal System, in Klerer and Reinfelds, Interactive Systems for Experimental Applied Mathematics.* New York: Academic, 1968.

[31] D. A. Fischer, "A common programming language for the department of defense, background and technical requirements," IDA Sci. Technol. Division, paper P-1191, June 1976.

[32] R. Griswold, J. Poage, and I. Polonsky, *The SNOBOL 4 Programming Language.* Englewood Cliffs, NJ: Prentice-Hall, 1971.

[33] J. Gimpel, "A theory of discrete patterns and their implementation in SNOBOL 4," *Commun. Ass. Comput. Mach.,* Feb. 1973.

[34] L. Gilman and A. J. Rose, *APL, an Interactive Approach,* 2nd Ed. New York: Wiley, 1974.

[35] J. B. Goodenough and S. L. Gerhard, "Towards a theory of test data selection," *ICRS,* Apr. 1975.

[36] C. A. R. Hoare, "An axiomatic basis for computer programming," *Commun. Ass. Comput. Mach.,* Oct. 1969.

[37] C. A. R. Hoare and N. Wirth, "An axiomatic definition of the programming language PASCAL," *Acta Inform.,* vol. 2, no. 4, 1973.

[38] ——, *Notes on Data Structuring, In Dahl, Dijkstra and Hoare, Structured Programming.* New York: Academic, 1972.

[39] ——, "Data reliability," *ICRS,* Apr. 1975.

[40] K. E. Iverson, *A Programming Language.* New York: Wiley, 1962.

[41] *Proc. Int. Conf. Reliable Software,* Apr. 1975; also *SIGPLAN Notices,* June 1975.

[42] J. Johnston, "The contour model of block structured processes," *DSIPL,* Feb. 1971.

[43] D. E. Knuth, "The Semantics of Context Free Languages," in *Mathematical Systems Theory,* vol. II, no. 2, 1968.

[44] ——, "The remaining trouble spots in ALGOL 60," *Commun. Ass. Comput. Mach.,* Oct. 1967.

[45] ——, *The Art of Computer Programming Volume III, Sorting and Searching,* 1973.

[46] ——, "Structured programming with go to statements," *Comput. Surveys,* Dec. 1974.

[47] J. C. King, "Symbolic execution and program testing," *Commun. Ass. Comput. Mach.,* July 1976.

[48] J. G. Kemeny and T. E. Kurtz, *Basic Programming.* New York: Wiley, 1967.

[49] P. Lucas and K. Walk, "On the formal description of PL/I," *Annu. Rev. Automatic Programming,* vol. 6, pt 3. New York: Pergamon, 1969.

[50] R. L. London, "A view of program verification," *ICRS,* Apr. 1975.

[51] B. H. Liskov, "A note on CLU," Computation Structures Group Memo 112, Nov. 1974.

[52] B. M. Leavenworth, "Syntax macros and extended translation," *Commun. Ass. Comput. Mach.,* Nov. 1966.

[53] B. H. Liskov and S. N. Zillies, "Specification techniques for data abstractions," *ICRS,* Apr. 1975.

[54] M. D. McIlroy, "Macro instruction extensions to compiler languages," *Commun. Ass. Comput. Mach.,* Apr. 1960.

[55] C. N. Mooers, "TRAC-A procedure-describing language for a reactive typewriter," *Commun. Ass. Comput. Mach.,* Mar. 1976.

[56] J. McCarthy *et al.*, *LISP 1.5 Programmers Manual.* Cambridge, MA: MIT Press, 1965.

[57] J. McCarthy, "Towards a mathematical science of computation," in *Proc. IFIP Congr.*, 1962.

[58] W. M. McKeeman, J. H. Horning, and D. B. Wortman, *A Compiler Generator.* Englewood Cliffs, NJ: Prentice-Hall, 1970.

[59] Z. Manna, *Mathematical Theory of Computation.* New York: McGraw-Hill, 1974.

[60] H. D. Mills, "Mathematical foundations for structured programming," IBM Corp., Gaithersburg, MD, FSC 72-6012, 1972.

[61] J. H. Morissey, "The QUIKTRAN system," *Datamation*, Feb. 1964.

[62] P. Naur, Ed., "Report on the algorithmic language ALGOL 60," *Commun. Ass. Comput. Mach.*, May 1960.

[63] ——, "Revised report on the algorithmic language ALGOL 60," *Commun. Ass. Comput. Mach.*, Jan. 1963.

[64] ——, Proofs of Algorithms by General Snapshots, BIT 6, 1966.

[65] Newell *et al.*, *Information Processing Language V Manual*, 2nd Ed. Englewood Cliffs, NJ: Prentice-Hall, 1965.

[66] E. I. Organick and J. G. Cleary, "A data structure model of the B6500 computer system," *DSIPL*, Feb. 1971.

[67] *PL/I, Current IBM System 360 Reference Manual*, (or Bates and Douglas), 2nd Ed. Englewood Cliffs, NJ: Prentice-Hall, 1975.

[68] D. I. Parnas, "A technique for software module specification with examples," *Commun. Ass. Comput. Mach.*, May 1972.

[69] B. Randell and L. J. Russell, *ALGOL 60 Implementation.* New York: Academic, 1964.

[70] D. J. Reifer, "Automated aids for reliable software," *ICRS*, Apr. 1975.

[71] D. Scott and S. Strachey, "Towards a mathematical semantics for computer languages," PRG 6, Oxford Univ. Comput. Lab., 1971.

[72] J. Sammet, *Programming Languages, History and Fundamentals.* Englewood Cliffs, NJ: Prentice-Hall, 1969.

[73] C. E. Shannon and W. Weaver, *The Mathematical Theory of Communications.* Urbana, IL: Univ. Illinois Press, 1962.

[74] N. F. Schneiderwind, "Analysis of error processes in computer software," *ICRS*, 1975.

[75] C. J. Shaw, "JOSS, a designers view of an experimental on-line system," in *Proc. FJCC*, 1964.

[76] ——, "A specification of JOVIAL," *Commun. Ass. Comput. Mach.*, Dec. 1963.

[77] E. H. Sibley, Ed., "Special issue: Data base management systems," *Comput. Surveys*, Mar. 1976.

[78] A. M. Turing, "On computable numbers with an application to the entscheidungsproblem," in *Proc. London Math. Soc.*, 1936.

[79] J. Thomas, "Module interconnection in programming systems supporting abstractions," Ph.D. dissertation, Brown Univ., Providence, RI, May 1976.

[80] R. D. Tennent, "The denotational semantics of programming languages," *Commun. Ass. Comput. Mach.*, Aug. 1976.

[81] J. Von Neumann, "The EDVAC report," in *Computer from PASCAL to Von Neumann*, H. Goldstein, Ed. Princeton, NJ: Princeton Univ. Press, 1972, Ch. 7, discussion.

[82] V. Wingaarden *et al.*, "Report on the algorithmic language ALGOL 68," *Numer. Math.*, Feb. 1969; also revised report, *Numer. Math.*, Feb. 1975.

[83] M. V. Wilkes, D. J. Wheeler, and S. Gill, *The Preparation of Programs for a Digital Computer.* New York: Addison-Wesley, 1951 (revised Ed., 1957).

[84] P. Wegner, *Programming Languages, Information Structures and Machine Organization.* New York: McGraw-Hill, 1968.

[85] W. Waite, "A language independent macro processor," *Commun. Ass. Comput. Mach.*, July 1967.

[86] P. Wegner, "Three computer cultures, computer technology, computer mathematics and computer science," in *Advances in Computers*, vol. 10. New York: Academic, 1972.

[87] ——, "Data structure models in programming languages," *DSIPL*, Feb. 1971.

[88] ——, "The Vienna definition language," *Comput. Surveys*, Mar. 1972.

[89] N. Wirth and H. Weber, "Euler—A generalization of ALGOL and its formal definition," *Commun. Ass. Comput. Mach.*, Jan. and Feb. 1966.

[90] N. Wirth, "Program development by stepwise refinement," *Commun. Ass. Comput. Mach.*, Apr. 1971.

[91] P. Wegner, "Abstraction—A tool in the management of complexity," in *Proc. 4th Texas Symp. Comput.*, Nov. 1975.

[92] N. Wirth, "The programming language PASCAL," *Acta Inform.*, 1971.

[93] P. Wegner, "Structured model building," Brown Univ., Providence, RI, Rep., 1974.

[94] W. Wulf, R. L. London, and M. Shaw, "Abstraction and verification in ALPHARD, introduction to language and methodology," Carnegie-Mellon Univ., Dep. Comput. Sci. Rep., June 1976.

[95] P. Wegner, "Operational semantics of programming languages," in *Proc. Symp. Proving Assertions about Programs*, Jan. 1972.

[96] ——, "Research paradigms in computer science," in *Proc. 2nd Int. Conf. Reliable Software*, Nov. 1976.

[97] N. Wirth, "Modula: A language for modular multiprogramming," ETH Institute for Informatics, TR18, Mar. 1976.

[98] P. Wegner, "Structured programming, program synthesis and semantic definition," Brown Univ. Rep., Providence, RI, 1972.

[99] V. Yngve, "COMIT as an IR language," *Commun. Ass. Comput. Mach.*, Jan. 1962.

[100] M. Zloof, "Query by example," in *Proc. Nat. Comput. Conf.*, 1975.

Peter Wegner received the B.Sc. degree in mathematics from the Imperial College, London, England, the Diploma in numerical analysis and automatic computing from Cambridge University, Cambridge, England, the M.A. degree in economics from Penn State University, and the Ph.D. degree in computer science from London University, London, England.

He has taught at the London School of Economics, Penn State, Cornell University, and Brown University and has been on the staff of the Computation Center at the Massachusetts Institute of Technology, and Harvard University. He is currently with the Division of Applied Mathematics, Brown University, Providence, RI. His publications are primarily in the programming language area but include papers in operations research and statistics.

Dr. Wegner has been consultant to the ACM Curriculum Committee (1965–1968), SIGPLAN Chairman (1969–1971) and is presently a member of the ACM Council.

Achieving Quality Software:
Reflections on the Aims and Objectives
of Alphard

William A. Wulf, Mary Shaw and Ralph L. London[1]

Reprinted with permission from the Carnegie-Mellon University Department of Computer Science Annual Report 1975-1976, pp. 7-15.

Introduction

The Alphard effort is focused on approaches to reducing the cost of software and improving its quality. In recent years many people have become seriously concerned about the increasing proportion of computing costs spent on software development and maintenance, and about the poor quality of much of the software which is produced. Software is delivered late, fails to perform as specified, costs too much to maintain and enhance, and so on. The phrase "software crisis" has been coined to describe this situation. It is quite possible that the phrase has been overused and the situation exaggerated, for the fact is that large software systems are produced and used effectively. Nevertheless, improvements of several orders of magnitude in both cost and quality ought to be possible.

One might consider any of a number of approaches to achieving a significant improvement in the software situation, including better management and training of personnel, standardization of programming languages and/or computer designs, application of improved programming methodologies, fully "automatic" programming, and so on. In many cases these approaches are complementary, and an ultimate "solution" depends upon progress in all the areas.

In the Alphard project, however, we have chosen to focus on program development tools and to bring together recent developments in the areas of programming methodology and program verification. There has been significant progress in both of these areas during the past five years, and both speak directly to the underlying causes of current software problems. It seems to us that the time is ripe to merge their results in a practical tool which, in turn, can be used to construct high quality software systems.

Our ultimate concern in this effort is with *real* programs—those of significant size and complexity. Moreover, we are concerned with the entire lifetime of these software products; the fact that the cost of software maintenance and enhancement often exceeds that of development, and frequently by a large factor, seems to be ignored by much of current software technology.

The Alphard project can be characterized as an attempt to construct a programming tool with four important properties:

(1) It supports, in a natural way, contemporary programming methodology, e.g., "structured programming".

(2) The resulting programs can be verified. That is, we can find mathematical proofs that the programs perform as specified.

(3) It produces programs which are both understandable and modifiable because the structure envisioned by the original designers is retained in the final program.

(4) The compiler can generate compact, efficient object code.

We shall see below how these goals and approaches have influenced the design at various points.

Structured programming deals with those aspects of the software problem which result from our human limitations in dealing with complexity [Dahl72, Dijkstra68a,68b, Gries74, Naur69, Parnas72a, Wirth71, Wulf72]. Perhaps the most profound insight which has emerged from the "software crisis" is that the fundamental difficulty with large software is our human inability to understand it. If we really understood our programs (and we should), then we would know why they were correct or incorrect, how their performance could be improved, how they could be enhanced to include new features, and so on.

Program verification is concerned with proving mathematically that a program performs the function stated by its specifications [London75]. The specifications are supplied as part of the program and are

---

[1]USC Information Sciences Institute, supported by Defense Advanced Research Projects Agency under contract DAHC-15-72-C-0308.

needed both as an essential element of a verification and as documentation of the program. The inclusion of verifiability as a central goal of the Alphard effort has two effects. The first, and most direct, is that it provides the opportunity for future large systems to be proved correct, thus largely eliminating the long shakedown period often required for new systems. Second, and somewhat more subtly, the discipline of designing a program as if it would be verified has a positive effect on its structure, even if the verification is never actually carried out. Anticipating this kind of program design has a similar positive effect on language structure.

Recognizing that programs exist for long periods of time and are altered by programmers other than their authors adds a new dimension, maintenance and enhancement, to the software development problem. It is not adequate for the program to be developed in a well-structured manner: if it is to be understandable and modifiable, the structure of the development must be retained in the ultimate program text.

Well-structured, understandable, verifiable, and easily modified programs can in principle be written in any programming language. In practice, however, we know that the presence of certain features in a language can materially affect all these desirable properties. We also know, from both natural and artificial languages, that the language we use to express our ideas can shape the ideas themselves [Whorf56]. By choosing features and structure properly we can therefore hope to exert a positive influence on the programs which are written. Instead of starting with an existing language and focusing individually on methodology, understandability, or verification, we chose to address these issues jointly in a new language design.

The targets of our concerns, *real* programs, demand more than correctness and modifiability; they must also execute with reasonable efficiency. The preoccupation with efficiency in the past has led to something of a "backlash" in which many (academics in particular) have chosen to condemn efficiency, claiming that advances in hardware technology will obliterate any need for concern with the speed or size of programs. We disagree on two grounds. First, if we have learned anything from the history of computing, it should be that our aspirations have grown faster than even the phenomenal increase in speed and decrease in cost of hardware. No one has yet built a computer that is too big! Second, any particular computer has a fixed and finite capacity; an inefficient program may (or may not)

cost much to run, but it consumes a portion of that fixed resource; that is, it prevents another program from being run. Thus in the Alphard design, efficient object code is considered to be as important as correctness and modifiability; fortunately, we do *not* believe that we must make a choice between these goals.

In the remainder of this paper we shall discuss some of the major features of Alphard, but our primary goals will be to emphasize the impact of the above concerns on the design and to show the relation between the design approach and the general goals of reducing the cost and improving the quality of programs. The picture we shall present is one taken in midstride. Alphard is still a paper design; it has been neither implemented nor used to construct and verify the real programs which are our target. In spite of this, the evolution of the design has produced a number of insights which seem worth capturing in print.

A Bit About the Alphard Language and the Verification Approach

The key concept in structured programming is *abstraction*: the retention of only the essential properties of an object and the corollary neglect of inessential details. Several abstraction techniques have appeared in the programming literature [Dijkstra72, Parnas72a,72b, Wirth71], and language mechanisms have been designed to support these techniques. The version which appears in Alphard is called a **form.** It is derived from Simula *classes* [Dahl72]; a similar adaptation has also appeared in CLU [Liskov74], and related features are beginning to appear in other languages [DataConference76]. We shall only introduce the general nature of the construct; more details may be found in [Wulf76, Shaw76].

In Alphard, the **form** is a syntactic device for encapsulating a set of data declarations, function definitions, and other information about implementation details while revealing to the user only selected information about the behavior of the abstraction. The resulting localization has several advantages over more traditional organizations:

—The user of the abstraction may ignore the details of the implementation.
—The programmer's abstractions are easier to discover in the final program because their data and function definitions are grouped together.
—The places where modifications must be made are more likely to be close together.

—A smaller portion of the program will be likely to require reverification when a change is made.

—It becomes possible to make *absolute* statements which are independent of even the most perverse programmers.

The Alphard **form** permits the programmer to introduce a new abstraction into the program. In most ways the newly introduced abstraction will resemble a new *type* as that term is used in other programming languages. Thus, an Alphard program might contain a definition such as:

```
form set =
    beginform
        . . .
    endform
```

This definition introduces a new abstract notion, "set". The **form** contains all the information relevant to the use, verification, and implementation of the abstract notion. In this case, for example, we would find in the **form** both the definition of the data structure to be used in representing a set (e.g., a list structure) and the definitions of some operations on sets (union, intersection, membership, etc.). The **form** also gives a formal specification of the abstract properties of these sets.

Once such a definition is written, a programmer can write an *abstract* program using the newly defined notion. Variables of the new type may be declared, the defined operations may be performed, and so on. We may, for example, write:

```
local x,y,z : set;
    . . .
x := x+y*z;
    . . .
```

because certain features of the language allow new functions to be associated with the infix operators. (In this case we might associate union with + and intersection with *.)

Our strategy for verifying Alphard programs parallels the program decomposition implicit in the notion of a **form**. We shall presume a relatively small main program expressed in terms of abstract objects and operations natural to the problem. The program may already express an algorithm with well-known properties; if so, it does not require (re)verification. If not, the main program is verified by traditional methods (e.g., inductive assertions), treating the specifications of the abstract objects and operations as if they were primitive. Then, to justify the use of the abstract objects, we verify that the concrete implementation of each abstraction is consistent with its specifications. (In general the implementation of an abstraction will be given in terms of further, *lower-level*, abstract objects and operations on them.) Thus the verification of the algorithms used to implement an abstraction will be similar to the verification of the most abstract (top level) program. An obvious requirement of this approach is that each of the implementations be *correct*, or verified, if the ultimate program is to be verified. Roughly speaking, the verification will show that the specified relations exist between all abstractions and their implementations so that each implementation behaves like, or *models* its abstraction.

Why This Approach?

Our goal here is to explain how several lines of research have impacted the Alphard design. To do this, we need not explicate the details of either the Alphard language or the verification approach further. It is sufficient to understand that

(1) An Alphard program is constructed as a number of units, called **forms.**
(2) Each **form** corresponds to an intuitively natural abstraction in the context of a given program.
(3) The properties of each abstraction, or **form,** are precisely specified.
(4) All information about how the abstraction is implemented is encapsulated within the **form** definition.
(5) It is possible to construct a mathematical proof that a specific implementation of a **form** conforms to its specifications.

The rationale for this approach arises generally from the programming milieu, but most strongly from the emerging understanding of programming methodology and program verification. In this section we shall summarize the direct impact of these lines of research on the language.

A later section will focus on the symbiosis of these concerns in the language design process.

1. Alphard and Programming Methodology

As mentioned earlier, the (sub)field now called programming methodology arose in an atmosphere of increasingly complex programs which, by-and-large, did not work. The realization which has evolved in the field is that it is our human inability to deal with complexity which gave rise to the symptoms of late, unreliable, slow, unmodifiable systems. Points (1)-(4) are direct responses to this problem. In order to control complexity we must, at the very least, organize programs into units of manageable intellectual size. The traditional mechanism for achieving this has been the subroutine, but subroutines are primarily useful for purely computational abstractions. Our intent with the **form** mechanism, on the other hand, is to capture a much broader class of abstractions—covering, insofar as we are able, the spectrum encompassed by the intuitive connotations of the word.

Early in the development of programming methodology it was common to hear the admonition to "subroutine" your program by breaking it into many small (less than one page) subroutines. Slightly later a similar admonition was to avoid, or eliminate, the **goto** [Dijkstra68b]. Although both of these are simplistic, they illustrate an important point: In a **goto**-less program, the text can be grouped into nested regions with the property that each region has a single entry and a single exit. To the extent that such a region corresponds to an abstract computation, especially one whose effect is easily verbalized, it represents a significant aid to understanding because a reader may ignore its internal details. A well-subroutined program has similar desirable properties, at least to the extent that each subroutine implements a single abstract computation. Of course, it will be of little help if the single entry/single exit regions of a **goto**-less program or the subroutines correspond to several abstractions or to an ill-conceived abstraction. Nevertheless, the computational abstractions realized in these ways localize all, or almost all, of the information related to how the abstraction is realized. Unfortunately this localization is not easily achieved for other kinds of abstractions (in conventional programming languages).

Localizing implementation information supports not only abstraction, but also *information hiding*. Abstraction is useful to the extent that it allows us to ignore inessential detail; the principle of information hiding asserts that we are better off if these inessential details are made *inaccessible*. So long as the details are accessible there will be a temptation to use the knowledge of these details—for example to gain some local efficiency. In the long range context of program reliability and modifiability, however, such exploitation of detailed knowledge almost always has a net negative consequence.

Except for the desire to broaden the class of abstractions handled, these same considerations drive the design of the form mechanism: (a) we intend **forms** to correspond to intellectually manageable abstractions so that they may be understood in terms of their behavioral properties rather than their implementations, (b) we demand a precise specification of these properties to avoid ambiguity, and (c) we force textual localization and information hiding so that inadvertent misuse of the knowledge of the implementation of an abstraction cannot subvert the benefits obtained by abstraction.

2. Alphard and Verification

Now let us turn to the contribution of verification, or mathematical proof of consistency between specification and implementation. Points (3)-(5) are responses to these ideas. The technology now exists to convert an arbitrarily large program into a set of theorems which, if shown valid, will establish that the program and its specifications are consistent (provided that the program is written in a programming language whose semantics are precisely defined). To a first approximation, the total size of these theorems is comparable to the size of the program. Thus, the theorems corresponding to a modern operating system (50,000-1,000,000 lines) would be truly immense: far larger than it is practical to verify by either manual or (current) automatic means. Indeed, no projections of breakthroughs in proof technology forecast that it will ever be possible to prove theorems of this magnitude directly.

The Alphard **form** mechanism has been designed so that a single **form** may be verified in isolation—that is, the consistency of its specifications and its implementation can be proved without reference either to its use or to the implementation of the lower level abstractions (**forms**) used in its implementation. This is ensured by the scope rules which encapsulate the implementation of the **form.** Thus, the **form** mechanism reduces the size of the theorems to be proved to within practical bounds while retaining the validity of the proof.

The explicit distinction between the abstract behavior of a data type and the concrete program which happens to implement that behavior provides an ideal setting in which to apply Hoare's techniques for proving data representations correct [Hoare72]. In the Alphard adaptation, we show that the concrete representation is adequate to represent the abstract type, that it is initialized properly, and that each operator provided for the type both preserves the integrity of the representation and does what it is claimed to do (in terms of both its abstract behavior and the concrete procedure that happens to implement the operator).

3. Modification Issues

It is only within the past few years that the programming research community has recognized that the important measure of program quality is its "cradle-to-grave" cost [Goldberg73]. No single component of this total cost should be weighted more heavily than all the others, for many tradeoffs are then available to mask the true costs. For example, with the advent of compilers we learned that programming cost can be reduced at the expense of execution cost (a lesson we have more recently had to unlearn). The methodologies of structured programming formalized the folklore that increasing design effort can reduce debugging time, and we have realized the value of clean and flexible programming when systems must be adapted to new requirements.

Most large programs are not simply written and run; rather, they are continually modified and enhanced. The same limitations which effectively prevent humans from dealing with the complexity of large programs also prevent them from anticipating all the ways their programs will be used. Thus, the initial program is seldom adequate for all its eventual uses, and it experiences constant pressure for improvement and expansion. Indeed, the more successful a program is, the more likely it is to be modified: only programs no longer in use are safe from this pressure. In many cases the cost of modification exceeds that of initial development, often by a large amount [Goldberg73].

Although modification issues have not received the attention we believe they deserve, the concerns of programming methodology are especially relevant to solving them. Much of the effort involved in modifying an extant program is devoted to simply understanding what is already there. If what is there is overly complex, modifying it can be difficult, time consuming, and susceptible to errors.

Responding to the modification issue adds a dimension to programming methodology. It is no longer adequate for the original programmer to develop the program in a well-structured manner; if the program is to be modifiable, the structure of the development must be retained in the ultimate program text. The future reader must be able to perceive the structure and use it to understand what the program is doing. A major objective of the Alphard design is precisely retention of this structure, and the **form,** particularly through points (1), (2), and (4), provides the vehicle for this retention.

In addition, as a program is modified the problem of reverification arises. In a large, monolithic program, it would be necessary to reverify the entire program each time any change was made. Generally this is not the case with Alphard programs. Most modifications will occur in a small number of **forms.** Of course, these **forms** will need to be reverified, but if their specifications are unchanged, no other reverification will be necessary. If the specifications of a **form** are altered, those other **forms** which use the altered one will, of course, need to be reverified, but that is all. Thus reverification effort should generally be proportional to the amount of code affected by the modification.

Interaction of Goals in the Language Design

In this section we turn to the way a number of concerns, especially methodology and verification, have interacted in the language design process, and to why we believe the resulting design could not have arisen from either set of considerations alone. We will begin by reviewing the features that have been used in programming languages to support various kinds of abstractions. We then illustrate the interaction of these concerns by tracing the evolution of one particular language construct, the iteration statement, and noting the reasons for various changes in its definition.

The notion of control, the sequence in which operations are to be performed, has always been central to programming. Its most primitive manifestations were explicit jumps, the infamous **gotos.** However, even the earliest programming languages recognized that certain control patterns appear so frequently that it is advantageous to provide explicit abstractions for these patterns in the form of special language syntax. The most notable examples are DO (or FOR) loops and subroutines. The kinds of abstractions achievable with these two constructs are very different: the subroutine allows the details of a general calculation to be encapsulated under a single name, and the loop allows a calculation to be performed repeatedly with certain *very regular* systematic changes in the interpretation of its body.

1. Early Control Abstractions in Alphard

When we introduced the **form** to encapsulate data abstractions in Alphard, we found that the systematic variation permitted by the traditional counting loop is too rigid to support our abstractions. All the variation in such a loop must be encoded in terms of a counter, usually an integer, and the (sometimes complex) computations which express that encoding of the data structure must then appear in *every use* of a loop—a clear violation of the principles that underlie the introduction of the **form.**

Thus we knew from the outset that expressing abstractions in terms of procedures and data structures would not be enough; we would have to find a way to associate a "natural" sequencing order with a data structure. As early as 1972 our notes referred to "implicit sequencing", in which this "natural" order would be deduced from the structure of the data. At about the same time, we were thinking of control as having the properties of a separable module, with well-known external properties and an unknown specific implementation.

By early 1973, when the **form** concept was emerging, we realized that the "natural" sequencing order is a property of the abstraction being designed, not of the particular representation chosen to implement it. Yet, the manner in which this sequencing order is achieved *is* a property of the particular implementation. As a consequence, information about iteration patterns must be elicited from the programmer along with the other properties of his abstraction. That is, it must be defined in the **form.**

Thus by 1974 we had arrived at the position expressed in this except from [Wulf74, pp. 2-3]:

Data Structures and Sequencing Abstractions: In this section I would like to deal with two related issues—abstraction mechanisms for data structures and abstraction mechanisms for sequencing. In many ways the weakest aspect of abstraction mechanisms in current languages relates to data structures and their manipulation. With the exception of Simula, most languages provide only the ability to specify the (static) format of a structure; correlated manipulation of the structure and/or its elements is physically and conceptually separated from the structure definition. This point may be illustrated in many ways, but we shall focus on one—sequencing.

Most sequencing in a program is related to the data structures on which that program operates. Consider, for example, the following simple Algol 60 program:

> **begin**
> **array** A[0:N]; **real** S; **integer** i;
>   . . .
> S := 0;
> **for** i := 1 **step** 1 **until** N **do** S := S + A[i];
>   . . .
>   **end**;

Clearly in such a case the **for** clause is intimately related to the array A—its intent is to step through A performing the statement "S := S + A[i]" once, and only once, for each element of the index set. What we intended, but had no way to say in Algol, was:

> **forall** a ϵ A **do** S : = S+a;

Our inability to express ourselves this way in Algol has several unfortunate consequences:

— We were forced to say too much. For example, the order of the evaluation had to be specified when, in fact, it was immaterial.

— Changes are difficult. Any change in the representation of the conceptual entity denoted by A would require locating and altering the control used to sequence through A.

— Proofs are difficult. Although conceptually trivial, the formal proof of this simple loop using the inductive assertion method is not. At least in part the reason for this lies in the fact that the proof involves the dummy control variable "i"; in part the difficulties arise because extraneous detail, e.g., the sequencing order, is explicit.

Note that, except for the final paragraph of the excerpt, the entire concern here is methodological. We were primarily concerned with the notion that the order of sequencing through a data structure should be "natural" to that structure, and that irrelevant details of the implementation should, somehow, be submerged. Specifically, it seemed that this would allow rather free modification of the representation of the data structure without altering the statement which sequenced through it. At this point, however, we did not have a solid proposal for how these goals were to be achieved.

About this time, several things happened. One was a recognition that the **form** concept, if it were to be strong enough to support a wide variety of abstractions, ought to be able to support control abstractions as well. (If it did not, or could not, it would reflect a weakness in the mechanism.) The second was a substantial elaboration of the simple **for** statement to cater to common special cases— e.g., the first and last times a loop is executed. The third was formalization of the proof technique for **forms,** including the nature of their specifications. Let us examine each of these lines of development.

2. Evolution of the Iteration Statement

In early 1974 we participated in a study of computer description languages. We concluded that computer descriptions should generally rely on abstractions in much the same way that programs do, and we learned in particular that, at the hardware level, the programmer's intuitive ideas (e.g., his normal abstractions) about control constructs can be implemented in a large variety of ways. For example, programmers normally regard sequential statement execution as primitive, but hardware designers must choose from a wide spectrum of synchronous and asynchronous implementations with various degrees of overlapped processing. Indeed, the implementation of operation sequencing may differ from one part of a machine to another. When we translated this insight back to the programming language domain, we realized that the customary policy of building all the knowledge about control into the compiler can preclude efficient implementation of certain abstractions. In response to this problem we developed the concept of *control specialization*: the implementor of a data type may wish to provide information to tailor the actions of the language's control syntax to the requirements of that type. We concentrated on specializations for iteration, and found we could achieve them by allowing the implementor of a data abstraction to provide information on how initialization, "next-element" selection, and the completion test are to be performed when a loop operates on a structure of that type. This information is provided by a **form** which meets certain special requirements; such a **form** is called a *generator*. Thus the statement

    for aϵ A **do** S := S+a

acts very much like the loop

    begin local a: generate(A);
    π := a.&init;
    while π **do**
      (S:= S+a; π:=a.&next)
    end

where generate(A) denotes the loop control information for A and the functions a.&init and a.&next respectively produce the first and each successive element of A and return a Boolean to show whether they succeed in doing so.

At about the same time, we realized that programmers often write incomplete loops, for example by processing the initial element separately or executing a loop on an n-element vector only n-1 times (because the loop body performs a pairwise operation on adjacent elements). The statement we had devised, however, required a complete generation of all the elements of the structure—and it did so precisely because the integer encoding of the "next-element" operation was *not* available to the programmer who wrote the loop. We responded by adding mechanism in the loop statement (i.e., the language semantics) to accommodate these cases. By the summer of 1975, the loop statement was

    for a: generate(A) **do**
      firstime S := a   ! for the first element
                          generated
      repeat S := S+a ! for all elements except
                          the first
      ifnull S := O   ! if there were no elements
                          in the structure A
      finally   ! after all elements (if any)
                          had been processed

where the bodies of the four clauses were executed as indicated by the comments (! . . .). We also found a number of other deserving special cases (e.g., the boundaries of a matrix). All of this seemed plausible on methodological grounds.

3. Proof Rule Considerations

In the fall of 1975, we tried to write an axiomatic proof rule in the manner of [Hoare73] for the complex style of the **for**. We disliked all our attempts because of either extreme bulkiness or perceived problems in using the rule in verifying **for** statements. The plausibility of this **for** statement evaporated under this graphic demonstration that the number of paths through a loop was just too large. Whereas the simpler **for** has the flowchart of Figure 3.1, the statement with special processing for the first element and the empty structure has the flowchart of Figure 3.2

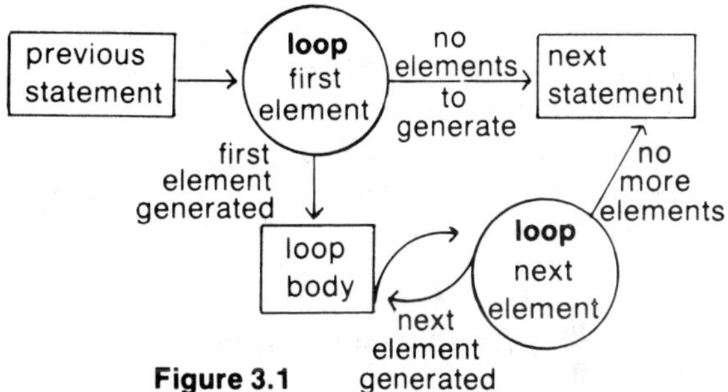

Figure 3.1

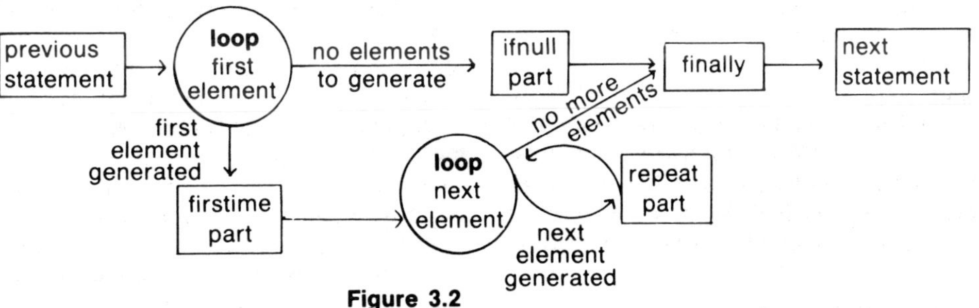

Figure 3.2

and the other "deserving special cases" were correspondingly more complex. The crucial insight from verification was that the proof rule for each statement needed a clause for each of several paths in the diagram, and notational manipulation was not going to reduce the complexity. It then became apparent that the complexity of the rule(s) was symptomatic of a difficulty which any programmer would have in attempting to understand the statement or its use.

Even though we realized the statement was too complex, the concerns which led to that complexity were real. We therefore could not simply retreat to the simpler style. While trying to solve the problem by changing the syntax of the **for** statement, we realized that the decisions about which special cases or boundary conditions to handle were properly in the domain of the programmer of the abstraction, not of the language designer. We also discovered that features already in the **form** mechanism were strong enough to provide what we needed. Thus, in fact, we were able to retreat to the simpler **for** syntax, and its simpler proof rule, without losing the flexibility (power) needed.

Even with the simpler syntax, certain difficult cases arise. For example, the loop body and the generator may both need to modify the data structure. We were reluctant to preclude general mechanisms, yet common instances of those general mechanisms had to be simple. Proof rule considerations showed us one way to understand the dilemma. Full generality of the **for** statement, if it is needed, is still possible but requires a complex proof rule. With two sets of successive reasonable simplifying assumptions in the clauses of the proof rule, we were led to appropriately simple proof rules for those desired common cases. In particular, the simplest case yields the proof rule for the Pascal **for** statement [Hoare73]. The details of this development are given in [Shaw76]. We do not believe we would have discovered these relationships without verification considerations; we certainly would not have expressed the simplifications properly.

We see in this evolution a pattern that has occurred repeatedly in the language: we realize the inadequacy of a traditional construct and grope for a solution (sometimes far afield). After using the solution, we find that it is too baroque, we eliminate the rare cases, and finally we fold the remainder in with some other construct, often to the benefit of the latter as well.

The usefulness of this type of iteration statement is not restricted to Alphard. The Euclid programming language is intended for the expression of system programs which are to be verified [Lampson76]. Even though Euclid is deliberately restricted to current knowledge of programming languages and compilers, the Euclid designers have included control abstractions closely analogous to the Alphard functions &init and &next and a portion of the iteration facility. Accordingly, the Alphard construction and verification experience will be applicable to Euclid as well.

Conclusions

The Alphard effort evolved from a desire to alleviate the manifest problems of constructing high quality software systems, and to do so within a time scale consistent with a realistic evaluation of the state of scientific knowledge. This generalized desire was transformed into the more specific goal of designing a program development tool with the four properties listed in the introduction; namely, the programs written using the tool should be:

(1) well-structured
(2) verifiable
(3) understandable and modifiable
(4) efficient

Whether or not we have achieved all of these goals is still an open question, for Alphard is still a paper design. The experience to date, however, is encouraging.

Several standard examples from the literature have been written and verified. Several cascaded examples which use verified **forms** as primitives have also been verified. Our claims about modifiability have been experimentally confirmed for those examples which we have modified. The lengths of the programs and their proofs are within reasonable limits and indeed quite satisfying.

While we find this evidence pleasing, perhaps the most exciting aspect of the effort to date has been the symbiotic interaction of the attempt to simultaneously achieve these goals. Although we initially had reason to suspect that structure, verifiability, modifiability, and efficiency could be *compatible* within a design, we have been surprised, and extremely pleased, at the degree to which the interaction of these concerns has influenced the design process itself. In a short paper it is impossible to enumerate all of the manifestations of this interaction, but we have tried to say enough to indicate its pervasiveness.

Before concluding we would like to acknowledge another form of interaction which has made this research possible. The astute reader will have noted that two of the authors are physically separated from the third by several thousand miles. Yet we have been in daily, often hourly contact. Even the draft of this paper has been physically located, and relocated, at the home sites of the various authors at various times—often changing location within a few minutes when one or another of us wished to make a minor (or major) revision. The technology which made this interaction possible is the ARPANET which links the computers at the authors' home sites, among others. Without this technology it would have been virtually impossible to conduct this research; and we gratefully acknowledge it.

References

Dahl [72] Dahl, O.-J. and Hoare, C. A. R. Hierarchical program structures, in *Structured Programming* (Dahl, O.-J., Dijkstra, E. W., and Hoare, C. A. R.) Academic Press, 1972, pp. 175-220.

DataConference [76] *Proc. of the SIGPLAN/ SIGMOD Conference on Data: Abstraction, Definition, and Structure* and *Supplement to the Proc.*, March 1976.

Dijkstra [68a] Dijkstra, E. W. A constructive approach to the problem of program correctness, *BIT 8*, (July 1968) 174-186.

Dijkstra [68b] Dijkstra, E. W. Go to statement considered harmful, *Comm. ACM 11*, 3, (March 1968) 147-148.

Dijkstra [72] Dijkstra, E. W. Notes on structured programming, in *Structured Programming* (Dahl, O.-J., Dijkstra, E. W., and Hoare, C. A. R.) Academic Press, 1972, pp. 1-82.

Goldberg [73] Goldberg, J. (Ed.) *Proc. of a Symposium on the High Cost of Software*, SRI, September 1973.

Gries [74] Gries, D. On structured programming— A reply to Smoliar, *ACM Forum, Comm. ACM 17*, 11, (November 1974) 655-657.

Hoare [72] Hoare, C. A. R. Proof of correctness of data representations, *Acta Informatica 1*, 4, (1972) 271-281.

Hoare [73] Hoare, C. A. R. and Wirth, N. An axiomatic definition of the programming language Pascal, *Acta Informatica 2*, 4, (1973) 335-355.

Lampson [76] Lampson, B. W., Horning, J. J., London, R. L., Mitchell, J. G., and Popek, G. J. Report on the programming language Euclid, August 1976.

Liskov [74] Liskov, B. and Zilles, S. Programming with abstract data types, *SIGPLAN Notices 9*, 4, (April 1974) 50-59.

London [75] London, R. L. A view of program verification, *Proc. International Conference on Reliable Software*, April 1975, pp. 534-545.

Naur [69] Naur, P. and Randell, B. (Eds.) *Software Engineering, Report on a Conference Sponsored by the NATO Science Committee, Garmisch, Germany, October 7-11, 1968*, NATO, January 1969.

Parnas [72a] Parnas, D. L. On the criteria to be used in decomposing systems into modules, *Comm. ACM 15*, 12, (December 1972) 1053-1058.

Parnas [72b] Parnas, D. L. A technique for software module specification with examples, *Comm. ACM 15*, 5, (May 1972) 330-336.

Shaw [76] Shaw, M., Wulf, W. A., and London, R. L. Abstraction and verification in Alphard: Iteration and generators, Carnegie-Mellon University and USC Information Sciences Institute Technical Reports, 1976.

Whorf [56] Whorf, B. L. A linguistic consideration of thinking in primitive communities, in *Language, Thought, and Reality* (Carroll, J. B., Ed.) MIT Press, 1956.

Wirth [71] Wirth, N. Program development by stepwise refinement, *Comm. ACM 14*, 4, (April 1971) 221-227.

Wulf [72] Wulf, W. A. Shaw, M. Global variables considered harmful, *SIGPLAN Notices 8*, 2, (February 1973) 28-34.

Wulf [74] Wulf, W. A. Alphard: Toward a language to support structured programming, Carnegie-Mellon University Technical Report, April 1974.

Wulf [76] Wulf, W. A., London, R. L., and Shaw, M. Abstraction and verification in Alphard: Introduction to language and methodology, Carnegie-Mellon University and USC Information Sciences Institute Technical Reports, 1976. *Also* Wulf, W. A., London, R. L., and Shaw, M. An introduction to the construction and verification of Alphard programs, *IEEE Transactions on Software Engineering SE*-2, 4, (December 1976).

Section 2
Programming Language Design

This section addresses general issues of programming language design. It also contains guidelines for language design written by two of the best programming language designers, Hoare and Wirth.

The brief paper by Wasserman on issues in programming language design was the focal point for a panel discussion at the 1975 National Computer Conference. (See *ACM SIGPLAN Notices,* vol. 10, no. 7, July, 1975, for the edited discussion.) The paper points out the key areas of debate in the language design field and provides a number of references to important work in the field (many of which are reprinted in this volume).

The paper by Hoare, previously available only as a technical report from Stanford, was presented as an invited talk at the First ACM Principles of Programming Languages Conference in 1973. A very effective statement of the "small is beautiful" school of programming language design, it remains timely today. Indeed, Hoare declined the opportunity to revise the paper for this volume, preferring to let his original words stand the test of time.

Niklaus Wirth, although best known for the design of Pascal, has designed a large number of languages, including ALGOL-W, Modula, and, most recently, Modula 2. His paper on language design, originally presented at the 1974 IFIP Congress in Stockholm, provides some general principles of design; it is interesting to contrast his design objectives with those of Hoare, noting that they agree to a rather large extent but differ in several key respects.

In the next paper, Wasserman considers the problem of validating programs in Pascal-like languages through testing or verification. He points out some of the trouble spots in Pascal (as is also done in the section on Pascal later in the book), and provides some guidelines for programming in Pascal and similar languages to enhance the comprehensibility and the correctness of programs.

In the final paper in this section, Tennent shows that some of the principles of formal semantics can be applied to the language design process itself. Indeed, there is a strong interaction between the language design process and the formal definition process. Until now, there has been relatively little attempt to formalize some of the practical programming languages because they contain types of statements that are difficult to formalize, including input/output, file processing, and exception-handling statements. Furthermore, the ability to pass parameters in a variety of ways and to create side effects complicates the formal definition process.

Increasingly now, however, formal definitions and language design are proceeding in parallel. Language constructs are only included in a language if they can be formalized. As more and more effective means are found for defining the semantics of programming languages, it will become possible to define formally the semantics of larger classes of languages. Furthermore, increased efforts to do so will point out additional trouble spots in languages, since inability to describe the actions of a language statement in a formal sense is usually an indication of a serious problem with the language itself.

Issues in programming language design—
An overview*

by ANTHONY I. WASSERMAN
*University of California at San Francisco***
San Francisco, California

Reprinted from *Proceedings, National Computer Conference*, 1975, pp. 297-299, ©
AFIPS Press. Reprinted by permission.

The past few years have witnessed an increased understanding of the relationship between programming languages and problem solving. Programming is now understood to be a rather difficult task which requires the simultaneous application of principles, skills, and art.[1,2,3] Computer scientists have recognized that the features of a programming language can have a significant effect upon the ease with which reliable programs can be developed. It has also been observed that certain languages and language features are particularly well suited for the use of systematic programming techniques, while others hinder or discourage such discipline.[4,5,6] Of course, it is possible to write well-structured, clearly organized programs in any programming language, but such programs have often been the exception rather than the rule.

As a result of this work, there have been numerous developments in the general area of programming languages. Among these are the following:

(1) a significant number of new programming languages have been designed and/or implemented,[7] with several developed principally to promote proper programming practices;[8,9,10]

(2) the general features of existing and proposed languages have been analyzed in an attempt to identify desirable characteristics of programming languages;[11,12,13,14] strong criticism has been directed at those languages which do not appear to contain the requisite features for the systematic development of reliable software;[15,16]

(3) preprocessors have been implemented for several programming languages, thereby allowing programmers to use "structured programming" techniques;

(4) direct modifications have been designed and/or implemented for several programming languages, in order to enhance their suitability for program development;

(5) general design criteria for programming languages have been advanced, with attention focused on the need for a language to have a sound theoretical basis;[17,18]

Although the design goals for the individual language modifications and language developments vary considerably, there are a number of common objectives which can be identified. First, the value of linear flow of control was recognized, primarily for its value in program debugging and verification, and powerful control structures were proposed and added to promote such a flow.[19,20,21,22] Second, the value of abstraction was recognized as a way to develop a representation of information which is more closely related to the application being programmed than exists in any programming language with a fixed number of data types.[23,24] Third, the scope and binding of variables was studied as a technique which simplifies program verification and which reduces programming errors caused by side effects.[25,26] Fourth, it was recognized that a language must be comprehensible, so that programs written in the language can be read and maintained. Fifth, efforts were made to limit the size of languages, in order to make them easier to implement and to make it possible for a programmer to thoroughly understand the tool. Finally, modular program structures were observed to make an important contribution to the production of large software systems.

These design objectives are reflected in a variety of decisions which are made in designing programming languages. Since the universe of design objectives is somewhat self-contradictory, as is immediately evident from a comparative analysis of languages, the language designer must consider the tradeoffs among the various possible features for a language, and give more emphasis to some of these objectives than others. It is agreed, however, that the language designer must have a thorough understanding of the goals of the language prior to commencing a specification of the syntax and semantics of the language.

Although there are a large number of closely related issues involved in the design of a language, much of the current work in language design is focused on three areas: language extensibility, data types and abstraction, and control structures.

Language extensibility refers to the ability of the programmer to modify the language being used, with the intent of extending the power of the language.[23,27,28] A relatively small "base" language is defined, along with capabilities to add features such as new data types, new

* This work was supported in part by the Commonwealth Fund.
** Graduate Program in Medical Information Science. The author is also affiliated with the Computer Science Division, University of California at Berkeley.

operators, new syntax, and new control structures in order to enable the program to more closely correspond to the problem domain.[29] The derived language or "task language" which thereby results can allow programs to be written in such a way that they are comprehensible to almost anyone familiar with the application area of the program. Persons working on the development of extensible languages foresee the establishment of a higher level language which could evolve gracefully via packages of definitions. The availability of such packages for particular task areas could then greatly increase programmer productivity.

Data types and abstraction refers to the number of predefined data types which are available in a language, the means available for combining the primitive types to create more complex types, and the way in which new abstractions may be introduced into the language.[24] The notion of an abstract data type has been advanced to define a class of abstract objects which is completely characterized by the operations available on those objects.[30] The means by which a variable takes on a given type and has a value assigned to it are extremely important issues in language design.[31,32]

Control structures are the means by which the order of execution of statements in a program is determined. While it has been formally shown that only sequential control, a conditional statement, and iterative control are necessary to describe any computation,[20] it is also understood that restricted use of the *go to* statement may result in greater program clarity.[33] Much of the work in control structures has dealt with the definition of mechanisms for conditional testing and iteration which reduce the need for the *go to* statement, and which produce dynamic program behavior closely resembling the static program structure. Because of the need to permit communication among tasks, various control structures have been proposed which permit coroutines,[34] parallel processing, synchronization, and monitoring.[35,36,37] A wide variety of proposals for improving control structures of existing and new languages have been suggested, including forms of nondeterministic control,[38,39] and the relative power and merits of these alternatives have been discussed extensively.

Although these three issues are at the heart of much of the work on programming language design, there are a number of other issues which have received attention. First, the rapid growth of interactive systems and their use by non-programmers has identified a need for string processing facilities and exception handling capabilities.[40,41] Second, the development of conversational programs for access to large data bases has focused attention on the need for capabilities in the area of data management and the need for more powerful input/output facilities.[42] Third, there are standardization efforts in progress for a number of programming languages in order to improve program transferability. Fourth, research into program proving and verification has led to additional proposals for programming languages.[43] Finally, there is also a need to simplify the task of program documentation, so that one can easily understand how a program works.

The language designer must then be able to synthesize all of these various concepts in such a way as to produce a language which is defined in a uniform way, which has a logical relationship between the syntax and the semantics, which allows an efficiently executing program to be produced, and which permits programmers to conceptualize a solution to a problem in a straightforward manner. The interrelationships among these design criteria are extremely complex, and it appears that it will be some time before a language emerges which can satisfy all of the needs of a broad class of programming applications.

Beyond that point, there are a number of political and economic issues which will affect the eventual acceptance of such a language. The primary determinants appear to be the support given to the language through implementation by major vendors of computer hardware and software, and the ease by which programmers and programming management can be attracted away from their present language and trained in the new language. Until then, most programmers will be left to work with tools which are now recognized to be somewhat inadequate for the effective solution of programming problems.

In conclusion, then, several key questions can be raised concerning the design of programming languages. How do we develop a programming mechanism which can accurately mirror logical thinking?[44] Furthermore, how do we develop a tool which is suitable for stepwise refinement of the problem from its abstract form to its "elaborated" form in a "natural" way? Last, how then does such a language get introduced and accepted by the general programming community so that it raises the quality of software production? These are the main questions which underlie present research and development in the field of programming languages.

REFERENCES

1. Dijkstra, E. W., "The Humble Programmer," *CACM*, Vol. 15, No. 10, October 1972, pp. 859-866.
2. Knuth, D. E., "Computer Programming as an Art," *CACM*, Vol. 17, No. 12, December 1974, pp. 667-673.
3. Dennis, J. B., "The Design and Construction of Software Systems," in *Advanced Course on Software Engineering*, ed. M. Beckmann *et al.* Berlin: Springer Verlag, 1973, pp. 12-28.
4. Dahl, O-J., E. W. Dijkstra and C. A. R. Hoare, *Structured Programming*, London: Academic Press, 1972.
5. Dijkstra, E. W., "GOTO Statement Considered Harmful," *CACM*, Vol. 11, No. 3, March 1968, pp. 147-8.
6. Wulf, W. A., "A Case Against the GOTO," *ACM SIGPLAN Notices*, Vol. 7, No. 11, November 1972, pp. 63-69.
7. Sammet, J., "Roster of Programming Languages for 1973," *Computing Reviews*, Vol. 15, No. 4, April 1974, pp. 147-160.
8. Wirth, N., "The Programming Language PASCAL (Revised Report)," Berichte der Fachgruppe Computer-Wissenschaften, Eidgenossische Technische Hochschule, Zurich, 1973.
9. Wulf, W. A., "BLISS: A Language for Systems Programming," *CACM*, Vol. 14, No. 12, December 1971, pp. 780-790.
10. Liskov, B., "A Note on CLU," Computation Structures Group Memo 112, MIT Project MAC, 1974.
11. Cheatham, T. E., Jr., "The Recent Evolution of Programming Languages," *Proceedings IFIP Congress 71*, Amsterdam: North-Holland, 1972, pp. 298-313.

12. Elson, M., *Concepts of Programming Languages,* Palo Alto: Science Research Associates, 1973.

13. Ledgard, H. F., "Ten Mini-Languages: a Study of Topical Issues in Programming Languages," *Computing Surveys,* Vol. 3, No. 3, September 1971, pp. 115-146.

14. Wasserman, A. I., "Online Programming Systems and Languages: a History and Appraisal," University of California at San Francisco Laboratory of Medical Information Science Technical Report No. 6, July 1974.

15. Aiello, J. M., "An Investigation of Current Language Support for the Data Requirements of Structured Programming," MAC Technical Memorandum 51, MIT Project MAC, 1974.

16. Sherertz, D. D., A. I. Wasserman and D. R. Allison, "Some Critical Comments Concerning MUMPS," *Proceedings 1974 MUMPS Users' Group Meeting,* St. Louis: MUMPS Users' Group, Biomedical Computing Laboratory, Washington University, pp. 173-190.

17. Wirth, N., "On the Design of Programming Languages," *Information Processing 74.* Amsterdam: North Holland, 1974, pp. 386-393 (preprints).

18. Hoare, C. A. R., "Hints on Programming Language Design, " Stanford University Computer Science Department Technical Report CS-73-403, December 1973.

19. Fisher, D. A., "A Survey of Control Structures in Programming Languages," *ACM SIGPLAN Notices,* Vol. 7, No. 11, November 1972, pp. 1-13.

20. Bohm, C. and G. Jacopini, "Flow Diagrams, Turing Machines, and Languages with only Two Formation Rules," *CACM,* Vol. 9, No. 5, May 1966, pp. 366-371.

21. Herriot, R., "A Uniform View of Control Structures in Programming Languages," *Information Processing 74,* Amsterdam: North Holland, 1974, pp. 331-335 (preprints).

22. Zahn, C. T., "A Control Statement for Natural Top-Down Structured Programming," in *Programming Symposium: Proceedings, Colloque sur la Programmation,* ed. B. Robinet. Berlin: Springer-Verlag, 1974, pp. 170-180.

23. Cheatham, T. E., Jr., "Motivation for Extensible Languages," *ACM SIGPLAN Notices,* Vol. 4, No. 8, August 1969, pp. 45-48.

24. Flon, L., "A Survey of Some Issues Concerning Abstract Data Types," Carnegie-Mellon University, Department of Computer Science Technical Report, September 1974.

25. George, J. E. and G. R. Sager, "Variables—Bindings and Protection," *ACM SIGPLAN Notices,* Vol. 8, No. 12, December 1973, pp. 18-29.

26. Presser, L. and J. R. White, "Making Global Variables Beneficial," *Information Processing 74,* Amsterdam: North-Holland, 1974, pp. 413-418 (preprints).

27. Galler, B., "Extensible Languages," *Information Processing 74,* Amsterdam: North Holland, 1974, pp. 313-316 (preprints).

28. Schuman, S., (ed.) Proceedings of the International Symposium on Extensible Languages, *ACM SIGPLAN Notices,* Vol. 6, No. 12, December 1971.

29. Wegbreit, B., "The ECL Programming System," *Proceedings AFIPS 1971 FJCC,* Vol. 39, pp. 253-262.

30. Liskov, B. and S. Zilles, "Programming with Abstract Data Types," *ACM SIGPLAN Notices,* Vol. 9, No. 4, April 1974, pp. 50-60.

31. Morris, J. H., Jr., "Types are not Sets," *Conference Record of ACM Symposium on Principles of Programming Languages,* 1973, pp. 120-124.

32. Wegbreit, B., "The Treatment of Data Types in EL1," *CACM,* Vol. 17, No. 5, May 1974, pp. 251-264.

33. Knuth, D. E., "Structured Programming with *GOTO* Statements," *Computing Surveys,* Vol. 6, No. 4, December 1974, pp. 261-301.

34. Conway, M. E., "Design of a Separable Transition-Diagram Compiler," *CACM,* Vol. 6, No. 7, July 1963, pp. 396-408.

35. Brinch Hansen, P., *Operating System Principles,* Englewood Cliffs, Prentice-Hall, Inc., 1973.

36. Dijkstra, E. W., "Hierarchical Ordering of Sequential Processes," in *Operating System Techniques,* ed. Hoare and Perrott, London: Academic Press, 1973, pp. 72-93.

37. Hoare, C. A. R., "Monitors: an Operating System Structuring Concept," *CACM* Vol. 17, No. 10, October 1974, pp. 549-557.

38. Floyd, R. W., "Nondeterministic Algorithms," *JACM,* Vol. 14, No. 4, October 1967, pp. 636-644.

39. Dijkstra, E. W., "Guarded Commands, non-determinacy, and a Calculus for the Derivation of Programs," Report EWD418, Burroughs, Nuenen, the Netherlands, 1974.

40. Wasserman, A. I., "Some Principles of User Software Engineering for Information Systems," *IEEE COMPCON Spring 75 Conference Digest* (in press).

41. Goodenough, J. B., "Structured Exception Handling," *Conference Record of the Second ACM Symposium on Principles of Programming Languages,* 1975, pp. 204-224.

42. Codd, E. F., "Recent Investigations in Relational Data Base Systems," *Information Processing 74,* Amsterdam: North-Holland Publishing Co, 1974, pp. 1017-1021 (preprints).

43. Kosy, D. K., "Approaches to Improved Program Validation through Programming Language Design," in *Program Test Methods,* ed. W. Hetzel. Englewood Cliffs: Prentice-Hall, Inc., 1973, pp. 75-92.

44. Wirth, N., "On the Composition of Well-Structured Programs," *Computing Surveys,* Vol. 6, No. 4, December 1974, pp. 247-260.

Hints on Programming Language Design*

C. A. R. Hoare
Oxford University Computing Laboratory

Introduction

I would like in this paper to present a philosophy of the design and evaluation of programming languages which I have adopted and developed over a number of years, namely that the primary purpose of a programming language is to help the programmer in the practice of his art. I do not wish to deny that there are many other desirable properties of a programming language—for example, machine independence, stability of specification, use of familiar notations, a large and useful library, existing popularity, or sponsorship by a rich and powerful organization. These aspects are often dominant in the choice of a programming language by its users, but I wish to argue that they ought not to be. I shall therefore express myself strongly. I fear that each reader will find some of my points wildly controversial; I expect he will find other points that are obvious and even boring; I hope that he will find a few points which are new and worth pursuing.

My approach is first to isolate the most difficult aspects of the programmer's task, and state in general terms how a programming language design can assist in meeting these difficulties. I discuss a number of goals which have been followed in the past by language designers, and which I regard as comparatively irrelevant or even illusory. I then turn to particular aspects of familiar high-level programming languages and explain why they are in some respects much better than machine code programming, and in certain cases worse. Finally, I draw a distinction between language feature design and the design of complete languages. The appendix contains an annotated reading list; I recommend it as a general educational background for language designers of the future.

Principles

If a programming language is regarded as a tool to aid the programmer, it should give him the greatest assistance in the most difficult aspects of his art, namely program design, documentation, and debugging.

*First published as Stanford University Computer Science Department Technical Report No. CS-73-403, Dec. 1973.

Program design. The first and very difficult aspect of design is deciding what the program is to do, and formulating this as a clear, precise, and acceptable specification. Often just as difficult is deciding how to do it—how to divide a complex task into simpler subtasks, specify the purpose of each part, and define clear, precise, and efficient interfaces between them. A good programming language should give assistance in expressing not only how the program is to run, but what it is intended to accomplish; and it should enable this to be expressed at various levels, from the overall strategy to the details of coding and data representation. It should assist in establishing and enforcing the programming conventions and disciplines which will ensure harmonious cooperation of the parts of a large program when they are developed separately and finally assembled together.

Programming documentation. The purpose of program documentation is to explain to a human reader the way in which a program works, so that it can be successfully adapted after it goes into service, either to meet the changing requirements of its users, to improve it in the light of increased knowledge, or just to remove latent errors and oversights. The view that documentation is something that is added to a program after it has been commissioned seems to be wrong in principle and counterproductive in practice. Instead, documentation must be regarded as an integral part of the process of design and coding. A good programming language will encourage and assist the programmer to write clear self-documenting code, and even perhaps to develop and display a pleasant style of writing. The readability of programs is immeasurably more important than their writeability.

Program debugging. Program debugging can often be the most tiresome, expensive, and unpredictable phase of program development, particularly at the stage of assembling subprograms written by many programmers over a long period. The best way to reduce these problems is by successful initial design of the program and by careful documentation during the construction of code. But even the best designed and documented programs will contain errors and inadequacies which the computer itself can help to eliminate. A good programming language will give maximum assistance in this. First, the notations should be designed to reduce as far as possible the scope for coding error; or at least to guarantee that such errors can be detected by a compiler, before the program even begins to run. Certain programming errors cannot always be detected in this way, and must be cheaply detectable at run time; in no case can they be allowed to give rise to machine or implementation dependent effects, which are inexplicable in terms of the language itself. This is a criterion to which I give the name ''security.'' Of course, the compiler itself must be utterly reliable, so that its user has complete confidence that any unexpected effect was obtained by his own program. And the compiler must be compact and fast, so that there is no appreciable delay or cost involved in correcting a program in source code and resubmitting for another run; and the object code too should be fast and efficient, so that extra instructions can be inserted even in large and time-consuming programs in order to help detect their errors or inefficiencies.

A necessary condition for the achievement of any of these objectives is the utmost simplicity in the design of the language. Without simplicity, even the language designer himself cannot evaluate the consequences of his design decisions. Without simplicity, the compiler writer cannot achieve even reliability, and certainly cannot construct compact, fast, and efficient compilers. But the main beneficiary of simplicity is the user of the language. In all spheres of human intellectual and practical activity, from carpentry to golf, from sculpture to space travel, the true craftsman is the one who thoroughly understands his tools. And this applies to programmers too. A programmer who fully understands his language can tackle more complex tasks, and complete them more quickly and more satisfactorily than if he did not. In fact, a programmer's need for an understanding of his language is so great that it is almost impossible to persuade him to change to a new one. No matter what the deficiencies of his current language, he has learned to live with them; he has learned how to mitigate their effects by discipline and documentation, and even to take advantage of them in ways which would be impossible in a new and cleaner language which avoided the deficiency.

It therefore seems especially necessary in the design of a new programming language, intended to attract programmers away from their current high-level language, to pursue the goal of simplicity to an extreme, so that a programmer can readily learn and remember all its features, can select the best facility for each of his purposes, can fully understand the effects and consequences of each decision, and can then concentrate the major part of his intellectual effort on understanding his problem and his programs rather than his tool.

A high standard of simplicity is set by the machine or assembly code programming for a small computer. Such a machine has an extremely uniform structure—for example, a main store consisting of 2^m words numbered consecutively from zero up, a few registers, and a simple synchronous standard interface for communication and control of peripheral equipment. There is a small range of instructions, each of which has a uniform format; and the effect of each instruction is simple, affecting at most one register and one location of store or one peripheral. Even more important, this effect can be described and understood quite independently of every other instruction in the repertoire. And finally, the programmer has an immediate feedback on the compactness and efficiency of his code. Enthusiasts for

high-level languages are often surprised at the complexity of the problems which have been tackled with such simple tools.

On larger modern computers, with complex instruction repertoires and even more complex operating systems, it is especially desirable that a high-level language design should aim at the simplicity and clear modular description of the best hardware designs. But the only widely used languages which approach this ideal are Fortran, LISP, and Algol 60, and a few languages developed from them. I fear that most more modern programming languages are getting even more complicated; and it is particularly irritating when their proponents claim that future hardware designs should be oriented toward the implementation of this complexity.

Discussion

The previous two sections have argued that the objective criteria for good language design may be summarized in five catch phrases: simplicity, security, fast translation, efficient object code, and readability. However desirable these may seem, many language designers have adopted alternative principles which belittle the importance of some or all of these criteria, perhaps those which their own languages have failed to achieve.

Simplicity. Some language designers have replaced the objective of simplicity by that of modularity, by which they mean that a programmer who cannot understand the whole of his language can get by with a limited understanding of only part of it. For programs that work as the programmer intended this may be feasible; but if his program does not work, and accidentally invokes some feature of the language which he does not know, he will get into serious trouble. If he is lucky, the implementation will detect his mistake, but he will not be able to understand the diagnostic message. Otherwise, he is even more helpless. If to the complexity of his language is added the complexity of its implementation, the complexity of its operating environment, and even the complexity of institutional standards for the use of the language, it is not surprising that when faced with a complex programming task, so many programmers are overwhelmed.

Another replacement of simplicity as an objective has been orthogonality of design. An example of orthogonality is the provision of complex integers, on the argument that we need reals and integers and complex reals, so why not complex integers? In the early days of hardware design, some very ingenious but arbitrary features turned up in order codes as a result of orthogonal combinations of the function bits of an instruction, on the grounds that some clever programmer would find a use for them—and some clever programmer always did. Hardware designers have now learned more sense; but language designers are clever programmers and have not.

The principles of modularity, or orthogonality, insofar as they contribute to overall simplicity, are an excellent means to an end; but as a substitute for simplicity they are very questionable. Since in practice they have proved to be a technically more difficult achievement than simplicity, it is foolish to adopt them as primary objectives.

Security. The objective of security has also been widely ignored; it is believed instead that coding errors should be removed by the programmer with the assistance of a so-called "checkout" compiler. But this approach has several practical disadvantages. For example, the debugging compiler and the standard compiler are often not equally reliable. Even if they are, it is impossible to guarantee that they will give the same results, especially on a subtly incorrect program; and when they do not, there is nothing to help the programmer find the mistake. For a large and complex program, the extra inefficiency of the debugging runs may be serious; and even on small programs, the cost of loading a large debugging system can be high. You should always pity the fate of the programmer whose task is so difficult that his program will not fit into the computer together with your sophisticated debugging package. Finally, it is absurd to make elaborate security checks on debugging runs, when no trust is put in the results, and then remove them in production runs, when an erroneous result could be expensive or disastrous. What would we think of a sailing enthusiast who wears his lifejacket when training on dry land, but takes it off as soon as he goes to sea? Fortunately, with a secure language the security is equally tight for production and for debugging.

Fast translation. In the early days of high-level languages, it was openly stated that speed of compilation was of minor importance, because programs would be compiled only once and then executed many times. After a while it was realized that the reverse was often true, that a program would be compiled frequently while it was being debugged. But instead of constructing a fast translator, language designers turned to independent compilation, which permits a programmer to avoid recompiling parts of his program which he has not changed since the last time. But this is a poor substitute for fast compilation, and has many practical disadvantages. Often it encourages or even forces a programmer to split a large program into modules which are too small to express properly the structure of his problem. It entails the use of wide interfaces and cumbersome and expensive parameter lists at inappropriate places. And even worse, it prevents the compiler from adequately checking the validity of these interfaces. It requires additional file space to store bulky intermediate code, in addition to source code which must, of course, never be thrown away. It discourages the programmer from making changes in his data structure or representation, since this would involve a heavy burden of recompilation. And, finally, the linkage editor is often cumbersome to invoke and expensive to execute. And it is all so unnecessary, if the compiler for a good language can work faster than the linkage editor anyway.

If you want to make a fast compiler even faster still, I can suggest three techniques which have all the benefits of independent compilation and none of the disadvantages.

(1) Prescan. The slowest part of a modern fast compiler is the lexical scan which inputs individual characters, assembles them into words or numbers, identifies basic symbols, removes spaces and separates the comments. If the source text of the program can be stored in a compact form in which this character handling does not have to be repeated, compilation time may be halved, with the added advantage that the original source program may still be listed (with suitably elegant indentation); and so the amount of file storage is reduced by a factor considerably greater than two. A similar technique was used by the PACT I assembler for the IBM 701.

(2) Precompile. This is a directive which can be given to the compiler after submitting *any* initial segment of a large program. It causes the compiler to make a complete dump of its workspace, including dictionary and object code, in a specified user file. When the user wishes to add to his program and run it, he directs the compiler to recover the dump and proceed. When his additions are adequately tested, a further precompile instruction can be given. If the programmer needs to modify a precompiled procedure, he can just redeclare it in the block containing his main program, and normal Algol-like scope rules will do the rest. An occasional complete recompilation will consolidate the changes after they have been fully tested. The technique of precompilation is effective only on single-pass compilers; it was successfully incorporated in the Elliott Algol programming system.

(3) Dump. This is an instruction which can be called by the user program during execution, and causes a complete binary dump of its code and workspace into a named user file. The dump can be restored and restarted at the instruction following the dump by an instruction to the operating system. If all necessary data input and initialization is carried out before the dump, the time spent on this as well as recompilation time can be saved. This provides a simple and effective way of achieving the Fortran effect of block data, and was successfully incorporated in the implementation of Elliott Algol.

The one remaining use of independent compilation is to link a high-level language with machine code. But even here independent compilation is the wrong technique, involving all the inefficiency of procedure call and all the complexity of parameter access at just the point where it hurts most. A far better solution is to allow machine code instructions to be inserted in-line within a high-level language program, as was done in Elliott Algol; or better, provide a macro facility for machine code, as in PL/360.

Independent compilation is a solution to yesterday's problems; today it has grown into a problem in its own right. The wise designer will prefer to avoid rather than solve such problems.

Efficient object code. There is another argument which is all too prevalent among enthusiastic language designers—that efficiency of object code is no longer important, that the speed and capacity of computers is increasing and their price is coming down, and the programming language designer might as well take advantage of this. This is an argument that would be quite acceptable if used to justify an efficiency loss of 10 or 20 percent, or even 30 and 40 percent. But all too frequently it is used to justify an efficiency loss of a factor of two, or 10, or even more; and worse, the overhead is not only in time taken but in space occupied by the running program. In no other engineering discipline would such avoidable overhead be tolerated, and it should not be in programming language design, for the following reasons:

- The magnitude of the tasks we wish computers to perform is growing faster than the cost-effectiveness of the hardware.
- However cheap and fast a computer is, it will be cheaper and faster to use it more efficiently.
- In the future we must hope that hardware designers will pay increasing attention to reliability rather than to speed and cost.
- The speed, cost, and reliability of peripheral equipment is not improving at the same rate as those of processors.

- If anyone is to be allowed to introduce inefficiency, it should be the user programmer, not the language designer. The user programmer can take advantage of this freedom to write better structured and clearer programs, and should not have to expend extra effort to obscure the structure and write less clear programs just to regain the efficiency which has been so arrogantly preempted by the language designer.

There is a widespread myth that a language designer can afford to ignore machine efficiency, because it can be regained, when required, by the use of a sophisticated optimizing compiler. This is false; there is nothing that the good engineer can afford to ignore. The only language which has been optimized with general success is Fortran, which was very specifically designed for that very purpose. But even in Fortran, optimization has grave disadvantages:

- An optimizing compiler is usually large, slow, unreliable, and late.
- Even with a reliable compiler, there is no guarantee that an optimized program will have the same results as a normally compiled one.
- A small change in an optimized program may switch off optimization with an unpredictable and unacceptable loss of efficiency.
- The most subtle danger is that optimization tends to remove from the programmer his fundamental control over and responsibility for the quality of his programs.

The solution to these problems is to produce a language for which a simple straightforward "non-pessimising" compiler will produce straightforward object programs of acceptable compactness and efficiency—similar to those produced by a resolutely non-clever (but also non-stupid) machine code programmer. Make sure that the language is sufficiently expressive that most other optimizations can be made in the language itself; and, finally, make the language so simple, clear, regular, and free from side effects that a general machine-independent optimizer can simply translate an inefficient program into a more efficient one with guaranteed identical effects, expressed in the same source language. The fact that the user can inspect the results of optimization in his own language mitigates many of the defects listed above.

Readability. The objective of readability by human beings has sometimes been denied in favor of readability by a machine; and sometimes it has even been denied in favor of abbreviation of writing, achieved by a wealth of default conventions and implicit assumptions. It is, of course, possible for a compiler or service program to expand the abbreviations, fill in the defaults, and make explicit the assumptions. But in practice, experience shows that it is very unlikely that the output of a computer will ever be more readable than its input, except in such trivial but important aspects as improved indentation. Since, in principle, programs should be read by others, or reread by their authors, *before* being submitted to the computer, it would be wise for the programming language designer to concentrate on the easier task of designing a readable language to begin with.

Comment conventions

If the purpose of a programming language is to assist in the documentation of programs, the design of a superb comment convention is obviously our most important concern. In low-level programming, the greater part of the space on each line is devoted to comment. A comment is always terminated by an end of line, and starts either in a fixed column, or with a special symbol allocated for this purpose:

LDA X [THIS IS A COMMENT

The introduction of free format into high-level languages prevents the use of the former method; but it is surprising that few languages have adopted the latter.

Algol 60 has two comment conventions. One is to enclose the text of a comment between the basic word *comment* and a semicolon:

comment this is a comment;

This has several disadvantages over the low-level comment convention:

(1) The basic word *comment* is too long. It occupies space which would be better occupied by the text of the comment and is particularly discouraging to short comments.

(2) The comment can appear only after a *begin* or a semicolon, although it would sometimes be more relevant elsewhere.

(3) If the semicolon at the end is accidentally omitted, the compiler will without warning ignore the next following statement.

(4) One cannot put program text within a comment, since a comment must not contain a semicolon.

The second comment convention of Algol 60 permits a comment between an *end* and the next following semicolon, *end* or *else*. This has proved most unfortunate, since omission of a semicolon has frequently led to ignoring the next following statement:

... end this is a mistake A[i] : = x;

The Fortran comment convention defines as comment the whole of a line containing a C in the first column:

C   THIS IS A COMMENT

Its main disadvantages are that it does not permit comments on the same line as the code to which they refer, and that it discourages the use of short comments. An unfortunate consequence is that a well-annotated Fortran program occupies many pages, even though the greater part of each page is blank. This in itself makes the program unnecessarily difficult to read and understand.

The comment convention of Cobol suffers from the same disadvantages as Fortran, since it insists that commentary should be a separate paragraph.

More recently designed languages have introduced special bracketing symbols (e.g., /* and */) to enclose comments, which can therefore be placed anywhere in the program text where they are relevant:

/*THIS IS A COMMENT */ .

But there still remains the awkward problem of omitting or mispunching one of the comment brackets. In some languages, this will cause omission of statements between two comments; in others it may cause the whole of the rest of the program to be ignored. Neither of these disasters are likely to occur in low-level programs, where the end of line terminates a comment.

46

Syntax

Another aspect of programming language design which is often considered trivial or arbitrary is its syntax. But this is also a mistake; the designer should select and observe the best possible syntactic framework for his language, for two important practical reasons:

(1) In a modern fast compiler, a significant time can be taken in assembling characters into meaningful symbols —identifiers, numbers, and basic words—and in checking the context-free structure of the program.

(2) When a program contains a syntactic error, it is important that the compiler should be able to pinpoint the error accurately, to diagnose its cause, recover from it, and continue checking the rest of the program. Recall the first American space probe to Venus, reportedly lost because Fortran cannot recognize a missing comma in a DO statement. In Fortran the statement

$$DO\ 17\ I = 1\ 10$$

looks to the compiler like an assignment to a (probably undeclared) variable DO17I:

$$DO17I = 110$$

In low-level programming, the use of fixed field format neatly solves both problems. The position and length of each meaningful symbol is known, and it can be copied and compared as a whole without even examining the individual characters; and if one field contains an error, it can be immediately pinpointed, and checking can be resumed at the very next field.

Fortunately, free format techniques have been discovered which solve the problems nearly as neatly as fixed format. The use of a finite state machine to define the assembly of characters into symbols, and one of the more restrictive forms of context-free grammars (e.g., precedence or top-down or both) to define the structure of a program—these must be recommended to every language designer. It is certainly possible for a machine to analyze more complex grammars, but there is every indication that the human programmer will find greater difficulty, particularly if an error is present or even only suspected. If a compiler cannot diagnose the syntax of an individual statement until it reaches the end of the program, what hope has a poor human?

As an example of what happens when a language departs from the best known technology, that of context-free syntax, consider the case of the labeled END. This is a convention in PL/I whereby any identifier between an END and its semicolon automatically signals the end of the procedure with that name, and of any enclosed program structure, even if it has no END of its own. At first sight this is a harmless notational convenience which Peter Landin might call "syntactic sugar"; but in practice the consequences are disastrous. If the programmer accidentally omits an END anywhere in his program, it will automatically and without warning be inserted just before the next following labeled END, which is very unlikely to be where it was wanted. Landin's phrase for this would be "syntactic rat poison." Wise programmers have therefore learned to avoid the labeled END, which is a great pity, since if the labeled END was used merely to *check* the correctness of the nesting of statements, it would have been very useful, and permitted earlier and cleaner error recovery, as well as remaining within the disciplines of context-free languages. Here is a classic example of a language feature which combines danger to the programmer with difficulty for the implementor. It is all too easy to reconcile criteria of demerit.

Arithmetic expressions

A major feature of Fortran, which gives it the name FORmula TRANslator, is the introduction of the arithmetic expression. Algol 60 extends this idea by the introduction of a conditional expression. Why is this such an advance over assembly code? The traditional answer is that it appeals to the programmer's familiarity with mathematical notation. But this only leads to the more fundamental question, why is the notation of arithmetic expressions of such benefit to the mathematician? The reason seems to be quite subtle and fundamental. It embodies the principles of structuring, which underlie all our attempts to master a complex problem or control a complex situation by analyzing it into simpler subproblems with clean and narrow interfaces between them.

Consider an arithmetic expression of the form

$$E + F,$$

where E and F may themselves be simple or complex arithmetic expressions. (1) The meaning of this whole expression can be understood wholly in terms of an understanding of the meanings of E and F; (2) the purpose of each part consists solely in its contribution to the purpose of the whole; (3) the meaning of the two parts can be understood wholly independently of each other; (4) if E or F is itself an arithmetic expression, the same structuring principle can be applied to the analysis of the parts as is applied to the understanding of the whole; (5) the interface between the parts is clear, narrow, and well controlled—in this case just a single number. And, finally, (6) the separation of the parts and their relation to the whole is clearly apparent from their written form.

These seem to be six fundamental principles of structuring—transparency of meaning and purpose, independence of parts, recursive application, narrow interfaces, and manifestness of structure. In the case of arithmetic expressions, these six principles are reconciled and achieved together with very high efficiency of implementation. But the applicability of the arithmetic expression is seriously limited by the extreme narrowness of the interface. Often the programmer wishes to deal with much larger data structures—for example, vectors or matrices or lists; and languages such as APL and LISP have permitted the use of expressions with these structures as operands and results. This seems to be an excellent direction of advance in programming language design, particularly for special-purpose languages. But the advance is not purchased without some penalty in efficiency and programmer control. The very reason why arithmetic expressions can be evaluated with such efficiency is that the operands and results of each subexpression are sufficiently small to be held in a high-speed register, or stored and recovered from a mainstore location in a single instruction. When the operands are too large, and especially when they may be partially or wholly stored on backing store, it becomes much more efficient to use updating operations, since then the space occupied by one of the operands can be used to hold the result. It would therefore seem advisable to introduce special notations into a language to denote such operations as adding one matrix to another, appending one list to another, or making a new entry in a file. For example,

> $A. + B$ instead of $A := A + B$ if A and B are matrices
> Ll.append(L2)   if L1 and L2 are lists.

Another efficiency problem which arises from the attempt of a language to provide large data structures and built-in operations on them is that the implementation must select a particular machine representation for the data, and use it uniformly, even in cases where other representations might be considerably more efficient. For example, the APL representation is fine for small matrices, but is very inappropriate or even impossible for large and sparse ones. The LISP representation of lists is very efficient for data held wholly in main store, but becomes inefficient when the lists are so long that they must be held on backing store, particularly disks and tapes. Often the efficiency of a representation depends on the relative frequency of various forms of operation, and therefore should be different in different programs, or even be changed from one phase of a program to another.

A solution to this problem is to design a general-purpose language which provides the programmer with the tools to design and implement his own representation for data and code the operations upon it. This is the main justification for the design of "extensible" languages, which so many designers have aimed at, with rather great lack of success. In order to succeed, it will be necessary to recognize the following:

(1) The need for an exceptionally efficient base language in order to define the extensions.

(2) The avoidance of any form of syntactic extension to the language. All that is needed is to extend the meaning of the existing operators of the language, an idea which was called "overloading" by McCarthy.

(3) The complete avoidance of any form of automatic type transfer, coercion, or default convention, other than those implemented as an extension by the programmer himself.

I fear that most designers of extensible languages have spurned the technical simplifications which make them feasible.

Program structures

However far the use of expressions and functional notations may be extended, a programmer will eventually require the capability of updating his environment. Sometimes this will be because he wants to perform input and output, sometimes because it is more efficient to store the results of a computation so that the stored value can be used rather than recomputed at a later time, and sometimes because it is a natural way of representing his problem—for example, in the case of discrete event simulation or the monitoring and control of some real world process.

Thus it is necessary to depart from the welcome simplicity of the mathematical expression, but to attempt to preserve as far as possible the structuring principles which it embodies. Fortunately, Algol 60 (in its compound, conditional, for, and procedure statements) has shown the way in which this can be done. The advantages of the use of these program structures is becoming apparent even to programmers using languages which do not provide the notations to express them.

The introduction of program structures into a language not only helps the programmer, but does not injure the efficiency of an implementation. Indeed, the avoidance of wild jumping will be of positive benefit on machines with slave stores or paging hardware; and if a compiler makes any attempt at optimization, the clear indication of the control structure of a program can only simplify this task.

There is one case where Algol 60 does not provide an appropriate structure, and that is when a selection must be made from more than two alternatives in accordance with some integer value. In this case, the programmer must declare a switch, specifying a list of labels, and then jump to the ith label in this list.

> $switch$ SS = L1, L2, L3;
>
> . . .
> $go\ to$ SS[i];
> L1: Q_1; $go\ to$ L;
> L2: Q_2; $go\ to$ L;
> L3: Q_3;
> L:

Unfortunately, introduction of the switch as a nameable entity is not only an extra complexity in the language and implementation, but gives plenty of scope for tricky programming and even trickier errors, particularly when jumping to some common continuation point on completion of the alternative action.

The first language designers to deal with the problem of the switch proposed to generalize it by providing the concept of the label array, into which the programmer could store label values. This has some peculiarly unpleasant consequences in addition to the disadvantages of the switch. First, it obscures the program, so that its control structure is not apparent from the form of the program, but can be determined only by a run-time trace. And second, the programmer is given the power to jump back into the middle of a block he has already exited, with unpredictable consequences unless a run-time check is inserted. In Algol 60 the scope rules make this error detectable at compile time.

The way to avoid all these problems is a very simple extension to the Algol 60 conditional notation, a construction which I have called the case construction. In this notation, the example of the switch shown above would take the form

> $case$ i of
> $\{Q_1,$
> $Q_2,$
> $Q_3\};$

This was my first programming language invention, of which I am still most proud, since it appears to bear no trace of compensating disadvantage.

Variables

One of the most powerful and most dangerous aspects of machine code programming is that each individual instruction of the code can change the content of any register, any location of store, and alter the condition of any peripheral; it can even change its neighboring instructions or itself. Worse still, the identity of the location changed is not always apparent from the written form of the instruction; it cannot be determined until run time, when the values of base registers, index registers, and indirect addresses are known. This does not matter if the program is correct, but if there is the slightest error, even only in a single bit, there is no limit to the damage which may be done, and no limit to the difficulty of tracing the cause of the damage. In summary, the interface between every two consecutive instructions in a machine code program consists of the state of the entire machine—registers, mainstore, backing stores and all peripheral equipment.

In a high-level language, the programmer is deprived of the dangerous power to update his own program while it is running. Even more valuable, he has the power to split his machine into a number of separate variables, arrays, files, etc. When he wishes to update any of these, he must quote its name explicitly on the left of the assignment so that the identity of the part of the machine subject to change is immediately apparent. And, finally, a high-level language can guarantee that all variables are disjoint, and that updating any one of them cannot possibly have any effect on any other.

Unfortunately, many of these advantages are not maintained in the design of procedures and parameters in Algol 60 and other languages. But instead of mending these minor faults, many language designers have preferred to extend them throughout the whole language by introducing the concept of reference, pointer, or indirect address into the language as an assignable item of data. This immediately gives rise in a high-level language to one of the most notorious confusions of machine code, namely that between an address and its contents. Some languages attempt to solve this by even more confusing automatic coercion rules. Worse still, an indirect assignment through a pointer, just as in machine code, can update any store location whatsoever, and the damage is no longer confined to the variable explicitly named as the target of assignment. For example, in Algol 68, the assignment

$$x := y;$$

always changes x, but the assignment

$$x := y + 1;$$

if x is a reference variable, may change any other variable (of appropriate type) in the whole machine. One variable it can *never* change is $x!$. Unlike all other values (integers, strings, arrays, files, etc.) references have no meaning independent of a particular run of a program. They cannot be input as data, and they cannot be output as results. If either data or references to data have to be stored on files or backing stores, the problems are immense. And on many machines they have a surprising overhead on performance; for example, they will clog up instruction pipelines, data lookahead, slave stores, and even paging systems. References are like jumps, leading wildly from one part of a data structure to another. Their introduction into high-level languages has been a step backward from which we may never recover.

Block structure

In addition to the advantages of disjoint named variables, high-level languages provide the programmer with a powerful tool for achieving even greater security, namely the scope and locality associated with block structure. In Fortran or Algol 60, if the programmer needs a variable for the purposes of a particular part of his program, he can declare it locally to that part of the program. This enables the programmer to make manifest in the structure of his program the close association between the variable and the code which uses it; and he can be absolutely confident that no other part of the program, whether written by himself or another, can ever interfere with, or even look at, the variable without his written permission, i.e., unless he passes it as a parameter to a particular named procedure. The use of locality also greatly reduces the width of the interfaces between parts of the program; the fact that programmers no longer need to tell each other the names of their working variables is only one of the beneficial consequences.

Like all the best programming language features, the locality and scope rules of Algol 60 are not only of great assistance to the programmer in the decomposition of his task and the implementation of its subtasks; they also permit economy in the use of machine resources, for example main store. The fact that a group of variables is required for purposes local only to part of a program means that their values will usually be relevant only while that part of the program is being executed. It is therefore possible to reallocate to other purposes the storage assigned to these variables as soon as they are no longer required. Since the blocks of a program in Algol 60 are always completed in the exact reverse of the order in which they were entered, the dynamic reallocation of storage can be accomplished by stack techniques, with small overhead of time and space, or none at all in the case of blocks which are not procedure bodies, for which the administration can be done at compile time. Finally, the programmer is encouraged to declare at the same time those variables which will be used together, and these will be allocated in contiguous locations, which will increase the efficiency of slave storage and paging techniques.

It is worthy of note that the economy of dynamic reallocation is achieved without any risk that the programmer will accidentally refer to a variable that has been reallocated, and this is guaranteed by a compile-time and not a run-time check. All these advantages are achieved in Algol 60 by the close correspondence between the statically visible scope of a variable in a source program and the dynamic lifetime of its storage when the program is run. A language designer should therefore be extremely reluctant to break this correspondence, which can easily be done, for example, by the introduction of references which may point to variables of an exited block. The rules of Algol 68, designed to detect, such so-called "dangling references" at compile time, are both complicated and ineffective; and PL/I does not bother at all.

Procedures and parameters

According to current theories of structured programming, every large-scale programming project involves the design, use, and implementation of a special-purpose programming language, with its own data concepts and primitive operations, specifically oriented to that particular project. The procedure and parameter are the major tool provided for this purpose by high-level languages since Fortran. In itself, this affords all the major advantages claimed for extensible languages. Furthermore, in its implementation as a closed subroutine, the procedure can achieve very great economies of storage at run time. For these reasons, the language designer should give the greatest attention to this feature of his language. Procedure calls and parameter passing should produce very compact code. Lengthy preludes and postludes must be avoided. The effect of the procedure on its parameters should be clearly manifest from its syntactic form, and should be simple to understand and resistant to error. And, finally, since the procedure interface is so often the interface between major parts of a program, the correctness of its use should be subjected to the most rigorous compile-time check.

The chief defects of the Fortran parameter mechanism are:

(1) It fails to give a notational distinction at the call side between parameters that convey values into a procedure, that convey values out of a procedure, and that do both. This negates many of the advantages which the assignment statement has over machine code programming.

(2) The shibboleth of independent compilation prohibits compile-time checks on parameter passing, just where interface errors are most likely and most disastrous and most difficult to debug.

(3) The ability to define side effects of function calls negates many of the advantages of arithmetic expressions.

At least Fortran permits efficient implementation, unless a misguided but all too frequent attempt is made to permit a mixture of languages across the procedure interface. A subroutine that does not know whether it is being called from Algol or from Fortran has a hard life.

Algol 60 perpetuates all these disadvantages, but not the advantage. The difficulty of compile-time parameter checking is due to the absence of parameter specifications. Even if an implementation insists on full specification (and most do), the programmer has no way of specifying the parameters of a formal procedure parameter. This is one of the excuses for the inefficiency of many Algol implementations. The one great advance of Algol 60 is the value parameter, which is immeasurably superior to the dummy parameter of Fortran and PL/I. What a shame that the name parameter is the default!

But perhaps the most subtle defect of the Algol 60 parameter is that the user is permitted to pass the same variable twice as an actual parameter corresponding to two distinct formal parameters. This immediately violates the principle of disjointness and can lead to many curious, unexpected effects. For example, if a procedure

$$\text{matrix multiply } (A, B, C)$$

is intended to have the effect

$$A := B \times C,$$

it would seem reasonable to square A by

$$\text{matrix multiply } (A, A, A).$$

This error is prohibited in standard Fortran, but few programmers realize it, and it is rarely enforced by compile-time or run-time check. No wonder the procedure interface is the one on which run-time debugging aids have to concentrate.

Types

Among the most trivial but tiresome errors of low-level programming are type errors—for example, using a fixed-point operation to add floating-point numbers, using an address as an integer or vice versa, or forgetting the position of a field in a data structure. The effects of such errors, although fully explicable in terms of bit patterns and machine operations, are so totally unrelated to the concepts in terms of which the programmer is thinking that the detection and correction of such errors can be exceptionally tedious. The trouble is that the hardware of the computer is far too tolerant and forgiving. It is willing to accept almost any sequence of instructions and make sense of them at its own level. That is the secret of the power, flexibility, simplicity, and even reliability of computer hardware, and should therefore be cherished.

But it is also one of the main reasons why we turn to high-level languages, which can eliminate the risk of such error by a compile-time check. The programmer declares the type of each variable, and the compiler can work out the type of each result; it therefore always knows what type of machine code instruction to generate. In cases where there is no meaningful operation (for example, the addition of an integer and a Boolean), the compiler can inform the programmer of his mistake, which is far better than having to chase its curious consequences after the program has run.

However, not all language designers would agree. Some languages, by complex rules of automatic type transfers and coercions, prefer the dangerous tolerance of machine code, but with the following added disadvantages:

(1) The result will often be ''nearly'' right, so that the programmer has less warning of his error.

(2) The inefficiency of the conversion is often a shock.

(3) The language is much complicated by the rules.

(4) The introduction of genuine language extensibility is made much more difficult.

Apart from the elimination of risk of error, the concept of type is of vital assistance in the design and documentation phases of program development. The design of abstract and concrete data structures is one of the first tools for refining our understanding of problems, and for defining the common interfaces between the parts of a large program. The declaration of the name and structure or range of values of each variable is a most important aspect of clear programming, and the formal description of the relationship of each variable to other program variables is a most important part of its annotation. Finally, an informal description of the purpose of each variable and its manner of use is a most important part of program documentation. In fact, I believe a language should enable the programmer to declare the units in which his numbers are expressed, so that a compiler can check that he is not confusing radians and degrees, adding heights to weights, or comparing meters with yards.

Again not all language designers would agree. Many languages do not require the programmer to declare his variables at all. Instead they define complex default rules which the compiler must apply to undeclared variables. But this can only encourage sloppy program design and documentation, and nullify many of the advantages of block structure and type checking; the default rules soon get so complex that they are very likely to give results not expected by the programmer, and as ludicrously or subtly inappropriate to his intentions as a machine code program which contains a type error.

Of course, wise programmers have learned that it is worthwhile to expend the effort to avoid these dangers. They eagerly scan the compiler listings to ensure that every variable has been declared, and that all the characteristics assigned to it by default are acceptable. What a pity that the designers of these languages take such trouble to give such trouble to their users and themselves.

Language feature design

This paper has given many practical hints on how *not* to design a programming language. It has even suggested that many recent languages have followed these hints. But there are very few positive hints on what to put into your next language design. Nearly everything I have ever published is full of positive and practical suggestions for programming language features, notations, and implementation methods; furthermore, for the last 10 years, I have tried to pursue the same objectives in language design that I have expounded here, and I have tried to make my proposals as convincing as I could. And yet I have never designed a programming language—only programming language features. It is my belief that these two design activities should be more clearly separated in the future.

(1) The designer of a new feature should concentrate on one feature at a time. If necessary, he should design it in the context of some well known programming language which he likes. He should make sure that his feature mitigates some disadvantage or remedies some incompleteness of the language, without compromising any of its existing merits. He should show how the feature can be simply and efficiently implemented. He should write a section of a user manual, explaining clearly with examples how the feature is intended to be used. He should check carefully that there are not traps lurking for the unwary user, which cannot be checked at compile time. He should write a number of example programs, evaluating all the consequences of using the feature, in comparison with its many alternatives. And, finally, if a simple proof rule can be given for the feature, this would be the final accolade.

(2) The language designer should be familiar with many alternative features designed by others, and should have excellent judgment in choosing the best and rejecting any that are mutually inconsistent. He must be capable of reconciling, by good engineering design, any remaining minor inconsistencies or overlaps between separately designed features. He must have a clear idea of the scope and purpose and range of application of his new language, and how far it should go in size and complexity. He should have the resources to implement the language on one or more machines, to write user manuals, introductory texts, advanced texts; he should construct auxiliary programming aids and library programs and procedures; and, finally, he should have the political will and resources to sell and distribute the language to its intended range of customers. One thing he should not do is to include untried ideas of his own. His task is consolidation, not innovation.

Conclusion

A final hint: listen carefully to what language users *say* they want, until you have an understanding of what they *really* want. Then find some way of achieving the latter at a small fraction of the cost of the former. This is the test of success in language design, and of progress in programming methodology. Perhaps these two are the same subject anyway. ■

Appendix: Annotated reading list

"Report on the Algorithmic Language ALGOL 60," ed. P. Naur, *Comm. ACM*, Vol. 3, 1960, pp. 299-314. The more I ponder the principles of language design and the techniques which put them into practice, the more is my amazement and admiration of Algol 60. Here is a language so far ahead of its time, that it was not only an improvement on its predecessors, but also on nearly all its successors.

Of particular interest are its introduction of all the main program structuring concepts, the simplicity and clarity of its description, rarely equalled and never surpassed. Consider especially the avoidance of abbreviation in the syntax names and equations, and the inclusion of examples in every section.

D. E. Knuth, "The Remaining Troublespots in ALGOL 60," *Comm. ACM*, Vol. 10, No. 10, Oct. 1967, pp. 611-618. Most of these troublespots have been eliminated in the widely used subsets of the language. When you can design a language with so few troublespots, you can be proud. The real remaining troublespot is the declining quality of implementations.

N. Wirth and C. A. R. Hoare, "A Contribution to the Development of ALGOL," *Comm. ACM*, Vol. 9, No. 6, June 1966, pp. 413-432. This language is widely known as Algol W. It remedies many of the defects of Algol 60 and includes many of the good features of Fortran IV and LISP. Its introduction of references avoids most of the defects described above under "Block structure." It has been extremely well implemented on the IBM 360 and has a small and scattered band of devoted followers.

N. Wirth, "PL/360," *J. ACM*, Vol. 15, No. 1, Jan. 1968. This introduces the benefits of program structures to low-level programming for the IBM/360. It was hastily designed and implemented as a tool for implementing Algol W; it excited more interest than Algol W and has been widely imitated on other machines.

N. Wirth, "The Programming Language PASCAL," *Acta Informatica*, Vol. 1, No. 1, 1971, pp. 35-63. Designed to combine the machine-independence of Algol W with the efficiency and control of PL/360. New features are the simple but powerful and efficient type-definition capabilities, including sets and a very clean treatment of files. When used to write its own translator, it achieves a remarkable combination of clarity of structure and detail together with high efficiency in producing good object code.

O-J. Dahl, E. W. Dijkstra, and C. A. R. Hoare, *Structured Programming*, Academic Press, New York, 1972. Expounds a systematic approach to the design and development and documentation of computer programs. The last section is an excellent introduction to SIMULA 67 and the ideas which underlie it.

J. McCarthy, "Recursive Functions of Symbolic Expressions and Their Computation by Machine, Part 1," *Comm. ACM*, Vol. 3, No. 4, Apr. 1960. Describes a beautifully simple and powerful, fully functional language for symbol manipulation. Introduces the scan-mark garbage collection technique, which makes such languages feasible. LISP has some good interactive implementations, widely used in artificial intelligence projects. It has also been extended in many ways, some good and some bad, some local and some short-lived.

"ASA Standard FORTRAN," *Comm. ACM*, Vol. 7, No. 10, Oct. 1964. This language had the right objectives. It introduces the array, the arithmetic expression, and the procedure. The parameter mechanism is very efficient and potentially secure. It has some very efficient implementations for numerical applications. When used outside this field, it is little more helpful or machine-independent than assembly code, and can be remarkably inefficient. Its input/output is cumbersome, prone to error, and surprisingly inefficient. The standardizers have maintained the horrors of early implementations (the equivalence algorithm, second-level definition), and have resolutely set their face against the advance of language design technology, thereby saving it from many later horrors.

"ASA Standard COBOL," *Codasyl COBOL J. Development*, 1968 (National Bureau of Standards Handbook 106). Describes a language suitable for simple applications in business data processing. It contains good data structuring capability, but poor facilities for abstraction. It aimed at readability, but unfortunately achieved only prolixity; it aimed to provide a complete programming tool, in a way few languages have since. It is poor for variable format processing. The primacy of the character data item makes it rather inefficient on modern machines; and the methods provided to regain efficiency (e.g., SYNCHRONIZED) often introduce machine-dependency and insecurity.

Acknowledgments

The form of this paper owes much to the kind suggestions of Don Knuth.

The work on this paper was supported in part by the National Science Foundation under grant number GJ 36473X and by ARPA Research Contract DAHC 15-73-C-0435.

INFORMATION PROCESSING 74 – NORTH-HOLLAND PUBLISHING COMPANY (1974)

ON THE DESIGN OF PROGRAMMING LANGUAGES

Niklaus WIRTH

*Institut für Informatik, Eidg. Technische Hochschule
Zürich, Switzerland*

(INVITED PAPER)

Reprinted with permission from *Information Processing 74*, pp. 386-393. Copyright
1974 North Holland Publishing Company.

This paper reports on some past experiments in the design of programming languages. It
presents the view that a language should be simple, and that simplicity must be achieved
by transparence and clarity of its features and by a regular structure, rather than by
utmost conciseness and unwanted generality. The paper contains an overview of the
language designer's problems and dilemmas, and ends with some hints drawn from past
experience.

In order to prevent misunderstanding or even
disappointment, I should like to warn the
reader not to interpret this title as an
announcement of a general critique of commonly used languages. Although this might be
a very entertaining subject, probably all
that can be said about it has been said and
heard by those willing to listen. There is
no reason to repeat it now. Neither do I
intend to present an objective assessment of
the general situation in the development of
programming languages, the technical trends,
the commercial influences, and the psychology
of their users. The activities in this field
were enormous over the past years, and it
would be presumptuous to believe that a
single person could present a comprehensive,
objective picture. Moreover, many aspects
have been aptly reviewed and commented elsewhere (1–3).

Instead, I should like to convey a view of
the development of design attitudes, of the
shift of emphasis in design goals over the
past decade. Also, I will try to provide
some insight into the multitude of problems
aspects, and demands that the designer of a
language is facing, and to woo gently for
recognition of the difficulties of this
profession. Let me start by recalling some
of my own reminiscences of incidents that
caused me to end up in this role of language
designer.

AN EXCURSION INTO "HISTORY"

My interest in computers had been awakened
when I was an engineering student in the
late 1950s; I was fascinated on the one hand
by simplicity and inherent reliability of
the basic building blocks, the digital
circuits, and on the other hand by the
astounding variety of effects that could be
obtained by combining many of them in different ways. Moreover, these combinations could
be varied not by extensive and cumbersome
use of the soldering iron, but by merely
composing ingenious sequences of hexadecimal
digits placed on a magnetic drum. As the
general task of an engineer is the improvement of his technical gadgets, I perceived
that computers were an ideal ground for
engineering activities, and felt that there
was ample room for further improvement. This
assessment turned out to be correct up to

the present day. But how was progress to be
achieved? One way was by enhancing the reliability and effectiveness of their electronic components. The other – hazily defined
path – seemed to be to make computers more
conveniently usable, to make them less of an
exclusive domain of the highly trained
specialist.

This was the situation when I entered graduate school at Berkeley: In one room there
stood a huge prototype of a computer with a
bewildering number of wires and tubes. In a
much smaller room nearby there were a few
such specialists, talking about a "language"
and a "translator". Luckily for me, a student
helping to bring the big monster of a computer into operation didn't report too
enthusiastically about that project, and I
perceived the feeling that the future of
computer hardware design did not lie in a
university department anyway. Hence, I
decided to explore the other alley, although
that group was surrounded by skepticism, as
word passed that some of these people did
neither know Ohm's law nor Maxwell's equations.

The new and fascinating project under the
direction of H.D. Huskey consisted in adding
facilities to the programming language NELIAC
by extending the translator program. This
program was, remarkably, coded in the very
language that it was compiling and, in retrospect, quite advanced for its time (4).
Indeed, the fascination of the project
originated much more from the sense of
adventurousness than from the satisfaction
of achieved perfection. For, although programming in NELIAC proved to be considerably
more convenient than exercises in the
cryptology of hexadecimal codes, the room
for still further improvements continued to
appear unlimited. Looking at it from the
distance, that compiler was a horror; the
excitement came precisely from having insight
into a machinery that nobody understood
fully. There was the distinct air of sorcery.

Then Algol 60 appeared in the literature and
– after the difficulties of learning the new
syntactic formalism were mastered – began to
provide some relief from the oppressive
feeling that there was no way to bring order
into large languages and compilers. Yet even
then, the task of constructing an Algol

compiler generating acceptably good code appeared enormous. The more the Algol compiler project neared completion, the more vanished order and clarity of purpose. It was then that I clearly felt the distinct yearning for <u>simplicity</u> for the first time. I became convinced that we should learn to master simpler tasks before tackling big ones, and that we need to be equipped with much better linguistic and mental tools. But apparently "useful" languages had to be big.

SIMPLICITY IN GENERALITY

In this situation, A. van Wijngaarden appeared like a prophet with his idea of Generalised Algol (5). His point was that languages were not only too complex, but due to this very complexity also too restrictive. "In order that a language be powerful and elegant it should not contain many concepts and it should not be defined with many words." The new trend was to discover the fundamental concepts of algorithms, to extract them from their various incarnations in different language features, and to present them in a pure, distilled form, free from arbitrary and restrictive rules of applicability.

The following short example may illustrate the principle. In Algol 60, the concept of a subprogram appears in two features: as declared procedure, and as name parameter to procedures. The passing of a parameter is realised as an assignment of an object (the actual parameter) to a variable (the formal parameter). A simplification and concurrent increase in power and flexibility of Algol can therefore be obtained by unifying the notions of procedure and parameter, by letting them become objects that can be assigned to variables like numbers or logical values. Let such an object be denoted by the program text enclosed by quote marks; the correspondence between constructs of Algol 60 and the generalised notation are shown by the following table:

Algol 60	Generalisation
<u>procedure</u> P; <statement>	P := `<statement>`
Q(<expression>)	Q(`<expression>`)

The gain in simplicity of language is obvious and the resulting gain in flexibility is striking. For example, it is now possible to assign different subroutines to a variable at different times, or even to replace a function subroutine by a constant! We are suddenly offered the power so far reserved to the assembly language coder letting his program modify some of its own instructions.

Implementation of such far reaching generalisations were on open challenge. I decided to investigate, whether these concepts could be condensed into a minimal language and compiler, as a language without compiler seemed to be of marginal value to me. This effort resulted in my first programming language, called Euler (5). It was a success in several ways, certainly if measured by the number of subsequent implementations on a wide variety of computers. The language was accepted as an intellectual challenge, a

flexible and powerful vehicle. Its simplicity and compactness made it an ideal implementation exercise for many prospective compiler engineers. Its greatest value, however, lay in revealing how simplicity should <u>not</u> be understood and achieved.

The premise that a language should not be burdened by (syntactical) rules that define meaningful texts (5) led to a language where it was difficult and almost impossible to detect a flaw in the logic of a program. It led to what I like to call a high-level Turing machine. Making mistakes is human (particularly in programming), and we need all the help possible to avoid committing them. But how can one expect a language to aid in avoiding mistakes, if it is even incapable of assisting in their detection.

The lesson is, then, that if we try to achieve simplicity through generality of language we may end up with programs that through their very conciseness and lack of redundancy elude our limited intellectual grasp. It is a mistake to consider the prime characteristic of high-level languages to be that they allow to express programs merely in their shortest possible form and in terms of letters, words, and mathematical symbols instead of coded numbers. Instead, the language is to provide a framework of abstractions and structures that are appropriately adapted to our mental habits, capabilities, and limitations. The "distance" of these abstractions from the actual realisation in terms of a computer is an established measure for the "height" of a language's level.

The key, then, lies not so much in minimising the number of basic features of a language, but rather in keeping the included facilities simple to understand in all their consequences of usage and free from unexpected interactions when they are combined. A form must be found for these facilities which is convenient to remember and intuitively clear to a programmer, and which acts as a natural guidance in the formulation of his ideas. The language should not be <u>burdened</u> with syntactical rules, it must be <u>supported</u> by them. They must therefore be purposeful, and prohibit the construction of ambiguities. It is a good idea to employ adequate, concise key words, and to forbid that they can be used in any other way. Prolixity is to be avoided, as it introduces a wrong kind of redundancy.

LEVELS OF ABSTRACTIONS

One of the most crucial steps in the design of a language is the choice of the abstraction upon which programs are to base. They can be selected only if the designer has a clear picture of the purpose of his language, of the area of its intended application. But all too often that purpose is not neatly specified and includes so many diverse aspects that a designer is given only inadequate guidance from prospective users. But at least he should restrict his selection to <u>abstractions from the same level</u> which are in some sense compatible with each other. I should like to offer three examples to this topic.

Algol 60 has chosen a well-defined set of abstract objects of computation: numbers and logical values, replacing bits and words as used on a lower level. The operations that are applicable to them are governed by mathematical laws and axioms which can be understood without referring to the number's representation in terms of bits and words. In the realm of control structures, the language introduces the operations of selective execution and repetition in the form of neatly structured statements. But their form was not sufficiently flexible - e.g. repetition is intimately coupled with a variable progressing through an arithmetic series of values, and selection s only provided among two alternatives. To provide the user with a facility for cases not covered by these control structures, the designers of Algol resorted to borrowing the universally applicable jump order from the lower level of machine coding. The <u>goto</u> statement is but a polished form of the jump.

This may not seem too serious in itself. But consider that now the programmer is able to use these facilities combined. The following example - which an honest Algol programmer will refrain from using, or otherwise will at least get a bad conscience - shows the point.

<u>for</u> i := 1 <u>step</u> 1 <u>until</u> 100 <u>do</u>
<u>begin</u> S; <u>if</u> p <u>then</u> <u>goto</u> L <u>end</u>

The whole purpose of the for clause is to proclamate to the reader: "the qualified statement is going to be executed once for every i = 1,2,3,...,100". The jump, however, may sneakily cause this promise to be broken! Whereas jumping out of a substructure may be considered to be a matter of morale only, jumping back into a structure even raises technical problems. They require the establishment of protective rules and restrictions which are afflicted by the stigma of improvisation and afterthought. They complicate the language by burdening its definition, its comprehension, and its compiler.

The second example concerns the notion of <u>pointers</u> or <u>references</u> in high-level languages. When programming in assembly code, probably the most powerful pitfall is the possibility to compute the address of a storage cell that is to be changed. The effective address may range over the entire store (and even be that of the instruction itself). A very essential feature of high-level languages is that they permit a conceptual dissection of the store into disjoint parts by declaring distinct variables. The programmer may then rely on the assertion that every assignment affects only that variable which explicitly appears to the left of the assignment operator in his program. He may then focus his attention to the change of that single variable, whereas in machine coding he always has - in principle - to consider the entire store as the state of the computation. The necessary prerequisite for being able to think in terms of safely independent variables is of course the condition that no part of the store may assume more than a single name. Whereas this highly desirable property is sacrificed in Fortran by the use of the "equivalence" statement,

Algol loses it through its generality of parameter mechanism and rule of scope. Even if the sensible rule is observed that a procedure's parameters must denote disjoint variables, one and the same variable may be referred to under more than one name, as shown by the following example.

<u>begin</u> <u>integer</u> a;
   <u>procedure</u> S(x); <u>integer</u> x;
   <u>begin</u> a := a+1; x := x ↑2
   <u>end</u>;
   a := 1; S(a); write(a)
<u>end</u>

This design partly stems from the failure to separate the roles of textual abbreviation and of parametric program decomposition, both projected onto the same facility of the procedure. For mere textual abbreviations, one might be more willing to refrain from the use of parameters; in the case of program decomposition, communication with the environment might advantageously be restricted to explicit parameters. Hence, the notion of simplicity and frugality was rather counterproductive when viewed from the point of programming security.

We note that a **parameter** substitution represents an assignment of the storage <u>address</u> of the actual variable (a) to the formal parameter (x). In the spirit of generalisation it appeared as highly logical to admit the address into the society of computable objects. The address of a variable a - now called a reference - was thus introduced in the language Euler and denoted by @ a . It can be assigned to any other variable, say x . The variable a is then openly available under two names, a and x., and there is no limit to the number of further names that can be given to a . This experiment of reopening Pandora's box of storage addresses in Euler provided a clear warning of their undesirability, but didn't prevent the introduction of references into Algol 68 in their fullest flexibility.

The concept of <u>data type</u> provides added security insofar as a compiler may check against inadvertant use of incompatible variables in, for instance, assignments. This is, in itself, introducing another restriction unknown at the level of machine code, where every cell can be loaded with a copy of every other cell's content. The idea of simplicity through generality again led to the elimination of restrictive type rules, and of the data type in general. It was adopted by a family of languages designed to fill the apparent gap between high-level languages and assembly code, which are now known as machine oriented higher order languages (Mohols). They permit the construction of expressions with "untyped" operands and the application of both arithmetic and logical operations on the same variables. The result of programs written in such languages can only be understood through knowledge of the particular storage representation of data in terms of bits and words. Although effects may be produced that turn out to be the desired ones, they force the programmer to leave the realm of abstraction that a language is pretending to offer him.

So much for the third example of transgression of levels of abstraction in languages.

THE THREE EXAMPLES REVISITED

I do not deny that there are situations in programming which call for facilities not present in Algol-like languages. But they should not be met by compromising on the level of abstraction. The sneaky reintroduction of patently pernicious facilities from the era of machine coding is not an **acceptable** solution. In order to establish remedies, we must discover the true reasons for the programmers wish of such facilities. The language designer must not ask "what do you want?", but rather "how does your problem arise?" For, the answer to the first question will inevitably be "jumps, type-less operands, and addresses".

To convey an idea of the spirit in which a designer ought to approach such problems, I will sketch possible solutions to the three mentioned cases. The presented features do <u>not</u> provide the full flexibility inherent in jumps, type-less operands, and free address manipulation. But this is precisely their virtue; they still impose certain sensible restrictions of usage, and help maintain a programming discipline. In particular, they do not compromise the language's high level of abstraction; they do not introduce notions which can be explained only in terms of an underlying machine.

In the case of the for statement, what the programmer really needs is not necessarily a jump order, but merely a more flexible way to express termination of a repetition. The solution consists in providing a simpler form of repetitive statement whose termination does not necessarily depend on a variable moving through·an arithmetic progression. Widely accepted forms are the while- and repeat statements, for example

<u>while</u> B <u>do</u> S
<u>repeat</u> S <u>until</u> B

The important point is that now the total effect of the composite statement can be deduced solely from the properties of the repeated component. The pertinent deduction rule can be formally expressed, for instance in Hoare's formalism (7). If P and Q denote any assertions on the state of the computation, then $P\{S\}Q$ means: if P holds before the execution of S , and this execution terminates, then Q holds after termination. The two deduction rules governing the above statement forms are (8):

$$\frac{P\wedge B \ \{S\} \ P}{P\{\underline{while} \ B \ \underline{do} \ S\} \ P\wedge\neg B}$$

$$\frac{P\{S\}Q \ , \ \neg B\wedge Q\{S\}Q}{P\{\underline{repeat} \ S \ \underline{until} \ B\} \ Q\wedge B}$$

Another situation requiring the use of a jump in Algol arises when one statement has to be selected among many. A feature invented by Hoare in exactly the same spirit, that not only replaces a jump and a switch declaration, but expresses the selection of one case among many in a structured, orderly way, is the case statement (9).

As for the second example, one may ask why addresses or pointers are needed anyway. I do not intend to pursue this argument here, but claim that if one consents to their necessity, they should be admitted only in a considerably tamed form. Security in pointer handling can be improved drastically by the following measures:

1. Every pointer variable is allowed to point to objects of a single type only (or to none); it is said to be <u>bound</u> to that type. This rule allows to maintain a compiler's capability of full type checking.

2. Pointers may only refer to variables that have no explicit name declared in the program, that is, they point exclusively to anonymous variables allocated when needed during execution. This rule protects the programmer from the dangers arising when variables are accessible under different names.

3. The programmer must explicitly specify whether he refers to a pointer itself or to the object to which the pointer refers (no automatic "coercion"). This rule helps to avoid ambiguous constructs and complicated default conventions liable to misunderstanding.

The reasons ~~why programmers~~ sometimes wish to deal with type-less variables are more difficult to pinpoint. The most frequent one is probably the necessity to pack different kinds of data densely into a single word, which the available language always regards as an indivisible entity. For instance, we might have to pack a triple r - say a file descriptor - consisting of a name x of 6 characters, a 5-bit status information s , and a 2-digit length count n . (The 5 status bits may, for example, indicate a tape's loadpoint, end of tape, and end of record positions, its density mode and parity check status.) A pictorial representation might be

<table>
<tr><td></td><td>x</td><td>s</td><td>n</td></tr>
<tr><td>r</td><td>A B C D E F</td><td>10001</td><td>89</td></tr>
<tr><td></td><td>36</td><td>5</td><td>7</td></tr>
</table>

and a common way to denote the value of such a triple is as an octal (or hexadecimal) number, because the word is available in the language under the misnomer "integer". In order to determine this number, the programmer must forget his original abstractions and perform the binary encoding "by hand". If he is lucky, he obtains

$$r = 0102030405064331_8 \quad \text{or} \quad r = 0420C41468C9_{16}$$

Part of the true information is arithmetic in its nature (n), another is logical (s), and a third alphabetic (x). Hence, all kinds of orders must be applicable. But this is only possible, if the operand is not restricted by its characterisation through an associated type. What the programmer really needs in this case is a data structuring facility relieving him from the tedious and errorprone labor of data encoding and packing.

As an illustration, in the programming language Pascal the triple r can be directly declared as a structured variable, yielding the dense packing indicated by the picture above (10). The first component of r is declared to be an array of 6 characters, the second to be a set of status indicators, and the third a number in the range of 0 to 99.

```
type string = packed array[0..5] of char;
   indicator = (loadpoint,eof,eor,pchk,
               highdensity);
var r: packed record
         x: string;
         s: set of indicator;
         n: 0 .. 99
      end
```

Assignments, instead of involving obscure arithmetic operations expressing shifts etc., are simply written as

```
r.x := 'ABCDEF';
r.s := [loadpoint,highdensity];
r.n := 89
```

Each of the three components has a distinct name and a distinct type. Its proper usage can be completely checked by compiler and program reader alike. Naturally, such a structuring facility complicates a compiler considerably, much depending on the quality of the underlying hardware architecture. It even increases the "volume" of a language; but significantly, it does not reduce its conceptual simplicity.

The proposed solutions to the three mentioned problem areas lie in introducing restrictive rules, and are contrary to the spirit of "power through simplicity" and "simplicity through generality". But they have already proven to be wisely chosen precautions and have aided tremendously in practical programming. The additional burden of type checking by the compiler has been much more than compensated by the amount of confidence gained in the final programs. And this is what good language design should mainly aim for.

COMBINING FEATURES INTO A LANGUAGE

A characteristic of a well-designed feature is that is does not imply any unexpected, hidden inefficiencies of implementation. The packed record structure shown above displays this property: a compiler has full knowledge of the address of each such variable and of the position of the components within a word. It can therefore generate appropriate and efficient instructions for access, packing and unpacking. The whole advantage of this scheme, however, immediately vanishes, if, for example, we introduce so-called dynamic arrays, that is, if we allow information about the actual dimensions of an array to

be withheld from the compiler. The textual scan of the program does not reveal the amount of storage needed; as a consequence dynamic allocation must be used involving indirect addressing. This not only impairs the efficiency of the code, but – more importantly – destroys the whole scheme of storage economy.

This is but one example for many that could be listed to show how the combination of two seemingly harmless and well-understood features may suddenly have disastrous effects. A capable language designer must not only be able to select appropriate features, but must also be able to foresee all effects of their being used in combination.

Naturally, one might suggest that a compiler be designed that generates efficient and dense code when the component sizes are known, and less effective code otherwise. But this attitude leads to the optimising monster compilers so well known for their bulkiness and unreliability. Even more significant is the consideration that a good language should not only aid the programmer in avoiding mistakes, but that it must also give him an idea of the complexity and effectiveness of the features it offers. However, if the use of the same feature under only slightly different circumstances yields widely different factors of economy, then the language clearly lacks this highly desirable property. It is very important that the basic method of implementation of each feature can be explained independently from all other features in a manner sufficiently precise to give the programmer a good estimate of the computational effort involved. Some modern languages fail miserably when measured on this criterion.

Transparence is particularly vital with respect to storage allocation and access technique, since storage access is such a frequent operation that any unanticipated, hidden complexity can have disastrous effects of the performance on a whole program. In fact, I found that a large number of programs perform poorly because of the language's tendency to hide "what is going on" with the misguided intention of "not bothering the programmer with details". Transparence of access mechanism can be achieved by neatly categorising data structuring facilities with respect to applicable access technique. This rule was taken as a guiding principle in the design of the language Pascal, which offers the following structuring facilities:

1. Arrays. Components are selected by computable index. Their offset calculation must in general be deferred until execution time (using index registers if available).

2. Records. Components are selected by a fixed selector name. Their address can therefore be evaluated entirely at compile time. As the compiler may retain their offsets individually in a table, the components are not restricted to be of the same size and type, as in the case of arrays.

3. Sets. Components are not individually selectable at all. Instead, the membership operator _in_ allows to test for their presence or absence. If the size of sets is sufficiently small, they can be represented by their characteristic function fitting into a single word.

4. Files (sequences). Since the length of a sequence may vary during program execution, a dynamic allocation mechanism is required. But it is considerably simplified, because only sequential access is permitted through a "window" displaying the component at the current position.

Variables of these fundamental structures can either be declared explicitly, or they may be invoked dynamically. In the first case they are known by their identifier, in the latter they must be accessed via pointer.

Knowledge of these access characteristics is vital for the programmer, as it is indispensible for the selection of data representation suitable for the algorithm. Regrettably, the current trend in language design seems to move in the opposite direction, namely to obscure these differences. The common excuse is that through the development of more suitable and more efficient hardware these differences would gradually disappear. The fact remains, however, that supposedly more suitable hardware becomes phenomenally complex. It is no longer economical to realise it directly in terms of electronic circuitry, and a new technique has therefore been invented – microprogramming. The essence of this development is that complicated features become the standard with their weird complexity well disguised, and that the programmer is denied the possibility to solve his tasks by simpler means. He doesn't even have a possibility to measure the built-in inefficiencies through quantitative comparisons!

LANGUAGE DESIGN IS DECISION MAKING

From the foregoing it may appear that the secret of good language design lies in a few rules and a sound attitude. In pracitce, of course, the designer is confronted with a bewildering variety of demands from various agents ranging from theoreticians to practitioners, from novices to experts, from revolutionaries crying for innovations to conservatives emphasising compatibility. Let me list a few of the most frequently encountered demands.

- The language must be easy to learn and easy to use.

- It must be safe from misinterpretation and misuse.

- It must be extensible without change of existing features.

- There must be a rigorous, mathematical definition, based on axioms and withstanding the scrutiny of logicians.

- The notation must be convenient and compatible with widely used (and sometimes not so logical) standards.

- The definition must be machine independent, that is without reference to a particular mechanism.

- The language must allow to make efficient use of the facilities of the available computer.

- The compiler must be able to generate efficient code and economise storage.

- The compiler must be fast and compact; it should be void of complex optimisation routines that are rarely used.

- The definition must be self-contained and complete. A reader must easily be able to identify the facilities needed for his purpose.

- The implementation must provide ready access to other facilities available on the system, such as program libraries and (therefore) subprograms written in different languages.

- The language and its compiler must be easily adaptable to different environments with different character sets and different operating system facilities.

- The compiler must be easily portable to other computers. Almost all of it should be conceived without specific reliance on a given order code and storage organisation.

- Time and cost for developing compiler and documentation must be minimal.

It is plain that several of these points are contradictory, but certainly not all of them. The designer must decide where he wishes to place emphasis. It is his task to find a carefully balanced compromise. In fact, the reconciliation of conflicting demands by well chosen compromises is an essential part of every engineering profession; language design should therefore be regarded as a typical engineering discipline. It can be mastered only by experience, and experience is usually gained only after a few failures! The designer's task is even aggravated by the fact that the conflicting demands come from different people whom he is supposed to serve. Whatever he decides, he should never expect unanimous approval.

However, I do not wish to convey the impression that sytisfying one criterion must necessarily mean sacrificing another. True progress appears through the invention of facilities that cater to several seemingly contradictory aims. The three examples mentioned before demonstrate that such progress is indeed feasible.

LANGUAGE DESIGN IS COMPILER CONSTRUCTION

In practice, a programming language is as good as its compiler(s).The believe that it should first be designed entirely in the abstract realm of, say, a set of axioms or an official document, is equally mistaken as the opinion that it must grow out of a practical experiment of implementation before being neatly documented. A successful language must grow out of clear ideas of design goals and of _simultaneous_ attempts to define it in terms of abstract structures, and to implement it on a computer, or preferably even on several computers. It

follows that experience in compiler construction is a prerequisite to successful language
design. Compiler design courses have indeed
appeared in the curricula of many computer
science department, and seem to be regarded
as the epitome of the software craft. Unfortunately they are often strongly biased
toward the aspect of syntax analysis, since
much theoretical work has been done in this
subject. However, the deep penetration of
this branch of theory has been of rather
small benefit to language design and sometimes was even detrimental. I am afraid that
it has misled many language designers to
believe that the complexity of a language's
syntax was of no concern, since an appropriate
parsing algorithm, if not already available,
could readily be found for any construction
introduced. But it is evident that a language
that is simple to parse for the compiler, is
also simple to parse for the human programmer,
and that can only be an asset. Moreover, the
real challenge in compiling is not the
detection of correct sentential forms, but
coping with ill-formed, erroneous programs,
in diagnosing the mistakes and in being able
to proceed in a sensible way.

The really essential prerequisite for
successful compiler construction is experience in the development of large, complex
programs. This includes mastery of techniques
in structuring programs and data in general,
and in selecting methods for various tasks in
particular, such as for scanning of text,
construction and search of symbol tables, and
composition of code sequences.

One is inclined to wonder where the training
of so many compiler and language designers
will lead, and whether it is justified. Here
I should like to point out that a general
appreciation of compiler principles will help
the understanding of computer operations and
promote the state of the art of programming
at large. But there is no reason to believe
that the growth rate of the population of
programming languages is thereby going to
decrease. The emphasis in new developments,
however, is gradually shifting from general
purpose toward application oriented languages.
It is precisely toward this trend that design
courses should be directed: exposition of
features and presentation of techniques that
are common to most areas amenable to algorithmic solution. Such features are, for
instance, the fundamental control concepts of
sequencing, conditioning, selection, repetition, and recursion. They form a well
established basis from which a designer can
proceed to fill the given framework with
specific facilities oriented toward his
particular task and area of application (11).

CONCLUSIONS

I have tried to convey a picture of the
problems, challenges, and ordeals facing a
language designer, and to draw some lessons
from experience gained in the design of a
series of languages and compilers. To con-
clude, let me summarise these lessons
learned.

- If you wish to develop a language, you must
  have a clear idea of how it is intended to
  be used.

- Keep in mind that a programming language is
  of no use without an efficient, reliable
  compiler and a clear, readable documentation.
  This should provide sufficient incentive to
  keep the language as simple as ever
  possible.

- Do not equate simplicity with lack of
  structure or limitless generality, but
  rather with transparence, clarity of
  purpose, and integrity of concepts.

- Adhere to a syntactic structure that can be
  analysed by simple techniques such as
  recursive descent with one-symbol lookahead.
  This not only aids a compiler, but also the
  programmer, and is vital for successful
  diagnosis of errors.

- Identify the basic abstractions on which
  the language is to be based. Try to define
  the language in terms of a mathematical
  formalism. This may help to detect hidden
  inconsistencies and to eliminate notions
  that cannot be understood in terms of the
  given abstractions.

- Do not consider the establishment of a
  formal definition as an end in itself. In
  particular, the formal definition cannot be
  a substitute for an informal presentation
  and for tutorial material. It is mostly an
  aid to the designer but not a user's
  document, in which mathematical rigor will
  contribute to volume but seldom serves the
  programmer's needs.

- Choose the basic features from the same
  level of abstraction. Obtain a clear idea
  on how to represent them in terms of a
  computer's order code and store. Be aware
  of the consequences arising from the
  coexistence of all the various features.
  They can sometimes be surprising and
  disastrous.

- Do not hesitate to exclude certain features
  that prove to be incompatible and too costly
  in terms of implementation. The fact that
  other languages include them is no guarantee
  for their indispensability.

- Obtain a sketch of the complete language
  before starting work on the compiler.
  Refrain from adopting highly controversial
  features; language changes are usually
  costly in time and effort even during
  development, and are virtually impossible
  after a compiler's release, if the language
  is successful.

- Design the language such that most checking
  operations can be performed at compile time
  and need not be deferred until execution.
  The concept of static data types of
  variables is essential in this respect, and
  enhances both programming security and
  system efficiency.

- Keep the responsability for the design of
  the language (and possible changes) confined
  to a single person. If implementation work
  is delegated, keep closely in touch with it,
  and make sure to obtain adequate feedback.
  Beware of programmers who will quietly find
  solutions no matter what they cost.

And finally, when the project is at its end,
carefully reassess it, recognise that many
aspects could be improved, and do it all
over again.

REFERENCES

[1] T.E. Cheatham, Jr., The recent evolution
of programming languages, <u>Information
Processing 71</u> (ed. C.V. Freimann),
North-Holland Publ. Co., Amsterdam,
1972, 298-313.

[2] J. Sammet, Programming languages:
history and fundamentals, Prentice-Hall,
Englewood-Cliffs, 1969.

[3] P. Naur, Programming languages - Status
and trends, <u>Proc. NordDATA 72</u>, Helsinki
1972, 36-38.

[4] H.D. Huskey, R. Love, N. Wirth, A syntactic description of BC NELIAC, <u>Comm.
ACM</u> vol. <u>6</u>, no. 7, 367-375 (July 1963).

[5] A. van Wijngaarden, Generalised ALGOL,
Ann. Rev. in <u>Autom. Programming</u> <u>3</u>,
(1963) 17-26.

[6] N. Wirth, H. Weber, EULER, A generalization of ALGOL, and its formal description, <u>Comm. ACM</u> vol. <u>9</u>, no. 1 and
2, 13-23, 89-99, and no. 12, 878 (Jan.,
Feb., Dec. 1966).

[7] C.A.R. Hoare, An axiomatic basis for
computer programming, <u>Comm. ACM</u> vol. <u>12</u>,
no. 10, (Oct. 1969) 576-581.

[8] C.A.R. Hoare, N. Wirth, An axiomatic
definition of the programming language
Pascal, <u>Acta Informatica</u> vol. <u>2</u>, (1973)
335-355.

[9] C.A.R. Hoare, Hints on programming
language design, SIGACT/SIGPLAN Symposium on priciples of programming
languages, Boston, Oct. 1973.

[10] N. Wirth, The programming language
Pascal, <u>Acta Informatica</u> vol. <u>1</u>, (1971)
35-63.

[11] M.V. Wilkes, The outer and inner syntax
of a programming language, <u>Comp. J.</u>
vol. <u>11</u>, no. 3, (Nov. 1968) 260-263.

TESTING AND VERIFICATION ASPECTS OF PASCAL-LIKE LANGUAGES

ANTHONY I. WASSERMAN

Medical Information Science, University of California, San Francisco, San Francisco, CA 94143 U.S.A.

(*Received 29 November* 1978)

Abstract—This paper addresses aspects of programming language design that affect the ease with which programs written in a language can be subjected to systematic testing and/or program verification. The discussion focuses of Pascal and on several languages that have been derived primarily from Pascal, particularly Euclid and PLAIN. Specific language issues addressed include translation-time checking, program readability, flow of control, support for program modularity, data flow, and program immutability. The relative ease of validating such programs is then determined by the style in which the programs are written. The paper presents some guidelines for writing programs in Pascal-like languages for testability and verifiability.

Programming languages Testing Verification Pascal Type checking Programming style Aliasing

1. INTRODUCTION

A MAJOR theme in current software engineering research and development is software reliability. One key aspect of this area focuses upon techniques for determining the correctness of programs, i.e. the extent to which they satisfy their specifications, either through testing or verification. Testing is a collection of activities that provides a practical demonstration of conformity between the program and the specification, based upon systematic selection of test cases, execution of program paths and segments, and inference based upon test results. Verification is a formal mathematical proof that the program conforms to its specification.

Both of these approaches have met with some success. Testing techniques successfully uncovered large numbers of program errors that could be fixed on a one-by-one basis; the vast majority of useful programs in existence today were developed in this manner [1]. More recently, automated tools for testing have been developed, providing environments for testing individual modules and for systematically executing the various paths of a program symbolically [2, 3]. Work has progressed toward developing a theoretical basis for testing, to complement the more pragmatic techniques of the past [4, 5]. Program verification techniques have come into practice more slowly. It is fair to say that the biggest impact of verification has been the *recognition* that one might want to verify a program, rather than actual program proofs.

There are indications that work in verification and testing are increasingly overlapping. Some of the symbolic execution systems, for example, were developed by groups with a professed interest in formal proofs of programs. Indeed, it has been suggested that future demonstrations of program correctness will draw on both techniques of testing and verification [6]. Accordingly, the term "validation" will be used in this paper to refer to both the testing and the verification approaches to determination of program correctness.

Program validation is extremely dependent upon other stages of the software development life cycle. For example, it is extremely difficult to prove anything about a program in the absence of a precise, unambiguous statement of what it is to do, an observation that has led to extensive work in the area of formal specifications [7–9]. Similarly, considerable attention has been given to programming language design and to programming methodology, since the structure and use of programming languages determines the ease with which validation can be carried out.

These developments tie together the various aspects of the software life cycle. Testing and verification cannot simply be applied after the fact, but must be an integral part of the entire software development process [10]. Requirements definition and system specification must be reviewed for conformity to the wishes of the user/customer. The system must then be designed and implemented in such a way that it is feasible to validate the actions of the program against the existing specification.

The design stage and the implementation stage separate the specification stage from the validation stage. The ease with which the specification may be transformed into an executable program and the ease with which the implemented program may be checked for correctness is strongly affected by the characteristics of the programming language used.

As a result, research in programming language design and use has aimed at discovering those languages and language features that assist program validation, as well as the proper ways to use those languages. One visible outcome of this research has been the development of programming language features that force a greater degree of discipline upon the programmers and thus reduce the number of errors that can occur during program execution, thereby mitigating some of the testing and verification difficulties. As an example, the degree of resemblance between the specification and the actual code has an impact upon the relative ease of validation. Similarly, issues of programming style involving control flow and data flow have a significant impact upon the validation process.

The goal of this paper is to examine certain language features with an eye toward understanding their role in the testing and verification activities. We shall see those features that complicate the process, as well as those that provide support for testing and verification, giving attention to Pascal [11] and to languages derived from Pascal since those languages most clearly reflect the current trends in language design.

A secondary goal is to provide some guidance to other programming language designers so that they may gain better understanding of the way that language design decisions interact with program validation. Language design is not merely the assemblage of a number of language features in support of a consistent set of language design goals. Instead, it is the *synthesis* of features from existing languages, combined with the judicious inclusion of new features *and* the exclusion of unnecessary frills, to create a syntactically and semantically unambiguous notation. In this respect, it is often the *interactions* among language features that present difficulties for validation rather than the individual features themselves.

2. PASCAL AND PASCAL-LIKE LANGUAGES

The development of Pascal was motivated both by the desire for a new language to teach programming and as "an efficient tool to write large programs." Concern was given to keeping the language fairly small, to providing a "simple and systematic language structure," and to permitting efficient implementations [11]. By most measures, Pascal has served this purpose well; the number of implementations and the size of the user community have continued to grow, despite ongoing debate over some of the fine points of the language. Furthermore, several mechanized verification aids have been developed to assist in the proof of programs written in Pascal or a Pascal subset (see [12], for example).

Hoare and Wirth have axiomatized the language [13], thereby providing a formal semantic description of each syntactic construct in the language. This axiomatization is of major importance for compiler implementation and program verification, since it provides a precise specification of the language actions in a non-deterministic, machine independent way. Such a specification, for example, makes it possible to prove the correctness of the implementation of Pascal or a Pascal subset.

In addition, Pascal has spawned a number of other programming languages, including Euclid, PLAIN, Concurrent Pascal and, most recently, Ada, a language designed to meet U.S. Department of Defense requirements for a "Common High Order Language."

Euclid [14] is primarily intended as a tool for the construction of verifiable systems programs. It eliminates input/output and floating point arithmetic from Pascal while adding stronger rules for data types, improved access rules for variables, and a module definition facility that supports data abstraction concepts. As a system implementation language, it also permits the creation of machine dependent program modules, incorporating some carefully constrained loopholes to provide access to low level machine primitives. Euclid also introduces some constructs representing revisions to Pascal, enhancing the ability of compilers to analyze the program and simplifying program verification. The most significant of these changes is the prohibition of aliasing (see below). A set of proof rules, resembling the Pascal axiomatization, has been developed for Euclid [15].

PLAIN [16] is primarily intended as a tool for the construction of interactive information systems, typically involving conversational access to a data base. Unlike Euclid, support for program verification was not a primary goal in the design of PLAIN; nonetheless, some of its features contribute to ease of testing and verification. It adds strings and relations, with their associated operations to Pascal, contains a module declaration facility for data abstraction, supports a rudimentary pattern specification and pattern-matching capability, and provides an exception-handling facility. Some of these language features, particularly those for exception-handling and data base management, go beyond the state of the art in program testing and verification; the design of PLAIN was driven primarily by application needs. As with Euclid, PLAIN incorporates some revisions to Pascal, mainly intended to enhance program uniformity and readability, and to encourage a systematic approach to program construction [17]. Both Euclid and PLAIN strive for greater support for program modularity than is present in Pascal.

Concurrent Pascal [18] is primarily intended as a tool for writing operating systems and other software systems exhibiting parallelism in execution. Concurrent Pascal supports the concept of monitors [19] and provides for an explicit hierarchy of access rights to shared data structures. Otherwise, it sticks more closely to Pascal than does either Euclid or PLAIN.

The Department of Defense effort involved a set of attempts to design a language meeting a set of requirements known as "STEELMAN" [20]. The language, Ada, was designed competitively, with each of the four original language designs based upon Pascal. Two of these designs were then selected for further work and redesign, and one was selected as Ada [21]. Ada is intended to support the creation of programs for embedded computer systems, typically those found in military communications, guidance, and weapons systems. However, the language is suitable for a considerably broader range of applications, including those of systems programming.

In the following discussion, then, we shall identify specific aspects of programming languages and describe the ways in which they aid or hinder the processes of testing and verification, drawing as required upon these various languages. The key point to observe throughout is the significance of various language design decisions with respect to both testing and verification.

3. LANGUAGE FEATURES AFFECTING TESTING AND VERIFICATION

The ease of testing and verification is influenced both by *static* and *dynamic* program characteristics. Static factors are those features that may be easily checked automatically by a compiler at translation time, those that are independent of the execution characteristics of the program. Dynamic factors are those aspects of the program which are dependent upon its execution properties. The correspondence between the dynamic behavior of a program and its static properties is significant. It is highly desirable to have the execution of a program proceed in linear fashion, thereby resembling its listing, since that characteristic enhances program readability and simplifies "desk checking" by a programmer or programming group in the process of code review.

As a general goal, a programming language should support static checking to the greatest extent possible. Two principal design goals are critical to this objective:

(1) Program readability—The ease with which a program can be read and understood is fundamental to the process of uncovering errors.
(2) Translation time checking—The extent to which the language translator detects both syntactic and semantic errors in the language affects the difficulty of dynamic checking. The language should permit as many errors as possible to be caught before an executable object program is produced.

Dynamic checking is heavily dependent upon techniques of path testing and runtime error detection. Suitable language control structures may make it possible to sharply reduce the number of discrete execution paths that may be taken during program execution. In addition, the ability to trap and handle runtime errors can guarantee successful program operation under a number of exceptional conditions.

Attempts to aid testing and verification activities place numerous constraints upon language design and usage. Programmers who are used to coding in less restrictive languages will undoubtedly have difficulty in adjusting to languages that address these issues or program reliability. In short, these languages must enforce a discipline that will often seem unnatural and unnecessary to programmers who are not accustomed to such controls.

On the other hand, though, such discipline is consistent with modern software development methods and is intended to result in better structured, more readable programs. Indeed, it is intended to impose restraints on those programmers who have an uncontrollable urge to write code prior to solving the problem at hand and who tend to write ill-structured, difficult to maintain programs. On balance, then, these languages may be "just what the doctor ordered" to improve the quality of programs and the determination of their correctness.

Furthermore, language features that provide support for testing and verification also provide support for other aspects of a systematic programming methodology. For example, the desirability of testing program modules individually fits in well with the desirability of system design at the module level, using techniques such as program design languages and structure charts [22].

4. STATIC CHECKING

4.1. *Program readability*

Pascal and its descendants generally provide for a high degree of program readability, particularly if the programmer uses a consistent scheme of program indentation (or has access to a "prettyprinter"). Programmers can easily use mnemonic names for types, variables, and routines (functions and procedures) and incorporate comments freely. Complete declarations are required and are presented at the head of each routine. Compound statements and blocks provide for the special symbols **begin** and **end** to bracket groups of statements.

For most programmers, the most immediate readability problem is to discern the overall program structure. Unlike FORTRAN and PL/I, which may have their main programs appear first, in Pascal-like languages, the main program is placed last, since all of the various other routines are only declarations until they are invoked. Thus, the reader of a Pascal program must begin near the end and must then locate all of the invoked program units, eventually piecing together the program's calling structure. While this problem can be mitigated with the aid of a cross reference program or a software tool that generates a calling tree, it still remains a shortcoming of these languages. Related problems are to locate all of the different names used in the program, to locate all of the program units (functions, procedures, or modules) in which a given variable is used, and to identify correspondences between actual and formal parameters, especially where parameters are passed by reference.

Euclid makes an improvement over Pascal in this area by requiring identifiers used in a routine or module to explicitly *imported* into its scope. The effect of this requirement is that imported names and declared names appear in the heading of each routine and module. This rule provides greater control over the use of globally declared identifiers and makes it easier to determine by straightforward inspection where identifiers are declared and used. Furthermore, imported variables that are modified within a routine must be prefixed with the special symbol **var** to highlight that fact. Constants are excepted from this importing requirement, since they may be declared **pervasive** throughout a scope.

PLAIN handles the situation similarly, requiring the use of an **imports** declaration. Identifiers are characterized as **readonly, modified,** or **invoked.** The identification of invoked program units simplifies the problem of building a calling tree in the absence of an automated aid. However, PLAIN goes even further in pursuit of readability. For example, the **restricted to** clause defines the routines that may import that variable. This restriction, associated with the declaration of the variable, assists in locating all uses of such variables, controlling the routines into which they may be imported. In addition, PLAIN requires use of the separator "—>" in both actual and formal parameter lists to distinguish those parameters which are not modified from those which may be.

Euclid, PLAIN, Ada all permit variables to be initialized, a feature not present in Revised Pascal. This capability, while having the disadvantage of integrating executable actions into declarative statements, offers a couple of significant advantages. By associating a declaration and an initialization, the reader of the program can distinguish initialization of a variable from modifications to the variable or to some component of the variable. In addition, the number of executable statements is reduced by the number of initializations. Finally, PLAIN provides a shorthand notation for the initialization of structured variables, eliminating the need for a sequence of assignments or an iterative statement to assign those values.

The importance of readability cannot be overemphasized. Software systems have a long lifetime, typically go through many versions, requiring changes and enhancements, and thus must be read by humans as well as by machines. Hoare has noted, for example, that the readability of programs is much more important than their writeability [23]. It should be apparent that all manual forms of debugging, testing, and verification are greatly aided by comprehensible programs. Readability, though, is only one characteristic of a language supporting efforts to determine program correctness. Indeed, it can also be a very subjective measure, since languages and programs considered to be cryptic to some are eminently readable to others.

4.2. *Type checking*

A more important aspect of static analysis is the degree to which errors beyond straightforward syntax errors may be detected by the language translator. Again, Pascal is quite strong in this regard, with its descendants making some improvements from the standpoint of verification and type checking. Language features that determine the ease of translation time checking are type checking and coercion rules and the ability to create self-modifying programs.

A language with strict type checking requires, for example, that actual and formal parameters be of the same type and that the operands for given operators be of a designated type; otherwise runtime errors can arise. Closely related to the issue of data types is the issue of naming and the rules for naming objects in the program, particularly the ability to refer to an object by more than one name, termed *aliasing*.

Rules concerning the formation of expressions and the communication of variables between modules require type checking. Every identifier in a Pascal-like program is declared with its type within the program text. Unlike the "typeless" languages where variables may be coerced automatically to different types to fit their use in a given expression, variables in these languages retain their type throughout the program. (Note that the same *name* may be reused within a single program, but that such use represents a *different* variable.) As long as all of the various program units are presented to the translator together (no separate compilations), it is possible to carry out this type checking in a straightforward manner. Furthermore, the Ada language has developed a separate compilation facility that preserves the same degree of type safety as is present when all units are presented together.

The most serious problem with type checking in Pascal arises from the ability to pass procedures and functions as parameters. There is no requirement to provide information about the parameters of the procedure and function parameters in Pascal, making it infeasible to check at compile-time for a match upon the number of type of parameters.

Consider the Pascal function shown in Fig. 1. If one incorporates them in a program and makes the function call

$$trap\ (0, 1, 100, \sin)$$

the program will operate properly, since the call of f within *trap* expects a single parameter of type real, as does the built-in sin function. However, if one makes the function call

$$trap\ (0, 1, 100, g)$$

using the following definition of g

```
function g (a, b: real): real;
begin
    g: = a + b
end;
```

a runtime error will occur, since g has two parameters rather than the desired one. These flaws are carried over in Concurrent Pascal, but are absent from Euclid, which forbids the use of procedures and functions as parameters.

Euclid has a couple of places where the type-checking may be relaxed. First, a type reference may be of type **any** within variant records. Although plenty of checking is available, such a facility can be used, if so desired, to bypass some of the more rigorous type checking. Also, objects may be introduced and used within machine dependent

```
function trap (x, y: real; n: integer; function f: real): real;
{trap uses the trapezoidal method to compute the approximate
integral of the function f over the interval [x,y]. The approximation
fails if f is discontinuous on the interval.}
var i: integer;
sum, z, width: real;
begin
    width:= (y − x)/n;
    i:= 1;
    sum:= 0;
    while i < n do
    begin
        z:= x + i* width;
        sum:= sum + f(z);
        i:= i + 1
    end
    trap:= width*(sum + (f(x) + f(y))/2)
end;
```

Fig. 1. Function parameters in Pascal.

modules, possibly using the assembly language of the host machine; clearly, these cannot be checked.

4.3. *Aliasing*

Another serious problem in analysis is caused by aliasing, since use of aliasing creates side effects when an assignment to x results in the modification of some other variable y. Consider the Pascal program shown in Fig. 2. The vectors are passed by reference to procedure sum in order to avoid the overhead of copying the vectors, as is required in a call by value. In normal use, the actual parameters would be three different vectors. In this case, however, sum is called with the same first and third parameter. Accordingly, the original values for elements in x are destroyed as an effect of the call to sum. Numerous other examples of this situation can be given (see [24] for example).

```
const max = 200;
type vector = array [1..max] of integer;
var x, y: vector;
    procedure sum (var a, b, c: vector);
    {sum adds vectors a and b, storing the result in c}
    var i: integer;
    begin
      for i:= 1 to max do
      c[i]:= a[i] + b[i]
    end;
begin
    {main program}
       .

       .

    {obtain values for x and y}
       .

       .

    sum (x, y, x);
       .

       .

end.
```

Fig. 2. Aliasing in Pascal.

Euclid goes to considerable effort to disallow those programming constructs that permit aliasing. Among other reasons, these steps are taken to overcome some of the difficulties that can arise in program verification if aliasing is permitted. Two major techniques are used: "overlapping variable detection" and "extended parameter lists."

Overlapping variable detection identifies those situations in which two names are used refer to the same object. In Euclid, all of the actual **var** parameters in a procedure call must be nonoverlapping. If the actual parameters are simple names, then they must be distinct, thereby prohibiting a procedure call such as *sum* (x, y, x) above. However, if the actual parameter is a structured variable, it is also necessary to check for overlap among the components of the variable, such as an array a and one of its elements $a[i]$. It is important to observe that not all of this checking can be done statically. For example, if a procedure call contains the actual parameters $a[i]$ and $a[j]$, there is no aliasing unless $i = j$, a situation that can usually be determined only during program execution.

Overlapping variable detection applies not only to the **var** parameters in the actual procedure list, but also to interactions between parameters and global variables. The "extended parameter list" consists of the actual parameters, imported variables and constants, and pervasive constants (those constants declared global to a scope that·need

67

not be explicitly imported). Then, the check for overlapping variables is applied to the union of variables and parameters; no two variables in this extended parameter list may overlap. In effect, Euclid does not place any restriction on the language *syntax*; however, it checks the language *usage* to locate those situations where aliasing occurs, forbidding those cases that can be detected at compilation time and generating legality assertions for the verifier to prove for those cases that must be determined at runtime.

4.4. *Self-modifying programs*

Pascal and its descendants all make a distinction between programs and data. This distinction is an important one from the standpoint of testing and verification, since it may be used to prevent the creation of self-modifying programs. Historically, the concept of a Von Neumann machine relies on the notion of a stored program where the program to be executed occupies storage locations in much the same way as does the data to be manipulated. Thus, most assembly language programs routinely perform address modifications and other "programming tricks" to reduce the amount of memory required for the program.

In high level languages, though, the ability to create programs that modify themselves means that one cannot determine the program to be executed until execution time. If a program can create new control paths, then various path testing algorithms are hopelessly complicated. If a program can create new variables (with different names on different executions), then monitoring of variables is more complex. While the use of assertions can help to overcome the effects of such usage, self-modifying programs are much more susceptible to run-time errors than are static programs and are frequently cryptic to the reader.

Neither Pascal, nor any of its descendants, incorporate features like the ALTER statement of COBOL or the indirection features of MUMPS and SNOBOL4. The absence of such features is of great assistance to program validation. The only loopholes of this nature are the ability to insert machine dependent code in the Pascal-like system implementation languages (Euclid and Ada). Since there is no way to predict the action of this code, it is necessary to determine its correctness in other ways.

5. DYNAMIC CHECKING

While a great deal of support for program testing and verification is present in the static structure of a language, most static checking serves to validate the use of the language and the overall program structure, checking for consistency and completeness rather than for the desired results of program execution. Virtually all of the checking for semantic correctness is performed during program execution. Here too, however, the features of the programming language are of great help, despite the fact that the program may be represented by an object program (the compiled version).

The most significant factors are the ability to cause side effects and the extent to which flow of control is restrained. The control structures reflected in the high level language are the primary determinant of this control flow. Dynamic data structures, involving modification of pointer structures and storage allocation/deallocation, are also important areas for checking. Other dynamic checking involves the handling of exceptional conditions and the evaluation of assertions.

5.1. *Side effects*

A side effect is a program action that occurs automatically as the result of some other program action. Side effects are normally caused when a program unit modifies some program variable other than a parameter to that unit. The hazards of modifying global variables in this way are well understood [25]. Side effects are a persistent source of errors in programs and are often among the most difficult problems to detect.

Consider the Pascal program segment shown in Fig. 3. In the function f, the parameter a is passed by reference. A side effect of the function is to modify the value of a. When the function call is used in an expression, a side effect of the *expression evaluation* is a modification of the value of the function parameter. Hence, the values assigned to y and z within the main program will be different, merely as a result of reordering the expression, if we assume that expression evaluation is performed consistently left-to-right or right-to-left. This kind of side effect is not only poor programming practice (since it makes errors hard to find), but allowing such side effects also complicates the implementation, since expressions must be evaluated in a given order rather than leaving freedom for the compiler writer to effect certain optimizations on expressions.

```
program fig3;
var x, y, z: real;


    function f (var a: real): real;
    begin
        f := 2*a;
        a := a + 1
    end;


begin


    {assume x initialized prior to following statement}
    z := x + f(x);


    {assume x not modified between the two assignment statements}


    y := f(x) + x;


end.
```

Fig. 3. Pascal function with side effect.

Side effects are disallowed in functions in most decendants of Pascal, including Euclid, PLAIN, and Ada. Enforcement of this rule requires considerable checking, particularly in PLAIN, which permits procedure and function parameters. In addition to forbidding parameters from being modified within the function body, it is also necessary to prevent assignments to globals imported into the function. If a function calls a procedure, the called procedure must be checked to make certain that the effect of the procedure does not cause the constraints on side effects to be violated. Accordingly, the called procedure may not modify any global variables, nor may it modify the value of one of the function parameters that has been passed to it in turn.

Thus, at translation time, all procedure calls within functions must be checked to see if the called procedure modifies any globals or any of the function's parameters. The list of imported variables present in the heading of PLAIN and Euclid procedures simplifies this checking. However, the scheme can break down in PLAIN, since a procedure or function may be a parameter to a function, making it impossible to make the determination concerning side effects prior to program execution; these checks must be made at execution time in PLAIN.

An additional problem in PLAIN is that strict interpretation of the rules against side effects would also prohibit all input/output and file operations, along with many database operations. For example, routine output messages (of the type commonly used in debugging) could not be included in functions.

Instead of imposing these lengthy restrictions on functions with the attendant checking, some derivatives of Pascal, including some of the preliminary designs of Ada, returned to the ALGOL 60 idea of a value-returning procedure, which combines the value-returning ability of a function with the generalized ability of a procedure to cause side effects.

5.2. *Control structures*

Minimization of paths of control flow is an important aid in simplifying the extent of program testing or verification conditions. Techniques such as symbolic execution require checking of every class of control flow. Similarly, program verification requires separate proof segments for each path.

Features for control flow are slightly different among the various languages. Both Pascal and Ada contain a **goto** statement, while Euclid and PLAIN do not. These control structures, except for the **goto,** support the structured programming concept of "single-entry, single-exit", thereby serving to reduce the number of paths that must be tested and the number of assertions that must be checked.

Both Euclid and PLAIN have replaced the Pascal **for, while-do,** and the **repeat-until** with a single statement type. Both have loop bodies introduced by the symbol **loop.** In the most basic form, control enters the loop and exits upon executing an **exit** statement. In both languages, the loop may be preceded by a clause to control the number of executions of the scope. In PLAIN, the **foreach** clause generates elements out of a named set, perhaps a range of integers or the tuples of a relation. In Euclid, the **for** statement not only permits selection out of a named set, but also provides for the dynamic generation of values from a module type generator.

From a validation standpoint, both of these schemes overcome the deficiency of earlier languages by making the control variable of the loop a *constant*, prohibiting assignments to it within the scope of the loop and preventing the exportation of the value of the control variable upon loop termination. One can thus guarantee termination of loops, a critical step in strong verification.*

One of the most basic checks that can be made through testing of control paths is to make certain that all variables have defined values prior to their use in an expression. Variables may obtain values through read statements, through initialization (in Euclid, PLAIN, and Ada), through a procedure setting a **var** parameter (in Pascal and Euclid), a **modified** parameter (PLAIN), or through explicit assignment. However, testing programs must check all possible control paths to ascertain that there is no situation in which control flow may reach an expression where a variable does not have an appropriate value. This check is one of the most important benefits of minimizing control paths and eliminating unrestricted flow of control.

Path testing strategies are complicated by the inclusion of parallelism and coroutines, as they exist in Concurrent Pascal and in Ada. In such situations, variables may be shared among two or more concurrently executing processes. The test procedure must make certain that problems of mutual exclusion and synchronization are satisfactorily handled and that concurrent updates, if they exist, do not affect program correctness. The notion of a **monitor** in Concurrent Pascal is designed to eliminate the potential hazards that can occur. Processes may gain exclusive access to shared objects and thereby achieve mutual exclusion. Otherwise, program results will not be determinate and may render testing and verification techniques totally useless.

---

* Strong verification requires proof of program termination in addition to proof of the verification conditions.

5.3. *Dynamic data structures*

In addition to static variables declared within a program and referenced by an identifier, Pascal and its descendants permit variables to be generated dynamically and referenced by a pointer. This mechanism requires the presence of facilities to allocate and deallocate storage dynamically during program execution, since the structure to which a pointer points must be able to change.

As Hoare, among others, has noted [26], the use of pointers presents some serious problems for program validation, comparable in many ways to the unconstrained use of the **goto** statement. The first problem is that repeated calls upon the allocation mechanism may exhaust the available storage and thereby cause program termination. A second problem is that use of pointers is an easy way to effect aliasing, and that it can only be detected at runtime. The third problem is that the pointer mechanism, as it exists in Pascal can lead to a "dangling reference", whereby a pointer can point to a non-existent object. In Fig. 4, the pointer type p is declared to point to objects of type letters, and pp is declared to be of type p. In **procedure** build, a linked list of characters is built from characters read from an input line, using the variables first and last of type p, as well as the globally declared variable pp. The variables first, last, and pp are all of type p, and point to objects of type letters. Space for the next letter is allocated before that letter is read. When the end of line is reached, the unneeded cell is disposed and last↑. next is set to **nil**, denoting the end of the string. However, when build terminates, pp continues to exist and points to the nonexistent object. According to the rules of Pascal, one could use pp in the main program following the call to build, but the effect would be unpredictable, even though the program would be syntactically valid. It can be seen that the heart of this problem is the interaction between the pointer mechanism and the use of global variables in Pascal.

```pascal
program fig4 (input);
  type p = ↑letters;
    letters = record
                  letter: char;
                  next: p
                end;
  var pp: p;
  procedure build;
  var first, last: p;
    ltr: char;
  begin
    new (first); {allocate space for the first letter}
    last:= first;
    while eoln (input) do
    begin
      read (ltr);
      last↑. letter: = ltr;
      new (pp); {allocate space for the next letter}
      last↑. next:= pp; {point to the new cell}
      last:= pp
    end;
    dispose (pp);
    last↑. next: = nil {clean up pointer}
  end;
begin
  build {the use of pp here would be a dangling reference}
end.
```

Fig. 4. Dangling reference in Pascal.

The problems of pointers have been addressed in PLAIN and Euclid, with PLAIN making only a minor restriction, while Euclid attacks the roots of the difficulty directly. PLAIN simply limits the use of pointer types to those modules defining data abstractions. In that way, the number of program units that actually manipulated pointers is reduced and the size of the program units using them directly is small enough that they can be carefully checked. Such restrictions can prevent the use of dangling references, for example.

Euclid's solution is aimed at all three of the problems mentioned above: storage allocation, dangling references, and aliasing. Briefly, pointers are associated with a **collection,** which is in turn associated with a zone providing storage for its variables. Since all items in a collection are of the same type, there can be no overlapping variables, and hence no aliasing, unless two pointers to the same collection are equal. Furthermore, the scope of declaration of collections, combined with restrictions on the Free operation, assures that the dangling reference situation cannot occur. Thus, pointer variables, critical components of systems programs to be written in Euclid, can be made much more safe than they are in Pascal.

5.4. *Exceptions*

Other control flow problems arise as a result of runtime conditions. There are a large number of exceptional conditions that may arise during program execution, including arithmetic underflow and overflow, invalid subscript values, attempting to read beyond an end-of-file, and various hardware errors. In Pascal and Euclid, these conditions normally lead to program termination. From a verification standpoint, one can say that the program fails to meet its output assertion. In other words, a program that raises an exceptional condition is not a legal program; of course, one tries to make certain that such exceptional conditions do not happen.

In PLAIN, however, there exists a systematic exception-handling mechanism [27], whereby exceptions may be raised both automatically by the runtime system of the program and explicitly by the programmer with a **signal** statement. An exception may be handled through a call to a **handler procedure,** which can permit continued execution of the program upon handling the exception, repetition of the operation that led to the exception, or program termination. The procedure call mechanism makes it possible to test the program in the presence of exceptions or to attempt verification through the use of assertions upon entry to and exit from the handler. One way to view this mechanism is as an expansion of the input assertion, i.e. a procedure will operate properly in the case of certain classes of exceptions, as well as in the "normal" case. The exception handling mechanism in Ada is quite similar.

5.5. *Assertions*

Assertions are valuable aids in several respects. First, they are useful to both mechanical verifiers and to test data generators in generating verification conditions and test cases. Next, they are useful in prohibiting program execution from continuing in those situations where a critical assumption is not met, possibly preserving the reliability of the program or the integrity of associated files and data bases. Most important, though, is that the *creation* of the assertions by the programmer forces a thorough analysis of the program logic and can lead to programs that are easier to validate.

Although Pascal does not include assertions, many of its descendants do. Furthermore, many of the automated program verification systems added assertions to Pascal. The simplest facility is the **assert** statement, as it exists in Euclid, Ada, and PLAIN. Every time that control reaches an **assert** statement, the associated condition is examined. If it is a Boolean expression, it must evaluate to true; otherwise the condition is treated as a comment. (In Euclid, the assertion is only verified if the check option is on.)

Euclid also includes three special kinds of assertions. The first **two,** known as **pre** and **post,** are assertions that must be true upon entry to and exit from a routine or module, respectively. The third assertion is an **invariant,** which must be true throughout the execution of a module "except perhaps when one of the procedures of the module has been called and has not yet returned" ([14], Section 6.2.3). It may be necessary to check the associated Boolean expression a number of times, normally whenever an assignment is made to a variable present in the expression.

6. PROGRAMMING FOR VERIFIABILITY AND TESTABILITY

The insights that have been gained into the influence of language features for static and dynamic checking can be turned around and viewed as some programming principles, some stylistic guidelines aimed at reducing the effort required to validate programs. At the same time, language designers can identify those language features that should be avoided or modified if program validation is a key goal of the language design.

Many of these points have been mentioned elsewhere in the paper. Furthermore, many of them are well known to persons who have adopted a disciplined approach to coding, including many Pascal programmers. They are collected here for convenience and for reference, as such a list does not seem to exist elsewhere. Furthermore, the efforts to design Euclid, Ada, PLAIN, and many other languages, including CLU [28], Alphard [29], and Gypsy [30] have yielded new insights into the interrelationships between language features, language use, and program validation.

(1) Modularize the system—construct modules that are small in size, that hide a single design decision or carry out a single function, and that have clearly defined interfaces, passing data explicitly wherever possible. These steps aid comprehensibility of the system, permit testing and verification of small program units, and support team development of software systems.

(2) Strive for program readability—use mnemonic names for variables, procedures, functions, data types, and other program objects; annotate the code with comprehensive comments, making sure that they agree with the specification; use consistent indentation practices so that code groupings can be easily seen; construct programs so that control flow within each program unit is linear; provide sufficient external documentation in the form of cross reference tables, calling diagrams, and design representations to assist the reader.

(3) Avoid programming tricks—side effects and aliasing can be used to produce unexpected results, causing programs to do the unexpected and complicating the validation effort; machine-dependent code, particularly at the instruction level of the host computer, should be avoided wherever possible.

(4) Restrict use of global data—data should be explicitly passed between program units wherever possible; the number of parameters may be minimized by judicious use of structured objects, such as arrays and records. Excessive use of global variables permits more units to access and/or modify those variables, complicating the problem of identifying faulty program units when a global variable obtains an incorrect value.

(5) Use data abstraction concepts—construct functions and procedures (or abstract data types for those languages providing them) for commonly used classes of objects and define the necessary operations upon those objects. This step restricts access to the representation of objects, thereby simplifying modification of the program and alteration of representation decisions. It also permits the data types with their operations to be separately validated and the relatively small size of the code effecting the operation simplifies the validation process.

(6) Miminize the number of paths through programs—both testing and verification strategies rely upon coverage of the different paths of control flow through a program. Deeply nested **if-then-else-end if** statements, for example, cause exponential growth in the number of such paths. Simple control paths also reduce the complexity of verification conditions that must be proved at different program points; elimination of the **goto** and similar constructs can assure a linear flow of control.

(7) Give preference to static data structures—data objects based upon fixed storage allocation not only eliminate some of the execution time overhead, but minimize the likelihood of errors caused by lack of available storage or by references to nonexistent objects.

It should be noted that these suggestions are almost evenly balanced between process design and data design. Language design and programming methodology have long given primary attention to process decomposition and to control flow issues. However, it now appears that aspects of data design are equally as important.

7. CONCLUSION

Programming language design, after a period of stagnation in the late 1960s, has once again become an extremely popular activity in the research community, driven heavily by the notions of systematic software development. The requirement of supporting the software development process has resulted in extensive study of those programming language features most likely to cause difficulties in determining program correctness.

At this stage, there is still much to be done. The merits and shortcomings of Pascal, both as an expressive tool and as a vehicle for program testing and verification, have been thoroughly discussed. The languages treated here, along with a substantial number of other new languages, have explored the issues even further. However, there is still relatively little practical experience with any of the Pascal descendants.

While one would like to believe that these new languages, with their strict rules on program structure, lead to higher quality, i.e., more reliable, programs, there is only a little bit of evidence in support of that belief [31]. A thorough evaluation will have to study several large software systems written in these languages throughout their life cycle in order to determine the distribution of effort throughout the development stages and the extent of required corrections after the systems become operational. If these language features have the desired effect, that effect should be determinable from several factors:

(1) it will be possible to construct formal proofs for a larger class of programs;
(2) the time spent in the testing stage will decrease as a result of fewer programming errors and fewer paths to test;
(3) the cost of maintenance will decrease since the testing and verification activities can be more thorough;
(4) the languages producing these results will receive widespread acceptance and considerable usage, perhaps replacing some of the languages in heavy use at the moment.

In the next couple of years, it will be necessary to design and build testing and verification tools for these languages in order to provide answers to these outstanding questions and to provide the hard data that is needed to validate (or perhaps invalidate) the current trends in language design.

Acknowledgements—The author gratefully acknowledges the careful reading and detailed comments provided by Ralph London, along with his clarification of some aspects of Euclid. The referee comments on an earlier draft of this paper were also helpful. Computing support was provided by National Institutes of Health grant RR-1081, to the UCSF Computer Graphics Laboratory, Principal Investigator: Robert Langridge.

REFERENCES

1. E. F. Miller, Jr., Program testing technology in the 1980s, *The Oregon Report: Proceedings of the Conference on Computing in the 1980s*, pp. 72–79 (1978).
2. J. C. King, Symbolic execution and program testing, *Comm. ACM* **19**, 385–394 (1976).
3. L. A. Clarke, A system to generate test data and symbolically execute programs, *IEEE Transactions on Software Engineering* **SE-2**, 215–222 (1976).
4. J. B. Goodenough and S. L. Gerhart, Toward a theory of test data selection, *IEEE Transactions on Software Engineering* **SE-1**, 156–173 (1975).

5. W. E. Howden, Theoretical and empirical studies of program testing, *IEEE Transactions on Software Engineering* **SE-4**, 293–298 (1978).
6. S. L. Gerhart, Program verification in the 1980s, *The Oregon Report: Proc. of the Conference on Computing in the 1980s.* pp. 80–89 (1978).
7. B. Liskov and S. N. Zilles, Specification techniques for data abstractions, *IEEE Transactions on Software Engineering* **SE-1**, 7–19 (1975).
8. J. A. Goguen, J. W. Thatcher and E. G. Wagner, An initial algebra approach to the specification, correctness, and implementation of abstract data types, In *Current Trends in Programming Methodology* (ed. R. T. Yeh) vol. 4, pp. 80–149. Prentice–Hall, Englewood Cliffs, NJ (1978).
9. O. Roubine and L. Robinson, SPECIAL reference manual, Technical Report CSG-45, SRI International, Menlo Park, CA (1976).
10. W. C. Cave and A. B. Salisbury, Controlling the software life cycle—the project management task, *IEEE Transactions on Software Engineering* **SE-4**, 326–334 (1978).
11. N. Wirth, The programming language Pascal, *Acta Informatica* **1**, 35–63 (1971).
12. D. I. Good, R. L. London, and W. W. Bledsoe, An interactive program verification system, *IEEE Transactions on Software Engineering* **SE-1**, 59–67 (1975).
13. C. A. R. Hoare and N. Wirth, An axiomatic definition of the programming language Pascal, *Acta Informatica* **2**, 335–355 (1973).
14. B. W. Lampson *et al.*, Report on the programming language Euclid, *ACM SIGPLAN Notices* **12**(2) (1977).
15. R. L. London *et al.*, Proof rules for the programming language Euclid, *Acta Informatica* **10**, 1–26 (1978).
16. A. I. Wasserman, D. D. Sherertz and E. F. Handa, Report on the programming language PLAIN, Technical Report #34, Laboratory of Medical Information Science, University of California, San Francisco, CA, 1978.
17. A. I. Wasserman, The design of PLAIN—support for systematic programming, Technical Report # 40, Laboratory of Medical Information Sciences, University of California, San Francisco, CA, 1979.
18. P. Brinch Hansen, The programming language Concurrent Pascal, *IEEE Transactions on Software Engineering* **SE-1**, 199–206 (1975).
19. C. A. R. Hoare, Monitors: an operating system structuring concept, *Comm. ACM* **17**, 549–557 (1974).
20. Department of Defense Advanced Research Projects Agency, Requirements for high order computer languages—'STEELMAN', June, 1978.
21. J. D. Ichbiah (ed.), Preliminary Ada Reference Manual, *ACM SIGPLAN Notices,* **14**(6) (1979).
22. E. Yourdon and L. L. Constantine, *Structured Design.* Prentice-Hall, Englewood Cliffs, NJ (1979).
23. C. A. R. Hoare, Hints on programming language design, Technical Report CS-73-403, Computer Science Department, Stanford University, Palo Alto, CA (1973).
24. T. Venema and J. des Rivieres, Euclid and Pascal, *ACM SIGPLAN Notices* **13**(3), 57–69 (1978).
25. W. A. Wulf and M. Shaw, Global variables considered harmful, *ACM SIGPLAN Notices* **8**(2), 28–32 (1973).
26. C. A. R. Hoare, Data Structures, In *Current Trends in Programming Methodology* (Edited by R. T. Yeh) vol. 4, pp. 1–11. Prentice-Hall, Englewood Cliffs, NJ (1978).
27. A. I. Wasserman, Design and evaluation of a procedure-oriented exception-handling mechanism, submitted for publication, 1980.
28. B. Liskov *et al.*, CLU reference manual, Computation Structures Group Memorandum 161, MIT Laboratory for Computer Science, Cambridge MA (1978).
29. W. A. Wulf *et al.*, An informal description of Alphard (preliminary), Technical Report, Department of Computer Science, Carnegie-Mellon University, Pittsburgh, PA (1978).
30. A. L. Ambler *et al.*, Gypsy: a language for specification and implementation of verifiable programs. *Proc. of ACM Conference on Language Design for Reliable Software, ACM SIGPLAN Notices* **12**(3), 1–10 (1977).
31. J. D. Gannon, An experimental evaluation of data types on programming reliability *Comm. ACM* **20**, 584–595 (1977).

About the Author—Anthony I. Wasserman is an Associate Professor of Medical Information Science at the University of California, San Francisco, and a Lecturer in the Computer Science Division at the University of California, Berkeley. He has a Ph.D. degree in Computer Sciences from the University of Wisconsin—Madison (1970). In addition to editing three books and writing more than 30 technical articles in the areas of programming languages, software engineering, and data base management, Prof. Wasserman has been active in professional societies. He has served as an ACM National Lecturer (1973–1976), as Chairman of ACM's Special Interest Group on Software Engineering (1976–1979), and as a Technical Program Committee member of numerous conferences.

Acta Informatica 8, 97–112 (1977)

Language Design Methods Based on Semantic Principles

R. D. Tennent

Department of Computing and Information Science, Queen's University,
Kingston, Ontario, Canada

Summary. Two language design methods based on principles derived from the denotational approach to programming language semantics are described and illustrated by an application to the language Pascal. The principles are, firstly, the correspondence between parametric and declarative mechanisms, and secondly, a principle of abstraction for programming languages adapted from set theory. Several useful extensions and generalizations of Pascal emerge by applying these principles, including a solution to the array parameter problem, and a modularization facility.

"At first sight, the idea of any rules or principles being superimposed on the creative mind seems more likely to hinder than to help, but this is really quite untrue in practice. Disciplined thinking focusses inspiration rather than blinkers it."

G. L. Glegg: "The Design of Design"

1. Introduction

1.1. Semantic Principles

One of the motivations for the development of mathematical semantic models for practical programming languages has been to provide tools, concepts, and principles to assist designers of new languages and language features. The aim of this paper is to propose and illustrate systematic approaches to the design of two important aspects of programming languages. The methods are based on principles which derive from the approach to programming language semantics of D. Scott and C. Strachey and followers; the modern form of this theory is described in Milne and Strachey [28], but many of the concepts may be traced back to earlier work, such as McCarthy [26], Landin [21], and Strachey [34]. Tennent [36] is a tutorial introduction to the approach.

The first principle, which we term the principle of *correspondence*, was first stated and exploited by Landin [23]:

"In almost every language a user can coin names, obeying certain rules about the contexts in which the name is used and their relation to the textual segments that introduce, define, declare, or otherwise constrain its use. These rules vary considerably from one language to another, and frequently even within a single language there may be different conventions for different classes of names, with near-analogies that come irritatingly close to being exact. So rules about user-coined names is an area in which we might expect to see the history of computer applications give ground to their logic. Another such area is in specifying functional relations. In fact these two areas are closely related since any use of a user-coined name implicitly involves a functional relation; e.g. compare

$$x(x+a) \qquad\qquad f(b+2c)$$
$$\textbf{where } x = b+2c \qquad\qquad \textbf{where } f(x) = x(x+a)."$$

The correspondence between the semantics of declarative and parametric mechanisms has significantly influenced the design of only a small number of languages [23, 9, 39, 31, 35]. In the next section, a simple and useful design discipline is proposed which is based on the correspondence principle.

The second semantic principle will be termed the principle of *abstraction*. "Abstraction" is usually understood as a process of extracting general structural properties in order to allow relatively inessential details to be disregarded, and in this sense it is familiar to every mathematician and programmer. The term also has a technical sense in certain branches of mathematics and the theory of computation. In set theory [e.g. 33], the principle of abstraction is that any property (i.e. one-place predicate formula) $P[x]$ defines a set $\{x \mid P[x]\}$. Other forms of abstraction are also possible; for $R[x, y]$ a two-place predicate, $\{\langle x, y \rangle : R[x, y]\}$ might be a binary relational abstraction [30], and for $E[x]$ a term (expression) with free variable x, $\lambda x. E[x]$ might be a functional abstraction [5]. In this paper, the term "abstraction" will always have this technical significance.

In set theory, the principle of abstraction is of critical importance because were it to be used in the unfettered "naive" form stated above, it would lead to inconsistencies such as the well-known "paradox" of B. Russell. What this has to do with programming language design is that Scott's theory of computation and denotational semantic models of programming languages have shown that the meanings of reasonable programming language features satisfy a continuity condition, and that within this theory "unrestricted" abstraction *is* permissible.

This theoretical result motivates the following principle of abstraction for programming languages: an abstraction facility may be provided for any semantically-meaningful category of syntactic constructs. Procedure definitions for abstraction from statements in ALGOL 60 and lambda expressions for abstraction from forms in LISP are familiar examples of such facilities.

The principles of correspondence and abstraction are independent semantic concepts; however, for their application to language design it is necessary to consider them jointly, because parametric mechanisms are always involved in abstraction and, in almost all languages, the only abstraction facilities are declarations.

1.2. Design Methodology

The principles discussed in the preceding section are not principles of design, but rather of formal semantics; however, they do suggest and legitimize systematic approaches which can help to achieve design ends. From the principle of correspondence it may be concluded that the declarative and parametric mechanisms of a language should be designed together by comparing and reconciling corresponding declarative and parametric forms. This discipline helps in both discovering and correcting unnecessary restrictions, "missing" facilities, irregularities in the syntax, semantics, or terminology, unexpected interactions or complications, and so on.

The design approach suggested by the principle of abstraction is based on identifying all of the semantically-meaningful syntactic categories of the language and then designing a coherent set of abstraction facilities for each of these.

The rest of this paper describes an experiment in language design illustrating these semantically-based methods. The starting point will be the language Pascal [18] which is well documented and widely used, so that we may assume familiarity with it. Analysis of the declarative, parametric, and abstraction mechanisms of Pascal along the lines described above will point out many minor problems in the language, but will also suggest revisions which would rectify these problems without requiring any major changes to the underlying concepts of the language.

2. Terminology and Meta-Variables

2.1. Syntax

(i) The left-hand side and right-hand side of a definition or comparable construction will be referred to as its *formal parameter* and *actual parameter*, respectively.
(ii) Capital Greek letters, possibly with primes or subscripts, will be used as syntactic meta-variables, as specified in Table 1.
(iii) A *sequencer* [28] is a syntactic construct whose interpretation always results in a "jump"; in Pascal, the only sequencers have the form:

Γ; **go to** N

Table 1. Syntactic categories and meta-variables

Syntactic category	Meta-variable	Comments
Numerals	N	
Identifiers	I	
Formal parameters	Φ	
Specifiers	Π	To be discussed in Section 4.2
Type expressions	T	e.g. the actual parameter of a type definition
Static expressions	Σ	Statically-evaluable
Variable expressions	Ξ	e.g. the left-hand side of an assignment
Expressions	E	e.g. the right-hand side of an assignment
Declarations	Δ	Including definitions and declaration-lists
Statements	Γ	Including blocks and statement-lists

2.2. Semantics

The conventional value of an expression will be termed an *R-value*; for a static expression, this will be qualified as being a *static R*-value. The denotation of a variable expression (without coercion) will be termed an *L-value*. The values of type expressions and labels will be termed *type values* and *label values*, respectively. Functions, procedures, and so on will be termed *abstraction values*.

3. Analysis

3.1. Correspondence

In this section the declarative and parametric forms in Pascal are systematically compared in the manner suggested by the principle of correspondence. This analysis is summarized in Table 2 and motivates the following critical comments:

(i) There are no "static" (**const** and **type**) parametric forms. A very serious consequence of this is that a programmer cannot define an abstraction to operate on array parameters with arbitrary index types or bounds; other commentators have attributed this to the lack of dynamic array bounds [11], or to constraints imposed by static type-checking [19, 24, 43, 3].

(ii) According to Jensen and Wirth [18] the control identifier of a **for** statement cannot be updated in the controlled statement, and its value is undefined on normal exit from the iteration. This is as close as Pascal gets to allowing an identifier to be bound directly to a non-static *R*-value. Some of the advantages of a general mechanism for *R*-value binding have been pointed out by Wirth and Hoare [44]:

"The intention of the programmer can be made explicit for the benefit of the reader, and the translator is capable of checking that the assumption of constancy is in fact justified. Furthermore, the translator can sometimes takes advantage of the declaration of constancy to optimize a program."

An additional advantage is that without it, a programmer cannot pass the *R*-value of a non-assignable structure such as a file to an abstraction and must use a

Table 2. Parameter and declaration correspondence in Pascal

Denotation	Declarative construct	Parametric construct	
		Formal parameter	Actual parameter
Static R-value	**const** $I = \Sigma$		
Type value	**type** $I = T$		
Non-static R-value	**for** $I := E \ldots$		
New L-value	**var** $I : T$	$I : I'$	E
Existing L-value	**with** Ξ **do** $\ldots$	**var** $I : I'$	Ξ
Abstraction value	**function** $I(\ldots; \Phi_i; \ldots):I'; \ldots$	**function** $I : I'$	I
Label value	**label** $N; \ldots; N : I'; \ldots$		

var parameter. An earlier version of Pascal [40] had a parametric mechanism for R-value binding (inconsistently termed the **const** parameter), but it was replaced by the "value" parameter [1].

(iii) The **for** statement is not really a declarative construction because the control identifier must be declared in an enclosing procedure heading and outside of **for** loops can be used as an ordinary variable. The advantages of making the control identifier local to the **for** statement are discussed in [13].

(iv) There is a misleading notational irregularity in the use of **var** for binding an identifier to a *new* L-value in declarations and to an *existing* L-value as a parameter; furthermore, the terminology of "value" parameter is inconsistent with the corresponding **var** declaration.

(v) Any data type may be specified for a **var** declaration, but the type of a "value" parameter must be assignable.

(vi) The restriction to a type identifier (I') rather than a general type expression (T) at four places in Table 2 is unnecessary; this restriction apparently originates in an earlier implementation of Pascal in which **type** definitions were interpreted somewhat differently.

(vii) There is no explicit actual parameter in a **var** declaration, so that there is no mechanism for initializing the new L-value at the time of allocation.

(viii) There is no general declarative mechanism for binding identifiers to existing L-values.

(ix) The **with** statement in Pascal allows abbreviated references to the fields of a record; however, the "formal parameters" (the field names for the record type) are implicit, and this seems to impair program readability in non-trivial applications.

(x) The types of parameters of abstractional parameters cannot be specified, preventing complete static type-checking.

(xi) There is no parametric mechanism for label values.

This list of irregularities, missing or overly-specialized facilities, unnecessary restrictions, and so on is fairly lengthy, but the problems are quite minor and easily rectified. Many have been pointed out before in commentaries on Pascal [11, 19, 24, 43, 10, 4]; the significance of this analysis is that it exemplifies a *systematic* approach to discovering imperfections and flaws in a design of declarative and parametric mechanisms which does not require a complete semantic definition or implementation. For further evidence of the usefulness of this approach, the reader is invited to carry out a similar analysis of ALGOL 60, and compare the results with the trouble-spots, mistakes, and features that could have been in ALGOL 60 discussed by Wichmann [38].

3.2. Abstraction

Identification of the semantically-meaningful syntactic categories of a language is not as straightforward as in may seem. Many distinctions necessary in a concrete

Table 3. Abstraction in Pascal

Syntactic category	Abstraction values
Statements	Procedures
Expressions	Functions
Type expressions	
Static expressions	
Variable expressions	
Declarations	
Sequencers	

syntactic specification (such as among expression, factor, term, etc.) have only syntactic significance; on the other hand, a syntactic specification may not need to make a subtle distinction with semantic significance. For example, the **go to** construct is usually termed a statement, but from a semantic point of view it is more properly classified as a sequencer because of the nature of its interpretation.

As a last example, we mention the guarded command concept introduced by Dijkstra [8]; this might seem to be a semantically-meaningful category, but the paper does not give a semantic interpretation for guarded commands themselves. The non-deterministic **if** ... **fi** and **do** ... **od** constructs are defined by breaking up the constituent guarded commands into guards and statement-lists. If semantic meanings were assigned to guarded commands per se, this would suggest an abstraction facility with guarded commands as bodies.

The semantically-meaningful categories in Pascal and the associated abstraction facilities are summarized in Table 3. In addition to the obvious observation that five out of seven possibilities do not exist in Pascal, the only remark that needs to be made is that the body of a function is actually a statement rather than an expression, and its value is obtained by using the name of the function as a write-only variable (in L-value contexts).

4. Synthesis

4.1. Introduction

In this section the use of the proposed methods in language design will be illustrated by outlining one possible revision of Pascal which avoids the difficulties discussed in the preceding analysis, yet does not make any significant change in the underlying conceptual framework. We have tried to keep the notation as close as possible to that of Pascal; the following simple extensions and modifications will be assumed in the examples:

(i) A static expression is allowed to be any statically-evaluable expression.

(ii) A block (qualified statement) has the general form:

with Δ
do Γ

and can appear in any appropriate context, and not just as a procedure body.

(iii) Abstraction definitions will have the forms

$$\textbf{procedure } I(\ldots; \Phi_i; \ldots) = \Gamma$$
$$\text{or: } \textbf{function } I(\ldots; \Phi_i; \ldots): T = E$$

The use of expressions rather than statements as function bodies is more consistent with the principle of abstraction and avoids many semantic complications [29, 25]. Although our examples will not require it, a block expression construction (as in [44]) would be needed to allow imperative computation in function bodies.

(iv) A qualified declaration construction adapted from [23] will be used to provide a set of abstractions with "own" variables:

$$\textbf{private } \Delta$$
$$\textbf{within } \Delta'$$

The effect is that the scope of Δ is limited to Δ'; however, the dynamic lifetimes of L-values allocated in Δ continue until exit of the block in which the construction appears.

(v) The statement

$$\textbf{loop } \Gamma \textbf{ end}$$

is executed by repeatedly executing Γ, presumably until an appropriate jump out of the construct.

4.2. Correspondence

The "theoretical" ideal suggested by the principle of correspondence may be summed up as follows: for any formal parameter Φ and compatible actual parameter A, the effect on a block body of the qualifying declaration $\Phi = A$ should be identical to the effect on an abstraction body having Φ in its formal parameter list when A is the corresponding argument. The proposed declarative and parametric forms summarized in Table 4 (which should be compared with Table 2) achieve this ideal almost completely. The fine points of this proposal are explained in the following remarks, but the reader may want to skip ahead to the examples in Figures 1 to 5.

(i) A **type** or **const** parameter form binds occurrences of its identifier in subsequent formal parameters of the declaration list or parameter list, as well as in the body of the block or abstraction.

Table 4. Proposed parameter and declaration correspondence

Denotation	Formal parameter	Actual parameter
Static R-value	**const** $I:T$	Σ
Type value	**type** I	T
Non-static R-value	**val** $I:T$	E
New L-value	**new** $I:T$	E
Existing L-value	**var** $I:T$	Ξ
Abstraction value	**function** $I(\ldots; \Pi_i; \ldots):T$	I

(ii) Static parameters can be implemented by generating a separate code segment for every distinct actual parameter. This approach would allow efficient Pascal-like storage access and complete static type-checking. The code produced would not be any more space-consuming than for a comparable Pascal program; in Pascal, the multiple copies of the abstraction would have to appear in the source program as well as the object code. Of course, this is only the simplest possible implementation approach; in many situations an optimizing compiler would be able to merge together the code segments. For an obvious reason, the use of static parameters in recursive abstractions would have to be restricted, for example by requiring that the actual parameter in a recursive call be identical to the corresponding formal parameter.

(iii) The actual parameter corresponding to a **new** formal parameter form whose data type is *not* assignable is a special kind of procedure call. The procedure must be one whose last formal parameter is a **var** parameter of that type. The call supplies arguments for all but the last of the procedure's parameters; the newly-allocated L-value becomes the last argument of the initializing procedure. Wang [37] termed this mechanism "call-by-initialize". A simple example is:

> **new** f: **file of** *char = rewrite*.

For **new** declarations, the actual parameter may be omitted as in Pascal.

(iv) Restrictions on **var** declarations analogous to those on **var** parameters in Pascal would be necessary to preserve disjointness of variables [41, 42, 17, 15, 25].

(v) If the type of a **val** formal parameter form is not assignable, then the actual parameter must not be selectively updated in the scope of the binding. This would allow a call-by-reference implementation and is similar to a restriction suggested by Hoare [12].

(vi) Specifiers (meta-variable Π) are provided to allow complete type specification of abstractional parameters. A specifier has the form of a formal parameter without an identifier; for example, **val**: T. There seems to be no reason not to allow **var** specifiers in procedural parameters, but other possible specifier forms such as **const**: T, **type**, and higher-order abstractions might be excluded to simplify implementation.

(vii) An ALGOL 60-like **label** parameter would be possible, but it would not correspond to Pascal's **label** declarations; furthermore, a corresponding **label** declaration would be a useless facility without more extensive label-valued expressions. We have chosen to avoid the well-known problems that would arise by following this line of thought; instead, we adopt the long-advocated [22, 6] and currently fashionable approach of getting rid of labels and **go to**s entirely, in favour of sequencers whose targets are determined by the structure of the program text. There are several possibilities: **stop** (exit program), **return** (exit procedure body), **break** (exit loop), and so on. We adopt just one: **exit**, which exits the current block; an abstraction facility to be discussed later will permit parameterization and "labelling" of exits.

(viii) The **for** statement is easily modified to be a declarative construct (using R-value binding) as follows:

for $I:T=E_1$ **to** E_2 **do** Γ

There would also be an analogous **downto** form and we will also use the simplified form:

for $I:T$ **do** Γ

for the very common case that the identifier is to be bound to every value in a type T.

(ix) **val** and **var** parameters should not be identified with call-by-value and call-by-reference implementations, respectively; these would always be correct, but other implementations may be more convenient or efficient in some cases [12]. Since the proof rules for Pascal [17] require disjointness of variables, call-by-value/result will also be a correct implementation for **var** parameters; also, if the compiler knows that an actual **val** parameter cannot be updated in the scope of the binding (for example, in a function, which according to the proof rules must be free of side effects), then call-by-reference would also be correct.

Examples of the proposed parametric and declarative forms are given in Figures 1 to 5. Figure 1 is the heading of a procedural realization of the prime-finding algorithm in Dijkstra [7, Section 9]. This should be compared to [41, p. 141]; *primes* is a general procedure rather than a specialized program. Note the use of the generalized forms of static expressions and parameter specifications, and the similarity between the bindings of n in the parameter list and m in the declaration list.

```
procedure primes (const n: integer; var p: array [1..n] of integer)
= begin
    with const m: integer = round (sqrt(n)):
        new mult: array [1..m] of integer
            ⋮
    do
            ⋮
Fig. 1   end
```

Procedure *order* in Figure 2 takes advantage of the polymorphism of the operator $\geq$; some legal calls are:

$$order\ (integer,\ i, j)$$
$$order\ (colour,\ c, d)$$
$$order\ (real,\ x, y)$$
$$order\ (\textbf{set of}\ colour,\ s, t)$$

but: $order\ (\uparrow person,\ p, q)$

would be a compiler-detectable error.

```
procedure order (type t; var x, y:t);
= if x ≥ y then
    begin
      with val z:t = x
      do x := y; y := z
    end
```
Fig. 2

Procedure *maparray* in Figure 3 illustrates the use of a specifier in an abstractional parameter. In Figure 4 a single stack is represented by private array A and depth index p; the scope of these identifiers is limited to the bodies of the abstractions. Procedure *matmply* in Figure 5 is for multiplying matrices and illustrates the use of **val** and **var** parameters, **var** declarations, the simplified **for** statement, and generalized parameter specifications.

```
procedure maparray (type ind, d;
                    var A: array [ind] of d;
                    procedure p(var: d))
= for i: ind do p(A[i])
```
Fig. 3

```
with
  private
    new A: array [1..n] of d;
    new p:0..n = 0
  within
    procedure push (val x:d)
    = begin p := p + 1; A[p] := x end;
    procedure pop (var x:d)
    = begin x := A[p]; p := p - 1 end;
    function empty: Boolean = (p = 0)
  do
    ... push( ) ... pop( ) ... empty ...
```
Fig. 4

```
procedure matmply (type ind 1, ind 2, ind 3;
                   var A: array [ind 1, ind 2] of real;
                   val B: array [ind 1, ind 3] of real;
                   val C: array [ind 3, ind 2] of real)
= for i: ind 1 do
   for j: ind 2 do
   begin
     with var A ij: real = A[i, j]
     do A ij := 0;
       for k: ind 3 do
         A ij := A ij + B[i, k] * C[k, j]
   end
```
Fig. 5

4.3. Abstraction

In this section we will describe a "full complement" of abstraction facilities for the syntactic categories in Pascal; these are summarized in Table 5. Abstractions from expressions and statements are, of course, functions and procedures; for the other syntactic categories, the following proposals are made:

Table 5. Proposed abstractions

Syntactic category	Abstraction values
Expressions	Functions
Statements	Procedures
Static expressions	Static functions
Type expressions	Type functions
Variable expressions	Selectors
Declarations	Modules
Sequencers	Sequels

(i) Static and Type Expressions

Incorporating a facility for abstraction from statically-evaluable forms such as static and type expressions is particularly straightforward; there are no implicit dynamic parameters so that there is no need to make a distinction analogous to the one between:

function $I:T=E$

and: **val** $I:T=E$

Hence, **const** and **type** definitions can be generalized to have optional parameters; we call the abstracted entities *static functions* and *type functions*, respectively. Examples are given in Figure 6, which also shows how such functions would be invoked by supplying actual parameters.

const *sum* (**const** n: *integer*): *integer* $= n*(n+1)$ **div** 2;
type *vector* (**const** n: *integer*; **type** d) $=$ **array** $[1..n]$ **of** d;

Fig. 6

new V: *vector* (*sum* (*m*), *real*)

Static function and type function parameters are conceivable, but would not be possible if **const** and **type** specifiers were not allowed.

(ii) Variable Expressions

An abstraction from a variable expression will be termed a *selector*, after Hoare [14]. To preserve disjointness and stack implementability, the L-value returned by a selector must be a component of either a **var** parameter of the selector or a private variable accessible to it; furthermore, a selector should have no side effects. An example of a (parameter-less) selector is given in Figure 7; *top* allows the top of the stack to be accessed and updated, without any pushing or popping. Selectors can be composed with other selectors, including built-in mechanisms such as array indexing and record field selection. The selector facility is a safe way of providing some of the power of computed references, as recommended by Hoare [16].

Selector parameters would make disjointness checking much more difficult, and should probably not be allowed.

(iii) Declarations

In our "stack" example (Figs. 4 and 7), the definition of the concept is tied to its actual creation and use. A separation can be achieved by means of a facility for

```
            with
               private
                  new A: array [1..n] of d;
                  new p:0..n=0
               within
                  procedure push (val x:d) = ...
                  procedure pop (var x:d) = ...
                  function empty: Boolean = ...
                  selector top:d = A[p]
            do
               ⋮
               top := y
               ⋮
```

Fig. 7

```
         with
            module stack (const n:integer; type d)
            =(private
                  new A: array [1..n] of d;
                  new p:0..n=0
               within
                  procedure push ...
                  procedure pop ...
                  function empty ...
                  selector top ...);
               ⋮
         do
               ⋮
            begin
               with stack (100, real) do
                  ⋮
            end
```

Fig. 8

abstracting from the declarations to yield an entity we term a *module*, after Schuman [32]; the result is shown in Figure 8.

The module *stack* can be invoked in the heading of any contained block and this would bind free occurrences of the public identifiers *push*, *pop*, etc. in the body of that block; a separate "stack" would be allocated for each such invocation (necessarily in distinct blocks). A useful compiler action would be to make explicit in the output listing the identifiers which become bound by a module invocation, and their specifications. The module facility is similar to the block prefixing mechanism in SIMULA [2].

Module parameters would allow a kind of dynamic scope convention and should probably not be allowed.

(iv) Sequencers

An abstraction from a sequencer will be termed a *sequel*[1]. After getting rid of **goto** s, the only sequencer construct that remains has the general form: Γ; **exit**. We may therefore adopt the convention that in the body of a **sequel** definition the terminating **exit** may be left implicit; that is, the body is a statement, and after its execution control transfers to the end of the block in which the sequel is

---

[1]   These are not related to the sequels of Milne [27]

```
        begin
          with sequel found (val j:1..m) = B[j]:= B[j]+1
          do
            with new i:0..m = hash(x);
              sequel present = found(i);
              sequel absent = begin A[i]:= x; found (i) end
            do loop
                if A[i] = x then present;
                if A[i] = 0 then absent;
                i:= i-1; if i=0 then i:= m
            end
          end
```
Fig. 9

declared. The resulting language facility is a special case of Landin's [23] "program-points" and essentially similar to Zahn [45] and Knuth's [20] "events".

Figure 9 is an example adapted from Knuth [20]. The hash table A is to be searched using an index computed from the search argument x by the function *hash*; the sequels *present* and *absent* represent success or failure of the search, and the sequel *found* represents the action to be taken when an index for x is finally established.

Sequel parameters would be similar to label parameters in ALGOL 60 and would be useful though somewhat difficult to implement on some machines.

4.4. Discussion

As an illustration of the proposed design methods the presentation of the revisions and extensions has emphasized the objectives of better correspondence between parameters and declarations, and completeness of the abstraction facilities. In practice these must not be regarded as design ends, but merely as means; although detailed description of a proposed revision of Pascal is not the main purpose of this paper, it is appropriate at this point to evaluate the proposal in order to emphasize that while a systematic method can be used "as a reliable and inspiring guide" (Dijkstra), it does not relieve a designer of the responsibility to critically evaluate a design. We use the design goals expounded in [15, 42, 43].

(i) Flexibility

Notwithstanding the conservative opinions expressed by its designer [43], Pascal has been shown to be susceptible to some useful and clean extensions and generalizations. The features of the proposal that seem to contribute most to expressivity as compared to Pascal are static parameters, which provide a simple, secure, efficient, and general solution to the notorious array parameter problem, and the new abstractions, especially the **module** concept. None of Pascal's capabilities have been taken away except the **go to** sequencer, which few will lament, and the original form of the **with** statement, which might be advantageously replaced by a record constructor notation.

(ii) Security

No aspect of the proposal would compromise security in any way; indeed, features such as **val** parameters, specifiers, and **private** declarations would significantly improve it.

(iii) Readability and (iv) Efficiency
All aspects of the proposal are at least as good as Pascal in these respects.

(v) Simplicity
This objective is of primary importance, yet it is the most difficult to evaluate objectively; many of the issues have been discussed by Hoare [15] and Wirth [42, 43]. The proposed revision is certainly a "larger" language than Pascal, in that there are more facilities and a compiler for it would be somewhat more complicated; all the same, we do not regard the revised language as significantly more complex. Firstly, it is evident that exactly the same semantic and syntactic concepts underlie both, as well as the same approaches to type checking, coercions, storage management, data structuring, and control structuring.

Secondly, the total number of parametric *and* declarative forms in the revision is essentially the same as in Pascal. Or course, it might be desirable to have fewer such mechanisms, but it seems that provision of an explicit choice among a variety of simple and essentially different forms is as important to transparence, efficiency, and security for binding mechanisms as it is for control structures, data structures, and coercion conventions, and we believe the approach described to be consistent with Pascal's general design philosophy.

Finally, the regularity and conceptual coherence of the abstraction facilities, as well as their usefulness, compensate for the increased volume of the language.

In summary, the proposed changes and extensions would seem to be worthy of consideration for future versions of Pascal or new Pascal-like languages. It should also be noted that many of the facilities could even be accomodated into current Pascal implementations as local extensions, since no significant conceptual change would be involved.

5. Concluding Remarks

Recent interest in programming style and methodology has had the effects of, firstly, confirming the considerable practical importance of language design issues, and, secondly, demonstrating the usefulness of systematic and disciplined approaches to design problems. In this paper, two language design methods have been shown to be helpful both in analyzing language features in order to discover irregularities, unnecessary restrictions, and missing facilities, and also in synthesizing coherent, consistent and complete language features. There has been space to consider only one linguistic framework and a single design approach, but the generality of the semantic principles of correspondence and abstraction on which the methods are based suggests that they would be equally useful in other frameworks.

Perhaps the most important contribution of the methodological approach is that while mainly intended to help a designer to cope with the detailed problems of achieving consistency, completeness, and regularity in the design of specific language features, it also has the effect of drawing his attention to deeper structural issues, such as the nature of the denotable values and semantically-meaningful syntactic categories of the language under study. Significant progress in language design will require new concepts and the methods discussed in this paper should contribute to the future development of such concepts by focussing attention on structural aspects of programming languages.

Acknowledgements. The suggestions and encouragement of Robert Milne and other members of the Oxford University Programming Research Group are gratefully acknowledged. Comments by Mike Jenkins and Mike Symes on an earlier version were very helpful in improving the presentation. This research was supported by the National Research Council of Canada, grant A8990.

References

1. Ammann, U., Wirth, N.: Advantages of the value parameter over the constant parameter. Unpublished memo, Eidgenössische Technische Hochschule, Zürich, 1972
2. Birtwistle, G. M., Dahl, O.J., Myrhaug, B., Nygaard, K.: SIMULA BEGIN. Philadelphia: Auerbach 1973. Also Lund: Studentlitteratur 1974
3. Brinch Hansen, P.: Universal types in Concurrent Pascal. Information Processing Letters **3**, 165–166 (1975)
4. Bron, C., de Vries, W.: A Pascal compiler for PDP-11 mini-computers. Software Practice and Experience **6**, 109–116 (1976)
5. Church, A.: The calculi of lambda conversion. Princeton: Princeton University Press 1941
6. Dijkstra, E. W.:.*Goto* statement considered harmful. Comm. ACM **11**, 147–148, 538, 541 (1968)
7. Dijkstra, E.W.: Notes on structured programming. In: Structured programming (O.J. Dahl, E. W. Dijkstra, C.A.R. Hoare, eds.). London: Academic Press 1972
8. Dijkstra, E.W.: Guarded commands, non-determinacy, and formal derivation of programs. Comm. ACM **18**, 453–457 (1975)
9. Evans, A.: PAL – a language for teaching programming linguistics. Proc. 23rd ACM National Conference, Princeton: Brandin Systems Press 1968
10. Grosse-Lindemann, C.O., Nagel, H.H.: Postlude to a Pascal compiler bootstrap on a DEC system 10. Software Practice and Experience **6**, 29–42 (1976)
11. Habermann, A.N.: Critical comments on the programming language Pascal. Acta Informatica **3**, 47–57 (1973)
12. Hoare, C.A.R.: Procedures and parameters: an axiomatic approach. In: Symposium on Semantics of Algorithmic Languages (E. Engeler, ed.), Lecture Notes in Mathematics, Vol. 188. Berlin-Heidelberg-New York: Springer 1971
13. Hoare, C.A.R.: A note on the *for* statement. BIT **12**, 334–341 (1972)
14. Hoare, C.A.R.: Notes on data structuring. In: Structured programming (O.J. Dahl, E. W. Dijkstra, C.A.R. Hoare, eds.). London: Academic Press 1972
15. Hoare, C.A.R.: Hints on programming language design. Computer Science Department, Stanford University, CS-403, 1973
16. Hoare, C.A.R.: Recursive data structures. International J. Computer and Systems Sciences **4**, 105–132 (1975)
17. Hoare, C.A.R., Wirth, N.: An axiomatic definition of the programming language Pascal. Acta Informatica **2**, 335–355 (1973)
18. Jensen, K., Wirth, N.: Pascal: User manual and report. Lecture Notes in Computer Science, Vol. 18. Berlin-Heidelberg-New York: Springer 1974
19. Knobe, B., Yuval, G.: Towards Pascal II. The Hebrew University of Jerusalem, 1974
20. Knuth, D.E.: Structured programming with *goto* statements. Computing Surveys **6**, 261–301 (1974)
21. Landin, P.J.: The mechanical evaluation of expressions. Computer J. **6**, 308–320 (1964)
22. Landin, P. J.: Getting rid of labels. Univac Systems Programming Research Report, New York, 1965
23. Landin, P.J.: The next 700 programming languages. Comm. ACM **9**, 157–164 (1966)
24. Lecarme, O., Desjardins, P.: More comments on the programming language Pascal. Acta Informatica **4**, 231–243 (1975)
25. Ligler, G.T.: A mathematical approach to language design. Conference Record of the Second ACM Symposium on Principles of Programming Languages, Palo Alto, 1975

26. McCarthy, J.: A basis for a mathematical theory of computation. In: Computer programming and formal systems (P. Braffort, D. Hirschberg, eds.). Amsterdam: North-Holland 1963
27. Milne, R. E.: The formal semantics of computer languages and their implementations. Oxford University Computing Laboratory, Programming Research Group, technical microfiche TCF-2, 1974
28. Milne, R. E., Strachey, C.: A theory of programming language semantics. London: Chapman and Hall. Also New York: Wiley 1976
29. Mosses, P.: The mathematical semantics of ALGOL 60. Oxford University Computing Laboratory, Programming Research Group, technical monograph PRG-12, 1974
30. Quine, W. O.: Set theory and its logic. Cambridge (Mass.): Harvard University Press 1963
31. Reynolds, J. C.: Gedanken — a simple typeless language based on the principle of completeness and the reference concept. Comm. ACM **13**, 308–319 (1970)
32. Schuman, S. A.: Towards modular programming in high-level languages. Algol Bulletin **37**, 12–23 (1974)
33. Stoll, R. R.: Set theory and logic. San Francisco: Freeman 1963
34. Strachey, C.: Towards a formal semantics. In: Formal language description languages (T. Steel, ed.). Amsterdam: North-Holland 1966
35. Tennent, R. D.: Mathematical semantics and design of programming languages. University of Toronto, Ontario, Canada, Ph. D. thesis, 1973
36. Tennent, R. D.: The denotational semantics of programming languages. Comm. ACM **19**, 437–453 (1976)
37. Wang, A.: Generalized types in high-level programming languages. Institute of Mathematics, University of Oslo, Norway, Research Reports in Informatics, No. **1**, 1975
38. Wichmann, B. A.: ALGOL 60: Compilation and assessment. London: Academic Press 1973
39. van Wijngaarden, A., et al.: Report on the algorithmic language ALGOL 68. Numer. Math. **14**, 79–218 (1969)
40. Wirth, N.: The programming language Pascal. Acta Informatica **1**, 35–63 (1971)
41. Wirth, N.: Systematic programming — an introduction. Englewood Cliffs (N. J.): Prentice-Hall 1973
42. Wirth, N.: On the design of programming languages. In: Proc. IFIP Congress 74 (J.L. Rosenfeld, ed.), Stockholm. Amsterdam: North-Holland 1974
43. Wirth, N.: An assessment of the programming language Pascal. IEEE Trans. Software Engineering 1, pp. 192–198 (1975)
44. Wirth, N., Hoare, C. A. R.: A contribution to the development of ALGOL. Comm. ACM **9**, 413–431 (1966)
45. Zahn, C. J.: A control statement for natural top-down structured programming. In: Programming Symposium Proceedings, Colloque sur la Programmation, Paris (1974). Lecture Notes in Computer Science, Vol. 19. Berlin-Heidelberg-New York: Springer 1974

Received June 1, 1976

Section 3
Control Structures

Control structures form one of the key issues in programming language design. Much of the effort in the field in the early 1970's was directed at attempting to find a suitable set of control structures to support linear flow of control within a program module. More recently, considerable attention has been given to the design of language features suitable for expressing concurrency.

The tutorial paper by Wasserman surveys the topic of control structures and shows the relationship between sequential control structures and structured programming. The article also briefly urges the need for concurrent control structures.

The brief letter by Dijkstra, "Go To Statement Considered Harmful," as it was entitled by a *Communications of the ACM* editor, is among the most widely cited references in the programming languages literature. Little more than a page long, it was the first widely circulated statement that pointed out the hazards of indiscriminate use of the **goto** statement. Note that Dijkstra's objections were esthetic as well as technical.

The **goto** debate went on for several years and reached a peak in 1972 when there were several public debates over the relative merits of programming with and without the **goto** statement. Indeed, in many circles, the whole issue of sructured programming came down to the **goto** debate, which missed Dijkstra's entire original intent in using the term "structured programming."

Into this debate came Knuth with a voice of reason. His paper, entitled "Structured Programming with **goto** Statements," long available as a technical report and widely circulated in that form, was finally published in late 1974. Knuth points out that while it is nice to program without the **goto** statement, such a practice occasionally leads to rather convoluted program structures, and the resulting program is often less comprehensible than an equivalent program having a well placed **goto**. Knuth also reviews a number of alternative control structures that provide a more "structured" way to provide a branch in control flow. This excellent paper covered both sides of the debate accurately and evenly, and served to lay the debate pretty much to rest.

The concepts of iterators and generators were introduced into a number of programming languages, notably CLU and Alphard, as a replacement for the traditional **for** statement. The paper by Shaw, Wulf, and London describes the Alphard facility and shows how it supports the Alphard goal of program verification. Some additional information on Alphard's specification and verification methodology may be found in "An Introduction to the Construction and Verification of Alphard Programs," by Wulf, London, and Shaw, *IEEE Transactions on Software Engineering,* Vol. SE-2, No. 4, December, 1976.

Two papers by Hoare deal with concurrency and with language features to support concurrent programming. The paper on monitors is important in both the programming languages and operating systems fields, since a monitor is used to provide mutually exclusive access to shared objects. As such, it is valuable for organizing operating systems, as a mechanism for ensuring mutual exclusion and synchronization among processes in an operating system. Brinch Hansen designed monitors into Concurrent Pascal, and then used Concurrent Pascal in the design of the Solo operating system. (See Brinch Hansen's *The Architecture of Concurrent Programs,* Prentice-Hall, 1977.)

Hoare's paper on communicating sequential processes provides a different look at concurrent programming. Most other concurrent programming mechanisms are based on the assumptions that processes are loosely connected and that they only need to communicate at occasional moments. In such a setting, one process may receive a message from another, and carry out some activity, without having to communicate directly back to the sender. Hoare's proposal assumes a more active interprocess communication, wherein two processes intentionally set up communication with one another. Although this idea has not been extensively utilized as yet, it has appeal when one considers the needs of working on distributed systems with a number of small interrelated concurrent processes.

Dijkstra's paper on guarded commands is based on the use of nondeterministic control structures. His development of guarded commands was part of a method for the formal derivation of programs, whereby a program and its proof should be developed together. The notion of a "predicate transformer" is associated with each statement in the language and provides the basis for working backward from a postcondition, i.e., a statement that is true after execution of the statement, to the "weakest precondition" that guarantees the validity of the postcondition. In Dijkstra's book, *A Discipline of Programming* (Prentice-Hall, 1976), he defines a small programming language in which the guarded commands serve as the *only* control structures, with the two forms of guarded command serving in place of conditional and iterative control statements.

Thus, the papers in this section run the gamut between the practical and the theoretical, covering both sequential and concurrent programming.

Introduction to Sequential Control Structures

Anthony I. Wasserman

Structured programming considerations

There is presently considerable interest in the development of tools and techniques that lead to better programs. Among the principal concerns in this field is the relationship between features of a programming language and the construction of good programs.

Historically, ''good'' programs were efficient programs, in terms either of execution time or of use of space. While efficiency is still an important consideration, it must be balanced against such other factors as program reliability and correctness. It makes little difference how efficient a program is if the answers which it produces are unreliable or incorrect.

Another important consideration is that of program maintenance. Because most programs written for production usage have a lifetime of 10 years or more, they will go through a number of modifications throughout their lifetimes and will exist in a number of different versions. They will be changed when they are to run on different computer systems, when users request modifications, and when programmers or users find errors. Thus, a program must be written so that the person(s) maintaining the program can easily comprehend and change it. The use of cryptic coding methods and programming tricks detracts from program understandability and is therefore not considered to be good programming practice.

In the past, however, these factors of correctness and maintenance were not given adequate attention. Particularly in the early days of computers and programming languages, the challenge was to write programs in the first place and then to make them execute properly with the relatively limited resources that were available. Main memory size was limited, and execution speeds were rather slow, especially in comparison with the machines available today. As people gained experience in building software systems, people attempted to build increasingly sophisticated programs.

By the late 1960's, a number of these software development efforts had failed catastrophically because intellectual complexity of the problems had outstripped the ability of the software designer to solve the problem at hand. As a result of these failures—which included such programs as medical information systems, airline reservation systems, real-time command and control systems, and operating systems—attention focused upon the practices of program production.

One of the early discoveries was that the coding practices used by programmers have a major impact upon the quality of the resulting program. Programmers needed to be able to isolate parts of a program from one another, to test these program units independently, to minimize interactions between program units, and to determine that each unit worked properly. This discovery led to the development of *structured programming,* a methodology which combines the process of problem solution with the process of writing a correctly executing program to implement the solution. The discovery also led to the development of rules for writing programs so as to simplify a reader's determination of their functions. Finally, it led to a great deal of research in programming languages, research which is reflected in the design of a number of programming languages and features. The discussion of control structures in this section is heavily influenced by the issues of structured programming.

Linear flow of control. One characteristic of a well-written program is that its static appearance, i.e., the listing, closely resembles the dynamic action, i.e., the program's execution. It is possible to read such a program line-by-line and follow the logic of the program, which is not the case if the execution of the program skips around from one part of the progrm to the other in a haphazard manner. Under these circumstances, it becomes difficult to determine the conditions under which execution reaches particular points of the program. Futhermore, the number of test cases required to check out such a program becomes quite high. Most readers feel more confident about the accuracy of a program if they can look at it and feel intuitively that all of the cases have been checked and that the program works correctly.

Accordingly attention was focused primarily on restricting the unrestrained branching within a program, mostly upon use of the the **goto** statement and its variants in different programming languages. The **goto** statement gave the programmer the ability to branch virtually anywhere within a program. The Algol 60 programmer, for example, could branch out of several blocks to a label in a surrounding block. Worse, the **goto** statement could be used to implement a form of particularly convoluted logic. The more primitive the control constructs in a language, the more the **goto** statement is needed.

The language features which are used to control program flow and logical branching and to determine the sequence of statment execution are termed *control structures.* These structures range from **goto** through **if** statements, **do** loops, and subprogram calls. Much of the work done in this area can be characterized as trying to provide a rich enough set of control structures to eliminate the need for the use of the **goto** statement. There was, of course, much debate over this subject, with various people presenting cases for and against the **goto** statement.

An unfortunate result of the extended debate was the loss of much of the original meaning of the term "structured programming." In the minds of many people, structured programming came to be identified with the attempt to purge the **goto** statement from programs rather than with the broader goal of a systematic approach to program development which began with a problem-solving activity and terminated with a correctly functioning program.

The Bohm-Jacopini result. In 1966, Bohm and Jacopini published a paper which showed that it was theoretically possible to construct all programs with only three kinds of statements: composition, an **if-then-else,** and a **while-do.** All flowcharts could be converted to contain only those three statement forms. Theoretically, then, if a programming language had a mechanism for executing statements in order (composition), an **if-then-else** statement, and **while-do** statement or its equivalent, then all programs in that language could be written without the **goto** statement. If there was no way of branching outside one of these three statements, then all programs would exhibit linear flow of control.

Using the Bohm-Jacopini result, it becomes possible to think in terms of "one-in, one-out control flow." There is only one path into each of these statements and only one path out of each, as shown below.

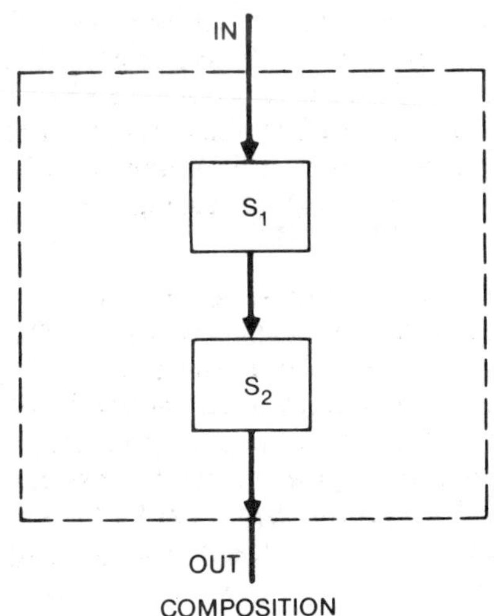

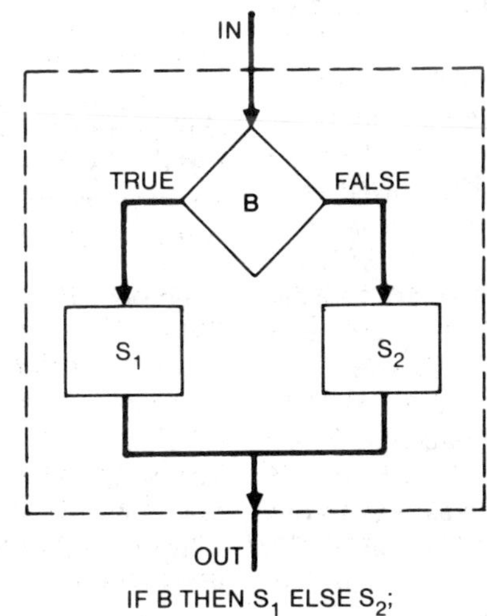

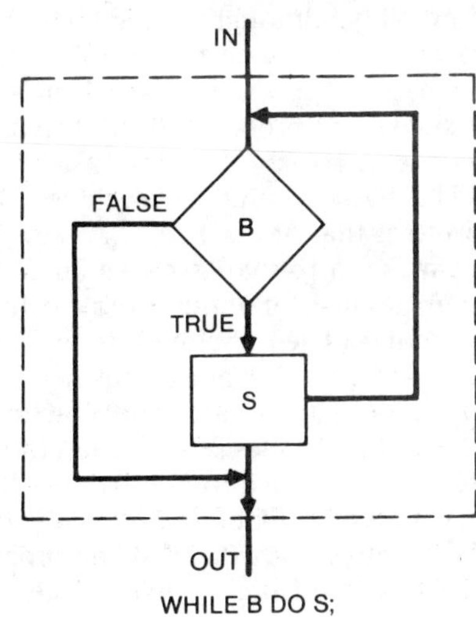

Each statement may be any one of the three forms. Thus, a valid flow diagram would be

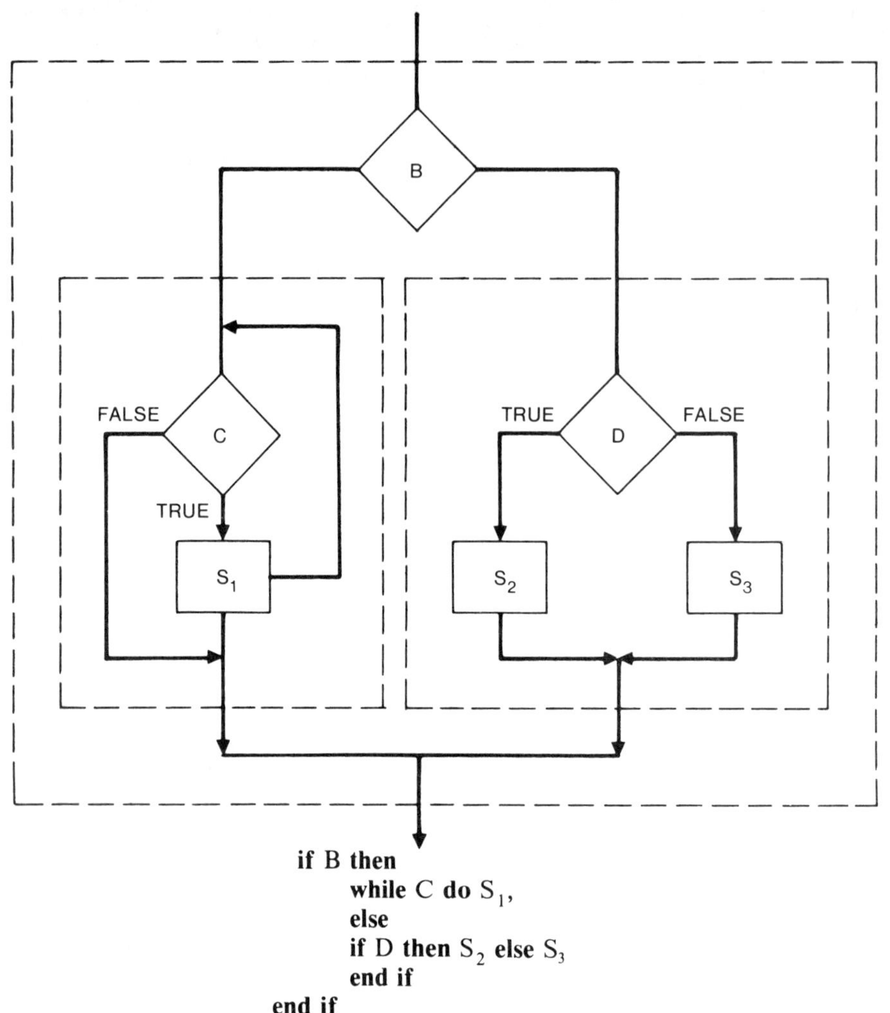

if B then
  while C **do** S_1,
else
  if D **then** S_2 **else** S_3
  end if
end if

since the one-on, one-out control flow can be applied.

Program verification. The ability to construct programs which exhibit this linear flow of control makes it easier to formally prove properties about them. One approach to seeing if a program operates correctly is to test it thoroughly, although testing has traditionally been used to search for errors rather than to ascertain correctness. An alternative approach, one which is gradually becoming feasible, is to prove in a mathematical sense that the program is correct.

The basic technique developed for proving programs correct is that of *assertions*. At key points in the program, one makes a formal assertion about the properties of program variables or about other conditions which are true at that point. Then one must prove formally that the assertion is correct. If one can further prove that the program does indeed terminate, and that the final assertion corresponds to the desired function of the program, then the program is verified to be correct.

A successful proof requires the proof of an assertion for each control path through the program. If a program is relatively free from branching, then the complexity of the various assertions is reduced because the number of control paths is reduced. If one subdivides a large program into a number of smaller parts, one can prove the smaller parts independently and combine their proofs into a proof of the large program, in much the same way that mathematicians prove a number of lemmas which are then used in the proof of a more complex theorem.

When it became apparent that certain language features either assist or hinder the development of proofs, the issue of program verification emerged as a driving force in the development of new control sturctures and in the design of programming languages. Some newer research-oriented languages include a form of statement intended for use by computer-based systems for program verification. Generally treated by computers as comments, these assertions state the conditions which are to be proved at a given point.

The objective of this work on verification is to be able to certify that a program correctly does what its specification claims. Verification techniques are still in their infancy, however, since there are a number of sizeable research problems to be solved first. Among these problems are techniques for dealing with systems in which multiple processes are executing concurrently and techniques for formally specifying what a program is to do, since a formal specification is required if one is to prove that a program corresponds precisely to its specification. In short, verification issues have prompted an overwhelming percentage of recent work on control structures and have led to a much better understanding of program construction.

Program organization

The most global unit of execution is a program, an autonomous unit. A program is composed of a number of program subunits or modules. Each module in turn is composed of statements. Statements are typically of two kinds: declarative, which provide information about the data to be used or about the execution environment; and executable, which cause a computation to be performed or some logical action to be taken. Declarative statements include all of the variable and type declarations in a block, COBOL Data Divisions, and FORTRAN FORMAT statements and COMMON blocks. Executable statements include assignment statements, procedure or subroutine calls, input/output commands, and branching statements.

One of the modules in a program is designated the ''main program'' or the ''external module.'' Program execution begins with the first executable statement in that module, with further execution determined by the control flow specified by the executable statements.

We shall use the term ''module'' to refer to a program unit, generally a procedure, a function, or a subroutine, although the term can be applied to an abstract data type declaration as well. We must note, however, that this use does not correspond precisely to the more general concept of a module. That concept considers a module to be a collection of data and statements that forms a coherent logical unit, carrying out a single function or a set of related activities. While a good program design will lead to the construction of program units that meet this concept of a module, there is no requirement that they do so. Thus, our use of the term ''module'' is partly for convenience—one term to encompass functions, subroutines, and procedures—and partly an indication that such program units should conform to the traditional notion of a module.

Control statements

Control statements determine which statements in a program are executed and the order in which they are executed. Some executable statements result in branching out of normal execution sequence, while others do not. In the presence of a sequence of assignment statements without function calls, no branching occurs—each statement is executed in order. Other control statements lead to some kind of testing and branching, to iteration, or to a branch to another program statement or module.

It should be noted that when we write,

$$Y := F(X) + 2;$$
$$Z := Z - Y;$$

where F is a function call, there is a call to another program module, namely, the module for function F, embedded within the first assignment statement. The module is called, a value is returned for F, and execution of the first assignment statement is completed, with control then passing to the second assignment statement.

An unconstrained branch occurs when the program makes a transfer of control without a return point. The primary language construction for such transfers is the **goto** statement, although we can achieve similar effects with other language features as well.

The unconstrained branch permits control to be transferred to any statement within a module, as long as the destination is an executable statement with an associated label to serve as a target. If the module is an internal one, the transfer can be to any point within the module or within a surrounding external module. There is a general agreement now that proper programming practices minimize use of the **goto.**

Conditional branching. Much of the logic of computer programs is based on the ability to perform alternative sequences of steps based upon the result of a test. For example, a statement requires comparison of two numbers. If one number is greater than the other, then one set of steps is taken; otherwise, a different set of steps is taken. We can generalize this notion to N alternatives as well. A variable can take on any integer value from 1 to N. Depending upon that value at a given point, the sequence can follow any of N different control paths. This ability to branch on conditions is encompassed in programming languages by the **if-then-else** construct and by the **case** statement.

We have already seen that the **if-then-else** statement conforms to the one-in, one-out control flow of structured programs. The following diagram indicates that the **case** statement meets this requirement as well. Thus, the **if** statement and the **case** statement provide the basis for a large portion of conditional testing and branching.

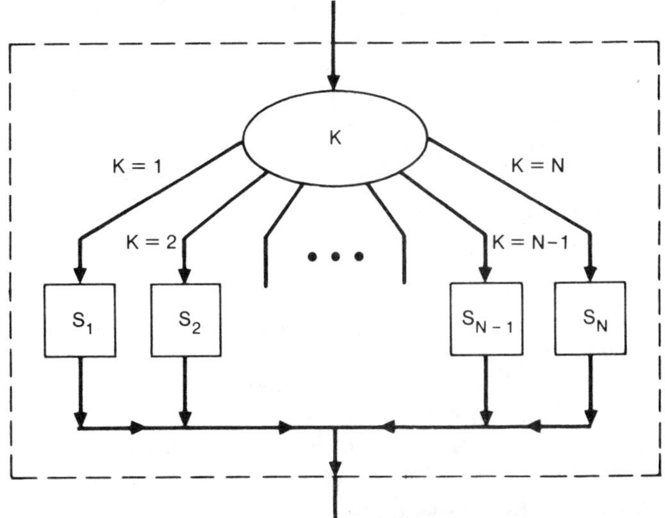

Iteration. Repetitive execution of a statement or a sequence of statements characterizes much of computing. For example, a large number of data processing tasks, including payroll processing and billing, fall into this category, as do many numerical problems as well, including assigning values to elements of vectors and arrays. Thus, iterative statements, for managing repetitive execution of a group of statements, are essential for a high-level programming language. Iterative statements fall into two categories: those in which the iteration is carried out while a boolean condition remains true, and those in which the iteration is carried out while some control variable remains within a given range of values.

Iteration with a control variable. On the surface, it would appear that iteration with a control variable is rather straightforward. As we shall quickly see, however, a number of issues must be resolved in developing an iteration mechanism for a programming language.

In its simplest form, an iterative statement with a control variable designates the number of times that an action is to be performed.

for i: = 1 **to** 100 **do** S;

is an example of such a statement, where i is an integer

variable and S is a statement, possibly a compound statement. If we desired to iterate over the odd numbers, we could write

for i: = 1 **by 2 to** 99 **do** S;

Instead of using integer literals in the **for** statement, it is possible to use arbitrary expressions. Thus, one can write

for i : = k **by** (j + k)/2 **to** sqrt(m) **do** S;

and the basic effect is still the same. However, some questions immediately arise. In this statement, j, k, and m are variables. Is it permissible to make assignments to them within the body of the loop? For that matter, is it permissible to explicitly change the value of i within the loop? What is the effect of doing so? Does the control variable i have a value upon termination of the loop, or is it undefined?

The language designer must resolve all of these points, and the programmer and implementer must follow them. Answers to these questions vary from one language to another, but recent language designs have tended to be more restrictive. A common approach in several newly designed languages is to treat the control variable as a local readonly variable. Thus, the use of i introduces a new variable and a new program scope. No assignment can be made to i within the loop, since it is readonly, and i ceases to exist upon exit from the loop. If there were a variable named i in the surrounding scope, it could not be accessed within the loop (since the variable i is effectively redeclared), but becomes accessible again upon exit from the scope of the loop.

Iteration without a control variable. The other major approach to programmed iteration is to execute a statement repeatedly while a boolean condition is met, until a boolean condition is met, or until an explicit exit statement is encountered. Two of the most common language constructs for this purpose are termed the **while-do** and the **repeat-until.** We may rewrite the statement

for i : = 1 **by 2 to** 99 **do** S;

to show how they work.

```
i : = 1;                    i : = 1;
  while i ⩽ 99 do             repeat
  begin                        S;
    S;                         i : = i + 2
    i : = i + 2              until i>99;
  end;
while-do statement          repeat-until statement
```

The article by Knuth in this section illustrates these statements further and shows several variations upon them. A large number of variations have been proposed and incorporated into various programming languages.

As mentioned earlier, one of the primary reasons for the interest in different conditional and iterative control structures has been to develop a set of control structures which were sufficiently powerful and expressive to eliminate the need for and use of the **goto** statement. There are some strong arguments in favor of programming without the **goto**, but the reader is cautioned against rewriting existing programs to eliminate the **goto** statements within them. Such an exercise may lead to hopelessly confusing programs and more involuted control structures than were present before. Reformulation of intricately entwined masses of **goto** statements still tends to leave intricately entwined program logic.

What we are really after is clarity of thought and algorithm. We must attempt the valuable programming discipline of avoiding **goto**'s at the level of the initial algorithm formualtion, not at the stage of reprogramming. At the program development level, this discipline is tremendously attractive and can lead to lucid and easily readable programs once the programmer overcomes the initial trauma associated with this way of thinking.

Communication among modules

The previous section dealt with the different control structures available for coding a single module. We covered the types of branching that typically occur in such modules and some of the available language features for handling this branching. As we noted earlier, however, a program typically consists of a number of different modules joined together. Information can be communicated between modules by the use of commonly accessible data or by having one module call upon another. In this way, we will see a model of program execution and control flow on a larger scale.

Transfer of control between program units. Program units may be connected in a number of different ways. A particularly simple way is to think of a program as consisting of a number of routines with some physical ordering that determines the sequence in which the routines will be executed. Such an approach closely resembles the method used in some programming systems where the amount of memory available for a program is quite small. In that case, the compiler breaks the program up into a number of pieces, each of which will fit into the available space. The last statement in each of the pieces (except for the last) chains execution to the next piece. This approach is a very low-level form of transferring control between program units, since it is little more than a **goto** statement.

In general, we would like a module to be able to call another module, cause that module to be executed, and then resume execution immediately after the call in the original module. Furthermore, we would often like to communicate information between the two modules, perhaps in the nature of results. Finally, we would like the calling sequence to be of arbitrary length so that one module may call another, which in turn calls a third module, and so on, with the status of all of the suspended modules properly preserved so that execution will continue at the appropriate point when control is finally returned to the first module.

We thus see the concept of transferring control between modules. When one module invokes (or calls) another executable module, it causes control to be passed to that other module. When that module has finished executing, possibly after calling other modules, control will be returned to the first module so that it may continue its execution. When execution of a module is interrupted by a call to another module, it is necessary to preserve the status of the first module for later execution, storing the names and values of variables accessible in that module and the location at which execution must begin upon return of control.

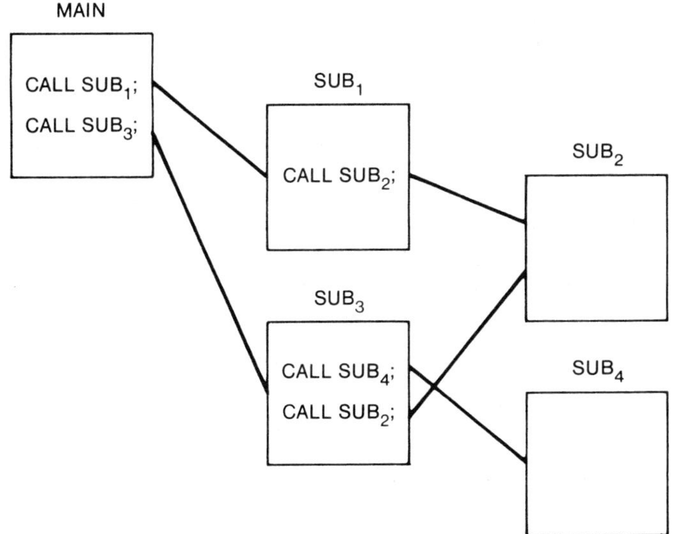

If each of the modules in this diagram exhibits linear flow of control, then the modules will be executed in the order MAIN, SUB1, SUB2, SUB1, MAIN, SUB3, SUB4, SUB3, SUB2, SUB3, MAIN.

Parameter passing mechanisms. A module is a collection of program steps gathered together to perform, in general, a single operation, such as computing a mathematical function or sorting a set of numbers. We have observed the need to transmit information to and from a module and have seen how this can be implicitly accomplished with the use of COMMON blocks or global variables. At the same time, however, there are some shortcomings associated with the use of those mechanisms. Accordingly, in this section, we will examine approaches to passing needed information explicitly between modules.

We can place the information communicated between modules into two broad categories: input information, which provides data needed for the module's action, and output information, which transmits results produced by the module's action. Rather than assigning storage for this data in a commonly accessible location, we associate a *parameter list* with the module containing the required input and output information. When the module is invoked from an external module, the call must include a parameter list to correspond with the module's parameter list.

The use of input parameters gives us the ability to generalize the action of a module. Consider a sorting module which sorts an array A of 100 elements and places the sorted elements in B, where A and B are in commonly accessible areas. There would be no immediately available method to sort an array X with 50 elements without rewriting the module. Alternatively, we can think of three parameters: AIN, AOUT, and N, where AIN and AOUT are arrays and N is the size of the array. AIN is an input parameter which holds the array to be sorted; AOUT is an output parameter which holds the sorted array; N is an input parameter telling the number of elements in AIN and AOUT to be sorted.

Rather than simply writing **module** SORT to define the module and

SORT

to invoke it, where there are no parameters, the analogous form with parameters would define

module SORT (AIN, AOUT, N)

and a call to that module for arrays A and B of size 100 would be

SORT (A, B, 100)

The advantages and disadvantages of this approach are immediately apparent. The biggest advantage is that we can make the action of the module very obvious in terms of its relationships to other modules. First, we prominently display all of the shared data elements in a module definition with parameters. Next, we give other modules an unambiguous form of communication to that module. Input parameters will likewise be returned in a certain form. In that way, there is no need for any module to know anything about the inside of any other module. We are not really concerned about how the SORT module works, as long as we know that the array AOUT will produce the correct output when we give it the correct inputs for AIN and N. For medium-to-large programming problems, the logical separation of modules resulting offers us the benefits of being able to divide up the project among a number of programmers and of being able to simplify the complexity of the problem by making it possible to focus on modules individually. These benefits are of immense importance in program design and development; parameters are crucial to our being able to develop workable modular program structures.

Some disadvantages must also be noted. As we shall observe, there is some execution time overhead associated with the use of parameters, primarily involving the time and space required to establish the communication between modules. We shall see that some of this potential overhead depends upon the method by which parameters are passed.

To this point, we have been rather sketchy about the mechanics of parameter passing and the way in which a correspondence is established between parameters in a given module and parameters in the calling module, choosing instead to advocate the use of parameters as a valuable programming tool. We shall now take up the details of parameter passing.

When we develop a module that will have parameters, it is necessary to identify those parameters, as to their number, their type, their usage, and their method of transmission. The parameter list accompanies the declaration of the module itself. The parameters declared here are called *formal parameters*. We define each of them as having a type and give each a name. This name is local to the module in which it is defined; the existence of other program variables with the same name is not relevant. Within that module, we use the formal parameter as a normal variable of the declared type.

When the module is invoked, the call will contain a set of *actual parameters*. In most languages, the number of actual parameters must agree with the number of formal parameters. Furthermore, the actual and formal parameters must agree as to type. If the formal parameter is an integer, the actual parameter cannot be an array of real numbers.

This is the basis for establishing correspondence between actual and formal parameters. Suppose that we have declared a procedure in Pascal:

procedure XYZ (LETTER: char; SIZE: integer; EPS:
real);

and have declared variables in another procedure (or the
main program) as follows:

var SYMBOL: char;
       NUM: integer;
     DELTA: real;

We could then write

XYZ (SYMBOL, NUM, DELTA)

as an invocation of procedure XYZ, establishing correspondence between SYMBOL and LETTER, NUM and
SIZE, and DELTA and EPS. Note that if we had declared
SYMBOL, NUM, or DELTA to be of different types, we
would not have properly established the correspondence,
since the type checking rules would have been violated.
Similarly, if the call to XYZ did not have three parameters,
the correspondence would not be correctly made, and a
compilation error would result.

We should also note that the declarations in the main
program or module might have been

var LETTER: char;
      SIZE: integer;
      EPS: real;

However, these names would *not* be the same as the names
in the formal parameter list. It would still be necessary to
establish the correspondence in the call

XYZ (LETTER, SIZE, EPS)

since there is no guarantee that variables of the same name
are of the same type. Use of the same name is a fairly common programming practice and offers the advantage of
improving program comprehensibility, but it should not
obscure the fact that the actual and formal parameters are
distinct items.

As noted earlier, parameters can be used for input, output, or both input and output. An input parameter provides a value to a module which is used within the module;
an output parameter is assigned a value within the module.
Clearly, a parameter can be used in both capacities. A simple example appears in the SORT procedure above. Instead of storing the sorted array in AOUT, we could perform sorting within AIN. Thus, the array AIN would be
both an input and output parameter, eliminating the need
for AOUT. The original array A would be taken as an input parameter (corresponding to AIN). Unless the input
array had already been sorted, an assignment would be
made to one or more elements of AIN within SORT, so
that it would serve as both an input and output parameter.
N, the number of elements, would remain strictly an input
parameter.

Call by value, call by reference, call by name. Three
basic forms of transmission are used between actual and
formal parameters: call by *value,* call by *reference,* and call
by *name.* We shall now compare and contrast these three
approaches to parameter passing, noting first that different languages support one or more of these methods.

Call by value is a method of parameter transmission
whereby the value of the actual parameter is evaluated
once upon entry to the module. Its value is assigned to the
corresponding formal parameter, which is then used as a

local variable within the module.

Value parameters are generally used to transmit information which is to be unchanged in a module, such as
number of iteration steps for an approximation procedure,
the number of records for some data processing or sorting
procedure, or the boundaries and step size for a numerical
integration problem. Numeric constants are typically passed by value; problems can arise if they are transmitted in
other ways.

Call by reference is a method of parameter transmission
whereby the address of the actual parameter is associated
with the formal parameter. The effect of this correspondence is that assignment of a value to the formal parameter
results in assignment of that value to the actual parameter.
With call by value, we create a new local variable with appropriate local storage set aside. With call by reference, the
parameter mechanism only serves to point to an existing
variable in the calling module. Output parameters are effectively treated this way, since they provide the transmission of values back to the calling module.

We can offer a comparison between the two forms of
transmission with an example (using Pascal):

```
program TEST;
var X,Y: real;
procedure F (X: real; var Y: real);
   begin
      X: = 4;
      Y: = 5
   end;
begin
   X : = 3; Y : = 6;
   F (X,Y);
   write (X,Y);
end.
```

The values of X and Y are initialized to 3 and 6 respectively
in the main program. F is called. X is called by value and Y
is called by reference, as denoted by the word **var**
preceding the appearance of Y in the formal parameter list.
Thus, X is a local variable in F, while Y refers to the same
object as does Y as in the call to F. Accordingly, the assignment to X in F is local, but the assignment to Y is not. The
values printed for X and Y by the write statement in the
main program are 3 and 5, respectively.

Call by reference is used frequently for output
parameters, when the object in the parameter list is to be
modified by the module. Its overhead is very low, since
there is no need for local storage and the mapping simply
takes the formal parameter and produces a pointer to the
address of the actual parameter. When we contrast this approach with the creation of local storage for parameters
which are passed by value, it is apparent that there are
other instances in which call by reference is also useful.

When one wishes to transmit a large block of data,
perhaps an array or a group of records, both space and
time requirements can be significant—the space needed for
implementation of call by value and the time required to
make the assignment at execution time. Thus, it is frequently desirable to transmit such data by reference rather
than by value, even though the data may not be modified
within the module. The alternative is to place the large data
objects in a common or global storge area; however, the
overhead of call by reference is sufficiently low that little is
to be gained from bypassing the parameter approach.

However, we should note here that parameters called by value are not strictly input parameters in all languages, and parameters called by reference are not strictly output parameters or input/output parameters. Pragmatic programming considerations frequently take precedence over the pure concepts.

Call by name is a method of parameter passing whereby we substitute the actual parameter for the formal parameter at every point where the formal parameter appears in a module. Call by name was devised for Algol 60 as a technique for passing the names of functions and procedures. Because alternative mechanisms for passing function and procedure names have since been developed, however, call by name is now simply an Algol 60 artifact. Nonetheless, it sheds some additional light on the parameter passing problems.

Suppose that we wish to evaluate a mathematical function $F(Y)$ at $N+1$ equidistant points between A and B, where $A<B$, and that we wish to store those values in a real array RES. In Algol 60, we can write

```
procedure EVAL (A,B,N,F,Y,RES); value A,B,N;
real A,B,F,Y;
integer N;
real array RES;
comment in the main program, the actual parameter
        for RES must be of size N + 1 or greater;
begin
    integer I; real SS;
    SS := (B − A)/N;
    for I := 0 step 1 until N + 1 do
    begin
        Y := A + I*SS;
        RES [I] := F;
    end
end;
```

In order to compute the value for SIN(Y) for 180 different values of Y from 0 through 180 degrees, one could write

```
EVAL (0, 3.14159265, 180,SIN(Y),Y,TABLE);
```

where TABLE has been declared

```
real array TABLE [0:180];
```

F is called by name, so that SIN(Y) is inserted where F appears in the body of EVAL. Y is given differing values in the preceding line, the effect of which is to assign 181 different values to RES. Note that RES is also called by name, since everything not explicitly called by value is called by name, so TABLE replaces RES upon the call, thereby accomplishing the desired information transmission.

In Algol 60, F is a real quantity and the actual parameter SIN(Y) is substituted. At first glance, it appears that this approach is very similar to call by reference, but this is not really the case. Consider the following procedure in Algol 60,

```
procedure SWAP (A,B);
integer A,B;
begin
    integer TEMP;
    TEMP := A; A := B; B := TEMP
end;
```

which appears to exchange two numbers. Now look at the following program:

```
begin
    integer array A [1:10];
    integer I,J;
        for J := 1 step 1 until 10 do A[J] := J + 1;
        I := 4; SWAP (A[I],I);
        I := 6; SWAP (I,A[I]);
end;
```

In the first call to SWAP, things work as expected, with A[4] getting the value 4 and I getting the value 5. In the second call, though, I gets the value of A[I], namely 7; then A[7] gets the value of TEMP, namely 6. The value of A[6] is not changed. This surprise occurs because the subscript I was changed before the formal parameter B, corresponding to A[I], appeared on the left-hand side of the assignment.

In short, call by name must be used with some caution, as it presents substantial overhead in implementation, since a text substitituion must be made for *every* use of formal parameter. Furthermore, it leads to some subtle programming errors such as the one associated with SWAP above. Finally, more efficient ways exist for accomplishing the goals of call by name. As a result, the common parameter mechanisms in programming languages are call by reference and call by value.

Summary

We have examined several of the issues in sequential control structures and in passing information between modules via parameters. The availability of control structures within a language plays a large role in determining how well a particular language supports the concepts and the goals of structured programming.

We can see that the various basic control structures for logical branching, repetition, and module invocation determine the extent to which programmers can write readable programs that exhibit a linear flow of control. The statements for module invocation (function and procedure calls) and the associated rules for information sharing and transmission determine the extent to which a programmer can break down a problem into different modules. Ideally, these modules can be separately programmed and effectively united into a complete program that represents a solution to the original problem.

The whole area of control structures is still an active research subject, particularly with respect to language support for concurrent processing. If we consider a program in execution to be regarded as a *process,* we can see the need for processes to communicate with one another, to be able to initiate the execution of other processes, and to terminate themselves or other processes. An entirely different set of control structures is needed to support this parallelism, along with appropriate facilities for sharing of data among a number of processes. Several of the articles in this section deal with solutions to these problems of concurrency.

Go To Statement Considered Harmful

Reprinted from *Communications of the ACM*, March 1968, pp. 147-148. Copyright 1968 Association for Computing Machinery, Inc. Reprinted by permission.

Key Words and Phrases: go to statement, jump instruction, branch instruction, conditional clause, alternative clause, repetitive clause, program intelligibility, program sequencing
CR Categories: 4.22, 5.23, 5.24

EDITOR:

For a number of years I have been familiar with the observation that the quality of programmers is a decreasing function of the density of **go to** statements in the programs they produce. More recently I discovered why the use of the **go to** statement has such disastrous effects, and I became convinced that the **go to** statement should be abolished from all "higher level" programming languages (i.e. everything except, perhaps, plain machine code). At that time I did not attach too much importance to this discovery; I now submit my considerations for publication because in very recent discussions in which the subject turned up, I have been urged to do so.

My first remark is that, although the programmer's activity ends when he has constructed a correct program, the process taking place under control of his program is the true subject matter of his activity, for it is this process that has to accomplish the desired effect; it is this process that in its dynamic behavior has to satisfy the desired specifications. Yet, once the program has been made, the "making" of the corresponding process is delegated to the machine.

My second remark is that our intellectual powers are rather geared to master static relations and that our powers to visualize processes evolving in time are relatively poorly developed. For that reason we should do (as wise programmers aware of our limitations) our utmost to shorten the conceptual gap between the static program and the dynamic process, to make the correspondence between the program (spread out in text space) and the process (spread out in time) as trivial as possible.

Let us now consider how we can characterize the progress of a process. (You may think about this question in a very concrete manner: suppose that a process, considered as a time succession of actions, is stopped after an arbitrary action, what data do we have to fix in order that we can redo the process until the very same point?) If the program text is a pure concatenation of, say, assignment statements (for the purpose of this discussion regarded as the descriptions of single actions) it is sufficient to point in the program text to a point between two successive action descriptions. (In the absence of **go to** statements I can permit myself the syntactic ambiguity in the last three words of the previous sentence: if we parse them as "successive (action descriptions)" we mean successive in text space; if we parse as "(successive action) descriptions" we mean successive in time.) Let us call such a pointer to a suitable place in the text a "textual index."

When we include conditional clauses (**if** B **then** A), alternative clauses (**if** B **then** $A1$ **else** $A2$), choice clauses as introduced by C. A. R. Hoare (case[i] of $(A1, A2, \cdots, An)$), or conditional expressions as introduced by J. McCarthy ($B1 \rightarrow E1, B2 \rightarrow E2, \cdots, Bn \rightarrow En$), the fact remains that the progress of the process remains characterized by a single textual index.

As soon as we include in our language procedures we must admit that a single textual index is no longer sufficient. In the case that a textual index points to the interior of a procedure body the dynamic progress is only characterized when we also give to which call of the procedure we refer. With the inclusion of procedures we can characterize the progress of the process via a sequence of textual indices, the length of this sequence being equal to the dynamic depth of procedure calling.

Let us now consider repetition clauses (like, **while** B **repeat** A or **repeat** A **until** B). Logically speaking, such clauses are now superfluous, because we can express repetition with the aid of recursive procedures. For reasons of realism I don't wish to exclude them: on the one hand, repetition clauses can be implemented quite comfortably with present day finite equipment; on the other hand, the reasoning pattern known as "induction" makes us well equipped to retain our intellectual grasp on the processes generated by repetition clauses. With the inclusion of the repetition clauses textual indices are no longer sufficient to describe the dynamic progress of the process. With each entry into a repetition clause, however, we can associate a so-called "dynamic index," inexorably counting the ordinal number of the corresponding current repetition. As repetition clauses (just as procedure calls) may be applied nestedly, we find that now the progress of the process can always be uniquely characterized by a (mixed) sequence of textual and/or dynamic indices.

The main point is that the values of these indices are outside programmer's control; they are generated (either by the write-up of his program or by the dynamic evolution of the process) whether he wishes or not. They provide independent coordinates in which to describe the progress of the process.

Why do we need such independent coordinates? The reason is—and this seems to be inherent to sequential processes—that we can interpret the value of a variable only with respect to the progress of the process. If we wish to count the number, n say, of people in an initially empty room, we can achieve this by increasing n by one whenever we see someone entering the room. In the in-between moment that we have observed someone entering the room but have not yet performed the subsequent increase of n, its value equals the number of people in the room minus one!

The unbridled use of the **go to** statement has an immediate consequence that it becomes terribly hard to find a meaningful set of coordinates in which to describe the process progress. Usually, people take into account as well the values of some well chosen variables, but this is out of the question because it is relative to the progress that the meaning of these values is to be understood! With the **go to** statement one can, of course, still describe the progress uniquely by a counter counting the number of actions performed since program start (viz. a kind of normalized clock). The difficulty is that such a coordinate, although unique, is utterly unhelpful. In such a coordinate system it becomes an extremely complicated affair to define all those points of progress where, say, n equals the number of persons in the room minus one!

The **go to** statement as it stands is just too primitive; it is too much an invitation to make a mess of one's program. One can regard and appreciate the clauses considered as bridling its use. I do not claim that the clauses mentioned are exhaustive in the sense that they will satisfy all needs, but whatever clauses are suggested (e.g. abortion clauses) they should satisfy the requirement that a programmer independent coordinate system can be maintained to describe the process in a helpful and manageable way.

It is hard to end this with a fair acknowledgment. Am I to

judge by whom my thinking has been influenced? It is fairly obvious that I am not uninfluenced by Peter Landin and Christopher Strachey. Finally I should like to record (as I remember it quite distinctly) how Heinz Zemanek at the pre-ALGOL meeting in early 1959 in Copenhagen quite explicitly expressed his doubts whether the **go to** statement should be treated on equal syntactic footing with the assignment statement. To a modest extent I blame myself for not having then drawn the consequences of his remark.

The remark about the undesirability of the **go to** statement is far from new. I remember having read the explicit recommendation to restrict the use of the **go to** statement to alarm exits, but I have not been able to trace it; presumably, it has been made by C. A. R. Hoare. In [1, Sec. 3.2.1.] Wirth and Hoare together make a remark in the same direction in motivating the case construction: "Like the conditional, it mirrors the dynamic structure of a program more clearly than **go to** statements and switches, and it eliminates the need for introducing a large number of labels in the program."

In [2] Guiseppe Jacopini seems to have proved the (logical) superfluousness of the **go to** statement. The exercise to translate an arbitrary flow diagram more or less mechanically into a jumpless one, however, is not to be recommended. Then the resulting flow diagram cannot be expected to be more transparent than the original one.

REFERENCES:
1. WIRTH, NIKLAUS, AND HOARE, C. A. R.   A contribution to the development of ALGOL. *Comm. ACM 9* (June 1966), 413–432.
2. BÖHM, CORRADO, AND JACOPINI, GUISEPPE.   Flow diagrams, Turing machines and languages with only two formation rules. *Comm. ACM 9* (May 1966), 366–371.

EDSGER W. DIJKSTRA
Technological University
Eindhoven, The Netherlands

Structured Programming with **go to** Statements

DONALD E. KNUTH

Stanford University, Stanford, California 94305

Reprinted from *Computing Surveys,* December 1974, pp. 261-301. Copyright 1974
Associatiion for Computing Machinery, Inc. Reprinted by permission.

A consideration of several different examples sheds new light on the problem of creating reliable, well-structured programs that behave efficiently. This study focuses largely on two issues: (a) improved syntax for iterations and error exits, making it possible to write a larger class of programs clearly and efficiently without **go to** statements; (b) a methodology of program design, beginning with readable and correct, but possibly inefficient programs that are systematically transformed if necessary into efficient and correct, but possibly less readable code. The discussion brings out opposing points of view about whether or not **go to** statements should be abolished; some merit is found on both sides of this question. Finally, an attempt is made to define the true nature of structured programming, and to recommend fruitful directions for further study.

Keywords and phrases: structured programming, **go to** statements, language design, event indicators, recursion, Boolean variables, iteration, optimization of programs, program transformations, program manipulation systems searching, Quicksort, efficiency

CR categories: 4.0, 4.10, 4.20, 5.20, 5.5, 6.1 (5.23, 5.24, 5.25, 5.27)

> You may go when you will go,
> And I will stay behind.
> *—Edna St. Vincent Millay* [66]

> Most likely you go your way and I'll go mine.
> *—Song title by Bob Dylan* [33]

> Do you suffer from painful elimination?
> *—Advertisement, J. B. Williams Co.*

INTRODUCTION

A revolution is taking place in the way we write programs and teach programming, because we are beginning to understand the associated mental processes more deeply. It is impossible to read the recent book *Structured programming* [17; 55] without having it change your life. The reasons for this revolution and its future prospects have been aptly described by E. W. Dijkstra in his 1972 Turing Award Lecture, "The Humble Programmer" [27].

As we experience this revolution. each of us naturally is developing strong feelings one way or the other, as we agree or disagree with the revolutionary leaders. I must admit to being a non-humble programmer, egotisti-

This research was supported in part by the National Science Foundation under grant number GJ 36473X, and by IBM Corporation.

CONTENTS

cal enough to believe that my own opinions of the current trends are not a waste of the reader's time. Therefore I want to express in this article several of the things that struck me most forcefully as I have been thinking about structured programming during the last year; several of my blind spots were removed as I was learning these things, and I hope I can convey some of my excitement to the reader. Hardly any of the ideas I will discuss are my own; they are nearly all the work of others, but perhaps I may be presenting them in a new light. I write this article in the first person to emphasize the fact that what I'm saying is just one man's opinion; I don't expect to persuade everyone that my present views are correct.

Before beginning a more technical discussion. I should confess that the title of this article was chosen primarily to generate attention. There are doubtless some readers who are convinced that abolition of **go to** statements is merely a fad, and they may see this title and think, "Aha! Knuth is rehabilitating the **go to** statement, and we can go back to our old ways of programming again." Another class of readers will see the heretical title and think, "When are diehards like Knuth going to get with it?" I hope that both classes of people will read on and discover that what I am really doing is striving for a reasonably well balanced viewpoint about the proper role of **go to** statements. I argue for the elimination of **go to**'s in certain cases, and for their introduction in others.

I believe that by presenting such a view I am not in fact disagreeing sharply with Dijkstra's ideas, since he recently wrote the following: "Please don't fall into the trap of believing that I am terribly dogmatical about [the **go to** statement]. I have the uncomfortable feeling that others are making a religion out of it, as if the conceptual problems of programming could be solved by a single trick, by a simple form of coding discipline!" [29]. In other words, it seems that fanatical advocates of the New Programming are going overboard in their strict enforcement of morality and purity in programs. Sooner or later people are going to find that their beautifully-structured programs are running at only half the speed —or worse—of the dirty old programs they used to write, and they will mistakenly blame the structure instead of recognizing what is probably the real culprit—the system overhead caused by typical compiler implementation of Boolean variables and procedure calls. Then we'll have an unfortunate counter-revolution, something like the current rejection of the "New Mathematics" in reaction to its over-zealous reforms.

It may be helpful to consider a further analogy with mathematics. In 1904, Bertrand Russell published his famous paradox about the set of all sets which aren't members of themselves. This antinomy shook the foundations of classical mathematical reasoning, since it apparently brought very simple and ordinary deductive methods into question. The ensuing crisis led to the rise of "intuitionist logic", a school of thought championed especially by the Dutch mathematician, L. E. J. Brouwer; intuitionism abandoned all deductions that were based on questionable nonconstructive ideas. For a while it appeared that intuitionist logic would cause a revolution in mathematics. But the new approach angered David Hilbert, who was perhaps the leading mathematician of the time; Hilbert said that "Forbidding a mathematician to make use of the principle of the excluded middle is like forbidding an astronomer his telescope or a boxer the use of his fists." He characterized the intuitionist approach as seeking "to save mathematics by throwing overboard all that is troublesome. . . . They would chop up and mangle the science. If we would follow such a reform as they suggest, we could run the risk of losing a great part of our most valuable treasures" [80, pp. 98–99, 148–150, 154–157, 184–185, 268–270].

Something a little like this is happening in computer science. In the late 1960's we witnessed a "software crisis", which many people thought was paradoxical because programming was supposed to be so easy. As a result of the crisis, people are now beginning to renounce every feature of programming that can be considered guilty by virtue of its association with difficulties. Not only **go to** statements are being questioned; we also hear complaints about floating-point calculations, global variables, semaphores, pointer variables, and even assignment statements. Soon we might be restricted to only a dozen or so programs that are sufficiently simple to be allowable; then we will be almost certain that these programs cannot lead us into any trouble, but of course we won't be able to solve many problems.

In the mathematical case, we know what happened: The intuitionists taught the other mathematicians a great deal about deductive methods, while the other mathematicians cleaned up the classical methods and eventually "won" the battle. And a revolution did, in fact, take place. In the computer science case, I imagine that a similar thing will eventually happen: purists will point the way to clean constructions, and others will find ways to purify their use of floating-point arithmetic, pointer variables, assignments, etc., so that these classical tools can be used with comparative safety.

Of course all analogies break down, including this one, especially since I'm not yet conceited enough to compare myself to David Hilbert. But I think it's an amusing coincidence that the present programming revolution is being led by another Dutchman (although he doesn't have extremist views corresponding to Brouwer's); and I do consider assignment statements and pointer variables to be among computer science's "most valuable treasures".

At the present time I think we are on the verge of discovering at last what programming languages should really be like. I look forward to seeing many responsible experiments with language design during the next few years; and my dream is that by 1984 we will see a consensus developing for a really good programming language (or, more likely, a coherent family of languages). Furthermore, I'm guessing that people will become so disenchanted with the languages they are now using—even Cobol and Fortran— that this new language, Utopia 84, will have a chance to take over. At present we are far from that goal, yet there are indications that such a language is very slowly taking shape.

Will UTOPIA 84, or perhaps we should call it NEWSPEAK, contain **go to** statements? At the moment, unfortunately, there isn't even a consensus about this apparently trivial issue, and we had better not be hung up on the question too much longer since there are only ten years left.

I will try in what follows to give a reasonably comprehensive survey of the **go to** controversy, arguing both pro and con, without taking a strong stand one way or the other until the discussion is nearly complete. In order to illustrate different uses of **go to** statements, I will discuss many example programs, some of which tend to negate the conclusions we might draw from the others. There are two reasons why I have chosen to present the material in this apparently vacillating manner. First, since I have the opportunity to choose all the examples, I don't think it's fair to load the dice by selecting only program fragments which favor one side of the argument. Second, and perhaps most important, I tried this approach when I lectured on the subject at UCLA in February, 1974, and it worked beautifully: nearly everybody in the audience had the illusion that I was largely supporting his or her views, regardless of what those views were!

1.   ELIMINATION OF go to STATEMENTS

Historical Background

At the IFIP Congress in 1971 I had the pleasure of meeting Dr. Eiichi Goto of Japan, who cheerfully complained that he was always being eliminated. Here is the history of the subject, as far as I have been able to trace it.

The first programmer who systematically began to avoid all labels and **go to** statements was perhaps D. V. Schorre, then of UCLA. He has written the following account of his early experiences [85]:

> Since the summer of 1960, I have been writing programs in outline form, using conventions of indentation to indicate the flow of control. I have never found it necessary to take exception to these conventions by using *go statements*. I used to keep these outlines as original

> documentation of a program, instead of using flow charts . . . Then I would code the program in assembly language from the outline. Everyone liked these outlines better than the flow charts I had drawn before, which were not very neat—my flow charts had been nick-named "balloon-o-grams".

He reported that this method made programs easier to plan, to modify and to check out.

When I met Schorre in 1963, he told me of his radical ideas, and I didn't believe they would work. In fact, I suspected that it was really his rationalization for not finding an easy way to put labels and **go to** statements into his META-II subset of ALGOL [84], a language which I liked very much except for this omission. In 1964 I challenged him to write a program for the eight-queens problem without using **go to** statements, and he responded with a program using recursive procedures and Boolean variables, very much like the program later published independently by Wirth [96].

I was still not convinced that all **go to** statements could or should be done away with, although I fully subscribed to Peter Naur's observations which had appeared about the same time [73]. Since Naur's comments were the first published remarks about harmful **go to**'s, it is instructive to quote some of them here:

> If you look carefully you will find that surprisingly often a **go to** statement which looks back really is a concealed **for** statement. And you will be pleased to find how the clarity of the algorithm improves when you insert the **for** clause where it belongs. . . . If the purpose [of a programming course] is to teach ALGOL programming, the use of flow diagrams will do more harm than good, in my opinion.

The next year we find George Forsythe also purging **go to** statements from algorithms submitted to *Communications of the ACM* (cf. [53]). Incidentally. the second example program at the end of the original ALGOL 60 report [72] contains four **go to** statements, to labels named AA, BB, CC, and DD, so it is clear that the advantages of ALGOL's control structures weren't fully perceived in 1960.

In 1965, Edsger Dijkstra published the following instructive remarks [21]:

> Two programming department managers from

107

different countries and different backgrounds —the one mainly scientific, the other mainly commercial—have communicated to me, independently of each other and on their own initiative, their observation that the quality of their programmers was inversely proportional to the density of goto statements in their programs. . . . I have done various programming experiments . . . in modified versions of ALGOL 60 in which the goto statement was abolished. . . . The latter versions were more difficult to make: we are so familiar with the jump order that it requires some effort to forget it! In all cases tried, however, the program without the goto statement turned out to be shorter and more lucid.

A few months later, at the ACM Programming Languages and Pragmatics Conference, Peter Landin put it this way [59]:

> There is a game sometimes played with ALGOL 60 programs—rewriting them so as to avoid using **go to** statements. It is part of a more embracing game—reducing the extent to which the program conveys its information by explicit sequencing. . . . The game's significance lies in that it frequently produces a more "transparent" program—easier to understand, debug, modify, and incorporate into a larger program.

Peter Naur reinforced this opinion at the same meeting [74, p. 179].

The next chapter in the story is what many people regard as the first, because it made the most waves. Dijkstra submitted a short article to *Communications of the ACM*, devoted entirely to a discussion of **go to** statements. In order to speed publication, the editor decided to publish Dijkstra's article as a letter, and to supply a new title, "Go to statement considered harmful". This note [23] rapidly became well-known; it expressed Dijkstra's conviction that **go to**'s "should be abolished from all 'higher level' programming languages (i.e., everything except, perhaps, plain machine code). . . . The **go to** statement as it stands is just too primitive; it is too much an invitation to make a mess of one's program." He encouraged looking for alternative constructions which may be necessary to satisfy all needs. Dijkstra also recalled that Heinz Zemanek had expressed doubts about **go to** statements as early as 1959; and that Peter Landin, Christopher Strachey, C. A. R. Hoare and others had been of some influence on his thinking.

By 1967, the entire XPL compiler had been written by McKeeman, Horning, and Wortman, using **go to** only once ([65], pp. 365–458; the **go to** is on page 385). In 1971, Christopher Strachey [87] reported that "It is my aim to write programs with no labels. I am doing quite well. I have got the operating system down to 5 labels and I am planning to write a compiler with no labels at all." In 1972, an entire session of the ACM National Conference was devoted to the subject [44; 60; 100]. The December, 1973, issue of *Datamation* featured five articles about structured programming and elimination of **go to**'s [3; 13; 32; 64; 67]. Thus, it is clear that sentiments against **go to** statements have been building up. In fact, the discussion has apparently caused some people to feel threatened; Dijkstra once told me that he actually received "a torrent of abusive letters" after publication of his article.

The tide of opinion first hit me personally in 1969, when I was teaching an introductory programming course for the first time. I remember feeling frustrated on several occasions, at not seeing how to write programs in the new style; I would run to Bob Floyd's office asking for help, and he usually showed me what to do. This was the genesis of our article [52] in which we presented two types of programs which did not submit gracefully to the new prohibition. We found that there was no way to implement certain simple constructions with **while** and conditional statements substituted for **go to**'s, unless extra computation was specified.

During the last few years several languages have appeared in which the designers proudly announced that they have abolished the **go to** statement. Perhaps the most prominent of these is BLISS [98], which originally replaced **go to**'s by eight so-called "escape" statements. And the eight weren't even enough; the authors wrote, "Our mistake was in assuming that there is no need for a label once the **go to** is removed," and they later [99, 100] added a new statement "**leave** ⟨label⟩ **with** ⟨expression⟩" which goes to the place *after* the statement identified by the ⟨label⟩. Other **go to**-less languages for systems programming have

Computing Surveys, Vol. 6, No. 4, December 1974

similarly introduced other statements which provide "equally powerful" alternative ways to jump.

In other words, it seems that there is widespread agreement that **go to** statements are harmful, yet programmers and language designers still feel the need for some euphemism that "goes to" without saying **go to.**

A Searching Example

What are the reasons for this? In [52], Floyd and I gave the following example of a typical program for which the ordinary capabilities of **while** and **if** statements are inadequate. Let's suppose that we want to search a table $A[1] \cdots A[m]$ of distinct values, in order to find where a given value x appears; if x is not present in the table, we want to insert it as an additional entry. Let's suppose further that there is another array B, where $B[i]$ equals the number of times we have searched for the value $A[i]$. We might solve such a problem as follows:

Example 1:

```
for i := 1 step 1 until m do
  if A[i] = x then go to found fi;
not found: i := m+1; m := i;
  A[i] := x; B[i] := 0;
found: B[i] := B[i]+1;
```

(In the present article I shall use an ad hoc programming language that is very similar to ALGOL 60, with one exception: the symbol **fi** is required as a closing bracket for all **if** statements, so that **begin** and **end** aren't needed between **then** and **else.** I don't really like the looks of **fi** at the moment; but it is short, performs a useful function, and connotes finality, so I'm confidently hoping that I'll get used to it. Alan Perlis has remarked that **fi** is a perfect example of a cryptic notation that can make programming unnecessarily complicated for beginners; yet I'm more comfortable with **fi** every time I write it. I still balk at spelling *other* basic symbols backwards, and so do most of the people I know; a student's paper containing the code fragment "esac; **comment bletch tnemmoc;**" is a typical reaction to this trend!)

There are ways to express Example 1 without **go to** statements, but they require

more computation and aren't really more perspicuous. Therefore, this example has been widely quoted in defense of the **go to** statement, and it is appropriate to scrutinize the problem carefully.

Let's suppose that we've been forbidden to use **go to** statements, and that we want to do *precisely* the computation specified in Example 1 (using the obvious expansion of such a **for** statement into assignments and a **while** iteration). If this means not only that we want the same results, but also that we want to do the same operations in the same order, the mission is impossible. But if we are allowed to weaken the conditions just slightly, so that a relation can be tested twice in succession (assuming that it will yield the same result each time, i.e., that it has no side-effects), we can solve the problem as follows:

Example 1a:

```
i := 1;
while i ≤ m and A[i] ≠ x do i := i+1;
if i > m then m := i; A[i] := x; B[i] := 0 fi;
B[i] := B[i]+1;
```

The **and** operation used here stands for McCarthy's sequential conjunction operator [62, p. 185]; i.e., "p **and** q" means "**if** p **then** q **else false fi**", so that q is not evaluated when p is false. Example 1a will do exactly the same sequence of computations as Example 1, except for one extra comparison of i with m (and occasionally one less computation of $m+1$). If the iteration in this **while** loop is performed a large number of times, the extra comparison has a negligible effect on the running time.

Thus, we can live without the **go to** in Example 1. But Example 1a is slightly less readable, in my opinion, as well as slightly slower; so it isn't clear what we have gained. Furthermore, if we had made Example 1 more complicated, the trick of going to Example 1a would no longer work. For example, suppose we had inserted another statement into the **for** loop, just before the **if** clause; then the relations $i \leq m$ and $A[i] = x$ wouldn't have been tested consecutively, and we couldn't in general have combined them with **and.**

John Cocke told me an instructive story

relating to Example 1 and to the design of languages. Some PL/I programmers were asked to do the stated search problem without using jumps, and they came up with essentially the following two solutions:

```
a)      DO I = 1 to M WHILE A(I) ¬ = X;
        END;
        IF I > M THEN
            DO; M = I; A(I) = X; B(I) = 0; END;
        B(I) = B(I) + 1;
b)      FOUND = 0;
        DO I = 1 TO M WHILE FOUND = 0;
            IF A(I) = X THEN FOUND = 1;
        END;
        IF FOUND = 0 THEN
            DO; M = I; A(I) = X; B(I) = 0; END;
        B(I) = B(I) = 1;
```

Solution (a) is best, but since it involves a null iteration (with no explicit statements being iterated) most people came up with Solution (b). The instructive point is that Solution (b) doesn't work; there is a serious bug which caused great puzzlement before the reason was found. Can the reader spot the difficulty? (The answer appears on page 141.)

As I've said, Example 1 has often been used to defend the **go to** statement. Unfortunately, however, the example is totally unconvincing in spite of the arguments I've stated so far, because the method in Example 1 is almost *never* a good way to search an array for x! The following modification to the data structure makes the algorithm much better:

Example 2:

```
A[m+1] := x; i := 1;
while A[i] ≠ x do i := i+1;
if i > m then m := i; B[i] := 1;
else B[i] := B[i]+1 fi;
```

Example 2 beats Example 1 because it makes the inner loop considerably faster. If we assume that the programs have been handcoded in assembly language, so that the values of i, m, and x are kept in registers, and if we let n be the final value of i at the end of the program, Example 1 will make $6n + 10$ (+3 if not found) references to memory for data and instructions on a typical computer, while the second program will make only $4n + 14$ (+6 if not found). If, on the other hand, we assume that these programs are translated by a typical "90% efficient compiler" with bounds-checking suppressed, the corresponding run-time figures are respectively about $14n + 5$ and $11n + 21$. (The appendix to this paper explains the ground rules for these calculations.) Under the first assumption we save about 33% of the run-time, and under the second assumption we save about 21%, so in both cases the elimination of the **go to** has also eliminated some of the running time.

Efficiency

The ratio of running times (about 6 to 4 in the first case when n is large) is rather surprising to people who haven't studied program behavior carefully. Example 2 doesn't look *that* much more efficient, but it is. Experience has shown (see [46], [51]) that most of the running time in non-IO-bound programs is concentrated in about 3% of the source text. We often see a short inner loop whose speed governs the overall program speed to a remarkable degree; speeding up the inner loop by 10% speeds up everything by almost 10%. And if the inner loop has 10 instructions, a moment's thought will usually cut it to 9 or fewer.

My own programming style has of course changed during the last decade, according to the trends of the times (e.g., I'm not quite so tricky anymore, and I use fewer **go to**'s), but the major change in my style has been due to this inner loop phenomenon. I now look with an extremely jaundiced eye at every operation in a critical inner loop, seeking to modify my program and data structure (as in the change from Example 1 to Example 2) so that some of the operations can be eliminated. The reasons for this approach are that: a) it doesn't take long, since the inner loop is short; b) the payoff is real; and c) I can then afford to be less efficient in the other parts of my programs, which therefore are more readable and more easily written and debugged. Tools are being developed to make this critical-loop identification job easy (see for example [46] and [82]).

Thus, if I hadn't seen how to remove one of the operations from the loop in Example 1 by changing to Example 2, I would probably (at least) have made the **for** loop run from m to 1 instead of from 1 to m, since it's usually easier to test for zero than to compare with m. And if Example 2 were really critical, I would improve on it still more by "doubling it up" so that the machine code would be essentially as follows.

Example 2a:

```
A[m+1] := x; i := 1; go to test;
loop:  i := i+2;
test:    if A[i] = x then go to found fi;
         if A[i+1] ≠ x then go to loop fi;
         i := i+1;
found: if i > m then m := i; B[i] := 1;
       else B[i] := B[i]+1 fi;
```

Here the loop variable i increases by 2 on each iteration, so we need to do that operation only half as often as before; the rest of the code in the loop has essentially been duplicated to make this work. The running time has now been reduced to about $3.5n + 14.5$ or $8.5n + 23.5$ under our respective assumptions—again this is a noticeable saving in the overall running speed, if, say, the average value of n is about 20, and if this search routine is performed a million or so times in the overall program. Such loop-optimizations are not difficult to learn and, as I have said, they are appropriate in just a small part of a program, yet they very often yield substantial savings. (Of course if we want to improve on Example 2a still more, especially for large m, we'll use a more sophisticated search technique; but let's ignore that issue, at the moment, since I want to illustrate loop optimization in general, not searching in particular.)

The improvement in speed from Example 2 to Example 2a is only about 12%, and many people would pronounce that insignificant. The conventional wisdom shared by many of today's software engineers calls for ignoring efficiency in the small; but I believe this is simply an overreaction to the abuses they see being practiced by penny-wise-and-pound-foolish programmers, who can't debug or maintain their "optimized" programs. In established engineering disciplines a 12% improvement, easily obtained, is never considered marginal; and I believe the same viewpoint should prevail in software engineering. Of course I wouldn't bother making such optimizations on a one-shot job, but when it's a question of preparing quality programs, I don't want to restrict myself to tools that deny me such efficiencies.

There is no doubt that the grail of efficiency leads to abuse. Programmers waste enormous amounts of time thinking about, or worrying about, the speed of noncritical parts of their programs, and these attempts at efficiency actually have a strong negative impact when debugging and maintenance are considered. We *should* forget about small efficiencies, say about 97% of the time: premature optimization is the root of all evil.

Yet we should not pass up our opportunities in that critical 3%. A good programmer will not be lulled into complacency by such reasoning, he will be wise to look carefully at the critical code; but only *after* that code has been identified. It is often a mistake to make a priori judgments about what parts of a program are really critical, since the universal experience of programmers who have been using measurement tools has been that their intuitive guesses fail. After working with such tools for seven years, I've become convinced that all compilers written from now on should be designed to provide all programmers with feedback indicating what parts of their programs are costing the most; indeed, this feedback should be supplied automatically unless it has been specifically turned off.

After a programmer knows which parts of his routines are really important, a transformation like doubling up of loops will be worthwhile. Note that this transformation introduces **go to** statements—and so do several other loop optimizations; I will return to this point later. Meanwhile I have to admit that the presence of **go to** statements in Example 2a has a negative as well as a positive effect on efficiency; a non-optimizing compiler will tend to produce awkward code, since the contents of registers can't be assumed known when a label is passed. When I computed the running times cited above by looking at a typical compiler's output for this example, I found that the improvement in performance was not quite as much as I had expected.

Error Exits

For simplicity I have avoided a very important issue in the previous examples, but it must now be faced. All of the programs we have considered exhibit bad programming practice, since they fail to make the necessary check that m has not gone out of range. In each case before we perform "$m := i$" we should precede that operation by a test such as

if $m = max$ **then go to** memory overflow;

where max is an appropriate threshold value. I left this statement out of the examples since it would have been distracting, but we need to look at it now since it is another important class of **go to** statements: an *error exit*. Such checks on the validity of data are very important, especially in software, and it seems to be the one class of **go to**'s that still is considered ugly but necessary by today's leading reformers. (I wonder how Val Schorre has managed to avoid such **go to**'s during all these years.)

Sometimes it is necessary to exit from several levels of control, cutting across code that may even have been written by other programmers; and the most graceful way to do this is a direct approach with a **go to** or its equivalent. Then the intermediate levels of the program can be written under the assumption that nothing will go wrong.

I will return to the subject of error exits later.

Subscript Checking

In the particular examples given above we can, of course, avoid testing m vs. max if we have dynamic range-checking on all subscripts of A. But this usually aborts the program, giving us little or no control over the error recovery; so we probably want to test m anyway. And ouch, what subscript checking does to the inner loop execution times! In Example 2, I will certainly want to suppress range-checking in the **while** clause since its subscript can't be out of range unless

$A[m+1]$ was already invalid in the previous line. Similarly, in Example 1 there can be no range error in the **for** loop unless a range error occurred earlier. It seems senseless to have expensive range checks in those parts of my programs that I *know* are clean.

In this respect I should mention Hoare's almost persuasive arguments to the contrary [40, p. 18]. He points out quite correctly that the current practice of compiling subscript range checks into the machine code while a program is being tested, then suppressing the checks during production runs, is like a sailor who wears his life preserver while training on land but leaves it behind when he sails! On the other hand, that sailor isn't so foolish if life vests are extremely expensive, and if he is such an excellent swimmer that the chance of needing one is quite small compared with the other risks he is taking. In the foregoing examples we typically are much more certain that the subscripts will be in range than that other aspects of our overall program will work correctly. John Cocke observes that time-consuming range checks can be avoided by a smart compiler which first compiles the checks into the program then moves them out of the loop. Wirth [94] and Hoare [39] have pointed out that a well-designed **for** statement can permit even a rather simple-minded compiler to avoid most range checks within loops.

I believe that range checking should be used far more often than it currently is, but not everywhere. On the other hand I am really assuming infallible hardware when I say this; surely I wouldn't want to remove the parity check mechanism from the hardware, even under a hypothetical assumption that it was slowing down the computation. Additional memory protection is necessary to prevent my program from harming someone else's, and theirs from clobbering mine. My arguments are directed towards compiled-in tests, not towards the hardware mechanisms which are really needed to ensure reliability.

Hash Coding

Now let's move on to another example, based on a standard hashing technique but otherwise designed for the same application as the above. Here $h(x)$ is a hash function which takes on values between 1 and m; and $x \neq 0$. In this case m is somewhat larger than the number of items in the table, and "empty" positions are represented by 0.

Example 3:

```
i := h(x);
while A[i] ≠ 0 do
  begin if A[i] = x then go to found fi;
    i := i−1; if i = 0 then i := m fi;
  end;
  not found: A[i] := x; B[i] := 0;
  found: B[i] := B[i]+1;
```

If we analyze this as we did Example 1, we see that the trick which led to Example 2 doesn't work any more. Yet if we want to eliminate the **go to** we can apply the idea of Example 1a by writing

$$\text{while } A[i] \neq 0 \text{ and } A[i] \neq x \text{ do } \ldots$$

and by testing afterwards which condition caused termination. This version is perhaps a little bit easier to read; unfortunately it makes a redundant test, which we would like to avoid if we were in a critical part of the program.

Why should I worry about the redundant test in this case? After all, the extra test whether $A[i]$ was $\neq 0$ or $\neq x$ is being made outside of the **while** loop, and I said before that we should generally confine our optimizations to inner loops. Here, the reason is that this **while** loop *won't* usually be a loop at all; with a proper choice of h and m, the operation $i := i-1$ will tend to be executed very infrequently, often less than once per search on the average [54, Section 6.4]. Thus, the entire program of Example 3, except perhaps for the line labeled "not found", must be considered as part of the inner loop, if this search process is a dominant part of the overall program (as it often is). The redundant test will therefore be significant in this case.

Despite this concern with efficiency, I should actually have written the first draft of Example 3 without that **go to** statement, probably even using a **while** clause written in an extended language, such as

$$\text{while } A[i] \notin \{0, x\} \text{ do } \ldots$$

since this formulation abstracts the *real* meaning of what is happening. Someday there may be hardware capable of testing membership in small sets more efficiently than if we program the tests sequentially, so that such a program would lead to better code than Example 3. And there is a much more important reason for preferring this form of the **while** clause: it reflects a symmetry between 0 and x that is not present in Example 3. For example, in most software applications it turns out that the condition $A[i] = x$ terminates the loop far more frequently than $A[i] = 0$; with this knowledge, my second draft of the program would be the following.

Example 3a:

```
i := h(x);
while A[i] ≠ x do
  begin if A[i] = 0
    then A[i] := x; B[i] := 0;
      go to found;
    fi;
    i := i−1; if i = 0 then i := m fi;
  end;
  found: B[i] := B[i]+1;
```

This program is easy to derive from the **go to**-less form, but not from Example 3; and it is better than Example 3. So, again we see the advantage of delaying optimizations until we have obtained more knowledge of a program's behavior.

It is instructive to consider Example 3a further, assuming now that the **while** loop is performed many times per search. Although this should not happen in most applications of hashing, there are other programs in which a loop of the above form is present, so it is worth examining what we should do in such circumstances. If the **while** loop becomes an inner loop affecting the overall program speed, the whole picture changes; that redundant test outside the loop becomes utterly negligible, but the test "**if** $i = 0$" suddenly looms large. We generally want to avoid testing conditions that are almost always false, inside a critical loop. Therefore, under these new assumptions I would change the data structure by adding a new element $A[0] = 0$ to the array and eliminating the test for $i = 0$ as follows.

Example 3b:

```
    i := h(x);
    while A[i] ≠ x do
      if A[i] ≠ 0
      then i := i−1
      else if i = 0
        then i := m;
        else A[i] := x; B[i] := 0;
          go to found;
        fi;
      fi;
    found: B[i] := B[i]+1;
```

The loop now is noticeably faster. Again, I would be unhappy with slow subscript range checks if this loop were critical. Incidentally, Example 3b was derived from Example 3a, and a rather different program would have emerged if the same idea had been applied to Example 3; then a test "**if** $i = 0$" would have been inserted *outside* the loop, at label "not found", and another **go to** would have been introduced by the optimization process.

As in the first examples, the program in Example 3 is flawed in failing to test for memory overflow. I should have done this, for example by keeping a count, n, of how many items are nonzero. The "not found" routine should then begin with something like "$n := n+1$; **if** $n = m$ **then go to** memory overflow".

Text Scanning

The first time I consciously applied the top-down structured programming methodology to a reasonably complex job was in the late summer of 1972, when I wrote a program to prepare the index to my book *Sorting and Searching* [54]. I was quite pleased with the way that program turned out (there was only one serious bug), but I did use one **go to** statement. In this case the reason was somewhat different, having nothing to do with exiting from loops; I was exiting, in fact, from an **if-then-else** construction.

The following example is a simplified version of the situation I encountered. Suppose we are processing a stream of text, and that we want to read and print the next character from the input; however, if that character is a slash ("/") we want to "tabulate" instead (i.e., to advance in the output to the next tab-stop position on the current line); however, two consecutive slashes means a

"carriage return" (i.e., to advance in the output to the beginning of the next line). After printing a period (".") we also want to insert an additional space in the output. The following code clearly does the trick.

Example 4:

```
    x := read char;
    if x = slash
    then x := read char;
      if x = slash
      then return the carriage;
        go to char processed;
      else tabulate;
      fi;
    fi;
    write char (x);
    if x = period then write char (space) fi;
  char processed:
```

An abstract program with similar characteristics has been studied by Peterson et al. [77; Fig. 1(a)]. In practice we occasionally run into situations where a sequence of decisions is made via nested **if-then-else's**, and then two or more of the branches merge into one. We can manage such decision-table tasks without **go to**'s by copying the common code into each place, or by defining it as a **procedure**, but this does not seem conceptually simpler than to make **go to** a common part of the program in such cases. Thus in Example 4 I could avoid the **go to** by copying "*write char (x)*; **if** $x = period$ **then** *write char (space)* **fi**" into the program after "*tabulate;*" and by making corresponding changes. But this would be a pointless waste of energy just to eliminate a perfectly understandable **go to** statement: the resulting program would actually be harder to maintain than the former, since the action of printing a character now appears in two different places. The alternative of declaring procedures avoids the latter problem, but it is not especially attractive either. Still another alternative is:

Example 4a:

```
    x := read char;
    double slash := false;
    if x = slash
    then x := read char;
      if x = slash
      then double slash := true;
      else tabulate;
      fi;
```


114

fi;
if *double slash*
then *return the carriage*;
else *write char* (x);
  if $x = period$ **then** *write char* (space) **fi**;
fi;

I claim that this is conceptually no simpler than Example 4; indeed, one can argue that it is actually more difficult, because it makes the *entire* routine aware of the "double slash" exception to the rules. instead of dealing with it in one exceptional place.

A Confession

Before we go on to another example, I must admit what many readers already suspect, namely, that I'm subject to substantial bias because I actually have a vested interest in **go to** statements! The style for the series of books I'm writing was set in the early 1960s, and it would be too difficult for me to change it now; I present algorithms in my books using informal English language descriptions, and **go to** or its equivalent is almost the only control structure I have. Well, I rationalize this apparent anachronism by arguing that: a) an informal English description seems advantageous because many readers tell me they automatically read English, but skip over formal code; b) when **go to** statements are used judiciously together with comments stating nonobvious loop invariants, they are semantically equivalent to **while** statements, except that indentation is missing to indicate the structure; c) the algorithms are nearly always short, so that accompanying flowcharts are able to illustrate the structure; d) I try to present algorithms in a form that is most efficient for implementation, and high-level structures often don't do this; e) many readers will get pleasure from converting my semiformal algorithms into beautifully structured programs in a formal programming language; and f) we are still learning much about control structures, and I can't afford to wait for the final consensus.

In spite of these rationalizations, I'm uncomfortable about the situation, because I find others occasionally publishing examples of algorithms in "my" style but without the important parenthesized comments and/or with unrestrained use of **go to** statements. In addition, I also know of places where I have myself used a complicated structure with excessively unrestrained **go to** statements, especially the notorious Algorithm 2.3.3A for multivariate polynomial addition [50]. The original program had at least three bugs; exercise 2.3.3-14, "Give a formal proof (or disproof) of the validity of Algorithm A", was therefore unexpectedly easy. Now in the second edition, I believe that the revised algorithm is correct, but I still don't know any good way to prove it; I've had to raise the difficulty rating of exercise 2.3.3-14, and I hope someday to see the algorithm cleaned up without loss of its efficiency.

My books emphasize efficiency because they deal with algorithms that are used repeatedly as building blocks in a large variety of applications. It is important to keep efficiency in its place, as mentioned above, but when efficiency counts we should also know how to achieve it.

In order to make it possible to derive quantitative assessments of efficiency, my books show how to analyze machine language programs; and these programs are expressed in MIXAL, a symbolic assembly language that explicitly corresponds one-for-one to machine language. This has its uses, but there is a danger of placing too much stress on assembly code. Programs in MIXAL are like programs in machine language, devoid of structure; or, more precisely, it is difficult for our eyes to perceive the program structure. Accompanying comments explain the program and relate it to the global structure illustrated in flowcharts, but it is not so easy to understand what is going on; and it is easy to make mistakes, partly because we rely so much on comments which might possibly be inaccurate descriptions of what the program really does. It is clearly better to write programs in a language that reveals the control structure, even if we are intimately conscious of the hardware at each step; and therefore I will be discussing a structured assembly language called PL/MIX in the fifth volume of *The art of computer programming*. Such a language (analogous to Wirth's PL360 [95]) should really be supported by each manufacturer for each machine in place of the old-fashioned structureless assemblers that still proliferate.

On the other hand I'm not really unhappy that MIXAL programs appear in my books, because I believe that MIXAL is a good example of a "quick and dirty assembler", a genre of software which will always be useful in its proper role. Such an assembler is characterized by language restrictions that make simple one-pass assembly possible, and it has several noteworthy advantages when we are first preparing programs for a new machine: a) it is a great improvement over numeric machine code; b) its rules are easy to state; and c) it can be implemented in an afternoon or so, thus getting an efficient assembler working quickly on what may be very primitive equipment. So far I have implemented six such assemblers, at different times in my life, for machines or interpretive systems or microprocessors that had no existing software of comparable utility; and in each case other constraints made it impractical for me to take the extra time necessary to develop a good, structured assembler. Thus I am sure that the concept of quick-and-dirty-assembler is useful, and I'm glad to let MIXAL illustrate what one is like. However, I also believe strongly that such languages should never be improved to the point where they are too easy or too pleasant to use; one must restrict their use to primitive facilities that are easy to implement efficiently. I would never switch to a two-pass process, or add complex pseudo-operations, macro-facilities, or even fancy error diagnostics to such a language, nor would I maintain or distribute such a language as a standard programming tool for a real machine. All such ameliorations and refinements should appear in a structured assembler. Now that the technology is available, we can condone unstructured languages only as a bootstrap-like means to a limited end, when there are strong economic reasons for not implementing a better system.

Tree Searching

But, I'm digressing from my subject of **go to** elimination in higher level languages. A few weeks ago I decided to choose an algorithm at random from my books, to study its use of **go to** statements. The very first example I encountered [54, Algorithm 6.2.3C] turned out to be another case where existing programming languages have no good substitute for **go to**'s. In simplified form, the loop where the trouble arises can be written as follows.

Example 5:

```
compare:
 if A[i] < x
 then if L[i] ≠ 0
   then i := L[i]; go to compare;
   else L[i] := j; go to insert fi;
 else if R[i] ≠ 0
   then i := R[i]; go to compare;
   else R[i] := j; go to insert fi;
 fi;
 insert: A[j] := x;
 L[j] := 0; R[j] := 0; j := j+1;
```

This is part of the well-known "tree search and insertion" scheme, where a binary search tree is being represented by three arrays: $A[i]$ denotes the information stored at node number i, and $L[i]$, $R[i]$ are the respective node numbers for the roots of that node's left and right subtrees; empty subtrees are represented by zero. The program searches down the tree until finding an empty subtree where x can be inserted; and variable j points to an appropriate place to do the insertion. For convenience, I have assumed in this example that x is not already present in the search tree.

Example 5 has four **go to** statements, but the control structure is saved from obscurity because the program is so beautifully symmetric between L and R. I know that these **go to** statements can be eliminated by introducing a Boolean variable which becomes true when $L[i]$ or $R[i]$ is found to be zero. But I don't want to test this variable in the inner loop of my program.

Systematic Elimination

A good deal of theoretical work has been addressed to the question of **go to** elimination, and I shall now try to summarize the findings and to discuss their relevance.

S. C. Kleene proved a famous theorem in 1956 [48] which says, in essence, that the set of all paths through any flowchart can be represented as a "regular expression" R built up from the following operations:

s	the single arc s of the flowchart
$R_1; R_2$	concatenation (all paths consisting of a path of R_1 followed by a path of R_2)
$R_1 \cup R_2$	union (all paths of either R_1 or R_2)
R^+	iteration (all paths of the form p_1; p_2; $\cdots$; p_n for some $n \geq 1$, where each p_i is a path of R)

These regular expressions correspond loosely to programs consisting of statements in a programming language related by the three operations of sequential composition, conditionals (**if-then-else**), and iterations (**while** loops). Thus, we might expect that these three program control structures would be sufficient for all programs. However, closer analysis shows that Kleene's theorem does not relate directly to control structures; the problem is only superficially similar. His result is suggestive but not really applicable in this case.

The analogous result for control structures was first proved by G. Jacopini in 1966, in a paper written jointly with C. Böhm [8]. Jacopini showed, in effect, that any program given, say, in flowchart form can be transformed systematically into another program, which computes the same results and which is built up from statements in the original program using only the three basic operations of composition, conditional, and iteration, plus possible assignment statements and tests on auxiliary variables. Thus, in principle, **go to** statements can always be removed. A detailed exposition of Jacopini's construction has been given by H. D. Mills [69].

Recent interest in structured programming has caused many authors to cite Jacopini's result as a significant breakthrough and as a cornerstone of modern programming technique. Unfortunately, these authors are unaware of the comments made by Cooper in 1967 [16] and later by Bruno and Steiglitz [10], namely, that from a practical standpoint the theorem is meaningless. Indeed, any program can obviously be put into the "beautifully structured" form

```
p := 1;
while p > 0 do
  begin if p = 1 then perform step 1;
    p := successor of step 1 fi;
  if p = 2 then perform step 2;
    p := successor step 2 fi;
  ...
  if p = n then perform step n;
    p := successor of step n fi;
  end.
```

Here the auxiliary variable p serves as a program counter representing which box of the flowchart we're in, and the program stops when p is set to zero. We have eliminated all **go to**'s, but we've actually lost all the structure.

Jacopini conjectured in his paper that auxiliary variables are necessary in general, and that the **go to**'s in a program of the form

```
L₁: if B₁ then go to L₂ fi;
      S₁;
    if B₂ then go to L₂ fi;
      S₂;
      go to L₁;
L₂: S₃;
```

cannot always be removed unless additional computation is done. Floyd and I proved this conjecture with John Hopcroft's help [52]. Sharper results were later obtained by Ashcroft and Manna [1], Bruno and Steiglitz [10], Kosaraju [57], and Peterson, Kasami, and Tokura [77].

Jacopini's original construction was not merely the trivial flowchart emulation scheme indicated above; he was able to salvage much of the given flowchart structure if it was reasonably well-behaved. A more general technique of **go to** elimination, devised by Ashcroft and Manna [1], made it possible to capture still more of a given program's natural flow; for example, their technique applied to Example 5 yields

Example 5a:

```
t := true;
while t do
  begin if A[i] < x
    then if L[i] ≠ 0 then i := L[i];
      else L[i] := j; t := false fi;
    else if R[i] ≠ 0 then i := R[i];
      else R[i] := j; t := false fi;
  end;
A[j] := x;
```

But, in general, their technique may cause a program to grow exponentially in size; and when error exits or other recalcitrant **go to**'s are present, the resulting programs will indeed look rather like the flowchart emulator sketched above.

If such automatic **go to** elimination procedures are applied to badly structured programs, we can expect the resulting programs to be at least as badly structured. Dijkstra pointed this out already in [23], saying:

> The exercise to translate an arbitrary flow diagram more or less mechanically into a jumpless one, however, is not to be recommended. Then the resulting flow diagram cannot be expected to be more transparent than the original one.

In other words, we shouldn't merely remove **go to** statements because it's the fashionable thing to do; the presence or absence of **go to** statements is not really the issue. The underlying structure of the program is what counts, and we want only to avoid usages which somehow clutter up the program. Good structure can be expressed in FORTRAN or COBOL, or even in assembly language, although less clearly and with much more trouble. The real goal is to formulate our programs in such a way that they are easily understood.

Program structure refers to the way in which a complex algorithm is built up from successively simpler processes. In most situations this structure can be described very nicely in terms of sequential composition, conditionals, simple iterations, and with **case** statements for multiway branches; undisciplined **go to** statements make program structure harder to perceive, and they are often symptoms of a poor conceptual formulation. But there has been far too much emphasis on **go to** elimination instead of on the really important issues; people have a natural tendency to set up an easily understood quantitative goal like the abolition of jumps, instead of working directly for a qualitative goal like good program structure. In a similar way, many people have set up "zero population growth" as a goal to be achieved, when they really desire living conditions that are much harder to quantify.

Probably the worst mistake any one can make with respect to the subject of **go to** statements is to assume that "structured programming" is achieved by writing programs as we always have and then eliminating the **go to**'s. Most **go to**'s shouldn't be there in the first place! What we really want is to conceive of our program in such a way that we rarely even *think* about **go to** statements, because the real need for them hardly ever arises. The language in which we express our ideas has a strong influence on our thought processes. Therefore, Dijkstra [23] asks for more new language features—structures which encourage clear thinking—in order to avoid the **go to**'s temptations toward complications.

Event Indicators

The best such language feature I know has recently been proposed by C. T. Zahn [102]. Since this is still in the experimental stage, I will take the liberty of modifying his "syntactic sugar" slightly, without changing his basic idea. The essential novelty in his approach is to introduce a new quantity into programming languages, called an *event indicator* (not to be confused with concepts from PL/I or SIMSCRIPT). My current preference is to write his event-driven construct in the following two general forms.

A) **loop until** $\langle event \rangle_1$ **or** $\cdots$ **or** $\langle event \rangle_n$:
$\langle$statement list$\rangle_0$;
repeat;
then $\langle event \rangle_1 => \langle$statement list$\rangle_1$;
$\vdots$
$\langle event \rangle_n => \langle$statement list$\rangle_n$;
fi;

B) **begin until** $\langle event \rangle_1$ **or** $\cdots$ **or** $\langle event \rangle_n$;
$\langle$statement list$\rangle_0$;
end;
then $\langle event \rangle_1 => \langle$statement list$\rangle_1$;
$\vdots$
$\langle event \rangle_n => \langle$statement list$\rangle_n$;
fi;

There is also a new statement, "$\langle event \rangle$", which means that the designated event has occurred: such a statement is allowed only within ⟨statement list⟩$_0$ of an **until** construct which declares that event.

In form (A), ⟨statement list⟩$_0$ is executed repeatedly until control leaves the construct entirely or until one of the named events occurs; in the latter case, the statement list corresponding to that event is executed. The behavior in form (B) is similar, except that no iteration is implied; one of the named events must have occurred before the **end** is reached. The **then** $\cdots$ **fi** part may be omitted when there is only one event name.

The above rules should become clear after looking at what happens when Example 5 above is recoded in terms of this new feature:

Example 5b:

```
loop until left leaf hit or
            right leaf hit:
   if A[i] < x
   then if L[i] ≠ 0 then i := L[i];
      else left leaf hit fi;
   else if R[i] ≠ 0 then i := R[i];
      else right leaf hit fi;
   fi;
   repeat;
   then left leaf hit => L[i] := j;
        right leaf hit => R[i] := j;
   fi;
   A[j] := x; L[j] := 0; R[j] := 0; j := j+1;
```

Alternatively, using a single event,

Example 5c:

```
loop until leaf replaced:
   if A[i] < x
   then if L[i] ≠ 0 then i := L[i]
      else L[i] := j; leaf replaced fi;
   else if R[i] ≠ 0 then i := R[i]
      else R[i] := j; leaf replaced fi;
   fi;
   repeat;
   A[j] := x; L[j] := 0; R[j] := 0; j := j+1;
```

For reasons to be discussed later, Example 5b is preferable to 5c.

It is important to emphasize that the first line of the construct merely declares the event indicator names, and that event indicators are *not* conditions which are being tested continually; ⟨event⟩ statements are simply transfers of control which the compiler can treat very efficiently. Thus, in Example 5c the statement "leaf replaced" is essentially a **go to** which jumps out of the loop.

This use of events is, in fact, semantically equivalent to a restricted form of **go to** statement, which Peter Landin discussed in 1965 [58] before most of us were ready to listen. Landin's device has been reformulated by Clint and Hoare [14] in the following way: Labels are declared at the beginning of each block, just as procedures normally are, and each label also has a ⟨label body⟩ just as a procedure has a ⟨procedure body⟩. Within the block whose heading contains such a declaration of label L, the statement **go to** L according to this scheme means "execute the body of L, then leave the block". It is easy to see that this is exactly the form of control provided by Zahn's event mechanism, with the ⟨label body⟩s replaced by ⟨statement list⟩s in the **then** $\cdots$ **fi** postlude and with ⟨event⟩ statements corresponding to Landin's **go to**. Thus, Clint and Hoare would have written Example 5b as follows.

```
while true do
   begin label left leaf hit; L[i] := j;
      label right leaf hit; R[i] := j;
      if A[i] < x
      then if L[i] ≠ 0 then i := L[i];
         else go to left leaf hit fi;
      else if R[i] ≠ 0 then i := R[i];
         else go to right leaf hit fi;
   end;
   A[j] := x; L[j] := 0; R[j] := 0; j := j+1;
```

I believe the program reads much better in Zahn's form, with the ⟨label body⟩s set in the code between that which logically precedes and follows.

Landin also allowed his "labels" to have parameters like any other procedures; this is a valuable extension to Zahn's proposal, so I shall use events with value parameters in several of the examples below.

As Zahn [102] has shown, event-driven statements blend well with the ideas of structured programming by stepwise refinement. Thus, Examples 1 to 3 can all be cast into the following more abstract form, using an event "found" with an integer parameter:

```
begin until found:
   search table for x and
   insert it if not present;
end;
then found (integer j) => B[j] := B[j]+1;
fi;
```

This much of the program can be written before we have decided how to maintain the table. At the next level of abstraction, we might decide to represent the table as a sequential list, as in Example 1, so that "search table $\cdots$" would expand into

```
for i := 1 step 1 until m do
    if A[i] = x then found(i) fi;
m := m+1; A[m] := x; found(m);
```

Note that this **for** loop is more disciplined than the one in our original Example 1, because the iteration variable is not used outside the loop; it now conforms to the rules of ALGOL W and ALGOL 68. Such **for** loops provide convenient documentation and avoid common errors associated with global variables; their advantages have been discussed by Hoare [39].

Similarly, if we want to use the idea of Example 2 we might write the following code as the refinement of "search table $\cdots$":

```
begin integer i;
    A[m+1] := x; i := 1;
    while A[i] ≠ x do i := i+1;
    if i > m then m := i; B[m] := 0 fi;
    found(i);
end;
```

And finally, if we decide to use hashing, we obtain the equivalent of Example 3, which might be written as follows.

```
begin integer i;
    i := h(x);
    loop until present or absent:
        if A[i] = x then present fi;
        if A[i] = 0 then absent fi;
        i := i − 1;
        if i = 0 then i := m fi;
    repeat;
    then present => found(i);
        absent => A[i] := x; found(i);
    fi;
end;
```

The **begin until** ⟨event⟩ construct also provides a natural way to deal with decision-table constructions such as the text-scanning application we have discussed.

Example 4b:

```
begin until normal character input
    or double slash:
    char x;
    x := read char;
    if x = slash
    then x := read char;
```

```
        if x = slash
        then double slash;
        else tabulate;
            normal character input (x);
        fi;
    else normal character input (x);
    fi;
end;
then normal character input (char x) =>
    write char (x);
        if x = period then write char (space) fi;
    double slash => return the carriage,
fi;
```

This program states the desired actions a bit more clearly than any of our previous attempts were able to do.

Event indicators handle error exits too. For example, we might write a program as follows.

```
begin until error or normal end:
    . . .
    if m = max then error ('symbol table full') fi;
    . . .
    normal end;
end;
then error (string S) =>
    print ('unrecoverable error,' S);
    normal end =>
        print ('computation complete');
fi;
```

Comparison of Features

Of course, event indicators are not the only decent alternatives to **go to** statements that have been proposed. Many authors have suggested language features which provide roughly equivalent facilities, but which are expressed in terms of **exit, jump-out, break,** or **leave** statements. Kosaraju [57] has proved that such statements are sufficient to express all programs without **go to**'s and without any extra computation, but only if an exit from arbitrarily many levels of control is permitted.

The earliest language features of this kind (besides Landin's proposal) provided essentially only one exit from a loop; this means that the code appearing in the **then** $\cdots$ **fi** postlude of our examples would be inserted into the body itself before branching. (See Example 5c.) The separation of such code as in Zahn's proposal is better, mainly because the body of the construct corresponds to code that is written under different "invariant assumptions" which are inoperative after a particular event has occurred.

Thus, each event corresponds to a particular set of assertions about the state of the program, and the code which follows that event takes cognizance of these assertions, which are rather different from the assertions in the main body of the construct. (For this reason I prefer Example 5b to Example 5c.)

Language features allowing multiple exits have been proposed by G. V. Bochmann [7], and independently by Shigo et al. [86]. These are semantically equivalent to Zahn's proposals, with minor variations; but they express such semantics in terms of statements that say "exit to ⟨label⟩". I believe Zahn's idea of event indicators is an improvement on the previous schemes, because the specification of events instead of labels encourages a better *conception* of the program. The identifier given to a label is often an imperative verb like "insert" or "compare", saying what action is to be done next, while the appropriate identifier for an event is more likely to be an adjective like "found". The names of events are very much like the names of Boolean variables, and I believe this accounts for the popularity of Boolean variables as documentation aids, in spite of their inefficiency.

Putting this another way, it is much better from a psychological standpoint to write

> **loop until** found $\cdots$; found; $\cdots$ **repeat**

than to write

```
search: while true do
   begin ··· ; leave search; ··· end.
```

The **leave** or **exit** statement is operationally the same, but intuitively different, since it talks more about the program than about the problem.

The PL/I language allows programmer-defined ON-conditions, which are similar in spirit to event indicators. A programmer first *executes* a statement "ON CONDITION (identifier) block" which specifies a block of code that is to be executed when the identified event occurs, and an occurrence of that event is indicated by writing SIGNAL CONDITION (identifier). However, the analogy is not very close, since control returns to the statement following the SIGNAL statement after execution of the specified block of code, and the block may be dynamically respecified.

Some people have suggested to me that events should be called "conditions" instead, by analogy with Boolean expressions. However, that terminology would tend to imply a relation which is continually being monitored, instead of a happening. By writing "**loop until** *yprime* is near *y:* $\cdots$" we seem to be saying that the machine should keep track of whether or not y and *yprime* are nearly equal; a better choice of words would be an event name like "**loop until** convergence established: $\cdots$" so that we can write "**if** $abs(yprime - y) < epsilon \times y$ **then** convergence established". An event occurs when the program has *discovered* that the state of computation has changed.

Simple Iterations

So far I haven't mentioned what I believe is really the most common situation in which **go to** statements are needed by an ALGOL or PL/I programmer, namely a simple iterative loop with one entrance and one exit. The iteration statements most often proposed as alternatives to **go to** statements have been "**while** B **do** S" and "**repeat** S **until** B". However, in practice, the iterations I encounter very often have the form

```
A: S;
   if B then go to Z fi;
   T; go to A;
Z:
```

where S and T both represent reasonably long sequences of code. If S is empty, we have a **while** loop, and if T is empty we have a **repeat** loop, but in the general case it is a nuisance to avoid the **go to** statements.

A typical example of such an iteration occurs when S is the code to acquire or generate a new piece of data, B is the test for end of data, and T is the processing of that data. Another example is when the code preceding the loop sets initial conditions for some iterative process; then S is a computation of quantities involved in the test for convergence, B is the test for convergence, and T is the adjustment of variables for the next iteration.

Dijkstra [29] aptly named this a loop

which is performed "*n* and a half times". The usual practice for avoiding **go to**'s in such loops is either to duplicate the code for S, writing

S; **while** $\bar{B}$ **do begin** T; S **end**;

where $\bar{B}$ is the negation of relation B; or to figure out some sort of "inverse" for T so that "T^{-1}; T" is equivalent to a null statement, and writing

T^{-1}; **repeat** T; S **until** B;

or to duplicate the code for B and to make a redundant test, writing

repeat S; **if** $\bar{B}$ **then** T **fi**; **until** B;

or its equivalent. The reader who studies **go to**-less programs as they appear in the literature will find that all three of these rather unsatisfactory constructions are used frequently.

I discussed this weakness of ALGOL in a letter to Niklaus Wirth in 1967, and he proposed two solutions to the problem, together with many other instructive ideas in an unpublished report on basic concepts of programming languages [94]. His first suggestion was to write

repeat begin S; **when** B **exit**; T; **end**;

and readers who remember 1967 will also appreciate his second suggestion,

turn on begin S; **when** B **drop out**; T; **end.**

Neither set of delimiters was felt to be quite right, but a modification of the first proposal (allowing one or more single-level **exit** statements within **repeat begin** ··· **end**) was later incorporated into an experimental version of the ALGOL W language. Other languages such as BCPL and BLISS incorporated and extended the **exit** idea, as mentioned above. Zahn's construction now allows us to write, for example,

loop until all data exhausted:
  S;
  if B **then** all data exhausted **fi**;
  T;
repeat;

and this is a better syntax for the $n + \frac{1}{2}$ problem than we have had previously.

On the other hand, it would be nicest if our language would provide a single feature which covered all simple iterations without going to a rather "big" construct like the event-driven scheme. When a programmer uses the simpler feature he is thereby making it clear that he has a simple iteration, with exactly one condition which is being tested exactly once each time around the loop. Furthermore, by providing special syntax for this common case we make it easier for a compiler to produce more efficient code, since the compiler can rearrange the machine instructions so that the test appears physically at the end of loop. (Many hours of computer time are now wasted each day executing unconditional jumps to the beginning of loops.)

Ole-Johan Dahl has recently proposed a syntax which I think is the first real solution to the $n + \frac{1}{2}$ problem. He suggests writing the general simple iteration defined above as

loop; *S*; **while** $\bar{B}$: *T;* **repeat**;

where, as before, S and T denote sequences of one or more statements separated by semicolons. Note that as in two of our original **go to**-free examples, the syntax refers to condition $\bar{B}$ which represents staying *in* the iteration, instead of condition B which represents exiting; and this may be the secret of its success.

Dahl's syntax may not seem appropriate at first, but actually it reads well in every example I have tried, and I hope the reader will reserve judgment until seeing the examples in the rest of this paper. One of the nice properties of his syntax is that the word **repeat** occurs naturally at the end of a loop rather than at its beginning, since we read the actions of the program sequentially. As we reach the end, we are instructed to repeat the loop, instead of being informed that the *text* of the loop (not its execution) has ended. Furthermore, the above syntax avoids ALGOL's use of the word **do** (and also the more recent unnatural delimiter **od**); the word **do** as used in ALGOL has never sounded quite right to native speakers of English, it has always been rather quaint for us to say "**do** *read* (A[*i*])" or "**do begin**"! Another feature of Dahl's proposals is that it is easily axiomatized along the lines proposed by Hoare [37, 41]:

$$\frac{\{P\}S\{Q\}}{\{Q \wedge \bar{B}\}T\{P\}}$$
$$\{P\} \textbf{ loop: } S; \textbf{ while } \bar{B}: T; \textbf{ repeat}; \{Q \wedge \neg \bar{B}\}$$

(Here I am using braces around the assertions, as in Wirth's PASCAL language [97], instead of following Hoare's original notation "P {S} Q", since assertions are, by nature, parenthetical remarks.)

The nicest thing about Dahl's proposal is that it works also when S or T is empty, so that we have a uniform syntax for all three cases; the **while** and **repeat** statements found in ALGOL-like languages of the late 1960s are no longer needed. When S or T is empty, it is appropriate to delete the preceding colon. Thus

> **loop while** $\bar{B}$:
>   T;
> **repeat**;

takes the place of "**while** $\bar{B}$ **do begin** T **end**;" and

> **loop**:
>   S
> **while** $\bar{B}$ **repeat**;

takes the place of "**repeat** S **until** B;". At first glance these may seem strange, but probably less strange than the **while** and **repeat** statements did when we first learned them.

If I were designing a programming language today, my current preference would be to use Dahl's mechanism for simple iteration, plus Zahn's more general construct, plus a **for** statement whose syntax would be perhaps

> **loop for** $1 \leq i \leq n$:
>   S;
> **repeat**;

with appropriate extensions. These control structures, together with **if** $\cdots$ **then** $\cdots$ **else** $\cdots$ **fi**, will comfortably handle all the examples discussed so far in this paper, without any **go to** statements or loss of efficiency or clarity. Furthermore, none of these language features seems to encourage overly-complicated program structure.

2. INTRODUCTION OF go to STATEMENTS

Now that I have discussed how to remove **go to** statements, I will turn around and show why there are occasions when I actually wish to *insert* them into a **go to**-less program. The reason is that I like well-documented programs very much, but I dislike inefficient ones; and there are some cases where I simply seem to need **go to** statements, despite the examples stated above.

Recursion Elimination

Such cases come to light primarily when I'm trying to optimize a program (originally well-structured), often involving the removal of implicit or explicit recursion. For example, consider the following recursive procedure that prints the contents of a binary tree in symmetric order. The tree is represented by L, A, and R arrays as in Example 5, and the recursive procedure is essentially the *definition* of symmetric order.

Example 6:

```
procedure treeprint(t); integer t; value t;
    if t ≠ 0
    then treeprint(L[t]);
        print(A[t]);
        treeprint(R[t]);
    fi;
```

This procedure may be regarded as a model for a great many algorithms which have the same structure, since tree traversal occurs in so many applications; we shall assume for now that printing is our goal, with the understanding that this is only one instance of a general family of algorithms.

It is often useful to remove recursion from an algorithm, because of important economies of space or time, even though this tends to cause some loss of the program's basic clarity. (And, of course, we might also have to state our algorithm in a language like FORTRAN or in a machine language that doesn't allow recursion.) Even when we use ALGOL or PL/I, every compiler I know imposes· considerable overhead on procedure calls; this is to a certain extent inevitable because of the generality of the parameter mechanisms, especially call by name and the maintenance of proper dynamic environments. When procedure calls occur in an inner loop the overhead can slow a program down by a factor of two or more. But if we hand tailor our own implementation of recursion instead of relying on a general mechanism we can usually find worthwhile simplifications, and in the process we occasionally get a deeper insight into the original algorithm.

There has been a good deal published about recursion elimination (especially in the work of Barron [4], Cooper [15], Manna and Waldinger [61], McCarthy [62], and Strong [88; 91]); but I'm amazed that very little of this is about "down to earth" problems. I have always felt that the transformation from recursion to iteration is one of the most fundamental concepts of computer science, and that a student should learn it at about the time he is studying data structures. This topic is the subject of Chapter 8 in my multi-volume work; but it's only by accident that recursion wasn't Chapter 3, since it conceptually belongs very early in the table of contents. The material just wouldn't fit comfortably into any of the earlier volumes; yet there are many algorithms in Chapters 1–7 that are recursions in disguise. Therefore it surprises me that the literature on recursion removal is primarily concerned with "baby" examples like computing factorials or reversing lists, instead of with a sturdy toddler like Example 6.

Now let's go to work on the above example. I assume, of course, that the reader knows the standard way of implementing recursion with a stack [20], but I want to make simplifications beyond this. Rule number one for simplifying procedure calls is:

> If the last action of procedure p before it returns is to call procedure q, simply **go to** the beginning of procedure q instead.

(We must forget for the time being that we don't like **go to** statements.) It is easy to confirm the validity of this rule, if, for simplicity, we assume parameterless procedures. For the operation of calling q is to put a return address on the stack, then to execute q, then to resume p at the return address specified, then to resume the caller of p. The

above simplification makes q resume the caller of p. When $q = p$ the argument is perhaps a bit subtle, but it's all right. (I'm not sure who originated this principle; I recall learning it from Gill's paper [34, p. 183], and then seeing many instances of it in connection with top-down compiler organization. Under certain conditions the BLISS/11 compiler [101] is capable of discovering this simplification. Incidentally, the converse of the above principle is also true (see [52]): **go to** statements can always be eliminated by declaring suitable procedures, each of which calls another as its last action. This shows that procedure calls include **go to** statements as a special case; it cannot be argued that procedures are conceptually simpler than **go to**'s, although some people have made such a claim.)

As a result of applying the above simplification, and adapting it in the obvious way to the case of a procedure with one parameter, Example 6 becomes

Example 6a:

```
procedure treeprint(t); integer t; value t;
L: if t ≠ 0
   then treeprint(L[t]);
      print(A[t]);
      t := R[t]; go to L;
   fi;
```

But we don't really want that **go to**, so we might prefer to write the code as follows, using Dahl's syntax for iterations as explained above.

Example 6b:

```
procedure treeprint(t); integer t; value t;
loop while t ≠ 0:
   treeprint(L[t]);
   print(A[t]);
   t := R[t];
repeat;
```

If our goal is to impress somebody, we might tell them that we thought of Example 6b first, instead of revealing that we got it by straightforward simplification of the obvious program in Example 6.

There is still a recursive call in Example 6b; and this time it's embedded in the procedure, so it looks as though we have to go to the general stack implementation. However, the recursive call now occurs in only one place, so we need not put a return address on the stack; only the local variable t needs to be saved on each call. (This is another simplification which occurs frequently.) The program now takes the following nonrecursive form.

Example 6c:

```
procedure treeprint(t); integer t; value t;
  begin integer stack S; S := empty;
L1: loop while t ≠ 0:
       S <= t; t := L[t]; go to L1;
L2:    t <= S;
       print(A[t]);
       t := R[t];
    repeat;
    if nonempty(S) then go to L2 fi;
    end.
```

Here for simplicity I have extended ALGOL to allow a "stack" data type, where $S <= t$ means "push t onto S" and $t <= S$ means "pop the top of S to t, assuming that S is nonempty".

It is easy to see that Example 6c is equivalent to Example 6b. The statement "**go to** L1" initiates the procedure, and control returns to the following statement (labeled L2) when the procedure is finished. Although Example 6c involves **go to** statements, their purpose is easy to understand, given the knowledge that we have produced Example 6c by a mechanical, completely reliable method for removing recursion. Hopkins [44] has given other examples where **go to** at a low level supports high-level constructions.

But if you look at the above program again, you'll probably be just as shocked as I was when I first realized what has happened. I had always thought that the use of **go to** statements was a bit sinful, say a "venial sin"; but there was one kind of **go to** that I certainly had been taught to regard as a mortal sin, perhaps even unforgivable, namely one which goes into the middle of an iteration! Example 6c does precisely that, and it is perfectly easy to understand Example 6c by comparing it with Example 6b. In this particular case we can remove the **go to**'s without difficulty; but in general when a recursive call is embedded in general when a recursive call is embedded in several complex levels of control, there is no equally simple way to remove the recursion without resorting to something like Example 6c. As I say, it was a shock when I first ran across such an example. Later, Jim Horning confessed to me that he also was guilty, in the syntax-table-building program for the XPL system [65, p. 500], because XPL doesn't allow recursion; see also [56]. Clearly a new doctrine about sinful **go to**'s is needed, some sort of "situation ethics".

The new morality that I propose may perhaps be stated thus: "Certain **go to** statements which arise in connection with well-understood transformations are acceptable, provided that the program documentation explains what the transformation was." The use of four-letter words like **goto** can occasionally be justified even in the best of company.

This situation is very similar to what people have commonly encountered when proving a program correct. To demonstrate the validity of a typical program Q, it is usually simplest and best to prove that some rather simple but less efficient program P is correct and then to prove that P can be transformed into Q by a sequence of valid optimizations. I'm saying that a similar thing should be considered standard practice for all but the simplest software programs: A programmer should create a program P which is readily understood and well-documented, and then he should optimize it into a program Q which is very efficient. Program Q may contain **go to** statements and other low-level features, but the transformation from P to Q should be accomplished by completely reliable and well-documented "mechanical" operations.

At this point many readers will say, "But he should only write P, and an optimizing compiler will produce Q." To this I say, "No, the optimizing compiler would have to be so complicated (much more so than anything we have now) that it will in fact be *un*reliable." I have another alternative to propose, a new class of software which will be far better.

Program Manipulation Systems

For 15 years or so I have been trying to think of how to write a compiler that really produces top quality code. For example, most of the MIX programs in my books are considerably more efficient than any of today's most visionary compiling schemes would be able to produce. I've tried to study the various techniques that a hand-coder like myself uses, and to fit them into some systematic and automatic system. A few years ago, several students and I looked at a typical sample of FORTRAN programs [51], and we all tried hard to see how a machine could produce code that would compete with our best hand-optimized object programs. We found ourselves always running up against the same problem: the compiler needs to be in a dialog with the programmer; it needs to know properties of the data, and whether certain cases can arise, etc. And we couldn't think of a good language in which to have such a dialog.

For some reason we all (especially me) had a mental block about optimization, namely that we always regarded it as a behind-the-scenes activity, to be done in the machine language, which the programmer isn't supposed to know. This veil was first lifted from my eyes in the Fall of 1973, when I ran across a remark by Hoare [42] that, ideally, **a** language should be designed so that an optimizing compiler can describe its optimizations in the *source* language. Of course! Why hadn't I ever thought of it?

Once we have a suitable language, we will be able to have what seems to be emerging as the programming system of the future: an interactive *program-manipulation system*, analogous to the many symbol-manipulation systems which are presently undergoing extensive development and experimentation. We are gradually learning about program transformations, which are more complicated than formula manipulations but really not very different. A program-manipulation system is obviously what we've been leading up to, and I wonder why I never thought of it before. Of course, the idea isn't original with me; when I told Hoare, he said, "Exactly!" and referred me to a recent paper by Darlington and Burstall [18]. Their paper describes a system which removes some recursions from a LISP-like language (curiously, without introducing any **go to**'s), and which also does some conversion of data structures (from sets to lists or bit strings) and some

restructuring of a program by combining similar loops. I later discovered that program manipulation is just part of a much more ambitious project undertaken by Cheatham and Wegbreit [12]; another paper about source-code optimizations has also recently appeared [83]. Since LISP programs are easily manipulated as LISP data objects, there has also been a rather extensive development of similar ideas in this domain, notably by Warren Teitelman (see [89, 90]). The time is clearly ripe for program-manipulation systems, and a great deal of further work suggests itself.

The programmer using such a system will write his beautifully-structured, but possibly inefficient, program P; then he will interactively specify transformations that make it efficient. Such a system will be much more powerful and reliable than a completely automatic one. We can also imagine the system manipulating measurement statistics concerning how much of the total running time is spent in each statement, since the programmer will want to know which parts of his program deserve to be optimized, and how much effect an optimization will really have. The original program P should be retained along with the transformation specifications, so that it can be properly understood and maintained as time passes. As I say, this idea certainly isn't my own; it is so exciting I hope that *everyone* soon becomes aware of its possibilities.

A "calculus" of program transformations is gradually emerging, a set of operations which can be applied to programs without rethinking the specific problem each time. I have already mentioned several of these transformations: doubling up of loops (Example 2a), changing final calls to **go to**'s (Example 6a), using a stack for recursions (Example 6c), and combining disjoint loops over the same range [18]. The idea of macro-expansions in general seems to find its most appropriate realization as part of a program manipulation system.

Another well-known example is the removal of invariant subexpressions from loops. We are all familiar with the fact that a program which includes such subexpressions is more readable than the corresponding program with invariant subexpressions moved out of their loops; yet we consciously remove them when the running time of the program is important.

Still another type of transformation occurs when we go from high-level "abstract" data structures to low-level "concrete" ones (see Hoare's chapter in [17] for numerous examples). In the case of Example 6c, we can replace the stack by an array and a pointer, arriving at

Example 6d:

```
procedure treeprint(t); integer t; value t;
  begin integer array S[1:n]; integer k; k := 0;
L1: loop while t ≠ 0:
       k := k+1; S[k] := t;
       t := L[t]; go to L1;
L2:    t := S[k]; k := k−1;
       print(A[t]);
       t := R[t];
    repeat;
    if k ≠ 0 then go to L2 fi;
  end.
```

Here the programmer must specify a safe value for the maximum stack size n, in order to make the transformation legitimate. Alternatively, he may wish to implement the stack by a linked list. This choice can usually be made without difficulty, and it illustrates another area in which interaction is preferable to completely automatic transformations.

Recursion vs. Iteration

Before leaving the *treeprint* example, I would like to pursue the question of **go to** elimination from Example 6c, since this leads to some interesting issues. It is clear that the first **go to** is just a simple iteration, and a little further study shows that Example 6c is just one simple iteration inside another, namely (in Dahl's syntax)

Example 6e:

```
  procedure treeprint(t); integer t; value t;
    begin integer stack S; S := empty;
      loop:
        loop while t ≠ 0:
          S <= t;
          t := L[t];
        repeat;
        while nonempty(S):
        t <= S;
        print(A[t]);
        t := R[t];
      repeat;
    end.
```

Furthermore, there is a rather simple way to understand this program, by providing suitable "loop invariants". At the beginning of the first (outer) loop, suppose the stack contents from top to bottom are $t_n, \cdots, t_1$ for some $n \geq 0$; then the procedure's remaining duty is to accomplish the effect of

$$
\begin{aligned}
&treeprint(t); \\
&print(A[t_n]);\ treeprint(R[t_n]); \\
&\cdots; \\
&print(A[t_1]);\ treeprint(R[t_1]); \qquad (*)
\end{aligned}
$$

In other words, the purpose of the stack is to record postponed obligations to print the A's and right subtrees of certain nodes. Once this concept is grasped, the meaning of the program is clear and we can even see how we might have written it without ever thinking of a recursive formulation or a **go to** statement: The innermost loop ensures $t = 0$, and afterwards the program reduces the stack, maintaining (*) as the condition to be fulfilled, at key points in the outer loop.

A careful programmer might notice a source of inefficiency in this program: when $L[t] = 0$, we put t on the stack, then take it off again. If there are n nodes in a binary tree, about half of them, on the average, will have $L[t] = 0$ so we might wish to avoid this extra computation. It isn't easy to do that to Example 6e without major surgery on the structure; but it *is* easy to modify Example 6c (or 6d), by simply bracketing the source of inefficiency, including the **go to**, and the label, and all.

Example 6f:

```
  procedure treeprint(t); value t; integer t;
    begin integer stack S; S := empty;
L1:   loop while t ≠ 0:
L3:      if L[t] ≠ 0
         then S <= t; t := L[t]; go to L1;
L2:         t <= S;
         fi;
         print(A[t]);
         t := R[t];
      repeat;
      if nonempty(S) then go to L2 fi;
    end.
```

Here we notice that a further simplification is possible: **go to** L1 can become **go to** L3 because t is known to be nonzero.

An equivalent **go to**-free program analogous to Example 6e is

127

Example 6g:

```
procedure treeprint(t); value t; integer t;
  begin integer stack S; S := empty;
    loop until finished:
      if t ≠ 0
      then
        loop while L[t] ≠ 0:
          S <= t;
          t := L[t];
        repeat;
      else
        if nonempty(S)
        then t <= S;
        else finished;
        fi;
      fi;
      print(A[t]);
      t := R[t];
    repeat;
  end.
```

I derived this program by thinking of the loop invariant (*) in Example 6e and acting accordingly, *not* by trying to eliminate the **go to**'s from Example 6f. So I know this program is well-structured, and I therefore haven't succeeded in finding an example of recursion removal where **go to**'s are strictly necessary. It is interesting, in fact, that our transformations originally intended for efficiency led us to new insights and to programs that still possess decent structure. However, I still feel that Example 6f is easier to understand than 6g, given that the reader is told the recursive program it comes from and the transformations that were used. The recursive program is trivially correct, and the transformations require only routine verification; by contrast, a mental leap is needed to invent (*).

Does recursion elimination help? Clearly there won't be much gain in this example if the *print* routine itself is the bottleneck. But let's replace *print*(A[t]) by

$$i := i+1; B[i] := A[t];$$

i.e., instead of printing the tree, let's assume that we merely want to transfer its contents to some other array B. Then we can expect to see an improvement.

After making this change, I tried the recursive Example 6 vs. the iterative Example 6d on the two main ALGOL compilers available to me. Normalizing the results so that 6d takes 1.0 units of time per node of the tree, with subscript checking suppressed, I

found that the corresponding recursive version took about 2.1 units of time per node using our ALGOL W compiler for the 360/67; and the ratio was 1.16 using the SAIL compiler for the PDP-10. (Incidentally, the relative run-times for Example 6f were 0.8 with ALGOL W, and 0.7 with SAIL. When subscript ranges were dynamically checked, ALGOL W took 1.8 units of time per node for the nonrecursive version, and 2.8 with the recursive version; SAIL's figures were 1.28 and 1.34.)

Boolean Variable Elimination

Another important program transformation, somewhat less commonly known, is the removal of Boolean variables by code duplication. The following example is taken from Dijkstra's treatment [26, pp. 91–93] of Hoare's "Quicksort" algorithm. The idea is to rearrange array elements $A[m] \cdots A[n]$ so that they are partitioned into two parts: The left part $A[m] \cdots A[j-1]$, for some appropriate j, will contain all the elements less than some value, v; the right part $A[j+1] \cdots A[n]$ will contain all the elements greater than v; and the element $A[j]$ lying between these parts will be equal to v. Partitioning is done by scanning from the left until finding an element greater than v, then scanning from the right until finding an element less than v, then scanning from the left again, and so on, moving the offending elements to the opposite side, until the two scans come together; a Boolean variable up is used to distinguish the left scan from the right.

Example 7:

```
i := m; j := n;
v := A[j]; up := true;
loop:
  if up
  then if A[i] > v
    then A[j] := A[i]; up := false fi;
  else if v > A[j]
    then A[i] := A[j]; up := true fi;
  fi;
  if up then i := i+1 else j := j-1 fi;
while i < j repeat;
A[j] := v;
```

The manipulation and testing of up is rather time-consuming here. We can, in general, eliminate a Boolean variable by storing its current value in the program counter, i.e., by duplicating the program, letting one part of the text represent **true** and the other part **false**, with jumps between the two parts in appropriate places. Example 7 therefore becomes

Example 7a:

```
        i := m; j := n;
        v := A[j];
        loop: if A[i] > v
          then A[j] := A[i]; go to upf fi;
   upt: i := i+1;
        while i < j repeat; go to common;
        loop: if v > A[j]
          then A[i] := A[j]; go to upt fi;
   upf: j := j−1;
        while i < j repeat;
        common: A[j] := v;
```

Note that again we have come up with a program which has jumps into the middle of iterations, yet we can understand it since we know that it came from a previously understood program, by way of an understandable transformation.

Of course this program is messier than the first, and we must ask again if the gain in speed is worth this cost. If we are writing a sort procedure that will be used many times, we will be interested in the speed. The average running time of Quicksort was analyzed by Hoare in his 1962 paper on the subject [36], and it turns out that the body of the loop in Example 7 is performed about $2N \ln N$ times while the statement $up :=$ **false** is performed about $\frac{1}{3}N \ln N$ times, if we are sorting N elements. All other parts of the overall sorting program (not shown here) have a running time of order N or less, so when N is reasonably large the speed of the inner loop governs the speed of the entire sorting process. (Incidentally, a recursive version of Quicksort will run just about as fast, since the recursion overhead is not part of the inner loop. But in this case the removal of recursion is of great value for another reason, because it cuts the auxiliary stack space requirement from order N to order $\log N$.)

Using these facts about inner loop times, we can make a quantitative comparison of Examples 7 and 7a. As with Example 1, it seems best to make two comparisons, one with the assembly code that a decent programmer would write for the examples, and the other with the object code produced by a typical compiler that does only local optimizations. The assembly-language programmer will keep i, j, v, and up in registers, while a typical compiler will not keep variables in registers from one statement to another, except if they happen to be there by coincidence. Under these assumptions, the asymptotic running time for an entire Quicksort program based on these routines will be

	assembled	compiled
Example 7	$20\frac{2}{3}N \ln N$	$55\frac{1}{3}N \ln N$
Example 7a	$15\frac{1}{3}N \ln N$	$40N \ln N$

expressed in memory references to data and instructions. So Example 7a saves more than 25 % of the sorting time.

I showed this example to Dijkstra, cautioning him that the **go to** leading into an iteration might be a terrible shock. I was extremely pleased to receive his reply [31]:

> Your technique of storing the value of up in the order counter is, of course, absolutely safe. I did not faint! I am in no sense "afraid" of a program constructed that way, but I cannot consider it beautiful: it is really the same repetition with the same terminating condition, that "changes color" as the computation proceeds.

He went on to say that he looks forward to the day when machines are so fast that we won't be under pressure to optimize our programs; yet

> For the time being I could not agree more with your closing remarks: if the economies matter, apply "disciplined optimalization" to a nice program, the correctness of which has been established beyond reasonable doubt. Your massaging of the program text is then no longer trickery ad hoc, it is perfectly safe and sound.

It is hard for me to express the joy that this letter gave me; it was like having all my sins forgiven, since I need no longer feel guilty about my optimized programs.

Coroutines

Several of the people who read the first draft of this paper observed that Example 7a can perhaps be understood more easily as the result of eliminating *coroutine* linkage instead of Boolean variables. Consider the following program:

Example 7b:

```
coroutine move i;
  loop: if A[i] > v
          then A[j] := A[i];
            resume move j;
        fi;
        i := i+1;
    while i < j repeat;
coroutine move j;
  loop: if v > A[j]
          then A[i] := A[j];
            resume move i;
        fi;
        j := j−1;
    while i < j repeat;
i := m; j := n; v := A[j];
call move i;
A[j] := v;
```

When a coroutine is "resumed", let's assume that it begins after its own **resume** statement; and when a coroutine terminates, let's assume that the most recent **call** statement is thereby completed. (Actual coroutine linkage is slightly more involved, see Chapter 3 of [17], but this description will suffice for our purposes.) Under these conventions, Example 7b is precisely equivalent to Example 7a. At the beginning of *move i* we know that $A[k] \leq v$ for all $k < i$, and that $i < j$, and that $\{A[m], \cdots, A[j-1], A[j+1], \cdots, A[n]\} \cup v$ is a permutation of the original contents of $\{A[m], \cdots, A[n]\}$; a similar statement holds at the beginning of *move j*. This separation into two coroutines can be said to make Example 7b conceptually simpler than Example 7; but on the other hand, the idea of coroutines admittedly takes some getting used to.

Christopher Strachey once told me about an example which first convinced him that coroutines provided an important control structure. Consider two binary trees represented as in Examples 5 and 6, with their A array information in increasing order as we traverse the trees in symmetric order of their nodes. The problem is to *merge* these two A array sequences into one ordered sequence. This requires traversing both trees more or less asynchronously, in symmetric order, so we'll need two versions of Example 6 running cooperatively. A conceptually simple solution to this problem can be written with

coroutines, or by forming an equivalent program which expresses the coroutine linkage in terms of **go to** statements; it appears to be cumbersome (though not impossible) to do the job without using either feature.

Quicksort: A Digression

Dijkstra also sent another instructive example in his letter [30]. He decided to create the program of Example 7 from scratch, as if Hoare's algorithm had never been invented, starting instead with modern ideas of semi-automatic program construction based on the following *invariant* relation:

$$
\begin{aligned}
&v = A[n] \wedge \\
&\forall k(m \leq k < i => A[k] \leq v) \wedge \\
&\forall k(j < k \leq n => A[k] \geq v).
\end{aligned}
$$

The resulting program is unusual, yet perhaps cleaner than Example 7:

```
i := m; j := n−1; v := A[n];
loop while i ≤ j;
  if A[j] ≥ v then j := j−1;
  else A[i] := : A[j]; i := i+1;
  fi;
repeat;
if j ≤ m then A[m] := : A[n]; j := m fi;
```

Here "$:= :$" denotes the interchange (i.e., swap) operation. At the conclusion of this program, the A array will be different than before, but we will have the array partitioned as desired for sorting (i.e., $A[m] \cdots A[j]$ are $\leq v$ and $A[j+1] \cdots A[n]$ are $\geq v$).

Unfortunately, however, this "pure" program is less efficient than Example 7, and Dijkstra noted that he didn't like it very much himself. In fact, Quicksort is really quick in practice because there is a method that is even better than Example 7a: A good Quicksort routine will have a faster inner loop which avoids most of the "$i < j$" tests. Dijkstra recently [31] sent me another approach to the problem, which leads to a much better solution. First we can abstract the situation by considering any notions "small" and "large" so that: a) an element $A[i]$ is never both small and large simultaneously; b) some elements might be neither small nor large; c) we wish to rearrange an array so that all small elements precede all large ones; and d) there is at least one element which is not small, and at least one which is not large. Then we can write the

130

following program in terms of this abstraction.

Example 8:

$$i := m; j := n;$$
loop:
  loop while A$[i]$ is small:
    $i := i+1;$ **repeat;**
  loop while A$[j]$ is large:
    $j := j-1;$ **repeat;**
  while $i < j$:
    A$[i] :=: A[j];$
    $i := i+1; j := j-1;$
  repeat;

At the beginning of the first (outer) loop we know that A$[k]$ is not large for $m \leq k < i$, and that A$[k]$ is not small for $j < k \leq n$; also that there exists a k such that $i \leq k \leq n$ and A$[k]$ is not small, and a k such that $m \leq k \leq j$ and A$[k]$ is not large. The operations in the loop are easily seen to preserve these "invariant" conditions. Note that the inner loops are now extremely fast, and that they are guaranteed to terminate; therefore the proof of correctness is simple. At the conclusion of the outer loop we know that A$[m] \cdots$ A$[i-1]$ and A$[j]$ are not large, that A$[i]$ and A$[j+1] \cdots$ A$[n]$ are not small, and that $m \leq j \leq i \leq n$.

Applying this to Quicksort, we can set $v := $ A$[n]$ and write

"A$[i] < v$" in place of "A$[i]$ is small"
"A$[j] > v$" in place of "A$[j]$ is large"

in the above program. This gives a very pretty algorithm, which is essentially equivalent to the method published by Hoare [38] in his first major application of the idea of invariants, and discussed in his original paper on Quicksort [36]. Note that since $v = $ A$[n]$, we know that the first execution of "**loop while** A$[j] > v$" will be trivial; we could move this loop to the end of the outer loop just before the final **repeat**. This would be slightly faster, but it would make the program harder to understand, so I would hesitate to do it.

The Quicksort partitioning algorithm actually given in my book [54] is better than Example 7a, but somewhat different from the program we have just derived. My version can be expressed as follows (assuming that A$[m-1]$ is defined and $\leq$A$[n]$):

$$i := m-1; j := n; v := A[n];$$
loop until pointers have met:
  loop: $i := i+1;$ **while** A$[i] < v$ **repeat;**
  if $i \geq j$ **then** pointers have met; **fi**
  A$[j] := A[i];$
  loop: $j := j-1;$ **while** A$[j] > v$ **repeat;**
  if $i \geq j$ **then** $j := i;$ pointers have met; **fi**
  A$[i] := A[j];$
repeat;
A$[j] := v;$

At the conclusion of this routine, the contents of A$[m] \cdots$ A$[n]$ have been permuted so that A$[m] \cdots$ A$[j-1]$ are $\leq v$ and A$[j+1] \cdots$ A$[n]$ are $\geq v$ and A$[j] = v$ and $m \leq j \leq n$. The assembled version will make about $11N \ln N$ references to memory on the average, so this program saves 28% of the running time of Example 7a.

When I first saw Example 8 I was chagrined to note that it was easier to prove than my program, it was shorter, and (the crushing blow) it also seemed about 3% faster, because it tested "$i < j$" only half as often. My first mathematical analysis of the average behavior of Example 8 indicated that the asymptotic number of comparisons and exchanges would be the same, even though the partitioned subfiles included all N elements instead of $N-1$ as in the classical Quicksort routine. But suddenly it occurred to me that my new analysis was incorrect because one of its fundamental assumptions breaks down: the elements of the two subfiles after partitioning by Example 8 are not in random order! This was a surprise, because randomness *is* preserved by the usual Quicksort routine. When the N keys are distinct, v will be the largest element in the left subfile, and the mechanism of Example 8 shows that v will tend to be near the left of that subfile. When that subfile is later partitioned, it is highly likely that v will move to the extreme right of the resulting right sub-subfile. So that right sub-subfile will be subject to a trivial partitioning by its largest element; we have a subtle loss of efficiency ‛on the third level of recursion. I still haven't been able to analyze Example 8, but empirical tests have borne out my prediction that it is in fact about 15% slower than the book algorithm.

Therefore, there is no reason for anybody to use Example 8 in a sorting routine;

though it is slightly cleaner looking than the method in my book, it is noticeably slower, and we have nothing to fear by using a slightly more complicated method once it has been proved correct. Beautiful algorithms are, unfortunately, not always the most useful.

This is not the end of the Quicksort story (although I almost wish it was, since I think the preceding paragraph makes an important point). After I had shown Example 8 to my student, Robert Sedgewick, he found a way to modify it, preserving the randomness of the subfiles, thereby achieving both elegance and efficiency at the same time. Here is his revised program.

Example 8a:

```
i := m−1; j := n; v := A[n];
loop:
  loop: i := i+1; while A[i] < v repeat;
  loop: j := j−1; while A[j] > v repeat;
  while i < j:
    A[i] := : A[j];
  repeat;
  A[i] := : A[n];
```

(As in the previous example, we assume that $A[m-1]$ is defined and $\leq A[n]$, since the j pointer might run off the left end.) At the beginning of the outer loop the invariant conditions are now

$$m-1 \leq i < j \leq n;$$
$$A[k] \leq v \text{ for } m-1 \leq k \leq i;$$
$$A[k] \geq v \text{ for } j \leq k \leq n;$$
$$A[n] = v.$$

It follows that Example 8a ends with

$$A[m]\cdots A[i-1] \leq v = A[i] \leq A[i+1]\cdots A[n]$$

and $m \leq i \leq n$; hence a valid partition has been achieved.

Sedgewick also found a way to improve the inner loop of the algorithm from my book, namely:

```
i := m−1; j := n; v := A[n];
loop:
  loop: i := i+1; while A[i] < v repeat;
  A[j] := A[i]:
  loop: j := j−1; while A[j] > v repeat;
  while i < j:
    A[i] := A[j];
  repeat;
  if i ≠ j then j := j+1;
  A[j] := v;
```

Each of these programs leads to a Quicksort routine that makes about $10\frac{2}{3}N \ln N$ memory references on the average; the former is preferable (except on machines for which exchanges are clumsy), since it is easier to understand. Thus I learned again that I should always keep looking for improvements, even when I have a satisfactory program.

Axiomatics of Jumps

We have now discussed many different transformations on programs; and there are more which could have been mentioned (e.g., the removal of trivial assignments as in [50, exercise 1.1-3] or [54, exercise 5.2.1-33]). This should be enough to establish that a program-manipulation system will have plenty to do.

Some of these transformations introduce **go to** statements that cannot be handled very nicely by event indicators, and in general we might expect to find a few programs in which **go to** statements survive. Is it really a formidable job to understand such programs? Fortunately this is not an insurmountable task, as recent work has shown. For many years, the **go to** statement has been troublesome in the definition of correctness proofs and language semantics; for example, Hoare and Wirth have presented an axiomatic definition of Pascal [41] in which everything but **real** arithmetic and the **go to** is defined formally. Clint and Hoare [14] have shown how to extend this to event-indicator **go to**'s (i.e., those which don't lead into iterations or conditionals), but they stressed that the general case appears to be fraught with complications. Just recently, however, Hoare has shown that there is, in fact, a rather simple way to give an axiomatic definition of **go to** statements; indeed, he wishes quite frankly that it hadn't been quite so simple. For each label L in a program, the programmer should state a logical assertion $\alpha(\text{L})$ which is to be true whenever we reach L. Then the axioms

$$\{\alpha(\text{L})\} \text{ \textbf{go to} L } \{\textbf{false}\}$$

plus the rules of inference

$$\{\alpha(\text{L})\} \text{ S}\{\text{P}\} \vdash \{\alpha(\text{L})\} \text{ L:S }\{\text{P}\}$$

are allowed in program proofs, and all properties of labels and **go to**'s will follow if the $\alpha(L)$ are selected intelligently. One must, of course, carry out the entire proof using the same assertion $\alpha(L)$ for each appearance of the label L, and some choices of assertions will lead to more powerful results than others.

Informally, $\alpha(L)$ represents the desired state of affairs at label L; this definition says essentially that a program is correct if $\alpha(L)$ holds at L and before all "**go to** L" statements, and that control never "falls through" a **go to** statement to the following text. Stating the assertions $\alpha(L)$ is analogous to formulating loop invariants. Thus, it is not difficult to deal formally with tortuous program structure if it turns out to be necessary; all we need to know is the "meaning" of each label.

Reduction of Complication

There is one remaining use of **go to** for which I have never seen a good replacement, and in fact it's a situation where I still think **go to** is the right idea. This situation typically occurs after a program has made a multiway branch to a rather large number of different but related cases. A little computation often suffices to reduce one case to another; and when we've reduced one problem to a simpler one, the most natural thing is for our program to **go to** the routine which solves the simpler problem.

For example, consider writing an interpretive routine (e.g., a microprogrammed emulator), or a simulator of another computer. After decoding the address and fetching the operand from memory, we do a multiway branch based on the operation code. Let's say the operations include no-op, add, subtract, jump on overflow, and unconditional jump. Then the subtract routine might be

$$operand := -\ operand;\ \textbf{go to}\ \text{add};$$

the add routine might be

$$accum := accum + operand;$$
$$tyme := tyme + 1;$$
$$\textbf{go to}\ \text{no op};$$

and jump on overflow might be

```
if overflow
then overflow := false; go to jump;
else go to no op;
fi;
```

I still believe that this is the correct way to write such a program.

Such situations aren't restricted to interpreters and simulators, although the foregoing is a particularly dramatic example. Multiway branching is an important programming technique which is all too often replaced by an inefficient sequence of **if** tests. Peter Naur recently wrote me that he considers the use of tables to control program flow as a basic idea of computer science that has been nearly forgotten; but he expects it will be ripe for rediscovery any day now. It is the key to efficiency in all the best compilers I have studied.

Some hints of this situation, where one problem reduces to another, have occurred in previous examples of this paper. Thus, after searching for x and discovering that it is absent, the "not found" routine can insert x into the table, thereby reducing the problem to the "found" case. Consider also our decision-table Example 4, and suppose that each period was to be followed by a carriage return instead of by an extra space. Then it would be natural to reduce the post-processing of periods to the return-carriage part of the program. In each case, a **go to** would be easy to understand.

If we need to find a way to do this without saying **go to**, we could extend Zahn's event indicator scheme so that some events are allowed to happen in the **then** $\cdots$ **fi** part after we have begun to process other events. This accommodates the above-mentioned examples very nicely; but of course it can be dangerous when misused, since it gives us back all the power of **go to**. A restriction which allows ⟨statement list⟩$_i$ to refer to ⟨event⟩$_j$ only for $j > i$ would be less dangerous.

With such a language feature, we can't "fall through" a label (i.e., an event indicator) when the end of the preceding code is reached; we must explicitly name each event when we go to its routine. Prohibiting

133

"fall through" means forcing a programmer to write "**go to** common" just before the label "common:" in Example 7a; surprisingly, such a change actually makes that program more readable, since it makes the symmetry plain. Also, the program fragment

> subtract: *operand* := − *operand*; **go to** add;
> add: *accum* := *accum* + *operand*;

seems to be more readable than if "**go to** add" were deleted. It is interesting to ponder why this is so.

3. CONCLUSIONS

This has been a long discussion, and very detailed, but a few points stand out. First, there are several kinds of programming situations in which **go to** statements are harmless, even desirable, if we are programming in ALGOL or PL/I. But secondly, new types of syntax are being developed that provide good substitutes for these harmless **go to**'s, and without encouraging a programmer to create "logical spaghetti".

One thing we haven't spelled out clearly, however, is what makes some **go to**'s bad and others acceptable. The reason is that we've really been directing our attention to the wrong issue, to the objective question of **go to** elimination instead of the important subjective question of program structure. In the words of John Brown [9], "The act of focusing our mightiest intellectual resources on the elusive goal of **go to**-less programs has helped us get our minds off all those really tough and possibly unresolvable problems and issues with which today's professional programmer would otherwise have to grapple." By writing this long article I don't want to add fuel to the controversy about **go to** elimination, since that topic has already assumed entirely too much significance; my goal is to lay that controversy to rest, and to help direct the discussion towards more fruitful channels.

Structured Programming

The real issue is structured programming, but unfortunately this has become a catch phrase whose meaning is rarely understood in the same way by different people. Everybody knows it is a Good Thing, but as McCracken [64] has said, "Few people would venture a definition. In fact, it is not clear that there exists a simple definition as yet." Only one thing is really clear: Structured programming is *not* the process of writing programs and then eliminating their **go to** statements. We should be able to define structured programming without referring to **go to** statements at all; then the fact that **go to** statements rarely need to be introduced as we write programs should follow as a corollary.

Indeed, Dijkstra's original article [25] which gave Structured Programming its name never mentions **go to** statements at all; he directed attention to the critical question, "For what program structures can we give correctness proofs without undue labor, even if the programs get large?" By correctness proofs he explained that he does not mean formal derivations from axioms, he means any sort of proof (formal or informal) that is "sufficiently convincing"; and a proof really means an understanding. By program structure he means data structure as well as control structure.

We understand complex things by systematically breaking them into successively simpler parts and understanding how these parts fit together locally. Thus, we have different levels of understanding, and each of these levels corresponds to an *abstraction* of the detail at the level it is composed from. For example, at one level of abstraction, we deal with an integer without considering whether it is represented in binary notation or two's complement, etc., while at deeper levels this representation may be important. At more abstract levels the precise value of the integer is not important except as it relates to other data.

Charles L. Baker mentioned this principle as early as 1957, as part of his 8-page review [2] of McCracken's first book on programming:

> Break the problem into small, self-contained subroutines, trying at all times to isolate the various sections of coding as much as possible ... [then] the problem is reduced to many much smaller ones. The truth of this seems

very obvious to experienced coders, yet it is hard to put across to the newcomer.

Abstraction is easily understood in terms of BNF notation. A metalinguistic category like ⟨assignment statement⟩ is an abstraction which is composed of two abstractions (a ⟨left part list⟩ and an ⟨arithmetic expression⟩), each of which is composed of abstractions such as ⟨identifier⟩ or ⟨term⟩, etc. We understand the program syntax as a whole by knowing the structural details that relate these abstract parts. The most difficult things to understand about a program's syntax are the identifiers, since their meaning is passed across several levels of structure. If all identifiers of an ALGOL program were changed to random meaningless strings of symbols, we would have great difficulty seeing what the type of a variable is and what the program means, but we would still easily recognize the more local features, such as assignment statements, expressions, subscripts, etc. (This inability for our eyes to associate a type or mode with an identifier has led to what I believe are fundamental errors of human engineering in the design of ALGOL 68, but that's another story. My own notation for stacks in Example 6c suffers from the same problem; it works in these examples chiefly because t is lower case and S is upper case.) Larger nested structures are harder for the eye to see unless they are indented, but indentation makes the structure plain.

It would probably be still better if we changed our source language concept so that the program wouldn't appear as one long string. John McCarthy says "I find it difficult to believe that whenever I see a tree I am really seeing a string of symbols." Instead, we should give meaningful names to the larger constructs in our program that correspond to meaningful levels of abstraction, and we should define those levels of abstraction in one place, and merely use their names (instead of including the detailed code) when they are used to build larger concepts. Procedure names do this, but the language could easily be designed so that no action of calling a subroutine is implied.

From these remarks it is clear that sequential composition, iteration, and conditional statements present syntactic structures that the eye can readily assimilate; but a **go to** statement does not. The visual structure of **go to** statements is like that of flowcharts, except reduced to *one* dimension in our source languages. In two dimensions it is possible to perceive **go to** structure in small examples, but we rapidly lose our ability to understand larger and larger flowcharts; some intermediate levels of abstraction are necessary. As an undergraduate, in 1959, I published an octopus flowchart which I sincerely hope is the most horribly complicated that will ever appear in print; anyone who believes that flowcharts are the best way to understand a program is urged to look at this example [49]. (See also [32, p. 54] for a nice illustration of how **go to**'s make a PL/I program obscure, and see R. Lawrence Clark's hilarious spoof about linear representation of flowcharts by means of a "**come from** statement" [13].)

I have felt for a long time that a talent for programming consists largely of the ability to switch readily from microscopic to macroscopic views of things, i.e., to change levels of abstraction fluently. I mentioned this [55] to Dijkstra, and he replied [29] with an excellent analysis of the situation:

I feel somewhat guilty when I have suggested that the distinction or introduction of "different levels of abstraction" allow you to think about only one level at a time, ignoring completely the other levels. This is not true. You are trying to organize your thoughts; that is, you are seeking to arrange matters in such a way that you can concentrate on some portion, say with 90% of your conscious thinking, while the rest is temporarily moved away somewhat towards the background of your mind. But that is something quite different from "ignoring completely": you allow yourself temporarily to ignore details, but some overall appreciation of what is supposed to be or to come there continues to play a vital role. You remain alert for little red lamps that suddenly start flickering in the corners of your eye.

I asked Hoare for a short definition of structured programming, and he replied that it is "the systematic use of abstraction to control a mass of detail, and also a means of documentation which aids program design."

I hope that my remarks above have made the abstract concept of abstraction clear; the second part of Hoare's definition (which was also stressed by Dijkstra in his original paper [25]) states that a good way to express the abstract properties of an unwritten piece of program often helps us to write that program, and to "know" that it is correct as we write it.

Syntactic structure is just one part of the picture, and BNF would be worthless if the syntactic constructs did not correspond to semantic abstractions. Similarly, a good program will be composed in such a way that each semantic level of abstraction has a reasonably simple relation to its constituent parts. We noticed in our discussion of Jacopini's theorem that every program can trivially be expressed in terms of a simple iteration which simulates a computer; but that iteration has to carry the entire behavior of the program through the loop, so it is worthless as a level of abstraction.

An iteration statement should have a purpose that is reasonably easy to state; typically, this purpose is to make a certain Boolean relation true while maintaining a certain invariant condition satisfied by the variables. The Boolean condition is stated in the program, while the invariant should be stated in a comment, unless it is easily supplied by the reader. For example, the invariant in Example 1 is that $A[k] \neq x$ for $1 \leq k < i$, and in Example 2 it is the same, plus the additional relation $A[m+1] = x$. Both of these are so obvious that I didn't bother to mention them; but in Examples 6e and 8, I stated the more complicated invariants that arose. In each of those cases the program almost wrote itself once the proper invariant was given. Note that an "invariant assertion" actually does vary slightly as we execute statements of the loop, but it comes back to its original form when we repeat the loop.

Thus, an iteration makes a good abstraction if we can assign a meaningful invariant describing the local states of affairs as it executes, and if we can describe its purpose (e.g., to change one state to another). Similarly, an **if** $\cdots$ **then** $\cdots$ **else** $\cdots$ **fi** statement will be a good abstraction if we can state an overall purpose, for the statement as a whole.

We also need well-structured *data;* i.e., as we write the program we should have an abstract idea of what each variable means. This idea is also usually describable as an invariant relation, e.g., "m is the number of items in the table" or "x is the search argument" or "$L[t]$ is the number of the root node of node t's left subtree, or 0 if this subtree is empty" or "the contents of stack S are postponed obligations to do such and such".

Now let's consider the slightly more complex case of an event-driven construct. This should also correspond to a meaningful abstraction, and our examples show what is involved: For each event we give an (invariant) assertion which describes the situation which must hold when that event occurs, and for the **loop until** we also give an invariant for the loop. An event statement typically corresponds to an abrupt change in conditions so that a different assertion from the loop invariant is necessary.

An error exit can be considered well-structured for precisely this reason—it corresponds to a situation that is impossible according to the local invariant assertions; it is easiest to formulate assertions that assume nothing will go wrong, rather than to make the invariants cover all contingencies. When we jump out to an error exit we go to another level of abstraction having different assumptions.

As another simple example, consider binary search in an ordered array using the invariant relation $A[i] < x < A[j]$:

```
loop while i+1 < j;
  k := (i+j) ÷ 2;
  if A[k] < x then i := k;
  else if A[k] > x then j := k;
    else cannot preserve the invariant fi;
  fi;
repeat;
```

Upon normal exit from this loop, the conditions $i+1 \geq j$ and $A[i] < x < A[j]$ imply that $A[i] < x < A[i+1]$, i.e., that x is not present. If the program comes to "cannot preserve the invariant" (because $x = A[k]$), it wants to **go to** another set of assumptions. The event-driven construct provides a level at which it is appropriate to specify the other assumptions.

Another good illustration occurs in Example 6g; the purpose of the main **if** statement is to find the first node whose A value should be printed. If there is no such t, the event "finished" has clearly occurred; it is better to regard the **if** statement as having the stated abstract purpose without considering that t might not exist.

With go to Statements

We can also consider **go to** statements from the same point of view; when do they correspond to a good abstraction? We've already mentioned that **go to**'s do not have a syntactic structure that the eye can grasp automatically; but in this respect they are no worse off than variables and other identifiers. When these are given a meaningful name corresponding to the abstraction (N.B. *not* a numeric label!), we need not apologize for the lack of syntactic structure. And the appropriate abstraction itself is an invariant essentially like the assertions specified for an event.

In other words, we can indeed consider **go to** statements as part of systematic abstraction; all we need is a clearcut notion of exactly what it means to **go to** each label. This should come as no great surprise. After all, a lot of computer programs have been written using **go to** statements during the last 25 years, and these programs haven't all been failures! Some programmers have clearly been able to master structure and exploit it; not as consistently, perhaps, as in modern-day structured programming, but not inflexibly either. By now, many people who have never had any special difficulty writing correct programs have naturally been somewhat upset after being branded as sinners, especially when they know perfectly well what they're doing; so they have understandably been less than enthusiastic about "structured programming" as it has been advertised to them.

My feeling is that it's certainly possible to write well-structured programs with **go to** statements. For example, Dijkstra's 1965 program about concurrent process control [24] used three **go to** statements, all of which were perfectly easy to understand; and I think at most two of these would have disappeared from his code if ALGOL 60 had had a **while** statement. But **go to** is hardly ever the best alternative now, since better language features are appearing. If the invariant for a label is closely related to another invariant, we can usually save complexity by combining those two into one abstraction, using something other than **go to** for the combination.

There is also another problem, namely at what level of abstraction should we introduce a label? This however is like the analogous problem for variables, and the general answer is still unclear in both cases. Aspects of data structure are often postponed, but sometimes variables are defined and passed as "parameters" to other levels of abstraction. There seems to be no clearcut idea as yet about a set of syntax conventions, relating to the definition of variables, which would be most appropriate to structured programming methodology; but for each particular problem there seems to be an appropriate level.

Efficiency

In our previous discussion we concluded that premature emphasis on efficiency is a big mistake which may well be the source of most programming complexity and grief. We should ordinarily keep efficiency considerations in the background when we formulate our programs. We need to be subconsciously aware of the data processing tools available to us, but we should strive most of all for a program that is easy to understand and almost sure to work. (Most programs are probably only run once; and I suppose in such cases we needn't be too fussy about even the structure, much less the efficiency, as long as we are happy with the answers.)

When efficiencies do matter, however, the good news is that usually only a very small fraction of the code is significantly involved. And when it is desirable to sacrifice clarity for efficiency, we have seen that it *is* possible to produce reliable programs that can be maintained over a period of time, if we start with a well-structured program and then use well-understood transformations that can be applied mechanically. We shouldn't attempt to understand the resulting program as it appears in its final form; it should be thought of as the result of the original program modified by specified transformations. We can envision program manipulation systems which will facilitate making and documenting these transformations.

In this regard I would like to quote some observations made recently by Pierre-Arnoul de Marneffe [19]:

> In civil engineering design, it is presently a mandatory concept known as the "Shanley Design Criterion" to collect several functions into one part . . . If you make a cross-section of, for instance, the German V-2, you find external skin, structural rods, tank wall, etc. If you cut across the Saturn-B moon rocket, you find only an external skin which is at the same time a structural component and the tank wall. Rocketry engineers have used the "Shanley Principle" thoroughly when they use the fuel pressure inside the tank to improve the rigidity of the external skin! . . . People can argue that structured programs, even if they work correctly, will look like laboratory prototypes where you can discern all the individual components, but which are not daily usable. Building "integrated" products is an engineering principle as valuable as structuring the design process.

He goes on to describe plans for a prototype system that will automatically assemble integrated programs from well-structured ones that have been written top-down by stepwise refinement.

Today's hardware designers certainly know the advantages of integrated circuitry, but of course they must first understand the separate circuits before the integration is done. The V-2 rocket would never have been airborne if its designers had originally tried to combine all its functions. Engineering has two phases, structuring and integration; we ought not to forget either one, but it is best to hold off the integration phase until a well-structured prototype is working and understood. As stated by Weinberg [93], the former regimen of analysis/coding/debugging should be replaced by analysis/coding/debugging/improving.

The Future

It seems clear that languages somewhat different from those in existence today would enhance the preparation of structured programs. We will perhaps eventually be writing only small modules which are identified by name as they are used to build larger ones, so that devices like indentation, rather than delimiters, might become feasible for expressing local structure in the source language. (See the discussion following Landin's paper [59].) Although our examples don't indicate this, it turns out that a given level of abstraction often involves several related routines and data definitions; for example, when we decide to represent a table in a certain way, we simultaneously want to specify the routines for storing and fetching information from that table. The next generation of languages will probably take into account such related routines.

Program manipulation systems appear to be a promising future tool which will help programmers to improve their programs, and to enjoy doing it. Standard operating procedure nowadays is usually to hand code critical portions of a routine in assembly language. Let us hope such assemblers will die out, and we will see several levels of language instead: At the highest levels we will be able to write abstract programs, while at the lowest levels we will be able to control storage and register allocation, and to suppress subscript range checking, etc. With an integrated system it will be possible to do debugging and analysis of the transformed program using a higher level language for communication. All levels will, of course, exhibit program structure syntactically so that our eyes can grasp it.

I guess the big question, although it really shouldn't be so big, is whether or not the ultimate language will have **go to** statements in its higher levels, or whether **go to** will be confined to lower levels. I personally wouldn't mind having **go to** in the highest level, just in case I really need it; but I probably would never use it, if the general iteration and event constructs suggested in this paper were present. As soon as people learn to apply principles of abstraction consciously, they won't see the need for **go to**, and the issue will just fade away. On the other hand, W. W. Peterson told me about his experience teaching PL/I to beginning programmers: He taught them to use **go to** only in unusual special cases where **if** and **while** aren't right, but he found [78] that "A disturbingly large percentage of the students ran into situations that require **go to**'s, and sure enough, it was often because **while** didn't work well to their plan, but almost invariably because their plan was poorly thought out." Because of arguments like this. I'd say we should, indeed, abolish **go to** from the high-level language, at least as an experiment in training people to formulate their abstractions more carefully. This does have a beneficial effect on style, although I would not make such a prohibition if the new language features described above were not available. The question is whether we should ban it, or educate against it; should we attempt to legislate program morality? In this case I vote for legislation, with appropriate legal substitutes in place of the former overwhelming temptations.

A great deal of research must be done if we're going to have the desired language by 1984. Control structure is merely one simple issue, compared to questions of abstract data structure. It will be a major problem to keep the total number of language features within tight limits. And we must especially look at problems of input/output and data formatting, in order to provide a viable alternative to COBOL.

ACKNOWLEDGMENTS

I've benefited from a truly extraordinary amount of help while preparing this paper. The individuals named provided me with a total of 144 pages of single-spaced comments, plus six hours of conversation, and four computer listings:

Frances E. Allen
Forest Baskett
G. V. Bochmann
Per Brinch Hansen
R. M. Burstall
Vinton Cerf
T. E. Cheatham, Jr.
John Cocke
Ole-Johan Dahl
Peter J. Denning
Edsger Dijkstra
James Eve
K. Friedenbach
Donald I. Good
Ralph E. Gorin
Leo Guibas
C. A. R. Hoare
Martin Hopkins
James J. Horning
B. M. Leavenworth
Henry F. Ledgard
Ralph L. London
Zohar Manna
W. M. McKeeman
Harlan D. Mills
Peter Naur
Kjell Overholt
James Peterson
W. Wesley Peterson
Mark Rain
John Reynolds
Barry K. Rosen
E. Satterthwaite, Jr.
D. V. Schorre
Jacob T. Schwartz
Richard L. Sites
Richard Sweet
Robert D. Tennent
Niklaus Wirth
M. Woodger
William A. Wulf
Charles T. Zahn

These people unselfishly devoted hundreds of man-hours to helping me revise the first draft; and I'm sorry that I wasn't able to reconcile all of their interesting points of view. In many places I have shamelessly used their suggestions without an explicit acknowledgment; this article is virtually a joint paper with 30 to 40 co-authors! However, any mistakes it contains are my own.

APPENDIX

In order to make some quantitative estimates of efficiency, I have counted memory references for data and instructions, assuming a multiregister computer without cache memory. Thus, each instruction costs one unit, plus another if it refers to memory; small constants and base addresses are assumed to be either part of the instruction or present in a register. Here are the code sequences developed for the first two examples, assuming that a typical assembly-language programmer or a very good optimizing compiler is at work.

LABEL	INSTRUCTION	COST	TIMES
Example 1:	$r1 \leftarrow 1$	1	1
	$r2 \leftarrow m$	2	1
	$r3 \leftarrow x$	2	1
	to test	1	1
loop:	$A[r1]: r3$	2	$n-a$
	to found **if** $=$	1	$n-a$
	$r1 \leftarrow r1+1$	1	$n-1$
test:	$r1: r2$	1	n
	to loop **if** $\leq$	1	n
notfound:	$m \leftarrow r1$	2	a
	$A[r1] \leftarrow r3$	2	a
	$B[r1] \leftarrow 0$	2	a
found:	$r4 \leftarrow B[r1]$	2	1
	$r4 \leftarrow r4+1$	1	1
	$B[r1] \leftarrow r4$	2	1

LABEL	INSTRUCTION	COST	TIMES
Example 2:	$r2 \leftarrow m$	2	1
	$r3 \leftarrow x$	2	1
	$A[r2+1] \leftarrow r3$	2	1
	$r1 \leftarrow 0$	1	1
loop:	$r1 \leftarrow r1+1$	1	n
	$A[r1]: r3$	2	n
	to loop **if** $\neq$	1	n
	$r1: r2$	1	1
	to found if $\leq$	1	1
notfound:	$m \leftarrow r1$	etc. as in Example 1.	

A traditional "90% efficient compiler" would render the first example as follows:

LABEL	INSTRUCTION	COST	TIMES
Example 1:	$r1 \leftarrow 1$	1	1
	to test	1	1
incr:	$r1 \leftarrow i$	2	$n-1$
	$r1 \leftarrow r1+1$	1	$n-1$
test:	$r1 : m$	2	n
	to notfound **if** $>$	1	n
	$i \leftarrow r1$	2	$n-a$
	$r2 \leftarrow A[r1]$	2	$n-a$
	$r2 : x$	2	$n-a$
	to found **if** $=$	1	$n-a$
	to incr	1	$n-1$
notfound:	$r1 \leftarrow m$	2	a
	$r1 \leftarrow r1 + 1$	1	a
	$i \leftarrow r1$	2	a
	$m \leftarrow r1$	2	a
	$r1 \leftarrow x$	2	a
	$r2 \leftarrow i$	2	a
	$A[r2] \leftarrow r1$	2	a
	$B[r2] \leftarrow 0$	2	a
found:	$r1 \leftarrow i$	2	1
	$r2 \leftarrow B[r1]$	2	1
	$r2 \leftarrow r2+1$	1	1
	$B[r1] \leftarrow r2$	2	1

***

Answer to PL/I Problem, page 110.

The variable I is increased before FOUND is tested. One way to fix the program is to insert "I = I − FOUND;" before the last statement.

***

BIBLIOGRAPHY

[1] ASHCROFT, EDWARD, AND MANNA, ZOHAR. "The translation of 'go to' programs to 'while' programs," *Proc. IFIP Congress 1971* Vol. 1, North-Holland Publ. Co., Amsterdam, The Netherlands, 1972, 250–255.

[2] BAKER, CHARLES L. "Review of D. D. McCracken, *Digital computer programming*," *Math. Comput.* 11 (1957), 298–305.

[3] BAKER, F. TERRY, AND MILLS, HARLAN D. "Chief programmer teams," *Datamation* 19, 12 (December 1973), 58–61.

[4] BARRON, D. W. *Recursive techniques in programming*, American Elsevier, New York, 1968, 64 pp.

[5] BAUER, F. L. "A philosophy of programming," University of London Special Lectures in Computer Science (October 1973): Lecture notes published by Math. Inst., Tech. Univ. of Munich, Germany.

[6] BERRY, DANIEL M. "Loops with normal and abnormal exits," *Modeling and Measurement Note 23*, Computer Science Department, Univ. California, Los Angeles, Calif. 1974, 39 pp.

[7] BOCHMANN, G. V. "Multiple exits from a loop without the GOTO," *Comm. ACM 16*, 7 (July 1973), 443–444.

[8] BÖHM, CORRADO AND JACOPINI, GUISEPPE. "Flow-diagrams, Turing machines, and languages with only two formation rules," *Comm. ACM 9*, 5 (May 1966), 366–371.

[9] BROWN, JOHN R. "In memoriam . . .", unpublished note, January 1974.

[10] BRUNO J., AND STIEGLITZ, K. "The expression of algorithms by charts," *J. ACM* **19**, 3 (July 1972), 517–525.

[11] BURKHARD, W. A. "Nonrecursive tree traversal algorithms," in *Proc. 7th Annual Princeton Conf. on Information Sciences and Systems*, Princeton Univ. Press, Princeton, N.J., 1973, 403–405.

[12] CHEATHAM, T. E., JR., AND WEGBREIT, BEN. "A laboratory for the study of automating programming," in *Proc. AFIPS 1972 Spring Joint Computer Conf.*, Vol. **40**, AFIPS Press, Montvale, N.J., 1972, 11–21.

[13] CLARK, R. LAWRENCE. "A linguistic contribution to GOTO-less programming," *Datamation* **19**, 12 (December 1973), 62–63.

[14] CLINT, M., AND HOARE, C. A. R. "Program proving: jumps and functions," *Acta Informatica* **1**, 3 (1972), 214–224.

[15] COOPER, D. C. "The equivalence of certain computations," *Computer J.* **9**, 1 (May 1966), 45–52.

[16] COOPER, D. C. "Böhm and Jacopini's reduction of flow charts," *Comm. ACM* **10**, 8 (August 1967), 463, 473.

[17] DAHL, O.-J., DIJKSTRA, E. W., AND HOARE, C. A. R. *Structured programming*, Academic Press, London, England, 1972, 220 pp.

[18] DARLINGTON, J., AND BURSTALL, R. M. "A system which automatically improves programs," in *Proc. 3rd Interntl. Conf. on Artificial Intelligence*, Stanford Univ., Stanford, Calif., 1973, 479–485.

[19] DE MARNEFFE, PIERRE-ARNOUL. "Holon programming: A survey," Universite de Liege, Service Informatique, Liege, Belgium, 1973, 135 pp.

[20] DIJKSTRA, E. W. "Recursive programming," *Numerische Mathematik* **2**, 5 (1960), 312–318.

[21] DIJKSTRA, E. W. "Programming considered as a human activity," in *Proc. IFIP Congress 1965*, North-Holland Publ. Co., Amsterdam, The Netherlands, 1965, 213–217.

[22] DIJKSTRA, E. W. "A constructive approach to the problem of program correctness," *BIT* **8**, 3 (1968), 174–186.

[23] DIJKSTRA, E. W. "Go to statement considered harmful," *Comm. ACM* **11**, 3 (March 1968), 147–148, 538, 541. [There are two instances of pages 147–148 in this volume; the *second* 147–148 is relevant here.]

[24] DIJKSTRA, E. W. "Solution of a problem in concurrent programming control," *Comm. ACM* **9**, 9 (September 1968), 569.

[25] DIJKSTRA, E. W. "Structured programming," in *Software engineering techniques*, J. N. Buxton and B. Randell [Eds.] NATO Scientific Affairs Division, Brussels, Belgium, 1970, 84–88.

[26] DIJKSTRA, E. W. "EWD316: A short introduction to the art of programming," Technical University Eindhoven, The Netherlands, August 1971, 97 pp.

[27] DIJKSTRA, E. W. "The humble programmer," *Comm. ACM* **15**, 10 (October 1972), 859–866.

[28] DIJKSTRA, E. W. "Prospects for a better programming language," in *High level languages*, C. Boon [Ed]., Infotech State of the Art Report 7, 1972, 217–232.

[29] DIJKSTRA, E. W. personal communication, January 3, 1973.

[30] DIJKSTRA, E. W. personal communication, November 19, 1973.

[31] DIJKSTRA, E. W. personal communication, January 30, 1974.

[32] DONALDSON, JAMES R. "Structured programming," *Datamation* **19**, 12 (December 1973), 52–54.

[33] DYLAN, BOB. *Blonde on blonde*, record album produced by Bob Johnston, Columbia Records, New York, March 1966, Columbia C2S 841.

[34] GILL, STANLEY. "Automatic computing: Its problems and prizes," *Computer J.* **8**, 3 (October 1965), 177–189.

[35] HENDERSON, P. AND SNOWDON, R. "An experiment in structured programming," *BIT* **12**, 1 (1972), 38–53.

[36] HOARE, C. A. R. "Quicksort," *Computer J.* **5**, 1 (1962), 10–15.

[37] HOARE, C. A. R. "An axiomatic approach to computer programming," *Comm. ACM* **12**, 10 (October 1969), 576–580, 583.

[38] HOARE, C. A. R. "Proof of a program: FIND," *Comm. ACM* **14**, 1 (January 1971), 39–45.

[39] HOARE, C. A. R. "A note on the for statement," *BIT* **12**, 3 (1972), 334–341.

[40] HOARE, C. A. R. "Prospects for a better programming language," in *High level languages*, C. Boon [Ed.], Infotech State of the Art Report 7, 1972, 327–343.

[41] HOARE, C. A. R., AND WIRTH, N. "An axiomatic definition of the programming language PASCAL," *Acta Informatica* **2**, 4 (1973), 335–355.

[42] HOARE, C. A. R. "Hints for programming language design," Computer Science report STAN-CS-74-403, Stanford Univ., Stanford, Calif., January 1974, 29 pp.

[43] HOPKINS, MARTIN E. "Computer aided software design," in *Software engineering techniques*, J. N. Buxton and B. Randell [Eds.] NATO Scientific Affairs Division, Brussels, Belgium, 1970, 99–101.

[44] HOPKINS, MARTIN E. "A case for the GOTO," *Proc. ACM Annual Conference* Boston, Mass., August 1972, 787–790.

[45] HULL, T. E. "Would you believe structured FORTRAN?" *SIGNUM Newsletter* **8**, 4 (October 1973), 13–16.

[46] INGALLS, DAN. "The execution time profile as a programming tool," in *Compiler optimization*, 2d Courant Computer Science Symposium, Randall Rustin [Ed.], Prentice-Hall, Englewood Cliffs, N. J., 1972, 107–128.

[47] KELLEY, ROBERT A., AND WALTERS, JOHN R. "APLGOL-2, a structured programming system for APL," IBM Palo Alto Scientific Center report 320-3318 (August 1973), 29 pp.

[48] KLEENE, S. C. "Representation of events in nerve nets," in *Automata Studies*, C. E. Shannon and J. McCarthy [Eds.], Princeton University Press, Princeton, N.J., 1956, 3–40.

[49] KNUTH, DONALD E. "RUNCIBLE—Algebraic translation on a limited computer," *Comm. ACM* **2**, 11 (November, 1959), 18–21.

[There is a bug in the flowchart. The arc labeled "2" from the box labeled "θ:" in the upper left corner should go to the box labeled $R_M = 8003$.]

[50] KNUTH, DONALD E. *Fundamental algorithms, The art of computer programming*, Vol. 1, Addison-Wesley, Reading, Mass. 1968 2d ed., 1973, 634 pp

[51] KNUTH, DONALD E. "An empirical study of FORTRAN programs," *Software—Practice and Experience* 1, 2 (April–June 1971), 105–133.

[52] KNUTH, DONALD E., AND FLOYD, ROBERT W. "Notes on avoiding 'go to' statements," *Information Processing Letters* 1, 1 (February 1971), 23–31, 177.

[53] KNUTH, DONALD E. "George Forsythe and the development of Computer Science," *Comm. ACM* 15, 8 (August 1972), 721–726.

[54] KNUTH, DONALD E. *Sorting and searching, The art of computer programming*, Vol. 3, Addison-Wesley, Reading, Mass., 1973, 722 pp.

[55] KNUTH, DONALD E. "A review of 'structured programming'," Stanford Computer Science Department report STAN-CS-73-371, Stanford Univ., Stanford, Calif., June 1973, 25 pp.

[56] KNUTH, DONALD E., AND SZWARCFITER, JAYME L. "A structured program to generate all topological sorting arrangements," *Information Processing Letters* 2, 6 (April 1974) 153–157.

[57] KOSARAJU, S. RAO. "Analysis of structured programs," *Proc. Fifth Annual ACM Symp. Theory of Computing*, (May 1973), 240–252; also in *J. Computer and System Sciences*, 9, 3 (December 1974).

[58] LANDIN, P. J. "A correspondence between Algol 60 and Church's lambda-notation: part I," *Comm. ACM* 8, 2 (February 1965), 89–101.

[59] LANDIN, P. J. "The next 700 programming languages," *Comm. ACM* 9, 3 (March 1966), 157–166.

[60] LEAVENWORTH, B. M. "Programming with(out) the GOTO," *Proc. ACM Annual Conference*, Boston, Mass., August 1972, 782–786.

[61] MANNA, ZOHAR, AND WALDINGER, RICHARD J. "Towards automatic program synthesis," in Symposium on Semantics of Algorithmic Languages, *Lecture Notes in Mathematics* 188, E. Engeler [Ed.], Springer-Verlag, New York, 1971, 270–310.

[62] MCCARTHY, JOHN. "Recursive functions of symbolic expressions and their computation by machine, part I," *Comm. ACM* 3, 4 (April 1960), 184–195.

[63] MCCARTHY, JOHN. "Towards a mathematical science of computation," in *Proc. IFIP Congress 1962, Munich, Germany*, North-Holland Publ. Co., Amsterdam, The Netherlands, 1963, 21–28.

[64] MCCRACKEN, DANIEL D. "Revolution in programming," *Datamation* 19, 12 (December 1973), 50–52.

[65] MCKEEMAN, W. M.; HORNING, J. J.; AND WORTMAN, D. B. *A compiler generator*, Prentice-Hall, Englewood Cliffs, N. J., 1970, 527 pp.

[66] MILLAY, EDNA ST. VINCENT. "Elaine"; cf. Bartlett's *Familiar Quotations*.

[67] MILLER, EDWARD F., JR., AND LINDAMOOD, GEORGE E. "Structured programming: top-down approach," *Datamation* 19, 12 (December 1973), 55–57.

[68] MILLS, H. D. "Top-down programming in large systems," in *Debugging techniques in large systems*, Randall Rustin [Ed.], Prentice-Hall, Englewood Cliffs, N. J., 1971, 41–55.

[69] MILLS, H. D. "Mathematical foundations for structured programming," report FSC 72-6012, IBM Federal Systems Division, Gaithersburg, Md. (February 1972), 62 pp.

[70] MILLS, H. D. "How to write correct programs and know it," report FSC 73-5008, IBM Federal Systems Division, Gaithersburg, Md. (1973), 26 pp.

[71] NASSI, I. R., AND AKKOYUNLU, E. A. "Verification techniques for a hierarchy of control structures," Tech. report 26, Dept. of Computer Science, State Univ. of New York, Stony Brook, New York (January 1974), 48 pp.

[72] NAUR, PETER [Ed.] "Report on the algorithmic language ALGOL 60," *Comm. ACM* 3, 5 (May 1960), 299–314.

[73] NAUR, PETER. "Go to statements and good Algol style," *BIT* 3, 3 (1963), 204–208.

[74] NAUR, PETER. "Program translation viewed as a general data processing problem," *Comm. ACM* 9, 3 (March 1966), 176–179.

[75] NAUR, PETER. "An experiment on program development," *BIT* 12, 3 (1972), 347–365.

[76] PAGER, D. "Some notes on speeding up certain loops by software, firmware, and hardware means," in *Computers and automata*, Jerome Fox [Ed.], John Wiley & Sons, New York 1972, 207–213; also in *IEEE Trans. Computers*, C-21, 1 (January 1972), 97–100.

[77] PETERSON, W. W.; KASAMI, T.; AND TOKURA, N. "On the capabilities of **while, repeat**, and **exit** statements," *Comm. ACM* 16, 8 (August 1973), 503–512.

[78] PETERSON, W. WESLEY. personal communication, April 2, 1974.

[79] RAIN, MARK AND HOLAGER, PER. "The present most recent final word about labels in MARY," *Machine Oriented Languages Bulletin* 1, Trondheim, Norway (October 1972), 18–26.

[80] REID, CONSTANCE. *Hilbert*, Springer-Verlag, New York, 1970, 290 pp.

[81] REYNOLDS, JOHN. "Fundamentals of structured programming," Systems and Info. Sci. 555 course notes, Syracuse Univ., Syracuse, N.Y., Spring 1973.

[82] SATTERTHWAITE, E. H. "Debugging tools for high level languages," *Software—Practice and Experience* 2, 3 (July–September 1972), 197–217.

[83] SCHNECK, P. B., AND ANGEL, ELLINOR. "A FORTRAN to FORTRAN optimizing compiler," *Computer J.* 16, 4 (1973), 322–330.

[84] SCHORRE, D. V. "META-II—a syntax-directed compiler writing language," *Proc. ACM National Conference*, Philadelphia, Pa., 1964, paper D1.3.

[85] SCHORRE, D. V. "Improved organization for procedural languages," Tech. memo TM 3086/002/00, Systems Development Corp., Santa Monica, Calif., September 8, 1966, 8 pp.

[86] SHIGO, O.; SHIMOMURA, T.; FUJIBAYASHI S.; AND MAEJIMA, T. "SPOT: an experimental system for structured programming" (in Japanese), *Conference Record*, Information Processing Society of Japan, 1973. [Translation available from the authors, Nippon Electric Company Ltd., Kawasaki, Japan.]

[87] STRACHEY, C. "Varieties of programming language," in *High level languages*, C. Boon [Ed.], Infotech State of the Art Report 7, 1972, 345–362.

[88] STRONG, H. R. JR. "Translating recursion equations into flowcharts," *J. Computer and System Sciences* **5**, 3 (June 1971), 254–285.

[89] TEITELMAN, W. "Toward a programming laboratory," in *Software Engineering Techniques*, J. N. Buxton and B. Randall [Eds.], NATO Scientific Affairs Division, Brussels, Belgium, 1970, 137–149.

[90] TEITELMAN, W. et al. "INTERLISP reference manual," Xerox Palo Alto Research Center, Palo Alto, Calif., and Bolt Beranek and Newman, Inc., 1974.

[91] WALKER, S. A., AND STRONG, H. R. "Characterizations of flowchartable recursions," *J. Computer and System Sciences* **7**, 4 (August 1973), 404–447.

[92] WEGNER, EBERHARD. "Tree-structured programs," *Comm. ACM* **16**, 11 (November 1973), 704–705.

[93] WEINBERG, GERALD M. "The psychology of improved programming performance," *Datamation* **17**, 11 (November 1972), 82–85.

[94] WIRTH, N. "On certain basic concepts of programming languages," Stanford Computer Science Report CS 65, Stanford, Calif. (May 1967), 30 pp.

[95] WIRTH, N. "PL 360, a programming language for the 360 computers," *J. ACM* **15**, 1 (January 1968), 37–74.

[96] WIRTH, N. "Program development by stepwise refinement," *Comm. ACM* **14**, 4 (April 1971), 221–227.

[97] WIRTH, N. "The programming language Pascal," *Acta Informatica* **1**, 1 (1971), 35–63.

[98] WULF, W. A.; RUSSELL, D. B.; AND HABERMANN, A. N. "Bliss: A language for systems programming," *Comm. ACM* **14**, 12 (December 1971), 780–790.

[99] WULF, W. A. "Progamming without the goto," *Information Processing 71, Proc. IFIP Congress*, Vol. 1, North-Holland Publ. Co., Amsterdam, The Netherlands, 1971, 408–413.

[100] WULF, W. A. "A case against the GOTO," *Proc. ACM 1972 Annual Conference*, Boston, Mass. (August 1972), 791–797.

[101] WULF, W. A.; JOHNSON, RICHARD K.; WEINSTOCK, CHARLES P.; AND HOBBS, STEVEN O. "The design of an optimizing compiler," Computer Science Department report, Carnegie-Mellon Univ., Pittsburgh, Pa., (December 1973), 103 pp.

[102] ZAHN, CHARLES T. "A control statement for natural top-down structured programming," presented at Symposium on Programming Languages, Paris, 1974.

Abstraction and Verification in Alphard: Defining and Specifying Iteration and Generators

Mary Shaw and William A. Wulf
Carnegie-Mellon University

Ralph L. London
University of Southern California

Reprinted from *Communications of the ACM*, August 1977, pp. 553-564. Copyright 1977 Association for Computing Machinery, Inc. Reprinted by permission.

The Alphard "form" provides the programmer with a great deal of control over the implementation of abstract data types. In this paper the abstraction techniques are extended from simple data representation and function definition to the iteration statement, the most important point of interaction between data and the control structure of the language itself. A means of specializing Alphard's loops to operate on abstract entities without explicit dependence on the representation of those entities is introduced. Specification and verification techniques that allow the properties of the generators for such iterations to be expressed in the form of proof rules are developed. Results are obtained that for common special cases of these loops are essentially identical to the corresponding constructs in other languages. A means of showing that a generator will terminate is also provided.

Key Words and Phrases: abstraction and representation, abstract data types, assertions, control specialization, correctness, generators, invariants, iteration statements, modular decomposition, program specifications, programming languages, programming methodology, proofs of correctness, types, verification
CR Categories: 4.20, 5.24

Introduction

This paper is one in a series describing the Alphard programming system and its associated verification methods. It presumes that the reader is familiar with the material in [16, 17], particularly the use of **forms** for abstraction and the verification methodology for **forms.** The summary of the verification methodology in the Appendix also provides the reader with a brief glimpse of **forms.**

The primary goal of the **form** mechanism is to permit and encourage the localization of information about a user-defined *abstraction.* Specifically, the mechanism is designed to localize both verification and modification. Other reports on Alphard have discussed ways to isolate specific information about representation and implementation; in this paper we deal with localizing another kind of information.

Suppose that S is a "set-of-integers" and that we wish to compute the sum of the integers in this set. In most contemporary programming languages, we would have to write a statement such as

sum ← 0; **for** i ← 1 **step** 1 **until** S.size **do** sum ← sum + S[i]

or possibly

p ← S; sum ← 0;
while p ≠ **nil do** (sum ← sum + p.value; p ← p.next)

or, if we knew that the set elements all lie in the range [lb..ub], we might write

sum ← 0; **for** i ← lb **to** ub **do if** i∈S **then** sum ← sum + i

None of these statements is really satisfactory. First, they all seem to imply an order to the summation, whereas the abstract computation does not. Next, the first statement strongly suggests a vector implementation of the set and the second a list implementation. (Although other implementations are not excluded, the resulting loops will probably be unacceptably inefficient.) The third statement does not suggest an implementation of the set, but may be too inefficient if the cardinality of the set is much smaller than ub − lb + 1.

It would be much better if we could write something like

sum ← 0; **for** x∈S **do** sum ← sum + x

which implies nothing about either the order of processing or the representation of sets. Except for notational differences, this latter example illustrates our goal. We want to encourage suppression of the details of how iteration over that abstract data structure is actually implemented. The difficulty in doing this is that the abstract objects are not predefined in Alphard. Hence it is the author of the abstraction who must specify the implementation of (the analog of) "x∈S."

We resolve the problem by separating the responsibility for defining the meaning of a loop into three parts: (1) Alphard defines the (fixed) syntax and the broad outline of the semantics. (2) The definition of the abstraction that is controlling the iteration fills in the details of the loop control (in particular, the algorithms for selecting the next element and terminating the loop). (3) The user supplies the loop body. Conventional languages provide only a small fixed number of alternatives (usually one) for the second part of this information. In Alphard it is supplied by the **form** that defines the abstraction; we say this part of the definition *specializes* the iteration statement to that abstraction. Related constructs appear in IPL-V as generators

[11] and in Lisp as the mapping functions [10, 15].

One of the major goals of Alphard is to provide mechanisms to support the use of good programming methodology. The rationale for generators given above is based on methodological considerations; that is, it is generally *good* to abstract from the implementation and hide its details. Generators permit us to do this for control constructs much as the **functions** in a **form** permit abstraction of operations [16, 17].

A second major goal is to provide the ability to specify precisely the effect of a program and then prove the program implements that specification. To meet this goal, we must provide more than just the language mechanism for generators: we must also provide both a way to specify their effects and a corresponding proof methodology. A natural means of doing this for **generators** is somewhat different from one for **functions**. Functions are naturally characterized by predicates which relate the state of the computation before their invocation to its state afterward. Generators, however, are not *invoked* in the usual sense; rather they are used to control the repeated execution of an arbitrary "body" of an iteration statement. Thus a natural specification of a generator is in terms of a "proof rule" which permits the effect of the entire iteration statement to be expressed.

This paper contains two strongly related components: First we introduce the language mechanism for generators; then we turn to the specification and verification of generators and of the iteration statements which use them. We begin with a digression on a language feature which is not discussed elsewhere, but is needed for the definition of generators. We then introduce the two Alphard iteration statements and show how they can be specialized by the user. One of these is an iteration construction designed for searching a series of values for an element with a desired property. It should replace most of the loop-exit **gotos** used in current languages. (Interlisp [14] contains a wide variety of iteration statements, one of which specializes to this construct.)

We obtain general proof rules for the two loop constructs and then state a series of simplifying assumptions that certain generators may satisfy. We obtain a corresponding series of proof rules whose simplicity increases with the restrictiveness of the assumptions we make about the generators. These assumptions lead both to rules that correspond directly to familiar rules for iteration (e.g. those of Pascal [4, 6]) and to simple rules for a substantial number of interesting abstract structures (e.g. those given by Hoare [2]).

Finally, we show how to use proof rules instead of functional descriptions to specify many of the **forms** which define generators. We also give a technique for showing that loops using a generator will halt (assuming the loop body terminates). We prove, with one application of this technique, that many common generators have this property.

Form Extensions

In this section we introduce another language facility which makes it more convenient to define certain abstractions and to manage the definitions after they are written. The facility allows a programmer to define one **form** as an *extension* of another. The new **form** will have most or all of the properties of the old one, plus some additional ones. (This mechanism is similar to, and derived from, the *class concatenation* mechanism of Simula [1].) We introduce this mechanism at this point because it is needed for generator definitions, which will be discussed in the next section.

The following skeletal **form** definition is an illustration of most of the major attributes of the extension mechanism:

```
form counter extends i: integer =
  beginform
  specifications
    initially counter = 1;
    inherits ⟨ =, ≠, <, >, ≤, ≥ ⟩;
    function
       inc(x: counter) . . .,
       dec(x: counter) . . .;
  representation
    init i ← 1;
  implementation
    body inc = x.i ← x.i + 1;
    body dec = x.i ← x.i − 1;
  endform
```

The general flavor of the mechanism is that the new abstraction, "counter" in this case, is to be an extension of a previously defined one called its *base type*, here "integer." As such, the new abstraction inherits the indicated properties specified for the base type and may appear in contexts where the base type was permitted (e.g. as an actual parameter where the formal specifies the base **form**). Further, the new abstraction has the additional properties specified in the extension **form**, "inc" and "dec" in this case.

Even though the newly defined **form** is an extension of another, the body of the new **form** is not granted access to the **representation** of the old one; the only access rights granted to the body of the new **form** are those defined in the **specifications** of the one being extended. Thus, although the extension may add (and delete, see below) properties of the extended abstraction, it *cannot* affect the correctness of its implementation, and we ned not reverify the properties of the original. (Indeed, since these properties are identical we do not demand that they even be specified.)

In this example, and indeed more generally, it is not desirable for *all* of the properties of the old abstraction to be inherited by the new one. The "⟨ ⟩" notation may be used as in [16, 17] to list the rights that the instantiation of the new abstraction is *allowed* to inherit. Thus the maximum set of rights permitted to the instantiation of a "counter" is the union of the inherited rights $(=, ≠, <, >, ≤, ≥)$ and the newly defined rights (inc and dec). Note in particular that assignment to a counter is *not* one of the inherited rights; thus the only way to achieve a side effect on a counter is through the operations "inc" and "dec." The *implementation* of the extension **form** may, of course, use all operations on the base type.

As a practical matter, the instantiation of the base **form** ("i" from "i: integer" in this example) may be considered a part of the **representation** part of the extended **form**. Note, however, that this need not be the entire **representation** part of the extension; in many cases the extension will involve additional data.

Iteration Constructs in Alphard

Alphard provides two iteration commands: The **for** statement is used for iteration over a complete data structure, and the **first** statement is used (primarily) for search loops. As mentioned above, each of these commands may be *specialized* for each use. Specialization information is provided through a standard interface called a *generator*. A generator is itself simply a **form**, but it must adhere to certain special requirements that make it mesh with the semantics of iteration statements:

(a) It must provide two functions (named &init and &next) with properties described below.

(b) Invocation of these functions in a prescribed order must produce a sequence of values to bind to the loop variable.[1]

(c) It must be an *extension* whose base type is the same as the type of the elements being supplied to the loop body.

Before we discuss generators intended for specific structures, we illustrate the use of the **for** and **first** statements with simple counting loops.

The "for" Statement

We shall begin with the **for** statement. The syntax for the statement is[2]

for x: gen(y) **while** β(x) **do** ST(x,y,z)

where β(x) is an expression, the statement ST(x,y,z) is the loop body, x is the instantiation of the generator "gen," y is the set of instantiation parameters to the generator, and z is the set of other variables used in the statement. The phrase "x: gen," which is our notational analog of the "x $\in$ S" in the introduction, means "bind x to an instantiation of the generator named gen intended specifically to generate the elements specified by y." Then x may appear free in β and ST; like any loop variable, x is rebound for each pass through the loop.

The meaning of the **for** loop is given by

begin local x: gen(y), π: boolean;
   π ← x.&init;
  while π *cand* β(x) **do**
    (ST(x,y,z); π ← x.&next)
end

Here, *cand* is the "conditional and" operator: "b_1 *cand* b_2" ≡ "**if** b_1 **then** b_2 **else** false." Also, β and ST are taken from the **for** statement, and x.&init and x.&next are functions supplied by the generator as described below.[3] The compiler-generated variable π is not accessible to the programmer.

One of the generators defined in Alphard's standard prelude is

upto(lb,ub: integer) **extends** k: integer

This generator produces the sequence of values ⟨lb, lb + 1, lb + 2, . . . , ub − 1, ub⟩, or the empty sequence if lb > ub. This generator, in combination with the **for** statement, provides the familiar "stepping" loop found in nearly all programming languages; for example, an Alphard loop for summing the integers from 1 to n is

sum ← 0; **for** j: upto(1, n) **do** sum ← sum + j

Note that *two* types are involved in this example. We said in earlier contexts that the notation "j: upto(. . .)" means "bind j to an instantiation of upto." This implies that the type of j is "upto." However, notice that j is used in the body of the loop as though it were an integer. This is possible because of the extension mechanism described in the previous section. Although the apparent type of j is upto, **form** upto extends integers, inheriting all operations except assignment (the definition is given in the next section). As a result, integer operations on j are legal and behave as expected.

The "first" Statement

One of the common uses of loops is for searching a sequence of values for the first one which passes some test. The use of an ordinary loop construct for this purpose is probably the most common cause of *necessary* **gotos** in conventional programming languages: Once the test has been satisfied, there is no reason to continue executing the loop. Since this case occurs so often, Alphard provides a special syntax for it. We may write[4]

first x: gen(y) **suchthat** β(x) **then** S_1(x,y,z) **else** S_2(y,z)

where S_1 and S_2 are statements and β is an expression. Again, x is an instantiation of generator gen and may appear free in β and S_1 (but *not* in S_2). The meaning of the **first** loop is given by the statement

---

[1] Although we call this a "loop variable," it will not normally be possible to alter its value within the loop body.

[2] Either "**for** x: gen(y)" or "**while** β(x)" may be omitted, yielding the pure **while** and pure **for** statements, respectively. If "**while** β(x)" is omitted, β is assumed to be identically true. If "**for** x: gen(y)" is omitted, no x is declared or set, β and ST (clearly) cannot depend on x, and &init and &next are assumed to be the constant true. β may depend on y and z in addition to x; for simplicity we write β(x) instead of the more exact β(x, y, z).

[3] In Alphard, certain functions are given names beginning with "&." These are usually functions provided by the user to perform operations that correspond to special constructs of the language. Outside the **form** in which they are defined, they may *not* be called by user programs. In this case, the **for** loop expects to call functions named &init and &next with certain specified properties. Alphard prevents a user from calling them explicitly — to skip iterations in a loop, for example.

[4] Either "**then** S_1" or "**else** S_2" may be omitted; an omitted clause is assumed to denote the empty statement.

```
begin label λ;
  begin local x: gen(y), π: boolean;
    π ← x.&init;
    while π do
      if β(x) then (S₁(x,y,z); goto λ) else π ← x.&next
  end;
  S₂(y,z);
λ: end
```

As above, the compiler-generated names π and λ are not accessible to the programmer.

In [16] we presented a subroutine to compare two vectors of arbitrary (but identical) types and index sets. The subroutine presented there was phrased in terms of an Algol-like **for** loop. It can now be written in real Alphard by using the **first** statement[5]:

```
function eqvecs(A, B: vector(?t ⟨≠⟩, ?lb, ?ub))
  returns (eq: boolean) =
  first i: upto(lb,ub) suchthat A[i] ≠ B[i]
  then eq ← false
  else eq ← true
```

It does not matter what the bounds of the two vectors are, as long as they are the same. In this case, we are not relying on the procedure return or an explicit escape to terminate the loop early in the case of inequality; that is handled by the **first** statement. The proof of "eqvecs" will be given in a later section.

We have introduced Alphard loop constructs by comparing them to simple counting loops. This is the first step toward solving the problem of sequencing over arbitrary structures under the control of the defining type. We now show how generators and loops are verified.

Defining and Verifying Generators

We said that a generator is a **form** which supplies special functions and performs a sequence of bindings to the control variable of the loop. In this section we show how a generator is defined and invoked, still using "upto" as an example. We first present its definition, then add assertions, verify it as a **form**, and establish its special properties as a generator.

The definition of the "upto" generator, without verification information, is

```
form upto(lb,ub: integer) extends k: integer =
  beginform
  specifications
    inherits ⟨allbut ←⟩;
    function
      &init(u: upto) returns b:boolean,
      &next(u: upto) returns b:boolean;
  implementation
    body &init = (u.k ← u.lb; b ← u.lb ≤ u.ub);
    body &next = (u.k ← u.k + 1; b ← u.k ≤ u.ub);
  endform
```

---

[5] In this example the function specification and the function body are given as one declaration. This is an obvious abbreviation of the notation used elsewhere. The *?identifier* notation is used to indicate that the values of these parameters must be identical for A and B and that specific values will be supplied implicitly with the vectors. This is explained in [16, 17].

Since no variables other than k are needed, the **representation** part is empty at this point. This **form** extends integers, but does not pass along the right to assign to an "upto"[6]; this prevents the user from changing the loop variable during the iteration.

Using this **form** and the meaning of the **for** statement given in the previous section, we can exhibit a loop that corresponds to the expansion of the "upto" functions in the statement for summing integers. This code is, of course, only suggestive, but it illustrates an expansion which a compiler might reasonably produce. Note that an obvious optimization has been applied; later, when we exhibit the formal specifications of "upto," the value of the iteration variable x will turn out to be irrelevant when &init or &next returns false.

```
sum ← 0;
begin
  local x: upto(lb,ub);
    x ← x.lb;
    while x ≤ x.ub do (sum ← sum + κ; κ ← x + 1);
end
```

Since "upto" is a **form**, we can verify the **form** properties as described in [16, 17] and summarized in the Appendix. With verification information added in italics, the definition of "upto" becomes

```
form upto(lb,ub: integer) extends k: integer =
  beginform
  specifications
    requires true;
    inherits ⟨allbut ←⟩;
    let upto = [lb..ub] where lb ≤ ub ⊃ upto =
      [lb..k − 1][k][k + 1..ub];
    invariant true;
    initially true;
    function
      &init(u: upto) returns b:boolean
        post (b ≡ lb ≤ ub) ∧ (b ⊃ lb = k ≤ ub),
      &next(u: upto) returns b:boolean
        pre lb ≤ k ≤ ub
        post (b ≡ k' < ub) ∧ (b ⊃ k = k' + 1 ∧ lb ≤ k ≤ ub);
  representation
    rep(k) = if lb ≤ ub then [lb..k − 1][k][k + 1..ub] else [];
    invariant true;
  implementation
    body &init out (b ≡ lb ≤ ub) ∧ (b ⊃ lb = k ≤ ub) =
      (u.k. ← u.lb; b ← u.lb ≤ u.ub);
    body &next in lb ≤ k ≤ ub out (b ≡ k' < ub)
      ∧ (b ⊃ k = k' + 1 ∧ lb ≤ k ≤ ub) =
      (u.k ← u.k + 1; b ← u.k ≤ u.ub);
  endform
```

The abstract specifications describe an "upto" as an interval [lb..ub]; since the **form** upto extends the integer k, a direct reference to a loop variable of type upto will access k, the current value of the loop counter. We shall find it useful later to view the upto as the concatenation of the interval already processed ([lb..k − 1]), the current element ([k]), and the interval yet to be

---

[6] The phrase "**allbut** ←" means that all integer functions *except* ← are applicable to the upto.

generated ($[k + 1..ub]$). Either k stays between the endpoints of the interval $[lb..ub]$ or the interval is empty. This is enforced by the phrase $lb \leq k \leq ub$ which appears in the **pre** condition for &next and both **post** conditions. The notation k' denotes the value of k upon entry to &next.

Note that no promise about the value of k is made before the loop starts (i.e. before &init is called) or after it has run to completion (either &init or &next returns false). The **rep** function shows how an interval is represented by its two endpoints and the loop variable. The **post** condition on &init guarantees that the first element generated is lb, but only if $lb \leq ub$. The **pre** condition on &next prevents &next from being executed when there is no valid current element (in particular, &init must be called first). The **post** condition on &next guarantees that generated values are consecutive and that the generator stops at ub.

For "upto" the four steps which are required to verify the **form** properties are quite simple. (Note that the "u." qualification on u.lb, u.k, and u.ub is omitted for simplicity.)

For the **form**
1. Representation validity
   Show: true $\supset$ true
   Proof: clear
2. Initialization
   Show: true { } true $\wedge$ true
   Proof: clear

For the function &init
3. Concrete operation
   Show: true $\{k \leftarrow lb; b \leftarrow lb \leq ub\}$
   $(b \equiv lb \leq ub) \wedge (b \supset lb = k \leq ub)$
   Proof: Using the assignment axiom, the expression becomes
   true $\supset$ ($lb \leq ub \equiv lb \leq ub) \wedge (lb \leq ub \supset lb = lb \leq ub)$
   which surely holds.
4. Relation between abstract and concrete
   Corresponding abstract and concrete assertions are identical and the **rep** function performs a direct mapping, so the proofs are clear.

For the function &next
3. Concrete operation
   Show: $lb \leq k \leq ub \{k \leftarrow k + 1; b \leftarrow k \leq ub\}$
   $(b \equiv k' < ub) \wedge (b \supset k = k' + 1 \wedge lb \leq k \leq ub)$

   Proof: With the assignment axiom, the expression becomes
   $lb \leq k \leq ub \supset (k + 1 \leq ub \equiv k' < ub) \wedge$
   $(k + 1 \leq ub \supset k + 1 = k' + 1 \wedge lb \leq k + 1 \leq ub)$
   which holds because $k' = k$ is an implicit hypothesis of the antecedent.
4. Relation between abstract and concrete
   Same as &init.4.

Proof Rules for Loops

In this section we consider the verification of Alphard's two iteration constructs, **for** and **first**. Specifically, we develop proof rules for these statements, discovering in the process certain desirable properties for **forms** which are intended to be used as generators. Some of these properties will be required of all genera-

tors; others will be considered optional, but their presence will substantially simplify proof rules and proofs.

The development will proceed as follows. First we consider a proof rule for the **for** statement which makes minimal assumptions about the generator. This rule is derived directly from the statement's meaning as given earlier. As a consequence, it is rather bulky. Then we make a small number of basic assumptions about the generator. For the purposes of this paper, these assumptions will be required of all generators and hence will have to be discharged when the generator is verified as a **form**. They will allow us to simplify substantially the proof rules for the **for** and **first** statements. Next we consider a further set of assumptions about generators; these assumptions are not mandatory, but they are satisfied by typical generators. These will allow us to obtain still simpler proof rules for particular generators. Finally, we consider the properties that a generator must have in order to be a *terminating generator*.

Development of the "for" Rule
Suppose that we wish to prove

P{**for** x: gen(y) .**while** $\beta(x)$ **do** ST(x,y,z) | I(x,y,z)}Q

where x, y, and z are as defined earlier and the notation "P {loop | I} Q" is used to denote "P {loop} Q using I as the loop assertion (invariant) placed *after* the loop body." Further, suppose that we make only the minimal assumptions about the **form** "gen," namely that it has been verified as a **form** and that it supplies two functions, &init and &next, each of which takes a single parameter of type gen and returns a boolean result. We also assume that $\beta(x)$ has no side effects. We adopt the following notation in the iteration proof rules:

G = abstract invariant of the generator. G may depend on x and y but not on z.

β_{req} = the usual **requires** clause of the generator, stating restrictions on y so that the generator can be instantiated.[7]

$\beta_{f,j}$ = the j-condition for generator function f; e.g. $\beta_{init.post}$ is the post condition for &init. $\beta_{f,j}$ depends on x and y only.

$x_0, \ldots, x_p$ denotes the previously generated values of x, if any.

Since the generator has been verified as a **form**, we know

$G \wedge \beta_{init.pre}\{\pi \leftarrow x.\&init\} \ G \wedge \beta_{init.post}$
$G \wedge \beta_{next.pre}\{\pi \leftarrow x.\&next\} \ G \wedge \beta_{next.post}$
$\beta_{req}\{init \ clause\} \ G$

where *init clause* denotes the **init** clause of the **representation** part.

The expansion of

for x: gen(y) **while** $\beta(x)$ **do** ST(x,y,z)

as a standard **while** statement, including the assertions which will be required for verification in the most general case, is

---

[7] We conventionally use "β" to name predicates. Hence, e.g. β_{req} is unrelated to $\beta(x)$.

```
assert P ∧ β_req;
begin local x: gen(y), π: boolean;
assert P ∧ G ∧ β_init.pre;
π ← x.&init;
while π cand β(x) do
  begin
    ST(x,y,z);
    assert I ∧ G ∧ β_next.pre;
    π ← x.&next;
  end;
end;
assert Q
```

We shall give from this expansion a proof rule for the most general Alphard **for** statement. The standard **while** rule is not directly applicable to this expansion because the loop-cutting assertion is located in the middle of the loop body rather than before the test. This assertion placement means the test does not always appear just before or just after an assertion; in two control paths through the expansion (the third and fifth lines in the proof rule below), the test π *cand* $\beta(x)$ appears between either the statements $\pi \leftarrow$ x.&init or $\pi \leftarrow$ x.&next and ST(x,y,z). To indicate in these paths that π *cand* $\beta(x)$ may be assumed between the statements, the **assume** clause is introduced.[8] Its proof rule is

$$\frac{P \wedge Q \supset R}{P \ \{\textbf{assume } Q\} \ R}.$$

Using the **assume** clause and considering the five control paths between assertions, we have the general proof rule for the **for** statement,

$$
\begin{array}{l}
P \wedge \beta_{req} \ \{init\ clause\} \ P \wedge \beta_{init.pre} \\[2pt]
P \wedge G \wedge \beta_{init.pre} \ \{\pi \leftarrow \text{x.\&init}\} \ \neg\,(\pi \wedge \beta(x)) \supset Q \\[2pt]
P \wedge G \wedge \beta_{init.pre} \ \{\pi \leftarrow \text{x.\&init}; \ \textbf{assume } \pi \wedge \beta(x); \ ST(x,y,z)\} \\
\hfill I \wedge G \wedge \beta_{next.pre} \\[2pt]
I \wedge G \wedge \beta_{next.pre} \ \{\pi \leftarrow \text{x.\&next}\} \ \neg\,(\pi \wedge \beta(x)) \supset Q \\[2pt]
I \wedge G \wedge \beta_{next.pre} \ \{\pi \leftarrow \text{x.\&next}; \ \textbf{assume } \pi \wedge \beta(x); \ ST(x,y,z)\} \\
\hfill I \wedge G \wedge \beta_{next.pre}
\end{array}
$$
$$\overline{\qquad P \wedge \beta_{req} \ \{\textbf{for } x\colon \text{gen}(y) \ \textbf{while } \beta(x) \ \textbf{do} \ ST(x,y,z) \mid I\}Q \qquad}$$

This formulation, because of its generality, may appear formidable. The main difficulty appears to be that the *init clause*, the two generator functions, and the loop body may each change y in various ways even though P and I hold at the places required by the rule. The *init clause* and the generator functions are therefore involved in the verification of each use of a generator. However, the following three reasonable assumptions about the generator will simplify matters a good deal.

Basic Generator Assumptions

(a) The post conditions on &init and &next are of the form

$$(b \equiv \pi_i) \wedge \beta_i \quad \text{and} \quad (b \equiv \pi_n) \wedge \beta_n,$$

respectively, where b is the result parameter of these functions.

(b) $G \supset \beta_{init.pre}$, $G \wedge (\pi_i \wedge \beta_{init.post} \vee \pi_n \wedge \beta_{next.post}) \supset \beta_{next.pre}$.

(c) The *init clause* and the functions &init and &next terminate. (This does not simplify the proof rule. It is, however, a desirable property, and it becomes especially relevant in the discussion of generator termination below.)

(d) The generator and the loop body are *independent*. That is, for arbitrary predicates R and S

R(y,z) {*init clause*} R(y,z),
R(y,z) {$\pi \leftarrow$ x.&init} R(y,z),
R(y,z) {$\pi \leftarrow$ x.&next} R(y,z), and
S(x,y) {ST(x,y,z)} S(x,y).

Point (a) is a minor restriction and can be checked syntactically. Point (b) requires two proofs. The first is usually trivial since $\beta_{init.pre}$ is generally omitted (defaulted to true) and $\beta_{next.pre}$ is usually included in both **post** conditions. G may often be strong enough by itself, but we may not want to commit the generator to provide a value at all times. In the latter case we therefore require that &init and &next make it possible for &next to be executed. Point (c) can be proved independently of the use of the generator. The proofs should usually be easy (see the section below on termination).

Point (d) requires four proofs; in the typical case, however, the first three are trivial. Because of the scope restrictions mentioned in [16, 17], the only ways the *init clause*, &init, or &next could affect the predicate R(y,z) are through y, which is explicitly passed as a parameter to the **form** gen, and through side-effect-producing operations of &init and &next. Thus the proof can be carried out locally for the generator definition—generally by inspection. The fourth proof is more difficult. Because of the scope restrictions, the only way that the loop body could affect the loop variable x is for the generator to provide a function which could have a side effect on x (for example, by exporting assignment rights). This proof should be local to the generator definition. However, the independence of y from ST cannot in general be shown for the generator and must be treated as a restriction on its use.

Simplified Rules for Iteration Statements

If the generator and its use meet the four basic generator assumptions given above, a simplified proof rule applies to the **for** statement[9]:

$$
\frac{
\begin{array}{c}
G \wedge [P \wedge \beta_i \wedge \neg(\pi_i \wedge \beta(x)) \vee I \wedge \beta_n \wedge \neg(\pi_n \wedge \beta(x))] \supset Q \\
G \wedge \beta(x) \wedge [P \wedge \beta_i \wedge \pi_i \vee I \wedge \beta_n \wedge \pi_n] \ \{ST(x,y,z)\}I
\end{array}
}{
P \wedge \beta_{req} \ \{\textbf{for } x\colon \text{gen}(y) \ \textbf{while } \beta(x) \ \textbf{do} \ ST(x,y,z) \mid I\}Q
}
$$

Note that the first line establishes that Q holds when (if) the loop terminates—which may happen immediately after the invocation of &init (handled by the first term of the disjunction in [ ]'s), or after an invocation

---

[8] The **assume** clause appears in [5, p. 164] as the "marked" assertion using the notation Q-if in place of **assume** Q.

[9] The justifications of this and the **first** rule, from the corresponding general rules and the basic generator assumptions, are given in [13].

of &next (handled by the second term of the disjunction). In both cases termination may result either because the relevant generator function returned false or because $\beta(x)$ failed — hence the terms of the form "$\neg(\pi \wedge \beta(x))$". The second line ensures that the invariant is established after each application of the loop body.

Under the same assumptions, the following proof rule applies to the **first** statement:

$$\frac{G \wedge P\, [\beta_i \wedge \pi_i \vee \beta_n \wedge \pi_n \wedge \neg\beta(x_0..x_p)] \wedge \beta(x)\, \{S_1(x,y,z)\}Q \qquad G \wedge P \wedge [\neg\pi_i \wedge \beta_i \vee \neg\pi_n \wedge \beta_n \wedge \neg\beta(x_0..x_p)]\, \{S_2(y,z)\}Q}{P \wedge \beta_{req}\{\textbf{first } x:\ gen(y)\ \textbf{suchthat}\ \beta(x)\ \textbf{then}\ S_1(x,y,z)\ \textbf{else}\ S_2(y,z)\}Q}$$

where "$\neg\beta(x_0..x_p)$" is an abbreviation for "$\neg\beta(x_0) \wedge \ldots \wedge \neg\beta(x_p)$." Note that the second line handles the "else" cases, where no match is found; the two terms of the disjunction are the case where the generator terminates immediately and the case where every element generated fails the **suchthat** test $\beta(x)$. The first line handles the case where a match is found. Note also that the presumed independence of the generator and the user program means that P is not affected by &init and &next.

Simplified Rules for Typical Generators

Most generators are far more stylized than the simple assumptions above require. The following assumptions about standard aggregates used in typical generators allow us to obtain proof rules of further simplicity.

Standard Aggregate Assumptions

(a) The additional abstraction provided by the generator is explicated in terms of an aggregate (of objects of the base type) for which the following are defined:

@ = an operator to combine (e.g. concatenate) two aggregates,
$\langle\rangle$ = the empty aggregate,
lead(S) = first element of S to be generated.

Examples of such aggregates are sets, sequences, and intervals. The corresponding empty aggregates are { }, $\langle\rangle$, and [ ]; the corresponding @ operators are union, concatenation, and merging adjacent intervals.

(b) The instantiation of the generator will produce the complete aggregate T of objects to be generated. Further, a nonempty T can be decomposed as

$$T = s\ @\ \langle x\rangle\ @\ t$$

where $\langle x\rangle$ is the unit aggregate consisting of the current element x; s and t are (possibly empty) aggregates — s, those elements previously generated and t, those remaining to be generated; and s, $\langle x\rangle$, and t are mutually disjoint.

(c) The specifications on &init and &next have the form

```
functions
   &init(&g: gen) returns &b:boolean
      post (&b ≡ T ≠ ⟨⟩) ∧ (&b ⊃ x = lead(T) ∧ D₁(x))
   &next(&g: gen) returns &b:boolean
      pre D₂(x)
      post (&b ≡ t' ≠ ⟨⟩) ∧ (&b ⊃ x=lead(t') ∧ D₃(x))
```

where &g is an instantiation of gen corresponding to the aggregate T and the $D_i(x)$ guarantee that the decomposition of T specified in (b) is legal and can be found.

The standard aggregate assumptions subsume points (a) and (b) of the basic generator assumptions, but points (c) and (d) of the latter must still be demonstrated in addition to the standard aggregate assumptions.

If these assumptions hold, we can derive several simpler proof rules. The rule for the **for** statement becomes

$$\frac{\begin{array}{l} G \wedge [P \wedge (T = \langle\rangle \vee \neg\beta(\text{lead}(T))) \\ \qquad\qquad \vee T \neq \langle\rangle \wedge I(s) \wedge (s = T \vee \neg\beta(x))] \supset Q \\ G \wedge T \neq \langle\rangle \wedge [P \wedge \beta(\text{lead}(T)) \\ \qquad\qquad \vee (s \neq T \wedge I(s) \wedge \beta(x))]\, \{ST\}\ I(s\ @\ \langle x\rangle) \end{array}}{P \wedge \beta_{req}\, \{\textbf{for } x:\ gen(y)\ \textbf{while}\ \beta(x)\ \textbf{do}\ ST(x,y,z)\ |\ I\}Q}$$

and the **first** rule simplifies to

$$\frac{G \wedge P \wedge \forall w \in s\ \neg\beta(w) \wedge \beta(x)\, \{S_1(x,y,z)\}Q \qquad G \wedge P \wedge \forall w \in T\ \neg\beta(w)\, \{S_2(y,z)\}Q}{P \wedge \beta_{req}\, \{\textbf{first } x:\ gen(y)\ \textbf{suchthat}\ \beta(x)\ \textbf{then}\ S_1(x,y,z)\ \textbf{else}\ S_2(y,z)\}Q}$$

We call these two rules the standard aggregate rules.

Special Cases and Examples

The Pure "for" Rule

In many cases the programmer may wish to drop the **while** clause, treating $\beta(x)$ as identically true. In addition, he will often wish to choose $P = I(\langle\rangle)$ and $Q = I(T)$. (Until now the major reason for distinguishing between P, Q, and I was that if $\beta(x)$ terminates the loop before the generator signals termination, I(T) is probably not true.) If these decisions are made, the proof rule simplifies further since the first premise reduces to true and several terms drop out of the second. Making the substitutions yields a generic rule similar to those of various **for** statements given by Hoare [2]:

$$\frac{G \wedge T = s\ @\ \langle x\rangle\ @\ t \wedge I(s)\, \{ST(x,y,z)\}\ I(s\ @\ \langle x\rangle)}{I(\langle\rangle) \wedge \beta_{req}\, \{\textbf{for } x:\ gen(y)\ \textbf{do}\ ST(x,y,z)\}\ I(T)}$$

Proof Rules for "upto"

To use one of these rules with a particular generator, we must "instantiate" it with the particulars of the generator in question. We illustrate this by developing the proof rules for upto. First, we discharge parts (c) and (d) of the basic generator assumptions:

(c) The bodies consist of simple assignment statements, and thus clearly terminate.

(d) There is no *init clause* and functions &init and &next change only local data and their return values; thus the first three parts of independence are satisfied. For the fourth part, note that no means is provided for the user of the **form** to alter k; the user is expected to refrain from altering lb and ub.

Next, we discharge the standard aggregate assumptions:

(a) Integer intervals are used.

(b) $[lb..ub] = [lb..k - 1][k][k + 1..ub]$ when $lb \leq k \leq ub$.

(c) **pre** and **post** conditions have the required form. Substituting the interval definitions into the standard aggregate rules and simplifying, we obtain

$$\frac{\begin{array}{c} P \wedge (lb > ub \vee \neg\beta(lb)) \vee lb \leq k \leq ub \wedge I[lb..k - 1] \\ \wedge \neg\beta(k) \vee lb \leq ub \wedge I[lb..ub] \supset Q \\ lb \leq ub \wedge (P \wedge \beta(lb) \vee lb \leq k \leq ub \wedge I[lb..k - 1] \\ \wedge \beta(k)) \{ST(k,y,z)\}\, I[lb..k] \end{array}}{P\ \{\textbf{for}\ k:\ \text{upto}(lb, ub)\ \textbf{while}\ \beta(k)\ \textbf{do}\ ST(k,y,z) \mid I(k,y,z)\}\ Q}$$

and

$$\frac{\begin{array}{c} P \wedge lb \leq k \leq ub \wedge (\forall w \in [lb..k - 1]\ \neg\beta(w)) \wedge \beta(k) \{S_1(k,y,z)\}\ Q \\ P \wedge \forall w \in [lb..ub]\ \neg\beta(w) \{S_2(y,z)\}\ Q \end{array}}{P\ \{\textbf{first}\ k:\ \text{upto}(lb,ub)\ \textbf{suchthat}\ \beta(k)\ \textbf{then}\ S_1(k,y,z)\ \textbf{else}\ S_2(y,z)\}\ Q}$$

where the y parameters are $\langle lb, ub \rangle$. In the special case $P = I[]$, $Q = I[lb..ub]$, and $\beta \equiv$ true, we obtain the Pascal rule for the **for** statement [2, 4]:

$$\frac{lb \leq k \leq ub \wedge I[lb..k - 1] \{ST(k,y,z)\}\ I[lb..k]}{I[]\ \{\textbf{for}\ k:\ \text{upto}(lb,ub)\ \textbf{do}\ ST(k,y,z)\}\ I[lb..ub]}$$

As must be the case, this rule is also obtained from the pure **for** rule by instantiating gen(y) with upto(lb,ub).

The Pure "while" Rule

We showed above that when the **while** clause is dropped, the **for** proof rule resembles Hoare's. We now show how to eliminate the loop variable and obtain the standard proof rule for the pure **while** statement.

Suppose we had a **form** named "forever" which extended type boolean and which satisfied the requirements above by using the value "true" for all the predicates involved. The aggregate T would be an infinite sequence of "true"s, and the standard aggregate **for** rule would become

$$\text{true} \wedge [P \wedge (\text{false} \vee \neg\beta(\text{true})) \vee \text{true} \\ \wedge I(\text{true*}) \wedge (\text{false} \vee \neg\beta(\text{true}))] \supset Q$$

$$\frac{\begin{array}{c} \text{true} \wedge [P \wedge \beta(\text{true}) \vee \text{true} \wedge I(\text{true*}) \\ \wedge \beta(\text{true})] \{ST(\text{true},,z)\}\ I(\text{true*}) \end{array}}{P\ \{\textbf{for}\ x:\ \text{forever}\ \textbf{while}\ \beta(\text{true})\ \textbf{do}\ ST(\text{true},,z) \mid I(\text{true*})\}\ Q}$$

where "true*" denotes a sequence of "true"s and the adjacent commas indicate the absence of the parameters y. By choosing $P = I$ and $Q = I \wedge \neg\beta$, eliminating the vacuous dependencies on "true," dropping the useless **for** clause, and simplifying, we obtain

$$\frac{I \wedge \beta \{ST(z)\}\ I}{I\ \{\textbf{while}\ \beta\ \textbf{do}\ ST(x)\}\ I \wedge \neg\beta}$$

which is the conventional **while** rule.

Generator Specifications by Proof Rules

We have shown how two sets of assumptions about the properties of a generator lead to very simple proof rules for the iteration statements. Notice now that if a generator satisfies these assumptions, the specifications for &init and &next can be *reconstructed* or *obtained*

from the proof rules. As a result, the author of the generator can perform the substitutions and simplifications, then give the proof rules in the specifications instead of giving the **pre** and **post** conditions. When this is possible, we use the keyword **generator** in place of **form** in the specification to alert the user.

To illustrate this, we write the generator for a counting loop that uses an integer step size greater than 1. This will provide the Alphard equivalent of Algol's

for i := a **step** j **until** b **do** S

for positive values of j. We first augment the interval notation $[a..b]$ to include a step size:

$$[a(j)b] \equiv_{\text{df}} \langle a, a + j, a + 2 * j, \ldots, b - (b - a)\ \text{mod}\ j \rangle\ \textbf{where}\ j > 0$$

If $a > b$, then $[a(j)b]$ is $\langle\ \rangle$. Note that $[a(1)b] = [a..b]$. The following rule allows us to merge two intervals:

$$[a(j)b][b + j(j)c] = [a(j)c]\ \text{provided}\ (b - a)\ \text{mod}\ j = 0$$

Using this notation, we can define the generator *stepup*:

```
generator stepup (lb,j,ub: integer) extends k: integer =
  beginform
  specifications
    requires j > 0;
    inherits ⟨allbut ←⟩;
    let stepup = [lb(j)ub] where lb ≤ ub ⊃ stepup
        = [lb(j)k − j][k][k + j(j)ub];
    rule forwhile(P ∧ j > 0, k, ⟨lb,j,ub⟩,
        β, ST(k,⟨lb,j,ub⟩,z), I, Q) =
      premise P ∧ (lb > ub ∨ ¬β(lb)) ∨
        lb ≤ k ≤ ub − d ∧ I[lb(j)k − j] ∧ ¬β(k) ∨
        lb ≤ ub ∧ I[lb(j)ub] ⊃ Q,
      premise lb ≤ ub ∧ (P ∧ β(lb) ∨
        lb ≤ k ≤ ub − d ∧ I[lb(j)k − j] ∧ β(k))
        {ST(k, ⟨lb,j,ub⟩,z)}
        I[lb(j)k] where d = (ub − lb) mod j;
    rule first(P ∧ j > 0, k, ⟨lb,j,ub⟩, β, S₁(k,⟨lb,j,ub⟩,z),
        S₂(⟨lb,j,ub⟩,z), Q) =
      premise P ∧ lb ≤ k ≤ ub ∧ (∀w ∈ [lb(j)k − j] ¬β(w)) ∧
        β(k) {S₁(k,⟨lb,j,ub⟩,z)} Q,
      premise P ∧ ∀w ∈ [lb(j)ub] ¬β(w)
        {S₂(⟨lb,j,ub⟩,z)} Q;
    rule for(I ∧ j > 0, k, ⟨lb,j,ub⟩, ST(k, ⟨lb,j,ub⟩,z)) =
      premise lb ≤ k ≤ ub − d ∧ I[lb(j)k − j]
        {ST(k,⟨lb,j,ub⟩,z)} I[lb(j)k]
        where d = (ub − lb) mod j;
  representation
    !
    ! same as upto
    !
  implementation
    !
    ! same as upto, except in &next "+1" becomes
    ! "+j" and k' < ub becomes k' + j ≤ ub
    !
  endform
```

Example of Loop Verification

In this section we illustrate the use of the proof rules given above by verifying the "eqvecs" function given earlier. With **pre** and **post** assertions, the function is

```
function eqvecs(A,B: vector(?t⟨≠⟩,?lb,?ub))
  returns (eq: boolean) =
  pre true post (eq ≡ (∀j ∈ [lb..ub]A[j] = B[j])) =
```

first i: upto(lb,ub) **suchthat** $A[i] \neq B[i]$
    then eq $\leftarrow$ false
    else eq $\leftarrow$ true

If the upto **first** rule is used, the proof requires that we establish the two premises:

Show: true $\wedge$ lb $\leq$ i $\leq$ ub $\wedge$ ($\forall$w $\in$ [lb..i $-$ 1] $\neg$ (A[y] $\neq$ B[y])) $\wedge$ A[i] $\neq$ B[i] {eq $\rightarrow$ false} eq $\equiv$ $\forall$j $\in$ [lb..ub] A[j] = B[j].
Proof: This simplifies to lb $\leq$ i $\leq$ ub $\wedge$ A[i] $\neq$ B[i] $\supset$ $\exists$j $\in$ [lb..ub] A[j] $\neq$ B[j]. Choose j = i.
Show: true $\wedge$ $\forall$w $\in$ [lb..ub] $\neg$ (A[w] $\neq$ B[w]) {eq $\rightarrow$ true} eq $\equiv$ $\forall$j $\in$ [lb..ub] A[j] = B[j].
Proof: clear.

Comparison with the Lisp Mapping Functions

Other examples of generators, in addition to those in this paper, may be found in [8] and [13]. In particular, the latter paper contains a generator of the elements from integer sequences where the sequences are represented by a restricted, but not uncommon, style of list processing. This generator may be easily and directly transformed into generators for use in Alphard iteration statements that express (some of) the Lisp mapping functions. The two functions map and mapc, which generate from the input list the tails or cdrs, and the elements or cars, respectively, are expressible as **for** statements whose body is the functional argument to map or mapc. The collecting, or consing, in maplist and mapcar must be done by the body of the **for** statement.

Termination of Generators

A major advantage of the **for** statements in many of the more recent programming languages, such as Pascal, is that they are guaranteed to terminate (provided, of course, that the statement which is the loop body terminates for each value of the **for** statement). As a result the programmer using them never need explicitly demonstrate termination. We would like to be able to make similar claims about the loops utilizing at least some generators; the generators having this property will be called *terminating generators*.

We can now present a technique for demonstrating this property.[10] Although the general **for** statement is

for x: gen(y) **while** β(x) **do** ST(x,y,z)

the clause "**while** β(x)" can only reduce the number of times ST(x,y,z) is executed. Hence it suffices to show

for x: gen(y) **do** ST(x,y,z)

terminates. Further, the generator and loop body, ST(x,y,z), are independent; so we know that as long as the body itself terminates for each x, it cannot cause the **for** statement to fail to terminate. Thus, if we can show the termination of the above statement for all possible

---

parameters of the generator and some *particular* loop body, we shall have shown that use of the generator cannot cause nontermination for any body.

Consider the statement

i $\leftarrow$ 0; **for** x: gen(y) **do** i $\leftarrow$ i + 1

If we could find: (1) a (nonnegative) value M_y depending only on y for which i $\leq$ M_y after executing the statement, and (2) a loop invariant which allowed us to prove that the loop terminated with such a value of i, then we would have proved termination of all loops using gen.

Clearly, the choice of M_y will depend on the instantiation parameters of the generator, i.e. on the data structure from which the elements are being generated. The loop invariant will have to assert that M_y bounds i; it will also have to relate the value of i to progress through the loop. The term that accomplishes the latter task, which we shall call $I_y(x)$, must be chosen for each generator whose termination is to be proved. Thus the loop invariant is of the form i $\leq$ M_y $\wedge$ $I_y(x)$. If we can associate with a generator a rule for determining M_y for any particular instantiation, and if we can find a suitable $I_y(x)$, then it suffices to show[11]

i = 0 {**for** x: gen(y) **do** i $\leftarrow$ i + 1 | i $\leq$ M_y $\wedge$ $I_y(x)$} i $\leq$ M_y

Note that the clause "i $\leq$ M_y" in this loop invariant ensures that the loop will terminate since i is strictly increasing from 0.

Although this must potentially be proved for each generator, we can show the termination of every generator which satisfies the standard aggregate assumptions (with a finite aggregate), provided only that it is possible to measure the size of an aggregate. To demonstrate this, we use the pure **for** rule, taking I(s) as i $\leq$ size(T) $\wedge$ i = size(s), where "size" is defined appropriately for the aggregate. The only premise

$$G \wedge T = s@\langle x\rangle@t \wedge i \leq \text{size}(T) \wedge i = \text{size}(s)$$
$$\{i \leftarrow i + 1\} i \leq \text{size}(T) \wedge i = \text{size}(s@\langle x\rangle)$$

follows since s and $\langle x\rangle$ are disjoint, whence size(s) $<$ size(T) and size(s@$\langle x\rangle$) = size(s) + 1. Hence the conclusion of the pure **for** rule is

$$i \leq \text{size}(T) \wedge i = \text{size}(\langle\ \rangle) \{\textbf{for } x: \text{gen}(y) \textbf{ do } i \leftarrow i + 1\}$$
$$i \leq \text{size}(T) \wedge i = \text{size}(T)$$

This then implies the desired result with M_y = size(T) and $I_y(x)$ = size(s).

Conclusions

The ultimate goal of the Alphard project is to increase the quality and reduce the total lifetime cost of *real* programs. Of the many alternative approaches to this goal, we have chosen one in which recent results

---

[10] Note that nontermination of the loop might also be caused by nontermination of the *init clause* or the functions &init and &next in the generator. This is explicitly ruled out by the basic generator assumptions, but must be treated as an additional requirement for proof of termination of generators which do not satisfy those assumptions.

[11] This method for showing termination is a simple instance of the commonly used well-founded set notion [7, 9]. Here the well-founded set is the nonnegative integers bounded by M_y.

from programming methodology and program verification are merged in a programming language design.

The key component of this merger is the introduction of a language mechanism, the **form**, to provide explicit support for the development of conceptual *abstractions*. The close association between **forms** and our intuitive notion of abstraction seems sound on methodological grounds, for it permits the programmer to concentrate on abstractions instead of their implementations. It also seems sound in terms of current (and projected) verification technology in that it permits isolated proofs of manageable size which collectively verify the entire program.

The success of this approach to improving quality and reducing costs depends, in large measure, on the degree to which the proposed language mechanism is able to express natural abstractions. In a previous paper [16, 17], we dealt with abstractions whose behavior is naturally expressed as a collection of operations defined over an abstract data structure. This is *not*, however, the full range of behaviors implicit in our understanding of the concept of "abstraction." Thus in this paper we concerned ourselves with that class of behaviors corresponding to the notion of enumerating the elements of an abstract aggregate (i.e. data structure).

The specific content of this paper has dealt with two related issues: the language features for defining and using such abstractions and the development of specification and verification techniques to accompany the language features. It is reassuring to us that the existing **form** mechanism is adequate to capture the new class of abstractions introduced here. We also find it interesting that the **forms** which define generators can be specified quite naturally in terms of proof rules instead of the usual functional specifications. Despite the complexity of the full generator mechanism and associated proof rules, a chain of simplifying assumptions yields the simple rules for common types of loops in other languages; furthermore, these common loops terminate.

A number of open problems remain. The loop specialization facility in Alphard described in this paper has made it possible to encapsulate iteration patterns along with other properties of an abstraction, but it has also made it awkward to write certain kinds of loops, including those which operate on only part of a structure and those in which a structure is modified by the loop which operates on it.

We may wish to eliminate many such irregular loops on methodological grounds, but others seem to be reasonable, understandable, and hence safe. For example, it seems acceptable to write loops for:

— recurrence relations in which the first k elements of a vector are treated individually and the rest uniformly.

— operations on matrices in which the boundary values receive special treatment,

— tree walks in which data values at the nodes, but not the tree structure, are changed,

— list processing operations when the loop body is making insertions and deletions to the list from which elements are being generated, and

— operations in which the loop body may wish to request early loop termination (without the distributed cost and complexity of including the test in the **while** clause).

Since a generator is in fact a **form**, the ability to write some of these loops may be provided by defining functions other than &init and &next in the generator. Operations on the structure would then still be performed only by the generator, which could presumably keep matters in hand. The restrictions under which this is reasonable are a subject for further research. This is not, however, an acceptable general solution, for it would require the generator to provide its own versions of all interesting operations on the structures for which it generates elements.

A general solution for the problem of permitting interactions between the generator and the loop body can be found by returning to the original proof rule, without even the basic generator assumptions. This rule assumes only an *init clause* and that &init and &next are functions provided by the generator. This solution is too general — it is too unwieldy for any but the most intricate of interactions. We believe that a promising path for further research is the search for sets of reasonable assumptions which permit interesting interactions and also, like the two sets of assumptions made in this paper, lead to vastly simplified proof rules. We also believe that some of these new assumptions can be stated in terms of additional invariant properties of the generator specifications and the operations on the structure. We expect to explore these topics in future papers.

Appendix. Informal Description of Verification Methodology

Alphard's verification methodology is designed to determine whether a **form** will actually behave as promised by its abstract specifications. The methodology depends on explicitly separating the description of how an object behaves from the code that manipulates the representation in order to achieve that behavior. It is derived from Hoare's technique for showing correctness of data representations [3].

The abstract object and its behavior are described in terms of some mathematical entities natural to the problem domain. Graphs are used in [12] to describe binary trees; sequences are used in [16] to describe queues and stacks and in [8] to describe list processing, and so on. We appeal to these abstract types:

— in the **invariant**, which explains that an instantiation of the **form** may be viewed as an object of the abstract type that meets certain restrictions,

— in the **initially** clause, where a particular abstract object is displayed, and

— in the **pre** and **post** conditions for each function, which describe the effect the function has on an abstract object which satisfies the invariant.

The **form** contains a parallel set of descriptions of the concrete object and how it behaves. In many cases this makes a function's effect much easier to specify and verify than would the abstract description alone.

Now, although it is useful to distinguish between the behavior we want and the data structures we operate on, we also need to show a relationship that holds between the two. This is achieved with the representation function **rep**(x), which gives a mapping from the concrete representation to the abstract description. A **form** verification is to ensure that the two invariants and the **rep**(x) relation between them are preserved.

In order to verify a **form** we must therefore prove four things. Two relate to the representation itself and two must be shown for each function. Informally, the four required steps are[12]:

For the **form**
   1. Representation validity
      $I_c(x) \supset I_a(rep(x))$
   2. Initialization
      requires {*init clause*} **initially**(rep(x)) $\wedge$ $I_c(x)$
For each function
   3. Concrete operation
      in(x) $\wedge$ $I_c(x)$ {*function body*} **out**(x) $\wedge$ $I_c(x)$
   4. Relation between abstract and concrete
      4a. $I_c(x)$ $\wedge$ **pre**(rep(x)) $\supset$ **in**(x)
      4b. $I_c(x)$ $\wedge$ **pre**(rep(x′)) $\wedge$ **out**(x) $\supset$ **post**(rep(x))

---

[12] We use $I_a(rep(x))$ to denote the abstract invariant of an object whose concrete representation is x, $I_c(x)$ to denote the corresponding concrete invariant, italics to refer to code segments, and the names of specification clauses and assertions to refer to those formulas. In step 4b, "**pre**(rep(x′))" refers to the value of x *before* execution of the function. A complete development of the **form** verification methodology appears in [16, 17].

Step 1 shows that any legal state of the concrete representation has a corresponding abstract object (the converse is deducible from the other steps). Step 2 shows that the initial state created by the **representation** section is legal. Step 3 is the standard verification formula for the concrete operation as a simple program; note that it enforces the preservation of I_c. Step 4 guarantees (a) that the concrete operation is applicable whenever the abstract **pre** condition holds and (b) that if the operation is performed, the result corresponds properly to the abstract specifications.

Acknowledgments. We owe a great deal to our colleagues at Carnegie-Mellon University and the University of Southern California Information Sciences Institute, especially Mario Barbacci, Neil Goldman, Donald Good, John Guttag, Paul Hilfinger, David Jefferson, Anita Jones, David Lamb, David Musser, Karla Perdue, Kamesh Ramakrishna, and David Wile. We would also like to thank James Horning and Barbara Liskov and their groups at the University of Toronto and M.I.T., respectively, for their critical reviews of Alphard. We also appreciate very much the perceptive responses that a number of our colleagues have made on an earlier draft of this paper. Finally, we are grateful to Raymond Bates, David Lamb, Brian Reid, and Martin Yonke for their expert assistance with the document formatting programs.

References
1. Dahl, O.-J., and Hoare, C.A.R. Hierarchical program structures. In *Structured Programming*, O.-J. Dahl, E.W. Dijkstra, and C.A.R. Hoare, Academic Press, New York, 1972, pp. 175–220.
2. Hoare, C.A.R. A note on the for statement. *BIT 12* (1972), 334–341.
3. Hoare, C.A.R. Proof of correctness of data representations. *Acta Informatica 1*, 4 (1972), 271–281.
4. Hoare, C.A.R., and Wirth, N. An axiomatic definition of the programming language Pascal. *Acta Informatica 2*, 4 (1973), 335–355.
5. Igarashi, S., London, R.L., and Luckham, D.C. Automatic program verification I: a logical basis and its implementation. *Acta Informatica 4*, 2 (1975), 145–182.
6. Jensen, K., and Wirth, N. *PASCAL User Manual and Report*. Lecture Notes in Computer Science, No. 18, Springer-Verlag, 1974.
7. Katz, S., and Manna, Z. A closer look at termination. *Acta Informatica 5*, 4 (1975), 333–352.
8. London, R.L., Shaw, M., and Wulf, W.A. Abstraction and verification in Alphard: a symbol table example. Tech. Reports, Inform. Sci. Inst., U. of Southern California, Marina del Rey, Calif., and Carnegie-Mellon U., Pittsburgh, Pa., 1976.
9. Luckham, D.C., and Suzuki, N. Automatic program verification IV: Proof of termination within a weak logic of programs. Memo AIM-269, Stanford University, Stanford, Calif., Oct. 1975.
10. McCarthy, J., Abrahams, P.W., Edwards, D.J., Hart, T.P., and Levin, M.I. *LISP 1.5 Programmer's Manual*. MIT Press, 1962.
11. Newell, A., Tonge, F., Feigenbaum, E.A., Green, B.F. Jr., and Mealy, G.H. *Information Processing Language-V Manual*. Prentice-Hall, Englewood Cliffs, N.J., Sec. Ed. 1964.
12. Shaw, M. Abstraction and verification in Alphard: design and verification of a tree handler. Proc. Fifth Texas Conf. on Computing Systems, 1976, pp. 86–94.
13. Shaw, M., Wulf, W.A., and London, R.L. Abstraction and verification in Alphard: Iteration and generators. Tech. Reports, Inform. Sci. Inst., U. of Southern California, Marina del Rey, Calif., and Carnegie-Mellon U., Pittsburgh, Pa., 1976.
14. Teitelman, W. Interlisp Reference Manual. Xerox Palo Alto Res. Ctr., Palo Alto, Calif., 1975.
15. Weissman, C. *LISP 1.5 Primer*, Dickenson, Encino, Calif., 1967.
16. Wulf, W.A., London, R.L., and Shaw, M. Abstraction and verification in Alphard: Introduction to language and methodology. Tech. Reports, Inform. Sci. Inst., U. of Southern California, Marina del Rey, Calif., and Carnegie-Mellon U., Pittsburgh, Pa., 1976.
17. Wulf, W.A., London, R.L., and Shaw, M. An introduction to the construction and verification of Alphard programs. *IEEE Trans. on Software Eng. SE-2*, 4 (Dec. 1976), 253–265.

Operating   C. Weissman
Systems   Editor

Monitors: An Operating System Structuring Concept

C.A.R. Hoare
The Queen's University of Belfast

This paper develops Brinch-Hansen's concept of a monitor as a method of structuring an operating system. It introduces a form of synchronization, describes a possible method of implementation in terms of semaphores and gives a suitable proof rule. Illustrative examples include a single resource scheduler, a bounded buffer, an alarm clock, a buffer pool, a disk head optimizer, and a version of the problem of readers and writers.

Key Words and Phrases: monitors, operating systems, scheduling, mutual exclusion, synchronization, system implementation languages, structured multiprogramming
   CR Categories: 4.31, 4.22

This paper is based on an address delivered to IRIA, France, May 11, 1973. Author's address: Department of Computer Science, The Queen's University of Belfast, Belfast BT7 1NN, Northern Ireland.

1. Introduction

A primary aim of an operating system is to share a computer installation among many programs making unpredictable demands upon its resources. A primary task of its designer is therefore to construct resource allocation (or scheduling) algorithms for resources of various kinds (main store, drum store, magnetic tape handlers, consoles, etc.). In order to simplify his task, he should try to construct separate schedulers for each class of resource. Each scheduler will consist of a certain amount of local administrative data, together with some procedures and functions which are called by programs wishing to acquire and release resources. Such a collection of associated data and procedures is known as a *monitor*; and a suitable notation can be based on the *class* notation of SIMULA67 [6].

```
monitorname: monitor
  begin ... declarations of data local to the monitor;
    procedure procname (... formal parameters ...);
      begin ... procedure body ... end;
    ... declarations of other procedures local to the monitor;
    ... initialization of local data of the monitor ...
  end;
```

Note that the procedure bodies may have local data, in the normal way.

In order to call a procedure of a monitor, it is necessary to give the name of the monitor as well as the name of the desired procedure, separating them by a dot:

```
monitorname.procname(... actual parameters ...);
```

In an operating system it is sometimes desirable to declare several monitors with identical structure and behavior, for example to schedule two similar resources. In such cases, the declaration shown above will be preceded by the word **class**, and the separate monitors will be declared to belong to this class:

```
monitor 1, monitor 2: classname;
```

Thus the structure of a class of monitors is identical to that described for a data representation in [13], except for addition of the basic word *monitor*. Brinch-Hansen uses the word *shared* for the same purpose [3].

The procedures of a monitor are common to all running programs, in the sense that any program may at any time attempt to call such a procedure. However, it is essential that only one program at a time actually succeed in entering a monitor procedure, and any subsequent call must be held up until the previous call has been completed. Otherwise, if two procedure bodies were in simultaneous execution, the effects on the local variables of the monitor could be chaotic. The procedures local to a monitor should not access any nonlocal variables other than those local to the same monitor, and these variables of the monitor should be inaccessible from outside the monitor. If these restrictions are imposed, it is possible to guarantee against certain of the more obscure forms of time-dependent coding error; and this guarantee could be underwritten by a visual scan of the text of the program, which could readily be automated in a compiler.

Any dynamic resource allocator will sometimes need to delay a program wishing to acquire a resource which is not currently available, and to resume that program after some other program has released the resource required. We therefore need: a "wait" operation, issued from inside a procedure of the monitor, which causes the calling program to be delayed; and a "signal" operation, also issued from inside a procedure of the same monitor, which causes exactly one of the waiting programs to be resumed immediately. If there are no waiting programs, the signal has no effect. In order to enable other programs to release resources during a wait, a wait operation must relinquish the exclusion which would otherwise prevent entry to the releasing procedure. However, we decree that a signal operation be followed immediately by resumption of a waiting program, without possibility of an intervening procedure call from yet a third program. It is only in this way that a waiting program has an absolute guarantee that it can acquire the resource just released by the signalling program without any danger that a third program will interpose a monitor entry and seize the resource instead.

In many cases, there may be more than one reason for waiting, and these need to be distinguished by both the waiting and the signalling operation. We therefore introduce a new type of "variable" known as a "condition"; and the writer of a monitor should declare a variable of type condition for each reason why a program might have to wait. Then the wait and signal operations should be preceded by the name of the relevant condition variable, separated from it by a dot:

condvariable.wait;
condvariable.signal;

Note that a condition "variable" is neither true nor false; indeed, it does not have any stored value accessible to the program. In practice, a condition variable will be represented by an (initially empty) queue of processes which are currently waiting on the condition; but this queue is invisible both to waiters and signallers. This design of the condition variable has been deliberately kept as primitive and rudimentary as possible, so that it may be implemented efficiently and used flexibly to achieve a wide variety of effects. There is a great temptation to introduce a more complex synchronization primitive, which may be easier to use for many purposes. We shall resist this temptation for a while.

As the simplest example of a monitor, we will design a scheduling algorithm for a single resource, which is dynamically acquired and released by an unknown number of customer processes by calls on procedures

procedure *acquire*;
procedure *release*;

A variable[1]

busy: *Boolean*

determines whether or not the resource is in use. If an attempt is made to acquire the resource when it is busy, the attempting program must be delayed by waiting on a variable

nonbusy: *condition*

which is signalled by the next subsequent release. The initial value of busy is false. These design decisions lead to the following code for the monitor:

```
single resource: monitor
begin busy: Boolean;
      nonbusy: condition;
   procedure acquire;
      begin if busy then nonbusy.wait;
               busy := true
      end;
   procedure release;
      begin busy := false;
            nonbusy.signal
      end;
      busy := false; comment initial value;
end single resource
```

Notes

1. In designing a monitor, it seems natural to design the procedure headings, the data, the conditions, and the procedure bodies, in that order. All subsequent examples will be designed in this way.

2. The acquire procedure does not have to retest that busy has gone false when it resumes after its wait, since the release procedure has guaranteed that this is so; and as mentioned before, no other program can intervene between the signal and the continuation of exactly one waiting program.

3. If more than one program is waiting on a condition, we postulate that the signal operation will reactivate the longest waiting program. This gives a simple neutral queuing discipline which ensures that every waiting program will eventually get its turn.

4. The single resource monitor simulates a Boolean semaphore [7] with *acquire* and *release* used for *P* and *V* respectively. This is a simple proof that the monitor/condition concepts are not in principle less powerful than semaphores, and that they can be used for all the same purposes.

---

[1] As in PASCAL [15], a variable declaration is of the form:
⟨*variable identifier*⟩: ⟨*type*⟩;

2. Interpretation

Having proved that semaphores can be implemented by a monitor, the next task is to prove that monitors can be implemented by semaphores.

Obviously, we shall require for each monitor a Boolean semaphore *"mutex"* to ensure that the bodies of the local procedures exclude each other. The semaphore is initialized to 1; a $P(mutex)$ must be executed on entry to each local procedure, and a $V(mutex)$ must usually be executed on exit from it.

When a process signals a condition on which another process is waiting, the signalling process must wait until the resumed process permits it to proceed. We therefore introduce for each monitor a second semaphore *"urgent"* (initialized to 0), on which signalling processes suspend themselves by the operation $P(urgent)$. Before releasing exclusion, each process must test whether any other process is waiting on *urgent*, and if so, must release it instead by a $V(urgent)$ instruction. We therefore need to count the number of processes waiting on *urgent*, in an integer *"urgentcount"* (initially zero). Thus each exit from a procedure of a monitor should be coded:

if *urgentcount* > 0 **then** $V(urgent)$ **else** $V(mutex)$

Finally, for each condition local to the monitor, we introduce a semaphore *"condsem"* (initialized to 0), on which a process desiring to wait suspends itself by a $P(condsem)$ operation. Since a process signalling this condition needs to know whether anybody is waiting, we also need a count of the number of waiting processes held in an integer variable *"condcount"* (initially 0). The operation *"cond.wait"* may now be implemented as follows (recall that a waiting program must release exclusion before suspending itself):

condcount := *condcount* $+$ 1;
if *urgentcount* > 0 **then** $V(urgent)$ **else** $V(mutex)$;
$P(condsem)$;
comment This will always wait;
condcount := *condcount* $-$ 1

The signal operation may be coded:

urgentcount := *urgentcount* $+$ 1;
if *condcount* > 0 **then** $\{V(condsem); P(urgent)\}$;
urgentcount := *urgentcount* $-$ 1

In this implementation, possession of the monitor is regarded as a privilege which is explicitly passed from one process to another. Only when no one further wants the privilege is *mutex* finally released.

This solution is not intended to correspond to recommended "style" in the use of semaphores. The concept of a condition-variable is intended as a substitute for semaphores, and has its own style of usage, in the same way that while-loops or coroutines are intended as a substitute for jumps.

In many cases, the generality of this solution is unnecessary, and a significant improvement in efficiency is possible.

1. When a procedure body in a monitor contains no wait or signal, exit from the body can be coded by a simple $V(mutex)$, since *urgentcount* cannot have changed during the execution of the body.

2. If a *cond.signal* is the last operation of a procedure body, it can be combined with monitor exit as follows:

if *condcount* > 0 **then** $V(condsem)$
else if *urgentcount* > 0 **then** $V(urgent)$
else $V(mutex)$

3. If there is no other wait or signal in the procedure body, the second line shown above can also be omitted.

4. If *every* signal occurs as the last operation of its procedure body, the variables *urgentcount* and *urgent* can be omitted, together with all operations upon them. This is such a simplification that O-J. Dahl suggests that signals should always be the last operation of a monitor procedure; in fact, this restriction is a very natural one, which has been unwittingly observed in all examples of this paper.

Significant improvements in efficiency may also be obtained by avoiding the use of semaphores, and by implementing conditions directly in hardware, or at the lowest and most uninterruptible level of software (e.g. supervisor mode). In this case, the following optimizations are possible.

1. *urgentcount* and *condcount* can be abolished, since the fact that someone is waiting can be established by examining the representation of the semaphore, which cannot change surreptitiously within noninterruptible mode.

2. Many monitors are very short and contain no calls to other monitors. Such monitors can be executed wholly in noninterruptible mode, using, as it were, the common exclusion mechanism provided by hardware. This will often involve *less* time in noninterruptible mode than the establishment of separate exclusion for each monitor.

I am grateful to J. Bezivin, J. Horning, and R.M. McKeag for assisting in the discovery of this algorithm.

3. Proof Rules

The analogy between a monitor and a data representation has been noted in the introduction. The mutual exclusion on the code of a monitor ensures that procedure calls follow each other in time, just as they do in sequential programming; and the same restrictions are placed on access to nonlocal data. These are the reasons why the same proof rules can be applied to monitors as to data representations.

As with a data representation, the programmer may associate an invariant $\mathcal{I}$ with the local data of a monitor, to describe some condition which will be true of this data before and after every procedure call. $\mathcal{I}$ must also be made true after initialization of the data, and before *every* wait instruction; otherwise the next following procedure call will not find the local data in a state which it expects.

With each condition variable b the programmer may associate an assertion B which describes the condition under which a program waiting on b wishes to be resumed. Since other programs may invoke a monitor procedure during a wait, a waiting program must ensure that the invariant $\mathcal{I}$ for the monitor is true beforehand. This gives the proof rule for waits:

$$\mathcal{I} \; \{b.wait\} \; \mathcal{I} \& B$$

Since a signal can cause immediate resumption of a waiting program, the conditions $\mathcal{I} \& B$ which are expected by that program must be made true before the signal; and since B may be made false again by the resumed program, only $\mathcal{I}$ may be assumed true afterwards. Thus the proof rule for a signal is:

$$\mathcal{I} \& B\{b.signal\}\mathcal{I}$$

This exhibits a pleasing symmetry with the rule for waiting.

The introduction of condition variables makes it possible to write monitors subject to the risk of deadly embrace [7]. It is the responsibility of the programmer to avoid this risk, together with other scheduling disasters (thrashing, indefinitely repeated overtaking, etc. [11]). Assertion-oriented proof methods cannot prove absence of such risks; perhaps it is better to use less formal methods for such proofs.

Finally, in many cases an operating system monitor constructs some "virtual" resource which is used in place of actual resources by its "customer" programs. This virtual resource is an abstraction from the set of local variables of the monitor. The program prover should therefore define this abstraction in terms of its concrete representation, and then express the intended effect of each of the procedure bodies in terms of the abstraction. This proof method is described in detail in [13].

4. Example: Bounded Buffer

A bounded buffer is a concrete representation of the abstract idea of a sequence of portions. The sequence is accessible to two programs running in parallel: the first of these (the producer) updates the sequence by appending a new portion x at the end; and the second (the consumer) updates it by removing the first portion. The initial value of the sequence is empty. We thus require two operations:

(1) $append(x:portion)$;

which should be equivalent to the abstract operation

$$sequence := sequence \; \cap \; \langle x \rangle;$$

where $\langle x \rangle$ is the sequence whose only item is x and $\cap$ denotes concatenation of two sequences.

(2) $remove(\mathbf{result} \; x:portion)$;

which should be equivalent to the abstract operations

$$x := first(sequence); \; sequence := rest(sequence);$$

where $first$ selects the first item of a sequence and $rest$ denotes the sequence with its first item removed. Obviously, if the sequence is empty, $first$ is undefined; and in this case we want to ensure that the consumer waits until the producer has made the sequence nonempty.

We shall assume that the amount of time taken to produce a portion or consume it is large in comparison with the time taken to append or remove it from the sequence. We may therefore be justified in making a design in which producer and consumer can both update the sequence, but not simultaneously.

The sequence is represented by an array:

$$buffer :\mathbf{array} \; 0..N - 1 \; \mathbf{of} \; portion;$$

and two variables:

(1) $lastpointer:0..N - 1$;

which points to the buffer position into which the next append operation will put a new item, and

(2) $count:0..N$;

which always holds the length of the sequence (initially 0).

We define the function

$$seq \; (b,l,c) =_{df} \mathbf{if} \; c = 0 \; \mathbf{then} \; empty$$
$$\mathbf{else} \; seq(b,l \ominus 1, c-1) \; \cap \langle b[l \ominus 1] \rangle$$

where the circled operations are taken modulo N. Note that if $c \neq 0$,

$$first(seq(b,l,c)) = b[l \ominus c]$$

and

$$rest(seq(b,l,c)) = seq(b,l,c-1)$$

The definition of the abstract sequence in terms of its concrete representation may now be given:

$$sequence =_{df} seq(buffer, lastpointer, count)$$

Less formally, this may be written

$$sequence =_{df} \langle buffer[lastpointer \ominus count],$$
$$buffer[lastpointer \ominus count \oplus 1],$$
$$\ldots,$$
$$buffer[lastpointer \ominus 1] \rangle$$

Another way of conveying this information would be by an example and a picture, which would be even less formal.

The invariant for the monitor is:

$$0 \leq count \leq N \; \& \; 0 \leq lastpointer \leq N - 1$$

There are two reasons for waiting, which must be represented by condition variables:

$$nonempty:condition;$$

means that the count is greater than 0, and

$$nonfull:condition;$$

means that the count is less than N.

With this constructive approach to the design [8], it is relatively easy to code the monitor without error.

```
bounded buffer:monitor
  begin buffer:array 0..N − 1 of portion;
        lastpointer:0..N − 1;
        count:0..N;
        nonempty,nonfull:condition;
    procedure append(x:portion);
      begin if count = N then nonfull.wait;
            note 0 ≤ count < N;
            buffer[lastpointer] := x;
            lastpointer := lastpointer ⊕ 1;
            count := count+1;
            nonempty.signal
      end append;
    procedure remove(result x:portion);
      begin if count = 0 then nonempty.wait;
            note 0 < count ≤ N;
            x := buffer[lastpointer⊖count];
            nonfull.signal
      end remove;
      count := 0; lastpointer := 0;
  end bounded buffer;
```

A formal proof of the correctness of this monitor with respect to the stated abstraction and invariant can be given if desired by techniques described in [13]. However, these techniques seem not capable of dealing with subsequent examples of this paper.

Single-buffered input and output may be regarded as a special case of the bounded buffer with $N = 1$. In this case, the array can be replaced by a single variable, the *lastpointer* is redundant, and we get:

```
iostream:monitor
begin buffer:portion;
      count:0..1;
      nonempty,nonfull:condition;
    procedure append(x:portion);
      begin if count = 1 then nonfull.wait;
        buffer := x;
        count := 1;
        nonempty.signal
      end append;
    procedure remove(result x:portion);
      begin if count = 0 then nonempty.wait;
        x := buffer;
        count := 0;
        nonfull.signal
      end remove;
      count := 0;
end iostream;
```

If physical output is carried out by a separate special purpose channel, then the interrupt from the channel should simulate a call of *iostream.remove(x)*; and similarly for physical input, simulating a call of *iostream.append(x)*.

5. Scheduled Waits

Up to this point, we have assumed that when more than one program is waiting for the same condition, a signal will cause the longest waiting program to be resumed. This is a good simple scheduling strategy, which precludes indefinite overtaking of a waiting process.

However, in the design of an operating system, there are many cases when such simple scheduling on the basis of first-come-first-served is not adequate. In order to give a closer control over scheduling strategy, we introduce a further feature of a conditional wait, which makes it possible to specify as a parameter of the wait some indication of the priority of the waiting program, e.g.:

busy . wait (p);

When the condition is signalled, it is the program that specified the lowest value of p that is resumed. In using this facility, the designer of a monitor must take care to avoid the risk of indefinite overtaking; and often it is advisable to make priority a nondecreasing function of the time at which the wait commences.

This introduction of a "scheduled wait" concedes to the temptation to make the condition concept more elaborate. The main justifications are:
1. It has no effect whatsoever on the *logic* of a program, or on the formal proof rules. Any program which works without a scheduled wait will work with it, but possibly with better timing characteristics.
2. The automatic ordering of the queue of waiting processes is a simple fast scheduling technique, except when the queue is exceptionally long—and when it is, central processor time is not the major bottleneck.
3. The maximum amount of storage required is one word per process. Without such a built-in scheduling method, each monitor may have to allocate storage proportional to the number of its customers; the alternative of dynamic storage allocation in small chunks is unattractive at the low level of an operating system where monitors are found.

I shall yield to one further temptation, to introduce a Boolean function of conditions:

condname.queue

which yields the value true if anyone is waiting on *condname* and false otherwise. This can obviously be easily implemented by a couple of instructions, and affords valuable information which could otherwise be obtained only at the expense of extra storage, time, and trouble.

A trivially simple example is an *alarmclock* monitor, which enables a calling program to delay itself for a stated number n of time-units, or "*ticks*". There are two entries:

```
procedure wakeme (n:integer);
procedure tick;
```

The second of these is invoked by hardware (e.g. an interrupt) at regular intervals, say ten times per second. Local variables are

now:integer;

which records the current time (initially zero) and

wakeup:**condition**;

on which sleeping programs wait. But the *alarmsetting* at which these programs will be aroused is known at the time when they start the wait; and this can be used to determine the correct sequence of waking up.

```
alarmclock:monitor
begin now:integer;
    wakeup:condition;
  procedure wakeme(n:integer);
    begin alarmsetting:integer;
      alarmsetting := now + n;
      while now < alarmsetting do wakeup.wait(alarmsetting);
      wakeup.signal;
      comment In case the next process is due to wake up at the
      same time;
    end;
  procedure tick;
    begin now := now + 1;
      wakeup.signal
    end;
  now := 0
end alarmclock
```

In the program given above, the next candidate for wakening is actually woken at every tick of the clock. This will not matter if the frequency of ticking is low enough, and the overhead of an accepted signal is not too high.

I am grateful to A. Ballard and J. Horning for posing this problem.

6. Further Examples

In proposing a new feature for a high level language it is very difficult to make a convincing case that the feature will be both easy to use efficiently and easy to implement efficiently. Quality of implementation can be proved by a single good example, but ease and efficiency of use require a great number of realistic examples; otherwise it can appear that the new feature has been specially designed to suit the examples, or vice versa. This section contains a number of additional examples of solutions of familiar problems. Further examples may be found in [14].

6.1 Buffer Allocation

The bounded buffer described in Section 4 was designed to be suitable only for sequences with small portions, for example, message queues. If the buffers contain high volume information (for example, files for pseudo offline input and output), the bounded buffer may still be used to store the *addresses* of the buffers which are being used to hold the information. In this way, the producer can be filling one buffer while the consumer is emptying another buffer of the same sequence. But this requires an allocator for dynamic acquisition and relinquishment of *buffer addresses*.

These may be declared as a type

type *bufferaddress* = 1..B;

where *B* is the number of buffers available for allocation.

The buffer allocator has two entries:

procedure *acquire* (**result** *b*:*bufferaddress*);

which delivers a free *buffer address b*; and

procedure *release*(*b*:*bufferaddress*);

which returns a *bufferaddress* when it is no longer required. In order to keep a record of free buffer addresses the monitor will need:

freepool:**powerset** *bufferaddress*;

which uses the *PASCAL* powerset facility to define a variable whose values range over all sets of *buffer addresses*, from the empty set to the set containing all *buffer addresses*. It should be implemented as a *bitmap* of *B* consecutive bits, where the *i*th bit is 1 if and only if *i* is in the set. There is only one condition variable needed:

nonempty:**condition**

which means that *freepool* $\neq$ *empty*. The code for the allocator is:

```
buffer allocator:monitor
begin freepool:powerset bufferaddress;
    nonempty:condition;
  procedure acquire (result b:bufferaddress);
    begin if freepool = empty then nonempty.wait;
      b := first(freepool);
      comment Any one would do;
      freepool := freepool − {b};
      comment Set subtraction;
    end acquire;
  procedure release(b:bufferaddress);
    begin freepool := freepool − {b};
      nonempty.signal
    end release;
  freepool := all buffer addresses
end buffer allocator
```

The action of a producer and consumer may be summarized:

```
producer: begin b:bufferaddress; ...
            while not finished do
              begin bufferallocator.acquire(b);
                ... fill buffer b ...;
                bounded buffer.append(b)
              end; ...
          end producer;

consumer: begin b:bufferaddress; ...
            while not finished do
              begin bounded buffer.remove(b);
                ... empty buffer b ...;
                buffer allocator.release(b)
              end; ...
          end consumer;
```

This buffer allocator would appear to be usable to share the buffers among several streams, each with its own producer and its own consumer, and its own instance of a bounded buffer monitor. Unfortunately, when the streams operate at widely varying speeds, and when the freepool is empty, the scheduling algorithm can exhibit persistent undesirable behavior. If two producers are competing for each buffer as it becomes free, a first-come-first-served discipline of allocation will ensure (apparently fairly) that each gets alternate buffers; and they will consequently begin to produce at equal speeds. But if one consumer is a 1000 lines/min printer and the other is a 10 lines/min teletype, the faster consumer will be eventually reduced to the speed of the slower, since it cannot forever go faster than its producer. At this stage nearly all buffers will belong to the slower stream, so the situation could take a long time to clear.

A solution to this is to use a scheduled wait, to ensure that in heavy load conditions the available buffers will be shared reasonably fairly between the streams that are competing for them. Of course, inactive streams need not be considered, and streams for which the consumer is currently faster than the producer will never ask for more than two buffers anyway. In order to achieve fairness in allocation, it is sufficient to allocate a newly freed buffer to that one among the competing producers whose stream currently owns fewest buffers. Thus the system will seek a point as far away from the undesirable extreme as possible.

For this reason, the entries to the allocator should indicate for what stream the buffer is to be (or has been) used, and the allocator must keep a count of the current allocation to each stream in an array:

count:**array** *stream* **of** *integer*;

The new version of the allocator is:

```
bufferallocator:monitor
  begin freepool:powerset bufferaddress;
      nonempty:condition
      count:array stream of integer;
    procedure acquire(result b:bufferaddress; s:stream);
      begin if freepool = empty then nonempty.wait(count[s]);
        count[s] := count[s] + 1;
        b := first(freepool);
        freepool := freepool − {b}
      end acquire;
    procedure release(b:bufferaddress; s:stream)
      begin count[s] := count[s] − 1;
        freepool := freepool − {b};
        nonempty·signal
      end;
    freepool := all buffer addresses;
    for s:stream do count[s] := 0
  end bufferallocator
```

Of course, if a consumer stops altogether, perhaps owing to mechanical failure, the producer must also be halted before it has acquired too many buffers, even if no one else currently wants them. This can perhaps be most easily accomplished by appropriate fixing of the size of the bounded buffer for that stream and/or by ensuring that at least two buffers are reserved for each stream, even when inactive. It is an interesting comment on dynamic resource allocation that, as soon as re-

sources are heavily loaded, the system must be designed to fall back toward a more static regime.

I am grateful to E.W. Dijkstra for pointing out this problem and its solution [10].

6.2 Disk Head Scheduler

On a moving head disk, the time taken to move the heads increases monotonically with the distance traveled. If several programs wish to move the heads, the average waiting time can be reduced by selecting, first, the program which wishes to move them the shortest distance. But unfortunately this policy is subject to an instability, since a program wishing to access a cylinder at one edge of the disk can be indefinitely overtaken by programs operating at the other edge or the middle.

A solution to this is to minimize the frequency of change of direction of movement of the heads. At any time, the heads are kept moving in a given direction, and they service the program requesting the nearest cylinder in that direction. If there is no such request, the direction changes, and the heads make another sweep across the surface of the disk. This may be called the "elevator" algorithm, since it simulates the behavior of a lift in a multi-storey building.

There are two entries to a disk head scheduler:

(1)   *request(dest:cylinder)*;

where

    type *cylinder* = 0..*cylmax*;

which is entered by a program just *before* issuing the instruction to move the heads to cylinder *dest*.

(2)   *release*;

which is entered by a program when it has made all the transfers it needs on the current cylinder.

The local data of the monitor must include a record of the current headposition, *headpos*, the current direction of *sweep*, and whether the disk is *busy*:

    headpos:*cylinder*;
    direction:(*up, down*);
    busy:*Boolean*

We need two conditions, one for requests waiting for an *upsweep* and the other for requests waiting for a *downsweep*:

    upsweep, downsweep:*condition*

```
dischead:monitor
begin headpos:cylinder;
    direction:(up, down);
    busy:Boolean;
    upsweep,downsweep:condition;
    procedure request(dest:cylinder);
    begin if busy then
      {if headpos < dest ∨ headpos = dest & direction = up
        then upsweep·wait(dest)
        else downsweep.wait(cylmax-dest)};
      busy := true; headpos := dest
    end request;
```

```
procedure release;
  begin busy := false;
    if direction = up then
      {if upsweep.queue then upsweep.signal
                   else {direction := down;
                         downsweep.signal}}
      else if downsweep.queue then downsweep.signal
                   else {direction := up;
                         upsweep.signal}
    end release;
    headpos := 0; direction := up; busy := false
end dischead;
```

6.3 Readers and Writers

As a more significant example, we take a problem which arises in on-line real-time applications such as airspace control. Suppose that each aircraft is represented by a record, and that this record is kept up to date by a number of "writer" processes and accessed by a number of "reader" processes. Any number of "reader" processes may simultaneously access the same record, but obviously any process which is updating (writing) the individual components of the record must have exclusive access to it, or chaos will ensue. Thus we need a class of monitors; an instance of this class local to *each* individual aircraft record will enforce the required discipline for that record. If there are many aircraft, there is a strong motivation for minimizing local data of the monitor; and if each read or write operation is brief, we should also minimize the time taken by each monitor entry.

When many readers are interested in a single aircraft record, there is a danger that a writer will be indefinitely prevented from keeping that record up to date. We therefore decide that a new reader should not be permitted to start if there is a writer waiting. Similarly, to avoid the danger of indefinite exclusion of readers, all readers waiting at the end of a write should have priority over the next writer. Note that this is a very different scheduling rule from that propounded in [4], and does not seem to require such subtlety in implementation. Nevertheless, it may be more suited to this kind of application, where it is better to read stale information than to wait indefinitely!

The monitor obviously requires four local procedures:

startread	entered by reader who wishes to read.
endread	entered by reader who has finished reading.
startwrite	entered by writer who wishes to write.
endwrite	entered by writer who has finished writing.

We need to keep a count of the number of users who are reading, so that the last reader to finish will know this fact:

readercount:*integer*

We also need a *Boolean* to indicate that someone is actually writing:

busy:*Boolean*;

We introduce separate conditions for readers and writers to wait on:

OKtoread, OKtowrite:*condition*;

The following annotation is relevant:

$$OKtoread \equiv \neg\ busy$$
$$OKtowrite \equiv \neg\ busy\ \&\ readercount = 0$$
$$invariant: busy \Rightarrow readercount = 0$$

```
class readers and writers: monitor
  begin readercount: integer;
        busy: Boolean;
        OKtoread, OKtowrite: condition;
        procedure startread;
        begin if busy ∨ OKtowrite.queue then OKtoread.wait;
            readercount := readercount + 1;
            OKtoread.signal;
            comment Once one reader can start, they all can;
          end startread;
        procedure endread;
        begin readercount := readercount − 1;
            if readercount = 0 then OKtowrite.signal
          end endread;
        procedure startwrite;
          begin
            if readercount ≠ 0 ∨ busy then OKtowrite.wait
            busy := true
          end startwrite;
        procedure endwrite;
          begin busy := false;
            if OKtoread.queue then OKtoread.signal
                        else OKtowrite.signal
          end endwrite;
        readercount := 0;
        busy := false;
  end readers and writers;
```

I am grateful to Dave Gorman for assisting in **the** discovery of this solution.

7. Conclusion

This paper suggests that an appropriate structure for a module of an operating system, which schedules resources for parallel user processes, is very similar to that of a data representation used by a sequential program. However, in the case of monitors, the bodies of the procedures must be protected against re-entrance by being implemented as critical regions. The textual grouping of critical regions together with the data which they update seems much superior to critical regions scattered through the user program, as described in [7, 12]. It also corresponds to the traditional practice of the writers of operating system supervisors. It can be recommended without reservation.

However, it is much more difficult to be confident about the condition concept as a synchronizing primitive. The synchronizing facility which is easiest to use is probably the conditional *wait* [2, 12]:

wait(B);

where B is a general Boolean expression (it causes the given process to wait until B becomes true); but this may be too inefficient for general use in operating systems, because its implementation requires re-evaluation of the expression B after every exit from a procedure of the monitor. The condition variable gives the programmer better control over efficiency and over scheduling; it was designed to be very primitive, and to have a simple proof rule. But perhaps some other compromise between convenience and efficiency might be better. The question whether the signal should always be the last operation of a monitor procedure is still open. These problems will be studied in the design and implementation of a pilot project operating system, currently enjoying the support of the Science Research Council of Great Britain.

Another question which will be studied will be that of the disjointness of monitors: Is it possible to design a separate isolated monitor for each kind of resource, so that it will make sensible scheduling decisions for that resource, using only the minimal information about the utilization of that resource, and using no information about the utilization of any resource administered by other monitors? In principle, it would seem that, when more knowledge of the status of the entire system is available, it should be easier to take decisions nearer to optimality. Furthermore, in principle, independent scheduling of different kinds of resource can lead to deadly embrace. These considerations would lead to the design of a traditional "monolithic" monitor, maintaining large system tables, all of which can be accessed and updated by any of the procedures of the monitor.

There is no a priori reason why the attempt to split the functions of an operating system into a number of isolated disjoint monitors should succeed. It can be made to succeed only by discovering and implementing good scheduling algorithms in each monitor. In order to avoid undesirable interactions between the separate scheduling algorithms, it appears necessary to observe the following principles:

1. Never seek to make an optimal decision; merely seek to avoid persistently pessimal decisions.

2. Do not seek to present the user with a virtual machine which is better than the actual hardware; merely seek to pass on the speed, size, and flat unopiniated structure of a simple hardware design.

3. Use preemptive techniques in preference to non-preemptive ones where possible.

4. Use "grain of time" [9] methods to secure independence of scheduling strategies.

5. Keep a low variance (as well as a low mean) on waiting times.

6. Avoid fixed priorities; instead, try to ensure that every program in the system makes reasonably steady progress. In particular, avoid indefinite overtaking.

7. Ensure that when demand for resources outstrips the supply (i.e. in overload conditions), the behavior of the scheduler is satisfactory (i.e. thrashing is avoided).

8. Make rules for the correct and sensible use of monitor calls, and assume that user programs will obey them. Any checking which is necessary should be done not by a central shared monitor, but rather by an algorithm (called "user envelope") which is local to each process executing a user program. This algorithm should be implemented at least partially in the hardware (e.g. base and range registers, address translation mechanisms, capabilities, etc.).

It is the possibility of constructing separate monitors for different purposes, and of separating the scheduling decisions embodied in monitors from the checking embodied in user envelopes, that may justify a hope that monitors are an appropriate concept for the structuring of an operating system.

Acknowledgments. The development of the monitor concept is due to frequent discussions and communications with E.W. Dijkstra and P. Brinch-Hansen. A monitor corresponds to the "secretary" described in [9], and is also described in [1, 3].

Acknowledgment is also due to the support of IFIP WG.2.3., which provides a meeting place at which these and many other ideas have been germinated, fostered, and tested.

Received February 1973; revised April 1974

References
1. Brinch-Hansen, P. Structured multiprogramming. *Comm. ACM 15*, 7 (July 1972), 574–577.
2. Brinch-Hansen, P. "A comparison of two synchronizing concepts," *Acta Information 1* (1972), 190–199.
3. Brinch-Hansen, P. *Operating System Principles*. Prentice-Hall, Englewood Cliffs, N.J., 1973.
4. Courtois, P. J., Heymans, F., Parnas, D.L. Concurrent control with readers and writers. *Comm. ACM 14*, 10 (Oct. 1971), 667–668.
5. Courtois, P.J., Heymans, F., Parnas, D.L. Comments on [2]. *Acta Informatica 1* (1972), 375–376.
6. Dahl, O.J. Hierarchical program structures. In *Structured Programming*, Academic Press, New York, 1972.
7. Dijkstra, E.W. Cooperating Sequential Processes. In *Programming Languages* (Ed. F. Genuys), Academic Press, New York, 1968.
8. Dijkstra, E.W. A constructive approach to the problem of program correctness. *BIT 8* (1968), 174–186.
9. Dijkstra, E.W. Hierarchical ordering of sequential processes. In *Operating Systems Techniques*, Academic Press, New York, 1972.
10. Dijkstra, E.W. Information streams sharing a finite buffer. *Information Processing Letters 1*, 5 (Oct. 1972), 179–180.
11. Dijkstra, E.W. A class of allocation strategies inducing bounded delays only. Proc AFIPS 1972 SJCC, Vol. 40, AFIPS Press, Montvale, N.J., pp. 933–936.
12. Hoare, C.A.R. Towards a theory of parallel programming. In *Operating Systems Techniques*, Academic Press, New York, 1972.
13. Hoare, C.A.R. Proof of correctness of data representations. *Acta Informatica 1* (1972), 271–281.
14. Hoare, C.A.R. A structured paging system. *Computer J. 16*, 3 (1973), 209–215.
15. Wirth, N. The programming language PASCAL. *Acta Informatica 1*, 1 (1971), 35–63.

Programming Languages

T.A. Standish
Editor

Guarded Commands, Nondeterminacy and Formal Derivation of Programs

Edsger W. Dijkstra
Burroughs Corporation

Reprinted from *Communications of the ACM*, August 1975, pp. 453-457. Copyright 1975 Association for Computing Machinery, Inc. Reprinted by permission.

So-called "guarded commands" are introduced as a building block for alternative and repetitive constructs that allow nondeterministic program components for which at least the activity evoked, but possibly even the final state, is not necessarily uniquely determined by the initial state. For the formal derivation of programs expressed in terms of these constructs, a calculus will be be shown.

Key Words and Phrases: programming languages, sequencing primitives, program semantics, programming language semantics, nondeterminacy, case-construction, repetition, termination, correctness proof, derivation of programs, programming methodology

CR Categories: 4.20, 4.22

1. Introduction

In Section 2, two statements, an alternative construct and a repetitive construct, are introduced, together with an intuitive (mechanistic) definition of their semantics. The basic building block for both of them is the so-called "guarded command," a statement list prefixed by a boolean expression: only when this boolean expression is initially true, is the statement list eligible for execution. The potential nondeterminacy allows us to map otherwise (trivially) different programs on the same program text, a circumstance that seems largely responsible for the fact that programs can now be derived in a manner more systematic than before.

In Section 3, after a prelude defining the notation, a formal definition of the semantics of the two constructs is given, together with two theorems for each of the constructs (without proof).

In Section 4, it is shown how, based upon the above, a formal calculus for the derivation of programs can be founded. We would like to stress that we do not present "an algorithm" for the derivation of programs: we have used the term "a calculus" for a formal discipline—a set of rules—such that, if applied successfully: (1) it will have derived a correct program; and (2) it will tell us that we have reached such a goal. (We use the term as in "integral calculus.")

2. Two Statements Made from Guarded Commands

If the reader accepts "other statements" as indicating, say, assignment statements and procedure calls, we can give the relevant syntax in BNF [2]. In the following we have extended BNF with the convention that the braces {...} should be read as "followed by zero or more instances of the enclosed."

⟨guarded command⟩ ::= ⟨guard⟩ → ⟨guarded list⟩
⟨guard⟩ ::= ⟨boolean expression⟩
⟨guarded list⟩ ::= ⟨statement⟩ {; ⟨statement⟩}
⟨guarded command set⟩ ::= ⟨guarded command⟩
        {▯ ⟨guarded command⟩}
⟨alternative construct⟩ ::= **if** ⟨guarded command set⟩ **fi**
⟨repetitive construct⟩ ::= **do** ⟨guarded command set⟩ **od**
⟨statement⟩ ::= ⟨alternative construct⟩ |
        ⟨repetitive construct⟩ | "other statements"

The semicolons in the guarded list have the usual meaning: when the guarded list is selected for execution its statements will be executed successively in the order from left to right; a guarded list will only be selected for execution in a state such that its guard is true. Note that a guarded command by itself is *not* a statement: it is a component of a guarded command set from which statements can be constructed. If the guarded command set consists of more than one guarded command, they are mutually separated by the separator $[]$; our text is then an arbitrarily ordered enumeration of an unordered set; i.e. the order in which the guarded commands of a set appear in our text is semantically irrelevant.

Our syntax gives two ways for constructing a statement out of a guarded command set. The alternative construct is written by enclosing it by the special bracket pair **if** ... **fi**. If in the initial state none of the guards is true, the program will abort; otherwise an arbitrary guarded list with a true guard will be selected for execution.

Note. If the empty guarded command set were allowed **if fi** would be semantically equivalent to "abort". (End of note.)

An example—illustrating the nondeterminacy in a very modest fashion—would be the program that for fixed x and y assigns to m the maximum value of x and y:

```
if x ≥ y → m := x
[] y ≥ x → m := y
fi.
```

The repetitive construct is written down by enclosing a guarded command set by the special bracket pair **do** ... **od.** Here a state in which none of the guards is true will not lead to abortion but to proper termination; the complementary rule, however, is that it will only terminate in a state in which none of the guards is true: when initially or upon completed execution of a selected guarded list one or more guards are true, a new selection for execution of a guarded list with a true guard will take place, and so on. When the repetitive construct has terminated properly, we know that all its guards are false.

Note. If the empty guarded command set were allowed **do od** would be semantically equivalent to "skip". (End of note.)

An example—showing the nondeterminacy in somewhat greater glory—is the program that assigns to the variables $q1$, $q2$, $q3$, and $q4$ a permutation of the values $Q1$, $Q2$, $Q3$, and $Q4$, such that $q1 \leq q2 \leq q3 \leq q4$. Using concurrent assignment statements for the sake of convenience, we can program

```
q1, q2, q3, q4 := Q1, Q2, Q3, Q4;
do q1 > q2 → q1, q2 := q2, q1
[] q2 > q3 → q2, q3 := q3, q2
[] q3 > q4 → q3, q4 := q4, q3
od.
```

To conclude this section, we give a program where not only the computation but also the final state is not necessarily uniquely determined. The program should determine k such that for fixed value n ($n > 0$) and a fixed function $f(i)$ defined for $0 \leq i < n$, k will eventually satisfy: $0 \leq k < n$ and $(\forall i: 0 \leq i < n: f(k) \geq f(i))$. (Eventually k should be the place of a maximum.)

```
k := 0; j := 1;
do j ≠ n → if f(j) ≤ f(k) → j := j + 1
           [] f(j) ≥ f(k) → k := j; j := j + 1
           fi
od.
```

Only permissible final states are possible and each permissible final state is possible.

3. Formal Definition of the Semantics

3.1 Notational Prelude

In the following sections we shall use the symbols P, Q, and R to denote (predicates defining) boolean functions defined on all points of the state space; alternatively we shall refer to them as "conditions," satisfied by all states for which the boolean function is true. Two special predicates that we denote by the reserved names T and F play a special role: T denotes the condition that, by definition, is satisfied by all states; F denotes, by definition, the condition that is satisfied by no state at all.

The way in which we use predicates (as a tool for defining sets of initial or final states) for the definition of the semantics of programming language constructs has been directly inspired by Hoare [1], the main difference being that we have tightened things up a bit: while Hoare introduces sufficient pre-conditions such that the mechanisms will not produce the wrong result (but may fail to terminate), we shall introduce necessary and sufficient—i.e. so-called "weakest"—pre-conditions such that the mechanisms are guaranteed to produce the right result.

More specifically: we shall use the notation $wp(S, R)$, where S denotes a statement list and R some condition on the state of the system, to denote the weakest precondition for the initial state of the system such that activation of S is guaranteed to lead to a properly terminating activity leaving the system in a final state satisfying the post-condition R. Such a wp—which is called "a predicate transformer" because it associates a pre-condition to any post-condition R—has, by definition, the following properties.

1. For any S, we have for all states: $wp(S,F) = F$ (the so-called Law of the Excluded Miracle).
2. For any S and any two post-conditions, such that for all states $P \Rightarrow Q$, we have for all states: $wp(S,P) \Rightarrow wp(S,Q)$.
3. For any S and any two post-conditions P and Q, we have for all states $(wp(S,P) \text{ and } wp(S,Q)) = wp(S,P \text{ and } Q)$.
4. For any deterministic S and any post-conditions P

and Q, we have for all states $(wp(S,P)$ **or** $wp(S,Q))$ $= wp(S, P$ **or** $Q)$.

For nondeterministic mechanisms S, the equality has to be replaced by an implication; the resulting formula follows from the second property.

Together with the rules of propositional calculus and the semantic definitions to be given below, the above four properties take over the role of the "rules of inference" as introduced by Hoare [1].

We take the position that we know the semantics of a mechanism S sufficiently well if we know its predicate transformer, i.e. can derive $wp(S,R)$ for any post-condition R.

Note. We consider the semantics of S only defined for those initial states for which has been established a priori that they satisfy $wp(S,T)$, i.e. for which proper termination is guaranteed (even in the face of possibly non-deterministic behavior); for other initial states we don't care. By suitably changing S, if necessary, we can always see to it that $wp(S,T)$ is decidable. (End of note.)

Example 1. The semantics of the empty statement, denoted by "skip" are given by the definition that for any post-condition R, we have wp ("skip", R) $= R$.

Example 2. The semantics of the assignment statement "$x := E$" are given by $wp("x := E", R) = R_E^x$, in which R_E^x denotes a copy of the predicate defining R in which each occurrence of the variable x is replaced by (E).

Example 3. The semantics of the semicolon ";" as concatenation operator are given by
$$wp("S1 ; S2", R) = wp(S1, wp(S2,R)).$$

3.2 The Alternative Construct

In order to define the semantics of the alternative construct we define two abbreviations.

Let *IF* denote

if $B_1 \rightarrow SL_1 \, \square \, \ldots \, \square \, B_n \rightarrow SL_n$ **fi**;

let BB denote

$$(\exists i : 1 \leq i \leq n : B_i);$$

then, by definition

$$wp(IF, R) = (BB \textbf{ and } (\forall i : 1 \leq i \leq n : B_i \Rightarrow wp(SL_i, R)),.$$

(The first term BB requires that the alternative construct as such will not lead to abortion on account of all guards false; the second term requires that each guarded list eligible for execution will lead to an acceptable final state.) From this definition we can derive—by simple substitutions:

THEOREM 1. *From $(\forall i : 1 \leq i \leq n : (Q \textbf{ and } B_i) \Rightarrow wp(SL_i, R))$ for all states we can conclude that $(Q \textbf{ and } BB) \Rightarrow wp(IF, R)$ holds for all states.*

Let t denote some integer function, defined on the state space, and let $wdec(S,t)$ denote the weakest pre-condition such that activation of S is guaranteed to lead to a properly terminating activity leaving the system in a final state such that the value of t is decreased by at least 1 (compared to its initial value). In terms of $wdec$ we can formulate the very similar:

THEOREM 2. *From $(\forall i : 1 \leq i \leq n : (Q \textbf{ and } B_i) \Rightarrow wdec(SL_i, t))$ for all states we can conclude that $(Q \textbf{ and } BB) \Rightarrow wdec(IF, t)$ holds for all states.*

Note (which can be skipped at first reading). The relation between wp and $wdec$ is as follows. For any point X in state space we can regard $wp(S, t \leq t_0)$ as an equation with t_0 as the unknown. Let its smallest solution for t_0 be $tmin(X)$. (Here we have added the explicit dependence on the state X.) Then $tmin(X)$ can be interpreted as the lowest upper bound for the final value of t if the mechanism S is activated with X as initial state. Then, by definition, $wdec(S, t) = (tmin(X) \leq t(X) - 1) = (tmin(X) < t(X))$. (End of note.)

3.3 The Repetitive Construct

As is to be expected, the definition of the repetitive construct

do $B_1 \rightarrow SL_1 \, \square \, \ldots \, \square \, B_n \rightarrow SL_n$ **od**,

that we denote by DO, is more complicated. Let

$$H_0(R) = (R \textbf{ and non } BB)$$

and for $k > 0$,

$$H_k(R) = (wp(IF, H_{k-1}(R)) \textbf{ or } H_0(R))$$

(where IF denotes the *same* guarded command set enclosed by "if fi"). Then, by definition

$$wp(DO, R) = (\exists k : k \geq 0 : H_k(R)).$$

(Intuitively, $H_k(R)$ can be interpreted as the weakest pre-condition guaranteeing proper termination after at most k selections of a guarded list, leaving the system in a final state satisfying R.) Via mathematical induction we can prove:

THEOREM 3. *If we have for all states $(P \textbf{ and } BB) \Rightarrow (wp(IF, P) \textbf{ and } wdec(IF, t) \textbf{ and } t \geq 0)$ we can conclude that we have for all states $P \Rightarrow wp(DO, P \textbf{ and non } BB)$.*

Note. The antecedent of Theorem 3 is of the form of the consequents of Theorems 1 and 2. (End of note.)

Because T is the condition by definition satisfied by all states, $wp(S,T)$ is the weakest pre-condition guaranteeing proper termination for S. This allows us to formulate an alternative theorem about the repetitive construct, viz.:

THEOREM 4. *From $(P \textbf{ and } BB) \Rightarrow wp(IF, P)$ for all states, we can conclude that we have for all states $(P \textbf{ and } wp(DO, T)) \Rightarrow wp(DO, P \textbf{ and non } BB)$.*

Note. In connection with the above theorems, P is called "the invariant relation" and t is called "the variant function." Theorems 3 and 4 are easily proved by mathematical induction, with k as the induction variable. (End of note.)

4. Formal Derivation of Programs

The formal requirement of our program performing $m := max(x,y)$—see above—is that for fixed x and y it establishes the relation

R: $(m = x$ or $m = y)$ and $m \geq x$ and $m \geq y$.

Now the Axiom of Assignment tells us that "$m := x$" is the standard way of establishing the truth of $m = x$ for fixed x, which is a way of establishing the truth of the first term of R. Will "$m := x$" do the job? In order to investigate this, we derive and simplify:

$$wp(\text{"}m := x\text{"}, R) = (x = x \text{ or } x = y)$$
$$\text{and } x \geq x \text{ and } x \geq y$$
$$= x \geq y.$$

Taking this weakest pre-condition as its guard, Theorem 1 tells us that

if $x \geq y \rightarrow m := x$ **fi**

will produce the correct result if it terminates successfully. The disadvantage of this program is that $BB \neq T$; i.e. it might lead to abortion; weakening BB means looking for alternatives which might introduce new guards. The obvious alternative is the assignment "$m := y$" with the guard $wp(\text{"}m := y\text{"}, R) = y \geq x$; thus we are led to our program

if $x \geq y \rightarrow m := x$
$\square$ $y \geq x \rightarrow m := y$
fi

and by this time $BB = T$, and therefore we have solved the problem. (In the meantime we have proved that the maximum of two values is always defined, viz. that R considered as equation for m has always a solution.)

As an example of the derivation of a repetitive construct we shall derive a program for the greatest common divisor of two positive numbers; i.e. for fixed, positive X and Y we have to establish the final relation $x = gcd(X,Y)$.

The formal machinery only gets in motion, once we have chosen our invariant relation and our variant function. The program then gets the structure

"establish the relation P to be kept invariant";
do "decrease t as long as possible under variance of P"
od.

Suppose that we choose for the invariant relation

P: $gcd(X,Y) = gcd(x,y)$ and $x > 0$ and $y > 0$,

a relation that has the advantage of being easily established by $x := X; y := Y$.

The most general "something" to be done under invariance of P is of the form $x, y := E1, E2$, and we are interested in a guard B such that

$$(P \text{ and } B) \Rightarrow wp(\text{"}x, y := E1, E2\text{"}, P)$$
$$= (gcd(X, Y) = gcd(E1, E2)$$
$$\text{and } E1 > 0 \text{ and } E2 > 0).$$

Because the guard must be a computable boolean expression and should not contain the computation of $gcd(X, Y)$—for that was the whole problem—we must see to it that the expressions E1 and E2 are so chosen, that the first term $gcd(X, Y) = gcd(E1, E2)$ is implied by P, which is true if $gcd(x, y) = gcd(E1, E2)$. In other words we are invited to massage the value pair (x,y) in such a fashion that their gcd is not changed. Because—and this is the place at which to mobilize our mathematical knowledge about the gcd-function—$gcd(x, y) = gcd(x - y, y)$, a possible guarded list would be $x := x - y$. Deriving $wp(\text{"}x := x - y\text{"}, P) = (gcd(X, Y) = gcd(x - y, y)$ and $x - y > 0$ and $y > 0)$ and omitting all terms of the conjunction implied by P, we find the guard $x > y$ as far as the invariance of P is concerned. Besides that we must require guaranteed decrease of the variant function t. Let us investigate the consequences of the choice $t = x + y$. From

$$wp(\text{"}x := x - y\text{"}, t \leq t_0)$$
$$= wp(\text{"}x := x - y\text{"}, x + y \leq t_0) = (x \leq t_0),$$

we conclude that $tmin = x$; therefore $wdec(\text{"}x := x - y\text{"}, t) = (x < x + y) = (y > 0)$.

The requirement of monotonic decrease of t imposes no further restriction of the guard because $wdec(\text{"}x := x - y\text{"}, t)$ is fully implied by P, and at our first effort we come to

$x := X; y := Y;$
do $x > y \rightarrow x := x - y$ **od**.

Alas, this single guard is insufficient: from P **and non** BB we are not allowed to conclude $x = gcd(X,Y)$. In a completely analogous manner, the alternative $y := y - x$ will require as its guard $y > x$, and our next effort is

$x := X; y := Y;$
do $x > y \rightarrow x := x - y$
$\square$ $y > x \rightarrow y := y - x$
od.

Now the job is done, because with this last program **non** $BB = (x = y)$ and $(P$ **and** $x = y) \Rightarrow (x = gcd(X,Y)$, because $gcd(x,x) = x$.

Note. The choice of $t = x + 2y$ and the knowledge of the fact that the gcd is a symmetric function could have led to the program

$x := X; y := Y;$
do $x > y \rightarrow x := x - y$
$\square$ $y > x \rightarrow x, y := y,x$
od.

The swap $x,y := y,x$ can never destroy P: the guard of the last guarded list is fully caused by the requirement that t is effectively decreased. (End of note.)

In both cases the final game has been to find a large enough set of such guarded lists that BB, the disjunction of their guards, was sufficiently weak: in the case of the alternative construct the purpose is avoiding abortion, in the case of the repetitive construct the goal is getting BB weak enough such that P **and non** BB is strong enough to imply the desired post-condition R.

It is illuminating to compare our first version of Euclid's Algorithm with what we would have written down with the traditional clauses:

$x := X; y := Y;$ (version A)
while $x \neq y$ **do if** $x > y$ **then** $x := x - y$
       else $y := y - x$ **fi od**

and

$x := X; y := Y;$ (version B)
while $x \neq y$ **do while** $x > y$ **do** $x := x - y$ **od**;
     while $y > x$ **do** $y := y - x$ **od**
   od.

In the fully symmetric version with the guarded commands the algorithm has been reduced to its bare essentials, while the traditional clauses force us to choose between versions A and B (and others), a choice that can only be justified by making assumptions about the time taken for tests and about expectation values for traversal frequencies. (But even taking the time taken for tests into account, it is not clear that we have lost: the average number of necessary tests per assignment ranges with guarded commands from 1 to 2, equals 2 for version A and ranges from 1 to 2.5 for version B. If the guards of a guarded command set are evaluated concurrently—nothing in our semantics excludes that— the new version is time-wise superior to all the others.) The virtues of the *case*-construction have been extended to repetition as well.

5. Concluding Remarks

The research, the outcome of which is reported in this article, was triggered by the observation that Euclid's Algorithm could also be regarded as synchronizing the two cyclic processes "**do** $x := x - y$ **od**" and "**do** $y := y - x$ **od**" in such a way that the relation $x > 0$ **and** $y > 0$ would be kept invariantly true. It was only after this observation that we saw that the formal techniques we had already developed for the derivation of the synchronizing conditions that ensure the harmonious cooperation of (cyclic) sequential processes, such as can be identified in the total activity of operating systems, could be transferred lock, stock, and barrel to the development of sequential programs as shown in this article. The main difference is that while for sequential programs the situation "all guards false" is a desirable goal—for it means termination of a repetitive construct—one tries to avoid it in operating systems—for there it means deadlock.

The second reason to pursue these investigations was my personal desire to get a better appreciation, which part of the programming activity can be regarded as a formal routine and which part of it seems to require "invention." While the design of an alternative construct now seems to be a reasonably straightforward activity, that of a repetitive construct requires what I regard as "the invention" of an invariant relation and a variant function. My presentation of this calculus should, however, not be interpreted as my suggestion that all programs should be developed in this way: it just gives us another handle.

The calculus does, however, explain my preference for the axiomatic definition of programming language semantics via predicate transformers above other definition techniques: the definition via predicate transformers seems to lend itself most readily to being forged into a tool for the goal-directed activity of program composition.

Finally, I would like to add a word or two about the potential nondeterminacy. Having worked mainly with hardly self-checking hardware, with which nonreproducing behavior of user programs is a very strong indication of a machine malfunctioning, I had to overcome a considerable mental resistance before I found myself willing to consider nondeterministic programs seriously. It is, however, fair to say that I could never have discovered the calculus before having taken that hurdle: the simplicity and elegance of the above would have been destroyed by requiring the derivation of deterministic programs only. Whether nondeterminacy is eventually removed mechanically—in order not to mislead the maintenance engineer—or (perhaps only partly) by the programmer himself because, at second thought, he does care—e.g. for reasons of efficiency— which alternative is chosen is something I leave entirely to the circumstances. In any case we can appreciate the nondeterministic program as a helpful stepping stone.

Acknowledgments. In the first place my acknowledgments are due to the members of the IFIP Working Group W.G.2.3 on "Programming Methodology." Besides them, W.H.J. Feijen, D.E. Knuth, M. Rem, and C.S. Scholten have been directly helpful in one way or another. I should also thank the various audiences— in Albuquerque (courtesy NSF), in San Diego and Luxembourg (courtesy Burroughs Corporation)— that have played their role of critical sounding board beyond what one is entitled to hope.

Received July 1974; revised January 1975

References
1. Hoare, C.A.R. An axiomatic basis for computer programming. *Comm. ACM 12*, 10 (Oct. 1969), 576–583.
2. Naur, Peter (Ed.). Report on the algorithmic language ALGOL 60. *Comm. ACM 3*, (May 1960), 299–314.

Programming   S. L. Graham, R. L. Rivest
Techniques   Editors

Communicating Sequential Processes

C.A.R. Hoare
The Queen's University
Belfast, Northern Ireland

This paper suggests that input and output are basic primitives of programming and that parallel composition of communicating sequential processes is a fundamental program structuring method. When combined with a development of Dijkstra's guarded command, these concepts are surprisingly versatile. Their use is illustrated by sample solutions of a variety of familiar programming exercises.

Key Words and Phrases: programming, programming languages, programming primitives, program structures, parallel programming, concurrency, input, output, guarded commands, nondeterminacy, coroutines, procedures, multiple entries, multiple exits, classes, data representations, recursion, conditional critical regions, monitors, iterative arrays
CR Categories: 4.20, 4.22, 4.32

1. Introduction

Among the primitive concepts of computer programming, and of the high level languages in which programs are expressed, the action of assignment is familiar and well understood. In fact, any change of the internal state of a machine executing a program can be modeled as an assignment of a new value to some variable part of that machine. However, the operations of input and output, which affect the external environment of a machine, are not nearly so well understood. They are often added to a programming language only as an afterthought.

Among the structuring methods for computer pro-

This research was supported by a Senior Fellowship of the Science Research Council.

Author's present address: Programming Research Group, 45, Banbury Road, Oxford, England.

grams, three basic constructs have received widespread recognition and use: A repetitive construct (e.g. the **while** loop), an alternative construct (e.g. the conditional **if..then..else**), and normal sequential program composition (often denoted by a semicolon). Less agreement has been reached about the design of other important program structures, and many suggestions have been made: Subroutines (Fortran), procedures (Algol 60 [15]), entries (PL/I), coroutines (UNIX [17]), classes (SIMULA 67 [5]), processes and monitors (Concurrent Pascal [2]), clusters (CLU [13]), forms (ALPHARD [19]), actors (Hewitt [1]).

The traditional stored program digital computer has been designed primarily for deterministic execution of a single sequential program. Where the desire for greater speed has led to the introduction of parallelism, every attempt has been made to disguise this fact from the programmer, either by hardware itself (as in the multiple function units of the CDC 6600) or by the software (as in an I/O control package, or a multiprogrammed operating system). However, developments of processor technology suggest that a multiprocessor machine, constructed from a number of similar self-contained processors (each with its own store), may become more powerful, capacious, reliable, and economical than a machine which is disguised as a monoprocessor.

In order to use such a machine effectively on a single task, the component processors must be able to communicate and to synchronize with each other. Many methods of achieving this have been proposed. A widely adopted method of communication is by inspection and updating of a common store (as in Algol 68 [18], PL/I, and many machine codes). However, this can create severe problems in the construction of correct programs and it may lead to expense (e.g. crossbar switches) and unreliability (e.g. glitches) in some technologies of hardware implementation. A greater variety of methods has been proposed for synchronization: semaphores [6], events (PL/I), conditional critical regions [10], monitors and queues (Concurrent Pascal [2]), and path expressions [3]. Most of these are demonstrably adequate for their purpose, but there is no widely recognized criterion for choosing between them.

This paper makes an ambitious attempt to find a single simple solution to all these problems. The essential proposals are:
(1) Dijkstra's guarded commands [8] are adopted (with a slight change of notation) as sequential control structures, and as the sole means of introducing and controlling nondeterminism.
(2) A parallel command, based on Dijkstra's *parbegin* [6], specifies concurrent execution of its constituent sequential commands (processes). All the processes start simultaneously, and the parallel command ends only when they are all finished. They may not communicate with each other by updating global variables.
(3) Simple forms of input and output command are introduced. They are used for communication between concurrent processes.

(4) Such communication occurs when one process names another as destination for output *and* the second process names the first as source for input. In this case, the value to be output is copied from the first process to the second. There is *no* automatic buffering: In general, an input or output command is delayed until the other process is ready with the corresponding output or input. Such delay is invisible to the delayed process.

(5) Input commands may appear in guards. A guarded command with an input guard is selected for execution only if and when the source named in the input command is ready to execute the corresponding output command. If several input guards of a set of alternatives have ready destinations, only one is selected and the others have *no* effect; but the choice between them is arbitrary. In an efficient implementation, an output command which has been ready for a long time should be favored; but the definition of a language cannot specify this since the relative speed of execution of the processes is undefined.

(6) A repetitive command may have input guards. If all the sources named by them have terminated, then the repetitive command also terminates.

(7) A simple pattern-matching feature, similar to that of [16], is used to discriminate the structure of an input message, and to access its components in a secure fashion. This feature is used to inhibit input of messages that do not match the specified pattern.

The programs expressed in the proposed language are intended to be implementable both by a conventional machine with a single main store, and by a fixed network of processors connected by input/output channels (although very different optimizations are appropriate in the different cases). It is consequently a rather static language: The text of a program determines a fixed upper bound on the number of processes operating concurrently; there is no recursion and no facility for process-valued variables. In other respects also, the language has been stripped to the barest minimum necessary for explanation of its more novel features.

The concept of a communicating sequential process is shown in Sections 3–5 to provide a method of expressing solutions to many simple programming exercises which have previously been employed to illustrate the use of various proposed programming language features. This suggests that the process may constitute a synthesis of a number of familiar and new programming ideas. The reader is invited to skip the examples which do not interest him.

However, this paper also ignores many serious problems. The most serious is that it fails to suggest any proof method to assist in the development and verification of correct programs. Secondly, it pays no attention to the problems of efficient implementation, which may be particularly serious on a traditional sequential computer. It is probable that a solution to these problems will require (1) imposition of restrictions in the use of the proposed features; (2) reintroduction of distinctive no-tations for the most common and useful special cases; (3) development of automatic optimization techniques; and (4) the design of appropriate hardware.

Thus the concepts and notations introduced in this paper (although described in the next section in the form of a programming language fragment) should not be regarded as suitable for use as a programming language, either for abstract or for concrete programming. They are at best only a partial solution to the problems tackled. Further discussion of these and other points will be found in Section 7.

2. Concepts and Notations

The style of the following description is borrowed from Algol 60 [15]. Types, declarations, and expressions have not been treated; in the examples, a Pascal-like notation [20] has usually been adopted. The curly braces { } have been introduced into BNF to denote none or more repetitions of the enclosed material. (Sentences in parentheses refer to an implementation: they are not strictly part of a language definition.)

```
<command> ::= <simple command>|<structured command>
<simple command> ::= <null command>|<assignment command>
        |<input command>|<output command>
<structured command> ::= <alternative command>
        |<repetitive command>|<parallel command>
<null command> ::= skip
<command list> ::= {<declaration>; |<command>;} <command>
```

A command specifies the behavior of a device executing the command. It may succeed or fail. Execution of a simple command, if successful, may have an effect on the internal state of the executing device (in the case of assignment), or on its external environment (in the case of output), or on both (in the case of input). Execution of a structured command involves execution of some or all of its constituent commands, and if any of these fail, so does the structured command. (In this case, whenever possible, an implementation should provide some kind of comprehensible error diagnostic message.)

A null command has no effect and never fails.

A command list specifies sequential execution of its constituent commands in the order written. Each declaration introduces a fresh variable with a scope which extends from its declaration to the end of the command list.

2.1 Parallel Commands

```
<parallel command> ::= [<process>{||<process>}]
<process> ::= <process label> <command list>
<process label> ::= <empty>|<identifier> ::
        |<identifier>(<label subscript>{,<label subscript>}) ::
<label subscript> ::= <integer constant>|<range>
<integer constant> ::= <numeral>|<bound variable>
<bound variable> ::= <identifier>
<range> ::= <bound variable>:<lower bound>..<upper bound>
<lower bound> ::= <integer constant>
<upper bound> ::= <integer constant>
```

Each process of a parallel command must be *disjoint* from every other process of the command, in the sense that it does not mention any variable which occurs as a target variable (see Sections 2.2 and 2.3) in any other process.

A process label without subscripts, or one whose label subscripts are all integer constants, serves as a name for the command list to which it is prefixed; its scope extends over the whole of the parallel command. A process whose label subscripts include one or more ranges stands for a series of processes, each with the same label and command list, except that each has a different combination of values substituted for the bound variables. These values range between the lower bound and the upper bound inclusive. For example, $X(i:1..n) :: CL$ stands for

$$X(1) :: CL_1 || X(2) :: CL_2 ||...|| X(n) :: CL_n$$

where each CL_j is formed from CL by replacing every occurrence of the bound variable i by the numeral j. After all such expansions, each process label in a parallel command must occur only once and the processes must be well formed and disjoint.

A parallel command specifies concurrent execution of its constituent processes. They all start simultaneously and the parallel command terminates successfully only if and when they have all successfully terminated. The relative speed with which they are executed is arbitrary. *Examples:*

(1) [cardreader?cardimage||lineprinter!lineimage]

Performs the two constituent commands in parallel, and terminates only when both operations are complete. The time taken may be as low as the longer of the times taken by each constituent process, i.e. the sum of its computing, waiting, and transfer times.

(2) [west :: DISASSEMBLE||X :: SQUASH||east :: ASSEMBLE]

The three processes have the names "west," "X," and "east." The capitalized words stand for command lists which will be defined in later examples.

(3) [room :: ROOM||fork(i:0..4) :: FORK||phil(i:0..4) :: PHIL]

There are eleven processes. The behavior of "room" is specified by the command list ROOM. The behavior of the five processes fork(0), fork(1), fork(2), fork(3), fork(4), is specified by the command list FORK, within which the bound variable i indicates the identity of the particular fork. Similar remarks apply to the five processes PHIL.

2.2 Assignment Commands

```
<assignment command> ::= <target variable> := <expression>
<expression> ::= <simple expression>|<structured expression>
<structured expression> ::= <constructor>(<expression list>)
<constructor> ::= <identifier>|<empty>
<expression list> ::= <empty>|<expression>{,<expression>}
<target variable> ::= <simple variable>|<structured target>
<structured target> ::= <constructor>(<target variable list>)
<target variable list> ::= <empty>|<target variable>
        {,<target variable>}
```

An expression denotes a value which is computed by an executing device by application of its constituent operators to the specified operands. The value of an expression is undefined if any of these operations are undefined. The value denoted by a simple expression may be simple or structured. The value denoted by a structured expression is structured; its constructor is that of the expression, and its components are the list of values denoted by the constituent expressions of the expression list.

An assignment command specifies evaluation of its expression, and assignment of the denoted value to the target variable. A simple target variable may have assigned to it a simple or a structured value. A structured target variable may have assigned to it a structured value, with the same constructor. The effect of such assignment is to assign to each constituent simpler variable of the structured target the value of the corresponding component of the structured value. Consequently, the value denoted by the target variable, if evaluated *after* a successful assignment, is the same as the value denoted by the expression, as evaluated *before* the assignment.

An assignment fails if the value of its expression is undefined, or if that value does not *match* the target variable, in the following sense: A *simple* target variable matches any value of its type. A *structured* target variable matches a structured value, provided that: (1) they have the same constructor, (2) the target variable list is the same length as the list of components of the value, (3) each target variable of the list matches the corresponding component of the value list. A structured value with no components is known as a "signal."

Examples:

(1) $x := x + 1$	the value of x after the assignment is the same as the value of $x + 1$ before.
(2) $(x, y) := (y, x)$	exchanges the values of x and y.
(3) $x := cons(left, right)$	constructs a structured value and assigns it to x.
(4) $cons(left, right) := x$	fails if x does not have the form $cons(y, z)$; but if it does, then y is assigned to left, and z is assigned to right.
(5) $insert(n) := insert(2*x + 1)$	equivalent to $n := 2*x + 1$.
(6) $c := P()$	assigns to c a "signal" with constructor P, and no components.
(7) $P() := c$	fails if the value of c is not $P()$; otherwise has no effect.
(8) $insert(n) := has(n)$	fails, due to mismatch.

Note: Successful execution of both (3) and (4) ensures the truth of the postcondition $x = cons(left, right)$; but (3) does so by changing x and (4) does so by changing left and right. Example (4) will fail if there is *no* value of left and right which satisfies the postcondition.

2.3 Input and Output Commands

```
<input command> ::= <source>?<target variable>
<output command> ::= <destination>!<expression>
<source> ::= <process name>
```

<destination> ::= <process name>
<process name> ::= <identifier>|<identifier>(<subscripts>)
<subscripts> ::= <integer expression>{,<integer expression>}

Input and output commands specify communication between two concurrently operating sequential processes. Such a process may be implemented in hardware as a special-purpose device (e.g. cardreader or lineprinter), or its behavior may be specified by one of the constituent processes of a parallel command. Communication occurs between two processes of a parallel command whenever (1) an input command in one process specifies as its source the process name of the other process; (2) an output command in the other process specifies as its destination the process name of the first process; and (3) the target variable of the input command matches the value denoted by the expression of the output command. On these conditions, the input and output commands are said to *correspond*. Commands which correspond are executed simultaneously, and their combined effect is to assign the value of the expression of the output command to the target variable of the input command.

An input command fails if its source is terminated. An output command fails if its destination is terminated or if its expression is undefined.

(The requirement of synchronization of input and output commands means that an implementation will have to delay whichever of the two commands happens to be ready first. The delay is ended when the corresponding command in the other process is also ready, or when the other process terminates. In the latter case the first command fails. It is also possible that the delay will never be ended, for example, if a group of processes are attempting communication but none of their input and output commands correspond with each other. This form of failure is known as a deadlock.)

Examples:

(1) cardreader?cardimage	from cardreader, read a card and assign its value (an array of characters) to the variable cardimage
(2) lineprinter!lineimage	to lineprinter, send the value of lineimage for printing
(3) $X?(x, y)$	from process named X, input a pair of values and assign them to x and y
(4) DIV!($3*a + b$, 13)	to process DIV, output the two specified values.

Note: If a process named DIV issues command (3), and a process named X issues command (4), these are executed simultaneously, and have the same effect as the assignment: $(x, y) := (3*a + b, 13)$ ($\equiv x := 3*a + b; y := 13$).

(5) console(i)?c	from the ith element of an array of consoles, input a value and assign it to c
(6) console($j - 1$)!"A"	to the $(j - 1)$th console, output character "A"
(7) $X(i)?V( )$	from the ith of an array of processes X, input a signal V( ); refuse to input any other signal
(8) sem!P( )	to sem output a signal P( )

2.4 Alternative and Repetitive Commands

<repetitive command> ::=*<alternative command>
<alternative command> ::= [<guarded command>
    {☐<guarded command>}]
<guarded command> ::= <guard> → <command list>
    |(<range>{,<range>})<guard> → <command list>
<guard> ::= <guard list>|<guard list>;<input command>
    |<input command>
    <guard list> ::= <guard element>{;<guard element>}
<guard element> ::= <boolean expression>|<declaration>

A guarded command with one or more ranges stands for a series of guarded commands, each with the same guard and command list, except that each has a different combination of values substituted for the bound variables. The values range between the lower bound and upper bound inclusive. For example, $(i:1..n)G \rightarrow CL$ stands for

$$G_1 \rightarrow CL_1 [] G_2 \rightarrow CL_2 [] ... [] G_n \rightarrow CL_n$$

where each $G_j \rightarrow CL_j$ is formed from $G \rightarrow CL$ by replacing every occurrence of the bound variable i by the numeral j.

A guarded command is executed only if and when the execution of its guard does not fail. First its guard is executed and then its command list. A guard is executed by execution of its constituent elements from left to right. A Boolean expression is evaluated: If it denotes false, the guard fails; but an expression that denotes true has no effect. A declaration introduces a fresh variable with a scope that extends from the declaration to the end of the guarded command. An input command at the end of a guard is executed only if and when a corresponding output command is executed. (An implementation may test whether a guard fails simply by trying to execute it, and discontinuing execution if and when it fails. This is valid because such a discontinued execution has no effect on the state of the executing device.)

An alternative command specifies execution of exactly one of its constituent guarded commands. Consequently, if all guards fail, the alternative command fails. Otherwise an arbitrary one with successfully executable guard is selected and executed. (An implementation should take advantage of its freedom of selection to ensure efficient execution and good response. For example, when input commands appear as guards, the command which corresponds to the earliest ready and matching output command should in general be preferred; and certainly, no executable and ready output command should be passed over unreasonably often.)

A repetitive command specifies as many iterations as possible of its constituent alternative command. Consequently, when all guards fail, the repetitive command terminates with no effect. Otherwise, the alternative command is executed once and then the whole repetitive command is executed again. (Consider a repetitive command when all its true guard lists end in an input guard. Such a command may have to be delayed until either (1) an output command corresponding to one of the input guards becomes ready, or (2) all the sources named by the input guards have terminated. In case (2), the repetitive command terminates. If neither event ever occurs, the process fails (in deadlock.)

Examples:

(1) $[x \geq y \rightarrow m := x [] y \geq x \rightarrow m := y]$

If $x \geq y$, assign x to m; if $y \geq x$ assign y to m; if both $x \geq y$ and $y \geq x$, either assignment can be executed.

(2) $i := 0; *[i < \text{size}; \text{content}(i) \neq n \rightarrow i := i + 1]$

The repetitive command scans the elements content(i), for $i = 0, 1, \ldots$, until either $i \geq$ size, or a value equal to n is found.

(3) $*[c:\text{character}; \text{west}?c \rightarrow \text{east}!c]$

This reads all the characters output by west, and outputs them one by one to east. The repetition terminates when the process west terminates.

(4) $*[(i:1..10)\text{continue}(i); \text{console}(i)?c \rightarrow X!(i, c); \text{console}(i)!\text{ack}();$
   $\text{continue}(i) := (c \neq \text{sign off})]$

This command inputs repeatedly from any of ten consoles, provided that the corresponding element of the Boolean array continue is true. The bound variable i identifies the originating console. Its value, together with the character just input, is output to X, and an acknowledgment signal is sent back to the originating console. If the character indicated "sign off," continue(i) is set false, to prevent further input from that console. The repetitive command terminates when all ten elements of continue are false. (An implementation should ensure that no console which is ready to provide input will be ignored unreasonably often.)

(5) $*[n:\text{integer}; X?\text{insert}(n) \rightarrow \text{INSERT}$
   $[]n:\text{integer}; X?\text{has}(n) \rightarrow \text{SEARCH}; X!(i < \text{size})$
   $]$

(Here, and elsewhere, capitalized words INSERT and SEARCH stand as abbreviations for program text defined separately.)

On each iteration this command accepts from X *either* (a) a request to "insert(n)," (followed by INSERT) *or* (b) a question "has(n)," to which it outputs an answer back to X. The choice between (a) and (b) is made by the next output command in X. The repetitive command terminates when X does. If X sends a nonmatching message, deadlock will result.

(6) $*[X?V() \rightarrow \text{val} := \text{val} + 1$
   $[]\text{val} > 0; Y?P() \rightarrow \text{val} := \text{val} - 1$
   $]$

On each iteration, accept *either* a V() signal from X and increment val, *or* a P() signal from Y, and decrement val. But the second alternative cannot be selected unless val is positive (after which val will remain invariantly nonnegative). (When val > 0, the choice depends on the relative speeds of X and Y, and is not determined.) The repetitive command will terminate when both X and Y are terminated, or when X is terminated and val ≤ 0.

3. Coroutines

In parallel programming coroutines appear as a more fundamental program structure than subroutines, which can be regarded as a special case (treated in the next section).

3.1 COPY

Problem: Write a process X to copy characters output by process west to process east.

Solution:

$X :: *[c:\text{character}; \text{west}?c \rightarrow \text{east}!c]$

Notes: (1) When west terminates, the input "west?c" will fail, causing termination of the repetitive command, and of process X. Any subsequent input command from east will fail. (2) Process X acts as a single-character buffer between west and east. It permits west to work on production of the next character, before east is ready to input the previous one.

3.2 SQUASH

Problem: Adapt the previous program to replace every pair of consecutive asterisks "**" by an upward arrow "↑". Assume that the final character input is not an asterisk.

Solution:

```
X :: *[c:character; west?c →
  [c ≠ asterisk → east!c
  []c = asterisk → west?c;
      [c ≠ asterisk → east!asterisk; east!c
      []c = asterisk → east!upward arrow
  ]] ]
```

Notes: (1) Since west does not end with asterisk, the second "west?c" will not fail. (2) As an exercise, adapt this process to deal sensibly with input which ends with an odd number of asterisks.

3.3 DISASSEMBLE

Problem: to read cards from a cardfile and output to process X the stream of characters they contain. An extra space should be inserted at the end of each card.

Solution:

```
*[cardimage:(1..80)character; cardfile?cardimage →
    i:integer; i := 1;
    *[i ≤ 80 → X!cardimage(i); i := i + 1]
    X!space
]
```

Notes: (1) "(1..80)character" declares an array of 80 characters, with subscripts ranging between 1 and 80. (2) The repetitive command terminates when the cardfile process terminates.

3.4 ASSEMBLE

Problem: To read a stream of characters from process X and print them in lines of 125 characters on a lineprinter. The last line should be completed with spaces if necessary.

Solution:

```
lineimage:(1..125)character;
i:integer; i := 1;
*[c:character; X?c →
    lineimage(i) := c;
    [i ≤ 124 → i := i + 1
    ▯i = 125 → lineprinter!lineimage; i := 1
]   ];
[i = 1 → skip
▯i > 1 → *[i ≤ 125 → lineimage(i) := space; i := i + 1];
    lineprinter!lineimage
]
```

Note: (1) When X terminates, so will the first repetitive command of this process. The last line will then be printed, if it has any characters.

3.5 Reformat
Problem: Read a sequence of cards of 80 characters each, and print the characters on a lineprinter at 125 characters per line. Every card should be followed by an extra space, and the last line should be completed with spaces if necessary.
Solution:

```
[west::DISASSEMBLE||X::COPY||east::ASSEMBLE]
```

Notes: (1) The capitalized names stand for program text defined in previous sections. (2) The parallel command is designed to terminate after the cardfile has terminated. (3) This elementary problem is difficult to solve elegantly without coroutines.

3.6 Conway's Problem [4]
Problem: Adapt the above program to replace every pair of consecutive asterisks by an upward arrow.
Solution:

```
[west::DISASSEMBLE||X::SQUASH||east::ASSEMBLE]
```


4. Subroutines and Data Representations

A conventional nonrecursive subroutine can be readily implemented as a coroutine, provided that (1) its parameters are called "by value" and "by result," and (2) it is disjoint from its calling program. Like a Fortran subroutine, a coroutine may retain the values of local variables (*own* variables, in Algol terms) and it may use input commands to achieve the effect of "multiple entry points" in a safer way than PL/I. Thus a coroutine can be used like a SIMULA class instance as a concrete representation for abstract data.

A coroutine acting as a subroutine is a process operating concurrently with its user process in a parallel command: [subr::SUBROUTINE||X::USER]. The SUBROUTINE will contain (or consist of) a repetitive command: *[X?(value params) → ... ; X!(result params)], where ... computes the results from the values input. The subroutine will terminate when its user does. The USER will call the subroutine by a pair of commands: subr!(arguments); ... ; subr?(results). Any commands between these two will be executed concurrently with the subroutine.

A multiple-entry subroutine, acting as a representation for data [11], will also contain a repetitive command which represents each entry by an alternative input to a structured target with the entry name as constructor. For example,

```
*[X?entry1(value params) → ...
▯X?entry2(value params) → ...
]
```

The calling process X will determine which of the alternatives is activated on each repetition. When X terminates, so does this repetitive command. A similar technique in the user program can achieve the effect of multiple exits.

A recursive subroutine can be simulated by an array of processes, one for each level of recursion. The user process is level zero. Each activation communicates its parameters and results with its predecessor and calls its successor if necessary:

```
[recsub(0)::USER||recsub(i:1..reclimit)::RECSUB].
```

The user will call the first element of

```
recsub: recsub(1)!(arguments); ... ; recsub(1)?(results);.
```

The imposition of a fixed upper bound on recursion depth is necessitated by the "static" design of the language.

This clumsy simulation of recursion would be even more clumsy for a mutually recursive algorithm. It would not be recommended for conventional programming; it may be more suitable for an array of microprocessors for which the fixed upper bound is also realistic.

In this section, we assume each subroutine is used only by a *single* user process (which may, of course, itself contain parallel commands).

4.1 Function: Division With Remainder
Problem: Construct a process to represent a function-type subroutine, which accepts a positive dividend and divisor, and returns their integer quotient and remainder. Efficiency is of no concern.
Solution:

```
[DIV::*[x,y:integer; X?(x,y) →
    quot,rem:integer;quot := 0; rem := x;
    *[rem ≥ y → rem := rem − y; quot := quot + 1];
    X!(quot,rem)
    ]
||X::USER
]
```


4.2 Recursion: Factorial
Problem: Compute a factorial by the recursive method, to a given limit.
Solution:

```
[fac(i:1..limit)::
*[n:integer;fac(i − 1)?n →
    [n = 0 → fac(i − 1)!1
```

```
[]n > 0 → fac(i + 1)!n − 1;
    r:integer;fac(i + 1)?r;fac(i − 1)!(n ∗ r)
]]
||fac(0)::USER
]
```

Note: This unrealistic example introduces the technique of the "iterative array" which will be used to a better effect in later examples.

4.3 Data Representation: Small Set of Integers [11]

Problem: To represent a set of not more than 100 integers as a process, S, which accepts two kinds of instruction from its calling process X: (1) S!insert(n), insert the integer n in the set, and (2) S!has(n); ... ; S?b, b is set true if n is in the set, and false otherwise. The initial value of the set is empty.

Solution:

```
S::
content:(0..99)integer; size:integer; size := 0;
*[n:integer;X?has(n) → SEARCH;X!(i < size)
[]n:integer;X?insert(n) → SEARCH;
    [i < size → skip
    []i = size; size < 100 →
        content (size) := n; size := size + 1
]   ]
```

where SEARCH is an abbreviation for:

```
i:integer; i := 0;
*[i < size; content(i) ≠ n → i := i + 1]
```

Notes: (1) The alternative command with guard "size < 100" will fail if an attempt is made to insert more than 100 elements. (2) The activity of insertion will in general take place concurrently with the calling process. However, any subsequent instruction to S will be delayed until the previous insertion is complete.

4.4 Scanning a Set

Problem: Extend the solution to 4.3 by providing a fast method for scanning all members of the set without changing the value of the set. The user program will contain a repetitive command of the form:

```
S!scan( ); more:boolean; more := true;
*[more;x:integer; S?next(x) → ... deal with x ....
[]more; S?noneleft( ) → more := false
]
```

where S!scan( ) sets the representation into a scanning mode. The repetitive command serves as a **for** statement, inputting the successive members of x from the set and inspecting them until finally the representation sends a signal that there are no members left. The body of the repetitive command is *not* permitted to communicate with S in any way.

Solution: Add a third guarded command to the outer repetitive command of S:

```
... []X?scan( ) → i:integer; i := 0;
            *[i < size → X!next(content(i)); i := i + 1];
            X!noneleft( )
```

4.5 Recursive Data Representation: Small Set of Integers

Problem: Same as above, but an array of processes is to be used to achieve a high degree of parallelism. Each process should contain at most one number. When it contains no number, it should answer "false" to all inquiries about membership. On the first insertion, it changes to a second phase of behavior, in which it deals with instructions from its predecessor, passing some of them on to its successor. The calling process will be named S(0). For efficiency, the set should be sorted, i.e. the ith process should contain the ith largest number.

Solution:

```
S(i:1..100)::
*[n:integer; S(i − 1)?has(n) → S(0)!false
[]n:integer; S(i − 1)?insert(n) →
    *[m:integer; S(i − 1)?has(m) →
        [m ≤ n → S(0)!(m = n)
        []m > n → S(i + 1)!has(m)
        ]
    []m:integer; S(i − 1)?insert(m) →
        [m < n → S(i + 1)!insert(n); n := m
        []m = n → skip
        []m > n → S(i + 1)!insert(m)
] ] ]
```

Notes: (1) The user process S(0) inquires whether n is a member by the commands S(1)!has(n); ... ; [(i:1..100)S(i)? b → skip]. The appropriate process will respond to the input command by the output command in line 2 or line 5. This trick avoids passing the answer back "up the chain." (2) Many insertion operations can proceed in parallel, yet any subsequent "has" operation will be performed correctly. (3) All repetitive commands and all processes of the array will terminate after the user process S(0) terminates.

4.6 Multiple Exits: Remove the Least Member

Exercise: Extend the above solution to respond to a command to yield the least member of the set and to remove it from the set. The user program will invoke the facility by a pair of commands:

```
S(1)!least( ); [x:integer;S(1)? x → ... deal with x ...
                []S(1)?noneleft( ) → ...
                ]
```

or, if he wishes to scan and empty the set, he may write:

```
S(1)!least( );more:boolean; more := true;
            *[more; x:integer; S(1)?x → ... deal with x ... ; S(1)!least( )
            []more; S(1)?noneleft( ) → more := false
            ]
```

Hint: Introduce a Boolean variable, b, initialized to true, and prefix this to all the guards of the inner loop. After responding to a !least( ) command from its predecessor, each process returns its contained value n, asks its successor for its least, and stores the response in n. But if the successor returns "noneleft( )," b is set false and the inner loop terminates. The process therefore returns to its initial state (solution due to David Gries).

5. Monitors and Scheduling

This section shows how a monitor can be regarded as a single process which communicates with more than one user process. However, each user process must have a different name (e.g. producer, consumer) or a different subscript (e.g. $X(i)$) and each communication with a user must identify its source or destination uniquely.

Consequently, when a monitor is prepared to communicate with *any* of its user processes (i.e. whichever of them calls first) it will use a guarded command with a range. For example: $*[(i:1..100)X(i)?(\text{value parameters}) \rightarrow ... ; X(i)!(\text{results})]$. Here, the bound variable i is used to send the results back to the calling process. If the monitor is not prepared to accept input from some particular user (e.g. $X(j)$) on a given occasion, the input command may be preceded by a Boolean guard. For example, two successive inputs from the same process are inhibited by $j = 0; *[(i:1..100)i \neq j; X(i)?(\text{values}) \rightarrow ... ; j := i]$. Any attempted output from $X(j)$ will be delayed until a subsequent iteration, after the output of some other process $X(i)$ has been accepted and dealt with.

Similarly, conditions can be used to delay acceptance of inputs which would violate scheduling constraints— postponing them until some later occasion when some other process has brought the monitor into a state in which the input can validly be accepted. This technique is similar to a conditional critical region [10] and it obviates the need for special synchronizing variables such as events, queues, or conditions. However, the absence of these special facilities certainly makes it more difficult or less efficient to solve problems involving priorities—for example, the scheduling of head movement on a disk.

5.1 Bounded Buffer

Problem: Construct a buffering process X to smooth variations in the speed of output of portions by a producer process and input by a consumer process. The consumer contains pairs of commands $X!\text{more}( )$; $X?p$, and the producer contains commands of the form $X!p$. The buffer should contain up to ten portions.
Solution:

```
X::
buffer:(0..9) portion;
in,out:integer; in := 0; out := 0;
comment 0 ≤ out ≤ in ≤ out + 10;
    *[in < out + 10; producer?buffer(in mod 10) → in := in + 1
    [out < in; consumer?more( ) → consumer!buffer(out mod 10);
        out := out + 1
    ]
```

Notes: (1) When out < in < out + 10, the selection of the alternative in the repetitive command will depend on whether the producer produces before the consumer consumes, or vice versa. (2) When out = in, the buffer is empty and the second alternative cannot be selected even if the consumer is ready with its command $X!\text{more}( )$.

However, after the producer has produced its next portion, the consumer's request can be granted on the next iteration. (3) Similar remarks apply to the producer, when in = out + 10. (4) X is designed to terminate when out = in and the producer has terminated.

5.2 Integer Semaphore

Problem: To implement an integer semaphore, S, shared among an array $X(i:1..100)$ of client processes. Each process may increment the semaphore by S!V( ) or decrement it by S!P( ), but the latter command must be delayed if the value of the semaphore is not positive.
Solution:

```
S::val:integer; val := 0;
    *[(i:1..100)X(i)?V( ) → val := val + 1
    [(i:1..100)val > 0; X(i)?P( ) → val := val − 1
    ]
```

Notes: (1) In this process, no use is made of knowledge of the subscript i of the calling process. (2) The semaphore terminates only when all hundred processes of the process array X have terminated.

5.3 Dining Philosophers (Problem due to E.W. Dijkstra)

Problem: Five philosophers spend their lives thinking and eating. The philosophers share a common dining room where there is a circular table surrounded by five chairs, each belonging to one philosopher. In the center of the table there is a large bowl of spaghetti, and the table is laid with five forks (see Figure 1). On feeling hungry, a philosopher enters the dining room, sits in his own chair, and picks up the fork on the left of his place. Unfortunately, the spaghetti is so tangled that he needs to pick up and use the fork on his right as well. When he has finished, he puts down both forks, and leaves the room. The room should keep a count of the number of philosophers in it.

Fig. 1.

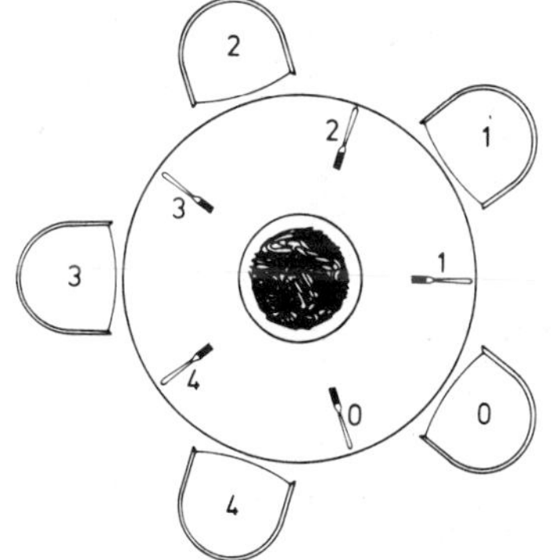

Solution: The behavior of the *i*th philosopher may be described as follows:

```
PHIL = *[... during ith lifetime ... →
        THINK;
        room!enter( );
        fork(i)!pickup( ); fork((i + 1) mod 5)!pickup( );
        EAT;
        fork(i)!putdown( ); fork((i + 1) mod 5)!putdown( );
        room!exit( )
        ]
```

The fate of the ith fork is to be picked up and put down by a philosopher sitting on either side of it

```
FORK =
  *[phil(i)?pickup( ) → phil(i)?putdown( )
  []phil((i − 1)mod 5)?pickup( ) → phil((i − 1) mod 5)?putdown( )
  ]
```

The story of the room may be simply told:

```
ROOM = occupancy:integer; occupancy := 0;
  *[(i:0..4)phil(i)?enter( ) → occupancy := occupancy + 1
  [](i:0..4)phil(i)?exit( ) → occupancy := occupancy − 1
  ]
```

All these components operate in parallel:

```
[room::ROOM||fork(i:0..4)::FORK||phil(i:0..4)::PHIL].
```

Notes: (1) The solution given above does not prevent all five philosophers from entering the room, each picking up his left fork, and starving to death because he cannot pick up his right fork. (2) Exercise: Adapt the above program to avert this sad possibility. Hint: Prevent more than four philosophers from entering the room. (Solution due to E. W. Dijkstra).

6. Miscellaneous

This section contains further examples of the use of communicating sequential processes for the solution of some less familiar problems; a parallel version of the sieve of Eratosthenes, and the design of an iterative array. The proposed solutions are even more speculative than those of the previous sections, and in the second example, even the question of termination is ignored.

6.1 Prime Numbers: The Sieve of Eratosthenes [14]

Problem: To print in ascending order all primes less than 10000. Use an array of processes, SIEVE, in which each process inputs a prime from its predecessor and prints it. The process then inputs an ascending stream of numbers from its predecessor and passes them on to its successor, suppressing any that are multiples of the original prime. Solution:

```
[SIEVE(i:1..100)::
  p,mp:integer;
  SIEVE(i − 1)?p;
  print!p;
  mp := p; comment mp is a multiple of p;
  *[m:integer; SIEVE(i − 1)?m →
      *[m > mp → mp := mp + p];
      [m = mp → skip
      []m < mp → SIEVE(i + 1)!m
  ]  ]
||SIEVE(0)::print!2; n:integer; n := 3;
      *[n < 10000 → SIEVE(1)!n; n := n + 2]
||SIEVE(101)::*[n:integer;SIEVE(100)?n → print!n]
||print::*[(i:0..101) n:integer; SIEVE(i)?n → ...]
]
```

Note: (1) This beautiful solution was contributed by David Gries. (2) It is algorithmically similar to the program developed in [7, pp. 27–32].

6.2 An Iterative Array: Matrix Multiplication

Problem: A square matrix A of order 3 is given. Three streams are to be input, each stream representing a column of an array IN. Three streams are to be output, each representing a column of the product matrix IN $\times$ A. After an initial delay, the results are to be produced at the same rate as the input is consumed. Consequently, a high degree of parallelism is required. The solution should take the form shown in Figure 2. Each of the nine nonborder nodes inputs a vector component from the west and a partial sum from the north. Each node outputs the vector component to its east, and an updated partial sum to the south. The input data is produced by the west border nodes, and the desired results are consumed by south border nodes. The north border is a constant source of zeros and the east border is just a sink. No provision need be made for termination nor for changing the values of the array A.

Fig. 2.

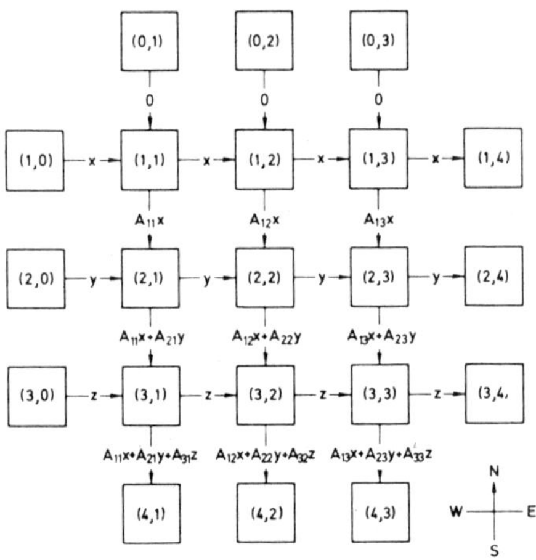

Solution: There are twenty-one nodes, in five groups, comprising the central square and the four borders:

```
[M(i:1..3,0)::WEST
||M(0,j:1..3)::NORTH
||M(i:1..3,4)::EAST
||M(4,j:1..3)::SOUTH
||M(i:1..3,j:1..3)::CENTER
]
```

The WEST and SOUTH borders are processes of the user program; the remaining processes are:

```
NORTH = *[true → M(1,j)!0]
EAST = *[x:real; M(i,3)?x → skip]
CENTER = *[x:real; M(i,j − 1)?x →
        M(i, j + 1)!x; sum:real;
        M(i − 1, j)?sum; M(i + 1,j)!(A(i,j)*x + sum)
    ]
```

7. Discussion

A design for a programming language must necessarily involve a number of decisions which seem to be fairly arbitrary. The discussion of this section is intended to explain some of the underlying motivation and to mention some unresolved questions.

7.1 Notations

I have chosen single-character notations (e.g. !,?) to express the primitive concepts, rather than the more traditional boldface or underlined English words. As a result, the examples have an APL-like brevity, which some readers find distasteful. My excuse is that (in contrast to APL) there are only a very few primitive concepts and that it is standard practice of mathematics (and also good coding practice) to denote common primitive concepts by brief notations (e.g. $+,\times$). When read aloud, these are replaced by words (e.g. plus, times).

Some readers have suggested the use of assignment notation for input and output:

<target variable> := <source>
<destination> := <expression>

I find this suggestion misleading: it is better to regard input and output as distinct primitives, justifying distinct notations.

I have used the same pair of brackets ([...]) to bracket all program structures, instead of the more familiar variety of brackets (**if..fi**, **begin..end**, **case...esac**, etc.). In this I follow normal mathematical practice, but I must also confess to a distaste for the pronunciation of words like **fi**, **od**, or **esac**.

I am dissatisfied with the fact that my notation gives the same syntax for a structured expression and a subscripted variable. Perhaps tags should be distinguished from other identifiers by a special symbol (say #).

I was tempted to introduce an abbreviation for combined declaration and input, e.g. $X?(n{:}\text{integer})$ for $n{:}\text{integer}; X?n$.

7.2 Explicit Naming

My design insists that every input or output command must name its source or destination explicitly. This makes it inconvenient to write a library of processes which can be included in subsequent programs, independent of the process names used in that program. A partial solution to this problem is to allow one process (the *main* process) of a parallel command to have an empty label, and to allow the other processes in the command to use the empty process name as source or destination of input or output.

For construction of large programs, some more general technique will also be necessary. This should at least permit substitution of program text for names defined elsewhere—a technique which has been used informally throughout this paper. The Cobol COPY verb also permits a substitution for formal parameters within the copied text. But whatever facility is introduced, I would recommend the following principle: Every program, after assembly with its library routines, should be printable as a text expressed wholly in the language, and it is this printed text which should describe the execution of the program, independent of which parts were drawn from a library.

Since I did not intend to design a complete language, I have ignored the problem of libraries in order to concentrate on the essential semantic concepts of the program which is actually executed.

7.3 Port Names

An alternative to explicit naming of source and destination would be to name a *port* through which communication is to take place. The port names would be local to the processes, and the manner in which pairs of ports are to be connected by channels could be declared in the head of a parallel command.

This is an attractive alternative which could be designed to introduce a useful degree of syntactically checkable redundancy. But it is semantically equivalent to the present proposal, provided that each port is connected to exactly one other port in another process. In this case each channel can be identified with a tag, together with the name of the process at the other end. Since I wish to concentrate on semantics, I preferred in this paper to use the simplest and most direct notation, and to avoid raising questions about the possibility of connecting more than two ports by a single channel.

7.4 Automatic Buffering

As an alternative to synchronization of input and output, it is often proposed that an outputting process should be allowed to proceed even when the inputting process is not yet ready to accept the output. An implementation would be expected automatically to interpose a chain of buffers to hold output messages that have not yet been input.

I have deliberately rejected this alternative, for two reasons: (1) It is less realistic to implement in multiple disjoint processors, and (2) when buffering is required on a particular channel, it can readily be specified using the given primitives. Of course, it could be argued equally well that synchronization can be specified when required by using a pair of buffered input and output commands.

7.5 Unbounded Process Activation

The notation for an array of processes permits the same program text (like an Algol recursive procedure) to have many simultaneous "activations"; however, the exact number must be specified in advance. In a conventional single-processor implementation, this can lead to inconvenience and wastefulness, similar to the fixed-length array of Fortran. It would therefore be attractive to allow a process array with no a priori bound on the number of elements; and to specify that the exact number of elements required for a particular execution of the program should be determined dynamically, like the maximum depth of recursion of an Algol procedure or the number of iterations of a repetitive command.

However, it is a good principle that every actual run of a program with unbounded arrays should be identical to the run of some program with all its arrays bounded in advance. Thus the unbounded program should be defined as the "limit" (in some sense) of a series of bounded programs with increasing bounds. I have chosen to concentrate on the semantics of the bounded case—which is necessary anyway and which is more realistic for implementation on multiple microprocessors.

7.6 Fairness
Consider the parallel command:

```
[X:: Y!stop( )|| Y::continue:boolean; continue := true;
   *[continue; X ?stop( ) → continue := false
     []continue → n := n + 1
     ]
].
```

If the implementation always prefers the second alternative in the repetitive command of Y, it is said to be *unfair*, because although the output command in X could have been executed on an infinite number of occasions, it is in fact always passed over.

The question arises: Should a programming language definition specify that an implementation must be *fair*? Here, I am fairly sure that the answer is NO. Otherwise, the implementation would be obliged to successfully complete the example program shown above, in spite of the fact that its nondeterminism is unbounded. I would therefore suggest that it is the programmer's responsibility to prove that his program terminates correctly—without relying on the assumption of fairness in the implementation. Thus the program shown above is incorrect, since its termination cannot be proved.

Nevertheless, I suggest that an efficient implementation should try to be reasonably fair and should ensure that an output command is not delayed unreasonably often after it first becomes executable. But a proof of correctness must not rely on this property of an efficient implementation. Consider the following analogy with a sequential program: An efficient implementation of an alternative command will tend to favor the alternative which can be most efficiently executed, but the programmer must ensure that the logical correctness of his program does not depend on this property of his implementation.

This method of avoiding the problem of fairness does not apply to programs such as operating systems which are intended to run forever because in this case termination proofs are not relevant. But I wonder whether it is ever advisable to write or to execute such programs. Even an operating system should be designed to bring itself to an orderly conclusion reasonably soon after it inputs a message instructing it to do so. Otherwise, the *only* way to stop it is to "crash" it.

7.7 Functional Coroutines
It is interesting to compare the processes described here with those proposed in [12]; the differences are most striking. There, coroutines are strictly deterministic: No choice is given between alternative sources of input. The output commands are automatically buffered to any required degree. The output of one process can be automatically fanned out to any number of processes (including itself!) which can consume it at differing rates. Finally, the processes there are designed to run forever, whereas my proposed parallel command is normally intended to terminate. The design in [12] is based on an elegant theory which permits proof of the properties of programs. These differences are not accidental—they seem to be natural consequences of the difference between the more abstract applicative (or functional) approach to programming and the more machine-oriented imperative (or procedural) approach, which is taken by communicating sequential processes.

7.8 Output Guards
Since input commands may appear in guards, it seems more symmetric to permit output commands as well. This would allow an obvious and useful simplification in some of the example programs, for example, in the bounded buffer (5.1). Perhaps a more convincing reason would be to ensure that the externally visible effect and behavior of every parallel command can be modeled by some sequential command. In order to model the parallel command

$$Z :: [X!2||Y!3]$$

we need to be able to write the sequential alternative command:

$$Z :: [X!2 → Y!3[]Y!3 → X!2]$$

Note that this *cannot* be done by the command

$$Z :: [true → X!2; Y!3[]true → Y!3; X!2]$$

which can fail if the process Z happens to choose the first alternative, but the processes Y and X are synchronized with each other in such a way that Y must input from Z before X does, e.g.

```
  Y :: Z?y; X!go( )
||X :: Y?go( ); Z?x
```

7.9 Restriction: Repetitive Command With Input Guard
In proposing an unfamiliar programming language feature, it seems wiser at first to specify a highly restrictive version rather than to propose extensions—especially when the language feature claims to be primitive. For example, it is clear that the multidimensional process array is not primitive, since it can readily be constructed in a language which permits only single-dimensional arrays. But I have a rather more serious misgiving about the repetitive command with input guards.

The automatic termination of a repetitive command on termination of the sources of all its input guards is an extremely powerful and convenient feature but it also involves some subtlety of specification to ensure that it

is implementable; and it is certainly not primitive, since
the required effect can be achieved (with considerable
inconvenience) by explicit exchange of "end()" signals.
For example, the subroutine DIV(4.1) could be rewritten:

```
[DIV :: continue:boolean; continue := true;
*[continue; X?end() → continue := false
[]continue; x,y:integer; X?(x,y) → ... ; X!(quot,rem)
||X :: USER PROG; DIV!end()
 ]
```

Other examples would be even more inconvenient.

But the dangers of convenient facilities are notorious.
For example, the repetitive commands with input guards
may tempt the programmer to write them without making adequate plans for their termination; and if it turns
out that the automatic termination is unsatisfactory,
reprogramming for explicit termination will involve severe changes, affecting even the interfaces between the
processes.

8. Conclusion

This paper has suggested that input, output, and
concurrency should be regarded as primitives of programming, which underlie many familiar and less familiar programming concepts. However, it would be unjus-
tified to conclude that these primitives can wholly replace
the other concepts in a programming language. Where
a more elaborate construction (such as a procedure or a
monitor) is frequently useful, has properties which are
more simply provable, and can also be implemented
more efficiently than the general case, there is a strong
reason for including in a programming language a special
notation for that construction. The fact that the construction can be defined in terms of simpler underlying primitives is a useful guarantee that its inclusion is logically
consistent with the remainder of the language.

Acknowledgments. The research reported in this paper has been encouraged and supported by a Senior
Fellowship of the Science Research Council of Great
Britain. The technical inspiration was due to Edsger W.
Dijkstra [9], and the paper has been improved in presentation and content by valuable and painstaking advice
from D. Gries, D. Q. M. Fay, Edsger W. Dijkstra, N.
Wirth, Robert Milne, M. K. Harper, and its referees.
The role of IFIP W.G.2.3 as a forum for presentation
and discussion is acknowledged with pleasure and grat-
itude.

Received March 1977; revised August 1977

References
1. Atkinson, R., and Hewitt, C. Synchronisation in actor systems.
Working Paper 83, M.I.T., Cambridge, Mass., Nov. 1976.
2. Brinch Hansen, P. The programming language Concurrent
Pascal. *IEEE Trans. Software Eng. 1*, 2 (June 1975), 199–207.
3. Campbell, R.H., and Habermann, A.N. The specification of
process synchronisation by path expressions. *Lecture Notes in
Computer Science 16*, Springer, 1974, pp. 89–102.
4. Conway, M.E. Design of a separable transition-diagram
compiler. *Comm. ACM 6*, 7 (July 1963), 396–408.
5. Dahl, O-J., et al. SIMULA 67, common base language.
Norwegian Computing Centre, Forskningveien, Oslo, 1967.
6. Dijkstra, E.W. Co-operating sequential processes. In
Programming Languages, F. Genuys, Ed., Academic Press, New
York, 1968, pp. 43–112.
7. Dijkstra, E.W. Notes on structured programming. In *Structured
Programming*, Academic Press, New York 1972, pp. 1–82.
8. Dijkstra, E.W. Guarded commands, nondeterminacy, and formal
derivation of programs. *Comm. ACM 18*, 8 (Aug. 1975), 453–457.
9. Dijkstra, E.W. Verbal communication, Marktoberdorf, Aug.
1975.
10. Hoare, C.A.R. Towards a theory of parallel programming. In
Operating Systems Techniques, Academic Press, New York, 1972, pp.
61–71.
11. Hoare, C.A.R. Proof of correctness of data representations. *Acta
Informatica 1*, 4 (1972), 271–281.
12. Kahn, G. The semantics of a simple language for parallel
programming. In *Proc. IFIP Congress 74*, North Holland, 1974.
13. Liskov, B.H. A note on CLU. Computation Structures Group
Memo. 112, M.I.T., Cambridge, Mass, 1974.
14. McIlroy, M.D. Coroutines. Bell Laboratories, Murray Hill, N.J.,
1968.
15. Naur, P., Ed. Report on the algorithmic language ALGOL 60.
Comm. ACM 3, 5 (May 1960), 299–314.
16. Reynolds, J.C. COGENT. ANL-7022, Argonne Nat. Lab.,
Argonne, Ill., 1965.
17. Thompson, K. The UNIX command language. In *Structured
Programming*, Infotech, Nicholson House, Maidenhead, England,
1976, pp. 375–384.
18. van Wijngaarden, A. Ed. Report on the algorithmic language
ALGOL 68. *Numer. Math. 14* (1969), 79–218.
19. Wulf, W.A., London, R.L., and Shaw, M. Abstraction and
verification in ALPHARD. Dept. of Comptr. Sci., Carnegie-Mellon
U., Pittsburgh, Pa., June 1976.
20. Wirth, N. The programming language PASCAL. *Acta
Informatica 1*, 1 (1971), 35–63.

Section 4
Data Types

The notion of a data type serves to distinguish programming languages from one another in a very strong way. Many programming languages are essentially typeless — variables in those languages are automatically converted to whatever form is needed to carry out an associated operation. Such languages are typically declaration-free, and variables can alternately represent string values, numeric values, or boolean variables.

On the other hand, languages such as those derived from Algol 60 insist that all variables have a well-defined type and that this type not be changed throughout the scope of the variable. The type notion is extended to subtype, which may be used to define new types, such as subrange types, based upon existing types.

These typed languages then check type usage throughout the program. Operators may be applied only to objects of certain type, so that it becomes impossible to perform multiplication on two variables of type string or concatenation on integers. Similarly, type checking is applied on parameters, so that the actual and formal parameters for a function, procedure, or subroutine must agree in the number and type of parameters. It has been shown that typed languages provide certain advantages over untyped languages with respect to programming reliability; at the same time, however, the type system of a language occasionally complicates the programming task, and most system implementation languages, used for programming operating systems, routinely provide ways to escape from the type checking system of the language.

Languages typically provide a set of built-in data types based upon the intended range of applications of the language. But an important feature in many new programming languages is the ability to extend programming languages by defining and using new data types built upon the existing types, and then to be able to declare variables of these new types. This section deals almost exclusively with this notion of "abstract data types."

The first paper, by Wasserman, discusses these points and the motivation for the introduction of new data types. The second paper, by Liskov and Zilles, is a classic that shows the use of abstract types and provides the motivation for the design of the programming language CLU.

Guttag shows the relationship between formal specifications of data types and the development of data structures in programs. From there, it is a short step to see how to realize these notions in a programming language.

Finally, Wegbreit discusses the mode facility of EL1, an extensible language that formed the heart of the ECL programming system. EL1 provides a greater variety of extensions than does Pascal or its relatives. The paper is particularly interesting because EL1 predated the current vogue of encapsulated data types, yet still provided most of the desired capabilities.

Introduction to Data Types

Anthony I. Wasserman

Data Types and Associated Operations

In solving a problem, one normally devises a representation for the problem and for the objects to be manipulated in solving the problem. If we are thinking about chess, for example, we mentally represent the board and all the pieces. Similarly, we are able to describe the appropriate operations on (or moves of) the pieces.

If, on the other hand, we are trying to simulate lines at a supermarket, a completely different kind of representation comes to mind. We abstract the actual situation into a number of "servers" (the cashiers), and a queue associated with each server. The meaningful operations in such a system are rather limited: a person joins a queue; a person is served, thereby shortening a queue; a person leaves the queue (for any of several reasons); a new queue is formed (by a cashier opening a new checkout line), or the number of queues is reduced (by closing a line).

Thus, in solving a problem, we create some type of representation of the problem and of the associated information. If the solution to the problem is to be programmed on a computer, we then have to be able to devise representations of objects and operations for machine processing. Most important, the machine representation of our objects should closely resemble the way we have conceived of the object. For example, the availability of a two-dimensional array of size 8×8 would be extremely useful for representing the chess board mentioned above.

The types of data objects available in a programming language have a major impact on the suitability of a programming language for a particular application, since these data-object types provide a representation which is meaningful *in terms of the problem which is being solved*. One could successfully write all programs in assembly language, using the primitive data types of bits, bytes, integers, and (occasionally) floating point numbers available there. But the mental effort required to transform a meaningful object into the limited kinds of representations offered in assembly languages can be difficult.

After all, high level languages were invented so that the programmer could work with notation that was more familiar to humans than the notation of machine instructions. In the same sense, one wants to avoid working with primitive data types. If a program involves queues, it would be ideal to have queues as part of the host language in which the application will be programmed. The same can be said for records, trees, stacks, complex numbers, sets, directed graphs, sparse matrices, and all of the other kinds of data objects of which a programmer can conceive.

Thus, the collection of data types within a programming language is extremely important in determining the ease with which a programmer can write a particular application in that language. Although this distinction is not important at a theoretical level, at a practical level it can be of the utmost importance. For example, FORTRAN is weak for file processing and business data processing because it does not support the concept of a record containing logical subfields. COBOL is weak for numerical computation because representation of floating point numbers is difficult and because COBOL does not have the set of built-in functions present in FORTRAN for performing operations upon floating point numbers. The most significant basis for the claim that PL/I can service all applications is the broad range of data types: fixed and floating point numeric quantities, fixed and variable length character strings, structures for record processing, arrays, pointers, and so on.

The programming language treatment of data types varies considerably. In a number of untyped languages, such as APL and MUMPS, objects can be coerced automatically from one type to another. In MUMPS, for example, if we add an object to another object, then we treat each as an integer-valued expression, and the result of the addition, if assigned to another variable, is an integer. If a string operation is involved, then the objects are treated as strings.

It is much more common for data objects (variables) to have known data types. In many languages, the number of data types is fixed. BASIC, for example, supports a very small number of data types, while FORTRAN supports somewhat more. It is also possible to define structured data types, such as arrays of integers.

Newer languages support not only a fixed number of built-in data types, but also the ability to introduce a number of new data types. In Pascal, for example, built in types include integer, real, boolean, char, arrays of those types, and sets. In addition, however, one can define new types in several ways. An enumeration type can be defined by simply naming the type and the values that it can accept:

type color = (blue, green, yellow, red, purple, brown, black, chartreuse);

If one then declares a variable

var stripe: color;

it is then possible to make assignments of the form

stripe : = red;

at any point where the type color and the variable stripe are known.

Another powerful type extension facility is that of records. A record type allows one to group together a number of related objects by a common name. A record object has a number of fields that may be accessed separately. One might write, for example:

type emp = **record**
        name: **array** [1..25] **of** char;
        department: 101..999;
        title: array [1..20] **of** char;
        salary: 8000..99999;
        {other fields}
        end record;

Then one could declare, for example:

var personnel: **array** [1..2000] **of** emp;

to hold the information on up to 2000 employees. The salary of employee 315 could be accessed with the expression personnel [315]. salary.

Thus, we have considerable ability to introduce new types that are appropriate for a given application. The data types available in Pascal are a significant step beyond those available in many other previously developed languages. A major reason for this is that Pascal makes the type declaration facility visible, separating the definition of a type from the declaration of a variable of a given type. Furthermore, Pascal supports extensive checking of variable use to see that variables of the proper type are used throughout the program. (A couple of loopholes exist in Pascal's type checking system, but the idea is sound, and the loopholes have been closed in some of Pascal's descendants.) It is safe to say that the basic set of data types supported by Pascal, combined with the ability to define new types, has been a significant factor in the acceptance and widespread use of Pascal.

In addition to the types of data supported by a language, it is important to consider the kinds of operations performed on data. Meaningful operations on numeric data include addition, subtraction, multiplication, division, exponentiation, relational operators, and a variety of algebraic functions. The operation of concatenation may not be meaningful in the context of numeric data, although it has a perfectly understandable meaning in the context of character string data.

If the data object is a push-down stack, the valid operations might include pushing a value onto the stack, popping a value off the stack, testing to see if the stack is empty or full, and (possibly) examining the top value on the stack without removing the value. If an operation such as looking at the sixth value from the stack were permitted, then the object would no longer be a stack in the true sense of the term. Similarly, the operation of multiplying two stacks together does not appear to have a practical meaning.

In summary, then, it is generally useful to think about data types *with a set of associated operations*. It is not necessary that the data types conceived in this way be restricted to those that are available in a given programming language; on the contrary, it is generally useful to think about abstract objects *independent* of their representation in a programming language.

When one studies data types in programming languages, it becomes clear that some languages restrict the legal operations upon objects of given types, while other languages do not. Some languages, including CLU and Ada, provide a mechanism whereby a programmer can build new data types from old in order to be able to represent a desired set of data objects more easily. This ability to introduce a new data type permits the programmer to carry a specific abstract object from the problem-solving stage through the programming stage.

It is important for the programmer to have available a set of data types which are appropriate for the application to be programmed. Rather than restricting our thinking to the built-in types of a particular language, it is valuable to permit *any* data type and associated set of operations that a programmer envisions. Then the programmer can define those data objects and operations in terms of the built-in data types and composite types within a language.

This notion gets to the heart of the way that people approach the solution of programming problems. When someone presents a programmer with a problem, the presentation is usually rather abstract, e.g., "Write a program to find the first 1000 prime numbers," or "Write a compiler for the FORTRAN language." Nothing is said in the problem statement about the structure of the program to be built or the data objects that will be created and manipulated in solving the problem.

Instead, the programmer must analyze the problem and must gradually define the program structure and the data structures, supplying more detail as the solution to the problem becomes clearer. This process of problem solution often involves splitting a large problem into smaller pieces, and possibly splitting those pieces up still further, until the programmer gains a full understanding of the problem. At that point, each of the pieces is small enough that it is intellectually manageable, so that the programmer can proceed with the solution.

This approach to problem-solving, known as *stepwise refinement* or *hierarchical decomposition,* involves two parallel definitional activities: definition of the individual program modules required to carry out each of the identified functions for the solution, and definition of the data objects upon which the operations will be performed. These activities are closely related, since they take place jointly and since some of the program modules will carry out an operation on a data object.

In the early stages of this process, the data structures are usually ambiguous. If we have 1000 prime numbers, it is not immediately clear whether we will store them in an array, group them into a set, or define some other kind of data structure for them. If our problem involves the simulation of lines in a supermarket, it is clear that we will be working with queues, but it is not relevant how we represent those queues in terms of available data structures. We will make that choice of data structure at a later level of program refinement, when it has become clear what the operations on that structure will be and when we can make an intelligent decision as to representation. In the interim, however, it is possible, indeed desirable, to visualize the queue *as if it were a built-in data type.* In that way, the programmer can determine the proper set of operations on that data type. Then the programmer can choose the representation for the queue and program the operations in terms of that representation.

If the rest of the programming has proceeded without knowledge of the representation, the other program modules only know the names of the operations. In that way, the only way that they access the data object is through the known set of operations. Suppose that it then became necessary to change the representation of the data object. It would clearly also be necessary to change the program for the operations upon the object, but *nothing else in the program would have to be changed,* since no other program modules made use of the physical representation of the object. This characteristic is termed *data independence.*

To some extent, we can achieve data independence in program construction in a large number of programming languages if we take some care. We simply define a data structure and a set of subprograms representing the operations on that structure, then are careful to use only the defined operations on the data structure.

Consider as an example the case of a linear list of items. We may choose to represent that list with an array or with some linked structure. However, the operations can be identical and would include

SEARCH (L, VAL)	Search list L for item with value VAL
INSERT (L, POS, VAL)	Insert value VAL after position POS in list L
REMOVE (L, VAL)	Remove value VAL from list L
DELETE (L, POS)	Delete the item in position POS from list L
ASSIGN (L, POS, VAL)	Assign value VAL to item in position POS in list L

It is clear that none of these function or procedure calls provides the caller with any information about the choice of representation for the list.

So far, so good. However, most widely used languages do not provide any means for truly hiding the representation of the object (although one can come close in PL/I). The entire mechanism presented here could be undermined by a single assignment or a single reference anywhere in the program which uses the actual representation of the object rather than the defined operations. If L were represented by an array in PL/I, for example, we might write

$$L(J) = L(J + 1);$$

In that case, we would have violated the access rules for data independence and might also have performed an "illegal" operation, i.e., one which is not equivalent to one of the defined operators on L.

What we need, then, is a form of enforcement mechanism that guarantees that no outside modules can gain access to the representation of some object. In that way, we can define an object and a set of operations upon that object with full assurance that only those operations will be used. This definition is equivalent to providing a new data type for the host language. Hence, we shall use the term *abstract data type* to refer to a new data type created in this way.

Several concepts come into play here. First, we build upon the existing data types in a language. Next, we build upon the mechanisms for defining operators, i.e., functions and procedures. Finally, we add to the ability to define new data types within a language. Now we will extend that to let the programmer define a new type by specifying a set of operations, a representation for the data type in terms of existing types in the language, and the program code to carry out the operations upon the chosen representation. This new type definition is *encapsulated* within a single program unit, so that only the names of the operations and the name of the type are visible to external program units.

We can illustrate these ideas through use of the stack example mentioned above. Suppose that we wish to introduce the data type stack into a language that supports the data types of Pascal, including integers, booleans, arrays, and records. We wish to be able to create stacks holding up to some predefined number max of integers. We will define a **module** consisting of four parts:

1) The **exports** part, in which we give the names of externally visible operations and exceptions. Only names in this list may be considered to be usable operations by other program modules. The exceptions may result from improper application of the operations, such as trying to pop something from an empty stack, in much the same way that a divide-by-zero exception may be raised while doing numeric operations on the built-in type integer.

2) The **rep** part, in which we give the actual representation of the data type. The associated operations within this module will use this data representation, but it is not accessible elsewhere. For a stack, we could select a record structure consisting of an array of stack values and a pointer to the top of the stack. Alternatively, we could use a linked list structure with a pointer mechanism, or any of several other distinct possibilities as well. Not that the use of a record/array representation imposes a maximum size on the stack, whereas a linked list is essentially boundless.

3) The **ops** part, in which we give the functions and procedures to carry out the operations.

4) The module body, in which we give the initializing operations.

The module, written in the programming language PLAIN, can then be used within a program body. Since it represents a data type, variables can be declared to be of that type, as in the table.

```
type stack = module { assume max is defined as a constant elsewhere }
            exports
                function empty (x:stack): boolean;
                procedure push (val: integer -> x:stack);
                procedure pop (-> x:stack, val:integer);
                function top(x:stack): integer;
                exception stkfull, stkempty;
            rep record
                    stktop: 0..max;
                    elements: array [1..max] of integer;
                end record;

            ops
                function empty (x:stack): boolean;
                begin empty := x.stktop = 0 end;

                procedure push (val: integer -> x:stack);
                exception stkfull;
                begin
                    if x.stktop >= max then signal stkfull
                    else
                        x.stktop := x.stktop + 1;
                        assert (x.stktop >= 1) & (x.stktop <= max);
                        x.elements[x.stktop] := val;
                    end if
                end;

                procedure pop (-> x:stack, val:integer);
                imports stack.empty: invoked;
                exception stkempty;
                begin
                    if stack.empty(x) then signal stkempty
                    else
                        assert (x.stktop >= 1) & (x.stktop <= max);
                        val := x.elements[x.stktop];
                        x.stktop := x.stktop - 1;
                    end if
                end;

                function top(x:stack): integer;
                 { push and pop guarantee that 0<=stktop<=max }
                imports empty: invoked;
                exception stkempty;
                begin
                    if empty(x) then signal stkempty
                    else top:= x.elements[x.stktop]
                    end if
                end;
            begin { initialize stack }
                stktop := 0
end module;
```

Table. Module stack written in PLAIN

var ss: stack;

This declaration creates a new stack, initialized to be empty.

Then ss may be used along with the stack operations, wherever objects of type stack may be used, including, for example:

if stack.empty (ss) **then** . . .

If we also declare an integer variable i

var i: integer;

we can then write

stack. push (i → ss)

where the arrow denotes that the push operation modifies ss.

The declaration shown here is quite restrictive, since our declaration of the stack module restricts it; it must be of a fixed size and must only hold objects of type integer. With this declaration, it would be necessary to declare a new module type for stacks of characters or other objects. Furthermore, some parameterization mechanism is essential if one wishes to be able to dynamically declare objects of different sizes.

In short, one might want a *generic* data type definition facility, where we might use a notation similar to the following:

```
type generator stacks [size: integer; content: type] =
    exports
        {as above}
    rep record
            stktop: 0..size;
            elements: array [1..size] of content
        end record;
```

ops
   {same operations as above, except that uses of max are replaced by size and that uses of integer are replaced by content}
begin
   stktop : = 0
end module;

This type generator would serve as the basis for creating specific data types. If we had declared

const max = 100;

we could then use the type generator facility to create a specific data type to hold max integers in a stack, that is, to be equivalent to the module shown above.

type stack = **generate** stacks [max, integer];

where max and integer are taken as actual parameters to the type generator stacks. We could then declare ss as a variable of type stack as before.

This type definition facility is essentially equivalent to the *generic package* facility of Ada. It is apparent that this feature is quite powerful, but that it encompasses some implementation overhead above and beyond the simpler facility which creates a single type.

These data type concepts are extremely important in computer science and programming language research. They provide a degree of modularization and structuring not previously found in data structures and data types, and make it possible to formalize the operations on data objects. Some of the other papers in this section use the stack example or similar examples to show how one can algebraically specify the properties of new objects (data types) and then implement them so that the correspondence between the data type specification and implementation can be formally verified.

Barbara Liskov
Massachusetts Institute of Technology
Project MAC
Cambridge, Massachusetts

Stephen Zilles
Cambridge Systems Group
IBM Systems Development Division
Cambridge, Massachusetts

Reprinted from *ACM SIGPLAN Notices,* April 1974, pp. 50-59. Copyright 1974
Association for Computing Machinery, Inc. Reprinted by permission.

Abstract

The motivation behind the work in very-high-level languages is to ease the programming task by providing the programmer with a language containing primitives or abstractions suitable to his problem area.
The programmer is then able to spend his effort in the right place; he concentrates on solving his problem,
and the resulting program will be more reliable as a result. Clearly, this is a worthwhile goal.

Unfortunately, it is very difficult for a designer to select in advance all the abstractions which the
users of his language might need. If a language is to be used at all, it is likely to be used to solve
problems which its designer did not envision, and for which the abstractions embedded in the language are
not sufficient.

This paper presents an approach which allows the set of built-in abstractions to be augmented when the
need for a new data abstraction is discovered. This approach to the handling of abstraction is an outgrowth
of work on designing a language for structured programming. Relevant aspects of this language are described,
and examples of the use and definitions of abstractions are given.

Introduction

This paper describes an approach to computer
representation of abstraction. The approach, developed while designing a language to support structured programming, is also relevant to work in very-
high-level languages. We begin by explaining its
relevance and by comparing work in structured programming and very-high-level languages.

The purpose of structured programming is to
enhance the reliability and understandability of
programs. Very-high-level languages, while primarily intended to increase programmer productivity
by easing the programmer's task, can also be expected to enhance the reliability and understandability of code. Thus, similar benefits can be expected from work in the two areas.

Work in the two areas, however, proceeds along
different lines. A very-high-level language attempts to present the user with the abstractions
(operations, data structures, and control structures) useful to his application area. The user
can use these abstractions without being concerned
with how they are implemented -- he is only con-

cerned with what they do. He is thus able to ignore details not relevant to his application area,
and to concentrate on solving his problem.

Structured programming attempts to impose a
discipline on the programming task so that the resulting programs are "well-structured." In this
discipline, a problem is solved by means of a process of successive decomposition. The first step
is to write a program which solves the problem but
which runs on an abstract machine, one which provides just those data objects and operations which
are ideally suited to solving the problem. Some or
all of those data objects and operations are truly
abstract, i.e., not present as primitives in the
programming language being used. We will, for the
present, group them loosely together under the term
"abstraction."

The programmer is initially concerned with
satisfying himself (or proving) that his program
correctly solves the problem. In this analysis he
is concerned with the way his program makes use of
the abstractions, but not with any details of how
those abstractions may be realized. When he is
satisfied with the correctness of his program, he
turns his attention to the abstractions it uses.
Each abstraction represents a new problem, requiring
additional programs for its solution. The new program may also be written to run on an abstract

Work reported herein was supported in part by the
National Science Foundation under research grant
GJ-34671.

189

machine, introducing further abstractions. The original problem is completely solved when all abstractions generated in the course of constructing the program have been realized by further programs.

It is clear now that the approaches of very-high-level languages and structured programming are related to one another: each is based on the idea of making use of those abstractions which are correct for the problem being solved. Furthermore, the rationale for using the abstractions is the same in both approaches: to free the programmer from concern with details not relevant to the problem he is solving.

In very-high-level languages, the designers attempt to identify the set of useful abstractions in advance. A structured programming language, on the other hand, contains no preconceived notions about the particular set of useful abstractions, but, instead, must provide a mechanism whereby the language can be extended to contain the abstractions which the user requires. A language containing such a mechanism can be viewed as a general-purpose, indefinitely-high-level language.

In this paper we describe an approach to abstraction which permits the set of built-in abstractions to be augmented when the need for new abstractions is discovered. We begin by analyzing the abstractions used in writing programs, and identify the need for data abstractions. A language supporting the use and definition of data abstractions is informally described, and some example programs are given. Remaining sections of the paper discuss the relationship of the approach to previous work, and some aspects of the implementation of the language.

The Meaning of Abstraction

The description of structured programming given in the preceding section is vague because it is couched in such undefined terms as "abstraction" and "abstract machine." In this section we analyze the meaning of "abstraction" to determine what kinds of abstraction a programmer requires, and how a structured programming language can support these requirements.

What we desire from an abstraction is a mechanism which permits the expression of relevant details and the suppression of irrelevant details. In the case of programming, the use which may be made of an abstraction is relevant; the way in which the abstraction is implemented is irrelevant. If we consider conventional programming languages, we discover that they offer a powerful aid to abstraction: the function or procedure. When a programmer makes use of a procedure, he is (or should be) concerned only with what it does -- what function it provides for him. He is not concerned with the algorithm executed by the procedure. In addition, procedures provide a means of decomposing a problem -- performing part of the programming task inside a procedure, and another part in the program which calls the procedure. Thus, the existence of procedures goes quite far toward capturing the meaning of abstraction.

Unfortunately, procedures alone do not provide a sufficiently rich vocabulary of abstractions. The abstract data objects and control structures of the abstract machine mentioned above are not accurately represented by independent procedures. Because we are considering abstraction in the context of structured programming, we will omit discussion of control abstractions.

This leads us to the concept of abstract data type which is central to the design of the language. An <u>abstract</u> <u>data</u> <u>type</u> defines a class of abstract objects which is completely characterized by the operations available on those objects. This means that an abstract data type can be defined by defining the characterizing operations for that type.

We believe that the above concept captures the fundamental properties of abstract objects. When a programmer makes use of an abstract data object, he is concerned only with the behavior which that object exhibits but not with any details of how that behavior is achieved by means of an implementation. The behavior of an object is captured by the set of characterizing operations. Implementation information, such as how the object is represented in storage, is only needed when defining how the characterizing operations are to be implemented. The user of the object is not required to know or supply this information.

Abstract types are intended to be very much like the built-in types provided by a programming language. The user of a built-in type, such as <u>integer</u> or <u>integer</u> <u>array</u>, is only concerned with creating objects of that type and then performing operations on them. He is not (usually) concerned with how the data objects are represented, and he views the operations on the objects as indivisible and atomic when in fact several machine instructions may be required to perform them. In addition, he is not (in general) permitted to decompose the objects. Consider, for example, the built-in type <u>integer</u>. A programmer wants to declare objects of type <u>integer</u> and to perform the usual arithmetic operations on them. He is usually not interested in an integer object as a bit string, and cannot make use of the format of the bits within a computer word. Also, he would like the language to protect him from foolish misuses of types (e.g., adding an integer to a character) either by treating such a thing as an error (strong typing), or by some sort of automatic type conversion.

In the case of a built-in data type, the programmer is making use of a concept or abstraction which is realized at a lower level of detail -- the programming language itself and its compiler. Similarly, an abstract data type is used at one level and realized at a lower level, but the lower level does not come into existence automatically by being part of the language. Instead, an abstract data type is realized by writing a special kind of program, called an <u>operation</u> <u>cluster</u>, or cluster for short, which defines the type in terms of the operations which can be performed on it. The language facilitates this activity by allowing the use of an abstract data type without requiring its on-the-spot definition. The language processor supports abstract data types by building links between the use of a type and its definition (which may be provided either earlier or later), and by enforcing the view

of a data type as equivalent to a set of operations
by a very strong form of data typing.

We observe that a consequence of the concept of
abstract data types is that most of the abstract operations in a program will belong to the sets of operations characterizing abstract types. We will use
the term _functional abstraction_ to denote those abstract operations which do not belong to any characterizing set. A functional abstraction will be
implemented as a composition of the characterizing
operations of one or more data types, and will be
supported in the usual way by a procedure. A sine
routine might be an example of such a functional abstraction. The implementation of the sine routine
could be a Taylor series expansion expressed in
terms of characterizing operations of the type _real_.

The Programming Language

We now give an informal description of a programming language which permits the use and definition of abstract data types. This language is a
simplified version of a structured programming language that is under development at M.I.T. It is
derived primarily from PASCAL[1] and is conventional
in many respects, but it differs from conventional
languages in several important ways.

The language provides _two_ forms of modules corresponding to the two forms of abstraction: procedures, which support functional abstractions, and
operation clusters, which support abstract data
types. Each module is translated (compiled) by itself.

The language has no free variables in the conventional sense. Within a module, the only names
that are free, and therefore are defined externally,
are the names of other modules; that is, cluster
names and procedure names. These names are bound at
translation time by means of a directory of module
names created by the programmer expressly for this
purpose. No names remain to be bound in the translated module.

The language has only structured control.
There are no _goto_'s or labels, but merely variants
of concatenation, selection (_if_, _case_) and iteration
(_while_) constructions. A structured error-handling
mechanism is under development. In this paper, it
is represented only by the presence of the reserved
word _error_.

The way in which the language permits the use
and definition of abstract data types can best be
illustrated by an example. We have chosen the following problem: Write a program, Polish_gen, which
will translate from an infix language to a Polish
post-fix language. Polish_gen is to be a general-
purpose program which makes no assumptions about
input or output devices (or files). It makes only
the following assumptions about the input language:

1. The input language has an operator precedence grammar.

2. A symbol of the input language is either an
   arbitrary string of letters and numbers, or
   a single, non-alphanumeric character; blanks
   terminate symbols but are otherwise ignored.

For example, if Polish_gen received the string

$$a + b * (c + d)$$

as input, it would produce the string

$$a\ b\ c\ d + * +$$

as output. We have chosen this problem as our example because the problem and its solution are
familiar to people interested in programming languages, and the problem is sufficiently complex to
illustrate the use of many abstractions.

Using Abstract Data Types

The procedure Polish_gen, shown in Figure 1,
performs the translation described above. It takes
three arguments: input, an object of abstract type
infile which holds the sentence of the input language; output, an object of abstract type outfile
which will accept a sentence of the output language;
and g, an object of abstract type grammar which can
be used to recognize symbols of the input language
and determine their precedence relations. In addition, Polish_gen makes use of local variables of abstract types stack and token. Note that all the
data-type-names appear free in Polish_gen, as does
"scan," which names the single functional abstraction used by Polish_gen.

The language uses the same syntax to declare
variables of abstract data type as to declare variables of primitive type. The syntax distinguishes
between declarations which involve the creation of
an object and those which do not. For example,

    t: token

states that t is the name of a variable which holds
an object of abstract type token, but that no token
object is to be created, so that the value of t is
initially undefined. Thus the variable t is being

```
Polish_gen: procedure(input: infile,
                       output: outfile, g: grammar);

t: token;
mustscan: boolean;
s: stack(token);

mustscan := true;
stack$push(s, token(g, grammar$eof(g)));
while stack$empty(s) do
    if mustscan
        then t := scan(input, g)
        else mustscan := true;
    if token$is_op(t)
        then
            case token$prec_rel(stack$top(s), t) of
              "<":: stack$push(s, t);
              "=":: stack$erasetop(s);
              ">":: begin
                      outfile$out_str(output,
                        token$symbol(stack$pop(s)));
                      mustscan := false;
                    end
            otherwise error;
        else outfile$out_str(output, token$symbol(t));
end
outfile$close(output);
return;
end Polish_gen
```

Figure 1

declared in the same way as mustscan in

    mustscan: <u>boolean</u>

The presence of parentheses following the type name signals creation of an object. For example,

    s: stack(token)

states that s is the name of a variable which holds an object of abstract type stack, and a stack object is to be created and stored in s. Information required for creating the object is passed in a parameter list; in the example, the only parameter, token, defines the type of element which may be placed on the stack s. The declaration of a stack is similar to an array declaration, such as "<u>array</u>[1..10] <u>of</u> characters," in that they both require the type of elements to be specified.

The language is strongly typed; thus there are only three ways in which an abstract object can be used:

1. An abstract object may be operated upon by the operations which define its abstract type.

2. An abstract object may be passed as a parameter to a procedure. In this case, the type of the actual argument passed by the calling procedure must be identical to the type of the corresponding formal parameter in the called procedure.

3. An abstract object may be assigned to a variable, but only if the variable is declared to hold objects of that type.

Application of a defining operation to an abstract object is indicated by an <u>operation call</u> in which a compound name is used: for example,

    grammar$eof(g)
    stack$push(s, t)
    token$is_op(t)

The first part of the compound name identifies the abstract type to which the operation belongs while the second component identifies the operation. An operation call will always have at least one parameter -- an object of the abstract type to which the operation belongs.

There are several reasons why the type-name is included in the operation call. First, since an operation call may have several parameters of different abstract types, the absence of the type-name may lead to an ambiguity as to which object is actually being operated on. Second, use of the compound name permits different data types to use the same names for operations without any clash of identifiers arising. Third, we believe that the type-name prefix will enhance the understandability of programs, once the reader is used to the notation. Not only is the type of the operation immediately apparent, but operation calls are clearly distinguished from procedure calls.

The statement

    t := scan(input, g)

illustrates both passing abstract objects as parameters, and assigning an abstract object to a variable. The procedure scan, shown in Figure 2, expects objects of type infile and grammar as its arguments, and returns an object of type token,

scan: <u>procedure</u>(input: infile, g: grammar)
    <u>returns</u> token;

  newsymb: <u>string</u>;
  ch: <u>char</u>;

  ch := infile$get(input)
  <u>while</u> ch=" " <u>do</u> ch := infile$get(input); <u>end</u>
  <u>if</u> infile$eof(input)
    <u>then return</u> token(g, grammar$eof(g));
  newsymb := <u>unit string</u>(ch);
  <u>if</u> alphanumeric(ch) <u>then</u>
    <u>while</u> alphanumeric(infile$peek(input)) <u>do</u>
      newsymb := newsymb <u>concat</u> infile$get(input);
    <u>end</u>
  <u>return</u> token(g, newsymb);

<u>end</u> scan

Figure 2

which is then stored in the token variable t.

We have explained that objects can be created in conjunction with variable declaration. It is also possible for objects to be created independently of variable declaration. Object creation is specified (whether inside a declaration or not) by the appearance of the type-name followed by parentheses. For example, in the last line of scan

    token(g, newsymb)

states that a token object, representing the symbol just scanned, is to be created; the information required to create the object (the grammar and the symbol just scanned) is passed in a parameter list.

A brief description of the logic of Polish_gen can now be given. Polish_gen uses the functional abstraction scan to obtain a symbol of the grammar from the input string. Scan returns the symbol in the form of a token -- a type introduced to provide efficient execution without revealing information about how the grammar represents symbols. Polish_gen stores the token containing the newly scanned symbol in variable t. If t holds a token representing an identifier (like "a") rather than an operator (like "+"), that identifier is put in the output file immediately. Otherwise, the token on top of the stack is compared with t to determine the precedence relation between them. If the relation is "<", t is pushed on the stack (e.g., "+" < "*"). If the relation is "=", both t and the top-of-stack token are discarded (e.g., "("=")"). If the relation is ">", the operator held in the top-of-stack token is appended to the output file, exposing a new top-of-stack token. Since that operator token may have a higher precedence than t, the boolean variable mustscan is used to prevent a new symbol from being scanned and to insure the next comparison is with the current value of t. Because a grammar-dependent representation of the end of file symbol (grammar$eof(g)) is initially pushed onto the stack, the stack will become empty causing Polish_gen to complete only when a matching eof token is generated by exhausting the input. (We have made the simplifying assumption that the input is a legitimate sentence of the infix language.)

The scan procedure obtains characters from the input file via the operations defining the abstract type infile. It makes use of the data types <u>char</u> and <u>string</u>, and operations on objects of these types. Although these types are shown as built-in, they

192

could easily have been abstract types instead. In that case, the built-in predicate _alphanumeric_, for example, would have been expressed as char$alphanumeric. Only the syntax would change; the meaning and use of the types would be the same in either case.

To sum up, Polish_gen makes use of five data abstractions, infile, outfile, grammar, token and stack, plus one functional abstraction, scan. The power of the data abstractions is illustrated by the types infile and outfile, which are used to shield Polish_gen from any physical facts concerning its input and output, respectively. Polish_gen does not know what input and output devices are being used, when the I/O actually takes place, nor does it know how characters are represented on the devices. What it does know is just enough for its needs: For parameter output it knows how to add a string of characters (outfile$out_str) and how to signify that the output is complete (outfile$close). For parameter input, it knows how to obtain the next character (infile$get), how to look at the next character without removing it from input (infile$peek), and how to recognize the end of input (infile$eof). (Note that for scan to operate correctly, infile must provide a non-blank, non-alphanumeric character on any call on infile$get or infile$peek after the end of file has been reached.) In every case its knowledge consists of the names of the operations which provide these services.

Defining Abstract Data Types

In this section, we describe the programming object -- the operation cluster -- whose translation provides an implementation of a type. The cluster contains code implementing each of the characterizing operations and thereby embodies the idea that a data type is defined by a set of operations.

As an example, consider the abstract data type stack used by Polish_gen. A cluster supporting stacks is shown in Figure 3. This cluster implements a very general kind of stack object in which the type of the stack elements is not known in advance. The cluster parameter element_type indicates the type of element a particular stack object is to contain.

The first part of a cluster definition provides a very brief description of the interface which the cluster presents to its users. The cluster interface defines the name of the cluster, the parameters required to create an instance of the cluster (an object of the abstract type which the cluster implements), and a list of the operations defining the type which the cluster implements, e.g.,

       stack: _cluster_(element-type: _type_)
          _is_ push, pop, top, erasetop, empty

The use of the reserved word _is_ underlines the idea of a data type being characterized by a group of operations.

The remainder of the cluster definition, describing how the abstract type is actually supported, contains three parts: the object representation, the code to create objects and the operation definitions.

```
stack: cluster(element_type: type)
           is push, pop, top, erasetop, empty;

    rep(type_param: type) = (tp: integer;
                             e_type: type;
                             stk: array[1..]
                                  of type_param;

    create

        s: rep(element_type);

        s.tp := 0;
        s.e_type := element_type;
        return s;
        end

    push: operation(s: rep, v: s.e_type);

        s.tp := s.tp+1;
        s.stk[s.tp] := v;
        return;
        end

    pop: operation(s: rep) returns s.e_type;

        if s.tp = 0 then error;
        s.tp := s.tp-1;
        return s.stk[s.tp+1];
        end

    top: operation(s: rep) returns s.e_type;

        if s.tp = 0 then error;
        return s.stk[s.tp];
        end

    erasetop: operation(s: rep);

        if s.tp = 0 then error;
        s.tp := s.tp-1;
        return;
        end

    empty: operation(s: rep) returns boolean;

        return s.tp = 0;
        end

    end stack
```

Figure 3

Object Representation. Users of the abstract data type view objects of that type as indivisible entities. Inside the cluster, however, objects are viewed as decomposable into elements of more primitive type. The _rep_ description

    rep{ (⟨rep-parameters⟩)} = ⟨type-definition⟩

defines a new type, denoted by the reserved word _rep_, which is accessible only within the cluster and describes how objects are viewed there. The ⟨type-definition⟩ defines a template which permits objects of that type to be built and decomposed. In general, it will make use of the data structuring methods provided by the language: arrays (possibly unbounded) or PASCAL records. The optional ("{}") ⟨rep-parameters⟩ make it possible to delay specifying some aspects of the ⟨type definition⟩ until an instance of the _rep_ is created. Consider the rep description of the stack cluster:

rep(type_param: type) = (tp: integer; e_type: type;
                         stk: array[1..] of type_param)

The ⟨type-definition⟩ specifies that a stack object is represented by a record containing three components named tp, stk, and e_type. The parameter, type_param, specifies the type of element which may be stored in the unbounded array named stk which will hold the elements pushed onto a stack object. This same type will also be stored in the e_type component, and is used for type checking as will be described below. The tp component holds the index of the topmost element of the stack.

Object Creation. The reserved word create marks the create_code, the code to be executed when an object of the abstract type is created. The cluster may be viewed as a procedure whose procedure body is the create-code. When a user indicates that an object of abstract type is to be created, for example,

                    s: stack(token)

one thing that happens (at execution time) is a call on the create-code, causing that procedure body to be executed. The parameters of the cluster are actually parameters of the create-code. Since free variables, other than references to externally defined modules, are not provided, these parameters are not accessible either to the operations or to the ⟨type definition⟩ in the rep. Therefore, any information about the parameters that is to be saved must be explicitly inserted into each instance of the rep.

The code shown in the stack cluster is typical of create-code. First, an object of type rep is created; that is, space is allocated to hold the object as defined by the rep. Then, some initial values are stored in the object. Finally, the object is returned to the caller. When the object is returned, its type is changed from type rep to the abstract type defined by the cluster.

Operations. The remainder of the cluster consists of a group of operation definitions, which provide implementations of the permissible operations on the data type. Operation definitions are like ordinary procedure definitions except that they have access to the rep of the cluster, which permits them to decompose objects of the cluster type. Operations are not themselves modules; they will be accepted by the translator only as part of a cluster.

Operations always have at least one parameter -- of type rep. Because the cluster may simultaneously support many objects of its defined type, this parameter tells the operation the particular object on which to operate. Note that the type of this parameter will change from the abstract type to type rep as it is passed between the caller and the operation.

Because the language is strongly typed, the type of objects pushed on a given stack must be checked for consistency with the type of elements the stack can hold. This consistency requirement is specified syntactically by declaring that the type of the second argument of push is to be the same as the e_type component of the rep of the stack object which is the first argument of push. The translator

can generate code to verify that the types match at run time and to raise an error if they don't.

Controlling the Use of Information

Abstract data types were introduced as a way of freeing a programmer from concern about irrelevant details in his use of data abstractions. But in fact we have gone further than that. Because the language is strongly typed, the user is unable to make use of any implementation details. In this section we discuss the benefits that accrue from this limitation: the programs which result are more modular, and easier to understand, modify, maintain and prove correct.

Token is a good example of a type created to control access to implementation details. Instead of introducing a new type, Polish_gen could have been written to accept strings from scan, to store strings on the stack, and to compare strings to determine the precedence relation (via an appropriate operation grammar$prec_rel). Such a solution would be inefficient. Since the precedence matrix can be indexed by the positions of the operators in the reserved word table of the grammar, an efficient implementation would look up the character string only once to find out if it is an operator symbol and, if so, use the index of the operator in Polish_gen.

This, however, exposes information about the representation of the grammar. If Polish_gen or some other module which uses the grammar makes use of this information, normal maintenance and modification of the grammar cluster can introduce errors which are difficult to track down.[2] Therefore, the new type, token, is introduced to limit the distribution of information about how the grammar is represented. Now a redefinition of the grammar cluster can affect only the token cluster -- which makes no assumptions about the index it receives from grammar. If an error occurs while looking up a precedence relation (like an index out of bounds), the error can only have been caused by something in the token or grammar cluster.

Actually, the selection of an implementation of tokens -- for example, whether a token is represented by an integer or a character string -- involves a design decision. This decision can be delayed until the cluster for tokens is defined and need not be made during the coding of Polish_gen. Therefore, the programming of Polish_gen can be done according to one of Dijkstra's programming principles: build the program one decision at a time.[3] Following this principle leads to a simplified logic for Polish_gen, making it easier to understand and maintain.

Making the representation inaccessible also results in a program which is easier to prove correct. The proof of a program is divided into two parts: a proof that the cluster correctly implements the type, and a proof that the program using the type is correct. Only in the former proof need details of the implementation of type objects be considered; the latter proof is based only on the abstract properties of the types, which may be expressed in terms of relations among the characterizing operations for each type.

Relationship to Previous Work

Much work has been done in the area of creating
suitable mechanisms for defining data types. There
is no hope of surveying all that work here, nor is
it all relevant to this paper. In this section we
outline the areas of work that are most closely related to clusters in that they provide some tools
for defining abstract data types, and we discuss
how the cluster approach differs from that work.
The related work can be roughly divided into three
categories: extensible languages, implementation
specifications for a set of standard abstract operators, and SIMULA 67 class definitions.

Extensible Languages

Much of the work and much of the success with
extensible languages[4] has been in the area of data
type definition. This work, however, has been primarily oriented toward defining representations
rather than abstract types. New data representations, or modes as they are frequently called, are
created by constructing the representation in terms
of existing modes using the primitive mode construction facilities of the language. Mode construction
facilities provided by an extensible language typically include mechanisms for defining pointers to
objects, for defining unions of distinct mode classes, and for constructing aggregates (arrays and
records) of objects. These correspond closely to
the facilities used in this paper to define reps.
The use of these mode definition mechanisms implies
the definition of a set of constructors, selectors
and predicates which may be applied to objects of
the mode being defined. In some languages, the mode
definitions may allow this set of operations to be
augmented by certain operations, such as assignment,
which are expressly provided for in the language.

The main problem with extensible languages is
that they do not encourage the use of data abstractions. It is, in general, impossible to define all
the operations characterizing an abstract data type
within the mode definition. As we noted, only the
representation of a data type is defined using the
mode extension mechanism. Any abstract operation
which is not equivalent to a constructor, selector
or predicate for the representation must be defined
outside the mode definition by a procedure or macro
which can be made to appear like an operator by
using the syntax extension facility. Therefore, a
user must learn two different mechanisms; and the
definition, instead of being collected in one place,
as it is in an operation cluster, is split into distinct parts. Furthermore, it is difficult to restrict access to the representation solely to the
characterizing operations of the abstract data type.

Standard Abstract Operations

The work derived from the earlier work of
Mealy[5] and Balzer[6] is much closer in spirit to the
approach taken here. Mealy established the view
that a data collection is a map from a set of selectors to a set of values, and that operations on
data collections are either transformations on the
map or uses of the map to access elements. This
view has led to attempts to standardize a set of abstract operators for data collections. For example,
Balzer proposed a particular abstraction for such
collections which defines a set of four abstract operators to create, access, modify, and destroy ab-

stract data collections. The user would define a
particular collection by specifying how each abstract operation was to be implemented. This work
has been extended (e.g., Earley[7]), but its primary
emphasis has remained on defining a standard set of
abstract operations. More complex operations are
defined as procedures written in terms of these abstract operations.

Although it is useful to distinguish some abstract operations, such as "create," which have a
high probability of being applicable to every abstract data type, it seems unreasonable to expect
that a predetermined set of operations will suffice
to manipulate every abstract data object. Therefore,
leaving the selection of the operations to the crea-
tor of the type, as is done with operation clusters,
provides a more closely tailored abstraction.

SIMULA Classes

The language which most closely resembles, in
form, the language presented here is SIMULA 67.[8]
SIMULA class definitions have many similarities with
cluster definitions. There is, however, a very important philosophical difference in these two languages which leads to several important linguistic
differences. The classes of SIMULA were designed to
represent and provide full accessibility to data objects. Every attribute and function in a class is
accessible in the block in which the class definition
is embedded. Therefore, the actual form of the representation is always known to the user.

In contrast to this, the rep of a cluster is
not accessible outside the cluster. Operations in
the cluster provide the only way to access the contents of the rep and, even then, only a subset of
the operations defined in the cluster may be externally accessible. As a result of this philosophical
difference, the mechanisms for referencing data, the
use of non-local variable references, and the use of
blocks and block structuring are quite different in
the two languages.

Implementation Considerations

Most aspects of the implementation of clusters
will be handled in a conventional manner. There
are, however, several aspects of the implementation
which deserve special mention because they are nonstandard or have a significant impact on the practicality of using clusters to represent abstract
data.

Modules and Module-Names

The compiler accepts a module as input. A
module will usually be a cluster, but will sometimes be a procedure like Polish_gen or scan. In
the course of module translation, externally defined
module-names, used to refer to procedures and data
types, will be encountered. (Note that the references to operations on abstract data types do not
introduce any additional external references because
they are relative to the abstract type with which
the operation name is prefixed.)

When the compiler processes a module it builds
or adds to a description-unit containing information
about the module. Information held in the
description-unit includes:

1. The location of the object code generated by the compiler.

2. A description of the interface which the module makes available to its users. In particular, complete information about types of all parameters and values expected by the module is maintained. If the module is a cluster, information will be kept for each operation in the cluster.

3. A list of all modules which use the module.

Obviously much more information can be stored in the description-unit: debugging information in the form of symbol tables, etc., documentation information, specification information in the form of predicate calculus descriptions of input/output relationships, and even an analysis of the rationale for the decisions made in designing the module.

The description unit is the focus for all information about a module. It can be created when the module is processed or it can be created to be the target of references from other modules. Creating a description unit before the module it represents is processed supports top-down design and provides a simple way to define recursion. Since the description unit holds a list of all uses of the module, the consistency of the uses and the definition can be checked when the module is actually defined and appropriate error messages can be generated at that time. The actual definition can be delayed for quite some time as the description unit can be used to locate code to simulate the behavior of the module for debugging purposes.

In the course of translating a module, the translator must give a meaning to each module name by binding it to the code of the corresponding module. This is done via the description unit. The translator obtains access to description units by means of a directory, containing a set of module-name/description unit pairs, which it receives as an argument. All external references must be resolved by means of this directory; if they cannot be resolved, an appropriate error message is generated.

The directory is a user-constructed object which is, in general, built to control the translation of a specific set of related modules. The actual description units are stored in a multilevel, tree structured file system similar to the MULTICS file system,[9] and the references to description units in a directory are actually references into this file system. The primitives for constructing directories and for manipulating the file system are independent of the language, forming the "file system cluster" and the "directory cluster."

Type Checking

The language described in this paper is based on the idea of strong type checking, and the language translator is supposed to enforce strong type checking even across the interface between two separately compiled procedures. In this section we discuss some of the problems arising from strong type checking.

Strong type checking means that whenever an object is passed from a calling function to a called function, its type must be compatible with the type declared in the called function. If the called function is a procedure, the types must match identically. If the called function is an operation, then the types must match identically unless the object is of the abstract type defined by the cluster to which the operation belongs. In this case, the type of the object is changed to the type _rep_ for that cluster. Thus, the type checking mechanism controls whether the representation of an object is visable to a given operation. If a type error were undetected in this case, information supposed to have been inaccessible outside of the cluster, will become accessible, and program modularity will be destroyed.

Type checking in this language is more complex than in most conventional languages. This is because user-defined abstractions, both data types and procedures, may have types as parameters. Consider the data type stack defined above. We have noted the similarity between stacks and arrays: In each case, a type specification for the components of the structure must be supplied before an instance can be created. Constructs, such as stack and array, are called _type generators_ because they define a class of types rather than a single type. Each individual type in the class is generated by supplying type definitions for each of the type parameters of the type generator. A type generator, like stack, which is built to serve the needs of future users, defines an open-ended class of types, and the members of its type class are _not_ known at the time the stack cluster is compiled.

One of the effects of allowing user defined type generators is that some of the operations in the cluster for that "type" are polymorphic; that is, the operations may be defined over many different type domains, subject to the constraint that the types of any given set of arguments are type-consistent. An example of such an operation is push in the stack cluster. Push takes as its operands a stack and a value. The type consistency requirement for push is that, if the type of the stack is "stack of T," the value pushed must be of type T; thus, strong type checking for the operation push involves determining that its stack argument really is a stack, determining the type of the stack argument, determining the type of the value being pushed and determining that they satisfy the consistency requirement.

It is desirable to do compile-time type checking, since type errors are detected as early as possible. Because of the freedom with which types can be used in the language, however, it is not clear how complete the compile time type checking can be. Therefore, the design of the language is based on a run-time type checking mechanism which is augmented by as much compile-time checking as is possible.

It is clear that given a suitable representation of types, a run time check for identically matching types can be programmed. The kind of type checking which results in the representation of an object being exposed to an operation can be handled at run-time by a technique described by Morris[10] which is an outgrowth of the work on protection in operating systems. (There is a strong correlation between clusters and protected subsystems; clusters provide a natural mechanism for encapsulating private information.)[11]

In the future we may be able to dispense with the run time mechanism, since recent work by John Reynolds[12] indicates that complete compile-time type checking may be possible. We look forward to the completion of Reynolds' work, and intend to design a version of the language based on compile-time type checking in the near future.

Retention

The language has been designed to permit activations of clusters, procedure and operation to be implemented using a stack discipline. Clusters, procedures and operations have no free variables at execution time, and all variables defined therein are purely local. All information that is to be retained or shared must be stored in the rep of an object. The objects are allocated in a heap where the retention strategy is used. In practice, there are a number of easily identified cases where objects need not be placed in the heap but can instead be allocated on the stack, either because the object is not shared or because once it has been allocated its content never changes. These cases may be optimized by the language translator.

Efficiency

We believe it is helpful to associate two structures with a program: its logical structure and its physical structure. The primary business of a programmer is to build a program with a good logical structure -- one which is understandable and leads to ease in modification and maintenance.[13] However, a good logical structure does not necessarily imply a good physical structure -- one which is efficient to execute. In fact, the techniques employed to achieve good logical structure (hierarchy, access to data only through functions, etc.) in many cases seem to imply bad physical structure.

We believe it is the business of the compiler to map good logical structure into good physical structure. The fact that the two structures may diverge is acceptable provided that the compiler is verified, and that all programming tools (for example, the debugging aids) are defined to hide the divergence.

The language is intended to be compiled by an optimizing compiler which achieves a good physical structure in the output code. An important efficiency can be obtained from the fact that the language is flexible with respect to the meaning of an operation call. Each operation call may be replaced either by an actual call upon the corresponding operation or by inline code for the operation. Two aspects of the language design make this flexibility possible:

1. Because the syntax for an operation call is identical in both cases, it is possible to change the compiling technique that is used without rewriting the procedure in which the operator is used.

2. The invariant portion of the cluster -- the code for the operations -- has been carefully separated from the rep, which holds the object dependent information; thus, inline insertion of the code is possible.

Inline insertion of the code for an operation allows that code to be subject to the optimization transformations available in the compiler. Optimizing transformations, such as compile-time evaluation and common subexpression elimination, remove redundant computations, thereby decreasing the time needed to execute the operation. For example, all error checks in the stack cluster operations could be eliminated if those operations were inserted inline in Polish_gen. These standard optimization techniques should be extremely effective because the compiler is dealing with a structured program; the lack of free variables, and of goto's and other confusing control structures implies that a thorough data and control flow analysis can be performed. In other words, the compiler can benefit from the good logical structure of the program to obtain a thorough understanding of it, just as a person can.

The price paid to obtain this execution time optimization is an increase in the cost of redefining or modifying a module. Each such modification may require the recompilation of the modules which use the modified functions inline. Since the decision to use inline code can be delayed until performance measurements indicate which sections of a system are critical, one need relinquish the flexibility of easy program modification only where a positive performance benefit would result from inline code. Note that the list of the uses of the module, kept in the description-unit, can be used to cause automatic recompilation when changes are made.

Conclusions

This paper described a new kind of abstraction, the abstract data type, which augments our ability to make use of abstraction in building programs. The approach was discussed both as a concept and as a part of a programming language. Several examples of its use were given. An abstract data type was defined to be a class of objects which is completely characterized by the operations which may be performed on those objects. A new linguistic construct, the operation cluster, was introduced to provide programming language support for abstract data types.

The rationale behind undertaking to develop the language was to make the practice of structured programming more understandable by providing a langauge in which the abstractions uncovered in the course of program design could be expressed. We believe that the concept of abstract data type provides data abstraction in a form most useful to the programmer: he need only be aware of the behavior of an abstract object, which is precisely the information he needs to write his program, and irrelevant details about how the object is represented in storage and how the operations are implemented, are hidden from him. In fact, he is unable to make use of implementation details, leading to an improvement in program quality: programs will be more modular, and easier to understand, modify, maintain, and prove correct.

Of course, program quality is most dependent on good program design. Although a language can never teach a programmer what constitutes a well-designed program, it can guide him into thinking about the right things. We believe that abstraction is the key to good design,[13] and we have discovered in our experiments in using the language that it encourages the programmer to consciously search for abstractions, especially data abstractions, and to think very hard about their use and definition.

We believe that the approach to abstraction discussed in the paper can be usefully incorporated in many different kinds of languages. It is unlikely that any language, no matter how high-level, contains all the abstractions which any person working in it would require. Therefore, the abstraction-building-mechanism described in this paper would be a useful feature of a very-high-level language.

Acknowledgements

The authors gratefully acknowledge the helpful comments on the content and structure of the paper made by Jack Dennis, Austin Henderson, Greg Pfister, and the referees.

References

1. Wirth, N. The programming language PASCAL. *Acta Informatica*, *Vol.* 1 (1971), pp 35-63.

2. Parnas, D. L. Information distribution aspects of design methodology, *Proceedings of the IFIP Congress*, August 1971.

3. Dijkstra, E. W. Notes on structured programming. *Structured Programming*, A.P.I.C. Studies in Data Processing, No. 8, Academic Press, New York, 1972, pp 1-81.

4. Schuman, S. A. and P. Jorrand. Definition mechanisms in extensible programming languages. *Proceedings of the AFIPS*, Vol. 37, 1970, pp 9-19.

5. Mealy, G. Another look at data. *Proceedings of the AFIPS*, *Vol.* 31, 1967, pp 525-534.

6. Balzer, R. M. Dataless programming. *Proceedings of the AFIPS*, *Vol.* 31, 1967, pp 557-566.

7. Earley, J. Toward an understanding of data structures. *Comm. of the ACM*, Vol. 14, *No.* 10 (October 1971), pp 617-627.

8. Dahl, O.-J., B. Myhrhaug, and K. Nygaard. *The SIMULA 67 Common Base Language*. Norwegian Computing Center, Oslo, Publication S-22, 1970.

9. Daley, R. C., and P. G. Neumann. A general-purpose file system for secondary storage. *Proceedings of the AFIPS*, Vol. 27, 1965, pp 213-229.

10. Morris, J. H., Jr. Protection in programming languages. *Comm. of the ACM*, Vol. 16, *No.* 1 (January 1973), pp 15-21.

11. Zilles, S. N. Procedural encapsulation: a linguistic protection technique. *SIGPLAN Notices*, Vol. 8, *No.* 9 (September 1973), pp 140-146.

12. Reynolds, J. Personal communication.

13. Liskov, B. H. A design methodology for reliable software systems. *Proceedings of the AFIPS*, Vol. 41, 1972, pp 191-199.

Data: Abstraction,   B. Wegbreit
Definition, and Structure Editor

Abstract Data Types and the Development of Data Structures

John Guttag
University of Southern California

Reprinted from *Communications of the ACM*, June 1977, pp. 396-404. Copyright 1977 Association for Computing Machinery, Inc. Reprinted by permission.

Abstract data types can play a significant role in the development of software that is reliable, efficient, and flexible. This paper presents and discusses the application of an algebraic technique for the specification of abstract data types. Among the examples presented is a top-down development of a symbol table for a block structured language; a discussion of the proof of its correctness is given. The paper also contains a brief discussion of the problems involved in constructing algebraic specifications that are both consistent and complete.

Key Words and Phrases: abstract data type, correctness proof, data type, data structure, specification, software specification

CR Categories: 4.34, 5.24

This work was supported in part by the National Science Foundation under grant number MCS76-06089.

A version of this paper was presented as the SIGPLAN/SIGMOD Conference on Data: Abstraction, Definition, and Structure, Salt Lake City, Utah, March 22–24, 1976.

Author's address: Computer Science Department, University of Southern California, Los Angeles, CA 90007.

1. Introduction

Dijkstra [4] and many others have made the point that the amount of complexity that the human mind can cope with at any instant in time is considerably less than that embodied in much of the software that one might wish to build. Thus the key problem in the design and implementation of large software systems is reducing the amount of complexity or detail that must be considered at any one time. One way to do this is via the process of abstraction.

One of the most significant aids to abstraction used in programming is the self-contained subroutine. At the point where one decides to invoke a subroutine, one can (and most often should) treat it as a "black box." It performs a specific arbitrarily abstract function by means of an unprescribed algorithm. Thus, at the level where it is invoked, it separates the relevant detail of "what" from the irrelevant detail of "how." Similarly, at the level where it is implemented, it is usually unnecessary to complicate the "how" by considering the "why," i.e. the exact reasons for invoking a subroutine often need not be of concern to its implementor. By nesting subroutines, one may develop a hierarchy of abstractions.

Unfortunately, the nature of the abstractions that may be conveniently achieved through the use of subroutines is limited. Subroutines, while well suited to the description of abstract events (operations), are not particularly well suited to the description of abstract objects. This is a serious drawback, for in a great many applications the complexity of the data objects to be manipulated contributes substantially to the overall complexity of the problem.

2. The Abstraction of Data

The large knot of complexly interrelated attributes associated with a data object may be separated according to the nature of the information that the attributes convey regarding the data objects that they qualify. Two kinds of attributes, each of which may be studied in isolation, are:

(1) those that describe the representation of objects and the implementations of the operations associated with them in terms of other objects and operations, e.g. in terms of a physical store and a processor's order code;

(2) those that specify the names and define the abstract meanings of the operations associated with an object. Though these two kinds of attributes are in practice highly interdependent, they represent logically independent concepts.

The emphasis in this paper is on the second kind of attribute, i.e. on the specification of the operations associated with classes of data objects. At most points in a program one is concerned solely with the behav-ioral characteristics of a data object. One is interested in what one can do with it, not in how the various operations on it are implemented. The analogy with a closed procedure is exact. More often than not, one need be no more concerned with the underlying representation of the object being operated on than one is with the algorithm used to implement an invoked procedure.

If at a given level of refinement one is interested only in the behavioral characteristics of certain data objects, then any attempt to abstract data must be based upon those characteristics, and only those characteristics. The introduction of other attributes, e.g. a representation, can only serve to cloud the relevant issues. We use the term "abstract data type" to refer to a class of objects defined by a representation-independent specification.

The class construct of SIMULA 67 [3] has been used as the starting point for much of the more recent work on embedding abstract types in programming languages, e.g. [14, 16, 18]. While each of these offers a mechanism for binding together the operations and storage structures representing a type, they offer no representation-independent means for specifying the behavior of the operations. The only representation-independent information that one can supply are the domains and ranges of the various operations. One could, for example, define a type Queue (of Items) with the operations

```
NEW:                    → Queue
ADD:          Queue × Item → Queue
FRONT:        Queue → Item
REMOVE:       Queue → Queue
IS_EMPTY?:    Queue → Boolean
```

Unfortunately, however, short of supplying a representation, the only mechanism for denoting what these operations "mean" is a judicious choice of names. Except for intuitions about the meaning of such words as Queue and FRONT, the operations might just as easily be defining type Stack as type Queue. The domain and range specifications for these two types are isomorphic. To rely on one's intuition about the meaning of names can be dangerous even when dealing with familiar types [19]. When dealing with unfamiliar types it is almost impossible. What is needed, therefore, is a mechanism for specifying the semantics of the operations of the type.

There are, of course, many possible approaches to the specification of the semantics of an abstract data type. Most, however, can be placed in one of two categories: operational or definitional. In an operational specification, instead of trying to describe the properties of the abstract data type, one gives a recipe for constructing it. One begins with some well-understood language or discipline and builds a model for the type in terms of that discipline. Wulf [24], for example, makes good use of sequences in modeling various data structures.

The operational approach to formal specification has many advantages. Most significantly, operational specifications seem to be relatively (compared to definitional specifications) easily constructed by those trained as programmers — chiefly because the construction of operational specifications so closely resembles programming. As the operations to be specified grow complex, however, operational specifications tend to get too long (see, for example, Batey [1]) to permit substantial confidence in their aptness. As the number of operations grows, problems arise because the relations among the operations are not explicitly stated, and inferring them becomes combinatorially harder.

The most serious problem associated with operational specifications is that they almost always force one to overspecify the abstraction. By introducing extraneous detail, they associate nonessential attributes with the type. This extraneous detail complicates the problem of proving the correctness of an implementation by introducing conditions that are irrelevant, yet nevertheless must be verified. More importantly, the introduction of extraneous detail places unnecessary constraints on the choice of an implementation and may potentially eliminate the best solutions to the problem.

Axiomatic definitions avoid this problem. The algebraic approach used here owes much to the work of Hoare [13] (which in turn owes much to Floyd [5]) and is closely related to Standish's "axiomatic specifications" [22] and Zilles' "algebraic specifications" [25]. Its formal basis stems from the heterogeneous algebras of Birkhoff and Lipson [2]. An algebraic specification of an abstract type consists of two pairs: a syntactic specification and a set of relations. The syntactic specification provides the syntactic information that many programming languages already require: the names, domains, and ranges of the operations associated with the type. The set of relations defines the meanings of the operations by stating their relationships to one another.

3. A Short Example

Consider type Queue (of Items) with the operations listed in the previous section. The syntactic specification is as above:

```
NEW:                    → Queue
ADD:          Queue × Item → Queue
FRONT:        Queue → Item
REMOVE:       Queue → Queue
IS_EMPTY?:    Queue → Boolean
```

The distinguishing characteristic of a queue is that it is a first in–first out storage device. A good axiomatic definition of the above operations must therefore assert that and only that characteristic. The relations (or axioms) below comprise just such a definition. The meanings of the axioms should be relatively clear. ("=" has its standard meaning, "q" and "i" are typed free variables, and "error" is a distinguished value with the property that the value of any operation applied to an argument list containing error is error, e.g. $f_n(x_1, \ldots, x_i, \text{error}, x_{i+2}, \ldots, x_n) = \text{error}$.)

(1) IS_EMPTY? (NEW) = true
(2) IS_EMPTY? (ADD(q,i)) = false
(3) FRONT(NEW) = error
(4) FRONT (ADD(q,i)) = **if** IS_EMPTY? (q)
                       then i
                       else FRONT(q)
(5) REMOVE(NEW) = error
(6) REMOVE (ADD(q,i)) = **if** IS_EMPTY? (q)
                        then NEW
                        else ADD(REMOVE(q),i)

Note that this set of axioms involves no assumption about the attributes of type Item. In effect Item is a parameter of type Type, and the specification may be viewed as defining a type schema rather than a single type. This will be the case for many algebraic type specifications.

With some practice, one can become quite adept at reading algebraic axiomatizations. Practice also makes it easier to construct such specifications; see Guttag [11]. Unfortunately, it does not make it trivial. It is not always immediately clear how to attack the problem. Nor, once one has constructed an axiomatization, is it always easy to ascertain whether or not the axiomatization is consistent and sufficiently complete. The meaning of the operations is supplied by a set of individual statements of fact. If any two of these are contradictory, the axiomatization is inconsistent. If the combination of statements is not sufficient to convey all of the vital information regarding the meaning of the operations of the type, the axiomatization is not sufficiently complete.[1]

Experience indicates that completeness is, in a practical sense, a more severe problem than consistency. If one has an intuitive understanding of the type being specified, one is unlikely to supply contradictory axioms. It is, on the other hand, extremely easy to overlook one or more cases. Boundary conditions, e.g. REMOVE(NEW), are particularly likely to be overlooked.

In an attempt to ameliorate this problem, we have devised heuristics to aid the user in the initial presentation of an axiomatic specification of the operations of an abstract type and a system to mechanically "verify" the sufficient-completeness of that specification. As the first step in defining a new type, the user would supply the system with the syntactic specification of the type and an axiomatization constructed with the aid of the heuristics mentioned above. Given this preliminary specification, the system would begin to prompt the user to supply the additional information necessary for the system to derive a sufficiently complete axiom set

---

[1] Sufficiently complete is a technical notion first developed in Guttag [8]. It differs considerably from both the notion of completeness commonly used in logic and that used in Zilles [25].

for the operations. A detailed look at sufficient-completeness is contained in Guttag [8, 9].

4. An Extended Example

A common data structuring problem is the design of the symbol table component of a compiler for a block structured language. Many sources contain good discussions of various symbol table organizations. Setting aside variations in form, the basic operations described vary little from source to source. They are:

INIT:	Allocate and initialize the symbol table.
ENTERBLOCK:	Prepare a new local naming scope.
LEAVEBLOCK:	Discard entries from the most recent scope entered, and reestablish the next outer scope.
IS_INBLOCK?:	Has a specified identifier already been declared in this scope? (Used to avoid duplicate declarations.)
ADD:	Add an identifier and its attributes to the symbol table.
RETRIEVE:	Return the attributes associated (in the most local scope in which it occurs) with a specified identifier.

Though many references provide insights into how these operations can be implemented, none presents a formal definition (other than implementations) of exactly what they mean. The abstract concept "symbol table" thus goes undefined. Those who attempt to write compilers in a top-down fashion suffer from a similar problem. Early refinements of parts of the compiler make use of the basic symbol table operations, but the "meaning" of these operations is provided only by subsequent levels of refinement. This is infelicitous in that the clear separation of levels of abstraction is lost and with it many of the advantages of top-down design. By providing axiomatic semantics for the operations, this problem can be avoided.

The thought of providing rigorous definitions for so many operations may, at first, seem a bit intimidating. Nevertheless, if one is to understand the refinement, one must know what each operation means. The following specification of abstract type Symboltable supplies these meanings.

Type: Symboltable

Operations:

INIT:	$\rightarrow$ Symboltable
ENTERBLOCK:	Symboltable $\rightarrow$ Symboltable
LEAVEBLOCK:	Symboltable $\rightarrow$ Symboltable
ADD:	Symboltable $\times$ Identifier $\times$ Attributelist $\rightarrow$ Symboltable
IS_INBLOCK?:	Symboltable $\times$ Identifier $\rightarrow$ Boolean
RETRIEVE:	Symboltable $\times$ Identifier $\rightarrow$ Attributelist

Axioms:

(1) LEAVEBLOCK(INIT) = error

(2) LEAVEBLOCK(ENTERBLOCK(symtab)) = symtab

(3) LEAVEBLOCK(ADD(symtab, id, attrs)) = LEAVEBLOCK(symtab)

(4) IS_INBLOCK? (INIT, id) = false

(5) IS_INBLOCK? (ENTERBLOCK(symtab), id) = false

(6) IS_INBLOCK? (ADD(symtab, id, attrs), idl) =
    if IS_SAME? (id, idl)[2]
      then true
      else IS_INBLOCK? (symtab, id)

(7) RETRIEVE(INIT, id) = error

(8) RETRIEVE(ENTERBLOCK(symtab), id) =
    RETRIEVE(symtab, id)

(9) RETRIEVE(ADD(symtab, id, attrs), idl)=
    if IS_SAME? (id, idl)
      then attrs
      else RETRIEVE(symtab, idl)

This set of relations serves a dual purpose. Not only does it define an abstract type that can be used in the specification of various parts of the compiler, but it also provides a complete self-contained specification for a major subsystem of the compiler. If one wished to delegate the design and implementation of the symbol table subsystem, the algebraic characterization of the abstract type would (unlike the informal description in, say, McKeeman [15]) be a sufficient specification of the problem. In fact, the procedure discussed earlier can be used to formally prove the sufficient-completeness of this specification.

The next step in the design process is to further refine type Symboltable, i.e. to provide implementations of the operations of the type. These implementations will implicitly furnish representation for values of type Symboltable.

A representation of a type T consists of (i) any interpretation (implementation) of the operations of the type that is a model for the axioms of the specification of T, and (ii) a function Φ that maps terms in the model domain onto their representatives in the abstract domain. (This is basically the abstraction function of Hoare [12].)

It is important to note that Φ may not have a proper inverse. Consider, for example, type Bounded Queue (with a maximum length of three). A reasonable representation of the values of this type might be based on a ring-buffer and top pointer. Given this representation, the program segment:

```
x := EMPTY.Q
x := ADD.Q(x, A)
x := ADD.Q(x, B)
x := ADD.Q(x, C)
x := REMOVE.Q(x)
x := ADD.Q(x, D)
```

would translate to a representation for x of the form:

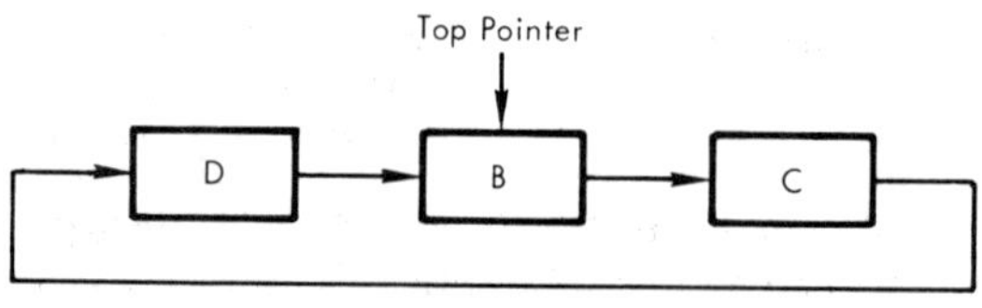

---

[2] The definition of IS_SAME? is part of the specification of an independently defined type Identifier.

Similarly:

x := EMPTY.Q
x := ADD.Q(x, B)
x := ADD.Q(x, C)
x := ADD.Q(x, D)

would yield a representation for x of the form:

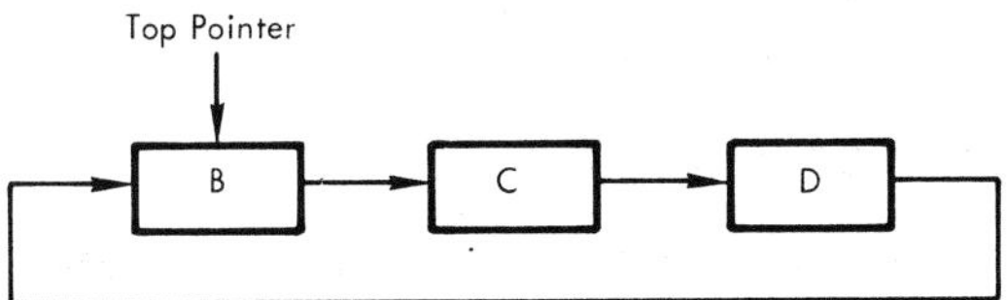

It is clear that these two representations though not identical, refer to the same abstract value. That is to say, the mapping from values to representations, Φ^{-1}, may be one-to-many.

The representation of type Symboltable will make use of the abstract data types Stack (of arrays) and Array (of attributelists) as defined below.

Type: Stack

Operations:

NEWSTACK: $\rightarrow$ Stack
PUSH: Stack $\times$ Array $\rightarrow$ Stack
POP: Stack $\rightarrow$ Stack
TOP: Stack $\rightarrow$ Array
IS_NEWSTACK?:   Stack $\rightarrow$ Boolean
REPLACE: Stack $\times$ Array $\rightarrow$ Stack

Axioms:

(10) IS_NEWSTACK? (NEWSTACK) = true
(11) IS_NEWSTACK? (PUSH(stk, arr)) = false
(12) POP(NEWSTACK) = error
(13) POP(PUSH(stk, arr)) = stk
(14) TOP(NEWSTACK) = error
(15) TOP(PUSH(stk, arr)) = arr
(16) REPLACE(stk, arr) = **if** IS_NEWSTACK? (stk)
          then error
          else PUSH(POP(stk), arr)

Type: Array

Operations:

EMPTY: $\rightarrow$ Array
ASSIGN: Array $\times$ Identifier $\times$ Attributelist $\rightarrow$ Array
READ: Array $\times$ Identifier $\rightarrow$ Attributelist
IS_UNDEFINED?:   Array $\times$ Identifier $\rightarrow$ Boolean

Axioms:

(17) IS_UNDEFINED? (EMPTY, id) = true
(18) IS_UNDEFINED? (ASSIGN(arr, id, attrs), idl) =
    if IS_SAME? (id, idl)
        then false
          else IS_UNDEFINED? (arr, idl)
(19) READ(EMPTY, id) = error
(20) READ(ASSIGN(arr, id, attrs), idl) = **if** IS_SAME? (id, idl)
               then attrs
               else READ(arr, idl)

The general scheme of the representation of type Symboltable is to treat a value of the type as a stack of arrays (with index type Identifier), where each array contains the attributes for the identifiers declared in a single block. For every function f in the more abstract domain (e.g. type Symboltable), a function f' is defined in the lower-level domain; thus we have:

INIT': $\rightarrow$ Stack
ENTERBLOCK':   Stack $\rightarrow$ Stack
LEAVEBLOCK':   Stack $\rightarrow$ Stack
ADD':   Stack $\times$ Identifier $\times$ Attributelist $\rightarrow$ Stack
IS_INBLOCK?':   Stack $\times$ Identifier $\rightarrow$ Boolean
RETRIEVE':   Stack $\times$ Identifier $\rightarrow$ Attributelist

The "code" for each of these functions is ("::" means "is defined as"):

INIT' :: PUSH(NEWSTACK, EMPTY)
ENTERBLOCK'(stk) :: PUSH(stk, EMPTY)
LEAVEBLOCK'(stk) :: **if** IS_NEWSTACK? (POP(stk))
             then error
             else POP(stk)
ADD'(stk, id, attrs) :: REPLACE(stk, ASSIGN(TOP(stk), id, attrs))
IS_INBLOCK?'(stk, id) :: **if** IS_NEWSTACK? (stk)
             then false
             else $\neg$ IS_UNDEFINED? (TOP(stk), id)
RETRIEVE'(stk, id) :: **if** IS_NEWSTACK? (stk)
             then error
             else $\neg$ IS_UNDEFINED? (TOP(stk), id)
               then RETRIEVE'(POP(stk), id)
               else READ(TOP(stk), id)

The interpretation function Φ is defined by:

(a) $\Phi(\text{error}) = \text{error}$
(b) $\Phi(\text{NEWSTACK}) = \text{error}$
(c) $\Phi(\text{PUSH(stk, EMPTY)}) = $ **if** IS_NEWSTACK? (stk)
                  then INIT
                  else ENTERBLOCK(Φ(stk))
(d) $\Phi(\text{PUSH(stk, ASSIGN(arr, id, attrs))}) = $ ADD(ΦPUSH(stk, arr)), id, attrs))

Before continuing to refine these operations, i.e. before supplying representations for types Array and Stack, let us consider the problem of proving that the above implementation of type Symboltable is correct.

In the course of such a proof two kinds of invariants may have to be verified: inherent invariants and representation invariants. The inherent invariants represent those invariant relationships that must be maintained by any representation of the type. They correspond to the axioms used in the specification of the type. A representation invariant, on the other hand, is peculiar to a particular representation of a type.

The basic procedure followed in verifying the inherent invariants is to take each axiom for type Symboltable and replace all instances of each function appearing in the axiomatization with its interpretation. Then, by using the axiomatizations of the operations used in constructing the representations, it is shown that the left-hand side of each axiom is equivalent to the right-hand side of that axiom. That is to say, they represent the same abstract value.

What must be shown therefore is that for every relation $f'(x^*) = z$ (where x^* is a list, possibly empty, of arguments), derived from the axiomatization of type Symboltable,

(a) if the range of f is the type being defined (i.e., Symboltable), $\Phi(f'(x^*)) = \Phi(z)$ for all legal assignments to the free variables of x^* and z, or

(b) if the range of f is a type other than that being defined, $f'(x^*) = z$ for all legal assignments to the free variables of x^* and z.

To show this, we have at our disposal a proof system consisting of the axioms and rules of inference of our programming language plus the axioms defining the abstract types used in the representation.

The proof depends upon the assumption that objects of type Symboltable are created and manipulated only via the operations defined in the specification of that type. (The use of classes as described in Palme [18] makes this assumption relatively easy to verify.) All that need be shown is that INIT' establishes the invariants and that if on entry to an operation all invariants hold for all objects of type Symboltable to be manipulated by that operation, then all invariants on those objects hold upon completion of that operation. More complete discussions of how this may be done are contained in Guttag [8], Spitzen [21], and Wegbreit [23] (where it is called generator induction).

To verify that the implementation is consistent with Axioms 1 through 8 is quite straightforward. (It has, in fact, been done completely mechanically by David Musser [17] using the program verification system at the University of Southern California Information Sciences Institute [7]. Thus the proofs will not be presented here. Axiom 9, on the other hand, presents some problems that make the portion of the proof pertinent to that axiom worth examining.

The proof that the implementation satisfies Axiom 9 is based upon an assumption about the environment in which the operations of the type are to be used. In effect, the assumption asserts that an identifier is never added to an empty symbol table, i.e. a scope must have been established (on a more concrete level, an array must have been pushed onto the stack) before an identifier can be added. The concrete manifestation of this assumption is formally expressed:

Assumption 1. For any term, ADD'(symtab, id, attrs), IS_NEWSTACK? (symtab) = false.

The validity of the above assumption can be assured by adding to the implementation of ADD' a check for this condition and having it execute an ENTER-BLOCK' if necessary. This would make it possible to construct a completely self-contained proof of the correctness of the representation. In most cases, however, it would also introduce needless inefficiency. The compiler must somewhere check for mismatched (i.e. extra) "end" statements. Any check in ADD' would therefore be redundant.

This observation leads to a notion of conditional correctness, i.e. the representation of the abstract type is correct if the enclosing program obeys certain constraints. In practice, this is often an extremely useful notion of correctness, especially if the constraint is easily checked. If, on the other hand, the environment in which the abstract type is to be used is unknown (e.g. if the type is to be included in a library), this is probably unacceptably dangerous. Given the above assumption, the verification of Axiom 9 is straightforward but lengthy and will therefore not be presented here. It does appear in Guttag [8].

Now we know that, given implementations of types Stack and Array that are consistent with their specifications, the implementation of type Symboltable is "correct." Assuming PL/I-like based variables, pointers, and structures, the implementation of type Stack is trivial. The basic scheme is to represent a stack as a pointer to a list of structures of the form:

```
1. stack elem based,
   2. val Array,
   2. prev pointer.
```

The operations may be implemented as follows (PL/I keywords have been boldfaced):

```
NEWSTACK' :: null
PUSH'(symtab, newblock) ::
  procedure(symtab: pointer, newblock: Array) returns(pointer)
    declare elem_ptr pointer
    allocate(stack_elem) set(elem_ptr)
    elem_ptr → prev := symtab
    elem_ptr → val := newblock
    return(elem_ptr)
  end
POP'(symtab) ::
  procedure(symtab: pointer) returns(pointer)
    if symtab = null
      then return(error)
      else return(symtab → prev)
  end
TOP'(symtab) ::
  procedure(symtab: pointer) returns(Array)
    if symtab = null
      then return(error)
      else return(symtab → val)
  end
IS_NEWSTACK?'(symtab) :: symtab = null
REPLACE'(symtab, newblock) ::
  procedure(symtab: pointer, newblock: Array) returns(pointer)
    if symtab = null
      then return(error)
      else symtab → val := newblock
        return(symtab)
  end
```

Φ is defined by the mapping:

```
Φ(symtab) :: if symtab = null
               then NEWSTACK
               else PUSH(Φ(symtab → prev), symtab → val))
```

The implementation chosen for type Array is a bit more complicated. The basic scheme is to represent an array as a PL/I-like array, hash_tab, of n pointers to lists of structures of the form:

```
1. entry based,
   2. id Identifier
   2. attributes Attributelist,
   2. next pointer.
```

The correct element of hash_tab is selected by performing a hash on values of type Identifier. Therefore, in addition to the operations used in the code above, the implementation of type Array uses an operation

$$\text{HASH:Identifier} \rightarrow \{1, 2, \ldots, n\}$$

which is assumed to be defined in the type Identifier specification. The "code" implementing type Array is:

```
declare hash_tab(n) pointer based

EMPTY' ::
  procedure returns(pointer)
    declare new_hash_tab pointer
    allocate (hash_tab) set (new_hash_tab)
    do i := 1 to n
      new_hash_tab → hash_tab(i) := null
    end
    return(new_hash_tab)
  end
ASSIGN'(arr, indx, atr) ::
  procedure(arr: pointer, indx: Identifier, atr: Attributelist)
        returns(pointer)
    declare new_entry pointer
    allocate(entry) set (new_entry)
      new_entry → id := indx
      new_entry → attributes := atr
      new_entry → next := arr → hash_tab(HASH(indx))
      arr → hash_tab(HASH(indx)) := new_entry
    return(arr)
  end
READ'(arr, indx) ::
  procedure(arr: pointer, indx: Identifier) returns(Attributelist)
    declare bucket_ptr pointer
      bucket_ptr := arr → hash_tab(HASH(indx))
    do while(bucket_ptr ≠ null & ¬ IS_SAME?(bucket_ptr → id,
      indx))
      bucket_ptr := bucket_ptr → next
    end
    if bucket_ptr = null
      then return(error)
      else return (bucket_ptr → attributes)
  end
IS_UNDEFINED?'(arr, indx) ::
  procedure(arr: pointer, indx: Identifier) returns(Boolean)
    declare bucket_ptr pointer
      bucket_ptr := arr → hash_tab(HASH(indx))
    do while (bucket_ptr ≠ null & ¬ IS_SAME? (bucket_ptr → id,
      indx))
      bucket_ptr := bucket_ptr → next
    end
    return (bucket_ptr = null)
  end
```

As one might expect, Φ is a bit more complex for this representation. It is defined by using two intermediate functions: $\Phi 1$ to construct a union over all the entries in the hash table, and $\Phi 2$ to construct a union over the elements of an individual bucket.

```
(a) Φ(hash_tab_ptr) = Φ1(hash_tab_ptr, EMPTY, 1)
(b) Φ1(hash_tab_ptr, arr, i) =
      if i > n
        then arr
        else Φ1(hash_tab_ptr, Φ2(hash_tab_ptr → hash_tab(i), arr),
          i + 1)
(c) Φ2(bucket_ptr, arr) =
      if bucket_ptr = null
        then arr
        else ASSIGN(Φ2(bucket_ptr → next, arr), bucket_ptr → id,
          bucket_ptr → attributes)
```

The design of the symbol table subsystem of the compiler is now essentially complete. Given implementations of types Identifier and Attributelist and some obvious syntactic transformations, the above code could be compiled by a PL/I compiler. Before doing so, however, it would be wise to prove that the implementations of types Stack and Array are consistent with the specifications of those types. While such a proof would involve substantial issues related to the general program verification problem (e.g. vis à vis the integrity of the pointers and the question of modifying shared data structures), it would not shed further light on the role of abstract data types in program verification and is not presented in these pages.

The ease with which algebraic specifications can be adapted for different applications is one of the major strengths of the technique. Because the relationships among the various operations appear explicitly, the process of deciding which axioms must be altered to effect a change is straightforward. Let us consider a rather substantial change in the language to be compiled. Assume that the language permits the inheritance of global variables only if they appear in a "knows list," which lists, at block entry, all nonlocal variables to be used within the block [6]. The symbol table operations in a compiler for such a language would be much like those already discussed. The only difference visible to parts of the compiler other than the symbol table module would be in the ENTERBLOCK operation: It would have to be altered to include an argument of abstract type Knowlist. Within the specification of type Symboltable, all relations, and only those relations, that explicitly deal with the ENTERBLOCK operation would have to be altered. An appropriate set of axioms would be:

```
IS_INBLOCK?(ENTERBLOCK(symtab, klist), id) = false
LEAVEBLOCK(ENTERBLOCK(symtab, klist)) = symtab
RETRIEVE(ENTERBLOCK(symtab, klist), id) =
  if IS_IN?(klist, id)
    then RETRIEVE(symtab, id)
    else error
```

Note that the above relations are not well defined. The undefined symbol IS_IN?, an operation of the abstract type Knowlist, appears in the third axiom. The solution to this problem is simply to add another level to the specification by supplying an algebraic specification of the abstract type Knowlist. An appropriate set of operations might be:

```
CREATE:              → Knowlist
APPEND:   Knowlist × Identifier → Knowlist
IS_IN?:   Knowlist × Identifier → Boolean
```

These operations could then be precisely defined by the following axioms:

```
IS_IN?(CREATE) = false
IS_IN?(APPEND(klist, id), idl) = if IS_SAME?(id, idl)
                                   then true
                                   else IS_IN?(klist, idl)
```

The implementation of abstract type Knowlist is trivial. The changes necessary to adapt the previously presented implementation of abstract type Symboltable would be more substantial. The kind of changes necessary can, however, be inferred from the changes made to the axiomatization.

5. Conclusions

We have not yet applied the techniques discussed in this paper to realistically large software projects. Nevertheless, there is reason to believe that the techniques demonstrated will "scale up." The size and complexity of a specification at any level of abstraction are essentially independent of both the size and complexity of the system being described and of the amount of mechanism ultimately used in the implementation. The independence springs in large measure from the ability to separate the precise meaning of a complex abstract data type from the details involved in its implementation. It is the ability to be precise without being detailed that encourages the belief that the approach outlined here can be applied even to "very large" systems can and perhaps reduce systems that were formerly "very large" (i.e. incomprehensible) to more manageable proportions.

Abstract types may thus play a vital role in the formulation and presentation of precise specifications for software. Many complex systems can be viewed as instances of an abstract type. A database management system, for example, might be completely characterized by an algebraic specification of the various operations available to users. For those systems that are not easily totally characterized in terms of algebraic relations, the use of algebraic type specifications to abstract various complex subsystems may still make a substantial contribution to the design process. The process of functional decomposition requires some means for specifying the communication among the various functions — data often fulfills this need. The use of algebraic specifications to provide abstract definitions of the operations used to establish communication among the various functions may thus play a significant role in simplifying the process of functional abstraction.

The extensive use of algebraic specifications of abstract types may also lead to better-designed data structures. The premature choice of a storage structure and set of access routines is a common cause of inefficiencies in software. Because they serve as the main means of communication among the various components of many systems, the data structures are often the first components designed. Unfortunately, the information required to make an intelligent choice among the various options is often not available at this stage of the design process. The designer may, for example, have poor insight into the relative frequency of the various operations to be performed on a data structure. By

providing a representation-free, yet precise, description of the operations on a data structure, algebraic type definitions enable the designer to delay the moment at which a storage structure must be designed and frozen.

The second area in which we expect the algebraic specification of abstract types to have a substantial impact is on proofs of program properties. For verifications of programs that use abstract types, the algebraic specification of the types used provides a set of powerful rules of inference that can be used to demonstrate the consistency of the program and its specification. That is to say, the presence of axiomatic definitions of the abstract types provides a mechanism for proving a program to be consistent with its specifications, provided that the implementations of the abstract operations that it uses are consistent with their specifications. Thus a technique for factoring the proof is provided, for the algebraic type definitions serve as the specification of intent at a lower level of abstraction. For proofs of the correctness of representations of abstract types, the algebraic specification provides exactly those assertions that must be verified. The value of having such a set of assertions available should be apparent to any one who has attempted to construct, *a posteriori*, assertions appropriate to a correctness proof for a program. A detailed discussion of the use of algebraic specifications in a semiautomatic program verification system is contained in Guttag [10].

Given suitable restrictions on the form that axiomatizations may take, a system in which implementations and algebraic specifications of abstract types are interchangeable can be constructed. In the absence of an implementation, the operations of the algebra may be interpreted symbolically. Thus, except for a significant loss in efficiency, the lack of an implementation can be made completely transparent to the user. Such a system should prove valuable as a vehicle for facilitating the testing of software.

The ability to use specifications for testing is closely related to the policy of restricted information flow advocated in Parnas [20]. If a programmer is supplied with algebraic definitions of the abstract operations available to him and forced to write and test his module with only that information available to him, he is denied the opportunity to rely intentionally or accidentally upon information that should not be relied upon. This not only serves to localize the effect of implementation errors, but also to increase the ease with which one implementation may be replaced by another. This should, in general, serve to limit the danger of choosing a poor representation and becoming inextricably locked into it.

Before ending this paper, it seems fitting to mention some of the failings and problems associated with the work described. The specification technique presented here requires that all operations be specified as functions, i.e. as mappings from a cross product of values to a single value. Most programs, on the other hand, are laden with procedures that return several values (via parameters) or no value at all. (The latter kind of procedure is invoked purely for its side effects.) The inability to specify such procedures is a serious problem, but one that we believe can be solved with only minor changes to the specification techniques [10].

The value of abstraction in general and abstraction of data types in particular has been stressed throughout this paper. Nevertheless, the process is not without its dangers. It is all too easy to create abstractions that ignore crucial distinctions or attributes. The specification technique presented here, for example, provides no mechanism for specifying performance constraints and thus encourages one to ignore distinctions based on such criteria. In some environments, such considerations are crucial, and to abstract them out can be disastrous.

Another problem with algebraic specifications is that they supply little direction to implementors. Only experience will tell how easy it is to go from an algebraic specification to an implementation. It is clear, however, that the transition is less easy than from an operational specification.

Our most important reservation pertains to the ease with which algebraic specifications can be constructed and read. They should present no problem to those with formal training in computer science. At present, however, most people involved in the production of software have no such training. The extent to which the techniques described in this paper are generally applicable is thus somewhat open to conjecture.

Acknowledgment. The author is greatly indebted to J.J. Horning of the University of Toronto, who, as the author's thesis supervisor, provided three years of good advice.

References
1. Batey, M., Ed. Working Draft of ECMA/ANSI PL/I Standard Tenth Rev., ANSI, New York, (Sept. 1973).
2. Birkhoff, G., and Lipson, J.D. Heterogeneous algebras. *J. Combinatorial Theory 8* (1970), 115–133.
3. Dahl, O.-J., Nygaard, K., and Myhrhaug, B. The SIMULA 67 Common Base Language. Norwegian Comptng. Centre, Oslo, 1968.
4. Dijkstra, E.W. Notes on structured programming. In *Structured Programming*, Academic Press, New York, 1972.
5. Floyd, R.W. Assigning Meaning to Programs. Proc. Symp. in Applied Math., Vol. XIX, AMS, Providence, R.I., 1967, pp. 19–32.
6. Gannon, J.D. Language design to enhance programming reliability. Ph.D. Th., Comptr. Syst. Res. Group Tech. Rep. CSRG-47, Dept. Comptr. Sci., U. of Toronto, Ontario, 1975.
7. Good, D.I., London, R.L., and Bledsoe, W.W. An interactive program verification system. *IEEE Trans. on Software Engineering SE-1*, 1 (March 1975), 59–67.
8. Guttag, J.V. The specification and application to programming of abstract data types. Ph.D. Th., Comptr. Syst. Res. Group Tech. Rep. CSRG-59, Dept. Comptr. Sci. 1975, U. of Toronto, Ontario, 1975.
9. Guttag, J.V. and Horning, J.J., The algebraic specifications of abstract data types. *Acta Informatica* (to appear).
10. Guttag, J.V., Horowitz, E., and Musser, D.R. Abstract data types and software validation. Tech. Rep., Inform. Sci. Inst., U. of Southern California, Los Angeles, 1976.
11. Guttag, J.V., Horowitz, E., and Musser, D.R. The design of data type specifications. Proc. Second Int. Conf. on Software Eng., San Francisco, Oct. 1976, pp. 414–420.
12. Hoare, C.A.R., Proof of correctness of data representations. *Acta Informatica 1* (1972), 271–281.
13. Hoare, C.A.R., and Wirth, N. An axiomatic definition of the programming language PASCAL. *Acta Informatica 2* (1973), 335–355.
14. Liskov, B.H., and Zilles, S.N. Programming with abstract data types. Proc. ACM SIGPLAN Symp. on Very High Level Languages, SIGPLAN Notices (ACM) 9, 4 (April 1974), 50–59.
15. McKeeman, W.M., Symbol Table Access. In *Compiler Construction, An Advanced Course*, T.L. Bauer, and J. Eichel, Eds., Springer-Verlag, New York, 1974.
16. Morris, J.H. Types are not sets. Conf. Rec. ACM Symp. on the Principles of Programming Languages, Boston, Mass., Oct. 1973, pp. 120–124.
17. Musser, D. Private communication, 1975.
18. Palme, J. Protected program modules in SIMULA 67. FOAP Rep. C8372-M3(E5), Res. Inst. of National Defense, Stockholm, 1973.
19. Parnas, D.L. A technique for the specification of software modules with examples. *Comm. ACM 15*, 5 (May 1973), 330–336.
20. Parnas, D.L. Information distribution aspects of design methodology. Information Processing 71, North Holland Pub. Co., Amsterdam, 1971, pp. 339–344.
21. Spitzen, J., and Wegbreit, B. The verification and synthesis of data structures. *Acta Informatica 4* (1975), 127–144.
22. Standish, T.A. Data structures: An axiomatic approach. BBN Rep. No. 2639, Bolt, Beranek and Newman, Cambridge, Mass., (1973).
23. Wegbreit, B., and Spitzen, J. Proving properties of complex data structures. *J. ACM 23*, 2 (April 1976), 389–396.
24. Wulf, W.A., London, R.L., and Shaw, M. Abstraction and verification in Alphard: Introduction to language and methodology. USC Inform. Sci. Tech. Rep., U. of Southern California, Los Angeles, 1976.
25. Zilles, S.N. Abstract specifications for data types. IBM Res. Lab., San Jose, Calif., 1975.

Programming   T.A. Standish
Languages   Editor

The Treatment of Data Types in EL1

Ben Wegbreit
Harvard University

Reprinted from *Communications of the ACM,* May 1974, pp. 251-264. Copyright 1974 Association for Computing Machinery, Inc. Reprinted by permission.

In constructing a general purpose programming language, a key issue is providing a sufficient set of data types and associated operations in a manner that permits both natural problem-oriented notation and efficient implementation. The EL1 language contains a number of features specifically designed to simultaneously satisfy both requirements. The resulting treatment of data types includes provision for programmer-defined data types and generic routines, programmer control over type conversion, and very flexible data type behavior, in a context that allows efficient compiled code and compact data representation.

Key Words and Phrases: data types, modes, mode unions, type conversion, coercion, generic functions, extensible languages, data type definition, data description language, compilation

CR Categories: 4.12, 4.13, 4.22

This work was supported in part by the U.S. Air Force, Electronics System Division, under Contract F19628-71-C-0173 and by the Advanced Research Projects Agency under Contract F19628-71-C-0174. Author's present address: Computer Science Laboratory, Xerox Palo Alto Research Center, 3180 Porter Drive, Palo Alto, CA 94304.

[1] The present version of EL1 in the ECL programming system runs on the PDP-10 under the TOPS and TENEX monitors. Versions for other machines are contemplated.

1. Introduction

The prime function of a problem-oriented language is to provide a set of data types and associated operations sufficient to represent the unit objects and operations of its problem domain. This representation must on the one hand be very natural to the programmer and on the other be implementable on computing machines in a very efficient fashion. The success of Fortran, Snobol, Lisp, and Cobol is due principally to their respectively providing such representation for scalars and arrays of numbers, strings, lists, and data processing records. Each language has an envelope of applications in which program creation is natural and program execution is efficient. This envelope is determined primarily by the set of data types and operations it provides.

In recent years there has been considerable effort to construct languages with significantly larger performance envelopes [1, 2, 3, 4, 5, 6]. That is, languages to serve many or all problem domains. In constructing such languages, the principal problem is providing a sufficient set of data types and associated operations in a manner that affords both natural notation and efficient representation. It should be stressed that both considerations are important. Further, while either alone can be satisfied easily, *simultaneously* achieving very efficient representation and natural notation for a wide variety of data types is a quite difficult matter.

The purpose of this paper is to discuss how this problem is addressed in the programming language EL1. EL1 is a working programming language.[1] It is the language component of the ECL programming system which is currently under further development as part of a research project at Harvard University. It has a number of features specifically designed to make possible a flexible, yet efficient, treatment of data types. These features, their shaping of data type handling, and their interaction with other aspects of the language are the topics of this paper.

This paper is divided into nine sections. Section 2 is a brief sketch of the language EL1, outlining its main features and establishing the notation to be used in the rest of the paper. EL1 gives a somewhat unconventional treatment to the union of data types; since this concept arises in several contexts, it is examined in detail in Section 3. Section 4 describes the basic data type definition facilities of EL1. Section 5 discusses the evaluation of data type definitions and the implications of this to compilation. Section 6 discusses *generic* routines (routines whose action depends on the types of their arguments). Section 7 discusses type conversion and its interaction with generic routines. Section 8 treats the more sophisticated aspects of the EL1 data type definition facility: the mechanisms which allow the programmer detailed control over data type behaviors. Section 9 turns from the specific to the general—abstracting the techniques used in EL1 and examining to what extent they can be applied to other problem-oriented languages.

2. A Brief Sketch of EL1

In written appearance, EL1 is a fairly conventional programming language in the Algol 60 tradition. It includes variables and subscripted variables, prefix and infix operations, labeled statements and gotos, block structure, procedure calls, and assignments, all written in standard fashion. Many standard forms are somewhat generalized in EL1. For example, assignment is treated as a binary operator whose value is its left-hand operand. Also, blocks have values—the value of the last statement executed. Hence,

$$X \leftarrow \text{BEGIN } B[J \leftarrow J+1] \leftarrow \text{COS}(W); \, F(B[J],Y) \text{ END}$$

adds one to J, then assigns COS(W) to B[J], then applies F to B[J] and Y, and finally assigns the result of F to X. A conditional expression has the format $\mathcal{P} \rightarrow \mathcal{E}$. $\mathcal{E}$ is evaluated if and only if $\mathcal{P}$ is true. For example, in

```
BEGIN
     I ← O;
  L: A[I←I+1] ← O;
     I < N → GOTO L
END
```

the loop is repeated until I reaches N. There is a second sort of conditional—the conditional statement, written with a double-shafted arrow, interpreted as: if the left-hand side is true, execute the right-hand side and exit the block with that value. Hence, the Lisp conditional $(\text{COND } (\mathcal{P}_1\mathcal{E}_1)(\mathcal{P}_2\mathcal{E}_2) \ldots (\mathcal{P}_n\mathcal{E}_n))$ is written in EL1 as

```
BEGIN
   𝒫₁ ⇒ 𝒠₁;
   𝒫₂ ⇒ 𝒠₂;
     .
       .
     .
   𝒫ₙ ⇒ 𝒠ₙ
END
```

For example, the following block computes an approximate square root of a number A with initial approximation X to within EPS

```
BEGIN
  L: ABS(X**2−A) < EPS ⇒ X;
     X ← (X+A/X)/2;
     GOTO L
END
```

The block is exited only when the left-hand side of the first statement is *true*; when the exit is taken, the value of the block is X.

Variables are either formal parameters to a routine or variables local to a block. In either case, a variable is declared to be of some specific data type and is restricted to contain values of that type throughout its lifetime.

Data types, termed *modes* in EL1, include the following built-in types: BOOL (Boolean), CHAR (character), INT (fixed point), REAL (floating point), REF (pointer unrestricted as to the mode of the object it can point to), SYMBOL (corresponding to nonnumeric atoms in Lisp), MODE (the data type "data type"), FORM (the Lisp S-expression), and ROUTINE (procedure or operator). From the standpoint of creation, assignment, and use as arguments or formal parameters, all these modes are equally valid. Hence: DECL I,J: INT; creates integer-valued variables named I and J, while DECL M1, M2, COMPLEX: MODE; declares three mode-valued variables, and DECL F1, FOO, FUM, CSIGN: ROUTINE; creates four routine-valued variables. While all these modes are equally valid, they vary considerably in complexity. For example, a BOOL value is a single bit while a MODE value has associated with it all the information needed by the language to implement a data type. However, from the standpoint of the programmer, the complexity is largely invisible. He is concerned only with the behavior of values having these modes: a BOOL value can be used in the left arm of a conditional while a MODE value can be used in declaring the type of a variable.

Objects are distinct from variables in EL1. Variables may name objects, but the mapping is not one-to-one. That is, while each variable names some object, several variables may name the same object (e.g. when an argument is passed by reference to a routine), several variables may name different parts of a single object, and an object may be named by no variable. An object lies either on a block-structured *stack* (like that of Algol 60) or in the free storage region termed the *heap* (like that of Lisp or Algol 68). In the former case, the lifetime of an object is concomitant with that of the block in which it was created. In the latter case, an object remains until no variable names it and no pointers reference it. Garbage collection periodically reclaims objects in the heap no longer in use and returns them to the free storage pool.

An object has a mode determined at the time of object creation. An object is created in one of two ways, either implicitly as the result of a declaration, or explicitly by means of the generators CONST and ALLOC. Objects created implicitly by declaration reside on the *stack*. Objects created by the explicit generator CONST also reside on the *stack*; objects created by the explicit generator ALLOC reside in the *heap*. As an example, suppose that the mode COMPLEX has been defined (a definition in the language will be given in Section 3), then consider

```
CONST(COMPLEX OF X, Y)
ALLOC(COMPLEX OF X, Y)
```

The first line constructs a complex number on the *stack* and returns this complex as its value; the second line constructs a complex number in the *heap* and returns a *pointer* to the complex number as its value. As an example of how the latter value may be used, consider

DECL P:REF;

.
.

P ← ALLOC(COMPLEX OF 3, 4);

The first line creates a pointer-valued variable P unrestricted to the sort of object it can point to; the second line assigns to P a pointer to the complex number $3+4i$. Given a pointer such as P, the object pointed to can be accessed by applying the function VAL; e.g. VAL(P) is the complex number $3+4i$. The only means for creating a new pointer value is ALLOC. Hence, pointers point only to the heap, *never* to the stack.

In EL1, the notion of a *routine* embraces both procedures and operators. A routine-valued variable may be assigned a routine-value; e.g.

```
CSIGN← EXPR (X:REAL; CHAR)
      BEGIN
          X > 0 ⇒ %P;
          X < 0 ⇒ %N;
          %Z
      END
```

Here the routine has a single parameter[2] named X of mode REAL, delivers a CHAR value, and has a body consisting of a block which computes the sign of its argument and yields the charatcer P, the character N or the character Z. Any routine may be written as a function and applied to its arguments, e.g. CSIGN(A[J]).

A routine-valued variable can be declared to be an operator of several sorts, thereby establishing certain *syntactic* properties. A *routine-valued variable* declared to be a *prefix* operator can be applied to a single argument without enclosing the operand in parentheses. A routine taking two arguments declared as an *infix* operation can be used accordingly. (The standard operators such as $+$, $*$, $-$, $/$, $←$, $=$, and others are defined in this way as part of an initial, system-provided operator set.) A routine taking n arguments can be declared a *matchfix* operator, in conjunction with a right-matching token. For example, if ⟨ is a matchfix operator with right matching token ⟩, then ⟨X, Y+Z, F(A,B,2)⟩ denotes the application of the routine ⟨ to the three arguments X, Y+Z, and F(A,B,2).

The principal concern of this paper is with mode-valued constants, mode-valued variables, and mode-valued routines. The primitive data types (BOOL, CHAR, INT, REAL, and REF) described previously are examples or mode-valued constants. To make the notion clear, consider

DECL P: BOOL;

.
.

P ← TRUE;

This creates a *Boolean* valued variable P and later assigns it the Boolean value *true* (denoted by the Boolean constant TRUE). Analogously, consider

DECL M1: MODE;

.
.

M1 ← INT;

This creates a mode-valued variable M1 and later assigns it the mode-value *integer* (denoted by the mode constant INT). In addition to the mode constants mentioned earlier, there are two others: NONE and ANY. The former is the mode of the empty object. The latter is the union of all possible modes; Section 3 discusses this and other mode unions.

A mode-valued variable may be used in any position where a mode value is required. For example, suppose that after the above assignment has been executed the following block is entered

```
BEGIN
      DECL J: M1;

      .
      .

END
```

In this block, *J* is an *integer* valued variable. If M1 had some other mode value, say $\mathfrak{M}$, then J would be an $\mathfrak{M}$-valued variable.

The concept of mode-valued routine is a logical consequence of treating modes as values. The simplest such routine is MD which takes a single argument and delivers its *mode*. For example, MD(FALSE) = BOOL and MD(SIN(X)) = REAL. A more significant example of mode-valued routines is mode construction. That is, a set of primitive mode-valued routines provides the means for constructing new modes. These primitive mode constructors take modes as arguments and define new modes in terms of these. From the primitive mode constructors, the programmer can define other mode-constructing routines by means of functional composition, iteration, conditionals, and recursion. Mode constructors, primitive and programmer-defined, are discussed in Sections 4, 5, and 8.

The above sketch of EL1 treats those facets of the language required for the purposes of this paper. (A complete description of the language is given in the programmer's reference manual [7].) However, the traditional discussion of a language per se neglects many facets of its usage and implementation. For EL1 those considerations are particularly important, and an understanding of several extralingual facets is essential to an understanding of this paper.

EL1 is the language component of the ECL programming system.[3] The system is used on-line with two

---

[2] This is the simplest declarative structure for a formal parameter; it specifies the default binding. Additional declarative information can be given to specify that a private copy of the argument is to be made (binding by *value* in Algol 60) or that the argument be unevaluated (essentially, FEXPR of Lisp).

[3] The system includes the usual facilities for on-line interaction such as a text editor, a trace feature, and a debugging package. An overview of the system is given in [8].

fully compatible language processors—an interpreter and a compiler.[4] Compiled and interpreted routines may be freely intermixed with no restrictions. One key point of the ECL system is that there is no rigid "compile time," "load time," "run time" distinction. Routines are interpreted until explicitly compiled. Compilation is carried out by calling the compiler as a subroutine.

It is therefore possible to compile a routine several times with very precise control over the degree of "binding." For each compilation of a routine, one can compute certain invariants of that compilation instance and then compile code which reflects these invariants. That is, suppose P is a routine with free variables $I_1 \ldots I_n$. Suppose some k of these $I_{j_1} \ldots I_{j_k}$ are bound to specific values $V_1 \ldots V_k$ and the result is compiled. The code generated will be better, often substantially better, than the code for P had all variables been left free.

The compiler may be invoked with a procedure P and a set S of variables which are to be so bound. For each variable I in S, each free appearance of I in P is replaced by its value at the time of compilation. Such a variable is said to be *frozen*. If a routine identifier, the free variables of the routine, and the arguments to the routine are all frozen (or are otherwise constant) then, under appropriate circumstances, the routine may be evaluated during compilation, the value thus produced taking the place of the call. Hence, depending on S, compilation may leave none or all free variables in P and generate very tight or very loose bindings.

3. Mode Union

The concept of mode union is treated rather specially in EL1. As an example of this treatment, recall that the mode constant ANY denotes the "union" of all modes. Consider an assignment to the routine-valued variable F, e.g. F ← BXPR (X: ANY; BOOL) BEGIN . . . END;. F then takes as argument a value of any mode, e.g. F(3), F(3.), F("W"), F(TRUE), F(REAL) are all legal calls on F. In each case, the X of this invocation of F is bound to the argument. The critical point of the EL1 treatment of unions is as follows: in *each* case the X of this invocation of F takes on the mode of the argument and cannot change mode during its lifetime. Hence, in the first call on F, X is bound to 3 and becomes an

integer. The value of X can be changed by an assignment; e.g. X ← 4;, but the mode of X is fixed.[5]

In Section 4 we discuss modes which act as "restricted" unions, that is, mode$_1$ or mode$_2$ or . . . or mode$_n$. There, as here, a formal parameter declared to have such a mode is bound at the time of call to some *specific alternative* from the set of possibilities; just which alternative is determined by the argument. Subsequent to creation, the formal parameter cannot change from that alternative mode. For example, a negation routine may be defined to have a single parameter whose formal mode is *int* or *real* or *complex*. The mode of the argument determines which one of these is the actual mode.

The EL1 union differs from a set theoretic union in exactly one respect: after a variable is created, its mode is fixed to be a specific alternative. A set theoretic union would allow variables whose modes as well as values could be changed throughout their lifetime. (This is, for example, the treatment of mode union given in [9].) Clearly, the EL1 union is a subcase of the more general set theoretic union.[6] This restriction is imposed for two reasons: implementation efficiency and linguistic simplicity. By requiring variables to assume some definite (i.e. non-united) mode, there is never the need to allocate extra stack storage to provide for the contingency of a variable changing its mode and thereby assuming a larger size. Among other consequences, this makes possible a stack implementation of the mode ANY; (this, of course, would not be possible for a set theoretic ANY). Since union is treated as postponement of a mode choice, the concept of union does not exist for the evaluator; i.e. each object has a definite unchanging mode. Hence, there is no need for special semantic rules to deal with unions.[7] Finally, the treatment of union in EL1 integrates smoothly with the use of generic routines; this is discussed in Section 6.

---

[5] An analogy may be made with the length of an Algol 60 array. Consider, for example, the Algol 60 fragment **begin real array** $A[1:N]; \ldots$ **end**. A is declared to be an array of length N. For each instance of the block (i.e. block activation), the length of A is fixed to the then current value of N at the time of block entry. Subsequently, the value of A may change but not its length.

[6] It is possible to obtain many of the desirable features of a set theoretic union by using a pointer which, at different times, references objects of different modes. As discussed in Sections 7 and 8, an appropriate mode definition can be used to make the existence of the pointer relatively invisible; e.g. one can arrange that if X is a pointer referencing an integer, then 3+X is interpreted as 3+VAL(X).

[7] As an example of the sort of issue we thereby avoid, consider the following. Let A be a true set theoretic union of *int* and *bool* and let its current value be an *int*. Suppose A is passed by *reference* (in the sense of PL/I) to a routine F which takes an *int* formal parameter named X. Since A currently has an *int* value, presumably this is legal. What if F uses A free and assigns a *bool* value to it? Does this affect X? The difficulties raised by this example are complicated when a set theoretic union is taken where one or more alternatives is a compound object (e.g. set theoretic union of *int* and *complex*).

---

[4] Although there is an interpreter and compilation is optional, the language has been strongly shaped by the expectation that production programs will be eventually compiled. For example, an interpretable-only language could be "type-less" with all variables free to take on values of any type. However, efficiency considerations lead to a compiler and with it typed variables. Most of the declarative data type information is really of interest only to the compiler. However, to maintain compatibility between language processors, the interpreter verifies that the data type constraints are satisfied.

4. Mode Construction

Given sets $t_1, \ldots, t_n$, one can form new sets from these in several ways:

1. Cartesian product: $t_1 \times t_2 \times \ldots \times t_n$.
2. Union: $t_1 \cup t_2 \cup \ldots \cup t_n$.
3. Mappings: $(t_1 \times \ldots \times t_{n-1}) \rightarrow t_n$.
4. Self product—definite and indefinite: t_i^k and $\bigcup_{k=0}^{\infty} t_i^k$.

These have the natural interpretations: structures (in the sense of Cobol), unions, routines, and arrays, respectively. These four formation rules define four classes of modes and four classes of objects belonging to these modes. Corresponding to each of the first three formation rules, there is a primitive EL1 routine—STRUCT, ONEOF, PROC—which generates new modes of that class. Array modes are created by the routines VECTOR and SEQ, corresponding to definite and indefinite self product, respectively. The basic mode definition mechanism of EL1 is the set of primitive mode-valued constants and the set of primitive mode-valued routines. All other modes are generated from these.

STRUCT takes as arguments a list of pairs ($name_i$: $mode_i$), where $mode_i$ is the mode of the ith component and $name_i$ is the symbolic name. For example,[8]

```
LIGHT_BULB ← STRUCT(HOURS_USED:REAL,
                    WATTS:INT,
                    COLOR:CHAR,
                    BURNT_OUT:BOOL)
```

defines a mode of class *structure* consisting of four fields: a real, an integer, a character, and a Boolean named HOURS_USED, WATTS, COLOR, and BURNT_OUT, respectively. The mode thus defined is assigned to the mode-valued variable LIGHT_BULB. Subsequent to the assignment, the variable may be used as a type declarer DECL X, Y, Z:LIGHT_BULB; creating variables X, Y, and Z of mode LIGHT_BULB, and three associated objects (in the stack) named by the identifiers. The individual components can be referred to by qualified naming (in the style of PL/1) so that Z.COLOR is a character field. Alternatively, a component can be selected by an integer subscript so that Z[J] is identical to Z.COLOR if and only if J has the value 3. The value of a component may be changed by assignment, e.g. Z.WATTS ← 60. Assignment of one LIGHT_BULB to another is denoted in the usual fashion X ← Z and copies all components of the structure.

VECTOR takes as arguments an integer K and a mode $\mathfrak{M}$; VECTOR(K, $\mathfrak{M}$) generates the mode $\mathfrak{M}^K$. SEQ takes a single mode argument $\mathfrak{M}$; SEQ($\mathfrak{M}$) generates the mode $\bigcup_{K=0}^{\infty} \mathfrak{M}^K$. In the latter case, the mode is said to be *length unresolved*. While the mode is length unresolved, any particular object of such a mode has a fixed length determined at the time the object is created.

For example, CARD □ VECTOR(80, CHAR); defines the mode "array of 80 characters" and assigns it to the mode-valued variable CARD. Any variable of mode CARD (e.g. DECL C: CARD) has exactly 80 components which may be accessed by subscripting (e.g. C[I]). The mode "length unresolved array of characters" may be defined by STRING ← SEQ(CHAR);. This creates a mode whose instances may be of any length. The length of each instance is, however, fixed at the time of creation, e.g. DECL S:STRING BYVAL CONST(STRING SIZE 200);. This creates a variable S of mode STRING and initializes it to a STRING of 200 components. Subsequently, the values of S's components may change but not the number of components. The number of components in an array may be determined by applying the primitive routine LENGTH; e.g. LENGTH(S) = 200. As with structures, assignment of arrays is written using the assignment operator and copies all components.

ONEOF($t_1, t_2, \ldots, t_n$) defines a "union" of n alternative modes $t_1 \ldots t_n$, where "union" is used in the sense described in Section 3. That is, a variable declared to be of such a mode takes on some specific alternative determined by its initial value. For example,

```
ARITH ← ONEOF(INT,REAL);
SIGN ← EXPR(X:ARITH; ARITH) BEGIN ... END
    .
    .
    .
SIGN(−13)
    .
    .
    .
DECL Y: ARITH BYVAL P(X)
```

In the second line, the routine is declared to take a single argument which is either INT or REAL. In the call to SIGN, in line 3 an INT is used so that X in this invocation of SIGN is an INT. In the fourth line, Y is declared to be either an INT or a REAL—which one is determined by the mode of P(X) on each execution of this line.

PROC($t_1, \ldots, t_{n-1}; t_n$) defines the mode "mapping from $t_1 \times \ldots \times t_{n-1}$ into t_n". For example, CODE ← PROC(CHAR;INT) defines the mode of routines which convert characters into integers.

In addition to the four classes of modes described above, there is a fifth class which arises from other than set theoretic considerations: the class *pointer*. PTR(t) is the mode "pointers restricted to point to objects of mode t" and PTR($t_1, \ldots, t_n$) is the mode "pointers restricted to point to t_1's or t_2's or $\ldots$ or t_n's." Here, unlike the situation with EL1 unions, no commitment is made when such a pointer is created. Such a variable may first point to a t_1, later to a t_n, and still later to a t_2.[9] For example, DECL SP: PTR(INT, REAL, COM-

---

[8] The promised definition of the data type *complex* is: COMPLEX ← STRUCT(RE: REAL, IM: REAL). If Z is a complex variable, then Z.RE and Z.IM denote its two REAL components.

[9] Hence, the built-in mode REF is equivalent to PTR($t_1, \ldots, t_n$) where $\{t_i\}$ is the set of modes used in a program.

PLEX); creates a variable SP whose mode is "pointer to INT or REAL or COMPLEX." Like all pointers, SP is given the default initial value NIL, meaning a pointer to nothing. Assignments to SP may change this value SP ← ALLOC(COMPLEX of 3, 4) so that SP points to a complex number whose value is $3+4i$.

5. The Evaluation of Mode Definitions

All the primitive mode generators are callable functions. They evaluate their arguments which may be *any* syntactic form which yields an appropriately typed value. This leads to multidimensional arrays such as REAL_MATRIX ← SEQ(SEQ(REAL)) arrays of structures such as VECTOR(4,STRUCT(RE: REAL, IM: REAL)) and structures of arrays and pointers such as STRUCT(A: INT, B: PTR(INT), C: SEQ(INT)). Mode-valued variables, conditionals, and other routines are equally acceptable as arguments to mode generators. For example, VECTOR(N**2, F(X)) defines the mode: "array of N^2 F(X)'s" where N and F(X) are determined at the point that VECTOR is called. Turning to a more complex example, the following loop computes the mode: "complete binary tree of depth N whose terminal nodes are integers"

```
BEGIN
    DECL TEMP:MODE BYVAL INT;
    DECL I:INT BYVAL N;
L:  (I ← I − 1) < 0 ⇒ TEMP;
    TEMP ← STRUCT(L: TEMP, R: TEMP);
    GOTO L
END
```

It should be noted that the EL1 treatment of mode definition is quite different from that found in other programming languages, such as Algol 68. Traditionally, mode definition has been a static operation carried out at compile time. By treating the mode-defining operators as executable routines which evaluate their arguments, EL1 obtains a more flexible and more powerful means of mode creation. The most important single consequence is the notion of programmer-defined, mode-valued routines. Consider, for example, converting the above binary tree generator into a routine.

```
TREE ← EXPR(I: INT BYVAL, M: MODE BYVAL; MODE)
    BEGIN
        L:  (I ← I − 1) < 0 ⇒ M;
            M ← STRUCT(L: M, R: M);
            GOTO L
END
```

TREE takes the depth (I) and leaf mode (M) as arguments—both passed by value. The loop is the same as before, except that now it generates the sequence depending on the value of the leaf mode. Hence, TREE(I,M) is the mode binary tree of depth I and leaves of mode M, for any integer I and mode M.

A second example may be of use. Consider defining the mode "multidimensional array of order K of M's."

```
MULTI_ARRAY ← EXPR(K: INT, M: MODE; MODE)
    BEGIN
        K = 0 ⇒ M;
        SEQ(MULTI_ARRAY(K − 1,M))
    END
```

MULTI_ARRAY of K M's is either M (if K is 0) or is a SEQuence of the result obtained by applying MULTI_ARRAY to K − 1 and M. The definition is obvious and would be somewhat uninteresting were it the only one possible. However, there are other ways of constructing multidimensional arrays which, for some purposes, are far superior to the one given above. If, for example, a frequent operation is exchanging entire rows, then it will be advantageous to use an array of *pointers* to the constituent rows. The generalization of this to order K is defined

```
P_ARRAY ← EXPR(K: INT, M: MODE; MODE)
    BEGIN
        K = 0 ⇒ M;
        K = 1 ⇒ SEQ(M);
        SEQ(PTR(P_ARRAY(K − 1,M)))
    END
```

The K = 0 case is obvious; for K = 1 we define a conventional array; for higher K's we construct a SEQ of PTR's to the result of P_ARRAY applied to K − 1 and M.

The point of programmer-defined mode routines is that they permit data type abstraction. Instead of talking loosely about some collection of related modes, one can define a collection precisely by means of a routine which generates it. *Mode sets* such as matrices, binary trees, lists, rings, etc., of various element types can be defined by their generators. This permits the creation of mode-definition libraries. More important, it allows the programming of algorithms which act on a class such as binary trees without regard to the constituent elements. Only during compilation is it necessary to freeze free variables to determine *which* specific sort of binary tree. Finally, it allows one to prove properties of mode sets independently of their particular elements by appealing to the properties of the mode set generating routine.

It must be stressed that the considerable generality provided by dynamic execution of mode definitions need *not* exact a price in inefficient code. It was explained in Section 2 that in compiling a routine R1, one could *freeze* the values of free variables to their current values. Suppose we execute M ← P_ARRAY($\mathcal{E}_1$, $\mathcal{E}_2$). M then assumes some definite mode value. If R1 uses M as a type declarer, leaving M as a free variable, then R1 may be compiled with M frozen. The specific mode value of M will be used. It is therefore possible for a program to *compute* the modes it uses and compile parts of itself specific to these computations.

6. Generic Routines

The main reason for having united modes (e.g. ANY and those generated by ONEOF) is to type formal parameters for routines which accept several distinct types of arguments. Such routines (e.g. the operator $+$ in Algol 60) do not convert these arguments to fixed types but rather perform different actions dependent on argument types. Such routines are termed *generic*. Almost all languages have such routines but almost always as built-in operations. In this section we discuss how the programmer defines his own generic routines in EL1.

The basics have already been discussed: one needs the ability to declare formal parameters having united modes and a means of testing the actual modes of these parameters. The latter is provided by the primitive routine MD; for any expression ε, $MD(\varepsilon)$ is the mode of the value of ε. To illustrate a possible, if far from satisfactory technique, consider defining $+$ to act on INTs, REALs, and COMPLEXs.

```
SCALAR ← ONEOF(INT, REAL, COMPLEX);
+ ← EXPR(X:SCALAR, Y:SCALAR; SCALAR)
    BEGIN
      (MD(X) = INT) AND (MD(Y) = INT)
        ⇒ FIXADD(X, Y);
      (MD(X) = COMPLEX) AND (MD(Y) = COMPLEX)
        ⇒ CONST(COMPLEX OF X.RE, +Y.RE,
    X.IM + Y.IM);
      (MD(X) = INT) AND (MD(Y) = REAL)
        ⇒ FLOATADD(FLOAT(X), Y);
      etc.
    END
```

The $+$ routine is here declared to take two arguments—each of which may be one of {INT, REAL, COMPLEX}. The routine body tests the types of its arguments on each invocation and dispatches to the appropriate code section.

This has two principal defects: (1) the type testings and their conjunctions are redundant and hence tedious to read and write; and (2) it is difficult for the compiler to exploit knowledge it may have concerning the modes of arguments. For example, if A has been declared to be an INT, then $A+3.2$ will invoke the third alternative, but how is the compiler to know this? It could, of course, make the deduction by "interpreting" the $+$ routine. While this will work in principle, it seems an unnecessarily difficult approach. Instead, we impose additional structure on the program—structure which simultaneously makes the code more readable by the programmer and more comprehensible by the compiler.

The traditional means for imposing structure in a programming language is with a new syntactic form, here the GENERIC form. A GENERIC form[10] is delimited by the brackets "GENERIC" and "END" and contains a set of arguments followed by a set of conditional-like statements whose left arm is a set of modes and whose right arm is an alternative value of the generic form. For example, the above $+$ routine may be

directly recoded using a GENERIC form as its body

```
+ ← EXPR(X:SCALAR, Y:SCALAR; SCALAR)
    GENERIC(X, Y)
      [INT, INT] ⇒ FIXADD(X, Y);
      [COMPLEX, COMPLEX] ⇒ CONST(COMPLEX OF
        X.RE+Y.RE, X.IM+Y.IM);
      [INT, REAL] ⇒ FLOATADD(FLOAT(X), Y);
    etc.
    END
```

The alternatives are considered in turn until one is found which matches the actual modes of the arguments to the GENERIC. (If none match, an error routine is called.) The importance of the GENERIC to compilation is, of course, that "considering the alternatives" may be carried out during compilation so that compiled calls on $+$ may be replaced by a call on the right-hand side of the appropriate alternative statement.

If there are several formals having united modes, the number of possible combinations can grow to unwieldy size. Even with a concise notation for expressing alternatives, this is unacceptable. It need not, however, arise. An element of the mode set of a GENERIC statement can be an arbitrary syntactic form, so long as the value it produces is a mode. Hence, a GENERIC statement such as: [CHAR, ONEOF(INT,STRING), ANY] ⇒ . . . will cover (i.e. match against) each of the following sets of argument modes {CHAR,INT,REAL} {CHAR,STRING,INT}, etc. In general, a mode G in a mode set *covers* an argument mode A if any of the following hold:

1. G = ANY.
2. G is a united mode ONEOF$(t_1 \ldots t_n)$ and A = t_i for some i.
3. G = A.

Even collections of modes will, in some cases, prove too restrictive in performing generic selection. Consider, for example, a print routine which takes a single argument X—an object to be printed
EXPR(X:ANY; NONE) . . . .
X can be of ANY mode and no result is returned. The routine is to print X in one of three formats, depending on whether X is a *structure*, an *array*, or a *pointer*. Testing this is straightforward: Consider a routine STRUCTP which is a predicate true of structures only. Hence, STRUCTP(X) is the test which checks for the first print class. The trick is to make the discrimination while compiling a call on the print routine.

This can be done if the left-hand side of a generic statement is generalized to: $[\mathfrak{M}_1, \ldots, \mathfrak{M}_N]\mathcal{P}$ where the $\mathfrak{M}$'s are forms which evaluate to modes to be compared to the argument modes and $\mathcal{P}$ is an arbitrary predicate.

---

[10] A GENERIC form may appear anywhere within a routine. This is useful for routines with one or more formal parameters having united modes but which contain substantial computation ε which does not depend on the modes of these arguments (e.g. computation based on the non-united arguments). Such routines can be written with an *embedded* GENERIC form. The code for ε is then effectively shared among the various generic alternatives.

An alternative is chosen only if all modes match and $\mathcal{P}$ is *true*.[11] For example, the desired print routine has the structure

```
EXPR(X:ANY; NONE)
GENERIC
    STRUCTP(X) ⇒ . . . ;
    ARRAYP(X) ⇒ . . . ;
    TRUE ⇒ . . .
END
```

Any predicate can be used as part of a generic alternative. Provided that the predicates can be evaluated during compilation, this provides a very general mechanism for the programmer to control compilation, i.e. to perform once at compile time a choice which would otherwise be made repeatedly during execution. Hence, the generalized GENERIC form is potentially quite powerful. The facility it provides is related to the freezing of free variables during compilation. The difference is this. *Freezing* allows one to produce individual compilations of a routine, each tailored to some specific environment; the GENERIC form allows a single routine to take several alternative actions, yet allows choice among the alternatives to be made when compiling a call on the routine.

Compilation should give special treatment to GENERICs under two circumstances: (1) in compiling a routine whose body is a single GENERIC form, and (2) in compiling another routine which contains one or more calls on routines of type 1. We consider these in turn.

Compilation of a routine, such as + whose body is a single GENERIC form, should produce: (1) *a main body* for the routine, and (2) a set of *alternative bodies*— one for each alternative GENERIC statement. The main body consists of: (1.1) a flag indicating that this is the main body of a GENERIC, (1.2) executable code, (1.3) a list of *alternative mode/predicate sets*, and (1.4) a list of pointers to the *alternative bodies*. The main body has the original formal mode set, e.g. for the + routine this is (SCALAR,SCALAR;SCALAR). It can be called

directly (e.g. from interpreted code), in which case it tests the alternative mode/predicate sets against the arguments and dispatches to the appropriate alternative body. That is, calling the main body simply invokes type testing during execution. The alternative bodies are themselves complete code blocks[12] which can be called directly.

Consider next the compilation of another routine, say FOO, which contains a call on a generic routine (e.g. the + routine in X+FUM(Z)). Since the + body is flagged as being GENERIC, an attempt should be made to discover which alternative would be chosen *were* the decision deferred until run-time. There are two possibilities: (1) some alternative is chosen, say the *i*th, in which case the compiler should generate a call directly on the *i*th body; and (2) the compiler discovers that it cannot make a choice, in which case it should generate a call on the main body. Which case applies is determined by the modes of the arguments and the alternative mode/predicate sets in the GENERIC.

Consider first the modes of the arguments. When the + routine is called, its two arguments will have some definite (i.e. nongeneric) mode. However, the compiler has access only to declarative information and from this must deduce what we shall term *compilation modes*. In some cases, these will be less precise than the actual argument mode. For example, a formal parameter, which is ONEOF(INT,REAL), has a united compilation mode. Similarly, a block such as

```
BEGIN  P(X) ⇒ "IN"; 0. END
```

returns either a SYMBOL or a REAL and hence has compilation mode ONEOF(SYMBOL,REAL).

Since the *compilation mode* of an argument may be united, the generic selection mechanism must admit a united argument mode. Hence, the definition of *covers* given above must be expanded to include this case. In general, a mode G in a mode set *covers* an argument mode A if any of the following hold:

1. G = ANY.
2. G is a united mode ONEOF($t_1 \ldots t_n$) and A = t_i for some *i*.
3. G = A.
4. G and A are both united and each alternative of A is an alternative of G (i.e. G ⊇ A).

Because of the fourth clause, it is possible that the choice cannot be made during compilation. If G is ONEOF($t_1 \ldots t_n$) and A is ONEOF($\hat{t}_1 \ldots \hat{t}_m$), it may be that G does not cover A but G covers one or more of the $\hat{t}$'s. We say that G *partially covers* A. If the *actual* mode is one of the t's in G, then G will cover the actual mode and the alternative may be chosen, otherwise it will not. The compiler cannot tell which will be the case and hence must postpone generic selection until execution of the function call.

Given a set of compilation modes $(\mathfrak{M}_1 \ldots \mathfrak{M}_n)$ for the arguments and a table of alternative mode/predicate sets each of the form $[\mathfrak{F}_{i1} \ldots \mathfrak{F}_{in}]\mathcal{P}_i$, choosing the

---

[11] $\mathcal{P}$ may be absent, in which case it is taken as TRUE. Similarly, any of the $\mathfrak{M}$s can be absent, in which case they are taken as ANY. Note that the mode set is semantically unnecessary since all mode checks could be carried out in the predicate. However, factoring the selection into two parts—a simple pattern match and an arbitrary predicate—is useful for pragmatic reasons.

[12] Mode information derived from the generic alternatives can be used to advantage in compiling these bodies. For example, consider

```
EXPR(X:ANY, Y:ONEOF(BOOL, CHAR, STRING); REAL)
GENERIC
    [INT,BOOL] ⇒ 𝔉₁;
    [ONEOF(REAL,CHAR), STRING] ⇒ 𝔉₂;
        .
        .
        .
END
```

The first alternative, $\mathfrak{F}_1$, is compiled under the assumption that X is an INT and Y is a BOOL. It may be that $\mathfrak{F}_1$ and $\mathfrak{F}_2$ are textually identical, yet the different assumptions of argument modes may lead to different compiled code, each block being tailored to its formal modes.

appropriate GENERIC alternative should proceed as follows. The alternative sets are considered in turn, starting with the first. If each formal mode $\mathfrak{F}_{ij}$ *covers* $\mathfrak{M}_j$ and if $\mathcal{P}_i$ is evaluatable and true, then the ith alternative is chosen. If for some j, $\mathfrak{F}_{ij}$ *partially covers* $\mathfrak{M}_j$, or if $\mathcal{P}_i$ is not evaluatable, then generic selection cannot be made during compilation. Otherwise, the next alternative set is considered.

7. Type Conversion

Type conversion provides a second means for dealing with a multiplicity of data types, a means orthogonal to generics. Both conversions and generics allow a routine to be called with arguments belonging to a set of possible modes, but here the similarity stops. With the generic mechanism, the routine has a corresponding *set* of possible parameter modes. With the type conversion mechanism, the routine has a *single* parameter mode and values of different modes are converted to that mode.

Traditionally, the choice of conversion routines to be used is fixed for all time by the language designer. Even in traditional languages, there is little reason for this early freezing. Where it is possible for the programmer to define new types, it becomes essential that he be permitted to specify the associated conversions.

Hence, the treatment of type conversion in EL1 is designed to satisfy two goals: (1) smoothly meshing type conversion with the generic mechanism, and (2) allowing the programmer to specify what the type conversion will be. In outline, the technique used in EL1 is as follows. First a test is made to see if the formal mode *covers* the argument mode (i.e. either the modes are equal or the formal is generic and one of its alternatives is equal to the argument mode). Failing this, the argument is converted to a value belonging to the formal mode using a type conversion routine associated with the argument mode. (If there is no type conversion routine, then an error results.)

For example, suppose that the + routine has been defined on pairs of SCALARS (defined as ONEOF(COMPLEX,REAL,INT)) and that + is called with a STRING-valued argument A. In computation tree terms, we have the direct tree for the computation, say $3+A$

```
        +
      /   \
    3       A.
```

Since the formal mode of the second parameter (SCALAR) does not cover the argument mode (STRING), the direct tree is replaced with the implicit tree

```
        +
      /   \
    3      ℂ(STRING)
          /        \
        A            SCALAR
```

where $\mathbb{C}$(STRING) is the conversion routine associated with string. As with all conversion routines, this takes two arguments: the object to be converted, and the desired mode of the converted result. Here, the desired mode is the formal mode of the second parameter—SCALAR. A possible conversion routine for STRING is:

```
EXPR(X:STRING, FM:MODE; FM)
GENERIC ( )
    FM COVERS INT ⇒ STRING_TO_INT(X);
    FM COVERS SYMBOL ⇒ HASH(X);
          .
          .
END
```

Like most conversion routines, this is a GENERIC. The first alternative consists of a single predicate which uses the infix operator COVERS. This is *true* iff its left-hand operand is a mode which covers its right-hand operand. Hence, the first alternative is chosen whenever the desired mode includes INT. This is the case in the above call on +, so STRING_TO_INT is applied to A. The result, an integer, is taken as the actual argument to the + routine.

One could apply this schema of point-to-point conversion between actual value and target mode to all (source, destination) pairs for which conversion was desired. However, even using generic destination modes to cut down on the number of distinct destinations, the number of pairs could be undesirably large. Further, when defining a new mode $\mathfrak{M}_A$, it would be necessary to explicitly define each desired conversion to an existing mode. Again, the number of such conversions may be undesirably large.

Such an exhaustive enumeration of point-to-point conversions can be avoided by judicious use of functional composition. Consider, for example, the conversion from a CHAR argument to a REAL formal mode. The conversion CHAR → REAL is almost surely the composition of CHAR → INT and INT → REAL. Similarly, COMPLEX → INT is surely COMPLEX → REAL followed by REAL → INT. This suggests an analogous functional composition of conversion routines. For example, the conversion routine for CHAR might be written

```
EXPR(X:CHAR, FM:MODE; FM)
GENERIC
    FM COVERS STRING ⇒ CONST(STRING OF X);
    FM COVERS INT ⇒ CHAR_CODE(X);
    (FM COVERS REAL) OR (FM COVERS COMPLEX) ⇒
      INT_CONVERT(CHAR_CODE(X), FM);
          .
          .
END
```

The third alternative tests whether either REAL or COMPLEX is acceptable; if so, X is converted to an INT, and the INT conversion routine is called to complete the work.

In general, specifying conversion by composition allows the programmer to factor the conversion bush stemming from a data type. This does *not* address the question of what the paths should be when there is more than one path logically possible. An answer to the question can only come from a knowledge of what the data types represent; i.e. a decision must be based on the specific application. The point of the factoring scheme is to provide a concise notation for expressing the desired paths, once a decision has been made.

Thus far the discussion has centered around a hypothetical evaluator with an actual argument requiring conversion in hand. That is, we have described the actions of the interpreter and neglected the compiler. In explaining the semantics of type conversion, this model is quite appropriate. One general rule of EL1 semantics is that the evaluator model dictates actions in complex circumstances; the compiler is constrained to produce code that does the same thing. Applying the general rule to type conversion, the compiler must generate code for type conversions which has results identical to those which would have been obtained using the interpreter.

To take a concrete example, consider a function call FOO(MUMBLE(X)) where the formal parameter of FOO has mode $\mathfrak{M}_F$ and the formal result type of the MUMBLE routine is $\mathfrak{M}_R$. There are three cases:

1. $\mathfrak{M}_F$ covers $\mathfrak{M}_R$.
2. $\mathfrak{M}_F$ does not cover $\mathfrak{M}_R$ and $\mathfrak{M}_R$ is nongeneric.
3. $\mathfrak{M}_F$ does not cover $\mathfrak{M}_R$ and $\mathfrak{M}_R$ is generic.

In case 1, no conversion is required.

In case 2, the function call is treated as if the program had read FOO($\mathcal{C}(\mathfrak{M}_R)$(MUMBLE(X),$\mathfrak{M}_F$)) where $\mathcal{C}(\mathfrak{M}_R)$ is the conversion routine for $\mathfrak{M}_R$.

Case 3 is somewhat subtle. It is known that the actual result mode, $\mathfrak{M}_A$, will be one of the alternatives of $\mathfrak{M}_R$. Either (1) $\mathfrak{M}_F$ covers $\mathfrak{M}_A$, in which case no type conversion is required; or (2) it does not, in which case the conversion routine $\mathcal{C}(\mathfrak{M}_A)$ must be invoked. However, the compiler has no way of determining what $\mathfrak{M}_A$ will be. Hence, it generates code which tests the mode of MUMBLE(X) at run time and invokes the conversion routine for that mode if (2) holds.

The case of a generic compilation mode $\mathfrak{M}_R$ which is not covered by a formal mode $\mathfrak{M}_F$ is not confined to the values of routines. Similar situations are produced by blocks, variables, etc.—wherever the compiler cannot completely determine the data type of a construct. In the important case of blocks, the different data types frequently arise from different block exits; here, the compiler can distribute the type conversion in space so as to use the efficient case 2 treatment. For example, suppose that FOO is called with the argument

BEGIN (PX) $\Rightarrow$ Y; J END

where MD(Y) = REAL, MD(J) = INT, so that the compilation mode $\mathfrak{M}_R$ of the block is ONEOF(REAL,INT).

Suppose $\mathfrak{M}_F$ does not cover this. A commonly used technique in language design is to "widen" the result of the block to REAL and compile in code for REAL to $\mathfrak{M}_F$ conversion. However, this can result in unnecessary conversion steps. A better solution is to treat each statement that can lead out of a block independently, and compile the block as if it had been

BEGIN P(X) $\Rightarrow \mathcal{C}$(REAL)(Y,$\mathfrak{M}_F$); $\mathcal{C}$(INT)(J,$\mathfrak{M}_F$) END

This is particularly attractive when $\mathfrak{M}_F$ covers either REAL or INT so that the appropriate conversion routine is omitted.

8. Programmer Specified Mode Behavior

The treatment of mode definition given in Section 4 centered on the construction of modes. That is, a mode WALDO can be defined to be a set of objects having fields A, B, C of types t_1, t_2, t_3, etc. Such a syntactic specification is, however, only one aspect of mode definition. Indeed, at a sufficiently high level of abstraction,[13] a level which is often only implicit in programming, the syntactic specification is irrelevant; what is of interest is how an object *behaves*. In this view of programming, a syntactic mode specification is a lower level concept which serves to implement some higher level set of behavioral laws. The definition mechanism of Section 4 is then a necessary prerequisite, but only as a basis on which to build a sophisticated mode definition mechanism. Given that this is the direction to be taken in providing a truly problem-oriented language, the issue is what constitutes a higher level mode definition and how to state such a definition in a convenient way.

Section 6 has shown the approach to be taken. Consider two modes M1 and M2, defined

M1 $\leftarrow$ SI::VECTOR(16, BOOL);
M2 $\leftarrow$ MANT::VECTOR(16, BOOL);

This introduces a sixth primitive mode constructor denoted by the infix operator ": :". Here it is given a name as its left-hand operand and a mode as its right-hand operand and constructs a new *labeled* mode distinct from all modes which may be structurally similar but have different or no labels. In the above example, SI and MANT serve as labels for their respective modes, so that the two modes are not equal and neither is equal to VECTOR(16,BOOL). Since M1 and M2 are different modes, they can be assigned different conversion routines, say C1 and C2, respectively. Suppose X1 and X2 are variables of modes M1 and M2, respectively. Structurally, they are identical. However, if used in a position where conversion is required (e.g. 3+X1 or

---

[13] Such layers of abstraction are directly related to the strata of Dijkstra's structured programming [10]. We pursue this point later.

$3+X2$), they may act quite differently. To take a simple example, $SI::VECTOR(16,BOOL)$ may represent a signed integer whose magnitude is less than 2^{15} using 16 bits in two's complement notation, while
$MANT::VECTOR(16,BOOL)$
may represent a real number between 1 and 0. These facts about representation are stored in the routines that handle conversion from these modes to other modes (here, SCALAR). The algorithm which uses X1 and X2 itself displays none of these representational issues. It performs the abstract operation of addition and the data type definitions of X1 and X2 determine the rest. It should be noted that two mechanisms are employed— the implicit type conversion for the arguments to the + routine, and the GENERIC mechanism in the + routine itself. For the purpose of this discussion, the former is the more important since it is more global in scope— the conversion routine for M1 will be applied in *any* situation where a value of mode M1 causes a type mismatch.

This separation of abstract process-oriented algorithm from detailed mode-dependent manipulations is a first step in the direction we wish to take. To push this further, we need only find other "global" situations in which mode-specific manipulations should be called into play. Four[14] others have been chosen for consideration in EL1—assignment, selection, printing, and generation. To pursue the above example, programmer control over the meaning of assignment would allow one to specify that $X1 \leftarrow -34.2$ is to cause the real value to be converted to an integer and that value packed into 16 bits.

A second example may be useful to illustrate the power of this technique. For debugging and other purposes, it is frequently useful to be able to monitor the value of a variable and take some special action (e.g. output an error message) under certain abnormal conditions (e.g. when its value exceeds the value of another variable). Let X be such a variable of mode M, let P(X) be a predicate which tests for abnormal conditions, and let A(X) be the action to be taken. One can define a new mode M' in terms of M, P, and A as follows:
1. M''s are structurally identical to M's.
2. Whenever a formal mode M is required and an actual value of mode M' is in hand, the M' is copied and the copy treated as if it were an M.
3. Whenever an object of mode M' is assigned a new value X, the predicate P(X) is evaluated; if the result is *true*, A(X) is executed.
One can go further and automate this process by defining a routine SENSITIVE_MODE (as a function of one mode M and two routines P and A) that constructs the new mode M'. Having written this one routine, the programmer has at his disposal the notion of "sensitive object" for any mode M. Redeclaring any variable to be

a SENSITIVE_MODE(M,P,A) inserts the monitoring probes with no other changes to the program required.

To provide some substance to the discussion, we turn to a third example which we treat in detail. Consider defining the mode "ring buffer of characters." If X is such a buffer, its chief characteristics are:
1. An assignment of a CHAR value to X pushes the character onto the back end of the buffer if there is room, else error.
2. Use of X where formal mode CHAR is desired pops a character from the front end of the buffer if the buffer is nonempty, else error.
Very likely, other properties would be desirable:
3. The buffer can be treated *as if* it maintained at all times a correct count of the number of characters it holds and X.COUNT accesses this component.
4. The top element of the buffer can be inspected without popping it by selecting the TOP element, i.e. X.TOP.

A possible structure for such buffers is
STRUCT(FRONT:INT,BACK:INT,
           BODY:VECTOR(K,CHAR));
where K is some constant—the maximum number of characters the buffer is to hold. (To simplify the discussion, we suppose a given value for K, say 200.) FRONT and BACK will be indices to the front and back ends of the buffer, with the convention that characters go *in* the back end and *out* the front end. Hence, FRONT chases BACK backward around the ring with modulo K arithmetic.

To establish the desired behavior, it is necessary to create a mode having the above structure but with special properties for conversion, assignment, selection, printing, and generation. A labeled mode with special properties can most conveniently be created by invoking the :: operator with a more complex left-hand argument. Consider
RB $\leftarrow$ ⟨"RBUF", RBC, RBA, RBS, RBP, RBG⟩::
       STRUCT(FRONT:INT, BACK:INT,
       BODY:VECTOR(K, CHAR))
Here the left-hand argument to :: is a list consisting of a name ("RBUF"), and routines for conversion, assignment, selection, printing, and generation, respectively. (The list is delimited by the matchfix operator pair ⟨ and ⟩, c.f. Section 2.) RB is a mode-valued variable. Its value is defined by the assignment to be
RBUF::STRUCT(FRONT:INT; BACK:INT,
       BODY:VECTOR(200,CHAR))
which differs from other modes having identical structure but different (or no) label.

The desired behavior of RB is established by the definitions of the routines RBC, RBA, RBS, RBP, and RBG. We consider the first three; the other two then become obvious.

With regard to selection, we have established that if X is an RB, there are to be two and only two "fields" which may be selected: X.COUNT, which gives the number of items in the buffer; and X.TOP, which

[14] It is possible to justify additional ones, such as storage reclamation. Some experience will perhaps be required before a completely satisfactory set is found.

gives the top item of the buffer. That these fields do not actually exist as such is irrelevant, so long as the mode definition creates the desired behavior (illusion if you will). Further, when using an RB *as* an RB, there is no need to directly access the fields FRONT, BACK, and BODY. The job of the selection routine is to define the desired fields "COUNT" and "TOP" in terms of the fields which actually exist and simultaneously render these latter fields unavailable to direct access. The language evaluator provides a triggering mechanism for this definition. It calls the selection routine[15] of RB on any selection of the form X . fieldname, where X is of mode RB. It will be passed two arguments—the object being selected from and the name of the field represented as a symbol. Consider the definition.

```
RBS ←
  EXPR(X:RB, FD:SYMBOL; INT)
  GENERIC ( )
      FD = "TOP"      ⇒ BEGIN
                         LOWER(X).FRONT ≠ LOWER
                           (X).BACK ⇒ LOWER(X).
                           BODY[LOWER(X).FRONT];
                         BUFF_EMPTY(X);
                         END
      FD = "COUNT" ⇒ BEGIN
                         DECL F:INT BYVAL LOWER(X).
                           FRONT;
                         DECL B:INT BYVAL LOWER(X).
                           BACK;
                         F>B ⇒ F−B;
                         F<B ⇒ 200−B+F;
                         ∅
                         END
         TRUE ⇒ SELECTION_FAULT(RB, FD)
  END
```

The routine tests the field name by comparing it to the symbol-valued constants "TOP" and "COUNT". Based on this comparison, the main conditional discriminates between three main cases: (1) the ⟨fieldname⟩ is TOP; (2) the ⟨fieldname⟩ is COUNT; and (3) neither of the above. The last case is treated as an error and a system error routine is called. Consider the case FD = "TOP". We adopt the convention that FRONT is the index of the first good element to be emptied on output and BACK is the index of the next element to be filled on input; hence the buffer is non-empty whenever FRONT ≠ BACK. However, it is *not* possible to make the required test by writing X . FRONT ≠ X . BACK. Since X is an RB, this would invoke the selection routine for RB recursively. What we need is the selection routine not for RB but rather for the underlying representation STRUCT(FRONT:INT,BACK:INT,

BODY:VECTOR(200,CHAR))

The primitive routine LOWER maps X onto an object having the same pattern of bit values but a different mode, the mode of the *underlying representation*. In fact, no copying need be done: X and LOWER(X)

refer to the same object; they just ascribe different *modes* to this object. With this explanation of LOWER, the rest of the code should be fairly clear: if the buffer is not empty, its top element is selected. As to the case F = "COUNT", the block uses two local variables simply to avoid writing LOWER(X) . FRONT and LOWER(X) . BACK repeatedly; the number of characters is calculated in the obvious way.

Consider next the conversion routine for RB. Assuming for the sake of simplicity that the only conversion to be considered is RB → CHAR, consider

```
RBC ←
  EXPR(X:RB, FM:MODE; CHAR)
  BEGIN
    DECL F:INT BYVAL LOWER(X).FRONT;
    DECL TEMP:CHAR;
    FM ≠ CHAR ⇒ TYPE_FAULT(RB, FM);
    F = LOWER(X).BACK ⇒ BUFF_EMPTY(X);
    TEMP ← LOWER(X).BODY[F];
    F ← LOWER(X).FRONT ←F−1;
    F = 0 → LOWER(X).FRONT ← 200;
    TEMP
  END
```

This creates a local variable F initialized to the value of LOWER(X).FRONT and a TEMP of mode CHAR to hold the result of the routine. The next two lines test that the desired mode is CHAR and that the buffer is not empty. Then TEMP is assigned the top element and LOWER(X).FRONT is decremented. If the new value is zero, LOWER(X).FRONT is wrapped around the buffer. Finally, the block (and hence routine) returns TEMP as its value.

The assignment routine is similar and should be self-explanatory:

```
RBA ←
  EXPR(X:RB, Y:CHAR; CHAR)
  BEGIN
    LOWER(X).BODY[LOWER(X).BACK] ← Y;
    LOWER(X).BACK ← LOWER(X).BACK−1;
    LOWER(X).BACK = 0 → LOWER(X).BACK ← 200;
    LOWER(X).BACK ≠ LOWER(X).FRONT ⇒ Y;
    BUFF_OVERFLOW(X)
  END
```

One point should be noted. Suppose B1 and B2 are both RB's, and consider the assignment B1 ← B2;. Since the left-hand operand is an RB, the RB assignment routine is called. Binding its formals to its arguments proceeds as follows. The formal X is an RB, so this is bound directly to B1. However, the formal Y is a CHAR, and the argument B2 is an RB. Hence, the conversion routine for RBs is called with arguments B2 and CHAR. The result is to pop an element from B2 and bind the formal Y to this. Hence, the assignment causes an element to be popped from the front of B2 and added to the back of B1.

Turning from the specific to the general, several points should be noted. (1) It is straightforward to treat the buffer size K and the mode M of its constituent elements as parameters and write a routine

BUFFER(K,M) that produces a mode for any values of K and M. Such a BUFFER routine can be viewed as a realization of one implementation technique of the concept of buffer. From another point of view, one can ignore the implementation and take BUFFER as an abstract set of data types with certain properties. (2) The notion of *underling representation* has a natural extension. We have jut used the mode
STRUCT(FRONT:INT,BACK:INT,
        BODY:VECTOR(200,CHAR))
as a basis for defining RB so that the former is the underlying representation of the latter; we could equally well use an RB as a basis for defining a new mode, for which RB would be the underlying representation.

We illustrate this notion with an example. A character stream is frequently used to encode a virtual character set greater than that actually available by using one or more characters as escape characters whose appearance changes the interpretation of characters which follow them. In such cases, a virtual character is an array of actual characters. It is then useful to consider a class of buffers into which single CHARs can be pushed at the back end but which deliver STRINGs at the front end. Let this mode be called STRB. One could in principle define STRB in terms of the underlying representation
STRUCT(FRONT:INT,BACK:INT,
        BODY:VECTOR(200,CHAR))
However, it is far more convenient to use RB as the underlying representation. Then STRB can be defined in terms of COUNT, TOP, and the operations of assigning to and converting from RB's. In this definition, if X is a STRB, then LOWER(X) is to be interpreted as an RB. In this fashion, any existing data type can be used as the basis for defining a new type.

The syntax for carrying this out is simple since the labeling of modes can be cascaded. If $\mathfrak{M}$ is a mode, and $\mathfrak{N}$ is an identifier, then $\langle$"$\mathfrak{N}$", ...$\rangle$ :: $\mathfrak{M}$ is a new mode with label $\mathfrak{N}$ based on the mode $\mathfrak{M}$. For example, $\langle$"STRBUF", ...$\rangle$ :: RB defines a new mode equal to
STRBUF::RBUF::STRUCT(FRONT:INT,
        BACK:INT, BODY:VECTOR(200, CHAR))
If X is an instance of this mode, LOWER(X) is an RB. This new mode can itself be used as the right-hand argument to the :: operator to build up a hierarchy of mode definitions. Such a definition scheme has a number of consequences closely related to Dijkstra's structured programming.

In writing a program in the style of structured programming, one builds a "string of pearls." Each pearl has its own set of abstract operations and data types defined in terms of lower level pearls. Realizing this for operations is straightforward; higher level routines are composed from lower level routines. Programmer control over mode behavior, as discussed in this section, provides an analogue for data. A mode $\mathfrak{M}_i$ at one level in the string can be *based on* one or more modes at

lower levels. A well-engineered definition set will use LOWER only in the mode specification routines (conversion, assignment, selection, printing, and generation). Operations at that level see *only* the behavior of the defined mode $\mathfrak{M}_i$, not its definitions in terms of lower level notions. Hence, the actual representation used to achieve this behavior is irrelevant at this and higher levels. Without changing other parts of the program, one can vary this representation at will. This affords a very powerful means to (1) optimize performance for a given task and (2) modify the program to perform related tasks.

9. Conclusion

The treatment of data types in EL1 rests on nine points:
1. Modes as values in the language,
2. The facility for freezing free variables during compilation.
3. The generic interpretation of mode union.
4. Routines as a unification of operators and procedures.
5. Inclusion of both generic routines and type conversion.
6. Programmer-defined generic routines and programmer control over type conversions.
7. Interpreter-based semantics for generic selection and type conversion which the compiler is constrained to follow.
8. Programmer control over mode behavior.
9. The notion of underlying representation and the basing of one mode on the behavior of another.
Some of these are independent of one another, of the EL1 language, and of the ECL system; these can be applied directly to other languages. Other points depend strongly on the language and system; carrying these over is a bit tricky.

The most radical points are the first and second. These are also the most significant. The inclusion of modes among the legitimate values in a language allows modes to be *computed*, providing a very powerful definitional capability. A direct consequence is the concept of programmer-defined, mode-valued routines and, hence, the functional abstraction these provide.

The first point demands the second (or some equivalent). Computed mode values are of interest only if they can be used as the types of variables in compiled routines. Hence, there must be some mechanism to specify that a particular nonprimitive mode value is to be used as a data type. An important notion here is the concept of evaluability during compilation and the upward propagation of computation-tree collapse. The utility of this mechanism goes beyond its use in connection with data types. It allows the programmer to nail down invariants of all sorts and have the program reflect the consequences of these invariants.

Turning to point 3 above, we note that there are

many possible interpretations of "union" as applied to data types. The one used in EL1 was chosen on the basis of simplicity, implementability, and because it meshes most smoothly with the generic routines. This interpretation of union—the generic—treats a united mode as the postponement of a commitment until execution. Hence, during execution the concept largely disappears, simplifying the semantic description.

The use of routines as a unification of operators and procedures hardly requires comment. Apart from external syntax, there is no real difference between the two. A language which allows the programmer to define both should surely provide identical semantics for the two. The alternative is harder to communicate, learn, and implement. Regrettably, it is the common practice.

Having both generic routines and type conversion is almost a necessity. Neither alone provides the right flexibility; neither is a good substitute for the other. The scheme used in EL1 may be briefly summarized as: if a formal mode covers the argument mode, binding is direct; otherwise, the argument is converted to some mode that is covered.

Given that a language includes generic routines and type conversion, it should follow that these be controllable by the programmer, i.e. that he be permitted to define generic routines (in addition to the built-in set) and that he be permitted to specify the type conversions. This is not hard to implement. Most of the necessary mechanisms are already present to handle the built-in definitions. Implementation of programmer control is mostly a matter of employing these mechanisms on programmer-supplied definitions.

The only subtle point is choosing a semantic model. Generic selection and type conversion can become complex, since conversions are typically cascaded and often applied to the arguments of generic routines. A compiler model is awkward, since it either imposes language restrictions to insure compile-time knowledge of modes or, lacking this, produces a description which depends not on modes but the compiler's knowledge of modes. The use of an interpreter (i.e. run-time) model greatly simplifies the descriptive task.

Giving the programmer control over the behavior of the modes he defines is again easy to implement, provided the implementation is done correctly. Any system which allows the definition of new data types must construct tables or their equivalent to give meaning to subsequent conversions, assignments, selections, generations, etc., of variables having these types. It is a short step and a considerable improvement from such tables to system-generated routines tailored to each new data type. The next step is to allow the programmer to specify the routines *he* wants invoked. His routines must define their operation in terms of a machine-independent underlying representation. If this is done correctly, the layering of underlying representations falls out naturally.

In summary, the treatment of data types in EL1 is based on a set of fairly straightforward notions, most of which are simple to implement. Much of this treatment can be carried over to other high level programming languages. The linguistic power they add is considerable.

Acknowledgments. The current implementation of the EL1 language and the ECL programming system is the work of many individuals. In particular, the author would like to acknowledge the contributions of W. Conrad, G. Holloway, and J. Spitzen.

Received June 1971; revised April 1973

References
1. PL I Language Reference Manual. Form C28-8201-2. IBM Syst. Ref. Lib. (1969).
2. Abrahams P.S. et al. The LISP2 programming language and system. Proc. AFIPS 1966 FJCC, Vol. 29, AFIPS Press, Montvale, N.J., pp. 661–676.
3. Van Wijngaargen, A.V., et al. Report on the algorithmic language ALGOL 68. *Numerische Mathematik 14* (1969), 79–218.
4. Garwick, J.V. GPL, a truly general purpose language. *Comm. ACM 11,* 9 (Sept. 1968), 634–638.
5. Hoare, C.A.R. Record handling. In *Programming Languages.* F. Genuys (Ed.) Academic Press, New York, 1968, pp. 291–347.
6. Standish, T.A. A data definition facility for programming languages. Doc. diss., Comput. Sci. Dep., Carnegie Institute of Technology, Pittsburgh, Pa., 1967.
7. Wegbreit, B., et al. The ECL programmer's manual, Technical Report 21-72, Center for Res. in Comput. Tech., Harvard U., Cambridge, Mass., 1972.
8. Wegbreit, B. The ECL programming system, Proc. AFIPS 1971 FJCC, Vol. 39, AFIPS Press, Montvale, N.J., pp. 253–262.
9. Reynolds, J.C. A set-theoretic approach to the concept of type. Working material for NATO Conf. on Techniques in Software Engineering, Rome, Italy, Oct. 1969.
10. Dijkstra, E.W. Notes on structured programming. T.H. Report 70-WSK-03, Technological U. Eindhoven, The Netherlands, Apr. 1970.

Section 5
Pascal: Pro and Con

The programming language Pascal was designed in the late 1960's by Prof. Niklaus Wirth at the Federal Technical University (ETH) in Zürich. Although he originally intended it primarily for teaching students to think about programming in a systematic way and to study ways in which programming languages could be efficiently implemented, its use and popularity have spread widely. Today, Pascal is available on nearly every computer system, from personal computer systems (such as the Apple) to microcomputer systems (many of which use the UCSD Pascal system) to minicomputers and mainframes.

In addition, Pascal has served as the basis for the design of a number of other programming languages, including Ada, Concurrent Pascal, Pascal/R, and PLAIN, all of which are the subjects of articles in succeeding chapters. Certainly an influence in the design of numerous other languages as well, Pascal has been adapted and/or extended for various systems programming applications. There are presently active groups in the U.K. and the U.S. working toward the definition of a standardized dialect of Pascal that addresses some of the trouble spots in the original definition of Pascal and that makes some extensions to Wirth's language.

Pascal, as a descendant of ALGOL 60, represents the basis for much of the current work in programming language design. In this section, we try to show the features of Pascal, followed by several articles that argue some of the technical issues in the language.

Wirth's "The Programming Language Pascal" is the first paper in the open literature that describes Pascal. The version of Pascal described here is the original; the Revised Report on the language made several minor changes, of which the most significant is the elimination of the **class** concept.

The paper by Habermann stirred up considerable controversy when published, since it strongly criticizes some of the key decisions made in the design of Pascal. Wirth's decision to require static array bounds, for example, makes it impossible to write a generalized matrix multiplication routine in which the size of the various matrices are supplied at execution time. While Wirth's decision is justified on implementation efficiency considerations, Habermann argues that many of the Pascal decisions complicate life for the programmer.

Lecarme and Desjardins wrote their paper as a response to Habermann and as a defense of Pascal.

Wirth's second paper, assessing Pascal, points out some modifications that he would make if he were to redesign Pascal, but expresses overall satisfaction with the design and implementation of the language.

Finally, Welsh, Sneeringer, and Hoare point out difficulties in the language and ambiguities in the Revised Report. Some of the problems with type checking, aliasing, and function and procedure parameters are also noted in Wasserman's paper on testing and verification aspects of Pascal-like languages in Section 2.

The Programming Language Pascal

N. Wirth *

Received October 30, 1970

Summary. A programming language called Pascal is described which was developed on the basis of Algol 60. Compared to Algol 60, its range of applicability is considerably increased due to a variety of data structuring facilities. In view of its intended usage both as a convenient basis to teach programming and as an efficient tool to write large programs, emphasis was placed on keeping the number of fundamental concepts reasonably small, on a simple and systematic language structure, and on efficient implementability. A one-pass compiler has been constructed for the CDC 6000 computer family; it is expressed entirely in terms of Pascal itself.

1. Introduction

The development of the language *Pascal* is based on two principal aims. The first is to make available a language suitable to teach programming as a systematic discipline based on certain fundamental concepts clearly and naturally reflected by the language. The second is to develop implementations of this language which are both reliable and efficient on presently available computers, dispelling the commonly accepted notion that useful languages must be either slow to compile or slow to execute, and the belief that any nontrivial system is bound to contain mistakes forever.

There is of course plenty of reason to be cautious with the introduction of yet another programming language, and the objection against teaching programming in a language which is not widely used and accepted has undoubtedly some justification —at least based on short-term commercial reasoning. However, the choice of a language for teaching based on its widespread acceptance and availability, together with the fact that the language most widely taught is thereafter going to be the one most widely used, forms the safest recipe for stagnation in a subject of such profound paedagogical influence. I consider it therefore well worth-while to make an effort to break this vicious circle.

Of course a new language should not be developed just for the sake of novelty; existing languages should be used as a basis for development wherever they meet the chosen objectives, such as a systematic structure, flexibility of program and data structuring, and efficient implementability. In that sense Algol 60 was used as a basis for Pascal, since it meets most of these demands to a much higher degree than any other standard language [1]. Thus the principles of structuring, and in fact the form of expressions, are copied from Algol 60. It was, however, not deemed appropriate to adopt Algol 60 as a subset of Pascal; certain construction principles, particularly those of declarations, would have been incom-

---

* Fachgruppe Computer-Wissenschaften, Eidg. Technische Hochschule, Zürich, Schweiz.

3*

patible with those allowing a natural and convenient representation of the additional features of Pascal. However, conversion of ALGOL 60 programs to Pascal can be considered as a negligible effort of transcription, particularly if they obey the rules of the IFIP ALGOL Subset [2].

The main extensions relative to ALGOL 60 lie in the domain of data structuring facilities, since their lack in ALGOL 60 was considered as the prime cause for its relatively narrow range of applicability. The introduction of record and file structures should make it possible to solve commercial type problems with Pascal, or at least to employ it successfully to demonstrate such problems in a programming course. This should help erase the mystical belief in the segregation between scientific and commercial programming methods. A first step in extending the data definition facilities of ALGOL 60 was undertaken in an effort to define a successor to ALGOL in 1965 [3]. This language is a direct predecessor of Pascal, and was the source of many features such as e.g. the while and case statements and of record structures.

Pascal has been implemented on the CDC 6000 computers. The compiler is written in Pascal itself as a one-pass system which will be the subject of a subsequent report. The "dialect" processed by this implementation is described by a few amendments to the general description of Pascal. They are included here as a separate chapter to demonstrate the brevity of a manual necessary to characterise a particular implementation. Moreover, they show how facilities are introduced into this high-level, machine independent programming language, which permit the programmer to take advantage of the characteristics of a particular machine.

The syntax of Pascal has been kept as simple as possible. Most statements and declarations begin with a unique key word. This property facilitates both the understanding of programs by human readers and the processing by computers. In fact, the syntax has been devised so that Pascal texts can be scanned by the simplest techniques of syntactic analysis. This textual simplicity is particularly desirable, if the compiler is required to possess the capability to detect and diagnose errors and to proceed thereafter in a sensible manner.

2. Summary of the Language

An algorithm or computer program consists of two essential parts, a description of *actions* which are to be performed, and a description of the *data* which are manipulated by these actions. Actions are described in Pascal by so-called *statements*, and data are described by so-called *declarations* and *definitions*.

The data are represented by values of *variables*. Every variable occuring in a statement must be introduced by a *variable declaration* which associates an identifier and a data type with that variable. The *data type* essentially defines the set of values which may be assumed by that variable. A data type may in Pascal be either directly described in the variable declaration, or it may be referenced by a type identifier, in which case this identifier must be described by an explicit *type definition*.

The basic data types are the *scalar* types. Their definition indicates an ordered set of values, i.e. introduces an identifier as a constant standing for each value in the set. Apart from the definable scalar types, there exist in Pascal four *standard scalar types* whose values are not denoted by identifiers, but instead by numbers and quotations respectively, which are syntactically distinct from identifiers. These types are: *integer, real, char*, and *alfa*.

The set of values of type *char* is the character set available on the printers of a particular installation. *Alfa* type values consist of sequences of characters whose length again is implementation dependent, i.e. is the number of characters packed per word. Individual characters are not directly accessible, but *alfa* quantities can be unpacked into a character array (and vice-versa) by a standard procedure.

A scalar type may also be defined as a *subrange* of another scalar type by indicating the smallest and the largest value of the subrange.

Structured types are defined by describing the types of their components and by indicating a *structuring method*. The various structuring methods differ in the selection mechanism serving to select the components of a variable of the structured type. In Pascal, there are five structuring methods available: array structure, record structure, powerset structure, file structure, and class structure.

In an *array structure*, all components are of the same type. A component is selected by an array selector, or computable *index*, whose type is indicated in the array type definition and which must be scalar. It is usually a programmer-defined scalar type, or a subrange of the type *integer*.

In a *record structure*, the components (called *fields*) are not necessarily of the same type. In order that the type of a selected component be evident from the program text (without executing the program), a record selector does not contain a computable value, but instead consists of an identifier uniquely denoting the component to be selected. These component identifiers are defined in the record type definition.

A record type may be specified as consisting of several *variants*. This implies that different variables, although said to be of the same type, may assume structures which differ in a certain manner. The difference may consist of a different number and different types of components. The variant which is assumed by the current value of a record variable is indicated by a component field which is common to all variants and is called the *tag field*. Usually, the part common to all variants will consist of several components, including the tag field.

A *powerset structure* defines a set of values which is the powerset of its base type, i.e. the set of all subsets of values of the base type. The base type must be a scalar type, and will usually be a programmer-defined scalar type or a subrange of the type *integer*.

A *file structure* is a sequence of components of the same type. A natural ordering of the components is defined through the sequence. At any instance, only one component is directly accessible. The other components are made accessible through execution of standard file positioning procedures. A file is at any time in one of the three modes called *input, output*, and *neutral*. According to the mode, a file can be read sequentially, or it can be written by appending components to the existing sequence of components. File positioning procedures may influence the mode. The file type definition does not determine the number of components, and this number is variable during execution of the program.

The *class structure* defines a class of components of the same type whose number may alter during execution of a program. Each declaration of a variable with class structure introduces a set of variables of the component type. The set is initially empty. Every activation of the standard procedure *alloc* (with the class as implied parameter) will generate (or allocate) a new component variable in the class and yield a value through which this new component variable may be accessed. This value is called a *pointer*, and may be assigned to variables of type pointer. Every pointer variable, however, is through its declaration bound to a fixed class variable, and because of this *binding* may only assume values pointing to components of that class. There exists a pointer value **nil** which points to no component whatsoever, and may be assumed by any pointer variable irrespective of its binding. Through the use of class structures it is possible to construct data corresponding to any finite graph with pointers representing edges and component variables representing nodes.

The most fundamental statement is the *assignment statement*. It specifies that a newly computed value be assigned to a variable (or component of a variable). The value is obtained by evaluating an *expression*. Pascal defines a fixed set of operators, each of which can be regarded as describing a mapping from the operand types into the result type. The set of operators is subdivided into groups of

1. arithmetic operators of addition, subtraction, sign inversion, multiplication, division, and computing the remainder. The operand and result types are the types *integer* and *real*, or subrange types of *integer*.

2. Boolean operators of negation, union (or), and conjunction (and). The operand and result types are *Boolean* (which is a standard type).

3. set operators of union, intersection, and difference. The operands and results are of any powerset type.

4. relational operators of equality, inequality, ordering and set membership. The result of relational operations is of type *Boolean*. Any two operands may be compared for equality as long as they are of the same type. The ordering relations apply only to scalar types.

The assignment statement is a so-called *simple statement*, since it does not contain any other statement within itself. Another kind of simple statement is the *procedure statement*, which causes the execution of the designated procedure (see below). Simple statements are the components or building blocks of *structured statements*, which specify sequential, selective, or repeated execution of their components. Sequential execution of statements is specified by the *compound statement*, conditional or selective execution by the *if statement* and the *case statement*, and repeated execution by the *repeat statement*, the *while statement*, and the *for statement*. The if statement serves to make the execution of a statement dependent on the value of a *Boolean* expression, and the case statement allows for the selection among many statements according to the value of a selector. The for statement· is used when the number of iterations is known beforehand, and the repeat and while statements are used otherwise.

A statement can be given a name (identifier), and be referenced through that identifier. The statement is then called a *procedure*, and its declaration a *procedure declaration*. Such a declaration may additionally contain a set of variable declarations, type definitions and further procedure declarations. The variables, types and procedures thus defined can be referenced only within the procedure itself, and are therefore called *local* to the procedure. Their identifiers have significance only within the program text which constitutes the procedure declaration and which is called the *scope* of these identifiers. Since procedures may be declared local to other procedures, scopes may be nested.

A procedure may have a fixed number of parameters, which are classified into constant-, variable-, procedure-, and function parameters. In the case of a variable parameter, its type has to be specified in the declaration of the formal parameter. If the actual variable parameter contains a (computable) selector, this selector is evaluated before the procedure is activated in order to designate the selected component variable.

Functions are declared analogously to procedures. In order to eliminate side-effects, assignments to non-local variables are not allowed to occur within the function.

3. Notation, Terminology, and Vocabulary

According to traditional Backus-Naur form, syntactic constructs are denoted by English words enclosed between the angular brackets $\langle$ and $\rangle$. These words also describe the nature or meaning of the construct, and are used in the accompanying description of semantics. Possible repetition of a construct is indicated by an asterisk (0 or more repetitions) or a circled plus sign (1 or more repetitions). If a sequence of constructs to be repeated consists of more than one element, it is enclosed by the meta-brackets {and}.

The basic *vocabulary* consists of basic symbols classified into letters, digits, and special symbols.

$$\langle\text{letter}\rangle ::= A|B|C|D|E|F|G|H|I|J|K|L|M|N|O|P|Q|R|S|T|U|V|W|X|Y|Z|$$
$$a|b|c|d|e|f|g|h|i|j|k|l|m|n|o|p|q|r|s|t|u|v|w|x|y|z$$

$$\langle\text{digit}\rangle ::= 0|1|2|3|4|5|6|7|8|9$$

$$\langle\text{special symbol}\rangle ::= +|-|*|/|\vee|\wedge|\neg|=|\neq|<|>|\leq|\geq|(|)|[|]|\{|\}|:=|$$
$$_{10}|\cdot|,|;|:|'|\uparrow|\textbf{div}|\textbf{mod}|\textbf{nil}|\textbf{in}|$$
$$\textbf{if}|\textbf{then}|\textbf{else}|\textbf{case}|\textbf{of}|\textbf{repeat}|\textbf{until}|\textbf{while}|\textbf{do}|$$
$$\textbf{for}|\textbf{to}|\textbf{downto}|\textbf{begin}|\textbf{end}|\textbf{with}|\textbf{goto}|$$
$$\textbf{var}|\textbf{type}|\textbf{array}|\textbf{record}|\textbf{powerset}|\textbf{file}|\textbf{class}|$$
$$\textbf{function}|\textbf{procedure}|\textbf{const}$$

The construct

$$\{\langle\text{any sequence of symbols not containing ''}\}\text{''}\rangle\}$$

may be inserted between any two identifiers, numbers (cf. 4), or special symbols. It is called a *comment* and may be removed from the program text without altering its meaning.

4. Identifiers and Numbers

Identifiers serve to denote constants, types, variables, procedures and functions. Their association must be unique within their scope of validity, i.e. within the procedure or function in which they are declared (cf. 10 and 11).

⟨identifier⟩ ::= ⟨letter⟩ ⟨letter or digit⟩*

⟨letter or digit⟩ ::= ⟨letter⟩ | ⟨digit⟩

The decimal notation is used for numbers, which are the constants of the data types *integer* and *real*. The symbol $_{10}$ preceding the scale factor is pronounced as "times 10 to the power of".

⟨number⟩ ::= ⟨integer⟩ | ⟨real number⟩

⟨integer⟩ ::= ⟨digit⟩$^{\oplus}$

⟨real number⟩ ::= ⟨digit⟩$^{\oplus}$. ⟨digit⟩$^{\oplus}$ |
    ⟨digit⟩$^{\oplus}$. ⟨digit⟩$^{\oplus}$ $_{10}$ ⟨scale factor⟩ | ⟨integer⟩$_{10}$ ⟨scale factor⟩

⟨scale factor⟩ ::= ⟨digit⟩$^{\oplus}$ | ⟨sign⟩ ⟨digit⟩$^{\oplus}$

⟨sign⟩ ::= + | −

Examples:

  1   100   0.1 $5_{10}{-}3$ $87.35_{10}{+}8$

5. Constant Definitions

A constant definition introduces an identifier as a synonym to a constant.

⟨unsigned constant⟩ ::= ⟨number⟩ | '⟨character⟩$^{\oplus}$' | ⟨identifier⟩ | **nil**

⟨constant⟩ ::= ⟨unsigned constant⟩ | ⟨sign⟩ ⟨number⟩

⟨constant definition⟩ ::= ⟨identifier⟩ = ⟨constant⟩

6. Data Type Definitions

A data type determines the set of values which variables of that type may assume and associates an identifier with the type. In the case of structured types, it also defines their structuring method.

⟨type⟩ ::= ⟨scalar type⟩ | ⟨subrange type⟩ | ⟨array type⟩ | ⟨record type⟩ |
    ⟨powerset type⟩ | ⟨file type⟩ | ⟨class type⟩ | ⟨pointer type⟩ |
    ⟨type identifier⟩

⟨type identifier⟩ ::= ⟨identifier⟩

⟨type definition⟩ ::= ⟨identifier⟩ = ⟨type⟩

6.1. Scalar Types

A scalar type defines an ordered set of values by enumeration of the identifiers which denote these values.

⟨scalar type⟩ ::= (⟨identifier⟩ **{**, ⟨identifier⟩**}***)

Examples:

(*red, orange, yellow, green, blue*)
(*club, diamond, heart, spade*)
(*Monday, Tuesday, Wednesday, Thursday, Friday, Saturday, Sunday*)

Functions applying to all scalar types are:

succ   the succeeding value (in the enumeration)
pred   the preceding value (in the enumeration)

6.1.1. Standard Scalar Types

The following types are standard in Pascal, i.e. the identifier denoting them is predefined:

integer   the values are the integers within a range depending on the particular implementation. The values are denoted by integers (cf. 4) and not by identifiers.

real   the values are a subset of the real numbers depending on the particular implementation. The values are denoted by real numbers as defined in paragraph 4.

Boolean   (*false, true*)

char   the values are a set of characters depending on a particular implementation. They are denoted by the characters themselves enclosed within quotes.

alfa   the values are sequences of n characters, where n is an implementation dependent parameter. If α and β are values of type alfa

$$\alpha = a_1 \dots a_k \dots a_n$$
$$\beta = b_1 \dots b_k \dots b_n,$$

then

$$\alpha = \beta, \quad \text{if and only if} \quad a_i = b_i \quad \text{for} \quad i = 1 \dots n,$$
$$\alpha < \beta, \quad \text{if and only if} \quad a_i = b_i \quad \text{for} \quad i = 1 \dots k-1 \quad \text{and} \quad a_k < b_k,$$
$$\alpha > \beta, \quad \text{if and only if} \quad a_i = b_i \quad \text{for} \quad i = 1 \dots k-1 \quad \text{and} \quad a_k > b_k.$$

Alfa values are denoted by sequences of (at most) n characters enclosed in quotes. Trailing blanks may be omitted. Alfa quantities may be regarded as a packed representation of short character arrays (cf. also 10.1.3.).

6.1.2. Subrange Types

A type may be defined as a subrange of another scalar type by indication of the least and the highest value in the subrange. The first constant specifies the lower bound, and must not be greater than the upper bound.

⟨subrange type⟩ ::= ⟨constant⟩ .. ⟨constant⟩

Examples:

> 1..100
>
> $-10..+10$
>
> *Monday..Friday*

6.2. Structured Types

6.2.1. Array Types

An array type is a structure consisting of a fixed number of components which are all of the same type, called the *component type*. The elements of the array are designated by indices, values belonging to the so-called *index type*. The array type definition specifies the component type as well as the index type.

⟨array type⟩ ::= **array** [⟨index type⟩ **{**, ⟨index type⟩**}***] **of** ⟨component type⟩

⟨index type⟩ ::= ⟨scalar type⟩ | ⟨subrange type⟩ | ⟨type identifier⟩

⟨component type⟩ ::= ⟨type⟩

If n index types are specified, the array type is called *n-dimensional*, and a component is designated by n indices.

Examples:

> **array** [1..100] **of** *real*
>
> **array** [1..10, 1..20] **of** 0..99
>
> **array** [−10..+10] **of** *Boolean*
>
> **array** [*Boolean*] **of** *Color*

6.2.2. Record Types

A record type is a structure consisting of a fixed number of components, possibly of different types. The record type definition specifies for each component, called *field*, its type and an identifier which denotes it. The scope of these so-called *field identifiers* is the record definition itself, and they are also accessible within a field designator (cf. 7.2) refering to a record variable of this type.

A record type may have several *variants*, in which case a certain field is designated as the *tag field*, whose value indicates which variant is assumed by the record variable at a given time. Each variant structure is identified by a case label which is a constant of the type of the tag field.

⟨record type⟩ ::= **record** ⟨field list⟩ **end**

⟨field list⟩ ::= ⟨fixed part⟩ | ⟨fixed part⟩; ⟨variant part⟩ | ⟨variant part⟩

⟨fixed part⟩ ::= ⟨record section⟩ **{**; ⟨record section⟩**}***

⟨record section⟩ ::= ⟨field identifier⟩ **{**, ⟨field identifier⟩**}***: ⟨type⟩

⟨variant part⟩ ::= **case** ⟨tag field⟩ : ⟨type identifier⟩ **of** ⟨variant⟩ **{**; ⟨variant⟩**}***

⟨variant⟩ ::= **{** ⟨case label⟩ :**}**$^{\oplus}$ (⟨field list⟩) | **{** ⟨case label⟩**}**$^{\oplus}$

⟨case label⟩ ::= ⟨unsigned constant⟩

⟨tag field⟩ ::= ⟨identifier⟩

Examples:

```
record day: 1..31;
       month: 1..12;
       year: 0..2000
end

record name, firstname: alfa;
       age: 0..99;
end

record x, y: real;
       area: real;
case s: Shape of
triangle:  (side: real;
            inclination, angle1, angle2: Angle);
rectangle: (side1, side2: real;
            skew, angle3: Angle);
circle:    (diameter: real)
end
```

6.2.3. Powerset Types

A powerset type defines a range of values as the powerset of another scalar type, the so-called *base type*. Operators applicable to all powerset types are:

- $\vee$ union
- $\wedge$ intersection
- —   set difference
- **in**   membership

⟨powerset type⟩ ::= **powerset** ⟨type identifier⟩ | **powerset** ⟨subrange type⟩

6.2.4. File Types

A file type definition specifies a structure consisting of a sequence of components, all of the same type. The number of components, called the *length* of the file, is not fixed by the file type definition, i.e. each variable of that type may have a value with a different, varying length.

Associated with each variable of file type is a *file position* or *file pointer* denoting a specific element. The file position or the file pointer can be moved by certain standard procedures, some of which are only applicable when the file is in one of the three *modes*: input (being read), output (being written), or neutral (passive). Initially, a file variable is in the neutral mode.

⟨file type⟩ ::= **file of** ⟨type⟩

6.2.5. Class Types

A class type definition specifies a structure consisting of a class of components, all of the same type. The number of components is variable; the initial number upon declaration of a variable of class type is zero. Components are created (allocated) during execution of the program through the standard procedure *alloc*. The maximum number of components which can thus be created, however, is specified in the type definition.

$\langle$class type$\rangle ::=$ **class** $\langle$maxnum$\rangle$ **of** $\langle$type$\rangle$

$\langle$maxnum$\rangle ::= \langle$integer$\rangle$

6.2.6. Pointer Types

A pointer type is associated with every variable of class type. Its values are the potential pointers to the components of that class variable (cf. 7.5), and the pointer constant **nil**, designating no component. A pointer type is said to be *bound* to its class variable.

$\langle$pointer type$\rangle ::= \uparrow\langle$class variable$\rangle$

$\langle$class variable$\rangle ::= \langle$variable$\rangle$

Examples of type definitions:

```
Color    = (red, yellow, green, blue)
Sex      = (male, female)
Charfile = file of char
Shape    = (triangle, rectangle, circle)
Card     = array [1..80] of char
Complex  = record realpart, imagpart: real end
Person   = record name, firstname: alfa;
                  age: integer;
                  married: Boolean;
                  father, youngestchild, eldersibling: ↑family;
           case s: Sex of
           male: (enlisted, bold: Boolean);
           female: (pregnant: Boolean;
                  size: array [1..3] of integer)
           end
```

7. Declarations and Denotations of Variables

Variable declarations consist of a list of identifiers denoting the new variables, followed by their type.

$\langle$variable declaration$\rangle ::= \langle$identifier$\rangle$ **{** , $\langle$identifier$\rangle$**}*** : $\langle$type$\rangle$

Two *standard file variables* can be assumed to be predeclared as

input, output: **file of** *char*

The file *input* is restricted to input mode (reading only), and the file *output* is restricted to output mode (writing only). A Pascal program should be regarded as a procedure with these two variables as formal parameters. The corresponding actual parameters are expected either to be the standard input and output media of the computer installation, or to be specifyable in the system command activating the Pascal system.

Examples:

x, y, z: *real*
u, v: *Complex*
i, j: *integer*
k: 0..9
p, q: *Boolean*
operator: (*plus, times, absval*)
a: **array** [0..63] **of** *real*
b: **array** [*Color, Boolean*] **of**
       record *occurrence*: *integer*;
           appeal: *real*
      end
c: *Color*
f: **file of** *Card*
hue1, hue2: **powerset** *Color*
family: **class** 100 **of** *Person*
p1, p2: ↑*family*

Denotations of variables either denote an entire variable or a component of a variable.

⟨variable⟩ ::= ⟨entire variable⟩ | ⟨component variable⟩

7.1. Entire Variables

An entire variable is denoted by its identifier.

⟨entire variable⟩ ::= ⟨variable identifier⟩
⟨variable identifier⟩ ::= ⟨identifier⟩

7.2. Component Variables

A component of a variable is denoted by the denotation for the variable followed by a selector specifying the component. The form of the selector depends on the structuring type of the variable.

⟨component variable⟩ ::= ⟨indexed variable⟩ | ⟨field designator⟩ |
        ⟨current file component⟩ | ⟨referenced component⟩

7.2.1. Indexed Variables

A component of an *n*-dimensional array variable is denoted by the denotation of the variable followed by *n* index expressions.

⟨indexed variable⟩ ::= ⟨array variable⟩ [⟨expression⟩ {,⟨expression⟩}*]
⟨array variable⟩ ::= ⟨variable⟩

The types of the index expressions must correspond with the index types declared in the definition of the array type.

Examples:

$a\,[12]$
$a\,[i+j]$
$b\,[red,\ true]$
$b\,[succ\,(c),\ p \wedge q]$
$f \uparrow [1]$

7.2.2. Field Designators

A component of a record variable is denoted by the denotation of the record variable followed by the field identifier of the component.

⟨field designator⟩ ::= ⟨record variable⟩ . ⟨field identifier⟩
⟨record variable⟩ ::= ⟨variable⟩
⟨field identifier⟩ ::= ⟨identifier⟩

Examples:

$u\,.\,realpart$
$v\,.\,realpart$
$b\,[red,\ true]\,.\,appeal$
$p2 \uparrow .\,size$

7.2.3. Current File Components

At any time, only the one component determined by the current file position (or file pointer) is directly accessible.

⟨current file component⟩ ::= ⟨file variable⟩ ↑
⟨file variable⟩ ::= ⟨variable⟩

7.2.4. Referenced Components

Components of class variables are referenced by pointers.

⟨referenced component⟩ ::= ⟨pointer variable⟩ ↑
⟨pointer variable⟩ ::= ⟨variable⟩

Thus, if $p1$ is a pointer variable which is bound to a class variable v, $p1$ denotes that variable and its pointer value, whereas $p1 \uparrow$ denotes the component of v referenced by $p1$.

Examples:

$p1 \uparrow .\ father$
$p1 \uparrow .\ eldersibling \uparrow .\ youngestchild$

8. Expressions

Expressions are constructs denoting rules of computation for obtaining values of variables and generating new values by the application of operators. Expressions consist of operands, i.e. variables and constants, operators, and functions.

The rules of composition specify operator *precedences* according to four classes of operators. The operator ¬ has the highest precedence, followed by the so-called multiplying operators, then the so-called adding operators, and finally, with the lowest precedence, the relational operators. Sequences of operators of the same precedence are executed from left to right. These rules of precedence are reflected by the following syntax:

⟨factor⟩ ::= ⟨variable⟩ | ⟨unsigned constant⟩ | ⟨function designator⟩ |
    ⟨set⟩ | (⟨expression⟩) | ¬ ⟨factor⟩

⟨set⟩ ::= [⟨expression⟩ {, ⟨expression⟩}*] | [ ]

⟨term⟩ ::= ⟨factor⟩ | ⟨term⟩ ⟨multiplying operator⟩ ⟨factor⟩

⟨simple expression⟩ ::= ⟨term⟩ |
    ⟨simple expression⟩ ⟨adding operator⟩ ⟨term⟩ |
    ⟨adding operator⟩ ⟨term⟩

⟨expression⟩ ::= ⟨simple expression⟩ |
    ⟨simple expression⟩ ⟨relational operator⟩
    ⟨simple expression⟩

Expressions which are members of a set must all be of the same type, which is the base type of the set. [ ] denotes the empty set.

Examples:

Factors:
$$x$$
$$15$$
$$(x + y + z)$$
$$sin(x + y)$$
$$[red, c, green]$$
$$¬p$$

Terms:
$$x * y$$
$$i/(1 - i)$$
$$p \wedge q$$
$$(x \leq y) \wedge (y < z)$$

Simple expressions:
$$x + y$$
$$-x$$
$$hue1 \vee hue2$$
$$i * j + 1$$

Expressions:
$$x = 1.5$$
$$p \leqq q$$
$$(i < j) = (j < k)$$
$$c \text{ \textbf{in} } hue1$$

8.1. Operators

8.1.1. The Operator ¬

The operator ¬ applied to a *Boolean* operand denotes negation.

8.1.2. Multiplying Operators

$$\langle\text{multiplying operator}\rangle ::= * \,|\, / \,|\, \textbf{div} \,|\, \textbf{mod} \,|\, \wedge$$

operator	operation	type of operands	type of result
*	multiplication	$\begin{cases}real \text{ or} \\ integer\end{cases}$	*integer*, if both operands are of type *integer*, *real* otherwise
/	division	$\begin{cases}real \text{ or} \\ integer\end{cases}$	*real*
div	division with truncation	*integer*	*integer*
mod	$m \textbf{ mod } n = $ $m - ((m \textbf{ div } n) * n)$	*integer*	*integer*
∧	$\begin{cases}\text{logical "and"} \\ \text{set intersection}\end{cases}$	*Boolean* any powerset type T	*Boolean* T

8.1.3. Adding Operators

$$\langle\text{adding operator}\rangle ::= + \,|\, - \,|\, \vee$$

operator	operation	type of operands	type of result
+	addition	*real* or *integer*	*integer*, if both operands are of type *integer*, *real* otherwise
−	subtraction	*real* or *integer*	
−	set difference	any powerset type T	T
∨	$\begin{cases}\text{logical "or"} \\ \text{set union}\end{cases}$	*Boolean* any powerset type T	*Boolean* T

When used as operators with one operand only, − denotes sign inversion, and + denotes the identity operation.

8.1.4. Relational Operators

$$\langle \text{relational operator} \rangle ::= = \mid \neq \mid < \mid \leqq \mid \geqq \mid > \mid \textbf{in}$$

operator	type of operands	result
$=$ $\neq$	any type, except file and class types	*Boolean*
$<$ $>$ $\leqq$ $\geqq$	any scalar or subrange type	*Boolean*
in	any scalar or subrange type and its powerset type respectively	*Boolean*

Notice that all scalar types define *ordered* sets of values. In particular, *false* $<$ *true*. The operators $\leqq$ and $\geqq$ may also be used for comparing values of powerset type, and then denote set inclusion $\subseteq$ and $\supseteq$ respectively.

8.2. Function Designators

A function designator specifies the activation of a function. It consists of the identifier designating the function and a list of actual parameters. The parameters are variables, expressions, procedures, and functions, and are substituted for the corresponding formal parameters (cf. 9.1.2., 10, and 11).

$$\langle \text{function designator} \rangle ::=$$
$$\langle \text{function identifier} \rangle \, (\langle \text{actual parameter} \rangle \, \{, \langle \text{actual parameter} \rangle\}*)$$
$$\langle \text{function identifier} \rangle ::= \langle \text{identifier} \rangle$$

Examples:

$Sum\,(a,\,100)$
$GCD\,(147,\,k)$
$sin\,(x+y)$
$eof\,(f)$

9. Statements

Statements denote algorithmic actions, and are said to be *executable*.

$$\langle \text{statement} \rangle ::= \langle \text{simple statement} \rangle \mid \langle \text{structured statement} \rangle$$

9.1. Simple Statements

A simple statement is a statement of which no part constitutes another statement.

$$\langle \text{simple statement} \rangle ::= \langle \text{assignment statement} \rangle \mid$$
$$\langle \text{procedure statement} \rangle \mid \langle \text{goto statement} \rangle$$

9.1.1. Assignment Statements

The assignment statement serves to replace the current value of a variable by a new value indicated by an expression. The assignment operator symbol is :=, pronounced as "becomes".

$$\langle \text{assignment statement} \rangle ::= \langle \text{variable} \rangle := \langle \text{expression} \rangle \mid$$
$$\langle \text{function identifier} \rangle := \langle \text{expression} \rangle$$

The variable (or the function) and the expression must be must be of identical type (but neither class nor file type), with the following exceptions permitted:

1. the type of the variable is *real*, and the type of the expression is *integer* or a subrange thereof.

2. the type of the expression is a subrange of the type of the variable.

Examples:

$$x := y + 2.5$$
$$p := (1 \leq i) \wedge (i < 100)$$
$$i := sqr(k) - (i * j)$$
$$hue := [blue, succ(c)]$$

9.1.2. Procedure Statements

A procedure statement serves to execute the procedure denoted by the procedure identifier. The procedure statement may contain a list of *actual parameters* which are substituted in place of their corresponding *formal parameters* defined in the procedure declaration (cf. 10). The correspondence is established by the positions of the parameters in the lists of actual and formal parameters respectively. There exist four kinds of parameters: variable-, constant-, procedure parameters (the actual parameter is a procedure identifier), and function parameters (the actual parameter is a function identifier).

In the case of variable parameters, the actual parameter must be a variable. If it is a variable denoting a component of a structured variable, the selector is evaluated when the substitution takes place, i.e. before the execution of the procedure. If the parameter is a constant parameter, then the corresponding actual parameter must be an expression.

$$\langle \text{procedure statement} \rangle ::= \langle \text{procedure identifier} \rangle \mid$$
$$\langle \text{procedure identifier} \rangle (\langle \text{actual parameter} \rangle$$
$$\{, \langle \text{actual parameter} \rangle\}^*)$$
$$\langle \text{procedure identifier} \rangle ::= \langle \text{identifier} \rangle$$
$$\langle \text{actual parameter} \rangle ::= \langle \text{expression} \rangle \mid \langle \text{variable} \rangle \mid$$
$$\langle \text{procedure identifier} \rangle \mid \langle \text{function identifier} \rangle$$

Examples:

$$next$$
$$Transpose\ (a, n, m)$$
$$Bisect\ (sin, -1, +2, x, q)$$

9.1.3. Goto Statements

A goto statement serves to indicate that further processing should continue at another part of the program text, namely at the place of the label. Labels can be placed in front of statements being part of a compound statement (cf. 9.2.1.).

⟨goto statement⟩ ::= **goto** ⟨label⟩

⟨label⟩ ::= ⟨integer⟩

The following restriction holds concerning the applicability of labels:

The scope (cf. 10) of a label is the procedure declaration within which it is defined. It is therefore not possible to jump into a procedure.

9.2. Structured Statements

Structured statements are constructs composed of other statements which have to be executed either in sequence (compound statement), conditionally (conditional statements), or repeatedly (repetitive statements).

⟨structured statement⟩ ::= ⟨compound statement⟩ |
      ⟨conditional statement⟩ | ⟨repetitive statement⟩ |
      ⟨with statement⟩

9.2.1. Compound Statements

The compound statement specifies that its component statements are to be executed in the same sequence as they are written. Each statement may be preceded by a label which can be referenced by a goto statement (cf. 9.1.3.).

⟨compound statement⟩ ::=
  begin ⟨component statement⟩ **{**;⟨component statement⟩**}* end**

⟨component statement⟩ ::=
  ⟨statement⟩ | ⟨label definition⟩ ⟨statement⟩

⟨label definition⟩ ::= ⟨label⟩ :

Example:

  begin $z := x$; $x := y$; $y := z$ **end**

9.2.2. Conditional Statements

A conditional statement selects for execution a single one of its component statements.

⟨conditional statement⟩ ::= ⟨if statement⟩ | ⟨case statement⟩

9.2.2.1. If Statements

The if statement specifies that a statement be executed only if a certain condition (*Boolean* expression) is *true*. If it is *false*, then either no statement is to be executed, or the statement following the symbol **else** is to be executed.

⟨if statement⟩ ::= **if** ⟨expression⟩ **then** ⟨statement⟩ |
      if ⟨expression⟩ **then** ⟨statement⟩ **else** ⟨statement⟩

The expression between the symbols **if** and **then** must be of type *Boolean*.

4•

Note: The syntactic ambiguity arising from the construct

if ⟨expression—1⟩ **then if** ⟨expression—2⟩ **then** ⟨statement—1⟩
    else ⟨statement—2⟩

is resolved by interpreting the construct as equivalent to

if ⟨expression—1⟩ **then**
    begin if ⟨expression—2⟩ **then** ⟨statement—1⟩ **else** ⟨statement—2⟩
    end

Examples:

if $x < 1.5$ **then** $z := x + y$ **else** $z := 1.5$
if $p \neq$ **nil then** $p := p\uparrow.father$

9.2.2.2. Case Statements

The case statement consists of an expression (the selector) and a list of statements, each being labeled by a constant of the type of the selector. It specifies that the one statement be executed whose label is equal to the current value of the selector.

⟨case statement⟩ ::= **case** ⟨expression⟩ **of**
      ⟨case list element⟩ **{**; ⟨case list element⟩**}* end**
⟨case list element⟩ ::= **{** ⟨case label⟩:**}**$^{\oplus}$ ⟨statement⟩ | **{** ⟨case label⟩:**}**$^{\oplus}$

Example:

case *operator* **of**
plus: $x := x + y$;
times: $x := x * y$;
absval: **if** $x < 0$ **then** $x := -x$
end

9.2.3. Repetitive Statements

Repetitive statements specify that certain statements are to be executed repeatedly. If the number of repetitions is known beforehand, i.e. before the repetitions are started, the for statement is the appropriate construct to express this situation; otherwise the while or repeat statement should be used.

⟨repetitive statement⟩ ::= ⟨while statement⟩ |
      ⟨repeat statement⟩ | ⟨for statement⟩

9.2.3.1. While Statements

⟨while statement⟩ ::= **while** ⟨expression⟩ **do** ⟨statement⟩

The expression controlling repetition must be of type *Boolean*. The statement is repeatedly executed until the expression becomes *false*. If its value is *false* at the beginning, the statement is not executed at all. The while statement

while e **do** S

is equivalent to

> **if** e **then**
>   **begin** S;
>   **while** e **do** S
>   **end**

Examples:

> **while** $(a[i] \neq x) \wedge (i < n)$ **do** $i := i + 1$
> **while** $i > 0$ **do**
> **begin if** $odd(i)$ **then** $z := z * x$;
> $i := i$ **div** 2;
> $x := sqr(x)$
> **end**

9.2.3.2. Repeat Statements

⟨repeat statement⟩ ::=
    repeat ⟨statement⟩ **{**;⟨statement⟩**}* until** ⟨expression⟩

The expression controlling repetition must be of type *Boolean*. The sequence of statements between the symbols **repeat** and **until** is repeatedly (and at least once) executed until the expression becomes *true*. The repeat statement

> **repeat** S **until** e

is equivalent to

> **begin** S;
>   **if** $\neg e$ **then**
>   **repeat** S **until** e
> **end**

Examples:

> **repeat** $k := i$ **mod** j;
> $i := j$;
> $j := k$
> **until** $j = 0$

> **repeat** $get(f)$
> **until** $(f \uparrow = a) \vee eof(f)$

9.2.3.3. For Statements

The for statement indicates that a statement is to be repeatedly executed while a progression of values is assigned to a variable which is called the *control variable* of the for statement.

> ⟨for statement⟩ ::= **for** ⟨control variable⟩ := ⟨for list⟩ **do** ⟨statement⟩
> ⟨for list⟩ ::= ⟨initial value⟩ **to** ⟨final value⟩ |
>   ⟨initial value⟩ **downto** ⟨final value⟩

⟨control variable⟩ ::= ⟨identifier⟩
⟨initial value⟩ ::= ⟨expression⟩
⟨final value⟩ ::= ⟨expression⟩

The control variable, the initial value, and the final value must be of the same scalar type (or subrange thereof).

A for statement of the form

for $v := e1$ **to** $e2$ **do** S

is equivalent to the statement

if $e1 \leq e2$ **then**
begin $v := e1$; S;
    for $v := succ(v)$ **to** $e2$ **do** S
end

and a for statement of the form

for $v := e1$ **downto** $e2$ **do** S

is equivalent to the statement

if $e1 \geq e2$ **then**
begin $v := e1$; S;
    for $v := pred(v)$ **downto** $e2$ **do** S
end

Note: The repeated statement S must alter neither the value of the control variable nor the final value.

Examples:

for $i := 2$ **to** 100 **do if** $a[i] > max$ **then** $max := a[i]$
for $i := 1$ **to** n **do**
for $j := 1$ **to** n **do**
begin $x := 0$;
    for $k := 1$ **to** n **do** $x := x + a[i, k] * b[k, j]$;
    $c[i, j] := x$
end
for $c := red$ **to** $blue$ **do** $try(c)$

9.2.4. With Statements

⟨with statement⟩ ::= **with** ⟨record variable⟩ **do** ⟨statement⟩

Within the component statement of the with statement, the components (fields) of the record variable specified by the with clause can be denoted by their field identifier only, i.e. without preceding them with the denotation of the entire record variable. The with clause effectively opens the scope containing the field identifiers of the specified record variable, so that the field identifiers may occur as variable identifiers.

Example:

```
with date do
begin
  if month = 12 then
  begin month := 1; year := year + 1
  end else month := month + 1
end
```

This statement is equivalent to

```
begin
  if date.month = 12 then
  begin date.month := 1; date.year := date.year + 1
  end else date.month := date.month + 1
end
```

10. Procedure Declarations

Procedure declarations serve to define parts of programs and to associate identifiers with them so that they can be activated by procedure statements. A procedure declaration consists of the following parts, any of which, except the first and the last, may be empty:

⟨procedure declaration⟩ ::=
  ⟨procedure heading⟩
  ⟨constant definition part⟩ ⟨type definition part⟩
  ⟨variable declaration part⟩
  ⟨procedure and function declaration part⟩ ⟨statement part⟩

The procedure heading specifies the identifier naming the procedure and the formal parameter identifiers (if any). The parameters are either constant-, variable, procedure-, or function parameters (cf. also 9.1.2.).

⟨procedure heading⟩ ::= **procedure** ⟨identifier⟩ ; |
  procedure ⟨identifier⟩ (⟨formal parameter section⟩
  { ; ⟨formal parameter section⟩}*) ;
⟨formal parameter section⟩ ::=
  ⟨parameter group⟩ |
  const ⟨parameter group⟩ { ; ⟨parameter group⟩}* |
  var ⟨parameter group⟩ { ; ⟨parameter group⟩}* |
  function ⟨parameter group⟩ |
  procedure ⟨identifier⟩ { , ⟨identifier⟩}*
⟨parameter group⟩ ::= ⟨identifier⟩ { , ⟨identifier⟩}* : ⟨type identifier⟩

A parameter group without preceding specifier implies constant parameters.

The constant definition part contains all constant synonym definitions local to the procedure.

⟨constant definition part⟩ ::= ⟨empty⟩ |
  const ⟨constant definition⟩ { , ⟨constant definition⟩}*;

The type definition part contains all type definitions which are local to the procedure declaration.

⟨type definition part⟩ ::= ⟨empty⟩ |
  type ⟨type definition⟩ **{**;⟨type definition⟩**}***;

The variable declaration part contains all variable declarations local to the procedure declaration.

⟨variable declaration part⟩ ::= ⟨empty⟩ |
  var ⟨variable declaration⟩ **{**;⟨variable declaration⟩**}***;

The procedure and function declaration part contains all procedure and function declarations local to the procedure declaration.

⟨procedure and function declaration part⟩ ::=
  { ⟨procedure or function declaration⟩;**}***
⟨procedure or function declaration⟩ ::=
  ⟨procedure declaration⟩ | ⟨function declaration⟩

The statement part specifies the algorithmic actions to be executed upon an activation of the procedure by a procedure statement.

⟨statement part⟩ ::= ⟨compound statement⟩

All identifiers introduced in the formal parameter part, the constant definition part, the type definition part, the variable-, procedure or function declaration parts are *local* to the procedure declaration which is called the *scope* of these identifiers. They are not known outside their scope. In the case of local variables, their values are undefined at the beginning of the statement part.

The use of the procedure identifier in a procedure statement within its declaration implies recursive execution of the procedure.

Examples of procedure declarations:

```
procedure readinteger (var x: integer);
    var i, j: integer;
begin i := 0;
    while (input↑ ≥ '0') ∧ (input↑ ≤ '9') do
    begin j := int (input↑) − int ('0');
            i := i * 10 + j;
            get (input)
    end;
    x := i
end

procedure Bisect (function f: real; const low, high: real;
    var, zero: real; p: Boolean);
    var a, b, m: real;
begin a := low;  b := high;
    if (f(a) ≥ 0) ∨ (f(b) ≤ 0) then p := false else
```

```
    begin p := true;
       while abs (a − b) > eps do
       begin m := (a + b)/2;
          if f(m) > 0 then b := m else a := m
       end;
       zero := a
    end
end

procedure GCD (m, n: integer; var, x, y, z: integer);  {m ≥ 0, n > 0}
var a1, a2, b1, b2, c, d, q, r: integer;
begin {Greatest Common Divisor x of m and n,
       Extended Euclid's Algorithm, cf. [4], p. 14}
   c := m;  d := n;
   a1 := 0;   a2 := 1;   b1 := 1;   b2 := 0;
   while d ≠ 0 do
   begin {a1*m + b1*n = d, a2*m + n2*n = c,
          gcd (c, d) = gcd (m, n)}
          q := c div d;  r := c mod d;
          {c = q*d + r, gcd (d, r) = gcd (m, n)}
          a2 := a2 − q*a1;  b2 := b2 − q*b1;
          {a2*m + b2*n = r, a1*m + b1*n = d}
          c := d;   d := r;
          r := a1;   a1 := a2;   a2 := r;
          r := b1;   b1 := b2;   b2 := r;
          {a1*m + b1*n = d, a2*m + b2*n = c,
          gcd (c, d) = gcd (m, n)}
   end;
   {gcd (c, 0) = c = gcd (m, n)}
   x := c;   y := a2;   z := b2
   {x = gcd (m, n), y*m + z*n = gcd (m, n)}
end
```

10.1. Standard Procedures

Standard procedures are supposed to be predeclared in every implementation
of Pascal. Any implementation may feature additional predeclared procedures.
Since they are, as all standard quantities, assumed as declared in a scope surrounding the Pascal program, no conflict arises form a declaration redefining
the same identifier within the program. The standard procedures are listed and
explained below.

10.1.1. File Positioning Procedures

put (f)   advances the file pointer of file *f* to the next file component. It is
only applicable, if the file is either in the output or in the neutral
mode. The file is put into the output mode.

get (*f*)   advances the file pointer of file *f* to the next file component. It is only applicable, if the file is either in the input or in the neutral mode. If there does not exist a next file component, the end-of-file condition arises, the value of the variable denoted by *f*↑ becomes undefined, and the file is put into the neutral mode.

reset (*f*)   the file pointer of file *f* is reset to its beginning, and the file is put into the neutral mode.

10.1.2. Class Component Allocation Procedure

alloc (*p*)   allocates a new component in the class to which the pointer variable *p* is bound, and assigns the pointer designating the new component to *p*. If the component type is a record type with variants, the form

alloc (*p, t*)   can be used to allocate a component of the variant whose tag field value is *t*. However, this allocation does not imply an assignment to the tag field. If the class is already compleately allocated, the value **nil** will be assigned to *p*.

10.1.3. Data Transfer Procedures

Assuming that *a* is a character array variable, *z* is an alfa variable, and *i* is an integer expression, then

pack (*a, i, z*)   packs the *n* characters $a[i] \ldots a[i+n-1]$ into the alfa variable *z* (for *n* cf. 6.1.1.), and

unpack (*z, a, i*)   unpacks the alfa value *z* into the variables $a[i] \ldots a[i+n-1]$.

11. Function Declarations

Function declarations serve to define parts of the program which compute a scalar value or a pointer value. Functions are activated by the evaluation of a function designator (cf. 8.2) which is a constituent of an expression. A function declaration consists of the following parts, any of which, except the first and the last, may be empty (cf. also 10.).

⟨function declaration⟩ ::=
  ⟨function heading⟩
  ⟨constant definition part⟩ ⟨type definition part⟩
  ⟨variable declaration part⟩
  ⟨procedure and function declaration part⟩ ⟨statement part⟩

The function heading specifies the identifier naming the function, the formal parameters of the function (note that there must be at least one parameter), and the type of the (result of the) function.

⟨function heading ::= **function** ⟨identifier⟩ (⟨formal parameter section⟩
                 {;⟨formal parameter section⟩}*) : ⟨result type⟩ ;
⟨result type⟩ ::= ⟨type identifier⟩

The type of the function must be a scalar or a subrange type or a pointer type. Within the function declaration there must be at least one assignment statement assigning a value to the function identifier. This assignment determines the result of the function. Occurrence of the function identifier in a function designator within its declaration implies recursive execution of the function. Within the statement part no assignment must occur to any variable which is not local to the function. This rule also excludes assignments to parameters.

Examples:

```
function Sqrt(x: real): real;
   var x0, x1: real;
begin x1 := x;   {x > 1, Newton's method}
   repeat x0 := x1; x1 := (x0 + x/x0)*0.5
      {x0² - 2*x1*x0 + x = 0}
   until abs(x1 - x0) ≤ eps;
   {(x0 - eps) ≤ x1 ≤ (x0 + eps),
   (x - 2*eps*x0) ≤ x0² ≤ (x + 2*eps*x0)}
   Sqrt := x0
end

function Max(a: vector; n: integer): real;
   var x: real;   i: integer;
begin x := a[1];
   for i := 2 to n do
   begin {x = max(a₁ ... a_{i-1})}
      if x < a[i] then x := a[i]
      {x = max(a₁ ... a_i)}
   end;
   {x = max(a₁ ... a_n)}
   Max := x
end

function GCD(m, n: integer): integer;
begin if n = 0 then GCD := m else GCD := GCD(n, m mod n)
end

function Power(x: real; y: integer): real;   {y ≥ 0}
   var w, z: real;   i: integer;
begin w := x;   z := 1;   i := y;
   while i ≠ 0 do
   begin {z*wⁱ = x^y}
      if odd(i) then z := z*w;
      i := i div 2;   {z*w^{2i} = x^y}
      w := sqr(w)   {z*wⁱ = x^y}
   end;
   {i = 0, z = x^y}
   Power := z
end
```

11.1. Standard Functions

Standard functions are supposed to be predeclared in every implementation of Pascal. Any implementation may feature additional predeclared functions (cf. also 10.1.).

The standard functions are listed and explained below:

11.1.1. Arithmetic Functions

abs (*x*) computes the absolute value of *x*. The type of *x* must be either *real* or *integer*, and the type of the result is the type of *x*.

sqr (*x*) computes x^2. The type of *x* must be either *real* or *integer*, and the type of the result is the type of *x*.

sin (*x*)
cos (*x*)
exp (*x*) | the type of *x* must be either *real* or *integer*, and the type of the result
ln (*x*) | is *real*
sqrt (*x*)
arctan (*x*)

11.1.2. Predicates

odd (*x*) the type of *x* must be *integer*, and the result is *x* **mod** $2 = 1$

eof (*f*) indicates, whether the file *f* is in the end-of-file status.

11.1.3. Transfer Functions

trunc (*x*) *x* must be of type *real*, and the result is of type *integer*, such that $abs(x) - 1 < trunc(abs(x)) \leq abs(x)$

int (*x*) *x* must be of type *char*, and the result (of type *integer*) is the ordinal number of the character *x* in the defined character set.

chr (*x*) *x* must be of type *integer*, and the result (of *type char*) is the character whose ordinal number is *x*.

11.1.4. Further Standard Functions

succ (*x*) *x* is of any scalar or subrange type, and the result is the successor value of *x* (if it exists).

pred (*x*) *x* is of any scalar or subrange type, and the result is the predecessor value of *x* (if it exists).

12. Programs

A Pascal program has the form of a procedure declaration without heading (cf. also 7.4.).

⟨program⟩ ::= ⟨constant definition part⟩⟨type definition part⟩
           ⟨variable declaration part⟩
           ⟨procedure and function declaration part⟩⟨statement part⟩.

13. Pascal 6000

The version of the language Pascal which is processed by its implementation on the CDC 6000 series of computers is described by a number of amendments to the preceding Pascal language definition. The amendments specify extensions and restrictions and give precise definitions of certain standard data types. The section numbers used hereafter refer to the corresponding sections of the language definition.

3. Vocabulary

Only capital letters are available in the basic vocabulary of symbols. The symbol **eol** is added to the vocabulary. Symbols which consist of a sequence of underlined letters are called *word-delimiters*. They are written in Pascal 6000 without underlining and without any surrounding escape characters. Blanks or end-of-lines may be inserted anywhere except within $:=$, word-delimiters, identifiers, and numbers. The symbol $_{10}$ is written as '.

4. Identifiers

Only the 10 first symbols of an identifier are significant. Identifiers not differing in the 10 first symbols are considered as equal. Word-delimiters must not be used as identifiers. At least one blank space must be inserted between any two word-delimiters or between a word-delimiter and an adjacent identifier.

6. Data Types

6.1.1. Standard Scalar Types

integer   is defined as
   type *integer* $= -2^{48} + 1 .. 2^{48} - 1$

real   is defined according to the CDC 6000 floating point format specifications. Arithmetic operations on real type values imply rounding.

char   is defined by the CDC 6000 display code character set. This set is incremented by the character denoted by **eol**, signifying end-of-line.

The ordered set is:

$$
\begin{array}{cccccccccc}
\textbf{eol} & A & B & C & D & E & F & G & H & I \\
J & K & L & M & N & O & P & Q & R & S \\
T & U & V & W & X & Y & Z & 0 & 1 & 2 \\
3 & 4 & 5 & 6 & 7 & 8 & 9 & + & - & * \\
/ & (&) & \$ & = & \sqcup & , & . & ' & [\\
] & : & \neq & \{ & \vee & \wedge & \uparrow & \} & < & > \\
\leq & \geq & \neg & ; & & & & & &
\end{array}
$$

(Note that the characters ' { } are special features on the printers of the ETH installation, and correspond to the characters $\equiv$ $\ulcorner$ $\downarrow$ at standard CDC systems.)

alfa   the number n of characters packed into an alfa value is 10 (cf. 6.1.1.).

6.2.3. Powerset Types

The base type of a powerset type must be either

1. a scalar type with less than 60 values, or

2. a subrange of the type *integer*, with a minimum element $min(T) \geqq 0$ and a maximum element $max(T) < 59$, or

3. a subrange of the type char with the maximum element $max(T) < \text{'}>\text{'}$.

6.2.4. and 6.2.5. File and Class Types

No component of any structured type can be of a file type or of a class type.

7. Variable Declarations

File variables declared in the main program may be restricted to either input or output mode by appending the specifiers

$$[in] \quad \text{or} \quad [out]$$

to the file identifier in its declaration. Files restricted to input mode (input files) are expected to be Permanent Files attached to the job by the SCOPE Attach command, and files restricted to output mode may be catalogued as Permanent Files by the SCOPE Catalog command. In both commands, the file identifier is to be used as the Logical File Name [5].

10. and 11. Procedure and Function Declarations

A procedure or a function which contains local file declarations must not be activated recursively.

14. Glossary

actual parameter	9.1.2.	field identifier	7.2.2.
adding operator	8.1.3.	field list	6.2.2.
array type	6.2.1.	file type	6.2.4.
array variable	7.2.1.	file variable	7.2.3.
assignment statement	9.1.1.	final value	9.2.3.3.
case label	6.2.2.	fixed part	6.2.2.
case list element	9.2.2.2.	for list	9.2.3.3.
case statement	9.2.2.2.	for statement	9.2.3.3.
class type	6.2.5.	formal parameter	
class variable	6.2.6.	section	10.
component statement	9.2.1.	function declaration	11.
component type	6.2.1.	function designator	8.2.
component variable	7.2.	function heading	11.
compound statement	9.2.1.	function identifier	8.2.
conditional statement	9.2.2.	goto statement	9.1.3.
constant	5.	identifier	4.
constant definition	5.	if statement	9.2.2.1.
constant definition part	10.	index type	6.2.1.
control variable	9.2.3.3.	indexed variable	7.2.1.
current file component	7.2.3.	initial value	9.2.3.3.
digit	3.	integer	4.
entire variable	7.1.	label	9.1.3.
expression	8.	label definition	9.2.1.
factor	8.	letter	3.
field designator	7.2.2.	letter or digit	4.

The author gratefully acknowledges his indeptedness to C. A. R. Hoare for his many valuable suggestions concerning overall design strategy as well as details, and for his critical scrutiny of this paper.

References

1. Naur, P.: Report on the algorithmic language ALGOL 60. Comm ACM **3**, 299–314 (1960).
2. Report on Subset ALGOL 60 (IFIP): Comm. ACM **7**, 626–628 (1964).
3. Wirth, N., Hoare, C. A. R.: A contribution to the development of ALGOL. Comm. ACM **9**, 413–432 (1966).
4. Knuth, D. E.: The art of computer programming, Vol. 1. Addison-Wesley 1968.
5. Control Data 6000 Computer Systems, SCOPE Reference Manual, Pub. No. 60189400.

Prof. Dr. N. Wirth
Eidgenössische Technische Hochschule
Fachgruppe Computer-Wissenschaften
Clausiusstraße 55
CH-8006 Zürich
Schweiz

Critical Comments on the Programming Language Pascal

A. N. Habermann

Received May 3, 1973

Summary. The programming language Pascal is claimed to be more suitable than other languages for "teaching programming as a systematic discipline". However, an investigation of the Reports on the Pascal language reveals that it suffers as much from ill-defined constructs as many of the languages to which it is supposed to offer an alternative. Problems with the language are caused primarily by the confusion of ranges, types and structures and by the phenomena associated with goto statements.

1. Introduction

The design of the programming language Pascal was based on the combination of two principal aims: to create "a language suitable to teach programming as a systematic discipline", but at the same time a language that can be implemented as a reliable and efficient programming system [1].

Pascal is supposed not to contain the features and constructs of other languages that are hard to explain and are said to be an "insult to minds trained in systematic reasoning". Contrary to this statement we will see that on the one hand some useful constructs of other languages that are not hard to explain have been left out of Pascal, whereas Pascal, on the other hand, has features that are hard to explain and hinder the user in systematic programming.

We argue first that some useful and well understood constructs have not been incorporated in Pascal. Secondly we go through a simple programming exercise which shows that using Pascal as a teaching tool causes problems similar to the ones caused by using any other language. Subsequently, we discuss the major inadequacies of the language which are found in labels and **goto** statements, in confusing ranges, types and structures, and in procedures, functions and parameter passing. Finally, we examine the presentation of the syntax definition and the description of the semantics in the Revised Report [2].

2. Useful Constructs Not Incorporated in Pascal

2.1. Block Structure

A sound programming principle is to declare a variable at the place where it is used. In a sorting program, for instance, a certain part of the program can be understood as "merge two ordered sections of length p and q into one ordered section of length $p + q$". The merging process needs some local pointers to carry out the ordering. Programming such a sorting problem in a constructive and systematic way requires that the action of merging two sections can be written as a module that fits in an environment to which only the external specification of that module is relevant. The internal structure (to which the declaration of such pointers clearly belongs) ought to be of no concern (and definitely not accessible) to the environment. The notion of a program block as defined in ALGOL 60 [3] is a clean and well-understood construct that is very useful for this purpose.

Runtime overhead of block entry and exit is sometimes mentioned as an argument against block-structure. Such overhead, however, is very small if erratic changes of control through **goto** statements are not possible. Moreover, there is no need for any overhead in the absence of dynamic arrays because space for local blocks can be fixed, overlaying parallel blocks, at procedure entry.

2.2. Dynamic Arrays

Changing the bounds of an array in Pascal implies recompilation of the program. It was conjectured that a resulting gain in execution speed would more than compensate for this inconvenience. Not only is this argument very doubtful, but the implications are much farther reaching than such a statement suggests.

It is well known that execution time for accessing array elements exceeds by far the time needed for processing an array declaration. Since the former hardly depends on whether or not an array can have variable bounds, a significant gain in execution speed is not to be expected.

The true reason for not incorporating dynamic arrays in Pascal is probably the fact that variable subranges can hardly be treated as a type.

The absence of dynamic arrays causes other inconveniences as well. Suppose we program a function LENGTH that computes the length of a vector.

```
type A = array [0 ... 63] of real; B = array [0 ... 100] of real;
var p: A; q: B;
function LENGTH (u: ...; n: integer): real;
    var sum: real;
begin sum: = 0;
    for i: = 0 to n do sum: = sum + u[i] * u[i];
    {Pascal has no operator for exponentiation}
    LENGTH: = sqrt (sum)
end
```

The problem with the definition of function LENGTH is that we *must* choose between specifying the formal parameter as either type A or type B and as a result the function can operate only on one of the two types. Thus, instead of one uniform function LENGTH for all vectors, we are forced to define as many different functions LENGTH as there are vectors with different numbers of elements. The choice of the procedure statement example Transpose (a, n, m) (Section 9.1.2) and of the function declaration Max (Section 11) suggests by lack of any further explanation that Pascal is in this respect as powerful as ALGOL 60. This is an unfair presentation of Pascal's reality.

2.3. **own** Variables

There are not many implementations of ALGOL 60 in existence that allow dynamic own arrays. If those are not implemented, storage allocation can be restricted to a mere stack discipline, whereas a heap in the ALGOL 68 sense is needed otherwise requiring considerable overhead at runtime for storage allocation and garbage collection [4]. But this is not to say that the concept of **own** is entirely useless. On the contrary, it serves the objective of writing well-structured programs and it can easily be defined as to allow an efficient implementation. The idea of specifying a named object as **own** is to make the name known only to the local environment, but in such a way that the last assigned value of the named object is retained across two successive activations of that local environment. Consider for instance the storage maintenance policy that uses the first fit algorithm as discussed in [5]. Storage consists of "free" and "used" blocks. When a request arrives for a free block of size s, the allocation agent searches for the first free block that is larger than s. Knuth observes that, if the agent starts at the beginning of the list of free blocks every time a request arrives, free blocks of small sizes tend to accumulate at the beginning of the list. But this can easily be avoided by resuming the search for a free block that is large enough at the very place where the search halted last time. The pointer that indicates this place is typically an object that should have been declared as an **own** variable of the allocation agent. Its value should not get lost in between two activations of the allocation agent, but the variable is of no concern to the environment in which the agent operates.

One can easily think of useful generalisations of the **own** concept to names that are shared by certain modules of a program, but which are inaccessible to other modules including the environment in which the former modules operate. It gives a module its private (or shared) section of global space. Observe that this **own** concept is basic to the structure and understanding of co-routines and concurrent processes.

Initialisation of an **own** object is rather inconvenient in ALGOL 60. This inconvenience can easily be eliminated by incorporating the initialisation in the declaration and placing the latter as a prefix of the environment in which the **own** object is used.

2.4. Conditional Expressions

ALGOL W has two sorts of conditional expressions, one of the form **if** BE **then** $e1$ **else** $e2$ and one of the form **case** IE **of** (expressionlist). It is conceivable that a teacher does not discuss these constructs when he goes through a first pass over a language with beginning programmers. But they do certainly make sense to a more advanced programmer who is concerned about a clear structure of his program. The statement

$$i := \textbf{if } i = 7 \textbf{ then } 1 \textbf{ else } i + 1$$

expresses more clearly that a value is assigned to i than the statement

$$\textbf{if } i = 7 \textbf{ then } i := 1 \textbf{ else } i := i + 1$$

in which it is more or less incidental that both alternative statements assign to i and do nothing else.

3. An Exercise in Programming in Pascal

A typical problem for an introductory programming course is the sieve of Eratosthenes, an algorithm for computing the prime numbers less than a given number N. The idea of Eratosthenes' algorithm is to place the numbers 2 to N in a row and then repeat the action of finding the leftmost number in the row followed by erasing it and all its multiples still left in the row. A prime number is found every time that the leftmost number in the row is determined.

The row of numbers 2 to N is naturally represented as an array A. Since the array bounds must be fixed, let us choose an arbitrary number for N, e.g., $N = 1999$. The elements of A are initialized with the value of their index. Erasing a number from the row can be implemented by assigning a zero to the corresponding element in A. Thus, a natural start of the program is:

```
begin var A : array [2 … 1999] of integer; i: 2 … 1999;
      for i := 2 to 1999 do A [i]:=i.
```

The innocent student in programming, for instance the one who studied program structuring as presented in [6], may think that the **for** statement could be replaced consistently by a **while** or **repeat** statement. But an unexpected difficulty shows up if i is declared of subrange type $2 … 1999$, because

```
begin var A : array [2 … 1999] of integer; i: 2 … 1999;
      i := 2; repeat A [i]:=i; i=i+1
         until i > 1999
```

results in an error indication at the operator $+$. Section 8.1.3 is clear at this point: it requires that both operands of an addition are of type integer or real and there are reasons to assume that a phrase as "or subrange thereof" has not accidently been omitted. For, Section 8.1.4 mentions subrange type explicitly in a similar place; furthermore, subrange type is not an instance of scalar type (see Section 6.1); finally, a type can hardly be associated with the result of an addition of two operands of subrange type.

It seems as if the problem can be avoided by writing $i := succ(i)$ instead of $i := i + 1$. But now the test $i > 1999$ fails at the very moment that the repeat statement is about to terminate, because $succ(i)$ is undefined when $i = 1999$ (Section 11.1.4). The proper solution is to declare variable i as integer instead of as subrange type. (A clever programmer will of course use the trick of declaring i of subrange $2 … 2000$ and not use element $A [2000]$).

However, the use of i as index expression is strictly speaking illegal when i is declared of type integer, because the type of i does not match the index type od array A (Section 6.2.1). If this were true, there is hardly a way around applying a trick as mentioned above. But the report is sufficiently vague at this point as to allow a different interpretation. The crucial phrase used in the report is that index expression and index type must "correspond" (Section 7.2.1), whereas in similar situations the phrasing "same type" or "identical type" is used (6.2.1, 8, 9.1.1, 9.2.3.3). The correct interpretation of the word "correspond" seems to be that at runtime the evaluated expression must happen to be in the subrange as determined by the array type definition. It will interest advocates of compile time checks to find out that this interpretation implies at least as much checking at runtime as when ranges are not considered as types.

Our previous experience suggests that we program the search for prime numbers by means of a **for** statement.

> **for** $i:=2$ **to** 1999 **do**
> **if** $A[i] \neq 0$ **then**
> **begin** $PRINT(i)$; erase all multiples of i **end**.

A new difficulty arises when we program "erase all multiples of i". We would like to go through array A in steps of i, but Pascal provides only a fixed step element of one or minus one. We can, of course, create a range that can be stepped through in steps of one and compute the index value into array A as a function of the successive elements of this range. We then get:

> **for** $k:=1$ **to** 1999 **div** i **do** $A[k*i]:=0$.

Programming "erase all multiples of i" this way incurs paying the price of an integer division and a multiplication that is repeatedly evaluated. We can avoid the latter at the cost of an additional variable that holds the value of the index expression. The declaration of this variable must be added to the program heading and it turns out that a subrange type cannot easily be used as type for any of the variables for which this would make sense.

A simpler program is obtained, after all, if "erase all multiples of i" is programmed as a **while** statement. We won't pursue, however, the details any further, because the program is not really important here. The purpose of the exercise was merely to show that a teacher who uses Pascal cannot avoid discussion of language peculiarities just as he would when he used another programming language.

4. Labels and **goto** statements

It is surprising that in the design of a tutorial language the issue of programming without **goto** statements is totally ignored. This does not seem to be very much in the spirit of structured programming as presented in [7]. But even so, the secondary aim of Pascal to provide a fast language system should have prevented inclusion of the **goto** statement because of the trouble it causes in a compiler, especially in a one pass compiler. An example of the difficulties a one pass compiler has to cope with because of labels and goto statements is sketched below.

> **procedure** P; **label** 1;
>   **procedure** Q;
>   **procedure** R; **begin** — **goto** 1; — **goto** 1; — **end** $\{R\}$;
>   **begin** — **goto** 1; — **goto** 1; — 1: **end** $\{Q\}$;
> **begin** — **goto** 1; — **goto** 1 — 1: **end** $\{P\}$;

A non-local label requires a forward declaration as in procedure P. It seems as if the goto statements in procedures Q and R refer to that label. However, the label at the end of Q definitely changes the interpretation of the goto statements in Q.

At this point we may conclude that the program is in error because label 1 should have been declared as global in the heading of procedure Q (Section 10). But further scanning leads ultimately to a label defined at the end of procedure P

4*

for which a global definition certainly makes sense, so the conclusion may be that no mistake was made after all. If the **goto** statement should be incorporated, it probably ought to be restricted to local labels. A separate provision can be made for jumping to error handling procedures that cause an automatic change of scope.

The Revised Report is sometimes vague and probably mistaken in other places about labels and the consequences of **goto** statements. First, it is doubtful whether or not a label in front of the statement part of a procedure declaration is considered as "in the procedure" or not (see 9.1.3). We assume it is, because otherwise the problem arises that control could be transferred to such a labelled statement without activation of the procedure. Second, in the Revised Report, the scope of a label is defined to be the procedure within which it is defined (Section 9.1.3). We assume that it is a mistake that functions are not mentioned in the scope rule for labels, because it seems at least as strange to jump into a function as into a procedure. Finally, the change in scope definition from compound statement, as in the original Report, to procedure and the absence of block structure together cause the notorious problem of jumping into a for statement. There is nothing in Pascal that prevents this and it seems hard to impose this restriction gracefully given the definition of Pascal.

The Revised Report resolves the ambiguity of labels and case labels as it existed in the original Report by using comma as separator between case labels, by using colon as separator between the rightmost case label and the statement label, and by restricting the number of statement labels to one.

The statement

```
4: case i of
   1, 2: 3: goto 3;
      4: goto 4;
   5: 6: goto 5;
   6: 5: goto 6
   end
```

is then correct according to the Revised Report, but realize that the first alternative is the only one that, once selected, repeats merely itself.

5. Subranges, Types, and Structures

The most unsatisfactory aspect of the Pascal language is the artificial unification of subranges, types and structures. This has a negative effect on the tutorial qualities of the language, it conveys a narrow view on types as merely ordered sets of values and it causes problems for the programmer as will be shown below.

It turns out that subranges cannot consistently be treated as types and vice-versa. E.g., using scalar types as subranges legalizes the declaration

var A: **array** [*real*] **of** *integer*.

The program exercise in the preceding section presented several examples of the difficulties that arise if subranges are strictly treated as types with respect to expressions, control ranges and index expressions. Such problems of interpretation are not just restricted to subranges of type integer as is shown in the example below.

> **case** *succ* (*d*) **of**
> Tuesday, Thursday, Friday: $S1$;
> Wednesday, Saturday: $S2$ **end**.

Suppose variable d is declared of subrange type workday, which is defined as subrange Monday ... Friday. The case expression *succ*(*d*) is also of type workday if we hold on to the strict interpretation, so the statement contains a type conflict because of label Saturday (Section 9.2.2.2). Another question is how *succ*(*d*) should be interpreted when $d =$ Friday, because Friday has no successor in type workday.

The idea of treating subranges as types is completely abandoned in case of assignment statements, because the type of the variable is even allowed to be a subrange of the type of the expression to be assigned (Section 9.1.1). One may expect that the same rules apply to value parameters, although nothing is said about subranges in Section 9.1.2.

Instead of considering subranges as types, the following rules should apply

a) the type of an object in Pascal declared of subrange type, st, is the type of the super-range of which st is a section;

b) ranges are evaluated and tested at runtime. It would be feasible to consider Pascal subrange declarations as type declarations with a range attribute for runtime checks.

Consider subsequently the treatment of structures as types. The Pascal language has four fixed structuring rules indicated by the word delimiters **array**, **record**, **set** and **file**. A useful rule in Pascal is the composition of array and record structures such as

> **type** $R =$ **record** *vec*: **array** $[1 \ldots 10]$ **of** integer **end**;
> $A =$ **array** $[1 \ldots 10]$ **of array** $[1 \ldots 10]$ **of** R; **var** $s:A$.

Although the Revised Report contains only one trivial example of accessing such structures or their components (Section 7.2.2), a Pascal compiler test showed that all useful constructs are accepted on the left hand side of an assignment statement: s, $s[i]$, $s[i][j]$, $s[i][j] \cdot vec$ and $s[i][j] \cdot vec[k]$.

However, the composition rule is not enough to justify the idea of treating structures as types. It turns out that in all relevant language constructs, except assignments, structures are, or ought to be, treated differently from simple type objects or pointers in Pascal. One has access to elements of a structure, but (of course) not to the structure of a simple typed object or pointer. Structured objects cannot be used as operands in algebraic expressions and should not be used as index expressions. The default parameter passing rule for simple types and pointers is by value, but the default rule for structures should be by reference. Range expressions in array declarations and control statements such as for statements or case statements can be of certain simple types, but should not be structures. So, the similarity of treatment in assignment statements does apparently not carry over to any other language construct.

The notion of simple type attempts to distinguish somewhat between types and structures, but, unfortunately, structures sneak in again by means of type identifiers. The declaration $v:A$ parses variable v as being of simple type (Section 6.1), so the declaration

$$\textbf{var } p\text{: } \textbf{array } [A] \textbf{ of } v$$

is legal in a procedure. Observe that this declaration is legal irrespective of how type A is defined! It could be defined as array or file or even a composition of those.

A useful distinction between types and structures is based on two principles a) a typed object is treated as an atomic entity, i.e. the type definition hides the structure of the objects, whereas elements of a structure can be accessed anywhere within the scope of existence; b) the major constituent of a structured type definition is the set of operations that can be performed on the objects of the type, whereas changes of structures are solely accomplished through operations on the elements.

Array and record are examples of structures, matrix and complex are examples of types. The representation of the latter can be changed radically without affecting the use of the typed objects.

The type hierarchy of Pascal is compared with the proper type hierarchy in the diagram below.

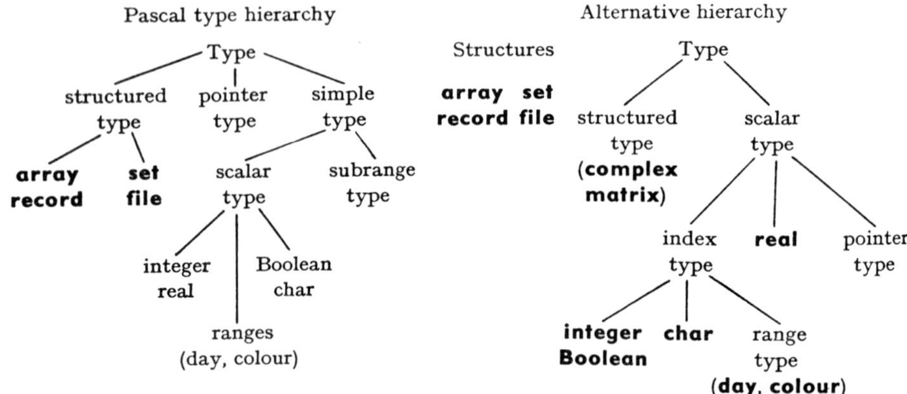

6. Procedures, Functions, and Parameters

In the original version of Pascal an attempt was made to avoid side-effects in functions by means of the rule that assignments to non-local variables were not allowed. This attempt failed, of course, because a side-effect could also be caused by a procedure call or by the use of pointer variables. The restriction has therefore been left out of the Revised Report (of which fact no notice is given in Section 11 in which functions are defined).

The difference between procedure and function is now so marginal that it is really not worth keeping. If it were useful to distinguish the two in the compiler in order to check whether or not an assignment to the function identifier occurs, the compiler could easily do so by means of the presence or absence of a function type identifier in the heading. A distinction, as in BLISS, between function and routine seems much more useful, because it serve two purposes, that of improving clarity of program structure and that of efficiency during compilation and execution [8].

We argued before that the default case of passing an array, file, set or record ought to be by reference, because call by value implies that a complete copy of the structure must be passed across to the procedure or function activation.

A concept that leads to much inefficiency, particularly at runtime, is the formal procedure or function parameter. Example

```
procedure P (procedure F);
    var p, q, r: integer; x, y, z: real;
begin — F (x, y, z); — F (p, q, z); — end;
procedure A (b, c, d: integer); begin — end {A};
procedure B (u: real; v: ↑R; w: f);
    begin — end {B};
P (A); — P (B); —
```

It is hardly possible to perform all the necessary type checking at compile time and therefore code must be generated to check the types at runtime. One solution is to require full specification of the formal procedure or function with respect to its type and the types of its parameters. This would be consistent with the requirement for full specification of any other formal. It would have made much more sense if attention had been paid to this kind of consideration and simple forms of procedures or functions than to eliminating side-effects or creating an artificial distinction between procedures and functions.

7. The Revised Report

The description of the semantics is rather inaccurate and incomplete at times. Some of the changes have been indicated, but several major revisions remain unmentioned. E.g.; the scope rules for labels in Section 9.1.3, the removal of the assignment restriction in functions, several type productions in Section 6.

The definition of ⟨base type⟩ is an example of the inaccuracy of the Report. The semantics of Section 6.2.3 describe ⟨base type⟩ as being not structured type. From the production ⟨type⟩ at the beginning of Section 6 we conclude that ⟨base type⟩ apparently goes to ⟨simple type⟩ or ⟨pointer type⟩; but the production in Section 6.2.3 for ⟨base type⟩ excludes ⟨pointer type⟩. And there are many more. The general experience is that one can start at an arbitrary point in the Revised Report on Pascal and will inevitably find a little mistake or a not precisely described notion after a while. A constant has no type; yet, the definitions of subrange and case statement depend on the type of constants. What are we to think of undefined notions as "corresponding types", "operations", "outside a procedure" etc. ? Right at the beginning the notation { } is introduced.

Yet, when it should be applied for the first time, the superfluous symbols * and $\oplus$ are used. First we learn that the functions succ and pred apply to arguments of scalar type. When subranges are introduced, nothing is said about these functions in spite of the fact that subrange type is not included in scalar type (Section 6.1). Yet in Section 11 we find that the functions succ and pred apply to both types. All these flaws, omissions and inconsistencies demonstrate that it may not be so easy to achieve precision and consistency in an informal description as was suggested in the introduction of the original Report (Section 1).

Conclusion

The result of designing the Pascal language is disappointing in view of the high spirits and strong statements in the introduction of the original Report. It is nice that a programmer can define types, but a type should not merely be viewed as a value range. We saw that subranges can hardly be treated as types, while structures and types do not allow a similar treatment in any language construct except, apparently, in assignments.

Paying attention to tutorial qualities of a language is laudable, but unacceptable in this regard are the confusion of subranges, types and structures, the inclusion of **goto** statements and the inferior presentation of the language in the Revised Report. It is worthwhile to strive for a language that can be supported by an efficient programming system, but this objective should not have led to the exclusion of some well-defined concepts present in other languages, whereas it should have resulted in better specification and substitution rules for parameters and a useful distinction between functions and procedures.

It would be regrettable if Pascal is going to be fixed in its present state, as the introduction of the Revised Report seems to do. There are still many fundamental language design issues to be discussed in general. Among the practical points are:

grouping of statements by means of bracket pairs or control delimiters;

initialisation in declarations;

simple assignment operations of the sort "add to variable".

Among the major issues are:

type definitions as a template for structured objects (cf. mode and operation definitions ALGOL 68 [4] and the class concept in SIMULA 67 [9]);

structure definitions as a description of the access algorithm to elements of an instance of a structure;

control statements and rules for leaving scopes of control.

A small language of the Pascal sort can, of course, provide only limited capabilities with regard to these major issues. It is therefore acceptable that Pascal has fixed structuring rules, but viewing subranges and structures as types is a deplorable oversimplication. The value of the Pascal design and implementation effort is in stimulating research and development of language constructs in view of the present state of the art of programming. However, the language will defeat its purpose if it is going to be consolidated in its present form with all its flaws and inconsistencies for the sake of compatibility. Instead of presenting a particular language as **the** solace, we had better continue a discussion on language issues and analyse their impact on programming systems.

Acknowledgement. Comment by Profs. D. Gries and J. J. Horning has been most helpful to improve the presentation of this study.

References

1. Wirth, N.: The programming language Pascal. Acta Informatica **1**, 35–63 (1971)
2. Wirth, N.: The programming language Pascal (Revised Report). Berichte der Fachgruppe Computer-Wissenschaften, Eidgenössische Technische Hochschule, Zürich 1972
3. Naur, P. (ed.): Revised report on the algorithmic language ALGOL 60. Comm. ACM **6**, 1–17 (1963)
4. van Wijngaarden, A. (ed.): Report on the algorithmic language ALGOL 68. Num. Math. **14**, 79–218 (1969)
5. Knuth, D. E.: The art of computer programming, Vol. 1 (ch. 2). Reading (Mass.): Addison-Wesley 1968
6. Dijkstra, E. W.: A short introduction to the art of programming. Dept. of Mathematics, Technological University. Eindhoven, EWD 316, 1971
7. Dijkstra, E. W.: Notes on structured programming. In: Dahl, O. J., Dijkstra, E. W., and Hoare, C. A. R.: Structured programming. London: Academic Press 1972
8. Wulf, W. A., *et al.*: BLISS: A language for systems programming. Comm. ACM **14**, 780–790 (1971)
9. Dahl, O., *et al.*: Simula 67: Common base language. Norwegian Computing Center, University of Oslo 1967

Professor A. N. Habermann
Department of Computer Science
Carnegie-Mellon University
Pittsburgh, Pa. 15213
USA

Reprinted with permission from *Acta Informatica,* Vol. 4, No. 3, 1975, pp. 231-243.

More Comments on the Programming Language Pascal

O. Lecarme and P. Desjardins

Received June 17, 1974

Summary. A. N. Habermann recently published some "Critical comments on the programming language Pascal". His reproaches are principally that numerous constructs are ill-defined, that there is "confusion" amongst ranges, types and structures, and that the **goto** statement should have been abolished. The present reply successively deals with points that are clearly refutable, those which are debatable and those which constitute valid criticism. Its principal aim is to encourage the reader to form his own opinion.

1. Introduction

We read with much interest and some miscontentment the paper "Critical comments on the programming language Pascal" by A. N. Habermann [6]. The interest was instigated by our current involvement with this language, and the miscontentment occasioned by the (sometimes unduly) strong attacks the paper makes on a language we like. We like it because, for three years now, we have been using it intensively, with complete success, as a support for teaching introductory and advanced courses in computer science (a first course on programming, and courses on data structures, compilers and operating systems design), and as an implementation tool for a compiler writing system [19] and for another Pascal compiler [2].

The aim of the present reply is to correct the unfavourable impression that readers, without any knowledge of Pascal, could get from Habermann's criticisms. We will not follow his argumentation point by point, but rather classify the subject matter into four parts: clearly refutable points, points which are at least debatable, valid criticisms and finally misunderstandings and minor errors. Although this plan may occasionally cause some problems to the reader who tries to go through Habermann's paper simultaneously, we believe it to be the only logical one. Thus, we strongly urge the reader to go through the whole of Habermann's paper first, so that he can see the debate in the proper perspective.

Since all the key texts on Pascal can now easily be obtained, we encourage the reader to mould his own opinion by reading references [16, 12] and [25]. One should notice, however, that Habermann based his paper exclusively on the first version of the Revised Report [26] and only it (the Revised Report is now a part of [16]). The Axiomatic Description [12] was not available at the time he wrote his comments; this would allow for certain misinterpretations.

2. Refutable Points

In this section, we deal with points which are, in our opinion, clearly refutable, i.e. criticisms which resulted from a misinterpretation of the basic aims of Pascal or a misunderstanding of some major aspects of the language itself. It is possible that some people might have preferred a different repartition of points between this section and the following one.

2.1. Useful Constructs Not Included in Pascal

Habermann suggests four such constructs, but it would be very easy to continue adding constructs to the language indefinitely: Pascal does not contain **all** the constructs which may be considered useful, nor even all those present in other programming languages. This is because creation of an endless list of constructs is clearly not the right direction to follow for the development of better programming languages. The most unfortunate attempt in this direction is that of PL/I [14], and even its most irreclaimable addicts and most enthusiastic eulogists always seem to find more constructs to incorporate in it [4, 13, 22].

In fact, one of the principal strengths of Pascal is that it is a simple and concise language, including only what is vital for reaching its aims. We remind the reader that there are only two of them: to allow the teaching of programming as a systematic discipline, and at the same time to be implementable in a reliable and efficient way. These objectives are precisely the most difficult ones to reach when using languages which try to incorporate all "useful constructs". The author of Pascal has therefore severely restricted the number of facilities, and it is quite sure that almost everyone will find missing certain of his favourite constructs. Consequently, we find not valid as a whole the criticism that Pascal does not contain some feature or other. The individual importance of the specific "left out" constructs Habermann regrets constitutes yet another point, less decidable, which is deferred until Section 3.

2.2. An Exercise in Programming in Pascal

The simple exercise worked out for the reader by Habermann is supposed to prove that Pascal is a poor tool for teaching programming. All that such an example demonstrates is simply that it is possible to misuse Pascal, which is of course true for any tool. Consequently, we prefer to rework the part of the example which is given, to show that in actual Pascal no difficulties arise.

The problem is to compute prime numbers using the sieve of Eratosthenes. A comparison of the different algorithms available, even superficially, should be useful before trying to put down a solution [5, 28], but this precise algorithm is not so bad, and it has been particularly well investigated by Dijkstra [5], Hoare [9] and Wirth [16, 27].

Habermann chooses to represent the numbers between 2 and n by an array of integers, in which every element contains its own index: to remove a number from the sieve, one assigns a zero to the corresponding element. Although using the set structure of Pascal should be far better [9, 16], we shall use simply a Boolean array, not only because it seems more natural but because we will encounter the same problems with indexes as Habermann did. A natural way to start-off the program is:

```
const n = 1999;
type index = 2 .. n;
var A : array [index] of Boolean; i : index;
begin for i := 2 to n do A [i] := true
```

The constant and type declarations for *n* and *index* are not mandatory but very useful: they contribute to the clarity of the program; the number *1999* textually appears in only one place; a modification of the program to deal with *3000* or *200* numbers would require modification of the constant declaration only.

Using as pretext the ideas of Dijkstra [3], Habermann then proposes to replace the **for** statement by a **repeat** statement. This modification is completely useless, since the **for** statement is perfectly adapted to situations where the number of iterations is known before entering the loop. Moreover, the program could become less efficient, and surely be less clear. But the modification brings forth an interesting point: in a **repeat** or **while** loop simulating a **for** loop, the control variable needs to take on one more value than in the **for** loop. This is not inherent to Pascal but to the meaning of these statements. The natural solution in Pascal is to declare *i* on a subrange longer by one than the index type of *A*:

```
const n = 1999;
type index = 2 .. n; extendedindex = 1 .. n;
var A : array [index] of Boolean; i : extendedindex;
begin i := 1;
        repeat i := i + 1; A [i] := true
        until i = n
```

Furthermore, there is no problem in using the operator $+$, since all operators which are defined on integer operands also accept operands whose type is a subrange of the type *integer*. This is quite obvious; otherwise, there would have been no point in defining subrange types. Furthermore, all the above is clearly stated in the Axiomatic Description of Pascal [12], as we shall see in Section 2.3. Habermann deserves credit for having pointed out the problem, without ever having read the Axiomatic Description. Similarly, there would be no problem if we choose to write $i := succ(i)$ instead of $i := i + 1$: as a general rule the *succ* function does not depend on whether or not its argument was declared to be of a scalar type or of a subrange of that type. So in the case of $succ(i)$ when $i = 1999$, the successor value is defined since *1999* does have a successor in the base type *integer*. Finally, the fact that the index type of *A* is not the same as the type of *i* is no problem either; both have the same base type, i.e. *integer*, and the only validity condition for array references is that index values fall within array bounds, as in all programming languages. Of course, if the programmer wishes to forego the advantages obtained by using subrange types—namely the implicit checks upon assignment—, he may also declare *i* to be of type *integer*.

The next section of the program deals with the search for prime numbers, and is straightforward. Add a variable *k* of type $0 .. n$ (which can, for the sake of simplicity, serve also for i) then:

```
for i:= 2 to n do
if A [i] then
begin write (i);
      {erase all multiples of i:}
      k:= 0;
      while k≤n−i do
      begin k:= k+i; A [k]:= false end
end
```

Habermann's example stops here, consequently so does ours. The conclusion derived by Habermann was that "a teacher who uses Pascal cannot avoid discussion of language peculiarities just as he would when he used another programming language". We have already said at the beginning of the present section that one can, without proving anything, misuse any language. What seems more serious to us is that this section, as well as the remainder of Habermann's paper, places criticisms of the style of the Report, and criticisms of the language itself, on the same level, and incorrect interpretations which may result from the former are used to try to discredit the latter, by systematically using its possibilities at the wrong time.

2.3. Subranges and Types

One of the most original aspects of Pascal is the whole notion of type. To use the same terminology as Habermann, this one notion unifies different concepts which may be named "type" (the manner in which bit patterns must be interpreted), "range" (the set of possible values for a variable of the given type) and "structure" (a template for storing data). It is our intention to put off the discussion on structured types until Section 3.5, and to tackle here the rest of the question.

One must not fear that declaring a variable of subrange type makes that variable lose all the properties of the base type from which the subrange is taken. On the contrary, this variable inherits all the properties of the base type, plus the possibility of having run-time checks performed whenever values are assigned to that variable and also the property of possibly taking up less space in memory. Another most important point to understand is that the type of an expression is not always the same as the types of variables in it. This is true even in Fortran or Algol 60: for example, in Algol 60, $1/2$ is of type **real** while its operands are of type **integer**, and $1 < 2$ is of type **Boolean**. The Axiomatic Description of Pascal is perfectly clear on the matter. Given a scalar type T and a subrange type S extracted from T, if a and b are variables of type S and $\otimes$ an operator defined on type T, then the expression $a \otimes b$ is legal, and yields a result of type T. The assignment statement is handled in a similar way, but assignment of a value of type T to a variable of type S is not always legal.

Of course it is true that most of the validity checks involved in subrange types must be made at run time, but it is an easy thing to have them performed only when the user requests so (or better still, always have them made, unless the user explicitly says otherwise); moreover, they constitute an invaluable security device. It would be best to view such a dynamic check as nothing but application of the type transfer function into the subrange type, a function which happens to be only partial. Subranges have other important qualities. Their mnemonic and descriptive value is such that a well-written Pascal program generally does not contain integer variables: they are replaced by variables whose type is a subrange of type integer. Another important aspect is that they allow the user to control the space occupied by a variable of subrange type, for example when he includes one as an element of a packed structured type; this is much more general than the **long** and **short** attributes of **real** and **int** types in Algol 68 [23].

Section 5 of Habermann's paper concludes with a tree diagram supposed to represent the type hierarchy in Pascal. A more correct version of this diagram follows. It uses Hoare's terminology [7], since Pascal implements most of the ideas presented in this paper. Of course, this hierarchy is not **the** "proper" one, but only that of Pascal.

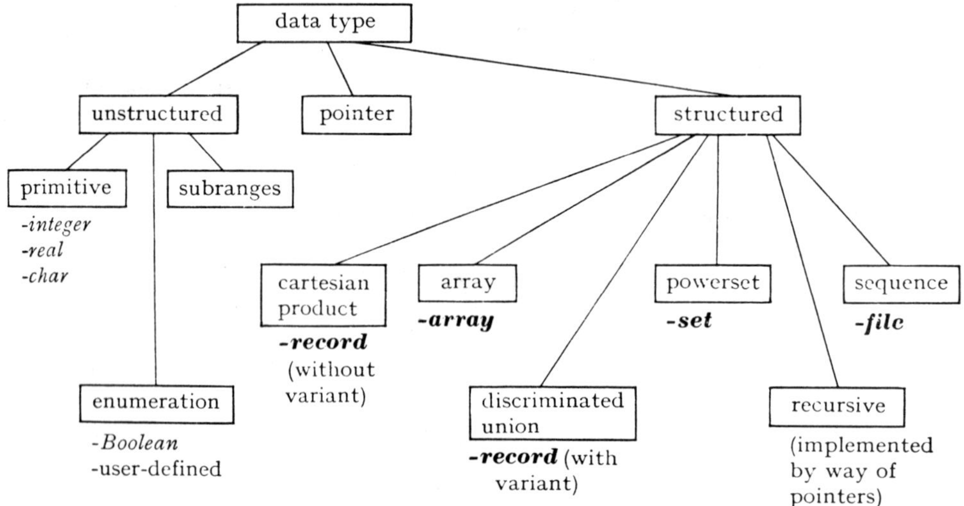

2.4. Miscellaneous

In Section 2.2, Habermann writes in an example the expression $u[i] * u[i]$, and adds as comment that Pascal has no operator for exponentiation. Precisely to cover this case, Pascal offers the function $sqr(x)$, which squares its argument (*real*, *integer* or subrange thereof). For most compilers, the generated code for a multiplication would be better than the one for $u[i]\uparrow 2$, which would probably require evaluation of a logarithm and an exponential. More generally, the exponentiation operator was not made a part of Pascal for the sake of simplicity and clarity. If one tries to completely describe it, for all valid and invalid combinations of operand types, signs and precisions, one inevitably obtains several pages of complicated explanations and tables [15]. Moreover, the ground rule that the type of all results must be evident at compile time would be violated in the case $i\uparrow j$, at least if one insists that it be *integer* if $j \geq 0$.

16*

Another clearly refutable suggestion is the one which is made in Section 6, to have a default passing mode for structured values in procedure calls. Such a proposal would only introduce an incoherent particular case into the language, making programs less clear. The example of PL/I clearly shows the danger of default options which depend on context and on the nature of objects, especially in parameter passing. One of the basic principles of Pascal is to hide nothing from its user, and to do nothing in his place, as would be the case if a parameter was supposed to be variable simply because it was a structured one. The precise choice of the best suited passing mode is another problem, which must be decided by the user himself, taking into account the type of the parameters and their utilization within the procedure.

3. Debatable Points

In this section, we deal with points on which reasonable people can disagree in all honesty. Generally, the direction chosen in Pascal is clearly not the only reasonable one, and a different approach would surely have its qualities. However, the solutions taken for Pascal generally fit well in the whole philosophy of the language, especially as to clarity and simplicity.

3.1. Block Structure

Pascal does not provide a block structure in exactly the same sense as Algol 60 [20], since all declarations are made at the procedure level, the program itself being a degenerate procedure. Therefore, it is not possible to open a block in the middle of another, simply by introducing some declarations after the **begin** symbol. However, it is important to clearly distinguish between the different possibilities given by the block structure of Algol 60, and to see which possibilities Pascal lacks because of its different approach. Both languages provide dynamic storage allocation of variables, as well as the notion of locality of declarations. Only Algol 60 offers the possibility of including two disjoint blocks within a single other one, thus saving storage by assigning variables of both blocks to the same area. In Pascal, this economy is only possible at the procedure level.

The advantage of the approach taken in Pascal is, once more, that of simplicity. Declarations are clearly separated from instructions, being grouped between the heading and the body of procedures (and functions). The **begin** symbol has only one purpose, which cannot be modified by what follows it. Another source of difficulty is the fact that the introduction of a declaration at the beginning of a compound statement changes the scope of every label defined within this construct.

In fact, the resulting simplification and clarification in Pascal has not proven to be disadvantageous, and our experience tends to show that for a program built in a modular and systematic way, the need for disjoint blocks which are not procedures seldom occurs. When it does, the price to pay is not heavy: define two procedures without parameters, one for each block, and call them in place of the blocks. The block then becomes a particular case of a more general construct. To define as procedures the modules used during program design is more general and natural than to replace them with disjoint blocks. In fact, it is a logical consequence of top-down design, which is one of the bases of structured and systematic programming. Habermann argues that the block of Algol 60 allows better locality of declarations, which is of course true. But what he fails to mention is that this type of structuring concept can also have harmful effects [21]. One intermediate solution could be a syntactic device similar to the monitor [10], which Brinch-Hansen proposes to implement in Pascal [1].

3.2. Dynamic Arrays

The bounds of an array declared in Pascal must be known at compilation time, so changing these bounds implies recompilation of the program. Although generations of programmers have submitted daily to this constraint when using Fortran, it is true it is an inconvenience. However, it is worth examining the magnitude of this inconvenience, and to see whether it is not compensated by some advantages. The problem of array parameters is yet another issue, the discussion of which is deferred until Section 4.1.

It is true that the cost of dynamic local arrays is quite small on machines with displacement addressing and good integer multiplication. Nevertheless it is also true that in this case, the compiler has to generate code in order to check that the index expression in $a[3]$ is within bounds; that compilers working on computers having immediate-type instructions cannot make use of those time-saving instructions in code sequences involved with array bounds checking.

One of the most important aspect to be considered is the consequences involved in allowing dynamic arrays as components of other arrays, records or files: in a language striving to be both general and simple, the added complexity in the behaviour of such structures would certainly not be helpful to the user. Furthermore, the implementor would have the choice either to ignore the special case of fixed bounds and thus deteriorate performances of all programs, including those not using dynamic arrays, or to try to optimize when possible, obtaining an optimizing compiler hampered with bulkiness, unreliability and consequently higher maintenance cost [29].

The facilities for constant and type declarations in Pascal make it extremely easy to simultaneously change the bounds of one or several arrays, subrange declarations, limits of loops and any other points regarding the arrays involved; see for example the partial programs in Section 2.2 of the present paper. Moreover, to be able to choose array bounds at run time frequently leads the programmer to leave the user with the responsibility of choosing sufficient limits, checking that they are not overflowed, and even of counting his data by hand.

3.3. Conditional Expressions

Habermann judges that the statement $i := $ **if** $i = 7$ **then** 1 **else** $i + 1$ expresses more clearly than the statement **if** $i = 7$ **then** $i := 1$ **else** $i := i + 1$ that a certain value is assigned to i. This point seems to be at the very least debatable, and our experience suggests that Algol 60 programmers use almost exclusively the second form, which has the advantage of allowing the replacement of either of the two assignments by a compound statement without modifying the other. Of course, there exist some other Algol 60 styles, à la Lisp, which use a great deal of embedded constructs, but readability rapidly becomes a problem.

Algol 60 gives an intermediate and quite acceptable solution, but with the inconvenience that the same basic words have different syntactic functions. The only way to allow full generality in that sense would be (depending on the chosen point of view) to unify or to confuse the notions of statement and expression, yielding an expression language like Algol 68 [23] or Bliss [30]. The consequences of such a decision for the language structure and for its compilation are very complex, and exceed by far the doubtful advantage quoted before. As may be seen in several examples in [23] or [30], the normal use of an expression language may yield formulas which are much too deeply parenthesized (be it explicitly or not) to be easily understandable. Just as the human mind can manage only small amounts of program at a time [5], it seems to have a mental stack of a very limited depth. This may be a more important reason for the lack of understandability of APL programs than the plethora of different operators, and it is another case of the situation where generality is contradictory with simplicity [29].

3.4. Labels and Goto Statement

This point is the most characteristic of those aspects of programming languages about which reasonable people may disagree in all honesty, as may be seen in [18]. Knuth is even able to disagree with himself on this issue [17]! However, let us remark that Pascal restricts the use of labels severely. They are not at all manipulable objects, they must be declared in all cases, and the effect of jumping from outside of a structured statement into that statement is not defined (although compilers will not necessarily indicate an error) [16], and so on. Since you cannot prevent the users from writing bad programs if they like to do so, and since a **goto** exiting a procedure is the simplest way to handle error cases where the structure of the program must be irreparably broken [8], the choice to maintain labels and **goto**'s in Pascal is as well defensible as the other solutions currently proposed [30, 18].

3.5. Structured Types

As we said in Section 2.3, the notion of type in Pascal includes three different concepts, which we call type, range and structure, to use the same terminology as Habermann. The decision to name "type" that information which is used by compilers to determine a storage template, is indeed debatable, but the important question is not the appropriateness of the particular labels chosen. More important is the fact that a structured object can, in all sensible situations, be handled as an unstructured one. For example, an array may be a component of a file or another array, or a field of a record; assignments are valid for almost all objects, provided that the left-hand and right-hand sides have the same type, consequently one can in a single statement copy a record (without variant) or an array; some operators may have structured operands, for example the comparison operators for packed arrays of characters (called "strings").

The result of the approach chosen in Pascal is that the whole notion of a data type is simple and coherent, as may be seen in the tree diagram at the end of Section 2.3. In this schema, all structured types are made from other types, which can themselves often be structured, but ultimately lead to unstructured types, and from there to either primitive types or enumeration-defined types. Of course, compilers may enforce some restrictions to facilitate implementation, for example they may forbid files as components of other structures, especially files of files.

The set of primitive types could indeed be extended to include, for example, complex numbers, but they have no counterpart in most hardware, and may be simulated at a very small cost using the data structuring tools offered by Pascal, with the important restriction that functions cannot return a structured result. We do not think that the lack of distinction between types, ranges and structures, by labelling all of them as type, is a source of confusion, although it may hinder somewhat the understanding and explanation of subrange type particularities.

3.6. Side-Effect in Functions

While the original Report on Pascal [24] recommended that a function make no modification to non-local variables (but did not pretend that they could not), the Revised Report does not say anything on the matter, which is regrettable. In fact, to enforce such a restriction would be extremely difficult and costly, if · not impossible, unless one forbids variable parameters and procedure calls within the body of a function. This is another instance of the situation where you cannot prevent the user from writing silly programs, unless you prevent him from writing any program at all. Moreover, the Revised Report allows declaration and call of a parameterless function, which is of no use if it cannot modify any non-local variable. Such functions **are** useful in some cases, and several standard functions have (or sometimes have) no parameter.

4. Valid Criticisms

This section deals with points which are indeed deficiencies in Pascal, and should perhaps be changed in a future version of the language (if possible). The brevity of this section is in itself a good argument in favour of Pascal.

4.1. Array Parameters

Since the bounds of an array are part of its type (or, more exactly, of the type of its indexes), it is impossible to define a procedure or function which applies to arrays with differing bounds. Although this restriction may appear to be a severe one, the experiences we have had with Pascal tend to show that it occurs very infrequently. The reason is probably that, because array bounds are static, different arrays which have components of the same type and which have to be handled in the same way generally have the same bounds, not exactly fitted to the set of data during a particular run. However, the need to bind the size of parametric arrays is a serious defect in connection with the use of program libraries.

4.2. Variable Initialization

Pascal does not presently allow initialization of variables at compilation time, at least in its official version. The richness of data structuring tools makes such a possibility very difficult to define. A possible solution would be to define constructors for structured data types [7], as in the following example:

> **type** $r =$ **record** *name:* **packed array** $[1 .. 10]$ **of** *char; age: integer; male:*
>   *Boolean* **end**;
> **var** *x:r;*
> **begin** *x:* $=r$ *('B. Pascal', 42, true);*

4.3. Parametric Procedures

Pascal presently contains, in one respect, a lack of rigorous specification which either leads to a certain inefficiency, if one wants to do all the necessary checks, or to a certain insecurity if they are not all done. In the specification of a function or procedure passed as a parameter (we shall say "parametric procedure"), the type and number of parameters are not specified at all, so it is generally impossible to easily detect at compile time the following error (this example is ours):

> **procedure** *P* **(procedure** *Q);* **begin** *Q(1, "A")* **end**;
> **procedure** *R (x: Boolean);* **begin** *write (x)* **end**;
> **begin** *P(R)* **end**.

Although Pascal, in this respect, strictly adopted the rules of Algol 60, some restrictions have already been made to the use of parametric procedures: a parametric procedure was at first not allowed to have procedure of function parameters [24], and now it cannot have variable parameters either [16], leaving only value parameters. While useful and not constricting, these restrictions do not suffice to ensure complete security, and they are not made explicit in the syntax. However, it is easy to make the simple syntactic modification which appears below, redefining the non-terminal ⟨*formal parameter section*⟩ in Section 10 of the Revised Report.

> ⟨*formal parameter section*⟩ $::=$ ⟨*parameter group*⟩ |
>   **var** ⟨*parameter group*⟩ |
>   **function** ⟨*procedure skeleton*⟩ : ⟨*type identifier*⟩
>   {, ⟨*procedure skeleton*⟩ : ⟨*type identifier*⟩} |
>   **procedure** ⟨*procedure skeleton*⟩ {, ⟨*procedure skeleton*⟩}
> ⟨*procedure skeleton*⟩ $::=$ ⟨*identifier*⟩ |
>   ⟨*identifier*⟩ (⟨*type identifier*⟩ {, ⟨*type identifier*⟩ })

With this modification, the restrictions quoted before appear explicitly in the syntax, and the heading of our procedure P must be either

> **procedure** *P* **(procedure** *Q(integer, char))*

which will allow detection of an error when P is called with R as a parameter, or

> **procedure** *P* **(procedure** *Q(Boolean))*

which will allow rejection of the call to Q in the body of P. The verification of compatibility between formal and actual parameters of parametric procedures can thus be made completely (and cheaply) at compile time, even with a one-pass compiler, if it adopts the convention of pre-declaring procedures (see [26], Section 13).

5. Misunderstandings and Minor Errors

We shall consider in this section only the misunderstandings and errors made by Habermann which may lead the reader to a false idea of Pascal. We shall ignore many obvious points, which any serious reader can easily rectify by himself.

5.1. Syntactic Errors in Examples

In Pascal, all declarations precede the body of a procedure or of the program. Thus, in both examples of Section 3, **begin** should occur after the declarations. Similarly, a **begin** should be placed in front of the last line of the example in Section 6. In Section 2.2, however, this is done correctly.

One error is repeated consistently throughout the whole paper: the lower and upper limits of a subrange (in a type declaration or as an index type) should be separated by "`..`" instead of "`...`".

In fact, when it is said in Section 3 that a program "results in an error indication at the operator $+$", an actual Pascal compiler would have indicated four errors before encountering this operator (**begin** before declarations; "`...`" in a subrange, twice; and $i = i + 1$ instead of $i := i + 1$), and none at that point.

5.2. Errors Concerning the Notion of Type

At the beginning of Section 5, it is said that , since scalar types are subranges, the declaration

var A : **array** [*real*] **of** *integer*

is legal. Of course, this is false: the type *real* constitutes a singular case of scalar type, since the number of values of this type is unknown. This however, is not clearly stated in the Revised Report.

Similarly, it is said near the end of the same section that, since a simple type may be represented by a type identifier, a file or array type may serve as index for an array. This is patently absurd, and it is evident that a type identifier does not **always** represent a simple type.

In Section 7, it is said that "a constant has no type". This is obviously false, and the Report clearly specifies in Section 4 the type of the value represented by each kind of constant.

5.3. Miscellaneous Errors

In the middle of Section 4, a question is asked "whether or not a label in front of the statement part of a procedure declaration is considered as in the procedure or not". The answer is that a label is forbidden in such a place, as the Report clearly states.

6. Conclusion

The main point to note in conclusion of this reply is that the Report on Pascal is aimed to serve both as a defining document and as a manual and tutorial for programmers. Such a paper must necessarily rely on some natural good will on the part of the reader, unless it is to grow into PL/I like dimensions [14, 15] or Algol 68 unreadability [23].

The second point is that the Report has an indispensable complement and companion, the Axiomatic Description [12], which defines in a rigorous manner all the semantics of Pascal and occupies only nine printed pages. Moreover, it is quite readable.

Acknowledgments. Our colleague Neil Stewart was most helpful in improving the style of this paper. Jim Horning was particularly helpful by strongly criticizing the emotional and technical contents of a first version. Finally, we must thank Dave Gries and the referee for pertinent suggestions and thorough study of our argumentation.

References

1. Brinch Hansen, P.: A programming methodology for operating system design. In: Rosenfeld, J. L. (ed.): Information Processing 74. Amsterdam: North-Holland 1974
2. Desjardins, P.: A Pascal compiler for the Xerox Sigma 6. *Sigplan Notices* **8**: 6, 34–36 (1973)
3. Dijkstra, E. W.: A short introduction to the art of programming. Department of Mathematics, Technische Hogeschool Eindhoven, EWD-316, 1971
4. Dijkstra, E. W.: The humble programmer. *Comm. ACM* **15**, 859–866 (1972)
5. Dijkstra, E. W.: Notes on structured programming. In: Dahl, O.-J. *et al.*: *Structured programming.* London: Academic Press 1972
6. Habermann, A. N.: Critical comments on the programming language Pascal. *Acta Informatica* **3**, 47–57 (1973)
7. Hoare, C. A. R.: Notes on data structuring. In: Dahl, O.-J. *et al.*: *Structured programming.* London: Academic Press 1972
8. Hoare, C. A. R.: Recursive data structures. Computer Science Department, Stanford University, CS-400, October 1973
9. Hoare, C. A. R.: Prof of a structured program: the sieve of Eratosthenes. *Computer J.* **15**, 321–325 (1974)
10. Hoare, C. A. R.: Monitors: an operating system structuring concept. Computer Science Department, Stanford University, CS-401, Noevmber 1973. Also published in *Comm. ACM* **17**, 549–557 (1974)
11. Hoare, C. A. R.: Hints on programming language design. Computer Science Department, Stanford University, CS-403, December 1973
12. Hoare, C. A. R., Wirth, N.: An axiomatic definition of the programming language Pascal. Eidgenössische Technische Hochschule Zürich, Berichte der Fachgruppe Computer-Wissenschaften 6, November 1972. Also published in *Acta Informatica* **2**, 335–355 (1973)
13. Holt, R. C.: Teaching the fatal disease (or) introductory computer programming using PL/I. *Sigplan Notices* **8**: 5, 8–23 (1973)
14. PL/I language specifications. IBM Corporation, Form C28–6571
15. PL/I (F) reference manual. IBM Corporation, Form C28–8201
16. Jensen, K., Wirth, N.: Pascal-User manual and Report. *Lecture Notes in Computer Science* 18. Berlin-Heidelberg-New York: Springer 1974
17. Knuth, D. E.: Structured programming with *goto* statements. Computer Science Department, Stanford University, CS-416, May 1974. Also published in *Computing Surveys* **6**, 261–301 (1974)
18. Leavenworth, B. (ed): Control structures in programming languages. The goto controversy. *Sigplan Notices* **7**: 11, 53–91 (1972)
19. Lecarme, O., Bochmann, G. V.: A (truly) usable and portable compiler writing system. In: Rosenfeld, J. L. (ed): Information Processing 74. Amsterdam: North-Holland 1974

20. Naur, P. (ed.): Revised report on the algorithmic language Algol 60. *Comm. ACM* **6**, 1–17 (1963)
21. Shaw, M., Wulf, W. A.: Global variables considered harmful. *Sigplan Notices* **8**: 2, 28–34 (1973)
22. Sykes, J. M.: Languages: the user's view of the computer. In: Boon, C. (ed.): High level languages. International Computer State of the Art Report 7. Maidenhead: Infotech Information Ltd 1972
23. van Wijngaarden, A. *et al.*: Report on the algorithmic language Algol 68. *Numer. Math.* **14**, 79–218 (1969)
24. Wirth, N.: The programming language Pascal. Berichte der Fachgruppe Computer-Wissenschaften 1, Eidgenössische Technische Hochschule Zürich, November 1970. Also published in *Acta Informatica* **1**, 35–63 (1971)
25. Wirth, N.: The design of a Pascal compiler. *Software Practice and Experience* **1**, 309–333 (1971)
26. Wirth, N.: The programming language Pascal (Revised report). Berichte der Fachgruppe Computer-Wissenschaften 5, Eidgenössische Technische Hochschule Zürich, November 1972. Also published in: Jensen, K., Wirth, N.: Pascal—User manual and Report. *Lecture Notes in Computer Science* **18**. Berlin-Heidelberg-New York: Springer 1974
27. Wirth, N.: *Systematic programming—An introduction*. Englewood Cliffs (N. J.): Prentice-Hall 1973
28. Wirth, N.: From programming techniques to programming methods. In: Günther A., Levrat B., Lipps H., *et al.* (eds.): International Computing Symposium 1973. Amsterdam: North-Holland 1974
29. Wirth, N.: On the design of programming languages. In: Rosenfeld, J. L. (ed.): Information Processing 74. Amsterdam: North-Holland 1974
30. Wulf, W. A., Russell, D. B., Habermann, A. N.: Bliss: a language for systems programming. *Comm. ACM* **14**, 780–790 (1971)

Professor O. Lecarme ·
Laboratoire d'Informatique
Université de Nice
Parc Valrose, 06034 Nice
France

P. Desjardins
Groupe de Recherches sur les
Systèmes et Langages de Programmation
Département d'Informatique
Université de Montréal
C.P. 6128, Montréal 101
Canada

An Assessment of the Programming Language Pascal

NIKLAUS WIRTH

Reprinted from *IEEE Transactions on Software Engineering,* June 1975, pp. 192-198. Copyright © 1975 by The Institute of Electrical and Electronics Engineers, Inc.

Abstract—The programming language Pascal is assessed in the light of "reliable programming" and with the background of five years of experience with the language. Some features are selected to point out remaining problems, either inherent or specific, from which some guidelines for the design or choice of languages for reliable programming are derived. Among the discussed features are the concept of data type, the sequential file structure, and the type union.

Index Terms—Data types, files and sequences, language evaluation, language and reliable programming, parametrized types, Pascal, program correctness versus reliability, type union.

WHAT IS RELIABLE SOFTWARE?

RELIABLE is the attribute for a person, an organization, or a mechanism that you can trust, that you can depend on, that is worthy of your confidence. For example, a reliable clock is one that indicates accurate time even during an earthquake, a reliable railway system is one where trains run punctually even during a snowstorm, a reliable bridge is a bridge that does not crack even under heavy load, and a reliable transistor is one that operates for years, possibly under extreme temperature and radiation. The common enemy of reliability in these examples are adverse circumstances and influences that may cause a deterioration of the physical properties of material. The accumulation of these influences is called aging. Reliability is achieved by dimensioning the mechanisms properly, taking such adverse conditions into consideration. In a railway system the schedule is arranged such that it leaves room for catching up on lost time, and an ample supply of spare engines is kept on the alert for emergencies. A bridge is built stronger than actually needed most of the time—and a transistor is equipped with cooling devices and radiation shields.

What does this all have to do with software? Well, we all have experienced failures of computer systems; and we all would like them to be reliable too. When a computer fails, the first question among its intimates is usually: is the hardware or the software the culprit? Most customers of a computation center show signs of relief when the latter is announced, for the disruption of service is then quickly ended by a so-called dead start, and life goes on as if (almost) nothing had occurred. Indeed there had been neither an earthquake, nor a snowstorm, nor a weighty load, nor heat or radiation. Instead, merely unpredictable circumstances had led to a state of computation for which the logical structure of the program had not

Manuscript received February 1, 1975.
The author is with the Federal Institute of Technology (ETH), Zürich, Switzerland.

been designed, which the system's designers did not anticipate. And when pressing the dead start button, the computer operator is reasonably confident that these circumstances would not reoccur too soon.

What must we conclude? We understand by the term software the collection of programs that deterministically prescribe a system's detailed behavior and transitions of state. These programs are constants and are independent of any "adverse conditions" of an environment. Hence, software cannot fail because of unpredictable happenings and age, but only due to defects in its logical design. This leads us to a replacement of the attribute "reliable" by "correct."

We may be accused of nitpicking with words. To this I can only reply that the choice of words often reveals a speaker's *attitude* more profoundly than is dear to him. The attitude through which we content ourselves at producing "reliable" software instead of correct software, bears the danger that we may also consider various *degrees* of reliability. Software may then be termed reliable and "more reliable"; we may also call it correct, but certainly not "more correct."

The difference in these words is also manifested in the techniques to be employed in producing reliability in software versus in clocks, bridges, and transistors. In most technical phenomena, reliability is achieved by over dimensioning the components, by using high-quality material, or by supplying standby equipment that automatically goes into action when a failure occurs. In programs, merely repeating a logical test 18 times instead of performing it once does not help, if the logical structure is correct and the underlying hardware is reliable. In fact, the degree to which a program is unreliable is exactly the probability with which its incorrect parts are executed. But this measure is *not* a property of the program itself.

Reconciling ourselves with the word correct in place of reliable has the advantage that we more readily identify the causes of failures of our products to meet their goal. They are not to be sought in external, unforeseeable, adverse circumstances, but solely in our own inadequate minds, and in our failure to communicate, if several people participate in a program's design. The advantage of this recognition is that we know where to concentrate our efforts; its unpleasant part is the fact that it will be a never-ending crusade, because committing mistakes is a truly human characteristic.

The most sensible targets in our drive at producing correct software are evidently *the programmers themselves.* Nothing whatsoever can replace a sound, systematic training in precise reasoning. Other sensible targets are the tools that we employ to assist our reasoning. These include primarily the *formal languages* in which we express our thoughts and abstractions, and by which we transmit them to other people. We have directed our efforts to improve our programming tools for more than a decade, and I will therefore devote the main part of this paper to a report and an evaluation of the latest product, the language Pascal, in the light of the topic "reliable software" [13].

The justification to discuss Pascal in the context of the issue of reliable software is derived from the fact that several large programs have been written in this language. They include several compilers which have been widely distributed and thus can be considered as genuine software engineering products. The value of using a high-level language for such systems has been demonstrated most convincingly in the first effort to transport the compiler onto another computer [11], which I consider a landmark in the technology of software engineering.

The following brief assessment of Pascal begins with an enumeration of features that proved to be valuable in constructing correct programs and at the same time do not impair the conceptual simplicity and efficient implementability of the language. It is followed by a short selection of features that give rise to some issues and even controversies [3], [9]. Intentionally we refrain, however, from suggesting extensions to the language, although we fully recognize the legitimacy of many wishes in view of certain areas of application. The aim is to evaluate a language that was designed in 1969 and has been in practical use for five years, as we feel that it is more important to report about factual experiences than to postulate additional, unproven, and sophisticated facilities at a time when the large majority of programmers and engineers still operate with languages and techniques conceived 20 years ago. For a general overview and details of the language we refer to the published literature [8].

IMPORTANT FEATURES OF PASCAL WHICH CONTRIBUTE TO TRANSPARENT PROGRAMMING

Experience with Pascal has shown the following features to be essential in making programs transparent and in avoiding and detecting mistakes. Their common and distinguishing characteristic is that they provide a compiler with redundant information that is used in checking for consistency of the program, without causing appreciable overhead in program execution. The most essential facility in this respect is the type definition, and in particular the distinction between *types* and *variables*. In fact, declarative features contribute not only to transparence and reliability, but also to the efficiency of the compiled code.

1) Symbolic Scalar Types:
Example:

type color = (red, yellow, green, blue)

This declaration lets the compiler check against inconsistent use of variables of this type, and it prohibits the application of incompatible operations (such as arithmetic to colors). The use of suggestive names for constants is particularly helpful. The above declaration is easily processed by a compiler into a mapping of colors onto a suitable subset of the integers.

2) Record Types:
Example:

type person = **record** name: alfa;

        age: integer;

        sex: (male, female);

        ...

end

A sensible generalization of the array which allows to introduce compound data with components of different types (heterogeneous structures).

3) Set Types:
Example:

type tint = **set of** color

The set provides for an appealing formulation of what so far had been expressed in terms of *bitstrings*. The representation of sets by their characteristic function assures utmost simplicity and efficiency of implementation [4], [12]. Together with 1) this feature has proven to be an invaluable asset in the description of compilers and operating systems.

4) Subrange Types:
Example:

type index = 0. .99

A variable of this type possesses the properties of variables of the base type (integer in the example) under the restriction that its value remains within the specified range. The declaration provides a compiler with information that may be used to choose a most economical use of storage (e.g., a variable of type index can be represented by 7 bits only) and to accompany each assignment with the necessary checks against violation of the specified invariant property. In practice, this facility has turned out to be equally helpful in detecting logical flaws as built-in bound checks upon array indexing.

5) Simple Forms of Iterative and Selective Statements: In the realm of control structures, the simple and flexible <u>while</u>, <u>repeat</u>, and <u>case</u> statements are a great asset. Together with the <u>if</u> statement and a drastically trimmed version of the <u>for</u> statement of Algol 60 they suffice to formulate the vast majority of programs as a nested, hierarchical structure of these fundamental composition schemes. This contributes in a most essential way to the ease of understanding and verifying programs, and greatly facilitates the task of code optimization for compilers.

FACILITIES AND CONVENTIONS THAT HAMPER THE CLARITY OF PROGRAMS

1) Operator Precedence: In the interest of simplicity and efficient translatability, Pascal aimed at a reasonably small number of operator precedence levels. Algol 60's hierarchy of 9 levels seemed clearly too baroque. An additional incentive for change was the replacement of the equivalence operator for Boolean expressions by the equality operator. Since these two operators reside on different priority levels in Algol 60, some departure from the old rules were mandatory. In retrospect, however, the decision to break with a widely used tradition seems ill-advised, particularly with the growing significance of complicated Boolean expressions in connection with program verification.

Algol 60	Pascal	
↑		¬
* / ÷	* / div mod	∧
+ −	+ −	∨
= ≠ < ≤ ≥ >	= ≠ < ≤ ≥ >	
¬		
∧		
∨		
⊃		
≡		

Examples of expressions in Algol 60 and Pascal:

$$\neg\, x < y \qquad\qquad \neg\,(x < y)$$

$$x < y \wedge y < z \qquad (x < y) \wedge (y < z)$$

$$x < y \equiv y < z \qquad (x < y) = (y < z)$$

2) The GOTO *Statement:* There is hardly any doubt that the use of GOTO statements which disassociate the control structure of a process with the textual structure of its program is a frequent source of mistakes and impairs the verifiability of programs. This was perfectly clear even when the decision to include the GOTO statement in Pascal was taken [2]. Yet even now there is no general agreement on an adequate replacement. Placing further restrictions upon the GOTO statement—for instance, allowing only forward jumps—may be one solution. But clearly, allowing integers only instead of identifiers as labels is no sufficient deterrent to programmers who have previously worked with Fortran! In teaching programming, the use of a subset Pascal system *without* GOTO statement is strongly recommended.

THE EXPLICIT DISTINCTION BETWEEN "TYPES" AND "VARIABLES"

The most widely used technique of program verification is based on the explicit statement of assertions about the state of the computation at different points in the program. Recently, it has been recognized that it would be even more useful to attach assertions to specific variables rather than program points.

Declarations are essentially a statement of invariant properties of the respective variables. In Pascal, every variable is said to be of a certain *type*, and a data type can be defined explicitly by the programmer. It implies essential invariants needed for the verification of programs, and it moreover supplies a compiler with sufficient information to decide on a suitable storage representation. In essence, a compiler translates a type definition into a storage template to be used upon allocation of each variable of this type.

Moreover, the type definition determines the set of operators that are applicable to variables (sometimes called "instances") of that type.

It follows that a type definition should combine all attributes of a variable that are constant and known at the time of compilation (static). In fact, Pascal goes so far as to exclude *all* information from a type definition that cannot be determined from a simple textual scan. This rule has its important merits, but also bears some inconveniences, as shall be explained below. Our experience shows that the advantages of explicit type definitions are enormous and indispensible, if program transparence and efficiency of compiled code are both an issue.

Unfortunately, the Pascal concept of type has also stirred some controversy [3]. It seems to be largely originating from a too strict interpretation of the word *type* based on its use in the world of mathematics. There, the concept of types distinguishes between numbers and truth values, between numbers and sets of numbers, or between sets and sets of sets, but not between integers and natural numbers (a subrange of the former) or between small sets and larger sets. In the world of programming it is both natural and necessary to extend this concept of type, because objects can become different (types) because of far more (detailed) reasons than in abstract mathematics, where problems of representation are immaterial.

Which were, then, the negative consequences of adhering to the rule of strictly static type definitions? They became manifest in the form of two restrictions in the use of arrays, as compared to Algol 60. The first is the exclusion of so-called *dynamic arrays*, because the array type definition includes the specification of its size. There are good reasons for wanting dynamic arrays, but also convincing arguments against them [9]. The fact remains that dynamic arrays in the sense of Algol 60 are sort of a hermaphroditic (hybrid) species: their size can neither be determined at compile time, nor can it be changed during program execution. Instead, it is fixed upon block entry.

The second drawback is in practice much more severe. It originates from the essential requirement that formal procedure parameters specify their types. But in the case of *array parameters*, this once again includes their size. As a consequence, a given procedure can only be applied to arrays of one fixed size. This rule hardly contributes to program security and transparence, but seriously impairs the highly desirable flexibility of procedures.

Both problems can be overcome by allowing type definitions—in particular array types—to be parametrized. The following example shows the use of such a *parametrized type*.

```
type table(m,n) = array[m...n] of integer;
var t1: table(1,100);
    t2: table(0,999);
function sum (t: table; u,v: integer): integer;
   var i,s: integer;
begin s := 0;
   for i := u to v do s := t[i] + s;
   sum := s
end;
begin . . .
   s1 := sum(t1,1,100);
   s2 := sum(t2,0,999);
      . . .
end.
```

From this example we can see both the utility and the dangers of such a generalization, and possibly also the consequences upon a compiler. A most sensible decision is to restrict parametrization to the index bounds of array types, and to allow for constants only as actual parameters (in variable declarations). This already solves the dilemma of array parameters. If dynamic arrays are to be allowed, the latter rule may be relaxed. I would caution, however, against any further generalization: allowing the component type of an array to be a parameter too, for example, would destroy many advantages of the Pascal type concept at once.

AN IMPORTANT CONCEPT AND A PERSISTENT SOURCE OF PROBLEMS: FILES

In Pascal, files are understood to be strictly sequential files, and are defined in terms of the mathematical notion of a *sequence*. Like the array, they are homogeneous structures, but in contrast to the array, their size changes (truly) dynamically. Naturally, we not only aimed at a simple and consistent mathematical definition of files and their operators, but also kept in mind their efficient realization, particularly with a view towards the involvement of secondary storage media. As it turned out, the original file concept was right in terms of implementation, but not in terms of mathematical axiomatization which seemed highly desirable for a tool to construct reliable software. Therefore, the file scheme was slightly modified in a revision of the language made in 1973 that is summarized in [6]. Although the revised file facility proved to be a definite improvement, some inherent difficulties became evident only after extended usage. This may be the reason that the file concept had never been mentioned in any critical commentary about Pascal.

What are these deficiencies, and where do they have their roots? I presume that the main culprit is the attempt to hide from the programmer and the verifier the fact that files must be allocatable on secondary storage media. In this case, an efficient buffering mechanism is involved. Indeed, such technicalities may well be withheld from the programmer who is concerned with correctness only, if the scheme presented to him is rigorously defined and faultless, and if the consequences on efficiency are fully understood and accepted.

Originally, a file f was viewed as a sequence in which at any time only a single element was accessible, if there existed one. Conceptually, one could think of a *window*, through which that element, denoted by $f\uparrow$, could be seen (the arrow denotes the "window position"). But that description is not honest, of course, if $f\uparrow$ actually represents a buffer variable in primary store, via which data are transferred to and from secondary stores (tapes, disks). Therefore the appealing fiction of a sliding window was dropped in favor of a distinct *buffer variable*. But of course, also this is not quite honest, if the true buffer comprises several logical file elements, such that the operation $put\ (f)$ will actually be effectuated by a mere pointer updating until the buffer is full. For then it is difficult to explain why $f\uparrow$ suddenly changes its value during the operation $put\ (f)$. In reality we now have a buffer of which a single component is visible through a sliding window; and this situation is slightly too complicated to be neatly expressed by a simple scheme of axioms.

I wish to suggest two possible solutions to this dilemma. Characteristically, the choice depends on the intended application of the language. If Pascal is to serve for system construction purposes, then the file facility might be dropped entirely, because the very purpose would be the description of possible file mechanisms in terms of more primitive concepts. If, however, Pascal is viewed as a general purpose language in which files are an indispensible concept, then the basic operators *get* and *put* might be replaced by *read* and *write* statements defined in terms of the former as follows:

$$read\ (f,x) \equiv x := f\uparrow\ ; get\ (f)$$
$$write\ (f,x) \equiv f\uparrow\ := x;\ put\ (f)$$

This makes it possible to hide the chosen buffering mechanism entirely, and to ignore the existence of a window or of a buffer variable. (Incidentally, Pascal states exactly these abbreviations, but allows them only for textfiles. The relaxation of this restriction is an obvious step.)

A premise of the axiomatic scheme was that the predicate $eof(f)$ be always defined (true, if the part of the file to the right of the reading position is empty, false otherwise). This implies that a file access must be made before the program actually specifies any reading. The solution lies in combining the rewinding of the file with the initial loading of the buffer. Emptiness can be recognized during this operation. The unpleasant consequence is that a program can never leave a file in a properly rewound state. This may itself not be of any concern, as long as we remain strictly in the world of the Pascal program; but if this program is considered as one action upon a more permanent environment, it must be considered as a deficiency. Indeed, the appropriateness of the primitive *rewrite*(*f*) appears at least questionable. It is, from a theoretical point of view, indispensible, because it is the only operation by which a file variable can be given an initial value, namely the empty sequence (see [6]). In practice, however, rewinding (a tape) is considered as the basic operation, and rewinding does *not* cause the tape to be erased. An obvious "solution" consists in splitting *reset*(*f*) and *rewrite*(*f*) into the "more primitive" operations as follows:

$$reset(f) \equiv rewind(f); openread(f)$$
$$rewrite(f) \equiv rewind(f); openwrite(f)$$

The drawbacks are that the state of the predicate *eof*(*f*) and the buffer *f* ↑ are undetermined in between, and that a programmer is liable to forget to specify the openread or openwrite operation.

The most unsatisfactory consequences of the Pascal file concept lie in the area of substructures, and in particular textfiles. Originally, the idea of substructures could well be ignored. Texts were considered as sequences of characters, separated into lines by control characters. This concept is also embodied by the ISO (and ASCII) conventions, and proved to be most conveniently implementable. On a CDC 6000 computer with 6-bit characters and a set of 63 printing characters, the obvious choice was to introduce a 64th control character **eol** to signal the end of a line.

A program reading a textfile *f*, performing an operation *L* at the beginning of each line and an operation *P* after reading each character, is easily expressed by the following schema:

```
while ¬eof( f) do
   begin L; read( f,ch);
      while ch ≠ eol do
         begin P(ch); read ( f,ch)
         end
   end                                    (1)
```

But then, alas, a new operating system came along with a set of 64 characters. It supposedly incorporates a true miracle: the coding of 64 characters *and* a line separation within 6 bits only! How can reliable software be constructed at all on the basis of such premises?

The new situation left no escape from providing textfiles with an explicit substructure: a textfile was to be considered as a sequence of lines, each line being itself a sequence of characters. In analogy to the predicate *eof*(*f*), a predicate *eoln*(*f*) was introduced to indicate the end of a line. Evidently, also a pair of new operators became necessary, *writeln*(*f*) to terminate the generation of a line, and *readln*(*f*) to initiate the reading of a next line.

Another problem arose simultaneously. At the end of a line, the predicate *eoln*(*f*) becomes true. Should at the end of the last line the predicate *eof*(*f*) also become true simultaneously? Probably so, because evidently the end of the last line is also the end of the text. Once again, we are faced with a dilemma: when reading the end of a line, we either find out whether there exists a next line, and we therefore read on (which may not be the intent of the programmer), or we refrain from looking ahead, and must leave the definition of *eof*(*f*) up to a further explicit *readln* instruction. Neither solution is fully satisfactory.

In the latter case (as in rev. Pascal), the program corresponding to schema (1) is

```
while ¬eof( f)do
begin L;
   while ¬eoln( f) do
      begin read( f,ch); P(ch)
      end;
   readln( f)
end                                       (2)
```

In the former case, the resulting program is slightly but significantly different:

```
while ¬eof( f) do
   begin readln( f); L;
      while ¬eoln( f) do
         begin read( f,ch); P(ch)
         end
   end                                    (3)
```

The difference may appear to be minimal, even negligible. It lies not so much in the form of the program but in the underlying concepts. And frequently such details decide ultimately about the acceptability—the healthiness—of a language. The issue of files is a typical case of the devil persistently and successfully hiding in the details.

SECURITY VERSUS FLEXIBILITY: TYPE UNIONS

It is sometimes desirable that a variable may assume values of different types. Its type is then said to be the *union* of these types. There appear to be three different motivations behind the desire for union types.

1) The need for *heterogeneous structures*. For example, in an interpreter a stack may have to consist of integer, real, and Boolean components. If the stack is represented by an array, its homogeneity is a hindrance. Although each "stack" element assumes only one fixed type during its lifetime, the underlying (static) array element appears to have a varying type.

2) *Storage sharing* (overlays). This implies the use of the same storage area—expressed in the language as "the same actual variable"—for different purposes, i.e., for representing different abstract variables whose lifetimes are disjoint.

3) Realization of implicit *type transfer functions*. For instance, a variable of type real is interpreted as being of type integer for the purpose of printing the internal representation in, say, octal form.

The dangers of the type union facility lie in the possibility to err about the current type of a variable and in the difficulty to identify the mistake. If it occurs in an assignment, the consequences may be disastrous. Efforts must be made to provide automatic checking facilities. We therefore distinguish between *discriminated* and *free unions* [5]. In the former case, the variable carries along a tag which indicates the currently valid type (which is one among the types specified in the definition of the union type). In the latter case, no such direct information is stored. Clearly, the latter provides greater freedom in programming, the former increased security through automatic consistency checks.

In Pascal, the concept of type union is embodied in the form of *variants of record structures*. The discriminated union inherently dictates a record structure, because every value consists of (at least) two components: the actual value and the tag value identifying its current type.

Example:

```
type stackelement =
  record
    case tag: (A,B,C) of
      A: (i: integer);
      B: (r: real);
      C: (b: Boolean)
  end;

var s: array[1..100] of stackelement
```

In a program with these declarations, the occurrence of a variable designator $s[i].r$ is only valid if at this point that variable is of type real. It is so, if and only if $s[i].tag = B$. A compiler may generate this test automatically, provided that it also ensures an appropriate setting of the tag upon assignment. This, however, implies an appreciable, although worthwhile overhead. Suggestions have been made to provide syntactic structures which let the compiler determine the current tag value from context. One such feature is the *inspect when* statement of Simula [1]. But these constructs sometimes turn out to leave insufficient freedom to express a given situation in a natural way.

No such facility was included in Pascal; to the contrary, in its revised version (1973) the tagfield of a variant record definition was declared to be optional. If it is omitted, we obtain the equivalent of a free type union, and a compiler has *no* chance of checking consistency in its application. One may rightly criticize this development which clearly opens the door for a very dangerous sort of programming errors, but there seem to exist applications where the discriminated union is insufficiently flexible. (Even so, my advice is to refrain from using variants without tagfield.)

The issue of type unions is a clear example of a case where a language may offer added security only at the expense of flexibility, or vice versa. The programmer must make his own choice. Yet, we have the impression that a more satisfactory solution must be found. It will not necessarily be found in new language facilities, but may lie in a different approach to data organization.

The truly disconcerting fact is that facilities such as the record variant, provided for a genuine need for flexibility (motivation 1 above), can be (and are!) easily misused. The example for the third motivation (see above) is characteristic for programmers who (habitually) think in terms of machine facilities and assembly code, and (love to) show that their techniques can also be expressed in a higher level language. It is probably the most disheartening experience for a language designer to discover how features provided with honest intentions are "ingeniously" misused to betray the language's very principles.

SUMMARY AND CONCLUSIONS

We have argued that the concept of a *degree of program reliability* is ill conceived and helps to foster a mistaken attitude in software engineering. Instead, a program can be called *correct*, if and only if its operations are fully consistent with static specifications of the expected results of the dynamic process. As programs used in practice are enormously complex and have a tendency to become even more complex in future applications, programming errors will always be with us. Instead of relying too much on either antiquated "debugging tools" or on futuristic automatic program verifiers, we should give more emphasis to the systematic construction of programs with languages that facilitate transparent formulation and automatic consistency checks.

The language Pascal was designed with exactly these aims. Five years of experience in its use have proven its significant merits with respect to ease of programming, suitability for formal program verification [7], [10], efficient implementability, and practical portability. They have also revealed some weaknesses and some remaining difficulties. After analyzing the roots of these problems, we are tempted to list a few conclusions about the design and the choice of languages for "reliable programming."

The language must rest on a foundation of simple, flexible, and neatly axiomatized features, comprising the basic structuring techniques of data and program.

Language rules must not deviate from widely accepted traditions of formal notations, even if these traditions are sometimes inconsistent or inconvenient. More importantly, *new* features must be designed with utmost care to notational regularity and consistency.

The urge to gain flexibility and "power" through generalizations must be restrained. A generalization may easily be carried too far and have revolutionary consequences on implementation (e.g., full parametrization of types).

Every basic feature is to be governed by a consistent set of "obvious" rules (axioms). The rules must be such that efficient implementability does not depend on particular (or even peculiar) properties of a specific computer system (e.g., on the existence of a line-end-character).

In many cases, security and flexibility are antagonistic

properties. Security is obtained through redundancy which is used by the system to perform consistency checks. Often, redundancy is cumbersome to provide, and the programmer must decide whether to choose a straightjacket providing relative security, or a free language where the responsibility is entirely his own (e.g., discriminated versus free type unions).

Every rule of the language must be enforceable by the system. It follows that rules should preferably be checkable by a mere textual scan, but also run-time checks should become widely used.

A rich language may be welcome to the professional program *writer* who's principle delight is his familiarization with all its intricate facets. But the interests of the program *reader* dictate a reasonably frugal language. People who want to understand a program (including their own), compilers, and automatic verification aids all belong to the class of readers.

In the interest of increased quality of software products, we may be well advised to get rid of many facilities of modern, baroque programming languages that are widely advertised in the name of "user-orientation," "scientific sophistication," and "progress."

ACKNOWLEDGMENT

The author wishes to acknowledge the criticism and suggestions of members of the International Federation of Information Processing Working Group 2.3 which helped to clarify this presentation.

REFERENCES

[1] Birtwistle, Dahl, Myhrhaug, Nygaard, "SIMULA Begin," *Studentlitteratur*, Univ. Lund, Lund, Sweden, 1974.
[2] E. W. Dijkstra, "GOTO statements considered harmful," *Commun. Ass. Comput. Mach.*, vol. 11, pp. 147–148, Mar. 1968.
[3] A. N. Habermann, "Critical comments on the programming language PASCAL," *Acta Informatica*, vol. 3, pp. 47–58, 1973.
[4] C. A. R. Hoare, "Set manipulation," *Algol Bulletin*, vol. 27, pp. 29–37, Dec. 1967.
[5] O.-J. Dahl, E. W. Dijkstra, and C. A. R. Hoare, "Notes on data structuring," in *Structured Programming*. New York: Academic, 1972.
[6] C. A. R. Hoare and N. Wirth, "An axiomatic definition of the programming language PASCAL," *Acta Informatica*, vol. 2, pp. 335–355, 1973.
[7] S. Igarashi, R. L. London, and D. C. Luckham, "Automatic program verification: a logical basis and its implementation," Dep. Comput. Sci., Stanford Univ., Stanford, Calif., Comput. Sci. Rep. 73-365, May 1973.
[8] K. Jensen and N. Wirth, "PASCAL—User Manual and Report," in *Lecture Notes in Computer Science*, vol. 18, New York: Springer-Verlag, 1974.
[9] O. Lecarme and P. Desjardins, "Reply to a paper by A. N Habermann on the programming language PASCAL," *SIGPLAN Notices*, vol. 9, pp. 21–27, Oct. 1974.
[10] E. Marmier, "A program verifier for Pascal," in *Proc. Int. Fed. Inform. Processing Congr.*, Inform. Processing 74. Amsterdam, The Netherlands: North-Holland, 1974.
[11] J. Welsh and C. Quinn, "A PASCAL compiler for ICL 1900 series computers," *Software—Practice and Experience*, vol. 2, pp. 73–77, 1972.
[12] N. Wirth, "The design of a Pascal compiler," *Software—Practice and Experience*, vol. 1, pp. 309–333, 1971.
[13] ——, "The programming language PASCAL," *Acta Informatica*, vol. 1, pp. 35–63, 1971.

SOFTWARE—PRACTICE AND EXPERIENCE, VOL. 7, 685–696 (1977)

Reprinted with permission from *Software—Practice and Experience,* Vol. 7, No. 6,
November 1977, pp. 685-696 and *Pascal—The Language and Its Implementation,*
D.W. Barron, ed. Copyright by John Wiley & Sons Ltd.

Ambiguities and Insecurities in Pascal

J. WELSH, W. J. SNEERINGER* AND C. A. R. HOARE†
Department of Computer Science, Queen's University, Belfast BT7 1NN, N. Ireland

SUMMARY

Ambiguities and insecurities in the programming language Pascal are discussed.

KEY WORDS Pascal Language design Language definition Security

INTRODUCTION

On rare occasions in programming language development there appears a programming
language which is widely recognized as superior, and which propagates itself among dis-
cerning implementors and users solely by its merits, and without any political or commercial backing. ALGOL 60[1] was such a language. Pascal[2] is another.

One characteristic of such superior languages is that they rapidly give rise to a host of
suggested extensions, improvements and imitations. From ALGOL 60 came ALGOL D,[3]
ALGOL W,[4] ALGOL 68,[5] PL/I,[6] Simula 67[7] and Pascal itself. Pascal has been followed by
the critique by Habermann,[8] Concurrent Pascal,[9] Pasqual,[10] Modula[11] and Euclid.[12] It is
one of the symptoms of the superiority of these languages that their original design remains
superior to many of their successors, and even the authors themselves can find little to
improve in formulating a revised version.[13–15] Thus the very superiority of the language
may inhibit for a while the further progress of the art of language design.

One reason for this is that there is no immediate recognition of exactly what constitute
the merits of the language. Indeed, the merits of ALGOL 60 have only recently been
appreciated under the new name of *structured programming.* Similarly, most criticism of the
language is rather superficial, concentrating on critics' favourite 'features' and 'facilities'
which have been left out.

If future language designs, and indeed future users, are to benefit fully from the significant
advances made by Pascal, it is essential that its defects, as well as its virtues, should be
carefully identified and catalogued. The detailed, almost pettifogging nature of the
criticisms in this paper may be taken as a testimony to a belief that Pascal is at the present
time the best language in the public domain for purposes of systems programming and
software implementation. Nevertheless, these criticisms may lead to a better understanding
of the definitional problems created in Pascal, and to a better treatment of these problems
in the languages which must inevitably follow it.

No consideration is given to changes to Pascal other than those necessary to overcome
the ambiguities and insecurities identified.

---

* Present address: IBM Corporation, 11400 Burnet Road, Austin, Texas 78759, U.S.A.
† Address from October 1977: Programming Research Group, Oxford University, 45 Banbury Road, Oxford.

Received 27 May 1977

Throughout this paper, the abbreviations *User Manual* and *Report* are used to stand for the first and second parts, respectively, of the *Pascal User Manual and Report.*[15] There are several earlier versions of the *Report.*[14] The abbreviation *Axiomatic Definition* is also used for the formal definition of Pascal's semantics given by Hoare and Wirth.[17]

AMBIGUITIES

Ambiguities and omissions in the *Report* or *User Manual* are not mentioned in what follows if they can be easily resolved. The objective is to criticize the language, not the *Report* or the *User Manual*; but insofar as the language's features (or apparent intentions) create problems of definition, the *Report* must be considered as well.

Equivalence of types

Section 9.1.1 of the *Report* states that the two sides of an assignment statement 'must be of identical type', with certain exceptions involving reals and subranges. The phrase *identical type* is not defined and its meaning is not obvious. Much of Habermann's criticism of Pascal hinged on the omission from the *Report* of similar exception rules for other contexts in which subrange or real variables might or might not appear. As the Axiomatic Definition shows, the subrange problem can be resolved by the systematic introduction of implicit subrange–range transfers as context requires. However, the notion of type equivalence creates problems for other Pascal types too.

In the declarations,

```
type T    = array [1..10] of INTEGER;
var A, B:   array [1..10] of INTEGER;
    C:      array [1..10] of INTEGER;
    D:      T;
    E:      T;
```

consider the following two possible definitions of equivalence of types.

Name equivalence

Two variables are considered to be of the same type only if they are declared together (as A and B) or if they are declared using the same type identifier (as D and E). Any type specification other than a type identifier creates a new type which is not equivalent to any other type. Thus A, C and D all have different types. Notice that primitive types are specified using type identifiers, so two variables will have the same type if they are both declared INTEGER. This is called *name equivalence* because two variables that are not declared together can have the same type only if they are declared using the same type name.

Structural equivalence

Two variables are considered to be of the same type whenever they have components of the same type structured in the same way. Using this definition, all of the variables in the example above have the same type.

Name equivalence is quite a nuisance to the programmer, since he or she must often make up extra type names. On the other hand, name equivalence provides extra protection against type errors. Furthermore, structural equivalence causes a logical problem. Consider this example using structural equivalence.

```
var K: (MALE, FEMALE);
    L: (MALE, FEMALE);
```

Clearly the types of K and L are equivalent, since they have the same structure. However,
>   **var** M: (MALE, FEMALE);
>   N: (FEMALE, MALE);

is illegal because the identifiers MALE and FEMALE are not unique. Distinguishing between these two cases will be difficult for the compiler. It cannot simply consider the construct (MALE, FEMALE) to be a declaration of the identifiers MALE and FEMALE as it could in the case of name equivalence. If it did, it would reject the legal declaration of identifier L.

Even worse, suppose that the type (MALE, FEMALE) is created and then the identifier MALE is used for an unrelated purpose in an inner block. Then, in a block inside both of these, the construct (MALE, FEMALE) is used again. Is it a reference to the first type ? A new type ? An error ? There seems to be no good answer.

The use of structural equivalence also creates a problem with record types, which is illustrated by the following:
>   **var** F: **record** T, U: REAL **end**;
>   G: **record** V, W: REAL **end**;

Do F and G have the same type ? Either answer seems reasonable and consistent.

Structural equivalence creates a further dilemma for the implementor in relation to the **packed** prefix for structured types. Section 6.2 of the *Report* states that the prefix 'has no effect on the meaning of the program but is a hint to the compiler that storage should be economized even at the price of some loss in efficiency of access'. Presumably therefore a packed type is equivalent to an otherwise structurally equivalent unpacked one, and the compiler must permit, and generate code for, assignment or, worse still, actual-formal parameter correspondence between them. This problem does not arise with name equivalence since the syntax of $\langle$type$\rangle$ excludes the form **packed** $\langle$*type identifier*$\rangle$.

Name equivalence is not, however, without its problems. It precludes, for example, the assignment of a string constant to a variable of a corresponding string type. Section 4 of the *Report* states that a string constant of *n* characters has an implicit type
>   **packed array** [1..*n*] **of** *char*

With name equivalence, however, this implied type cannot be equivalent to any other so the string may only appear in certain limited contexts such as calls on the built-in procedure *write*. A similar problem arises with constructed sets, whose type is also implicitly specified; this problem is considered further in a later section of this paper.

Name equivalence also creates a potential confusion for the user of the type definition
>   **type** T1 = T2;

where T2 is the name of a type defined elsewhere. With name equivalence this will not produce a convenient local synonym for type T2 as might be expected, but a new type T1 which is not equivalent to type T2 in any context.

Clearly the current features of Pascal do not permit a simple choice between name or structural equivalence as defined. Some alternative or compromise equivalence definition must be adopted. In practice of course each implementation of Pascal has already made some choice. The ETH compiler (the compiler described by the *User Manual*) uses structural equivalence in most cases.[16] However, a scalar type declaration such as (MALE, FEMALE) is taken to be a declaration of the identifiers MALE and FEMALE, and therefore causes a message about a duplicate declaration if repeated in the same block. (It will create a new type equivalent to the first if used in an inner block.) Record types are equivalent if the corresponding field types are the same, but packed structured types are not equivalent to corresponding unpacked ones.

It is unsatisfactory that implementors should be left to make such decisions, since any divergence in their choice imperils the portability of Pascal programs. The authors of Euclid, Pascal's most recent derivative, were clearly conscious of Pascal's deficiencies in this area. Although the definition of Euclid has been modelled on the Pascal *Report*, it incorporates an explicit definition of type equivalence based on the repeated replacement of type identifiers by the sequence of symbols appearing in their definition. Two types are equivalent if, in the sequences of symbols which they produce,

> (a) corresponding occurrences of free constant identifiers (i.e. those not declared by these types) denote the same value;
> (b) corresponding symbols are otherwise identical.

The resultant definition of type equivalence is close to the structural equivalence suggested above. Whether this particular definition is the best for the language remains an open question, but the provision of *some* such explicit definition is an important requirement, both for Pascal and for any language which imitates its repertoire of data types.

Scope rules and one-pass compilation

One of the design objectives stated for Pascal was to enable efficient compilation of its programs. Although the *Report* does not say so explicitly, the language features appear to favour one-pass compilation as a means to this end, and implementors have assumed this to be the designer's intent. However, this implicit one-pass compilation capability creates some traps for the unwary, into which implementors have duly fallen.

In general, one-pass compilation requires that the declaration of an identifier precede all other references to that identifier. The Pascal *Report* does not specify at any point that an identifier's declaration must precede its use. It does, however, impose a rigid order on the different classes of declaration which are made within a block, thus:

$\langle block \rangle ::= \langle label\ declaration\ part \rangle$
$\qquad\qquad\quad \langle constant\ definition\ part \rangle$
$\qquad\qquad\quad \langle type\ definition\ part \rangle$
$\qquad\qquad\quad \langle variable\ declaration\ part \rangle$
$\qquad\qquad\quad \langle procedure\ and\ function\ declaration\ part \rangle$
$\qquad\qquad\quad \langle statement\ part \rangle$

This has the effect of ensuring that constant identifiers are defined before they can be used in type definitions, that type identifiers are defined before they can be used in variable declarations and that variable identifiers are declared before they can be used in the statement part or as non-locals in nested procedures and function. However, it does not guarantee declaration before use *within* the type definition or procedure declaration parts. For example, the following program segment is unacceptable to a one-pass compiler because the use of the identifier COMPLEX to declare type MATRIX precedes the declaration of COMPLEX.

```
type MATRIX = array [1..10, 1..10] of COMPLEX;
     COMPLEX = record REALPART, IMAGPART: REAL end;
var  M: MATRIX;
       ⋮
     WRITE(M[2, 2].REALPART);
```

Now consider the same program segment and assume that this declaration is in the containing block:

```
type COMPLEX = record RE, IM: REAL end;
```

There are at least two possible interpretations of this program by a one-pass system:

(1) The elements of M each have two real components with names RE and IM, since the outer declaration of COMPLEX was current when the declaration of MATRIX was scanned. (2) The program is in error because the inner declaration of COMPLEX is the one that should apply, and it follows the declaration of MATRIX.

This program is incorrect in either case. Under interpretation (1), the call to WRITE is incorrect because the REALPART is not a valid field name for variable M. We are not just haggling over which statement gets the error message, however. If the field name REAL-PART in the call to WRITE were replaced by RE, the resulting program would be correct according to interpretation (1) and incorrect according to (2).

Notice that (1) is the easier interpretation to implement. Each reference to an identifier is simply bound to the most recent declaration of that identifier. One way to implement (2) might be to bind the element type of MATRIX to the outer definition of COMPLEX, but record this binding so that an error can be declared when the inner definition of COMPLEX is scanned. The recorded binding has to be applied not only in the current scope but also in any enclosing scopes between it and the outer definition.

Unfortunately, interpretation (1) has some problems involving pointer types, and (2) is the better interpretation. Consider the following example:

```
type FLIGHT =
        record
          NUMBER: 0..999;
          FIRSTPAS: ↑PASSENGER;
            ...
        end;

      PASSENGER =
      record
        FLIGHTBOOKED: ↑FLIGHT;
        NEXTPAS: ↑PASSENGER
          ...
      end;
```

Each of the two types in the example refers to the other, so whichever type is declared second in the program will have its identifier referenced before it is declared. This is a case where the rule that identifiers must be declared before they are used is too restrictive to be practical, and Pascal implementations make an exception to accommodate this case. Pointer declarations, such as ↑PASSENGER, are allowed to precede the declaration of the identifier used. Fortunately, the compiler can allocate storage for a pointer without knowing what type of thing it will reference, since the size of a pointer does not depend on what it points at.

The problem with interpretation (1) is illustrated by the example above if there happens to be a type PASSENGER declared in an outer block. In that case, interpretation (1) demands that the name PASSENGER in field FIRSTPAS be bound to the outer definition of type PASSENGER. This is very bad, because the meaning of a valid block can be changed by declaring an identifier in an outer block.

In fact the *Report* does exclude interpretation (1) since Section 4 states that the 'association (of identifiers) must be unique within their scope of validity, i.e. within the procedure or function in which they are declared'. (No explicit definition of scope for main program identifiers is given.) However, the significance of Section 4 is clearly not apparent to its implementors, since the ETH compiler itself follows interpretation (1), even to the extent of binding the pointer type ↑ PASSENGER to a non-local instance of PASSENGER if one exists.

A similar difficulty arises with mutually recursive procedures and functions. To retain one-pass compilation with checking of parameters the ETH compiler requires a FORWARD declaration, which is not described in the *Report* or included in the syntax diagrams or BNF. It is described only in Section 11.C of the *User Manual*, from which we take the following example.

```
procedure Q(X:T); FORWARD;
procedure P(Y:T);
begin
    Q(A)
  end;
procedure Q; (* PARAMETERS NOT REPEATED *)
  begin
    P(B)
  end;
begin
  P(A);
  Q(B)
end.
```

The line

```
procedure Q(X:T); FORWARD;
```

which must precede the procedure P, provides enough information so that the call to Q from within P can be compiled.

These problems arise because the *Report* does not define any precise rules for the relative positions of the declaration and use of identifiers. Implementors of one-pass compilers must impose additional restrictions on the language definition, or create the unsatisfactory implementation effects outlined above. If one-pass compilation is to be a language objective it should be made explicit in the language definition and an explicit declaration-before-use rule should be adopted, with whatever exceptions the language features may require.

With such a rule the rigid order which Pascal imposes on the constant, type, variable and procedure declaration parts could be relaxed, allowing natural groupings of the types, variables and procedures which manipulate them. The inability to make such groupings in structuring large programs is one of Pascal's most frustrating limitations.

Given such groupings, or modules, of course the additional controls on their mutual interaction such as those which Modula and Euclid provide are clearly desirable. The control over the use of identifiers which these languages offer is a clear indication that the current needs of programming have moved well beyond the implicit scope rules of simple block structure, and Pascal.

Set constructors

As was indicated earlier, the implicit types of string constants and constructed sets create problems in defining type equivalence. However, the implicit type definition creates additional problems in the representation of sets.

According to Section 8 of the *Report*, 'Expressions which are members of a set must all be of the same type, which is the base type of the set.' This leads to the conclusion that the type of the set constructor [1, 5, 10..19, 23] is **set of** INTEGER, since Section 4 makes it clear that the types of 1, 5, 10, 19 and 23 are INTEGER. However, Section 14 states that 'The implementer may set a limit to the size of a base type over which a set can be defined.

(Consequently, a bit pattern representation may reasonably be used for sets).' Since the apparent base type in the example is INTEGER and the size of type INTEGER is larger than any reasonable limit, one might conclude that the example is illegal in at least some implementations. The example comes from Section 8 of the *Report*, so it seems fair to say that the *Report* is confusing, if not ambiguous.

In practice the conflict is yet another which is resolved by an implicit range to subrange transfer. Given that a limit on the size of base types exists, the compiler may assume that the intended base type of [1, 5, 10..19, 23] is some subrange of the integers, and apply an implicit range to subrange transfer to its member values. The problem is that the intended subrange is not apparent, which in turn has consequences for the representation of the set.

Using a bit pattern representation for sets, the type

set of 20..29

is represented by a bit pattern very much like the type

packed array [20..29] **of** BOOLEAN

where element N of the array is TRUE if and only if N is in the set. The trouble is that the base type of [1, 5, 10..19, 23] has not been specified, so the compiler does not know what the bounds of its Boolean array should be.

Implementations overcome this problem by imposing an additional limit on the base types of sets. For example, in the ETH compiler the limit on the size of a base type is 59, so the compiler knows that the Boolean array can be no larger than 59. However, the compiler also needs its upper and lower bounds. The ETH compiler therefore adds the restriction that each element of any set of integers must be between 0 and 58. This rule allows any set of integers to be represented by an array with bounds 0 and 58. A similar rule applies to sets of non-integers. In that case, no element E is allowed unless $ORD(E) \leqslant 58$. This solution has the consequence that apparently representable set types such as

DATES = **set of** 1939..1945

are excluded by current implementations.

For implementations which choose, or are forced by short word lengths or byte orientation, to use multilength representations of sets the implicit type of the set constructor presents an additional problem. Either all sets over subranges of a given type must use the same length of representation, or the required length of a constructed set must be deduced from context. The extreme case occurs when the empty set [ ] (which has no implicit base type at all) occurs as an actual parameter of a formal procedure or function (which provides no contextual indication of the representation required).

All these problems can be avoided by requiring an explicit specification of the base type of every set constructor. For example, given a set type

DIGITS = **set of** 0..9

the constructor notation used might be

DIGITS (1, 3, 5)

This makes the programmer write a bit more, but allows the base type of a set to be any scalar type that does not have too many elements. Not only are the restrictions simpler and less constraining, but the language is cleaner because every set constructor has a type which can be determined during compilation without any use of context. A version of Pascal using such a constructor, and a multiword representation of sets, has been implemented[18] and shown to provide a more flexible, and more efficient, set manipulation facility. A similar notation has now been adopted in Euclid.

This notation also reconciles the set constructor with the name equivalence convention for types discussed earlier. A similar solution for string constants might be considered. Given a string type

MESSAGE = **packed array** [1..16] **of** *char*

a constant of the type might be written thus

MESSAGE('ILLEGAL OPERANDS')

In this case the additional burden on the programmer may be unacceptable in contexts where named type specification is unecessary, e.g. in calls to the built-in procedure *write*, and some default for omitting the type name and parentheses may be appropriate.

INSECURITIES

For the purposes of this discussion, an insecurity is a feature that cannot be implemented without either (1) a risk that violations of the language rules will go undetected, or (2) run-time checking that is comparable in cost to the operation being performed.

Pascal has fewer insecurities than most comparable languages. For example, it is not possible to use a pointer to access a dynamic variable of the wrong type. This error is caught during compilation because each pointer can only point at variable or a single type. The remarkable thing about Pascal is that the number of insecurities is small enough to make it worthwhile to prepare a list in the hope that future research will lead to languages with even fewer or perhaps no insecurities.

Variant records

Pascal allows variant records with and without tag fields. An example of a variant record with a tag field is

```
V: record AREA:REAL;
      case S:SHAPE of
         TRIANGLE: (SIDE:REAL;
                    INCLINATION, ANGLE1, ANGLE2:REAL);
         CIRCLE:    (DIAMETER:REAL)
   end
```

The field *AREA* always exists, but whether *DIAMETER* exists or not depends on whether the value of the tag field, *S*, is *CIRCLE* or not. A version of this record without a tag field can be created by omitting 'S' after the symbol *case*.

If there is no tag field, then the variant record is inevitably insecure. Either ANGLE1 or ANGLE2 could be referenced when it is not present, and there is no way to catch the error, even at run-time. This is bad, because such an error is likely to be difficult to find.

The compiler could insert a tag field even when the programmer does not request it, but it would be misleading and pointless to allow the programmer to omit the tag field if the compiler included it anyway. The introduction to Pascal of variant records without tag fields must be regarded as a retrograde step, to be regretted by Pascal users, and avoided by the designers of future languages.

Given that a tag field is present in all variant records, a run-time check is still required to achieve security. However, the run-time check can be avoided when code like the following is used to reference the variant part

```
case V.S of
    TRIANGLE: begin (references to V.SIDE, etc.) end;
    CIRCLE:     begin (references to V.DIAMETER) end
end
```

since the value of the tag field when the references occur is known when the program is compiled. This is done in Simula 67 with an **inspect when** statement, which is similar to the **case** statement above. A similar modification to Pascal has been investigated,[19] which showed that direct violations from within the **case** construct were easily detected, but that detection of indirect changes of the variant by reassignment of the entire record variable, possibly during procedure calls from within the case, was impractical. The *Report* does outlaw such changes with a **with** statement (Section 9.2.4) but this restriction is equally impractical to enforce by compile-time or run-time checking.

Euclid incorporates an explicit construct which enables direct variant violations to be detected at compile-time. For more general reasons of program verification Euclid's definition also goes to considerable lengths to enable variable overlaps, such as might cause an implicit change of variant, to be detected. Whether the added complexity of the rules required, and the added restrictions which they impose on the programmer, are an acceptable price to pay for variable access security, may be shown by experience of implementing and using Euclid. The rules and restrictions involved cannot be readily added to current framework of Pascal.

Functions and procedures as parameters

When a Pascal formal parameter is a function or a procedure, the language does not require or even permit the programmer to specify the number and types of any parameters. The following example, which is due to Lecarme and Desjardins,[20] illustrates a program which contains an error that cannot reasonably be detected at compile-time:

```
procedure P(procedure Q);
    begin Q(2, 'A') end;
procedure R(X:BOOLEAN);
    begin WRITE(X) end;
begin P(R) end.
```

The apparent solution is to allow full specification of parameters in this case, as is done in ALGOL 68. The normal syntax for parameter specification is excessive for this purpose since it includes specification of names of the formal parameters, and these names are not required. Lecarme and Desjardins proposed a syntax for specifying the types without giving names. With their syntax, the first line of the example above is written

```
procedure P(procedure Q(INTEGER, CHAR));
    begin Q(2, 'A') end;
```

which gives enough information for the error to be detected during compilation.

To enable the correct parameter passing code to be generated for their calls, Pascal currently allows procedures and functions passed as parameters to take value parameters only. Given an adequate notation for expressing the parameter requirements of formal procedures or functions, this restriction can in principle be relaxed. The notation required is more complicated than that of Lecarme and Desjardins, however, since it must distinguish between variable and value parameters. If procedure parameters which themselves

45

take procedure parameters are allowed the notation must also provide a nested, and potentially recursive, specification of parameter requirements.

The Pascal compiler for UNIVAC 1100 computers, developed at DIKU in Copenhagen, incorporates an extension which meets these requirements.[21] Formal parameter lists can be defined and named in a separate parameter declaration part of each block. The parameter requirements of actual procedures may then be specified by reference to a named parameter list, and those of formal procedures must be specified in this way. In the DIKU system formal parameter names are always included in the parameter list specification, so that procedures sharing a parameter specification must use the same formal parameter names as well.

Range violations

As in most compiled languages, accessing an element of a Pascal array is insecure if an index is out of bounds. Since almost all languages have this problem, it is appropriate to try to solve it with hardware. The extra hardware cost is quite small. The descriptor mechanism of the ICL 2900 series computers provides an implicit bound check during array access but, while it works well for the arrays allowed in languages such as FORTRAN or ALGOL 60, it is inadequate for some of the array structures permitted in Pascal.[22]

Array access is just one of a number of contexts in which a value outside a permitted range can arise in Pascal. Others are assignment to a subrange variable, case selection, set membership creation and testing, and indeed overflow in integer and real arithmetic. While it is unreasonable to hope to exclude by language design the possibility of all such violations, designers must aim to reduce the cost of their run-time detection. It should be noted that Pascal's provision of enumerated and subrange types is a significant step in this direction. Each use of a variable of an enumerated type removes a potential insecurity by ensuring that the finite set of values which the variable may take is verified at compile-time. For a subrange variable run-time verification of the values taken may be necessary but, assuming these checks are made, other more frequent and hence more expensive checks may be avoided at each point where the variable value is used. A Pascal compiler which exploits this technique has been constructed[23] for ICL 1900 computers, and has shown that for simple array manipulations run-time subscript checking can be eliminated, or reduced to insignificance.

Uninitialized variables

Uninitialized variables are also difficult to detect, and all hardware detection mechanisms known to us are quite expensive. Possible solutions are to require that every variable be initialized when it is declared or that every variable be assigned in such a way that the compiler can easily verify that there are no references to uninitialized variables. The latter might work very well in a language without jumps, and deserves further investigation.

Dangling references

Accessing of dynamic variables (those found via pointers) is not secure because the storage for the dynamic variable may have been released. This is a very common insecurity for which Pascal allows no obvious solution.

It can be argued that Pascal's pointer is a low-level facility provided for use in those situations for which the high-level data constructs are inadequate, and that it is unreasonable to expect security from a low-level facility. Whatever the philosophical validity of this argument it is little consolation to a programmer whose pointers go wrong!

Euclid offers an optional security against such errors by enabling reference counts to be maintained for collections of dynamically allocated variables. Storage release is then an implicit operation occurring when a reference count reaches zero, rather than an explicit programmable action. Maintaining reference counts is, of course, a considerable overhead if applied to every pointer variable assignment. The success of the Euclid proposal depends on the degree to which the compiler can detect those program segments which use local pointer variables to trace a dynamically allocated structure without altering the non-local reference pattern in any way. Reference counting code can then be avoided for the pointer manipulation within the segment.

CONCLUSION

At the time that Pascal was first designed and developed, the most fashionable languages in the learned and practical world were ALGOL 68 and PL/I. The discovery that the advantages of a high-level language could be combined with high efficiency in such a simple and elegant manner as in Pascal was a revelation that deserves the title of breakthrough. Because of the very success of Pascal, which greatly exceeded the expectations of its author, the standards by which we judge such languages have also risen. It is grossly unfair to judge an engineering project by standards which have been proved attainable only by the success of the project itself, but in the interests of progress, such criticism must be made.

Of the criticisms made in this paper, some identify shortcomings of Pascal which can readily be made good by minor changes to the language or its definition. Others indicate problems for which there is no easy solution within the current framework. As a language which attempts to overcome most of the problems listed, Euclid deserves special mention, though it should also be pointed out that no implementation of Euclid has yet been reported. Unfortunately, Euclid achieves its goals at the expense of a significant loss of simplicity and elegance in the language definition. Whether this trade-off is inevitable or whether some future breakthrough can restore elegance and simplicity without loss of security is a question which language designers must ponder for some time to come.

ACKNOWLEDGEMENTS

The research on this paper was supported in part by a grant from the Science Research Council of Great Britain.

REFERENCES

1. P. Naur (Ed.), 'Report on the algorithmic language ALGOL 60', *Comm. ACM*, **3**, 299–314 (1960).
2. N. Wirth, 'The programming language Pascal', *Acta Informatica*, **1**, 35–63 (1971).
3. B. A. Galler and A. J. Perlis, 'A proposal for definitions in ALGOL', *Comm. ACM*, **10**, 204–219 (1967).
4. N. Wirth and C. A. R Hoare, 'A contribution to the development of ALGOL', *Comm. ACM*, **9**, 413–432 (1966).
5. A. van Winjngaarden (Ed.), 'Report on the algorithmic language ALGOL 68', *Numerische Mathematik*, **14**, 79–218 (1969).
6. IBM, *PL/I(F) Language Reference Manual, Order Number C28–8201*, IBM, 1969.
7. G. Birtwistle *et al.*, *Simula Begin*, Auerbach, 1975.
8. A. N. Habermann, 'Critical comments on the programming language Pascal', *Acta Informatica*, **3**, 47–57 (1973).

9. P. Brinch Hansen, 'The programming language Concurrent Pascal', *IEEE Trans. Software Engng*, **1**, 2 (1975).

10. R. D. Tennent, 'Pasqual: a proposed generalisation of Pascal', *Technical Report No. 75–32*, Department of Computing and Information Science, Queen's University, Kingston, Ontario, Canada.

11. N. Wirth, 'Modula: a language for modular multiprogramming', *Software—Practice and Experience*, **7**, 3–35 (1977).

12. B. W. Lampson *et al.*, 'Report on the programming language Euclid', *ACM Sigplan Notices*, **12**, 2 (1977).

13. P. Naur, 'Revised report on the algorithmic language ALGOL 60', *Comm. ACM*, **6**, 1 (1963).

14. N. Wirth, 'The programming language Pascal (Revised Report)', *Berichte der Fachgruppe Computer-Wissenschaften Nr. 5*, ETH Zurich (1973).

15. K. Jensen and N. Wirth, 'Pascal—User Manual and Report', *Lecture Notes in Computer Science*, **18**, Springer Verlag, 1974.

16. U. Ammann, 'The Zurich implementation', *Proc. Symp. on Pascal—the language and its implementation, Southampton* (1977).

17. C. A. R. Hoare and N. Wirth, 'An axiomatic definition of the programming language Pascal', *Acta Informatica*, **2**, 335–355 (1973).

18. C. J. Copeland, 'Extensions to Pascal', *MSc. dissertation*, Queen's University, Belfast (1975).

19. P. W. C. Sinte, 'Recursive data structures in Pascal', *MSc. dissertation*, Queen's University, Belfast (1975).

20. O. Lecarme and P. Desjardins, 'More comments on the programming language Pascal', *Acta Informatica*, **4**, 231–243 (1975).

21. J. Steensgaard-Madsen, *Procedures as Monitors in Sequential Programming*, DIKU, Copenhagen, Denmark, 1977.

22. M. Rees, 'Pascal on an advanced architecture', *Proc. Symp. on Pascal—the language and its implementation, Southampton* (1977).

23. J. Welsh, 'Two ICL 1900 Pascal compilers', *Proc. Symp. on Pascal—the language and its implementation, Southampton* (1977).

Section 6
The Design of Ada

The U.S. Department of Defense directed the systematic design of the programming language Ada, named for Lady Lovelace, who may be considered the first programmer by virtue of her work with Charles Babbage. The design of Ada resulted from the DoD's desire to have a standard high order language for the implementation of embedded computer systems, such as those on shipboard and in aircraft.

Most systems written for the DoD were either in assembler language or in one of a host of relatively obscure programming languages for which there exist only a couple of machines and compilers capable of translating the languages. Furthermore, there were a relatively small number of expert programmers for these languages, thereby complicating the problem of evolving these programs as errors appeared or enhancements were needed.

The Department of Defense, in recognition of the very large sum of money being spent on software and of the relatively fragile state of some of that software, established a High Order Language Working Group (HOLWG) to look into the problem. They established a set of criteria that an ideal high order language should have ("Strawman,") and then refined this set of characteristics ("Woodenman," "Tinman").

The "Tinman" document was used as a basis for evaluating existing languages to see which, if any, satisfied the criteria. Because the document proposed a set of almost 100 characteristics, it was clear at the outset that no language would come close to satisfying the entire set, although LIS and Algol 68 rated quite highly.

Accordingly, the HOLWG went ahead with its plan to design a new language for embedded computer systems that embodied the advances of programming languages of the 1970's. The new language also could represent an order of magnitude improvement in the quality of language used, with the intent of obtaining significant improvements in software quality, system evolvability, and programmer productivity.

Four organizations—SRI International, SofTech, Intermetrics, and Honeywell-Bull-CII—received contracts to carry out a preliminary design of a language satisfying the latest set of requirements ("Ironman"). Curiously, when these preliminary designs—known, respectively, as Yellow, Blue, Red, and Green—were evaluated, despite the DoD's effort to separate the contractors from the individual language designs by use of the colors, astute reviewers were able to associate the design teams with their respective designs in a matter of minutes.

The DoD selected two of the preliminary designs (Red and Green); a revised set of criteria was produced ("Steelman"); and both languages were revised. Although the contractor redesigned the Red language virtually from scratch using a new design team, the Green language was selected as the preliminary design of Ada. Subsequent redesign of this language, completed in the summer of 1980, represents the Ada language.

Based on the state of the art in programming language technology, Ada incorporates features for encapsulated (abstract) data types, exception handling, modularization with separate compilation of modules, and concurrent programming, including asynchronous interrupt handling. It incorporates a number of relatively untested language design ideas based upon a Pascal and LIS framework.

At this time, there is no fully operational Ada compiler and hence almost no experience in the use of Ada. It is too early to tell whether Ada will be widely adopted and used, or whether it will have the desired effects on program quality. All that is certain is that the sponsor, the Department of Defense, is strong enough to encourage the use of the language and its implementation by a large number of hardware and software vendors.

Meanwhile, the Department of Defense and the HOLWG have pursued the goal of programmer productivity by turning their attention to programming environments and software tools to support the Ada programmer, and have developed a set of criteria to form the basis for programming environments ("Pebbleman," "Stoneman"). Future work should see the development of experimental software tools covering large parts of the software development and evolution life cycle, including both technical and managerial aspects. These tools will then be integrated into programming environments.

The papers in this section trace the development of Ada, providing additional detail on the above historical account as seen from the Department of Defense perspective. The "Steelman" requirements show the basis for the language design, indicating the concern of the HOLWG not only with the characteristics of the language itself but also with matters of language and compiler control. The final paper in the section, by Peter Wegner, gives a brief overview of the preliminary version of Ada. His book of the same title, published by Prentice Hall, gives a more thorough introduction.

DEPARTMENT OF DEFENSE

REQUIREMENTS FOR HIGH ORDER

COMPUTER PROGRAMMING LANGUAGES

"STEELMAN"

June 1978

PREFACE

The Department of Defense Common High Order Language program was
established in 1975 with the goal of establishing a single high order computer
programming language appropriate for DoD embedded computer systems. A
High Order Language Working Group (HOLWG) was established to formulate the
DoD requirements for high order languages, to evaluate existing languages
against those requirements, and to implement the minimal set of languages
required for DoD use. As an administrative initiative toward the eventual goal,
DoD Directive 5000.29 provides that any new defense systems should be
programmed in a DoD approved and centrally controlled high order language.
DoD Instruction 5000.31 gives an interim list of approved languages: COBAL,
FORTRAN, TACPOL, CMS-2, SPL/1, and JOVIAL J3 and J73. Economic
analyses that were used to quantify the benefits from increased use of high
order languages, also showed that the rapid introduction of a single modern
language would increase the benefits considerably. The requirements have
been widely distributed for comment throughout the military and civil
communities, producing successively more refined versions from STRAWMAN
through WOODENMAN, TINMAN, IRONMAN, and the present STEELMAN.
During the requirement development process, it was determined that the single
set of requirements generated was both necessary and sufficient for all major
DoD applications. Formal evaluation was performed on dozens of existing
languages concluding that no existing language could be adopted as a single
common HOL for the DoD but that a single language meeting essentially all the
requirements was both feasible and desirable. Four contractors were funded
to produce competing prototype designs. After analysis of these preliminary
designs the number of design teams was reduced to two. Their designs will be
completed and a single language will emerge. Further steps in the program will
include test and evaluation of the language, production of compilers and other
tools for software development and maintenance, control of the language, and
validation of compilers. Government-funded compilers and software tools, as
well as the compiler validation facility, will be widely and inexpensively
available and well maintained.

THE TECHNICAL REQUIREMENTS

The technical requirements for a common DoD high order programming language given here are a synthesis of the requirements submitted by the Military Departments. They specify a set of constraints on the design of languages that are appropriate for embedded computer applications (i.e., command and control, communications, avionics, shipboard, test equipment, software development and maintenance, and support applications). We would especially like to thank the phase one analysis teams, the language design teams, and the many other individuals and organizations that have commented on the Revised Ironman and have identified weaknesses and trouble spots in the technical requirements. A primary goal in this revision has been to reduce the complexity of the resulting language.

This revision incorporates the following changes. Care has been taken to ensure that the paragraph numbers remain the same as in the Revised Ironman. There have been several changes in terminology and many changes in wording to improve the understandability and preciseness of the requirements. Several requirements have been restated to remove constraints that were, unintended but were implied because the requirement suggested a particular mechanism rather than giving the underlying requirement. The requirements for embedded comments (2I), unordered enumeration types (3-2B), associative operator specifications (7D), dynamic aliasing of array components (10B), and multiple representations of data (11B) have been deleted because they have been found unnecessary or are not adequately justified. The minimal source language character set has been reduced to 55 characters to make it compatible with the majority of existing input devices (2A). The do together model for parallel processing has been found inadequate for embedded computer applications and has been replaced by a requirement for parallel processes (section 9). The preliminary designs have demonstrated the need for additional requirements for explicit conversion between types (3B), subtype constraints (3D), renaming (3-5B), a language distinction between open and closed scopes (5G), and the ability, but preferably not special mechanisms, to pass data between parallel processes (9H), to write nonverifiable assertions (10F), to wait for several signals simultaneously (9J), and to mark shared variables (9C).

The Steelman is organized with an outline similar to that expected in a language defining document. Section 1 gives the general design criteria. These provide the major goals that influenced the selection of more specific requirements in later sections and provide a basis for language design decisions that are not otherwise addressed in this document. Sections 2 through 12 give more specific constraints on the language and its translators. The Steelman calls for the inclusion of features to satisfy specific needs in the design, implementation, and maintenance of military software, specifies both general and specific characteristics desired for the language, and calls for the exclusion of certain undesirable characteristics. Section 13 gives some of the intentions and expectations for development, control, and use of the language. The intended use and environment for the language has strongly influenced the requirements, and should influence the language design.

A precise and consistent use of terms has been attempted throughout the document. Many potentially ambiguous terms have been defined in the text. Care has been taken to distinguish between requirements, given as text, and comments, given as bracketed notes.

The following terms have been used throughout the text to indicate where and to what degree individual constraints apply:

shall	indicates a requirement placed on the language or translator
should	indicates a desired goal but one for which there is no objective test
shall attempt	indicates a desired goal but one that may not be achievable given the current state-of-the-art, or may be in conflict with other more important requirements
shall require	indicates a requirement placed on the user by the language and its translators (language is subject)
shall permit	indicates a requirement placed on the language to provide an option to the user (language is subject)
must	indicates a requirement placed on the user by the language and its translators (user is subject)
may	indicates a requirement placed on the language to provide an option to the user (user is subject)
will	indicates a consequence that is expected to follow or indicates an intention of the DoD; it does not in any case by itself constrain the design of the language
translation	refers to any processing applied to a program by the host or object machine before execution; it includes lexical analysis, syntactic error checking, program analyses, optimization, code generation, assembly, and loading
execution	refers to the processing by the object machine to carry out the actions prescribed by the program.

1. General Design Criteria

1A. Generality. The language shall provide generality only to the extent necessary to satisfy the needs of embedded computer applications. Such applications involve real time control, self diagnostics, input-output to nonstandard peripheral devices, parallel processing, numeric computation, and file processing.

1B. Reliability. The language should aid the design and development of reliable programs. The language shall be designed to avoid error prone features and to maximize automatic detection of programming errors. The language shall require some redundant, but not duplicative, specifications in programs. Translators shall produce explanatory diagnostic and warning messages, but shall not attempt to correct programming errors.

1C. Maintainability. The language should promote ease of program maintenance. It should emphasize program readability (i.e., clarity, understandability, and modifiability of programs). The language should encourage user documentation of programs. It shall require explicit specification of programmer decisions and shall provide defaults only for instances where the default is stated in the language definition, is always meaningful, reflects the most frequent usage in programs, and may be explicitly overridden.

1D. Efficiency. The language design should aid the production of efficient object programs. Constructs that have unexpectedly expensive implementations should be easily recognizable by translators and by users. Features should be chosen to have a simple and efficient implementation in many object machines, to avoid execution costs for available generality where it is not needed, to maximize the number of safe optimizations available to translators, and to ensure that unused and constant portions of programs will not add to execution costs. Execution time support packages of the language shall not be included in object code unless they are called.

1E. Simplicity. The language should not contain unnecessary complexity. It should have a consistent semantic structure that minimizes the number of underlying concepts. It should be as small as possible consistent with the needs of the intended applications. It should have few special cases and should be composed from features that are individually simple in their semantics. The language should have uniform syntactic conventions and should not provide several notations for the same concept. No arbitrary restriction should be imposed on a language feature.

1F. Implementability. The language shall be composed from features that are understood and can be implemented. The semantics of each feature should be sufficiently well specified and understandable that it will be possible to predict its interaction with other features. To the extent that it does not interfere with other requirements, the language shall facilitate the production of translators that are easy to implement and are efficient during translation. There shall be no language restrictions that are not enforceable by translators.

1G. Machine Independence. The design of the language should strive for machine independence. It shall not dictate the characteristics of object machines or operating systems except to the extent that such characteristics are implied by the semantics of control structures and built-in operations. It shall attempt to avoid features whose semantics depend on characteristics of the object machine or of the object machine operating system. Nevertheless, there shall be a facility for defining those portions of programs that are dependent on the object machine configuration and for conditionally compiling programs depending on the actual configuration.

1H. Complete Definition. The language shall be completely and unambiguously defined. To the extent that a formal definition assists in achieving the above goals (i.e., all of section 1), the language shall be formally defined.

2. General Syntax

2A. Character Set. The full set of character graphics that may be used in source programs shall be given in the language definition. Every source program shall also have a representation that uses only the following 55 character subset of the ASCII graphics:

```
%&' ()*+,-./:;<=>?
0123456789
ABCDEFGHIJKLMNOPQRSTUVWXYZ_
```

Each additional graphic (i.e., one in the full set but not in the 55 character set) may be replaced by a sequence of (one or more) characters from the 55 character set without altering the semantics of the program. The replacement sequence shall be specified in the language definition.

2B.   Grammar.   The language should have a simple, uniform, and easily parsed grammar and lexical structure.   The language shall have free form syntax and should use familiar notations where such use does not conflict with other goals.

2C.   Syntactic Extensions.   The user shall not be able to modify the source language syntax.   In particular the user shall not be able to introduce new precedence rules or to define new syntactic forms.

2D.   Other Syntactic Issues.   Multiple occurrences of a language defined symbol appearing in the same context shall not have essentially different meanings.   Lexical units (i.e., identifiers, reserved words, single and multicharacter symbols, numeric and string literals, and comments) may not cross line boundaries of a source program.   All key word forms that contain declarations or statements shall be bracketed (i.e., shall have a closing as well as an opening key word).   Programs may not contain unmatched brackets of any kind.

2E.   Mnemonic Identifiers.   Mnemonically significant identifiers shall be allowed. There shall be a break character for use within identifiers.   The language and its translators shall not permit identifiers or reserved words to be abbreviated.   [Note that this does not preclude reserved words that are abbreviations of natural language words.]

2F.   Reserved Words.   The only reserved words shall be those that introduce special syntactic forms (such as control structures and declarations) or that are otherwise used as delimiters.   Words that may be replaced by identifiers, shall not be reserved (e.g., names of functions, types, constants, and variables shall not be reserved).   All reserved words shall be listed in the language definition.

2G.   Numeric Literals.   There shall be built-in decimal literals.   There shall be no implicit truncation or rounding of integer and fixed point literals.

2H.   String Literals.   There shall be a built-in facility for fixed length string literals. String literals shall be interpreted as one-dimensional character arrays.

2I.   Comments.   The language shall permit comments that are introduced by a special (one or two character) symbol and terminated by the next line boundary of the source program.

3.   Types

3A.   Strong Typing.   The language shall be strongly typed.   The type of each variable, array and record component, expression, function, and parameter shall be determinable during translation.

3B.   Type Conversions.   The language shall distinguish the concepts of type (specifying data elements with common properties, including operations), subtype (i.e., a subset of the elements of a type, that is characterized by further constraints), and representations (i.e., implementation characteristics).   There shall be no implicit conversions between types.   Explicit conversion operations shall be automatically defined between types that are characterized by the same logical properties.

3C.   Type Definitions.   It shall be possible to define new data types in programs.   A type may be defined as an enumeration, an array or record type, an indirect type, an existing type, or a subtype of an existing type.   It shall be possible to process type definitions entirely during translation. An identifier may be associated with each type. No restriction shall be imposed on user defined types unless it is imposed on all types.

3D. Subtype Constraints. The constraints that characterize subtypes shall include range, precision, scale, index ranges, and user defined constraints. The value of a subtype constraint for a variable may be specified when the variable is declared. The language should encourage such specifications. [Note that such specifications can aid the clarity, efficiency, maintainability, and provability of programs.]

3.1. Numeric Types

3-1A. Numeric Values. The language shall provide distinct numeric types for exact and for approximate computation. Numeric operations and assignment that would cause the most significant digits of numeric values to be truncated (e.g., when overflow occurs) shall constitute an exception situation.

3-1B. Numeric Operations. There shall be built-in operations (i.e., functions) for conversion between the numeric types. There shall be operations for addition, subtraction, multiplication, division, negation, absolute value, and exponentiation to integer powers for each numeric type. There shall be built-in equality (i.e., equal and unequal) and ordering operations (i.e., less than, greater than, less than or equal, and greater than or equal) between elements of each numeric type. Numeric values shall be equal if and only if they have exactly the same abstract value.

3-1C. Numeric Variables. The range of each numeric variable must be specified in programs and shall be determined by the time of its allocation. Such specifications shall be interpreted as the minimum range to be implemented and as the maximum range needed by the application. Explicit conversion operations shall not be required between numeric ranges.

Approximate Arithmetic

3-1D. Precision. The precision (of the mantissa) of each expression result and variable in approximate computations must be specified in programs, and shall be determinable during translation. Precision specifications shall be required for each such variable. Such specifications shall be interpreted as the minimum accuracy (not significance) to be implemented. Approximate results shall be implicitly rounded to the implemented precision. Explicit conversions shall not be required between precisions.

3-1E. Approximate Arithmetic Implementation. Approximate arithmetic will be implemented using the actual precisions, radix, and exponent range available in the object machine. There shall be built-in operations to access the actual precision, radix, and exponent range of the implementation.

Exact Arithmetic

3-1F. Integer and Fixed Point Numbers. Integer and fixed point numbers shall be treated as exact numeric values. There shall be no implicit truncation or rounding in integer and fixed point computations.

3-1G. Fixed Point Scale. The scale or step size (i.e., the minimal representable difference between values) of each fixed point variable must be specified in programs and be determinable during translation. Scales shall not be restricted to powers of two.

3-1H. Integer and Fixed Point Operations. There shall be integer and fixed point operations for modulo and integer division and for conversion between values with different scales. All built-in and predefined operations for exact arithmetic shall apply between arbitrary scales. Additional operations between arbitrary scales shall be definable within programs.

3.2. Enumeration Types

3-2A. Enumeration Type Definitions. There shall be types that are definable in programs by enumeration of their elements. The elements of an enumeration type may be identifiers or character literals. Each variable of an enumeration type may be restricted to a contiguous subsequence of the enumeration.

3-2B. Operations on Enumeration Types. Equality, inequality, and the ordering operations shall be automatically defined between elements of each enumeration type. Sufficient additional operations shall be automatically defined so that the successor, predecessor, the position of any element, and the first and last element of the type may be computed.

3-2C. Boolean Type. There shall be a predefined type for Boolean values.

3-2D. Character Types. Character sets shall be definable as enumeration types. Character types may contain both printable and control characters. The ASCII character set shall be predefined.

3.3. Composite Types

3-3A. Composite Type Definitions. It shall be possible to define types that are Cartesian products of other types. Composite types shall include arrays (i.e., composite data with indexable components of homogeneous types) and records (i.e., composite data with labeled components of heterogeneous type).

3-3B. Component Specifications. For elements of composite types, the type of each component (i.e., field) must be explicitly specified in programs and determinable during translation. Components may be of any type (including array and record types). Range, precision, and scale specifications shall be required for each component of appropriate numeric type.

3-3C. Operations on Composite Types. A value accessing operation shall be automatically defined for each component of composite data elements. Assignment shall be automatically defined for components that have alterable values. A constructor operation (i.e., an operation that constructs an element of a type from its constituent parts) shall be automatically defined for each composite type. An assignable component may be used anywhere in a program that a variable of the component's type is permitted. There shall be no automatically defined equivalence operations between values of elements of a composite type.

3-3D. Array Specifications. Arrays that differ in number of dimensions or in component type shall be of different types. The range of subscript values for each dimension must be specified in programs and may be determinable at the time of array allocation. The range of each subscript value must be restricted to a contiguous sequence of integers or to a contiguous sequence from an enumeration type.

3-3E. Operations on Subarrays. There shall be built-in operations for value access, assignment, and catenation of contiguous sections of one-dimensional arrays of the same component type. The results of such access and catenation operations may be used as actual input parameter.

3-3F. Nonassignable Record Components. It shall be possible to declare constants and (unary) functions that may be thought of as record components and may be referenced using the same notation as for accessing record components. Assignment shall not be permitted to such components.

3-3G. Variants. It shall be possible to define types with alternative record structures (i.e., variants). The structure of each variant shall be determinable during translation.

3-3H. Tag Fields. Each variant must have a nonassignable tag field (i.e., a component that can be used to discriminate among the variants during execution). It shall not be possible to alter a tag field without replacing the entire variant.

3-3I. Indirect Types. It shall be possible to define types whose elements are indirectly accessed. Elements of such types may have components of their own type, may have substructure that can be altered during execution, and may be distinct while having identical component values. Such types shall be distinguishable from other composite types in their definitions. An element of an indirect type shall remain allocated as long as it can e referenced by the program. [Note that indirect types require pointers and sometimes heap storage in their implementation.]

3-3J. Operations on Indirect Types. Each execution of the constructor operation for an indirect type shall create a distinct element of the type. An operation that distinguishes between different elements, an operation that replaces all of the component values of an element without altering the element's identity, and an operation that produces a new element having the same component values as its argument, shall be automatically defined for each indirect type.

3.4. Sets

3-4A. Bit Strings (i.e., Set Types). It shall be possible to define types whose elements are one-dimensional Boolean arrays represented in maximally packed form (i.e, whose elements are sets).

3-4B. Bit String Operations. Set construction, membership (i.e., subscription), set equivalence and nonequivalence, and also complement, intersection, union, and symmetric difference (i.e., component-by-component negation, conjunction, inclusive disjunction, and exclusive disjunction respectively) operations shall be defined automatically for each set type.

3.5. Encapsulated Definitions

3-5A. Encapsulated Definitions. It shall be possible to encapsulate definitions. An encapsulation may contain declarations of anything (including the data elements and operations comprising a type) that is definable in programs. The language shall permit multiple explicit instantiations of an encapsulation.

3-5B. Effect of Encapsulation. An encapsulation may be used to inhibit external access to implementation properties of the definition. In particular, it shall be possible to prevent external reference to any declaration within the encapsulation including automatically defined operations such as type conversions and equality. Definitions that are made within an encapsulation and are externally accessable may be renamed before use outside the encapsulation.

3-5C. Own Variables. Variables declared within an encapsulation, but not within a function, procedure, or process of the encapsulation, shall remain allocated and retain their values throughout the scope in which the encapsulation is instantiated.

4. Expressions

4A. Form of Expressions. The parsing of correct expressions shall not depend on the types of their operands or on whether the types of the operands are built into the language.

4B. Type of Expressions. It shall be possible to specify the type of any expression explicitly. The use of such specifications shall be required only where the type of the expression cannot be uniquely determined during translation from the context of its use (as might be the case with a literal).

4C. Side Effects. The language shall attempt to minimize side effects in expressions, but shall not prohibit all side effects. A side effect shall not be allowed it it would alter the value of a variable that can be accessed at the point of the expression. Side effects shall be limited to own variables of encapsulations. The language shall permit side effects that are necessary to instrument functions and to do storage management within functions. The order of side effects within an expression shall not be guaranteed. [Note that the latter implies that any program that depends on the order of side effects is erroneous.]

4D. Allowed Usage. Expressions of a given type shall be allowed wherever both constants and variables of the type are allowed.

4E. Translation Time Expressions. Expressions that can be evaluated during translation shall be permitted wherever literals of the type are permitted. Translation time expressions that include only literals and the use of translation time facilities (see 11C) shall be evaluated during translation.

4F. Operator Precedence Levels. The precedence levels (i.e., binding strengths) of all (prefix and infix) operators shall be specified in the language definition, shall not be alterable by the user, shall be few in number, and shall not depend on the types of the operands.

4G. Effect of Parentheses. If present, explicit parentheses shall dictate the association of operands with operators. The language shall specify where explicit parentheses are required and shall attempt to minimize the psychological ambiguity in expressions. [Note that this might be accomplished by requiring explicit parentheses to resolve the operator-operand association whenever a nonassociative operator appears to the left of an operator of the same precedence at the least-binding precedence level of any subexpression.]

5. Constants, Variables, and Scopes

5A. Declarations of Constants. It shall be possible to declare constants of any type. Such constants shall include both those whose values are determined during translation and those whose value cannot be determined until allocation. Programs may not assign to constants.

5B. Declarations of Variables. Each variable must be declared explicitly. Variables may be of any type. The type of each variable must be specified as part of its declaration and must be determinable during translation. [Note, "variable" throughout this document refers not only to simple variables but also to composite variables and to components of arrays and records.]

5C. Scope of Declarations. Everything (including operators) declared in a program shall have a scope (i.e., a portion of the program in which it can be referenced). Scopes shall be determinable during translation. Scopes may be nested (i.e., lexically embedded). A declaration may be made in any scope. Anything other than a variable shall be accessable within any nested scope of its definition.

5D. Restrictions on Values. Procedures, functions, types, labels, exception situations, and statements shall not be assignable to variables, be computable as values of expressions, or be usable as nongeneric parameters to procedures or functions.

5E. Initial Values. There shall be no default initial values for variables.

5F. Operations on Variables. Assignment and an implicit value access operation shall be automatically defined for each variable.

5G. Scope of Variables. The language shall distinguish between open scopes (i.e., those that are automatically included in the scope of more globally declared variables) and closed scopes (i.e., those in which nonlocal variables must be explicitly imported). Bodies of functions, procedures, and processes shall be closed scopes. Bodies of classical control structures shall be open scopes.

6. Classical Control Structures

6A. Basic Control Facility. The (built-in) control mechanisms should be of minimal number and complexity. Each shall provide a single capability and shall have a distinguishing syntax. Nesting of control structures shall be allowed. There shall be no control definition facility. Local scopes shall be allowed within the bodies of control statements. Control structures shall have only one entry point and shall exit to a single point unless exited via an explicit transfer of control (where permitted, see 6G), or the raising of an exception (see 10C).

6B. Sequential Control. There shall be a control mechanism for sequencing statements. The language shall not impose arbitrary restrictions on programming style, such as the choice between statement terminators and statement separators, unless the restriction makes programming errors less likely.

6C. Conditional Control. There shall be conditional control structures that permit selection among alternative control paths. The selected path may depend on the value of a Boolean expression, on a computed choice among labeled alternatives, or on the true condition in a set of conditions. The language shall define the control action for all values of the discriminating condition that are not specified by the program. The user may supply a single control path to be used when no other path ·is selected. Only the selected branch shall be compiled when the discriminating condition is a translation time expression.

6D. Short Circuit Evaluation. There shall be infix control operations for short circuit conjunction and disjunction of the controlling Boolean expression in conditional and iterative control structures.

6E. Iterative Control. There shall be an iterative control structure. The iterative control may be exited (without reentry) at an unrestricted number of places. A succession of values from an enumeration type or the integers may be associated with successive iterations and the value for the current iteration accessed as a constant throughout the loop body.

6G. Explicit Control Transfer. There shall be a mechanism for control transfer (i.e., the go to). It shall not be possible to transfer out of closed scopes, into narrower scopes, or into control structures. It shall be possible to transfer out of classical control structures. There shall be no control transfer mechanisms in the form of switches, designational expressions, label variables, label parameters, or alter statements.

7. Functions and Procedures

7A. Function and Procedure Definitions. Functions (which return values to expressions) and procedures (which can be called as statements) shall be definable in programs. Functions or procedures that differ in the number or types of their parameters may be denoted by the same identifier or operator (i.e., overloading shall be permitted). [Note that redefinition, as opposed to overloading, of an existing function or procedure is often error prone.]

7B. Recursion. It shall be possible to call functions and procedures recursively.

7C. Scope Rules. A reference to an identifier that is not declared in the most local scope shall refer to a program element that is lexically global, rather than to one that is global through the dynamic calling structure.

Functions

7D. Function Declarations. The type of the result for each function must be specified in its declaration and shall be determinable during translation. The results of functions may be of any type. If a result is of a nonindirect array or record type then the number of its components must be determinable by the time of function call.

Parameters

7F. Formal Parameter Classes. There shall be three classes of formal data parameters: (a) input parameters, which act as constants that are initialized to the value of corresponding actual parameters at the time of call, (b) input-output parameters, which enable access and assignment to the corresponding actual parameters, either throughout execution or only upon call and prior to any exit, and (c) output parameters, whose values are transferred to the corresponding actual parameter only at the time of normal exit. In

the latter two cases the corresponding actual parameter shall be determined at time of
call and must be a variable or an assignable component of a composite type.

7G. Parameter Specifications. The type of each formal parameter must be explicitly
specified in programs and shall be determinable during translation. Parameters may be
of any type. The language shall not require user specification of subtype constraints for
formal parameters. If such constraints are permitted they shall be interpreted as
assertions and not as additional overloading. Corresponding formal and actual
parameters must be of the same type.

7H. Formal Array Parameters. The number of dimensions for formal array parameters
must be specified in programs and shall be determinable during translation.
Determination of the subscript range for formal array parameters may be delayed until
invocation and may vary from call to call. Subscript ranges shall be accessible within
function and procedure bodies without being passed as explicit parameters.

7I. Restrictions to Prevent Aliasing. The language shall attempt to prevent aliasing
(i.e., multiple access paths to the same variable or record component) that is not intended,
but shall not prohibit all aliasing. Aliasing shall not be premitted between output
parameters nor between an input-output parameter and a nonlocal variable. Unintended
aliasing shall not be permitted between input-output parameters. A restriction limiting
actual input-output parameters to variables that are nowhere referenced as nonlocals
within a function or routine, is not prohibited. All aliasing of components of elements of
an indirect type shall be considered intentional.

8. Input-Output, Formating and Configuration Control

8A. Low Level Input-Output. There shall be a few low level input-output operations
that send and receive control information to and from physical channels and devices.
The low level operations shall be chosen to insure that all user level input-output
operations can be defined within the language.

8B. User Level Input-Output. The language shall specify (i.e., give calling format and
general semantics) a recommended set of user level input-output operations. These
shall include operations to create, delete, open, close, read, write, position, and
interrogate both sequential and random access files and to alter the association between
logical files and physical devices.

8C. Input Restrictions. User level input shall be restricted to data whose record
representations are known to the translator (i.e., data that is created and written entirely
within the program or data whose representation is explicitly specified in the program).

8D. Operating System Independence. The language shall not require the presence of
an operating system. [Note that on many machines it will be necessary to provide
run-time procedures to implement some features of the language.]

8E. Resource Control. There shall be a few low level operations to interrogate and
control physical resources (e.g., memory or processors) that are managed (e.g., allocated
or scheduled) by built-in features of the language.

8F. Formating. There shall be predefined operations to convert between the symbolic
and internal representation of all types that have literal forms in the language (e.g., strings
of digits to integers, or an enumeration element to its symbolic form). These conversion
operations shall have the same semantics as those specified for literals in programs.

9. Parallel Processing

9A. Parallel Processing. It shall be possible to define parallel processes. Processes (i.e., activation instances of such a definition) may be initiated at any point within the scope of the definition. Each process (activation) must have a name. It shall not be possible to exit the scope of a process name unless the process is terminated (or uninitiated).

9B. Parallel Process Implementation. The parallel processing facility shall be designed to minimize execution time and space. Processes shall have consistent semantics whether implemented on multicomputers, multiprocessors, or with interleaved execution on a single processor.

9C. Shared Variables and Mutual Exclusion. It shall be possible to mark variables that are shared among parallel processes. An unmarked variable that is assigned on one path and used on another shall cause a warning. It shall be possible efficiently to perform mutual exclusion in programs. The language shall not require any use of mutual exclusion.

9D. Scheduling. The semantics of the built-in scheduling algorithm shall be first-in-first-out within priorities. A process may alter its own priority. If the language provides a default priority for new processes it shall be the priority of its initiating process. The built-in scheduling algorithm shall not require that simultaneously executed processes on different processors have the same priority. [Note that this rule gives maximum scheduling control to the user without loss of efficiency. Note also that priority specification does not impose a specific execution order among parallel paths and thus does not provide a means for mutual exclusion.]

9E. Real Time. It shall be possible to access a real time clock. There shall be translation time constants to convert between the implementation units and the program units for real time. On any control path, it shall be possible to delay until at least a specified time before continuing execution. A process may have an accessible clock giving the cumulative processing time (i.e., CPU time) for that process.

9G. Asynchronous Termination. It shall be possible to terminate another process. The terminated process may designate the sequence of statements it will execute in response to the induced termination.

9H. Passing Data. It shall be possible to pass data between processes that do not share variables. It shall be possible to delay such data transfers until both the sending and receiving processes have requested the transfer.

9I. Signalling. It shall be possible to set a signal (without waiting), and to wait for a signal (without delay, if it is already set). Setting a signal, that is not already set, shall cause exactly one waiting path to continue.

9J. Waiting. It shall be possible to wait for, determine, and act upon the first completed of several wait operations (including those used for data passing, signalling, and real time).

10. Exception Handling

10A. Exception Handling Facility. There shall be an exception handling mechanism for responding to unplanned error situations detected in declarations and statements during execution. The exception situations shall include errors detected by hardware, software errors detected during execution, error situations in built-in operations, and user defined exceptions. Exception identifiers shall have a scope. Exceptions should add to the execution time of programs only if they are raised.

10B. Error Situations. The errors detectable during execution shall include exceeding the specified range of an array subscript, exceeding the specified range of a variable, exceeding the implemented range of a variable, attempting to access an uninitialized variable, attempting to access a field of a variant that is not present, requesting a resource (such as stack or heap storage) when an insufficient quantity remains, and failing to satisfy a program specified assertion. [Note that some are very expensive to detect unless aided by special hardware, and consequently their detection will often be suppressed (see 10G).]

10C. Raising Exceptions. There shall be an operation that raises an exception. Raising an exception shall cause transfer of control to the most local enclosing exception handler for that exception without completing execution of the current statement or declaration, but shall not of itself cause transfer out of a function, procedure, or process. Exceptions that are not handled within a function or procedure shall be raised again at the point of call in their callers. Exceptions that are not handled within a process shall terminate the process. Exceptions that can be raised by built-in operations shall be given in the language definition.

10D. Exception Handling. There shall be a control structure for discriminating among the exceptions that can occur in a specified statement sequence. The user may supply a single control path for all exceptions not otherwise mentioned in such a discrimination. It shall be possible to raise the exception that selected the current handler when exiting the handler.

10E. Order of Exceptions. The order in which exceptions in different parts of an expression are detected shall not be guaranteed by the language or by the translator.

10F. Assertions. It shall be possible to include assertions in programs. If an assertion is false when encountered during execution, it shall raise an exception. It shall also be possible to include assertions, such as the expected frequency for selection of a conditional path, that cannot be verified. [Note that assertions can be used to aid optimization and maintenance.]

10G. Suppressing Exceptions. It shall be possible during translation to suppress individually the execution time detection of exceptions within a given scope. The language shall not guarantee the integrity of the values produced when a suppressed exception occurs. [Note that suppression of an exception is not an assertion that the corresponding error will not occur.]

11. Representation and Other Translation Time Facilities

11A. Data Representation. The language shall permit but not require programs to specify a single physical representation for the elements of a type. These specifications shall be separate from the logical descriptions. Physical representation shall include object representation of enumeration elements, order of fields, width of fields, presence of "don't care" fields, positions of word boundaries, and object machine addresses. In particular, the facility shall be sufficient to specify the physical representation of any record whose format is determined by considerations that are entirely external to the program, translator, and language. The language and its translators shall not guarantee any particular choice for those aspects of physical representation that are unspecified by the program. It shall be possible to specify the association of physical resources (e.g., interrupts) to program elements (e.g., exceptions or signals).

11C. Translation Time Facilities. To aid conditional compilation, it shall be possible to interrogate properties that are known during translation including characteristics of the object configuration, of function and procedure calling environments, and of actual parameters. For example, it shall be possible to determine whether the caller has suppressed a given exception, the caller's optimization criteria, whether an actual parameter is a translation time expression, the type of actual generic parameters, and the values of constraints characterizing the subtype of actual parameters.

11D. Object System Configuration. The object system configuration must be explicitly specified in each separately translated unit. Such specifications must include the object machine model, the operating system if present, peripheral equipment, and the device configuration, and may include special hardware options and memory size. The translator will use such specifications when generating object code. [Note that programs that depend on the specific characteristics of the object machine, may be made more portable by enclosing those portions in branches of conditionals on the object machine configuration.]

11E. Interface to Other Languages. There shall be a machine independent interface to other programming languages including assembly languages. Any program element that is referenced in both the source language program and foreign code must be identified in the interface. The source language of the foreign code must also be identified.

11F. Optimization. Programs may advise translators on the optimization criteria to be used in a scope. It shall be possible in programs to specify whether minimum translation costs or minimum execution costs are more important, and whether execution time or memory space is to be given preference. All such specifications shall be optional. Except for the amount of time and space required during execution, approximate values beyond the specified precision, the order in which exceptions are detected, and the occurrence of side effects within an expression, optimization shall not alter the semantics of correct programs, (e.g., the semantics of parameters will be unaffected by the choice between open and closed calls).

12. Translation and Library Facilities.

12A. Library. There shall be an easily accessible library of generic definitions and separately translated units. All predefined definitions shall be in the library. Library entries may include those used as input-output packages, common pools of shared declarations, application oriented software packages, encapsulations, and machine configuration specifications. The library shall be structured to allow entries to be associated with particular applications, projects, and users.

12B. Separately Translated Units. Separately translated units may be assembled into operational systems. It shall be possible for a separately translated unit to reference exported definitions of other units. All language imposed restrictions shall be enforced across such interfaces. Separate translation shall not change the semantics of a correct program.

12D. Generic Definitions. Functions, procedures, types, and encapsulations may have generic parameters. Generic parameters shall be instantiated during translation and shall be interpreted in the context of the instantiation. An actual generic parameter may be any defined identifier (including those for variables, functions, procedures, processes, and types) or the value of any expression.

13. Support for the Language

13A. Defining Documents. The language shall have a complete and unambiguous defining document. It should be possible to predict the possible actions of any syntactically correct program from the language definition. The language documentation shall include the syntax, semantics, and appropriate examples of each built-in and predefined feature. A recommended set of translation diagnostic and warning messages shall be included in the language definition.

13B. Standards. There will be a standard definition of the language. Procedures will be established for standards control and for certification that translators meet the standard.

13C. Completeness of Implementations. Translators shall implement the standard definition. Every translator shall be able to process any syntactically correct program. Every feature that is available to the user shall be defined in the standard, in an accessible library, or in the source program.

13D. Translator Diagnostics. Translators shall be responsible for reporting errors that are detectable during translation and for optimizing object code. Translators shall be responsible for the integrity of object code in affected translation units when any separately translated unit is modified, and shall ensure that shared definitions have compatible representations in all translation units. Translators shall do full syntax and type checking, shall check that all language imposed restrictions are met, and should provide warnings where constructs will be dangerous or unusually expensive in execution and shall attempt to detect exceptions during translation. If the translator determines that a call on a routine will not terminate normally, the exception shall be reported as a translation error at the point of call.

13E. Translator Characteristics. Translators for the language will be written in the language and will be able to produce code for a variety of object machines. The machine independent parts of translators should be separate from code generators. Although it is desirable, translators need not be able to execute on every object machine. The internal characteristics of the translator (i.e., the translation method) shall not be specified by the language definition or standards.

13F. Restrictions on Translators. Translators shall fail to translate otherwise correct programs only when the program requires more resources during translation than are available on the host machine or when the program calls for resources that are unavailable in the specified object system configuration. Neither the language nor its translators shall impose arbitrary restrictions on language features. For example, they shall not impose restrictions on the number of array dimensions, on the number of identifiers, on the length of identifiers, or on the number of nested parentheses levels.

13G. Software Tools and Application Packages. The language should be designed to work in conjunction with a variety of useful software tools and application support packages. These will be developed as early as possible and will include editors, interpreters, diagnostic aids, program analyzers, documentation aids, testing aids, software maintenance tools, optimizers, and application libraries. There will be a consistent user interface for these tools. Where practical software tools and aids will be written in the language. Support for the design, implementation, distribution, and maintenance of translators, software tools and aids, and application libraries will be provided independently of the individual projects that use them.

DoD's common programming language effort is aimed at reducing the development and maintenance cost and improving the quality of software for embedded computer systems. Here is a brief review of the background, scope, goals, and methods of that effort.

DoD's Common Programming Language Effort

David A. Fisher
Institute for Defense Analyses

As long as there were no machines, programming was no problem at all; when we had a few weak computers, programming became a mild problem, and now that we have gigantic computers, programming has become an equally gigantic problem. In this sense the electronic industry has not solved a single problem, it has only created them—it has created the problem of using its products.

E. W. Dijkstra
Turing Award Lecture

As has often been noted, the past 25 years of digital computing have been characterized by striking increases in computing speed, memory capacity, and hardware reliability, with simultaneous decreases in power consumption and hardware cost. What is perhaps not so widely recognized is that these trends have led to inflated expectations for automating not only those tasks that had been previously performed manually, but also for automating some tasks that hadn't even been attempted before. Much of the burden of these increased expectations has fallen on software.

Within the Department of Defense, systems requirements for software have been expanded, as exemplified by automation of control functions in systems such as Tacfire, the Safeguard ballistic missile defense system, the Airborne Warning and Control System, the Trident ballistic missile system, and the Minuteman system.

Costs. Studies conducted in 1973 and 1974 provide some quantitative data on the size and makeup of the software problem.[1,2] Although little information is available, these studies give some conservative estimates that provide reliable lower bounds on the cost of software in the DoD. For example, in 1973 digital computer software costs were estimated at $3 billion to $3.5 billion annually and were growing in dollars and in proportion to other computer costs. An additional $2 to $3 billion were spent in the same year for the support and operation of computer systems. These studies also showed that the greatest software problems in the DoD, as measured by their cost, are associated with so-called embedded computer systems (Figure 1), and that the majority of costs are incurred in software maintenance rather than development.

The rising cost of computer resources has resulted in increased attention by the highest levels of management, and a number of technical and managerial procedures have been undertaken.[3] Initial guidance was provided by DoD Directive 5000.29, Management of Computer Resources in Major Defense Systems.[4]

At one time DoD was a major innovator and consumer of the most sophisticated computer hardware, but now it represents only a small fraction of the total market. In software, that unique position still remains: a significant fraction of the total software industry is devoted to DoD-related programs—and this is true in even larger proportion for the more advanced and demanding systems. Thus, as it once had for hardware technology, DoD now has the opportunity and responsibility to ensure that its influence on software technology is beneficial.

Common language effort. One of the major tasks undertaken by DoD to alleviate software problems has been the common programming language effort. This effort is based on the idea that many of the support costs for software increase with the number of languages, and that languages must be suited to their applications. Furthermore, with a common programming language, a software development and maintenance environment could be built, providing centralized support and common libraries, that could be shared by several projects working in the same application area. Ideally, support software, including translators, could be developed in the source language so that any existing tools could be made available on a new machine at the cost of developing a new code generator for a standard compiler.

Embedded computer systems. Because the majority of software costs in the DoD are associated with embedded computer systems, the common language effort is concerned primarily with embedded computer software. The term "embedded computer system" was first used in 1974[5] to denote one that is logically incorporated in a larger system—e.g., an electromechanical device, a tactical system, a ship, an aircraft, or a communications system—whose primary function is not computation. Included in the concept of embedded computer systems is the support software necessary to design, develop, and maintain them. Computers used primarily for data processing, scientific, or research applications are not normally included in the embedded computer systems category.

Embedded computer software often exhibits characteristics that are strikingly different from those of other computer applications. The programs are frequently large (50,000 to 100,000 lines of code) and long-lived (10 to 15 years). Personnel turnover is rapid, typically two years. Outputs are not just data, but also control signals. Change is continuous because of evolving system requirements—annual revisions are often of the same magnitude as the original development.

Mission relationships. Software requirements vary from system to system depending upon the mission. The relative importance of execution efficiency, memory utilization, program modifiability, reliability, and program production time vary widely among applications and among components of a single system. Many embedded computer applications require software that will continue to operate in the presence of faults, whether the faults are in the computer hardware, input data, operator procedures, or the software.

At least 200 models of computers are used in embedded computer systems at DoD. In many applications, the computers must be installed in configurations that are incompatible with general-purpose installations. For example, the applications may require monitoring of sensors, control of equipment, display, or operator input processing. They must interface special peripheral equipment like radar, real-time clocks, and analog devices. Software must some-

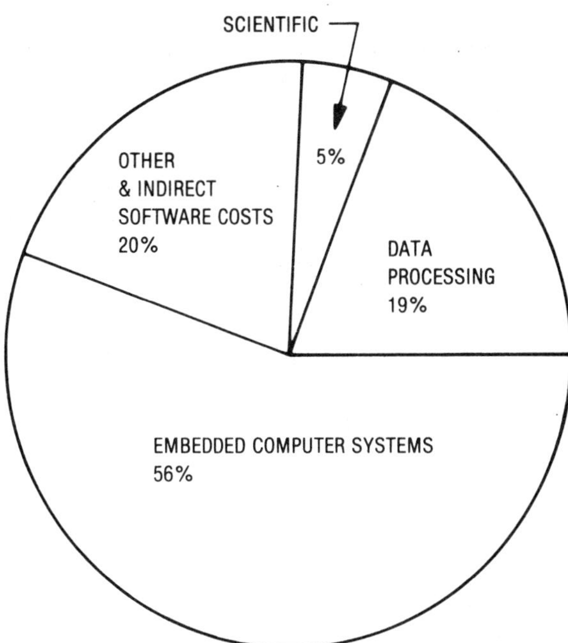

Figure 1. Breakdown of estimated $3 billion annual DoD software costs.

times be able to respond at periodic (real time) intervals, to service interrupts within limited times, and to predict computation times. The time intervals vary from microseconds in device interface handling, through milliseconds in sensor monitoring, and seconds in control applications, to days in report generation.

Special-purpose executive programs must be developed for many applications that cannot afford the overhead (and do not require the generality) of general-purpose operating systems. Systems programming capability is also needed to develop and maintain support software, including translators, software development tools, and testing aids, as well as their host operating systems.

In many applications, including command and control, training, and software development, it is necessary to access, manipulate, and display large quantities of data. Much of this data is symbolic or textual rather than numeric, and must be organized in an orderly and accessible fashion. Memory space rather than execution time is often the critical resource. On the other hand, a substantial numeric processing capability may still be essential, especially in simulation, sensor processing, and equipment control.

Software problems. Difficulties with embedded computer software are not atypical. Software problems that require or are susceptible to technical solution arise primarily from the nonsuitability of existing languages for embedded computer applications, from inadequate tools for software development and maintenance, and from insufficient concern for maintenance during software development.

Others, listed below, suggest management solutions in conjunction with technology.

Software development and maintenance are constrained by the availability of dollars, development time, machine resources, competent personnel, and useful programming tools. As with any activity in which expectations exceed the available capability, something must give. In this case, the symptoms appear in the form of software that is nonresponsive to user needs, unreliable, excessively expensive, untimely, inflexible, difficult to maintain, and not reusable.

Much has been said about the problems of software reliability. DoD software has all the common symptoms—occasional system crashes, inability to deal with user errors and ill-formed data, and errors which occur so frequently in a complex program from an apparently minor change. Software reliability, however, is particularly important in the military environment where errors can have severe consequences.

One little-recognized problem is that few useful software tools are available to the embedded software developer and maintainer. One reason is that resource limitations on hardware have led to an over-reliance on assembly language programming. There has been little incentive for individual projects to expend the effort and resources necessary to provide facilities that would be generally useful, especially when there are few, if any, other projects using the same programming language. This may also account for the lack of off-the-shelf software.

Finally, there is little cost accountability. This situation has been created by the lack of visibility of software to management, inaccessibility of software costs, and failure to give software the same scrutiny as hardware.

At least 450 general-purpose programming languages and (incompatible) dialects are used in DoD embedded computer applications—and none is widely used. With few exceptions the only common (i.e., widely-used) languages are Cobol (in data processing applications) and Fortran (in scientific and engineering applications). The remaining languages are used almost exclusively in embedded computer applications.

Programming languages

The present diversity of programming languages used in embedded computer systems did not cause most of the problems—nor would a common programming language cause them to disappear. Nevertheless, the existing language situation unquestionably aggravates them and inhibits some potential solutions.

The programming language is the central element in the design, development, and maintenance of software. It is the one software component that pervades all software component activity. It provides the building blocks from which software is constructed.

Together with its implementation (as a compiler), it acts as the final arbitrator for the behavior of application software and associates an interpretation with each program. The programming language is a major concern when developing software tools and aids, when communicating techniques and algorithms, when writing manuals, and when training personnel.

Ill effects. The large number of programming languages and the lack of any widely-used language have had many ill-effects:

Excessive cost. There is enormous duplication of costs for the design, implementation, testing, maintenance, and training that must be repeated for the translators, software tools, application software, and support packages for each language.

Slow communication. Transfer of new software technology to practical use is severely retarded. The diversity of languages creates artificial boundaries that complicate communication, reduce understanding, and lead to mutual mistrust among users.

Scattered research. There is little research on the problems of software for embedded computer systems. Lack of programming language commonality makes it nearly impossible to gather quantitative data about problems that are unique to these applications.

Unnecessary ties to vendors. When a language is unique to a single project, so must be the support software. In consequence, the software maintenance is tied to the original vendor. This tendency is strengthened in the common situation in which the translator and support tools for the language are written in still another language that remains the property of the vendor.

Diversion from important tasks. The development of a new programming language for each project diverts energy from the real task. Of necessity, projects are concerned with their own application; their primary goal must be to develop the application software. Project personnel may have neither the inclination, time, funds, nor expertise to develop more powerful or more generally useful software tools that are needed to support their language.

Diffused expenditures. The large number of languages diffuses the available funds so that only the most primitive software aids can be afforded. Potentially useful software tools are limited to users of the associated language and, thus, provide little leverage.

Risk in using existing languages. When the existing languages are poorly supported (as they must be when there is no widely used language) and a new compiler must be developed for each new system (as is typical in embedded computer applications), the adoption of an existing language by a new project is often more risky and less cost effective (at least during development) than it is to develop a new language specialized to the application.

History

The common language effort has had a short but lively history. It began in 1974 when groups in each of the military departments independently proposed the adoption of a common programming language for developing major defense systems. Those efforts included the Army "Implementation Language for Real-Time Systems" study, the Navy CS-4 effort, and the "High Order Language Standardization for the Air Force" study. In January 1975 a joint service program was formulated on the advice of the Director of Defense Research and Engineering.* He also instructed that no further funds be expended for the implementation of new programming languages in major defense systems until the problem of software commonality (i.e., of insufficient sharing of software resources) had been resolved.[6]

Working group. To coordinate the activities of the common language effort, a high order language working group was subsequently formed with official members from the Army, Navy, Air Force, Marine Corps, Defense Communications Agency, National Security Agency, and Defense Advanced Research Projects Agency. NASA and other offices within DoD have also participated. A representative of the British Ministry of Defence has been working full time in the United States since January 1977. The author acts as technical advisor. The high-order language working group is chaired by a representative of the Undersecretary of Defense, Research and Engineering.

The working group is chartered to "investigate the establishment of a minimal number of common high-order computer programming languages to be used in the development, acquisition, and support of computer resources embedded within Defense Systems."[7] In particular, it is to define the technical requirements for a common language, compare them with existing languages, recommend adoption or implementation of the necessary languages, and to monitor and assist any such actions. Thus, the working group coordinates all the activities of the common language effort but does not participate directly in the design or implementation of programming languages or their associated software.

The major concerns of the common language effort are to reduce the number of programming languages and to provide a useful, well supported environment for those that remain. The working group realized early that it would be impractical to convert existing programs to a common language;

hence the common language effort applies only to new systems.

Interim list. A first step in reducing the number of programming languages was to adopt an interim list of approved languages. The military departments each nominated a limited number of languages. Those nominations resulted in the issuance of DoD Instruction 5000.31.[8] This instruction specifies that only approved high-order languages (Table 1) will be used to develop new defense system software, unless another language can be shown to be more cost effective over the system life cycle.

Table 1. Interim list of approved programming languages.

CMS-2
SPL-1
Tacpol
J3 Jovial
J73 Jovial
ANSI Cobol
ANSI Fortran

Generating the requirements. In the spring of 1975, the working group began the process of determining the characteristics of a general-purpose programming language suitable for embedded computer applications. The characteristics were to be given in the form of requirements which would act as constraints on the acceptability of a language, but would not dictate specific language features. The requirements are not a language specification; instead, they attempt to rigorously define the needed characteristics in a form that can be critically reviewed.

STRAWMAN. Although there are several widely accepted general goals and criteria (such as efficiency, reliability, readability, simplicity, and implementability), they do not lend themselves to quantifiable assessment. At the opposite extreme are specific language features, advocated by some, which if adopted as requirements would impose strong constraints on the form but not necessarily increase the effectiveness of the language. The arguments for or against any specific language feature are often applicable to a class of features sharing certain properties, and they often depend on other characteristics of the language. The requirements attempt to isolate the needed properties from the features that implement them. Initially, rigorous definition at the level of requirements proved difficult, so a STRAWMAN of preliminary requirements was established. STRAWMAN was widely circulated within the military departments and to a lesser extent in the academic community and industry.

WOODENMAN. The reviews of STRAWMAN resulted in inputs which were formed into a fairly complete, but still tentative, set of requirements

called WOODENMAN.[9] This document contained
descriptions of the general (i.e., nonquantifiable)
characteristics which were desired; it also contained
many other desirable characteristics whose feasibility, practicality, and mutual compatibility had
not been tested. WOODENMAN, too, was widely
distributed, not only within the military departments but also to other government agencies, the
computer science research community, and industry.
Additionally, a number of technical experts outside
the United States were solicited for comments, the
European community being especially responsive.

TINMAN. Based on the various inputs and the
official responses from each of the military departments, a TINMAN[10,11] set of requirements was
derived. TINMAN removed former requirements for
which there was no sound rationale, restricted
unnecessarily general requirements, and modified
others to be practical within existing technology.
Each requirement in TINMAN had its own justification. TINMAN requirements were officially approved by the assistant secretary for research and
development of each of the military departments
in January 1976.

The document was circulated widely for comment,
and in October of that year a workshop[12] was held
at Cornell University to discuss the technical issues
that had been raised by the requirements and to
further investigate their feasibility.

IRONMAN. A new version of the requirements,
called IRONMAN,[13] was issued in January 1977.
IRONMAN requirements were substantially the
same as those of TINMAN, but modified for feasibility
and clarity and presented in an entirely different
format. TINMAN was discursive and organized
around general areas of discussion. IRONMAN, on
the other hand, is very brief and is organized like
a language description or manual. It is essentially
a specification with which to initiate the design of
a language. However, it is still sufficiently general
to constrain the structure of a language without
dictating the details of its design. A more recent
revision, the Revised IRONMAN,[14] was issued in
July 1977 and is available for comment.

At each iteration, comments were gathered and co-
ordinated by the services and their working group
representatives, then analyzed and reformulated as
requirements by the Institute for Defense Analyses.
In all, 74 commands and offices within DoD, 66 individuals outside of DoD, and 43 companies and organizations (not counting the workshop at Cornell
or the language evaluation efforts) have contributed
over 2000 pages of commentary on the requirements.
Not all of the suggestions have been adopted, and
many have been modified before acceptance, but
each has been considered in sufficient detail to determine why it should or should not be followed.

Beginning with WOODENMAN, each iteration has
reduced the number and generality of the capabilities requested. As the needs of the application
have become better understood, as the application
needs have been examined with respect to known
language features, and as more emphasis has been
placed on the general requirements for reliability,
maintainability, and efficiency, many of the requirements have become both more precise and less
restrictive.

Similarity of requirements. One surpising result
of the requirements effort has been the similarity
of the requirements among the different application
areas. Early in this program, it appeared that different user communities might have fundamentally
different requirements with insufficient overlap to
justify a common language or might have critical
requirements that were incompatible. Such communities include avionics, guidance, command and
control, communications, and training simulators.
However, it has been impossible to single out different sets of requirements for particular communities.
Almost all the potential users had the same
requirements, although priorities differed. Often
the priorities varied among segments of a task. All
users needed input-output, real-time facilities, strong
data typing, etc.

Upon reflection, the technical rationale for this
outcome was clear. The surprise was historical and
was based on the observation that in the past the
different communities have favored different language
approaches. Further investigation showed that the
origin of this disparity was primarily administrative
rather than technical. This did not, however, establish that a single language could meet all the stated
requirements, only that, if a language meeting all
requirements were found, it would satisfy the perceived needs.

Language evaluation. During 1976, 23 programming languages (Table 2) were evaluated against
the developing requirements. These evaluations
were performed by 16 companies and organizations.

Most of the languages received at least two
evaluations. In several cases the designers of a
language were included among its evaluators. The
report[15] consolidating the evaluations includes the
following findings:

- No language satisfied the requirements so well
that it could be adopted as a common language.

- Several of the languages were sufficiently compatible with the technical requirements so that
they could be modified to produce an acceptable
language. All of the languages in this group are
derivatives of Algol-68, Pascal, or PL/I.

- Without exception, the evaluators found all the
interim approved languages to be inappropriate as
a basis for developing a common language.

- It was the consensus of the evaluators that it
is currently possible to produce a single language
that would meet essentially all the requirements.

The latter finding means that no technological impediment to a single language was found and that it is likely that divergent requirements, such as those for readable programs, avoidance of unnecessary complexity, implementable compilers, semantic and syntactic consistency, machine independence, and object code efficiency, can be met.

As might be expected, the more modern languages tended to satisfy the requirements for reliability and maintainability, while languages intended for process control and DoD applications satisfied the requirements that reflect the special needs of embedded computer applications.

Design competition. Since no existing language simultaneously satisfied the needs of embedded computer applications, of reliable and maintainable software, and of machine independence, and since it appeared feasible to satisfy all the requirements without new technology, the services undertook a joint engineering design effort to produce a common language that would satisfy the requirements. Because all the languages that were identified as appropriate for modification are derivatives of Algol-68, Pascal, or PL/I, it was decided that the common language also should be a derivative of (but not necessarily upward compatible with) one of those three. Several competing designs were planned. Most of the fifteen proposals received, including the four best, were based on Pascal. These four—CII-Honeywell Bull, Intermetrics, SofTech, and SRI International—began parallel design efforts in August 1977.

We know that we design a language to simplify the expression of an unbounded number of algorithms created by an important class of problems. The design should be performed only when the algorithms for this class impose, or are likely to impose, after some cultivation, considerable traffic on computers as well as considerable composition time by programmers using existing languages. The language, then, must reduce the cost of a set of transactions to pay the cost of its design, maintenance, and improvement.

Alan J. Perlis
1966 Turing Award Lecture

The philosophy of the technical requirements

The technical requirements for the common language reflect six major goals: (1) that it be suitable for software in DoD embedded computer applications; (2) that it be appropriate for the design, development, and maintenance of reliable software for systems that are large, long-lived, and continually undergoing change; (3) that it be suitable as a common language (i.e., complete, unambiguous, and machine-independent standards can be established); (4) that it will not impose execution costs in applications where it provides unused or unneeded generality; (5) that it provide a base around which a useful software development, maintenance, and support environment can be built; and (6) that it be an example of good current language design practice. At the highest level, the requirements take the form of general design criteria (i.e., constraints) that are most strongly influenced by the first three goals.

Application needs. Many facilities must be provided in a language that is suitable for embedded computer applications, but four stand out because they are not usually provided in general-purpose languages for data processing and scientific applications:

User input-output interface specification. These applications use specialized input-output devices whose characteristics may not be known at the time of language design.

Exception handling. It must be possible to write programs that will automatically recover from errors, whether in the hardware, software, or data.

Real-time control. It must be possible to access real-time clocks, to control external devices in real time, and to respond within real-time constraints.

Parallel processing. It must be possible to write programs that control many devices in parallel, that share processors through interleaved execution, and whose parts may be executed concurrently on multiprocessors.

Needs of environment. The characteristics of military software and its environment impose several general design criteria on a suitable language:

Reliability. The combination of extremely complex systems with life-and-death implications may not be unique to the military, but it certainly requires that language characteristics which promote the production of reliable software be weighted very highly.

Modifiability. Perhaps as much as 90 percent of software costs in embedded computer systems go for software maintenance. Language features that contribute to the maintainability of reliable and efficient programs should have a major impact on software costs.

Efficiency. Physical limitations of military systems (e.g., an airplane) may impose limitations on the time and space for computations. In consequence, the efficiency of object programs is a legitimate and sometimes critical concern in military applications. Software that cannot meet these constraints may be, in effect, worthless.

Needs of commonality. Moreover, the desire for a language that can be widely used throughout DoD adds still more design criteria:

Machine independence. With over 200 computer models used in DoD, the language must be sufficiently machine-independent that it can be made available on a variety of object machines.

Practicality. The language must be sufficiently easy and inexpensive to implement that its wide use will be encouraged.

Complete definition. The language must have a complete and unambiguous definition to assure that software can be shared and incompatible implementations can be avoided.

Easily accessible support software. The availability of useful and easily accessible support software is, of course, the ultimate technical goal of the common language effort, but the ability to build such a support environment can be strongly influenced by the language characteristics.

General requirements. The design criteria were then translated into eight formal requirements dealing with the generality, reliability, maintainability, efficiency, simplicity, implementability, machine-independence, and formal definability of a suitable language. These eight, which constitute the first chapter of the technical requirements,[14] are further expanded into specific constraints on the design in the remaining chapters.

Attempts to expand the general requirements to a more detailed level where quantifiable measures could be applied, raised questions about the relative priorities of the general requirements and about how conflicts in requirements should be resolved. Some of the tradeoffs that were considered are outlined below. Others are given in references 11 and 16. Together they constitute a design philosophy for a common language, a philosophy of not making concessions on the general requirements unless absolutely necessary, and only after careful consideration of the implications.

Safety vs. efficiency. Intuition and historical observation tell us that there is a tradeoff between safety and efficiency in programs. Languages such as Euclid have emphasized safety but do not have efficient implementations. At the same time there are numerous examples in language designs of concessions to efficiency at the expense of safety (e.g., the "free union" in Pascal). The apparent tradeoff may not be inherent. Euclid was a vehicle for research and was not intended for use in large software efforts. The information needed to guarantee safety includes the type and ranges of values of variables (to limit their use in a program). That is, safety requires the same information as is needed by an optimzing compiler to determine what optimizations can be safely applied. This suggests that the same answer (i.e., languages that provide more information in programs) may provide partial solutions to the problems of safety, maintainability, and efficiency. This idea was pursued in the requirements development phase, and thus far no case has been found in which the efficiency of a correct program must be reduced in order to guarantee safety (although the compiler may be more complex).

Generalization vs. specialization. A general-purpose language can satisfy a variety of needs and can be applied to meet many, possibly unforeseen, situations, while a special-purpose language with built-in facilities for a particular application is often more efficient and therefore less expensive in use. The question is how to achieve both in the same programming language. The approach taken was to aim for a simple general-purpose language that would have the power needed for the intended applications, but would not yet be specialized for any particular application.

Such a language should have a few general-purpose structures, each providing a single primitive capability that can be combined with the others to form more specialized structures. Predefined application-oriented library definitions should be available in the language. As definitions made within the language, they can be independently controlled, need not add to the complexity of other applications, and need not affect the implementation of the language itself.

Programming ease vs. program safety. The more tolerant the programming language, the less it imposes on the programmer to specify his intent and assumptions in his programs, and thus the coding task is easier.

The safety of programs, on the other hand, is enhanced by requiring specification of the programmer's intent (e.g., specifying the range and types of variables), allowing redundant specifications (e.g., types determinable from either the formal or actual parameters), restricting the mixing of data types (e.g., prohibiting implicit type conversions), permitting restricted access to program components (e.g., specifying the scope of access for variables), and denying access to non-essential properties of data and programs (e.g., encapsulated type definitions).

A safe language allows the translator to check for program consistency and to verify that the programmer has, in fact, conformed to his stated intent and his own conventions in each program.

Considering that coding is a tiny fraction of the total software cost and that there are major software reliability and maintenance problems in embedded computer systems, the tradeoff between programming ease and program safety has been resolved in favor of safety.

Achieving efficiency. The desire for efficiency in software is often in conflict with other important goals such as minimal development cost, timely delivery, reliability, and functional utility. Systems requirements for efficiency ultimately take the form of space and time constraints imposed by the computer hardware. No additional benefit is derived from failure to use available space or failure to use an idle processor. Consequently, efficiency should be viewed as a constraint and not as an optimization criterion when developing programs.

Without automated software tools to identify which parts of a program are consuming the computational resources, the whole program must be optimized. Without efficient high-level languages suited to the task, the most capable programmers must be used to hand-tailor the machine code. The complexity of the task coupled with other constraints when developing a system seldom permits an optimal solution. More important, because a military system undergoes change throughout its lifetime, what may have initially been an efficient implementation becomes inefficient when changes occur in the assumptions and system characteristics against which it was optimized.

To be efficient, a high-order language must contain features that are appropriate to the applications. That is, it must have features that permit the user to express what is to be accomplished by the computation without dictating the details of how it is to be implemented. The translator can then select the most efficient implementation as a function of the generality and context of its use.

The language must be built from features that have efficient implementations on most machines; if the features are too general or too specialized, they often will not have efficient representations. It must be possible to combine built-in features to produce higher-level mechanisms that are specialized to a particular application, task, or program without imposing run-time cost for multiple levels of procedure calls. An efficient language will require the programmer to provide more formal documentation and will encourage the use of structured control primitives. Finally, whenever possible, features should be chosen to maximize the amount of processing that can be done during translation.

Current activities and plans

Three phases are planned for the design and implementation of the common language. The first phase or preliminary designs will be completed in February 1978. The preliminary designs will be incomplete but are supposed to be sufficiently detailed to determine the likelihood of their satisfying the major goals for the language. In particular, they are to address the most difficult design issues and to explain the rationale for each design decision.

The preliminary designs will be analyzed by a variety of teams from the military, industrial, and research communities on a voluntary basis between February 16 and March 13, 1978 (i.e., 390 individuals from 125 teams). The aim of the analyses[17] is to identify the major weaknesses, errors, and oversights in the preliminary designs and to determine their severity. The analyses will be used to identify the strengths and weaknesses of the individual designs, to obtain independent appraisals of the preliminary designs with respect to a number of specific design criteria, to help determine which subset of the design efforts will be continued into the second phase, and to provide feedback to the design contractors as they complete their designs. It is anticipated that the preliminary designs, the results of the individual analyses, and a summary evaluation report will be publicly available.

The candidate language designs will be completed in 1979, after which there will be an analysis and review of each design, leading to selection of one as the common language. A complete prototype translator (possibly in the form of an interpreter) will be available at that time.

The technical requirements continue to be refined with minor revisions issued at 6-month to 1-year intervals. The final version of the requirements and the final language design will be consistent with one another. Inconsistencies discovered during the preliminary design efforts are expected to impose changes in the requirements. A revised version, STEELMAN, is planned for late spring 1978.

During the remainder of 1978, the primary concern of the high-order language working group will be with the support and environment for a common language. Possible approaches will be identified and plans laid for language standards; translator certification; a root compiler; a common library; automated tools for software design, development, and maintenance; and a common (host) user-interface. A working paper outlining alternatives and initial positions will be issued by the working group in the spring of 1978. Further input will be provided by the National Bureau of Standards technical symposium on "Tools for Improved Computing in the 80's" to be held in June 1978, and by a proposed workshop to be sponsored by the military departments following the NBS symposium.

Several parallel activities are planned for the third phase (i.e., the year following selection of the common language). These include test programming of DoD applications; fine tuning of the language design; and development of production compilers, the common library, support facilities, software development and maintenance tools, translator certification and test facilities, and special-purpose application libraries.

The language will not be made available for production use in DoD applications until the testing and implementation phase has been completed (i.e., 1980 in the current schedule). The common language, upon nomination by the military services, would then be added to the list of languages that are approved for use in DoD systems. No compiler will be certified until a standard definition of the language is adopted at the end of the third phase.

If the common language effort is successful (1) there will be a reduction in the number and a rise in the level of the general-purpose languages used for new software in DoD embedded computer systems, (2) there will be an effective and useful software development and maintenance environment built around the languages that remain, and (3) duplicate efforts to develop and maintain similar software tools and support systems will be reduced. The wider the acceptance and use of the language (inside and outside DoD), the greater will be the benefits to DoD. Its acceptance and usefulness, in turn, depend on its appropriateness for potential applications; on the quality of its design, implementation, and support; and on the economic implications of its use as seen by potential users. Consequently, the effort has encouraged and continues to encourage active participation from industry as well as from potential users within DoD. Interested organizations are encouraged to contribute to the continuing revision of the technical requirements, the development of a strategy to assure commonality among implementations of the language, and the planning and construction of a suitable environment for the language. ■

Acknowledgement

The work reported here was conducted under contract DAHC1573 C 0200 for the Department of Defense. The publication of this paper does not indicate endorsement by DoD, nor should the contents be construed as reflecting the official position of that agency.

Some of the material presented here has also appeared in reference 18.

References

1. Barry W. Boehm et al., *Information Processing/Data Automation Implication of Air Force Command and Control Requirements in the 1980s (CCIP-85)*, Vol. I, *Highlights* (Revised Edition), February 1972, and Vol. IV, *Technology Trends: Software*, October 1973, Space and Missile Systems Organization, AFSC, Los Angeles, California.

2. D. A. Fisher, "Automatic Data Processing Costs in the Defense Department," Institute for Defense Analysis, Paper P-1046, AD-A004841, October 1974.

3. Barry C. DeRoze, "An Introspective Analysis of DoD Weapon System Software Management," *Defense Management Journal*, Vol. 11, No. 4, pp. 2-7, October 1975.

4. Department of Defense Directive 5000.29, "Management of Computer Resources in Major Defense Systems," April 26, 1976.

5. John H. Manley, "Embedded Computers—Software Cost Considerations," *AFIPS Conf. Proc., Vol. 41, 1974 NCC*, pp. 343-347.

6. Malcom R. Currie, "DoD Higher Order Programming Language." Memorandum issued by Director, Defense Research and Engineering (DDR&E), January 28, 1975.

7. "Charter for the High Order Language Working Group," Management Steering Committee for Embedded Computer Resources, Barry C. DeRoze, Chairman.

8. Department of Defense Instruction Number 5000.31, "Interim List of DoD High Order Programming Languages (HOL)," (signed) Frank A. Shrontz, Assistant Secretary of Defense (Installation and Logistics); Frank P. Wacher, Assistant Secretary of Defense (Comptroller); Richard M. Shriver, Director Telecommunication and Command and Control Systems; and Malcom R. Currie, Director of Defense Research and Engineering, November 24, 1976.

9. David A. Fisher, "*WOODENMAN*—Set of Criteria and Needed Characteristics for a Common DoD High Order Programming Language," Institute for Defense Analyses, Working Paper, August 13, 1975.

10. High Order Language Working Group, "Department of Defense Requirements for High Order Computer Programming Languages—TINMAN," June 1976.

11. D. A. Fisher, "A Common Programming Language for the Department of Defense—Background and Technical Requirements," Institute for Defense Analyses, Paper P-1191, AD-A028297, June 1976.

12. John H. Williams and David A. Fisher, Eds., *Lecture Notes in Computer Science, Vol. 54, Design and Implementation of Programming Languages—Proceedings of a DoD Sponsored Workshop*, October 1976, 496 pp., Springer-Verlag, 1977.

13. High Order Language Working Group, "Department of Defense Requirements for Higher Order Computer Programming Languages-IRONMAN," January 14, 1977.

14. High Order Language Working Group, "Department of Defense Requirement for High-Order Computer Programming Languages—Revised IRONMAN," July 1977.

15. S. Amoroso, P. Wegner, D. Morris, D. White, "Language Evaluation Coordinating Committee Report to the High-Order Language Working Group (HOLWG)," AD-A037634, 2617 pp., January 14, 1977, with appendices by

  a. Lloyd Campbell, Army Ballistic Research Laboratory, Aberdeen, Maryland;

  b. P. Parayre, Centre de Programmation de la Marine, Paris, France;

  c. J. D. Ichbiah, CII-Honeywell Bull, Louveciennes, France;

  d. Computer Sciences Corporation, Falls Church, Virginia;

  e. A. Demers and J. Williams, Cornell University, Ithaca, New York;

  f. Jean E. Sammet, Maurice Ackroyd, Michael L. Bell, I. Gray Kinnie, and Richard S. Kopp; IBM Federal Systems Division, Gaithersburg, Maryland;

  g. Brian L. Marks, and Robert F. Maddock, IBM United Kingdom Laboratories, Winchester, England; and Tom C. Spillman, IBM Federal Systems Division;

  h. J. G. P. Barnes, Imperial Chemical Industries Limited, Slough, England;

  i. B. M. Brosgol, R. E. Hartman, J. R. Nestor, M. S. Roth, and L. M. Weissman, Intermetrics, Inc., Cambridge, Massachusetts;

  j. National Security Agency, Ft. Meade, Maryland;

  k. Dr. Tomas Martin, PEARL Development Board, c/o Gesellschaft fur Kernforschung MBH, Karlsruhe, W. Germany;

  l. RLG Associates, Inc., Reston, Virginia;

  m. E. F. Miller and A. I. Wassermann, Science Applications, Inc., San Francisco, California;

  n. John B. Goodenough, Clement L. McGowan, and John R. Kelly, SofTech, Inc., Waltham, Massachusetts;

  o. Software Sciences Limited, Farnborough, Hampshire, England;

  p. Texas Instruments Incorporated, Huntsville, Alabama.

16. David A. Fisher and Philip R. Wetherall "Rationale for Fixed-Point and Floating-Point Computational Requirements for A Common Programming Language," Institute for Defense Analyses, Paper P-1305, January 1978.

17. Defense Advanced Research Projects Agency, "Plan for the Analyses of the Preliminary Designs for A Common Programming Languages for the Department of Defense," December 30, 1977.

18. Lt. Col. William A. Whitaker, "The U. S. Department of Defense High Order Language Effort," Unpublished paper, 11 pp., Defense Advanced Research Projects Agency, November 9, 1977.

David A. Fisher is a member of the research staff at the Institute for Defense Analyses in Arlington, Virginia, where he has studied software costs in the DoD and provided technical assistance to the Common Programming Language Effort. He has been an assistant professor at Vanderbilt University and the University of Delaware. Previously he was a staff engineer at Burroughs Corporation where he was involved in the design of microprogrammable computers, of programming languages, of operating systems, and of military software.

His areas of publications include software costs, bounded-workspace algorithms, control structures, and parallel processing.

Fisher received a PhD in computer science from Carnegie-Mellon University in 1970, an MSE from Moore School of Electrical Engineering, University of Pennsylvania in 1967, and a BS in mathematics from Carnegie Institute of Technology in 1964. He is a senior member of IEEE and a member of AIAA and ACM.

PROGRAMMING WITH ADA: AN INTRODUCTION
BY MEANS OF GRADUATED EXAMPLES
Peter Wegner
Department of Computer Science
Brown University, Providence, R. I. 02912

Reprinted from *ACM SIGPLAN Notices,* December 1979, pp. 1-46. Copyright 1978
Association for Computing Machinery, Inc. Reprinted by permission.

Chapter 1. AN OVERVIEW OF ADA

Ada is a programming language for numerical applications, system program-
ming applications and embedded computer applications with real-time requirements.
The language was designed to satisfy the Steelman requirements (SIGPLAN Notices,
December 1978). This overview supplements the Ada reference manual and rationale
(SIGPLAN Notices, June 1979). It is the first chapter of a book to be published
in December 1979 by Prentice-Hall, and is included here with the permission of
Prentice-Hall, Inc. Its purpose is to provide an overview of Ada for programmers
with previous programming experience in a higher-level language like Fortran.
Subsequent chapters include a more detailed discussion of the features of Ada as
well as some longer programming examples.

The material in this chapter falls naturally into three parts. Sections
1.1-1.6 develop the "classical" features of the language, which are closely
related to features already present in languages like Pascal. Sections 1.7-
1.12 describe "novel" language features which facilitate modularity and concurrent programming. Sections 1.13-1.18 describe program structure and compilation issues necessary to understand how large programs fit together.

Ada was named after Ada Lovelace who was a leading computer pioneer of the
nineteenth century, a colleague of Charles Babbage, and the daughter of Lord
Byron. It was designed at CII-Honeywell-Bull by a Paris-based design team
led by Jean Ichbiah.* The design team has included Bernd Krieg-Brueckner,
Brian A. Wichman, Henry F. Ledgard, Jean-Claude Heliard, Jean-Raymond Abrial,
John G.P. Barnes, and Olivier Roubine.

---

*The author wishes to thank Jean Ichbiah for taking a personal interest
in the development of this introduction to Ada.

CHAPTER 1

AN OVERVIEW OF ADA

1.1 A Simple Ada Program

Chapter 1 presents an overview of Ada as a whole so that the reader can view the forest before examining individual trees. The principal concepts and features are illustrated by means of graduated examples at a level of detail that should be sufficient to read and understand most Ada programs. A more detailed presentation sufficient for writing programs in the language is given in later chapters.

Our first example is a procedure called SIMPLE_ADD which reads two numbers, computes their sum, and prints the result. Each line includes a comment using the Ada notation for comments ("--" followed by the text of the comment).

Example 1.1. A very simple program

```
procedure SIMPLE_ADD is    -- a procedure called SIMPLE_ADD
   X,Y,Z: INTEGER;          -- which has three declared variables X,Y,Z
begin                       -- and a sequence of statements which consists of
   GET(X);                  -- a GET statement which reads a value into X
   GET(Y);                  -- a GET statement which reads a value into Y
   Z := X+Y;                -- an assignment statement which assigns a value to Z
   PUT(Z);                  -- a PUT statement which prints the value of Z
end SIMPLE_ADD;             -- and which is terminated by the keyword end
```

The first line specifies that this program is a procedure called SIMPLE_ADD. The second line declares the three "identifiers" X, Y, Z to be integer variables. These two lines together constitute the declarative part of the procedure and are followed by a sequence of executable statements enclosed by the keywords begin..end. The statement sequence contains two input statements which read data from an input medium into X and Y, an assignment statment which computes the sum of X and Y, and an output statement which outputs the result.

The structure of this program is as follows:

Example 1.2. Program structure

```
procedure name is           ] declarative part
   declarations of variables   (describes data)
begin
   statements that may use the variables   ] statement part
end;                                          (describes computation)
```

This program structure is a prototype for the structure of
all programs in the language. Every program contains a declarative part which names and describes variables and other program
entities, and a sequence of statements which specify computations
using the entities introduced in the declarative part. Section
1.2 below further explores constructs that occur in the statement
part of an Ada program, while section 1.3 further explores constructs that may occur in the declarative part.

Names introduced by the programmer in a declarative part are
called identifiers. Each declaration introduces one or more identifiers and specifies a set of attributes for each identifier.
The declaration for X, Y, Z specifies the attributes of X, Y, Z
in terms of the data type INTEGER. The attributes in this case
include the set of values which may be taken by the variables
X, Y, Z and the operations applicable to X, Y, Z.

Ada is a strongly typed language in the sense that every
identifier used in a program must be defined by a declaration.
The declaration imposes restrictions on the way in which an identifier may be used, which may be checked at compile time. Such
checks allow many programming errors to be caught earlier than
would otherwise be possible.

In describing computations performed by programs it is convenient to use the terminology that declarations are elaborated,
statements are executed and expressions are evaluated. Thus the
procedure SIMPLE_ADD is performed by first elaborating the declarations for X, Y, Z and then executing the four statements of
the procedure body. Execution of the third statement "Z := X+Y;"
involves evaluation of the expression X+Y and assignment of the
resulting value to Z.

1.2   Programming Examples

Programs generally contain control structures which control
the order of execution of statements of a program. The two most
important kinds of control statements in Ada are conditional
statements (which select among alternative actions) and loop
statements (which specify controlled repetition of an action).

Conditional statements are illustrated by the following if
statement for computing the absolute value of X.

Example 1.3. Simple if statement

```
if X < 0 then           -- if X is less than zero then
   X := -X;             -- replace X by -X
end if;                 -- otherwise do nothing
```


   Loop statements are illustrated by the following for statement, which sums the first ten elements of the vector V.

Example 1.4. Simple loop statement

```
SUM := 0;                   -- initialize variable SUM to zero
for I in 1..10 loop         -- loop for successive values of I
   SUM := SUM + V(I);       -- add Ith element of vector V to SUM
end loop;                   -- end of loop
```


   The following program fragment for computing the maximum of the first ten elements of V contains an if statement nested in a for statement.

Example 1.5. Loop with embedded if statement

```
MAX := V(1);                -- initialize MAX to first element of V
for I in 2..10 loop         -- loop for successive values of I
   if V(I) > MAX then       -- if new V(I) > maximum so far
      MAX := V(I);          -- V(I) becomes new provisional maximum
   end if;                  -- end of if statement
end loop;                   -- end of loop
```


   Nesting of statements within other statements is typical of the structure of Ada programs. The nested structure of the above program fragment is as follows:

Example 1.6. Nested control structures

```
assignment statement
for statement (special kind of loop statement)
   if statement nested in the for statement
      assignment statement nested in the if statement
   end of nested if statement
end of loop statement (for statement)
```


   This program fragment performs a well-defined function (the function of computing the maximum of a vector of values). The facility of computing the maximum of a vector can be provided in a modular fashion to an arbitrary number of users by embedding the code for computing the maximum in a function definition.

<u>Example 1.7. Function definition for computing the maximum</u>

```
function MAX_TEN(V: VECTOR) return INTEGER is  -- a function called MAX_TEN
                               -- which has parameter V of type VECTOR and returns
                               -- an INTEGER result
   MAX: INTEGER;               -- it has a local variable MAX
 begin                         -- and a sequence of statements
   MAX := V(1);                -- which assigns V(1) to MAX
   for I in 2..10 loop         -- and then loops
     if V(I) > MAX then        -- and tests if V(I) > MAX
       MAX := V(I);            -- if so, V(I) is maximum so far
     end if;                   -- if V(I) <= MAX take no action
   end loop;                   -- end of loop
   return MAX;                 -- when loop is completed, return with value MAX
 end MAX_TEN;                  -- end of MAX_TEN function definition
```


The above function provides a computational resource to the
user (for computing the maximum of a ten-element vector). The
following statement computes the sum of a ten-element vector A and
a ten-element vector B and assigns the result to the variable Y.

<u>Example 1.8. Function call</u>

```
Y := MAX_TEN(A) + MAX_TEN(B);
```


Calls of a function like MAX_TEN may appear in an expression
on the right-hand side of an assignment statement anywhere that a
constant or variable may appear.

The function MAX_TEN above illustrates the basic idea of
defining a computational resource and subsequently using it. But
MAX_TEN has the following imperfections:

1. The restriction that vectors have precisely ten elements
    is unrealistic. A resource for computing the maximum of
    a vector should work for vectors of any "reasonable" size.
2. It is sometimes necessary to know not only the value of
    the maximum element but also its location (index) within
    the vector, so that further operations on the maximum
    element can be performed.

The following function MAX_INDEX computes the index of the
maximum element for vectors of arbitrary length. It has a parameter V of the type VECTOR which is assumed to have been previously
defined by the programmer as a one-dimensional array of integers
(see section 1.3). It makes use of the "attribute enquiries"
V'FIRST and V'LAST which yield as their values the indices of the
first and last elements of the vector V. It also makes use of the
Ada facility for initializing declarations.

Example 1.9. Function definition for computing the maximum index

```
function MAX_INDEX(V: VECTOR) return INTEGER is  -- a function MAX_INDEX with
   MAX: INTEGER := V(1);          -- a local variable MAX initialized to V(1)
   INDEX: INTEGER := 1;           -- a local variable INDEX initialized to 1
begin                             -- and a body which iterates
   for I in V'FIRST..V'LAST loop   -- over elements of the vector
     if V(I) > MAX then           -- tests if V(I) > MAX
       MAX := V(I);               -- if so sets MAX to V(I)
        INDEX := I;               -- and remembers value of INDEX
     end if;                      -- if V(I) <= MAX takes no action
   end loop;                      -- ends the loop
   return INDEX;                  -- and returns with index of maximum element
end MAX_INDEX;
```

The call "MAX_INDEX(A)" returns the index of the maximum
element. Thus the maximum element of A is given by
"A(MAX_INDEX(A))". The difference of the maxima of two vectors
A, B (possibly of different lengths) may be computed as follows:

Example 1.10. Call of MAX INDEX function

```
DIFF := A(MAX_INDEX(A)) - B(MAX_INDEX(B));
```

The usefulness of returning the index of the maximum element
rather than its value is illustrated by the following program
fragment for interchanging the values of the first element and
maximum element of a vector.

Example 1.11. Use of MAX INDEX

```
K := MAX_INDEX(A);
TEMP := A(K);
A(K) := A(1);
A(1) := TEMP;
```

This mechanism can be used as a basis for sorting by finding
successive maxima of subvectors, as illustrated for the following
vector with the five elements 3, 1, 7, 6, 4.

Example 1.12. Example of sorting by successive maxima

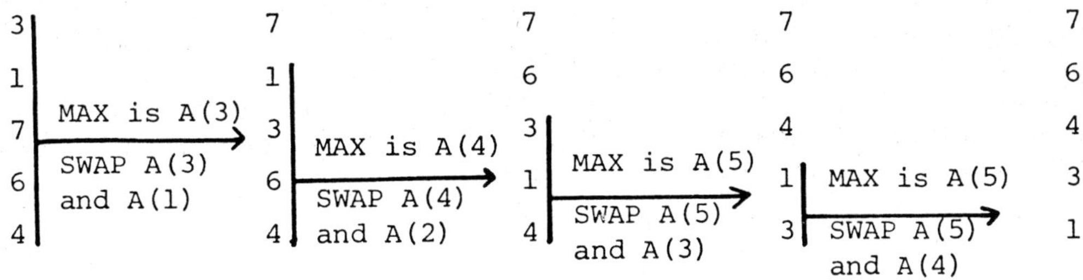

In order to performing sorting by successive maxima using
the MAX_INDEX subprogram we must permit parameters that are subarrays (slices) of contiguous elements of the array being sorted.
Ada permits slices (subarrays) of contiguous elements of an array
to be specified by the notation A(I..J), which denotes the sub-
array consisting of the contiguous array elements A(I) through
A(J).

In the next example the call "MAX_INDEX(A(I..N))" yields
the index of the maximum element of the slice A(I..N). It is
assumed that the vector A to be sorted has A'FIRST = 1.

Example 1.13. Sorting by successive maxima

```
N := A'LAST;                      -- assign array size to N
for I in 1..N loop                -- and iterate
   K := MAX_INDEX(A(I..N));       -- find MAX_INDEX of slice A(I..N)
   TEMP := A(K);                  -- interchange maximum element A(K)
   A(K) := A(I);                  -- with first element A(I)
   A(I) := TEMP;                  -- of the slice A(I..N)
end loop;                         -- and repeat for next value of I
```


Sorting is a well-defined task that may conveniently be
specified by a procedure. Procedures, like functions, are
defined by a definition which specifies the task to be performed,
and may subsequently be called by a procedure call. Unlike
functions, procedures do not return a result but instead perform
their task by modifying values of variables whose names are known
to users of the procedure. The following procedure SORT has a
parameter of the type VECTOR whose value is modified (sorted) as
a result of executing the procedure.

Example 1.14. Sort procedure

```
procedure SORT(A: in out VECTOR) is
   N: constant INTEGER := A'LAST;
   K, TEMP: INTEGER;
begin
   for I in 1..N loop
      K := MAX_INDEX(A(I..N));
      TEMP := A(K);
      A(K) := A(I);
      A(I) := TEMP;
   end loop;
end SORT;
```


The SORT program makes use of two language features we have
not previously encountered:

1. Constant declaration. The local identifier N is initial-
    ized each time the procedure is entered to a constant
    (the length of the vector A) and is therefore introduced

by a constant declaration. The constant N may have different values for different invocations of the SORT
procedure but is constant during any given invocation.

2. Input-output parameters. The vector parameter A of the
SORT procedure is both accessed and modified during
execution of the SORT procedure and therefore must be
specified by the binding mode in out. This contrasts
with the parameter V of the function MAX_INDEX which was
used purely for input and never modified. Input parameters in Ada need not have their mode explicitly specified so that "V: VECTOR" is a sufficient parameter
specification for V although "V: in VECTOR", which
explicitly specifies that V is an input parameter, is
more complete. However, for input-output parameters
the binding mode in out must be explicitly specified.

The SORT procedure may be called by a procedure call
statement as follows.

Example 1.15. Call of SORT procedure

```
SORT(INT_VECT);
```

Note that a call of the SORT procedure affects the environment by changing the order of the elements of its vector parameter, while the MAX_INDEX function cannot affect its environment by changing values of its parameters, but affects its environment only by the result which it returns. It is true in
general that functions have only input parameters and can affect
their environment only by returning a result, while procedures
do not return a result and must affect their environment by
modifying parameter values.

The SORT procedure may be used without any knowledge about
how sorting is implemented. If the SORT procedure is replaced by
a functionally equivalent procedure which performs sorting in an
entirely different way, it will not affect the user.

Sorting is in fact one of the most intensively studied problems in the literature, and there are literally hundreds of essentially different ways of sorting a vector. Sorting by successive
maxima was chosen for purposes of illustration because it is one
of the simplest to explain and because it allows us to illustrate
some interesting features of Ada.

1.3 Type and Object Declarations

Now that we have seen some examples of Ada programs, we
shall examine in greater detail the Ada facilities for data
description. The key notion for data description is the notion
of a data type. A data type determines a set of values which may
be taken by identifiers declared to be of the data type, and a
set of operations applicable to objects of the data type.

Ada supports the <u>predefined</u> data types INTEGER, FLOAT, BOOLEAN and CHARACTER. However, the power of Ada lies in the programmer's ability to define <u>programmer-defined data types</u> tailored to particular applications by means of <u>type definitions</u>.

One reason for defining a new type is simply to prevent mixing of operations on logically distinct kinds of objects. For example, if we want to count apples and oranges, but avoid mixing apples and oranges, we can introduce the two programmer-defined integer types APPLES and ORANGES, as in the following example.

Example 1.16. Type compatibility and type conversion

```
procedure DERIVED_TYPES is          -- a procedure
   type APPLES is new INTEGER;      -- which defines a new type APPLES
   type ORANGES is new INTEGER;     -- and a new type ORANGES
   A: APPLES;                       -- an object of the type APPLES
   B: ORANGES;                      -- an object of type ORANGES
   I: INTEGER;                      -- and an object of type INTEGER
begin
   A := 0;        -- integer literal assigned to object of type APPLES
   B := 0;        -- and to object of type ORANGES
   A := A+A;      -- apples can be added to each other
   I := A+B;      -- but apples cannot be added to oranges (illegal statement)
   I := INTEGER(A) + INTEGER(B);    -- unless forcibly converted to integers
end DERIVED_TYPES;
```

The types APPLES and ORANGES in the above example are called <u>derived types</u> because they are derived from an existing type INTEGER. Derived types inherit literals from their defining type. Thus the statement "A := 0;" which assigns the literal "0" to a variable of the type APPLES, is legal. They also inherit operations from their defining type. Thus the expression "A + A" which applies the "+" operator to variables of the type APPLES is legal. So is "A + 1". However, the addition operator requires its two operands to be of the same type (so that "A + B" and "A + I" are illegal). The assignment operator requires the expressions on the right-hand side to have the same type as the name on the left-hand side (so that "I := A;" is illegal). However, explicit conversion is possible between a derived type and its defining type (INTEGER(A) is of type INTEGER while APPLES(I) would be of type APPLES). Thus "I := INTEGER(A) + INTEGER(B);" is legal since both operands of the addition operator are of type INTEGER, the sum is of type INTEGER, and the type of the value on the left-hand side is compatible with the type of the variable on the right-hand side.

The declaration of the derived type APPLES automatically extends the meaning of the addition operator + so that it can be used to add not only integers but also apples. Extending the meaning of an operator to operands of a new type is referred to as <u>overloading</u> the operator. Ada permits operators to be overloaded both implicitly by defining a new type derived from a type for which that operator is meaningful, and explicitly by a function definition (see section 1.8).

The "+" operator is already overloaded because addition is
defined for both fixed- and floating-point operands (fixed- and
floating-point addition is in fact implemented by different
machine-language instructions on most computers). The type declarations for APPLES and ORANGES overload the "+" operator with
additional programmer-defined meanings. The meaning of any particular occurrence of the operator "+" depends on the types of
its operands. Since the types of the operands of any operator
are always known at compile time, the compiler can always determine which of the several meanings of + is intended and can compile code which reflects the desired meaning.

The predefined data type INTEGER has an implicit (implementation-defined) range of values. Explicit control over the range
of values of integer variables may be accomplished by a type
definition with an explicit range constraint, as in the following
example.

Example 1.17. Programmer-defined integer type

```
procedure FIBONACCI is     -- a procedure for computing Fibonacci numbers
   type SHORT_INT is range -32768..32767;  -- with a type SHORT_INT
   J: SHORT_INT := 0;      -- two variables of the type SHORT_INT
   K: SHORT_INT := 1;      -- initialized for generating Fibonacci numbers
begin                      -- and a statement sequence
   while K < 10000 loop    -- which tests if last Fibonacci number < 10000
     PUT(K);               -- outputs the current Fibonacci number
     K := J+K;             -- sets K to the next Fibonacci number
     J := K-J;             -- sets J to previous value of K
   end loop;               -- and repeats this process
end FIBONACCI;
```

This example declares a programmer-defined type SHORT_INT
and two initialized objects J, K of the type SHORT_INT. The
programmer-defined type has an explicitly defined range which
ensures that the program will be portable among implementations.
Moreover, the range may be implemented in a 16-bit word, ensuring both time and space efficiency on computers whose hardware
supports implementation of 16-bit integers.

There is a fundamental distinction between the type declaration of SHORT_INT which creates a new type from which an arbitrary number of instances can be created by subsequent declarations, and the object declaration of J, K which creates objects
of the data type that can be used in subsequent computations.

The data types INTEGER and SHORT_INT are referred to as
scalar types because objects of the type have no components.
Another important class of scalar types is enumeration types.
Enumeration types have finite value sets which may be explicitly
enumerated, as in the following example.

<u>Example 1.18.</u> <u>Enumeration types</u>

```
procedure ENUMERATION_TYPES is
   type COLOR is (RED,GREEN,YELLOW,BLUE);     -- COLOR has four possible values
   ADA: COLOR;                                -- ADA is object of type COLOR
begin
   ADA := GREEN;            -- value GREEN of type COLOR is assigned to ADA
end;
```

Enumeration types are very useful for defining finite sets of everyday objects such as colors, weekdays (MON, TUE,..), directions (N, E, S, W), digits (0, 1, 2,..), computer op codes (ADD, MULT,..), etc. Ada supports iteration over enumeration types and the use of enumeration types as index sets for arrays.

Scalar types have no components and may be contrasted with <u>structured types</u> such as arrays whose components are selectable by indexing. The next example declares a programmer-defined array type VECTOR, two objects V, W of the type VECTOR, and illustrates assignment to vector components and complete vectors.

<u>Example 1.19.</u> <u>Array data types</u>

```
procedure ARRAY_TYPES is      -- a procedure called ARRAY_TYPES
   type VECTOR is array(1..5) of INTEGER;   -- with type declaration for VECTOR
   V,W: VECTOR;                  -- and object declarations for V, W
begin                           -- and a sequence of statements
   V(5) := 8;                   -- which assigns to element of vector
   W := (2,4,6,8,10);           -- assigns aggregate to complete vector
   V := W;                      -- assigns value of vector W to vector V
end;                            -- and then is terminated
```

The type declaration for VECTOR defines a <u>template</u> from which an arbitrary number of vector objects can be created by object declarations. Array objects have components (elements) which may be individually accessed by indexing (V(5), W(I)), which may be initialized to array aggregates (W := (2,4,6,8,10);) or which may be assigned values of compatible array variables (V := W;). Thus array data structures may be viewed as abstract entities which have aggregate values as well as individual values.

The bounds of an array type definition may be left unspecified by using a type definition (INDEX) rather than a range specification (1..5) to specify the index type of the array. Array types whose bounds are unspecified must have their bounds specified at object declaration time.

<u>Example 1.20.</u> <u>Vectors with unspecified bounds</u>

```
type INDEX is range 1..1000;           -- type INDEX is used to define
type VECTOR is array(INDEX) of INTEGER; -- array type VECTOR with unspecified bounds
U, V: VECTOR(1..20);                    -- 20-element vector objects
W: VECTOR(1..10);                       -- 10-element vector object
```

The type VECTOR above has unspecified bounds and allows
vector objects of any size between 1 and 1000 to be created. In
general, the bounds may be any subrange of the range determined
by the index type of the type definition.

Array types with unspecified bounds are particularly important in subprograms with array parameters such as the SORT procedure and MAX_INDEX function discussed in the previous section.
The parameter VECTOR in these subprograms must have unspecified
bounds to allow calls for vectors of different sizes. Another
example of a subprogram requiring vector parameters of unspecified bounds is the following vector multiplication (inner product) function.

Example 1.21. Vector multiplication

```
function VECMULT(X,Y: VECTOR) return INTEGER is  -- vector multiplication function
  RESULT: INTEGER := 0;                -- which initializes result to zero
begin                                  -- and has a statement sequence
  assert X'FIRST = Y'FIRST;            -- with two assert statements
  assert X'LAST = Y'LAST;              -- that check compatibility of vectors
  for I in X'FIRST..X'LAST loop        -- which iterates over vector elements
    RESULT := RESULT+X(I)*Y(I);        -- accumulates inner product
  end loop;                            -- repeats for successive vector elements
  return RESULT;                       -- and returns value of inner product
end VECMULT;
```

The VECMULT function, like the SORT and MAX_INDEX subprograms
of the previous section, make use of attribute enquiries to determine the bounds of actual vector parameters. The attribute enquiries X'FIRST, X'LAST yield the index of the first and last
components and are used to control iteration.

This example illustrates the use of assert statements. An
assert statement may occur in either the declarative part or the
body of a program unit, and is conceptually elaborated in line
during execution, although its truth may sometimes be verified
at compile time by an optimizing compiler. If the condition
determined by the assert statement is true, the computation may
continue. If it is false, then an error action is executed.

Array types have components which must all be of the same
type and which may be accessed by indices. Ada supports a
second important class of programmer-defined data structures
called records whose components may be of different type and are
accessed by a selector name qualified by the name of the record.

Example 1.22. Record data types

```
procedure RECORD_TYPES is
   type COMPLEX is              -- the programmer-defined type COMPLEX is
     record                     -- a record with
       RE: INTEGER;             -- a component named RE of type INTEGER
       IM: INTEGER;             -- and a component IM of type INTEGER
     end record;                -- end of record type definition
   C,C1: COMPLEX;               -- two objects C, C1 of the type COMPLEX
begin
   C.RE := 2;                   -- assign to RE component of C
   C.IM := C.RE+1;              -- assign to IM component of C
   C1  := (0,0);                -- assign aggregate to complete record C1
   C1  := C;                    -- assign value of C to complete record C1
   C  := (C.RE*C1.RE-C.IM*C1.IM,C.RE*C1.IM+C.IM*C1.RE); -- product C*C1
end RECORD_TYPES;
```

Records, like arrays, may be manipulated not only by accessing individual record components (such as C.RE) but also by the
assignment of record aggregates to record variables (C1 := (0,0);)
and by direct assignment between compatible record variables
(C1 := C;).

The record COMPLEX in the previous example has two components
of type INTEGER. Ada permits record types to have components of
undetermined size and/or type. The following record type has a
dynamic array component whose size is determined by the value of
a second component whose value is a constant determined at the
time of creation of instances of the record.

Example 1.23. Record types of varying size

```
type BUFFER is
   record
     SIZE: constant INTEGER range 1..N;  -- discriminant component
     BLOCK: array(1..SIZE) of INTEGER;   -- array whose size depends on
   end record;                           -- discriminant
```

Record types having components of varying size or type are
called variant records. Such records must contain an explicit
constant component in which the size is explicitly specified at
record allocation time. The constant component is called a
discriminant because it discriminates among records of different
sizes.

Ada permits variant records with components whose type and
component name vary for different objects of the type. The
following type PERSON has a second component whose type and component name depend on whether the person is male or female.

<u>Example 1.24.</u> <u>Components of varying type</u>

```
type PERSON is
  record
    SEX: constant (M,F);   -- discriminant component (deferred constant)
    case SEX of      -- component whose name and type depend on discriminant
      when M => BEARDED: BOOLEAN;
      when F => CHILDREN: INTEGER range 0..100;
    end case;
  end record;
```

The record PERSON has a discriminant SEX which is an enumeration type and may take one of the two values M or F. The discriminant is said to be a <u>deferred constant</u> because assignment of a value is deferred from <u>type declaration</u> time to the time that values are assigned to record variables. Assignment to a discriminant is possible only when assigning a value to the complete record.

The discriminant components of a record are in a sense redundant because the information they contain is already present in the components which they discriminate. However, a discriminant makes explicit the structure variation of a record in a form in which it can be used to check the validity and security of operations on a record.

From another point of view, a discriminant of a variant record may be viewed as a <u>parameter</u> whose value is supplied at object creation time rather than type definition time. Ada allows discriminants of variant records to be specified by a parametric notation.

<u>Example 1.25.</u> <u>Parametrized types</u>

```
B: BUFFER (N);
P: PERSON (M);
```

Records of varying size, such as BUFFER, may have "dynamic" parameters whose value is determined at the time the declaration is elaborated. Records of varying type require the parameter to be statically determined, so that type compatibility can be checked at compile time.

1.4 Program Structure

Now that statements and data declarations have been introduced, we are ready to discuss the overall structure of Ada programs.

In describing how an Ada program is constructed from its constituents, we can identify the following levels of program structure:

Characters, which are the lowest-level atomic constituents
    of a program;
Lexical units, which are the atomic units of meaning
    (semantic units);
Expressions, which specify a computation that computes a
    "value";
Assignment statements, which assign the value computed by
    an expression to a variable;
Control structures, which control the sequence in which
    assignment statements and other statements of the program
    are executed;
Declarations, which define the attributes of identifiers
    used in the statements of a program;
Program units, which associate declarations defining the
    attributes of identifiers with statements which use them;
Compilation units, which are the units of structure for
    program development and separate compilation.

A compilation unit may be a subprogram or a module. Subprograms include procedures and functions, while modules include
packages and tasks, as illustrated in figure 1.

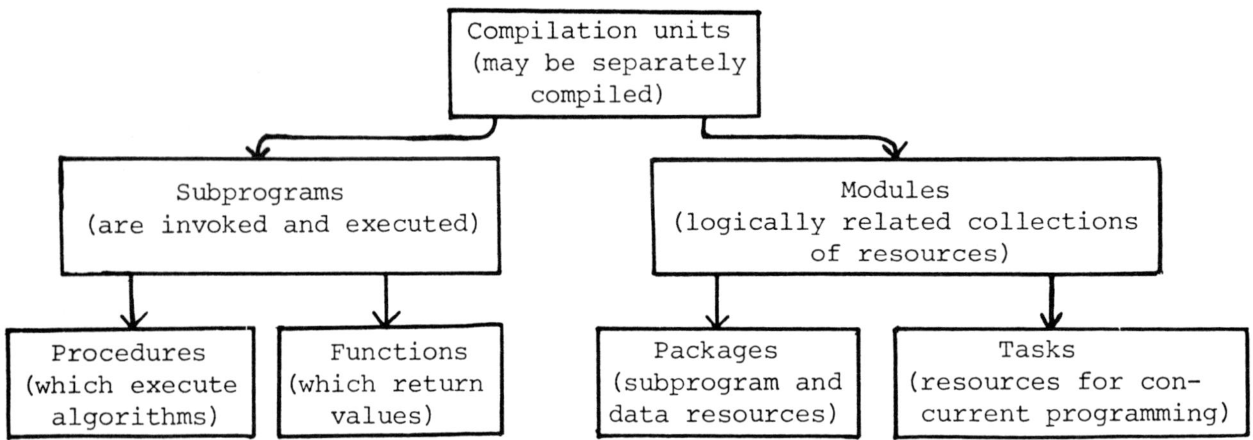

Figure 1. Classification of compilation units.

Procedures and functions are "traditional" programming language constructs taken from earlier higher-level languages like
Fortran and Pascal. Packages and tasks are novel language constructs which reflect recent advances in language design.

Packages support the modular specification of logically
related collections of computational resources. For example, a
matrix package provides a logically related collection of computational resources for performing computations on matrices, while
an input-output package provides a logically related collection
of computational resources for performing input-output. Tasks
are the modular units for concurrent programming. They support
communication among concurrently executing tasks by a novel
mechanism called the rendezvous mechanism which requires synchronization between a called task and a calling task whenever messages
between tasks are communicated.

Subprograms and modules may be compilation units (they may
be separately compiled) as well as program units (they associate
identifier declarations with statements which use them). In
fact, every compilation unit is automatically a program unit.
However, not every program unit is a compilation unit. In particular, subprograms and modules defined in a declarative part
of an enclosing compilation unit are not compilation units. The
nesting of subprogram definitions in enclosing compilation units
is illustrated in the next section.

1.5 Subprograms

Subprograms were introduced informally in section 1.2. In
this and the next section we consider in greater detail the
nested declaration of subprograms and the nature of subprogram
parameters.

Subprograms are defined by a subprogram declaration which
specifies the subprogram name, formal parameters, local declarations and statement sequence. They are invoked by a subprogram
call which specifies the name and actual parameters to be used
in place of the formal parameters for the given instance of invocation. Function declarations, which return a result, specify
in addition the type of the result that will be returned by the
function.

The following function F has an integer input parameter and
a local variable called LOCAL, and returns an integer result.

Example 1.26. Function declarations

```
function F(N: INTEGER) return INTEGER is  -- F has integer parameter and result
   LOCAL: INTEGER;              -- and local variable of type INTEGER
begin                          -- and two statements which
   LOCAL := N**2+N+1;          -- use local variable for intermediate result
   return LOCAL;               -- return value of type integer
end F;
```

The first line of this function declaration specifies its
name, its formal parameter, and the type of its result, and constitutes the complete user interface specification. The second
line specifies an internal local variable (inaccessible to the
user of F). The two statements make use of the local variable
and parameter, and compute the function $F(N) = N^2 + N + 1$.

This function may be called by a function call which has
the same syntactic status as a variable appearing on the right-
hand side of an assignment statement.

Example 1.27. Function calls

```
I := F(3)               -- the value 13 is assigned to I
J := F(3)+F(4);         -- the value 34 (13 + 21) is assigned to J
```

Function declarations and calls can be put together into a
single program in which both the integer variables I, J and the
function F are declared in the declarative part of an enclosing
procedure.

Example 1.28. Nested function declaration

```
procedure FUNCTIONS is                        ⎤            ⎤
   I,J: INTEGER;                               |            |
   function F(N: INTEGER) return INTEGER;   ⎤  |            |  declarative part
     LOCAL: INTEGER;                        |  n           |  of procedure
   begin                                    |  e           |
     LOCAL := N**2+N+1;                      |  s           |
     return LOCAL;                          |  t           |
   end;                                     ⎦  e           ⎦
begin                                          d
   I := F(3);          -- value is 13          f         ⎤
   J := F(3)+F(4);     -- value is 34          u         |  statements of
end FUNCTIONS;                                 n         |  procedure
                                               c         |
                                               t         |
                                               i         |
                                               o         |
                                               n         |
                                               F         ⎦
```

This example illustrates the nesting of subprogram declarations in the declarative part of other subprograms that is typical of the structure of Ada programs. The procedure FUNCTIONS
has the declarations for the integers I, J and the procedure F
nested in its declarative part. The function F in turn has the
parameter N and the integer variable LOCAL declared in its
declarative part. The function F could in turn have a function
nested in its declarative part so that nesting of subprogram
declarations in the declarative part of textually enclosing subprogram declarations is possible to an arbitrary level.

1.6   Subroutine Parameters

The parameters of a subprogram definition are said to be
formal parameters since they are "dummy" identifiers (bound
variables) which can be replaced by other non-conflicting identifiers without changing the meaning of the subprogram. For
example, the parameter N of F in the example above can be
replaced by M or X (but not by LOCAL) in its three occurrences
within F without changing the meaning of F.

The parameters which occur in a subprogram call are called
actual parameters because they determine the values actually used
in executing a given call of the subprogram. When a subroutine
is called, actual parameters of the call are "substituted" for
formal parameters of the definition in a manner constrained by
the binding mode of each parameter.

The binding mode of a formal parameter determines whether
corresponding actual parameters are read-only, write-only or
read-write. These three binding modes are respectively called
in, out and in out.

When no binding mode is specified the default binding mode

is <u>in</u>. Thus the parameter N of the function F above has the
default binding mode <u>in</u>.

Functions may have only <u>in</u> parameters because they are
allowed to affect their environment only by the result they
return. Procedures generally have at least one parameter with
the binding mode <u>out</u> or <u>in out</u> by means of which they produce
effects in their environment of call.*

The use of <u>in out</u> parameters is illustrated by the following
procedure for swapping (exchanging) the values of its two integer parameters.

<u>Example 1.29. In out procedure parameters</u>

```
procedure SWAP(X,Y: in out INTEGER) is      -- SWAP has two in out parameters
   LOCAL: INTEGER:              -- and a local variable
begin                          -- and three statements
   LOCAL := X;                  -- which use LOCAL for intermediate storage
   X := Y;                      -- while interchanging X and Y
   Y := LOCAL;
end;
```

The parameters X,Y above have the binding mode <u>in out</u>
because the procedure both uses the parameter values (X, Y occur
on the right-hand side of an assignment statement) and changes
the parameter values (X, Y occur on the left-hand side of an
assignment statement).

<u>In</u> parameters behave (within the procedure body) like local
constants whose value is provided by the corresponding actual
parameter at the point of call. The actual parameter can be a
literal, a variable, or an expression. Thus the function F
defined in example 1.8 can be called with the calls F(3), F(I),
F(I+J), etc.

Actual parameters of the <u>out</u> and <u>in out</u> modes must be variables. <u>Out</u> parameters act as local variables whose value is
assigned to the corresponding actual parameter as a result of
execution of the subprogram. <u>In out</u> parameters act as local
variables whose value is initialized from the actual parameter
at the time of call and assigned to the actual parameter as a
result of execution.

A call "SWAP(A,B);" of the procedure SWAP would cause the
parameters X, Y of the procedure declaration to act as local
variables initialized to the values of A, B at the time of call.

------

*Procedures can also affect their environments through non-
local variables and by output statements which are effectively
assignments to nonlocal storage in an output medium. However,
procedure parameters are the preferred mechanism for controlled
and flexible transfer of information between the calling and
called environments, and good programming practice dictates that
nonlocal variables be used with caution.

The final values of X, Y resulting from execution of the procedures would be assigned to A, B as a result of execution of the
procedure.

Use of the SWAP procedure may be illustrated by the following SORT procedure. It is assumed that the procedure SWAP, the
function MAX INDEX and the data type VECTOR are defined in a declarative environment that is textually accessible to the SORT
procedure.

Example 1.30. Sort procedure

```
procedure SORT(A: in out VECTOR) is   -- a sort procedure
  K: INTEGER;                          -- with a local variable K
begin                                  -- and a statement sequence
  for I in 1..A'LENGTH loop            -- which finds the maximum of
    K := MAX_INDEX(A(I..A'LENGTH));    -- successive subarrays of A
    SWAP (A(I),A(K));          -- and swaps first and max elements of subarray
  end loop;                    -- in order to sort the vector A
end SORT;
```

The above sorting routine can be used only for sorting integers. In many applications it is convenient to define subprograms for tasks such as swapping and sorting not just for a
single type such as integers but for a wide variety of types.
This can be done in Ada by means of generic subprograms.

1.7. Generic Subprograms

Subprograms may have formal parameters which are variables
of any defined data type, but cannot have formal parameters whose
"values" are procedures or type definitions. Generic clauses
provide a translation-time facility for parametrization of subprograms which allows both types and subprograms to appear as
"generic" subprogram parameters. The generic SWAP procedure
below illustrates the use of generic clauses in defining computational operations, such as swapping of two variables, which
have a common pattern for a wide variety of types.

Example 1.31. Generic swap procedure

```
generic (type T)                   -- a generic clause with type parameter T
procedure SWAP(X,Y: in out T) is   -- which becomes generic parameter of SWAP
  TEMP: T := constant X;           -- TEMP has type T, is initialized to X
begin              -- the three statements swap two objects of type T
  X := Y;          -- using a local object TEMP of type T
  Y := TEMP;       -- the required code may differ for different types T
end SWAP;
```

Generic procedures cannot be directly called. They may be
viewed as macro definitions which must be called with particular
values of generic parameters, and "expanded" at compile time,

before they can be executed. The compile-time process of calling
and "expanding" generic procedures is called instantiation. The
resulting procedures are called instances of the parent generic
procedure. The following example illustrates instantiation of
the generic SWAP procedure. Two instances of SWAP called
SWAP_INT and SWAP_VECT, which may respectively be used to swap
integer and vector objects, are created.

Example 1.32. Instantiation of generic procedures

procedure SWAP_INT is new SWAP(INTEGER);
procedure SWAP_VECT is new SWAP(VECTOR);

The SWAP procedure for vectors above will have very different code from the procedure for integers. Instantiation of
generic procedures in general may generate different code for
different instances, and may be viewed as a compile-time rather
than execution-time process. Generic procedures may be viewed
as macro definitions, and generic instantiations may be viewed
as macro calls which cause code to be generated.

The relation between translation-time instantiation with
specific values of generic parameters (by execution of a new
command) and run-time instantiation with specific actual parameters (by execution of a procedure call) is illustrated in
figure 2.

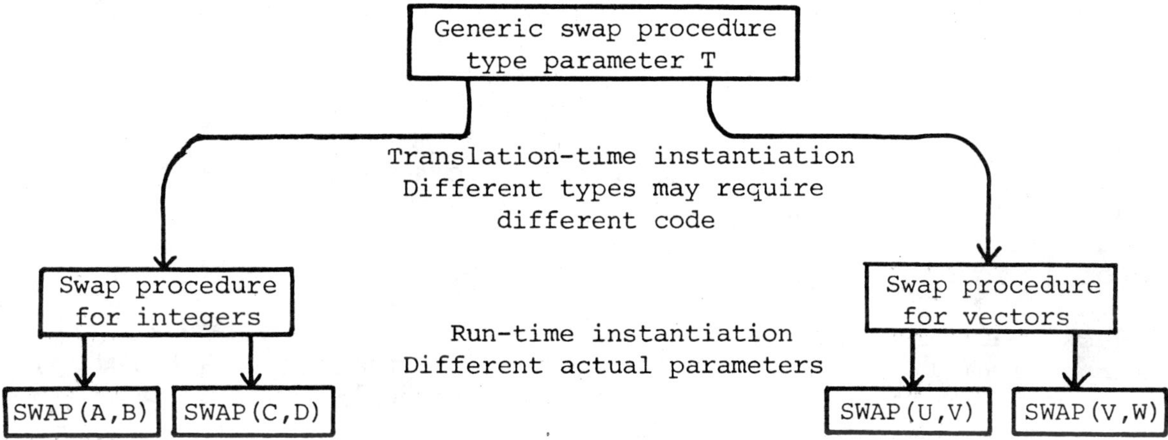

Figure 2. Relation between generic instantiation
and procedure calling.

Generic parameters may include subprogram parameters as
well as type parameters. Type and subprogram parameters must
have their values statically determined at compile time because
they may affect the code generated by the compiler when the
generic subprogram is instantiated at compile time.

<u>1.8   Packages</u>

Packages are a mechanism for providing a collection of logically related computational resources. The package DATA below provides the user with two integer objects, a data type VECTOR and two vector objects.

<u>Example 1.33.   Data packages</u>

```
package DATA is
   I,J: INTEGER;
   type VECTOR is array (1..100) of INTEGER;
   V,W: VECTOR;
end;
```

Packages are specified in the declarative part of a program unit. Components of the package DATA may be referred to by means of qualified names such as DATA.I, DATA.V(K). Components of a package may be made directly accessible and referred to by unqualified names by means of a <u>use</u> clause.

<u>Example 1.34.   The use clause</u>

```
procedure USE_DATA is
   use DATA;
begin
   I := 5;
   V(K) := 3;
end USE_DATA;
```

A use clause can occur only as the first statement in a declarative part (in order to ensure uniform name conventions throughout the associated program unit). There can be only one use clause in a declarative part but the use clause can contain names of several packages.

Packages which provide data objects and data types are similar to named common data pools of languages such as Fortran, but are more powerful because data types as well as data objects may be provided to the user. However, the computational resources provided by a package may in general include not only data resources but also program resources. The following spec- ification for a rational number package includes a record type which allows rational numbers (represented by integer pairs) to be created, an operation "=" which tests equality of rational numbers and two operations "+", "*" for addition and multipli- cation of rational numbers.

Example 1.35. Specification of a rational number package

```
package RATIONAL_NUMBERS is
  type RATIONAL is
    record
      NUMERATOR: INTEGER;
      DENOMINATOR: INTEGER range 1..INTEGER'LAST;
    end record;
  function "=" (X,Y: RATIONAL) return BOOLEAN;
  function "+" (X,Y: RATIONAL) return RATIONAL;
  function "*" (X,Y: RATIONAL) return RATIONAL;
end;
```

This specification is not complete, because it gives only
the form and not the semantics of the "=", "+" and "*" operations. However, it provides the user with complete information
concerning the form of user access to resources provided by the
package, and provides the compiler with sufficient information
to compile function calls, perform type checking, and allocate
storage for object declarations in the environment of the user.

The program resources provided by the rational number
packages are implemented in a package body whose details are
hidden from the user. The package body for the rational numbers
package given below includes a hidden procedure SAME_DENOMINATOR
(invisible to users of the package) which reduces the arguments
X and Y of the "=" and "+" operations to the same denominator
so that (3,4) and (6,8) are equal, and (3,2)+(1,4) becomes (7,4).

Example 1.36. Body of rational numbers package

```
package body RATIONAL_NUMBERS is
  procedure SAME_DENOMINATOR (X,Y: in out RATIONAL) is
  begin
    -- reduces X and Y to the same denominator
  end;
  function "=" (X,Y: RATIONAL) return BOOLEAN is
    U,V: RATIONAL;
  begin
    U := X;
    V := Y;
    SAME_DENOMINATOR (U,V);
    return (U.NUMERATOR = V.NUMERATOR);
  end "=";
  function "+" (X,Y: RATIONAL) return RATIONAL is   ... end "+";
  function "*" (X,Y: RATIONAL) return RATIONAL is   ... end "*";
end RATIONAL_NUMBERS;
```

The example below illustrates the creation of objects of
the type RATIONAL in a user environment, and the use of rational
number equality, addition, multiplication and assignment.

<u>Example 1.37. Use of rational numbers package</u>

```
declare                          -- rational number package must be visible
  use RATIONAL_NUMBERS;          -- allow unqualified use of +, *, =
  X,Y,Z: RATIONAL := (1,1);      -- declare three initialized RATIONAL objects
begin
  X := (3,4);                    -- rational number assignment
  Y := (6,8);                    -- equality was defined so that (6,8) = (3,4)
  if X = Y then                  -- rational number equality testing
    Z := X*X;                    -- rational number multiplication and assignment
  else
    Z := X+Y;                    -- rational number addition and assignment
  end if;
end;
```

In the statement "Z := X+Y;" above, + is interpreted as
rational number addition because the operands X, Y are rational
numbers, and := is interpreted as rational number assignment.
When a new type such as RATIONAL is introduced, assignment and
equality are automatically defined for objects of the type, but
all other operations (such as +, *) must be explicitly defined.
In the rational number package equality is redefined so that
(3,4) and (6,8) are equal. The explicitly-defined meaning of
equality supersedes the automatically-defined meaning.*

The rational number example illustrates that packages may
contain type declarations, and that objects of the type may be
created and manipulated using the operations for that type defined
within the module.

1.9 Abstract Data Types

The rational number package provides a resource for creating
objects of the type RATIONAL and for addition and multiplication
of rational numbers. However, the user can also manipulate the
components of objects of the type RATIONAL in a manner that is
totally unrelated to the fact that they are rational numbers.

---

*If equality had not been defined within the package, then
X=Y for rational number operands X, Y would be TRUE for identical
integer pairs but FALSE for X = (3,4) and Y = (6,8). Every definition of equality automatically causes the complementary operator /= to be defined. However, the other relatinal operators,
such as <, are not defined for new types and would have to be
explicitly defined, just as + and *.

Example 1.38. Direct operations on type components

```
procedure COMPONENTS is
  use RATIONAL_NUMBERS;
  X,Y,Z: RATIONAL := (1,2);
begin
  X.NUMERATOR := X.NUMERATOR+5;         -- X becomes (6,2)
  X.NUMERATOR := Y.DENOMINATOR;         -- X becomes (2,2)
end;
```

These operations treat rational numbers as records with two
components rather than as abstract objects subject to rational
number operations. Ada has a mechanism for hiding the record
representation of rational numbers so that it is accessible only
within the rational number package.

Example 1.39. Private data types

```
package RATIONAL_NUMBERS is
  type RATIONAL is private;                 -- hides representation of objects
  function "=" (X,Y: RATIONAL) return BOOLEAN;
  function "+" (X,Y: RATIONAL) return RATIONAL;
  function "*" (X,Y: RATIONAL) return RATIONAL;
  function "/" (X,Y: INTEGER) return RATIONAL;
private
  type RATIONAL is
    record
      NUMERATOR: INTEGER;
      DENOMINATOR: INTEGER range 1..INTEGER'LAST;
    end record;
end;
```

The above specification for rational numbers hides the representation of objects of the type RATIONAL, so that components
become inaccessible and can be manipulated only by rational number
operations defined within the package. Hiding of the representation makes it impossible to directly represent rational constants
as ordered pairs of integers. That is, "X := (3,4);" becomes
illegal, because the user can no longer assume that (3,4) is a
literal of the type RATIONAL.

This difficulty can be overcome by introducing a function
for creation of rational numbers from integer pairs into the
package body.

Example 1.40. Create function for private data type

```
function "/" (X,Y: INTEGER) return RATIONAL is
begin
  return (X,Y);
end "/";
```

If "/" is introduced into the package body (where the representation of RATIONAL) is known) and the function specification (first line above) is introduced into the specification part of the package, then "/" can be used to convert integer pairs into rationals without the user being aware of the representation of rationals.

Example 1.41. Use of the create function

    X := 3/4;   -- create rational number, assign to X

    The resulting package treats rational numbers as a true abstract data type. That is, rational number can be created from integer pairs, assigned to variables, tested for equality, added and multiplied, but the security of rational numbers cannot be violated by modifying their components.

    The operator "/" which is defined above for integer arguments and a rational result is an overloading of the predefined operator "/" for integer (and floating-point) arguments and results. This example illustrates that Ada permits overloading of operators which have the same argument types but different result types. When the compiler encounters a statement "X := 3/4;" then "/" is interpreted as integer division if X is an integer type and as the creation function for rational numbers when X has the type RATIONAL. Since the type of every variable and literal is known at compile time, the overloaded operator "/" can always be disambiguated at compile time and the proper machine-language code can be compiled. The rational number package might well include still a further overloading of "/" to represent division of two rational numbers. This operator would have rational operands and produce a rational result.

    In order to be truly useful a mechanism is required for printing rational numbers and possibly for converting rational numbers back into integer pairs. Such functions could be added to the rational number package in a straightforward manner.

    Abstract data types will be further illustrated by a package for realizing stacks with PUSH and POP operations and a hidden representation for the stack structure. Since assignment to stack variables as well as equality testing of stacks is inappropriate, it is desirable to suppress the automatic creation of assignment and equality testing for the stack data type. This is accomplished by the keyword restricted.

Example 1.42. Stack example

```
package ALL_ABOUT_STACKS is
  restricted type STACK is private;
  procedure PUSH (E: in ELEMENT; S: in out STACK);
  procedure POP (E: out ELEMENT; S: in out STACK);
private
  type STACK is
    record
      TOP: INTEGER range 0..1000 := 0;
      SPACE: array(1..1000) of ELEMENT;
    end record;
end;
```

The record in the above example contains an integer (stack
pointer) and an array with space for 1000 stack objects of type
ELEMENT. The operations PUSH and POP must be defined in the
package body (not given here) in terms of operations on the array.

The implementation of stacks by arrays is hidden from the
user. It could be changed to an implementation of stacks by lists
without affecting users. However, such a change in the representation of stacks would affect the data structures created in user
modules by elaboration of object declarations for the type stack.
It is for this reason that the "private part" of a module is
considered to be part of the package specification rather than
part of the package body.

Ada distinguishes between the logical interface of a package -
determined by the visible part of the module, and the physical
interface - which consists of the complete specification part
and includes both the visible and the private part. The logical
part includes everything the user needs to know in order to use
the module, while the physical part includes additional information needed by the compiler to support use of the module. The
private part is considered to be part of the physical interface
because the compiler must know this information to allocate
storage for objects of the private types created in the user
environment.

1.10   Tasks

Tasks are the program units for concurrent programming.
The task facilities of Ada will be illustrated by considering a
"mailbox" task which accepts messages from a number of "sender"
tasks S1, S2, ..., SM and can transmit messages to a number of
receiving tasks R1, R2, ..., RN, as illustrated in figure 3 below.

We shall consider the specification and implementation of
the mailbox task and the mechanisms required in sending and
receiving tasks to communicate with the mailbox task. In our
first example it is assumed that the mailbox task can handle
only a single message at a time which must be transmitted to a
receiving task before a second message can be accepted. A

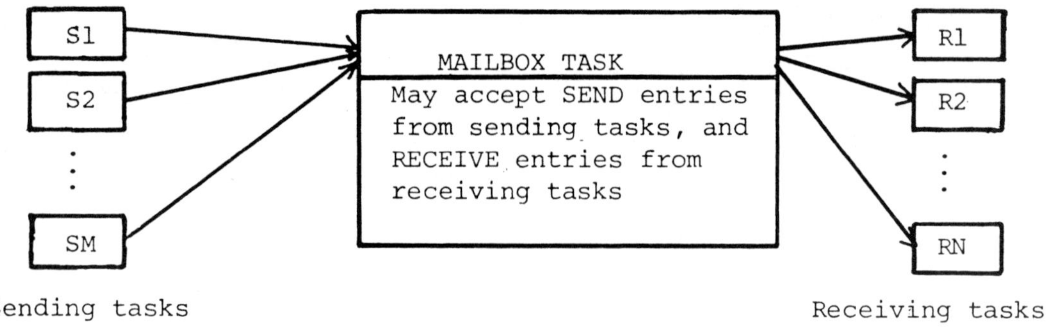

Figure 3.   Mailbox with multiple sending
and receiving tasks.

second example will consider the case when the mailbox has a
finite buffer of messages.

Tasks, like packages, have a specification part which specifies the resources made available to the user by a task, and a
body which defines the implementation of the resources. The
resources which can be provided to the user by a task include
entry resources which allow other tasks to communicate with the
given task. The following specification for a MAILBOX task has
an entry called SEND which allows other tasks to send mail to the
task and an entry called RECEIVE which allows other tasks to
receive mail from the task.

Example 1.43.   Specification for a MAILBOX task

```
task MAILBOX is
   entry SEND(INMAIL: in MESSAGE);      -- entry for sending mail to task
   entry RECEIVE(OUTMAIL: out MESSAGE);  -- entry for receiving mail from task
end;
```

The entries of a task may be called from other tasks by
entry calls which are syntactically just like procedure calls.
However, entry calls require synchronization between the calling
and called tasks before they can be executed. An entry call
in a calling task can be executed only if there is an accept
statement in the called task that is ready to accept it.

The mechanism for synchornizing an entry call in a calling
task and an accept statement in a called task will be illustrated
by considering the task body of the MAILBOX task.

Example 1.44. A task body

```
task body MAILBOX is
   BUFFER: MESSAGE;              -- local buffer, can store single message
begin
   loop
     accept SEND(INMAIL: in MESSAGE) do  -- accept SEND call from other task
        BUFFER := INMAIL;                 -- store message from sending task
     end;
     accept RECEIVE(OUTMAIL: out MESSAGE) do  -- accept RECEIVE call
        OUTMAIL := BUFFER;                -- transmit message to receiving task
     end;
   end loop;
end MAILBOX;
```

The MAILBOX task has a buffer in which messages may be
stored when SEND entries are accepted from sending tasks and
which serves as the message source when RECEIVE entries are
accepted from receiving tasks. Since messages must be sent to
the mailbox before they are transmitted and there is room for
only one message in the mailbox, SEND and RECEIVE entries must
be accepted in strictly alternating order.

The task may be initiated by the command "initiate MAILBOX;".
This will cause the MAILBOX task to start executing in parallel
with other tasks. The local variable BUFFER will be created and
the task will then go into an infinite loop which alternately
accepts SEND and RECEIVE entries from other tasks.

The structure of a program which defines and initiates the
MAILBOX task and a number of sending and receiving tasks might
be as follows.

Example 1.45. Task initiation

```
procedure TASK_EXAMPLE is
   specification of S1,S2..SM
   specification of R1, R2..RN
   specification of MAILBOX task
begin
   initiate S1, S2..SM;
   initiate R1,R2..RN;
   initiate MAILBOX;
end;
```

The specification of tasks must be defined in a declarative
part textually accessible at the point at which they are initiated. The bodies of the tasks may be separately compiled.

Tasks declared within a program unit must be completed before
that program unit may be exited. Thus if the procedure TASK_
EXAMPLE is called, exit from the procedure must wait until all
M+N+1 tasks declared and initiated within the procedure have terminated their execution.

We shall now examine more closely the mechanism for communication between the MAILBOX task and the sending and receiving tasks.

Execution of a call from a sending task for the entry SEND in the MAILBOX task requires both that the calling task is waiting to execute the entry call and that the called task (MAILBOX task) is waiting to execute an <u>accept</u> statement for that entry call, as illustrated in figure 4.

Figure 4. Rendezvous between calling and called tasks.

If the entry call occurs before the called task is ready to accept it, then the calling task is forced to wait until control in the called tasks reaches the <u>accept</u> statement. If the <u>accept</u> statement is reached before the entry call occurs, then the call can be handled immediately but the called task will be waiting on its <u>accept</u> statement until the entry call arrives. Acceptance of the entry call requires synchronization between the calling and the called tasks. When the synchronization is achieved we say that a <u>rendezvous</u> occurs. The rendezvous consists of executing statements between the <u>do</u> and <u>end</u> keywords following the <u>accept</u> statement. These statements may involve transfer of information between the calling and called tasks and require the calling task to be suspended while they are executed. When these statements have been executed we say that the rendezvous is complete and both tasks can proceed merrily on their way.

Thus a call of the SEND entry will result in a rendezvous during which the input mail transmitted from the calling task via the parameter INMAIL will be stored in a local buffer. A call of the RECEIVE entry results in a rendezvous during which the message in the buffer is transmitted to the calling program via the parameter OUTMAIL.

If entry calls for the entry SEND occur more rapidly than they can be accepted, they are placed in a queue and handled in a first-come-first-served order. In general, every entry of every task must have a queue to hold entry calls which have not yet been serviced.

The rendezvous mechanism is the basic Ada mechanism for synchronization between concurrently executing processes. It is a high-level structuring mechanism when compared to lower-level synchronization mechanisms such as semaphores. It imposes a

discipline of communication between tasks that is akin to the
discipline imposed by structured programming. It appears to be
a natural mechanism for communication, although escape to a lower-
level mechanism may sometimes be necessary, just as use of a goto
statement is sometimes necessary in structured programming.

1.11 Selection Among Task Entries

     The accept statement may be viewed as a mechanism which
enables a task to wait for a predetermined event, indicated by
the calling of an entry. However, in many parallel programming
applications we cannot predict the order in which entries will
occur, and wish to allow a task to choose its next action from
among several entry calls.

     Consider, for example, a mailbox whose buffer has a capacity
of n messages with the property that a message can be written
into the buffer provided it is not full and can be read from the
buffer provided it is not empty.

     In implementing such a mailbox we wish to execute SEND and
RECEIVE entries in the order in which they arrive provided the
buffer is not full when SEND is encountered and not empty when
RECEIVE is encountered. The conditional execution of entries can
be specified by conditional (guarded) accept statements as follows.

Example 1.46. Guarded accept statements

```
when NOT_FULL => accept SEND(..)..      -- SEND only when buffer not full
when NOT_EMPTY => accept RECEIVE(..).. -- RECEIVE only when buffer not empty
```

     We cannot predict the order in which SEND and RECEIVE entry
calls for a buffered mailbox task will occur. If the language is
to support execution of SEND and RECEIVE entries in the order of
their occurrence, it needs a mechanism for choosing among alternative accept statements depending on the order in which entry
calls occur. This mechanism is the select statement. Choice
between accepting a SEND call (providing the buffer is not full)
and accepting a RECEIVE call (provided the buffer is not empty)
can be specified as follows.

Example 1.47. Selection among guarded accept statements

```
select
   when NOT_FULL => accept SEND(..)..
or
   when NOT_EMPTY => accept RECEIVE(..)..
end select;
```

     A select statement is executed by first evaluating the when
conditions (NOT_EMPTY and NOT_FULL) to determine the set of
accept statements which are candidates for execution (called open
accept statements). The set of open accept statements is then

checked to determine if there are waiting entry calls. If one
or more open accept statements has a waiting entry call, then
one of them is chosen nondeterministically* for execution. If
no open accept statement has a waiting entry call, then execution
is suspended until an entry call for one of the open accept statements occurs.

The buffered mailbox task below is essentially an infinite
loop which repeatedly executes a select statement of the form given
in the previous example. The local variables SIZE and COUNT res-
psectively specify the buffer size and the number of elements in
the buffer, while the local variables NEXTIN, NEXTOUT indicate the
buffer index for the next SEND message and RECEIVE message.

Example 1.48. Buffered mailboxes

```
task body MAILBOX is
   SIZE: constant INTEGER := 20;                 -- buffer size
   BUFFER: array(1..SIZE) of MESSAGE;
   NEXTIN, NEXTOUT: INTEGER range 1..SIZE := 1;
   COUNT: INTEGER range 0..SIZE := 0;            -- number of items in buffer
begin
   loop
     select
       when COUNT < SIZE =>      -- guard which checks that buffer not full
         accept SEND(INMAIL: in MESSAGE) do  -- before accepting message
           BUFFER(NEXTIN) := INMAIL; -- critical section; must be executed
         end;                         -- before calling task resumes
         NEXTIN := NEXTIN mod SIZE + 1; -- statements outside critical section
         COUNT := COUNT+1;      -- may be executed concurrently with calling task
     or
       when COUNT > 0 =>
         accept RECEIVE(OUTMAIL: out MESSAGE) do
           OUTMAIL := BUFFER(NEXTOUT);
         end;
         NEXTOUT := NEXTOUT mod SIZE + 1;
         COUNT := COUNT - 1;
     end select;
   end loop;
end MAILBOX;
```

This task body illustrates that tasks are resources which
may have locally declared identifiers (such as buffers and
counters) required to implement the service provided by the task
to its users. When the buffer is neither empty nor full, which
is the usual case for a buffer of size 20, then both guarded
accept statements will be open and SEND and RECEIVE calls may
be accepted on a first-come-first-served basis.

----

*The choice among entry calls of open accept statements is
nondeterministic in the sense that user programs should not depend
on particular scheduling assumptions. However, the choice need
not be random. Any "fair" scheduling strategy, such as a "round-
robin" strategy, can be used by the system to implement nondeterministic choice among entry calls of open accept statements.

The program text between do and end following an accept statement is sometimes referred to as a critical section. A calling task cannot resume execution until execution of the critical section of the accept statement in the called task has been completed, and such critical sections should therefore be kept as short as possible. The present example illustrates that the statements executed in the called task as a result of rendezvous may include both statements within the critical section (which pass information between the calling and called task) and statements outside the critical section which may be executed concurrently with the calling task.

1.12   Generic Modules

Modules, like procedures, may be defined to be generic. Generic modules may have formal parameters and may be instantiated with different actual parameter values for different instances of the module.

A favorite example of generic modules is a stack package with push and pop operations.* In the following example both the stack size and the type of the stack elements are generic parameters.

Example 1.49.   A generic package

```
generic (SIZE: INTEGER; type ELEMENT)
package STACK is
   procedure PUSH(IN_ELEM: in ELEMENT);
   procedure POP(OUT_ELEM: out ELEMENT);
   FULL, EMPTY: exception;
end STACK;
```

This generic definition is a template. Instances of stacks each with a specific size and type may be created by instantiation.

Example 1.50.   Instantiation of a generic package

```
package STACK1 is new STACK(100, INTEGER);
package STACK2 is new STACK(50, INTEGER);
package STACK3 is new STACK(75, CHARACTER);
package STACK4 is new STACK(W, RATIONAL);
```

____

*A (pushdown) stack is a data structure in which elements can be stored by "push" operations and retrieved by subsequent "pop" operations. The pop operation retrieves the most recent element pushed onto the stack, so that information is retrieved in a last-in-first-out order. Nongeneric stack packages require elements to be of a specific type (such as INTEGER) and have a fixed maximum number of elements. The generic definition allows us to define as many different stacks as we want, each with its own size and element type.

The generic facility would be useful for creating multiple
instances of a package (or task) even in the absence of parameters. The previous example illustrates not only the ability
to vary stack attributes but also the ability to create multiple
stacks which could all have the same attributes.

The ability to create multiple instances of a module is particularly important in the case of task modules. Many concurrent
processing applications involve the modeling of situations where
there are multiple instances of a given object, such as a ship,
plane or radar monitor. In this case it is natural to create a
prototype generic task for the class of object introduced by a
declaration of the following form.

Example 1.51. Parameterless generic task module

```
generic task SHIP is
   specification of resources
   which constitute a ship
end SHIP;
```

Instantiations of this generic task may be defined by instantiation statements such as "task QE2 is new SHIP;".

Multiple instances of a task can be created either by instantiating a generic task as suggested above or by specifying a
one-dimensional array of tasks of a given type called a task
family. A one-dimensional array of ships could be specified as
follows.

Example 1.52. Task families

```
task SHIP(1..1000) is
   specification of resources
   which constitute a ship
end SHIP;
```

The above specification allows the user to refer to individual tasks as SHIP(55) or SHIP(I).

A task family should be regarded, for purposes of optimizing
storage space, as a potential rather than actual collection of
tasks. Execution of an initiate statement for a given member of
the family such as "initiate SHIP(55);" may be regarded as a
command not only to initiate the task but also to create an
instance of the task.

The generic mechanism for subprograms and modules is fundamentally the same, and provides a facility for both parametric
variation of templates and for the creation of multiple instances
of templates. However, the way in which the generic facility is
used is likely to differ for modules and procedures.

Procedures already have a parameter facility. Moreover, a
procedure call is effectively an instantiation of the procedure
for specific values of actual parameters. Thus the generic
facility for procedures duplicates many of the facilities already
provided by procedures, and is useful primarily as providing more
powerful parametrization (for types and subprograms) which may
require the generation of different code for different instances.

Modules do not have parameters and there is no mechanism
other than the generic mechanism for creating multiple instances.
Thus there is much less duplication of already-existing facilities in the case of modules. The use of parameterless generic
modules for creation of multiple instances of a prototype module
is likely to be widespread in large systems.

1.13 Blocks

We have completed our review of the principal language
features of Ada. In the remaining sections we shall consider
issues of program structure and other details necessary to understand how large programs fit together. The reader may feel that
the discussion in these sections is elementary and that they
should logically precede the sections on packages, tasks and
generics. However, this material was deliberately placed at the
end of this language overview so as to provide a minimum of
digression for the reader who wishes to proceed as quickly as
possible to the "meat" of the language. The remaining sections
of this overview may be skipped by the reader interested only
in what is in the language. They are concerned with developing
an understanding of the structure of the language rather than
with introducing new features.

In the present section the notion of a block is introduced
and the relation between blocks and other program units is considered. This leads into a discussion of separate compilation
and of the (scope) rules which determine textual accessibility to
declared identifiers.

There are three kinds of program units in Ada - subprograms,
modules and blocks. Subprograms and modules have been discussed
in some detail in earlier sections. They have _names_, and are
either stand-alone compilation units with no textual environment
or are specified in the declarative part of an enclosing program
unit. In contrast, blocks are _anonymous_ program units which have
the syntactic status of a statement and must occur _in line_ in the
statement _part_ of a program unit. The declarative _part_ of a
block is introduced by the keyword _declare_ and the sequence of
statements of a block are bracketed by the keywords _begin..end_.

Example 1.53. Syntax of blocks

```
[declare                         -- a block has an optional
   sequence of declarations]     -- declarative part
begin                            -- and a sequence of
   sequence of statements        -- statements bracketed by
end;                             -- the keywords begin..end
```

Blocks may be used to associate local nomenclature with a sequence of statements. There are also two other reasons for enclosing sequences of statements in a block which have nothing to do with nomenclature.

1. Blocks, just like other program units, cannot be exited until all tasks initiated in the block have completed execution. Thus initiate statements for a logically related set of tasks might be placed within a block to ensure that the set of tasks is completed before code following the block is executed.

2. Exception handlers may be associated with blocks (and other program units) in a manner described in section 1.18.

Thus blocks are a unit of program structure not only for purposes of nomenclature but also for purposes of task completion and exception handling.

In order to illustrate the relation between blocks and other program units, we shall start by considering the following simple block for interchanging the values of X and Y.

Example 1.54. Blocks

```
declare                 -- declarative part of block
   LOCAL: INTEGER;      -- with local variable
begin                   -- and a sequence of statements
   LOCAL := X;          -- which uses LOCAL
   X := Y;              -- and nonlocal variables X and Y
   Y := LOCAL;          -- and interchanges X and Y
end;                    -- and is then exited
```

The above block uses both the local variable LOCAL and the nonlocal variables X, Y in its body. The nonlocal variables of a block must be declared in a textually enclosing declarative part, as in the following example.

Example 1.55. Block nested in a procedure body

```
procedure BLOCKS is           -- a procedure called BLOCKS
  X,Y: INTEGER;                -- with local variables X, Y
begin                         -- and a sequence of statements
  X := 5;                     -- which initializes X
  Y := 7;                     -- and then initializes Y
  declare                     -- and then enters a nested block
    LOCAL: INTEGER;           -- with a local variable
  begin                       -- and a sequence of statements
    LOCAL := X;               -- which uses LOCAL
    X := Y;                   -- and nonlocal X, Y
    Y := LOCAL;               -- to interchange X, Y
  end;                        -- and is then exited
    -- do something useful
end BLOCKS;                   -- finally procedure is exited
```

The in-line occurrence of blocks with local nomenclature in
a procedure body makes the body difficult to read, and it is
likely that, for this and other reasons, they will not be used
very frequently in procedures. The block for interchanging two
variables can be rewritten as a procedure with formal parameters
X, Y, as in the following example.

Example 1.56. Replacement of blocks by procedures

```
procedure NO_BLOCKS is                        -- a procedure called NO_BLOCKS
  I,J: INTEGER;                               -- with local variables
  procedure SWAP(X,Y: in out INTEGER) is      -- and nested procedure declaration
    LOCAL: INTEGER;                           -- with a local variable
  begin                                       -- and a sequence of statements
    LOCAL := X;                               -- which uses LOCAL
    X := Y;                                   -- and parameters X, Y
    Y := LOCAL;                               -- to interchange X, Y
  end SWAP;                                   -- and is then exited
begin                                         -- the body of NO_BLOCKS
  I := 5;                                     -- initializes variables I,J of NO_BLOCKS
  J := 7;
  SWAP(I,J);                                  -- invokes procedure to interchange I,J
    -- do something useful
end;                                          -- and is eventually exited
```

The body of the procedure NO_BLOCKS may be read much more
easily than that of the procedure BLOCKS. Moreover, the procedure SWAP may be called at more than one textual point of the
body with different values of the parameters. Thus replacing
the block by a procedure increases both the readability and the
flexibility of the resulting program.

Replacement of an in-line block by a procedure call introduces additional overhead which may in certain critical situations be unacceptable. The overhead may be avoided by specifying a subprogram to be in-line.

Example 1.57. The pragma INLINE

pragma INLINE;

     Pragmas have no effect on the semantics of a program, but
are used to convey information to the compiler. The pragma
INLINE occurring in the declarative part of a subprogram definition suggests to the compiler that the subprogram body be expanded in line at all instances of call. The actual effect of
the pragma INLINE depends on the kinds of optimization built into
the compiler. Compilers may altogether ignore this pragma and
still be considered correct.

1.14   Separate Compilation

     Readers may object that the body of the NO_BLOCKS procedure
has been made more readable at the expense of cluttering up the
declarative part of the procedure. We can improve the readability of the procedure even further by declaring the SWAP procedure to be a separate compilation unit.

Example 1.58. Separately compiled procedure declaration

```
procedure SEPARATE_SWAP is
  I,J: INTEGER;
  procedure SWAP(X,Y: in out INTEGER) is separate;   -- SWAP is separately compiled
begin
  I := 5;
  J := 7;
  SWAP(I,J);
    -- do something useful
end;
```


     The text of procedures which are declared to be separate in
the context of an enclosing program unit must be introduced by a
restricted clause which specifies the program unit in which the
procedure is textually embedded, followed by the keyword separate.
Such procedure bodies may make use of identifiers declared in the
textual environment of declaration (such as I, J above). They
must be compiled after the program unit in which they are declared,
and recompiled if the enclosing program unit is redeclared. Such
procedures are dependent on a textual environment and must be
carefully distinguished from stand-alone separately compiled program units not dependent on textual environment (which are discussed in sections 1.16 and 1.17).

Example 1.59. Separately compiled procedure implementation

```
restricted(SEPARATE_SWAP);
separate procedure SWAP(X,Y: in out INTEGER) is
   TEMP: INTEGER;
begin
   TEMP := X;
   X := Y;
   Y := TEMP;
end SWAP;
```

The is separate declaration provides complete information
concerning the syntactic correctness of calls of the procedure
and allows the compiler to check the correctness of such calls.
Programs which use a separately specified procedure need not be
aware of its implementation. Moreover, changes in implementation
which do not affect its specification are guaranteed not to
require changes in program units which use the procedure. The
fact that changes in the implementation which do not affect the
specification are localized greatly enhances the maintainability
of large programs. The implementation of a procedure can be
changed even after programs which use it are running without
affecting other parts of the program. In this way program
changes which take advantage of a new hardware configuration or
of machine language optimizations can be introduced in a modular
fashion.

1.15 Scope of Identifiers

The scope of an identifier is the region of text over which
its declaration has an effect. The scope of an identifier
declared in the declarative part of a given program unit extends
from its point of declaration to the end of the program unit.
The following example has a procedure called OUTER with two local
integer variables, A, B and a nested procedure INNER with a redeclaration of B.

Example 1.60. Scope of identifiers

```
   procedure OUTER is            -- a procedure called OUTER
      A: INTEGER := 0;           -- with an integer variable A
      B: INTEGER := A+1;         -- and an integer variable B
      procedure INNER is         -- and a nested procedure called INNER
         B: BOOLEAN;             -- with B redeclared as BOOLEAN
      begin                      -- INNER has a statement sequence
         A := 1;                 -- which assigns an integer to A
         B := TRUE;              -- and assigns a BOOLEAN to the inner B
         OUTER.B := A+1;         -- and accesses the outer B by OUTER.B
      end;
   begin                         -- OUTER has a statement sequence
      A := 2;                    -- which assigns an integer to A
      B := TRUE;                 -- illegal assignment - can be caught by compiler
      B := A+1;                  -- and assigns to the outer B
   end;
```

In this example B is declared to be an integer variable in the outer procedure and a Boolean variable in the inner procedure. An unqualified reference to B in the inner procedure refers to the innter declaration of B, so that "B := TRUE;" is a valid statement of the inner procedure. However, the integer variable B may be referred to in the inner block by the qualified name OUTER.B so that the statement "OUTER.B := A+1;" is valid. The scope of the inner declaration of B does not extend to the sequence of statements of the outer procedure, so that the statement "B := TRUE;" in the outer procedure is illegal.

This example also illustrates that the outer declaration of B is in the scope of the outer A and can therefore use the value of A to initialize the declaration of B. Interchange of the declarations of A and B would be illegal because B would then no longer be declared in the scope of A and could not then use the value of A to initialize B.

1.16   Restricted Program Units

Program unit boundaries normally act like one-way membranes, allowing identifiers declared in textually enclosing units to be known within the program unit, but never allowing internally declared identifiers to be known outside the program unit. Thus a deeply nested program unit has access to several textually enclosing layers of environment and this could in some instances cause confusion.

Such free accessibility to the textually enclosing environment can be avoided by the <u>restricted</u> clause. The keyword <u>restricted</u> immediately preceding the program unit causes the textually enclosing environment to become inaccessible to the program unit.

Example 1.61. No access to textually enclosing environment

```
restricted procedure P (parameters) is
   -- declarations and statements which cannot access
   -- any nonlocal identifiers declared in the
   -- textual environment of P
end P;
```


A restricted clause of a given program unit may in general contain a <u>visibility list</u> of non-local program units accessible within the restricted program unit. The rules which determine the portion of the environment that becomes visible when a unit is mentioned in a visibility list depend on the textual relation between the restricted program unit and the program unit mentioned in the visibility list.

Figure 5 illustrates three possible textual relations between accessible program units mentioned in a visibility list and the restricted program unit P. That is, the accessible program unit may textually enclose P (like P1), may be declared

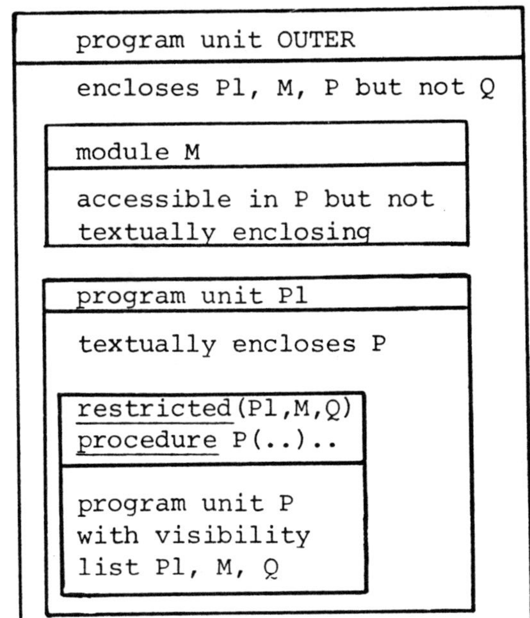

Figure 1.5. Textual relations among program units.

but not textually enclosing (like M), or may be a stand-alone
separately compiled module (like Q).

If P is textually nexted in Pl then occurrence of Pl in the
visibility list of P opens up accessibility of the textual environment as far out as Pl, but not beyond Pl. We can think of P as
being enclosed in a fog which allows everything to be seen as far
out as Pl but which is too thick for anything further out than Pl
to be visible.

If M is an accessible but not textually enclosing module,
then occurrence of M in the visibility list of P provides access
to the computational resources of M but not to other identifiers
in the declarative environment of M.

If Q is a stand-alone separately compiled module mentioned
in the visibility list of P, then P has access to the computational resources of Q.

The first name in a visibility list may, but need not, be the
name of an enclosing program unit. The remaining names (if any)
must be names of modules that are outside the restricted unit and
outside the enclosing program unit (if the first parameter defines
one). Thus the units which are made visible by a visibility list
are essentially modules which define collections of resources
rather than individual resources.

These rules are illustrated by the following example of a
restricted procedure P nested in a procedure Pl which is in turn
nested in a procedure OUTER containing a package M.

Example 1.62. Enclosing and non-enclosing program units

```
procedure OUTER is
   I: INTEGER;                        -- I is not accessible in P
   package M is                       -- M is accessible in P
      specification and body of M
   procedure Pl is                    -- Pl textually encloses P
      J: INTEGER;                     -- J is accessible in P
      restricted (Pl,M)               -- restricted clause for procedure P
      procedure P is                  -- P is restricted to Pl, M
      begin
        J := 5;                       -- legal, we can "see" out as far as Pl
        Pl;                           -- legal recursive call of Pl
        I := 5;                       -- illegal; we can see M but not I
      end;
   statements of Pl
statements of OUTER procedure
```

In this example the variable J declared in Pl is visible in
P, but the variable I declared in OUTER but not in M is not
visible in P.

1.17 Restricted Compilation Units and Libraries

Compilation units have no explicit textually enclosing environment, and it does not therefore make sense to impose
visibility restrictions relating to the textual environment.
However, there are implicit environments associated with compilation units whose visibility may be affected by restricted clauses.

1. The predefined environment which includes predefined
    types and other identifiers listed in the package
    STANDARD in appendix C of the language reference manual.
2. The "library" environment of compilation units which
    generally contain input-output packages, mathematical
    subroutine packages, and other standard library tools.
3. The set of stand-alone compilation units being defined
    by the user for the current application.

The visibility of identifiers of the predefined environment
is not affected by restricted clauses. Identifiers such as
INTEGER may be superseded by a redeclaration such as "type INTEGER
is SHORT_INTEGER;". However, even in this case access to the
original identifier is still possible by the qualified name
STANDARD.INTEGER.

Library compilation units and user-defined compilation units
may be made visible in a given user-defined compilation unit by
mentioning them in the restricted clause of the compilation unit.
Thus the input-output functions GET and PUT are in fact defined
in a library package TEXT_IO, and compilation units using GET and
PUT must include TEXT_IO in a restricted clause associated with
the compilation unit.

<u>Example 1.63.</u> <u>Communication among compilation units</u>

```
restricted (TEXT_IO)
procedure SIMPLE_ADD is
  use TEXT_IO;
  X,Y,Z: INTEGER;
begin
  GET(X);
  GET(Y);
  Z := X+Y;
  PUT(Z);
end;
```

Example 1.1 at the beginning of this chapter is, in fact, an incomplete program which would give rise to a compiler diagnostic indicating that GET and PUT are undefined. The above program is the complete version and could, with appropriate data, be executed.

User-defined compilation units have exactly the same status in the environment as library compilation units. The operating system for running Ada programs will generally contain a library file for each user which is updated whenever a compilation unit is compiled. Thus every compilation unit requires as input the text of the compilation unit and the library file and produces as output a compiled compilation unit and an updated library file (see figure 6).

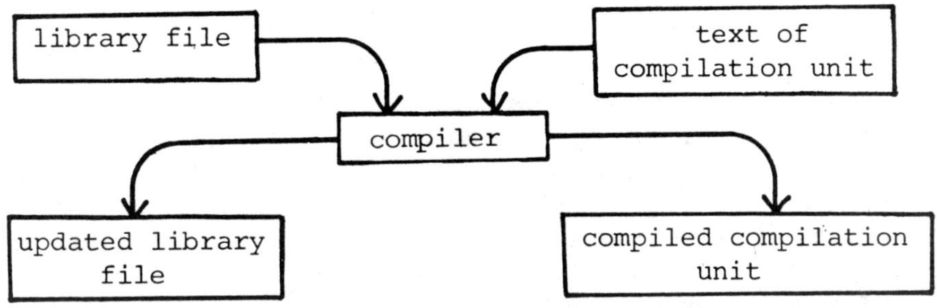

Figure 6. Effect of compiling a compilation unit.

Communication among compilation units of a user program requires mention of used compilation units in the visibility list of the restricted clause of the compilation unit in which they are used.

Mention of a compilation unit Cl in the restricted clause of a compilation unit C requires that the specification of Cl must already have been compiled at the time that C is compiled. The visibility dependencies determined by restricted clauses must determine a sequential (non-circular) hierarchy and must be compiled so that earlier program units of the hierarchy are compiled before later ones.

However, this dependency applies only to interface specifications of program units. Thus if Cl is a package, then the
specification of Cl must be compiled before any compilation units
which mention Cl in a restricted clause, but the package body of
Cl may be compiled and recompiled at any time without affecting
the compilation of compilation units which use Cl.

1.18   Exceptions

Exceptions provide a mechanism for the unusual termination
of program units. Normal termination of blocks and procedures
occurs by executing the last statement of the body, while normal
termination of functions is by executing a return statement.
Exceptions provide a dynamic mechanism for exit from program
units which bypasses the above normal termination mechanisms.

Exceptions may be defined by the user or predefined by the
system. Predefined exceptions may be illustrated by INDEX_ERROR
(when an index is outside the range specified by an array).
Since INDEX_ERROR is a predefined exception there is a system-
defined "default" action when an index error occurs. However,
this system-defined action may be superseded by user-defined
actions to handle index errors in specific parts of the program.

We shall illustrate below how exceptions may be declared,
raised and "handled" (by an exception handler). Declaration of
an exception is similar to declaration of a typed variable.

Example 1.64. Declaration of exceptions

```
OVERFLOW, UNDERFLOW: exception;      -- declare two exception identifiers
           SINGULAR: exception;      -- and another one
```


Exceptions may be raised by use of the keyword raise.

Example 1.65. Raising of exceptions

```
if DETERMINANT = 0 then              -- raise SINGULAR
   raise SINGULAR;                   -- if DETERMINANT is zero
end if;
```


Exceptions which are raised are handled by exception handlers. Exception handlers may appear only after the statement
sequence of a subprogram, module or block after the keyword
exception. Each individual exception handler is introduced by
the keyword when, followed by the exception name, followed by
the sequence of statements which handle the exception.

Example 1.66. Handling of exceptions

```
exception                            -- exception handler for SINGULAR
   when SINGULAR =>                  -- must appear at the end of
     PUT ("MATRIX IS SINGULAR");     -- a block, subprogram or module
```

Raising of an exception has some of the properties of a
parameterless procedure call, and an exception handler has some
of the properties of a parameterless procedure specification.
However, the mechanism for associating a handler with a raised
exception differs from the corresponding mechanism for procedures.

When an exception is raised during execution of a subprogram,
a handler is sought first local to the subprogram, then in the
environment of call of the subprogram, and then in successive
dynamically preceding program units. This dynamic criterion for
determining the handler associated with a raised exception contrasts with the static scope criterion of associating a procedure
with a procedure call.

The dynamic mechanism for associating handlers with raised
exceptions is illustrated by the following procedure P which has
a handler (the first handler) in the body of the main procedure
P and a second handler in the body of the procedure R.

Example 1.66. Dynamic search for exception handlers

```
procedure P is
   SINGULAR: exception;             -- declare exception SINGULAR in P
   procedure Q is
   begin
      ...
      if DETERMINANT = 0 then       -- code in Q which raises
        raise SINGULAR;             -- the exception SINGULAR
      end if;
      ...
   end Q;
   procedure R is
   begin
      ...Q...                       -- call of Q within R
   exception                        -- if exception occurs during this call
      when SINGULAR =>              -- of Q then second handler is selected
        -- second handler for SINGULAR
   end R;
begin -- P
   ...R...Q...                      -- call of Q in main body of P
exception                           -- if exception occurs during this call
   when SINGULAR =>                 -- of Q then first handler is selected
     -- first handler for SINGULAR
end P;
```

If, in the above example, the exception SINGULAR is raised
in the call of Q within R, a search is made first for a handler
within Q and then for a handler within R, so that the second
handler is selected. If SINGULAR is raised in a call of Q in
the main body of P, then the first handler is selected.

The action when handling of an exception has been completed differs from the corresponding procedure action of returning to the environment of call. An exception is regarded as an error. The environments in which the exception occurs and the environment in which it is handled are always abandoned. The exception handler is a mechanism for unusual completion of the subprogram in which the exception is handled. Thus, in the above example, raising of the exception SINGULAR within Q (within R) would cause the exception handler to terminate Q, and would cause the exception handler for SINGULAR within R to be executed in place of the normal sequence of code for completing the execution of R. On completion of the exception handler, control would be returned to the program which called R.

The process of terminating a subprogram because a raised exception is not handled, and then reraising the exception in the calling program, is called propagating the exception. Thus an exception raised in a given subprogram is propagated backwards through the dynamic chain of calls until a subprogram which handles the exception is found. The exception is then executed in the environment of the handler, constitutes unusual completion of that subprogram, and results in return to the point of call of the subprogram in which the handler is defined.

In addition to user-defined exceptions, there are predefined whose handlers are defined by the system. Some predefined exceptions such as DIVIDE_ERROR or INDEX_ERROR are automatically raised by the system (when an attempt is made to divide by zero or to access a nonexistent array element). Other predefined exceptions, such as FAILURE (raising of failure in task T2 within task T1) must be explicitly raised by the user to activate the system implementation. A complete list of predefined exceptions is given in the language reference manual (section 11).

The detection of exceptions may be suppressed. For example, if a time-critical computation wishes to save the time of checking for index errors in a given program unit, this can be accomplished by including the following pragma in the declarative part of the program unit.

Example 1.67. Suppression of implicit exceptions

pragma SUPPRESS (INDEX_ERROR);

This pragma allows the compiler to omit run-time checks for index errors in compiling the program unit but does not require the compiler to do so. Both the pragma SUPPRESS and the previously-discussed pragma INLINE are suggestions to the compiler to perform certain kinds of optimization, but may be ignored by the compiler. The pragma SUPPRESS should be used with caution, both because it can lead to uncontrolled program behavior when the suppressed exception occurs and is not properly handled, and because programs with suppressed exceptions may behave differently for different compilers.

Section 7
Language Issues: Data Base Management and Exception Handling

Although there is a great deal of experience and a considerable degree of consensus on issues such as data types and control structures, there is far less agreement and experience with some other aspects of programming language design. Among these areas are input/output, data base management, and exception handling. Recent work in language design for data base management and exception handling has produced a number of alternative proposals, some of which are examined in this section.

Work in programming languages and data base management proceeded separately for many years. Beginning with efforts of the CODASYL Data Base Task Group in 1971 [1], however, these areas have become more closely intertwined as writers consider the problem of preparing programs that involve access to data bases. Three basic approaches to the integration of programming languages and data base management have been taken [2]:

(1) embedding of a data base management query language in a conventional programming language;

(2) extension of a programming language to include data definition and manipulation facilities;

(3) design of new programming languages to incorporate some form of data base management facility as a basic component of the language.

The first of these approaches is exemplified by the embedding of the query language QUEL in the programming language C to provide access to the INGRES [3] relational database management system [4], and by the use of SQL in PL/1 to provide access to the relational database management system System R[5].

The second approach is exemplified in three ways: by the CODASYL Data Base Task Group's approach of defining a Data Definition Language (DDL) and Data Manipulation Language (DML) to provide access to network data base management systems through COBOL; by the DL/1 data manipulation facilities that can be incorporated in PL/1 programs to provide access to IBM's IMS data base management system; and by Pascal/R, an extension to Pascal that provides a nonprocedural set of operations for relational data base management in Pascal.

The paper by Schmidt in this section describes the Pascal/R features, which have been implemented in conjunction with a Pascal implementation for the Decsystem-10.

A number of newly designed programming languages — including PLAIN [6], Rigel [7], Aldat [8], Theseus [9], and ASTRAL [10] — exemplify the third approach. All of these incorporate relations and relational database management operations. The paper by Wasserman describes the data management facilities of PLAIN.

The need for exception handling arises when one wants to build robust programs — programs which are able to react to exceptional conditions, including errors, during program execution. Although several earlier programming languages, most notably PL/1, provided exception handling, the use of exception handling facilities often led to ill-structured programs. More recent effort in the area of exception handling provided better structured mechanisms which could be used in conjunction with structured programming practices and for which one could hope to establish program correctness, even in the presence of runtime exceptions. Such features are present in a number of modern languages, including CLU, Ada, and Plain.

The brief paper by Goodenough outlines the basic issues in exception handling, describing why one needs to have exception handling facilities and what these facilities should provide. The paper by Liskov and Snyder describes those facilities as they exist in CLU. The paper by Berry and colleagues describes another exception handling scheme, showing how it could be applied in conjunction with Alphard.

References

1. CODASYL Data Base Task Group. *April 71 Report.* (Available from ACM).

2. Wasserman, A.I., "Embedding Data Base Operations in Programming Languages," *IEEE COMPCON Spring 75 Conference Digest,* pp. 79-82.

3. Stonebraker, M.R., E. Wong, P. Kreps, and G.D. Held, "The Design and Implementation of INGRES," *Transactions on Database Systems,* vol. 1, no. 3 (September, 1976), pp. 189-222.

4. Allman, E., M.R. Stonebraker, and G.D. Held, "Embedding a Relational Data Sublanguage in a General Purpose Programming Language," *Proc. of Conference on Data: Abstraction, Definition, and Structure, ACM SIGPLAN Notices,* vol. 11, Special Issue (1976), pp. 25-35.

5. Astrahan, M.M., *et al.,* "System R: Relational Approach to Database Management," *Transactions on Database Systems,* vol. 1, no. 2 (June, 1976), pp. 97-137.

6. Wasserman, A.I., *et al.,* "Revised Report on the Programming Language PLAIN," Technical Report #42, Laboratory of Medical Information Science, University of California, San Francisco, 1980.

7. Rowe, L.A., and K. Shoens, "Data Abstraction, Views, and Updates in RIGEL," *Proc. ACM 1979 SIGMOD Conference,* pp. 71-81.

8. Merrett, T.H., "Relations as Programming Language Elements," *Information Processing Letters,* vol. 6, no. 1 (1977), pp. 29-33.

9. Shopiro, J.E., "Theseus — A Programming Language for Relational Databases," *Transactions on Database Systems,* vol. 4, no. 4 (December, 1979), pp. 493-517.

10. Amble, T., *et al.,* "Draft Report on the Programming Language ASTRAL," ASTRA-notat Nr. 31, Division of Computing Science, Norwegian Institute of Technology, Trondheim, Norway, April, 1979.

Some High Level Language Constructs for Data of Type Relation

JOACHIM W. SCHMIDT

Universität Hamburg, West Germany

Reprinted from *ACM Transactions on Data Base Systems,* September 1977, pp. 247-261. Copyright 1977 Association for Computing Machinery, Inc. Reprinted by permission.

For the extension of high level languages by data types of mode relation, three language constructs are proposed and discussed: a repetition statement controlled by relations, predicates as a generalization of Boolean expressions, and a constructor for relations using predicates. The language constructs are developed step by step starting with a set of elementary operations on relations. They are designed to fit into PASCAL without introducing too many additional concepts.

Key Words and Phrases: database, relational model, relational calculus, data type, high level language, nonprocedural language, language extension
CR Categories: 4.22, 4.33, 4.34

---

1. INTRODUCTION

A certain class of programming problems involves the processing of data with the following properties: there is a large amount of data, the data has internal connections, and the data must be made available to many users.

Since Codd's original paper [5], relations have been increasingly used in the solution of such database programming problems.

The "classical" language constructs for the processing of data organized around relations are by now accepted to be essentially: (a) primitive instructions for altering relations at the level of individual tuples: insertion, deletion, and modification; and (b) powerful retrieval facilities operating on relations at the level of sets of tuples: relational calculus- and algebra-oriented query languages.

In recent years numerous data sublanguages have been proposed, and some implemented, which contain these constructs to a greater or lesser extent. They differ from one another mainly in the conceptions of what user friendliness means [2, 4, 17].

A version of this paper was presented at the International Conference on the Management of Data, 1977, in Toronto, Canada—an annual conference of ACM SIGMOD.
Author's permanent address: Universität Hamburg, Institut für Informatik, Schlüterstrasse 70, D-2000 Hamburg 13, West Germany. Present address: University of Toronto, Computer Systems Research Group, Toronto M5S 1A4, Canada.

ACM Transactions on Database Systems, Vol. 2, No. 3, September 1977, Pages 247-261.

"

Traditionally a database with its associated data language is seen as an independent system; data is interchanged with users or with programmed systems through fixed interfaces in the form of I/O areas. Problems which arise from the integration of database language constructs, such as a data structure relation, in high level languages have up to now seldom been investigated [7, 1, 14]. Such investigations are of interest from at least two points of view: first for the extension of existing high level languages, and second for the further development of database concepts themselves, in particular the relation concept.

The currently prevalent high level programming languages have no constructs for the processing of large amounts of interrelated data. The file concept does not offer a general solution to this problem; files may be able to hold large quantities of data but the connections between data elements are inadequately handled, both at the level of high level language operations and at the level of access paths. As demonstrated by the example of the programming language SAIL [8] which contains ALGOL 60 and LEAP [12] data structures, there exists quite clearly a need for an algorithmic language with efficient constructs for handling intricately connected data.

Such investigations can also serve as a vehicle for the further development of the relation concept itself. The necessity for such development shows up, for example, in the previously mentioned difference in power between altering instructions and retrieval facilities. Whereas for a single retrieval command, all connections between relation tuples which are necessary for the answer to a query are evaluated, only a single tuple in a single relation can be inserted, deleted, or updated by an altering instruction. The user must therefore, in general, code a consistent database alteration transaction as a sequence of such altering instructions, each affecting a single relation. The user thereby bears most of the responsibility for the central problem of the integrity of the database.

A similar problem situation in general purpose programming languages led to the development of the concept of abstract data types [10]. A stack variable, for example, could be implemented in a high level programming language by means of an array variable, a Boolean variable, and an integer variable. These variables must be altered consistently when the value of the stack variable is changed (e.g. by push or pop). We could analogously define alterations in a database as operations on abstract data types and implement them as procedures on relations. In more recent work, Schmid and Swenson [13] for example, the beginnings of such a development can be discerned. The further development of database language constructs, however, cannot be discussed in the limited context of data sublanguages. On the contrary, this assumes to a great extent the concepts of high level programming languages.

These tendencies will not be further discussed in this paper (see e.g. [15]). In Section 2 the definition of types of mode relation and the declaration of relation variables are briefly described, together with the elementary read and write operations for relations. Section 3 introduces a repetition statement controlled by a relation variable. The generalization of Boolean expressions to predicates is handled in Section 4. In Section 5 the concept of a generalized relation constructor is discussed. Finally Section 6 outlines the state of the implementation and some further development. It should be noted that the language constructs have been designed to fit into PASCAL [16] without the introduction of too many additional concepts.

2. ELEMENTARY OPERATIONS ON RELATIONS

The definition of data types of mode relation is based upon data types of mode record. The value of a variable of a particular relation type is a set of tuples, each of which is in turn of the record type laid down in the definition of the relation type. The fields of these records will be taken to be of scalar type or of type string ("flat" records). Furthermore these types are presumed to be ordered types.

A second component of the definition of a relation type is the designation of certain fields of the relation tuples as a key. A key list characterizes a particular part of the tuple by enumerating the corresponding field identifiers. For these fields it holds that among the tuples of the relation a particular value assignation occurs at most once. The values of the key fields therefore uniquely determine a tuple in the relation. An ordering of the key values is defined by the presumed ordering on the values of the individual key fields and by the order of the key field identifiers in the key list.

Example 1.   If employees are characterized by the attributes employee number (unique), employee status, and employee name, then we can define relation variable *employees* as follows:

```
type erectype = record enr, estatus:integer; ename:string end;
     ereltype = relation ⟨enr⟩ of erectype;
var  employees:ereltype;
```

Along with data types of mode relation, operations are defined which allow values of relation variables to be altered and to be read tuple by tuple.

2.1 Elementary Altering Operations

A value change of a relation variable can occur through insertion, deletion, or modification of tuples. These operations are not in fact "elementary" insofar as through them not single tuples, but whole sets of tuples (i.e. again a relation variable), can be inserted, deleted, or modified. However, these operations alter at any given time the value of only one relation variable.

The *insertion operator* :+ brings about the insertion of tuples into the target operand to its left, dependent on the source operand to its right:

*rel*1 :+ *rel*2;

Source and target operands are relation variables of the same type. Into *rel*1 are inserted copies of those tuples of *rel*2 whose key values do not already occur in any tuple of *rel*1. The source operand *rel*2 remains unchanged.

The *deletion operator* :− brings about the deletion of tuples in the target operand dependent on the source operand:

*rel*1 :— *rel*2;

Source and target operands are relation variables of the same type. From *rel*1 are
deleted those tuples also contained in *rel*2. The source operand *rel*2 remains unchanged.

The *replacement operator* :& brings about the replacement of tuples in the target
operand dependent on the source operand:

*rel*1 :& *rel*2;

Source and target operands are relation variables of the same type. Each tuple of
*rel*1 whose key value occurs in a tuple of *rel*2 is replaced by a copy of the corresponding tuple in *rel*2. The source operand remains unchanged. Note that key
values cannot be changed with the aid of the replacement operator.

The *assignment operator* := assigns relation values between relation variables
of the same type:

*rel*1 := *rel*2;

A generalization of admissable source operands towards relational expressions will
be treated in Section 5.

2.2 An Elementary Relation Constructor

An anonymous 1-tuple relation can be constructed from a record variable with the
aid of the elementary relation constructor [..]. Of course any combination of fields
fulfills for this relation the requirements for a key; these relations are therefore
type-compatible with every relation variable whose type definition is based on the
type of the record variable, e.g.

rel := [*rec*];

The empty relation is denoted correspondingly by [ ].

Example 2. A tuple with employee number 2, employee name Nessie, and employee status 1 is to be inserted in the relation *employees*.

```
type   erectype = record enr, estatus: integer; ename: string end;
       ereltype = relation ⟨enr⟩ of erectype;
var    erec: erectype;
       employees: ereltype;
begin  .

       .
       erec.enr := 2;
       erec.estatus := 1;
       erec.ename := 'nessie';
       employees :+ [erec]
end.
```

Two standard procedures low(*rel*) and next(*rel*) are defined for the tuple-wise reading of relation variables. Furthermore the Boolean function aor(*rel*) (all of relation) and for each relation an implicitly declared buffer variable *rel*↑ are available.

The tuple of the relation *rel* with the lowest key value is assigned to the buffer *rel*↑ by the procedure call low(*rel*). The tuple with the next highest key value is assigned to *rel*↑ by the procedure call next(*rel*). If such a tuple does not exist then aor(*rel*) becomes true and *rel*↑ becomes undefined.

Example 3. Find those employees with the status of an assistant professor (employee status 2).

Solution 3.1.

```
type   erectype = record enr, estatus:integer; ename:string end;
       ereltype = relation ⟨enr⟩ of erectype;
var    employees, result:ereltype;
begin .
       :
       result := [ ];
       low(employees);
       while not aor(employees) do
       begin if employees ↑ .estatus = 2 then result :+ [employees ↑ ];
             next(employees)
       end
end.
```

The solution method underlying this example program accesses relations tuple-wise and in order, in the main controlled by the user. It is not generally satisfying for several reasons:

The ordering of tuple access by increasing key value is unnecessary from the point of view of program logic.

With respect to problem orientation the language constructs available for relations up to now are inadequate; this rapidly becomes evident with more complex examples. The above program is a solution in terms of the file concept and not in terms of relational databases.

For particular problems these elementary constructs are insufficient, e.g. nested loops accessing the same relation cannot be programmed.

The notation could be more concise.

There is little possibility for automatic optimization of accesses, for example by free choice of ordering or by processing of sets of tuples.

In the following sections we will develop step-by-step language constructs which should to a great extent overcome such objections.

3. THE REPETITION STATEMENT foreach

The foreach statement has the general form:

⟨*foreach statement*⟩ ::= **foreach** ⟨*control record variable*⟩
           in ⟨*range relation variable*⟩
           do ⟨*statement*⟩

The execution of a statement may be repeated with the aid of the foreach statement. For each repetition the control variable is assigned an arbitrary new tuple from the range relation until all tuples of the relation have been used. The control variable is declared implicitly to have the same record type that the range relation is based on. The scope of the control variable definition is the statement following **do**; within this scope the key values of the control variable and the range relation must not be altered. By using the foreach statement the solution for Example 3 becomes:

Solution 3.2.

```
{type definitions and variable declarations as in 3.1.}


begin .
    :
    result := [ ];
    foreach erec in employees do
        if erec.status = 2 then result :+ [erec]
end.
```

For a further example we introduce the relation *timetable* listing lectures held by employees and described by attributes employee number and course number, together with day, time, and place of each lecture.

Example 4. Find all those employees who lecture on Fridays.

Solution 4.1.

```
type    erectype = record enr, estatus:integer; ename:string end;
        ereltype = relation ⟨enr⟩ of erectype;
        trectype = record tenr, tcnr, ttime:integer;
                            tday, troom:string end;
        treltype = relation ⟨tenr, tcnr, tday⟩ of trectype;
var     employees, result:ereltype;
        timetable:treltype;
begin .
    :
    result := [ ];
    foreach erec in employees do
        foreach trec in timetable do
            if (erec.enr = trec.tenr) and (trec.tday = 'friday')
            then result :+ [erec]
end.
```

If we look at the example and its solution more closely we notice that:

The inner loop with range relation *timetable* is in general traversed too often; that is, whenever an entry for a particular employee's lecture held on Friday has been found, the remainder of the relation *timetable* is nevertheless processed.

If an employee lectures several times on a Friday, the corresponding employee record is inserted several times into the result. By virtue of the definition of the insertion operator this does not, however, affect the value of the target operand.

It would also be possible to avoid repeated insertions quite easily by programming an extra exit from the loop. In view of the developments in the following section, and for didactic reasons, we shall not bother to do this here.

The inner loop is only necessary to test a condition; in this particular case a condition on the value of the control variable *trec*. The control variable *erec* on the other hand is also needed for the construction of the result relation.

This state of affairs is more evident in the following solution for Example 4:
Solution 4.2.

```
{type definitions as in 4.1.}

var    employees, result:ereltype;
       timetable:treltype;
       some_trec_in_timetable:boolean;
begin .

       result := [ ];
       foreach erec in employees do
       begin some_trec_in_timetable := false;
         foreach trec in timetable do
           some_trec_in_timetable := some_trec_in_timetable or
           (erec.enr = trec.tenr) and (trec.tday = 'friday');
         if some_trec_in_timetable then result :+ [erec]
       end
end.
```

The additional exit from the inner loop is again omitted for didactic reasons.

Example 5. Find all employees who give no lectures.

This example contains a universal condition.

Solution 5.1.

```
{type definitions as in 4.1.}

var    employees, result:ereltype;
       timetable:treltype;
       all_trec_in_timetable:boolean;
begin .

       result := [ ];
       foreach erec in employees do
       begin all_trec_in_timetable := true;
         foreach trec in timetable do
           all_trec_in_timetable := all_trec_in_timetable and (erec.enr ≠ trec.tenr);
         if all_trec_in_timetable then result :+ [erec]
       end
end.
```

It seems natural for such problems, in which relations are used in testing one or all of their tuples against a certain condition, not to use repetition constructs but to introduce a special construct more related to this problem.

4. PREDICATES OVER RELATIONS

Examples 4 and 5 each require two nested loops. However, in both cases the outer loop and the inner loop have quite different significances in the logic of the program.

The outer loop over the range relation *employees* uses a logical condition evaluated by means of the inner loop—this is especially clear in Solutions 4.2 and 5.1. In both examples the condition governs the insertion of the value of the outer control variable into the result relation. Consequences will be discussed in Section 5.

The inner loop over the range relation *timetable* evaluates this condition. The condition itself is respectively an **or** connection (Example 4) or an **and** connection (Example 5) of Boolean terms involving tuples of the relation *timetable*, and is implemented by the foreach statement.

In the context of predicate logic these conditions are first-order predicates. This is more evident if one introduces range coupled quantifiers, i.e. quantifiers for which, together with the control variable (bound variable), the scope over which its value ranges must also be given (analogous to the foreach statement).

Predicates over relations will therefore be defined thus:

$\langle predicate \rangle ::= \langle quantifier \rangle \langle control\ record\ variable \rangle$
$\qquad\qquad$ **in** $\langle range\ relation\ variable \rangle$
$\qquad\qquad\quad$ $(\langle logical\ expression \rangle)$
$\langle logical\ expression \rangle ::= \langle term \rangle \mid \langle term \rangle \langle logical\ operator \rangle \langle logical\ expression \rangle$
$\langle quantifier \rangle ::=$ **some** $\mid$ **all**
$\langle logical\ operator \rangle ::=$ **and** $\mid$ **or**

Terms consist of components of the control variable, program variables, or constants, connected by the relational operators $=, <, >, \neq, \leq, \geq$; terms may also be predicates.

The implicitly declared control variable of the predicate is again of that record type in the range relation declaration.

4.1 The Existential Quantifier some

The predicate

$\quad$ **some** *rec* **in** *rel* $(\langle logical\ expression \rangle)$

is true iff at least one value of the control variable *rec* makes the logical expression true. The values of the control variable are defined by the tuples of the range relation *rel*. In general the logical expression will contain apart from bound variables further program variables and constants.

The solution for Example 4 using the **some** quantifier now looks like this:

Solution 4.3.

{*definitions and declarations as in 4.1.*}

begin .

    result := [ ];
    foreach *erec* **in** *employees* **do**
      if some *trec* **in** *timetable* ((*erec.enr* = *trec.tenr*) **and** (*trec.tday* = '*friday*'))
      then *result* :+ [*erec*]
end.

The tiresome problem of an additional exit from the loop has now disappeared for the user, and has been shifted on to the implementor responsible for the efficient implementation of predicates. An efficient implementation can above all exploit the fact that inside a predicate individual tuples of the range relation are not used as statement variables. The sequential processing of individual tuples can therefore be replaced by processing tuple sets in parallel. Comparing the three solutions developed for Example 4, we see that:

Solution 4.1, "**while not** aor(*timetable*) **do**," describes a sequential tuple-wise processing ordered by key values.

Solution 4.2, "**foreach** *trec* **in** *timetable* **do**," proceeds sequentially and tuple-wise but with no specific ordering.

Solution 4.3, "**some** *trec* **in** *timetable*," can be implemented by processing tuple sets in parallel.

If one considers that these tuple sets are so large in practice that they must be kept on secondary storage, these differences are highly significant.

4.2 The Universal Quantifier all

The predicate

    all *rec* **in** *rel* (⟨*logical expression*⟩)

is true iff all values of the control variable *rec* make the logical expression true. The values of the control variable are defined by the tuples of the range relation *rel*.

Using the **all** quantifier, the solution to Example 5 can be written thus:
Solution 5.2.

{*definitions and declarations as in 5.1.*}

begin .

    result := [ ];

```
        foreach erec in employees do
            if all trec in timetable (erec.enr ≠ trec.tenr)
            then result :+ [erec]
    end.
```

4.3 Nested Quantifiers

Predicates may contain several quantifiers. For an appropriate example we introduce a third relation that describes courses by their attributes course number (unique), course level, and course title.

Now an extension to Example 5:

Example 6.   Find those employees who give no lectures above the first year (course level 1).

This example requires both a universal and existential condition.

Solution 6.1.

```
        .
        .
type    erectype = record enr, estatus:integer; ename:string end;
        ereltype = relation ⟨enr⟩ of erectype;
        trectype = record tenr, tcnr, ttime:integer;
                            tday, troom:string end;
        treltype = relation ⟨tenr, tcnr, tday⟩ of trectype;
        crectype = record cnr, clevel:integer; cname:string end;
        creltype = relation ⟨cnr⟩ of crectype;
var     employees, result:ereltype;
        timetable:treltype;
        courses:creltype;
begin .
        .
        .
        result := [ ];
        foreach erec in employees do
            if all trec in timetable ((erec.enr ≠ trec.tenr) or
                some crec in courses ((trec.tcnr = crec.cnr) and (crec.clevel = 1)))
            then result :+ [erec]
    end.
```

It becomes evident with examples like this that data elements in a database are typically not processed in isolation but together with their mutual logical connections: A particular tuple of the relation *employees* is only further processed when it stands in a particular relation to the tuples of *timetable* and furthermore there is a particular tuple in the relation *courses* such that ... .

The actual processing of the tuples is so far identical in all examples: Dependent upon a predicate they are inserted into the result relation or not. The solutions to a large class of problems in retrieving data from databases can be programmed in this way.

We are now ready to go one step further and develop a specific language construct for this standard programming problem based on the constructs introduced so far.

5. GENERALIZING THE RELATION CONSTRUCTOR

With the concepts developed so far the value of a relation variable can be altered by deleting, inserting, or modifying tuples and by assigning a relation-valued expression. These expressions are, however, up to now limited to single relation variables and to the elementary relation constructor introduced in Section 2.2. The elementary constructor is only capable of making a 1-tuple relation $[x]$ from a record variable x. This restriction has led, in all the examples handled so far, to the construction of new relations according to the following schema: tuple-wise access to the source relation, sequential processing of these tuples as records, and tuple-wise construction of the result relation. On the other hand, in the quantifiers and the logical expressions we already have the necessary prerequisites for a generalization of the relation constructor along the lines

$$[x \text{ in } X: P(x, r, s, \ldots)]$$

where x is the free variable which describes the result tuple, X is a range relation which holds the possible value tuples for x, and P is some logical expression which depends on the free variable, and possibly on further bound variables r, s, etc., and on constants.

5.1 Construction of Subrelations

A first step in generalizing the relation constructor leads to the definition

$$\langle \textit{general relation constructor} \rangle ::= [\textbf{each} \ \langle \textit{control record variable} \rangle$$
$$\textbf{in} \ \langle \textit{range relation variable} \rangle:$$
$$\langle \textit{logical expression} \rangle]$$

The implicitly declared control variable is again of the same record type as that of the range relation. The logical expression has the usual logical and relational operators, and it may also contain quantifiers. As operands, the logical expression may contain components of the free control variable of the constructor and possibly of the bound variables of predicates, as well as program variables and constants.

With the aid of the general relation constructor, the solutions of the previous examples may be further simplified:

Solutions 3.3, 4.4, 5.3, 6.2.

```
type    erectype = record enr, estatus:integer; ename:string end;
        ereltype = relation ⟨enr⟩ of erectype;
        trectype = record tenr, tcnr, ttime:integer;
                          tday, troom:string end;
        treltype = relation ⟨tenr, tcnr, tday⟩ of trectype;
        crectype = record cnr, clevel:integer; cname:string end;
        creltype = relation ⟨cnr⟩ of crectype;
var     employees, result3, result4, result5, result6:ereltype;
        timetable:treltype;
```

```
          courses:creltype;
  begin .
          .
          .
          result3 := [each erec in employees:erec.estatus = 2];
          result4 := [each erec in employees:some trec in timetable ((erec.enr = trec.tenr) and
                         (trec.tday = 'friday'))];
          result5 := [each erec in employees:all trec in timetable (erec.enr ≠ trec.tenr)];
          result6 := [each erec in employees:all trec in timetable ((erec.enr ≠ trec.tenr) or
                         some crec in courses ((trec.tcnr = crec.cnr) and (crec.clevel = 1)))]
  end.
```

In the proposed form the relation constructor can only create subrelations from one relation variable. The general case of the construction of relations with the aid of several free variables and arbitrary result tuples made up of their components will be treated in the next section.

5.2 The General Relation Constructor

In its most general form a relation constructor can be defined using several free variables. Its value is a relation defined by tuples whose components come from components of the free variables of the constructor, and maybe program variables and constants:

```
⟨general relation constructor⟩ ::= [each (⟨target component list⟩)
                           for    ⟨control record variable list⟩
                           in     ⟨range relation variable list⟩:
                                  ⟨logical expression⟩]
⟨target component list⟩ ::= ⟨target component⟩ | ⟨target component⟩; ⟨target component list⟩
⟨target component⟩ ::= ⟨control record component variable⟩ | ⟨variable⟩ | ⟨constant⟩ | empty
```

The correspondence between the control variables and the range variables is implied by their position in the respective lists. The previously defined relation constructor of Section 5.1 is a special case of this more general constructor.

A fourth relation will be introduced for the last example; this relation contains the publications of the employees, described by the title, the year of publication, and, to identify the associated employee, an employee number.

Example 7. For those employees who give lectures, find the names and the title and year of their publications.

Solution 7.1.

```
          .
          .
  type    erectype = record enr, estatus:integer; ename:string end;
          ereltype = relation ⟨enr⟩ of erectype;
          prectype = record ptitle:string; pyear, penr:integer end;
          preltype = relation ⟨ptitle, penr⟩ of prectype;
          trectype = record tenr, tcnr, ttime:integer;
                            tday, troom:string end;
          treltype = relation ⟨tenr, tcnr, tday⟩ of trectype;
  var     employees:ereltype;
          papers:preltype;
```

```
        timetable: treltype;
        result: relation ⟨rname, rtitle⟩ of
                record rname, rtitle: string; ryear: integer end;
begin .
      .
      .

      result := [each (erec.ename; prec.ptitle; prec.pyear)
              for erec, prec in employees, papers:
              (prec.penr = erec.enr) and
              some trec in timetable (erec.enr = trec.tenr)]
end.
```

Specific problems with constructed relations, such as the definition of their keys and the possibility of checking keys at compilation time, will be treated elsewhere.

The relational constructor has certain advantages over the previous methods of solution:

It is a nonprocedural (very high level) language construct, in the sense that the user does not program a procedure which produces the result, but gives merely a declaration of certain properties of the result.

The notation is concise and keeps the important information textually together. This increases the readability for the user and facilitates a more efficient implementation.

The relation constructor may be given well-defined semantics in a similar way to predicate calculus.

The set of meaning preserving transformations of constructors is, in the context of predicate calculus, comprehensible. The freedom in the execution of the constructor thus obtained is very desirable for optimization.

At this point similarities to Codd's data sublanguage ALPHA [6] should be stressed. In particular the representation of queries in this calculus oriented language is closely akin to the relational constructor presented here. However, Codd considers relational calculus as an application of predicate calculus, whereas the relational constructor has been developed from, and integrated in, the concepts of a programming language.

6. SYSTEM IMPLEMENTATION AND FURTHER DEVELOPMENT

The various language constructs treated here are being incorporated into the PASCAL compiler for the DECsystem-10 [9] of the Institute for Informatics at Hamburg University. Apart from the necessary modifications to the compiler, a run-time system is being produced for the execution of the relational constructor and the predicates. This basically consists of an algorithm derived from that of Palermo [11] with additional optimization and supported by some advanced access methods. A first version of the system is expected to be available during the summer of 1977.

For the user, a relational database counts as an external variable and can—in analogy to external PASCAL files—be connected to a user program through a formal parameter in the program header. For the examples in this paper the program would appear thus:

```
program dbuser (informatics77);

type   .
       .

       .
       ereltype  = ... ;
       preltype  = ... ;
       creltype  = ... ;
       treltype  = ... ;
var    informatics77:database employees:ereltype; papers:preltype;
                              courses:creltype; timetable:treltype end;
       result1, result2, ...:ereltype;
       result7:relation ⟨rname, rtitle⟩ of record ... end;
begin with informatics77 do
       ⋮
end.
```

In parallel to the implementation of the constructs so far developed, we are
evaluating various further developments starting from standard Pascal with
respect to their applicability to database problems. With the aid of the **class**
concept in [3], objects in a database can be declared in a form which hides the
details of the database realization from the user, while improving data integrity
and data security (see [15]). Problems of simultaneous access can be investigated
using the **monitor** concept in [3].

7. SUMMARY

We have proposed three language constructs for use with data types of mode relation as extensions to a high level language, in particular to Pascal. These constructs
are: a repetition statement controlled by a relation; predicates, as extensions of
Boolean expressions; and a general relation constructor, dependent on predicates.
The language constructs have been developed stepwise from the most elementary
operations on relations.

For the purpose of information retrieval from a relational database the relation
constructor provides a solution which, in the context of a general purpose programming language, seems satisfactory.

For other questions, such as the problem of altering data consistently, or simultaneous processing of a database by several users, the proposals can serve as a
framework for further investigations.

ACKNOWLEDGMENTS

I would like to thank H. Fischer, M. Jarke, D. Meyer, H.-H. Nagel, and W. Ullmer
for their encouragement and the many critical and constructive comments.

REFERENCES

1. ALLMAN, E., STONEBRAKER, M., AND HELD, G. Embedding a relational data sublanguage
   in a general purpose programming language. SIGPLAN Notices (ACM) 8, 2 (Feb. 1976),
   25–35.

2. BOYCE, R.F., CHAMBERLIN, D.D., KING III, F.W., AND HAMMER, M.M. Specifying queries as relational expressions: The SQUARE data sublanguage. *Comm. ACM 18*, 11 (Nov. 1975), 621–628.

3. BRINCH HANSEN, P. The programming language Concurrent Pascal. *IEEE Trans. Software Eng. SE-1*, 2 (June 1975), 199–207.

4. CHAMBERLIN, D.D., AND BOYCE, R.F. SEQUEL: A structural English query language. Proc. ACM SIGMOD Workshop, Ann Arbor, Mich., May 1974, pp. 249–264.

5. CODD, E.F. A relational model of data for large shared data banks. *Comm. ACM 13*, 6 (June 1970), 377–387.

6. CODD, E.F. A data base sublanguage founded on the relational calculus. Proc. ACM SIGFIDET Workshop, San Diego, Calif., Nov. 1971, pp. 35–68.

7. EARLEY, J. Relational level data structures for programming languages. *Acta Informatica 2*, 4 (Dec. 1973), 293–309.

8. FELDMAN, J.A., LOW, J.R., SWINEHEART, D.C., AND TAYLOR, R.H. Recent developments in SAIL—an ALGOL-based language for artificial intelligence. Proc. AFIPS 1972 FJCC, Vol. 41, AFIPS Press, Montvale, N.J., pp. 1193–1202.

9. FRIESLAND, G., GROSSE-LINDEMANN, C.-O., LORENZ, F.H., NAGEL, H.-H., AND STIRL, P.-J. A PASCAL compiler bootstrapped on a DEC-system-10. 3. GI-Fachtagung über Programmiersprachen, *Lecture Notes in Computer Science, Vol. 7*, B. Schlender and W. Frielinghaus, Eds., Springer-Verlag, Berlin, 1974, pp. 101–113.

10. LISKOV, B., AND ZILLES, S. Programming with abstract data types. SIGPLAN Notices (ACM) *9*, 4 (April 1974), 50–59.

11. PALERMO, F.P. A data base search problem. Proc. 4th Comptr. and Inform. Sci. Symp., J.T. Tou, Ed., Plenum Press, New York, pp. 67–101.

12. ROVNER, P.D., AND FELDMAN, J.A. The LEAP language and data structure. Information Processing 68, North-Holland Pub. Co., Amsterdam, 1969, pp. 579–585.

13. SCHMID, H.A., AND SWENSON, J.R. On the semantics of the relational data model. Proc. ACM SIGMOD Conf., San Jose, Calif., May 1975, pp. 211–223.

14. SCHMIDT, J.W. Untersuchung einer Erweiterung von Pascal zu einer Datenbanksprache. Mitteilung Nr. 28, Inst. für Informatik., U. Hamburg, Hamburg, Germany, March 1976.

15. SCHMIDT, J.W. Type concepts for database definition: An investigation based on extensions to Pascal. Bericht Nr. 34, Inst. für Informatik., U. Hamburg, Hamburg, Germany, May 1977.

16. WIRTH, N. The programming language PASCAL. *Acta Informatica 1*, 1 (May 1971), 35–63.

17. ZLOOF, M.M. Query by example. Proc. AFIPS 1975 NCC, AFIPS Press, Montvale, N.J., pp. 431–438.

Received March 1977; revised May 1977

The Data Management Facilities of PLAIN

Anthony I. Wasserman

Medical Information Science
University of California, San Francisco
San Francisco, CA 94143 USA

Reprinted from *Proceedings, ACM 1979 SIGMOD International Conference on Data*, pp. 60-70. Copyright 1979 Association for Computing Machinery, Inc. Reprinted by permission.

Abstract

The programming language PLAIN has been designed to support the construction of interactive information systems within the framework of a systematic programming methodology. One of the key goals of PLAIN has been to achieve an effective *integration* of programming language and database management concepts, rather than either the functional interface to database operations or the low-level database navigation operations present in other schemes. PLAIN incorporates a relational database definitional facility, along with low-level and high-level operations on relations. This paper describes those features informally, showing how the database operations are combined with programming language notions such as type checking, block structure, expression evaluation, and iteration. A brief description of the implementation status is included.

Keywords: programming language design, database management, relations, type checking, relational algebra, abstract data types, interactive programs, information systems

Introduction

Over the past few years, there has been extremely rapid growth in the development and use of interactive information systems, spanning a broad range of applications. There is every indication that this area will continue to grow for the foreseeable future, fueled by both the increasing volume of information in modern societies and by the sharply reduced costs of most computing equipment.

An interactive information system (IIS) may be characterized as involving conversational access to data bases (or files) by persons unfamiliar with the technical aspects of computer systems, providing a predefined set of operations. Related systems provide various classes of users with facilities for accessing, modifying, and adding to a data base. In all of these cases, system

quality is of paramount importance. Systems must be reliable, must meet their specifications, must be tolerant of user errors, and must meet the needs of their users with respect to learnability, simplicity, and economy.

One of the key aids to building such systems is a programming environment for the applications programmer that provides a powerful and comprehensive set of tools for software design, development, and validation. A major component of this environment is the programming language to be used by the programmer, since the language can either support or hinder efforts to achieve the system design goals. It is therefore essential to give the programmer the greatest possible degree of support in the programming language.

With this need in mind, the design of the programming language PLAIN (Programming LAnguage for INteraction) was undertaken in 1975, following a thorough survey of languages and systems available for the construction of interactive programs [1]. Among the conclusions of this study was the observation that "the programming languages designed explicitly for interaction do not [have the structure] for creating modular, well-structured, reliable software." The idea behind PLAIN, then, was to provide a tool for the construction of interactive information systems that incorporates concepts of structured programming.

The design of PLAIN was carried out in parallel with a large number of other language designs, including CLU [2], Alphard [3], Gypsy [4], Euclid [5], and the Ada candidate languages [6]. All of these languages have similar objectives (with differing emphases, though) of support for data abstraction, support for system modularity, support for program readability, support for testing and/or verification of programs, and the imposition of greater discipline upon the programmer. All of these languages draw heavily upon Pascal [7], and have been additionally influenced by one another.

Of these languages, though, only PLAIN addresses the requirements of interactive programs and their developers. For example, stated requirements for the design of PLAIN included support for string handling, provision of a facility for pattern specification and matching to check user input and format output, a full complement of input/output operations, capabilities for handling exceptional conditions, and support for data base management, as well as the requirements for encouraging systematic programming practices [8]. Euclid and Alphard, by contrast, ignore input/output completely!

At the same time, techniques for incorporating data base management operations in programming languages were examined. Problems with embedded query languages and with host language interfaces were noted

387

and the need for a *unified* approach to programming languages and data base management was emphasized, so that "it becomes possible to achieve a level of consistency in syntax and semantics" and so that "both type checking and data independence can be achieved" [9]. Accordingly, PLAIN attempts to mesh language and data base management notions to provide a tightly integrated approach to data management.

There have been a couple of other efforts along the same general line as that taken by PLAIN. ASTRAL, being designed by Bratsbergsengen and Risnes [10], is philosophically closest to PLAIN; it is an extension of SIMULA with facilities for manipulation of relational data bases. Merrett's Aldat [11,12] is another language combining programming language and relational database concepts; the primary thrust of Merrett's work, however, is upon extensions to Codd's relational algebra and development of a "domain algebra." Merrett notes the different lines of work as part of his comparison of languages in [11].

These integrated approaches should be contrasted with other efforts that are purely extensions to existing languages, such as the Data Manipulation Language proposed by CODASYL for COBOL [13], the work of Summers, Coleman, and Fernandez to extend PL/1 [14], and Date's architecture to support language extensions for various data models [15]. As another example, Schmidt's Relational Pascal [16], provides for the definition of relations and for relational calculus operations upon relations, but has carefully separated data base statements so as to avoid some of the more unpleasant problems of language/data management interaction, such as those identified by Prenner and Rowe [17].

These problems include the non-procedurality of query languages contrasted to procedural programming languages, the difficulty of type checking, the tradeoffs between interpretation and compilation, and the need to support data abstractions, a need earlier noted by Minsky [18]. The design and implementation of PLAIN addresses all of these issues.

This paper will focus on the data definition and manipulation facilities of PLAIN, covering both the low-level and high-level operations, and concentrating upon the way in which they blend with programming language concepts of expressions, procedurality, iteration, and block structure. The presentation given here is neither complete nor formal, but is intended to illustrate the characteristics of PLAIN in order to permit contrast and comparison with other languages and to show its use for IIS construction. A more complete definition of PLAIN is given in [19].

Language Design Goals for Data Management

One of the key design goals for PLAIN was to support database management explicitly, rather than working with the lower-level concept of a file as it exists in many programming languages or relying upon traditional approaches to programming language/data base interfaces. As the design of PLAIN evolved, this goal was refined into a number of related goals that express the philosophy behind the design effort and help to explain some of the decisions taken. The most significant goals and decisions are presented in this section.

1) use existing language structures wherever possible

For the data management operations to blend cleanly with other language features, uniformity of syntax is important. Hence, a high-level non-procedural data management facility would not fit well in the context of a procedural language. Instead, database objects would be declared using the existing concepts of type and variable definition present in Pascal, and the control structures for branching (**if-then-else-end if** and **case**) and iteration (**foreach-loop-repeat**) would be applicable for database objects and operations, as well as for local variables and their operations.

2) minimize the number of features added to the language specifically for database management

This objective follows directly from the previous one. Not only should the design attempt to use existing language concepts wherever possible, but the number of *new* features added for databases should be kept to a minimum. Rather than providing a large and powerful set of database operations, the decision was made to strive for a compact, yet complete, set of operations. This decision was made with the understanding that the price of the language simplicity would be an increase in the amount of text needed to express complicated data management operations.

However, this decision was justified on a number of grounds, including the following:

A) the overall size of the language would be smaller, thereby simplifying the language definition, enhancing the likelihood of producing a formal definition of the language, and easing the problems of teaching people to program in PLAIN

B) implementation would be more straightforward with less effort required for optimizing the decomposition of high-level operations; some of the burden would be placed on the programmer, who might have to split a complex operation into two or more simpler operations to obtain the desired result

C) most routine database operations are quite simple anyway, often involving no more than the access or modification of a single item of data, or the addition of an entry to the database; it was assumed that the complicated queries presented in some of the literature about query languages are atypical of everyday database use, particularly for interactive information systems, where the typical pattern is repeated use of a relatively small number of operations.

D) it was felt that, insofar as possible, the complexity of code needed to program an operation should be proportional to the complexity of the operation itself.

3) apply systematic programming principles to data management operations

Work in the area of programming methodology has shown that both linear flow of program control within a module and disciplined use of data objects are valuable programming practices that increase the comprehensibility of software systems and reduce the number of program errors. As a result, several languages, including PLAIN, have eliminated the **go to** statement and have placed restrictions on the use of pointers.

A similar problem exists in database management with the notion of "navigating" through the database [20], whereby individual modules make use of information concerning the organization of the data base to follow pointer structures through a data base. A common consequence of this practice is an almost total loss of data independence, building the information about database organization so tightly into the fabric of the program logic that the cost of reorganizing the database would be prohibitive in terms of required program modifications. It is possible instead to hide some of the information concerning the definition of relations within procedures and functions, thereby restricting the number of modules that have access to the actual data base organization, with the ability to navigate through it.

Another aspect of systematic programming is the ability to determine that different objects are of the same data type, in order to validate operations involving those objects. As described below, type checking facilities can be used to define acceptable ranges for values, to make certain that actual and formal parameters correspond properly, and to constrain certain kinds of data base operations.

4) make the logical data model independent of its physical representation

Nothing in the language should imply or require that the representation of the data model take on a certain structure or that the data be stored using specific kinds of storage devices.

5) use the relational model of data

All of the preceding goals pointed clearly toward use of the relational model as the basis for database management in PLAIN. From a syntax standpoint, it is possible to exploit the similarity in notation between records and tuples, as was done by Schmidt. Similarly, an iterative statement can be used for tuple processing as a natural extension of other forms of iteration.

With respect to the second objective, the number of basic operations for the manipulation of relations has been shown to be quite small, especially in comparison with the set of operations used in some other data models. Furthermore, operations such as set union, intersection, and difference were already present in PLAIN (via Pascal) and could be directly extended to relations.

Next, mathematical formulations exist for relations and relational operations. Such formalizations would be useful in producing an axiomatization of the language, such as that produced for Pascal [21]. Finally, except for the notion of tuple processing, the concept of navigation is completely absent from the relational model of data.

It was recognized that the relational model of data has a number of shortcomings in terms of its ability to show hierarchies or other useful data base structures. However, the potential advantages of the model seemed to far outweigh the disadvantages for the purpose of design and implementation of a programming language. The decision was to provide for a specific well-known data model rather than to support a variety of data models with potential complications in language syntax and semantics.

6) permit alternative access to the data base

It is frequently desirable to obtain access to the relations other than through PLAIN. First, some form of data administration capability is necessary in order to define the relations which are to be used by the various programs, to define possible restrictions on access privileges, to perform routine maintenance of the data base, e.g., making incremental dumps, and to carry out other related functions.

Second, it is expected that the user will want to retrieve information from the data base through some other retrieval mechanisms, such as a query language, rather than having to write a program for that purpose. Although no effort has been made here to define such a query mechanism, efforts were made not to preclude that possibility.

Every effort was made to reflect these goals in the design of the data definition and manipulation facilities of PLAIN. The succeeding sections describe these facilities at greater length. The grammar is shown in a modified Backus-Naur Form (BNF) similar to that described by Wirth [22].

Data Definition

All objects used within PLAIN programs (with one minor exception) must be declared. There is no mechanism that permits names to be introduced dynamically, as is present in programming languages such as SNOBOL4 and MUMPS. Furthermore, as with Pascal, all objects must be declared to be of a given type. A number of different types are built into the language, including the simple types integer, float, boolean, char, and enumerated types, and the structured types **array, record, set, relation, file**, string, and pointer. Variables are declared and associated with a given type and are bound to that type throughout their existence. In general, a type characterizes the set of operations that are permissible upon an object of that type; thus, for example, one cannot multiply two strings.

In addition to the builtin types, it is possible to define new types and the operations upon them. This facility, termed *abstract data types* [23], permits a programmer to introduce new data types that are useful for a given application by defining the type, specifying its representation in terms of existing data types, creating functions or procedures to carry out the desired operations, and encapsulating this information so that the user of the data type (another program unit) has access to the operations, but *not to the representation.*[1] An abstract data type is a realization of a data abstraction, which provides a functional, formalizable, representation-free specification of the properties of an abstract object.

If one wished to define a stack type, for example, one could select a representation, define operations such as push, pop, top, create, and emptytest, and then allow the declaration of variables of type stack. In this scheme, it would be impossible to access the fifth element from the top of the stack since no explicit operation is provided for that.

A PLAIN data base type declaration specifies a structure consisting of an arbitrary number of record occurrences (tuples) where each tuple consists of a fixed number of components (attributes).

PLAIN supports two kinds of data base type declarations: **relation** and **marking**. A relation has the property that all tuples are unique, with the storage persistence of the relation potentially independent from the execution time or the block structure of the programs accessing or modifying them. Relations that exist within a database accessible from the executing PLAIN program may be "imported" into the execution environment and used; alternatively, it is possible to declare relations within a program in the same way that one declares variables, with the persistence of the relation determined by the lexical scope of the declaration.

Markings are used for intermediate results during operations on relations. Their persistence is determined solely by the lexical scope of their declaration. In no instance may they be shared between processes or exist beyond the termination of execution of the program in which they were created. A marking may or may not have duplicate tuples (depending on the way in that an assignment is made to it).

Thus, one may declare variables to be of type marking or relation, denoting the key attribute(s) for

---

[1]This notion is quite similar to the idea of *data independence* in database management, which seeks to hide representational details while providing suitable high level operations.

relations, following the Pascal syntax (similar to Schmidt [16]):

    databasetypedec ::= **type** typeidentifier "=" databasetype

    typeidentifier ::= identifier

    databasetype ::= relationtype | markingtype

    relationtype ::= **relation** "[" **key** keylist "]" **of** fielddesc

    fielddesc ::= recordtypeidentifier | fieldlist endrel

    recordtypeidentifier ::= typeidentifier

    keylist ::= identifierlist

    endrel ::= **end** dbname | **end relation** | **end** typeidentifier

The type declaration may be used to declare a data base structure. Then any number of variables may be declared to be of that type.

    dbvardec ::= **var** dbvaritem { ";" dbvaritem }

    dbvaritem ::= identifierlist ":" databasetype

This approach is consistent with the Pascal distinction between types and variables. An example of declaring a variable of type relation is as follows:

    var class: **relation** [**key** dept, number, section, term] **of**
            dept: char[4];
            number: char[4];
            section: 1..60;
            term: char[3];
            room: string;
            times: char[12];
            instructor: string
        end class;

Alternatively, one may define a record type and then declare a relation to be based upon that record type, as with

    type jrec = **record**
            jnum: char [2];
            jname: string;
            city: string
        end;

One may then declare

    var j: **relation** [**key** jnum] **of** jrec;

Note that j and class are variables, while jrec is a type identifier. One can declare a relation type and then declare several relation variables having similar structure. Attributes of a relation or marking must be of a simple type or string type, either fixed length (type char [n]) or variable length (type string).

A marking is created by assigning a data base expression to it. As with arithmetic assignment statements, the result of such an assignment gives the marking a new value, making its previous value inaccessible. A marking may only be assigned through a data base assignment statement. One may not append or delete individual tuples within a marking; locally declared relations should be used instead for those cases where modifications must be made to temporary objects. This approach preserves the concept of a marking as a "snapshot" of a relation or another marking.

Since markings are temporary objects, they need not be declared as fully as relations. Furthermore, the structure of a marking can be inferred from the operation(s) which create(s) it. The most important difference between relations and markings is that no key attributes are specified for markings. There are two major reasons for omitting key declarations in markings:

1   Some markings have duplicate tuples; the notion of a key is meaningless in that situation.

2   Key information is used in implementations for building efficient access paths to markings and is of no direct concern to the user.

The syntax for a marking declaration is then

    markingtype ::= **marking** [["[" atlist "]"] [**of** dbname]]

    atlist ::= identifierlist

    dbname ::= relationidentifier | markingidentifier

    relationidentifier ::= identifier

    markingidentifier ::= identifier

One could then declare, for example,

    var mathclass: **marking of** class;
            courses: **marking** [dept, number] **of** class;
            temp: **marking**;

Data Access

Tuple and Attribute Designators

At the lowest levels of relation access and manipulation, it is possible to name individual tuples within a relation through a *tuple designator*.

    tupledesignator ::= relationidentifier "[" keyvallist "]" | dbname "%"

    keyvallist ::= exprlist

If a relation of degree N has M key fields, where M ≤ N, the specification of the values for the M key fields designates a unique tuple of the relation (or no tuple at all). For example, the tuple designators j['j2'] and class ['math','101A',2,'F78'] designate specific tuples of the relations j and class declared above, using the ordering for attributes used in declaring the key attributes of the relation in the program. Note that the legal values for the section attribute of class are restricted to the range of 1 to 60 by the declaration of the relation.

It is also possible to denote a specific tuple within a relation with the tuple indicator "%". If one writes, for example,

    j% := j['j1']

then subsequent use of j% (prior to a new assignment to j%) will reference j['j1']. If j['j1'] does not exist, then j% obtains the value **nil**, and use of j% references no tuple, potentially an erroneous situation. The tuple indicator "%" should be viewed essentially as a place holder that provides a shorthand notation for successive referrals to a single tuple. Each relation has a single indicator; if more than one indicator is needed for a single relation, the general purpose iteration facility provided by the **foreach** clause (described below) will suffice.

Given the specification of a tuple, it is then possible to obtain the value of any of the attributes of that tuple and to assign values to individual attributes through an *attribute designator*, a tuple designator followed by an attribute.

    attributedesignator ::= tupledesignator "." attribute

    attribute ::= fieldidentifier

Note that the syntax is similar to that used to access a field within an array of records. It is also important to observe that the use of an attribute designator within an expression obtains a value from the relation or marking that may be used in the same manner as with other variables. Furthermore, the type of the attribute designator must be compatible with the type(s) of other variables in an expression.

For example, the expression

j['j3'].city

is of type string. Hence, it could be concatenated to other strings or have various string operations performed upon it, but could not be used in an arithmetic expression. One could write, for instance,

if j['j3'].city = 'Paris' **then** french **else** english **end if**

where french and english are procedure names.

In a similar fashion, one can assign values to specific elements within the relation, writing, for example,

class ['psyc','136B',1,'F78'].instructor := 'Freud'

These low level operations are effective for obtaining and updating specific data base elements.

This mechanism provides two important benefits. First, it is an *associative* addressing mechanism for data bases, comparable to the *indexed* addressing mechanism used for arrays of records. It is used to obtain single records (and thereby single values) from a relation, providing a clean solution to the problem of converting objects from type **relation** to their underlying record type. Although it can only be used for those cases where values for all key attributes can be specified, it is an effective means for denoting specific tuples or attributes in the data base.

Second, it achieves integration at the lowest level between language concepts and data base concepts, since an attribute designator may appear in arbitrary expressions throughout the program. Conceivably, information in the data base can be used to declare the dimensions of arrays, to provide a bound on the number of iterations of a loop, or to provide the text for a message.

Tuple Operations

At the tuple level, it is possible to insert tuples and to remove tuples one at a time. One may simply construct a new tuple by designating a record variable or by specifying values for the attributes, then enclosing that information in brackets to form a tuple constructor.

tuplestatement ::= relationidentifier tupleop tupleconstructor

tupleop ::= ":+" | ":-"

tupleconstructor ::= "[" recordname "]" | tupledesignator

recordname ::= recordvariable | "<" atvallist ">"

atvallist ::= atval { "," atval }

atval ::= expression | empty

In practice, then, new tuples may be added to a relation by assigning values to fields of a record, forming a tuple, and adding the new tuple to an existing relation. It is not necessary to define any attributes of the new tuple except for the key attribute(s); however, type checking is carried out so that the type of the record fields must correspond to the type of the relation attributes.

For example, if one declared

var project: jrec

and then assigned a value to project.jnum (and possibly other fields), one could write

j :+ [project]

to add the new tuple to relation j. (Of course, the value of project.jnum would have to be different from the value of jnum for any existing tuple, since jnum is the key attribute.)

Also, a tuple designator may be used to remove tuples, as follows:

j :- j['j1']

One may also iterate over the tuples of a relation or marking by use of the **foreach** clause in a **loop** statement. (The **foreach** and the **loop-repeat** are used for all iteration in PLAIN.) The effect of the **foreach** is to permit access to individual tuples, by controlling execution of a group of statements while a progression of values is assigned to an identifier called the *control variable*.

repetitivestatement ::= [foreach] **loop** statementlist **repeat**

foreach ::= **foreach** identifier **in** generator

generator ::= simpletypeidentifier | set | setidentifier | dbname

setidentifier ::= identifier

The **foreach** clause has the effect of creating a separate scope in which the control variable is automatically declared **as** a local variable. When iterating over a relation or a marking, the type of the control variable is that of the underlying record type.

As a simple example, consider the problem of writing out the jname values for all of the tuples in relation j (repeating any duplicates). One would write

foreach item **in** j **loop**
    write item.jname
repeat

The control variable item is of type jrec.

From a language design standpoint, it would have been possible to extend the syntax of the **foreach** clause substantially, permitting, for example, an arbitrary set or database expression as a generator. Since that generalization adds no inherent *power* to the language, it was decided not to provide it.

Relation Level Operations

High level operations on relations and markings permit the construction of data base expressions and the assignment of the expression to a relation or marking variable. The operations supported are selection, projection, and join, and the set-oriented operations of intersection, union, and difference.

These operations do not correspond precisely to either the relational algebra or the relational calculus. Nonetheless, combined with the other available operations on relations, they provide facilities that go beyond relational completeness as defined by Codd [24]. Since it is possible, if necessary, to perform tuple-at-a-time processing, one can carry out database operations that cannot be specified in the first-order predicate calculus.

It is important to note the strong preference given to the algebra-like operations, in contrast to the calculus-like operations of Relational Pascal and many of the query languages, such as QUEL [25] and SEQUEL2 [26]. There are several reasons for this decision, of which the following are the most important:

1   The operations are incorporated into a *procedural* language so that procedurality in the database operations is most consistent with the rest of the language.

2   Procedural operations can be split into steps (decomposed) very easily.

3   Procedurality suggests a direct implementation strategy requiring less analysis than required for some of the non-procedural schemes.

The non-procedural calculus-like languages mentioned above permit the construction of arbitrarily complex operations. From a programming language design standpoint, such complexity is inherently bad; simplicity is a critical goal in language design for ease of translation, ease of programming, and ease of program understanding. Complexity in query languages can occasionally be tolerated since the query is written by a single individual and used only a few times; programs, on the other hand, may be in use for a long time, where they must be understood by a number of programmers.

Accordingly, the approach taken in the design of the PLAIN operations was to provide all of the necessary computational power, but to force the programmer to decompose complicated operations into a sequence of simpler operations, creating intermediate results (markings) along the way. The following syntax is provided for database expressions:

```
dbexpression ::= dbexp  [ "=>" "(" targetlist ")" ]  |  "[]"

dbexp  ::= dbsetexp | dbrelexp

dbsetexp ::= dbvariable { dbop dbvariable }

dbrelexp ::= dbvariable [ where dbconditional ]

                |domain join domain

domain ::= dbvariable "." attribute

dbconditional ::= expression

targetlist ::= target  { "," target }

target ::= attribute  |  domain

dbop ::= "*"  |  "+"  |  "-"  .
```

Thus, the language syntax limits the complexity of data base expressions, forbidding the creation of arbitrarily complex expressions. For example, a single expression may contain a single selection or a join in combination with a projection. As a result, complex data base operations must be broken into several steps (perhaps creating markings). Experience in formulating many typical database operations using the data manipulation facilities of PLAIN has shown that it is extremely uncommon for such an operation to require more than two intermediate results to be created. The advantage of this approach is a simplification of the syntax, reduction of effort required to decompose the data base operations, and improved readability of the operations.

The resulting expression may be assigned to a relation or marking using the standard assignment operator (:=). Additionally, markings may be assigned with the assignment with duplicates operator (<-) to

prevent the elimination of duplicate tuples following an operation that projects out one of the key attributes of a relation.

```
dbassignment ::= dbvariable relassign dbexpression

relassign ::= ":="  |  "<-"

dbvariable ::= dbname [ "[" atlist "]" ]
```

Examples

In this example, we shall present a number of examples involving the use of the PLAIN data management operations. Although the primary purpose of *PLAIN* is different from that of database query languages, it is instructive to see how one could formulate such queries in PLAIN. Accordingly, we shall draw upon the database and some of the examples presented in [26]. The data base is defined as follows:

EMP	EMPNO	NAME	DNO	JOB	MGR	SAL	COMM

DEPT	DNO	DNAME	LOC

USAGE	DNO	PART

SUPPLY	SUPPLIER	PART

First, it is necessary to declare the database in PLAIN. Note that the above description provides no information about the domains for the attributes, the keys of the relations, or the extent to which the relations have been normalized. The following declarations make some assumptions about those aspects of the database.

```
imports dept, usage, supply: readonly; emp: modified;

type deptno = 1..200;   { valid department numbers }

var emp: relation [ key empno ] of
          empno: integer;
          name: string;
          dno: deptno;
          job: string;
          mgr: integer;
          sal: 7200..50000;
          comm: 0..0.2
      end emp;

    dept: relation [ key dno ] of
          dno: deptno;
          dname: string;
          loc: string
      end dept;

    usage: relation [key dno, part] of
          dno: deptno;
          part: string
      end usage;

    supply: relation [key supplier, part] of
          supplier: string;
          part: string
      end supply;
```

In most of these examples, the result will be assigned to a relation, whose name begins with "ans". In some cases, it will be necessary to create an intermediate marking, named temp, which is often reused on successive iterations through a loop, for example. Declarations for the answer relations are omitted for brevity, since they can be easily inferred. In all cases, the markings and the relations created may be assumed to be local to the program.

1) Find the names of employees in Dept. 50.

```
ans1 := emp where dno = 50 => (name)
```

2) What is the job title of employee number 334?

```
var position: string;

    position := emp[334].job;
    {associative access via key attribute}
```

3) What are the departments that employ more than 10 clerks?

```
ans3 := [];  {initialize to empty relation}
foreach d in dept   {d iterates over the tuples of dept}
loop
    temp :=  emp where dno = d.dno & job = 'clerk';
    if count (temp) > 10 then ans3 :+ [ < d.dname > ]
    end if
repeat
```

The solution taken here iterates over all departments, selects the clerks in each department, stores them in the marking temp, counts the number found, and then adds the department name to the unary relation ans3 if the number is greater than 10. It can be done more efficiently.

4) For each employee whose salary exceeds his manager's salary, list the employee's name and the manager's name.

```
ans4 := [];
foreach e in emp
loop
    if e.sal > emp [e.mgr].sal
    then ans4 :+ [ <e.name, emp[e.mgr].name > ]
    end if
repeat
```

Since employee number is the key attribute in emp, the employee number of an employee's manager, stored as the mgr attribute, can be used to associatively access the name and salary of the manager.

5) List the suppliers that supply any part used by Dept. 50.

```
temp := usage where dno=50 => (part);
ans5 := supply.part join temp.part => (supplier)
```

The marking temp contains those parts used by Dept. 50. That marking is joined with the supply relation on the common attribute part, and the join is projected onto the attribute supplier to obtain the answer. This is an instance where the available operations force the query to be decomposed into two steps with the creation of the intermediate marking temp.

If one wished, instead, to list the suppliers that supply all the parts used by Dept. 50, one first projects out the set of suppliers from relation supply. Following that, there are a number of ways to proceed. One way is to iterate over the suppliers, finding the parts that are supplied by a given supplier, and forming the difference with the parts used by Dept. 50, as stored in marking temp. If the difference is empty, then that supplier supplies all parts and can be appended to an answer relation. (In keeping with design goals 2C and 2D above, the code required to express this second query is relatively complicated, giving the programmer a more realistic view of the complexity of the operation itself, a complexity that is hidden in some query languages.)

6) Find the names of employees who have the same job and salary as Smith.

```
{Find the job title and salary of Smith}
tempr := emp where name = 'Smith' => (job,salary);
assert count(tempr)=1 ![assertion: message];
ans6 := emp where job=tempr%.job & sal=tempr%.sal
```

This query can not be properly answered if there is more than one employee named Smith, a situation which is ignored in the formulation of this query in [26]. Note that this solution uses the tuple indicator "%" with the relation tempr. This approach is satisfactory here since the assignment of tempr makes the current tuple indicator well-defined; in a relation with only one tuple, it clearly points to the desired tuple.

In this case, the assertion exception is raised if the **assert** statement returns false, and the **handler procedure** message is invoked, which presumably obtains the more specific information required and attempts another operation.

7) Give a 7.5% raise to all persons in Dept. 50 and a 5% raise to all buyers in departments other than 50.

```
foreach e in emp
loop
    if e.dno = 50
    then e.sal := 1.075 * e.sal
    else
        if job = 'buyer'
        then e.sal := 1.05 * e.sal
        end if
    end if
repeat
```

8) Read a department number from the terminal, then display the names of all employees in the given department.

```
program shownames;
imports emp: readonly;
type deptno = 1..200;
var input: deptno;
    emp: relation [key empno] of
            empno: integer;
            name: string;
            dno: deptno
        end emp;
    {unneeded attributes have been omitted from
        declaration of emp}
    temp: marking of emp;
begin
    write 'dno:';  { request department number input }
    read input ![range, ioerr, conversion, overflow: abort];
        {terminate program on invalid input}
    temp <- emp where dno=input => (name);
    foreach t in temp
    loop
        write t.name
    repeat
end shownames.
```

This program requests input from the terminal, then reads the resulting input as an integer. In this example, the program terminates abnormally in the event of input/output errors or erroneous user input; in an actual program, user errors would result in the invocation of a handler procedure to handle the exceptional condition. The notion of exception-handling is present in PLAIN as a way to permit the programmer to provide special purpose routines in the event of identified user errors or other unusual situations that may occur during program execution. Such facilities can be used to prevent the abnormal termination of programs with the resultant loss of time and/or work.

The marking temp is assigned with duplicates to take care of the case where two or more employees with the same name work in the same department. An alternative solution would have been to project empno and name after the selection so that no duplicates would exist and the normal assignment operator could be used.

It should be noted that the selection of tuples followed by iteration over the selected tuples is a decomposition of the facility provided by iterators and generators in programming languages such as CLU, Alphard, and Euclid. This approach is consistent with the rest of the language design philosophy of providing the building blocks to create even the most complex operations.

Finally, the comparison of dno and input in the selection clause should be noted. The attribute name dno is recognized as belonging to emp, while input is recognized as being a program variable. The use of the name dno is treated as a shorthand notation for emp.dno, in much the same way that one can omit record names within the scope of a **with** statement in Pascal. Both input and dno are of the same type, namely deptno.

These examples should not be regarded as a complete exposition of the capabilities of the language, but rather as an illustration of some of the most commonly used data management features.

A Longer Example

While the above examples illustrate many of the data management features of PLAIN, they do not represent a good illustration of the kinds of applications for which PLAIN is best suited. Indeed, it might be argued from these examples that PLAIN is esthetically less pleasing than are some of the query languages intended for use by "end users." (Of course, this conclusion is to be expected, since PLAIN is a programming language and not a query language.) Accordingly, this section provides a lengthier example, one that more clearly shows the type of problem for which PLAIN is best suited, one that could not be formulated using any of the widely known query languages.

The problem is to identify, for given departmental majors within a university, those students in that major whose grade point averages equal or exceed 3.5 out of 4.0, thereby qualifying them for the honor roll.

Information on students is kept in relation student. Information on courses is kept in relation course. Information on student enrollment in courses, along with grades, is kept in relation enroll. All of these relations, stored in the data base, are imported into **program** honorroll.

Grades are stored in a field of two characters in relation enroll, an alphabetic character optionally followed by a '+' or '-'. The value of grades is as follows: 'A' = 4, 'B' = 3, 'C' = 2, 'D' = 1, and 'F' = 0. A '+' appended to a 'B', 'C', or 'D' adds 0.3 to the value; a '-' appended to an 'A', 'B', 'C', or 'D' subtracts 0.3. A '+' or '-' used elsewhere is ignored. Students may also be assigned the grades 'I' for incomplete, 'S' for satisfactory, and 'U' for unsatisfactory. The 'I', 'S', and 'U' grades are not used in computing the grade point average. Courses in which the student is presently enrolled have an empty grade field.

A student may enroll in a course more than once; each enrollment is figured into the gradepoint average. No courses may be offered for a variable number of credits. (These last two constraints may represent a slight departure from the actual situation in many real-life instances.)

A PLAIN program to produce the desired reports follows.

```
program honorroll;
imports student, course, enroll: readonly; honors: invoked;
type  dabbr = char [4];
var   student: relation [key idnum] of
                    idnum: char [8];
                    name: string;
                    address: string;
                    college: char [2];
                    year: 0..5; {0 for special student;
                         5 for graduate student}
                    major: dabbr
                 end student;
      course: relation [key dept, number] of
                    dept: dabbr;
                    number: char [4]; {1 to 3 digits, possibly
                         followed by a letter}
                    credits: 0..8;
                    descrip: string;
                    incharge: string
                 end course;
      enroll: relation [key dept, number, section, term, pupil] of
                    dept: dabbr;
                    number: char [4];
                    section: 1..60;
                    term: char [3]; {sample: W78}
                    pupil: char [8];
                    grade: char [2]
                 end enroll;
      dept: dabbr;
pattern header ('Honor students in the department of ', 4A);
        item (25A, 5X, 8A, 5X, F);
   procedure honors (department: dabbr);
   {honors accepts a department name as input and computes
   the grade point average for all students in that department.
   For each student, it searches enroll to find the students in
   which that student is enrolled, computing a grade point
   average based on those courses for which an averageable
   grade has been assigned}
   imports student, enroll, course: readonly;
   {makes relations student, enroll, and course accessible within
   procedure honors}
   var  ncred: integer; {ncred is total number of averageable credits}
        entry: boolean;
        gpa, val, points: float;
        goodstudent: relation [key idnum] of
                    idnum: char [8];
                    name: string;
                    gradeavg: float
                 end goodstudent;
        {goodstudent is a local relation created and destroyed
            on each call to honors}
        st, temp: marking;
   begin
        goodstudent := [];
        {st obtains idnum and name for students majoring in the
        given department}
        st := student where major = department => (idnum, name);
        {for each student, find the student's enrollments}
        foreach s in st
        loop  bystudent:
             {hold the student's courses and grades; note that
             duplicates must be preserved, since a student may
             take a course more than once}
        temp <- enroll where pupil = s.idnum => (dept, number, grade);
        ncred := 0;
        points := 0.0;
        foreach t in temp
        loop byenroll:
             {total up grade points and credits for averageable courses}
             entry := true;  {set false if not an averageable grade}
             case t.grade[1] of   {look at first letter of grade}
                 when 'A': val := 4
                 when 'B': val := 3
                 when 'C': val := 2
                 when 'D': val := 1
                 when 'F': val := 0
                 else entry := false
             end case;
             if entry
             then
                 if (val >= 1) & (t.grade[2] = '-') then val :=
                 val - 0.3 end if;
                 if (val >= 1) & (val <= 3) & (t.grade[2] = '+')
```

```
            then val := val + 0.3 end if;
            {now find the number of credits for the given
            course, using an associative access to
            obtain the appropriate tuple}
            course% := course [t.dept, t.number];
            if course% ~= nil
            then    {add to the total number of credits}
                ncred := ncred + course%.credits
                {now add up the total number of grade points,
                    multiplying credits by grade value}
                points := points + course%.credits * val
            end if
            {if course% was nil, then there is an error
            in enroll relation; a production version of the
            program would note this fault}
        end if
    repeat byenroll;
    gpa := points / ncred;
    if gpa >= 3.5
    then
        {form a record with id number, name, and gra-
        depoint average, then append it to relation
        goodstudent}
        goodstudent :+ [ <s.idnum, s.name, gpa> ];
    end if
    repeat bystudent;
    {write out the honor roll students for department}
    foreach gs in goodstudent
    loop
        write <item> gs.name, gs.idnum, gs.gradeavg, \n
    repeat;
end honors; {all local variables, including relation goodstudent
                and markings st and temp, are destroyed}
begin   {main program}
    loop bydept:
        read dept;
        if dept = 'xxxx'
        then exit
        else
            write <header> dept, \n;
            honors (dept)
        end if
    repeat
end honorroll.
```

Type Checking

The concept of strong type checking is central to a number of programming languages derived from Pascal, including PLAIN. Similar notions exist in database systems that require adherence to domain definitions. Thus, it is conceptually straightforward to extend the type checking concept to the database environment, as has been shown above. Furthermore, Brodie has demonstrated that such type checking of database operations is of assistance in specifying and verifying the semantic integrity of database operations [27].

The type checking features of PLAIN are of help in constraining the permissible join operations and in thereby assisting in semantic integrity in the data base. In PLAIN, every type is treated as being distinct from every other type. Since a join can only be performed on attributes of the same type, the type definition facility provides a facility whereby invalid join operations can be prohibited. As an example, consider the relations emp and dept above. As presently declared, one could join emp.name with dept.loc, since both are of type string. However, if one made the following declarations:

```
type person = string;
     place = string;
```

and then declared the attribute name to be of type person and the attribute loc to be of type place, then the two relations could not be joined on those attributes. This type definition mechanism can be carried to any desired degree of detail.

It should also be noted that type checking applies to the use of attribute designators in expressions. For example, the term class%.room is of type string and therefore could not appear as part of an arithmetic expression.

In addition to declaring the type of an object, it is possible to apply additional constraints as well. One such instance in PLAIN involves use of a string pattern-matching facility. Without going into the details of the pattern specification and matching features, PLAIN contains the capability to specify and recognize strings conforming to a context-free grammar. Thus, for example, one could declare an item to be of type string and could then perform a pattern match upon the string to see that it contained only alphabetic characters or began with a specific letter. Such a facility is useful in the data base context for checking the integrity of objects to a greater extent than is provided by the type definition facility alone.

Type checking can also play a key role in constraining other kinds of operations through the use of abstract data types. The data abstraction facilities of PLAIN permit the programmer to introduce new data types, encapsulating the representation and the operations permissible upon that type in such a way as to hide the physical representation chosen for the data type. In addition, PLAIN permits exceptions raised by a data type to be included within the data type definition.

Because PLAIN contains relations as a builtin type, a relation may be used to define new data types. In this way, a set of operations upon a relation can be encapsulated into a new data type in order to restrict operations on a relation to a structured, predefined set, thereby providing a high-level view[2] (an extra level of abstraction) of the data base. PLAIN provides the necessary facilities to write programs to support the module-oriented view of database systems, as suggested by Weber [28]. Such a module may contain any valid operation on relations or upon markings known within that module, including updates. However, other operations within the module may serve to constrain the operation, to check data reliability, or possibly even some unrelated steps.

Using this idea of structured operations, one can build an IIS, giving different sets of operations to different classes of users, thereby restricting each user class to certain operations upon the data base. The users may invoke those operations indirectly through some form of interaction, possibly a command language. Suppose that we develop a system in which the valid user commands are 'hop', 'skip', 'jump', and 'stop', causing the execution of procedures c1, c2, and c3, and program termination, respectively. The basic program structure is as follows:

```
program iisschema;
    {names of imported relations declared in imports list}
var input: string;
    {data base declarations are included here}
pattern p1 ('hop'); p2 ('skip'); p3 ('jump'); stp ('stop');
patset p [p1,p2,p3,stp];
begin
    loop
        read input ![ioerr: abort];
            {terminate on hardware I/O error}
        case match (input, p) of
            when p1: c1
            when p2: c2
            when p3: c3
            when stp: exit
            else write 'illegal command'
        end case
    repeat;
    write 'byebye'
end iisschema.
```

---

[2]This use of the term "view" is somewhat different from its use elsewhere in the data base literature. In this case, the user does not "see" an artificial data base organization, but merely a set of permissible logical data base operations. The user does not see any data base organization.

The procedures c1, c2, and c3 may, of course, involve operations on the data base. For purposes of semantic integrity, we may say that the data base should be in a consistent state following the completion of any of these procedures. (Each procedure may correspond logically to an IIS transaction.)

Instead of declaring the relations within program iisschema, though, we might have declared, instead, a data type d that permitted operations c1, c2, and c3. In that case, the procedure calls to c1, c2, and c3 would be replaced by calls of d.c1, d.c2, and d.c3. The data base declarations would appear within the definition of type d rather than within program iisschema. Program iisschema would not have direct access to the data base and so could not carry out any unstructured operations upon it. More important, however, program iisschema would be totally independent of the representation chosen for the data type d, making it possible to change the representation without changing program iisschema, thereby adding a greater degree of flexibility to the program.

In a similar way, different abstract types could be declared for different classes of users, defining the operations that each could perform. Different programs could use these types and their associated operations to provide a different interface to each class of user, or even a choice of interfaces for a single user class. A single operation may potentially be provided for different user classes. All of these programs would be able to run concurrently in a multiprogrammed, shared data environment. (Note that the sharing and concurrency issues are handled at the data base management level, rather than at the programming language level.)

It is important to note that none of the type definitions nor the invoking program must specify the entire data base schema, but only that part of the data base that will be used. Effectively, different programs or data types may specify the data base slightly differently, using only those relations and attributes that are needed. (Weber [28] calls this a schema abstraction; it is conceptually very similar to the CODASYL subschema notion [13] as well.) In a traditional data base environment, such an approach would be unsatisfactory; however, within the environment envisioned here, all that is necessary is for the data base declarations to be consistent with the overall data base schema as defined by the data base administrator. In addition, users needing various unstructured operations on the data base (such as a generalized query facility) could access the data base through the query language, as well as writing special purpose programs in PLAIN to accomplish their task.

The extension of abstract data types to data base management and the use of PLAIN to achieve this extension is taken up in another paper [29], which describes the distinction between data abstractions and abstract data types, discusses the benefits of this approach for security and integrity, and provides a lengthier example applying these concepts.

Implementation Status

PLAIN is presently being implemented on the PDP-11 series of computers under the UNIX operating system [30]. The implementation strategy makes use of the compiler writing tools LEX and YACC [31] in order to produce a running version of the language in the shortest possible time. Implementation of the data base handler is separated from the implementation of the remainder of the language, since that simplifies the execution environment for those PLAIN programs that do not involve use of the data base operations.

The primary goal of the implementation of the data base handler is compactness. Along this line, only one storage structure, simple prefix B-trees [32], is being used in the first implementation. The data base handler communicates with the language runtime system through explicit calls involving passing segments of the runtime stack between the processes. The architecture of the PLAIN data base handler is described at greater length in [33]. That paper also provides some information on the implementation strategy for the data management facilities described in this paper.

Certain portions of the implementation are already operational. However, it is not expected that a running processor for the entire language will be available until the end of 1979.

Conclusion

PLAIN makes a number of advances toward achieving an effective integration between modern notions of programming languages and facilities for data base definition and manipulation. In particular, the use of an associative reference into relations provides a mechanism that binds the two together at the basic level of assignment and expression evaluation; the concept is basically an extension of associative data structure proposals for programming languages [34]. The associative access, as captured in the attribute designator, permits an attractive synthesis of procedural programming languages and data management operations.

The design of PLAIN satisfies the design goals for database management quite well. The number of new concepts and features added for this capability is quite small, while the number of existing features that could be extended to data management is quite substantial.

The design makes use of the following features already present in PLAIN prior to inclusion of the database features:

1) use of the record structure and syntax for definition of relations
2) use of the assignment statement for modifying relations
3) use of the **foreach** and **loop-repeat** constructs for iteration
4) use of the set operations of intersection, union, and difference
5) reliance upon the underlying concepts of type and variable
6) use of the abstract data type facility for relations
7) use of standard input/output statements of **read** and **write**
8) use of block structure to define the scope of markings
9) use of the **assert** statement for checking data base values

The number of new features added to PLAIN for data base management is limited to the following:

1) the use of tuple and attribute designators for associative access
2) the concept of a marking
3) the relational operations of **where**, **join**, and projection (=>)
4) the assignment with duplicates operator
5) tuple insertion and deletion operations
6) the current tuple indicator as a cursor for tuple processing
7) aggregation functions of count, sum, avg, min, max, and the exists function

Since PLAIN contains several innovations for achieving integration between programming languages and data base management, there are a number of problems to be addressed with respect to its suitability for solving a broad class of problems associated with the design and construction of interactive information systems and other related applications. It is expected that minor changes will be made in the language as work proceeds with the implementation and as experience is gained in use of the language. In addition, efforts to formalize the language definition will undoubtedly assist in removing any ambiguity or problems with the existing informal definition.

In summary, then, PLAIN is a vehicle for programmers to create well structured programs to be utilized primarily by parametric users. It will run within an environment that provides the programmer with a collection of programming tools and provides traditional data base management facilities as well. In this manner, a programmer can combine data base design with data structure and program design in a unified way, using software engineering practices.

Acknowledgments

Computing support was provided by National Institutes of Health grant RR-1081 to the UCSF Computer Graphics Laboratory, Principal Investigator: Robert Langridge. Martin Kersten and the referees made a number of constructive comments on an earlier draft of this paper.

References

[1] Wasserman, A.I., "Online Programming Systems and Languages: a History and Appraisal," Technical Report #6, Laboratory of Medical Information Science, University of California, San Francisco, 1974.

[2] Liskov, B. *et al.*, "Abstraction Mechanisms in CLU," *Comm. ACM*, vol. 20, no. 8 (August, 1977), pp. 564-576.

[3] Wulf, W.A. (ed.) *et al.*, "An Informal Description of Alphard (preliminary)", Technical Report CMU-CS-78-105, Department of Computer Science, Carnegie-Mellon University, 1978.

[4] Ambler, A.L. *et al.*, "Gypsy: a Language for Specification and Implementation of Verifiable Programs," *Proc. of ACM Conference on Language Design for Reliable Software, ACM SIGPLAN Notices*, vol. 12, no. 3 (March, 1977), pp. 1-10.

[5] Lampson, B.W. *et al.*, "Report on the Programming Language Euclid," *ACM SIGPLAN Notices*, vol. 12, no. 2 (February, 1977), pp. 1-79. (Revised report in preparation, 1979)

[6] Department of Defense Advanced Research Projects Agency, "Requirements for High Order Computer Programming Languages -- 'Steelman'", June, 1978.

[7] Wirth, N., "The Programming Language Pascal," *Acta Informatica*, vol. 1, no. 1 (1971), pp. 35-63.

[8] Wasserman, A.I., "PLAIN: Programming Language Design and Reliable Interactive Software," Technical Report #20, Laboratory of Medical Information Science, University of California San Francisco, March, 1976 (revised 1977).

[9] Wasserman, A.I., "Embedding Database Management Operations in Programming Languages," *Conference Digest -- IEEE COMPCON Spring 1976*, pp. 79-82.

[10] Bratsbergsengen, K. and O. Risnes, "ASTRAL -- a Structured Relational Applications Language, Technical Report 5/78, Division of Computing Science, University of Trondheim, Norway, June, 1978.

[11] Merrett, T.H., "Aldat- Augmenting the Relational Algebra for Programmers," Technical Report SOCS 78.1, School of Computer Science, McGill University, Montreal, P.Q., Canada, November, 1977.

[12] Merrett, T.H., "The Extended Relational Algebra, a Basis for Query Languages," in *Databases: Improving Usability and Responsiveness*, ed. B. Shneiderman. New York: Academic Press, 1978, pp. 99-128.

[13] CODASYL Data Base Task Group. April 71 Report. (available from ACM)

[14] Summers, R., C. Coleman, and E. Fernandez, "A Programming Language for Access to a Shared Data Base," *Proc. ACM Pacific 75 Conference*, pp. 114-118.

[15] Date, C.J., "An Architecture for High-Level Language Database Extensions," *Proc. ACM 1976 SIGMOD International Conference on Management of Data*, pp. 101-122.

[16] Schmidt, J.W., "Some High Level Language Constructs for Data of Type Relation," *ACM Transactions on Database Systems*, vol. 2, no. 3 (September, 1977), pp. 247-261.

[17] Prenner, C.J. and L.A. Rowe, "Programming Languages for Relational Database Management," *Proc. AFIPS 1978 NCC*, vol. 47, pp. 849-855.

[18] Minsky, N., "On Interaction with Data Bases," *Proc. ACM 1974 SIGFIDET Workshop on Data Description, Access, and Control*, pp. 52-62.

[19] Wasserman, A.I. *et al.*, "Report on the Programming Language PLAIN," Technical Report #34, Laboratory of Medical Information Science, University of California San Francisco, 1978.

[20] Bachman, C.W., "The Programmer as Navigator," *Comm. ACM*, vol. 16, no. 11 (November, 1973), pp. 653-658.

[21] Hoare, C.A.R. and N. Wirth, "An Axiomatic Definition of the Programming Language Pascal," *Acta Informatica*, vol. 2, no. 4 (1973), pp. 335-356.

[22] Wirth, N., "What Can We Do about the Unnecessary Diversity of Notation for Syntactic Definition?", *Comm. ACM*, vol. 20, no. 11 (November, 1977), pp. 822-823.

[23] Liskov, B. and S.N. Zilles, "Programming With Abstract Data Types," *ACM SIGPLAN Notices*, vol. 9, no. 4 (April, 1974), pp. 50-59.

[24] Codd, E.F., "Relational Completeness of Data Base Sublanguages," in *Data Base Systems*, ed. R. Rustin. Englewood Cliffs: Prentice-Hall, 1972, pp. 65-98.

[25] Stonebraker, M.R. *et al.*, "The Design and Implementation of INGRES," *ACM Transactions on Database Systems*," vol. 1, no. 3 (September, 1976), pp. 189-222.

[26] Chamberlin, D.D. *et al.*, "SEQUEL 2: A Unified Approach to Data Definition, Manipulation, and Control," *IBM Journal of Research and Development*, vol. 20, no. 6 (November, 1976), pp. 560-575.

[27] Brodie, M.R., "Specification and Verification of Database Semantic Integrity," Technical Report CSRG-91, Computer Systems Research Group, University of Toronto, Canada, April, 1978.

[28] Weber, H.J., "A Software Engineering View of Data Base Systems," *Proc. 4th International Conference on Very Large Data Bases*, 1978, pp. 36-50.

[29] Wasserman, A.I., "The Extension of Abstract Data Types to Data Base Management," in preparation.

[30] Ritchie, D.M. and K. Thompson, "The UNIX Time-Sharing System," *Comm. ACM*, vol. 17, no. 7 (July, 1974), pp. 365-375.

[31] Johnson, S.C. and M.E. Lesk, "Language Development Tools," *The Bell System Technical Journal*, vol. 57, no. 6 (July-August, 1978), part 2, pp. 2155-2175.

[32] Bayer, R. and K. Unterauer, "Prefix *B*-Trees", *ACM Transactions on Database Systems*, vol. 2, no. 1 (March, 1977), pp. 11-26.

[33] Kersten, M. and A.I. Wasserman, "The Architecture of the PLAIN Data Base Handler," submitted for publication.

[34] Feldman, J. and P. Rovner, "An Algol-Based Associative Language," *Comm. ACM*, vol. 12, no. 8 (August, 1969), pp. 439-449.

EXCEPTION HANDLING DESIGN ISSUES

John B. Goodenough
SofTech, Inc.
460 Totten Pond Road
Waltham, Mass. 02154

Exception handling design issues are reflected in discussions by Zahn [1], Parnas [2], Hill [3], Elson [4], Organick [5], and myself [6, 7]. The purpose of this paper is to summarize these issues. This summary can be used to evaluate the strengths and weaknesses of proposed or existing exception handling language features and as a guide in designing new features.

1. The Nature of Exception Conditions

Of the conditions detected while attempting to perform some operation, <u>exception conditions</u> are those brought to the attention of the operation's invoker. The invoker is then permitted (or required) to respond to the condition. Making the occurrence of an exception known outside the detecting operation is called <u>raising</u> the exception. Responding to a raised exception is called <u>handling</u> the exception.

Raising an exception is a means of parameterizing the response to certain conditions detected by an operation. This is useful if the appropriate response can vary so widely that building in any particular response would unduly limit the usability of the operation. In essence, exceptions serve to <u>generalize</u> operations, making them usable in a wider variety of contexts than would otherwise be the case. Exceptions can also be considered a means of supporting interactions between levels of abstraction. When an operation and its invoker exist at different levels of abstraction, raising an exception is a disciplined way of coordinating actions on different levels.

Exceptions are needed for three basically different purposes:

1) <u>to signify operation failure</u>, i.e., when an operation detects a condition whose occurrence implies potential or actual inability to produce a desired result, the operation's invoker must be informed so appropriate action can be taken. These exceptions are often called <u>error</u> conditions.

2) <u>to classify a valid result</u> of an operation so the result is used appropriately. For example, an operation for storing values in a data structure may raise an exception when the remaining amount of available space falls below some critical minimum. In this case, even though the operation has performed its function successfully, it is useful to raise this exception.

3) <u>to monitor</u> a computation's intermediate results or to request additional information that is too expensive to compute in advance of invoking the operation; it is more efficient for the invoker to provide the information on demand.

In short, exceptions are not raised just to deal with error conditions; the need
for interaction between an operation and its invoker arises for other reasons as
well.

2. Design Issues

Exception handling design issues can be classified as follows:

Requirements Issues
- What potentially useful <u>effects and behaviors</u> should a notation for
  exception handling be able to evoke? Resolution of these issues
  depends on one's conception of exception handling's role in programming.
- What <u>properties</u> of an exception handling notation are needed to
  satisfy general language design objectives and principles such as
  security from error, understandability, uniformity, simplicity, etc. ?

Evaluation Issues
- How are tradeoffs among conflicting requirements resolved?
  Deciding on the relative importance of different requirements is
  a design issue that leads to different notational proposals, but
  discussion of such design tradeoffs is beyond the scope of this paper.

In the remainder of the paper, I will list potential requirements to be satisfied
by proposed or existing exception handling language features.

2.1 Effects and Behaviors

Considering the role exception handling plays in programming, what effects
and behaviors should a programmer be able to evoke with a notation for exception
conditions? The following capabilities appear to be necessary or useful:
- <u>the ability to associate a handler with a raised exception</u>. When an
  exception is raised, some response to it is required. A language must
  provide some means of specifying what handler provides this response.
  The ability to associate different handlers with different invocations of
  the same operation is also required.
- <u>the ability to resume an operation</u>. The proper response to an exception may require taking some appropriate action and then continuing
  execution of the operation raising the exception from the point at which
  the exception was raised.
- <u>the ability to terminate an operation</u>. The decision to terminate an
  exception-raising operation may be made either from within the operation (in effect, the operation returns to its invoker and indicates that
  some exception condition has occurred; resuming the operation is not
  an option in this case), or the termination decision may be made from
  within a handler for the exception.
- <u>the ability to retry an operation</u>. The proper response to an exception
  may be to re-invoke the operation, after first terminating it. This
  seemingly trivial requirement may not be conveniently satisfied if the
  goto statement is not available [7].

- <u>the ability to associate parameters with exceptions</u>. The response to
an exception may depend on information accessible only at the point
from which the exception is raised. Means of supplying a handler with
this information is required. In addition, the handler may need to
supply the exception-raising operation with new or modified data
before the operation can be resumed (or terminated). In short, the
ability to transmit information to and from a handler is sometimes
essential in dealing with exceptions.

One design issue is whether or not this is a necessary and sufficient
set of capabilities needed to exploit the concept of exception conditions. Another
set of design issues concerns what properties an exception handling notation
should have to satisfy general language design objectives and principles. Listed
below are properties associated with software reliability, understandability,
uniformity, and efficiency.

2.2 Reliability

Designing language features so potential exception handling errors are
avoided, discouraged, or detected at compile-time is an important design
consideration. One set of design issues concerns how to facilitate or insure
detection of errors like the following:

- forgetting or not understanding what exceptions an operation can raise,
and so not giving these exceptions due consideration;
- associating the wrong handler with some invocation of an operation,
given that it's possible to associate different handlers with different
invocations of the operation;
- when an operation can raise more than one exception, associating a
handler with the wrong exception;
- attempting to resume an operation that cannot be resumed;
- attempting to terminate an operation that does not expect to be terminated after it raises a particular exception;
- insuring that when a handler terminates an operation, the operation is
not left in a state that causes an error when it is invoked later;
- violating an exception parameter's access constraints, e.g., modifying
read-only parameters or attempting to read parameters outside the
scope of their validity (e.g., in PL/I, attempting to read the ONCHAR
parameter outside the scope of a handler for a CONVERSION exception).

2.3 Understandability

Program understandability is enhanced by reducing the complexity of a
program. Exception handling complexity can be reduced by:
- eliminating useless redundancy, e.g.,
  - if an operation is used in several places in a program and the same
    response is always required to an exception it can raise, then it should
    be possible to write the handler for this exception only once instead
    of repeatedly.
  - when <u>different</u> exceptions are to be handled identically, it should be
    possible to write a handler only once and associate it implicitly with
    each of the exceptions.

- the ability to specify exception handlers by default makes it
  unnecessary to write exception handlers when the default action
  is appropriate. Suitable choice of default handlers can make
  programs more concise by eliminating programmer-defined
  handlers. This conciseness is helpful in making it easier to
  understand the "normal" effect of the program when exceptions
  are not raised.
- the notation should foster a disciplined and clear control flow structure.
  In particular, it should not be necessary to use an unconstrained
  goto statement to deal with exceptions.
- the notation should make it easy for a programmer to find out what
  handlers will be executed if a particular exception is raised.

2.4 Uniformity

To the extent language constructs are similar, they should be usable in
similar ways. Moreover, constraints on the use of a construct should apply uniformly in all contexts. When applied to exception handling, these principles suggest that language-defined operations (e.g., addition) and programmer-defined
operations (subroutines) should not have unnecessarily different exception handling capabilities. For example, if default exception handlers are provided for
language-defined operations, it should also be possible to provide default handlers
for programmer-defined operations. Moreover, the ability to use exception
conditions to enhance the generality of programmer-defined operations should be
paralleled by the existence of exceptions (e.g., OVERFLOW) that enhance the
generality of language-defined operations.

2.5 Efficiency

Language features should be designed so a programmer can avoid unacceptable
able run-time inefficiencies. One way to satisfy this objective is to provide
means of controlling the run-time overhead associated with language constructs.
Run-time exception handling efficiency can be controlled if:
- an exception handling notation is neutral with respect to a variety of
  implementation techniques, so a programmer can change a handler's
  implementation without having to change his program [see 6, 7].
- a program can defer the process of "cleaning up" [5, 6, 7] until it is
  known that an operation is to be terminated.
- a programmer can limit what parametric information is automatically
  supplied with language-defined exceptions.

3. Conclusion

This paper has not attempted an exhaustive survey of exception handling
language issues. The list given above does, however, constitute a representative
sampling of important issues pertaining to exception handling.

References

1. Zahn, C. T., Jr. A control statement for natural top-down structured programming. in <u>Programming Symposium</u>, Robinet, B. (ed.), Lecture Notes in Computer Science, vol. 19, Springer-Verlag, New York, 1974, 170-180.

2. Parnas, D. L. Response to detected errors in well-structured programs. Dept. of Comp. Sci., Carnegie-Mellon University, Pittsburgh, Pa., July 1972.

3. Hill, I. D. Faults in functions, in ALGOL and FORTRAN. <u>The Computer Journal</u> <u>14</u>, 3 (March 1972), 315-316.

4. Elson, M. <u>Concepts of Programming Languages</u>. Science Research Assoc., Chicago, Ill., 1973.

5. Organick, E. L. <u>The MULTICS System: An Examination of Its Structure</u>. MIT Press, Cambridge, Mass., 1972, 187-216.

6. Goodenough, J. B. Structured exception handling. <u>Conf. Record of the Second ACM Symposium on Principles of Programming Languages</u>, January 1975, 204-224.

7. Goodenough, J. B. Exception handling: Issues and a proposed notation. <u>Comm. ACM</u>, to appear.

Exception Handling in CLU

BARBARA H. LISKOV AND ALAN SNYDER

Reprinted from *IEEE Transactions on Software Engineering,* November 1979, pp. 546-558. Copyright © 1979 by The Institute of Electrical and Electronics Engineers, Inc.

Abstract—For programs to be reliable and fault tolerant, each program module must be defined to behave reasonably under a wide variety of circumstances. An exception handling mechanism supports the construction of such modules. This paper describes an exception handling mechanism developed as part of the CLU programming language. The CLU mechanism is based on a simple model of exception handling that leads to well-structured programs. It is engineered for ease of use and enhanced program readability. This paper discusses the various models of exception handling, the syntax and semantics of the CLU mechanism, and methods of implementing the mechanism and integrating it in debugging and production environments.

Index Terms—Exception handling, exit mechanisms, procedural abstractions, programming languages, structured programming.

I. INTRODUCTION

RECENTLY, there has been considerable emphasis on the development of programming language features that enhance the verifiability of programs [5]. While it is desirable that the task of developing correct programs be simplified as much as possible, another important goal of program construction is that programs behave "reasonably" under a wide range of circumstances. Such programs have been variously termed as reliable, robust, or fault tolerant.

In a reliable program, each procedure must be designed to behave as generally as possible. Its specifications should require a well-defined response to all possible combinations of legal inputs (inputs satisfying the type constraints), even when lower level modules on which this procedure is depending fail. Of course, different responses will be appropriate in the different cases. Note that even if the software has been verified, the possibility of hardware failure implies that software modules may fail, as does the presence of resource constraints.

This paper describes a linguistic mechanism that supports the construction of reliable software. The mechanism, called an *exception handling mechanism*, facilitates communication of certain information among procedures at different levels. The mechanism supports the view that different responses are appropriate in different situations. We assume that for each procedure there is a set of circumstances in which it will terminate "normally"; in general, this happens when the input arguments satisfy certain constraints and the lower level modules (implemented in both hardware and software) on which the procedure depends are all working properly. In other circumstances, the procedure is unable to perform any action that would lead to normal termination, but instead must notify some other procedure (for example, the invoking

Manuscript received March 8, 1979; revised June 25, 1979. This work was supported in part by the Advance Research Projects Agency of the Department of Defense, monitored by the Office of Naval Research under Contract N00014-75-C-0661, and in part by the National Science Foundation under Grants DCR74-21892 and MCS 74-21892.

B. H. Liskov is with the Laboratory for Computer Science, Massachusetts Institute of Technology, Cambridge, MA 02139.

A. Snyder is with the Hewlett-Packard Corporation, Palo Alto, CA 94304.

procedure) that an *exceptional condition* (or *exception*) has occurred.

For example, suppose *search* is a procedure that retrieves information associated with a given identifier in a symbol table. *Search* can return this information only if the identifier is present in the symbol table. The absence of the identifier constitutes an exceptional condition. Other exceptional conditions might also occur, for example, if the symbol table is implemented using a stack and the module implementing stacks is not working properly.

In referring to the condition as exceptions rather than errors we are following Goodenough [2]. The term "exception" is chosen because, unlike the term "error," it does not imply that anything is wrong; this connotation is appropriate because an event that is viewed as an error by one procedure may not be viewed that way by another. In fact, the term "exception" indicates that something unusual has occurred, and even this may be misleading: if the exception handling mechanism were efficient enough, exceptions might be used to convey information about normal and usual situations. For example, the *search* procedure might terminate normally only if the identifier were a local variable of the current block and use the exception handling mechanism to convey extra information about nonlocal variables.

Exception handling mechanisms have been largely ignored in programming languages. For a discussion of existing mechanisms, the reader is referred to [2] and [3]. In our opinion, the existing mechanisms are overly powerful and ill-structured. For example, in the on-condition mechanism of PL/I, on-units are associated with invocations dynamically rather than statically, and global variables must be used to communicate data between the procedure performing the **signal** and the on-unit. Goodenough [2] proposes a new mechanism that is more constrained and better structured. The mechanism presented in this paper is still more constrained. We also believe it to be more conducive to the development of well-structured programs.

The mechanism we describe facilitates communication of information that can be used to recover from faults such as erroneous data and failures of lower level modules. We do not discuss the methods, e.g., redundancy, that are used for fault detection and recovery. Mechanisms that are designed to facilitate fault detection and recovery, e.g., recovery blocks [8], are complementary to ours, as was noted in [7].

The mechanism we describe has been defined as part of the CLU programming language [4]. The mechanism is of general interest because it is constrained and simple. Its design was based on a tradeoff between simplicity and expressive power; major design goals were ease of use and program readability. The mechanism was designed for a sequential language (without coroutines or parallel processes). Otherwise, however, the mechanism is not dependent on CLU semantics, and could be incorporated in any procedure oriented language.

In the next section we discuss the main decisions that must be made in designing an exception handling mechanism and the exception handling models that result from these decisions; we also discuss our decisions and our reasons for making them. In Section III we describe the syntax and semantics of the CLU exception handling mechanism. In Section IV we discuss some methods of implementing the mechanism and also how the mechanism can enhance programmer effectiveness in a debugging and a production environment. In Section V, we discuss the expressive power of our mechanism and compare it with some other mechanisms of greater power. Finally, in Section VI we summarize and evaluate what we have done.

II. THE MODEL

To discuss exception handling we must first introduce some terminology about programs. The term *procedure* will be used to mean program text, either in a higher level language or in machine language. A procedure implements a *procedural abstraction*, which is a mapping from a set of argument objects to a set of result objects, possibly modifying some of the argument objects. A procedure may be *invoked* (or called) by an *invocation*, which is textually part of some procedure; that procedure is referred to as the *caller*. Invocation results in *activation* of the invoked procedure. An activation may *signal* an exception; the invocation that caused the activation *raises* that exception. The program text intended to be executed when an exception is raised is called the *handler*.

Our model of exception handling involves the communication of information from the procedure activation that detects an exceptional condition (the *signaler*) to some other procedure activation that is prepared to handle an occurrence of that condition (the *catcher*). In designing this model, we faced two major questions: 1) which procedure activations may catch an exception signaled by a procedure activation and 2) does the signaler continue to exist after signaling. These two questions are independent and may be addressed separately.

A. Single Versus Multilevel Mechanisms

The obvious candidates[1] for handling an exception signaled by some procedure activation are the activations in existence at the time the signal occurs. We can rule out the signaler itself, as exceptions are, by definition, conditions that the signaling procedure is unable to handle. The remaining question is whether to allow activations other than the immediate caller of the signaler to handle the exception.

Our answer to this question is based on the hierarchical program design methodology that CLU is intended to support [4]. As was explained above, each procedure implements a mapping. The caller of a procedure invokes the procedure to have the mapping performed; the caller need know only what the mapping is, and not how the procedure implements the mapping. Thus, while it is appropriate for the caller to know about the exceptions signaled by the procedure (and these are part of the abstraction implemented by that procedure), the caller should know nothing about the exceptions signaled by procedures used in the implementation of the invoked procedure.

The above considerations lead us to allow only the immediate caller of a procedure to handle exceptions signaled

[1]Levin [3] proposes an additional set of candidates. We will discuss Levin's work in Section V.

by that procedure. Of course, the handler in the caller can itself signal an exception, but that exception will then be part of the caller's abstraction.

We believe that the decision to limit handling of exceptions to the immediate caller is necessary for any well-structured exception handling mechanism. To maintain intellectual manageability of software, program structures that support understanding and verification through local code examination are needed. In particular, to understand how a procedure is implemented, one should not have to examine implementations of any other procedures. An understanding of the mappings performed by invoked procedures is needed, but this understanding should be obtained by reading specifications of those procedures and not their code. This requirement implies that specifications must describe all exceptions arising from invoking a procedure, including information about exceptions arising from procedures called at a lower level if the mechanism does not limit the handling of these exceptions. The point is that all exceptions that may be raised by a procedure, whether explicitly or implicitly, must be considered part of that procedural abstraction. Limiting the handling of exceptions to just the caller simply ensures that the linguistic constructs match the proper conceptual view. Note, however, that this constraint does *not* prevent the language designer from providing simplified ways of passing exceptions from one level to the next where appropriate.

The exception handling mechanism proposed by Goodenough [2] does impose our constraint on handling exceptions. The PL/I mechanism does not, nor does the mechanism in Mesa [6].

B. Resumption Versus Termination Model

The second question, whether the signaler should continue to exist after the exception is signaled, involves a tradeoff between expressive power and the complexity of the semantics. If the signaler can continue to exist after signaling, then it is possible that a catcher may fix up the exceptional condition so that processing of the signaler may be resumed. For this reason, we refer to this model as the *resumption model*. The model in which the signaling activation ceases to exist we refer to as the *termination model*. In this section we assume that the decision to support a one-level mechanism has been made, and we therefore limit our analysis to this case.

A one-level resumption model works as follows. Suppose that there are three procedures P, Q, and R, and that P invokes Q and Q invokes R. If R signals an exception r, then Q must handle it. Let H_r denote the statements in Q that handle r (H_r is the handler for r). In the course of handling r, H_r may signal an exception q, which must be handled by P (since P is the caller of Q).[2] Let H_q denote the statements in P that handle q (H_q is the handler for q). When H_q terminates, then

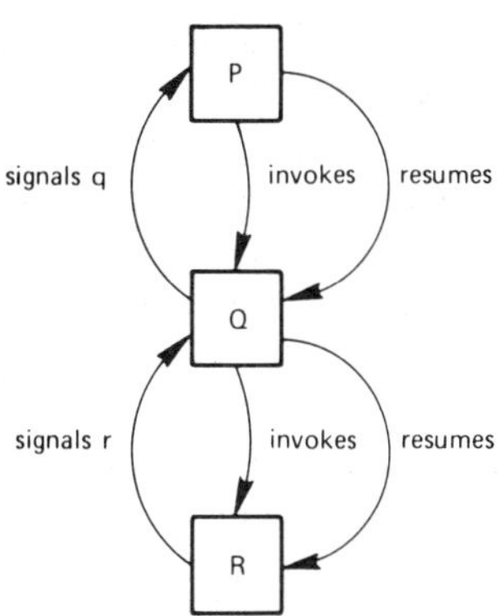

Fig. 1. Flow of control in the resumption model.

Q is resumed in the middle of H_r; only when H_r terminates is the execution of R continued. This situation is illustrated in Fig. 1. Note that information about signals flows upward one level at a time, while resumption flows downward one level at a time; multilevel flow is not permitted in either direction.

The resumption model is most easily understood by viewing the handler as an implicit procedure parameter of the signaler. The handler is called by the signaler when the exception it handles is signaled. The handler procedure is declared in the calling procedure, and its free variables get their meaning in the caller's environment, as do any exceptions it signals.[3]

In the termination model, occurrence of an exception causes the signaler to terminate. However, different kinds of behavior are expected of the called procedure under different conditions. The view taken is that a procedure may terminate in one of a number of conditions. One of these is the *normal condition*, while others are *exception conditions*. In each condition, it may be convenient to return a number of result objects; these will differ in number and type in the different conditions.

The resumption model is more complex than the termination model. This can be appreciated by considering how resumption affects the interrelationships among procedures, specifications of procedures, and linguistic mechanisms for exception handling.

The ordinary view of procedures is that, in the absence of recursion, the calling procedure is dependent on the called procedure but not vice versa. This view is upheld in the termination model. However, in the resumption model, the signaler and caller are mutually dependent: the caller invokes the signaler to perform some mapping, or satisfy some input/output relation, but the signaler depends on (the handler in) the caller to satisfy a similar relation when an exception is signaled.

Specifications of procedural abstractions in the termination model consist of a number of clauses, one specifying the behavior for the normal case and one for each exception case. Such clauses also exist in the resumption model, since it is still possible that the signaler is unable to terminate normally, for example, because a handler is unable to clear up the prob-

---

[2] If dynamic binding for exception names is used (as in PL/I), then R would be required to handle q. Making this assumption leads to a model at least as complex as the one we are considering. Furthermore, it is impossible under this assumption for H_r to raise exception in P without resorting to a multilevel mechanism.

[3] That is, exception names have static scope.

lem that led to the exception. In general, specifications have a termination model form (several termination states are defined) even when the resumption model is in use.

The interdependence between procedures in the resumption model show up in specifications as extra information. In addition to the clauses describing different termination states, it is also necessary to include descriptions of the behavior expected from the handlers when exceptions are signaled. Such descriptions are analogous to what must be given for a procedure taking procedure parameters, since handlers are implicit procedure parameters, as was discussed earlier.

The complexity of a linguistic mechanism supporting resumption is illustrated by Goodenough's proposal [2], which is a carefully considered design of a complete mechanism. Goodenough's design recognizes that to be really useful, termination must be supported as well as resumption. Three types of signals are recognized, corresponding to cases where the signaler may not be resumed, must be resumed, or where resumption is optional. In case the caller does not resume a signaler that must or could be resumed, a special ability is provided to permit the signaler to clean up (i.e., restore some nonlocal variables to a consistent state) before its activation is terminated. In addition, a default mechanism is provided to permit the signaler to handle its own exception in case the caller does not.

The termination model requires a simpler linguistic mechanism for its support than does the resumption model. Since a signal terminates the signaler, there is no need for multiple kinds of signals. Also, special mechanisms for cleaning up are not needed (the signaler must always clean up before signaling).

Since the termination model is simpler, it is preferable to the resumption model, provided it supplies adequate expressive power. We conjecture that the expressive power is adequate: that situations handled awkwardly by the termination model and simply by the resumption model are not frequent. We will discuss this conjecture further in Section V. In the next section we discuss the design of an exception handling mechanism based on the termination model.

III. Syntax and Semantics of the CLU Exception Mechanism

In Section II we explained the rationale for our major decisions.

1) The exceptions signaled by a procedure must be caught by the immediate caller.

2) Signaling an exception terminates the signaling procedure.

These two decisions lead to a single-level termination model of computation in which a procedure may terminate in one of a number of conditions. Thus, instead of a single return path, each procedure has several return paths. One of these is considered the normal path, while others are considered exceptional. In each case, result objects may be returned; the result objects may differ in number and type in the different cases.

An exception handling semantics that terminates execution of the signaling procedure could be incorporated in a programming language with no additional mechanism. The signaling procedure could simply return, passing back in addition to the real result objects a tag that identifies the reason for termination. Indeed, such a convention is often adopted as a way of dealing with exceptions in a language that has no exception handling mechanism. However, this approach has a major defect: every invocation must be followed by a conditional test to determine what the outcome was. This requirement leads to programs that are difficult to read, and probably inefficient as well, thus discouraging programmers from signaling and handling exceptions.

To aid programmers in building reliable software, an exception handling mechanism must be devised that can be implemented efficiently and that enhances program readability. In the remainder of this section we describe the CLU exception handling mechanism, which was developed to satisfy these goals. The discussion identifies some problems that arise in designing any such mechanism; the CLU mechanism provides a possible set of solutions to these problems.

A. Signaling

To provide a convenient method of signaling information about exceptions, we included directly in CLU the model of a procedure having many kinds of returns. A CLU procedure, therefore, can terminate in the normal way by returning and can terminate in an exceptional condition by signaling. In each case, result objects, differing in number and type, can be returned.

The information about the ways in which a procedure may terminate must be included in its heading. For example, the procedure performing integer division has the following heading:

$$\text{div} = \textbf{proc}\,(x, y: \text{int})\,\textbf{returns}\,(\text{int})\,\textbf{signals}\,(\text{zero\_divide})$$

which indicates that *div* may terminate by returning a single integer (the quotient of the two input arguments) or by signaling *zero_divide* (which indicates that the second argument was zero) and returning no results.

A CLU procedure terminates its execution by performing a *return statement* or a *signal statement.* The return statement terminates execution normally, while the signal statement terminates execution in the named exceptional condition. For example, the following (fairly useless) procedure determines the sign of an integer:

```
sign = proc(x: int) returns (int) signals (zero, neg (int))
    if x < 0 then signal neg (x)
        elseif x = 0 then signal zero
        else return (x)
    end
end sign
```

The information in the procedure heading is used to check that the exception names actually signaled are the correct ones and that the correct number and types of result objects are returned in both the normal and exceptional cases. This information is also used to determine that the exceptions handled by a calling procedure are named in the heading of the called procedure, and that, again, the number and types of result objects are correct in both the normal and exceptional cases.

B. Handling Exceptions

In CLU, exceptions arise only from invocations.[4] In particular, all uses of infix and prefix operators in CLU are considered to be "syntactic sugar" for invocations. For example, the expression

x + y

is syntactic sugar for the invocation

t$add (x, y)

where t is the type of x. Thus, if x is an integer, $x + y$ is an invocation of the integer addition operation. This viewpoint permits exceptions arising from built-in operations and user-defined procedures to be treated uniformly.[5]

In this section we discuss how handlers are associated with invocations. For usability and program readability, it is necessary to permit considerable flexibility in the placement of handlers. For example, requiring that the text of a handler be attached to the invocation that raises the exception would lead to unreadable programs in which expressions were broken up with handlers. Furthermore, the control flow of a program is often affected by the occurrence of an exception (for example, an *end_of_file* exception will terminate a loop). Therefore, our mechanism was designed to permit placement of a handler where the programmer deemed convenient, out of the main flow when possible to enhance readability, and altering the control flow when this was desired.

Two major decisions determined the form of CLU exception handling statements.

1) Handlers are statically associated with invocations.

2) Handlers may be attached only to statements, not to expressions.

Static association means that the handler associated with a particular exception condition that may be raised by a particular invocation can be determined by static analysis of the program text. This decision not only enhances program readability, but makes possible a more efficient implementation of the exception handling mechanism.

The decision to attach handlers only to statements and not expressions was made to simplify the mechanism. When a handler attached to an expression terminates, unless an explicit return, signal, or exit (see Section III-C) is performed, it must provide a value to be used as the value of the expression. By allowing handlers to be attached only to statements, we avoid providing a mechanism for substituting new values for expressions. We believe that the need to substitute a value for an expression is not great. In any case, the effect of attaching handlers to expressions can be obtained by breaking up complex expressions into sequences of assignment statements.

Handlers are placed in CLU programs by means of the *except statement*, which has the form

---

[4]Except for the special exception *failure* (described in Section III-D), which may be signaled at any point by the underlying implementation of CLU.

[5]The viewpoint does *not* require that a built-in operation be implemented by a closed routine; in-line code is perfectly permissible and consistent.

This statement has the following interpretation: the *statement* raises all the exceptions raised by the invocations it textually contains, excluding those handled by embedded except statements. The *handler list* will handle some subset (possibly all) of these exceptions. The except statement as a whole raises all the exceptions of the *statement* that are not handled by the *handler list* plus any exceptions raised by the *handler list*. Thus, when an exception is raised by an invocation, control goes to the innermost handler that handles that exception and is part of an except statement containing the invocation in its *statement* part.

Each handler in the *handler list* names one or more exceptions to be handled, followed by a list of statements (called the *handler body*) describing what to do. Permitting several exceptions to be named in the same handler avoids code duplication when the exceptions are all handled in the same way.

Several different forms are available for handlers depending on whether the named exceptions have associated result objects and whether those objects are used in the handler body. To handle one or more exceptions with no associated objects, the exception names are simply listed. For example,

when underflow, zero_divide: *body*

will handle exceptions named *underflow* and *zero_divide*, neither of which has any associated result objects.

To handle exceptions with result objects that are to be used in the handler body, names must be associated with the objects. Again a list of exception names is given, but it is followed by declarations of local variables to name the result objects, for example,

when e1, e2 (s: string, i: int): *body*

The scope of the declarations is the handler body. All of the named exceptions must return objects of the types listed in the declaration, in the order stated. When the handler is executed, these objects are bound to the declared variables and the body is executed. (This binding is similar to the binding of actual arguments to formal arguments that occurs when procedures are invoked. However, a return or signal in the handler body, rather than terminating just the handler, will instead terminate the entire enclosing procedure.)

To handle exceptions with result objects when the objects are not used in the handler body, the list of exception names is followed by (*) as shown below:

when neg, underflow (*): *body*

There need be no agreement between the number and types of result objects associated with the exceptions in this form; for example, the *neg* exception had a single argument, while *underflow* had none. This form encourages a programming style in which a procedure returns all possibly useful information when signaling; if this information is not needed in the calling procedure, it can easily be ignored.

If the programmer wishes to handle all remaining exceptions without listing their names, one of the following two forms can be used as the last handler in an except statement. The form

others: *body*

is used when information about exception names and result objects is not important. If information about the exception name is desired, the form

others (e_name: string): *body*

may be used. Here the name of the exception is given to the handler body as a string.

The handler body may contain any legal CLU statement. If the handler body returns or signals, then the containing procedure will be terminated as discussed in Section III-A. The handler body may also be terminated by an exit (see next section) or because an invocation within it raises an exception that is not handled within the handler body. Otherwise, when the handler body is finished, the next statement following the except statement in the normal flow will be executed.

The example below illustrates the association of handlers with exceptions:

```
begin % start of inner block
    S1 except
            when zero: S2
            end
    . . .
    end % end of inner block
    except
            when zero: S3
            others: S4
            end
```

If *zero* is raised by an invocation in *S1*, it will be handled by *S2*, not *S3*. However, if *zero* is raised by an invocation in *S2*, it will be handled by *S3*. All other exceptions raised in *S1* and *S2* will be handled by *S4*.

C. Exits and the Placement of Handlers

Our intention in defining the except statement is to permit the programmer to position handlers as is convenient. There are two constraints on the placement of handlers.

1) The handler must be placed on the statement whose execution is to be terminated if the handler body terminates without returning or signaling.

2) Suppose that an exception named e is raised by two invocations, and we wish to handle the occurrences of e differently. We do not permit multiple handlers to be provided for e in a single except statement. (This rule holds even if the invocations raising e provide different numbers or types of result objects; we do not allow such information to be used in selecting a handler.) Therefore, the two handlers must be in two except statements, each situated such that only one of the invocations raising e is in its scope.

These two constraints may conflict. For example, suppose that within a statement, S, the procedure *sign*, mentioned earlier, is invoked at two different points. Suppose also that the programmer wishes to handle the *neg* exception signaled

```
begin  % beginning of S
    a := sign(x)
        except when neg(i: int):
                    S1
                    exit done
        end
    b := sign(y)
        except when neg(i: int):
                    S2
                    exit done
        end
    ...
    end  % end of S
        except when done:
            ...
        end
```

Fig. 2. Example illustrating use of the exit mechanism.

by *sign* in a different manner for each of the two invocations, but in each case wishes execution to then continue with the statement following S. The first constraint would require that both handlers be placed on S, so that the execution of S would be terminated when the exceptions are raised. However, the second constraint requires that at least one handler be placed within S to resolve the ambiguous association between the invocations and the handlers.

We resolve this conflict in CLU by the addition of an exit mechanism, similar to those proposed by Zahn [9] and Bochmann [1]. The handlers are placed near the invocations. They terminate by exiting to a handler attached to the statement S. For example, one could handle the *neg* exceptions as shown in Fig. 2.

The exit statement can be used anywhere within a CLU procedure; its use is not restricted to handler bodies. The exit statement is similar to the signal statement, except that while the signal statement signals the condition to the calling procedure activation, the exit statement directly raises the condition so that it can be handled in the same procedure activation. The exit statement can specify a number of result objects to be passed to the handler.

We chose to have separate mechanisms for exits and exceptions (rather than using the signal statement for both exits and exceptions) because the two mechanisms capture different programmer intentions and thus naturally have different restrictions on their use. The intent of an exit is a local transfer of control. Thus, we require that exits be handled in the same procedure activation where they are raised. Furthermore, we require that exits be handled by a when arm (not an others arm), and if there are result objects, these must be accepted as arguments by the handler. The justification for these requirements is that exit names and result objects (unlike exception names and result objects) are under the control of the programmer of the procedure, and therefore should be chosen to mean something within that procedure.

The exit mechanism meshes nicely with the exception handling mechanism. In fact, the signal statement can be viewed simply as terminating a procedure invocation and exiting to the appropriate handler in the caller.

D. Uncaught Exceptions

Now we address the question of what happens if a procedure provides no handler for an exception raised by some contained invocation. One possibility is to consider the procedure to be illegal; checking for unhandled exceptions can be performed at compile-time. This approach is taken by Goodenough [2].

We have taken another approach. We felt it was unrealistic to require the programmer to provide handlers in situations where no meaningful action can be taken. Such situations will occur when a used abstraction is not working properly. For example, consider the statement

if ~ stack$empty (s) **then**

   . . .

   x := stack$pop (s)

   . . .

     end

Here the programmer invokes the *pop* operation for stacks only when the stack is nonempty. Now suppose that nevertheless stack underflow occurs. This situation is unlikely to arise in a debugged or verified program (but see Section IV). If it does arise, it indicates that the stack abstraction is not behaving correctly. Often there is no appropriate action for this procedure to take other than to report the fact to its caller. Since almost every abstraction can potentially behave incorrectly or in a way not expected by its caller, procedures must always be prepared to handle such cases. However, the action taken is almost always the same, and to require explicit handling of such cases would load every procedure with uninteresting code.

To facilitate reporting of failures and to relieve the programmer of the burden of handling such errors, CLU has one language-defined exception, named *failure*. *Failure* has one associated result object, a string that may contain some information about the cause of the failure. Every procedure can potentially signal *failure*; therefore *failure* is implicitly an exception of every procedure and may not be listed in the procedure heading explicitly. *Failure* may be signaled explicitly, however, in the usual way:

signal failure ("reason is . . . ")

The most common way that *failure* is signaled, however, is by an uncaught exception being automatically turned into a *failure* exception. For example, procedure *nonzero*

nonzero = **proc** (x: int) **returns** (int)

    return (sign (x))

       except

           when neg (y: int): **return** (y)

          end

    end nonzero

does not catch exception *zero* signaled by *sign*. If this exception is signaled, the invocation of *nonzero* will be terminated with the exception

   failure ("unhandled exception: zero")

The effect is equivalent to attaching a handler to the procedure body, e.g.,

   nonzero = · · ·

      . . .

     except

       others(s: string): **signal** failure (

           "unhandled exception: "|| s)

     end

   end nonzero

Here the symbol || is string concatenation.

A common case in which an exception will not be handled is when the unhandled exception is *failure*. Note that in this case it is the string argument of *failure* (rather than the string "failure") that is of interest. Therefore, this string is retained when *failure* is passed up to the next level. This effect is equivalent to attaching to the procedure body the handler

   except

       when failure (s: string): **signal** failure (s)

     end

Sometimes before signaling *failure* some cleaning up is needed. In this case, the others or when form is used explicitly, and after cleaning up, *failure* is signaled explicitly.

E. Example

We now present an example demonstrating the use of exception handlers. We will write a procedure, *sum_stream*, which reads in a sequence of signed decimal integers from a character stream and returns the sum of those integers. The input stream is viewed as containing a sequence of fields separated by spaces and newlines; each field must consist of a nonempty sequence of digits, optionally preceded by a single minus sign. *Sum_stream* has the form

   sum_stream = **proc** (s: stream) **returns** (int)

           signals (overflow,

               unrepresentable_integer (string),

               bad_format (string))

      . . .

     end sum_stream

Sum_stream will signal *overflow* if the sum of the numbers or an intermediate sum is outside the implemented range of integers. *Unrepresentable_integer* will be signaled if the stream contains an individual number that is outside the implemented range of integers. *Bad_format* will be signaled if the stream contains a field that is not an integer.

An implementation of *sum_stream* is presented in Fig. 3. It consists of a simple loop that accumulates the sum, using a procedure *get_number* to remove the next integer from the stream. *Get_number* will signal *end_of_file* if the stream contains no more fields, in which case *sum_stream* will return the accumulated sum. *Get_number* will also signal *bad_format* or *unrepresentable_integer* if an invalid field is encountered; these exceptions are passed upward by *sum_stream*. The *overflow* handler in *sum_stream* catches exceptions signaled by the *int$add* procedure, which is invoked using the infix + notation. We have placed the exception handlers on

```
sum_stream = proc (s: stream) returns (int)
                signals (overflow,
                         unrepresentable_integer (string),
                         bad_format (string))
    sum: int := 0
    while true do
            sum := sum + get_number (s)
            end
        except
          when end_of_file:
                return (sum)
          when unrepresentable_integer (f: string):
                signal unrepresentable_integer (f)
          when bad_format (f: string):
                signal bad_format (f)
          when overflow:
                signal overflow
          end
    end sum_stream
```

Fig. 3. The sum_stream procedure.

```
get_number = proc (s: stream) returns (int)
                signals (end_of_file,
                         unrepresentable_integer (string),
                         bad_format (string))
    field: string := get_field (s)
        except when end_of_file:
                signal end_of_file
            end
    return (s2i (field))
      except
        when unrepresentable_integer:
                signal unrepresentable_integer (field)
        when bad_format, invalid_character (*):
                signal bad_format (field)
        end
    end get_number
```

Fig. 4. The get_number procedure.

the while statement for readability; they could also have been placed directly on the assignment statement.

The procedure *get_number* is presented in Fig. 4. It calls a procedure *get_field* to obtain the next field in the stream and then uses *s2i* to convert the returned string to an integer. *S2i* has the following form:

```
s2i = proc (s: string) returns (int)
        signals (invalid_character (char),
                 bad_format,
                 unrepresentable_integer)
        . . .
        end s2i
```

S2i will signal *invalid_character* if the string *s* contains a character other than a digit or a minus sign. *Bad_format* will be signaled if *s* contains a minus sign following a digit, more than one minus sign, or no digits. *Unrepresentable_integer* will be signaled if *s* represents an integer that is outside the implemented range of integers. *Get_number* handles the excep-

tions signaled by *get_field* and *s2i* and signals them upward in terms that are meaningful to its callers. Although some of the names may be unchanged, the meanings of the exceptions (and even the number of arguments) are different in the two levels. Note the use of the (*) form in the handler for the *bad_format* and *invalid_character* exceptions since the signal arguments are not used.

The *get_field* procedure is presented in Fig. 5. It uses the following operation of the *stream* data type:

```
getc = proc (s: stream) returns (char) signals (end_of_file)
        . . .
        end getc
```

The *stream$getc* operation returns the next character from the stream and signals *end_of_file* if the stream is empty. Note that if *end_of_file* is signaled when a field is being accumulated, then that field is returned. Otherwise, *get_field* signals *end_of_file*.

Programming of the procedures in Figs. 3–5 would be

```
get_field = proc (s: stream) returns (string) signals (end_of_file)
    field: string := ""
    begin    % delimits scope of outermost end_of_file handler
        c: char := stream$getc (s)
        % search for field
        while c = ' ' cor c = '\n' do
                c := stream$getc (s)
                end
        % accumulate field
        while c ~= ' ' cand c ~= '\n' do
                field := string$append (field, c)
                c := stream$getc (s)
                    except when end_of_file:
                        return (field)
                        end
                end
        end
            except when end_of_file:
                signal end_of_file
                end
    return (field)
    end get_field
```

Fig. 5. The get_ field procedure.

simplified if the mechanism permitted implicit upward propagation of exceptions. This would permit arms of the form

```
when unrepresentable_ integer (f: string):
        signal unrepresentable_ integer (f)
```

to be omitted from the program text. As we gain experience in using the mechanism, we will learn how to modify it to enhance its convenience.

F. On Disabling Exceptions

One question that naturally arises about an exception handling mechanism is whether exceptions can be disabled. By disabling exceptions two kinds of savings can (potentially) be realized: the time spent detecting the occurrence of the exception can be saved, and the space used for the handlers and the information used to find the handlers can be saved. However, it is unacceptable if the result of disabling exceptions is that errors still occur, but are simply not recognized. Therefore, we do not believe that providing a means for programmer disabling of exceptions is consistent with encouraging good programming practice, and no such mechanism has been provided in CLU.

The situation still arises, however, in which it is possible to *guarantee* that the exception cannot occur, and it is desirable to take advantage of that guarantee to generate more efficient code. Looked at in this way, disabling of exceptions is seen as a kind of program optimization technique, since program optimization makes use of properties detected from program analysis to control the generation of code. There are two ways in which such properties can be detected. First, the combination of in-line substitution followed by analysis across module boundaries can result in more efficient code. For example, consider

```
if ~stack$empty (s) then x := stack$pop (s) · · ·
```

where s is a *stack*. If both *empty* and *pop* are expanded in-line, the result will be code roughly like

```
if s.size > 0 % body of empty
    then % body of pop
        if s.size > 0 then · · ·
```

Conventional techniques like redundant expression elimination and dead code removal can then be used to improve the code.

Alternatively, it would be fruitful to integrate the activities of a program verification system with the compiler. Then, for example, a verifier might prove of the user of s that *pop* is never called if s is empty. This assertion could then be used later to control the compilation of both the program using s, and the program implementing the *stack* module.

IV. Implementation, Debugging, and Diagnostics

In this section we discuss some implementation issues. First we sketch some methods for implementing the exception handling mechanism. Then we discuss how the mechanism can be incorporated in a debugging environment and in a production environment.

A. Implementation

There are several possible methods of implementing the exception handling mechanism. As usual, tradeoffs must be made between efficiency of space and time. We believe the following are appropriate criteria for an implementation:

1) normal case execution efficiency should not be impaired at all;

2) exceptions should be handled reasonably quickly, but not necessarily as fast as possible;

3) use of space should be reasonably efficient.

The tradeoff to be made is the speed with which exceptions are handled versus the space required for code or data used to locate handlers.

The implementation of signaling an exception involves the following actions:

1) discarding the activation record of the signaling activation (but saving the result objects associated with the exception),

2) locating the appropriate handler in the calling procedure,

3) adjusting the caller's activation record to reflect the possible termination of execution of expressions and statements,

4) copying the result objects into the caller's activation record,

5) transferring control to the handler.

Actions 3) and 5) are equivalent to a **goto** from the invocation to the handler. Actions 1) and 4) are similar to those occurring in normal procedure returns. Because the association between invocations and handlers is static, the compiler can provide the information needed to perform actions 2) and 3). Below we sketch two methods of providing this information; these methods differ considerably in their performance characteristics.

The first method, called the *branch table method*, is to follow each invocation with a branch table containing one entry for each exception that can be raised by the invocation. The

411

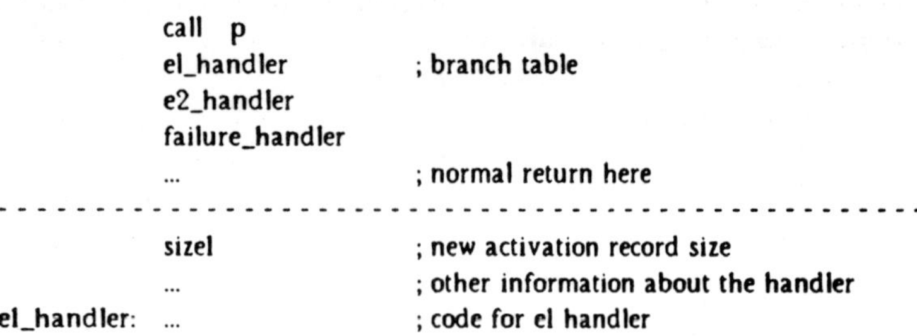

Fig. 6. Sketch of code generated by the branch table method.

invocation of a procedure whose heading lists n exceptions will have a branch table of $n + 1$ entries; the first n entries correspond to the exceptions listed in the heading, while the last entry is for *failure*. Each entry contains the location of a handler for the corresponding exception.

Using this method, return and signal are easy to implement: return transfers control to the location following the branch table, while signal transfers control to the location stored in the branch table entry for the exception being signaled. The information needed to adjust the caller's activation record could be stored with the handler, as could information about whether to discard the returned objects and whether this is an others handler; for example, this information could be stored in a table placed just before the first instruction of the handler. An example is given in Fig. 6 of the code generated by this method.

The branch table method provides for efficient signaling of exceptions, but at a considerable cost in space, since every invocation must be followed by a branch table (all invocations may at least signal *failure*). A second method, the *handler table method*, is the one used by the current CLU implementation. This method trades off some speed for space, and was designed under the assumption that there are many fewer handlers than invocations, which is consistent with our experience in using the mechanism.

The handler table method works as follows. Rather than build a branch table per invocation, the compiler builds a single table for each procedure. This table contains an entry for each handler in the procedure. An entry contains the following information: 1) a list of the exceptions handled by the handler (a null list can be used to indicate an **others** handler), 2) a pair of values defining the scope of the handler, that is, the object code corresponding to the statement to which the handler is attached, 3) the location of the code of the handler, 4) the new activation record size, and 5) an indicator of whether the returned objects are used in the handler. The scope and exceptions list together permit candidate handlers to be located: only an invocation occurring within the scope and raising an exception named in the exception list can possibly be handled by the handler (for an others handler, only the scope matters).

In this method, a return statement is implemented just as it would be in a language without exception handling. A signal statement requires searching the handler table to find entries for candidate handlers; if several candidates exist, the one with the smallest scope is selected. Placing the entries in the table in the (linear) order in which the corresponding handlers appear in the source text guarantees that the first candidate found is the handler to use. Unhandled exceptions can be recognized either by the absence of candidates or by storing one additional entry at the end of the handler table for this case.

B. Debugging and Diagnostics

Our exception handling mechanism is designed explicitly to provide information that programs, not programmers, can use to recover from exceptional conditions. However, the mechanism can also mesh smoothly with mechanisms intended to collect information of interest to programmers. The kind of behavior desired will differ, however, from a debugging environment to a production environment.

In an interactive debugging environment it is likely that a programmer would wish to be informed about the occurrence of some or all exceptions as they are signaled and be given a chance to handle them himself or take some other corrective action. Two possible modes might be useful here. The programmer may be interested only in signals of *failure* (especially those resulting from unhandled exceptions), or he may in addition name some particular exceptions of interest.

An exception handling mechanism running in such an environment, before locating a handler, would consult some debugging system information to determine if the current exception is one that the programmer wishes to know about. If the exception is of interest to the programmer, then system routines can be invoked to initiate a dialogue with the programmer. This dialogue may result in the program being continued or terminated.

It is worth noting that one argument in favor of the resumption model has been that it integrates debugging with program execution. The programmer (or actually the system as his representative) is thought of as the highest level activation, which will handle all exceptions not otherwise handled and which may later resume execution of some lower level activation. Note that this viewpoint allows the programmer to examine only unhandled exceptions. At any rate, we believe that it is not productive to try to merge debugging with ordinary processing, since the requirements in the two cases are quite different.

In a production environment, there is no programmer

available to interact with the program. Of course, there may be an operator present, and a program may attempt to recover by requesting some operator action (e.g., mounting a tape). This action can be accomplished by ordinary program structures (e.g., invoking a procedure to print a message on the operator's console).

When *failure* occurs in a production environment, there is still a good chance that program error is responsible. Therefore, it would be helpful if information about the failing program were collected for later examination by a programmer. This capability can easily be provided. Whenever *failure* is signaled, the exception handling mechanism can output information about each activation before terminating it. In the case of the first implicit signal of the "unhandled exception" failure, the mechanism should also provide information about the activation that signaled the unhandled exception. The information collected as *failure* propagates upwards will provide a trace of the failing program, which should be helpful for the programmer who determines later what the problem was. Debugging in a batch environment can be facilitated similarly, except that information about more exceptions than just *failure* may be of interest. Note that in either case the information being collected is *not* useful to programs (since it describes the states of implementations of other procedures) and therefore need not be made available to them.

V. EXPRESSIVE POWER

As we stated earlier, the decision to choose a termination model instead of a resumption model involves a tradeoff between the expressive power of the exception handling mechanism and its complexity. In our opinion, a more complex mechanism can be justified only if the additional expressive power it provides is frequently needed. In this section we explore this issue by considering examples of problems often put forth as justifying a resumption model.

The first problem concerns exceptions such as *underflow* that are generated by numeric operations. Often when an operation like *multiply* signals *underflow*, the desired action is to substitute a particular value (e.g., zero) for the result of the operation and continue the computation. In a resumption model, this behavior can be obtained by resuming the operation and passing it the value to be returned.

This behavior is equally easily obtained using a termination model. Because the *multiply* operation is not performing any computation after being resumed (it is merely returning the value provided), it is acceptable to terminate its activation. The only problem is for the handler to somehow substitute the new value for the result of the operation. For simple examples like

    z := x * y

"substituting" for the result of the invocation of *multiply* can be done simply by assigning to z. For more complicated examples, e.g.,

    z := x * y + z

using our mechanism it is necessary to introduce additional statements and temporary variables. However, such awkwardness is not a defect of the termination model but rather a result of our decision not to allow handlers to be attached to expressions. If such examples turned out to be frequent, our mechanism could be changed to accommodate them.

In fact, resumption is truly useful only in the following situation: when the exception is signaled, the signaler is in the middle of a computation that can be completed by performing additional computation upon receipt of a value from the handler. Resumption permits completion of the computation in this situation without redoing work already performed.

We can imagine that such a situation could arise during a numeric computation. If it did, and resumption were not available, then a default value (or, in the most general case, a procedure to compute a default value) could be passed as an extra input of the numeric routine.

This method is clearly not as convenient as using resumption; it becomes unacceptable if there are many default values or if there is deep nesting of procedures within the numeric routine, so that even a single default value must be passed down through many invocations. In our experience, neither of these characteristics hold for the routines in numeric libraries; on the contrary, default values are almost never of use, and the nesting is shallow.

The other example often used to support the choice of a resumption model is that of a storage pool that performs storage allocation for a number of objects in a program. If the amount of free storage in the storage pool becomes too low to satisfy a particular allocation request, it may still be possible to satisfy the request if some of the objects stored in the pool can be reorganized to use less storage. Many objects can be implemented in a number of ways, some that permit fast execution but use a lot of space and others that are slower but use less space. The idea would be to start out using fast representations but switch to more compact representations if free storage became too low. Note that this example is an instance of the general situation, described above, in which resumption is truly useful.

Levin [3] has designed an exception handling mechanism that directly supports the desired behavior. In Levin's mechanism, an exception can be associated with an object (the mechanisms discussed previously associate exceptions only with invocations). Thus, if the storage pool were unable to satisfy a request, it could signal an exception associated with the storage pool object. The mechanism would then allow all users of the object (in this case, modules that have objects allocated in the storage pool) to handle the exception. The handlers would attempt to free storage by reorganizing their associated objects.

Note that Levin's mechanism is strictly more powerful (in terms of expressive power) than the resumption models we discussed in Section II, since the users of the storage pool do not necessarily have any outstanding procedure activations at the time the exception is signaled. Furthermore, those objects that are in the middle of being operated upon are likely to be in an inconsistent state and thus not prepared for reorganization. Levin's mechanism makes it easy to inhibit the handling of an exception for objects in an inconsistent state.

In CLU, this recovery algorithm could be programmed by

having the storage pool explicitly maintain a collection of handler procedures to be invoked whenever free storage became too low.[6] The storage pool abstraction provides operations *alloc*, to add an object to a pool, and *delete*, to remove an object from a pool. *Alloc* would have an additional argument: the handler procedure to invoke if it becomes necessary to shrink the object being added to the pool. *Alloc* would add this procedure to the collection, while *delete* would remove from the collection the handler procedure associated with the object being deleted from the pool.

There is no doubt that the method sketched above is more complicated and more error prone than what could be done using Levin's mechanism. However, we believe that the storage pool example is both unusual and a special case. We doubt the existence of a large number of cases where the amount of storage freed would make the difference between successful and unsuccessful execution of a program.

In selecting examples for discussion, we examined those presented in papers favoring the resumption model [2], [3], and chose the ones that made the strongest case for resumption. In both examples, the solutions achieved using resumption were more natural than those possible without resumption. However, unless it is shown that such cases arise frequently, they do not justify the more complex mechanism.

VI. Discussion

In this paper we have discussed exception handling and described an exception handling mechanism. An exception handling mechanism is a tool for enhancing program reliability and fault tolerance. To enhance reliability procedures should be defined as generally as possible, that is, they should respond "reasonably" in as many situations as possible. An exception handling mechanism simplifies the writing of such procedures; it is primarily a mechanism for generalizing the behavior of procedures.

In Section II we discussed major decisions that must be made in designing an exception handling mechanism and the exception handling models that result from these decisions. We argued that any well-structured mechanism should be one-level: only the caller should handle exceptions raised by the invoked procedure. We further argued that the termination model, in which the signaling activation terminates, is better than the resumption model, in which the signaling activation continues to exist. The termination model is clearly simpler than the resumption model; we also believe that it has sufficient expressive power. Note that in our termination model, a procedure may terminate in one of a number of conditions (one of which is the so-called "normal" condition) and may return result objects differing in number and type for each condition. The ability to return objects provides a kind of expressive power not found in most other exception handling mechanisms.

Section III described the syntax and semantics of the CLU exception handling mechanism, which supports the termina-

tion model. While in Section II we were concerned primarily with interprocedure control and data flow, in Section III, we were concerned primarily with intraprocedure control and data flow. Our goal was to permit the programmer to place handlers where they are needed, without constraints due to conflict of exception names. This goal led to the introduction of an exit mechanism similar to those described by Zahn [9] and Bochmann [1]. Our design also acknowledged that many exceptions cannot be handled. These exceptions may not occur often, but they can potentially occur almost anywhere. The special exception named *failure*, which is signaled implicitly for all uncaught exceptions, was introduced to accommodate this situation. We also discussed why disabling exceptions is not a good idea, and suggested that research in program optimization techniques may be fruitful in avoiding the cost of checking for errors that are known not to occur.

In Section IV, we discussed two methods of implementing the exception handling mechanism, the branch table method and the handler table method. Both methods process normal returns as fast as possible; the branch table method also processes exceptions as fast as possible, while the handler table method is somewhat slower, but more space efficient. We also discussed the integration of the mechanism in debugging and production environments. The mechanism is defined to communicate information that can be used by *programs*, but this does not preclude an implementation that produces additional information for use by *programmers*.

In Section V, we discussed the expressive power of our exception handling model. We described two examples commonly put forward to justify the resumption model and discussed how they could be programmed in the termination model. The termination model solutions were inferior to the resumption model solutions. However, we believe that the examples under discussion occur very rarely, so a mechanism like the resumption model, which eases their programming at the cost of extra complexity, is not justified.

The CLU exception handling mechanism has been implemented by the handler table method. We have used the mechanism in writing many CLU programs (for example, most of the CLU compiler is written in CLU). We are convinced that our programs are better structured than they would be in the absence of the mechanism. Furthermore, we have not encountered any situations where a more powerful exception handling mechanism (e.g., resumption) was desired. Thus, our experience so far supports our belief that the mechanism is a good compromise between expressive power and simplicity. However, we have not written programs that attempt to handle the problem of resource constraints, a situation where resumption is most likely to be needed. Further experimentation is needed to reach a final conclusion on the wisdom of our choices.

Acknowledgment

The design of our exception handling mechanism was the work of the CLU design team, including R. Atkinson, T. Bloom, E. Moss, C. Schaffert, and R. Scheifler. This paper was improved by the comments of the referees and many others.

---

[6]Each procedure would have to be bound to the environment in which reorganization should be done. Since CLU procedures do not have free variables, the storage pool would have to maintain these environment objects also.

REFERENCES

[1] G. V. Bochmann, "Multiple exits from a loop without the GOTO," *Commun. Ass. Comput. Mach.*, vol. 16, pp. 443–444, July 1973.

[2] J. B. Goodenough, "Exception handling: Issues and a proposed notation," *Commun. Ass. Comput. Mach.*, vol. 18, pp. 683–696, Dec. 1975.

[3] R. Levin, "Program structures for exceptional condition handling," Ph.D. dissertation, Dep. Comput. Sci., Carnegie-Mellon Univ., Pittsburgh, PA, June 1977.

[4] B. Liskov, A. Snyder, R. Atkinson, and C. Schaffert, "Abstraction mechanisms in CLU," *Commun. Ass. Comput. Mach.*, vol. 20, pp. 564–576, Aug. 1977.

[5] *Proc. ACM Conf. on Language Design for Reliable Software, SIGPLAN Notices*, vol. 12, Mar. 1977.

[6] J. G. Mitchell, W. Maybury, and R. Sweet, "Mesa language manual," Xerox Res. Cent., Palo Alto, CA, Rep. CSL-78-1, Feb. 1978.

[7] P. M. Melliar-Smith and B. Randell, "Software reliability: The role of programmed exception handling," in *Proc. ACM Conf. on Language Design for Reliable Software, SIGPLAN Notices*, vol. 12, pp. 95–100, Mar. 1977.

[8] B. Randell, "System structure for software fault tolerance," *IEEE Trans. Software Eng.*, vol. SE-1, pp. 220–232, June 1975.

[9] C. T. Zahn, Jr., "A control statement for natural top-down structured programming," *Programming Symposium, Lecture Notes in Computer Science*, vol. 19, B. Robinet, Ed. New York: Springer-Verlag, 1974, pp. 170–180.

Barbara H. Liskov received the B.A. degree in mathematics from the University of California, Berkeley, and the M.S. and Ph.D. degrees in computer science from Stanford University, Stanford, CA.

From 1968 to 1972, she was associated with the Mitre Corporation, Bedford, MA, where she participated in the design and implementation of the Venus Machine and the Venus Operating System. She is presently Associate Professor of Electrical Engineering and Computer Science at the Massachusetts Institute of Technology, Cambridge. Her research interests include programming methodology, distributed systems, and the design of languages and systems to support structured programming.

Alan Snyder received the S.B., S.M., and Ph.D. degrees in computer science from the Massachusetts Institute of Technology, Cambridge.

He is currently a member of the Technical Staff in the Computer Research Laboratory at Hewlett-Packard Laboratories, Palo Alto, CA, working primarily in the area of integrated circuit design automation. His other interests include programming languages and machine architecture.

Dr. Snyder is a member of the Association for Computing Machinery.

TOWARD MODULAR VERIFIABLE EXCEPTION HANDLING*

D. M. Berry[1], R. A. Kemmerer[1]†, A. von Staa[2] and S. Yemini[1]

[1]Computer Science Department, University of California at Los Angeles,
Los Angeles, CA 90024, U.S.A. and
[2]Depto. de Informática, Pontifícia Universidade Católica, Rio de Janeiro, RJ, Brasil

(*Received* 1 *August* 1978; *revision received* 8 *October* 1979)

Reprinted from *Computer Languages,* Vol 5, 1980. Copyright 1980 by Pergamon
Press, Ltd.

Abstract—Recognizing that an error condition is an intrinsic part of the abstract type to which
the operation that detects the condition belongs, an attempt is made to specify and implement
error condition detection and handling within the framework of the Alphard form, a construct for
encapsulation of data type specification and implementation. The essence of the problem is this:
while error condition detection is done by the operation in the form, only the user of the type can
determine the meaning of the condition with respect to the way the type is used. Thus, the user
must be able to specify the handler. Unfortunately, programming the handler often requires
access to encapsulated implementation details which are hidden from the user.

After discussing the general issues of exception handling, modularity, and abstract data types,
this paper proposes a solution for one category of exceptions, namely errors. Specifically an
externally visible condition name is the link between an error's occurrence and some externally
visible but internally programmed handler for it. Issues raised by this partial solution, including
those of proof rules, are discussed.

Verification   Exception handling   Modularity   Structured programming   Software engineering   Assertions

1. INTRODUCTION

1.1. *Modularity*

The recognition has come to compter science that it is necessary that programmers
build upon the work of others when constructing complex software, if only to reduce the
complexity of the resulting software and thus to increase its reliability. The goal is to
allow development of independent program pieces, i.e., modules, each of which implements a single function or data abstraction. These pieces could be individually documented, programmed, tested, accepted, and then catalogued. Later, as more complex
modules are being developed, whenever a function or data abstraction is needed which is
implemented by a previously catalogued module, that module is used. Of course, the
newly developed module may also be catalogued for possible use in developing yet other
modules. In order for this process to work, it is necessary that the modules possess a high
degree of programming generality, data generality, implementation hiding, low coupling,
high strength, and composability. These properties have been thoroughly described in the
literature [1–5] and will be taken as well known here.

1.2 *Exception handling*

It is necessary first to agree upon some terminology. An *exception* or *exceptional
condition* is a condition that is detected while executing the body of a procedure or
attempting to perform an operation and which must be brought to the attention of the
invoker of the operation. When an exceptional condition is brought to the attention of

* This research was supported in part by the following: CNPq (BRASIL)-National Science Foundation
(USA) Interchange Program, Grant No. OIP 73-07346A02; the U.S. Energy Research and Development Ad-
ministration, Contract No. EY-76-S-03-0034, PA214; IBM do BRASIL; the Lady Davis Foundation, Hebrew
University, and the Weizmann Institute of Science in Israel; the Advanced Research Projects Agency of the
Department of Defense under Contract No. MDA 903-77-C-0211; FINEP (BRASIL) under Contract No.
CT-370.

† Present address: Computer Science Department, University of California at Santa Barbara, Santa Barbara,
CA 93106, U.S.A.

the invoker of the operation we say that the exceptional condition is *raised* or that the operation is *raising* the exception. The invoker's response to the raising of the exception is called *exception handling* and the software necessary to respond to the exception is called the *exception handler*.

Goodenough classifies the use of exceptions into three categories [6, 7]:

1. to deal with an operation's impending or actual failure,
2. to indicate the significance of a valid result or the circumstances under which it was obtained,
3. to permit an invoker to monitor an operation.

In this paper we focus our attention on the first category.

There are two kinds of failures: range failures and domain failures. Range failures occur when the result of an operation does not satisfy the operation's output assertion or when the operation decides it may never be able to satisfy its output assertion. An example of the first kind of range failure is when a read routine encounters an end-of-file mark instead of a record to be read. An example of the second kind is when a read routine encounters a parity error while reading a record. In this case it cannot be determined whether or not rereading the record will be successful.

In contrast to a range failure, a domain failure occurs when an input assertion of the operation cannot be satisfied. That is, the inputs fail to meet certain tests of acceptability. As an example of a domain failure, consider the case in which the input is supposed to be a string of numerals and blanks, and a letter appears in the input string.

A number of proposals for providing exception handling in programming languages exist [7–10], and one of these has actually been implemented [11]. However, none of these allow for fully modular composition of software primarily because in all of these schemes, the knowledge needed to detect and handle an exception is spread over parts of the program which would normally be in distinct modules.

The purpose, then, of this paper is to explore means to achieve modular exception handling. Our approach in the following sections is to note that exceptional conditions are an intrinsic part of data abstractions and then to try to deal with them within the linguistic frameworks already provided for dealing with data abstractions. Before this can be done, it is necessary to discuss abstract data types in general.

2. ABSTRACT DATA TYPES

2.1. *Specification*

An abstract data type, or more simply a data type, consists of

(1) a set of objects or values of the type together with
(2) a set of operations applicable to or yielding objects of the type.

A number of methods of specifying a type in this manner have been proposed. These include

(1) use of a higher level model [12–14],
(2) use of a state machine model [2],
(3) use of axiomatic descriptions [15, 16],
(4) use of algebraic descriptions [17–19].

These methods are described, compared, and contrasted in [20].

2.2. *Implementation*

One implements an abstract type by some closed scope construct providing a data structure to represent objects of the type and procedures operating on these structures to simulate the operations of the type. These include the Simula 67 class [21, 22], the von Staa module [23], the CLU cluster [24], the Euclid module [25], and the Alphard form [26, 27]. The construct generally contains provisions to hide from the user of the type all but the name of the type itself, the names of the operations, and if present, the specifications of the defining operations of the type. This constraint insures that the objects of the type can be manipulated only by the defining operations. Thus, if the operations are implemented correctly with respect to their specifications, the objects of the type will be used only in manners consistent with the specifications.

2.3. *Proof of correctness*

The benefit of hiding the implementation details from the user of a type is that it helps to decompose the proof of correctness of a program using the type. The implementor of a type needs to prove only that the operation procedures operating on the data structures behave as required by the specification. The user of the type may then assume the specifications in proving things about the program that uses the type.

Several methods have been proposed for proving the correctness of the implementation of a type with respect to its specification [15, 19, 26–28]. All the methods require that a mapping from the representation of an object to the object be found such that the mapping is preserved across the bodies of the operation procedures.

2.4. *Abstract data type as a module*

The closed construct implementing a type thus turns out to be the ideal module. Given several implementations of a particular type specification each in such a closed construct,

(1) the user need not change the format of operation calls as the implementation is changed,
(2) in any program assuming only the specification, apart from performance, the implementations appear no different in their effect,
(3) all implementations are hidden,
(4) the coupling between modules is low, as the only communication is through parameters of the operation,
(5) the strength of the module is high, as the constructs implement one "well-defined" data abstraction,
(6) each implementation may be freely composed with other modules as a unit to build higher level abstractions.

2.5. *Alphard*

In the sequel we will use Alphard [26, 27] as the medium for discussion and examples. Its closed construct, the **form**, provides the externally visible specification of the type, the implementing data structures and operation procedure bodies, and the mapping necessary to do the proof of correctness of the implementation. Furthermore, the language considers a form to be module.

3. APPROACH TO MODULAR EXCEPTION HANDLING

Parnas [29] observes that errors can be considered as happening during the application of an operation to some data and suggests that the specification of an operation of a type include a list of the possible errors and under what circumstances they are considered to have occurred. Thus, Parnas is suggesting that errors that can occur during the application of an operation of a type be considered as part of the type. For example, for the type integer, the divide operation is not applicable if the divisor is zero. The operation must detect and protect against attempts to divide by zero. Therefore, the zero-divide condition must be considered as a part of the type integer.

Guttag, Horowitz, and Musser and Goguen [30, 31] have incorporated errors into their algebraic specification techniques. An error is treated either as a special value of the type or as another operation of the type. The treatment of errors in the three references cited above is incomplete, as they deal only with the detection of domain failure errors and specification of a single response to an error. Other issues, i.e., detection of range failures, variable responses to an error, etc., are left unspecified. It may well be that only that which *has* been specified is all that should be part of the abstraction, but it is the purpose of our research to explore other possibilities.

Therefore the approach taken in this paper is to arbitrarily decide that

(1) all exceptions are an intrinsic part of some abstract data type just as are all operations, and in fact each is raised by some detecting operation of the type, and

(2) everything that one wishes to specify about an exception to a user of a data type, i.e.

    (a) when the exception is raised,
    (b) what a handler may do,
    (c) what a handler must do,
    (d) what information is passed to a handler, etc.,

is given as part of the data type's specification. This decision will give us an opportunity to explore such issues as

(1) what about exceptions really belong in the data abstraction,
(2) how the specifications of an exception should be stated,
(3) what language features are needed for implementing exceptions, and
(4) what proof rules are needed for dealing with abstract exceptions and their implementations.

All of this exploration is to be done with the goal of providing exception handling in as modular a manner as possible. In fact while we are restricting our considerations to type abstractions, what we say here should be applicable to any kind of abstraction so long as it is implemented by a closed scope module.

By making the arbitrary decision that we have, we have limited the apparent scope of what exceptions are, how they are detected, what they can do, and how they are handled. For example, by saying that all exceptions will be raised by some detecting operation, we are, in the terminology of Levin [10] restricting ourselves to *flow class* exceptions, i.e., those that get raised in attempts to apply an operation to data not in its domain, and are excluding *structure class* exceptions, i.e., those that get raised *whenever* the data structures implementing a particular abstraction satisfy a stated condition regardless of what operation is being performed. This exclusion makes sense from the modularity point of view since structure class exceptions produce a higher degree of coupling. It is less predictable when (i.e., where in the program) a structure class exception can get raised, as being notified of a structure class exception is not coupled to the use of any particular operation.

We are also saying, in effect, that all exceptions are *treated* as domain errors, i.e., some input data condition is detected which calls for handling other than that provided by the detecting operation. This is not to say that all exceptions are errors, but that all exceptions will be treated by the same constructs that are used to treat errors.

Treating an exception as an intrinsic part of some particular abstract data type solves the problem of exception propagation. In some languages, e.g., PL/1 and Ada [32], if the invoker of an operation (or routine) has not provided a handler for a condition that the operation has detected, the invoker's invoker is searched for a handler for the condition. If one is not found there, the invoker's invoker's invoker is searched, etc. In other words, the exceptional condition is *passed* from the routine to its invoker and from an invoker to its invoker. This passing of exceptional conditions gives rise to an expensive dynamic search of the activation record stack for a handler and, occasionally, to surprises as a handler in a statically invisible environment is found first (see the discussion in Section 9).

Our treatment of exceptions implies that an exceptional condition cannot just be passed on, because the condition has meaning only relative to the level of abstraction raising it. If an exceptional condition is to be passed on by the invoker to the invoker's invoker it must be rephrased into terms meaningful at the invoker's level of abstraction. For example, consider a matrix abstract type using the real number abstract type. A zero-divide detected by the real number type cannot just be passed to the matrix type's user; this user cannot adequately respond to the condition without more information. The real number type should report the condition in matrix-meaningful terms; e.g., "the matrix is singular", etc.

Another by-product of our treatment is that there need not be any dynamic search of the activation record stack for a handler for an exceptional condition. Since the handler for an exceptional condition must be provided by the detecting operation's invoker, the handler can in essence be treated as a parameter of the invocation. Searching for the handler for a condition can be implemented as simply as formal parameter access.

4. THE MODULARITY PROBLEM

The modularity problem of exception handling is the fact that proper handling sometimes requires a violation of the isolation of the levels of abstraction in a system. Consider a variation of Parnas's first example [29], "the bad tape block". A *tape file* type has among its operations an operation to *read* a record. In the implementation the read may be buffered so that an entire block is obtained from the tape file at once and records are peeled off from the buffer as they are requested; when all the records in a block have been read, another block is obtained from the file. The user of the file type is aware only of records and has no notion of buffering and of blocks.

Consider now the bad tape block condition. This condition may be detected only by the code of the *read* operation. It has no meaning to the invoker of the *read* who knows nothing about blocks. However, the response to the bad block, e.g., to retry, to ignore it, to terminate, etc., may be determined only by the invoker of the *read*. Only the invoker knows the use to which the records on the block would be put and thus how critical they are. Some of these response can be programmed without knowing how the file is implemented and thus outside the implementation of the file type e.g., terminating. Unfortunately other responses, such as retry and ignore the block, need access to the block buffer and other structures implementing the tape file. Unless the tape file type has provided *retry* and *ignore the block* operations as user invocable operations or has provided other means for programming these responses, there is no way for the user to dictate these responses. It is this kind of response that must be selected by the user of a type but which can be programmed only within an implementation of the type that creates the problem. At present, we see two solutions, one fully protected and the other not.

In the fully protected solution, the specification of a type must provide a variety of different handlers for each condition and/or a variety of different operations. The *user* of an operation that can raise a condition must be able to

(1) select which of several predefined handlers for the condition should be excercised in the event that the condition occurs during a particular application of the operation,

or

(2) program the desired response using only the operations visible to the user.

For this solution to work the type designer must have anticipated all possible responses sufficiently to have provided for each either a handler that does them or the operations needed to program them. An example is a handler for the integer zero-divide exception which just sets the result to some fixed number. This sort of handler can be programmed using operations already in the integer type.

The partially protected solution is to allow extension of types. The form must be opened to allow a new handler to be added to the type and to allow programming the new handler outside the form but with access to the representation of the type. Care must be taken that the specification of the type is not invalidated by the specification of the handler. Also care must be taken that the invariants of the representation and the preservation of the abstraction mapping are not violated by executing the handler body. Then the important issues are under what conditions may a form be modified and how to verify that the modifications preserve the correctness of the form.

420

Neither solution seems completely satisfactory. The first, while secure, places a heavy, if not impossible, burden of anticipation upon the type designer. The second requires extending the form and its proof rules in a manner which will guarantee that the security of the module is not compromised. It is not yet clear whether it is possible to design an extension that is flexible enough to allow practical exception handling and is at the same time verifiable.

For the fully protected solution, it might be that further study and classification of handlers will yield a set of guidelines for checking that all operations likely needed to support different handlers have been provided. For retry handlers, we may conclude that for each operation a corresponding inverse operation should be provided or that in each operation with side effects, copies of all modified data be saved until it is certain that the output assertion will be satisfied.

For the partially protected solution, rules are needed for making extensions in a manner which will not compromise security.

Our proposed constructs will be presented first in the fully anticipatory mode. Then the means for extension will be explained in terms of the full form the extensions yield.

5. THE FULLY PROTECTED PROPOSAL

5.1. *Preliminaries*

To allow forms to include exception handling in both the specification and the implementation parts, some notions defined earlier in Section 1 must be given more precise definitions:

A *condition* is any boolean valued expression. When a condition evaluates to true, the condition is said to have *occurred* or to have been *raised*.

A *handler* is a procedure possibly taking parameters and possibly returning a result. The handler may be *associated* with a particular condition, and to a condition may be associated several handlers. When a condition is raised, *one* of the handlers associated is called—parameters if any are passed and a return result if any is expected. Which of the associated handlers is executed is chosen by the user of the type. For each application of the operation which detects a condition c the user of the type *designates* which of c's handlers is to be called if c were to be raised during an execution of the application.

5.2. *Specification*

From the specification point of view, a *condition* is a boolean expression, and a *handler* is represented by a pair of assertions describing one particular response procedure to a particular condition.

As an example, consider the specification part of Fig. 1 giving a form for a stack type constructor. The form given here is similar to that of [26, 27], and in fact we assume the definitions and explanations given there except as noted herein.

The change in the basic type is that the maximum size of the stack is not considered a part of the type; rather it is taken as part of each value of the type. This change helps to preserve compile time checking of types. The manifestations of this change are that the maximum size is not a parameter of the type itself; there is a *create* operation which initializes its first parameter variable with an empty stack with the second parameter value as its maximum size; there is a *size* operation yielding the current size of whatever stack it is applied to; and there is a *maxsize* operation yielding the maximum size of whatever stack it is applied to.

The first line of the form says that stack is a type constructor whose argument is another type, t, having at least the := (assign) and the *undefined* operations. The specification part may be understood as follows:

(1) The **requires** clause says that to declare a variable of some stack type, e.g.,

     v:stack(integer)

there are *no* requirements to meet

form stack (t:**form** $<:=$,undefined $>$)
    beginform
    specifications
        requires true
        let stack $= <$stack$[1],\dots,$stack$[i],\dots,$stack$[n]>$
            where $(\forall i)\ ((2 \leqslant i \leqslant n \Rightarrow$ stack$[i]$ **is** t$) \wedge ($stack$[1]$ **is** integer$))$
        invariant $0 \leqslant$ truelength(stack) $\leqslant$ stack$[1]$
        initially true
        conditions tsmall,ovfl,popunfl,topunfl

    operations
        create(s:stack, n:integer)
            pre n > 0 **post** s $= <$n$>$
            pre n $\leqslant 0$ **post** tsmall(s,n)
        push(s:stack,x:t)
            pre truelength(s) $<$ s$[1]$ **post** s $=$ s' $_{(a}\ <$x$>$
            pre truelength(s) $\geqslant$ s$[1]$ **post** ovfl(s)
        pop(s:stack)
            pre truelength(s) > 0 **post** s $=$ leader(s')
            pre truelength(s) $\leqslant 0$ **post** popunfl(s)
        top(s:stack) **returns** x:t
            pre truelength(s) > 0 **post** x $=$ last(s')
            pre truelength(s) $\leqslant 0$ **post** topunfl(s)
        is_empty(s:stack)**returns** b:boolean
            pre true **post** b $=$ (truelength(s) $= 0$)
        size(s:stack)**returns** n:integer
            pre true **post** n $=$ truelength(s)
        maxsize(s:stack)**returns** n:integer
            pre true **post** n $=$ s$[1]$

    handlers
        toosmall(s:stack, n:integer)
            pre tsmall(s,n) **post** s $= <1>$
        toosmall_and_term(s:stack, n:integer)
            pre tsmall(s,n) **post** false
        overflow(s:stack, x:t)
            pre ovfl(s,x) **post** ovfl(s,x) ¢ i.e., does nothing ¢
        overflow_and_term(s:stack, x:t)
            pre ovfl(s,x) **post** false
        popunderflow(s:stack)
            pre popunfl(s) **post** popunfl(s)
        popunderflow_and_term(s:stack)
            pre popunfl(s) **post** false
        topunderflow(s:stack)**returns** x:t
            pre topunfl(s) **post** x $=$ undefined
        topunderflow_and_term(s:stack)**returns** x:t
            pre topunfl(s) **post** false
        defaults toosmall,overflow,popunderflow,topunderflow

    representation
        unique v:array(t), sp:integer
        rep(v,sp) $= <$upb(v),v$[1],\dots,$v$[$sp-1$]>$
        invariant $1 \leqslant$ sp $\leqslant$ upb(v) $+ 1$

    implementation
        body create **in** n > 0 **out** upb(s,v) $=$ n $\wedge$ s.sp $= 1$
            in n $\leqslant 0$ **out** tsmall(s,n):
            if n > 0
                 then makearray(s.v,1,n); s.sp $:= 1$
                 else tsmall(s,n)
            endif;
        body push **in** s.sp $\leqslant$ upb(s.v) **out** s.sp $=$ s.sp' $+ 1 \wedge$ s.v $= @$ (s.v',s.sp',x)
            in s.sp $>$ upb(s.v) **out** ovfl(s.x):
            if s.sp $>$ upb(s.v)
                 then ovfl(s,x)
                 else s.v$[$s.sp$] := $x; s.sp $:=$ s.sp $+ 1$
            endif;
        body pop **in** s.sp > 1 **out** s.sp $=$ s.sp - 1
            in s.sp $\leqslant 1$ **out** popunfl(s):
            if s.sp $\leqslant 1$
                 then popunfl(s)
                 else s.sp $:=$ s.sp - 1
            endif;

Fig. 1.

422

```
        body top in s.sp> 1 out x = s.v[s.sp - 1]
              in s.sp ≤ 1 out topunfl(s):
              if s.sp ≤ 1
                  then topunfl(s)
                  else x: = s.v[s.sp - 1]
              endif;
        body is_empty in true out b = (s.sp = 1):
              b: = (s.sp = 1);
        body size in true out n = s.sp - 1:
              n: = s.sp - 1;
        body maxsize in true out n = upb(s.v):
              n: = upb(s.v);
        body toosmall in tsmall(s,n) out upb(s.v) = 1 ∧ s.sp = 1:
              (makearray(s.v,1,1); s.sp: = 1);
        body toosmall_and_term in tsmall(s,n) out false:
              (print("attempt to create a stack with too small a size:", n, ".");
              halt);
        body overflow in ovfl(s,x) out ovfl(s,x):
              ¢ does nothing ¢;
        body overflow_and_term in ovfl(s,x) out false:
              (print("attempt to push into a full stack."); halt);
        body popunderflow in popunfl(s) out popunfl(s):
              ;
        body popunderflow_and_term in popunfl(s) out false:
              (print("attempt to pop an empty stack."); halt);
        body topunderflow in topunfl(s) out x = undefined:
              x: = undefined;
        body topunderflow_and_term in topunfl(s) out false:
              (print("attempt to take the top of an empty stack.");
              halt);
endform
```

Fig. 1.

(2) The **let** clause describes the abstract model of a bounded stack used to describe the operations. The bounded stack is actually an unbounded growing and shrinking sequence whose first element is the maximum size and whose second through last elements form the current stack with the last element being the top. The mathematical notion of sequence defined in [26, 27] is assumed. One additional operation of sequences is needed for our example namely that

$$\text{truelength}(s) = \text{length}(s) - 1.$$

Thus the maximum size is only artificially enforced since the sequence itself can model unbounded stacks.

(3) The **invariant** clause describes an invariant property of the abstraction, i.e., that the truelength of a sequence representing a stack lies between 0 and the value of the first element of the sequence inclusive.

(4) The **initially** clause says that one can assume nothing in particular about a variable which has been declared as a stack (but which has not yet been initialized by applying *create* to it).

(5) The **conditions** clause merely lists the conditions that the operations can detect.

(6) The **operations** clause (**functions** clause in [26, 27]) describes the behavior of each of the operations of the type. For each such operation, the following is given:

  (a) the operation name,
  (b) if the operation has parameters, the formal parameters and their types,
  (c) if the operation returns a value, the formal return variable (to which the value to be returned is assigned before returning) and its type,
  (d) at least one pair of **pre** and **post** assertions. At least one of these describes the "normal" input-output behavior of the operation (the first in all of our examples), and the rest describe the exceptional conditions requiring special handling. The convention used here is that for the "normal" behavior, the **pre**

and **post** assertions can be adapted for a particular call by some suitable procedure proof rule [33–35]. For the exceptional behavior pairs, the **pre** assertion is in fact the boolean expression defining a condition, and the **post** assertion is the parameterized *name* given to the condition; thus the **post** assertion is taken as an abbreviation of the **pre** assertion. The **post** assertion says, in effect, that the named condition has been raised. The actual parameters of the condition are exactly the formal parameters of the operation, and the name of the condition appears in the **conditions** clause. The effect of this convention is that, for example

    tsmall(s,n)

is logically equivalent to

    $n \leqslant 0$.

The disjunction of the **pre** assertions should be true but their pairwise conjunctions should be false. In this way, at any time, one and only one **pre - post** assertion pair is applicable.

(7) The **handlers** clause specifies the behavior of each handler associated with some condition. There is at least one handler for each condition. For each handler the following are given:

(a) the handler name,

(b) if the handler has parameters, then the formal parameters and their types. A handler has the same number and types, in order, of parameters as the condition to which it is associated and thus the same number and types, in order, of parameters as the operation that can detect the condition,

(c) if the handler returns a value, then the formal return variable and its type. The handler returns the same type result as the operation which can detect the condition with which the handler is associated,

(d) a **pre** assertion which is in fact the parameterized name of a condition with which the handler is associated. The actual parameters of the condition are the formals of the handler. The **pre** assertion serves two purposes: (1) its condition name identifies the condition to which the handler is associated; and (2) having been set up as equivalent to some logical expression involving the formal parameters of the condition's operation, it states what may be assumed about the formals of the handler upon entry to the handler. This works because of the conventions concerning the identity of the parameters of the operation, the condition, and the handler,

(e) a **post** assertion describing the net effect of the handler given the **pre** assertion. If the convention of the identity of the return types between the operation and handler is being followed, then the handler must, therefore compute a replacement value or effect for the operation. Therefore the handler's post assertion should imply that of the operation. Since false implies anything, this holds even for a terminating handler.

Note that in this example, there are two handlers, "x" and "x-and-term", for each condition. The first is a "forgiving" handler, either computing a replacement value for value returning operations or doing nothing or something innocuous for non-value returning operations. The second terminates the program, as indicated by the false **post** assertion (Termination is not in general a good idea, but we have used it here to simplify our example. A better idea would be to have the handler raise a condition to the invoker's invoker, thus passing the error indication through the invocation chain. An example is given later.).

(8) The **defaults** clause says that in the absence of a designation (to be described later) to the contrary, *toosmall, overflow, popunderflow,* and *topunderflow* are the handlers

to be used if and when their conditions occur. It is required that exactly one of the handlers associated with each condition be mentioned in this list.

5.3. *Use of defined types*

The user of the form of Fig. 1 may, for example,

(1) define the type *stack-of-ints* by applying the form to the type *integer*, which is assumed to have the := and *undefined* operations:
   type stack-of-ints = stack(integer),
(2) declare a variable *s* to be of type *stack-of-ints* by writing either of
   var s:stack(integer) or
   var s:stack-of-ints,
(3) apply any of the operations to variables and values of the right type:
   create(s,1024)
   push(s,1)
   i := top(s)
   pop(s)
   if is-empty(s) **then** ...
   if size(s) < maxsize(s) **then** ... ,
(4) designate a handler for a particular condition of a particular operation application. If a particular handler has been designated for a particular condition of a particular operation application, then if that condition were to occur during an execution of the application, the designated handler is executed. Returning from the handler results in an immediate return from the detecting application.

The designation is done syntactically in a compile time resolvable manner so as to allow for maximum optimization on the part of compilers.

A handler is designated for all occurrences of its condition and thus for all occurrences of its operation in a closed construct, except for those inner occurrences otherwise designated, by preceding the construct by a prefix containing the handler's name. Here a closed construct is a parenthesized expression, a statement, a conditional, a loop, a block, or a procedure. A prefix may list several handlers each for a different condition. Thus, the handler designated for a particular condition of a particular occurrence of an operation is the one which occurs innermost among the surrounding prefix lists. If no handler is designated by this method, then the default handler is considered designated.

In Fig. 2, there are two examples of prefixes, each designating one handler for the *popunfl* condition of the *pop* operation. The second of these in line 9 prefixes the statement *pop*(s) so that the *popunderflow* handler is designated for the one occurrence of *pop* in that statement. If the *popunfl* condition were to happen during an execution of this *pop*, then nothing would be popped, *s* would be left alone, i.e., empty, and the computation would continue as if nothing had happened. That this would come to pass can be deduced from the **pre** and **post** assertions of the *pop* operation and of the *popunderflow* handler. The first of the prefixes, in line 6, designates *popunderflow-and-term* as the

```
1       begin
2           var s:stack(integer);
3           create(s,10);
4           push(s,5);
5           pop(s);
6       [popunderflow_and_term]:begin
7               push(s,9);
8               pop(s);
9           [popunderflow]:pop(s);
10              pop(s);
11          end;
12          pop(s);
13      end
```

Fig. 2.

handler for all occurrences of *pop* in the region consisting of lines 6 through 11 except for the statement in line 9. Therefore, from the specifications of the *pop* operation and the *popunderflow-and-term* handler, we know that during the execution of any *pop* in this region, if the *popunfl* condition were to arise, the computation would terminate. Outside this region, the default handler for the *popunfl* condition, *popunderflow*, is designated. Thus during execution of any of these designated *pops* if the popunfl condition were to arise, the handler would result in the *pop* having done nothing to its argument. For all other conditions, the default handler is designated for the whole program.

(5) provide another handler for a particular condition and designate it for particular applications of the detecting operations. For example, suppose that line 9 of Fig. 2 were changed to

> [**handler** popunderflow_and_warn (s:stack)
>   **pre** popunfl(s) **post** popunfl(s)
> **body** popunderflow_and_warn
>   **in** popunfl(s) **out** popunfl(s):
>   print ("warning: a popunderflow has occurred")] :pop(s);

The user has provided another handler for the popunfl condition which is designated only for the *pop* in line 9. In general such a handler must have the properly parameterized condition as its **pre** and **in** assertions, and its body may be programmed using only operations visible to the user of the type.

5.4. *Implementation of types*

From the implementation point of view,

(1) a condition is a boolean expression to be calculated, preferably without side effects, during an operation application, and

(2) a handler is a procedure designed to be called in place of an operation if during the application of the operation the condition associated with the handler should evaluate to true.

These notions are easily incorporated into the representation and implementation parts of the form.

As an example, consider now the representation and implementation parts of the *stack* form of Fig. 1 that we have been examining.

(1) The **representation** clause describes how a stack is implemented in terms of objects of previously defined types. It consists of a number of subsidiary clauses.

(a) The **unique** clause says that *each* stack object consists of a one dimensional array v of elements of type t and an integer sp*. If there were some data that all stack objects shared, these data would be described in a **shared** clause. In effect these identifiers serve as a template for the allocation of an object of the abstract type. When one declares an abstract type, the variable is allocated space for the representing variables of the **unique** clause. The representation of an abstract object is thus a record with the **unique** variables as components.

(b) The **rep**(v,sp) clause shows what abstract stack, i.e., what sequence, a particular configuration of v and sp stand for. Specifically the upperbound of v, $upb(v)$, represents the first element of the sequence which is the maximum size of the stack. The elements of the stack from bottom to top are $v[1]$ through $v[sp-1]$ in that order. In other words, sp is the index of the first free slot on top of the stack. The **rep** serves merely to relate the concrete implementation to the abstract specification for the purpose of being able to prove the implementation correct with respect to the specification.

---

* The array type constructor we use here is similar to that of ALGOL 68 [36]—the bounds of an array are part of its value and not its type. The bounds of an array are provided as parameters of an array value creation operator, *makearray*, rather than as parameters of the type.

(c) The **invariant** clause describes a property of the components of the representation which is always true of the representation of a valid stack, namely that the value of sp always lies between 1 and 1 more than the maximum size of the stack.

(2) The **implementation** clause gives code bodies for the operations and handlers mentioned in the **specification** clause. The code body for each operation or handler assumes the formal parameters and formal return variable given in the specification of the operation or handler and is programmed using these formal identifiers, the shared implementation variable, if any, and whatever local variables that are needed. Whenever an identifier, say s, of the abstract type is used, the components of its representation are accessed by considering the **unique** variables as selectors in a dot notation, e.g., $s.v$ and $s.sp$ are the vector and top of stack index of s, respectively. For each operator the body consists of:

(a) **body** followed by the operation name,

(b) a list of **in** and **out** assertion pairs. Each such pair states that if the formal parameters and shared variables satisfy the **in** assertion then if the body halts, these parameters, and variables, and the formal return variable will satisfy the **out** assertion. Typically one of these pairs describes the "normal" operation of the body and each of the others describes when one condition is raised. To describe when a condition is raised, the **in** assertion should be a logical expression involving the formal parameters and shared variables stating when the condition is true, and the **out** assertion should be a parameterized condition name with some condition associated with the operation as the name and the formal parameters of the operation as the parameters. The parameterized condition name serves both as a call with parameters to the designated handler and as an abbreviation for the logical expression stating when the condition is raised.

It should be that the disjunction of the **in** assertions is true but that their pairwise conjunctions ard false, so that one and only one behavior is discernible in all cases,

(c) finally, one statement, conditional, loop, or block which is partially correct with respect to all of the pairs of **in** and **out** assertions. In the case that an **out** assertion of a pair is a parameterized condition name, the statement being partially correct with respect to the pair means that *if* the **in** assertion holds before the statement is executed, *then* the last thing the statement does before ending is to "call" the parameterized condition name *and* the **in** assertion still holds.

For each handler, the body consists of

(a) **body** followed by the handler name,

(b) a pair of **in** and **out** assertions. The **in** assertion is a parameterized condition name with the condition being that with which the handler is associated and the parameters being the same as those of the operation which can detect the condition. The **out** assertion describes the effect of the handler given that upon entry to the handler, the operation **in** assertion assumed equivalent to the parameterized condition name is true. In other words, if one **in-out** assertion pair for the operation that can detect condition C is

    in P **out** C(x)

and the **in-out** pair for a handler for C is

    in C(x) **out** Q

then the body is expected to cause Q to hold given that P holds,

(c) one statement, conditional, loop, or block partially correct with respect to P and Q described above. Note that if Q is false, the statement, conditional, loop or block must end with a **halt** (or a **goto**). However, it may do any number of other things, e.g., print out a message before it halts.

5.5. *What is required of proof rules*

The proof rules required for dealing with forms without exception handling have been described quite well in various Alphard reports [26, 27]. These allow one to prove that the implementation correctly implements the specifications and to use these specifications to prove things about programs using the defined type. The correctness proof is done by showing essentially that the representation map and the invariants are preserved across operation body execution. The proof of use is done by using a procedure proof rule such as adaptation [30, 33] to convert a **pre** and **post** pair of assertions about an operation into an assignment style axiom applicable at a particular call.

In our extended example we have introduced a number of other assertions and have hinted at some relationships these must satisfy for the form to make sense. While it is easy to see what should be demonstrated from the proof rules in specific cases, it is not so easy to see what the general proof rule should be. The development of appropriate proof rules is left as an area for further research.

Furthermore, the placement of assertions and the meanings attached to them suggests, as do Parnas and others [29, 31], that operation bodies cannot have any irreversible side effects on the parameters and shared variables until they have determined that no conditions are to be raised and that the operation will "succeed". In some cases, this is impractical, for a condition may be detectable only, or more conveniently, during the performance of the normal operation. In these cases, complete copies of the parameters would have to be saved just in case the operation were to fail. An example of this is a file merging operation which requires that the input files to be merged be sorted in the same order. Normally, one would simply start merging and during that process if no record is found out of order the operation succeeds. But suppose a record is found out of order. To meet the strict requirement of no side effects, either

(1) the files have to be unmerged (the new file keeps a record of the origin of its records),
(2) copies of the original files are made before or during the merging process, or
(3) the files have to be scanned completely before merging starts.

None of these are attractive due to the high space or time overhead.

Thus some way must be found to relax the no-side-effect requirement and to devise proof rules that can deal with the resultant operation and handler bodies. This is a topic for further research.

6. THE PARTIALLY PROTECTED SOLUTIONS

The ways of opening up a form to permit addition of unanticipated handlers are precisely the ways of opening up a form to permit any kind of variation.

(1) Have a language processing system, e.g., UNIX [37] which permits easy editing of program text and easy incorporation of developed modules into the programming library.
(2) As suggested by von Staa [23] make each part of a form that can vary be a parameter of the form.
(3) As suggested by Lauterbach [38], use a Module Interconnection Language [39, 40] to control construction of a complete type abstraction out of possibly separate pieces giving the specification, the representation, the operations and conditions, and the handlers of the type.

The first way is the least controlled, and we choose not to discuss it any further here.

The second way is already in wide use to define type constructors, e.g., *array* or our own *stack* example, which take types as parameters. Each time such a form name is applied to a type actual parameter, conceptually at least, a whole new form is produced with the actual substituted for each occurrence of the formal. In order to guarantee compile-time checkability these substitutions should be considered to be generated at compile time. Thus, no true type *variables* are allowed.

As long as substitution of actual parameters for formals in a form can be carried out at compile time, there is no reason not to permit objects other than types to be parameters of a type constructor form. Thus, we can permit parameters such as:

(1) constant values to permit definitions of a type constructor such as *array* capable of taking a constant integer dimensionality and an element type as parameters, or
(2) operation procedures to permit varying the meaning or implementation of one or more operations of the type.

To parameterize a handler for a condition is quite straightforward. As an example of the possibilities consider the modified *stack1* form of Fig. 3 which parameterizes the *overflow* handler which is still specified to be the default handler for the *ovfl* condition.

```
form stack1 (t:form < : = ,undefined > , overflow:handler)
    beginform
    specifications
        requires true
        let stack1 = <stack[1], ... ,stack1[i], ... ,stack1[n] >
            where (∀i) ((2 ≤ i ≤ n ⇒ stack1[i] is t) ∧ (stack1[1] is integer))
        invariant 0 ≤ truelength(stack1) ≤ stack1[1]
        initially true
        conditions tsmall,ovfl,popunfl, topunfl

    operations
        create(s:stack1, n:integer)
            pre n > 0 post s = <n >
            pre n ≤ 0 post tsmall(s,n)
        push(s:stack1,x:t)
            pre truelength(s) < s[1] post s = s' @ <x >
            pre truelength(s) ≥ s[1] post ovfl(s)
        pop(s:stack1)
            pre truelength(s) > 0 post s = leader(s')
            pre truelength(s) ≤ 0 post popunfl(s)
        top(s:stack1)returns x:t
            pre truelength(s) > 0 post x = last(s')
            pre truelength(s) ≤ 0 post topunfl(s)
        is_empty(s:stack1]returns b:boolean
            pre true post b = (truelength(s) = 0)
        size(s:stack1)returns n:integer
            pre true post n = truelength(s)
        maxsize(s:stack1)returns n:integer
            pre true post n = s[1]

    handlers
        toosmall(s:stack1, n:integer)
            pre tsmall(s,n) post s = <1 >
        toosmall_and_term(s:stack1, n:integer)
            pre tsmall(s,n) post false
        overflow_and_term(s:stack1, x:t)
            pre ovfl(s,x) post false
        popunderflow(s:stack1)
            pre popunfl(s) post popunfl(s)
        popunderflow_and_term(s:stack1)
            pre popunfl(s) post false
        topunderflow(s:stack1)returns x:t
            pre topunfl(s) post x = undefined
        topunderflow_and_term(s:stack1)returns x:t
            pre topunfl(s) post false
    defaults toosmall,overflow,popunderflow,topunderflow
```

Fig. 3.

```
representation
    unique v:array(t), sp:integer
    rep(v,sp) = <upb(v),v[1],...,v[sp-1]>
    invariant 1 ≤ sp ≤ upb(v) + 1

implementation
    body create in n>0 out upb(s.v)=n ∧ s.sp=1
        in n≤0 out tsmall(s,n):
        if n>0
            then makearray(s.v,1,n);s.sp:=1
            else tsmall(s,n)
        endif;
    body push in s.sp≤upb(s.v) out s.sp=s.sp' + 1 ∧ s.v=(a (s.v',s.sp',x)
        in s.sp>upb(s.v) out ovfl(s,x):
        if s.sp>upb(s.v)
            then ovfl(s,x)
            else s.v[s.sp]:=x; s.sp:=s.sp + 1
        endif;
    body pop in s.sp>1 out s.sp=s.sp' - 1
        in s.sp≤1 out popunfl(s):
        if s.sp≤1
            then popunfl(s)
            else s.sp:=s.sp - 1
        endif;
    body top in s.sp>1 out x=s.v[s.sp - 1]
        in s.sp≤1 out topunfl(s):
        if s.sp≤1
            then topunfl(s)
            else x:=s.v[s.sp - 1]
        endif;
    body is_empty in true out b=(s.sp=1):
        b:=(s.sp=1);
    body size in true out n=s.sp - 1:
        n:=s.sp - 1;
    body maxsize in true out n=upb(s.v):
        n:=upb(s.v);
    body toosmall in tsmall(s,n) out upb(s.v)=1 ∧ s.sp=1:
        (makearray(s.v,1,1); s.sp:=1);
    body toosmall_and_term in tsmall(s,n) out false:
        (print("attempt to create a stack with too small a size:", n, ".");
        halt);
    body overflow_and_term in ovfl(s,x) out false:
        (print("attempt to push into a full stack.");
        halt);
    body popunderflow in popunfl(s) out popunfl(s):
        ;
    body popunderflow_and_term in popunfl(s) out false:
        (print("attempt to pop an empty stack.");
        halt);
    body topunderflow in topunfl(s) out x=undefined:
        x:=undefined;
    body topunderflow_and_term in topunfl(s) out false:
        (print("attempt to take the top of an empty stack.");
        halt);

endform
```

Fig. 3.

Note that there are no specifications and body for the parameterized handler in the form. The first application of the form in Fig. 4 defines a *stack-of-ints* type identical to that defined in Section 5.3, as in this case the actual handler supplied is the same as in the original form of Fig. 1 with *integer* substituted for *t*. The second application in Fig. 4 defines a *more-informative-stack-of-ints* whose default handler for *ovfl* prints some useful information, i.e., what was going to be pushed and at which line the call to push occurred, before "ignoring" the operation request (*linenumber(y)* returns the line number containing the instruction pointed to by the current instruction pointer of the yth block, procedure, or operation activation down the dynamic chain).

```
type stack_of_ints = stack1(integer,
        handler overflow(s:stack1, x:t)
            pre ovfl(s,x) post ovfl(s,x)
        body overflow
            in ovfl(s,x) out ovfl(s,x): ;)

type more_informative_stack_of_ints = stack1(integer,
        handler overflow(s:stack1, x:t)
            pre ovfl(s,x) post ovfl(s,x)
        body overflow
            in ovfl(s,x) out ovfl(s,x):
        print("overflow while attempting to push", x,
            " at a call of push in line no.", linenumber(1));)
```

Fig. 4.

If the language permits partial parameter passing, even more flexibility can be obtained. For example,

```
stack1(,handler overflow(s:stack1,x:t)
            pre ovfl(s,x) post ovfl(s,x)
        body overflow
            in ovfl(s,x) out ovfl(s,x) : ;)
```

yields exactly the type constructor *stack* of Fig. 1.

Under the parameterization proposal as described above, one is required to supply an actual parameter each time the form is applied. A simple syntactic extension would be

(1) to allow a form to provide a default actual parameter for its own formal parameter which is used if no actual is supplied by the user of the form, and

(2) to allow the user to use **default** in place of an actual parameter to indicate that the form-supplied default is to be used.

Note finally that to preserve compile-time type checkability, variability involving actual parameters whose value cannot be resolved until run time, e.g., bounds of arrays as in ALGOL 60, must be done through parameters of the operations including *create* rather than through parameters of the form itself. Thus in the constructor form

```
form array(dimensionality:integer,elem-type:form)

        .

        .

        .

    endform;
```

the *create* operation would need to be able to take $2 * dimensionality$ integer values (lowerbound and upperbound for each dimension) as parameters to be able to allocate a specific array with specific bounds.

Finally, the third way of opening up a form merits careful consideration. It says simply that separate pieces of a form are brought together to build a single abstraction under the control of a module interconnection language (MIL) specification of the abstraction. A piece exists because it might be useful to some abstraction. Access to it by some abstraction is permitted only when granted by a MIL specification of the abstraction. Thus the notion of a fully closed form does not even exist in the first place to have to be broken up. Every piece is introduced as it is needed with access to whatever other pieces it needs access to.

Under this scheme, a new handler could be introduced to a type by specifying and implementing it in one piece. The code of this piece has access to the representation it needs to know. The piece is then checked and introduced to the type by modifying the MIL specification of the type to include the piece and to let the piece access other pieces.

This approach was proposed by Lauterbach as a solution to various other problems requiring violations of the strict encapsulation of complete forms. These include conver-

431

sion operations between two types, the addition of new operations to a type, and sharing of representations and/or code for operations among several types. For more details see [38].

In all of these partially protected solutions, a possible way to help insure that the security of a form is not compromised is to insist that, whatever additional conditions are detected and handlers are provided, the invariants of the representation of the data abstraction and the mapping from a representation state to the implemented abstract object are preserved. Also, if we view handlers as computing a replacement effect and/or returning a replacement value for the operation, it should be required to prove that the handler's output assertion implies that of the operation. Thus, we would be using the proof methodology to help achieve consistent extensions to data abstraction.

7. HANDLERS

We have seen several examples of handlers for exceptions. From these and from the literature [6–8, 10] we can identify five main possibilities for a handlers response to a condition.

(1) Do something and then return a substitute result for the operation giving rise to the condition; if the return type of operation is **void**, this reduces to doing something and returning to the instruction after the one calling the operation.
(2) Do something and explicitly transfer control to some labeled place. This includes doing something and halting the computation (**halt** is a **goto** to the end of the program).
(3) Do something, e.g., fix something, and then return to the calling program in such a way as to retry the operation detecting the condition that raised the exception.
(4) Notify the invoker of the invoker of the operation that the condition has occurred.
(5) Do something and resume the operation.

The first two we have seen before. They are useful where for the given parameters there is no way that the operation can "succeed", e.g., arithmetic underflow or division by zero. The first is useful when a reasonable replacement value can be found, e.g., often zero is a good substitute for an underflowed sum. The first is also useful in cases where something special has to be done in addition to the "normal" operation, some of the times that an operation is done. In this case, the condition is the detection of when the special thing must be done, and the substitute result is the original result itself. The second is useful when no replacement value is meaningful for the particular program and nothing can be done but give up, e.g., the result of the underflowed sum is going to be a denominator in a division.

In order for the first type of a handler to work, it is necessary that the handler have at the least the same parameters and the same return type as the operation that detects the condition of the exception. We also find it necessary, to permit orderly use of replacement handlers in the modification solution, that all handlers for a given condition take the same parameters and return a value of the same type. This is so that each mention of a condition within an operation body can pass the same parameters and be used in the same context regardless of which exception is being triggered at run time.

Also, observe that from an abstract point of view the parameters to the operation detecting the condition are all that any handler needs to know, since the condition name is equivalent to a logical expression involving only these parameters.

The third kind of handler is the most difficult to design properly. It is clear neither how to specify this kind of a response nor what constructs to provide to permit programming such a response. We suspect that some kind of coroutine-like behavior has to be established between the operation and the handler. This issue is left for future work.

The fourth kind of handler has a body which itself raises a condition defined in the module containing the invocation of the operation (which raised the condition which led to the handler's execution). This will require some kind of importation of condition names from the outside or condition name parameters.

Finally, the fifth kind of handler is no more than a subroutine which is called from the invoked operation and which returns to it.

8. DETECTION vs NONDETECTION OF CONDITIONS

The specification of a type determines whether or not a condition of the type will be detected. Thus, the user of a type has no choice as to which conditions are detected, he or she has a choice only of which handler to designate for a condition if the condition has more than one handler associated with it. To change the set of conditions detected by the operations of a type requires a change in the type and, at least conceptually, a new form.

In fact if one considers a type to be the sets of objects, conditions, and handlers described in the specifications of the type, any change in any of the sets is a change in type and a new form is required.

We have seen three ways of modifying a form to change handlers. These three ways can be used to change the conditions detected by the form. In particular, parameterization can be used.

```
form stack2 (t:form < : = ,undefined >, create:operation)
    beginform
    specifications
        requires true
        let stack2 = <stack2[1], ... ,stack2[i], ... ,stack2[n] >
            where (∀i) ((2 ≤ i ≤ n ⇒ stack2[i] is t) ∧ (stack2[1] is integer))
        invariant 0 ≤ truelength(stack2) ≤ stack2[1]
        initially true
            conditions tsmall,ovfl,popunfl,topunfl

    operations
        push(s:stack2,x:t)
            pre truelength(s)<s[1] post s=s' (a  <x>
            pre truelength(s)≥s[1] post ovfl(s)
        pop(s:stack2)
            pre truelength(s)>0 post s=leader(s')
            pre truelength(s)≤0 post popunfl(s)
        top(s:stack2) returns x:t
            pre truelength(s)>0 post x=last(s')
            pre truelength(s)≤0 post topunfl(s)
        is empty (s:stack2)returns b:boolean
            pre true post b=(truelength(s)=0)
        size(s:stack2)returns n:integer
            pre true post n=truelength(s)
        maxsize(s:stack2)returns n:inteter
            pre true post n=s[1]

    handlers
        toosmall(s:stack2,n:integer)
            pre tsmall(s,n) post s= <1>
        toosmall_and_term(s:stack2, n:integer)
            pre tsmall(s,n) post false
        overflow(s:stack2, x:t)
            pre ovfl(s,x) post ovfl(s,x) ¢ i.e., does nothing ¢
        overflow_and_term(s:stack2, x:t)
            pre ovfl(s,x) post false
        popunderflow(s:stack2)
            pre popunfl(s) post popunfl(s)
        popunderflow_and_term(s:stack2)
            pre popunfl(s) post false
        topunderflow(s:stack2)returns x:t
            pre topunfl(s) post x=undefined
        topunderflow_and_term(s:stack2)returns x:t
            pre topunfl(s) post false
        defaults toosmall,overflow,popunderflow,topunderflow

    representation
        unique v:array(t), sp:integer
        rep(v,sp) = <upb(v),v[1], ... ,v[sp-1] >
        invariant 1 ≤ sp ≤ upb(v) + 1
```

Fig. 5.

Fig. 5 (*continued*)

```
implementation
    body push in s.sp ≤ upb(s.v) out s.sp = s.sp' + 1 ∧ s.v = (a (s.v',s.sp',x)
              in s.sp > upb(s.v) out ovfl(s,x):
        if s.sp > upb(s.v)
            then ovfl(s,x)
            else s.v[s.sp]: = x; s.sp: = s.sp + 1
        endif;
    body pop in s.sp > 1 out s.sp = s.sp' - 1
             in s.sp ≤ 1 out popunfl(s):
        if s.sp ≤ 1
            then popunfl(s)
            else s.sp: = s.sp - 1
        endif;
    body top in s.sp > 1 out x = s.v[s.sp - 1]
             in s.sp ≤ 1 out topunfl(s):
        if s.sp ≤ 1
            then topunfl(s)
            else x: = s.v[s.sp - 1]
        endif;
    body is_empty in true out b = (s.sp = 1):
        b: = (s.sp = 1);
    body size in true out n = s.sp - 1:
        n: = s.sp - 1;
    body maxsize in true out n = upb(s.v):
        n: = upb(s.v);
    body toosmall in tsmall(s,n) out upb(s.v) = 1 ∧ s.sp = 1:
        (makearray(s.v,1,1); s.sp: = 1;
    body toosmall_and_term in tsmall(s,n) out false:
        (print("attempt to create a stack with too small a size:", n, ".");
        halt);
    body overflow in ovfl(s,x) out ovfl(s,x):
        ¢ does nothing ¢;
    body overflow_and_term in ovfl(s,x) out false:
        (print("attempt to push into a full stack.");
        halt);
    body popunderflow in popunfl(s) out popunfl(s):

    body popunderflow_and_term in popunfl(s) out false:
        (print("attempt to pop an empty stack.");
        halt);
    body topunderflow in topunfl(s) out x = undefined:
        x: = undefined;
    body topunderflow_and_term in topunfl(s) out false:
        (print("attempt to take the top of an empty stack.");
        halt);
endform
```

Fig. 5.

Parameterizing a condition requires parameterizing an operation, because it is the operation that detects the condition. As an example, consider the modified *stack2* form of Fig. 5 which parameterizes the *create* operation to parameterize the *tsmall* condition. Note that the form has no specification and no body for the parameterized operation. Figure 6 shows two types defined by application of the form. One is *stack-of-ints* which is identical to that of Section 5.3 because the actual *create* operation supplied is the same as for the form of Fig. 1. The second type defined is *large-stack-of-ints* which requires that the maximum size of the stack be greater than 100 and otherwise raises the *tsmall* condition.

9. PASSING EXCEPTIONAL CONDITIONS ON

It has already been mentioned that the treatment of an exceptional condition as an intrinsic part of the abstract type to which the detecting operation belongs imposes a certain discipline on passing an exceptional condition from the operation's invoker to its invoker's invoker. The exception, which is meaningful at the operation's level of abstraction must be rephrased to be meaningful at the invoker's level of abstraction. Further, it

434

```
type stack_of_ints = stack2(integer,
        operation create(s:stack2, n:integer)
            pre n>0 post s= <n>
            pre n≤0 post tsmall(s,n)
        body create
            in n>0 out upb(s.v)=n ∧ s.sp=1
            in n≤0 out tsmall(s,n):
        if n>0
            then makearray(s.v,1,n); s.sp:=1
            else tsmall(s,n)
        endif;)

type large_stack_of_ints = stack2(integer,
        operation create(s:stack2, n:integer)
            pre n>100 post s= <n>
            pre n≤100 out tsmall(s,n):
        body create
            in n>100 out upb(s.v)=n ∧ s.sp=1
            in n≤100 out tsmall(s,n):
        if n>100
            then makearray(s.v,1,n); s.sp:=1
            else tsmall(s,n)
        endif;)
```

Fig. 6.

has been indicated parenthetically that outright termination of a computation is not an appropriate response to many exceptional conditions, rather it may be more appropriate to pass the condition, albeit rephrased, on to one's invoker. This section considers as an example a condition reported by an operation of the *array* type to the *stack* form of Fig. 1 and shows several ways in which the *stack* form may deal with the condition.

Suppose that one-dimensional arrays of t's are defined by the form

form array(t:**form** < : =, ... >)

.

.

.

endform

and that among its operations is the *makearray* operation specified as follows:

makearray(a:array, l,u:integer)
        pre u-l+1⩾0 ∧ **not** insufficient_memory_for_array_of_length(u-l+1)
            post lwb(a)=1 ∧ upb(a)=u
        pre u-l+1⩾0 ∧ insufficient_memory_for_array_of_length(u-l+1)
            post nospace(a,l,u)
        pre u-l+1<0
            post lwb(a)=1 ∧ upb(a)=l-1.

That is, if an array with lower bound *l* and upper bound *u* would have nonnegative length then either *a* is set with an undefined array with those bounds or there is insufficient memory to allocate the requested array and the nospace(a,l,u) condition is raised. This is in fact the operation used in the implementation part of the *stack* form in Fig. 1. The other array operations were given with the usual syntactic sugar.

Suppose additionally, that in the *array* form there are two handlers supplied for the *nospace(a,l,u) condition.*

(1) outofspace_and_term(a:array, l,u:integer)

        pre nospace(a,l,u) **post** false

which prints an error message ("Insufficient memory for an array with bounds," , *l*, "," , u ".") and then halts.

435

(2) outofspace(a:array, l,u:integer)

> **pre** nospace(a,l,u) **post** lwb(a)=1 $\land$ upb(a)=l-1

which just gives to *a* an empty array with lower bound *l*.

In the *stack* form the bodies of the *create* operation and the *toosmall* handler make use of the *makearray* operation of the *array* form. Were these bodies to designate the *outofspace_and_term* handlers, then there is a possibility that creation of a stack would result in program termination plus a cryptic message about insufficient space for an array. This compromises modularity, for officially the user is not even aware that stacks are implemented with arrays. It has also become unpredictable as to whether or not the create operation will halt. Observe that in this case, the specifications of the *stack create* could be left as they are, for the meaning of a **pre-post** assertion pair is that if the **pre** assertion holds, and *if* execution ever arrives at the end of the operation, then the **post** assertion holds.

On the other hand, if the *outofspace* handler were to be designated by the bodies, there is a possibility that even when a stack of height greater than zero has been requested, a stack of height zero results. The specification of the *stack create* operation would now have to read

> create(s:stack, n:integer)
> > **pre** n>0 **post** s= $<$n$>$ $\lor$ s= $<$0$>$
> > **pre** n $\leqslant$ 0 **post** tsmall(s,n).

An element of unpredictability has been introduced; one cannot predict what size the stack will end up being.

The unpredictability that results from choosing either of the *array*-form-provided handlers is a direct consequence of leaving the handlers defined at the *array* level of abstraction to deal with the *nospace* condition. There is no way that these handlers can know about how the arrays are used, and thus, there is no way that they could consciously do something meaningful at the user's level of abstraction. In essence, their behavior is hidden from the user of the *stack* abstraction.

In order for the *nospace* condition to be reflected in a meaningful way to the user of the *stack* abstraction, it is necessary for the implementation of the *stack* form to provide its own handler for the array *nospace* condition and for this handler to raise a condition that is meaningful to the *stack* abstraction. For example, the condition *lackspace* could be added to the *stack* form's condition list and the handler,

> [**handler** pass_on_outofspace(a:array, l,u:integer)
> > **pre** nospace(a,l,u)
> > **post** lackspace(s,n)
>
> **body** pass_on_outofspace
> > **in** nospace(a,l,u)
> > **out** lackspace(s,n) :lackspace(s,n)],

could be prefixed to the bodies of the *stack* form's *create* operation and *toosmall* handler. When the *array nospace* condition is raised, this handler would simply raise the *stack* form's *lackspace* condition. The addition of this handler requires several other changes to the *stack* form. In the **specifications** part, one reads:

> create(s:stack, n:integer)
> > **pre** n>0 $\land$ **not** insufficient_memory_for_stack_of_height(n)
> > > **post** s= $<$n$>$
> >
> > **pre** n>0 $\land$ insufficient_memory_for_stack_of_height(n)
> > > **post** lackspace(s,n)
> >
> > **pre** n $\leqslant$ 0
> > > **post** tsmall(s,n)

and

toosmall(s:stack, n:integer)
     pre tsmall(s,n) $\wedge$ **not** insufficient_memory(1)
          post s = <1>
     pre tsmall(s,n) $\wedge$ insufficient_memory(1)
          post lackspace(s,n)

In the **implementation** part, one reads:

     body create
          in n>0 $\wedge$ **not** insufficient_memory_for_array_of_length(n)
               out upb(s,v)=n $\wedge$ s.sp=1
          in n>0 $\wedge$ insufficient_memory_for_array_of_length(n)
               out lackspace(s,n)
          in n$\leqslant$0
               out tsmall(s,n)
     ¢ pass_on_outofspace handler ¢:
          ¢ same body as before ¢

and

     body toosmall
          in tsmall(s,n) $\wedge$ **not** insufficient_memory(1)
               out upb(s.v)=1 $\wedge$ s.sp=1
          in tsmall(s,n) $\wedge$ insufficient_memory(1)
               out lackspace(s,n)
          ¢ pass_on_outofspace handler ¢
               ¢ same body as before ¢

At this point, whenever there is insufficient memory to allocate an array of the requested size, the *stack* form raises the *lackspace* condition. Three possible handlers for *lackspace* are specified and implemented below.

handlers

     lackspace_and_term(s:stack, n:integer)
          pre lackspace(s,n)
               post false
     lackspace_and_give_empty(s:stack, n:integer)
          pre lackspace(s,n)
               post s = <0>
     lackspace_and_give_what_is_possible(s:stack, n:integer)
          pre lackspace(s,n)
               post ($\exists$m) (0$\leqslant$m<n $\wedge$ s = <n>)

implementation

     body lackspace_and_term
          in lackspace(s,n) **out** false:
               (print("not enough space for stack of size", n, ".");
               halt);
     body lackspace_and_give_empty
          in lackspace(s,n) **out** upb(s.v)=0 $\wedge$ s.sp=1:
               (makearray(s.v,1,0); s.sp=1);

```
body lackspace_and_give_what_is_possible
    in lackspace(s,n) out (∃m) (0≤m<n ∧ upb(s.v)=m ∧ s.sp=1)
        (var succeed: boolean,
             i: integer;
         succeed := false; i :=n;
         [handler outofspace_indicate(a:array, l,u:integer)
             pre nospace(a,l,u) post succeed=false
         body outofspace_indicate
             in nospace(a.l.u) out succeed=false:
                 succeed := false;]:
         while i≥0 ∧ not succeed
             do succeed := true;
                makearray(s,v,l,i);
                i := i - 1
         endwhile;
         s.sp :=1);
```

The first handler is a terminating handler which prints a message relevant to *stack* creation. The second is a forgiving handler which just gives an empty stack. The third is also a forgiving handler. It finds the largest stack that can be given and gives it. Note the necessity of having a new handler for the *array nospace* condition within the body of the handler. If this new handler were not given, the program would go into an infinite loop alternately raising the *array nospace* condition and the *stack lackspace* condition. The scope of the internal handler is the **while** loop.

These examples demonstrate how conditions may be passed from one level of abstraction to another. The only requirement is that the condition be re-expressed in terms meaningful to the higher level abstraction.

10. CONCLUSIONS

It was first recognized that the very problem of verifiable, modular exception handling is that the information needed to implement a handler may not be visible at the spot where what the handler is supposed to do can be determined, i.e., at the spot of operation invocation.

Two classes of solutions were proposed. One requires full anticipation of all possible handlers or at least all operations that would be used to program these handlers. The needed proof rules and how the type designer might anticipate what is needed were briefly discussed. The other class of solutions require modification of the type defining form through either outright modification, parameterization, or MIL-directed assembling of the form. The merits and problems of each were briefly noted.

Also discussed were the kinds of things handlers are expected to be able to do in response to a condition in an operation. These include returning a substitute value for the operation, transferring control to some designated label, retrying the operation, and notifying the invoker of the invoker of the operation that the condition has occurred. The last two need more work to be able to specify and implement them in the context of our proposals.

Thus, in this paper only the surface has been scratched, and the issues have been identified. Further research should hopefully lead to their resolution.

REFERENCES

1. J. B. Dennis, Modularity, *Advanced Course in Software Engineering* (Edited by F. L. Bauer). Springer-Verlag, Berlin (1973).
2. D. L. Parnas, A technique for the specification of software modules, *CACM* **15** (1972).
3. D. L. Parnas, On the criteria to be used in decomposing systems into modules, *CACM* **15** (1972).
4. G. J. Myers, *Reliable Software through Composite Design*. Petrocelli/Charter, New York (1975).

5. D. D. Cowan, C. J. Lucena and A. von Staa, On the concept of modules in programming systems, *Report CS-76-05*, Faculty of Mathematics, University of Waterloo, January (1976).

6. J. B. Goodenough, Structured exception handling, *Second ACM Symposium on Principles of Programming Languages*, January (1975).

7. J. B. Goodenough, Exception handling: issues and a proposed notation, *CACM* **18** (1975).

8. J. M. Noble, The control of exceptional conditions in PL/1 object programs, *Proc. IFIP Congress 68* (1968).

9. R. A. Kemmerer, A STRIMULA 76 debugging system, Internal memo No. 149, Computer Science Dept., UCLA (1976).

10. R. Levin, Programming structures for exceptional condition handling, Ph.D. Thesis, Computer Science Department, Carnegie Mellon University (1977).

11. *OS Pl/1 Checkout and Optimizing Compilers: Language Reference Manual*, SC33-0009-2, IBM Corp. (1973).

12. J. T. Schwartz, On Programming, an Interim Report on the SETL Project. Department of Computer Science, Courant Institute, NYU, New York (1973).

13. J. B. Morris, A Comparison of MADCAP and SETL, Los Alamos Laboratory, University of California, Los Alamos, New Mexico (1973).

14. C. H. Lauterbach, M. A. Melkanoff and B. C. Moszkowski, Abstract data types in MADCAP-VI, Internal memo No. 140, Computer Science Dept., UCLA (1975).

15. C. A. R. Hoare, Proof of correctness of data representations, *Acta Inform.* **1** (1972).

16. C. A. R. Hoare and N. Wirth, An axiomatic definition of the programming language PASCAL, *Acta Inform.* **2** (1973).

17. S. N. Zilles, Algebraic Specification of Data Types. *MIT Project MAC Progress Report 11* (1975).

18. J. V. Guttag, The Specification and Application to Programming of Abstract Data Types, *CSRG-59*, University of Toronto (1975).

19. J. A. Goguen, J. W. Thatcher, E. G. Wagner and J. B. Wright, Abstract data types as initial algebras and correctness of data representations, *Proc. Conf. Computer Graphics, Pattern Recognition, and Data Structures*, (1975).

20. B. H. Liskov and S. N. Zilles, Specification techniques for data abstractions, *IEEE TSE* **1** (1975).

21. O. J. Dahl, B. Myhrhaug and K. Nygaard, Common base language, *Report S-22*, Norwegian Computing Center, Oslo, Norway (1970).

22. J. Palme, Protected program modules in SIMULA 67, *FOA-P Report C8372-M3(E5)*, Research Institute of National Defense, OR Center, Stockholm, Sweden (1973).

23. A. von Staa, Data transmission and modularity aspects of programming languages, Ph.D. Thesis, Department of Applied Analysis and Computer Science, University of Waterloo (1974).

24. B. H. Liskov and S. N. Zilles, Programming with abstract data types, *SIGPLAN Notices* **9** (1974).

25. B. W. Lampson, J. J. Horning, R. L. London, J. G. Mitchell and G. J. Popek, Report on the programming language Euclid, *SIGPLAN Notices* **12** (1977).

26. W. A. Wulf, R. L. London and M. Shaw, Abstraction and verification in Alphard: introduction to language and methodology. *USC ISI Tech. Report* (1976).

27. W. A. Wulf, R. L. London and M. Shaw, An introduction to the construction and verification of Alphard programs, *IEEE TSE* **2** (1976).

28. R. Milner, An algebraic definition of simulation between programs, *Report CS205*, Computer Science Dept., Stanford University (1971).

29. D. L. Parnas, Response to detected errors in well-structured programs, Computer Science Department, Carnegie-Mellon University (1972).

30. J. V. Guttag, E. Horowitz and D. R. Musser, Some extensions to algebraic specifications, *SIGPLAN Notices* **12** (1977).

31. J. A. Goguen, Abstract errors for abstract data types, *Formal Description of Programming Concepts* (Edited by E. Neuhold). North-Holland, Amsterdam (1978).

32. Preliminary Ada Reference Manual, *SIGPLAN Notices* **14** (1979).

33. S. Igarashi, R. L. London and D. C. Luckham, Automatic program verification I: a logical basis and its implementation, *Acta Inform.* **4** (1975).

34. C. A. R. Hoare, Procedures and parameters: an axiomatic approach, *Proceedings of the Symposium on Semantics of Algorithmic Languages* (Edited by E. Engler), Springer-Verlag, Berlin (1971).

35. J. V. Guttag, J. J. Horning and R. L. London, A proof rule for Euclid procedures, *Proc. IFIP Working Conference on Formal Description of Programming Concepts* (1977).

36. A. van Wijngaarden *et al.*, Revised report on the algorithmic language ALGOL 68, *Acta Inform.* **5** (1975).

37. D. M. Ritchie and K. Thompson, The UNIX time sharing system, *CACM* **17** (1974).

38. C. H. Lauterbach, Hierarchical organization of data types for program modularity, Ph.D. Thesis, Computer Science Department, UCLA (1977).

39. F. DeRemer and H. H. Kron, Programming-in-the-large versus programming-in-the-small, *IEEE TSE* **2** (1976).

40. J. W. Thomas, Module interconnection in programming systems supporting abstraction, *Computer Science Program Technical Report No. CS-16*, Division of Applied Mathematics, Brown University (1976).

About the Author—DANIEL M. BERRY was born in Cleveland Heights, Ohio in 1948. He received his B.S. in Mathematics from Rensselar Polytechnic Institute (1969). He went to graduate school at Brown University, during which time he worked at General Electric R&D Center in Schenectady, New York and taught at the Hebrew University in Jerusalem, Israel. He joined the UCLA faculty as an Acting Assistant Professor in September, 1972. After some delay he completed his Ph.D. Thesis in September, 1973 for his degree in Computer Science from Brown. Shortly thereafter he was promoted to Assistant Professor. In 1977 he became an Associate Professor. During the 1978–1979 academic year he spent a sabbatical at the Weizmann Institute and Hebrew University in Israel. At various times during his tenure at UCLA, he has visited Pontificia

Universidade Católica in Rio de Janeiro, Brasil, Pontifícia Universidad Católica in Santiago, Chile, Politecnico di Milano, Italia, Jet Propulsion Laboratory, Pasadena, California, and Tadiran and Israeli Aircraft Industries in Israel.

Dr Berry is a member of the ACM and of the IEEE.

About the Author—RICHARD A. KEMMERER was born in Allentown, Pennsylvania in 1943. He received his B.S. in Mathematics from the Pennsylvania State University (1966). From 1966 to 1974 he worked as a programmer and systems consultant for North American Rockwell and the Institute of Transportation and Traffic Engineering at UCLA. He began graduate school at UCLA in 1974 where he received his M.S. in Computer Science (1976) and his Ph.D. in Computer Science (1979). During his last year at UCLA he held an IBM fellowship. He is presently an Assistant Professor at the University of California, Santa Barbara. His research interests include formal verification, software engineering, and secure systems.

Dr Kemmerer is a member of the ACM.

About the Author—ARNDT VON STAA received the B.Eng. degree in Mechanical Engineering (1965) and the M.Sc. degree in Computer Science (1969), both from Pontifícia Universidade Católica do Rio de Janeiro, Brasil, (PUC/RJ) and the Ph.D. degree in Computer Science (1974) from University of Waterloo, Waterloo, Ontario, Canada. From 1962 to 1965 he worked as a programmer, later as an analyst at the Computing Center of PUC/RJ. In 1967 he joined the faculty of the Departamento de Informática at PUC/RJ, where he is an Associate Professor since 1975. His research activities center around software engineering and computer organization.

About the Author—SHAULA YEMINI received her B.S. (1971) and M.S. (1972), from the Hebrew University in Israel. She is currently a Ph.D. candidate in the Computer Science Department at UCLA. She is a member of the ACM.

Section 8
Programming Language Design Experience

One of the best ways to gain insight into the process of language design is to examine features of some recently designed languages in papers that include discussion of the design process, especially as to why certain features were incorporated into the respective languages. All of the languages described in this section have been designed and implemented within the past five years, each with somewhat different goals in mind.

CLU was the first language to incorporate the notion of data abstractions. In addition to that feature, CLU included numerous other design advances, among them the exception-handling facility described in the previous section and an abstraction mechanism for iteration. The paper by Liskov and colleagues describes the abstraction mechanisms of CLU, along with their design rationale.

Gypsy was designed by Don Good and colleagues to support the simultaneous specification and implementation of programs as a means to achieve verifiable software. Gypsy is intended primarily for realtime applications, such as communications systems. One of the interesting features of Gypsy is that it has no global variables and requires that all data be passed explicitly. Experience in the use of Gypsy has shown that the number of parameters passed between program units can be minimized through judicious use of structured variables.

Brinch Hansen's Concurrent Pascal is an extension of Pascal that incorporates data abstractions and monitors. It has been used to implement a well-structured operating system (Solo) for the PDP-11 operating system. The paper by Brinch Hansen describes those features of Concurrent Pascal that are extensions of Pascal.

PLAIN, designed by Wasserman and colleagues, is intended to support the systematic construction of interactive information systems, including string handling, data abstraction, and relational data base management facilities. Although based on Pascal, PLAIN addresses some of the trouble spots in Pascal, as Wasserman's paper explains.

Mesa, designed at Xerox Palo Alto Research Center, was intended as a system implementation language. Mesa has seen extensive use by the Xerox programmers to implement a variety of sophisticated systems. The paper by Geschke, Morris, and Satterthwaite describes some of that experience. It is particularly interesting to note those places where the Mesa programmers found it necessary to escape from the type checking requirements of the language and take advantage of loopholes.

Language Design for   S.L. Graham
Reliable Software   Editor

Abstraction Mechanisms in CLU

Barbara Liskov, Alan Snyder,
Russell Atkinson, and Craig Schaffert
Massachusetts Institute of Technology

Reprinted from *Communications of the ACM,* August 1977, pp. 564-576. Copyright
1977 Association for Computing Machinery, Inc. Reprinted by permission.

CLU is a new programming language designed to
support the use of abstractions in program
construction. Work in programming methodology has
led to the realization that three kinds of abstractions —
procedural, control, and especially data abstractions —
are useful in the programming process. Of these, only
the procedural abstraction is supported well by
conventional languages, through the procedure or
subroutine. CLU provides, in addition to procedures,
novel linguistic mechanisms that support the use of data
and control abstractions. This paper provides an
introduction to the abstraction mechanisms in CLU. By
means of programming examples, the utility of the
three kinds of abstractions in program construction is
illustrated, and it is shown how CLU programs may be
written to use and implement abstractions. The CLU
library, which permits incremental program
development with complete type checking performed
at compile time, is also discussed.

Key Words and Phrases: programming languages,
data types, data abstractions, control abstractions,
programming methodology, separate compilation
CR Categories: 4.0, 4.12, 4.20, 4.22

1. Introduction

The motivation for the design of the CLU programing language was to provide programmers with a tool that would enhance their effectiveness in constructing programs of high quality—programs that are reliable and reasonably easy to understand, modify, and maintain. CLU aids programmers by providing constructs that support the use of abstractions in program design and implementation.

The quality of software depends primarily on the programming methodology in use. The choice of programming language, however, can have a major impact on the effectiveness of a methodology. A methodology can be easy or difficult to apply in a given language, depending on how well the language constructs match the structures that the methodology deems desirable. The presence of constructs that give a concrete form for the desired structures makes the methodology more understandable. In addition, a programming language influences the way that its users think about programming; matching a language to a methodology increases the likelihood that the methodology will be used.

CLU has been designed to support a methodology (similar to [6, 22]) in which programs are developed by means of problem decomposition based on the recognition of abstractions. A program is constructed in many stages. At each stage, the problem to be solved is how to implement some abstraction (the initial problem is to implement the abstract behavior required of the entire program). The implementation is developed by envisioning a number of subsidiary abstractions (abstract objects and operations) that are useful in the problem domain. Once the behavior of the abstract objects and operations has been defined, a program can be written to solve the original problem; in this program, the abstract objects and operations are used as primitives. Now the original problem has been solved, but new problems have arisen, namely, how to implement the subsidiary abstractions. Each of these abstractions is considered in turn as a new problem; its implementation may introduce further abstractions. This process terminates when all the abstractions introduced at various stages have been implemented or are present in the programming language in use.

In this methodology, programs are developed incrementally, one abstraction at a time. Further, a distinction is made between an abstraction, which is a kind of behavior, and a program, or *module*, which implements that behavior. An abstraction isolates use from implementation: an abstraction can be used without knowledge of its implementation and implemented without knowledge of its use. These aspects of the methodology are supported by the CLU *library*, which maintains information about abstractions and the CLU modules that implement them. The library permits separate compilation of modules with complete type checking at compile time.

To make effective use of the methodology, it is necessary to understand the kinds of abstractions that are useful in constructing programs. In studying this question, we identified an important kind of abstraction, the data abstraction, that had been largely neglected in discussions of programming methodology.

A data abstraction [8, 12, 20] is used to introduce a new type of data object that is deemed useful in the domain of the problem being solved. At the level of use, the programmer is concerned with the *behavior* of these data objects, what kinds of information can be stored in them and obtained from them. The programmer is *not* concerned with how the data objects are represented in storage nor with the algorithms used to store and access information in them. In fact, a data abstraction is often introduced to delay such implementation decisions until a later stage of design.

The behavior of the data objects is expressed most naturally in terms of a set of operations that are meaningful for those objects. This set includes operations to create objects, to obtain information from them, and possibly to modify them. For example, push and pop are among the meaningful operations for stacks, while meaningful operations for integers include the usual arithmetic operations. Thus a data abstraction consists of a set of objects and a set of operations characterizing the behavior of the objects.

If a data abstraction is to be understandable at an abstract level, the behavior of the data objects must be *completely* characterized by the set of operations. This property is ensured by making the operations the *only direct means* of creating and manipulating the objects. One effect of this restriction is that, when defining an abstraction, the programmer must be careful to include a sufficient set of operations, since every action he wishes to perform on the objects must be realized in terms of this set.

We have identified the following requirements that must be satisfied by a language supporting data abstractions:

1. A linguistic construct is needed that permits a data abstraction to be implemented as a unit. The implementation involves selecting a representation for the data objects and defining an algorithm for each operation in terms of that representation.

2. The language must limit access to the representation to just the operations. This limitation is necessary to ensure that the operations completely characterize the behavior of the objects.

CLU satisfies these requirements by providing a linguistic construct called a *cluster* for implementing data abstractions. Data abstractions are integrated into the language through the data type mechanism. Access to the representation is controlled by type checking, which is done at compile time.

In addition to data abstractions, CLU supports two other kinds of abstractions: procedural abstractions and control abstractions. A procedural abstraction performs a computation on a set of input objects and produces a set of output objects; examples of procedural abstractions are sorting an array and computing a square root. CLU supports procedural abstractions by means of procedures, which are similar to procedures in other programming languages.

A control abstraction defines a method for sequencing arbitrary actions. All languages provide built-in control abstractions; examples are the **if** statement and the **while** statement. In addition, however, CLU allows user definitions of a simple kind of control abstraction. The method provided is a generalization of the repetition methods available in many programming languages. Frequently the programmer desires to perform the same action for all the objects in a collection, such as all characters in a string or all items in a set. CLU provides a linguistic construct called an *iterator* for defining how the objects in the collection are obtained. The iterator is used in conjunction with the **for** statement; the body of the **for** statement describes the action to be taken.

The purpose of this paper is to illustrate the utility of the three kinds of abstractions in program construction and to provide an informal introduction to CLU. We do not attempt a complete description of the language; rather, we concentrate on the constructs that support abstractions. The presence of these constructs constitutes the most important way in which CLU differs from other languages. The language closest to CLU is Alphard [24], which represents a concurrent design effort with goals similar to our own. The design of CLU has been influenced by Simula 67 [4] and to a lesser extent by Pascal [23] and Lisp [15].

In the next section we introduce CLU and, by means of a programming example, illustrate the use and implementation of data abstractions. Section 3 describes the basic semantics of CLU. In Section 4, we discuss control abstractions and more powerful kinds of data abstractions. We present the CLU library in Section 5. Section 6 briefly describes the current implementation of CLU and discusses efficiency considerations. Finally, we conclude by discussing the quality of CLU programs.

2. An Example of Data Abstraction

This section introduces the basic data abstraction mechanism of CLU, the cluster. By means of an example, we intend to show how abstractions occur naturally in program design and how they are used and implemented in CLU. In particular, we show how a data abstraction can be used as structured intermediate storage.

Consider the following problem: given some document, we wish to compute, for each distinct word in the document, the number of times the word occurs and its frequency of occurrence as a percentage of the total number of words. The document will be represented as a sequence of characters. A word is any nonempty sequence of alphabetic characters. Adjacent words are separated by one or more nonalphabetic characters such as spaces, punctuation, or newline characters. In recognizing distinct words, the difference between upper and lower case letters should be ignored.

The output is also to be a sequence of characters, divided into lines. Successive lines should contain an alphabetical list of all the distinct words in the document, one word per line. Accompanying each word should be the total number of occurrences and the frequency of occurrence. For example:

a	2	3.509%
access	1	1.754%
and	2	3.509%

Specifically, we are required to write the procedure *count_words*, which takes two arguments: an *instream* and an *outstream*. The former is the source of the document to be processed, and the latter is the destination of the required output. The form of this procedure will be

count_words = **proc** (i: instream, o: outstream);

   . . .

   end count_words;

Note that *count_words* does not return any results; its only effects are modifications of *i* (reading the entire document) and of *o* (printing the required statistics).

Instream and *outstream* are data abstractions. An *instream i* contains a sequence of characters. Of the primitive operations on *instreams*, only two will be of interest to us. *Empty* (*i*) returns **true** if there are no characters available in *i* and returns **false** otherwise. *Next* (*i*) removes the first character from the sequence and returns it. Invoking the *next* operation on an empty *instream* is an error.[1] An *outstream* also contains a sequence of characters. The interesting operation on *outstreams* is *put_string* (*s*, *o*), which appends the string *s* to the existing sequence of characters in *o*.

Now consider how we might implement *count_words*. We begin by deciding how to handle words. We could define a new abstract data type *word*. However, we choose instead to use strings (a primitive CLU type), with the restriction that only strings of lower case alphabetic characters will be used.[2]

Next we investigate how to scan the document. Reading a word requires knowledge of the exact way in which words occur in the input stream. We choose to isolate this information in a procedural abstraction, called *next_word*, which takes in the *instream i* and returns the next word (converted to lower case charac-

---

[1] The CLU error handling mechanism is discussed in [10].

[2] Sometimes it is difficult to decide whether to introduce a new data abstraction or to use an existing abstraction. Our decision to use strings to represent words was made partly to shorten the presentation.

ters) in the document. If there are no more words, *next_word* must communicate this fact to *count_words*. A simple way to indicate that there are no more words is by returning an "end of document" word, one that is distinct from any other word. A reasonable choice for the "end of document" word is the empty string.

It is clear that in *count_words* we must scan the entire document before we can print our results, and therefore we need some receptacle to retain information about words between these two actions (scanning and printing). Recording the information gained in the scan and organizing it for easy printing will probably be fairly complex. Therefore we defer such considerations until later by introducing a data abstraction *wordbag* with the appropriate properties. In particular, *wordbag* provides three operations: *create*, which creates an empty *wordbag*; *insert*, which adds a word to the *wordbag*; and *print*, which prints the desired statistical information about the words in the *wordbag*.[3]

The implementation of *count_words* is shown in Figure 1. The "%" character starts a comment, which continues to the end of the line. The "~" character stands for boolean negation. The notation *variable: type* is used in formal argument lists and declarations to specify the types of variables; a declaration may be combined with an assignment specifying the initial value of the variable. Boldface is used for reserved words, including the names of primitive CLU types.

The *count_words* procedure declares four variables: *i*, *o*, *wb*, and *w*. The first two denote the *instream* and *outstream* that are passed as arguments to *count_words*. The third, *wb*, denotes the *wordbag* used to hold the words read so far, and the fourth, *w*, the word currently being processed.

Operations of a data abstraction are named by a compound form that specifies both the type and the operation name. Three examples of operation calls appear in *count_words*: *wordbag$create( )*, *wordbag$insert (wb, w)* and *wordbag$print (wb, o)*. The CLU system provides a mechanism that avoids conflicts between names of abstractions; this mechanism is discussed in Section 5. However, operations of two different data abstractions may have the same name; the compound form serves to resolve this ambiguity. Although the ambiguity could in most cases be resolved by context, we have found in using CLU that the compound form enhances the readability of programs.

The implementation of *next_word* is shown in Figure 2. The *string$append* operation creates a new string by appending a character to the characters in the string argument (it does *not* modify the string argument). Note the use of the *instream* operations *next* and *empty*. Note also that two additional procedures have been used: *alpha (c)*, which tests whether a character is alphabetic or not, and *lower_case (c)*, which returns the lower case version of a character. The implementations

---

[3] The *print* operation is not the ideal choice, but a better solution requires the use of control abstractions. This solution is presented in Section 4.

Fig. 1. The *count_words* procedure.

```
count_words = proc (i: instream, o: outstream);
  % create an empty wordbag
  wb: wordbag := wordbag$create ( );
  % scan document, adding each word found to wb
  w: string := next_word (i);
  while w ~= " " do
    wordbag$insert (wb, w);
    w := next_word (i);
    end;
  % print the wordbag
  wordbag$print (wb, o);
  end count_words;
```

Fig. 2. The *next_word* procedure.

```
next_word = proc (i: instream) returns (string);
  c: char := '';
  % scan for first alphabetic character
  while ~alpha (c) do
    if instream$empty (i)
      then return " ";
      end;
    c := instream$next (i);
    end;
  % accumulate characters in word
  w: string := " ";
  while alpha (c) do
    w := string$append (w, c);
    if instream$empty (i)
      then return (w);
      end;
    c := instream$next (i);
    end;
  return (w);      % the nonalphabetic character c is lost
  end next_word;
```

of these procedures are not shown in the paper.

Now we must implement the type *wordbag*. The cluster will have the form

```
wordbag = cluster is create, insert, print;

  . . .

  end wordbag;
```

This form expresses the idea that the data abstraction is a set of operations as well as a set of objects. The cluster must provide a representation for objects of the type *wordbag* and an implementation for each of the operations. We are free to choose from the possible representations the one best suited to our use of the *wordbag* cluster.

The representation that we choose should allow reasonably efficient storage of words and easy printing, in alphabetic order, of the words and associated statistics. For efficiency in computing the statistics, maintaining a count of the total number of words in the document would be helpful. Since the total number of words in the document is probably much larger than the number of distinct words, the representation of a *wordbag* should contain only one "item" for each distinct word (along with a multiplicity count), rather than one "item" for each occurrence. This choice of representation requires that, at each insertion, we check whether the new word is already present in the *wordbag*. We would like a representation that allows the search for a matching "item" and the insertion of a not previously present "item" to be efficient. A binary tree representation [9] fits our requirements nicely.

Thus the main part of the *wordbag* representation consists of a binary tree. The binary tree is another data abstraction, *wordtree*. The data abstraction *wordtree* provides operations very similar to those of *wordbag*: *create* ( ) returns an empty *wordtree*; *insert* (*tr*, *w*) returns a *wordtree* containing all the words in the *wordtree tr* plus the additional word *w* (the *wordtree tr* may be modified in the process); and *print* (*tr*, *n*, *o*) prints the contents of the *wordtree tr* in alphabetic order on *outstream o* along with the number of occurrences and the frequency (based on a total of *n* words).

The implementation of *wordbag* is given in Figure 3. Following the header, we find the definition of the representation selected for *wordbag* objects:

rep = **record** [contents: wordtree, total: **int**];

The reserved type identifier **rep** indicates that the type specification to the right of the equal sign is the representing type for the cluster. We have defined the representation of a *wordbag* object to consist of two pieces: a *wordtree*, as explained above, and an integer, which records the total number of words in the *wordbag*.

A CLU record is an object with one or more named components. For each component name, there is an operation to select and an operation to set the corresponding component. The operation *get_n* (*r*) returns the *n* component of the record *r* (this operation is usually abbreviated *r.n*). The operation *put_n* (*r*, *x*) makes *x* the *n* component of the record *r* (this operation is usually abbreviated *r.n* := *x*, by analogy with the assignment statement). A new record is created by an expression of the form type${name_1: value_1, . . .}.

There are two different types associated with any cluster: the abstract type being defined (*wordbag* in this case) and the representation type (the record). Outside of the cluster, type checking ensures that a *wordbag* object will always be treated as such. In particular, the ability to convert a *wordbag* object into its representation is not provided (unless one of the *wordbag* operations does so explicitly).

Inside the cluster, however, it is necessary to view a *wordbag* object as being of the representation type, because the implementations of the operations are defined in terms of the representation. This change of viewpoint is signalled by having the reserved word **cvt** appear as the type of an argument (as in the *insert* and *print* operations). **Cvt** may also appear as a return type (as in the *create* operation); here it indicates that a returned object will be changed into an object of abstract type. Whether **cvt** appears as the type of an argument or as a return type, it stipulates a "conversion" of viewpoint between the external abstract type

Fig. 3. The *wordbag* cluster.

```
wordbag = cluster is
  create,      % create an empty bag
  insert,      % insert an element
  print;       % print contents of bag
  rep = record [contents: wordtree, total: int];
create = proc ( ) returns (cvt);
            return (rep${contents: wordtree$create ( ), total: 0});
          end create;
insert = proc (x: cvt, v: string);
            x.contents := wordtree$insert (x.contents, v);
            x.total := x.total + 1;
          end insert;
print = proc (x: cvt, o: outstream);
            wordtree$print (x.contents, x.total, o);
          end print;
end wordbag;
```

and the internal representation type. **Cvt** can be used only within a cluster, and conversion can be done only between the single abstract type being defined and the (single) representation type.[4]

The procedures in *wordbag* are very simple. *Create* builds a new instance of the **rep** by use of the record constructor

rep${contents: wordtree$create ( ), total: 0}

Here *total* is initialized to 0 and *contents* to the empty *wordtree* (by calling the *create* operation of *wordtree*). This **rep** object is converted into a *wordbag* object as it is being returned. *Insert* and *print* are implemented directly in terms of *wordtree* operations.

The implementation of *wordtree* is shown in Figure 4. In the *wordtree* representation, each node contains a word and the number of times that word has been inserted into the *wordbag*, as well as two subtrees. For any particular node, the words in the "lesser" subtree must alphabetically precede the word in the node, and the words in the "greater" subtree must follow the word in the node. This information is described by

node = **record** [value: **string**, count: **int**,
        lesser: wordtree, greater: wordtree];

which defines "node" to be an abbreviation for the information following the equal sign. (The reserved word **rep** is used similarly as an abbreviation for the representation type.)

Now consider the representation of *wordtrees*. A nonempty *wordtree* can be represented by its top node. An empty *wordtree*, however, contains no information. The ideal type to represent an empty *wordtree* is the CLU type **null**, which has a single data object **nil**. So the representation of a *wordtree* should be either a node or **nil**. This representation is expressed by

rep = **oneof** [empty: **null**, non_empty: node];

Just as the record is the basic CLU mechanism to

---

form an object that is a collection of other objects, the oneof is the basic CLU mechanism to form an object that is "one of" a set of alternatives. Oneof is CLU's method of forming a discriminated union, and is somewhat similar to a variant component of a record in Pascal [23].

An object of the type **oneof** $[s_1: T_1 \ldots s_n: T_n]$ can be thought of as a pair. The "tag" component is an identifier from the set $\{s_1 \ldots s_n\}$. The "value" component is an object of the type corresponding to the tag. That is, if the tag component is s_i, then the value is some object of type T_i.

Objects of type **oneof** $[s_1: T_1 \ldots s_n: T_n]$ are created by the operations $make\_s_i(x)$, each of which takes an object x of type T_i and returns the pair $\langle s_i, x \rangle$. Because the type of the value component of a oneof object is not known at compile time, allowing direct access to the value component could result in a run-time type error (e.g. assigning an object to a variable of the wrong type). To eliminate this possibility, we require the use of a special **tagcase** statement to decompose a oneof object:

```
tagcase e
    tag s₁ (id₁: T₁):    statements . . .
          . . .
    tag sₙ (idₙ: Tₙ):    statements . . .
    end;
```

This statement evaluates the expression e to obtain an object of type **oneof** $[s_1: T_1 \ldots s_n: T_n]$. If the tag is s_i, then the value is assigned to the new variable id_i and the statements following the ith alternative are executed. The variable id_i is local to those statements. If, for some reason, we do not need the value, we can omit the parenthesized variable declaration.

The reader should now know enough to understand Figure 4. Note, in the *create* operation, the use of the construction operation *make_empty* of the representation type of *wordtree* (the discriminated union **oneof** [empty: **null**, nonempty: node]) to create the empty *wordtree*. The **tagcase** statement is used in both *insert* and *print*. Note that if *insert* is given an empty *wordtree*, it creates a new top node for the returned value, but if *insert* is given a nonempty *wordtree*, it modifies the given *wordtree* and returns it.[5] The *insert* operation depends on the dynamic allocation of space for newly created records (see Section 3).

The *print* operation uses the obvious recursive descent. It makes use of procedure $print\_word(w, c, t, o)$, which generates a single line of output on o consisting of the word w, the count c, and the frequency of occurrence derived from c and t. The implementation of *print_word* has been omitted.

We have now completed our first discussion of the

---

[5] It is necessary for *insert* to return a value in addition having a side effect because in the case of an empty *wordtree* argument side effects are not possible. Side effects are not possible because of the representation chosen for the empty *wordtree* and because of the CLU parameter passing mechanism (see Section 3).

Fig. 4. The *wordtree* cluster.

```
wordtree = cluster is
   create,       % create empty contents
   insert,       % add item to contents
   print;        % print contents
   node = record [value: string, count: int,
                  lesser: wordtree, greater: wordtree];
   rep = oneof [empty: null, non_empty: node];
create = proc ( ) returns (cvt);
   return (rep$make_empty (nil));
   end create;
insert = proc (x: cvt, v: string) returns (cvt);
   tagcase x
      tag empty:
            n: node := node${value: v, count: 1,
                             lesser: wordtree$create ( ),
                             greater: wordtree$create ( )};
            return (rep$make_non_empty (n));
      tag non_empty (n: node):
            if v = n.value
                  then n.count := n.count + 1;
               elseif v < n.value
                  then n.lesser := wordtree$insert (n.lesser, v);
               else n.greater := wordtree$insert (n.greater, v);
               end;
            return (x);
      end;
   end insert;
print = proc (x: cvt, total: int, o: outstream);
   tagcase x
      tag empty: ;
      tag non_empty (n: node):
         wordtree$print (n.lesser, total, o);
         print_word (n.value, n. count, total, o);
         wordtree$print (n.greater, total, o);
      end;
   end print;
end wordtree;
```

court_words procedure. We return to this problem in Section 4, where we present a superior solution.

3. Semantics

All languages present their users with some model of computation. This section describes those aspects of CLU semantics that differ from the common Algol-like model. In particular, we discuss CLU's notions of objects and variables and the definitions of assignment and argument passing that follow from these notions. We also discuss type correctness.

3.1 Objects and Variables

The basic elements of CLU semantics are *objects* and *variables*. Objects are the data entities that are created and manipulated by CLU programs. Variables are just the names used in a program to refer to objects.

In CLU, each object has a particular *type*, which characterizes its behavior. A type defines a set of operations that create and manipulate objects of that type. An object may be created and manipulated only via the operations of its type.

An object may *refer* to objects. For example, a

record object refers to the objects that are the components of the record. This notion is one of logical, not physical, containment. In particular, it is possible for two distinct record objects to refer to (or *share*) the same component object. In the case of a cyclic structure, it is even possible for an object to "contain" itself. Thus it is possible to have recursive data structure definitions and shared data objects without explicit reference types. The *wordtree* type described in the previous section is an example of a recursively defined data structure. (This notion of object is similar to that in Lisp.)

CLU objects exist independently of procedure activations. Space for objects is allocated from a dynamic storage area as the result of invoking constructor operations of certain primitive CLU types. For example, the record constructor is used in the implementation of *wordbag* (Figure 3) to acquire space for new *wordbag* objects. In theory, all objects continue to exist forever. In practice, the space used by an object may be reclaimed when the object is no longer accessible to any CLU program.[6]

An object may exhibit time-varying behavior. Such an object, called a *mutable* object, has a state which may be modified by certain operations without changing the identity of the object. Records are examples of mutable objects. The record update operations (*put_s* (r, v), written as $r.s := v$ in the examples), change the state of record objects and therefore affect the behavior of subsequent applications of the select operations (*get_s* (r), written as $r.s$). The *wordbag* and *wordtree* types are additional examples of types with mutable objects.

If a mutable object m is shared by two other objects x and y, then a modification to m made via x will be visible when m is examined via y. Communication through shared mutable objects is most beneficial in the context of procedure invocation, described below.

Objects that do not exhibit time-varying behavior are called *immutable* objects, or *constants*. Examples of constants are integers, booleans, characters, and strings. The value of a constant object can not be modified. For example, new strings may be computed from old ones, but existing strings do not change. Similarly, none of the integer operations modify the integers passed to them as arguments.

Variables are names used in CLU programs to *denote* particular objects at execution time. Unlike variables in many common programming languages, which *are* objects that *contain* values, CLU variables are simply names that the programmer uses to refer to objects. As such, it is possible for two variables to denote (or *share*) the same object. CLU variables are much like those in Lisp and are similar to pointer variables in other languages. However, CLU variables are *not* objects; they cannot be denoted by other variables or

referred to by objects. Thus variables are completely private to the procedure in which they are declared and cannot be accessed or modified by any other procedure.

3.2 Assignment and Procedure Invocation

The basic actions in CLU are *assignment* and *procedure invocation*. The assignment primitive $x := E$, where x is a variable and E is an expression, causes x to denote the object resulting from the evaluation of E. For example, if E is a simple variable y, then the assignment $x := y$ causes x to denote the object denoted by y. The object is *not* copied; after the assignment is performed, it will be *shared* by x and y. Assignment does not affect the state of any object. (Recall that $r.s := v$ is not a true assignment, but an abbreviation for *put_s* (r, v).)

Procedure invocation involves passing argument objects from the caller to the called procedure and returning result objects from the procedure to the caller. The formal arguments of a procedure are considered to be local variables of the procedure and are initialized, by assignment, to the objects resulting from the evaluation of the argument expressions. Thus argument objects are shared between the caller and the called procedure. A procedure may modify mutable argument objects (e.g. records), but of course it cannot modify immutable ones (e.g. integers). A procedure has no access to the variables of its caller.

Procedure invocations may be used directly as statements; those that return objects may also be used as expressions. Arbitrary recursive procedures are permitted.

3.3 Type Correctness

Every variable in a CLU module must be declared; the declaration specifies the type of object that the variable may denote. All assignments to a variable must satisfy the variable's declaration. Because argument passing is defined in terms of assignment, the types of actual argument objects must be consistent with the declarations of the corresponding formal arguments.

These restrictions, plus the restriction that only the code in a cluster may use **cvt** to convert between the abstract and representation types, ensure that the behavior of an object is indeed characterized completely by the operations of its type. For example, the type restrictions ensure that the only modification possible to a record object that represents a *wordbag* (Figure 3) is the modification performed by the *insert* operation.

Type checking is performed on a module by module basis at compile time (it could also be done at run time). This checking can catch all type errors—even those involving intermodule references—because the CLU library maintains the necessary type information for all modules (see Section 5).

---

[6] An object is accessible if it is denoted by a variable of an active procedure or is a component of an accessible object.

4. More Abstraction Mechanisms

In this section we continue our discussion of abstraction mechanisms in CLU. A generalization of the *wordbag* abstraction, called *sorted_bag*, is presented as an illustration of parameterized clusters, which are a means for implementing more generally applicable data abstractions. The presentation of *sorted_bag* is also used to motivate the introduction of a control abstraction called an *iterator*, which is a mechanism for incrementally generating the elements of a collection of objects. Finally, we show an implementation of the *sorted_bag* abstraction and illustrate how *sorted_bag* can be used in implementing *count_words*.

4.1 Properties of the Sorted_bag Abstraction

In the *count_words* procedure given earlier, a data abstraction called *wordbag* was used. A *wordbag* object is a collection of strings, each with an associated count. Strings are inserted into a *wordbag* object one at a time. Strings in a *wordbag* object may be printed in alphabetical order, each with a count of the number of times it was inserted.

Although *wordbag* has properties that are specific to the usage in *count_words*, it also has properties in common with a more general abstraction, *sorted_bag*. A bag is similar to a set (it is sometimes called a multiset) except that an item can appear in a bag many times. For example, if the integer 1 is inserted in the set $\{1, 2\}$, the result is the set $\{1, 2\}$, but if 1 is inserted in the bag $\{1, 2\}$, the result is the bag $\{1, 1, 2\}$. A *sorted_bag* is a bag that affords access to the items it contains according to an ordering relation on the items.

The concept of a *sorted_bag* is meaningful not only for strings but for many types of items. Therefore we would like to parameterize the *sorted_bag* abstraction, the parameter being the type of item to be collected in the *sorted_bag* objects.

Most programming languages provide built-in parameterized data abstractions. For example, the concept of an array is a parameterized data abstraction. An example of a use of arrays in Pascal is

array 1..n **of integer**

These arrays have two parameters, one specifying the array bounds (1..n) and one specifying the type of element in the array (integer). In CLU we provide mechanisms allowing user-defined data abstractions (like *sorted_bag*) to be parameterized.

In the *sorted_bag* abstraction, not all types of items make sense. Only types that define a total ordering on their objects are meaningful since the *sorted_bag* abstraction depends on the presence of this ordering. In addition, information about the ordering must be expressed in a way that is useful for programming. A natural way to express this information is by means of operations of the item type. Therefore we require that the item type provide less than and equal operations

(called *lt* and *equal*). This constraint is expressed in the header for *sorted_bag*:

sorted_bag = **cluster** [t: **type**] **is** create, insert, . . .
   where t **has**
     lt, equal: **proctype** (t, t) **returns** (**bool**);

The item type *t* is a *formal parameter* of the *sorted_bag* cluster; whenever the *sorted_bag* abstraction is used, the item type must be specified as an *actual parameter*, e.g.

sorted_bag[**string**]

The information about required operations informs the programmer about legitimate uses of *sorted_bag*. The compiler will check each use of *sorted_bag* to ensure that the item type provides the required operations. The **where** clause specifies exactly the information that the compiler can check. Of course, more is assumed about the item type *t* than the presence of operations with appropriate names and functionalities: these operations must also define a total ordering on the items. Although we expect formal and complete specifications for data abstractions to be included in the CLU library eventually, we do not include in the CLU language declarations that the compiler cannot check. This point is discussed further in Section 7.

Now that we have decided to define a *sorted_bag* abstraction that works for many item types, we must decide what operations this abstraction provides. When an abstraction (like *wordbag*) is written for a very specific purpose, it is reasonable to have some specialized operations. For a more general abstraction, the operations should be more generally useful.

The *print* operation is a case in point. Printing is only one possible use of the information contained in a *sorted_bag*. It was the only use in the case of *wordbag*, so it was reasonable to have a *print* operation. However, if *sorted_bags* are to be generally useful, there should be some way for the user to obtain the elements of the *sorted_bag*; the user can then perform some action on the elements (for example, print them).

What we would like is an operation on *sorted_bags* that makes all of the elements available to the caller in increasing order. One possible approach is to map the elements of a *sorted_bag* into a sequence object, a solution potentially requiring a large amount of space. A more efficient method is provided by CLU and is discussed below. This solution computes the sequence one element at a time, thus saving space. If only part of the sequence is used (as in a search for some element), then execution time can be saved as well.

4.2 Control Abstractions

The purpose of many loops is to perform an action on some or all of the objects in a collection. For such loops, it is often useful to separate the selection of the next object from the action performed on that object.

```
count_numeric = proc (s: string) returns (int);
    count: int := 0;
    for c: char in string_chars (s) do
      if char_is_numeric (c)
        then count := count + 1;
        end;
      end;
    return (count);
    end count_numeric;
string_chars = iter (s: string) yields (char);
    index: int := 1;
    limit: int := string$size (s);
    while index < = limit do
      yield (string$fetch (s, index));
      index := index + 1;
      end;
    end string_chars;
```

CLU provides a control abstraction that permits a complete decomposition of the two activities. The **for** statement available in many programming languages provides a limited ability in this direction: it iterates over ranges of integers. The CLU **for** statement can iterate over collections of any type of object. The selection of the next object in the collection is done by a user-defined *iterator*. The iterator produces the objects in the collection one at a time (the entire collection need not physically exist); each object is consumed by the **for** statement in turn.

Figure 5 gives an example of a simple iterator called *string_chars*, which produces the characters in a string in the order in which they appear. This iterator uses string operations *size*(*s*), which tells how many characters are in the string *s*, and *fetch* (*s*, *n*), which returns the *n*th character in the string *s* (provided the integer *n* is greater than zero and does not exceed the size of the string).[7]

The general form of the CLU **for** statement is

for declarations **in** iterator_invocation **do**
   body
  end;

An example of the use of the **for** statement occurs in the *count_numeric* procedure (see Figure 5), which contains a loop that counts the number of numeric characters in a string. Note that the details of how the characters are obtained from the string are entirely contained in the definition of the iterator.

Iterators work as follows: A **for** statement initially invokes an iterator, passing it some arguments. Each time a **yield** statement is executed in the iterator, the objects yielded[8] are assigned to the variables declared in the **for** statement (following the reserved word **for**)

in corresponding order, and the body of the **for** statement is executed. Then the iterator is resumed at the statement following the **yield** statement, in the same environment as when the objects were yielded. When the iterator terminates, by either an implicit or explicit **return**, the invoking **for** statement terminates. The iteration may also be prematurely terminated by a **return** in the body of the **for** statement.

For example, suppose that *string_chars* is invoked with the string "a3". The first character yielded is 'a'. At this point, within *string_chars*, *index* = 1 and *limit* = 2. Next the body of the **for** statement is performed. Since the character 'a' is not numeric, *count* remains at 0. Next *string_chars* is resumed at the statement after the **yield** statement, and when resumed, *index* = 1 and *limit* = 2. Then *index* is assigned 2, and the character '3' is selected from the string and yielded. Since '3' is numeric, *count* becomes 1. Then *string_chars* is resumed, with *index* = 2 and *limit* = 2, and *index* is incremented, which causes the **while** loop to terminate. The implicit **return** terminates both the iterator and the **for** statement, with control resuming at the statement after the **for** statement, and *count* = 1.

While iterators are useful in general, they are especially valuable in conjunction with data abstractions that are collections of objects (such as sets, arrays, and *sorted_bags*). Iterators afford users of such abstractions access to all objects in the collection without exposing irrelevant details. Several iterators may be included in a data abstraction. When the order of obtaining the objects is important, different iterators may provide different orders.

4.3 Implementation and Use of Sorted_bag

Now we can describe a minimal set of operations for *sorted_bag*. The operations are *create*, *insert*, *size*, and *increasing*. *Create*, *insert*, and *size* are procedural abstractions that, respectively, create a *sorted_bag*, insert an item into a *sorted_bag*, and give the number of items in a *sorted_bag*. *Increasing* is a control abstraction that produces the items in a *sorted_bag* in increasing order; each item produced is accompanied by an integer representing the number of times the item appears in the *sorted_bag*. Note that other operations might also be useful for *sorted_bag*, for example, an iterator yielding the items in decreasing order. In general, the definer of a data abstraction can provide as many operations as seems reasonable.

In Figure 6, we give an implementation of the *sorted_bag* abstraction. It is implemented by using a sorted binary tree, just as *wordbag* was implemented. Thus a subsidiary abstraction is necessary. This abstraction, called *tree*, is a generalization of the *wordtree* abstraction (used in Section 2), which has been parameterized to work for all ordered types. An implementation of *tree* is given in Figure 7. Notice that both the *tree* abstraction and the *sorted_bag* abstraction place the same constraints on their type parameters.

---

[7] A **while** loop is used in the implementation of *string_chars* so that the example will be based on familiar concepts. In actual practice, such a loop would be written by using a **for** statement invoking a primitive iterator.

[8] Zero or more objects may be yielded, but the number and types of objects yielded each time by an iterator must agree with the number and types of variables in a **for** statement using the iterator.

Fig. 6. The *sorted_bag* cluster.

```
sorted_bag = cluster [t: type] is create, insert, size, increasing
   where t has equal, lt: proctype (t, t) returns (bool);
   rep = record [contents: tree[t], total: int];
create = proc ( ) returns (cvt);
   return (rep${contents: tree[t]$create ( ), total: 0});
   end create;
insert = proc (sb: cvt, v: t);
   sb.contents := tree[t]$insert (sb.contents, v);
   sb.total := sb.total + 1;
   end insert;
size = proc (sb: cvt) returns (int);
   return (sb.total);
   end size;
increasing = iter (sb: cvt) yields (t, int);
   for item: t, count: int
      in tree[t]$increasing (sb.contents) do
         yield (item, count);
         end;
      end increasing;
   end sorted_bag;
```

Fig. 7. The *tree* cluster.

```
tree = cluster [t: type] is create, insert, increasing
   where t has equal, lt: proctype (t, t) returns (bool);
   node = record [value: t, count: int,
                     lesser: tree[t], greater: tree[t]];
   rep = oneof [empty: null, non_empty: node];
create = proc ( ) returns (cvt);
   return (rep$make_empty (nil));
   end create;
insert = proc (x: cvt, v: t) returns (cvt);
   tagcase x
      tag empty:
         n: node := node${value: v, count: 1,
                        lesser: tree[t]$create ( ),
                        greater: tree[t]$create ( )};
         return (rep$make_non_empty (n));
      tag non_empty (n: node):
         if t$equal (v, n.value)
               then n.count := n.count + 1;
            elseif t$lt (v, n.value)
               then n.lesser := tree[t]$insert (n.lesser, v);
            else n.greater := tree[t]$insert (n.greater, v);
            end;
         return (x);
      end;
   end insert;
increasing = iter (x: cvt) yields (t, int);
   tagcase x
      tag empty: ;
      tag non_empty (n: node):
         for item: t, count: int
            in tree[t]$increasing (n.lesser) do
               yield (item, count);
               end;
         yield (n.value, n.count);
         for item: t, count: int
            in tree[t]$increasing (n.greater) do
               yield (item, count);
               end;
         end;
      end increasing;
   end tree;
```

An important feature of the *sorted_bag* and *tree* clusters is the way that the cluster parameter is used in places where the type **string** was used in *wordbag* and *wordtree*. This usage is especially evident in the implementation of *tree*. For example, *tree* has a representation that stores values of type *t*: the *value* component of a *node* must be an object of type *t*.

In the *insert* operation of *tree*, the *lt* and *equal* operations of type *t* are used. We have used the compound form, e.g. *t$equal* $(v, n.value)$, to emphasize that the *equal* operation of *t* is being used. The short form, $v = n.value$, could have been used instead.

The *increasing* iterator of *tree* works as follows: first it yields all items in the current tree that are less than the item at the top node; the items are obtained by a recursive use of itself, passing the *lesser* subtree as an argument. Next it yields the contents of the top node, and then it yields all items in the current tree that are greater than the item at the top node (again by a recursive use of itself). In this way it performs a complete walk over the tree, yielding the values at all nodes, in increasing order.

Finally, we show in Figure 8 how the original procedure *count_words* can be implemented in terms of *sorted_bag*. Note that the *count_words* procedure now uses *sorted_bag*[**string**] instead of *wordbag*. *Sorted_bag*[**string**] is legitimate since the type **string** provides both *lt* and *equal* operations. Note that two **for** statements are used in *count_words*. The second **for** statement prints the words in alphabetic order, using the *increasing* iterator of *sorted_bag*. The first **for** statement inserts the words into the *sorted_bag*; it uses an iterator

```
words = iter (i: instream) yields (string);

      . . .

      end words;
```

The definition of *words* is left as an exercise for the reader.

5. The CLU Library

So far, we have shown CLU modules as separate pieces of text, without explaining how they are bound together to form a program. This section describes the CLU library, which plays a central role in supporting intermodule references.

The CLU library contains information about abstractions. The library supports incremental program development, one abstraction at a time, and, in addition, makes abstractions that are defined during the construction of one program available as a basis for subsequent program development. The information in the library permits the separate compilation of single modules with complete type checking of all external references (such as procedure invocations).

The structure of the library derives from the fundamental distinction between abstractions and implementations. For each abstraction, there is a *description unit* which contains all system-maintained information about that abstraction. Included in the description unit are zero or more modules that implement the abstraction.[9]

The most important information contained in a description unit is the abstraction's *interface specification*, which is that information needed to type-check uses of the abstraction. For procedural and control abstractions, this information consists of the number and types of parameters, arguments, and output values, plus any constraints on type parameters (i.e. required operations, as described in Section 4). For data abstractions, it includes the number and types of parameters, constraints on type parameters, and the name and interface specification of each operation.

An abstraction is entered in the library by submitting the interface specification; no implementations are required. In fact, a module can be compiled before any implementations have been provided for the abstractions that it uses; it is necessary only that interface specifications have been given for those abstractions. Ultimately, there can be many implementations of an abstraction; each implementation is required to satisfy the interface specification of the abstraction. Because all uses and implementations of an abstraction are checked against the interface specification, the actual selection of an implementation can be delayed until just before (or perhaps during) execution. We imagine a process of binding together modules into programs, prior to execution, at which time this selection would be made.

An important detail of the CLU system is the method by which CLU modules refer to abstractions. To avoid problems of name conflicts that can arise in large systems, the names used by a module to refer to abstractions can be chosen to suit the programmer's convenience. When a module is submitted for compilation, its external references must be bound to description units so that type checking can be performed. The binding is accomplished by constructing an *association list*, mapping names to description units, which is passed to the compiler along with the source code when compiling the module. The mapping in the association list is stored by the compiler in the library as part of the module. A similar process is involved in entering interface specifications of abstractions, as these will include references to other (data) abstractions.

When the compiler type-checks a module, it uses the association list to map the external names in the module to description units and then uses the interface specifications in those description units to check that the abstractions are used correctly. The type correctness of the module thus depends upon the binding of

---

[9] Other information that may be stored in the library includes information about relationships among abstractions, as might be expressed in a module interconnection language [5, 21].

Fig. 8. The *count_words* procedure using iterators.

```
count_words = proc (i: instream, o: outstream);
  wordbag = sorted_bag[string];
  % create an empty wordbag
  wb: wordbag := wordbag$create ( );
  % scan document, adding each word found to wb
  for word: string in words (i) do
    wordbag$insert (wb, word);
    end;
  % print the wordbag
  total: int := wordbag$size (wb);
  for w: string, count: int in wordbag$increasing (wb) do
    print_word (w, count, total, o);
    end;
  end count_words;
```

names to description units and the interface specifications in those description units, and could be invalidated if changes to the binding or the interface specifications were subsequently made. For this reason, the process of compilation permanently binds a module to the abstractions it uses, and the interface description of an abstraction, once defined, is not allowed to change. (Of course, a new description unit can be created to describe a modified abstraction.)

6. Implementation

This section briefly describes the current implementation of CLU and discusses its efficiency.

The implementation is based on a decision to represent all CLU objects by *object descriptors*, which are fixed-size values containing a type code and some type-dependent information.[10] In the case of mutable types, the type-dependent information is a pointer to a separately allocated area containing the state information. For constant types, the information either directly contains the value (if the value can be encoded in the information field, as for integers, characters, and booleans) or contains a pointer to separately allocated space (as for strings). The type codes are used by the garbage collector to determine the physical representation of objects so that the accessible objects can be traced; they are also useful for supporting program debugging.

The use of fixed-size object descriptors allows variables to be fixed-size cells. Assignment is efficient: the object descriptor resulting from the evaluation of the expression is simply copied into the variable. In addition, a single size for variables facilitates the separate compilation of modules and allows most of the code of a parameterized module to be shared among all instantiations of the module. The actual parameters are made available to this code by means of a small parameter-dependent section, which is initialized prior to execution.

---

[10] Object descriptors are similar to capabilities [11].

452

Procedure invocation is relatively efficient. A single program stack is used, and argument passing is as efficient as assignment. Iterators are a form of coroutine; however, their use is sufficiently constrained that they are implemented using just the program stack. Using an iterator is therefore only slightly more expensive than using a procedure.

The data abstraction mechanism is not inherently expensive. No execution-time type checking is necessary. Furthermore, the type conversion implied by **cvt** is merely a change in the view taken of an object's type and does not require any computation.

A number of optimization techniques can be applied to a collection of modules if one is willing to give up the flexibility of separate compilation. The most effective such optimization is the inline substitution of procedure (and iterator) bodies for invocations [18]. The use of data abstractions tends to introduce extra levels of procedure invocations that perform little or no computation. As an example, consider the *wordbag$insert* operation (Figure 3), which merely invokes the *wordtree$insert* operation and increments a counter. If data abstractions had not been used, these actions would most likely have been performed directly by the *count_words* procedure. The *wordbag$insert* operation is thus a good candidate for being compiled inline. Once inline substitution has been performed, the increase in context will enhance the effectiveness of conventional optimization techniques [1–3].

7. Discussion

Our intent in this paper has been to provide an informal introduction to the abstraction mechanisms in CLU. By means of programming examples, we have illustrated the use of data, procedural, and control abstractions and have shown how CLU modules are used to implement these abstractions. We have not attempted to provide a complete description of CLU, but, in the course of explaining the examples, most features of the language have appeared. One important omission is the CLU exception handling mechanism (which does support abstractions); this mechanism is described in [10].

In addition to describing constructs that support abstraction, previous sections have covered a number of other topics. We have discussed the semantics of CLU. We have described the organization of the CLU library and discussed how it supports incremental program development and separate compilation and type checking of modules. Also we have described our current implementation and discussed its efficiency.

In designing CLU, our goal was to simplify the task of constructing reliable software that is reasonably easy to understand, modify, and maintain. It seems appropriate, therefore, to conclude this paper with a discussion of how CLU contributes to this goal.

The quality of any program depends upon the skill of the designer. In CLU programs, this skill is reflected in the choice of abstractions. In a good design, abstractions will be used to simplify the connections between modules and to encapsulate decisions that are likely to change [17]. Data abstractions are particularly valuable for these purposes. For example, through the use of a data abstraction, modules that share a system database rely only on its abstract behavior as defined by the database operations. The connections among these modules are much simpler than would be possible if they shared knowledge of the format of the database and the relationship among its parts. In addition, the database abstraction can be reimplemented without affecting the code of the modules that use it. CLU encourages the use of data abstractions and thus aids the programmer during program design.

The benefits arising from the use of data abstractions are based on the constraint, inherent in CLU and enforced by the CLU compiler, that only the operations of the abstraction may access the representations of the objects. This constraint ensures that the distinction made in CLU between abstractions and implementations applies to data abstractions as well as to procedural and control abstractions.

The distinction between abstractions and implementations eases program modification and maintenance. Once it has been determined that an abstraction must be reimplemented, CLU guarantees that the code of all modules using that abstraction will be unaffected by the change. The modules need not be reprogrammed or even recompiled; only the process of selecting the implementation of the abstraction must be redone. The problem of determining what modules must be changed is also simplified because each module has a well-defined purpose – to implement an abstraction – and no other module can interfere with that purpose.

Understanding and verification of CLU programs is made easier because the distinction between abstractions and implementations permits this task to be decomposed. One module at a time is studied to determine that it implements its abstraction. This study requires understanding the behavior of the abstractions it uses, but it is not necessary to understand the modules implementing those abstractions. Those modules can be studied separately.

A promising way to establish the correctness of a program is by means of a mathematical proof. For practical reasons, proofs should be performed (or at least checked) by a verification system, since the process of constructing a proof is tedious and error-prone. Decomposition of the proof is essential for program proving, which is practical only for small programs (like CLU modules). Note that when the CLU compiler does type checking, it is, in addition to enforcing the constraint that permits the proof to be decomposed, also performing a small part of the actual proof.

We have included as declarations in CLU just the information that the compiler can check with reasonable efficiency. We believe that the other information required for proofs (specifications and assertions) should be expressed in a separate "specification" language. The properties of such a language are being studied [7, 13, 14, 19]. We intend eventually to add formal specifications to the CLU system; the library is already organized to accommodate this addition. At that time various specification language processors could be added to the system.

We believe that the constraints imposed by CLU are essential for practical as well as theoretical reasons. It is true that data abstractions can be used in any language by establishing programming conventions to protect the representations of objects. However, conventions are no substitute for enforced constraints. It is inevitable that the conventions will be violated—and are likely to be violated just when they are needed most, in implementing, maintaining, and modifying large programs. It is precisely at this time, when the programming task becomes very difficult, that a language like CLU will be most valuable and appreciated.

Acknowledgments. The authors gratefully acknowledge the contributions made by members of the CLU design group over the last three years. Several people have made helpful comments about this paper, including Toby Bloom, Dorothy Curtis, Mike Hammer, Eliot Moss, Jerry Saltzer, Bob Scheifler, and the referees.

References

1. Allen, F.E., and Cocke, J. A catalogue of optimizing transformations. Rep. RC 3548. IBM Thomas J. Watson Res. Ctr., Yorktown Heights, N.Y., 1971.

2. Allen, F.E. A program data flow analysis procedure. Rep. RC 5278, IBM Thomas J. Watson Res. Ctr., Yorktown Heights, N.Y., 1975.

3. Atkinson, R.R. Optimization techniques for a structured programming language. S.M. Th., Dept. of Electr. Eng. and Comptr. Sci., M.I.T., Cambridge, Mass., June 1976.

4. Dahl, O.J., Myhrhaug, B., and Nygaard, K. The SIMULA 67 common base language. Pub. S-22, Norwegian Comptng. Ctr., Oslo, 1970.

5. DeRemer, F., and Kron, H. Programming-in-the-large versus programming-in-the-small. Proc. Int. Conf. on Reliable Software, SIGPLAN Notices 10, 6 (June 1975), 114–121.

6. Dijkstra, E.W. Notes on structured programming. *Structured Programming, A.P.I.C. Studies in Data Processing No. 8*, Academic Press, New York, 1972, pp. 1–81.

7. Guttag, J.V., Horowitz, E., and Musser, D.R. Abstract data types and software validation. Rep ISI/RR-76-48, Inform. Sci. Inst., U. of Southern California, Marina del Rey, Calif., Aug. 1976.

8. Hoare, C.A.R. Proof of correctness of data representations. *Acta Informatica 4* (1972), 271–281.

9. Knuth, D. *The Art of Computer Programming, Vol. 3: Sorting and Searching.* Addison Wesley, Reading, Mass., 1973.

10. Laboratory for Computer Science Progress Report 1974–1975. Comput. Structures Group. Rep. PR-XII, Lab. for Comptr. Sci., M.I.T. To be published.

11. Lampson, B.W. Protection. Proc. Fifth Annual Princeton Conf. on Inform. Sci. and Syst., Princeton U., Princeton, N.J., 1971, pp. 437–443.

12. Liskov, B.H., and Zilles, S.N. Programming with abstract data types. Proc. ACM SIGPLAN Conf. on Very High Level Languages, SIGPLAN Notices 9, 4 (April 1974), 50–59.

13. Liskov, B.H., and Zilles, S.N. Specification techniques for data abstractions. *IEEE Trans. Software Eng., SE-1* (1975), 7–19.

14. Liskov, B.H., and Berzins, V. An appraisal of program specifications. Comput. Structures Group Memo 141, Lab. for Comptr. Sci., M.I.T., Cambridge, Mass., July 1976.

15. McCarthy, J., et al. *LISP 1.5 Programmer's Manual.* M.I.T. Press, Cambridge, Mass., 1962.

16. Morris, J.H. Protection in programming languages. *Comm. ACM 16*, 1 (Jan. 1973), 15–21.

17. Parnas, D.L. Information distribution aspects of design methodology. Information Processing 71, Vol. 1, North-Holland Pub. Co., Amsterdam, 1972, pp. 339–344.

18. Scheifler, R.W. An analysis of inline substitution for the CLU programming language. Comput. Structures Group Memo 139, Lab. for Comptr. Sci., M.I.T., Cambridge, Mass., June 1976.

19. Spitzen, J., and Wegbreit, B. The verification and synthesis of data structures. *Acta Informatica 4* (1975), 127–144.

20. Standish, T.A. Data structures: an axiomatic approach. Rep. 2639, Bolt, Beranek and Newman, Cambridge, Mass., 1973.

21. Thomas, J.W. Module interconnection in programming systems supporting abstraction. Rep. CS-16, Comptr. Sci. Prog., Brown U., Providence, R.I., 1976.

22. Wirth, N. Program development by stepwise refinement. *Comm. ACM 14*, 4 (1971), 221–227.

23. Wirth, N. The programming language PASCAL. *Acta Informatica 1* (1971), 35–63.

24. Wulf, W.A., London, R., and Shaw, M. An introduction to the construction and verification of Alphard programs. *IEEE Trans. Software Eng. SE-2* (1976), 253–264.

GYPSY: A Language for Specification

and Implementation of Verifiable Programs

Allen L. Ambler
Amdahl Corporation

Donald I. Good, James C. Browne
Wilhelm F. Burger, Richard M. Cohen
Charles G. Hoch, Robert E. Wells

The University of Texas at Austin

Reprinted from *Proceedings, ACM Conference on Language Design for Reliable Software,* ACM SIGPLAN Notices, March 1977, pp. 1-10. Copyright 1977 Association for Computing Machinery, Inc. Reprinted by permission.

An introduction to the Gypsy programming and specification language is given. Gypsy is a high-level programming language with facilities for general programming and also for systems programming that is oriented toward communications processing. This includes facilities for concurrent processes and process synchronization. Gypsy also contains facilities for detecting and processing errors that are due to the actual running of the program in an imperfect environment. The specification facilities give a precise way of expressing the desired properties of the Gypsy programs. All of the features of Gypsy are fully verifiable, either by formal proof or by validation at run time. An overview of the language design and a detailed example program are given.

Key Words and Phrases: programming language, specification language, formal specification, verification, program proof, run time validation, concurrency, systems programming, communications processing.

CR Categories: 4.2, 4.22, 5.24

INTRODUCTION

The design of Gypsy was driven by the development of a comprehensive methodology for constructing verified programs oriented toward communications processing. This methodology consists of an integrated system of methods for formal program specification and verification either by formal proof or by validation at run time. The methodology also contains two tools for applying these methods: the program design language Gypsy, and an interactive system for the design and verification of Gypsy programs. Gypsy provides the means of expressing both programs and their formal specifications and is, therefore, the unifying element of the complete methodology. The language provides a precise means of expressing a program throughout all stages of its design -- from initial specification through implementation, verification, and subsequent evolution. The integration of programming and specification facilities into a common language is the most significant single characteristic of Gypsy. The merged syntax and semantics allows program proofs to be constructed rigorously in conjunction with program development, thereby bringing maximal benefit to the total programming process.

The incorporation of specifications and programming facilities into a single language provides three complementary approaches to program verification. First, formal proofs that the program will conform to specifications can be constructed before execution occurs. Second, specifications can be validated by actual evaluation at run time. Third, trace facilities provide a convenient mechanism for post-execution analysis if desired. The blending of these techniques (particularly the first two) produces desirable results. Those specifications that are to be validated at run time need not be proven and can be assumed to be valid in formal proofs. This, of course, increases program execution time, but an effective mixture of formal proof and run time validation can significantly reduce the size and complexity of formal proofs without creating intolerably inefficient programs.

A second significant characteristic of Gypsy is the inclusion of language features that allow for both the specification and the coding of concurrent processes. The original target of Gypsy was the expression of verifiable programs for communications processing such as those that might be found at the node of a computer network. This led to the incorporation of verifiable features for expressing concurrency and process synchronization and for expressing real-time dependencies. The result has been a high-level language for the development of general systems programs that can be verified to execute in conformity with precisely stated specifications.

A third significant characteristic is the provision for imperfect execution environments. While formal proofs usually assume a perfect execution environment, execution environments are rarely perfect. In recognition of this fact, the span of both specifications and program code has been extended to include facilities for correct execution in imperfect environments. Specifications and program code concerning data integrity, error monitoring, and error isolation and recovery are expressed directly in the language along with the error-free environment statements.

DESIGN OF GYPSY

Gypsy was developed as an integrated programming and specification language to support specification, coding and verification of systems software, with particular emphasis on communications software. Specific goals were:

1. Complete Verifiability. Every feature in the language must be rigorously verifiable, either by proof or run time validation.

2. Incremental Development. The language must support modular, incremental program development and verification. As best as possible, the language must simplify the verification process by encouraging small modules with tightly regulated interactions and by isolating and minimizing the effects of modifications to previously verified code. There must also be a facility for partial expression of program units.

3. Systems Programming. The language must support the development of systems software. There must be facilities for expressing process concurrency and synchronizing process communication. There must also be facilities for expressing real-time dependencies.

4. Imperfect Execution Environments. The language must support execution in imperfect environments. It must be possible to detect, isolate, and recover from run time anomalies as well as monitor the program state.

5. Specification Capability. The language must provide an extensive specification capability. For every property that is to be verified, there must be an adequate means of expressing it directly in the language. The integration of formal proof, run time validation, and monitoring must be consistent and provide a complete whole.

EXERCISING RESTRAINT

While we had great latitude in the design of Gypsy, we were constrained by the necessity of producing a usable system. This not only meant that we had to be able to implement and verify features of Gypsy, but that the amount of effort involved in utilizing the resulting product for the construction of actual application programs had to be kept reasonable. In effect, we faced a classical performance versus cost compromise. For each feature, we had to consider whether the merits of its inclusion outweighed the expense of verifying its properties. In many cases the decision was not easy.

Starting from Pascal [13], each existing Pascal construct was carefully analyzed and those which inhibited verification were modified or removed. The hierarchical definition structure was eliminated and protection lists were added to provide a tighter, more flexible environment for incremental program development and verification. Facilities for expressing concurrency, communication, synchronization, timing constraints, external events, error recovery, and monitoring were added, paying close attention to the requirements of the verification methodology. Each construct in the program code and the specification statements was designed to support the verification methodology. The program code syntax was modified to integrate the specification statements into a logically consistent and hopefully understandable language.

In the succeeding sections the salient features of Gypsy are discussed briefly, and are followed by an example program. The interested reader is refered to the "Report on the Language Gypsy" [1]. It may be helpful in reading the language features to flip back and forth between the examples as most, if not all, features are utilized there.

DESIGNING FOR VERIFICATION

A language which is to facilitate coding and specification must not only include capabilities necessary for expressing the problem domain of interest, but must exclude language constructs whose semantics defeat, or impede, verification. We defer a discussion of Gypsy's specification statements until a later section for pedagogical reasons. Their development was, however, closely interwoven with that of the coding statements.

Verification of program code has only recently become a prominent factor in programming language design. While Pascal was influenced by verification considerations [6], more recently Nucleus [11], Alphard [23], and Euclid [14] have been expressly designed for verification by formal proofs. Gypsy also is specifically designed for verification, but verification by run time validation as well as by formal proof. The first phase in the design of Gypsy was to develop a "conventional" language which was free from concepts known to render formal proof verification difficult. To this end, Pascal [13] was selected as a model and Gypsy was patterned after Pascal, but with significant differences.

Routines in Pascal can be nested to arbitrary depths which creates a hierarchy of nested "non-local" variables. Routines in Gypsy may not be nested and variables can only be defined within routines; hence, Gypsy has no non-local variables, i.e. all variables are either local variables or parameters. This simplifies verification as well as incremental program development, which will be discussed in the next section.

Functions in Pascal can take either variable or value parameters and can only return values of a simple type. In Gypsy, functions are allowed only constant and value parameters, but they can return values of most types. The restriction to non-variable parameters, together with the absence of non-local variables, guarantees that functions produce no side-effects. This simplifies verification considerably. It also increases the potential for optimization of expression evaluation.

Pascal allows routines to be included as parameters to other routines; Gypsy does not. This decision and the one not allowing non-local variables, are instances where the extra burden on the verification process did not appear worth the extra capability.

Certain of Pascal's data types do not appear at all in Gypsy. These are types "real", "class", "pointer", and "file".

Pascal has "if", "case", "for", "while", "repeat", and "goto" statements for execution control. Gypsy has a similar set of statements, "if", "case", "loop", and "leave", modified for proper placement of assertions and to eliminate the need for extra "begin-end" pairs. The "if" statement is conventional except for a trailing "end". The "case" statement has an additional keyword "is" and an optional "else" clause. The "loop" statement subsumes both the "while" and "repeat" constructs as well as the so-called "loop-and-a-half" construct and infinite loops. Termination and looping are controlled by "leave" statements. Gypsy has no "goto" statement.

DESIGNING FOR
INCREMENTAL DEVELOPMENT

A language that is to support the development and evolution of verified programs also must consider the practical aspects of verification. In developing a verified program of any significant size, it is necessary that the program be written as a large collection of small, independently verifiable units. Otherwise, a formal proof easily can expand into a mass of detail and become unmanageable. Also for proofs to be maximally effective they should be carried out on a unit-by-unit basis as the program is developed. Further, it is the nature of systems programs that they are continuously undergoing evolution, and with each modification some amount of reverification is necessary. It is, therefore, essential that the amount of reverification be kept to a minimum. For these reasons, we sought language features which supported unit-by-unit manipulation, increased unit independence, and isolated unit interactions.

A Gypsy program consists of a series of "routine", "macro", "constant", and "type" units; which may appear in any order. If a reference can not be resolved locally within a particular unit, a search of the other external unit names is made. When an unresolved local reference is found to be an external unit name, then the appropriate information is extracted and the analysis continued. Access rights to any unit may be stated in an "access list." These access lists will be checked during the process of resolving references. The combination of units and access lists provides a high degree of code independence, plus a tightly controlled environment.

A "routine" is a "function", a "procedure", a "process", or a "program". A "program" unit defines the initial program execution point. Routine declarations can only appear at the unit level; hence, Gypsy does not permit a nested hierarchy of routine definitions. Besides favoring unit independence, it was felt (1) that a hierarchical structure failed to provide adequate program protection without access lists and (2) that with access lists and without nonlocal variables a hierarchical structure was unnecessary. Routine calls may be recursive.

A macro unit binds a parameterized expression to a name. While macro expansions can be nested, they may not be recursively expanded as there would be no way to terminate a recursive expansion.

A constant unit parallels the constant declarations of Pascal except that a constant may be of any non-buffer type including a structured type. This provides the means for referencing global values without allowing global variables or requiring them to be passed as parameters if they are not to be modified.

A type unit declares a new type either by itemizing its value set or by composing existing types. A type unit which includes an access list is the equivalent of an abstract data structure [8] [15] [23] [5] [10]. The intent of an abstract data type is to be able to construct a new type and to restrict access to the components of that type to operations representative of the type. It is then possible, with a proper implementation, to alter the implementation of the abstract type and the corresponding operations without impacting the program. A comparison of the Gypsy access control to that of Pascal, Concurrent Pascal, Euclid, and CLU can be found in [2].

DESIGNING FOR CONCURRENCY
AND REAL-TIME

Programming languages have traditionally avoided concurrency; there have, however, been exceptions. The Burroughs family of extended Algol languages [16] provide processes and process communication, Bliss [21] provides coroutines and processes; Concurrent Pascal [5] combines processes and monitors, and Algol 68 [19] provides colateral elaboration of clauses. Several other languages have primitive means of accessing operating system functions which provide concurrency. Operating system research has generated a large number of concurrency and synchronization techniques which we will not attempt to reference. Two systems, RC4000 [3] and HYDRA [22], were significant factors in our decision on how to specify and implement concurrency.

Gypsy has a routine type called a "process". It differs from a "procedure" only in the types of parameters allowed and in the manner of its invocation. Processes communicate only through message buffers [4]. This is a natural choice for communications processing applications. A message "buffer" is a finite length queue on which there are only two operations defined, "send"(enqueue) and "receive"(dequeue). The queue is manipulated by a strict FCFS algorithm. Whenever a "send" is made on a full buffer the sending process is suspended until the condition is remedied. Likewise, a "receive" on an empty buffer will cause the process to be suspended. Associated with every buffer is a semaphore which guarantees mutually exclusive access to the buffer.

Concurrent processes are initiated by a "cobegin end" statement and may or may not terminate. Only when all processes called within a "cobegin" statement terminate will the statement following the "cobegin" be executed.

Polling is an important function of real-time systems; hence, it must be possible to poll a buffer without being suspended indefinitely trying to receive from an empty buffer. Gypsy has an "await" statement which allows the simultaneous waiting on the completion of any one of several buffer operations. An "await" is in many respects a guarded command [9], except that it has a very restricted set of guards and it has an optional time-out clause. The time-out clause specifies what is to be done if none of the requested operations completes by a certain time.

The concept of (real) time is provided by "clock" variables. A clock variable is a special variable which may not be modified by the program, but which is always changing. There may be any number of clocks in a program, but there is no guarantee that they will be synchronized. As Gypsy programs may be distributed across many machines, synchronization would be virtually impossible.

DESIGNING FOR IMPERFECT EXECUTION ENVIRONMENTS

An attribute of real-time software often overlooked in programming languages is the existence of both hardware and software faults. Fault detection, isolation, and recovery is an essential function in real-time software and consequently, languages for expressing such software should (1) provide capabilities for fault control programming and (2) provide an interface to the hardware which allows for the detection, isolation, and recovery of faults. The work of the Newcastle group [17] represents virtually all of the previous efforts on this topic.

A "condition" in Gypsy is an instantaneous event which may occur during the execution of a program. There is a large class of predefined "conditions" which correspond to hardware errors and dynamic language semantics errors, such as "caseerror". Programmers may, in addition, name and signal fault conditions by using a "signal" statement or an "otherwise" clause on a specification (discussed in the next section).

Any statement ending with the word "end", may optionally end with a "condition clause" followed by the word "end". The effect of the condition clause is that whenever a condition occurs, an immediate branch is taken to the condition clause, of the innermost containing statement, which specifies an action for that condition. Searching for the innermost condition clause may involve exiting a routine. After the condition clause is executed, control does not return to where it was before the fault, but instead drops out of the statement whose condition clause was executed. In some sense, a condition clause is a restricted version of a PL/I "on" condition which resembles one of Zahn's event driven case statements [24].

DESIGNING FOR SPECIFICATION

Gypsy plays the dual role of programming and specification language. The specification component of the language permits the precise expression of desired functional properties of key parts of the program. These properties are stated in terms of valid states that are to be maintained on the data objects of the program at various points in the program computation. The objective of a verification is to show that the computation always proceeds in conformity with the stated specifications. The conformity of the program with its specification can in most cases be either proved prior to execution or validated during execution. The same specification methods are used in both approaches to verification.

All specifications in Gypsy are stated as boolean-valued expressions. These specifications are designated to be verified either by proof, by run time validation, or both, or they may simply be assumed. Specifications that are proved or assumed need not be evaluated at run time, and therefore, they are permitted to contain special operations and types that could not otherwise be permitted. For example, boolean expressions may contain the logical quantifiers "for all" and "there exists" and refer to rational numbers and infinite sequences. These special operations and types may not be used in parts of the program that are to be executed, but they are assigned precise definitions for purposes of specification.

The most familiar kinds of specifications used in Gypsy are the "entry", "exit", and "assert" statements for procedures and functions. These follow the same form as that introduced by [12] for proving Pascal programs. The "exit" specification is interpreted in the weak sense, i.e. it holds if the program terminates.

"Entry", "exit", and "assert" specifications also can be used with processes. However, processes often are intentionally programmed never to terminate, and therefore an "exit" specification may be of no value. Specifications can be stated for non-terminating processes through "block" specifications. A "block" specification holds whenever the process is suspended by a buffer operation. This provides a temporary halting point.

Specifications for routines performing buffer manipulations normally are stated in terms of effects on buffer histories. In the terminology of [7], these are "mythical variables", but they are provided in a predefined way by the language rather than being installed by the programmer. Associated with every buffer b are several histories that are relevant to specifications and to the proof methodology. For example, "b.infrom" refers to the sequence of objects received "in" from the buffer by the process, and "b.outto" is the sequence of objects sent "out" to the buffer from the process.

Any sequence of "var" declarations in a routine can be followed by a "keep" specification. The "keep" expression must be maintained throughout the immediate scope of the "var" declaration. A procedure or function call releases the "keep", but the called unit must reestablish it before returning. This type of assertion is similar to those used by [18] for run time validation.

Any routine that is granted access to the concrete representation of an abstract type may have both unrestricted (entry, exit, block) and restricted (centry, cexit, cblock) external specifications. The external specifications of a routine are visible to the external environment of the routine; internal specifications (assert, keep) are not. Unrestricted external specifications are stated strictly in abstract terms and are visible to any calling routine. Restricted external specifications may be stated in both abstract and concrete terms and typically are used to define the desired relationship between the abstract and concrete. These restricted specifications are visible only to calling routines that also have access to the same set (or possibly a superset) or the abstract types that are accessible to the called routine. Thus, the concrete structure of an abstract type is revealed, through the restricted external specifications, only to other routines that also are granted access to the type. The centry and cexit types were motivated by similar specifications in Alphard.

Two kinds of specifications can be stated for Gypsy type definitions, "require" and "axiom". The require specification follows Alphard and is a precondition on the type parameters that is necessary for the proper creation of an object of that type. The axiom is a relation among the functions that have access to the type.

This set of specification methods provides powerful mechanisms for stating functional properties of programs, and formal proof methods have been defined for proving each of these types of properties. The specifications do not, at this time, directly permit the definition of quantitative aspects of program behavior such as resource utilization.

A MESSAGE SWITCHING NETWORK

The following example follows part of the development of a simple message switching network and illustrates many of the important features of Gypsy. Only the specification and implementation of the network will be discussed. Its verification is beyond the current scope. The development of the network will be top-down, but Gypsy admits any kind of program design strategy.

The top-level structure of the network is shown in Figure 1. network switches messages among a fixed number of users, each of which communicates with the network through a port. We will ignore protocols, and assume that each message is a separate, complete communication. Even at this early stage of development, the network can be written in Gypsy.

```
program Network(var upa:PortArray) = pending;

type PortArray = array(UserId) of Port;

type UserId = integer(1..NUsers);
const NUsers:integer = pending;

type Port = record(Get,Put:Line):
type Line = buffer(Csize) of Message:
const Csize:integer = pending;

type Message = pending;
```

This program gives a precise description of the lines of communication between the network and its external environment. Communication is through an "array(UserId) of Port." Each port is a record consisting of two buffers, and each buffer contains a maximum of Csize messages. The type UserId is an integer restricted to the range (1..NUsers). The actual number of users, the maximal buffer size, the structure of messages, and the implementation of the network are left pending.

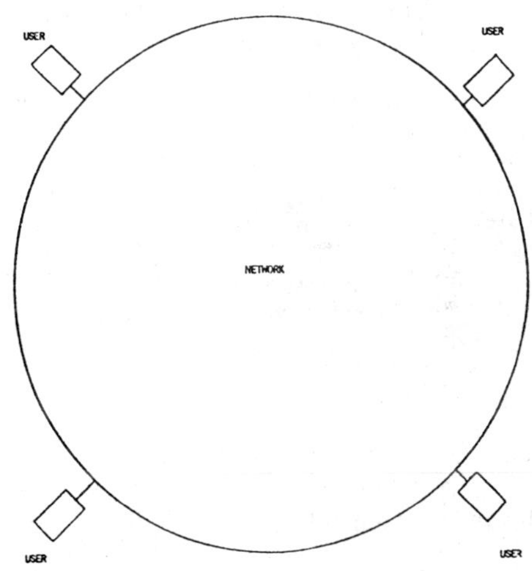

FIGURE 1. TOP LEVEL STRUCTURE OF NETWORK

In a simple network with no protocols, the fundamental specification that is desired is that messages are delivered properly among all possible pairs of users. This specification for the network can be written as

```
program Network(var upa:PortArray) =
begin
  block all i,j:UserId,
      ProperDelivery(i,j,upa);
  pending;
end;
```

The specification is written as a block, instead of
an exit, specification because we intend the
message network to be non-terminating. The network
being blocked means that all processes in the
network are blocked. This could happen for any
number of reasons, including deadlock, but in this
example, it will mean that there is no further
input available from any user.

Before we can proceed with the implementation
of the network, it is necessary that we be more
specific about the meaning of "ProperDelivery."
Loosely speaking, what we mean is that user j
receives only those messages that were intended for
j. We will make this definition precise with a
macro.

```
define ProperDelivery(i,j,pa) =
  mail(pa(j).Put.outto,i,j)
      sub mail(pa(i).Get.infrom,i,j);
```

(The macro definition was chosen to illustrate the
use of macros. ProperDelivery also could have been
defined using a function.) Pa(j).Put.outto is the
sequence of all messages sent out to buffer
pa(j).Put by the network, and pa(i).Get.infrom is
the sequence of messages received in from buffer
upa(i).Get. The function mail(ms,i,j) is the
subsequence of messages in message sequence ms that
are directed from port i to j.

The completion of the definition of
ProperDelivery requires a precise definition of the
mail function, and mail in turn will require some
additional information about messages.

```
function mail(ms:MessageSequence;i,j:UserId)
    MessageSequence =
begin
  exit (assume mail(ms,i,j) =
    if ms=MessageSequence()
    then MessageSequence()
    else if i = Source(first(ms)) and
           j = Destination(first(ms))
      then MessageSequence(first(ms))
         @ Mail(nonfirst(ms),i,j)
      else Mail(nonfirst(ms),i,j)
    fi   fi);
end;

type MessageSequence = sequence of Message;

type Message<Source,Destination,Text,Compose,
    Equal> =
begin
  axiom all m:Message,
      Equal(Compose(Source(m),Destination(m),
        Text(m)),m);
  pending;
end;

function Source(m:Message):UserId =
    pending;
function Destination(m:Message):UserId =
    pending;
```

```
function Text(m:Message):CString =
    pending;
function Compose(s,d:UserId;t:CString)
    :Message = pending;
function Equal(m1,m2:Message):boolean =
    pending;

type CString = sequence (100) of char;
```

The definition of mail(ms,i,j) is given as an
assumed exit specification which gives a complete
recursive definition of mail. The definition of
mail requires a new type, MessageSequence. The
type definition "sequence of Message" defines a
potentially infinite sequence of messages.
Sequences are given a precise meaning by the
semantics of Gypsy, but it is not necessary that
they be implemented. Gypsy has a number of these
kinds of constructs. They are included for
purposes of formal program analysis, and may appear
anywhere in a program where execution is not
required, such as in specifications that are proved
or assumed. In contrast, the type CString is a
sequence of ASCII characters of maximal size 100.
Normally a Gypsy implementation would contain
finite sequences but not infinite ones. Size
restrictions can be enforced by run time checks,
and both kinds of sequences share a common
semantics. MessageSequence() denotes the empty
sequence of messages. In general, type names can
be used to construct objects of that type. The @
operator is the sequence append operator.

The definition of mail makes use of two
functions on messages, Source and Destination. The
type definition of message permits these functions,
as well as Text, Compose, and Equal, access to the
internal structure of messages, which is
temporarily left pending. The axiom states an
identity relation that must be maintained among
this set of functions. This axiom implies that
three kinds of information can be extracted from a
message, a source, destination, and text part. The
source and destination are the means of directing a
message from one user to another, and the text is
the actual content of the message to be
transmitted. The Compose function builds a message
from these three parts, and Equal defines a message
equality. This is the only information that we
will need to know about messages to carry out the
full specification, implementation, and
verification of the network process. Eventually,
of course, we must choose a concrete representation
of messages and prove that the representation and
the implementation of the functions that can access
it satisfy the axioms.

Now we can give a completely precise
interpretation to ProperDelivery. For every i,j
pair, the mail from source i that is sent out to
port j must be a subsequence of the mail received
in from port i that is designated for destination
j. This requires that the messages be the same and
that they arrive in the same order that they were
sent. The subsequence relation permits the network
to drop messages. This is a concession to the
reality of potentially unrecoverable transmission
failures. This completes the specification of
network.

We can proceed with the top-down design at any place in the current Gypsy program where a pending appears. There are many ways this program could be implemented to satisfy the block specification, but we will choose the following:

```
program network(var upa:PortArray) =
begin
  block all i,j:UserId,
      ProperDelivery(i,j,upa);
  var npa:PortArray;
  cobegin
    Node(upa(i),npa(i),i) each i : UserId;
    switch(npa);
  end;
end;

process Node(var up,np:Port;i:UserId) =
begin
  block up.Put.outto sub np.Put.infrom
      and np.Get.outto sub up.Get.infrom;
  pending;
end;

process Switch(var npa:PortArray) =
begin
  block all i,j:UserId,
      ProperDelivery(i,j,npa);
  pending;
end;
```

This implements the program as a star network where each user is attached to exactly one node, and all of the nodes are connected to a single switch as shown in Figure 2. Each node is similar to a full-duplex channel program passing messages unaltered, and in sequence, between the user and the central switch. All of the nodes and the switch are set into concurrent execution by the cobegin in the network program.

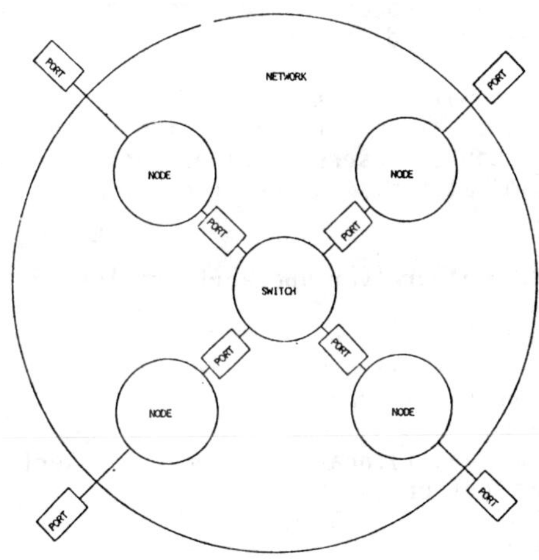

FIGURE 2. IMPLEMENTATION OF NETWORK

A node can be implemented by decomposing it into two one-way channels operating asychronously.

```
process Node(var up,np:Port;i:UserId) =
begin
  block up.Put.outto sub np.Put.infrom
      and np.Get.outto sub up.Get.infrom;
  cobegin
```

```
    Pass(np.Put,up.Put,i,Depart);
    Pass(up.Get,np.Get,i,Arrive);
  end;
end;

process Pass(var x,y:Line; i:UserId;
    d:Direction) =
begin
  block y.outto sub x.infrom;
  var m:Message;
  loop
    assert y.outto sub x.infrom
    receive m from x;
    trace i = if d = Depart
        then Destination(m)
        else Source(m) fi;
    send m to y;
  end;
end;

type direction = (Arrive, Depart);
```

Pass is intentionally programmed as a non-termination loop. The loop simply receives messages from line x and passes them on to line y performing a trace depending on the value of d. The send and receive statements are potential blockage points, and these are the points where the block specification must hold. A cobegin, as in node or network, also is a potential blockage point.

The Switch process also loops forever waiting on each buffer in its turn for a small time slice. If input is ready it will receive it; otherwise, it will time out and go on to the next buffer.

```
process Switch(var npa:PortArray) =
begin
  block all i,j:UserId,
      ProperDelivery(i,j,npa);
  var m:Message;
  var k:UserId;
  cond DestinationErr;
  keep Destination(m) in (1..NUsers)
      otherwise DestinationErr;
  loop
    k := 1;  .
    loop
      if k > NUsers then leave end;
      assert all i,j:UserId,
          ProperDelivery(i,j,npa);
      await
      on receive m from npa(k).Get:
          send m to npa(destination(m)).Put;
      after TimeSlice: ;
      when
      is DestinationErr: ;
      end;
      k := k + 1;
    end;
  end;
end;

const TimeSlice:integer = pending;
```

Switch repeatedly iterates through the Get buffers of the ports attempting to receive a message. Control leaves the inner loop at the leave statement, and the outer loop runs indefinitely.

461

If a message is not received in TimeSlice amount of time, the await is exited and the next buffer is considered. If a message is received within the allocated amount of time, it is sent to the appropriate destination. The keep specification of Switch is evaluated each time one of its variables is assigned a new value. If the specification ever is violated, a destination error is signalled. The keep prevents an invalid array index in the send statement. If the error occurs, control is transferred to the when clause of the await and the DestinationErr part of the when is performed. In this case, Switch does nothing, thus dropping the message. This conforms with the subsequence relation specified in ProperDelivery.

The process structure of the complete network is shown in Figure 3. All of these processes run concurrently. The intermediate level of a node process was not necessary. The Pass processes could have been invoked explicitly from the cobegin in Network. The extra level of decomposition is helpful conceptually and in breaking the network into small, individually verifiable components.

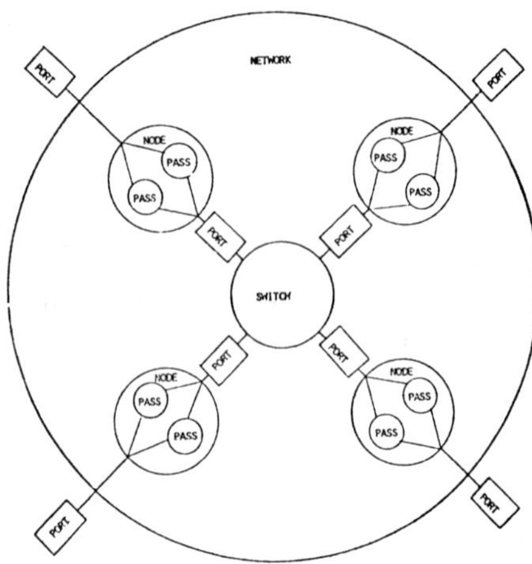

FIGURE 3. FULL NETWORK IMPLEMENTATION

Now let us return to the implementation of messages. They will be implemented in the obvious way as a record of three fields.

```
type Message<Source,Destination,Text,Compose,
    Equal> =
begin
  axiom all m:Message,
      Equal(Compose(Source(m),Destination(m),
          Text(m)),m);
  record(s,d:UserId; t:CString):
end;

function Source(m:Message):UserId =
begin
  cexit Source(m) = m.s;
  result := m.s;
end;

function Destination(m:Message):UserId =
begin
  cexit Destination(m) = m.d;
  result := m.d;
end;
```

```
function Text(m:Message):CString =
begin
  cexit Text(m) = m.t;
  result := m.t;
end;

function Compose(s,d:UserId; t:CString)
    :Message =
begin
  cexit Compose(s,d,t) = Message(s,d,t);
  result := Message(s,d,t);
end;

function Equal(m1,m2:Message):boolean =
begin
  exit Equal(m1,m2) iff Equal(m2,m1);
  cexit Equal(m1,m2) iff
      m1.s=m2.s and m1.d=m2.d and m1.t=m2.t;
  result := m1.s=m2.s and m1.d=m2.d
      and m1.t=m2.t;
end;
```

In the functions that are permitted access to the internal structure of messages, centry and cexit specifications also are permitted access to the internal structure, but entry and exit specifications are not. Entry and exit specifications are visible externally to all routines that call the functions, but the visibility of centry and cexit specifications is restricted. In this example, the cexits of Source, Destination, Text, Compose, and Equal are each visible to the other. This prevents the external specifications from revealing the internal structure of messages to the other routines in the program. In a function the local variable with the reserved name "result" is the value assigned to the function upon exit. It can be used in the same way as any other local variable. In the function Compose, Message(s,d,t) is another example of the type name used to construct an object of that type. Message(s,d,t) creates a message with successive fields equal to s, d, and t.

This completes the program and its specifications except for assigning values to the pending constants NUsers, Csize, and TimeSlice. The program at this stage of development can be written as

```
program network(var upa:PortArray) =
begin
  block all i,j:UserId,
      ProperDelivery(i,j,upa):
  var npa:PortArray;
  cobegin
    Node(una(i),npa(i),i) each i : UserId;
    switch(npa);
  end;
end;

type PortArray = array(UserId) of Port;

type UserId = integer(1..NUsers);
const NUsers:integer = pending;

type Port = record(Get,Put:Line);
type Line = buffer(Csize) of Message;
const Csize:integer = pending;
```

```
define ProperDelivery(i,j,pa) =
  mail(pa(j).put.outto,i,j)
     sub mail(pa(i).get.infrom,i,j);

function mail(ms:MessageSequence;i,j:UserId)
     :MessageSequence =
begin
  exit (assume mail(ms,i,j) =
    if ms=MessageSequence()
    then MessageSequence()
    else if i = Source(first(ms)) and
           j = Destination(first(ms))
      then MessageSequence(first(ms))
         @ Mail(nonfirst(ms),i,j)
      else Mail(nonfirst(ms),i,j)
    fi  fi);
end;

type MessageSequence = sequence of Message;

process Node(var up,np:Port;i:UserId) =
begin
  block up.Put.outto sub np.Put.infrom
    and np.Get.outto sub up.Get.infrom;
  cobegin
    Pass(np.Put,up.Put,i,Depart);
    Pass(up.Get,np.Get,i,Arrive);
  end;
end;

process Pass(var x,y:Line; i:UserId;
    d:Direction) =
begin
  block y.outto sub x.infrom;
  var m:Message;
  loop
    assert y.outto sub x.infrom;
    receive m from x;
    trace i = if d = Depart
       then Destination(m)
       else Source(m) fi
    send m to y;
  end;
end;

type direction = (Arrive, Depart);

process Switch(var npa:PortArray) =
begin
  block all i,j:UserId,
     ProperDelivery(i,j,npa);
  var m:Message;
  var k:UserId;
  cond DestinationErr;
  keep Destination(m) in (1..NUsers)
       otherwise DestinationErr;
  loop
   k := 1;
   loop
     if k > NUsers then leave end;
     assert all i,j:UserId,
        ProperDelivery(i,j,npa);
     await
     on receive m from npa(k).Get:
        send m to npa(destination(m)).Put;
     after Timeslice: ;
     when
     is DestinationErr: ;
     end;
     k := k + 1;
```

```
    end;
   end;
  end;

const TimeSlice:integer = pending;

type Message<Source,Destination,Text,Compose,
    Equal> =
begin
  axiom all m:Message,
    Equal(Compose(Source(m),Destination(m),
       Text(m)),m);
  record(s,d:UserId; t:CString);
end;

type CString = sequence (100) of char;

function Source(m:Message):UserId =
begin
  cexit Source(m) = m.s;
  result := m.s;
end;

function Destination(m:Message):UserId =
begin
  cexit Destination(m) = m.d;
  result := m.d;
end;

function Text(m:Message):CString =
begin
  cexit Text(m) = m.t;
  result := m.t;
end;

function Compose(s,d:UserId; t:CString)
    :Message =
begin
  cexit Compose(s,d,t) = Message(s,d,t);
  result := Message(s,d,t);
end;

function Equal(m1,m2:Message):boolean =
begin
  exit Equal(m1,m2) iff Equal(m2,m1);
  cexit Equal(m1,m2) iff
     m1.s=m2.s and m1.d=m2.d and m1.t=m2.t;
  result := m1.s=m2.s and m1.d=m2.d
     and m1.t=m2.t;
end;
```

There are many details of Gypsy that this example does not illustrate, but the development of this program and its specifications provides a good overview of the philosophy and capabilities of the language.

CONCLUSION

The initial design of Gypsy is complete. The design has been driven by the development of a comprehensive methodology for constructing verified communications processing software, and the trial application of the methodology to realistic problems [20]. A report on the full methodology is in preparation. It is expected that the language will continue to develop as methodology is tested and refined in further applications. A full report on the language can be found in [1]. This report gives a formal definition of the syntax, and an informal description of semantics. A formal definition of the semantics is in preparation. An interactive design and verification system for Gypsy programs is under construction. The system consists of a table-driven syntax analyzer, a verification condition generator, and an interactive theorem prover. First implementations of these components are operational for most of Gypsy. These components are being integrated under a program design management component that maintains a data base of Gypsy program units and supports incremental program development and verification. Implementation of Gypsy is planned, but has not yet begun.

Gypsy has a number of important and distinctive aspects. It is a high-level language for general purpose computing that also supports the development of systems programs. It includes facilities for concurrency and timing, execution in imperfect run time environments, and an access control mechanism. Gypsy includes extensive facilities for expressing functional specifications of its programs and of the units from which its programs are structured. All constructs in Gypsy are verifiable either by formal proof or run time validation. Run time validation can be used effectively to reduce the size and complexity of the formal proofs. Facilities are provided for decomposing both routines and data into small, logically meaningful, units that can be verified independently. This modularity greatly enhances the practical feasibility of formal proofs. We believe that integrating these features smoothly into a common language is a significant step in the design of languages to support the systematic development of highly reliable computer programs.

BIBLIOGRAPHY

[1] Ambler, A.L., Good, D.I., Burger, W.F. "Report on the Language Gypsy". ICSCA-CMP-1, The University of Texas at Austin, (1976).

[2] Ambler, A.L., Hoch, C.G.. "A Study of Protection in Programming Languages," ICSCA-CMP-3, The University of Texas at Austin, (1976).

[3] Brinch Hansen, P. "The Nucleus of a Multiprogramming System," CACM 13, 4 (1970).

[4] Brinch Hansen, P. "Operating Systems Principles," Prentice-Hall (1973).

[5] Brinch Hansen, P. "The Purpose of Concurrent Pascal," Proceedings ICRS (1975).

[6] Buxton, J.N. and Randell, B., eds. "Software Engineering Techniques", NATO Science Committee (1970).

[7] Clint, M. "Program Proving: Co-routines," Acta Informatica. 2 (1973).

[8] Dahl, O.J. "Notes on Data Structuring," Dahl, Dijkstra, and Hoare, Structured Programming, Academic Press (1972).

[9] Dijkstra, E.W. "Guarded Commands, Nondeterminacy, and Formal Derivation of Programs," CACM 18, 8 (1975).

[10] Flon, L. "A Survey of Some Issues Concerning Abstract Data Types," Technical Report, Carnegie-Mellon (1974).

[11] Good, D.I. and Ragland, L.C. "Nucleus--A Language for Provable Programs," Program Test Methods, Hetzel (ed.), Prentice-Hall (1973).

[12] Igarashi, S., London, R.L., and Luckham, D.C. "Automatic Program Verification I: A Logical Basis and Its Implementation," Report ISI/RR-73-11, USC, Information Science Institute (1973).

[13] Jensen, K. and Wirth, N. "Pascal User Manual and Report," Springer Verlag (1974).

[14] Lampson, B.W., Horning, J.J., London, R.L., Mitchell, J.G., and Popek, G.J. "Report on the Programming Language Euclid", Xerox Research Center, August, 1976.

[15] Liskov, B. and Zilles, S. "An Approach to Abstraction," Computation Structures Group Memo 88, MIT (1973).

[16] Lyle, D.M. "A Hierarchy of High Order Languages for Systems Programming," Proceeds of SIGPLAN Symposium on Languages for Systems Implementation (1971).

[17] Randell, B. "System Structure for Software Fault Tolerance," Proceedings ICRS (1975).

[18] Stucki, L.G. "Testing Impact on the Future of Software Engineering," Proceeds of Fourth Texas Conference on Computing Systems, University of Texas (1975).

[19] van Wijngaarden, A. "Report on the Algorithmic Language ALGOL 68," Numerische Mathematik, 14 (1969).

[20] Wells, R. "The Specification and Implementation of a Verifiable Communications System", Masters Thesis, The University of Texas at Austin, 1976.

[21] Wulf, W.A., Russell, D.B., and Habermann, A.N. "BLISS: A Language for Systems Programming," CACM 14, 12 (1971).

[22] Wulf, W.A., Levin, R., and Pierson, C. "Overview of the Hydra Operating System Development," Proceedings of Fifth Symposium on Operating Systems Principles, (1975).

[23] Wulf, W.A., London, R.L., and Shaw, M. "Abstraction and Verification in Alphard: Introduction to Language and Methodology," Research Report ISI/RR-76-46, ARPA, (1976).

[24] Zahn, C.T. "A Control Statement for Natural Top-Down Structured Programming," Symposium on Programming Languages (1974).

The Programming Language Concurrent Pascal

PER BRINCH HANSEN

Reprinted from *IEEE Transactions on Software Engineering,* June 1975, pp. 199-207. Copyright © 1975 by The Institute of Electrical and Electronics Engineers, Inc.

Abstract—The paper describes a new programming language for structured programming of computer operating systems. It extends the sequential programming language Pascal with concurrent programming tools called processes and monitors. Section I explains these concepts informally by means of pictures illustrating a hierarchical design of a simple spooling system. Section II uses the same example to introduce the language notation. The main contribution of Concurrent Pascal is to extend the monitor concept with an explicit hierarchy of access rights to shared data structures that can be stated in the program text and checked by a compiler.

Index Terms—Abstract data types, access rights, classes, concurrent processes, concurrent programming languages, hierarchical operating systems, monitors, scheduling, structured multiprogramming.

I. THE PURPOSE OF CONCURRENT PASCAL

A. Background

SINCE 1972 I have been working on a new programming language for structured programming of computer operating systems. This language is called Concurrent Pascal. It extends the sequential programming language Pascal with concurrent programming tools called processes and monitors [1]–[3].

This is an informal description of Concurrent Pascal. It uses examples, pictures, and words to bring out the creative aspects of new programming concepts without getting into their finer details. I plan to define these concepts precisely and introduce a notation for them in later papers. This form of presentation may be imprecise from a formal point of view, but is perhaps more effective from a human point of view.

B. Processes

We will study concurrent processes inside an operating system and look at one small problem only: how can large amounts of data be transmitted from one process to another by means of a buffer stored on a disk?

Fig. 1 shows this little system and its three components: a process that produces data, a process that consumes data, and a disk buffer that connects them.

The circles are *system components* and the arrows are the *access rights* of these components. They show that both processes can use the buffer (but they do not show that data flows from the producer to the consumer). This kind of picture is an *access graph*.

Manuscript received February 1, 1975. This project is supported by the National Science Foundation under Grant DCR74-17331.

The author is with the Department of Information Science, California Institute of Technology, Pasadena, Calif. 91125.

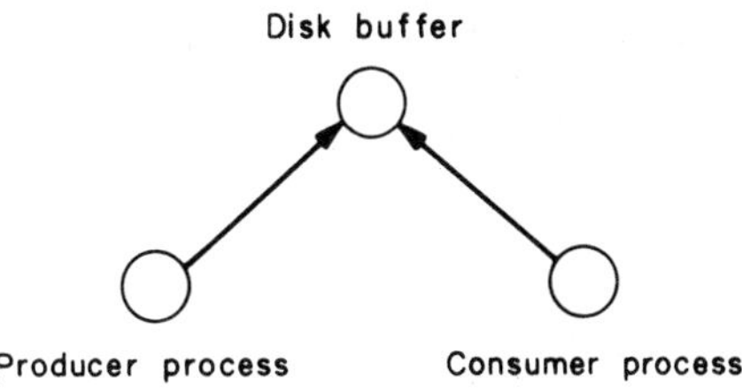

Fig. 1.   Process communication.

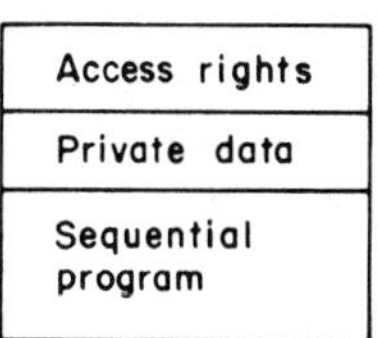

Fig. 2.   Process.

The next picture shows a process component in more detail (Fig. 2).

A *process* consists of a *private data* structure and a *sequential program* that can operate on the data. One process cannot operate on the private data of another process. But concurrent processes can share certain data structures (such as a disk buffer). The *access rights* of a process mention the shared data it can operate on.

C. Monitors

A disk buffer is a data structure shared by two concurrent processes. The details of how such a buffer is constructed are irrelevant to its users. All the processes need to know is that they can *send* and *receive* data through it. If they try to operate on the buffer in any other way it is probably either a programming mistake or an example of tricky programming. In both cases, one would like a compiler to detect such misuse of a shared data structure.

To make this possible, we must introduce a language construct that will enable a programmer to tell a compiler how a shared data structure can be used by processes. This kind of system component is called a monitor. A monitor can synchronize concurrent processes and transmit data between them. It can also control the order in which competing processes use shared, physical resources. Fig. 3 shows a monitor in detail.

A *monitor* defines a *shared data* structure and all the operations processes can perform on it. These synchronizing operations are called *monitor procedures*. A monitor also defines an *initial operation* that will be executed when its data structure is created.

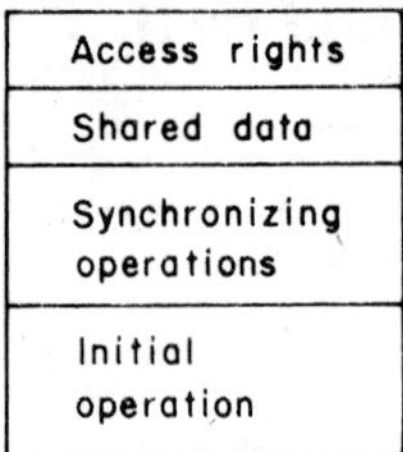

Fig. 3.   Monitor.

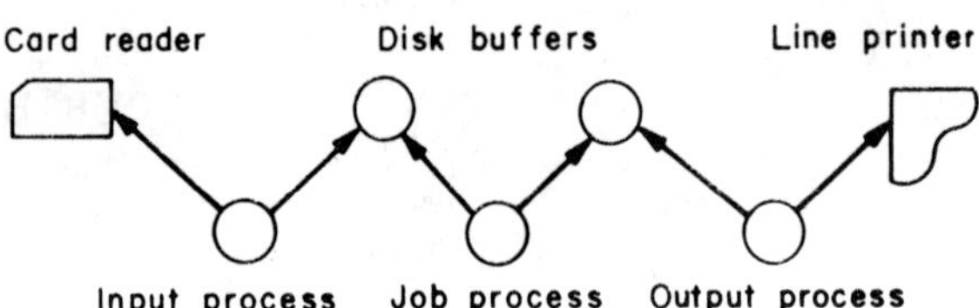

Fig. 4.   Spooling system.

We can define a *disk buffer* as a monitor. Within this monitor there will be shared variables that define the location and length of the buffer on the disk. There will also be two monitor procedures, *send* and *receive*. The initial operation will make sure that the buffer starts as an empty one.

Processes cannot operate directly on shared data. They can only call monitor procedures that have access to shared data. A monitor procedure is executed as part of a calling process (just like any other procedure).

If concurrent processes simultaneously call monitor procedures that operate on the same shared data these procedures must be executed strictly one at a time. Otherwise, the results of monitor calls will be unpredictable. This means that the machine must be able to delay processes for short periods of time until it is their turn to execute monitor procedures. We will not be concerned about how this is done, but will just notice that a monitor procedure has *exclusive access* to shared data while it is being executed.

So the (virtual) machine on which concurrent programs run will handle *short-term scheduling* of simultaneous monitor calls. But the programmer must also be able to delay processes for longer periods of time if their requests for data and other resources cannot be satisfied immediately. If, for example, a process tries to receive data from an empty disk buffer it must be delayed until another process sends more data.

Concurrent Pascal includes a simple data type, called a *queue*, that can be used by monitor procedures to control *medium-term scheduling* of processes. A monitor can either *delay* a calling process in a queue or *continue* another process that is waiting in a queue. It is not important here to understand how these queues work except for the following essential rule: a process only has exclusive access to shared data as long as it continues to execute statements within a monitor procedure. As soon as a process is delayed in a queue it loses its exclusive access until another process calls the same monitor and wakes it up again. (Without this rule, it would be impossible for other processes to enter a monitor and let waiting processes continue their execution.)

Although the disk buffer example does not show this yet, monitor procedures should also be able to call procedures defined within other monitors. Otherwise, the language will not be very useful for hierarchical design. In the case of a disk buffer, one of these other monitors could perhaps define simple input/output operations on the disk. So a monitor can also have *access rights* to other system components (see Fig. 3).

D. System Design

A process executes a sequential program—it is an active component. A monitor is just a collection of procedures that do nothing until they are called by processes—it is a passive component. But there are strong similarities between a process and a monitor: both define a data structure (private or shared) and the meaningful operations on it. The main difference between processes and monitors is the way they are scheduled for execution.

It seems natural therefore to regard processes and monitors as *abstract data types* defined in terms of the operations one can perform on them. If a compiler can check that these operations are the only ones carried out on the data structures, then we may be able to build very reliable, concurrent programs in which *controlled access* to data and physical resources is guaranteed before these programs are put into operation. We have then to some extent solved the *resource protection* problem in the cheapest possible manner (without hardware mechanisms and run time overhead).

So we will define processes and monitors as data types and make it possible to use several instances of the same component type in a system. We can, for example, use two disk buffers to build a *spooling system* with an input process, a job process, and an output process (Fig. 4). I will distinguish between definitions and instances of components by calling them *system types* and *system components*. Access graphs (such as Fig. 4) will always show system components (not system types).

Peripheral devices are considered to be monitors implemented in hardware. They can only be accessed by a single procedure *io* that delays the calling process until an input/output operation is completed. Interrupts are handled by the virtual machine on which processes run.

To make the programming language useful for stepwise system design it should permit the division of a system type, such as a disk buffer, into smaller system types. One of these other system types should give a disk buffer access to the disk. We will call this system type a *virtual disk*. It gives a disk buffer the illusion that it has its own private disk. A virtual disk hides the details of disk input/output from the rest of the system and makes the disk look like a data structure (an array of disk pages). The only operations on this data structure are *read* and *write* a page.

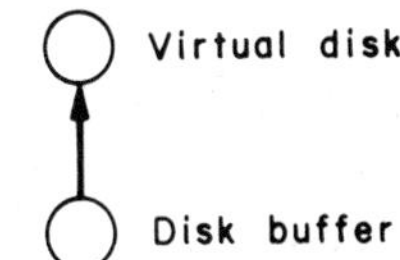

Fig. 5.   Buffer refinement.

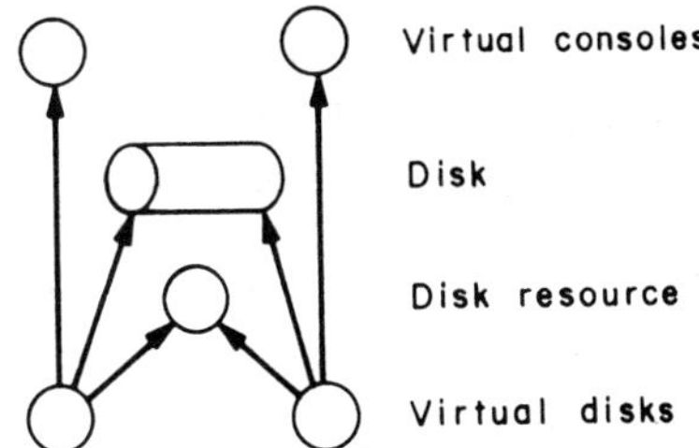

Fig. 6.   Decomposition of virtual disks.

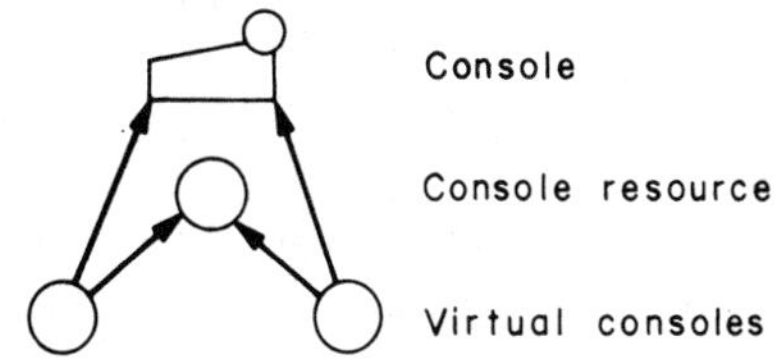

Fig. 7.   Decomposition of virtual consoles.

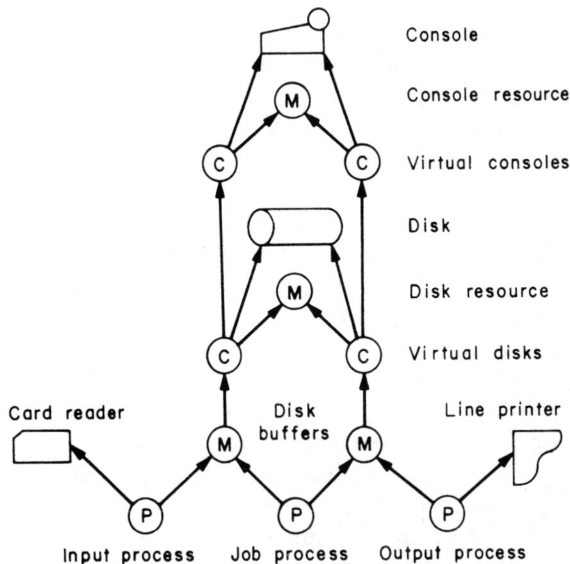

Fig. 8.   Hierarchical system structure.

Each virtual disk is only used by a single disk buffer (Fig. 5). A system component that cannot be called simultaneously by several other components will be called a *class*. A class defines a data structure and the possible operations on it (just like a monitor). The exclusive access of class procedures to class variables can be guaranteed completely at compile time. The virtual machine does not have to schedule simultaneous calls of class procedures at run time, because such calls cannot occur. This makes class calls considerably faster than monitor calls.

The spooling system includes two virtual disks but only one real disk. So we need a single *disk resource* monitor to control the order in which competing processes use the disk (Fig. 6). This monitor defines two procedures, *request* and *release* access, to be called by a virtual disk before and after each disk transfer.

It would seem simpler to replace the virtual disks and the disk resource by a single monitor that has exclusive access to the disk and does the input/output. This would certainly guarantee that processes use the disk one at a time. But this would be done according to the built-in short-term scheduling policy of monitor calls.

Now to make a virtual machine efficient, one must use a very simple short-term scheduling rule (such as first come, first served) [2]. If the disk has a moving access head this is about the worst possible algorithm one can use for disk transfers. It is vital that the language make it possible for the programmer to write a medium-term scheduling algorithm that will minimize disk head movements [3]. The data type *queue* mentioned earlier makes it possible to implement arbitrary scheduling rules within a monitor.

The difficulty is that while a monitor is performing an input/output operation it is impossible for other processes to enter the same monitor and join the disk queue. They will automatically be delayed by the short-term scheduler and only allowed to enter the monitor one at a time after each disk transfer. This will, of course, make the attempt to control disk scheduling within the monitor illusory. To give the programmer complete control of disk scheduling, processes should be able to enter the disk queue during disk transfers. Since *arrival* and *service* in the disk queueing system potentially are simultaneous operations they must be handled by different system components, as shown in Fig. 6.

If the disk fails persistently during input/output this should be reported on an operator's console. Fig. 6 shows two instances of a class type, called a *virtual console*. They give the virtual disks the illusion that they have their own private consoles.

The virtual consoles get exclusive access to a single, real console by calling a *console resource* monitor (Fig. 7). Notice that we now have a standard technique for dealing with virtual devices.

If we put all these system components together, we get a complete picture of a simple spooling system (Fig. 8). Classes, monitors, and processes are marked C, M, and P.

E. Scope Rules

Some years ago I was part of a team that built a multiprogramming system in which processes can appear and disappear dynamically [4]. In practice, this system was used mostly to set up a fixed configuration of processes. Dynamic process deletion will certainly complicate the semantics and implementation of a programming language considerably. And since it appears to be unnecessary for a large class of real-time applications, it seems wise to exclude it altogether. So an operating system written in Concurrent Pascal will consist of a fixed number of processes, monitors, and classes. These components and their data structures will exist forever after system initialization. An operating system can, however, be extended by recompilation. It remains to be seen whether this restriction will simplify or complicate operating system design. But the poor quality of most existing operating systems clearly demonstrates an urgent need for simpler approaches.

In existing programming languages the data structures of processes, monitors, and classes would be called "global data." This term would be misleading in Concurrent Pascal where each data structure can be accessed by a single component only. It seems more appropriate to call them *permanent data structures*.

I have argued elsewhere that the most dangerous aspect of concurrent programming is the possibility of *time-dependent programming errors* that are impossible to locate by program testing ("lurking bugs") [2], [5], [6]. If we are going to depend on real-time programming systems in our daily lives, we must be able to find such obscure errors before the systems are put into operation.

Fortunately, a compiler can detect many of these errors if processes and monitors are represented by a structured notation in a high-level programming language. In addition, we must exclude low-level machine features (registers, addresses, and interrupts) from the language and let a virtual machine control them. If we want real-time systems to be highly reliable, we must stop programming them in assembly language. (The use of hardware protection mechanisms is merely an expensive, inadequate way of making arbitrary machine language programs behave almost as predictably as compiled programs.)

A Concurrent Pascal compiler will check that the private data of a process only are accessed by that process. It will also check that the data structure of a class or monitor only is accessed by its procedures.

Fig. 8 shows that *access rights* within an operating system normally are not tree structured. Instead they form a directed graph. This partly explains why the traditional scope rules of block-structured languages are inconvenient for concurrent programming (and for sequential programming as well). In Concurrent Pascal one can state the access rights of components in the program text and have them checked by a compiler.

Since the execution of a monitor procedure will delay the execution of further calls of the same monitor, we must prevent a monitor from calling itself recursively. Otherwise, processes can become *deadlocked*. So the compiler will check that the access rights of system components are hierarchically ordered (or, if you like, that there are no cycles in the access graph).

The *hierarchical ordering* of system components has vital consequences for system design and testing [7].

A hierarchical operating system will be tested component by component, bottom up (but could, of course, be conceived top down or by iteration). When an incomplete operating system has been shown to work correctly (by proof or testing), a compiler can ensure that this part of the system will continue to work correctly when new untested program components are added on top of it. Programming errors within new components cannot cause old components to fail because old components do not call new components, and new components only call old components through well-defined procedures that have already been tested.

(Strictly speaking, a compiler can only check that single monitor calls are made correctly; it cannot check sequences of monitor calls, for example whether a resource is always reserved before it is released. So one can only hope for compile time assurance of *partial correctness*.)

Several other reasons besides program correctness make a hierarchical structure attractive:

1) a hierarchical operating system can be studied in a stepwise manner as a sequence of *abstract machines* simulated by programs [8];

2) a partial ordering of process interactions permits one to use *mathematical induction* to prove certain overall properties of the system (such as the absence of deadlocks) [2];

3) *efficient resource utilization* can be achieved by ordering the program components according to the speed of the physical resources they control (with the fastest resources being controlled at the bottom of the system) [8];

4) a hierarchical system designed according to the previous criteria is often *nearly decomposable* from an analytical point of view. This means that one can develop stochastic models of its dynamic behavior in a stepwise manner [9].

F. Final Remarks

It seems most natural to represent a hierarchical system structure, such as Fig. 8, by a two-dimensional picture. But when we write a concurrent program we must somehow represent these access rules by linear text. This limitation of written language tends to obscure the simplicity of the original structure. That is why I have tried to explain the purpose of Concurrent Pascal by means of pictures instead of language notation.

The class concept is a restricted form of the class concept of Simula 67 [10]. Dijkstra suggested the idea of monitors [8]. The first structured language notation for monitors was proposed in [2], and illustrated by examples in [3]. The queue variables needed by monitors for process scheduling were suggested in [5] and modified in [3].

The main contribution of Concurrent Pascal is to extend monitors with explicit access rights that can be checked at compile time. Concurrent Pascal has been implemented at Caltech for the PDP 11/45 computer. Our system uses sequential Pascal as a job control and user programming language.

II. THE USE OF CONCURRENT PASCAL

A. *Introduction*

In Section I the concepts of Concurrent Pascal were explained informally by means of pictures of a hierarchical spooling system. I will now use the same example to introduce the language notation of Concurrent Pascal. The presentation is still informal. I am neither trying to define the language precisely nor to develop a working system. This will be done in other papers. I am just trying to show the flavor of the language.

B. *Processes*

We will now program the system components in Fig. 8 one at a time from top to bottom (but we could just as well do it bottom up).

Although we only need one *input process*, we may as well define it as a general system type of which several copies may exist:

```
type inputprocess =
process(buffer: diskbuffer);
var block: page;
cycle
   readcards(block);
   buffer.send(block);
end
```

An input process has access to a *buffer* of type diskbuffer (to be defined later). The process has a private variable *block* of type page. The data type page is declared elsewhere as an array of characters:

```
type page = array (.1..512.) of char
```

A process type defines a *sequential program*—in this case, an endless cycle that inputs a block from a card reader and sends it through the buffer to another process. We will ignore the details of card reader input.

The *send* operation on the buffer is called as follows (using the block as a parameter):

```
buffer.send(block)
```

The next component type we will define is a *job process:*

```
type jobprocess =
process(input, output: diskbuffer);
var block: page;
cycle
   input.receive(block);
   update(block);
   output.send(block);
end
```

A job process has access to two disk buffers called *input* and *output*. It receives blocks from one buffer, updates them, and sends them through the other buffer. The details of updating can be ignored here.

Finally, we need an *output process* that can receive data from a disk buffer and output them on a line printer:

```
type outputprocess =
process(buffer: diskbuffer);
var block: page;
cycle
   buffer.receive(block);
   printlines(block);
end
```

The following shows a declaration of the main system components:

```
var buffer1, buffer2: diskbuffer;
   reader: inputprocess;
   master: jobprocess;
   writer: outputprocess;
```

There is an input process, called the *reader*, a job process, called the *master*, and an output process, called the *writer*. Then there are two disk buffers, *buffer1* and *buffer2*, that connect them.

Later I will explain how a disk buffer is defined and initialized. If we assume that the disk buffers already have been initialized, we can initialize the input process as follows:

```
init reader(buffer1)
```

The *init* statement allocates space for the *private variables* of the reader process and starts its execution as a sequential process with access to buffer1.

The *access rights* of a process to other system components, such as buffer1, are also called its *parameters*. A process can only be initialized once. After initialization, the parameters and private variables of a process exist forever. They are called *permanent variables*.

The init statement can be used to start concurrent execution of several processes and define their access rights. As an example, the statement

```
init reader(buffer1), master(buffer1, buffer2),
   writer(buffer2)
```

starts concurrent execution of the reader process (with access to buffer1), the master process (with access to both buffers), and the writer process (with access to buffer2).

A process can only access its own parameters and private variables. The latter are not accessible to other system components. Compare this with the more liberal scope rules of block-structured languages in which a program block can access not only its own parameters and local variables, but also those declared in outer blocks. In Concurrent Pascal, all variables accessible to a system component are declared within its type definition. This access rule and the init statement make it possible for a programmer to state access rights explicitly and have them checked by a compiler. They also make it possible to study a system type as a self-contained program unit.

Although the programming examples do not show this, one can also define constants, data types, and procedures within a process. These objects can only be used within the process type.

C. Monitors

The *disk buffer* is a monitor type:

```
type diskbuffer =
monitor(consoleaccess, diskaccess: resource;
   base, limit: integer);

   var disk: virtualdisk; sender, receiver: queue;
      head, tail, length: integer;

   procedure entry send(block: page);
   begin
      if length = limit then delay(sender);
      disk.write(base + tail, block);
      tail: = (tail + 1) mod limit;
      length: = length + 1;
      continue(receiver);
   end;

   procedure entry receive(var block: page);
   begin
      if length = 0 then delay(receiver);
      disk.read(base + head, block);
      head: = (head + 1) mod limit;
      length: = length - 1;
      continue(sender);
   end;

   begin "initial statement"
      init disk(consoleaccess, diskaccess);
      head: = 0; tail: = 0; length: = 0;
   end
```

A disk buffer has access to two other components, *consoleaccess* and *diskaccess*, of type resource (to be defined later). It also has access to two integer constants defining the *base* address and *limit* of the buffer on the disk.

The monitor declares a set of *shared variables:* the *disk* is declared as a variable of type virtualdisk. Two variables of type queue are used to delay the *sender* and *receiver* processes until the buffer becomes nonfull and nonempty. Three integers define the relative addresses of the *head* and *tail* elements of the buffer and its current *length*.

The monitor defines two *monitor procedures*, send and receive. They are marked with the word *entry* to distinguish them from local procedures used within the monitor (there are none of these in this example).

Receive returns a page to the calling process. If the buffer is empty, the calling process is *delayed* in the receiver queue until another process sends a page through the buffer. The receive procedure will then read and remove a page from the head of the disk buffer by calling a *read* operation defined within the virtual disk type:

$$disk.read(base + head, block)$$

Finally, the receive procedure will *continue* the execution of a sending process (if the latter is waiting in the sender queue).

Send is similar to receive.

The queuing mechanism will be explained in detail in the next section.

The *initial statement* of a disk buffer initializes its virtual disk with access to the console and disk resources. It also sets the buffer length to zero. (Notice, that a disk buffer does not use its access rights to the console and disk, but only passes them on to a virtual disk declared within it.)

The following shows a declaration of two system components of type resource and two integers defining the base and limit of a disk buffer:

```
var consoleaccess, diskaccess: resource;
   base, limit: integer;
   buffer: diskbuffer;
```

If we assume that these variables already have been initialized, we can initialize a disk buffer as follows:

```
init buffer(consoleaccess, diskaccess, base, limit)
```

The *init* statement allocates storage for the parameters and shared variables of the disk buffer and executes its initial statement.

A monitor can only be initialized once. After initialization, the parameters and shared variables of a monitor exist forever. They are called *permanent variables*. The parameters and local variables of a monitor procedure, however, exist only while it is being executed. They are called *temporary variables*.

A monitor procedure can only access its own temporary and permanent variables. These variables are not accessible to other system components. Other components can, however, call procedure entries within a monitor. While a monitor procedure is being executed, it has *exclusive access* to the permanent variables of the monitor. If concurrent processes try to call procedures within the same monitor simultaneously, these procedures will be executed strictly one at a time.

Only monitors and constants can be permanent parameters of processes and monitors. This rule ensures that processes only communicate by means of monitors.

It is possible to define constants, data types, and local procedures within monitors (and processes). The local procedures of a system type can only be called within the system type. To prevent *deadlock* of monitor calls and ensure that access rights are hierarchical the following rules are enforced: a procedure must be declared before it can be called; procedure definitions cannot be nested and cannot call themselves; a system type cannot call its own procedure entries.

The absence of recursion makes it possible for a compiler to determine the store requirements of all system components. This and the use of permanent components make it possible to use *fixed store allocation* on a computer that does not support paging.

Since system components are permanent they must be declared as permanent variables of other components.

D. Queues

A monitor procedure can delay a calling process for any length of time by executing a *delay* operation on a queue variable. Only one process at a time can wait in a queue. When a calling process is delayed by a monitor procedure it loses its exclusive access to the monitor variables until another process calls the same monitor and executes a continue operation on the queue in which the process is waiting.

The *continue* operation makes the calling process return from its monitor call. If any process is waiting in the selected queue, it will immediately resume the execution of the monitor procedure that delayed it. After being resumed, the process again has exclusive access to the permanent variables of the monitor.

Other variants of process queues (called "events" and "conditions") are proposed in [3], [5]. They are multi-process queues that use different (but fixed) scheduling rules. We do not yet know from experience which kind of queue will be the most convenient one for operating system design. A single-process queue is the simplest tool that gives the programmer complete control of the scheduling of individual processes. Later, I will show how multi-process queues can be built from single-process queues.

A queue must be declared as a permanent variable within a monitor type.

E. Classes

Every disk buffer has its own virtual disk. A virtual disk is defined as a class type:

```
type virtualdisk =
class(consoleaccess, diskaccess: resource);

var terminal: virtualconsole; peripheral: disk;

procedure entry read(pageno: integer; var block: page);
var error: boolean;
begin
  repeat
    diskaccess.request;
    peripheral.read(pageno, block, error);
    diskaccess.release;
    if error then terminal.write('disk failure');
  until not error;
end;

procedure entry write(pageno: integer; block: page);
begin "similar to read" end;

begin "initial statement"
  init terminal(consoleaccess), peripheral;
end
```

A virtual disk has access to a console resource and a disk resource. Its permanent variables define a virtual console and a disk. A process can access its virtual disk by means of *read* and *write* procedures. These procedure entries *request* and *release* exclusive access to the real disk before and after each block transfer. If the real disk fails, the virtual disk calls its virtual console to report the error.

The *initial statement* of a virtual disk initializes its virtual console and the real disk.

Section II-C shows an example of how a virtual disk is declared and initialized (within a disk buffer).

A class can only be initialized once. After initialization, its parameters and private variables exist forever. A class procedure can only access its own temporary and permanent variables. These cannot be accessed by other components.

A class is a system component that cannot be called simultaneously by several other components. This is guaranteed by the following rule: a class must be declared as a permanent variable within a system type; a class can be passed as a permanent parameter to another class (but not to a process or monitor). So a chain of nested class calls can only be started by a single process or monitor. Consequently, it is not necessary to schedule simultaneous class calls at run time—they cannot occur.

F. Input/Output

The real *disk* is controlled by a class

```
type disk = class
```

with two procedure entries

```
read(pageno, block, error)
write(pageno, block, error)
```

The class uses a standard procedure

```
io(block, param, device)
```

to transfer a block to or from the disk device. The io parameter is a record

```
var param: record
        operation: iooperation;
        result: ioresult;
        pageno: integer
      end
```

that defines an input/output operation, its result, and a page number on the disk. The calling process is delayed until an io operation has been completed.

A *virtual console* is also defined as a class

```
type virtualconsole =
class(access: resource);
var terminal: console;
```

It can be accessed by read and write operations that are similar to each other:

```
procedure entry read(var text: line);
begin
  access.request;
  terminal.read(text);
  access.release;
end
```

The real *console* is controlled by a class that is similar to the disk class.

G. Multiprocess Scheduling

Access to the console and disk is controlled by two monitors of type *resource*. To simplify the presentation, I will assume that competing processes are served in first-come, first-served order. (A much better disk scheduling algorithm is defined in [3]. It can be programmed in Concurrent Pascal as well, but involves more details than the present one.)

We will define a multiprocess queue as an array of single-process queues

```
type multiqueue = array (.0..qlength-1.) of queue
```

where $q$length is an upper bound on the number of concurrent processes in the system.

A first-come, first-served scheduler is now straightforward to program:

```
type resource =
monitor

var free: Boolean; q: multiqueue;
   head, tail, length: integer;

procedure entry request;
var arrival: integer;
begin
   if free then free:= false else
   begin
     arrival:= tail;
     tail:= (tail + 1) mod qlength;
     length:= length + 1;
     delay(q(.arrival.));
   end;
end;

procedure entry release;
var departure: integer;
begin
   if length = 0 then free:= true else
   begin
     departure:= head;
     head:= (head + 1) mod qlength;
     length:= length - 1;
     continue(q(.departure.));
   end;
end;

begin "initial statement"
   free:= true; length:= 0;
   head:= 0; tail:= 0;
end
```

H. Initial Process

Finally, we will put all these components together into a concurrent program. A Concurrent Pascal program consists of nested definitions of system types. The outermost system type is an anonymous process, called the initial process. An instance of this process is created during system loading. It initializes the other system components.

The initial process defines system types and instances of them. It executes statements that initialize these system components. In our example, the initial process can be sketched as follows (ignoring the problem of how base addresses and limits of disk buffers are defined):

```
type
   resource = monitor···end;
   console = class···end;
   virtualconsole =
     class(access: resource);···end;
   disk = class···end;
   virtualdisk =
     class(consoleaccess, diskaccess: resource);···end;
   diskbuffer =
     monitor(consoleaccess, diskaccess: resource;
       base, limit: integer);···end;
   inputprocess =
     process(buffer: diskbuffer);···end;
   jobprocess =
     process(input, output: diskbuffer);···end;
   outputprocess =
     process(buffer: diskbuffer);···end;
var
   consoleaccess, diskaccess: resource;
   buffer1, buffer2: diskbuffer;
   reader: inputprocess;
   master: jobprocess;
   writer: outputprocess;
begin
   init consoleaccess, diskaccess,
     buffer1(consoleaccess, diskaccess, base1, limit1),
     buffer2(consoleaccess, diskaccess, base2, limit2),
     reader(buffer1),
     master(buffer1, buffer2),
     writer(buffer2);
end.
```

When the execution of a process (such as the initial process) terminates, its private variables continue to exist. This is necessary because these variables may have been passed as permanent parameters to other system components.

ACKNOWLEDGMENT

It is a pleasure to acknowledge the immense value of a continuous exchange of ideas with C. A. R. Hoare on structured multiprogramming. I also thank my students L. Medina and R. Varela for their helpful comments on this paper.

REFERENCES

[1] N. Wirth, "The programming language Pascal," *Acta Informatica*, vol. 1, no. 1, pp. 35–63, 1971.
[2] P. Brinch Hansen, *Operation System Principles*. Englewood Cliffs, N. J.: Prentice-Hall, July 1973.
[3] C. A. R. Hoare, "Monitors: An operating system structuring concept," *Commun. Ass. Comput. Mach.*, vol. 17, pp. 549–557, Oct. 1974.
[4] P. Brinch Hansen, "The nucleus of a multiprogramming

system," *Commun. Ass. Comput. Mach.*, vol. 13, pp. 238–250, Apr. 1970.

[5] ——, "Structured multiprogramming," *Commun. Ass. Comput. Mach.*, vol. 15, pp. 574–578, July 1972.

[6] ——, "Concurrent programming concepts," *Ass. Comput. Mach. Comput. Rev.*, vol. 5, pp. 223–245, Dec. 1974.

[7] ——, "A programming methodology for operating system design," in *1974 Proc. IFIP Congr.* Stockholm, Sweden: North-Holland, Aug. 1974, pp. 394–397.

[8] E. W. Dijkstra, "Hierarchical ordering of sequential processes," *Acta Informatica*, vol. 1, no. 2, pp. 115–138, 1971.

[9] H. A. Simon, "The architecture of complexity," in *Proc. Amer. Philosophical Society*, vol. 106, no. 6, 1962, pp. 468–482.

[10] O.-J. Dahl and C. A. R. Hoare, "Hierarchical program structures," in *Structured Programming*, O.-J. Dahl, E. W. Dijkstra, and C. A. R. Hoare. New York: Academic, 1972.

Per Brinch Hansen was born in Copenhagen, Denmark, on November 13, 1938. He received the M.S. degree in electronic engineering from the Technical University of Denmark, Copenhagen, in 1963.

Afterwards he joined the Danish computer manufacturer, Regnecentralen, as a systems programmer and designer. In 1967 he became head of the department at Regnecentralen which developed the architecture of the RC 4000 computer and its multiprogramming system. From 1970 to 1972 he visited Carnegie-Mellon University, Pittsburgh, Pa., where he wrote the book *Operating System Principles* (Englewood Cliffs, N. J., Prentice-Hall, July 1973). This book contains the first proposal of the *monitor concept* on which the programming language Concurrent Pascal is based. In 1972 he became Associate Professor of Computer Science at the California Institute of Technology, Pasadena. He has been a consultant to Burroughs Corporation, Control Data Corporation, Jet Propulsion Laboratory, Philips, and Varian Data Machines. His main research interests are computer architecture and programming methodology.

Dr. Brinch Hansen is a member of the Working Group 2.3 on Programming Methodology sponsored by the International Federation for Information Processing.

The design of PLAIN—Support for systematic programming

by ANTHONY I. WASSERMAN*

Section on Medical Information Science
University of California, San Francisco
San Francisco, California

Reprinted from *Proceedings, National Computer Conference*, 1980, pp. 731-740, ©
AFIPS Press. Reprinted by permission.

DISCIPLINE IN SOFTWARE DEVELOPMENT

The successful construction of medium and large software systems requires the management of the complexity inherent in the problem being programmed. A well-disciplined approach to software development involves the production of a complete specification, a complete problem solution, and program design prior to the inception of actual coding. In practice, this requires the production of some form of program design representation [1] from the original specification, with the action of each module specified with a program design language [2]. Furthermore, data structures are specified and refined, in some cases to physical data structures, but more commonly to logical data structures.

It is from that point that coding begins. The information available to the coder should include, at a minimum, the input and output parameters for each independent program unit and an unambiguous description of the operations to be carried out by each. Analysis of information flow, performance or space requirements, and similar considerations lead to the identification of commonly used routines and data, yielding an initial program structure derived from the design.

A disciplined approach to software development, then, requires that the program *design stage* precede the program *construction stage*. The completed software design can be checked against the original specification by "walkthroughs" [3] or similar methods, with the resulting "software blueprints" providing the basis for implementation (or possibly redesign).

An important consideration in the target programming language, then, is the ease with which one can proceed from the design representation, with its modular structure and its degree of abstraction, to the program representation, i.e., executable code. A second key consideration is the ease with which one can determine the conformity between the completed program and the original specification, using testing and/or verification techniques.

* This work was supported in part by National Science Foundation grant MCS78-26287. Computing support for text preparation was provided by National Institutes of Health Grant RR-1081 to the University of California, San Francisco, Computer Graphics Laboratory, Principal Investigator: Robert Langridge.

PLAIN AND ITS DESIGN CONTEXT

The past few years have witnessed an increased understanding of the relationship between programming languages and problem solving [4,5]. As a result of this work in programming methodology, programming languages are no longer viewed as independent entities, but rather as an integral part of the problem-solving process. Programming languages are now seen as a mechanism for expressing a problem solution in a precise way for computer execution. As such, a given programming language may have a significant effect upon the ease with which the solution may be expressed. If the language does not easily support the abstractions used by the programmer in solving the problem, then the transformation from the problem solution to a correctly executing program will be complex, with the increased likelihood that errors will be introduced during this transformation process.

A number of new programming languages have been designed and/or implemented with a primary or secondary objective of promoting proper programming techniques [6,7, 8,9,10,11,12]. In addition, some general criteria for language designs have been advanced[13,14,15,16]. Design of the programming language PLAIN (Programming LAnguage for INteraction) has proceeded in parallel with these other efforts, commencing in 1975. Unlike the other languages, the intended application area for PLAIN is interactive information systems, typically programs whose end users will be application-knowledgeable and computer-naive. PLAIN is intended to provide the application programmer with a tool that supports the systematic construction of this class of programs. As such, it contains facilities for definition and use of relational data bases, modules for information hiding, string processing with a simple pattern-matching facility, and exception-handling, incorporated into a well-structured, Pascal-based language.

In this paper, however, we shall be concerned primarily with the support provided by PLAIN for concepts of systematic programming. We begin by presenting some goals that encourage a disciplined approach to software construction, commenting briefly on their contribution to the overall goals. Then, following a short survey of other languages, we examine PLAIN with respect to these design goals, particularly those of abstraction and modularity, and compare the approach of PLAIN with those of some other modern languages. Information on other aspects of the language and its implementation may be found in [11,17,18].

LANGUAGE DESIGN GOALS FOR SYSTEMATIC PROGRAMMING

Although the intended application areas and the relative priority of the goals vary considerably among the recently designed languages, there are a number of areas of general agreement that can be identified. These common objectives, taken together, provide a sound basis for programming language design. Languages that meet these objectives can be expected to provide an excellent framework for the systematic construction of high quality programs. These objectives are presented briefly and with only the most significant aspects of their rationale, as additional discussion of these issues may be found in the cited references.

1) Support for abstraction

Abstraction has been recognized as a means to develop a representation of concepts that relates closely to the application being programmed, to hide inessential details of the problem solution at various levels of the program development process, and to support the notion of "top-down" design. If a problem solution involves the use of queues or directed graphs, for example, one should be able to make use of those objects in the programming process.

The ability to define these abstract objects, along with appropriate operations on these objects, is extremely valuable. Such objects can be specified formally using algebraic techniques to define their behavior [19]. If the objects and their associated operators are *encapsulated* so that the representation of the object is isolated and inaccessible from other parts of the program, the facility for *data abstraction* is analogous to the facility for *procedural abstraction* provided by functions and procedures in many programming languages.

Such a programming language facility, generically termed *abstract data types* [20], provides the programmer with the opportunity to define behavioral characteristics of data objects and to refine program and data structures in parallel. It is then possible to create data objects within a program resembling those used in the problem solution, thereby easing the process of transforming the problem solution into a program.

2) Support for modularity

Although there are a number of different definitions of a "module," for purposes of this paper, one may consider a module to be an object, perhaps a procedure, function, or abstract data type, that carries out a well-defined operation, hides a design decision, or isolates information from other modules. Typically, the actions may be described in a sen-

tence or two of natural language. Furthermore, each module has well-defined interfaces to other modules. Modularity makes an important contribution to the overall comprehensibility of programs, to the practice of programming by levels of abstraction, and to the production of large software systems by allowing various pieces of a software system to be effectively isolated from one another [21,22,23].

The ability to decompose a large problem into a number of smaller ones and to delineate clearly the interactions among the pieces is an important tool in gaining intellectual mastery over complex problems. Software design aids such as HIPO charts [24] and structure charts [25] have been developed to help identify modules and to represent the total structure of the software system so that the decomposed modules can be integrated into a single integrated system. Furthermore, concepts of cohesion (unity of function) and coupling (module connections) [22,25] provide a basis for evaluating module designs.

3) Support for verification and testing

Program correctness, as determined through either formal verification or testing, has been a critical motivation for much of the work in software engineering and programming language design. Verification is a formal mathematically-based proof that a program conforms to its specification. Testing is a collection of activities that provides a practical demonstration of conformity between the program and its specification, based upon systematic selection of test cases and execution of program paths and segments.

Both the characteristics of a given programming language and the practices used to write programs in the language affect verification and testing. The ease of testing and verification is further influenced both by *static* and *dynamic* program characteristics [26]. Static factors are those features that may be automatically checked by a compiler at translation time, those that are independent of the execution characteristics of the program. Examples of static aspects include most type checking and some checking for the use of aliasing.

Dynamic factors are those aspects of the program that are dependent upon its execution properties, including control flow and response to exceptional conditions. Issues of programming style, such as the use of uncontrolled branches and pointer structures, clearly affect the complexity of checking required.

Support for verification and testing is closely tied to some of the other issues as well. For example, the desirability of testing or proving program modules individually fits in well with the desirability of system design at the module level. In addition, support for verification and testing implies the prior development of system specifications and hence a systematic approach to software creation. Finally, other issues such as modularity and readability are closely related to issues of program correctness, since the determination of correctness is greatly aided by module simplicity and comprehensibility.

4) Program readability

Program readability has been seen to be a valuable program property contributing to ease of program maintenance and modification [13]. The use of opaque programming "tricks" or the construction of cryptic programs is no longer considered to be an acceptable programming practice, as it has become recognized that programs must be read by humans as well as by machines during their increasingly long lifetimes.

Many properties combine to yield readable programs, including the use of mnemonic variable names, the presence of meaningful keywords, the liberal insertion of comments, and linear flow of program control. Here, too, programming practices are important, since it is possible to write a well-structured, highly understandable program in "poor" languages and a totally incomprehensible program in even the "best" language. Furthermore, program readability appears to be a highly personal and highly subjective quality, significantly influenced by the reader's previous programming experience and programming style.

5) Prevention of self-modifying programs

A number of languages, most notably LISP, treat programs and data interchangeably, in such a way as to permit the code being executed to vary dynamically, i.e., to be determined at execution time. Such an approach is entirely consistent with the concepts of stored programs and Von Neumann machines; unfortunately, though, this approach is in conflict with the goals of program readability and support for verification and testing, since the ability to create new variables and to alter the program dynamically makes verification and testing impossible unless one is able to test or prove all of the programs that can be generated. Furthermore, such programs are often difficult to comprehend, since the actual code is not totally visible. In Pascal and its descendants, procedures and data are separate entities, where data objects may change their values dynamically and procedures are static and immutable. Programs that permit "the execution of data" are forbidden.

6) Control of scope and binding of variables

Block-structured languages provide explicit control over the existence of variables. Space for declared variables is allocated upon entry to a block and deallocated (except for statically allocated variables) upon exit from that block. The set of known variables can be determined from observing the static structure of the program, with no ability to create variables dynamically.

Control of the scope and binding of variables has been identified as a technique that can reduce programming errors caused by side effects, particularly those resulting from indiscriminate use of global variables [27]. Such control is also needed to achieve modularity, since, without it, a programmer may easily circumvent restrictions concerning the proper use of input and output parameters for a module.

The use of pointers should also be noted here, since they may contribute to this problem. Many languages, such as PL/I and Pascal, permit the creation of "dangling references" by having an object in an outer block point to an object in an inner block. When control leaves the inner block, the object pointed to may disappear, but the pointer itself will remain.

7) Language size

Language size has also been seen to be important, since relatively small languages are easier to implement and can make it possible for the programmer to gain complete mastery of the programming language [13,14]. A number of different, albeit "rough," metrics can be used to estimate language size, including the number of keywords, the size of its grammar (in LALR form, for example), the number of statement types, or the size of the compiler or interpreter for a given computer.

There appears to be an optimal size for languages, with some languages being so small as to prohibit an adequate variety of control structures or data types, while other languages are so large as to prevent the average programmer from gaining a clear understanding of the entire language, with all of its syntactic and semantic subtleties.

These seven design objectives are not orthogonal. Indeed, there are numerous intricate connections among them, as well as some inherent conflicts. For example, control of scope and binding of variables is closely related to modularity. On the other hand, restrictions on language size may serve to limit the extent to which a language may support a variety of abstractions. Thus, the language designer seeking to achieve these design objectives must give higher priority to some objectives than to others and must trade off various alternatives judiciously.

LANGUAGES DESIGNED FOR SYSTEMATIC PROGRAMMING

As noted above, a number of different programming languages, including Pascal, CLU, Alphard, Gypsy, Euclid, LIS, PLAIN, Mesa, and Ada, have been designed with most or all of these design objectives in mind. (See [28] for example.) Even though the different languages are intended to serve a diversity of language requirements and applications areas, the languages have more similarities than differences when examined from the standpoint of support for systematic programming.

The most significant differences are those caused by different emphases in the design goals among the various languages. For example, Alphard and Euclid place a heavy stress on the goal of program verification, while the others might be said to *recognize* the importance of verification without the explicit requirement that programs in those languages *will* be verified. As another example, LIS and Euclid are seen as system implementation languages, to be used primarily for the development of operating systems, compilers, and similar programs, while CLU and PLAIN are application languages. (This is not to imply that the languages in one group *cannot* be used for other applications, but only the intent of their designers.)

In the remainder of this paper, we will examine the design decisions in PLAIN with respect to these objectives for supporting a systematic approach to program construction, assessing some of the decisions in comparison and contrast with those made for other programming languages. The intent of this discussion is to provide some insight into the design of PLAIN and into some of the tradeoffs that were made in that design; the reader is not expected to agree with all of these decisions—if there were unanimous agreement on these issues, there would not be so many languages! In short, one of the implicit goals of many of these new languages (as can be seen from their defining documents) is to gain additional understanding of programming methodology and the ways in which language features aid or hinder the programming process.

From a software engineering standpoint, each may be regarded as a tool that can be made available to the individual software development group as an instrument for building their product. It is to be expected that some of these tools will receive little use and little acceptance, while the use of others will be strongly encouraged and modified and/or enhanced over time.

Finally, it should be noted that the programming language is part of a complete problem-solving process, which is supported by a software development methodology and a programming environment. The environment and the methodology will vary among organizations and among languages, but it is really the programming language, in combination with the programming environment, that determines the full extent of support for systematic programming that is provided for the programmer.

PLAIN: A LANGUAGE DESIGNED FOR RELIABLE INTERACTIVE SOFTWARE

As noted above, PLAIN (Programming LAnguage for INteraction) is addressed to the dual goals of support for the construction of interactive programs, i.e., those programs that execute interactively and support for structured programming (in the original sense of that term [4]). PLAIN was designed with features to assist the development of programs involving conversational access to a data base.

These features include:

1) the data type **string** for variable length strings, along with appropriate operators and functions for string manipulation;
2) an elementary pattern specification facility along with pattern-matching operations, used both for validating user input and for formatting of input and output;
3) the data type **relation** and a set of operations to provide a facility for relational data base management [17,29];
4) a procedure-oriented exception-handling mechanism

for trapping errors and restricting control flow upon the occurrence of an exception, commonly used in the event of user input errors.

This set of features is largely missing from other programming languages that seek to support systematic programming. At the same time, those languages that are most heavily used for the construction of interactive program—BASIC, MUMPS [30], APL, LISP, and FORTRAN—are quite weak in meeting the design objectives stated above. PLAIN, by contrast, addresses both groups of design objectives.

From the outset, the original contribution of PLAIN was seen to be not so much the introduction of *new* language features, but rather a synthesis of features whose *interaction* would lead to a useful tool. In particular, the combination of relational data base management and facilities for data abstraction provides a powerful mechanism for structuring operations on data bases. Indeed, the design effort was undertaken with some reluctance, and only after a careful look at a number of other programming languages.

Given the planned number of innovations for supporting interactive programs, it was decided to be fairly conservative with respect to the inclusion of new features for systematic programming. The original intent was to remain fairly close to Pascal for these features; however, parallel developments in other language design efforts, including all of those mentioned above, were highly influential and the resulting language resembles Pascal somewhat less than was originally planned.

These new features are not only intended to support the creation of well-structured programs, but to go beyond that point so as to make a well-disciplined approach to program development a necessity for proper use of the language. In particular, it was considered extremely important to include features that aided modular decomposition of systems, with emphasis on intermodule communication [31], and to support joint refinement of procedures and data.

We now outline some features and design concepts of PLAIN that provide good problem-solving support and that impose various programming restrictions. The primary objective is not so much to present the PLAIN language in detail as to show the motivations of the design from the standpoint of programming discipline, with reference to the set of design objectives discussed above. Because of the interactions among these objectives, though, the subsequent discussion is structured along slightly different lines.

Abstraction and modularity in PLAIN

Abstraction and modular decomposition are two critical intellectual tools used by humans to solve problems. They are intricately related to one another, as each is intended to exhibit a *view* of a process or an object. For example, merely describing (at some level of abstraction) a process for sorting numbers into ascending order is inadequate for incorporating that process into a computer program; it is also essential to include a description of the interfaces between that operation and the host program.

To look at it another way, a module is a "black box" that provides an abstract view of a process or object to its invoker. Even though support for abstraction and support for modularity are presented as two separate design objectives, the extent to which one is achieved strongly affects the extent to which the other can be achieved. This is apparent if one considers the effect of being able to examine the internal structure of one module from another module; if one makes use of that internal information, then the abstraction is violated.

Many of the differences between Pascal and PLAIN are caused by the desire to provide better support for abstraction and modularity in PLAIN. Pascal has four key discernible weaknesses in this regard:

1) Unrestricted access to global variables—program units may freely access and/or modify variables declared in a containing lexical scope (unless the inner scope has a newly declared variable with the same name); thus, the use of specific variables is hidden, and a considerable amount of code inspection is required to determine the data flow. Access to dynamic structures via globally-declared pointers also makes it possible to create "dangling references," since the object being pointed to may be deallocated.

2) Absence of input/output parameters for modules—parameters in Pascal are passed by value and by reference (**var**). However, passing a variable by reference is no guarantee that it is an output parameter, since it is considered a good programming practice (and an efficient one) to pass structured variables by reference, thereby eliminating the space and time required to make a copy of the parameter. Nonetheless, neither the procedure heading nor the procedure call gives an indication as to input or output parameters. Indeed, the concept of passing parameters by value and by reference is an *implementation* concept rather than a *programming* concept.

3) Lack of support for data abstraction modules—Pascal supports procedural abstractions (procedures and functions), but has no facility for defining encapsulated data types, similar to those present in CLU (a cluster), Alphard (a form), Euclid (a module), or others.

4) Side effects in functions—it is possible for a Pascal function to accept parameters by reference and to modify them within the body of the function; similarly, it is permissible for a function to make an assignment to a global variable. Such a capability goes against the mathematical concept of a function, as well as breaking down the abstraction embodied in the function and (effectively) creating additional output parameters from the function module.

PLAIN attempts to overcome each of these weaknesses, thereby providing stronger support for abstraction and modularity. First, all use of global variables must be declared in the heading of the individual program unit (procedure, function, data abstraction module). The PLAIN **imports** list is similar to that of Euclid and the **glocon/glovar** declarations used by Dijkstra [32]. Some of these names are local declarations, some are parameters, but the rest are global variables or other program units. These nonlocal names must appear in the import list, along with a classification of their use, as **modified, readonly,** or **invoked**. This requirement does not apply to constants or to type declarations, which may be used freely. The effect of the imports list, though, is to increase the visibility of the use of variables throughout a program and to permit the reader of a module to determine the interrelationships between modules, both invocations and data connections.

In conjunction with use of the imports list to specify access to variables and program units, PLAIN contains the ability to restrict the use of a given variable to a designated set of program units. This feature, called the **restricted to** clause, controls the extent to which globally-declared variables may be used. With the imports clause alone, any global variable may be freely imported. However, there are many instances when it is desired to share a variable among a set of program units and to prevent it from being accessed by other units. (Labeled COMMON in FORTRAN can serve this same purpose.)

Consider, for example, a program in which routine main may call procedures $p1$, $p2$, and $p3$. Further, assume that $p2$ and $p3$ will both need the variable k, but that neither of them calls the other. Hence, communication of the value of k must occur through main. It is desired to prevent $p1$ from obtaining (and possibly modifying) k. Thus, one can declare

var k: integer **restricted to** $p2$, $p3$;

as a way of achieving the desired protection.

Furthermore, PLAIN, like Ada, overcomes the dangling reference problem by forbidding deallocation of dynamically allocated variables. While this is not an entirely satisfactory solution from the standpoint of storage utilization, it is the only solution that permits the use of pointers without resorting to garbage collection and without permitting dangling references. The use of objects of pointer type is restricted in PLAIN in order to limit the number of program units that are aware of the representation of dynamically allocated objects.

Next, PLAIN has different rules from Pascal concerning parameters. PLAIN parameters may be either **readonly** or **modified**. A readonly parameter is an input parameter to the procedure or function whose value is not changed by the procedure or function. A modified parameter is a parameter that may have a value assigned to it during the execution of a procedure (possibly as a result of a call to a procedure invoked from within that procedure); as such the actual parameter for a formal modified parameter must be a variable. It may or may not have an input value. (An alternative strategy would have been to follow LIS and Ada, which have *in*, *out*, and *inout* parameters. The readonly parameters and the modified parameters are separated, in both the procedure declaration *and* the procedure invocation by the symbol "→".

For example, one might declare a procedure for the greatest common denominator with the following heading:

procedure gcd (m,n: integer→*x,y,z*: integer);

with a valid call appearing as

gcd (59,93→*x,y,z*)

where *x, y,* and *z* have been declared as integers in the invoking routine.

This decision has several implications for implementation. First, conformity to the declaration must be checked to make sure that no assignment is made to readonly parameters. This involves making sure that the formal parameter does not appear on the left hand side of an assignment statement, in the modified part of an actual parameter list for a procedure called from within the given program unit, or as a modified variable imported into a lexically nested program unit. Although all of these checks can be made prior to execution time, they can involve a considerable amount of overhead.

An implementation advantage, however, is that it then becomes unnecessary to pass any of the parameters by value, thereby eliminating the overhead associated with copying of parameters. Because the use of the parameter can be checked from the program text, it is possible to pass all parameters by reference, regardless of whether they are readonly or modified. Thus, the programmer may accurately characterize all parameters as readonly or modified, depending upon their actual use. The overhead occurs at translation time and not during program execution.

The features described to this point have a significant impact upon the ease of transformation between the design phase and the program. Suppose that a system had been designed using the practices of Structured Design [19]. Part of the design representation is a structure chart showing the hierarchical structure of the system and the calls between modules. Each path between modules is numbered and an accompanying parameter table shows the input and output parameters for each module. For example, in Figure 1, the call to *A2* from *A* (path 5) provides *Y* as an input parameter and obtains *Z* as an output parameter; it can be seen that *Z* is then passed to MAIN as an output of *A* (path 1).

Third, PLAIN contains a facility for encapsulation, bearing some resemblance to similar features in CLU, Euclid, and Ada. In addition to defining new types, one can also encapsulate a set of related procedures and functions, providing a feature similar to that of the Ada **package**. Each encapsulated type declaration consists of a **rep** clause, in which the representation of the type is declared, an **ops** clause, in which the operators upon the type are declared, an **exports** clause, in which the names of externally visible operators are given, and an optional **exception** clause, in which one can name exceptions associated with the operations upon the type.

The procedures read and write may be defined in the type to extend the built-in **read** and **write** operations. The Boolean function equal may be defined to extend the built-in equal function for structured variables. The procedure init may be

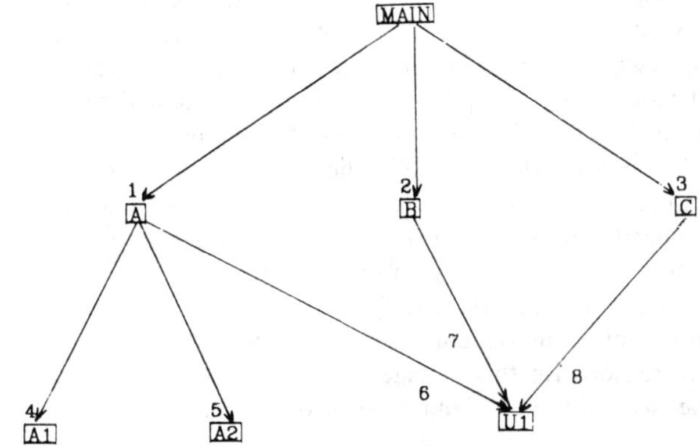

Path	Parameters Input	Output
1	X,Y	Z
2	D	SAFE
3		RES
4	X	
5	Y	Z
6	A	AQ
7	B	BQ
8	C	CQ

Figure 1—A structure chart

defined to specify actions to be carried out when a variable of that type is declared. The abstract type facility, along with several of the features previously described, can be illustrated by the familiar example of an integer stack.

The operations upon the stack may be specified as follows:

create:		→stack
push:	stack × integer	→stack U stackfull
pop:	stack	→stack U stackempty
top:	stack	→integer U stackempty
empty:	stack	→Boolean
equal:	stack × stack	→Boolean
size:	stack	→integer

Axioms:

$top(push(s,i)) = i$
$top(create) = stackempty$
$pop(push(s,i)) = $ if $size(s) < $ MAX then s else stackfull
$pop(create) = stackempty$
$equal(s1,s2) = $ if $empty(s1)$ & $empty(s2)$ then TRUE else
   if $empty(s1)$ | $empty(s2)$ then FALSE else
   $(top(s1) = top(s2))$ & $equal(pop(s1),pop(s2))$
$size(create) = 0$
$size(push(s,i)) = size(s) + 1$
$size(pop(s)) = size(s) - 1$

Before presenting the PLAIN module, it is important to make some observations about the specification. First, the create operation is carried out by the declaration of a variable of the type integerstack in the program using the data abstraction. Thus, there is no explicit create operation in the integerstack module. Next, the stack specification given here is somewhat different from the specification given elsewhere in the literature [19,33], primarily to accommodate the stack-full result caused by the finiteness of machine resources.

The code for the module is shown in Figure 2. It should be noted that the implementation is not a *direct* encoding of the specification (hinting at some problems that verifiers might have). The primary difference is that the specification of equal uses a recursive definition, while the implementation examines individual elements of the stack. There are three reasons for this change: 1) recursion is usually more expensive in terms of machine resources; 2) pop is a procedure, not a function, and so cannot be used in the language in the way that it is used in the specification, and; 3) naming rules complicate the means of referring to individual objects in each of two different stacks being compared. In addition, one would have to make copies of the stacks to use a recursive equal operation without destroying the stacks; that, too, is more expensive than a simple element-by-element comparison.

Limited parameterization of the type definition is permitted, as shown by the stack size parameter MAX. The formal parameters must be of a simple type. Thus, one can use a single data abstraction to define integer stacks of different sizes, but not to define a stack of integers and a stack of

```
type integerstack [MAX: integer] =
    module
        exports push, pop, top, empty, equal;
        exception stackfull, stackempty;
        rep
            record
                stktop: 0..MAX;
                elements: array [1..MAX] of integer
            end record;
        ops
            function size(s:integerstack): integer; {computes size of stack s}
            begin
                size := s.stktop
            end size;
            function empty (s:integerstack): boolean; {returns true iff stack s empty}
            imports size: invoked;
            begin
                empty := size(s)=0
            end empty;
            procedure push (val: integer -> s: integerstack); {pushes integer val onto stack s}
            exception stackfull;
            imports size: invoked;
            begin
                if size(s) >= MAX then signal stackfull
                else s.stktop := s.stktop + 1; s.elements [s.stktop] := val end if
            end push;
            procedure pop ( -> s: integerstack); {pops off top element of stack s}
            exception stackempty;
            imports empty: invoked;
            begin
                if empty(s) then signal stackempty else s.stktop := s.stktop -1 end if
            end pop;
            function top (s: integerstack): integer; {returns value on top of stack; no pop}
            exception stackempty;
            imports empty: invoked;
            begin
                if empty(s) then signal stackempty else top := s.elements [s.stktop] end if
            end top;
            function equal (s1,s2: integerstack): boolean; {returns true iff s1 = s2}
            imports size: invoked;
            var i: integer;
            begin
                if size(s1) ~= size(s2)
                then equal := false
                else
                    i := size(s1); equal := true;
                    loop
                        if i=0 then exit end if
                        if s1.elements[i]  = s2.elements[i]
                        then i := i - 1 else equal := false; exit
                        endif
                    repeat
                end if
            end equal;
                s.stktop := 0
    end integerstack;
```

Figure 2—Encapsulated type definition for integer stacks in PLAIN

strings. The reason for this restriction is that relation is a data type and it was desired to prevent abstract type definitions from accepting relation as a parameter; the cleanest solution was a complete prohibition of type parameters. The resulting facility is less powerful (but easier to implement) than the **generic package** facility of Ada. One can now declare, for example,

var *s*1: integerstack [50]; *s*2: integerstack [100].

As noted above, it is the intention of PLAIN to disallow side effects in functions. At the simplest level, it is possible to make certain that no globals are imported and modified, and that no readonly globals or parameters are used as modified parameters in procedures called from within the function. Also, the syntax of the language forbids the presence of modified parameters; in their absence, it is impossible to use aliasing to cause side effects.

In order to be *strict* about the side effects requirement, though, more checking is required. First, certain data base operations must be prohibited; specifically, those modifying the current tuple indicator or the data base itself, caused by iterating through a relation, can be considered a side effect. Second, input/output operations must be restricted, since alterations to a file may be considered a side effect, especially if the file can be read after termination of the function. Such a restriction can cause complications for the software developer desiring to place debugging messages within functions, for example. Third, since functions may call procedures, all of the procedures called during execution of a function (to an arbitrary number of levels of invocation) would have to be checked to make certain that they, too, do not violate these restrictions on side effects.

In short, even though it is highly desirable to prevent *all* side effects, the costs of doing so, both in execution overhead and programmer inconvenience, must be considered. The prevention of input/output operations is particularly problematical in this regard, and PLAIN relaxes the side effect restriction to permit input/output within the body of functions. Otherwise, PLAIN requires sufficient declarations by the programmer in the heading of each program unit that it is possible to check procedures to see if assignments to global variables are made.

From an implementation standpoint, it is straightforward to check the restrictions on the use of globals. A flag can be set to indicate whether or not the stack of activations includes a function call. If there is an active function call, i.e., the calling sequence of program units includes a function, then the procedure to be executed must be checked for modified globals. Otherwise, the call is disallowed and an exceptional condition is raised. Note, though, that this is only a partial solution to the problem, since the declaration (in an imports statement) that a procedure can modify a global variable does not necessarily mean that the global *is* modified on a particular call to the procedure, since control flow may bypass any statements causing a disallowed assignment. Without this compromise, however, it would be necessary to check *every* assignment within such procedures, and the overhead of making those checks would be enormous. In summary, the seemingly innocuous desire to prohibit side effects in functions can impose severe restrictions and execution overhead.

PLAIN, then, provides considerable support for abstraction and modularity, providing additional features beyond those of Pascal at some expense in language size and complexity. The provision for abstract data types and the strong requirements for module interfaces enhance the possibility of creating libraries of procedures, functions, and encapsulated type definitions that can be used as "software components" [34].

Support for verification

The design of PLAIN was motivated primarily by application needs; in the application areas addressed by PLAIN, there is a strong need for software and data reliability, particularly in areas such as medicine, where proper operation of a system may have life-critical importance. At the same time, though, the need for operational systems is so great that most developers of such systems tend to begin by writing code rather than by following any kind of coherent system design methodology. At present, there is almost no likelihood that anyone would attempt to prove the correctness of such a system, even had they produced a sufficiently rigorous specification.

Thus, support for program verification was not a major objective in the design of PLAIN, in the sense that it is in Alphard or Euclid. The assistance that PLAIN provides for program verification comes primarily through its resemblance to Pascal and to other modern languages. For example, PLAIN contains an **assert** statement that can be checked at execution time, but the statement only permits a Boolean expression, with no provision for such essential features as expressions involving universal or existential quantification. (Such quantification could be checked in a Boolean function that is part of the assertion.)

Along the same line, PLAIN is like Pascal with respect to aliasing, rather than including the features of Euclid that prevent aliasing. However, PLAIN improves upon Pascal with respect to the use of procedures and functions as parameters by requiring type information to be provided for the parameters of the procedure and function parameters. In this respect, it follows the proposal of the British Standards Institute for Pascal [35]. In this way, it is possible to perform a greater degree of type checking while still permitting function and procedure parameters.

This is not to say that the design of PLAIN ignores the possibility of verification, though, only that it was not a principal goal. A significant problem is that effective verification techniques have not yet been developed for the class of programs addressed by PLAIN. For example, very little has been done concerning verification of data base operations. Furthermore, even though the data base operations may be mechanically correct, it is impossible to guarantee with the present collection of facilities that the results are semantically meaningful.

PLAIN takes one small step in this regard, however, through its rules concerning type compatibility. In PLAIN, any two types having different names are different types. (The designers of Ada subsequently made the same definition.) Among the data base operations, the join operation of the relational algebra can only be performed on two objects of the same type. Thus, one can make judicious use of the data type facilities to assure that only meaningful joins can be performed.

As an example, consider two relations A and B, where A contains the attribute "age" and B contains the attribute "quantity^on^hand." If these attributes are both declared to be of type integer, then the relations A and B may be joined on these compatible attributes, however meaningless the result may be. If data types "agetype" and "amounttype" are defined in advance, though, with "age" declared to be of type "agetype" and "quantity^on^hand" declared to be of type "amounttype," then it becomes impossible to perform the join. In this manner, one may specify exactly which joins may occur and may verify their correctness from a logical standpoint.

Another verification problem is presented by the exception-handling mechanism. Once again, there are no practical methods for verifying programs in the presence of exceptional conditions; one might say that the occurrence of such a condition means that a program has failed to satisfy some input assertion and that the program therefore cannot be proved correct. Yet exception-handling is fundamental to PLAIN, since it is necessary to provide the programmer with facilities to prevent exceptional conditions from causing a program to terminate abnormally. The anticipated end users of PLAIN programs, being largely computer-naive, can be expected to make numerous errors, particularly in input, that must be properly trapped and handled; one simply cannot say that the program has failed to meet some input assertion and must therefore be terminated. Accordingly, the application programmers writing programs in PLAIN must be given the ability to trap and handle exceptions.

The PLAIN exception-handling mechanism, described at length in another paper [36], seeks to provide a well-structured flow of control following the occurrence of an exceptional condition. The programmer may create a **handler procedure** that can be associated with the occurrence of a specific exception at a specific program location. When an exception is raised, either through the **signal** statement, or through an automatic mechanism in the language processor, the handler procedure can carry out any required actions, potentially clear the offending exception, and then return control to normal program flow, to the beginning of the statement in which the exception occurred (**retry**) or to the invocation point of the procedure in which the exception occurred. In this way, exceptions can be passed through succeeding levels of invocation with any necessary actions being taken at each level. Since exception-handling is done with procedures, it is possible to pass parameters from the environment of the exception to the handler procedure, following the normal rules for scoping of declarations. At any point, the active exception may be cleared by the handler for that level so that normal program operation can continue.

The intent of this approach is to facilitate both the programming of exception-handling actions and the verification of programs in the presence of exceptions, since this method avoids the unrestrained flows of control and unrestricted access to variables that characterize some of the other exception-handling schemes. Although a more detailed approach to this verification is sketched out in [36], there has not yet been any practical experience with the application of verification techniques to such programs.

Support for program readability

Although, as previously noted, program readability is difficult to quantify and can be strongly affected by individual programming styles, it is possible to provide language features that enhance program comprehensibility. Many of these features provide support for other systematic programming goals as well. In general, the design of PLAIN attempts to follow Hoare's dictum that "the readability of programs is immeasurably more important than their writeability" [13].

As with many other language aspects, much of the readability of PLAIN programs results from its resemblance to Pascal. Among the common features supporting readability are:

—provision of appropriate keywords
—format free program structure permitting indentation on lines
—control structures supporting linear flow of program control within program units
—prevention of self-modifying programs
—straightforward provision for comments
—limited language size.

Similarly, the Pascal-like program structure retains the disadvantage of placing the main program at the end of the program text.

PLAIN incorporates some additional features intended to enhance program readability (as well as to help in achieving other goals). These features are the following:

—fully bracketed control structures
—explicit importing of global names into a module
—input/output parameter lists in both declaration and call of procedures.

The use of fully bracketed control structures permits a more consistent language definition and can reduce the use of **begin-end** pairs as separators. The reduction in **begin-end** pairs not only eliminates unnecessary program "clutter," but also removes a major source of programming errors, making the **begin-end** now serve only the single purpose of enclosing an entire executable program unit (main program, function, or procedure).

In Pascal, for example, the structure of the **if** statement is

    if Booleanexpression **then** statement [**else** statement].

In PLAIN, as well as in Ada and other newer languages, it is

    if Booleanexpression **then** statementlist
    [**else** statementlist] **end if**.

Similar gains are achieved with the **case** statement. The statement is terminated with an **end case** and individual cases are separated with the reserved word **when**. Again there can be a considerable reduction in the number of **begin-end** pairs, producing a situation in which both readability and writeability are improved.

The imports list, discussed above, in addition to helping enforce rules concerning modularity, is an aid to program readability. Because declarations and imported names are all visible in the heading of a program unit, it is easier to comprehend, modify, and/or validate units independently. The designers of Ada have taken the opposite view, claiming that importation of a large number of objects will *detract* from program readability and cause additional clutter. This author believes that the proper use of structured objects, combined with efforts to minimize coupling between modules, will prevent the imports list from becoming excessively long, and that its presence provides a good mechanism for specifying the interface between the PLAIN program and its execution environment. Further experience in the use of these languages may help to resolve this difference.

Another improvement to readability comes about from the restrictions on the use of pointer variables in PLAIN. Because pointer variable may only be used within modules, most program units are free of expressions involving complicated data access methods, such as multilevel pointer structures. While PLAIN does not achieve a uniform reference mechanism, the number of reference methods is quite small. Furthermore, function and procedure calls must be used to access the operations on the complex data structures defined in data abstractions. This restriction has several benefits:

—access to the physical representation of a data object is sharply restricted so that the reader of the program only needs to understand the logical operations on the object once the isolated representational information is understood
—the reader, typically performing a maintenance activity, needs to study much less of the program text in order to make changes to the data structures
—meaningful names can be chosen for the functions and procedures, thereby aiding reader understanding of the program.

It must also be recognized that some of these gains in readability come at the expense of some overhead in space or execution time as a result of the additional procedure and function calls needed to accomplish the encapsulation of data.

CONCLUSION

This paper has examined the design of the programming language PLAIN from the standpoint of the support that it provides for the notions of systematic programming, focusing on both its strengths and weaknesses. It can be seen that the design of PLAIN places major emphasis on the goals of abstraction, modularity, and readability, and that it makes advances over Pascal and features of some other modern languages with respect to supporting a well-disciplined approach to software construction.

At the same time, support for program verification and testing was consciously left at a lower level than is possible given the current technology of programming language design. The language size is moderate, containing more features and more syntax than Pascal, and being comparable to Ada in that respect. The goal of small language size was not achieved as fully as had been hoped, due to the apparent needs of the application area.

The implementation of PLAIN is presently under way on the PDP-11 computer under the UNIX operating system, and it is expected that an initial implementation will be operational in the summer of 1980. It is anticipated that implementation experience and increased use of the language will eventually lead to revisions in the language to provide improved support for the dual objectives of aiding the construction of interactive information systems and encouraging the use of systematic programming methodology.

REFERENCES

1. Peters, L. J. and Tripp, L. L., "Software Design Representation Schemes," *Proc. of the Symposium on Computer Software Engineering,* MRI Symposium Proceedings, vol. 24. Brooklyn: Polytechnic Press, 1976, pp. 31-56.
2. Caine, S. and Gordon, E., "PDL—a Tool for Software Design," *Proc. AFIPS 1975 NCC,* vol. 44, pp. 271-276.
3. Myers, G. J., "A Controlled Experiment in Program Testing and Code Walkthroughs/Inspections," *CACM,* vol. 21, no. 9 (September, 1978), pp. 760-768.
4. Dahl, O.-J., Dijkstra, E. W. and Hoare, C. A. R., *Structured Programming.* London: Academic Press, 1972.
5. Wirth, N., "Program Development by Stepwise Refinement," *CACM,* vol. 14, no. 4 (April, 1971), pp. 221-227.
6. Wirth, N., "The Programming Language Pascal," *Acta Informatica,* vol. 1, no. 1 (1971), pp. 35-63.
7. Wulf, W. A. (ed.) *et al.,* "An Informal Description of Alphard" (preliminary), Department of Computer Science, Carnegie-Mellon University, February, 1978.
8. Liskov, B., *et al.,* "CLU Reference Manual," MIT Laboratory for Computer Science, Computation Structures Group Memorandum 161, July 1978.
9. Lampson, B. W. *et al.,* "Report on the Programming Language Euclid," *ACM SIGPLAN Notices,* vol. 12, no. 2 (February, 1977), pp. 1-79.
10. Ambler, A. L. *et al.,* "Gypsy: a Language for Specification and Implementation of Verifiable Programs," *Proc. of ACM Conf. on Language Design for Reliable Software, ACM SIGPLAN Notices,* vol. 12, no. 3 (March, 1977), pp. 1-10.
11. Wasserman, A. I. *et al.,* "Revised Report on the Programming Language PLAIN," Laboratory of Medical Information Science, University of California San Francisco, Technical Report #34, July, 1978. (Revised Report in preparation).
12. Ichbiah, J. D. *et al.,* "Preliminary Ada Reference Manual," *ACM SIGPLAN Notices,* vol. 14, no. 6 (June, 1979), part A.
13. Hoare, C. A. R., "Hints on Programming Language Design," Stanford University Computer Science Department Technical Report CS-73-403, December, 1973.
14. Wirth, N., "On the Design of Programming Languages," *Information Processing 74.* Amsterdam: North-Holland, 1974, pp. 386-393.
15. Richard, F. and Ledgard, H., "A Reminder for Language Designers," *ACM SIGPLAN Notices,* vol. 12, no. 12 (December, 1977), pp. 73-82.
16. Department of Defense Advanced Research Projects Agency, "Requirements for High Order Computer Programming Languages—'STEELMAN'," June, 1978.
17. Wasserman, A. I., "The Data Management Facilities of PLAIN," *Proc. ACM 1979 SIGMOD Conference,* 1979, pp. 60-70.
18. Booster, T. W., "Implementation of Pattern Matching in PLAIN," M.S. Project Report, University of California, Berkeley, September, 1979.
19. Guttag, J. V., "Abstract Data Types and the Development of Data Structures," *CACM,* vol. 20, no. 6 (June, 1977), pp. 396-404.
20. Liskov, B. and Zilles, S. N., "Programming with Abstract Data Types," *ACM SIGPLAN Notices,* vol. 9, no. 4 (April, 1974), pp. 50-59.
21. Parnas, D. L., "On the Criteria to be Used in Decomposing Systems into Modules," *CACM,* vol. 15, no. 12 (December, 1972), pp. 1053-1058.
22. Myers, G. J. *Reliable Software through Composite Design.* New York: Petrocelli/Charter, 1975.
23. Liskov, B., "A Design Methodology for Reliable Software Systems," *Proc. AFIPS 1972 FJCC,* vol. 41, pp. 191-199.
24. HIPO—a Design Aid and Documentation Technique. White Plains: IBM Data Processing Division. Pub. GC20-1851.
25. Yourdon, E. and Constantine, L. L., *Structured Design.* Englewood Cliffs, NJ: Prentice-Hall, 1979.
26. Wasserman, A. I., "Testing and Verification Aspects of Pascal-like Languages," *Journal of Computer Languages,* vol. 4, no. 3/4 (1979), pp. 155-169.
27. Wulf, W. A. and Shaw, M., "Global Variables Considered Harmful," *ACM SIGPLAN Notices,* vol. 8, no. 2 (February, 1973), pp. 28-32.
28. Ichbiah, J. D. *et al.,* "Rationale for the Design of the Ada Programming Language," *ACM SIGPLAN Notices,* vol. 14, no. 6 (June, 1979), part B.
29. Codd, E. F., "A Relational Model of Data for Shared Data Banks," *CACM,* vol. 13, no. 6 (June, 1970), pp. 377-387.
30. American National Standards Institute. *MUMPS Language Standard.* ANSI X11.1-1977.
31. DeRemer, F. and Kron, H., "Programming-in-the-Large vs. Programming-in-the-Small," *IEEE Transactions on Software Engineering,* vol. SE-2, no. 2 (June, 1976), pp. 80-86.
32. Dijkstra, E. W. *A Discipline of Programming.* Englewood Cliffs: Prentice-Hall, 1976.
33. Wulf, W. A., London, R. L. and Shaw, M., "An Introduction to the Construction and Verification of Alphard Programs," *IEEE Transactions on Software Engineering,* vol. SE-2, no. 4 (December, 1976), pp. 253-264.
34. Belady, L. A., "Evolved Software for the 80's," *Computer,* vol. 12, no. 2 (February, 1979), pp. 79-82.
35. Ravenel, B., "Toward a Pascal Standard," *Computer,* vol. 12, no. 4 (April, 1979), pp. 68-82.
36. Wasserman, A. I., "Design and Evaluation of a Procedure-Oriented Exception-Handling Mechanism," in preparation, 1980.

Language Design for   S.L. Graham
Reliable Software   Editor

Early Experience with Mesa

Charles M. Geschke, James H. Morris Jr.,
and Edwin H. Satterthwaite
Xerox Palo Alto Research Center

Reprinted from *Communications of the ACM,*   August 1977, pp. 540-553
Copyright 1977 Association for Computing Machinery, Inc. Reprinted by permission.

The experiences of Mesa's first users — primarily its implementers — are discussed, and some implications for Mesa and similar programming languages are suggested. The specific topics addressed are: module structure and its use in defining abstractions, data-structuring facilities in Mesa, an equivalence algorithm for types and type coercions, the benefits of the type system and why it is breached occasionally, and the difficulty of making the treatment of variant records safe.

Key Words and Phrases: programming languages, types, modules, data structures, systems programming
CR Categories: 4.22

1. Introduction

What happens when professional programmers change over from an old-fashioned systems programming language to a new, modular, type-checked one like Mesa? Considering the large number of groups developing such languages, this is certainly a question of great interest.

This paper focuses on our experiences with strict type checking and modularization within the Mesa programming system. Most of the local structure of Mesa

A version of this paper was presented at the SIGPLAN/SIGOPS/SICSOFT Conference on Language Design for Reliable Software, Raleigh, N.C., March 28-30, 1977.

Authors' address: Computer Science Laboratory, Palo Alto Research Center, Xerox Corporation, 3333 Coyote Hill Road, Palo Alto CA 94304

was inspired by, and is similar to, that of Pascal [14] or Algol 68 [12], while the global structure is more like that of Simula 67 [1]. We have chosen features from these and related languages selectively, cast them in a different syntax, and added a few new ideas of our own. All this has been constrained by our need for a language to be used for the production of real system software right now. We believe that most of our observations are relevant to the languages mentioned above, and others like them, when used in a similar environment. We have therefore omitted a comprehensive description of Mesa and concentrated on annotated examples that should be intelligible to anyone familiar with a similar language. We hope that our experiences will help others who are creating or studying such languages.

An interested reader can find more information about the details of Mesa elsewhere. A previous paper [7] addresses issues concerning transfer of control. Another paper [3] discusses some more advanced data-structuring ideas. A paper on *schemes* [8] suggests another possible direction of advance. In this paper we restrain our desires to redesign or extend Mesa and simply describe how we are using the language as currently implemented.

The version of Mesa presented in this paper is one component of a continuing investigation into programming methodology and language design. Most major aspects of the language were frozen when implementation was begun in the autumn of 1974. Although we were dissatisfied with our understanding of certain design issues even then, we proceeded with implementation for the following reasons.

—We perceived a need for a "state of the art" implementation langauge within our laboratory. It seemed possible to combine some of our ideas into a design that was fairly conservative, but that would still dominate the existing and proposed alternatives.
—We wanted feedback from a community of users, both to evaluate those ideas that were ready for implementation and to focus subsequent research on problems actually encountered in building real systems.
—We had accumulated a backlog of ideas about implementation techniques that we were anxious to try.

It is important to understand that we have consciously decided to attempt a complete programming system for demanding and sophisticated users. Their own research projects were known to involve the construction of "state of the art" programs, many of which tax the limits of available computing resources. These users are well aware of the capabilities of the underlying hardware, and they have developed a wide range of programming styles that they have been loath to abandon. Working in this environment has had the following consequences.

—We could not afford to be too dogmatic. The language design is conservative and permissive; we have attempted to accommodate old methods of programming as well as new, even at some cost in elegance.

—Efficiency is important. Mesa reflects the general properties of existing machines and contains no features that cannot be implemented efficiently (perhaps with some microcode assistance); for example, there is no automatic garbage collection.

A cross-compiler for Mesa became operational in the spring of 1975. We used it to build a small operating system and a display-oriented symbolic debugger. By early 1976, it was possible to run a system built entirely in Mesa on our target machine, and rewriting the compiler in its own language was completed in the summer of 1976. The basic system, debugger, and compiler consist of approximately 50,000 lines of Mesa code, the bulk of which was written by four people. Since mid-1976, the community of users and scope of application of Mesa have been expanding rapidly, but its most experienced and demanding users are still its implementers. It is in this context that we shall try to describe our experiences and to suggest some tentative conclusions. Naturally, we have discovered some bugs and omissions in the design, and the implemented version of the language is already several years from the frontiers of research. We have tried to restrain our desire to redesign, however, and we report on Mesa as it is, not as we now wish it were.

The paper begins with a brief overview of Mesa's module structure. The uses of types and strict type checking in Mesa are then examined in some detail. The facilities for defining data structures are summarized, and an abstract description of the Mesa type calculus is presented. We discuss the rationale and methods for breaching the type system and illustrate them with a "type-strenuous" example that exploits several of the type system's interesting properties. A final section discusses the difficulties of handling variant records in a type-safe way.

2. Modules

Modules provide a capability for partitioning a large system into manageable units. They can be used to encapsulate *abstractions* and to provide a degree of *protection*. In the design of Mesa, we were particularly influenced by the work of Parnas [10], who proposes *information hiding* as the appropriate criterion for modular decomposition, and by the concerns of Morris [9] regarding protection in programming languages.

Module Structure

Viewed as a piece of source text, a *module* is similar to an Algol procedure declaration or a Simula class definition. It typically declares a collection of variables that provide a localized database and a set of procedures performing operations upon that database. Modules are designed to be compiled independently, but the declarations in one module can be made visible during the compilation of another by arranging to reference the first within the second by a mechanism called *inclusion*. To decouple the internal details of an implementation from its abstract behavior, Mesa provides two kinds of modules: *definitions* and *programs*.

A definitions module defines the interface to an abstraction. It typically declares some shared types and useful constants, and it defines the interface by naming a set of procedures and specifying their input/output types. Definitions modules claim no storage and have no existence at run time. Included modules are usually definitions modules, but they need not be.

Certain program modules, called *implementers*, provide the concrete implementation of an abstraction; they declare variables and specify bodies of procedures. There can be a one-to-many relation between definitions modules and concrete implementations. At run time, one or more instances of a module can be created, and a separate *frame* (activation record) is allocated for each. In this respect, module instances resemble Simula class objects. Unlike procedure instances, the lifetimes of module instances are not constrained to follow any particular discipline. Communication paths among modules are established dynamically as described below and are not constrained by, e.g., compile-time or run-time nesting relationships. Thus lifetimes and access paths are completely decoupled.

The following skeletal Mesa modules suggest the general form of a definitions module and one of its implementers:

```
Abstraction: DEFINITIONS =
  BEGIN
  . . .
  it: TYPE = . . .; rt: TYPE = . . .;
  . . .
  p: PROCEDURE;
  p1: PROCEDURE [INTEGER];
  . . .
  pi: PROCEDURE [it] RETURNS [rt];
  . . .
  END
```

```
Implementer: PROGRAM IMPLEMENTING Abstraction =
BEGIN
OPEN Abstraction;
x: INTEGER;
. . .
p: PUBLIC PROCEDURE = ⟨code for p⟩;
p1: PUBLIC PROCEDURE [i: INTEGER] = ⟨code for p1⟩;
. . .
pi: PUBLIC PROCEDURE [x: it] RETURNS [y: rt] =
      ⟨code for pi⟩;
. . .
END
```

Longer but more complete and realistic examples can be found in the discussion of *ArrayStore* below; *ArrayStoreDefs* and *ArrayStore* correspond to *Abstraction* and *Implementer,* respectively.

Mesa allows specification of attributes that can be used to control intermodular access to identifiers. In the definition of an abstraction, some types or record fields are of legitimate concern only to an implementer, but they involve or are components of other types that are parts of the advertised interface to the abstraction. Any identifier with the attribute PRIVATE is visible only in the module in which it is declared and in any module claiming to implement that module. Subject to the ordinary rules of scope, an identifier with the attribute PUBLIC is visible in any module that includes and *opens* the module in which it is declared. The PUBLIC attribute can be restricted by specifying the additional attribute READ-ONLY. By default, identifiers are PUBLIC in definitions modules and PRIVATE otherwise.

In the example above, *Abstraction* contains definitions of shared types and enumerates the elements of a procedural interface. *Implementer* uses those type definitions and provides the bodies of the procedures; the compiler will check that an actual procedure with the same name and type is supplied for each public procedure declared in *Abstraction*.

A module that uses an abstraction is called a *client* of that abstraction. Interface definitions are obtained by including the *Abstraction* module. Any instance of a client must be connected to an instance of an appropriate implementer before the actual operations of the abstraction become available. This connection is called *binding*, and there are several ways to do it.

Binding Mechanisms

When a relatively static and purely procedural interface between modules is acceptable, the connection can be made in a conventional way. Consider the following skeleton:

```
Client1: PROGRAM =
   BEGIN
   OPEN Abstraction;
   . . .
   px: EXTERNAL PROCEDURE;
   . . .
   p[ ]; px[ ];
   . . .
   END.
```

A client module can request a system facility called the *binder* to locate and assign appropriate values to all external procedure names, such as *px*. The binder follows a well-defined *binding path* from module instance to module instance. When the binder encounters an actual procedure with the same name as, and a type compatible with, an external procedure, it makes the linkage. The compiler automatically inserts an EXTERNAL procedure declaration for any procedure identifier, such as *p*, that is mentioned by a client but defined only in an included definitions module. The binder also checks that all identifiers from a single definitions module are bound consistently (that is, to a single implementer).

The observant reader will have noticed that this binding mechanism and the undisciplined lifetimes of module instances leave Mesa programs vulnerable to dangling reference problems. We are not happy about this, but so far we have not observed any serious bugs attributable to such references.

As an alternate binding mechanism, Mesa supports the Simula paradigm as suggested by the following skeleton (which assumes that *x* is a public variable):

```
Client2: PROGRAM =
   BEGIN
   OPEN Abstraction;
   frame: POINTER TO FRAME[Implementer] ←
          NEW Implementer;
   . . .
   frame ↑.x ← 0;
   frame ↑.p[ ];
   . . .
   END.
```

Here, the client creates an instance of *Implementer* directly. Through a pointer to the frame of that instance, the client can access any public variable or invoke any public procedure. Note that the relevant declarations are in *Implementer*; the *Abstraction* module is included only for type definitions. Some of the binding has been moved to compile time. In return for a wider, not necessarily procedural interface (and potentially more efficient code), the client has committed itself to using a particular implementation of the abstraction.

Because Mesa has procedure variables, it is possible for a user to create any binding regime he wishes simply by writing a program that distributes procedures. Some users have created their own versions of Simula classes. They have not used the binding mechanism described above for a number of reasons. First, the actual implementation of an abstract object is sometimes unknown when a program is compiled or instantiated; there might be several coexisting implementations, or the actual implementation of a particular object might change dynamically. Their binding scheme deals with such situations by representing objects as record structures with procedure-valued fields. The basic idea was described in connection with the implementation of streams in OS6 [11]: some fields of each record contain the state information necessary to characterize the object, while others contain procedure values that implement the set of operations. If the number of objects is much larger than the number of implementations, it is space-efficient to replace the procedure fields in each object with a link to a separate record containing the set of values appropriate to a particular implementation. When this binding mechanism is used, interface specifications consist primarily of type definitions, as suggested by the following skeleton:

```
ObjectAbstraction: DEFINITIONS =
  BEGIN
  Handle: TYPE = POINTER TO Object;
  Object: TYPE = RECORD [
    ops: POINTER TO Operations,
    state: POINTER TO ObjectRecord,
    ...];
  Operations: TYPE = RECORD [
    p1: PROCEDURE [Handle, INTEGER],
    ...];
  END.
```

A client invokes a typical operation by writing *handle* ↑ *.ops* ↑ *.p1* [*handle*, *x*], where *handle* is an object of type *Handle*.

Observations

We believe that we could not have built the current Mesa system if we had been forced to work with large logically monolithic programs. Assembly language programmers are well aware of the benefits of modularity, but many designers of high-level programming languages pay little attention to the problems of independent compilation and instantiation. Since these capabilities will be grafted on anyway, they should be anticipated in the original design. We have more to say about interface control in our discussion of types, but it is hard to overestimate the value of articulating abstractions, centralizing their definitions, and propagating them through the inclusion mechanism.

3. The Mesa Type System

Strict vs. Nonstrict Type Checking

A widely held view is that the purpose of type declarations is to allow one to write more succinct programs. For example, the Algol 60 declarations

real *x,y*; **integer** *i,j*;

allow one to attach two different interpretations to the symbol "+" in the expressions $x + y$ and $i + j$. Similarly, the declaration

x: RECORD[*a*: [0..7], *b*: [0..255]]

permits one to write *x.a* and *x.b* in place of descriptions of the shifting and masking that might occur. Descriptive declarations also allow utility programs such as debuggers to display values of variables in a helpful way when the type is not encoded as part of the value.

This view predominated in an earlier version of Mesa. Type declarations were used primarily as devices to improve the expressive power and readability of the language. Types were ignored by the compiler except to discover the number of bits involved in an operation. In contrast, the current version of Mesa checks type agreement as rigorously as languages such as Pascal or Algol 68, potentially rendering compile-time complaints in great volume. This means in effect that the language is more redundant since there are fewer programs acceptable to the compiler.

What benefit do we hope to gain by stricter checking and the attendant obligations on the programmer? We expect that imposing additional structure on the data space of the program and checking it mechanically will make the modification and maintenance of programs easier. The type system allows us to write down certain design decisions. The type checker is a tool that is used to discover violations of the conventions implied by those decisions without a great expenditure of thought.

Type Expressions

Mesa provides a fairly conventional set of expressions for describing types; detailed discussions of the more important constructors are available elsewhere [3]. We shall attempt just enough of an introduction to help in reading the subsequent examples and concentrate upon the relations among types.

There is a set of predefined basic types and a set of *type operators* which construct new types. The arguments of these operators may be other types, integer constants, or identifiers with no *a priori* meanings. Most of the operators are familiar from languages such as Pascal or Algol 68, and the following summary emphasizes only the differences.

Basic Types. The basic types are INTEGER, BOOLEAN, CHARACTER, and UNSPECIFIED, the last of which is a one-word, wild-card type.

Enumerated Types. If $a_1, a_2, \ldots, a_n$ are distinct identifiers, the form $\{a_1, a_2, \ldots, a_n\}$ denotes an ordered type of which the identifiers denote the allowed constant values.

Unique Types. If n is a manifest (compile-time) constant of type INTEGER, the form UNIQUE[n] denotes a type distinct from any other type. The value of n determines the amount of storage allocated for values of that type, which are otherwise uninterpreted. Its use is illustrated by the *ArrayStore* example in Section 4.

Record Types. If $T_1, T_2, \ldots, T_n$ are types and $f_2, \ldots, f_n$ are distinct identifiers, the the form RECORD[f_1: T_1, f_2: $T_2, \ldots, f_n$: T_n] denotes a record type. The f_i are called *field selectors*. As usual, the field selectors are used to access individual components; in addition, linguistic forms called *constructors* and *extractors* are available for synthesizing and decomposing entire records. The latter forms allow either keyword notation, using the field names, or positional notation. Intermodule access to individual fields can be controlled by specifying the attributes PUBLIC, PRIVATE, or READONLY; if no such attributes appear, they are inherited from the enclosing declaration. Some examples:

Thing: TYPE = RECORD [*n*: INTEGER, *p*: BOOLEAN];
v: *Thing*; *i*: INTEGER; *b*: BOOLEAN;
...

```
IF v.p THEN v.n ← v.n + 1;   --field selection
v ← [100, TRUE];             --a positional constructor
v ← [p:b, n:i];              --a keyword constructor
[n:i, p:b] ← v;              --the inverse extractor.
```

Pointer Types. If T is a type, the form POINTER TO T denotes a pointer type. If x is a variable of that type, then $x \uparrow$ *dereferences* the pointer and designates the object pointed to, as in Pascal. If v is of type T, then @v is its address with type POINTER TO T. The form POINTER TO READ-ONLY T denotes a similar type; however, values of this type cannot be used to change the indirectly referenced object. Such pointer types were introduced so that objects could be passed by reference across module interfaces with assurance that their values would not be modified.

Array Types. If T_i and T_c are types, the form ARRAY T_i OF T_c denotes an array type. T_i must be a finite ordered type. An array a maps an index i from the index type T_i into a value $a[i]$ of the component type T_c. If a is a variable, the mapping can be changed by assignment to $a[i]$.

Array Descriptor Types. If T_i and T_c are types, the form DESCRIPTOR FOR ARRAY T_i OF T_c denotes an array descriptor type. T_i must be an ordered type. An array descriptor value provides indirect access to an array and contains enough auxiliary information to determine the allowable indices as a subrange of T_i.

Set Types. If T is a type, the form SET OF T denotes a type, values of which are the subsets of the set of values of T. T must evaluate to an enumerated type.

Transfer Types. If $T_1, \ldots, T_i, T_j, \ldots, T_n$ are types and $f_1, \ldots, f_i, f_j, \ldots, f_n$ are distinct identifiers, then the form PROCEDURE $[f_1: T_1, \ldots, f_i: T_i]$ RETURNS $[f_j: T_j, \ldots, f_n: T_n]$ denotes a procedure type. Each nonlocal control transfer passes an argument record; the field lists enclosed by the paired brackets, if not empty, implicitly declare the types of the records accepted and returned by the procedure [7]. If x has some transfer type, a control transfer is invoked by the evaluation of $x[e_1, \ldots, e_i]$, where the bracketed expressions are used to construct the input record, and the value is the record constructed in preparation for the transfer that returns control.

The symbol PROCEDURE can be replaced by several alternatives that specify different transfer disciplines with respect to name binding, storage allocation, etc., but the argument transmission mechanism is uniform. Transfer types are full-fledged types; it is possible to declare procedure variables and otherwise to manipulate procedure values, which are represented by procedure descriptors. Indeed, some of the intermodule binding mechanisms described previously depend crucially upon the assignment of values to procedure variables.

Subrange Types. If T is INTEGER or an enumerated type, and m and n are manifest constants of that type, the form $T[m..n]$ denotes a finite, ordered subrange type for which any legal value x satisfies $m \leq x \leq n$. If T is INTEGER, the abbreviated form $[m..n]$ is accepted. These types are especially useful as the index types of arrays. Other notational forms, e.g. $[m..n)$, allow inter-vals to be open or closed at either endpoint.

Finally, Mesa has adapted Pascal's variant record concept to provide values whose complete type can only be known after a run-time discrimination. Because they are of more than passing interest, variant records are discussed separately in Section 5.

Declarations and Definitions

The form

$v\colon Thing \leftarrow e$

declares a variable v of type *Thing* and initializes it to the value of e; the form

$v\colon Thing = e$

is similar except that assignments cannot be made to v subsequently. When e itself is a manifest constant, this form makes v such a constant also.

This syntax is used for the introduction of new type names, using the special type TYPE. Thus

$Thing\colon \text{TYPE} = TypeExpression$

defines the type *Thing*. This approach came from ECL [13], in which a type is a value that can be computed by a running program and then used to declare variables. In Mesa, however, *TypeExpression* must be constant.

Recursive type declarations are essential for describing most list structures and are allowed more generally whenever they make sense. To accommodate a mutually recursive list structure, forward references to type identifiers are allowed and do not yield "uninitialized" values. (This is to be contrasted with forward references to ordinary variables.) In effect, all type expressions within a scope are evaluated simultaneously. Meaningful recursion in a type declaration usually involves the type constructor POINTER; in corresponding values, the recursion involves a level of indirection and can be terminated by the empty pointer value NIL. Recursion that is patently meaningless is rejected by the compiler; for example,

$r\colon \text{TYPE} = \text{RECORD} \ [left, right\colon r] \ \text{--not permitted}$
$a\colon \text{TYPE} = \text{ARRAY} \ [0..10) \ \text{OF} \ s;$
$s\colon \text{TYPE} = \text{RECORD} \ [i\colon \text{INTEGER}, m\colon a] \ \text{--not permitted}.$

Similar pathological types have been noted and prohibited in Algol 68 [6].

Equivalence of Type Expressions

One might expect that two identical type expressions appearing in different places in the program text would always stand for the same type. In Algol 68 they do. In Mesa (and certain implementations of Pascal) they do not. Specifically, the type operators RECORD, UNIQUE, and {...} generate new types whenever they appear in the text.

The original reasons for this choice are not very important, but we have not regretted the following consequences for records:

(a) All modules wishing to communicate using a shared record type must obtain the definition of that type from the same source. In practice, this means that all definitions of an abstraction tend to come from a single module; there is less temptation to declare scattered, partial interface definitions.

(b) Tests for record type equivalence are cheap. In our experience, most record types contain references to other record types, and this linking continues to a considerable depth. A recursive definition of equivalence would, in the worst case, require examining many modules unknown and perhaps unavailable to the casual user of a record type or, alternatively, copying all type definitions supporting a particular type into the symbol table of any module mentioning that type.

(c) The rule for record equivalence provides a mechanism for *sealing* values that are distributed to clients as passkeys for later transactions with an implementer. Suppose that the following declaration occurs in a definitions module:

Handle: PUBLIC TYPE = RECORD [*value*: PRIVATE *Thing*].

The PRIVATE attribute of *value* is overridden in any implementer of *Handle*. A client of that implementer can declare variables of type *Handle* and can store or duplicate values of that type, but there is no way for the client to construct a counterfeit *Handle* without violating the type system. Such sealed types appear to provide a basis for a compile-time capability scheme [2].

(d) Finally, this choice has not caused discomfort because programmers are naturally inclined to introduce names for record types anyway.

The case for distinctness of enumerated types is much weaker; we solved the problem of the exact relationships among such types of $\{a, b, c\}$, $\{c, b, a\}$, $\{a, c\}$, $\{aa, b, cc\}$, etc. by specifying that all these types are distinct. In this case, we are less happy that identical sequences of symbols construct different enumerated types.

Why did we not choose a similar policy for other types? It would mean that a new type identifier would have to be introduced for virtually every type expression, and we found it to be too tedious. In the case of procedures we went even further in liberalizing the notion of equivalence. Even though the formal argument and result lists are considered to be record declarations, we not only permit recursive matching but also ignore the field selectors in doing the match. We were unwilling to abandon the idea that procedures are mappings in which the identifiers of bound variables are irrelevant. We also had a pragmatic motivation. In contrast to records, where the type definitions cross interface boundaries, procedural communication among modules is based upon procedure values, not procedure types. Declaring named types for all interface procedures seemed tiresome. Fortunately all argument records are constructed in a standard way, so this view causes no implementation problems.

To summarize, we state an informal algorithm for testing for type equivalence. Given one or more program texts and two particular type expressions in them:

1. Tag each occurrence of RECORD, UNIQUE, and $\{\ldots\}$ with a distinct number.
2. Erase all the variable names in the formal parameter and the result lists of procedures.
3. Compare the two expressions, replacing type identifiers with their defining expressions whenever they are encountered. If a difference (possibly in a tag attached in step 1) is ever encountered, the two type expressions are not equivalent. Otherwise they are equivalent.

The final step appears to be a semidecision procedure since the existence of recursive types makes it impossible to eliminate all the identifiers. In fact, it is always possible to tell when one has explored enough (cf. [5], Section 2.3.5, Exercise 11).

Coercions

To increase the flexibility of the type system Mesa permits a variety of implicit type conversions beyond those implied by type equivalence. They fall into two categories: *free coercions* and *computed coercions*.

Free Coercions. Free coercions involve no computation whatsoever. For two types T and S, we write $T \subseteq S$ if any value of type T can be stored into a variable of type S without checking, change of representation, or other computation. (By "store" we mean to encompass assignment, parameter passing, result passing, and all other value transmission.) The following recursive rules show how to compute the relation $\subseteq$, assuming that equivalence has already been accounted for:

1. $T \subseteq T$.

In the following assume that $T \subseteq S$.

2. $T[i..j] \subseteq S$ if i is the minimum value of type S.

The restriction is necessary because we chose to represent values of a subrange type relative to its minimum value. Coercions in other cases require computation. Similarly,

3. $T[i..j] \subseteq S[i..k]$ iff $j \leq k$.
4. *var* $T \subseteq S$ if *var* is a variant of T (cf. Section 5).
5. RECORD$[f: T] \subseteq S$ for any field name f unless f has the PRIVATE attribute.
6. POINTER TO $T \subseteq$ POINTER TO READ-ONLY S.

In other words, one can always treat a pointer as a read-only pointer, but not vice versa.

7. POINTER TO READ-ONLY $T \subseteq$ POINTER TO READ-ONLY S.

The relation POINTER TO $T \subseteq$ POINTER TO S is *not* true because it would allow

ps: POINTER TO S;
pt: POINTER TO $T = @t$;
ps $\leftarrow pt$;
ps $\uparrow \leftarrow s$;

which is a sneaky way of accomplishing "$t \leftarrow s$," which is not allowed unless $S \subseteq T$.

8. ARRAY I OF T $\subseteq$ ARRAY I OF S.

Note that the index sets must be the same.

9. PROCEDURE [S'] RETURNS [T] $\subseteq$ PROCEDURE [T'] RETURNS [S] if T' $\subseteq$ S' as well.

Here the relation between the input types is the reverse of what one might expect.

Subrange Coercions. Coercions between subranges require further comment. As others have noted [4], associating range restrictions with types instead of specific variables leads to certain conceptual problems; however, we wanted to be able to fold range restrictions into more complex constructed types. We were somewhat surprised by the subtlety of this problem, and our initial solutions allowed several unintended breaches of the type system.

Values of an ordered type and all its subranges are interassignable even if they do not satisfy cases (2) or (3) above. This is an example of a computed coercion. Code is generated to check that the value is in the proper subrange and to convert its representation if necessary. It is important to realize that computed coercions cannot be extended recursively as was done above. Consider the declarations

```
x: [0..100] ← 15;
y: [10..20];
px: POINTER TO READ-ONLY [0..100] ← @x;
py: POINTER TO READ-ONLY [10..20];
```

The assignment $y \leftarrow x$ is permitted because x is 15; 5 is stored in y since its value is represented relative to 10. However, the assignment $py \leftarrow px$, which rule 7 might suggest, is not permitted because the value of x can change and there is no reasonable way to generate checking code. Even if the value of x cannot change, we could not perform any change in representation because the value 15 is shared. Similar problems arise when one considers rules 6, 8, and 9.

Other Computed Coercions. Research in programming language design has continued in parallel with our implementation work, and some proposals for dealing with uniform references [3] and generalizations of classes [8] suggested adding the following computed coercions to the language:

Dereferencing: POINTER TO $T \rightarrow T$
Deproceduring: PROCEDURE RETURNS $T \rightarrow T$
Referencing:　　$T \rightarrow$ POINTER TO T.

Initially we had intended to support contextually implied application of these coercions much as does Algol 68. Reactions of Mesa's early users to this proposal ranged from lukewarm to strongly negative. In addition, the data structures and accounting algorithms necessary to deduce the required coercions and detect pathological types substantially complicated the compiler. We therefore decided to reconsider our decision even after the design and some of the implementation had been done. The current language allows subrange coercion as described above. There is no uniform support for other computed coercions, but automatic dereferencing is invoked by the operators for field extraction and array indexing. Thus such forms as $p \uparrow .f$ and $a \uparrow \uparrow [i]$, which are common when indirection is used extensively, may be written as $p.f$ and $a[i]$.

There are hints of a significant problem for language designers here. Competent and experienced programmers seem to believe that coercion rules make their programs less understandable and thus less reliable and efficient. On the other hand, techniques being developed with the goal of decreasing the cost of creating and changing programs seem to build heavily upon coercion. Our experience suggests that such work should proceed with caution.

Why is coercion distrusted? Our discussions with programmers suggest that the reasons include the following:

- Mesa programmers are familiar with the underlying hardware and want to be aware of the exact consequences of what they write.
- Many of them have been burned by forgotten indirect bits and the like in previous programming and are suspicious of any unexpected potential for side effects.
- To some extent, coercion negates the advantages of type checking. One view of coercion is that it corrects common type errors, and some of the detection capability is sacrificed to obtain the correction.

We conjecture that the first two objections will diminish as programmers learn to think in terms of higher-level abstractions and to use the type checking to advantage.

The third objection appears to have some merit. We know of no system of coercions in which strict type checking can be trusted to flag all coercion errors, and such errors are likely to be especially subtle and persistent. The difficulties seem to arise from the interactions of coercion with generic operators. In Algol 68, there are rules about "loosely related" types that are intended to avoid this problem, but the identity operators still suffer. With the coercion rules that had been proposed for Mesa, the following trap occurs. Given the declaration p, q: POINTER TO INTEGER, the Mesa expressions $p \uparrow = q \uparrow$ and $2*p = 2*q$ would compare integers and give identical results; on the other hand, the expression $p = q$ would compare pointers and could give a quite different answer. In the presence of such traps, we believe that most programmers would resolve to supply the "$\uparrow$" always. If this is their philosophy, coercions can only hide errors. Even if such potentially ambiguous expressions as $p = q$ were disallowed, this example suggests that using coercion to achieve representational independence can easily destroy referential transparency instead.

4. Experiences with Strict Type Checking

It is hard to give objective evidence that increasing compile-time checking has materially helped the programming process. We believe that it will take more effort to get one's program to compile and that some of the effort eliminates errors that would have shown up during testing or later, but the magnitude of these effects is hard to measure. All we can present at the moment are testimonials and anecdotes.

A Testimonial

Programmers whose previous experience was with unchecked languages report that the usual fear and trepidation that accompanied making modifications to programs has substantially diminished. Under previous regimes they would never change the number or types of arguments that a procedure took for fear that they would forget to fix all of the calls on that procedure. Now they know that all references will be checked before they try to run the program.

An Anecdote

The following kind of record is used extensively in the compiler:

$RelativePtr$: TYPE = $[0..37777_8]$;
$TaggedPtr$: TYPE = RECORD$[tag$: $\{t_0,t_1,t_2,t_3\}$,
$\qquad\qquad\qquad\qquad ptr$: $RelativePtr]$

This record consists of a 2-bit tag and a 14-bit pointer. As an accident of the compiler's choice of representation, the expressions x and $TaggedPtr[t_0,x]$ generated the same internal value. The nonstrict type checker considered these types equivalent, and unwittingly we used $TaggedPtrs$ in many places actually requiring $RelativePtrs$. As it happened, the tag in these contexts was always t_0.

The compiler was working well, but one day we made the unfortunate decision to redefine $TaggedPtr$ as

RECORD$[ptr$: $RelativePtr$, tag: $\{t_0,t_1,t_2,t_3\}]$.

This caused a complete breakdown, and we hastily unmade that decision because we were unsure about what parts of the code were unintentionally depending upon the old representation. Later, when we submitted a transliteration of the compiler to the strict type checker, we found all the places where this error had been committed. At present, making such a change is routine. In general, we believe that the benefits of static checking are significant and cost-effective once the programmer learns how to use the type system effectively.

A Shortcoming

The type system is very good at detecting the difference in usage between T and POINTER TO T; however, programmers often use array indices as pointers, especially when they want to perform arithmetic on them. The difference between an integer used as a pointer and an integer used otherwise is invisible to the type checker. For example, the declaration

map: ARRAY $[i..j]$ OF INTEGER$[m..n]$;

defines a variable map with the property that compile-time type checking cannot distinguish between legitimate uses of k and $map[k]$. Furthermore, if $m \le i$ and $j \le n$, even a run-time bounds check could never detect a use of k when $map[k]$ was intended. We have observed several troublesome bugs of this nature and would like to change the language so that indices of different arrays can be made into distinct types.

Violating the Type System

One of the questions often asked about languages with compile-time type checking is whether it is possible to write real programs without violating the type system. It goes without saying that one can bring virtually any program within the confines of a type system by methods analogous to the silly methods for eliminating $gotos$; e.g. simulate things with integers. However, our experience has been that it is not always desirable to remain within the system, given the realities of programming and the restrictiveness of the current language. There are three reasons for which we found it desirable to evade the current type system.

Sometimes the violation is logically necessary. Fairly often one chooses to implement part of a language's run-time system in the language itself. There are certain things of this nature that cannot be done in a type-safe way in Mesa, or any other strictly type-checked language we know. For example, the part of the system that takes the compiler's output and creates values of type PROCEDURE must exercise a rather profound loophole in turning data into program. Another example, discussed in detail below, is a storage allocator. Most languages with compile-time checking submerge these activities into the implementation and thereby avoid the need for type breaches.

Sometimes efficiency is more important than type safety. In many cases the way to avoid a type breach is to redesign a data structure in a way that takes more space, usually by introducing extra levels of pointers. The section on variant records gives an example.

Sometimes a breach is advisable to increase type checking elsewhere. Occasionally a breach could be avoided by declaring two distinct types to be the same, but merging them would reduce a great deal of checking elsewhere. The $ArrayStore$ example below illustrates this point.

Given these considerations, we chose to allow occasional breaches of the type system, making them as explicit as possible. The advantages of doing this are twofold. First, making breaches explicit makes them less dangerous since they are clearer to the reader. Second, their occurrences provide valuable hints to a language designer about where the type system needs improvement.

One of the simplest ways to breach the Mesa type

system is to declare something to be UNSPECIFIED. The type checking algorithm regards this as a one-word don't-care type that matches any other one-word type. This is similar to PL/I UNSPEC. We have come to the conclusion that using UNSPECIFIED is too drastic in most cases. One usually wants to turn off type checking in only a few places involving a particular variable, not everywhere. In practice there is a tendency to use UNSPECIFIED in the worst possible way: at the interfaces of modules. The effect is to turn off type checking in other people's modules without their knowing it!

As an alternative, Mesa provides a general type transfer function, RECAST, that (without performing any computation) converts between any two types of equal size. It can often be used instead of UNSPECIFIED. In cases where we had declared a particular variable UNSPECIFIED, we now prefer to give it some specific type and to use RECAST whenever it is being treated in a way that violates the assumptions about that type.

The existence of RECAST makes many decisions much less painful. Consider the type CHARACTER. On the one hand we would like it to be disjoint from INTEGER so that simple mistakes would be caught by the type checker. On the other hand, one occasionally needs to do arithmetic on characters. We chose to make CHARACTER a distinct type and use RECAST in those places where character arithmetic is needed. Why reduce the quality of type checking everywhere just to accommodate a rare case?

Pointer arithmetic is a popular pastime for system programmers. Rather than outlawing it, or even requiring a RECAST, Mesa permits it in a restricted form. One can add or subtract an integer from a pointer to produce a pointer of the same type. One can subtract two pointers of the same type to produce an integer. The need for more exotic arithmetic has not been observed.

Here is a typical example: It is common to use a large contiguous area of memory to hold a data structure consisting of many records, e.g. a parse tree. To conserve space one would like to make all pointers relative to the start of the area, thus reducing the size of pointers that are internal to the structure. Furthermore, one might like to move the entire area, possibly via secondary storage. These needs would be met by an unimplemented feature called the *tied pointer*. The idea is that a certain type of pointer would be made relative to a designated base value and this value would be added just before dereferencing the pointer. In other words, if *ptr* were declared to be tied to *base* then *ptr* ↑ actually would mean (*base* + *ptr*) ↑ . Since tied pointers have not yet been implemented, this notation is in fact used extensively within the Mesa compiler. Subsequent versions of Mesa will include tied pointers, and this temporary loophole will be reconsidered.

The Skeleton Type System

Once we provided the opportunity for evading the official type system, we had to ask ourselves just why

we thought certain breaches were safe while others were not. Ultimately, we came to the conclusion that the only really dangerous breaches of the type systems were those that require detailed knowledge of the run-time environment. First and foremost, fabricating a procedure value requires a detailed understanding of how various structures in memory are arranged. Second, pointer types also depend on various memory structures' being set up properly and should not be passed through loopholes without some care. In contrast, the distinction between the two types RECORD [*a,b*: INTEGER] and RECORD [*c,d*: INTEGER] is not vital to the run-time system's integrity. To be sure, the user might wish to keep them distinct, but using a loophole to store one into the other would go entirely unnoticed by the system.

The present scheme that is used to judge the appropriateness of RECAST transformations merely checks to ensure that the source and destination types occupy the same number of bits. Since most of the code invoking RECAST has been written by Mesa implementers, this simplified check has proved to be sufficient. However, as the community of users has grown, we have observed a justifiable anxiety over the use of RECAST. Users fear that unchecked use of this escape will cause a violation of some system convention unknown to them.

We are in the process of investigating a more complete and formal skeletal type system that will reduce the hazards of the present RECAST mechanism. Its aim is to ensure that although a RECAST may do great violence to user-defined type conventions, the system's type integrity will not be violated.

Example – A Compacting Storage Allocator

A module that provides many arrays of various sizes by parceling out pieces of one large array is an interesting benchmark for a systems programming language for a number of reasons:

(a) It taxes the type system severely. We must deal with an array containing variable length heterogeneous objects, something one cannot declare in Mesa.

(b) The clients of the allocator wish to use it for arrays of differing types. This is a familiar polymorphism problem.

(c) As a programming exercise, the module can involve tricky pointer manipulations. We would like help to prevent programming errors such as the ubiquitous address/contents confusion.

(d) A nasty kind of bug associated with the use of such packages is the so-called dangling reference problem: variables or data structures might be used after their space has been relinquished.

(e) Another usage bug, peculiar to compacting allocators, is that a client might retain a pointer to storage that the compacter might move.

The first two problems make it impossible to stay entirely within the type system: One's first impulse is to

Fig. 1. Definitions module.

```
ArrayStoreDefs: DEFINITIONS =
BEGIN
 ArrayPtr: TYPE = POINTER TO PR;
 PR: TYPE = POINTER TO R;
 R: TYPE =
    RECORD [ p: Prefix,
             a: ARRAY [0..0] OF Thing ];
 Prefix: TYPE = RECORD [ backp: PRIVATE ArrayPtr,
                         length: READ-ONLY INTEGER ];
 Thing: TYPE = UNIQUE[16];
 AllocArray: PROCEDURE [length: INTEGER]
             RETURNS [new: ArrayPtr];
 FreeArray: PROCEDURE [dying: ArrayPtr];
END
```

Fig. 2. Implementation of a compacting storage allocator.

```
    DIRECTORY ArrayStoreDefs: FROM "ArrayStoreDefs";
    DEFINITIONS FROM ArrayStoreDefs.
 ArrayStore: PROGRAM IMPLEMENTING ArrayStoreDefs =
 BEGIN
 Storage: ARRAY [0..StorageSize) OF UNSPECIFIED;
 StorageSize: INTEGER = 2000;
 Table: ARRAY TableIndex OF PR;
 Table Index: TYPE = [0..TableSize);
 TableSize: INTEGER = 500;
 beginStorage: PR = @Storage[0];
             --the address of Storage[0]
 endStorage: PR = @Storage[StorageSize];
 nextR: PR ← beginStorage; --next space to put an R
 beginTable: ArrayPtr = @Table[0];
 endTable: ArrayPtr = @Table[TableSize];
 ovh: INTEGER = SIZE[Prefix]; --overhead
 AllocArray: PUBLIC PROCEDURE [n: INTEGER]
             RETURNS [new: ArrayPtr] =
 BEGIN i:TableIndex;
 IF n < 0 OR n > 77777B − ovh THEN ERROR;
 IF n + ovh > endStorage − nextR THEN
    BEGIN
    Compact[ ];
    IF n + ovh > endStorage − nextR THEN ERROR;
    END;
   --Find a table entry
 FOR i IN TableIndex DO
    IF Table[i] = NIL THEN GOTO found
    REPEAT
      found ⇒ new ← @Table[i];
      FINISHED ⇒ ERROR
    ENDLOOP;
 new ↑ ← nextR;
   --initialize the array storage
 new ↑ ↑ .p.backp ← new;
 new ↑ ↑ .p.length ← n;
 nextR ← nextR + (n + ovh);
 END;

 Compact: PROCEDURE = (omitted)

 FreeArray: PUBLIC PROCEDURE [dead: ArrayPtr] =
    BEGIN IF dead ↑ = NIL THEN ERROR; --array already free
    dead ↑ ↑ .p.backp ← NIL;
    dead ↑ ← NIL;
    END;
   --Initialization
 i: TableIndex;
 FOR i IN TableIndex DO Table[i] ← NIL ENDLOOP;
 END.
```

declare everything unspecified and proceed to program as in days of yore. The remaining problems are real ones, however, and we are reluctant to turn off the entire type system just when we need it most. The following is a compromise solution.

To deal with problem (a), we have two different ways of designating the array to be parceled out, which we call *Storage*. From a client's point of view, the storage is accessible through the definitions shown in the module *ArrayStoreDefs* (cf. Figure 1).

These definitions suggest that the client can get *ArrayPtrs* (i.e. pointers to pointers to array records) by calling *AllocArray* and can relinquish them by calling *FreeArray*. The PRIVATE attribute on *backp* means that the client cannot access that field at all. The READ-ONLY attribute on *length* means that the client cannot change it. Of course these restrictions do not apply to the implementing module. The type *Thing* occupies 16 bits of storage (one word) and matches no other type. Intuitively it is our way of simulating a type variable. The implementing module *ArrayStore* is shown in Figure 2. It declares the array *Storage* to create the raw material for allocation. We chose to declare its element type UNSPECIFIED. This means that every transaction involving *Storage* is an implicit invocation of a loophole. Specifically the initializations of *beginStorage* and *endStorage* store pointers to UNSPECIFIED into variables declared as pointers to *R*.

The general representation scheme is as follows: The storage area [*beginStorage..nextR*) consists of zero or more *R*s, each with the form $\langle backp, length, e_0, \ldots, e_{(length-1)}\rangle$, where *length* varies from sequence to sequence. The array represented by the record is $\langle e_0, \ldots, e_{(length-1)}\rangle$. If *backp* is not NIL then *backp* is an address in *Table* and *backp* ↑ is the address of *backp* itself. If *Table*[i] is not NIL, it is the address of one of these records (cf. Figure 3).

After the initialization, *Storage* is not mentioned again. All the subsequent type breaches in *ArrayStore* are of the pointer arithmetic variety. The expression *endStorage* − *nextR* in *AllocArray* subtracts two *PR's* to produce an integer. The type checker is not entirely asleep here: If we slipped up and wrote

IF n + ovh > endStorage − n

there would be a complaint because the left-hand side of the comparison is an integer and the right is a *PR*. The assignment

nextR ← nextR + (n + ovh)

at the end of *AllocArray* also uses the pointer arithmetic breach. The rule *PR* + INTEGER = *PR* makes sense here because n + ovh is just the right amount to add to *nextR* to produce the next place where an *R* can go.

Despite all these breaches, we are still getting a good deal of checking. The checker would point out (or correct) any address/contents confusions we had, manifested by the omission of ↑ 's or their unnecessary appearance. We can be sure that integers and *PR*s are not being mixed up. In the (unlikely) event that we wrote something like

$$new \uparrow .p.length \leftarrow new \uparrow .a[k]$$

we would be warned because the value on the left is an integer and the value on the right is a *Thing*. Notice that none of this checking would occur if *Thing* were replaced by UNSPECIFIED. Thus, even though the type system is not airtight, we are better off than we would be in a completely unchecked language (unless, perhaps, we get a false sense of security).

Now let us consider how this module is to be used by a client who wants to manipulate two different kinds of arrays: arrays of integers and arrays of strings. At first it looks as if the code is going to have a very high density of RECAST's. For example, to create an array and store an integer in it the client will have to say

```
IA: ArrayPtr = AllocArray[100];
IA ↑ ↑ .a[2] ← RECAST[6]
```

because the type of *IA* ↑ ↑ *.a*[2] is *Thing*, which does not match anything. Writing a loophole every time is intolerable, so we are tempted to replace *Thing* by UNSPECIFIED, thereby losing a certain amount of type checking elsewhere.

There are much nicer ways out of this problem. Rather than passing every array element through a loophole, one can pass the procedures *AllocArray* and *FreeArray* through loopholes (once, during initialization). The module *ArrayClient* (cf. Figure 4) shows how this is done. Not only does this save our having to make *Thing* UNSPECIFIED, it allows us to use the type checker to ensure that integer arrays contain only integers and that string arrays contain only strings. More precisely, the type checker guarantees that every store into *IA* stores ar integer. We must depend upon the correctness of the code in *ArrayStore*, particularly the compactor, to make sure that data structures stay well formed.

This scheme does not have any provisions for coping with problem (d), dangling reference errors. However, somewhat surprisingly, problem (e)—saving a raw pointer—cannot happen as long as the client does not commit any further breaches of the type system. The trick is in the way we declared *IntArray*—all in one mouthful. That makes it impossible to declare a variable to hold a raw pointer. This is because (as mentioned before) every occurrence of the type constructor RECORD generates a new type, distinct from all other types. Therefore, even if we should declare

```
rawPointer: POINTER TO RECORD [
  p: Prefix,
  a: ARRAY[0..0] OF INTEGER ];
```

we could not perform the assignment *rawpointer* ← *IA* ↑ because *IA* ↑ has a different type, even though it looks the same. If one cannot declare the type of *IA* ↑, it is rather difficult to hang onto it for very long. In fact,

the compiler has been carefully designed to ensure that no type-checked program can hold such a pointer across a procedure call.

Passing procedure values through loopholes is a rather frightening thing to do. What if, by some mischance, *AllocArray* doesn't have the number of parameters ascribed to it by the client? Since we have waved off the type checker to do the assignment of *AllocArray* to *AllocIntArray* and *AllocStrArray*, no compile-time type violation would be detected and some hard-to-diagnose disaster would occur at run time. To compensate for this, we introduce the curious procedure *Gedanken*, whose only purpose is to fail to compile if the number or size of *AllocArray*'s parameters change. The skeleton type system, discussed earlier in this section, would obviate the need for this foolishness.

We would like to emphasize that, although our examples focus on controlled breaches of the type system, many real Mesa programs do not violate the type system at all. We also expect the density of breaches to decrease as the descriptive powers of the type system increase.

5. Variant Records

Mesa, like Pascal, has variant records. The descriptive aspects of the two languages' notion of variant records are very similar. Mesa, however, also requires strict type checking for accessing the components of variant records. To illustrate the Mesa variant record facility consider the following example of the declaration for an I/O stream:

```
StreamHandle: TYPE = POINTER TO Stream;
StreamType: TYPE = {disk, display, keyboard};
Stream: TYPE = RECORD [
  Get: PROCEDURE[StreamHandle]RETURNS[Item],
  Put: PROCEDURE[StreamHandle, Item],
  body: SELECT type; StreamType FROM
    disk ⇒ [
      file: File Pointer,
      position: Position,
      SetPosition: PROCEDURE [
        POINTER TO disk Stream,
        Position],
      buffer: SELECT size:* FROM
        short ⇒ [b: ShortArray],
        long ⇒ [b: LongArray]
        ENDCASE ],
    display ⇒ [
      first: DisplayControlBlock,
      last: DisplayControlBlock,
      position: ScreenPosition,
      nLines: [0..100]],
    keyboard ⇒ NULL,
    ENDCASE];
```

The record type has three main variants; *disk*, *display*, and *keyboard*. Furthermore, the disk variant has two variants of its own: *short* and *long*. Note that the field names used in variant subparts need not be unique. The asterisk used in declaring the subvariant of

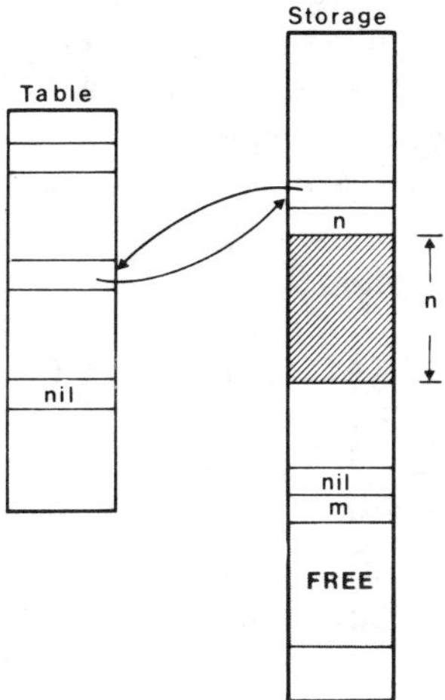

Fig. 3. *ArrayStore's* data structure.

disk is a shorthand mechanism for generating an enumerated type for tagging variant subparts.

The declaration of a variant record species a type, as usual; it is the type of the whole record. The declaration itself defines some other types: one for each variant in the record. In the above example, the total number of type variations is six, and they are used in the following declarations:

```
r: Stream;
rDisk: disk Stream;
rDisplay: display Stream;
rKeyb: keyboard Stream;
rShort: short disk Stream;
rLong: long disk Stream;
```

The last five types are called *bound variant types*. The rightmost name must be the type identifier for a variant record. The other names are adjectives modifying the type identified to their right. Thus *disk* modifies the type *Stream* and identifies a new type. Further, *short* modifies the type *disk Stream* and identifies still another type. Names must occur in order and may not be skipped. (For instance, *short Stream* would be incorrect since *short* does not identify a *Stream* variant.)

When a record is a bound variant, the components of its variant part may be accessed without a preliminary test. For example, the following assignments are legal:

```
rDisplay.last ← rDisplay.first;
rDisk.position ← rShort.position;
```

If a record is not a bound variant (e.g. *r* in the previous section), the program needs a way to decide which variant it is before accessing variant components. More importantly, the testing of the variant must be done in a formal way so that the type checker can verify that the programmer is not making unwarranted assumptions about which variant is in hand. For this purpose, Mesa uses a *discrimination* statement which resembles the declaration of the variant part. However, the arms in a discriminating SELECT contain statements; and, within a given arm, the discriminated record value is viewed as a bound variant. Therefore, within that arm, its variant components may be accessed using normal qualification. The following example discriminates on *r*:

```
WITH streamRec: r SELECT FROM
    display ⇒
        BEGIN streamRec.first ← streamRec.last;
        streamRec.position ← 73; streamRec.nLines ← 4;
        END;
    disk ⇒
    WITH diskRec: streamRec SELECT FROM
        short ⇒ diskRec.b[0] ← 10;
        long ⇒ diskRec.b[0] ← 100;
        ENDCASE;
ENDCASE ⇒ streamrec.put ← streamrec.newput;
```

The expression in the WITH clause must represent either a variant record (e.g. *r*) or a pointer to a variant record. The identifier preceding the colon in the WITH clause is a synonym for the record. Within each selection, the type of the identifier is the selected bound variant type, and fields specific to the particular variant can be mentioned.

In addition to the descriptive advantages of bound variant types, the Mesa compiler also exploits the more precise declaration of a particular variant to allocate the minimal amount of storage for variables declared to be of a bound variant type. For example, the storage for *r* above must be sufficient to contain any one of the five possible variants. The storage for *rKeyb*, on the other hand, need only be sufficient for storing a *keyboard Stream*.

The Mutable Variant Record Problem

The names *streamRec* and *diskRec* in the example above are really synonyms in the sense that they name the same storage as *r*; no copying is done by the discrimination operation. This decision opens a loophole in the type system. Given the declaration

```
Splodge: TYPE = RECORD [
    refcount: INTEGER;
    vp: SELECT t: * FROM
        blue ⇒
            [x: ARRAY[0..1000) OF CHARACTER],
        red ⇒
            [item: INTEGER, left, right: POINTER TO Splodge],
        green ⇒
            [item: INTEGER, next: POINTER TO green Splodge],
        ENDCASE];
```

one can write the code

```
t: Splodge;
P: PROCEDURE = BEGIN t ← Splodge[0, green[10, NIL]] END;
...
WITH s: t SELECT FROM
    red ⇒ BEGIN ... P[ ] .... s.left ← s.right END;
```

The procedure *P* overwrites *t*, and therefore *s*, with a *green Splodge*. The subsequent references to *s.left* and *s.right* are invalid and will cause great mischief.

Closing this breach is simple enough: we could have simply followed Algol 68 and combined the discrimination with a copying operation that places the entire

Fig. 4. Client of a compacting allocator.

```
        DIRECTORY ArrayStoreDefs: FROM "ArrayStoreDefs";
        DEFINITIONS FROM ArrayStoreDefs;
ArrayClient: PROGRAM =
  BEGIN
  --Integer array primitives
  IntArray: TYPE = POINTER TO POINTER TO
          RECORD[p: Prefix, a: ARRAY [0..0] OF INTEGER];
  AllocIntArray: PROCEDURE [INTEGER] RETURNS [IntArray]
          = RECAST[AllocArray];
  FreeIntArray: PROCEDURE [IntArray]
          = RECAST[FreeArray];

  --String array primitives
  StrArray: TYPE = POINTER TO POINTER TO
          RECORD[p: Prefix, a: ARRAY [0..0] OF STRING];
  AllocStrArray: PROCEDURE [INTEGER] RETURNS [StrArray]
          = RECAST[AllocArray];
  FreeStrArray: PROCEDURE [StrArray]
          = RECAST [FreeArray];

  Gedanken: PROCEDURE =
    --This procedure's only role in life is to fail to
    compile if ArrayStore does not have the right sort of
    procedures.
    BEGIN
    uAllocArray:
      PROCEDURE [INTEGER] RETURNS [UNSPECIFIED]
        = AllocArray;
      uFreeArray: PROCEDURE [UNSPECIFIED] = FreeArray;
      END;
  IA: IntArray = AllocIntArray[100];
  SA: StrArray = AllocStrArray[10];
  i: INTEGER;
  FOR i IN [0..IA↑↑.p.length) DO IA↑↑.a[i] ← i/3 ENDLOOP;
  SA↑↑.a[0] ← "zero"; SA↑↑.a[1] ← "one";
  SA↑↑.a[2] ← "two"; SA↑↑.a[3] ← "surprise";
  SA↑↑.a[4] ← "four";
  FreeIntArray[IA];
  FreeStrArray[SA];
  END.
```

Splodge in a new location (*s*) which is fixed to be *red*.
We chose not to do so for three reasons:
(1) Making copies can be expensive.
(2) Making a copy destroys useful sharing relations.
(3) This loophole has yet to cause a problem.

Consider the following procedure, which is representative of those found throughout the Mesa compiler's symbol table processor:

```
Add5: PROCEDURE[ x: POINTER TO Splodge] =
  BEGIN y: POINTER TO green Splodge;
  IF x = NIL THEN RETURN;
  WITH s: x↑ SELECT FROM
    blue ⇒ RETURN;
    red ⇒
      BEGIN s.item ← s.item + 5;
          Add5[s.left]; Add5[s.right] END;
    green ⇒
      BEGIN y ← @s; -- means y ← x
      UNTIL y = NIL DO
        y↑.item ← y↑.item + 5; y ← y↑.next;
        ENDLOOP;
      END
    ENDCASE
  END
```

As it stands, this procedure runs through a *Splodge*, adding 5 to all the integers in it. Suppose we chose to copy while discriminating: i.e. suppose $x\uparrow$ were copied into some new storage named *s*. In the *blue* arm a lot of space and time would be wasted copying a 1000-character array into *s*, even though it was never used. In the *red* arm the assignment to *s*'s *item* field is useless since it doesn't affect the original structure.

The *green* arm illustrates the usefulness of declaring bound variant types like *green Splodge* explicitly. If we had to declare *y* and the *next* field of a *green Splodge* to be simply *Splodges*, even though we knew they were always *green*, the loop in that arm would have to be rewritten to contain a useless discrimination.

To achieve the effect we desire under a copy-while-discriminating regime, we would have to redesign our data structure to include another level of pointers:

```
Splodge: TYPE = RECORD [
  refcount: INTEGER;
  vp: SELECT t: * FROM
    blue ⇒ [POINTER TO BlueSplodge],
    red ⇒ [POINTER TO RedSplodge],
    green ⇒ [POINTER TO GreenSplodge],
    ENDCASE];
  BlueSplodge: TYPE = RECORD[
    x: ARRAY[0..1000) OF CHARACTER];
  RedSplodge: TYPE = RECORD[
    item: INTEGER, left, right: POINTER TO Splodge];
  GreenSplodge: TYPE = RECORD[
    item: INTEGER, next: POINTER TO GreenSplodge];
```

Now we do not mind copying because it doesn't consume much time or space, and it doesn't destroy the sharing relations. Unfortunately, we must pay for the storage occupied by the extra pointers, and this might be intolerable if we have a large collection of *Splodges*.

How have we lived with this loophole so far without getting burnt? It seems that we hardly ever change the variant of a record once it has been initialized. Therefore the possible confusions never occur because the variant never changes after being discriminated. In light of this observation, our suggestion for getting rid of the breach is simply to invent an attribute IMMUT-ABLE whose attachment to a variant record declaration guarantees that changing the variant is impossible after initialization. This means that special syntax must be invented for the initialization step, but that is all to the good since it provides an opportunity for a storage allocator to allocate precisely the right amount of space.

6. Conclusions

In this paper, we have discussed our experiences with program modularization and strict type checking. It is hard to resist drawing parallels between the disciplines introduced by these features on the one hand and those introduced by programming without *goto*s on the other. In view of the great *goto* debates of recent memory, we would like to summarize our experiences with the following observations and cautions.

(1) The benefits from these linguistic mechanisms, large though they might be, do not come automatically. A programmer must learn to use them effectively. We are just beginning to learn how to do so.

(2) Just as the absence of *goto*s does not always make a program better, the absence of type errors does not make it better if their absence is purchased by sacrificing clarity, efficiency, or type articulation.

(3) Most good programmers use many of the techniques implied by these disciplines, often subconsciously, and can do so in any reasonable language. Language design can help by making the discipline more convenient and systematic, and by catching blunders or other unintended violations of conventions. Acquiring a particular programming style seems to depend on having a language that supports or requires it; once assimilated, however, that style can be applied in many other languages.

Acknowledgments. The principal designers of Mesa, in addition to the authors, have been Butler Lampson and Jim Mitchell. The major portion of the Mesa operating system was programmed by Richard Johnsson and John Wick of the System Development Division of Xerox. In addition to those mentioned above, Douglas Clark, Howard Sturgis, and Niklaus Wirth have made helpful comments on earlier versions of this paper.

References
1. Dahl, O.-J., Myhrhaug, B., and Nygaard, K. The SIMULA 67 common base language. Publ. No. S-2, Norwegian Comptng. Ctr., Oslo, May 1968.
2. Dennis, J.B., and Van Horn, E. Programming semantics for multiprogrammed computations. *Comm. ACM 9*, 3 (March 1966), 143–155.
3. Geschke, C., and Mitchell, J. On the problem of uniform references to data structures. *IEEE Trans. Software Eng. SE-1*, 2 (June 1975), 207–219.
4. Habermann, A.N. Critical comments on the programming language PASCAL. *Acta Informatica 3* (1973), 47–57.
5. Knuth, D. *The Art of Computer Programming, Vol. 1: Fundamental Algorithms.* Addison-Wesley, Reading, Mass., 1968.
6. Koster, C.H.A. On infinite modes. ALGOL *Bull. AB 30.3.3* (Feb. 1969), 109–112.
7. Lampson, B., Mitchell, J., and Satterthwaite, E. On the transfer of control between contexts. In *Lecture Notes in Computer Science, Vol. 19*, G. Goos and J. Hartmanis, Eds., Springer-Verlag, New York. (1974), 181–203.
8. Mitchell, J., and Wegbreit, B. Schemes: a high level data structuring concept. To appear in *Current Trends in Programming Methodologies*, R. Yeh, Ed., Prentice-Hall, Englewood Cliffs, N.J.
9. Morris, J. Protection in programming languages. *Comm. ACM 16*, 1 (Jan 1973), 15–21.
10. Parnas, D. A technique for software module specification. *Comm. ACM 15*, 5 (May 1972), 330–336.
11. Stoy, J.E., and Strachey, C. OS6 — an experimental operating system for a small computer, Part 2; input/output and filing system. *Computer J. 15*, 3 (Aug 1972), 195–203.
12. van Wijngaarden, A., Ed. A report on the algorithmic language ALGOL 68. *Num. Math. 14*, 2 (1969), 79–218.
13. Wegbreit, B. The treatment of data types in EL1. *Comm. ACM 17*, 5 (May 1974), 251–264.
14. Wirth, N. The programming language PASCAL. *Acta Informatica 1* (1971), 35–63.

Section 9
Axiomatic Definition of Programming Languages

Although techniques for specifying the syntax of languages are well understood and although general agreement exists about appropriate methods for syntax definition, such is not the case for programming language semantics. It is clear, however, that there are inherent problems with the kind of language definition used for most of the common programming languages today, including the definitions for American National Standard Fortran 77 and Cobol.

As long as the semantics of a language are presented in narrative form, there is an inherent danger of ambiguity or inconsistency. These problems will be reflected in implementation differences, thereby detracting from the portability of programs written in the "same" language for two different compilers. While compiler validation packages may serve to minimize the differences among implementations and programming conventions may further minimize portability problems, the fundamental problem remains the way in which the language is specified to the implementers.

Accordingly, a great deal of work has dealt with formal definition of programming languages. In general, this work has attempted to present either a mathematical formalization or an abstract machine model of the actions of language statements. Such techniques provide a basis for proving the correctness of a compiler and permit the programmer to determine *exactly* what various statements in the language do.

Of the languages for which there exist an American National Standard, only MUMPS has such a formal definition incorporated into the standard. This definition, based on transition diagrams, shows the semantic actions to be carried out when specific language constructs are encountered in a program. Because this formalization is based on an abstract machine model, it is possible to implement the language directly from the formal definition.

Numerous other formal definition techniques have been proposed and used. One that has received considerable attention is that of axiomatization, in which the effects of programming language statements are described in terms of axioms, along with sets of preconditions and postconditions to show the effect of each statement type. Hoare devised this technique and, with Wirth, applied it to the definition of Pascal. Both Hoare's original paper and the Wirth/Hoare axiomatization of Pascal appear in this section.

Other approaches to formal definition include the denotational semantics of Scott and Strachey, the Vienna Definition Language (applied to the PL/I definition), and two-level grammars (as used with Algol 68). Space limitations preclude the reprinting of more of these papers in this volume. However, the interested reader should refer to Marcotty, *et al.*, "A Sampler of Formal Definitions," *ACM Computing Surveys,* Vol. 8, No. 2 (June, 1976), pp. 191-276, which surveys several formal definition techniques and contains an excellent set of references.

An Axiomatic Basis for Computer Programming

C. A. R. HOARE

The Queen's University of Belfast, Northern Ireland*

In this paper an attempt is made to explore the logical foundations of computer programming by use of techniques which were first applied in the study of geometry and have later been extended to other branches of mathematics. This involves the elucidation of sets of axioms and rules of inference which can be used in proofs of the properties of computer programs. Examples are given of such axioms and rules, and a formal proof of a simple theorem is displayed. Finally, it is argued that important advantages, both theoretical and practical, may follow from a pursuance of these topics.

KEY WORDS AND PHRASES: axiomatic method, theory of programming' proofs of programs, formal language definition, programming language design, machine-independent programming, program documentation
CR CATEGORY: 4.0, 4.21, 4.22, 5.20, 5.21, 5.23, 5.24

1. Introduction

Computer programming is an exact science in that all the properties of a program and all the consequences of executing it in any given environment can, in principle, be found out from the text of the program itself by means of purely deductive reasoning. Deductive reasoning involves the application of valid rules of inference to sets of valid axioms. It is therefore desirable and interesting to elucidate the axioms and rules of inference which underlie our reasoning about computer programs. The exact choice of axioms will to some extent depend on the choice of programming language. For illustrative purposes, this paper is confined to a very simple language, which is effectively a subset of all current procedure-oriented languages.

2. Computer Arithmetic

The first requirement in valid reasoning about a program is to know the properties of the elementary operations which it invokes, for example, addition and multiplication of integers. Unfortunately, in several respects computer arithmetic is not the same as the arithmetic familiar to mathematicians, and it is necessary to exercise some care in selecting an appropriate set of axioms. For example, the axioms displayed in Table I are rather a small selection of axioms relevant to integers. From this incomplete set

* Department of Computer Science

of axioms it is possible to deduce such simple theorems as:

$$x = x + y \times 0$$

$$y \leqslant r \supset r + y \times q = (r - y) + y \times (1 + q)$$

The proof of the second of these is:

$$
\begin{aligned}
\text{A5} \quad (r - y) + y \times (1 + q) \\
&= (r - y) + (y \times 1 + y \times q) \\
\text{A9} \qquad &= (r - y) + (y + y \times q) \\
\text{A3} \qquad &= ((r - y) + y) + y \times q \\
\text{A6} \qquad &= r + y \times q \quad \text{provided } y \leqslant r
\end{aligned}
$$

The axioms A1 to A9 are, of course, true of the traditional infinite set of integers in mathematics. However, they are also true of the finite sets of "integers" which are manipulated by computers provided that they are confined to *nonnegative* numbers. Their truth is independent of the size of the set; furthermore, it is largely independent of the choice of technique applied in the event of "overflow"; for example:

(1) Strict interpretation: the result of an overflowing operation does not exist; when overflow occurs, the offending program never completes its operation. Note that in this case, the equalities of A1 to A9 are strict, in the sense that both sides exist or fail to exist together.

(2) Firm boundary: the result of an overflowing operation is taken as the maximum value represented.

(3) Modulo arithmetic: the result of an overflowing operation is computed modulo the size of the set of integers represented.

These three techniques are illustrated in Table II by addition and multiplication tables for a trivially small model in which 0, 1, 2, and 3 are the only integers represented.

It is interesting to note that the different systems satisfying axioms A1 to A9 may be rigorously distinguished from each other by choosing a particular one of a set of mutually exclusive supplementary axioms. For example, infinite arithmetic satisfies the axiom:

$$\text{A10}_I \quad \neg \exists x \forall y \qquad (y \leqslant x),$$

where all finite arithmetics satisfy:

$$\text{A10}_F \quad \forall x \qquad (x \leqslant \max)$$

where "max" denotes the largest integer represented.

Similarly, the three treatments of overflow may be distinguished by a choice of one of the following axioms relating to the value of $\max + 1$:

$$\text{A11}_S \quad \neg \exists x \quad (x = \max + 1) \qquad \text{(strict interpretation)}$$

$$\text{A11}_B \quad \max + 1 = \max \qquad \text{(firm boundary)}$$

$$\text{A11}_M \quad \max + 1 = 0 \qquad \text{(modulo arithmetic)}$$

Having selected one of these axioms, it is possible to use it in deducing the properties of programs; however,

A1	$x + y = y + x$	addition is commutative
A2	$x \times y = y \times x$	multiplication is commutative
A3	$(x + y) + z = x + (y + z)$	addition is associative
A4	$(x \times y) \times z = x \times (y \times z)$	multiplication is associative
A5	$x \times (y + z) = x \times y + x \times z$	multiplication distributes through addition
A6	$y \leqslant x \supset (x - y) + y = x$	addition cancels subtraction
A7	$x + 0 = x$	
A8	$x \times 0 = 0$	
A9	$x \times 1 = x$	

TABLE II

1. Strict Interpretation

+	0	1	2	3		$\times$	0	1	2	3
0	0	1	2	3		0	0	0	0	0
1	1	2	3	*		1	0	1	2	3
2	2	3	*	*		2	0	2	*	*
3	3	*	*	*		3	0	3	*	*

* nonexistent

2. Firm Boundary

+	0	1	2	3		$\times$	0	1	2	3
0	0	1	2	3		0	0	0	0	0
1	1	2	3	3		1	0	1	2	3
2	2	3	3	3		2	0	2	3	3
3	3	3	3	3		3	0	3	3	3

3. Modulo Arithmetic

+	0	1	2	3		$\times$	0	1	2	3
0	0	1	2	3		0	0	0	0	0
1	1	2	3	0		1	0	1	2	3
2	2	3	0	1		2	0	2	0	2
3	3	0	1	2		3	0	3	2	1

these properties will not necessarily obtain, unless the program is executed on an implementation which satisfies the chosen axiom.

3. Program Execution

As mentioned above, the purpose of this study is to provide a logical basis for proofs of the properties of a program. One of the most important properties of a program is whether or not it carries out its intended function. The intended function of a program, or part of a program, can be specified by making general assertions about the values which the relevant variables will take *after* execution of the program. These assertions will usually not ascribe particular values to each variable, but will rather specify certain general properties of the values and the relationships holding between them. We use the normal notations of mathematical logic to express these assertions, and the familiar rules of operator precedence have been used wherever possible to improve legibility.

In many cases, the validity of the results of a program (or part of a program) will depend on the values taken by the variables before that program is initiated. These initial preconditions of successful use can be specified by the same type of general assertion as is used to describe the results obtained on termination. To state the required connection between a precondition (P), a program (Q) and a description of the result of its execution (R), we introduce a new notation:

$$P \{Q\} R.$$

This may be interpreted "If the assertion P is true before initiation of a program Q, then the assertion R will be true on its completion." If there are no preconditions imposed, we write **true** $\{Q\}R$.[1]

The treatment given below is essentially due to Floyd [8] but is applied to texts rather than flowcharts.

3.1. Axiom of Assignment

Assignment is undoubtedly the most characteristic feature of programming a digital computer, and one that most clearly distinguishes it from other branches of mathematics. It is surprising therefore that the axiom governing our reasoning about assignment is quite as simple as any to be found in elementary logic.

Consider the assignment statement:

$$x := f$$

where

x is an identifier for a simple variable;

f is an expression of a programming language without side effects, but possibly containing x.

Now any assertion $P(x)$ which is to be true of (the value of) x *after* the assignment is made must also have been true of (the value of) the expression f, taken *before* the assignment is made, i.e. with the old value of x. Thus if $P(x)$ is to be true after the assignment, then $P(f)$ must be true before the assignment. This fact may be expressed more formally:

D0   Axiom of Assignment

$\vdash P_0 \{x := f\} P$

where

x is a variable identifier;

f is an expression;

P_0 is obtained from P by substituting f for all occurrences of x.

It may be noticed that D0 is not really an axiom at all, but rather an axiom schema, describing an infinite set of axioms which share a common pattern. This pattern is described in purely syntactic terms, and it is easy to check whether any finite text conforms to the pattern, thereby qualifying as an axiom, which may validly appear in any line of a proof.

---

[1] If this can be proved in our formal system, we use the familiar logical symbol for theoremhood: $\vdash P \{Q\} R$

3.2. Rules of Consequence

In addition to axioms, a deductive science requires at least one rule of inference, which permits the deduction of new theorems from one or more axioms or theorems already proved. A rule of inference takes the form "If $\vdash X$ and $\vdash Y$ then $\vdash Z$", i.e. if assertions of the form X and Y have been proved as theorems, then Z also is thereby proved as a theorem. The simplest example of an inference rule states that if the execution of a program Q ensures the truth of the assertion R, then it also ensures the truth of every assertion logically implied by R. Also, if P is known to be a precondition for a program Q to produce result R, then so is any other assertion which logically implies P. These rules may be expressed more formally:

> D1   Rules of Consequence
>
> If $\vdash P\{Q\}R$ and $\vdash R \supset S$ then $\vdash P\{Q\}S$
>
> If $\vdash P\{Q\}R$ and $\vdash S \supset P$ then $\vdash S\{Q\}R$

3.3. Rule of Composition

A program generally consists of a sequence of statements which are executed one after another. The statements may be separated by a semicolon or equivalent symbol denoting procedural composition: $(Q_1 ; Q_2 ; \cdots ; Q_n)$. In order to avoid the awkwardness of dots, it is possible to deal initially with only two statements $(Q_1 ; Q_2)$, since longer sequences can be reconstructed by nesting, thus $(Q_1 ; (Q_2 ; (\cdots (Q_{n-1} ; Q_n) \cdots)))$. The removal of the brackets of this nest may be regarded as convention based on the associativity of the ";-operator", in the same way as brackets are removed from an arithmetic expression $(t_1 + (t_2 + (\cdots (t_{n-1} + t_n) \cdots)))$.

The inference rule associated with composition states that if the proven result of the first part of a program is identical with the precondition under which the second part of the program produces its intended result, then the whole program will produce the intended result, provided that the precondition of the first part is satisfied.

In more formal terms:

> D2   Rule of Composition
>
> If $\vdash P\{Q_1\}R_1$ and $\vdash R_1\{Q_2\}R$ then $\vdash P\{(Q_1 ; Q_2)\}R$

3.4. Rule of Iteration

The essential feature of a stored program computer is the ability to execute some portion of program (S) repeatedly until a condition (B) goes false. A simple way of expressing such an iteration is to adapt the Algol 60 **while** notation:

$$\textbf{while } B \textbf{ do } S$$

In executing this statement, a computer first tests the condition B. If this is false, S is omitted, and execution of the loop is complete. Otherwise, S is executed and B is tested again. This action is repeated until B is found to be false. The reasoning which leads to a formulation of an inference rule for iteration is as follows. Suppose P to be an assertion which is always true on completion of S, provided that it is also true on initiation. Then obviously P will still be true after any number of iterations of the statement S (even

no iterations). Furthermore, it is known that the controlling condition B is false when the iteration finally terminates. A slightly more powerful formulation is possible in light of the fact that B may be assumed to be true on initiation of S:

> D3   Rule of Iteration
>
> If $\vdash P \wedge B\{S\}P$ then $\vdash P\{\textbf{while } B \textbf{ do } S\} \neg B \wedge P$

3.5. Example

The axioms quoted above are sufficient to construct the proof of properties of simple programs, for example, a routine intended to find the quotient q and remainder r obtained on dividing x by y. All variables are assumed to range over a set of nonnegative integers conforming to the axioms listed in Table I. For simplicity we use the trivial but inefficient method of successive subtraction. The proposed program is:

$$((r := x; \quad q := 0); \quad \textbf{while}$$
$$y \leqslant r \textbf{ do } (r := r - y; \quad q := 1 + q))$$

An important property of this program is that when it terminates, we can recover the numerator x by adding to the remainder r the product of the divisor y and the quotient q (i.e. $x = r + y \times q$). Furthermore, the remainder is less than the divisor. These properties may be expressed formally:

$$\textbf{true } \{Q\} \; \neg y \leqslant r \wedge x = r + y \times q$$

where Q stands for the program displayed above. This expresses a necessary (but not sufficient) condition for the "correctness" of the program.

A formal proof of this theorem is given in Table III. Like all formal proofs, it is excessively tedious, and it would be fairly easy to introduce notational conventions which would significantly shorten it. An even more powerful method of reducing the tedium of formal proofs is to derive general rules for proof construction out of the simple rules accepted as postulates. These general rules would be shown to be valid by demonstrating how every theorem proved with their assistance could equally well (if more tediously) have been proved without. Once a powerful set of supplementary rules has been developed, a "formal proof" reduces to little more than an informal indication of how a formal proof could be constructed.

4. General Reservations

The axioms and rules of inference quoted in this paper have implicitly assumed the absence of side effects of the evaluation of expressions and conditions. In proving properties of programs expressed in a language permitting side effects, it would be necessary to prove their absence in each case before applying the appropriate proof technique. If the main purpose of a high level programming language is to assist in the construction and verification of correct programs, it is doubtful whether the use of functional notation to call procedures with side effects is a genuine advantage.

Another deficiency in the axioms and rules quoted above

is that they give no basis for a proof that a program successfully terminates. Failure to terminate may be due to an infinite loop; or it may be due to violation of an implementation-defined limit, for example, the range of numeric operands, the size of storage, or an operating system time limit. Thus the notation "$P\{Q\}R$" should be interpreted "provided that the program successfully terminates, the properties of its results are described by R." It is fairly easy to adapt the axioms so that they cannot be used to predict the "results" of nonterminating programs; but the actual use of the axioms would now depend on knowledge of many implementation-dependent features, for example, the size and speed of the computer, the range of numbers, and the choice of overflow technique. Apart from proofs of the avoidance of infinite loops, it is probably better to prove the "conditional" correctness of a program and rely on an implementation to give a warning if it has had to abandon execution of the program as a result of violation of an implementation limit.

Finally it is necessary to list some of the areas which have not been covered: for example, real arithmetic, bit and character manipulation, complex arithmetic, fractional arithmetic, arrays, records, overlay definition, files, input/output, declarations, subroutines, parameters, recursion, and parallel execution. Even the characterization of integer arithmetic is far from complete. There does not appear to be any great difficulty in dealing with these points, provided that the programming language is kept simple. Areas which do present real difficulty are labels and jumps, pointers, and name parameters. Proofs of programs which made use of these features are likely to be elaborate, and it is not surprising that this should be reflected in the complexity of the underlying axioms.

5. Proofs of Program Correctness

The most important property of a program is whether it accomplishes the intentions of its user. If these intentions can be described rigorously by making assertions about the values of variables at the end (or at intermediate points) of the execution of the program, then the techniques described in this paper may be used to prove the correctness of the program, provided that the implementation of the programming language conforms to the axioms and rules which have been used in the proof. This fact itself might also be established by deductive reasoning, using an axiom set which describes the logical properties of the hardware circuits. When the correctness of a program, its compiler, and the hardware of the computer have all been established with mathematical certainty, it will be possible to place great reliance on the results of the program, and predict their properties with a confidence limited only by the reliability of the electronics.

The practice of supplying proofs for nontrivial programs will not become widespread until considerably more powerful proof techniques become available, and even then will not be easy. But the practical advantages of program proving will eventually outweigh the difficulties, in view of the increasing costs of programming error. At present, the method which a programmer uses to convince himself of the correctness of his program is to try it out in particular cases and to modify it if the results produced do not correspond to his intentions. After he has found a reasonably wide variety of example cases on which the program seems to work, he believes that it will always work. The time spent in this program testing is often more than half the time spent on the entire programming project; and with a realistic costing of machine time, two thirds (or more) of the cost of the project is involved in removing errors during this phase.

The cost of removing errors discovered after a program has gone into use is often greater, particularly in the case of items of computer manufacturer's software for which a large part of the expense is borne by the user. And finally, the cost of error in certain types of program may be almost

TABLE III

Line number	Formal proof	Justification
1	**true** $\supset x = x + y \times 0$	Lemma 1
2	$x = x + y \times 0 \{r := x\} x = r + y \times 0$	D0
3	$x = r + y \times 0 \; \{q := 0\} \; x = r + y \times q$	D0
4	**true** $\{r := x\} \; x = r + y \times 0$	D1 (1, 2)
5	**true** $\{r := x; \; q := 0\} \; x = r + y \times q$	D2 (4, 3)
6	$x = r + y \times q \wedge y \leqslant r \supset x = (r-y) + y \times (1+q)$	Lemma 2
7	$x = (r-y) + y \times (1+q)\{r := r-y\} x = r + y \times (1+q)$	D0
8	$x = r + y \times (1+q)\{q := 1+q\} x = r + y \times q$	D0
9	$x = (r-y) + y \times (1+q)\{r := r-y; \; q := 1+q\} \; x = r + y \times q$	D2 (7, 8)
10	$x = r + y \times q \wedge y \leqslant r \; \{r := r-y; \; q := 1+q\} \; x = r + y \times q$	D1 (6, 9)
11	$x = r + y \times q \; \{\textbf{while } y \leqslant r \textbf{ do} \; (r := r-y; \; q := 1+q)\} \; \neg y \leqslant r \wedge x = r + y \times q$	D3 (10)
12	**true** $\{((r := x; \; q := 0); \; \textbf{while } y \leqslant r \textbf{ do} \; (r := r-y; \; q := 1+q))\} \; \neg y \leqslant r \wedge x = r + y \times q$	D2 (5, 11)

NOTES

1. The left hand column is used to number the lines, and the right hand column to justify each line, by appealing to an axiom, a lemma or a rule of inference applied to one or two previous lines, indicated in brackets. Neither of these columns is part of the formal proof. For example, line 2 is an instance of the axiom of assignment (D0); line 12 is obtained from lines 5 and 11 by application of the rule of composition (D2).

2. Lemma 1 may be proved from axioms A7 and A8.

3. Lemma 2 follows directly from the theorem proved in Sec. 2.

incalculable—a lost spacecraft, a collapsed building, a crashed aeroplane, or a world war. Thus the practice of program proving is not only a theoretical pursuit, followed in the interests of academic respectability, but a serious recommendation for the reduction of the costs associated with programming error.

The practice of proving programs is likely to alleviate some of the other problems which afflict the computing world. For example, there is the problem of program documentation, which is essential, firstly, to inform a potential user of a subroutine how to use it and what it accomplishes, and secondly, to assist in further development when it becomes necessary to update a program to meet changing circumstances or to improve it in the light of increased knowledge. The most rigorous method of formulating the purpose of a subroutine, as well as the conditions of its proper use, is to make assertions about the values of variables before and after its execution. The proof of the correctness of these assertions can then be used as a lemma in the proof of any program which calls the subroutine. Thus, in a large program, the structure of the whole can be clearly mirrored in the structure of its proof. Furthermore, when it becomes necessary to modify a program, it will always be valid to replace any subroutine by another which satisfies the same criterion of correctness. Finally, when examining the detail of the algorithm, it seems probable that the proof will be helpful in explaining not only *what* is happening but *why*.

Another problem which can be solved, insofar as it is soluble, by the practice of program proofs is that of transferring programs from one design of computer to another. Even when written in a so-called machine-independent programming language, many large programs inadvertently take advantage of some machine-dependent property of a particular implementation, and unpleasant and expensive surprises can result when attempting to transfer it to another machine. However, presence of a machine-dependent feature will always be revealed in advance by the failure of an attempt to prove the program from machine-independent axioms. The programmer will then have the choice of formulating his algorithm in a machine-independent fashion, possibly with the help of environment enquiries; or if this involves too much effort or inefficiency, he can deliberately construct a machine-dependent program, and rely for his proof on some machine-dependent axiom, for example, one of the versions of A11 (Section 2). In the latter case, the axiom must be explicitly quoted as one of the preconditions of successful use of the program. The program can still, with complete confidence, be transferred to any other machine which happens to satisfy the same machine-dependent axiom; but if it becomes necessary to transfer it to an implementation which does not, then all the places where changes are required will be clearly annotated by the fact that the proof at that point appeals to the truth of the offending machine-dependent axiom.

Thus the practice of proving programs would seem to lead to solution of three of the most pressing problems in software and programming, namely, reliability, documentation, and compatibility. However, program proving, certainly at present, will be difficult even for programmers of high caliber; and may be applicable only to quite simple program designs. As in other areas, reliability can be purchased only at the price of simplicity.

6. Formal Language Definition

A high level programming language, such as ALGOL, FORTRAN, or COBOL, is usually intended to be implemented on a variety of computers of differing size, configuration, and design. It has been found a serious problem to define these languages with sufficient rigour to ensure compatibility among all implementors. Since the purpose of compatibility is to facilitate interchange of programs expressed in the language, one way to achieve this would be to insist that all implementations of the language shall "satisfy" the axioms and rules of inference which underlie proofs of the properties of programs expressed in the language, so that all predictions based on these proofs will be fulfilled, except in the event of hardware failure. In effect, this is equivalent to accepting the axioms and rules of inference as the ultimately definitive specification of the meaning of the language.

Apart from giving an immediate and possibly even provable criterion for the correctness of an implementation, the axiomatic technique for the definition of programming language semantics appears to be like the formal syntax of the ALGOL 60 report, in that it is sufficiently simple to be understood both by the implementor and by the reasonably sophisticated user of the language. It is only by bridging this widening communication gap in a single document (perhaps even provably consistent) that the maximum advantage can be obtained from a formal language definition.

Another of the great advantages of using an axiomatic approach is that axioms offer a simple and flexible technique for leaving certain aspects of a language *undefined*, for example, range of integers, accuracy of floating point, and choice of overflow technique. This is absolutely essential for standardization purposes, since otherwise the language will be impossible to implement efficiently on differing hardware designs. Thus a programming language standard should consist of a set of axioms of universal applicability, together with a choice from a set of supplementary axioms describing the range of choices facing an implementor. An example of the use of axioms for this purpose was given in Section 2.

Another of the objectives of formal language definition is to assist in the design of better programming languages. The regularity, clarity, and ease of implementation of the ALGOL 60 syntax may at least in part be due to the use of an elegant formal technique for its definition. The use of axioms may lead to similar advantages in the area of "semantics," since it seems likely that a language which can be described by a few "self-evident" axioms from which proofs will be relatively easy to construct will be preferable to a language with many obscure axioms which are difficult to apply in proofs. Furthermore, axioms enable the language designer to express his general *intentions* quite simply and directly, without the mass of detail which usually accompanies algorithmic descriptions. Finally, axioms can be formulated in a manner largely independent of each other, so that the designer can work freely on one axiom or group of axioms without fear of unexpected interaction effects with other parts of the language.

Acknowledgments. Many axiomatic treatments of computer programming [1, 2, 3] tackle the problem of proving the equivalence, rather than the correctness, of algorithms. Other approaches [4, 5] take recursive functions rather than programs as a starting point for the theory. The suggestion to use axioms for defining the primitive operations of a computer appears in [6, 7]. The importance of program proofs is clearly emphasized in [9], and an informal technique for providing them is described. The suggestion that the specification of proof techniques provides an adequate formal definition of a programming language first appears in [8]. The formal treatment of program execution presented in this paper is clearly derived from Floyd. The main contributions of the author appear to be: (1) a suggestion that axioms may provide a simple solution to the problem of leaving certain aspects of a language undefined; (2) a comprehensive evaluation of the possible benefits to be gained by adopting this approach both for program proving and for formal language definition.

However, the formal material presented here has only an expository status and represents only a minute proportion of what remains to be done. It is hoped that many of the fascinating problems involved will be taken up by others.

RECEIVED NOVEMBER, 1968; REVISED MAY, 1969

REFERENCES

1. YANOV, YU I. Logical operator schemes. *Kybernetika 1*, (1958).
2. IGARASHI, S. An axiomatic approach to equivalence problems of algorithms with applications. Ph.D. Thesis 1964. Rep. Compt. Centre, U. Tokyo, 1968, pp. 1–101.
3. DE BAKKER, J. W. Axiomatics of simple assignment statements. M.R. 94, Mathematisch Centrum, Amsterdam, June 1968.
4. MCCARTHY, J. Towards a mathematical theory of computation. Proc. IFIP Cong. 1962, North Holland Pub. Co., Amsterdam, 1963.
5. BURSTALL, R. Proving properties of programs by structural induction. Experimental Programming Reports: No. 17 DMIP, Edinburgh, Feb. 1968.
6. VAN WIJNGAARDEN, A. Numerical analysis as an independent science. *BIT 6* (1966), 66–81.
7. LASKI, J. Sets and other types. ALGOL Bull. 27, 1968.
8. FLOYD, R. W. Assigning meanings to programs. Proc. Amer. Math. Soc. Symposia in Applied Mathematics, Vol. 19, pp. 19–31.
9. NAUR, P. Proof of algorithms by general snapshots. *BIT 6* (1966), 310–316.

An Axiomatic Definition
of the Programming Language PASCAL

C. A. R. Hoare and N. Wirth

Received December 11, 1972

Summary. The axiomatic definition method proposed in reference [5] is extended and applied to define the meaning of the programming language PASCAL [1]. The whole language is covered with the exception of real arithmetic and go to statements.

Introduction

The programming language PASCAL was designed as a general purpose language efficiently implementable on many computers and sufficiently flexible to be able to serve in many areas of application. Its defining report [1] was given in the style of the ALGOL 60 report [2]. A formalism was used to define the syntax of the language rigorously. But the meaning of programs was verbally described in terms of the meaning of individual syntactic constructs. This approach has the advantage that the report is easily comprehensible, since the formalism is restricted to syntactic matters and is basically straightforward. Its disadvantage is that many semantic aspects of the language remain sufficiently imprecisely defined to give rise to misunderstanding. In particular, the following motivations must be cited for issuing a more complete and rigorous definition of the language:

1. PASCAL is being implemented at various places on different computers [3, 4]. Since one of the principal aims in designing PASCAL was to construct a basis for truly portable software, it is mandatory to ensure full compatibility among implementations. To this end, implementors must be able to rely on a rigorous definition of the language. The definition must clearly state the rules that are considered as binding, and on the other hand give the implementor enough freedom to achieve efficiency by leaving certain less important aspects undefined.

2. PASCAL is being used by many programmers to formulate algorithms as programs. In order to be safe from possible misunderstandings and misconceptions they need a comprehensive reference manual acting as an ultimate arbiter among possible interpretations of certain language features.

3. In order to prove properties of programs written in a language, the programmer must be able to rely on an appropriate logical foundation provided by the definition of that language.

4. The attempt to construct a set of abstract rules rigorously defining the meaning of a language may reveal irregularities of structure or machine dependent features. Thus the development of a formal definition may assist in better language design

Among the available methods of language definition the axiomatic approach proposed and elaborated by Hoare [5–7] seems to be best suited to satisfy the different aims mentioned. It is based on the specification of certain axioms and rules of inference. The use of notations and concepts from conventional mathematics and logic should help in making this definition more easily accessible and comprehensible. The authors therefore hope that the axiomatic definition may simultaneously serve as

1. a "contract" between the language designer and implementors (including hardware designers),

2. a reference manual for programmers,

3. an axiomatic basis for formal proofs of properties of programs, and

4. an incentive for systematic and machine independent language design and use.

This axiomatic definition covers exclusively the semantic aspects of the language, and it assumes that the reader is familiar with the syntactic structure of PASCAL as defined in [1]. We also consider such topics as rules about the scope of validity of names and priorities of operators as belonging to the realm of syntax.

The axiomatic method in language definition as introduced in [5] operates on four levels of discourse:

1. *PASCAL statements*, usually denoted by S.

2. *Logical formulas* describing properties of data, usually denoted by P, Q, R

3. *Assertions*, usually denoted by H, of which there are two kinds:

3 a) Assertions obtained by quantifying on the free variables in a logical formula. They are used to axiomatise the mathematical structures which correspond to the various data types.

3 b) Assertions of the form $P\{S\}Q$ which express that, if P is true before the execution of S, then Q is true after the execution of S. This kind of assertion is used to define the meaning of assignment and procedure statements. It is vacuously true, if the execution of S does not terminate.

4. *Rules of inference* of the form

$$\frac{H_1, \ldots, H_n}{H}$$

which state that whenever $H_1 \ldots H_n$ are true assertions, then H is also a true assertion, or of the form

$$\frac{H_1, \ldots, H_n \vdash H_{n+1}}{H}$$

which states that if H_{n+1} can be proven from $H_1 \ldots H_n$, then H is a true assertion. Such rules of inference are used to axiomatise the meaning of declarations and of structured statements, where $H_1 \ldots H_n$ are assertions about the components of the structured statements.

In addition, the notation

$$P_y^x$$

is used for the formula which is obtained by systematically substituting y for all free occurrences of x in P. If this introduces conflict between free variables of y and bound variables of P, the conflict is resolved by systematic change of the latter variables.

$$P_{y_1 \ldots y_n}^{x_1 \ldots x_n}$$

denotes simultaneous substitution for all occurrences of any x_i by the corresponding y_i. Thus occurrences of x_i within any y_j are *not* replaced. The variables $x_1 \ldots x_n$ must be distinct; otherwise the simultaneous substitution is not defined.

In proofs of PASCAL programs, it will be necessary to make use of the following two inference rules:

$$\frac{P\{S\}Q, \quad Q \supset R}{P\{S\}R}$$

$$\frac{P \supset Q, \quad Q\{S\}R}{P\{S\}R}$$

The axioms and rules of inference given in this article explicitly forbid the presence of certain "side-effects" in the evaluation of functions and execution of statements. Thus programs which invoke such side-effects are, from a formal point of view, undefined. The absence of such side-effects can in principle be checked by a textual (compile-time) scan of the program. However, it is not obligatory for a PASCAL implementation to make such checks.

The whole language PASCAL is treated in this article with the exception of real arithmetic and *go to* statements (jumps). Also the type *alfa* is not treated. It may be defined as

type *alfa* = **array** $[1 .. w]$ **of** *char*

where w is an implementation-defined integer.

The task of rigorously defining the language in terms of machine independent axioms, as well as experience gained in use and implementation of PASCAL have suggested a number of changes with respect to the original description. These changes are informally described in the subsequent section of this article, and must be taken into account whenever referring to [1]. For easy reference, the revised syntax is summarised in the form of diagrams in Appendix 1.

Many of the axioms have been explained in previous papers, e.g. [5, 8]. However, the axioms for procedures are novel; an informal explanation and example are given in Appendix 2.

The authors are not wholly satisfied with the axioms presented for classes, and for procedures and functions, particularly with those referring to global variables. This may be due either to inadequacy of the axiomatisation or to genuine logical complexity of these features of the language. The paper is offered as a first attempt at an almost complete axiomatisation of a realistic programming language, rather than as a definitive specification of a language especially constructed to demonstrate the definition method.

Changes and Extensions of PASCAL

The changes which were made to the language PASCAL since it was defined in 1969 and implemented and reported in 1970 can be divided into semantic and syntactic amendments. To the first group belong the changes which affect the meaning of certain language constructs and can thus be considered as essential changes. The second group was primarily motivated by the desire to simplify syntactic analysis or to coordinate notational conventions which thereby become easier to learn and apply.

File Types

The notion of the *mode* of a file is eliminated. The applicability of the procedures *put* and *get* is instead reformulated by antecedent conditions in the respective rules of inference. The procedure *reset* repositions a file to its beginning for the purpose of reading only. A new standard procedure *rewrite* is introduced to effectively discard the current value of a file variable and to allow the subsequent generation of a new file.

Parameters of Procedures

Constant parameters are replaced by so-called *value parameters* in the sense of ALGOL 60. A formal value parameter represents a variable local to the procedure to which the value of the corresponding actual parameter is initially assigned upon activation of the procedure. Assignments to value parameters from within the procedure are permitted, but do not affect the corresponding actual parameter. The symbol **const** will not be used in a formal parameter list.

Class and Pointer Types

The class is eliminated as a data structure, and pointer types are bound to a data type instead of a class variable. For example, the type definition and variable declaration

$$\textbf{type } P = \uparrow c;$$
$$\textbf{var } c: \textbf{class } n \textbf{ of } T$$

are replaced and expressed more concisely by the single pointer type definition

$$\textbf{type } P = \uparrow T.$$

This change allows the allocation of all dynamically generated variables in a single pool.

The for Statement

In the original report, the meaning of the for statement is defined in terms of an equivalent conditional and repetitive statement. It is felt that this algorithmic definition resulted in some undesirable overspecification which unnecessarily constrains the implementor. In contrast, the axiomatic definition presented in this paper leaves the value of the control variable undefined after termination of the for statement. It also involves the restriction that the repeated statement must not change the initial value [8].

Changes of a Syntactic Nature

Commas are used instead of colons to separate (multiple) labels in case statements and variant record definitions.

Semicolons are used instead of commas to separate constant definitions.

The symbol **powerset** is replaced by the symbols **set of**, and the scale symbol $_{10}$ is replaced by the capital letter E.

The standard procedure *alloc* is renamed *new*, and the standard function *int* is renamed *ord*.

Declarations of labels are compulsory.

Data Types

The axioms presented in this and the following sections display the relationship between a type declaration and the axioms which specify the properties of values of the type and operations defined over them. The treatment is not wholly formal, and the reader must be aware that

1. free variables in axioms are assumed to be universally quantified,

2. the expression of the "induction" axiom is always left informal,

3. the types of variables used have to be deduced either from the chapter heading or from the more immediate context,

4. the name of a type is used as a transfer function constructing a value of the type. Such a use of the type identifier is not available in PASCAL.

5. Axioms for a defined type must be modelled after the definition and be applied only in the scope (block) to which the definition is local.

6. A type name (other than that of a pointer type) may not be used directly or indirectly within its own definition.

Scalar Types

type $T = (c_1, c_2 \ldots c_n)$

1.1. $c_1, c_2 \ldots c_n$ are distinct elements of T.

1.2.   These are the only elements of T.

1.3. $c_{i+1} = succ\,(c_i)$ for $i = 1 \ldots n - 1$

1.4. $c_i = pred\,(c_{i+1})$ for $i = 1 \ldots n - 1$

1.5. $\neg\,(x < x)$

1.6. $(x < y) \wedge (y < z) \supset (x < z)$

1.7. $(x \neq c_n) \supset (x < succ\,(x))$

1.8. $x > y \equiv y < x$

1.9. $x \leq y \equiv \neg\,(x > y)$

1.10. $x \geq y \equiv \neg\,(x < y)$

1.11. $x \neq y \equiv \neg\,(x = y)$

We define $\min_T = c_1$ and $\max_T = c_n$ (not available to the PASCAL programmer)

The standard scalar type *Boolean* is defined as

$$\textbf{type } Boolean = (\textit{false, true}).$$

The standard type *integer* stands for a finite, coherent set of the whole numbers. The logical operators $\vee, \wedge, \neg$, and the arithmetic operators $+, -, *$, and **div**, are those of the conventional logical calculus and of whole number arithmetic. The modulus operator **mod** is defined by the equation

$$m \textbf{ mod } n = m - (m \textbf{ div } n) * n$$

whereas **div** denotes division with truncated fraction.

Implementations are permitted to refuse the execution of programs which refer to integers outside the range specified by their definition of the type *integer*.

The Type Char

2.1. The elements of the type *char* are the 26 (capital) letters, the 10 (decimal) digits, and possibly other characters defined by particular implementations. In programs, a constant of type *char* is denoted by enclosing the character in quote marks.

2.2.
$$\begin{array}{ll} \text{'A'} < \text{'B'} & \text{'1'} = succ\,(\text{'0'}) \\ \text{'B'} < \text{'C'} & \text{'2'} = succ\,(\text{'1'}) \\ \quad \cdots & \quad \cdots \\ \text{'Y'} < \text{'Z'} & \text{'9'} = succ\,(\text{'8'}). \end{array}$$

The sets of letters and digits are ordered, and the digits are coherent.

Axioms (1.5)–(1.11) apply to the *char* type. The functions *ord* and *chr* are defined by the following additional axioms:

2.3. if u is an element of *char*, then $ord\,(u)$ is a non-negative integer (called the *ordinal number* of u), and
$$chr\,(ord\,(u)) = u$$

2.4.
$$u < v \equiv ord\,(u) < ord\,(v).$$

These axioms have been designed to make possible an interchange of programs between implementations using different character sets. It should be noted that the function *ord* does not necessarily map the characters onto consecutive integers.

Subrange Types

$$\textbf{type } T = m \mathbin{..} n$$

Let a, m, n be elements of T_0 such that

$$m \leq a \leq n$$

and let x, y be elements of T. Then we define

$$\min_T = m \quad \text{and} \quad \max_T = n.$$

3.1. $T(a)$ is an element of T.

3.2. These are the only elements of T.

3.3. $T^{-1}(T(a)) = a$.

3.4. If $\ominus$ is a monadic operator defined on T_0, then
$$\ominus x \quad \text{means} \quad \ominus T^{-1}(x).$$

3.5. If $\bigcirc$ is a dyadic operator defined on $T_0 \times T_0$, then
$$x \bigcirc y \quad \text{means} \quad T^{-1}(x) \bigcirc T^{-1}(y)$$
$$x \bigcirc a \quad \text{means} \quad T^{-1}(x) \bigcirc a$$
$$a \bigcirc x \quad \text{means} \quad a \bigcirc T^{-1}(x).$$

Array Types

type $T = $ **array** $[I]$ **of** T_0

Let $m = min_I$ and $n = max_I$.

4.1. If x_i is an element of T_0 for all i such that $m \leq i \leq n$, then $T(x_m \ldots x_n)$ is an element of T.

4.2. These are the only elements of T.

4.3. $m \leq i \leq n \supset T(x_m \ldots x_n)[i] = x_i$.

4.4. **array** $[I_1, I_2 \ldots I_k]$ **of** T_0 $\quad$ means $\quad$ **array** $[I_1]$ **of array** $[I_2 \ldots I_k]$ **of** T_0.

4.5. $$x[i_1, i_2 \ldots i_k] \quad \text{means} \quad x[i_1][i_2] \ldots [i_k].$$

We introduce the following abbreviation for later use (see 11.1):

$(x, i:y)$ $\quad$ stands for
$T(x[m] \ldots x[pred(i)], y, x[succ(i)] \ldots x[n])$.

Record Types

type $T = $ **record** $s_1 : T_1; \ldots; s_m : T_m$ **end**

Let x_i be an element of T_i for $i = 1 \ldots m$.

5.1. $T(x_1, x_2 \ldots x_m)$ is an element of T.

5.2. These are the only elements of T.

5.3. $T(x_1 \ldots x_m) . s_i = x_i$ $\quad$ for $i = 1 \ldots m$.

Variant Records

type $T = $ **record** $s_1 : T_1; \ldots; s_{m-1} : T_{m-1};$
$\qquad\qquad$ **case** $s_m : T_m$ **of**
$\qquad\qquad\qquad k_1 : (s_1' : T_1');$
$\qquad\qquad\qquad k_2 : (s_2' : T_2');$
$\qquad\qquad\qquad \cdots$
$\qquad\qquad\qquad k_n : (s_n' : T_n')$
$\qquad\quad$ **end**

Let k_j be an element of T_m and let x_j' be an element of T_j' for $j = 1 \ldots n$. Then axiom 5.1 is rewritten as

5.1a $\quad T(x_1 \ldots x_{m-1}, k_j, x_j')\quad$ is an element of T.

Axioms 5.2 and 5.3 apply to this record type unchanged, and in addition the following axiom is given:

5.4. $\quad T(x_1 \ldots x_{m-1}, k_j, x_j').s_j' = x_j' \quad$ for $j = 1 \ldots n$.

We introduce the following abbrevation for later use (see 11.1):

$$(x, s_i : v) \quad \text{stands for} \quad T(x.s_1 \ldots x.s_{i-1}, y, x.s_{i+1} \ldots x.s_m)$$

and

$$(x, s_j' : y) \quad \text{stands for} \quad T(x.s_1 \ldots x.s_m, y)$$

The case with a field list containing several fields

$$k_j : (s_{j1} : T_{j1} : \ldots s_{jh} : T_{jh})$$

is to be interpreted as

$$k_j' : (s_j : T_j')$$

where s_j' is a fresh identifer, and T_j' is a type defined as

$$\textbf{type } T_j' = \textbf{record } s_{j1} : T_{j1}; \ldots; s_{jh} : T_{jh} \textbf{ end}$$

In this case $x \cdot s_{jt}$ is interpreted as $x \cdot s_j' \cdot s_{jt}$.

Set Types

$$\textbf{type } T = \textbf{set of } T_0$$

Let x_0, y_0 be elements of T_0.

6.1. $\quad [\ ]$ is an element of T.

6.2. $\quad$ If x is an element of T, then $x \vee [x_0]$ is a T.

6.3. $\quad$ These are the only elements of T.

6.4. $\quad [x_1, x_2, \ldots, x_n]$ means $\quad (([\ ] \vee [x_1]) \vee [x_2]) \vee \ldots \vee [x_n]$.

$[\ ]$ denotes the empty set, and $[x_0]$ denotes the singleton set containing x_0. The operators $\vee$, $\wedge$, and $-$, applied to elements of set type, denote the conventional operations of set union, intersection, and difference.

Note that PASCAL allows implementations to restrict set types to be built only on base types T_0 with a specified maximum number of elements.

File Types

$$\textbf{type } T = \textbf{file of } T_0$$

Let x_0 be an element of T_0.

7.1. $\quad \langle \rangle$ is an element of T.

7.2. $\quad$ If x is an element of T, then $x \& \langle x_0 \rangle$ is an element of T.

7.3. $\quad$ These are the only elements of T.

7.4. $\quad (x \& y) \& z = x \& (y \& z)$.

7.5. $\quad x \& \langle x_0 \rangle \ne \langle \rangle$.

$\langle\,\rangle$ denotes the empty file (sequence), and $\langle x_0\rangle$ the singleton sequence containing x_0. The operator & denotes concatenation such that $x \& y = \langle x_1 \dots x_m, y_1 \dots y_n\rangle$, if $x = \langle x_1 \dots x_m\rangle$ and $y = \langle y_1 \dots y_n\rangle$. Neither the explicit denotation of sequences nor the concatenation operator are available in PASCAL.

7.6. $first\,(\langle x_0\rangle \& x) = x_0,$ $rest\,(\langle x_0\rangle \& x) = x.$

The functions $first$ and $rest$ are not explicitly available in PASCAL. They will later be used to define the effect of file handling procedures.

Pointer Types

type $T = {\uparrow}T_0$

A pointer type consists of an arbitrary, unbounded set of values

$$\textbf{nil},\ \varphi_1,\ \varphi_2,\ \varphi_3 \dots$$

over which no operation except test of equality is defined. Associated with a pointer type T are a variable ξ of type *integer* (and initial value 0) and a variable τ with components $\tau_{\varphi_1},\ \tau_{\varphi_2},\ \dots$ which are all of type T_0. These components are the variables to which elements of T (other than **nil**) are "pointing". ξ is used in connection with the "generation" of new elements of T (see 11.7). ξ and τ are not available to the PASCAL programmer.

8.1. $x \neq \textbf{nil} \supset x{\uparrow} = \tau_x.$

Declarations

The purpose of a declaration is to introduce a named object (constant, type, variable, function, or procedure) and to prescribe its properties. These properties may then be assumed in any proof relating to the scope of the declaration.

Constant-, Type-, and Variable Declarations

If D is a sequence of declarations and S is a compound statement, then

$$D;\ S$$

is called a *block,* and the following is its rule of inference (expressed in the usual notation for subsidiary deductions):

9.1.
$$\frac{H \vdash P\{S\}Q}{P\{D;\ S\}Q}$$

H is the set of assertions describing the properties established by the declarations in D. P and Q may not contain any identifiers declared in D; if they do, the rule can be applied only after a systematic substitution of fresh identifiers local to the block. In the case of constant declarations the assertions in H are nothing but the list of equations themselves. In the case of type definitions they are the axioms derived from the declaration in the manner described above. In the case of a variable declaration $x:T$ it is the fact that x is an element of T.

514

File Variable Declarations

The declaration

$$\textbf{var } x:T$$

where

$$\textbf{type } T = \textbf{file of } T_0,$$

introduces the *two* variables x of type T and $x{\uparrow}$ of type T_0. $x{\uparrow}$ is called the *buffer variable* of x and is used implicitly by the standard file procedures. A so-called *file position* is associated with x; it splits x into a left part x_L and a right part x_R such that

9.2. x_L and x_R are of type T, and $x \equiv x_L \,\&\, x_R$.

x_L and x_R are not explicitly available to the programmer. Assignments to the buffer variable $x{\uparrow}$ are permitted only if $x_R = \langle\,\rangle$. This condition is denoted in PASCAL by the Boolean function *eof* (end of file):

9.3. $eof(x) \equiv x_R = \langle\,\rangle.$

In addition, the following axiom holds:

9.4. $x_R \neq \langle\,\rangle \supset x{\uparrow} = first\,(x_R).$

9.5.   The standard type *text*, and the standard variables *input*, and *output* are defined as follows:

$$\textbf{type } text = \textbf{file of } char$$
$$\textbf{var } input,\ output:text.$$

Function and Procedure Declarations

$$\textbf{function } f(L):T;\ S$$

Let **x** be the list of parameters declared in L, and let **y** be the set of global variables occuring within S (implicit parameters). Given the assertion $P\{S\}Q$, where f does not occur free in P, and none of the variables of **x** occurs free in Q, we may deduce the following implication:

10.1. $P \supset Q^f_{f(\mathbf{x},\mathbf{y})},$ for all values of the variables involved in this assertion

Note that the explicit parameter list **x** has been extended by the implicit parameters **y**, that **x** may not contain any variable parameters (specified by **var**), and that no assignments to nonlocal variables may occur within S. It is this property (10.1) that may be assumed in proving assertions about expressions containing calls of the function f, including those occuring within S itself and in other declarations in the same block. In addition, assertions generated by the parameter specifications in L may be used in proving assertions about S.

$$\textbf{procedure } p(L):S.$$

Let **x** be the list of explicit parameters declared in L; let **y** be the set of global variables occuring in S (implicit parameters), let $x_1 \ldots x_m$ be the parameters declared in L as variable parameters, and let $y_1 \ldots y_n$ be those global variables which are changed within S. Given the assertion $P\{S\}Q$ where none of the value parameters of $\mathbf{x}$ occurs free in Q, we may deduce the existence of functions f_i and g_j satisfying the following implication:

$$10.2. \quad P \supset Q^{x_1 \;\cdots\; x_m, \; y_1 \;\cdots\; y_n}_{f_1(\mathbf{x},\mathbf{y}) \;\cdots\; f_m(\mathbf{x},\mathbf{y}), \; g_1(\mathbf{x},\mathbf{y}) \;\cdots\; g_n(\mathbf{x},\mathbf{y})}$$

for all values of the variables involved in this assertion.

It is this property that may be assumed in proving assertions about calls of this procedure, including those occuring within S itself and in other declarations in the same block.

The functions f_i and g_j may be regarded as those which map the initial values of $\mathbf{x}$ and $\mathbf{y}$ on entry to the procedure onto the final values of $x_1 \ldots x_m$ and $y_1 \ldots y_n$ on completion of the execution of S.

Statements

Statements are classified into simple statements and structured statements. The meaning of simple statements is defined by axioms, and the meaning of structured statements is defined in terms of rules of inference permitting deduction of the properties of the structured statement from properties of its constituents. However, the rules of inference are formulated in such a way that the reverse process of deriving necessary properties of the constituents from postulated properties of the composite statement is facilitated. The reason for this orientation is that in deducing proofs of properties of programs it is most convenient to proceed in a "top-down" direction.

Simple Statements

Assignment Statements

$11.1. \quad P^x_y \{x := y\}\, P.$

We introduce the following conventions

(1)   If the type T of x is a subrange of the type of y,

$$P^x_y \quad \text{means} \quad P^x_{T(y)}.$$

(2)   If the type T of y is a subrange of the type of x,

$$P^x_y \quad \text{means} \quad P^x_{T^{-1}(y)}.$$

(3)   If x is an indexed variable

$$P^{a[i]}_y \quad \text{means} \quad P^a_{(a,i:y)}.$$

(4)   If x is a field designator

$$P^{r.s}_y \quad \text{means} \quad P^r_{(r,s:y)}.$$

Procedure Statements

$$11.2. \quad P^{x_1 \;\cdots\; x_m, \; y_1 \;\cdots\; y_n}_{f_1(\mathbf{x},\mathbf{y}) \;\cdots\; f_m(\mathbf{x},\mathbf{y}), \; g_1(\mathbf{x},\mathbf{y}) \;\cdots\; g_n(\mathbf{x},\mathbf{y})} \{p(\mathbf{x})\}\, P.$$

$\mathbf{x}$ is the list of actual parameters; $x_1 \ldots x_m$ are those elements of $\mathbf{x}$ which correspond to formal parameters specified as variable parameters, $\mathbf{y}$ is the set of all variables accessed nonlocally by the procedure p, and $y_1 \ldots y_n$ are those elements of $\mathbf{y}$ which are subject to assignments by the procedure.

$f_1 \ldots f_m$ and $g_1 \ldots g_n$ are the functions introduced and explained in 10.2. Note that $x_1 \ldots x_m$, $y_1 \ldots y_n$ must be all distinct (in the sense that none can contain or be a variable which is contained in another); otherwise the effect of the procedure statement is undefined. Rule 11.2 states that the procedure statement $p(\mathbf{x})$ is equivalent with the sequence of assignments (executed "simultaneously")

$$x_1 := f_1(\mathbf{x}, \mathbf{y}); \ldots x_m := f_m(\mathbf{x}, \mathbf{y});$$

$$y_1 := g_1(\mathbf{x}, \mathbf{y}); \ldots y_n := g_n(\mathbf{x}, \mathbf{y}).$$

Standard Procedures

The following inference rules specify the properties of the standard procedures *put*, *get*, *reset*, and *rewrite*. The assertion P in 11.3–11.6 must not contain x, x_L, x_R, $x{\uparrow}$, except in those cases where they occur explicitly in the list of substituends.

11.3. $eof(x) \wedge P^{x_L}_{x_L \& \langle x\uparrow\rangle} \{put(x)\}\, P\, eof(x).$

This axiom specifies that the procedure $put(x)$ is only applicable, if $eof(x)$ is true i.e. $x_R = \langle\ \rangle$. It thus leaves $eof(x)$ and $x_L = x$ invariant, makes $x{\uparrow}$ undefined, and corresponds to the assignment

$$x := x \,\&\, \langle x{\uparrow}\rangle.$$

11.4. $\neg eof(x) \wedge P^{x_L,\quad x\uparrow,\quad x_R}_{x_L \& \langle first(x_R)\rangle,\ first(rest(x_R)),\ rest(x_R)} \{get(x)\}\, P.$

The operation $get(x)$ is only applicable, if $\neg eof(x)$, i.e. $x_R \neq \langle\ \rangle$, and then corresponds to the three simultaneous assignments

$$x_L := x_L \,\&\, \langle first(x_R)\rangle; \quad x{\uparrow} := first(rest(x_R)); \quad x_R := rest(x_R).$$

11.5. $P^{x_L,\ x\uparrow,\quad x_R}_{\langle\ \rangle,\ first(x),\ x} \{reset(x)\}\, P.$

The operation $reset(x)$ corresponds to the three assignments

$$x_L := \langle\ \rangle; \quad x{\uparrow} := first(x); \quad x_R := x.$$

11.6. $P^{x}_{\langle\ \rangle} \{rewrite(x)\}\, P.$

The procedure statement $rewrite(x)$ corresponds to the assignment

$$x := \langle\ \rangle.$$

The following rule specifies the effect of the standard procedure *new*.

11.7. If t is a pointer variable of type T, then

$$new(t) \quad \text{means} \quad \xi := succ(\xi); \quad t := \varphi_\xi$$

where ξ is the hidden variable associated with the pointer type T.

Structured Statements

Compound Statements

12.1.
$$\frac{P_{i-1}\{S_i\}P_i \quad \text{for} \quad i = 1 \ldots n}{P_0\{\textbf{begin}\ S_1;\ S_2;\ \ldots;\ S_n\ \textbf{end}\}P_n}$$

If Statements

12.2.
$$\frac{P \wedge B\{S_1\}Q, \quad P \wedge \neg B\{S_2\}Q}{P\{\textbf{if } B \textbf{ then } S_1 \textbf{ else } S_2\}Q}$$

12.3.
$$\frac{P \wedge B\{S\}Q, \quad P \wedge \neg B \supset Q}{P\{\textbf{if } B \textbf{ then } S\}Q}$$

Case Statements

12.4.
$$\frac{P \wedge (x = k_i)\{S_i\}Q, \quad \text{for} \quad i = 1 \dots n}{(x \in [k_1 \dots k_n]) \wedge P\{\textbf{case } x \textbf{ of } k_1 : S_1; \dots; k_n : S_n \textbf{ end}\}Q}$$

Note: $k_a, k_b, \dots, k_m : S$ stands for $k_a : S; \ k_b : S; \dots; k_m : S$.

While Statements

12.5.
$$\frac{P \wedge B\{S\}P}{P\{\textbf{while } B \textbf{ do } S\}P \wedge \neg B}$$

Repeat Statements

12.6.
$$\frac{P\{S\}Q, \quad Q \wedge \neg B \supset P}{P\{\textbf{repeat } S \textbf{ until } B\}Q \wedge B}$$

For Statements

12.7.
$$\frac{(a \leq x \leq b) \wedge P\big([a \, .. \, x)\big)\{S\}P([a \, .. \, x])}{P([\ ])\{\textbf{for } x := a \textbf{ to } b \textbf{ do } S\}P([a \, .. \, b])}$$

$[u \, .. \, v]$ denotes the closed interval $u \dots v$, i.e. the set $\{i \mid u \leq i \leq v\}$ and $[u \, .. \, v)$ denotes the open interval $u \dots v$, i.e. the set $\{i \mid u \leq i < v\}$. Similarly, $(u \, .. \, v]$ denotes the set $\{i \mid u < i \leq v\}$. Note that $[u \, .. \, u) = (u \, .. \, u]$ is the empty set.

$$\frac{(a \leq x \leq b) \wedge P\big((x \, .. \, b])\big)\{S\}P([x \, .. \, b])}{P([\ ])\{\textbf{for } x := b \textbf{ downto } a \textbf{ do } S\}P([a \, .. \, b])}$$

Note that S must not change x, a, or b.

With Statements

12.9.
$$\frac{P^{r \cdot s_1 \dots r \cdot s_m}_{s_1 \quad\quad s_m}\{S\}Q^{r \cdot s_1 \dots r \cdot s_m}_{s_1 \quad\quad s_m}}{P\{\textbf{with } r \textbf{ do } S\}Q}$$

$s_1 \dots s_m$ are the field identifiers of the record variable r. Note that r must not contain any variables subject to change by S, and that

$$\textbf{with } r_1, \dots, r_n \textbf{ do } S$$

stands for

$$\textbf{with } r_1 \textbf{ do } \dots \textbf{ with } r_n \textbf{ do } S.$$

Appendix 1

Syntax Diagrams

identifier

unsigned integer

unsigned number

unsigned constant

constant

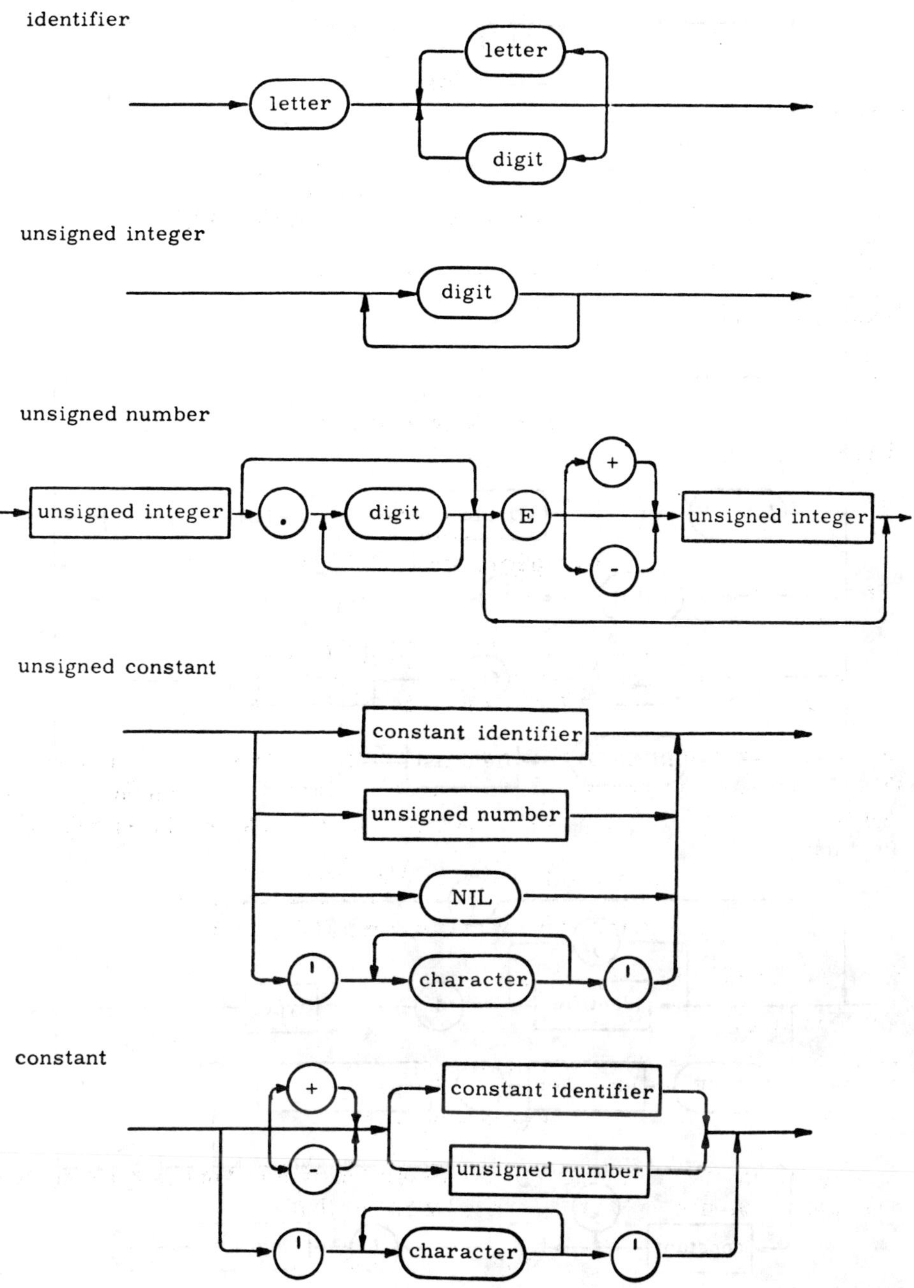

simple type

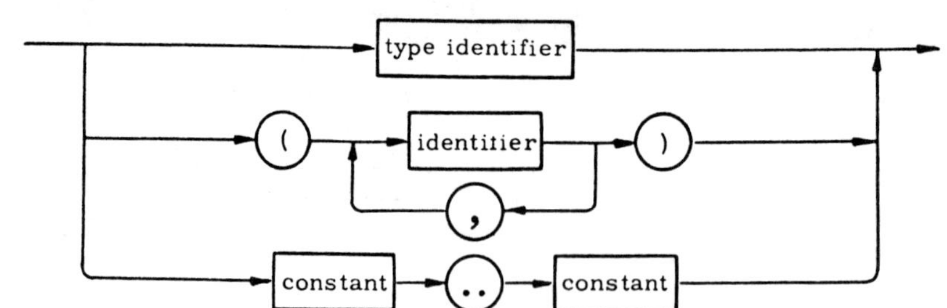

type

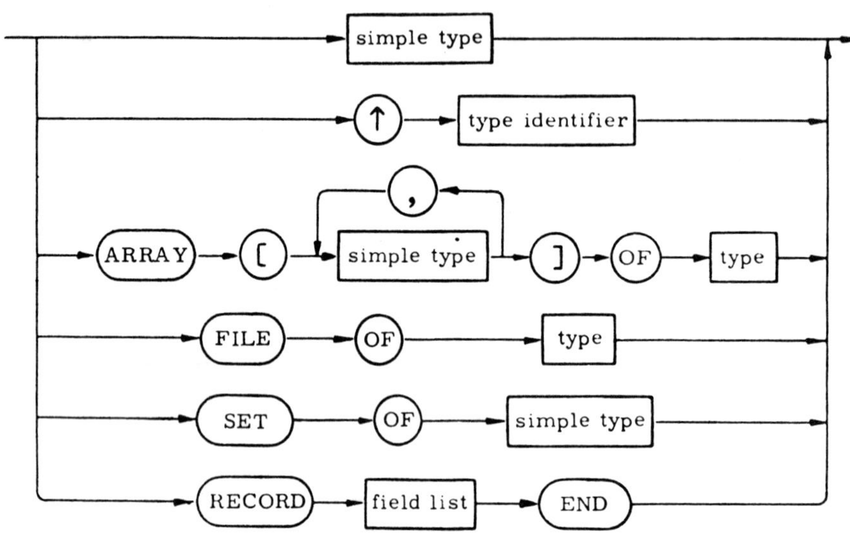

field list

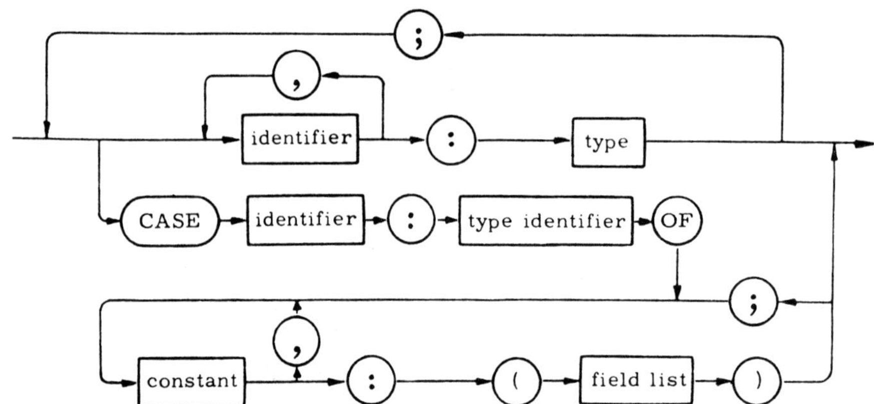

variable

factor

term

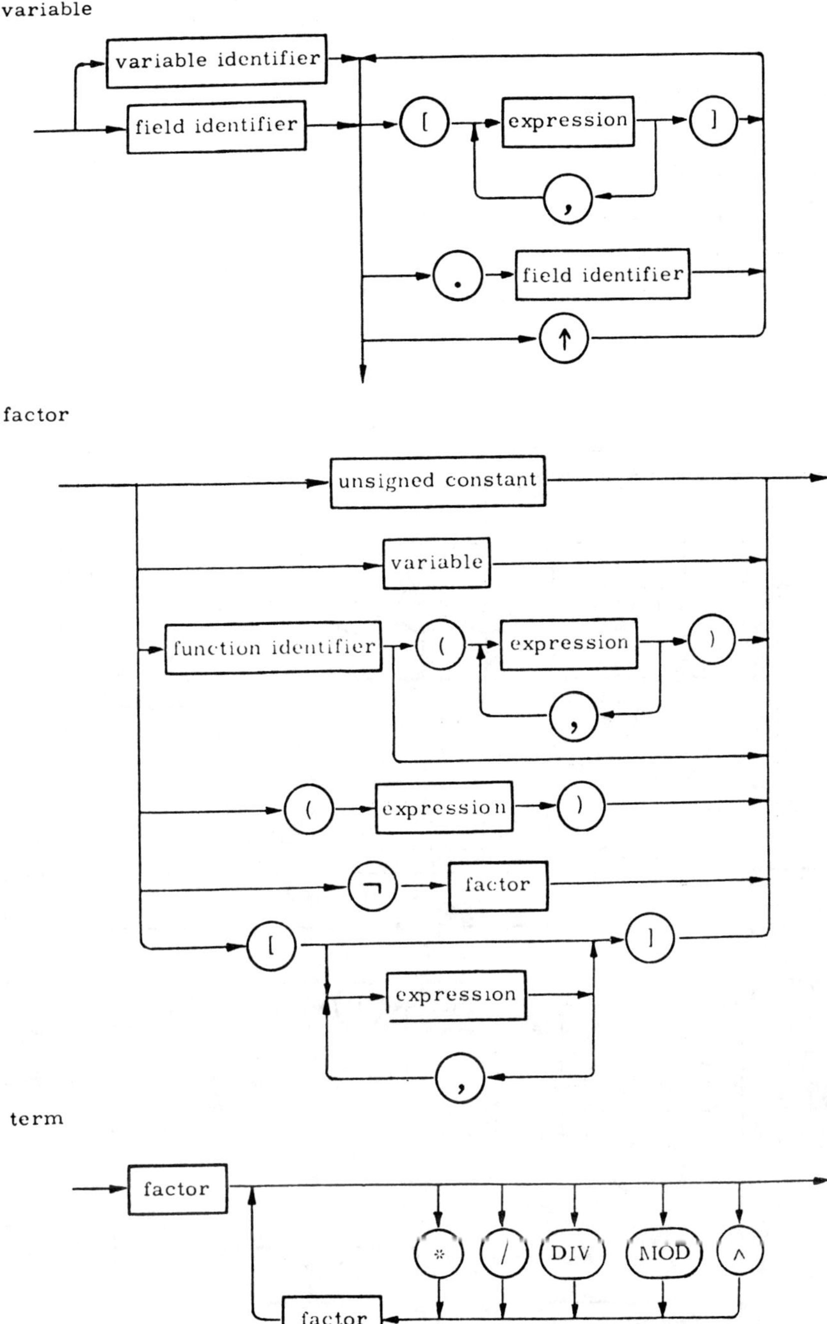

simple expression

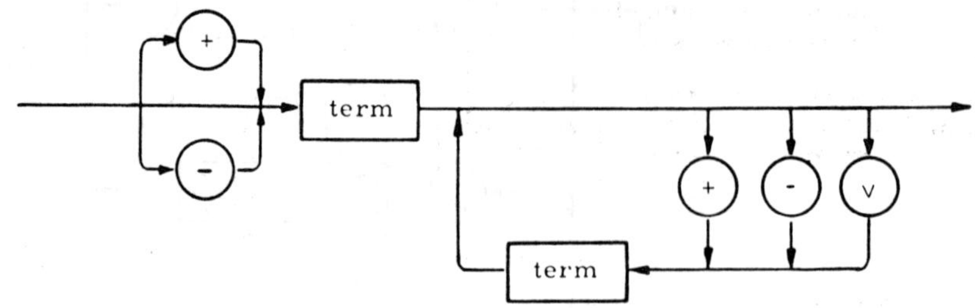

expression

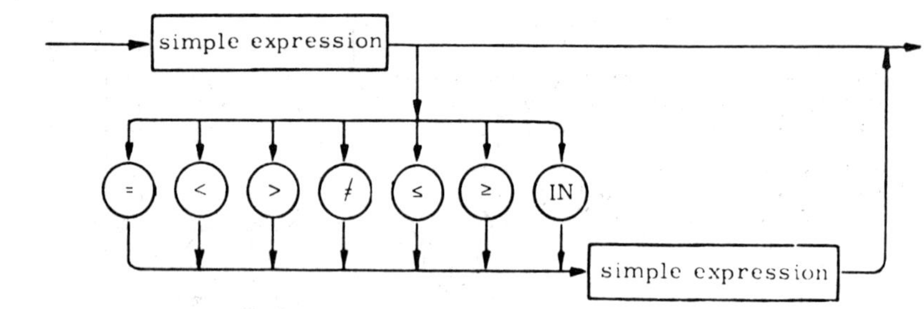

parameter list

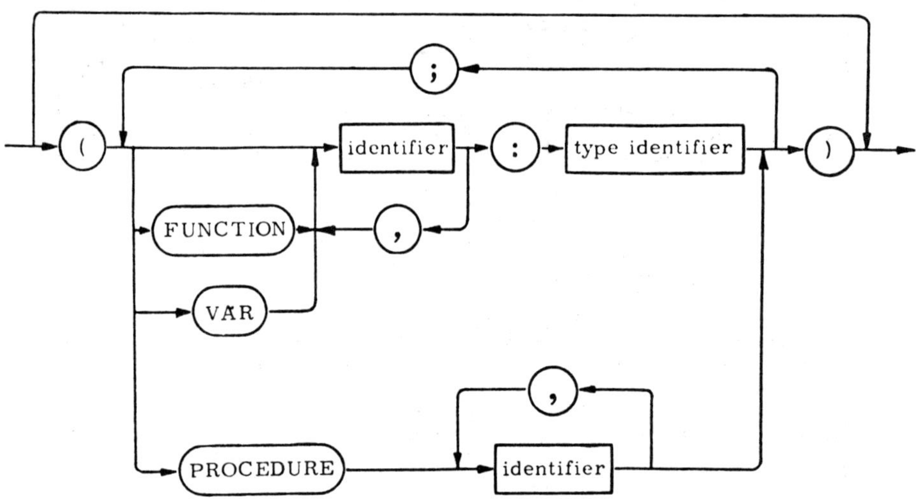

statement

unsigned integer
:
variable
function identifier
:=
expression
procedure identifier
(
,
expression
procedure identifier
)
BEGIN
statement
END
;
IF
expression
THEN
statement
ELSE
statement
CASE.
expression
OF
constant
:
statement
END
,
;
WHILE
expression
DO
statement
REPEAT
statement
UNTIL
expression
;
FOR
variable identifier
:=
expression
DOWNTO
TO
expression
DO
statement
WITH
,
variable
DO
statement
GOTO
unsigned integer

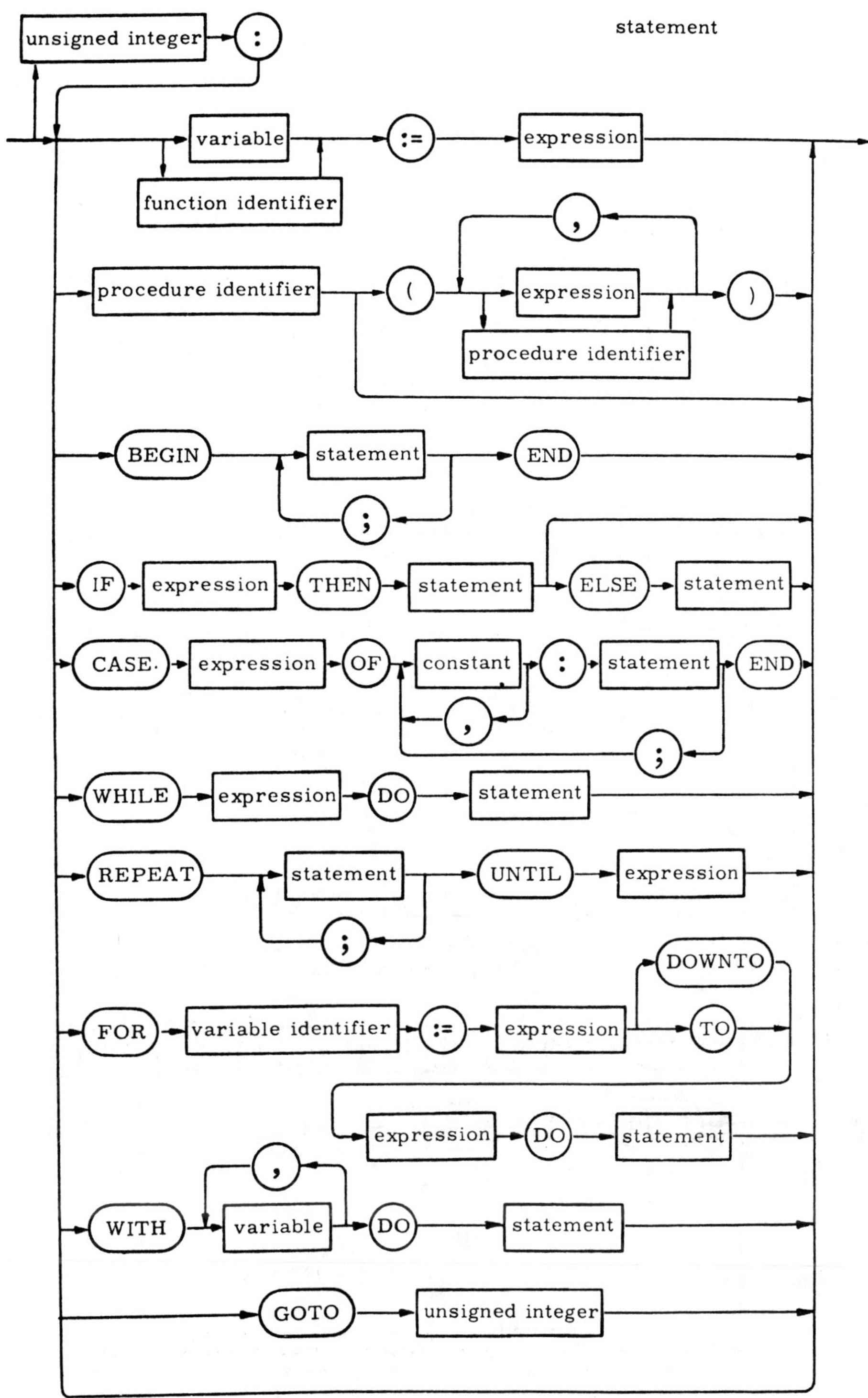

block

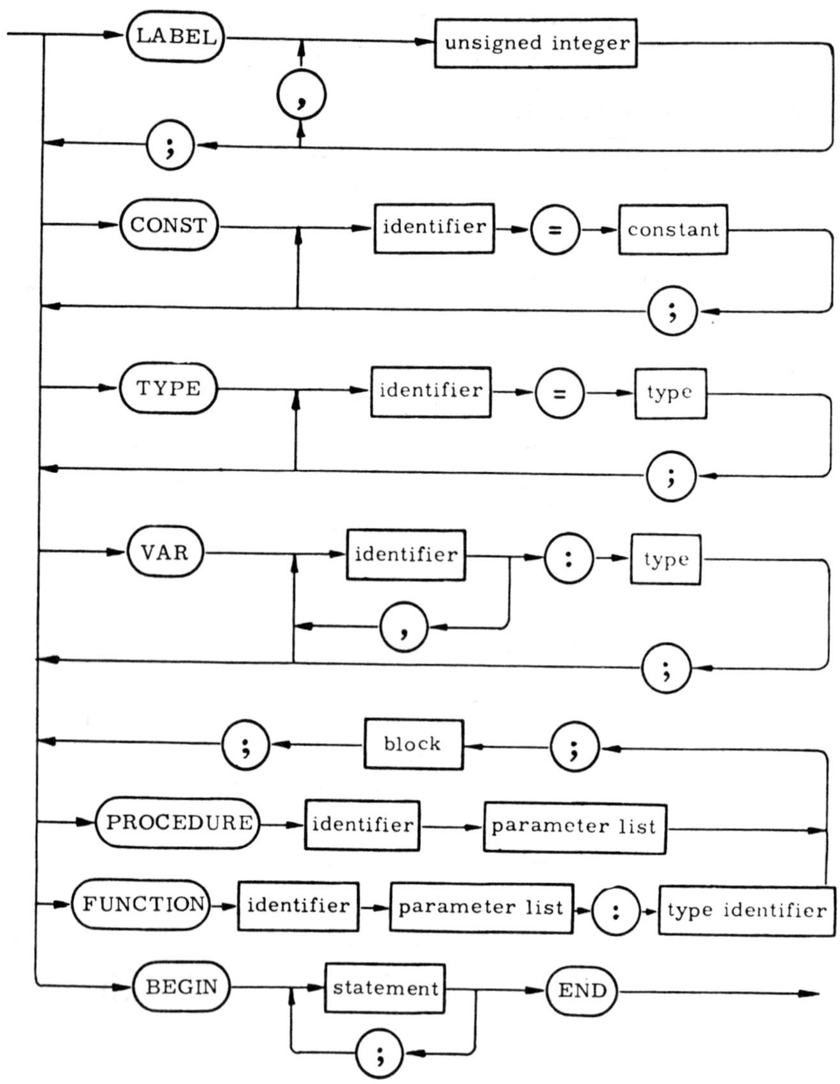

program

Appendix 2

Procedures

Consider the trivial procedure, with only one variable parameter, one value parameter, and no non-local references.

$$\textbf{procedure } p \textbf{ (var } a: integer; b: integer);$$
$$\textbf{begin} \quad b := 2*b; \textbf{ if } a > b \textbf{ then } a := b \textbf{ end}.$$

Letting S stand for the body of this procedure, it is easy to prove

$$(b = b_0) \wedge (b > 0)\{S\}a \leqq 2*b_0.$$

The invocation of this procedure will (in general) change the value of a in some manner dependent on the initial values of a and b (and initial values of non-local variables, if referenced from within S). Let us introduce a new function symbol f to denote this dependency, so that the final value of a can be denoted as

$$f(a, b).$$

Now the effect of any call of $P(x, y)$ is (by definition of f) equivalent to the simple assignment

$$x := f(x, y),$$

and using the axiom of assignment (11.1) we may idly conclude for any R that

$$R^x_{f(x,y)}\{f(x, y)\}R.$$

But by itself, application of this rule would be useless, since f has been introduced as an arbitrary function symbol. We need therefore to know at least something of the properties of f, and these can only be derived from the properties of the body of the procedure p. Suppose that we have proved

$$P\{S\}Q.$$

Occurrences of a in Q refer to the value of a *after* the execution of S, namely $f(a, b)$. Suppose that Q does not refer to any other program variable (in particular, does not refer to b). Then the values of all free variables of $Q^a_{f(a,b)}$ will be the same as they were in P, since the (a, b) in $f(a, b)$ also refer to the initial values of the parameters. Thus we may validly form the implication

$$P \supset Q^a_{f(a,b)},$$

and this implication will be true for all values of the variables involved in it. Thus, in the case shown above, we have

$$\forall a, b, b_0 ((b = b_0) \wedge (b > 0) \supset f(a, b) \leqq 2*b_0)$$

or more simply

$$\forall a, b (b > 0 \supset f(a, b) \leqq 2*b).$$

References

1. Wirth, N.: The programming language PASCAL. Acta Informatica **1**, 35–63 (1971)
2. Naur, P. (Ed.): Revised report on the algorithmic language ALGOL 60. Comm. ACM **6**, 1–17 (1963); Comp. J. **5**, 349–367 (1962/63); Numer. Math. **4**, 420–453 (1963)
3. Wirth, N.: The design of a PASCAL compiler. Software, Practice and Experience **1**, 309–333 (1971)
4. Welsh, J., Quinn, C.: A PASCAL compiler for the ICL 1900 Series Computers. Software, Practice and Experience **2**, 73–77 (1972)
5. Hoare, C. A. R.: An axiomatic basis for computer programming. Comm. ACM **12**, 576–581 (1969)
6. Hoare, C. A. R.: An axiomatic definition of the programming language PASCAL, Second Draft. Proc. Symposium on Theoretical Programming, Novosibirsk, Aug. 1972
7. Hoare, C. A. R.: Notes on data structuring. In: Dahl, O.-J., Dijkstra, E. W., and Hoare, C. A. R.: Structured programming. London und New York: Academic Press 1972
8. Hoare, C. A. R.: A note on the for statement. BIT **12**, 334–341 (1972)

C. A. R. Hoare
Computer Science Dept.
The Queen's University
Belfast BT7 1NN
Northern Ireland

N. Wirth
Eidgenössische Technische Hochschule
Fachgruppe Computer-Wissenschaften
CH-8006 Zürich
Clausiusstr. 55
Schweiz

 **Anthony I. Wasserman** is an Associate Professor of Medical Information Science at the University of California, San Francisco, and Adjunct Associate Professor of Computer Science at the University of California, Berkeley. His research interests center around the development of a methodology (user software engineering) and related tools to support the design and construction of interactive information systems. In 1970, he received his PhD in computer sciences from the University of Wisconsin, Madison, and has an AB in mathematics and physics from the University of California, Berkeley.

Wasserman has been active in professional organizations, serving as chairman of ACM SIGSOFT, the special interest group on software engineering, from 1976 to 1979, an ACM national lecturer from 1973 to 1976, and a member of numerous technical program committees. He is a member of IFIP WG 8.1 (Design and Evaluation of Information Systems) and WG 4.4 (Data Protection in Health Information Systems). He is the author of over 40 technical papers and co-editor of *Software Engineering Education—Needs and Objectives, Issues in Data Base Management,* and *Tutorial on Software Design Techniques.*

He is an Associate Editor of *Computing Surveys* and a member of the editorial advisory boards of *Information Systems* and *Transactions on Database Systems.*